PLAYS FOR THE COLLEGE THEATER

PLAYS FOR THE COLLEGE THEATER

COLLECTED AND EDITED

BY

GARRETT H. LEVERTON

Professor of Dramatic Production
Northwestern University

SAMUEL FRENCH

NEW YORK   LOS ANGELES

SAMUEL FRENCH LTD. LONDON

1941

Copyright, 1932, by Samuel French

ALL RIGHTS RESERVED

21855

To

E. S. L. AND E. B. L.

gratefully

INTRODUCTION

Plays for the College Theater represents an attempt to bring together a group of plays for classroom and laboratory use in the study of Stagecraft. Acting, and Directing. It is a book for the student of Dramatic Production, and it leaves to the many anthologies, already published, the task of selecting plays for study as literature; as specimens of a national drama; as representative of certain periods in the history of the theater; and the many other pegs around which collections of plays are grouped and published.

Several heretofore unpublished plays are included in this volume with the hope that college theaters will produce them and find both instruction and entertainment in their preparation. However, the presentation of fresh material is not the primary purpose of the book. Consideration of plays has been limited to those which provide scenes adaptable to class use as exercises in the many problems of Play Directing. No play is included which does not furnish good material in several of its scenes for the teaching of the major fundamentals of Direction and Production.

The book is the result of the editor's dissatisfaction with teaching from mimeographed scenes. The student cannot proceed intelligently when provided with only a short scene—he must have frequent access to the context of the entire play before he can decide on the staging of the scene which is being studied at the moment. Neither can he afford to buy single copies of all types and kinds of plays studied during the course; nor can Libraries furnish enough copies for use both in the classroom and in rehearsal. Hence the preparation of this volume.

The book provides scenes which may be prepared and presented by students to demonstrate the techniques of directing Farce, Comedy, Melodrama, and Tragedy. It offers material for the study and preparation of Satire, Burlesque, Fantasy, the Religious play, and the Folk play. Realism, Naturalism, Symbolism, Expressionism, and the Romantic play are represented, as are also plays from the various historical periods of the theater. There are plays in poetry and in prose—both in form and in conception. Many scenes furnish excellent exercises in the study of tempo, mood, atmosphere, climax, suspense, grouping, and the manipulation of large or small numbers of people in limited or full stage areas. A play in pantomime and a scenario from the Commedia dell' Arte provide material for the teaching of Acting as well as Directing and Production. Obviously the plays provide many problems in design, stage lighting, and costuming; and many characters which can be assigned as studies in make-up.

Scenes from most of these plays have been tried as teaching exercises in the courses at Northwestern University, and are presented herewith in the hope that they will prove to be both helpful and satisfactory as classroom and laboratory material.

I am most grateful to the authors and publishers represented in this volume for their assistance and courtesy in granting permission for the use of the plays.

I am confident that the students of the theater who use these pages will be as thankful as I am to Mrs. Richard Mansfield for her efforts to make available for them the prompt-book used by her famous husband in the portrayal of one of his greatest roles—Cyrano de Bergerac. This prompt-book now belongs to the Smithsonian Institution, and thanks are due its officials for loaning it so that it might be reprinted here.

The greatest debt is to Barrett H. Clark who has so generously given much time and many helpful suggestions toward the preparation of the volume. Really, he should be a co-editor of it. To Frank J. Sheil, general manager of Samuel French, I am greatly indebted for his help in securing material.

GARRETT H. LEVERTON.

Evanston, Illinois
May 1, 1932.

CONTENTS

THE YORK NATIVITY

A MIRACLE PLAY BASED ON TRANSLATIONS FROM THE YORK CYCLE AND FREELY
ARRANGED FOR PRODUCTION

By JOHN F. BAIRD

CHARACTERS

The Narrator
The Angel Gabriel
Mary
Joseph
First Shepherd
Second Shepherd
Third Shepherd
First King
Second King
Third King
Herod
Herod's Son
Herod's Two Advisers
Two Soldiers
Messenger

THE YORK NATIVITY

The setting, for a more formal production, duplicates as far as possible a religious picture in triptych form. This would make the set consist of three panels, the center one being larger than the two side ones. Rather than being actual scenery, the panels are simple Gothic frames. The floors of the panels are raised two steps above the level of the stage floor. The playing space of each panel is backed with black curtains. The panels may be lighted either from within the frames or from spotlights directed into them from a spot border downstage.

The action of the play is continuous and since the setting is formal, no front curtain need be used. At no time must the scenery, as such, obtrude. The entire pictorial effect must be gained from the grouping of the characters. The actual definition of each scene should be the light which illuminates it.

If it is impossible to use the triptych, the play can be enacted with each panel considered as a space at right, center, or left stage. Nearly every church contains the proper levels at the altar for staging this play.

A small platform, parallel with the footlights is used in the center panel. Steps from the panel floor lead up to it. The manger and HEROD'S throne are placed on this platform.

There is an organ prelude followed by a Gregorian chant which can only be faintly heard. Halfway through the chant, the NARRATOR appears and speaks throughout the remainder of it. He is costumed to suggest one of the prophets and speaks from a small lighted space.

The choir is invisible and is composed of mixed voices—male voices for the chants and mixed voices for the Allelujah choruses. It must be remembered that they are entirely subordinate to the play—so there should be no choral fire-works—please! The choir sings a capella throughout most of the play and must be well rehearsed in order to execute effectively the crescendo and diminuendo cues. In the last scene the choir is reenforced by the organ after the scene ends. Then the choir gradually fades out and the organ plays for a brief space of time. When it has finished, the performance is over.

The musical setting, notes on production, and costume plates may be had on application to the author, in care of the publisher.

PROLOGUE

NARRATOR [speaks from right stage].
And in the sixth month the angel Gabriel was sent from God unto a city of Galilee, named Nazareth.
To a virgin espoused to a man whose name was Joseph, of the house of David; and the virgin's name was Mary. And the angel came in unto her, and said, Hail, thou that art highly favoured; the Lord is with thee: blessed art thou among women.
And when she saw him she was troubled at his saying, and cast in her mind what manner of salutation this should be. And the angel said unto her, Fear not, Mary: for thou hast found favour with God.
And, behold, thou shalt conceive in thy womb, and bring forth a son, and shall call his name Jesus.
He shall be great, and shall be called the Son of the Highest: and the Lord God shall give unto him the throne of his father David.
And he shall reign over the house of Jacob for ever; and of his kingdom there shall be no end. Then said Mary unto the angel, How shall this be, seeing I know not a man?
And the angel answered and said unto her, The Holy Ghost shall come upon thee, and the power of the Highest shall overshadow thee: therefore also that holy thing which shall be born of thee shall be called the Son of God.
And behold, thy cousin Elizabeth, she hath also conceived a son in her old age: and this is the sixth month with her, who was called barren.
For with God nothing shall be impossible. And Mary said, Behold the handmaid of the Lord; be it unto me according to thy will.
And the angel departed from her. (Luke, 1, 26–38)
[Lights come up in left panel]

SCENE ONE

[MARY is discovered on her knees in silent prayer]
ANGEL.
Hail, thou Handmaid of Heaven high, Hail!
Thou that art highly favoured, hail! Blessed
Art thou among all women. Hail to thee!

3

MARY [*looks up, startled*]
What voice is this? And can it be that I,
A lowly maid, am so sought out? [*Turns her
head to the right so she can see* ANGEL]
　　　　　　　　　　　　Whence comes
This light as if from my celestial King. [*She
looks forward and sinks down so she is
sitting on her heels*]
I cannot be so nigh to this great light.
ANGEL.
Nor dread ye not, thou mild Marie. Hear ye;
Thy God has chosen thee for His. Of all
Who are women, blessed may thou be.
MARY [*rises slowly keeping her head bowed*].
　　　　　　　　　　　　Who art thou?
ANGEL.
I am a messenger of God, sent here
To tell to thee that thou art she whom God
Selects. Thy very chastity shall be
O'ershadowed by His mightiness. And from
This bliss shall spring a Child—The Son of God,
And thou shalt call Him Jesus. He will be
Thy Son, and still thy God,—a King! In
　　Heaven
He shall sit upon a throne and rule
Forever, far more time than man has known
Nor ever will.
MARY.
　　　　　　Oh, Angel, thou who greets
Me thus from God, how can I a barren
Maid conceive a child, or king, or God?
ANGEL.
Thy need is not to think in such a way,
But to have faith. Thy cousin, who is called
Elizabeth, is even now with child,
Though she is old, no longer barren. For,
With God nothing shall be impossible.
MARY [*facing down right, raises her head and
speaks, as if to Heaven*].
Thou Angel, blessèd messenger, God's will
I hold to be the highest, therefore I
Am glad, and in my gladness has my love
For Him increased a thousandfold. Behold
In me God's Handmaid, ready now to be
Engraved with Heaven's joy. Thy words are
　　each,
For me, commands. [*Kneels in prayerful atti-
tude*]
　　　　　My God, Thy will be done.
ANGEL.
Hail, thou Handmaid of Heaven high, hail!
Thou that art highly favoured, hail! Blessed
Art thou among all women. Hail to thee!
　　[*Dim out lights*]
　　CHANT
　　[*After chant,* NARRATOR *enters and speaks
　　from left stage*]
NARRATOR.
But while he thought on these things, Behold,
　　the Angel of the Lord appeared unto him
　　in a dream, saying, Joseph, thou son of
　　David, fear not to take unto thee Mary

thy wife: for that which is conceived in
　　her is of the Holy Ghost.
And she shall bring forth a son, and thou shalt
　　call his name Jesus: for he shall save his
　　people from their sins. Now all this was
　　done, that it might be fulfilled which was
　　spoken of the Lord by the prophet, say-
　　ing, Behold, a virgin shall be with child,
　　and shall bring forth a son, and they shall
　　call his name Emmanuel, which, being in-
　　terpreted, is God with us.
Then Joseph, being raised from sleep, did as the
　　Angel of the Lord had bidden him. (Mat-
　　thew, 1, 20–24)
　　[*Lights up in right panel*]

SCENE TWO

[JOSEPH *enters slowly and goes, during his
　　speech, to the right frame of the panel.
　　He leans on the staff which he carries*]
JOSEPH.
Oh, heavy is my step and wary is
My way, for I have need to care. I
Am old, and weak. Often do I ask
Myself why I have wedded one so young.
I repent me of my bargain. I
Am old, and weak. I should have led a single
Life. I am no longer as a boy,
Robust and full of spirits high. I
Am old, and weak. There in the temple where
I walked, the rod I carried, blossomed. They
Who saw this thing said I must marry. I
Am old, and weak. I cannot give Marie
The child which keeps her from full happiness.
Perhaps in sleep our God will show to me
The way. [*Slowly kneels*]
　　　　Great Sire, show me the way. Amen.
　　[*Lies down*]
ANGEL [*appears directly above* JOSEPH].
Awaken, Joseph, go to thy Marie.
One will be born to her which is conceived
From Heaven high. Such joy as shall be yours
Shall then descend to all mankind. For know
You, Mary's Son shall be thy God. As you
Shall see. He is thy Saviour. He shall rid
The world of evil. He shall be the highest.
JOSEPH.
Is this true that ye have told to me?
ANGEL.
Verily, Joseph, go to thy Marie.
　　[ANGEL *disappears*]
JOSEPH [*sits up*].
Was this a dream, or did I talk with one
Who came from God? He spoke, and I it was
Who answered him. [*Gets slowly to his feet,
　　in wonder. Goes center*]
　　　　　　　　But I am such a lowly
Carpenter. Around me, though, I feel
A gladness that is much too large to come
Of earth, or of some human word. It must

Be then that I have talked with one who comes
From God. Then all he spoke and promised will
Be true. This is too great a favour, Heaven
Sent. I will go to Mary and
Rejoice with her in her good fortune. Mary.
[*Starts left*]
[*Lights dim out, and come up in center
panel for*]

SCENE THREE

MARY [*kneeling up-stage center*].
I thank Thee, Lord, for all that Thou hast done.
Thy blessing to descend on such a humble
One as I is wonder. Too, I thank
Thee for Thy heavenly protection which
Has kept me in Thy way.
JOSEPH [*enters from the right*].
                  Hail thee, Mary,
Hail to thee! I was till now unknowing
What had come about. Lately I
Have talked with one who came from God and
made
It plain what has occurred. Forgive me for
Not knowing. I am but a humble man.
I dare not come too near to thee unless
I bow, and approach most reverently.
MARY [*rises*].
Forgiveness? Shame that thou shouldst think of
Such a thing. [*Goes a step toward* JOSEPH]
           I am thy wife and therefore there
Is nothing to forgive. Come near, and do
Not hold me in such awe.
JOSEPH [*goes to* MARY *and kneels, taking her
by the hand*].
               I thank thee for
These words. Since thou hast spoken I have
found
My courage once again. My purpose was
To ask if thou couldst make a journey. I
Must go to Bethlehem where Cæsar hath
Declared that all the house of David shall
Assemble. There a tax is laid upon
Us. We must go to meet his agents there.
[*Lights dim out*]
CHORUS, then
NARRATOR [*speaking at right stage*].
And it came to pass in those days, that there
    went out from Cæsar Augustus, a decree
    that all the world should be taxed.
And all went to be taxed, every one into his
    own city.
And Joseph also went up from Galilee, out of
    the city of Nazareth, into Judea, unto the
    city of David, which is called Bethlehem;
To be taxed with Mary, his espoused wife,
And so it was, that, while they were there, the
    days were accomplished that she should be
    delivered.
And she brought forth her first-born son,
    and wrapped him in swaddling clothes, and

laid him in a manger; because there was
no room for them in the inn. (Luke, 2,
1–7)
[*Lights up*]

SCENE FOUR

[JOSEPH *and* MARY *enter left stage and
move slowly toward center*]
JOSEPH.
Lord, grant to us good lodging for this night.
This place is poor, but we have sought both up
And down through divers streets in all this city.
    [*They arrive before center panel which
they regard*]
There is nothing left but this, a stable,
Such a throng of people is come here
To Bethlehem. What say ye, Mary, wife
And daughter, child? Can we here abide?
The walls are down, and mostly for a roof
Is nothing but the sky. What say ye, Mary?
MARY [*enters panel and turns to speak to
JOSEPH*].
God has brought us here, so shall we here
Abide. Therefore, Joseph, be of good cheer
For in this place the child will soon be born.
JOSEPH [*goes to* MARY]
The Child will soon be born? Then I must haste,
To find some fuel that will give us light
And warmth. [*Turns to survey the stable*]
             There is no light but murkiness
Which comes down from the sky. And warmth,
    we have
Naught else but that which comes from stabled
    beasts
    [*Indicates the manger up-stage*]
There by the manger. I will make all haste.
    [*Goes to manger and stands with his back
to the audience during* MARY'S *prayer*]
MARY [*kneeling*].
Almighty God, who governs and who gives,
Look on my joy and see the gladness in my
    soul.
Into thy hands I place my care. Amen.
    [JOSEPH *comes out of the panel and down-
stage*]
    [*Lights dim out*]
    [ANGEL CHORUS *very faintly heard*]
    [*Lights up*]

SCENE FIVE

JOSEPH [*down-stage center*].
The night is cold and dark. As far as I
Can see the barren earth gives up no faggots.
Perhaps the walls in yonder hut will keep
The night air out. But broken walls are poor
For such a purpose. They may keep out cold,
But they are powerless to provide the light.
The heavens do not help. They still are dark:

And being dark they hide the very thing
That is of great importance for this world.
Methinks that that is not the way to show
The earth the coming of its King. It is
So dark. [*The light from the star shines down
on* JOSEPH *as he stands looking upward.
The* ANGEL CHORUS *sings*]
       It lightens. Can this be the sign
Foretold by Balaam? It must be the star!
       [*Dim out*]

NARRATOR [*at left stage*].
And there were in the same country, shepherds
   abiding in the field; keeping watch over
   their flocks by night.
And, lo, the Angel of the Lord came upon them,
   and the Glory of the Lord shone round
   about them: and they were sore afraid.
And the Angel said unto them,
Fear not: for, Behold, I bring you good tidings
   of great joy, which shall be to all people.
For unto you is born this day in the city of
   David, a Saviour, which is Christ the Lord.
And this shall be a sign unto you;
Ye shall find the babe wrapped in swaddling
   clothes, lying in a manger.
And suddenly there was with the angel a multitude of the heavenly host, praising God
   and saying,
Glory to God in the highest, and on earth peace,
   good will toward men.
And it came to pass as the angels were gone
   away from them into Heaven, the Shepherds said one to another,
Let us now go even unto Bethlehem, and see
   this thing which is come to pass, which
   the Lord has made known unto us.
And they came with haste, and found Mary,
   and Joseph, and the babe lying in a
   manger. (Luke, 2, 8–16)
   [*Lights up in right panel*]

SCENE SIX

[THE FIRST SHEPHERD *is standing at center,
the* SECOND SHEPHERD *is reclining at
right, and the* THIRD SHEPHERD *is sitting
left*]

FIRST SHEPHERD.
Brothers, take heed and hear what I shall say.
Since there is naught to do but watch, we
   should
Be diligent and rehearse the sayings of
Our forefathers, Hosea and Isaiah,—
They who proved that to this world would
   come
A prince of higher rank than any king.
According to the prophecy, a virgin
Here on earth shall give Him life in Bethlehem.

SECOND SHEPHERD.
If that should be, then Balaam has
Told true. And it was he who prophesied

A star to know the birthplace of our Lord.

THIRD SHEPHERD.
'Tis true. If we should see that light then other
Shepherds, glad as we, would not exist.
For by that light shall all the children here
In Israel be free. But that was long
Ago. [*Rises*]
       Now, it were better that the three
Of us should seek our flocks and follow after
Them instead of some old prophecy.
       [*Start down stage. The star appears*]

OMNES.
The light!

FIRST SHEPHERD [*kneels*].
              It blinds.

SECOND SHEPHERD [*bows his head*].
              It saves.

THIRD SHEPHERD [*looks upward*].
                    It is the Lord.
       [*The* ANGEL CHORUS *is heard*]
       [*Lights dim out*]

NARRATOR [*at right*].
Now when Jesus was born in Bethlehem of
   Judea in the days of Herod the king, behold, there came wise men from the east
   to Jerusalem,
Saying, Where is he that is born King of the
   Jews? For we have seen his star in the
   east, and are come to worship him!
When Herod the king had heard these things,
   he was troubled, and all Jerusalem with
   him.
And when he had gathered all the chief priests
   and scribes of the people together, he de-
   manded of them where Christ should be
   born.
And they said unto him, In Bethlehem of
   Judea,—for thus it is written by the
   prophet.
Then Herod, when he had privily called the
   wise men, inquired of them diligently what
   time the star appeared.
And he sent them to Bethlehem, and said,
Go and search for the young child; and when
   ye have found him, bring me word again,
   that I may come and worship him also.
   (Matthew, 2, 1–8)
   [*Lights up in left panel*]

SCENE SEVEN

[*The* FIRST KING *is discovered kneeling*]

FIRST KING.
Lord, that giveth everlasting life,
My love is Thine, for giving me this chance
To be the first from my vast Eastern realm
To seek the star which was foretold. The jour-
   ney
I have made is long and it is strange
That I, a king, should be appointed by

My soul to follow after One who also
Is a king, but higher still. [*Rises and looks
about*]
But there
Should be some others on this road who also
Seek this king. [SECOND *and* THIRD KINGS *enter
from right*]
Here are two who come
As if in doubt as to the way.
[*Takes step toward them*]
Good Sirs.
SECOND KING.
God save you, Sir, and what may be your
errand
On this road at such a time of night?
FIRST KING.
I seek a star.
THIRD KING.
A star?
FIRST KING.
Aye, one that will
Make light the way to find a King, good Sirs.
SECOND KING.
But we are kings. We come in search of one
Predicted to be higher still than we.
FIRST KING.
Our journeys then must take a common pur-
pose,
I am likewise searching in that way
Which leads to Him. The star, of which I spoke,
Is heaven's sign which God will make apparent
When the time has come. Like you, I am
A king, but one of earth, so let us go
Together through this land.
THIRD KING.
Through this land?
I fear me that were not so easy. This
Is Herod's land. I think it better far
That we should gain permission from this king
Before we trespass farther in his realm.
We may have far to go before we find
This Child. The hovering star has likewise been
Foretold to us. It is the sign we seek.
SECOND KING.
Even in my country have we heard
The same. The warning which we know tells of
A mighty brilliance, how at night the sky
Shall be the equal of the day. The star
Shall shine so brightly that a path of light
Will lead all pilgrims to the shrine which is
His natal place.
FIRST KING.
Then it is the same.
THIRD KING.
Now let us go, rejoicing as we wend.
It is not far from here that Herod holds
His court, within a city which is called
Jerusalem.
[*Start forward but stop as light from star
bursts upon them*]
FIRST KING [*kneeling*].
This light!

SECOND KING [*crouches forward peering at
star*].
The star!
THIRD KING [*looking upward*].
Amen!
[CHORUS]
[*Lights dim out*]
[*After* CHORUS, *lights come up in center
panel*]

SCENE EIGHT

[HEROD *is sitting on his throne. His* SON
*is sitting on the steps at his feet. The
two* ADVISERS *are on either side. Two*
SOLDIERS *are on guard—one at each side
of the panel*]
HEROD.
The world is only where I choose to place
My feet. For if I touch the ground, then that
Must be the earth. So placed to hold my weight,
Which is not light, for I am mightier
Than all the gods. The one whose name is Jove
Must bow to me. Mars clanks his puny sword
And offers his salute as I pass by.
And Mercury, my messenger. Yet I
Am fleeter still than he. [*Stands*]
The stars which lie
Beyond this earth, I rule, and drive them, lag-
gards,
On their ceaseless round. And closer still
Than stars, the winds are subject unto me.
When I am calm they softly make sweet music.
But when I am angered they blow echoes
Of my rage throughout the world in order
That the people all may know and tremble.
I am he who throws the thunderbolts.
In day I use them as the terror of
My words. At night to strike the fire which is
The lightning wherefore I may see what pleases
Me. For, know you, I am Herod, King. [*Sits*]
Or in a softer humour I am beautiful
Beyond compare. I am more fair
Than gulls, and far more graceful. I am he
Who cannot be refused a boon by any
Man or lady, since I am so skilled
In manner. [*Sits forward on his throne*]
I am wise above all knowledge
In the world. The seer does not exist
Who can outwit me. If he threatens to,—
Off comes his head, and who is victor then?
A head should be close to the body for
Best thought. Since it is I who can control
The distance, it is I who can control
The thinking. [*Strokes his* SON'S *head*]
Tell us, pretty son, how it
Will be with thee when thou art king. Tell us.
HEROD'S SON.
I will be as Herod, fierce in all.
HEROD.
Aye.

HEROD'S SON.
I will wield the thunderbolts on high.
HEROD.
Aye.
HEROD'S SON.
I will make the earth to tremble when
I walk.
HEROD [sits back, well satisfied].
A pleasant thought, and one I had
Not heard before.
HEROD'S SON.
I shall strew death forever
In my path.
HEROD.
Aye, gentle son.
MESSENGER [runs on from left and kneels be-
fore HEROD].
O King.
HEROD.
Peace! We are engaged.
MESSENGER [raises one hand beseechingly].
O Herod, King.
HEROD.
Have done. We are not here to listen to
The prating of a messenger, but to
Sweet words of wisdom falling from the lips
Of my fair son.
MESSENGER [raises both arms to HEROD].
O hear me. Hear the news
That I have brought.
HEROD'S SON [springs up and comes down two
steps].
A curse upon you. Must I
Be interrupted by this noise? Ho! Guards!
Take this fellow out and flog him well.
MESSENGER [SOLDIERS step to center and each
takes one of the MESSENGER's arms, pull-
ing him to his feet].
The word I bring is not my blame. It is
The truth. If it does not contain what is
Of joy, then I am not the one to punish,
But let that be done to them who are
Responsible, to them who sent me here.
HEROD. [Son sits]
To them who sent you here? Who is this
"them"?
MESSENGER.
Three kings who wend within your realm.
HEROD.
Three kings?
MESSENGER [HEROD waves SOLDIERS to release
the MESSENGER. They go back to their
posts].
They come together, seemingly upon
Some peaceful purpose bent. And even now
They are outside the gates and ask admission
Here to speak with you, O Herod, King.
[Kneels]
HEROD [stands].
Upon some peaceful purpose? I do not
Believe this hoax. Some peaceful purpose? Pah!
I know their craftiness. They cannot sue

To Herod in this wise. Guards! Have them
bound!
FIRST ADVISER [taking a step toward HEROD].
Illustrious, great Herod, we admire
The wisdom of your orders. We are lowly
Men and therefore are our thoughts of little
Consequence.
HEROD [sits].
Your speech is true. Say on.
SECOND ADVISER.
O Herod, we had thought in our small way
That in the workings of your mind, your
thoughts
Had been so great that easily could one
So small be overlooked.
HEROD.
'Tis true. It might.
FIRST ADVISER.
Then hear us. Had you not perceived that it
Were better first to greet these kings on
friendly
Terms and learn the purpose of their journey?
HEROD.
True, I had some urge to do this thing,
But thought the plan too lacking in its show
Of kingly power. But since you, as lowly
Men, have garnered this small chaff that win-
nowed
From the working of my brain, and moulding
It have set it up as mine, I do
Perceive some virtue in the scheme. [Stands]
Guards! Show
These strangers here, and see that they are well
Convinced of friendliness, else it were hard
With you. [SOLDIERS and MESSENGER exeunt
left]
And all you others here, see that
There is some semblance hereabouts of peace.
[SOLDIERS enter escorting the THREE
KINGS. They take the KINGS to the
center]
FIRST KING.
God save you, sir, in His fair name.
HEROD.
I save
You in the name of Herod.
OMNES SED REGES [bowing].
Herod, King.
HEROD [sits].
What seek ye, pray, within my realm?
SECOND KING.
We ask
Permission to perform a pilgrimage
Which leads us through your land. Perhaps the
end
May be in your domain.
HEROD.
In my domain?
Then seek no further. You behold in me
The highest power and treasure to be found.
THIRD KING.
We seek no treasure.

HEROD.

       What then is your quest?

FIRST KING.

A child.

HEROD.

     A child? Then ye are mad to search.
Why, there are children everywhere.

SECOND KING.

         But not
A Child so signed and prophesied.

HEROD.

        So signed?
I do not understand.

FIRST KING.

       It has been said
Of old, a Star would lead the pilgrims to
His place of birth. And even now, at night,
Occurs a blinding light sent downward from
A star. It is this we follow.

HEROD.

           I
Am now quite certain that these men are jesting.
I have ordered nothing in the way
Of change between the night and day. Therefore,
It is dark without and only light
Here in my presence. Why should ye hunt out
A child?

SECOND KING.

     He is no common child. He has
Been born to rule the world, both here on earth,
And also in the highest heavens, where
His throne has been prepared for Him. For He
Will be a King, the highest over all.

HEROD [rises].

King? That cannot be. Here I am king,
This jesting goes too far. Guard! Seize these men
Who prate to me of Kings. [SOLDIERS start toward KINGS]

        I who am
A King.

FIRST ADVISER.

    O Herod! King! Remember now
Thy wisdom.

HEROD.

     Guards, unhand these men.
[SOLDIERS retire to their posts]

          My friends
I know will pardon me this little pleasantry.
[Sits]
The jest is over. Until now
I thought ye lightly spoke, but when I see
That ye are serious I bid ye go
Upon thy way with Herod's blessing. Go.

FIRST KING.

We thank you for this boon. [KINGS start to exit left]

HEROD.

        Stay yet a moment

Longer. [KINGS pause]
    By your story have you roused
My interest. I would know this king, perhaps
To do him honour. If ye find him, pray
Return and here acquaint me with his whereabouts.
[KINGS exeunt left]
Now go, and may ye three attain your purpose.
[The light from the Star floods in. HEROD stands]
What is that? That light! It blinds
Me when the doors are opened. Close them and
[HEROD'S SON, frightened, clings to back of throne]
Shut out this light.
       It is unearthly.
[HEROD sits and grabs at the sleeves of the ADVISERS to pull them closer to him]
          Counsel
Me and tell me, was there such a light
At Herod's birth? [ADVISERS shake heads "No"]
       Then can it be that these
Who lately went from here spoke true? This sign
Is great and therefore it portends calamity
To all my house. The child of which
They spoke may truly be a king. [Rises quickly]
          I will
Not have it so. [Looks up]
      The Heavens do not know
That they are reckoning with Herod. I
Will see that no child that was born within
The last two years shall grow to challenge Herod
For his throne. Guards! Kill them all. [SOLDIERS exeunt left]
         There can
Not be one higher in this land than I.
For I am highest. I will always be.
I am Herod, highest, Herod, King!
[The light from the star shines in again. HEROD sinks slowly into his throne, mumbling the last words of his speech]
[Lights dim out]

NARRATOR [at right].

When they had heard the king, they departed;
  and, lo, the Star, which they saw in the
  east, went before them,
  till it came and stood over where the
  young child was.
When they saw the star they rejoiced with
  exceeding great joy. (Matthew, 2, 9–10)
[Lights up]

SCENE NINE

[The THREE KINGS enter at left and start slowly across the stage]

FIRST KING.

Let us go forward now and finish out

Our quest!

SECOND KING.

       But which way must we go?

[*The* KINGS *stop and look up*]

THIRD KING.

                 The star

Is gone!

FIRST KING.

       Where is our sign?

SECOND KING.

It shone before us as we came.

THIRD KING.

I wonder. Can it be

That Herod's blaspheming has drawn a cloud

From Heaven which will hide this light from all

Mankind?

FIRST KING.

       I think the fault is not here in

The sky, but in our hearts. If we should pray

To God our faltering sight would be returned,

For it is with our souls that we are made

To see this light.

SECOND KING.

         Thou speakest true. [SECOND KING

kneels at center with FIRST *and* THIRD

KINGS *on either side of him*]

          O God,

Who gave to us this sign, give us again

The sight to see Thy pointing star. Amen.

[*The light from the star falls on them*]

THIRD KING.

Thy earnest prayer has gained for us the star's

Return. See where it shines. [SECOND KING

rises]

             May we go forward

And not stay another time; Amen.

[*The* KINGS *start off left*]

[*ANGEL CHORUS*]

[*Lights dim out*]

NARRATOR [*at right*].

And when they were come into the house, they
    saw the young child with Mary his mother,
    and fell down, and worshipped him: and
    when they had opened their treasures, they
    presented unto him gifts; gold, and frank-
    incense, and myrrh.

And being warned of God in a dream that they
    should not return to Herod, they departed
    into their own country another way.

And, behold, the angel of the Lord appeared
    to Joseph in a dream, saying, Arise, and
    take the young child and his mother, and
    flee into Egypt, and be thou there until I
    bring thee word: for Herod will seek the
    young child to destroy him. (Matthew, 2,
    11–13)

[*Lights come up in center panel*]

SCENE TEN

[MARY, *at right, and* JOSEPH, *at left of
manger, are bending over it with their*

*hands inside it as though they were low-
ering the Child into it. The* ANGEL
CHORUS *is heard throughout this scene*]

MARY.

Blessed Saviour, pardon us, we have

No other place to be Thy cradle but

This manger. It is Thy first bed and it

Is lowly. Still Thy presence makes it light

And bounds it with a glory far above

All earthly splendours. Thou art God in man.

So little, yet so great. So lowly as

To be a child to humble people, yet

So high Thou art a King of all. So little

As to be in this small manger, yet

So great Thou art a blessing to the world.

JOSEPH.

Though I am old, my eyes are gladdened by

Thy sight. My life is nearly over, still

I do not look to Thee to do again

What I have done. Thou art so young and
    being

So, are a Beginning! I am old

And am a finishing of all the ages

Past. The light that Heaven sends us from

This star shall mark the dawn of day which
    shall

Be everlasting. Even as the dark

Which was before the star, shall be the world's

Last night. So goes the old before the new.

[*The* ANGEL CHORUS *becomes louder*]

[*The* THREE SHEPHERDS *enter slowly from
left and make their way toward the
center panel*]

FIRST SHEPHERD.

Peace, Brothers, Peace. Here is the place

The star shines brightest. This must be the
    house.

A lowly stable. Can this be our Lord's

First earthly home? Let us approach and seek

The child within.

SECOND SHEPHERD.

           God's blessing rest on all

Within this house.

THIRD SHEPHERD.

It is the Lord. All hail! [*The* SHEPHERDS *enter
the panel, the* FIRST SHEPHERD *at center,
the* SECOND SHEPHERD *at left center, and the*
THIRD SHEPHERD *at right center*]

FIRST SHEPHERD [*kneels at center.* MARY *and*
JOSEPH *ascend a step at each side of the
manger and stand with clasped hands facing the manger and each other*].

Since I am but a simple shepherd, I

Look higher unto Thee than other men

Of gentler birth. Still I may look without

Offending Thee, and therein lies Thy greatest

Virtue. Thou art to all men a blessing!

They will hail Thee! I am poor, but I

Have brought a gift, however small. It is

A little bell. Its tinkling has till now

Made known the wanderings of each new born
    lamb.

But Thou art like unto a Lamb of God,—
So take it. It may show the world the way
To Thee.
> [*Rises, approaches the manger and lays
> his gift upon it and returns to his kneel-
> ing position. During this the music swells
> and subsides before* SECOND SHEPHERD'S
> *speech*]

SECOND SHEPHERD [*kneels at left.* THIRD SHEP-
HERD *kneels at right*].
Great Son, that shall save both the sea
And land, look down on me with favour. I
Am one who, like to Thee, am shepherd to
A flock. The charge Thou hast is mightier.
Thy flock shall be of men. But they will follow
Thee, and Thine will be the keeping of
Their paths in righteousness. And for Thy
office
I have brought a symbol. Here are acorns
Held upon a cord. They stand for future
Mightiness. For Thou art like them. From
These seeds will spring the strength which is
the oak.
Even as great power will spring from Thee.
> [*Rises. Places his gift on the manger and
> returns to kneeling position. Again the
> music swells and subsides*]

THIRD SHEPHERD.
Now look on me, my Lord, nor think me laggard
That I am the last one. Awed by what
I think the future holds for Thee I have
Till now remained as one apart. Think not
That I begrudge the praise the others here
Have given Thee. No. That is Thine. But I
Was wondering if Thy toil would be so effort-
less.
Such mighty things as Thou wilt do
Are more than even God could do without
A pause. So for that purpose I have brought
A horn. Its depth will hold cool waters when
Thou art athirst. Pray take it for the time
When Thou art weary. It will come too soon!
> [*Rises. Places his gift on the manger and
> returns to kneeling position. Music as
> before. Then the* THREE KINGS *enter
> right and come slowly to center*]

FIRST KING.
The path of light which we have followed seems
To make an ending hereabouts. It must
Be we approach the presence of our Lord.
SECOND KING.
The very air is charged with holiness
I think that we have found our journey's end.
What joy to be at last within the realm
Of our fair Saviour. We must lose no time.
THIRD KING.
But hereabouts are lowly houses. Can
It be that we will find our Saviour here?
FIRST KING.
The King we seek is not an earthly King.
His needs are not to have a court and rule
With all the trappings of a palace. He

It is who has his Kingdom everywhere.
He rules from hovel or from field and holds
His mighty sway o'er all, while we, with all
The pomp which makes us kings, can only hope
To do His bidding well.
SECOND KING.
> Is not the light
From yonder stable strong as though it did
Reflect the shining of the star? The meeting
Of these lights, the one from Heaven and
The other seemingly from here on earth,
Is as a sign to show to us that here
The power of sky and earth are met. It is
A God in Man!
THIRD KING.
> Then it is He! Come, let
Us go and worship Him!
> [*The* KINGS *go up to the panel. The
> SHEPHERDS stand—the* FIRST *and* THIRD
> *on the right; the* SECOND *on the left*]

FIRST KING.
Eternal blessings be to those within
This house.
JOSEPH [*coming down-stage center and ad-
dressing the* KINGS].
> Whom seek ye? This is but a lowly
Place, and by your habits, ye are kings.
SECOND KING.
We seek One higher still, and come as pilgrims
Who had hoped to find a place to worship
Here.
MARY. [*ascending the steps and standing up-
stage of the manger facing forward*]
> Sir kings, ye travel not in vain!
As ye have sought, here may ye find! Your
journeying
Has brought you to the highest Lord
On earth, as was foretold. [*Kneels*]
THIRD KING [JOSEPH *goes to the left where he
stands up-stage of the* SECOND SHEPHERD]
> Our solace here
Is found, as we had prayed. Our quest is here.
FIRST KING [*The* KINGS *kneel, the* FIRST KING
at center, the SECOND KING *at left center,
and the* THIRD KING *at right center*].
Hail, fairest One, of field or city, hail!
I have traveled far to look on Thee.
And seeing, I could wish that Thou wouldst
look
On me, and let Thy blessing fall on me.
The power I have here on earth is small—
But it is Thine, and to that end I bring
Thee gold. It is expression of my greatest
Privilege. I give it Thee. For, like
Thee, it is pure and carries in its gleam
A wealth of mightiness. Remember me.
> [*Rises and places his gift upon the manger
> and returns to kneeling position. Music
> for each* KING *as for the* SHEPHERDS]

SECOND KING.
Hail, thou Flower, that will never fade.
Hail, Son, whom God hath sent to save us from

All sin. I bid Thee hail, Thou God in Man!
And since Thou has descended, I bring Thee
Frankincense. It is sweet and like to Thee!
Its vapours are forever rising even
As Thy way is ever upward toward
Thy Father who is Heaven's king. Amen.

[*Rises. Places his gift on the manger and
returns to kneeling position*]

THIRD KING.

O Leader of a world which shall be henceforth
Saved. O Saviour of all men. All hail.
I dedicate my heart to Thee. This throbbing
Vessel into which at divers times
I have poured tinctures such as hate, ingratitude
And woe, is now full of a newer
Essence which is made of love and pity.
Both for Thee. Since Thou hast come among
Us as a man, and being born, so surely
Must Thy body die. And to that end
I bring Thee myrrh for burial. Amen.

[*Rises. Places gift and returns to his place
at right center. The* FIRST *and* SECOND
KINGS *rise. The music swells and sub-
sides*]

JOSEPH [*goes up to left of the manger*].

Ye Shepherds, ye who come to praise the Lord,
Pray come you near and make obeisance.
Here may worship everyone.

FIRST SHEPHERD.

            With Kings?

FIRST KING.

Aye, even so. Before our Lord are all
Men equal. Let us kneel together and
Rejoice!

[SHEPHERDS *and* KINGS *kneel—*FIRST KING
at left center; the FIRST SHEPHERD *at
right center, kneel upstage by the manger.
The* THIRD *and* SECOND SHEPHERDS *and
the* THIRD *and* SECOND KINGS *kneel
downstage, in this order, from right to
left*]

MARY [*coming down to the step at the right
of the manger, opposite* JOSEPH].

My Son, my Lord, the joy which thou
Hast brought to these shall be eternally
Thy gift to us. Thou gentle child!

ANGEL [*appears at center above the manger.
The grouping should be triangular*].

            Hail, Kings!

Be much intent on what I say! Return
Ye not to Herod! He means malice toward
Thee. Go back to thy realms another way.
Hark, Mary, Joseph! I am sent to thee
To tell thee Herod seeks to harm the Child.
Herod fears this little King! Take Him
And go to Egypt! There await the word
I bring to thee from God. Hear Gabriel!
Hail, thou Handmaid of Heaven high, hail
Thou that are highly favoured, hail! Blessed
Art thou among all women! Hail to thee!

[*The* ANGEL CHORUS *attains a crescendo,
the scene dims out, and the play ends*]

THE SUMMONING OF EVERYMAN

An Adapted Version from the Old Morality Play

By JOHN F. BAIRD

CHARACTERS

MESSENGER
THE VOICE OF GOD
DEATH
DECEIT
COWARDICE
FELLOW
EVERYMAN
CONSCIENCE
COUSIN
KINDRED
CONCEIT
MALICE
FAITH
EVIL
SERVANT
GOODS
GOOD DEEDS
KNOWLEDGE
CONFESSION
DISCRETION
BEAUTY
FIVE WITS
STRENGTH

The musical setting, costume and production notes may be had by addressing the author in care of the publisher.

THE SUMMONING OF EVERYMAN

The setting is a simple arrangement of levels. At centre of the unit which contains the levels, there should be a flight of six steps. On each side of this there need be only four steps. These steps rise toward up-stage. At the top of the center steps there should be a platform, and from this there should be an up-stage set of steps leading down and out of sight of the audience. This whole unit should be set with its down-stage edge about six feet from, and parallel to, the footlights. It should be surrounded on three sides by a black cyclorama of velvet or velours, or any material which reflects very little light. Directly up-stage at center may be a Gothic arched opening which is covered with paraffined muslin or tracing linen. Upon this, from the back, may be projected abstract forms and colours to form backgrounds for the various characters and scenes, and to heighten the emotional content. Neither the cyclorama nor the Gothic arch with its attendant projections need be used if the play is to be staged in a church; the steps which lead up to the altar would be sufficient.

Before the play itself opens there is a five- or six-minute musical prelude, preferably organ.

MESSENGER [*the* MESSENGER *is discovered in a spot, or comes out from between the curtains. He refers to a scroll and reads the passages inclosed in quotations. The prelude music softens as the light comes up*].
I pray you give your audience and hear
This matter reverently. By figures 'tis
A moral play. "The Summoning of Everyman"
It is, and of our lives it shows
Our endings and how transitory we be.
All this is wondrous precious. The intent
Is gracious and is sweet to bear away.
The story says, "Man in the beginning,"
Look you well and take good heed, "Ye think
In the beginning sin is full sweet," but
The end, 'twill cause thy soul to weep, "The body
Ends in clay." Here shall you see how Fellow,
Beauty, Pleasure, Jollity, and Strength
Will fade as doth the flower in May. And ye
Shall hear how Heaven's King calls Everyman
To fearful reckoning. Give audience,
And hear what He doth say.
[*The light fades and the* MESSENGER *exits in darkness*]
GOD [*a white spot slowly forms high in the*

background, *and after a slight pause* GOD *speaks. Only his voice is heard; the character is not seen*].
I see here in my majesty that all
The creatures in the world unmindful are,
And Living without dread in a prosperity
That worldly is. Their spirits are
So blind that, drowned in sin, they know me not
To be their God. Their minds all turn to riches.
To give them life I suffered to be dead.
I bathed their feet, and in return, upon
My head was set a crown of thorns. And I
Could do no more. But all forsake me now.
And therefore I will have a reckoning
From these, for if I leave the people thus
Alone they will become much worse than beasts
And out of envy one devour the other.
My hope had been for every man that in
My glory each should make his mansion. They
Alone elected, they alone have failed.
Their pleasure and their very beings I
Have lent to them. They thank me not. And I
Have offered them my mercy. There be few
That ask it. They are so encumbered with
Their gold that I must needs do justice unto
Them. On every man who lives and knows
Not fear. Where art thou, Death, thou mighty Messenger?
DEATH [*a spot from directly overhead dims up on* DEATH *as he slowly rises from a crouching to a kneeling position*].
Almighty God, at Thy commandment
I am here.
GOD.   Go thou to Everyman,
And tell him, in my name, that he must make
A pilgrimage. There is no escape.
He must bring a reckoning without
Delay or tarrying.
DEATH [*stands slowly*].
                Lord, I will in
The world outsearch both great and small, and cruelly
Come to him. Everyman will I
Beset, who lives, obeying not thy laws.
If he loves riches I will strike him with
My dart. Except that he hath alms to be
His friend, in Hell will he dwell. World without end.
[DEATH *starts to raise his arms and go up on his toes. The light fades while he is still in motion. The effect is one of continuous movement upward*]
DECEIT [DECEIT *and* COWARDICE *are discov-*

ered together as the lights come up. DE-
CEIT *is sitting on the second step at right
centre. The music stops*].

'Tis as I say, and have we, then, so hard
A life, good Cowardice?

COWARDICE [*is crouching and sitting on the
first step at the right of* DECEIT].

Deceit, I know
Not.

DECEIT. I will tell thee. No. We may appear
In mean attire, but that is to our gain.
The very lowness of our station profits
Us. When those on whom we prey look down
On us, marry, let them look a long
Way down. They think themselves the higher
for
The distance. When we flatter them they puff
Themselves like pigeons and, like pigeons, fly,
In their own minds, to higher perches where
They sit and preen their virtues until one
Appears who knows their weakness. Then the
fall
Occurs, and down they come. But we are
always
There to puff them up again with words.
And they go up again, and fall again.

COWARDICE. But even those who fall the lowest browbeat
Me.

DECEIT. Thy reason is beyond repair.
I make it plain. When one is fallen, first,
He looks about to find another lower.
He sees thee. He thanks God there are others
Still who must look up to him. Then, since
He must in some way prove superiority,
Thou it is who art belaboured.
And, since he is always victor over
Thee, his courage doth return, and who
Would not pay handsomely for that?

COWARDICE.   I would.

DECEIT. Aye, By my troth, I knew that thou
wouldst understand.
Thou art a faithful partner.

COWARDICE.   But
When I have drawn their blows on me . . .

DECEIT [*pantomimes the fight as he de-
scribes it*].

What blows?
I mentioned naught of fighting with a sword,
Or hand, or bludgeon. He belabours thee
With words, and roars fiercely, makes wide
gestures,
Swears by all the gods, and drags his honour
Out to be a shield whereon each blow
That falls is sacrilege. Noise? Aye. But
harmless.
And his movements, great enough to fight
An army. Aye. But forceless, counterfeit.
When thou hast done thy part and yielded up
The field to him, I come. I am at once
His cup and laurel bearer. He drinks deep,
And finds it sweet. 'Tis flattery. Then I place

The wreath of laurel on his head. He,
Thinking it a sign of victory, struts
And prances to the music I compose
With words. He thinks he is a hero, but
The woven wreath that I placed on his head,
I placed askew, which makes him look like
what
He is. A fool.

COWARDICE. Then I will not take hurt?

DECEIT. No more than I. But soft,
[*Rises and looks off left*]
is not the one
Approaching yonder Everyman? And with
Him Fellow. Look that thou art in accord
With what I say and we will earn some gold.

COWARDICE [*rises*].
Some gold? I could entreat for some of that.
[*Looks off left*]
But there is still a third who comes with
them,
And follows close to Everyman. The one
Who looks to be his shadow.
[*Points off left*]
There.

DECEIT.   I see
The one you mean. Aye. That is Conscience. He
Is ever at the side of Everyman.
[DECEIT *and* COWARDICE *give way to right
stage*]

EVERYMAN [FELLOW *enters first.* EVERYMAN
enters, closely followed by CONSCIENCE].
And tell me, Fellow, didst thou note how, when
The hoods were taken from the falcons, mine
Was swiftest in ascent, and flew the high-
est?

FELLOW [*stops at centre and turns left to
address* EVERYMAN].
Aye. But didst thou note that I released
The bird a moment in advance of all
The others there?

CONSCIENCE [*speaks into* EVERYMAN'S *ear
from over his left shoulder*].
And cried out, "Fraud,"
because
Ye thought that thou hadst seen another do
The same.

EVERYMAN [*pays no attention to* CON-
SCIENCE].
That was well done, good Fellow, but
In spite of all thy artifice, my bird
Was quickest to the kill, and swooping down
Upon his prey, was fiercest.

FELLOW.   Aye. A worthy
Bird, and owned by one who also is
The worthiest.

DECEIT.   This Fellow poaches on
Our ground. We must be quick or lose the game
To him.
[DECEIT, *followed by* COWARDICE, *comes
to the right of* FELLOW *and speaks to*
EVERYMAN]
God save you, sir.

EVERYMAN [*is facing forward; does not see* DECEIT*].*

                Did someone speak?

DECEIT. Aye, sir. I said, "God save you."

COWARDICE   Aye, sir, aye.

EVERYMAN [*looks at* DECEIT *and* COW-ARDICE].

Who are these beggars?

FELLOW.   Go your ways. Begone!

DECEIT. We ask no alms. We would admire the one

Who owns the bird which won to-day.

COWARDICE.   Aye, sir.

EVERYMAN [*crosses* FELLOW *to* DECEIT].

You saw my hawk? What thought you of it, pray?

DECEIT. 'Twas sheerest beauty, sir.

COWARDICE.   Aye, sir.

EVERYMAN.   Now here,

Good Fellow, is a man who knows a bird. Speak further.

CONSCIENCE [*crosses* FELLOW *to* EVERYMAN].

        This is flattery, Everyman.

DECEIT. When I first saw the falcon, hooded and

At rest, my thought was, "This bird has some strength.

It has much beauty, but in flight it may

Be clumsy."

COWARDICE. Aye, sir. . . .

    [DECEIT *nudges* COWARDICE *to make him correct his remark*]

                Nay, sir.

DECEIT.   When it darted

Upward, I thought, "There is magic."

EVERYMAN.   There.

Said I not the man was sane in judgement

Of such things?

FELLOW [*crosses* CONSCIENCE *to* EVERYMAN].

      But dost thou not forget

Thy purpose? We came here to find if any

In this market place had aught that thou

Wouldst buy.

EVERYMAN. Good Fellow, thou art right. My thoughts

Were led astray in talking to these men.

But where are they, these merchants? Know they not

That Everyman would trade with them?

FELLOW.   'Tis late.

Perhaps their day is finished.

EVERYMAN.   What? Then bring

Them back. Good Fellow, do you go and fetch

Them here.

FELLOW.   Most gladly, Everyman. For be

It never said that thou hast not a friend

In me.

EVERYMAN. And see they bring their richest treasures.

I would not buy trash.

FELLOW.   Rely on me.

I know thy taste. A moment's time and I

Will have them here.

    [FELLOW *exits right*]

EVERYMAN [*crosses* CONSCIENCE *to the right to look after* FELLOW].

         A faithful friend, and one

Who does my bidding well and honestly.

CONSCIENCE [*steps right to* EVERYMAN *and speaks over his right shoulder*].

And one who hopes to gain a gift thereby.

DECEIT [DECEIT *and* COWARDICE *step toward* EVERYMAN].

An't please you, sir, the merchants have not gone

Because the hour is late.

    [EVERYMAN *turns right to face* DECEIT]

COWARDICE.   Nay, sir.

DECEIT.   They went

To bolster up their wares with better things.

They said among themselves, "If Everyman

Is come to honour us by choosing of

Our stock, then what we show must be the best."

COWARDICE. Aye, sir.

EVERYMAN [*crosses to* DECEIT *at centre*].

        But we had only now decided

To come here.

DECEIT.   These merchants, sir, divine

Each wish of one of such importance as

Yourself.

COWARDICE. Aye, sir.

DECEIT.   They said among themselves,

"Is he a novice?"

COWARDICE.   Aye, sir.

EVERYMAN.   Am I then?

COWARDICE. Aye, sir.

EVERYMAN.   I like not this fellow's views.

DECEIT [*steps back upstage and to the right of* COWARDICE *whom he pushes a little toward* EVERYMAN *as he speaks*].

Good sir, think not upon his prating. He

Is far beneath your notice.

EVERYMAN.   Even so,

I do not gather insults from so low

A plane. Nor from any man. I

Am not so lightly taken by far greater

Men, much less this varlet here. A "novice."

I? You speak to Everyman, whose shrewd-ness

Is well known in all the markets in

The world. A "novice."

    [*Turns left toward* CONSCIENCE]

COWARDICE.   Aye, sir.

EVERYMAN [*wheels back on* COWARDICE *with renewed vigour*].

           Does the fellow

Still persist? I call on God to witness

How I am assaulted.

CONSCIENCE.   Vanity.

EVERYMAN. A "novice." I have power and wealth. If I

Should bring my might to bear on you for know

You I am influential, "novice," just

The sound of that small word would bring you
    quaking
To your knees.
    FELLOW [*enters from left followed by*
    COUSIN, *then* KINDRED].
                    I have told these merchants,
Everyman, and they are coming here
At once.
    [FELLOW *comes to the right of* EVERYMAN.
    COUSIN *and* KINDRED *go to the right of*
    DECEIT]
    But what is this? Hath any done
Thee wrong? Then it is well that I have
    brought
Thy kinsmen here.
    EVERYMAN.   I thank thee, Fellow.
    Too,
I thank thee, Cousin, and good Kindred. Here
Is one who doubts my means, and further slurs
My honour. But I have vanquished him, and
    that
Alone. It was a struggle.
    CONSCIENCE.   Had it been
A graver battle, not a sham, wherein
Thy life had been at stake, and thou hadst
    lost.
Everyman, look in thy soul, art thou
Prepared for such a time?
    EVERYMAN.   Good Conscience, goad
Me not. Good Fellow, give these men some gold
And say another time they may not come
So easy off.
    FELLOW. Right gladly, Everyman.
    [FELLOW, COWARDICE, DECEIT, COUSIN,
    and KINDRED *go off right*]
    EVERYMAN. Did not my Conscience say,
    "Thy soul?" My soul.
And is it ready for the time when I
Must leave this world? Such time is too far
    hence.
I must enjoy what I have here and now,
There still will be a time for thinking of
This soul.
    [*Goes up centre to call*]
            Where are these merchants? Fellow,
    Kindred,
Cousin! Where are ye? Come join me here.
    FELLOW [FELLOW, COUSIN, KINDRED, *and*
    CONCEIT *enter from right and go to* EVERY-
    MAN].
Aye, Everyman, we had but gone to do.
Thy bidding, and to pay those men who lately
Had disturbed thee here.
    COUSIN.   We made them understand
With whom they dealt.
    EVERYMAN [*comes downstage and the others*
    follow him. KINDRED, COUSIN, *and* CON-
    SCIENCE *come down at* EVERYMAN'S *left,*
    and FELLOW *and* CONCEIT *are at his right*].
            Where are these merchants?
    [*Stops*]
Just now, while ye left me, was my mind

Consumed with wretched thoughts, unseemly
    for
A man of my estate. Such thoughts that men
Of my age should not give much contemplation.
We are young. . . . Soft. . . . When I look
    at ye,
Ye all seem older. Am I, too . . . ?
    KINDRED.   Such humours
Must not cloud thy mind when there is trade
And sport in view.
    [MALICE *enters down right,* FAITH *down*
    left, and EVIL *enters from left and goes*
    up-stage centre]
                Come, Everyman, awaken.
Here are merchants with their wares.
    EVERYMAN.   Enough!
    [*Holds out a purse in front of him. All*
    the others except CONSCIENCE'S *grab at it.*
    Then, seeing EVERYMAN'S *questioning*
    look and realizing that they have forgot-
    ten themselves, they try to give it to
    each other and wander up-stage squab-
    bling over it. This leaves EVERYMAN *and*
    CONSCIENCE *down-stage centre*]
Here, take this gold and buy thyselves some
    trinkets
In the name of revelry.
    [*Followed by* CONSCIENCE, *crosses to*
    right to address MALICE *who is down*
    right]
                    What are
You called?
    MALICE. My name is Malice, and I barter
Friendship.
    [*Shows what looks to be a lump of gold,*
    the outer covering of which comes off
    and discloses a dirty green-grey mass]
                Here is some. 'Tis very like
To gold, and worth much more. The Friend-
    ship that
I offer here is tarnished, but some use
Will bring its brilliance back again.
    EVERYMAN.   I do
Not buy what has been damaged.
    [*Reaches for it and the cover comes off*
    in his hand]
                        Hold! The
    outer
Cover is but thin veneer. It comes
Apart and shows a snake-like substance here
    beneath.
I want none of it.
    [*Throws the cover at* MALICE]
                Go!
    [MALICE *exits right*]
    CONSCIENCE [*as* EVERYMAN *steps back*
    CONSCIENCE *speaks over his left shoulder*].
                    So always is
A human deed which must be bought with gold.
    EVERYMAN [*sees, and crosses left to* FAITH
    who is down left].
But what is offered here for sale? And what

May be your name?

FAITH. I am called Faith.

I have the Pearl of Virtue, Everyman.

[*Holds the pearl out for inspection*]

EVERYMAN. Of Virtue? Name its price.

FAITH. There is no price.

Thou hast but to stretch forth thy hand and take

It. Having gained it, thou must hold it fast.

CONSCIENCE [*speaks over* EVERYMAN'S *right shoulder*].

Pray take it, Everyman.

EVERYMAN. A thing so cheap

Must be of little worth. Away with pearls.

[*Steps back two or three steps, crossing* CONSCIENCE *and stopping at right centre*].

They are too flaccid and too small,

[FAITH *exits left*]

and none

Contains a colour bright enough to bring

Me pleasure.

[EVERYMAN *is still facing left*]

EVIL [*has been hidden up-stage by the group composed of* FELLOW, COUSIN, KINDRED, *and* CONCEIT. *Now he comes down centre and directly in back of* EVERYMAN].

If ye buy for colour and

For size, I have a stone to please thee, Everyman.

EVERYMAN [*merely glances over his right shoulder*].

Its name?

EVIL. It is the

[*He has had his cloak pulled closely about him, discloses a large red stone in his right hand*]

Stone of Folly.

EVERYMAN [*turns, is startled, and a little awed by the brilliance of the stone*].

Aye. This stone hath some life. But why

Are thy hands red?

EVIL. The colour doth infect

The one who owns it.

[*Reassures* EVERYMAN *with a gesture of his left hand*]

Pleasantly.

FELLOW [*comes down to the right of* EVIL; COUSIN *comes down to the right of* FELLOW; CONCEIT *to the right of* COUSIN. KINDRED *comes down left of* EVERYMAN; CONSCIENCE *to down left of* KINDRED. *All except* CONSCIENCE *have hands out toward stone*].

That

Stone must I have.

KINDRED. Await thy turn. The stone

Shall first be mine.

COUSIN. No, mine, for I would have it.

CONCEIT. Nay, The stone is much too great to be

In any hands but mine.

EVIL [*holds up his left hand to silence the fight*].

Peace, gentle sirs.

I will explain the stone. The weight is strong

Enough

[*Stoops forward and thrusts the stone out in front of him so it nearly touches the floor. All the others, except* CONSCIENCE, *crouch forward and, with extended arms, nearly succeed in touching the stone*]

to drag ye down and leave ye there

While falsely are your spirits

[*Stands quickly erect and holds the stone over his head. The hands still follow it*]

lifted up.

But being up, then down, is not monotonous.

This stone will lead a merry chase

[*Turns quickly and runs up to the top of the steps centre*]

For ye.

[*Turns quickly, facing forward, holding out the stone*]

What am I paid for it?

[*The others all follow to form a triangular grouping with* EVIL *at the top,* EVERYMAN *down left of* EVIL, KINDRED *down left of* EVERYMAN, CONSCIENCE *down left of* KINDRED, FELLOW *down right of* EVIL, COUSIN *down right of* FELLOW, *and* CONCEIT *down right of* COUSIN. *All except* CONSCIENCE *are reaching for the stone*]

CONCEIT. I am

Conceit. I give the privilege of my ownership.

EVIL. Too small by far. What higher price

Is offered?

COUSIN. I would give my raiment.

EVIL. Fool!

KINDRED. I will give my lands.

EVIL. Bid higher.

FELLOW. I

Will give thee ill-got gold.

EVIL. More.

EVERYMAN. I would give

[*Steps directly in front of* EVIL *and stretches his right hand upward*]

My soul

for . . .

[DEATH *appears. He comes up from in back of* EVIL *who immediately goes down and to the left, leaving* EVERYMAN *to throw up his other arm in a protective gesture as he faces* DEATH. *At the same time a path of light appears which has its up-stage end on* DEATH *and its down-stage end nearly at the edge of the stage. The general scene lighting dims down three-quarters*]

DEATH.

Everyman! Hast thou forgot thy God?

EVERYMAN.
Why askest thou,
 [*Bends slightly forward and turns to face down stage*]
    and by what right?
DEATH. Yea, I will show thee, Everyman, how I
Am sent in haste to thee from God out of
His majesty.
EVERYMAN [*comes down two steps*].
       Sent to me?
DEATH.   Sent
To thee.
EVERYMAN [*comes down two steps*].
     What desireth God of me?
DEATH. That thou must take a journey, long, and bring
Thy book of count with thee, for thou shalt not
Return. And look that thou be sure of all
Thy reckoning. 'Fore God thou shalt appear
And show thy every deed, for He would know
How thou hast spent thy life, and in what wise
Thou thinkst to enter paradise.
EVERYMAN.   But full
 [*Is all the way down the steps*]
Unready am I now to give such count.
 [*Turns to look up at* DEATH]
Who art thou?
DEATH. I am Death!
 [*All except* EVERYMAN *react away from* DEATH *without, however, moving from their places*]
      And it is God's
Command that every head to me is bent.
 [*All except* DEATH *and* EVERYMAN *leave hurriedly. All the lights, except the spotlight which throws the path, black out*]
EVERYMAN [*there is a pause during which* EVERYMAN *looks after the departing people. Then he turns slowly to* DEATH].
Oh, Death thou comest when I had thee least
In mind.
 [*Pleads, facing directly up-stage toward* DEATH]
   It lieth in thy power to intercede
For me. My goods I give thee, if
Ye will be kind, yea, many thousand crowns
I give to thee, if thou wilt but defer
This matter till another day.
DEATH.   Nay, Everyman,
 [EVERYMAN *cringes and turns slightly from* DEATH]
Not as you say. No gold nor silver,
Money's ring, nor pomp, nor influence,
A king could not from me my purpose take.
Come, you cannot stay.
EVERYMAN [*turns completely down-stage and kneels with clasped hands*].
     Oh, gracious God,
In heaven high, upon this awful road
May I not have some fellowman, to go
To thy high throne that I may show how, with

My life . . .
DEATH. Thy life, thou ownst it not. Why, hadst
Thou thought that these belonged to thee?
 [EVERYMAN *rises slowly*]
        Thy life,
Thy goods, thy everything . . . ?
EVERYMAN [*turns half-way up-stage*].
       So I had thought,
 [*Goes up on the second step, still only half facing* DEATH]
That I should bring all these 'fore God, so He
Might see . . .
DEATH. Nay, they were but lent to thee.
   [EVERYMAN *faces* DEATH]
As soon as thou art gone some other one
Awhile will have them, then go on, as I
Command.
EVERYMAN [*turns down-stage looking from side to side*].
   Oh, wretched, wretched, whither shall
I run or how escape this endless sorrow?
 [*Goes up several steps toward* DEATH]
Gentle Death, spare me until tomorrow
That I may . . .
DEATH.   Nay, thereto I will not
Consent. Nor to no man to whom this life
Is lent. For, know you, that this is the day
Which no man living 'scapes away.
 [DEATH *disappears during a black out*]
EVERYMAN [*sinks to a step facing right where he is lighted by a small spot*].
        And now
He's gone. The terrible one has made this day
A sombre night. Where shall I turn? But I
Have lived to such an end that all my works
Should speak for me. But what are they? A man
Like me? I'm rich. I do no wrong. But what
Of good?
    [*Stands*]
  I must not think this way.
 [*Sees* FELLOW *at right and takes a step toward him. The general stage lights come up*]
        Fellow,
Come make me merry.
FELLOW [*enters at right and goes to* EVERYMAN].
     Everyman, by this day
Why lookst thou piteously? If aught be wrong
I pray thee say.
 [*Looks around to make sure that* DEATH *has gone*]
     Thy visitor is gone?
EVERYMAN [*looks back up at the place where* DEATH *disappeared*].
But leaving me in danger still, my friend.
FELLOW [*since* EVERYMAN'S *back is toward him* FELLOW *sticks his tongue in his cheek and decides to make himself invaluable*].
My true friend, show to me thy mind, for I

Will not forsake thee till thy life doth end.
And, as good company, I am thy friend.
EVERYMAN [*turns to* FELLOW *and puts a hand upon his shoulder*].
That was spoken well, and lovingly.
FELLOW [*backs away as though insulted by* EVERYMAN'S *speech, and to make room for his heroic gestures.* EVERYMAN *at first thinks he is being deserted but as* FELLOW *warms to his task* EVERYMAN'S *face lights up again*].
Sir, I must know thy heaviness, I cannot
Stand and see thee in distress. If anyone
Has wronged you, sir, ye shall revengéd
Be. Though I am slain upon the ground,
For thee.
EVERYMAN. I thank thee, Fellowship, indeed.
FELLOW. Pah, thy thanks, they are no more to me, than is
The waving of a tree.
EVERYMAN [*comes down from the steps*].
But still I thank
Thee, Fellowship, for ten times sorrier
The day that thou shouldst fail to comfort me.
FELLOW. I say as I will do in deed.
EVERYMAN. Aye, then
Thou art a friend, and I have found thee true
Before.
FELLOW. So shall ye evermore. In faith
If you should go to Hell, then I would not
Forsake thee by the way.
EVERYMAN. Ye speak, and I
Believe thee well. Then I will show thee how
It is.
[*Sits on the second step and* FELLOW *stands looking down at him*]
A journey I am told to take,
A long way, hard and dangerous, to give
A straight account without delay before
Our Lord Almighty's throne, wherefore I pray
Thee, bear me company, as ye have promised,
On this journey.
FELLOW [*backs away*].
This is serious
Indeed. A promise is a duty, but
If I should take this voyage now, I know it well,
'Twill bring me pain. So strongly has thy story
Lain against my fear . . .
EVERYMAN [*rises and takes a step toward* FELLOW].
But said ye not,
If I had need . . .
FELLOW. Aye, that I did, indeed.
But as you've planned, when come we next into
This land.
EVERYMAN. Never, until the day of doom.
FELLOW [*backs a step away from* EVERYMAN].
In faith, I'll not come there.
[*Comes back to* EVERYMAN]

But who hath told
Thee this?
EVERYMAN. Death was with me here.
FELLOW. And yet
If thou wilt eat, and drink, and make good cheer
I'll not forsake thee while the day is clear.
[*Turns and gets three steps toward a hasty exit when he is stopped by* EVERYMAN'S *next speech*]
But this . . .
EVERYMAN [*takes a step toward* FELLOW].
I pray thee, pray thee, do so much
For me, and take me forward, for Saint Charity,
And comfort me until I am
Outside the town.
FELLOW. Not for a thousand crowns
[*Turns and walks half-way around* EVERYMAN *appraising him*]
Poor Everyman, farewell now at the end,
[*Crosses to exit at right, turns, tosses his last speech over his shoulder, and exits*]
And call me nevermore to be thy friend.
EVERYMAN [*goes a little toward the place where* FELLOW *made his exit*].
Good Fellow gone. Then they are right who say
That you can buy such friends when you have gold,
Such friends that drink your wine, but are not there
To light a torch and guide you through the cold
And darkness that surrounds the banquet hall.
KINDRED *and* COUSIN *enter stealthily from the left to retrieve* COUSIN'S *cloak which had been left on the steps at left centre during their hurried exit*]
And guide you through the cold, I know . . . the journey
Where shall I look, or call on whom to go . . .
[EVERYMAN *turns and discovers* KINDRED *and* COUSIN *who immediately assume servile kneeling positions*]
Why, Kinsmen, knew you of my need
That you should so return to go with me?
When you are here I do not feel alone
I should have known that you would go.
[EVERYMAN *kneels as* KINDRED *and* COUSIN *get uncertainly to their feet*]
Pray rise, or let it be that I should bend my knee
And thank thee for thy pains and company.
KINDRED [*tries to outbluster the situation*].
Here we are now at your commandment,
Cousin, pray you show us your intent
And do not spare
COUSIN [*is also helpful*].
Oh, yes, to us declare
What you would have us do, for we will live . . .

KINDRED. And eat together, by my faith, we will.

[*Approaches* EVERYMAN]

Because we are your kin you can be bold
To make of us requests and we will stay.

EVERYMAN. I do not ask for you to stay, but go
Upon a pilgrimage with me. I have
Been called to make accounting for my deeds.

COUSIN [*also approaches* EVERYMAN].

What count is this that you must give?

EVERYMAN. I must appear before the highest Judge
And use my works to argue for me there,
But if you attorneys are for me
I shall not want for better charity.

[*As* EVERYMAN *bows his head* KINDRED *and* COUSIN *exchange glances and make their decision*]

KINDRED. Go, and not return? I know that road;
I'd rather feed on bread and water for
A year than go with you. And, my account,
I have to see that it is full . . .

[*Pauses and pats his paunch*]

of wine . . .

EVERYMAN. My Cousin,

[*Stands*]

will you not accompany me?

COUSIN. No, No, No,

[*Suddenly thinks of an excuse and grabs his left foot*]

I have a cramp in my toe

KINDRED. At such a time these things are always bad.

COUSIN [*puts his foot back on the floor*].
This call of yours was a surprise?

KINDRED.   If we
Had had . . .

COUSIN.   It is too late by now, I fear

EVERYMAN [*approaches* KINDRED *and* COUSIN].
Kindred, Cousin, wilt thou go with me?

KINDRED [*backs away from* EVERYMAN].
If we had sooner known . . .

COUSIN. Yea, had we known. . . .

[KINDRED *and* COUSIN *flee in confusion. Left*]

EVERYMAN [*looks after them*].
This feignéd sympathy is not my need.
Still, Their going leaves a certain darkness.

[*Goes up to the second step at centre*]

Torches, torches. They should make more light.

[SERVANT *enters with torches. Right*]

This light is golden. It remindeth me. . . .
My Goods were better still, for if my life's
To be reviewed I shall depend upon
My Goods, since they are what I've laboured for.
I have of them such store that God must see
How diligent my life has been. That's it,

Bring forth my store of goods,

[SERVANT *exits at right*]

so I may count
And see the total mount so high that God
Himself will think me earnest in my life.

[GOODS *comes striding on from right carrying two large gold bags which he allows to drop heavily upon the stage. He is followed by the* SERVANT]

Come, bring it near, my Goods, my all.

GOODS. Everyman, to what good sport have I been called?
What would ye have, come, tell me lightly now.

EVERYMAN [*goes to* GOODS].
Oh Goods, some counsel would I have of thee.

GOODS [*puts an arm around* EVERYMAN'S *shoulders*].
Sir, if you have a trouble in this world
Pray tell me it that I may remedy . . .

EVERYMAN. It is not in this world, oh Goods, but in
The next, toward which I must in pilgrimage
Be gone, and take with me a reckoning
Of all my works, ambitions, and such things
As to my credit prove . . .

GOODS [*removes his arm from* EVERYMAN'S *shoulders.* EVERYMAN *backs away from* GOODS *and up onto the second step*].
And I should move
To go with thee. Such journeying is not
For me. Why, know you not that you yourself
Have made of me so great a thing, that I
Would be a weight and hold thee from thy goal?
Besides I am not yours, and I have heard
Through countless centuries the same plea made,
"Wilt thou go with me upon this road?"
They but mistake the shining of my substance
To be that light which is their soul's salvation.

EVERYMAN [*descends angrily to* GOODS].
False Goods, to think I treasured thee.

GOODS [*is quite indifferent*].
I know,
But from now on we'll each a different way.

EVERYMAN [*kneels to* GOODS *imploringly*].
I've loved thee much.

GOODS.   If that had not been so,
If to the poor thou hadst but thrown some part of me
I would not drag thee down as I do now.

EVERYMAN [*rises and backs away in a rage*].
Thou traitor to God thou hast caught me in thy snare.

GOODS. And did I ask for you to hold me dear?
Enough of this, I shall not tarry here,
But give myself in care of other fools
Who want me for their prey. Adieu, adieu,
Good Everyman, my blessings on thy way.

[GOODS *yawns heavily, picks up the bags*

and exits right. The Servant *follows him off*]

Everyman [*looks after* Goods].

Will no one help me on this pilgrimage?
First Fellow proved untrue and then my kin,
And now my Goods from which I'd thought that none
Could separate, has followed them.

[*Sits on the steps at right centre*]
Not one
Spoke civilly at parting. I must be weak
When such as they can overpower my every argument.
There must be something, someone who will go.
Whom have I known or what done that will
My credit swell? I think far in the past
I do remember some small good. It was,
It was . . .

[*Stands slowly*]
Good Deeds! Oh, Good Deeds,
Good Deeds, where
Art thou?

[Good Deeds *comes on at left leaning on* Knowledge's *shoulder. As soon as* Everyman *sees her, she sinks to the stage floor at left*]
If only thou wilt help me now.

Good Deeds. Here I am upon the cold harsh ground
Whereto I have been brought by thy neglect.
I cannot stir.

Everyman [*crosses to* Good Deeds].
Good Deeds, I stand in fear
For now right well thy counsel I should have.

Good Deeds. Everyman, I understand that you are summoned
Before Jerus'lem's King, and want me for
Thy company.

Everyman. Therefore I come to thee.
Good Deeds, I pray thee, wilt thou go with me?

Good Deeds. That I would, but see, I cannot stand.

Everyman. Hath something ill befallen thee?

Good Deeds. Yea, Sir.
And I may thank you for this woe. If you
Had cheered me perfectly your life's account
Would now be ready. Look, within this book
Are all the deeds and acts that do you credit.

[*Gives* Everyman *the book*]

Everyman [*falls back a step as he looks into the book*].

Oh, help me, Lord, I cannot see one letter here.

Good Deeds. Thy reckoning is poor for such a time.

Everyman. Help me, or I am forever damned.

Good Deeds. Everyman, I'm sorry of thy fall
And fain would help thee, but I cannot now.
Here is my sister, Knowledge, she will go
To help you make that dreadful reckoning.

Knowledge [*crosses to* Everyman].

I will go with thee, Poor Everyman,
And be thy guide in this thy greatest need.

Everyman. In good condition I am now in everything.
I am content. Thanks be to God.

Good Deeds. When Knowledge here hath brought thee to the place
Where thou shalt heal thee of thy sins,
Then come you with your reckoning, and your
Good Deeds will joyfully your servant be,
And stand with you before the Blessed Trinity.

Everyman [*crosses to* Good Deeds *and gives her the book*].

Good Deeds, I thank thee, now an hundred times,
Thy words have given me my courage back.

Knowledge [*crosses toward right leading* Everyman].

Now we will go together, Everyman,
To see Confession, and there be cleansed.

Everyman [*follows* Knowledge].

What joy this is, I would that we were there.
Tell me, Knowledge, where dwells this holy man?

Knowledge. Here in this house of salvation, you see,

[Confession *steps out on stage from right*]
He cometh from his place to comfort thee.
This is Confession, kneel down and mercy ask,
For he is high esteeméd by our God.

[Everyman *crosses* Knowledge *going to* Confession]

Everyman [*kneels to* Confession].

Oh, glorious fountain, that all sins doth clarify,
Wash from me the spots of vice unclean.
I come with Knowledge here to be redeemed,
So cleanse my heart with full contriteness now,
For I must go at God's command upon
A pilgrimage where I shall make account.
Oh, sweet Confession, help my Good Deeds,
That she may go and show the Lord my life . . .

Confession. Everyman, I know thy sorrow well. Because
With Knowledge thou hast come to me, thy comfort
I will be as best I can, and here
A precious jewel I will give to thee,

[*Gives a pendant jewel to* Everyman]
Called Penitance, voider of adversity.
Therewith shall your body chastened be
With abstinence and perseverance great.
And here you shall receive that scourge from me
Which is strong penance that ye must endure.
As did thy Saviour who was scourged for thee.

[*Gives the scourge to* Knowledge]
Good Knowledge, keep him in this voyage, and by
That time Good Deeds will be with thee.

Your time is going. If you would be saved,
From God seek mercy, He will grant it thee.
> [*Takes a step back and off-stage at right*]

EVERYMAN. May God be thanked for this,
his gracious work.
> [*Rises*]

Confession hath so rejoiced my heart
That any penance now will lightly fall.
Knowledge, give to me the scourge that I
May show this flesh how lowly is its place.

KNOWLEDGE. God give you time and space,
poor Everyman,
Thus I bequeath to you the scourge. Take it
> [*Gives the scourge to* EVERYMAN]

And make thy reck'ning sure before our God.

EVERYMAN [*Crosses* KNOWLEDGE *and goes to
centre*].
Now, in the Saviour's name, thou flesh, take
this.
> [*Strikes himself on the back with the
scourge*]

Because sins bodily from you have come.
And erstwhile as has been thy wont to be
So free, thou sufferest now,
> [*Again strikes himself on the back with
the scourge*]

                 and by thy pain
Do penance to our Lord, who suffered thee.

GOOD DEEDS. I thank God,
> [*Stands*]

            now that I can stand and walk
And am delivered of my weakening,
So I with Everyman may go, and tell
Of his good works before the throne of God.
> [GOOD DEEDS *crosses toward the right*]

KNOWLEDGE. Everyman, you can rejoice.
Now is your Good
Deeds whole and sound. See where she comes.

GOOD DEEDS.   Everyman,
Pilgrim, special friend,
> [*Kneels to* EVERYMAN]

            Blessed be thou,
I owe my mend to thee, and for this deed
Eternal glory is prepared for thee.
As ye have made me sound I will with thee
And bide by you in every step.

EVERYMAN.   Welcome,
My Good Deeds,
> [*Helps* GOOD DEEDS *to her feet*]

            for since I hear thy voice
I weep for very happiness and love.

KNOWLEDGE. Put on this garment wet with
all your tears,

EVERYMAN [*puts on the robe that* KNOWL-
EDGE *holds for him*].
Gentle Knowledge, what may be its name?

KNOWLEDGE. It is the robe of sorrow, and
from pain
It protects thee. Its very wearing is
Contrite, and asks forgiveness for thy sins.

EVERYMAN. Blessed be Jesus, Mary's son,
for now

I have contrition. Good Deeds, have we clear
My reckoning?

GOOD DEEDS.   God grant it that we have.

EVERYMAN. Then now I trust we need not
fear. My friends . . .
> [*Crosses to centre*]

May we go forward and not part again.

KNOWLEDGE [*follows* EVERYMAN].
Nay, Everyman, we will not leave thee now.

GOOD DEEDS [*follows* EVERYMAN].
Yet thou must take with thee three persons
more.

EVERYMAN. Who should they be?
> [*Turns toward* KNOWLEDGE *and* GOOD
DEEDS]

GOOD DEEDS.   Strength and Beauty take
With thee. Nor let Discretion bide behind.

KNOWLEDGE. Bring, too, thy Five Wits with
thee, Everyman,
For she will give good counsel on the way.

GOOD DEEDS. Be sure you have them ready
every hour.

EVERYMAN. I do not have them here.

KNOWLEDGE.   Then you must call.

EVERYMAN [*goes up to the second step at
centre*].
My friends, Discretion, Beauty, Five Wits,
Strength,
Be present here for I have need of thee.

GOOD DEEDS. Here at thy wish they all have
come, such as:

DISCRETION [*enters from right*].
Discretion.

BEAUTY [*enters from left*].
            Beauty.

FIVE WITS [*enters from right*].
               Five Wits.

STRENGTH [*enters from left*].
                 Strength.

GOOD DEEDS [*crosses to the left of* EVERY-
MAN].
                 Then come
You near and learn the length that you must
go
With Everyman upon his pilgrimage.

STRENGTH [*all come to* EVERYMAN *at centre*].
Aye, we will help him there, you may believe.

DISCRETION. Yea, we will all together go with
him.

EVERYMAN. Almighty God, loved may Thou
be, I give
Thee thanks, for Thou has brought to me these
friends,
Discretion, Five Wits, Beauty, Strength, I lack
No one,
> [EVERYMAN *comes down from the step
and faces up-stage*]

            Not even Knowledge and Good Deeds.

STRENGTH [*comes to just left of centre and
puts his hand on* EVERYMAN'S].
And I, your Strength, will ready be to fight
With anything that tries to bar the way.

FIVE WITS [*comes to just right of centre and puts her hand on* EVERYMAN'S].
And though you go throughout the world, I will
Not part from thee, for sweet nor sour.
BEAUTY [*comes to the left of* STRENGTH *and puts her hand on* EVERYMAN'S].
No more
Will I until death's hour, whatever shall
Befall.
DISCRETION [*comes to the right of* FIVE WITS *and puts his hand on* EVERYMAN'S].
I advise you first of all
To be deliberate and sure.
EVERYMAN. My friends,
May God reward you in his heav'nly sphere.
Now hearken all, for I will make my testament;
[*Turns, facing down-stage*]
Full half my goods in alms I give
By way of charity, the other half
Shall still remain in trust, to be returned
To whom it doth belong. All this I do
Despite the fiend of Hell, with whom, from this
Day forth I'm quit forever from his peril.
KNOWLEDGE [*goes to* EVERYMAN].
Everyman, hearken what I say; go you
To church and there receive the holy Sacrament.
GOOD DEEDS [*goes to* EVERYMAN].
Knowledge has advised you well,
There is no duke, nor emperor, nor king,
Whose station here on earth can equal be
Unto the church. Its doors are all the
Openings through which man goes to his
Redemption, which is a balm upon
The soul that God hath given us with pain
Out of His heart when He was crucified.
EVERYMAN. Oh, fain would I receive communion,
Then meekly to my Saviour I can go.
KNOWLEDGE [KNOWLEDGE *and* GOOD DEEDS *lead* EVERYMAN *to left where they kneel.* STRENGTH, BEAUTY, FIVE WITS, *and* DISCRETION *also kneel in such a way that the stage picture is semi-circular.* EVERYMAN *goes slowly off-stage at left*].
Everyman, that is the best that you can do.
Surely God will bring you to salvation.
EVIL [*comes on at right*].
But soft, who are these figures knelt as if
In prayer? What is this saintly crew? It can
Not be that they are here with Everyman.
Ah, no, for he keeps brighter company,
Such as the ones there in the market place
Who prompted him to offer me his soul.
Still they were with him as I came.
[*Goes to centre*]
I'll try
And see if they will say when he returns.
But which one shall I ask? And then will they
Reply?

[*Accosts* BEAUTY *and kneels down-stage left of her*]
Fair maid, behold thou one who, till
This hour has dwelt in Hell, in deepest Hell,
But who on seeing thee has risen up
To that sweet paradise which is thyself.
I hold thee in such awe that to aspire
To thee were rash and without hope. I will
Content myself with just a word from thee.
Your answer, pray, Oh, where is Everyman?
[*Stands*]
What, no reply? This one would seem to have
No tongue.
[*Comes to centre*]
But there are others here. I'll try
This one.
[*Indicates* STRENGTH]
It seemeth strange that one so strong
Should bend a knee beneath so light a weight
As is this faith. Why, one small hair could hold
It up. Did not Delilah clip the hair
That separated strength and faith? So then
Will I.
[*Crosses to* STRENGTH *whom he accosts in a most man-to-man manner*]
I see thou art a mighty man,
Yet can it be that all this muscled strength
Cannot so much as move thy tongue to tell
Me, where is Everyman? No answer here.
[*Decides on* DISCRETION *to whom he goes*]
I think that yonder man must know the law
He has a learnéd look, a legal aspect
Which I'll try conclusions with.
[*Assumes a pleading attitude as he comes up to* DISCRETION]
Oh, Sir,
I put my case to thee and plead that I
Have had most grievous wrongs at hands
Of those who do not know the law, or, knowing,
Do not hold respect for it. Is it
Not true that air is free, and is not owned
Nor bound? Yet here, within this hour, I am
Refused the small amount it takes to tell
Me, where is Everyman? No answer there.
[*Backs to centre*]
I wonder at this silence, all seem quite
Intent upon some thing.
[*Notices that they all kneel facing left*]
Their eyes are fastened
To a common point.
[*Turns to follow their gaze*]
It must be that . . .
[*Sees* EVERYMAN *off-stage left and evidently at some distance*]
What's this? Why, is not yonder Everyman?
But robed in white.
[*Goes a step toward the left*]
. . . Here's not the Everyman
I seek.
[*Takes a step back dismayed*]

What's in his face, not mirth from
pleasure. . . .
No . . .
[*Goes back another step*]
'Tis joy . . . in God!
[*Turns and goes quickly off right*]
He's not for me.
EVERYMAN [*enters slowly from left*].
I have received the Sacrament, thrice blessed
Be they that counseled me. I thank God ye
Have tarried here. Now, let us go without
Delay. God be our guide.
[*All rise as* EVERYMAN *gets to centre, and
start toward him*]
STRENGTH. Everyman,
We will not go from thee till thou hast done
This voyage long.
DISCRETION. And I, Discretion, will
Bide with thee, too.
KNOWLEDGE. And though this pilgrimage
Be long and hard, I will never part from thee.
EVERYMAN. Alas. I am so faint I cannot
stand.
[*Sinks to the stage at centre. All gather
around him in the following order from
left to right:* FIVE WITS, KNOWLEDGE,
BEAUTY, EVERYMAN, STRENGTH, GOOD
DEEDS, *and* DISCRETION]
Friends, let us not return into this land,
Not for great stores of gold. For I must creep
Into this cave and turn to earth, and sleep.
BEAUTY [*comes a step forward and onto the
second step*].
What! Into this grave?
EVERYMAN. Where ye shall be
Consumed.
BEAUTY. And should I smother here?
EVERYMAN. Yea,
And never more appear alive upon this earth,
But in heav'n before the highest Lord of all.
BEAUTY [*comes down two steps*].
I cross out all of this; adieu, then, by
Saint John.
[*Exits quickly left*]
EVERYMAN [*stands and goes a step after*
BEAUTY].
Alas! Whereunto may I trust?
Beauty gone. She promised me that she
Would live and die . . .
STRENGTH [*comes down two steps*].
Everyman, will I
Forsake thee too. Thy game, it likes me not.
EVERYMAN [*crosses back to centre*].
Why, wilt thou then deny me, Strength?
Stay but a little space.
STRENGTH. Nay, Sir, by
The rod of grace, I'll hie me from thee fast.
Though thou shouldst weep till thy heart burst.
EVERYMAN. Good Strength,
Ye said that you will ever bide by me.
STRENGTH. I have conveyed you far enough,
I understand

That ye be old enough to take
On hand thy pilgrimage, so I repent
Me that I came.
EVERYMAN [*crosses to* STRENGTH].
For your displeasure, Strength,
I am to blame. Yet promise is a debt.
STRENGTH. In faith, I care not. Thou art but
a fool
To make complaint. You spend your speech
and waste
Your brain. Go, thrust thee in the ground.
[*Exits right*]
EVERYMAN [*goes up two steps and looks
after* STRENGTH].
And I
Had thought to find thee surer. He that trust-
eth
In his Strength will find himself deceived,
It seems. Both Strength and Beauty have for-
saken
Me. They promised . . .
DISCRETION. I will after Strength
Be gone.
EVERYMAN [*crosses back to centre*].
Discretion, wilt thou too forsake
Me in this hour of need?
DISCRETION. In faith, I will
Be gone from thee, for without Strength, Dis-
cretion
Is but naught. To what end argument
If vigour lacks?
EVERYMAN. Yet, pray thee, for the love
Of holy Trinity, look piteously
Into my grave.
[*Indicates the grave up-stage*]
DISCRETION. Nay, so nigh I will
Not come. Farewell now, everyone.
[*Exits right*]
EVERYMAN [*turns and takes a step toward
left*].
Oh, all
Things fail, save God alone. These three are
gone . . .
FIVE WITS. And I will leave thee,
[EVERYMAN *turns toward* FIVE WITS]
Everyman, to follow
After them.
EVERYMAN [*takes a step toward* FIVE
WITS].
Alas!
[*Drops to his knee*]
Then may I weep.
I took you for my friend.
FIVE WITS. I will no longer
Stay, and there an end.
[*Exits at right. The music starts very
softly*]
EVERYMAN. Oh, Jesus, help
[*Faces down-stage*]
Me, now that all things have forsaken me.
GOOD DEEDS. Nay, Everyman, here I will
bide with thee,

For thou shalt find in me a friend.
> [*Takes* EVERYMAN'S *hand*]

EVERYMAN.   Thank thee,
Good Deeds. Knowledge, wilt thou go?

KNOWLEDGE.   Not yet,
Nor ever will I leave.
> [*Takes* EVERYMAN'S *hand*]

EVERYMAN [*rises*].

                          Then I must go,
To make my reckoning, and pay my debts,
Because I know my time is nearly spent,
Have mercy on me, God.
> [*Turns up-stage and starts up the first two steps*]

GOOD DEEDS.   Fear not, for we
Will speak for thee.
> [EVERYMAN *goes up two more steps*]

KNOWLEDGE.   Soon is our end, and small
Our pain.
> [EVERYMAN *gets to the top of the steps*]
>   Come, let us go,
> [KNOWLEDGE *and* GOOD DEEDS *face each other*]

                          and never come
Again.

> [KNOWLEDGE *and* GOOD DEEDS *face* EVERY-MAN *up-stage*]

EVERYMAN [*starts down the steps up-stage into the grave*].

                          Into Thy hands I now commend
My soul. Receive it, Lord, and there an end.
> [GOOD DEEDS *goes up the steps and then down into the grave following* EVERY-MAN]
> [KNOWLEDGE *goes to the top of the steps, faces down-stage, and crosses her hands on her breast*].

Now Everyman has gone to his eternal
Rest. Before the highest God of all
He stands with his Good Deeds, for only she
Can bide with him before that throne. His soul
Is saved because he had contrition for
His sins. So God forgives us evermore.
> [KNOWLEDGE *turns to face up-stage and as she does so she raises her hands forward and above her head. As she does this the cross of white light dims up in the background and the music reaches its climax. At the height of this the music suddenly stops and the light goes out leaving the stage in darkness and silence*]

THE PORTRAIT

A Commedia dell'Arte Scenario

By FLAMINIO SCALA

TRANSLATED FROM THE FRENCH BY GARRETT H. LEVERTON

CHARACTERS

Vittoria
Piombino
Pantalone
Gratiano
Isabella
Flaminia
Oratio
Flavio
Pedrolino
Arlecchino
Captain Spavento
Lesbino, *later Silvia*
A Rogue
Nobles and Civilians
Place: *Parma.*
Time: *Mid-Sixteenth Century.*

THE PORTRAIT

A troupe of actors were performing in Parma. According to the custom, the principal actress received many visitors, one of whom was a cavalier of the city named ORATIO. During his visit the cavalier exhibited a locket in which was hidden the portrait of the very beautiful woman who had given him this locket. During the course of the conversation, the actress —VITTORIA, by name—subtly removed the portrait from the locket before returning it, at the close of his visit. A few days later the husband of the beautiful woman came to see the actress. VITTORIA, not knowing who he was, chanced to show him the portrait of his wife. The husband, PANTALONE, was very much surprised, and at great length tried to persuade the actress to tell him the name of the man who had given her this portrait. PANTALONE concealed the reason for his interest in the affair and returned to his home in a fury to inflict exemplary chastisement on his culpable wife. However, on arriving there, the wife gave so many good excuses in support of her innocence that she succeeded in appeasing his anger.

The persons concerned in working out this situation are the actress, VITTORIA, and her comrade PIOMBINO; the two old men PANTALONE and GRATIANO; their wives, ISABELLA and FLAMINIA; and the wives's lovers, ORATIO and FLAVIO. PEDROLINO is valet to PANTALONE, and ARLECCHINO to CAPTAIN SPAVENTO. A young Milanese girl, disguised as a page, comes under the name of LESBINO to offer her services to the CAPTAIN, whom she loves.

ACT ONE

SCENE I

After the quarrel between ISABELLA and PANTALONE, her husband, over the portrait which was last seen in the hands of VITTORIA, ISABELLA begins to doubt ORATIO's love for her. She orders PEDROLINO to go to ORATIO and to demand from him the portrait which she had given him some time previously.

SCENE II

CAPTAIN SPAVENTO tells ARLECCHINO how through being obliged to assist in the play, he has fallen in love with the actress, VITTORIA. ARLECCHINO tells him he is wasting time.

SCENE III

Later, the CAPTAIN consents to take LESBINO as his page, after asking him many foolish questions about his bravery and his military talents.

SCENE IV

From her window, FLAMINIA calls to ARLECCHINO and asks him to carry a letter to a cavalier named FLAVIO, whom she will meet at the place where she conducts her rendezvous with gentlemen. ARLECCHINO takes the letter and promises to deliver it to the one to whom it is addressed. FLAMINIA gives him some money and withdraws. ARLECCHINO regards FLAMINIA's window knowingly.

SCENE V

DOCTOR GRATIANO, the husband of FLAMINIA, seeing ARLECCHINO with a letter in his hand and gazing at his wife's window, becomes suspicious, and demands to know what he is doing there and for whom the letter is intended. ARLECCHINO replies that a man named FLAVIO gave it to him to deliver to a lady. The DOCTOR takes the letter and raps ARLECCHINO with his cane.

SCENES VI TO X

PANTALONE comes between the DOCTOR and ARLECCHINO. FLAVIO presents himself. GRATIANO, furiously angry, returns the letter to him. FLAVIO receives it with profound humility. The others depart and FLAVIO reads the letter in which FLAMINIA begs him to frequent the theatre no longer.

SCENE XI

When PEDROLINO asks the return of the portrait of ISABELLA, ORATIO explains that it is impossible to return it to him because the locket is being repaired at the jeweler's. PEDROLINO smiles and asks him how long it has been since he has gone to the theatre, questions him about all the actors, and finally about the SIGNORA VITTORIA.

SCENE XII

At this moment ISABELLA arrives. She dissembles at first, then asks for the return of the portrait. But ORATIO repeats the same story he had already told PEDROLINO. She calls him a traitor and tells him she knows about his love for the actress to whom he has given her portrait. In her anger, she commands PEDROLINO to follow her and she leaves refusing to listen to ORATIO. ORATIO bemoans his ill luck and blames the presence of the actors as the reason for all his trouble. He is particularly discourteous in expressing his opinion of VITTORIA who has tricked him so deceitfully.

SCENE XIII

The CAPTAIN, hearing what ORATIO says about the actors, and particularly VITTORIA, comes to their defense. He argues that the theatre is a noble diversion and that the SIGNORA VITTORIA is an honorable lady. ORATIO, furious, calls him a liar and reaches for his sword. At this the CAPTAIN asks ORATIO if he wishes to fight a duel with him. ORATIO replies that he is ready. Then the CAPTAIN says he goes to write a letter which will remove from ORATIO the responsibility for his death in case he is killed, and will prevent the officers of justice from regarding him as an adversary. He asks ORATIO to do the same for him. Then he departs. ARLECCHINO observes that his master has the appearance of wishing to escape the affair. Thus ends the first act.

ACT TWO

SCENE I

VITTORIA, richly dressed, with gold necklaces and pearl bracelets, with diamonds and rubies on her fingers, engages herself through PIOMBINO to the DUKE OF PARMA, recalling the many courtesies which she was constantly receiving from the Parmesan nobility.

SCENES II TO V

PEDROLINO praises his master PANTALONE to VITTORIA. PANTALONE appears but he does not dare to approach the actress because he sees his wife at the window. PEDROLINO persuades PANTALONE that the actress is in love with him. PANTALONE, flattered, expresses the intention of giving her a present.

SCENE VI

While ORATIO recounts to his friend FLAVIO the unfortunate history of the portrait, ARLECCHINO brings him the CAPTAIN's letter of remission from blame. ORATIO strikes him with his fist and rushes off to the theatre.

SCENES VII TO XII

FLAVIO and PEDROLINO, and then FLAMINIA attempt to reconcile ISABELLA and ORATIO. ISABELLA softens but she declares that ORATIO shall get nothing from her so long as he does not return the portrait, and she forbids him, moreover, to go, himself, to negotiate for its return. PEDROLINO informs them how the two old men, PANTALONE and GRATIANO, are paying attention to the actress.

SCENE XIII

Now the DOCTOR arrives. PEDROLINO pretends to be arguing with FLAMINIA and is saying: "How do I know whether your husband goes to the theatre or not?" FLAMINIA, entering into the deception, pretends to be jealous of her husband. When she has withdrawn, PEDROLINO tells the DOCTOR of his visit to the SIGNORA VITTORIA and of how she is in love with the DOCTOR. GRATIANO is enchanted.

SCENE XIV

PIOMBINO greets the DOCTOR in behalf of SIGNORA VITTORIA. He begs him to take to the actress a silver pitcher and vase which she needs for a play which she is going to present. The DOCTOR replies that he will send these by PEDROLINO. PIOMBINO assures him that the actress is in love with him, and that because of him, she rejects the attentions of all the gentlemen who call on her at home or at the theatre. The DOCTOR is overjoyed and promises a reward to PIOMBINO.

SCENE XV

The CAPTAIN talks with his page, LESBINO, about the passion which the actress inspires in him. LESBINO tries to turn him away from this passion which he cannot make honorable. He asks him if he has never had another love. The CAPTAIN replies that he had been in love, in Milan, with a very beautiful young girl named SILVIA.

SCENE XVI

ARLECCHINO interrupts his master to tell him that VITTORIA is waiting for him at a nearby jeweler's. LESBINO, desperate, seeks to persuade ARLECCHINO that he ought to kill him, LESBINO, because he has conceived the intention of killing his master. ARLECCHINO beats and injures the page. FLAMINIA and ISABELLA intervene.

SCENE XVII

Suspecting that LESBINO is a woman in spite of her male attire, they take her to the residence of FLAMINIA. Thus ends the second act.

ACT THREE

SCENE I

VITTORIA and PIOMBINO go to dine at the house of a rich gentleman who gives them magnificent presents. They congratulate themselves because of the custom of making gifts to actors, a common custom in Italian cities and one which is seldom neglected by persons of distinguished rank. VITTORIA confesses that she laughs at all lovers who are not generous with her. PIOMBINO promises to provide well for her old age.

SCENES II AND III

PANTALONE comes to call on VITTORIA. She thanks him for the presents he has brought to her and invites him to be present at the theatre for the opening of her play. PANTALONE promises to be there. Presently FLAVIO arrives and the actress detains him with engaging conversation.

SCENE IV

But FLAMINIA sees them from her window. She is so angry that she goes out and slaps FLAVIO in the face and then returns to her house. FLAVIO, putting his hand to his smarting cheek, goes without saying a word. VITTORIA laughs heartily.

SCENE V

PANTALONE who has been a witness to this *coup de théâtre* blames FLAMINIA for her effrontery. He congratulates himself that he has such a modest and well-bred wife. After these musings, he exchanges compliments with the actress. But ISABELLA appears.

SCENE VI

She reproaches her husband for being gallant with other women while neglecting her. She lays all the facts before him and then adds that he does not deserve a wife like her. Finally, as her anger increases, she attacks him and puts him to flight. She turns to VITTORIA and tells her that if his honor does not prevent him from compromising himself with an actress, then he will have to be taught how to behave. ISABELLA then returns to her home. VITTORIA laughs and says that wherever one finds a troupe of actors, there also will be found married women with sour dispositions.

SCENE VII

GRATIANO now arrives. "Behold, the other pigeon waiting to have his feathers plucked," says PIOMBINO. The actress flirts with the DOCTOR. PIOMBINO reminds him of the silver pitcher and vase which he has promised her. GRATIANO joyfully takes PEDROLINO with him in order to bring back these presents. The actors ridicule his stupidity.

SCENE VIII

ORATIO arrives and greets VITTORIA. He demands the portrait of ISABELLA. She replies, with a laugh, that she hasn't the slightest idea what he is talking about. Then she departs with PIOMBINO.

SCENE IX

ISABELLA has seen ORATIO talking with the actress; she reproaches him for not keeping his promise. ARLECCHINO tells ORATIO that ISABELLA and FLAMINIA have taken his master's page away with them to their home, and are holding him there against his will. ISABELLA seizes the occasion to spite ORATIO and calls FLAMINIA, telling her to bring her new lover to the window. LESBINO appears and says to ISABELLA, "What do you wish of me, Signora?" ORATIO becomes enraged at the sight of this unknown person and withdraws, cursing ISABELLA.

SCENE X

PANTALONE asks the reason for all this noise. ISABELLA says that ORATIO wished to take her page away from her. "And what do you want with this page?" PANTALONE asks angrily. Then ISABELLA tells the story of SILVIA, the Milanese girl. She then urges PANTALONE to go to the theatre, find the CAPTAIN and bring him back if possible. PANTALONE sees at once that this is the chance he himself needed in order to get to go to the theatre.

SCENES XI TO XVII

The lovers begin to quarrel again. PEDROLINO observes that quarreling is a waste of time. Since their husbands are at the play which lasts for six hours, they could, therefore, use their time to much better advantage than quarreling. The lovers see the good sense in this remark and become reconciled. The valets try to decide on the best means to restore SILVIA to the CAPTAIN's good graces. The CAPTAIN appears.

SCENE XVIII

PEDROLINO tells the CAPTAIN that he will find VITTORIA at the home of PANTALONE. The CAPTAIN enters through the basement of the house where he comes upon SILVIA divested of her male attire.

Scene XIX

The two valets, Pedrolino and Arlecchino, are alone in the theatre. They sit on the floor and decide what they would say if the two old men were to return suddenly. At this moment in the scene there is some amusing pantomime. A rogue, carrying a lantern, sees the two valets. With many tears, he bemoans the fact that he has lost much money at cards. He does not have more than a dozen pieces of money left. The valets invite him to play with them. They play. The rogue wins the money and also the clothes of Pedrolino and Arlecchino. He leaves them sitting on the floor in their shirts. The valets are very despondent.

Scene XX

A great tumult arises in the theatre. Pantalone, Gratiano and Piombino rush in carrying Vittoria. She begs them to protect her from the dangers of a brawl which has broken out because of her. These gentlemen brawlers—the *bravi*—pour in, their swords bared. They see Vittoria, they seize her, and carry her out. Piombino follows them with gestures of despair.

Scene XXI

Pantalone and Gratiano find themselves face to face with the valets who are clad only in their shirts. They ask them to explain what has happened. The valets invent an explanation and say that the crowd which just left the theatre, robbed them of their money and clothes. They add, philosophically, that although the theatre brings pleasure, it is also the source of numerous scandals. While they are indulging in these wise reflections, Isabella and Flaminia come in and ask their husbands why the play is ended so soon.

Scene XXII

Pantalone replies that a brawl interrupted it and that he has not seen the Captain. Isabella tells how they informed the Captain that he would find Vittoria in the basement of their house, and that it is Silvia instead of the actress who is waiting there for him. Fearing however, that the Captain, thus deceived, might commit violence, they had asked Oratio and Flavio to take the trouble to stay with them. Pantalone and Gratiano approve.

Scene XXIII

The Captain leaves the house swearing he has been betrayed. Oratio and Flavio endeavor to calm him. Pantalone and all the others intercede in behalf of Silvia. The Captain listens. He admits that Silvia is honorably born; that she is the daughter of a rich Milanese merchant; and that he loves her. This diabolical actress had so far bewitched him that he had forgotten poor Silvia. But he returns to her and consents to marry her.

Scene XXIV

They bring in Silvia and she learns that her lover returns her affection.

Isabella and Flaminia urge their husbands to stay away from the theatre, and instead, to watch over their homes and the conduct of their wives. They reply that henceforth they will do as their wives ask. Everybody now goes to Pantalone's home to celebrate the wedding of Silvia and the Captain, and it is thus that the comedy of *The Portrait* ends.

GAMMER GURTON'S NEEDLE

A Modern Adaptation

By COLIN CAMPBELL CLEMENTS

CHARACTERS

DICCON
HODGE, *Gammer Gurton's Servant*
TIB, *Gammer Gurton's Maid*
GAMMER GURTON
COCK, *Gammer Gurton's Boy*
DAME CHAT
DOCTOR RAT, *The Curate*
MASTER BAILY
DOLL, *Dame Chat's Maid*
THE STAGE-MANAGER

GAMMER GURTON'S NEEDLE

PROLOGUE

[*Spoken before the curtain by the* STAGE-MANAGER]

As Gammer Gurton, with many wide stitches,
Sat piecing and patching Hodge's old breeches,
By chance, or misfortune, as she her work
    tossed,
In Hodge's old breeches her needle she lost.
When Diccon, the rascal, had heard by report,
That good Gammer Gurton was robbed in this
    sort,
He quietly persuaded, with her in this trouble,
That Dame Chat, an old gossip, the needle had
    found;
Yet knew she no more of this matter, alas!
Than knows Tom, the clerk, what the priest
    says at mass.
Hereof there began so fearful a fray
Doctor Rat was sent for, these gossips to stay—
But hold! Let's on with the play!

ACT ONE

SCENE: *The street before* GAMMER GURTON'S *house.*

DICCON [*he comes running out of the house at the back, in his hands he carries a side of bacon, which he quickly hides under his coat*].
Many a gossip's cup in my time have I tasted,
And many a broach and spit have I both turned
    and basted,
Many a piece of bacon have I had from out
    their balks
In running over the country with long and
    weary walks;
    [*He turns and looks at the house*]
Yet never came my foot within these door
    cheeks
To seek fish or flesh, garlic, onions or leeks,
That ever I saw such a sorry plight
As here within this house appeared to my
    sight!
There is howling, sobbing and prowling
Screaming, wailing and growling!
They are driven to such fits
I'm afraid the folks are not well in their wits!
    [HODGE *comes running in from the left*]
    HODGE.
See! Thus I come from dabbling! In the dirt
She set me digging! I'd like to tear her shirt!
    [*He looks down at his breeches*]

Gog's bones! See how the cloth tears!
By the mass, here's a gash! A shameful hole
    indeed,
Big enough, I swear, for a man to thrust in
    his head.
    DICCON.
The very best remedy, in such a case and hap,
Is to sew on a patch as big as your cap.
    HODGE.
Gog's soul, man, two days have not yet ended
Since Gammer Gurton, I'm sure, these breeches
    mended!
But I am made such a drudge, to trudge at
    every need
I would rip them though they were stitched
    with sturdy pack thread.
    DICCON.
Hodge, let your breeches go. Speak out and
    tell me,
What is the matter with Gammer Gurton and
    her maid, Tib?
    HODGE. What's the matter with them?
    DICCON.
First they yell, then sit still as stones in the
    street,
As though they had been taken with gnomes or
    some evil spirit.
    HODGE. Has someone stolen her ducks or
hens or taken Gib, her cat?
    DICCON.
How the devil can I tell, man? They gave me
    no word,
They gave no more heed to my talk than you
    would to a lord.
    HODGE.
Um . . . I cannot but muse what marvelous
    thing it is!
I shall go in and find out what matters are
    amiss.
    DICCON.
Then farewell, Hodge, since you must haste.
    [*He turns away and looks at a side of
    bacon which he has stolen from* GAM-
    MER GURTON'S *house*]
I will go to good-wife Chat's—and see how her
    ales taste.
    [*He hurries out right*]
    HODGE [*looking at his house*].
Perchance some evil spirit may haunt our
    house indeed,
    [*Backing away from the door*]
Ah, then I were a noddy to venture where I
    have no need!
    [TIB *comes running in from the house*]

TIB.

I am worse than mad, by the mass, much the
  worse for this fray!
I am chiden, I am blamed and beaten all the
  hours of the day!
Lamed and hunger-starved, pricked up all in
  jags,
With no patch to hide my back save a few
  rotten rags!
  HODGE. Tib . . . Tib, what has happened?
  TIB [looking up].
Old Gammer is in a terrible mood, and frantic
  all at once,
Cock, poor boy, and I, poor wench, have felt
  it in our bones!
  HODGE. What is the matter? Why does she
take on so?
  TIB. She is undone. Alas, her joy in life is
gone!
  HODGE. Oh! Oh!
  TIB.
If she does not have some comfort she is dead—
Swears between her lips she'll never take an-
  other inch of bread!
  HODGE.
By our lady! I am unhappy to see her in this
  dump,
Can it be that her stool broke and she had a
  mighty bump?
  TIB.
Oh, if it had only been *that* we would not
  greatly care
For breaking of her bones or smashing of her
  chair,
But greater is her grief! Oh, Hodge, we shall all
  feel!
  HODGE. Tib, she hasn't lost her—
  TIB. Um . . . my Gammer's lost her pre-
cious needle!
  HODGE [his hand goes flying to the seat of
his pants]. Her needle!
  TIB. Her needle.
  HODGE. Her needle?
  TIB. Her needle!
  HODGE. But how?
  TIB.
She was sitting down to rest, and bade me
  reach your breeches,
And by and by, a vengeance on it, before she
  had taken two stitches
To clap a patch upon your seat, by chance
  aside she leers
And Gib, our cat, in the milk-pan she spied
  over head and ears.
"Our cat! Stop, thief!" she cried aloud, and
  threw the breeches down,
Up went her staff, and out leapt Gib—out
  doors, into the town.
Since then we can't lay an eye on the needle!
  HODGE.
And my breeches, the ones I'm to wear to-
  morrow,

They're not yet sewed up?
  TIB.
No, Hodge, they lie with the same great tear!
  [GAMMER GURTON enters from the house]
  GAMMER.
Alas, Hodge, alas! I may well curse and ban
That ever I saw this day, with Gib in the milk-
  pan!
For these and ill-luck together, that maid and
  our boy,
Have took away my dear needle, and robbed
  me of my joy,
My fair long needle, that was my only treasure.
The first day of my sorrow is, and the last one
  of my pleasure!
  HODGE.
Might have kept it when you had it! But fools
  will be fools still!
Lose what is fast in your hands! You need not
  but you will!
  GAMMER.
Go quickly, Tib, run you jade, to the end there
  of the town,
There where you carried the dust, look where
  you poured it down.
  [TIB runs out left]
  HODGE.
Your needle lost! It's a pity you should lack
  care—and endless sorrow,
A pretty matter! How will my breeches be
  sewed! Must I go thus to-morrow?
  [He turns round and shows a great hole in
  the seat of his breeches]
  GAMMER.
Oh, Hodge, Hodge, if I could find my needle
  I'd sew it with a good, strong, double
  thread!
  HODGE.
Four of you sit idle at home—your needle to
  keep,
What the devil had you else to do? Four use-
  less sheep!
  GAMMER. I lost it, Hodge, trying to save the
milk which our cat, Gib, was wasting.
  HODGE. Where have you been fidgeting since
your needle got lost?
  GAMMER.
Within the house, near the door, sitting at my
  post
Where I have been looking for a long hour—
  before you came here,
But, alas! All was in vain, my needle is no-
  where near!
  HODGE. Get me a candle! I shall seek for it!
  GAMMER [calling]. Cock, come hither! Cock,
I say!
  COCK [entering from the house]. You called
me, Gammer?
  GAMMER.
Go grope behind the old brass pan.
There you will find an old shoe, wherein, if
  you look well,

You will find an inch or so of white tallow candle;
Light it and bring it as fast as you can.

COCK. All right, Gammer. [*He goes back into the house*]

GAMMER [*to* HODGE, *who is down on his hands and knees, before the door, searching for the needle*]. Wait, Hodge, till we have a light, then we can see better.

HODGE [*looking in at the door*]. Hurry, you worthless boy! Are you asleep?

COCK [*from within*]. I can't get the candle lighted. There is almost no fire.

HODGE [*rising*].
Are you deaf, stupid boy? Cock, I say, can't you hear?
I'll bet you a penny I'll make you come if I get hold of your ear.

GAMMER. Do not beat him, Hodge, but help him find the candle. [HODGE *goes into the house*. TIB *comes running in from the left*] Have you found it, Tib?

TIB [*shaking her head*]. I've tossed and tumbled over yonder heap to find your needle.

GAMMER [*wringing her hands*]. Alas! Alas!

TIB. 'Twas all in vain, without success, your needle is—where it was!

GAMMER. Alas, my needle! We shall never meet! Adieu! Adieu for aye!

TIB. Not so, Gammer, we might find it—if we knew where it lay.

[COCK, *doubled over with laughter, enters from the house*]

COCK.
Gog's sock, Gammer! If you will laugh look in at the door
And see how Hodge lies tumbling and tossing around the floor,
Raking there some fire to find among the ashes dead,
Where there's not a spark, even as big as a pin's head.
At last in a dark corner two sparks he thinks he spies
Which were, indeed, nothing but the cat, Gib's, two eyes!
"Puff," blows Hodge, thinking thereby to have fire without doubt;
With that Gib shut her two eyes—and so the fire was out!

GAMMER. No!

COCK [*still chuckling*].
At last Gib hopped up the stairs, among the posts and bins
Hodge running after her till broke were both his shins!

[*He lies down and rolls with laughter.* HODGE's *head appears at an upper window*]

HODGE.
Come up! Come up and help! Gib in her tail has fire

And is like to burn all if she gets any higher!

GAMMER. Where are you? Come down, Hodge, and let the cat alone!

HODGE.
Come down, you say? Nay, I'll watch that it don't catch;
The house comes down on your heads if fire gets in the thatch!

GAMMER. It's the cat's eyes, fool, that shine in the dark!

HODGE. Do you think that the cat has in every eye a spark?

GAMMER. No, but they shine like fire—as any man can see.

HODGE. But Gammer, if she burns the house you'll put the blame on me!

GAMMER.
Come down, and help to see that my needle is found
Down, Tib, on your knees I say! Down, Cock, to the ground.

[*They go down on their hands and knees to search for the lost needle.* HODGE *enters from the house*]

I'll find that lost needle in one place or another!

HODGE [*brushing the dust from his clothing*].
I hope a vengeance lights on Gib, and on Gib's mother
And all the families of cats and kittens, far and near!

GAMMER [*to* COCK]. Look on the ground, noddy! Do you think the needle is here?

COCK.
By my troth, Gammer, methought your needle I saw
But when I touched it, I knew it was straw!

TIB [*sitting down on the ground*]. Look! Whats' this? 'Tis it! By the mass!

[*They all gather round her*]

HODGE. Ah, throw it away. 'Tis nothing but a bit of grass!

[*During the last few minutes the lights have been growing dimmer*]

GAMMER. Come, my needle is where it was and it's as black as night.

HODGE. Let's come another time when we have more light.

[*They all go into the house. A light is set in the window of* GAMMER's *house.* DICCON *is heard coming down the street, singing:*]

DICCON.

Have I good drink, I surely think
Nothing can do me harm.
For truly then I fear no man,
Be he never so bold,
When I am armed, and thoroughly warmed
With jolly good ale and old.

Oh, back and side, go bare, go bare;

Both foot and hand, go cold:
But, belly, Gog send you good ale enough,
Whether it be new or old!

[*He comes staggering in from the right*]
Now a truly wise man by magic could divine
Which way my journey lies, or where I am to
    dine!
But one good turn I have: be it night or day,
South, East, North or West I am never out of
    my way.
[HODGE *enters from the house. He carries
    a piece of black bread in his hand*]
Oh, Hodge, have you had your dinner yet?
HODGE.
I am well rewarded, am I not? Don't you
    think?
I had a fine dinner—for all my work and
    swink!
Neither butter, cheese, milk, onions, flesh nor
    fish,
Nothing but a bit of barley-bread: a pleasant,
    costly dish!
DICCON. Oh, Hodge, will you share it with
    me?
HODGE.
Gog's name, man, save this bit of dry horse-
    bread
I've had no bite all day, no crumb has gone
    into my head!
DICCON. Was there no one at home to get
    dinner for you?
HODGE. Alas, Diccon, I came too late! There
    was nothing more to get!
DICCON. Nothing more to eat?
HODGE. Gib, a foul fiend light on her, licked
    the milk-pan dry!
DICCON. 'Twas not so well washed for many
    weeks, I'll bet my eye!
HODGE.
A pestilence light on all ill-luck! Still, I had
    thought, for all this
Of a side of bacon behind the door, at worst,
    I should not miss.
DICCON [*trying hard to keep his face
    straight*]. A side of bacon you say?
HODGE [*shaking his head*].
But when I went to cut a slip, as I very often
    do,
Gog's bones, Diccon, the cat had eat the bacon,
    too!
DICCON. Worse luck! Your bacon eaten, too!
    That was bad luck, Hodge.
HODGE.
Hungry . . . and see how I'm rent and torn,
    my heels and knees and breeches,
And I had hoped to sit by the fire and have a
    few stitches!
DICCON. Your Gammer can mend them.
HODGE [*sadly*].
No . . . no. Boots, man to tell.
I live with such fools I'd better be in hell!

My Gammer, alas, has not served me at all
    well.
DICCON. What do you mean by such talk,
    Hodge?
HODGE. What has she gone and done but
    lost her needle!
DICCON [*rubbing his stomach*]. Her milk,
    her bacon and her eel! And an eel is such a
    dainty dish.
HODGE. Tush! Her needle! Needle! Her
    needle, man! 'Tis neither flesh nor fish!
DICCON. What the devil is it then?
HODGE.
A little thing with a hole in the end, as bright
    as any silver,
Small, long, sharp at the point, and straight as
    any pillar.
DICCON [*scratching his head*]. You put me
    all in doubt.
HODGE. A needle! A needle! My Gammer's
    needle is gone!
DICCON. Her *needle!* Now I understand.
    [*Looking down at* HODGE's *breeches*] Oh, what
    a shameful loss for your breeches!
HODGE. I'd give a crown if they had but
    three stitches.
DICCON. Hodge, what will you give me if I
    find your needle?
HODGE. By m' father's soul, I'll give you . . .
    I'll give you a copper kettle.
DICCON. Can you keep your word?
HODGE. Else I'd wish my tongue were out.
DICCON [*shaking a dirty finger in* HODGE's
    face]. Just take my advice and I'll get your
    needle.
HODGE. You will?
DICCON. I will.
HODGE.
I'll run, I'll ride, I'll dig, I'll delve, I'll toil,
    you'll see,
I'll hold, I'll scrape, I'll pull, I'll pinch, I'll bend
    a knee;
I'll be your bondman, Diccon. I swear by
    moon and sun.
If nothing stops the gap in my seat, I'm utterly
    undone!
DICCON [*winking*]. Tell me. What is the real
    cause for all this sorrow?
HODGE [*shifting from one foot to the
    other*]. Kirstian Clack, Tom Simpson's maid,
    by the mass, comes here to-morrow!
DICCON. Ho-ho! So that's it? I thought as
    much.
HODGE. There's no telling what may happen
    between us.
DICCON [*poking* HODGE *in the ribs*]. Does she
    smile on you? Eh?
HODGE. She did. A week ago come Sunday.
DICCON. Will you swear to be no blab,
    Hodge?
HODGE. Yes . . . oh, yes . . . Diccon.
DICCON. Then lay your hand on your heart

and repeat after me— [*Suddenly*] Have you
no book?

HODGE. I have no book. I—

DICCON.

Then put your hand upon my heart
And repeat after me—mind your part—
[HODGE *repeats after* DICCON, *line for
line:*]
I, Hodge, breechless,
Swear to Diccon, richless,
By the hand that I shall kiss,
To keep his council close,
And always me to dispose
To work what his pleasure is.
[DICCON *pushes* HODGE, *who smacks
loudly, in the face with his open hand*]
Now, Hodge, mind you take heed
And do just as I say,
For so I judge it best;
This needle again to win,
There is no shift therein,
But conjure up a sprite.

HODGE [*trembling*]. You mean . . . you
mean the devil, Diccon! I say!

DICCON.

Yes, in good faith, that is the way—
We'll fetch him up with a pretty charm.

HODGE.

Wait, Diccon, do not be so hasty, yet,
By the mass, I'm beginning to sweat!
I'm afraid . . . afraid of some harm!

DICCON [*he takes* HODGE *by the shoulders
and stands him in the middle of the street, then
with his finger makes a big circle in the dust
around his frightened victim. In a deep voice:*]
There you are, Hodge, stir not, budge not,
Move not out of this circled plot.

HODGE. And shall I be safe here from his
claws?

DICCON.

The master-devil with his long paws
Cannot within this charmed circle reach.
[*He begins to hum softly*]

HODGE.

I say, Diccon, I say,
Go softly in this matter,
Oh, pray, go softly in this matter!

DICCON. What the devil, man, are you afraid
of nothing?

HODGE [*after a long pause*]. My nose, my
nose itches, Diccon.

DICCON. Do not budge! [*He goes on with
his strange noise*]

HODGE [*after another long pause*]. Can we
tarry a little—till I get a drink of water?

DICCON. Stand still to it! Why should you
fear him?

HODGE. Gog's sides, Diccon, I think I hear
him! Wait . . . wait . . . I shall mar all.

DICCON. The matter is no worse than I told.

HODGE.

My leg's asleep. I can no longer hold.

Too bad! I must move or I'll fall!

DICCON [*with a finger against his nose*].
Stand to it, Hodge! Oh—o-o-o-a boon!
I smell the devil! He'll be here soon!

HODGE. I'm gone! *I'm gone!* [*With a wild
whoop he breaks and runs into* GAMMER GUR-
TON'S *house*]

DICCON [*looking after him*].
Fie, dirty knave, and out upon you!
Above all other louts, fie on you!
[*He stands with his chin in his hand for a
moment thinking, then throws back his
head and laughs*]
Within a time quite short,
If you mark my words and note,
I will give you leave to cut my throat
If I do not have some sport.
[*He calls off right*]
Dame Chat! I say! Are you within?

DAME CHAT [*within*]. Who's out there making such a din?

DICCON. A right good fellow.

DAME CHAT [*she enters from the right*].
Well, Diccon, come in and rest.

DICCON.

Nay, nay, there is no time to tarry, I must say
ado,
[*He turns and goes close to her*]
But first, just for your ears, I have a word or
two.

DAME CHAT [*bending over*]. Oh, yes?

DICCON [*he glances over his shoulder at*
GAMMER GURTON'S *door, then, taking* DAME
CHAT *by the hand, leads her several paces
away. He whispers:*] I would not even tell my
sister, the matter is so great.

DAME CHAT [*her head bobbing*]. Yes . . .
yes.

DICCON.

First you must swear by our Lady of
Boulogne,
Saint Dunstan, and Saint Dominic, with the
three Kings of Cologne,
That you will keep what I have to tell you a
secret.

DAME CHAT.

That will I do! That will I do!
As secret as my own thoughts, by heaven—and
the devil, too!

DICCON.

Sh! Now Gammer Gurton, your neighbor, is in
a sad plight:
Her fair, fat, red rooster was stolen, yes, stolen
last night.

DAME CHAT. What! That rooster with the
yellow legs that crowed so much o' nights?

DICCON. Sh! . . . sh! Yes, that rooster was
stolen.

DAME CHAT. Was he taken out of the hens'
roost?

DICCON. I don't know where the devil he
was kept.

DAME CHAT. No-o.

DICCON. But Tib, the maid, has whispered in Gammer's ear that *you* stole the rooster!

DAME CHAT. That I—the fat jade! By bread and salt—

DICCON. Soft, Chat, I say! Be still! Don't say a word until—

DAME CHAT [*rolling up her sleeves*]. By the mass, I will! I'll have the young wench by the head, and the old trot by the throat!

DICCON [*enjoying the situation*]. Sh! Not a word, Dame Chat.

DAME CHAT [*shaking her head back and forth*].

Shall such a beggar's brawl as that, do you think, make me a thief?

The blight light on the jade's sides, a pestilence and mischief!

[*She calls:*]

Come out, you hungry, needy witch! Too bad my nails are short!

DICCON. Hold your tongue, woman!

DAME CHAT.

Would you allow, Diccon, such a sort to revile you,

With nasty words to blot your name, and so defile you?

DICCON. No. But you must see that I get no blame. You promised.

DAME CHAT. Your name will not be mentioned!

DICCON.

It's twenty pounds to a goose-quill Good Gammer will come

To fight about her rooster, for well I heard Tib say

That he was roasted in your house for breakfast yesterday!

DAME CHAT. By heavens, I'll break her head!

DICCON.

Sh! Give her your mind, and spare not,

Keep Diccon blameless, and then go to, I care not.

DAME CHAT [*shaking her fist at* GAMMER'S *house*]

Let the drab beware her throat! I can wait no longer!

In faith, old witch, it shall be seen, which of us is the stronger!

DICCON [*pushing* DAME CHAT *toward the right*].

Tush, go in the house, keep your words for an hour,

But when Gammer comes then let them pour. Now farewell.

[DAME CHAT *goes out, grumbling.* DICCON *laughs to himself*]

Now the fun has begun!

[HODGE *enters from the house. He stands near the door*

HODGE. Gog's soul, are you still alive?

DICCON. As you see.

HODGE. Dare I come?

DICCON. Yes, of course, why not?

HODGE [*in a subdued voice*]. Tush, man, is Gammer's needle found yet?

DICCON.

She can thank you it's not found, for if you had kept your stand

The devil would have brought it at your command.

HODGE [*coming closer*]. But—but could he not tell where the needle might be found?

DICCON. You foolish dolt, you wished to seek, even before we got our ground.

HODGE. But Diccon, Diccon, didn't the devil cry, "Ho . . . ho . . . ho"?

DICCON. If you had stayed where you stood you would have said so!

HODGE.

I'd swear on a book I heard him roar as I left. Tell me, Diccon, what did the knave have to say?

DICCON. The devil talked of many things. Sometimes of a cat, sometimes of a rat, but most of all I heard the word, "chat, chat."

HODGE. Oh!

DICCON.

This I understood, before off to hell he slid,

Between Chat, Doctor Rat and Gib, the cat, our needle is hid.

HODGE. Um . . . um . . .

DICCON.

Now whether Gib, the cat, has eaten it in her maw,

Or Doctor Rat, the curate, has found it in the straw,

Or old Dame Chat, your neighbor, has stolen it, only Gog knows,

But by to-morrow at this time, we shall learn how the matter goes.

HODGE. Can't you learn to-night, man? Don't you see what's here?

[*He turns round and shows the seat of his breeches*]

DICCON. Why, you've changed your breeches, Hodge!

HODGE [*a little shamefacedly*]. Yes . . . but this pair is as bad as the other. Now if we could find Gammer Gurton's needle—

DICCON [*scratching his head*]. I'm afraid we'll not be able to find it to-night.

HODGE. Alas, Diccon, then there is no hope?

DICCON. No-o-o.

HODGE. Then I'll get me along to Sim Glover's shop.

DICCON. For what?

HODGE. To seek a bit of string. I can tie up my breeches like a bag. There's nothing else to do.

DICCON. Then, to-morrow, perhaps, I'll have some news.

HODGE. Yes, I hope so, Diccon.

[*He goes out left.* GAMMER GURTON *enters from her house*]

GAMMER.
Good Lord, shall I ever have the luck my needle to spy?
What's that? Ho, Diccon! I am lost, man! Fie! Fie!

DICCON. Marry, tell me, Gammer, what is your trouble?

GAMMER.
Alas, the more I think of it, my sorrow becomes double!
My very goodly treasured needle I've lost: I know not where.

DICCON [*with pretended surprise*]. Your needle?

GAMMER [*wiping a tear from her eye*].
My needle, alas, I cannot well spare,
Oh, Diccon, I'm doubled with care.

DICCON. If it's only your needle, Gammer, I promise you all is safe.

GAMMER [*with new hope*]. Why, do you know which way my good needle is gone?

DICCON. Yes, that I do! And you shall hear anon.

GAMMER [*running to him*]. Tell me, Diccon, tell me!

DICCON. Sh! Sh! You promise not to tell who told you?

GAMMER. I'll promise anything, Diccon, anything.

DICCON [*he makes a horn of his hand and shouts into* GAMMER GURTON'S *anxious ear*].
Well, just as I was standing here, within these twenty hours—[*He points to the right*]—even at that gate before my face, a neighbor of yours—

GAMMER. Dame Chat!

DICCON. She stooped down, and took up a needle or a pin!

GAMMER. It was my needle, Diccon, I know!

DICCON.
And when she took it up, here before your very doors,
"Now wait, Dame Chat," said I, "that same is none of yours."
"Go 'way," said she, "you fool, for it is none of *yours!*"
Each other word I was a knave and you a queen of evil-doers.
Just because I up and spoke and said the needle was yours!

GAMMER [*indignantly*].
Thinks the callet by such a slight I'll my needle lack?
If she hopes to keep my needle . . . I'll break her wretched back!

DICCON [*shaking his finger*].
But, good Gammer Gurton, of this take heed, I'm not to be mentioned, no matter how fast you speed!

GAMMER. No, Diccon, I promise you.

DICCON. Remember that!

GAMMER [*she starts toward the house*].
I'll go in and put a clean apron on;
And if the needle I find, I'll well reward you, my son.

[*She goes into the house.* DICCON *stands looking after her and chuckling to himself as the curtains close. No sooner have they closed than* DICCON'S *head appears between them*]

DICCON [*whispering to the audience*].
My Gammer sure intends to break Chat's bones
With staffs or clubs or else with cobblestones.
[*To the musicians*]
In the meantime, fellows, wake up! Your fiddles! A tune, I say!
And let your friends hear such songs as you can play!

CURTAIN

ACT TWO

SCENE: *The same as the first act.*
[HODGE *enters from the left. In his hands he carries a nail and a long piece of string. Mumbles to himself:*]

HODGE.
Sim Glover, how I thank him! I'm mighty well fixed now,
Sim is as good a fellow as ever kissed a cow!
Here is a nail he gave me— I'll use it for a needle,
And here a piece of thong, as strong as any steel.

GAMMER [*she enters from her house*].
Now, Hodge! Come here, I have good news to give;
I know who has my needle; and soon I'll have it, as I live!

HODGE. The devil you do!

GAMMER. It's true . . . I do.

HODGE. Do you know where you lost it?

GAMMER. I know who found it!

HODGE. Oho! If that is true, farewell both nail and thong! [*He throws them away*] But who is it has your needle, Gammer?

GAMMER. That false vixen, Dame Chat, who counts herself so honest!

HODGE. Who told you so?

GAMMER. She picked it up. 'Twas Diccon who saw it done.

HODGE.
Diccon! That sly old knave? Gammer, he's a witch's son!
Of late I saw him call up a devil who bellowed and thundered,
"Ho-ho," he cried. I shook in my boots—and wondered!

GAMMER. Were you not afraid, Hodge, to see the devil in this place?

HODGE [*expanding his chest*]. No. If he had come near me I should have laid him on his face.

GAMMER. But, Hodge, had he no horns to push?

HODGE.

As long as your two arms. With a great long cow's tail,
And crooked, cloven feet, and many a hooked nail!

GAMMER [*lifting her hands*]. Gogamercy, Hodge!

HODGE.

The devil, when Diccon asked him—I heard him very well—
Said plainly, here before us, that Dame Chat had your needle.

GAMMER.

Then let us go and ask if she means to keep it;
Seeing we know so much 'twere madness to sleep on't.

HODGE [*edging around behind* GAMMER].

Go to her, Gammer, no doubt she's now indoors;
Bid her give you the needle. 'Tis none of hers but yours.

GAMMER [*she calls*].

Dame Chat, I ask you fairly, let me have what is mine!
I have not, these twenty years, taken one breath of thine;
Therefore, give me my needle and let me live beside thee.

DAME CHAT [*she enters from the right*].

Why have you crept from home here to my own door to chide me?
Go along, doting drab, begone, or I shall set you further!
Have you and that knave there come out to do murder?

GAMMER. Tush, do not gape at me so, woman! Do you wish to eat me?

DAME CHAT. Don't meddle with me . . . don't meddle!

GAMMER. Poor folks must have their rights. And I want my needle!

DAME CHAT.

Give you your rights and hang you up with all your beggar's broods!
What, will you make me a thief and say I stole your goods?

GAMMER [*shaking her stick*].

I'll say nothing, I warrant you, but what I can prove well—
You took my goods from in front of my house, that I can tell!

DAME CHAT. Did I, old witch, steal what was yours? How should her be known?

GAMMER. I cannot tell; but you took it up, as though it had been your own.

DAME CHAT [*taking a step forward*]. Marry, fie on you, you old gib, with all my very heart!

GAMMER [*taking a step forward*]. Nay, fie on you, you ramp, you rig, with all that take your part!

DAME CHAT. A vengeance on those lips that lay such things to my charge!

GAMMER. A vengeance? A vengeance on those callet's hips whose conscience is so large!

DAME CHAT. Come here, hog!

GAMMER. Come nearer, dog, and let me have a right.

DAME CHAT. You arrant witch!

GAMMER. You bawdy jade! I'll make you curse this night!

DAME CHAT. A bag and wallet!

GAMMER. A cart for a callet!

DAME CHAT.

I'll bet you a goat
I'll patch your coat.

GAMMER.

And I'll bury your bones in a pail!
You jade! You drab! You rake! You blab! Will not shame make you hide?

DAME CHAT. You scold! You bold! You rotten! You glutton! I'll no longer chide! But I will teach you to keep at home!

[*She lays a hand on* GAMMER'S *shoulder*]

GAMMER. Will you, you drunken beast!

[*With her left hand she pulls* DAME CHAT'S *cap down over her eyes and with the right hits her a sharp clap on the ear. Then the fight begins*]

HODGE [*jumping up and down with excitement*].

Stick to her, Gammer! Take her by the head! Punch her, Gammer!
Bite her, I say, Gammer! Oh, was ever such a fight seen!
Where are your nails? Claw her jaw! Pummel her old face green!
Gog's bones, Gammer, hold up your head!

DAME CHAT [*hits* GAMMER *full in the face*].

Take this, old trot, for amends, and learn your tongue to tame!

[*Hitting her again*]

And say you met at this pickering, not your fellow, but your dame!

[GAMMER *falls down on her hands and knees*, CHAT *gives her a kick which lays her flat on her stomach*]

HODGE [*wildly swings his arms*].

Where is the strong-armed drab? I'll give her a lasting mark!
Stand out of my way so that I kill none in the dark!

[DAME CHAT *chases him into the house and then walks away*]

GAMMER [*trying to get up*] Oh! Oh!

HODGE [*trying to reach* GAMMER].

Up, Gammer, if you are alive! I'll fight now for
us both.
You scald callet! I'll wring your neck as
though it were cloth!
DAME CHAT. Are you here again, you hoddy-
peg? Doll! Doll, fetch me my spit!
HODGE [*he picks up* GAMMER's *staff*].
By our father's spirit! I'll break you with it,
by cracky, by hoy—
Watch the door, Cock! Hold her out . . .
you ninish boy.
    [DOLL *runs in with* DAME CHAT's *spit*
    which she gives to her mistress and
    then turns to COCK]
DAME CHAT.
Hold the boy! Keep Hodge from running in!
I'll break all their heads, by sin!
    [*She hits* HODGE]
HODGE. Ouch! Ouch! Gog's wounds! Cock,
pull the latch! [*He runs into the house*]
DAME CHAT. In faith, Sir Loose-breech, had
you tarried, you should have found your
match!
GAMMER. Now beware your throat, fool,
you'll pay for all! [*She sneaks behind* DAME
CHAT *and grabbing her by the back of the neck
shakes her*]
HODGE [*from the window*].
Well said, Gammer, by my soul.
Hoist her, souse her, bounce her, trounce her,
pull out her throat-bole!
DAME CHAT.
You withered witch, if I once get my foot,
You old tar-leather, I'll teach you who belongs
to't!
    [*She hits* GAMMER *in the mouth*]
Take this one in the mouth! When I get my
breath I'll give you more.
    [*She runs out.* HODGE *hurries from the*
    house and helps GAMMER *to her feet*]
HODGE.
Up, Gammer, stand on your feet; are your
legs very sore?
Faith, if I had Chat by the face, I would
crack her bawdy crown!
GAMMER. Ho, Hodge, Hodge, where was
your help when the vixen had me down?
HODGE.
By the mass, Gammer, but for my staff, Chat
would have killed you!
I think the varlet would not have cared if
she'd stilled you!
But shall we lose our needle thus?
GAMMER.
No, Hodge, I shall never do so.
Do you think I'll take that at her hand?
No!
HODGE.
I wish this fight were settled, our needle safe
at home,
It's in my bones someone to kill, wherever it
be or whom!

GAMMER [*a little amazed at his words*].
We have a parson, Hodge, you know, a man
esteemed and wise,
Good Doctor Rat, I'll send for him and ask
for his advice.
He'll right this fight and clear this hate,
We'll have our needle or Chat never comes
within Heaven's gate.
HODGE.
Yes, marry, Gammer, I think it best some word
to send.
GAMMER.
The sooner Parson Rat comes, the sooner this
matter will end.
HODGE.
Listen, Gammer! Diccon's devil, as I remem-
ber well,
Of Doctor Rat, of Gib, our cat, and Chat a
felinous tale did tell.
I'll bet you forty pounds that is the way to get
your needle again.
GAMMER. Let's send for Doctor Rat! Call
out the boy. We'll make him take the pain.
HODGE [*calling*]. Hey, Cock! I say, come
out! What the devil! Can't you hear?
COCK [*he enters from the house*]. How now,
Hodge? Hello, Gammer! Is the weather now
clear? What is it? What would you have me
do?
GAMMER. Come here, Cock. Go swift to
Doctor Rat. And pray him come speak with
me; I am not well at ease.
COCK. Doctor Rat, the curate?
GAMMER [*nodding*].
You'll find him at his chamber, or else at
Mother Bee's;
Else seek him at Hob Filcher's shop, for I
have heard reported
There the ale is best of all in town, the place
is much frequented.
COCK. And shall I bring him with me, Gam-
mer?
GAMMER. Yea, good Cock.
COCK [*running out left*]. I'll have him here
before the clock has struck!
HODGE [*who is evidently a little weary*].
Now, Gammer, shall we go in and wait for his
coming?
What the devil? Pluck up! Take heart, leave
off this glooming.
Though she were stronger at the first, as I am
sure you found her,
Why, Gammer, you hit the drunken drab each
time you got behind her.
GAMMER [*shaking her head*].
Nay, nay, I'm sure she'll not forget from the
end to the beginning;
I do not doubt but that she will make great
boast of herself winning.
TIB [*she comes running in from the house*].
See, Gammer, Gammer, Gib, our cat, I'm afraid
she is ailing!

She stands behind the door gasping as though her wind were failing.

GAMMER. Poor Gib!

TIB. Poor Gib! What does it mean that she should so dote?

HODGE. Where is she? I'll bet twenty pounds your needle's in her throat! [*He runs into the house*]

GAMMER. Grab her, I say!

HODGE [*entering from the house with* GIB *in his arms*]. I believe I feel it! Does it prick your hand?

GAMMER [*feeling the cat*]. I cannot feel it.

HODGE [*feeling the cat from her nose to the tip of her tail*]. No . . . no. There's nothing in this land.

TIB.

Faith, she has eaten something that will not easily down;

I cannot tell whether she got it at home or abroad in the town.

GAMMER.

Alas, I fear it is some crooked pin!

Ah, then farewell, Gib! She's undone and lost—all save the skin!

HODGE.

'Tis your needle, woman, I say! Tib, go get me a knife

And I'll have it out of her maw, or else lose my life!

GAMMER. What! Nay! Hodge, fie! Kill not our cat, 'tis all the cat we have now!

HODGE. By the mass, Dame Chat has so moved me I care not what I kill now!

[*Giving* TIB *the cat*]

Here, then, Tib, hold up her head, so. There, take her.

I'll see what the devil is inside her. I'll rake her!

GAMMER. Rake a cat, Hodge? How can you?

HODGE.

Do you think I'm not able?

Doesn't Tom Tankard rake his cow in the stable?

[*COCK comes running in from the left*]

GAMMER. Quick! Let us hear what news you bring from Doctor Rat.

COCK.

Gammer, I've been there—you know well what about,

He is coming over at once, I'll swear to't.

GAMMER. Where did you find him, boy?

COCK.

At Hob Filcher's house—full of joy,

A cup of ale in his hand, and a crab lay in the fire;

I had much trouble going and coming, all was so of mire.

I'll lay a penny Doctor Rat will find your needle soon.

GAMMER.

I'm glad to hear that, Cock, for if he does 'twill prove a boon.

But come, let us go in, the Doctor will be here soon.

[*They all follow* GAMMER GURTON *into the house.* DOCTOR RAT *enters from the right*]

DOCTOR RAT [*mumbling to himself*].

A man were better twenty times a Cheshire cat and smirk

Than here among such a sort be parish priest or clerk,

Where he can never be at rest one minute of the day, .

But he must trudge about the town this way and that way.

I had not sit the space to drink two pots of ale

But Gammer's boy was straightway on my trail,

Saying she was sick, that I must come, to do I know not what!

If once her finger's end but ache, trudge! Call for Doctor Rat!

[*GAMMER GURTON enters from her house*]

What! Gammer Gurton? Here's your friend the curate, Doctor Rat.

GAMMER. Oh! Good Master Doctor! I have troubled you, I know well that!

DOCTOR RAT. How do you know, woman? Are you lusty or are you not well at ease?

GAMMER. By gab, Master, I am not sick . . . still I have a disease!

DOCTOR RAT. What is the matter?

GAMMER.

Alas! I have lost my needle! A drab came by and spied it,

But when I asked her for it she up and denied it!

DOCTOR RAT. What did she say?

GAMMER.

She began to scold and brawl—

Come hither, Hodge! This wretch can tell you all!

HODGE [*he enters from the house*]. Good morrow, Gaffer Vicar!

DOCTOR RAT. Come, fellow, tell your tale.

GAMMER. Tell him the truth, Hodge!

HODGE [*taking a long breath before he begins*].

My Gammer Gurton, here, see now,

Sat her down at this door, see now;

And as she began to bestir her, see now,

Her needle fell on the floor, see now;

And while her staff she took, see now,

At Gib, her cat, to fling, see now,

Her needle was lost on the ground, see now;

Then came a jade, Dame Chat, see now,

To ask for her black cup, see now;

And right here in this street, see now,

She picked our needle up, see now;

My Gammer then asked her, see now,

To give the needle back, see now,

Chat up and beat her head, see now!

Is not this a wondrous thing, see now?

She scratched my Gammer's face, see now!
I thought she'd stopped her throat, see now,
When I saw this I was mad, see now!
I jumped between the two, see now,
Else, I durst take an oath, see now,
My Gammer had been slain, see now.

GAMMER. It's the truth! Help us or we'll be beaten—and lose our needle, too!

DOCTOR RAT.
Tell me what you wish me to do—
Are you sure Dame Chat the lost needle found?

GAMMER [she sees DICCON coming down the street].
Oh, here comes the man who saw her take it from the ground.
Ask of him the truth—if you won't believe me.
Oh, help me get my needle, Doctor Rat, for Saint Charity!
[DICCON comes sauntering in]

DOCTOR RAT. Come here, Diccon.

DICCON. Aye, Doctor Rat.

DOCTOR RAT. Will you swear Dame Chat has Gammer's needle, lad?

DICCON. By Saint Benet, I will not! Do you think I am mad?

GAMMER. But you told me so! For shame! Can you deny it?

DICCON. But I said I'd not abide by it—not for heaven or hell!

DOCTOR RAT. Then we're no nearer the truth, for the truth you won't tell!

DICCON [looking to the right].
Sh! If Dame Chat sees us here she'll know what's the matter,
Faith, I advise you to go into the house, and pull the shutter.

DOCTOR RAT. 'Tis better so.

DICCON. And safer.

GAMMER. Yes.

DICCON.
I'll into Dame Chat's house and see the needle, no time to lose,
As soon as I learn, I'll come straight back with the news.

GAMMER [moving toward the house]. Now, gentle Diccon, do so; and, sir, let us trudge.

DOCTOR RAT [protestingly]. But Gammer, I can't stay long to be your judge.

DICCON [pleadingly].
Wait a little while, man. Pray take that much pain!
If I see no needle I'll come straight back again.

HODGE. Tarry awhile, good Master Doctor, out of gentleness!

DOCTOR RAT. Then let us get into the house. Diccon, hurry your business!

[GAMMER GURTON, with DOCTOR RAT and HODGE at her heels, goes into the house. DICCON moves away toward the right. The shutter of GAMMER's window is closed, which leaves the street in semi-darkness]

DICCON [talking to himself].
But with Dame Chat, my gossip, talk first I must,
For she must be the chief captain to lay Rat in the dust.
[DAME CHAT enters from the right]
Oh, good even, Dame Chat! Faith, we're well met in this place.

DAME CHAT. Good even, friend Diccon. Why are you walking this space?

DICCON. By my truth, to your house. To hear how the world goes—

DAME CHAT [she points with her thumb to GAMMER's house. Laughing]. Gog's legs, I wish you had seen! Oh, Lord, I gave them such blows!

DICCON.
Hodge, by heaven and hell, said he'd wreck his sorrow
And leave you never a hen alive by this time to-morrow.

DAME CHAT. The knave might as well hang himself as walk on my ground!

DICCON.
But let me help you save your hens while they are still sound.
Have you not behind your furnace or lead
A hole where a crafty knave could creep in of need?

DAME CHAT. Yes, my word, a hole broke there just these two days back!

DICCON [making sure that no one is about].
Hodge intends to slip in there this night with a sack!

DAME CHAT.
By Gog's bones, when he comes, now that I know the matter,
He shall crawl into a pot of boiling hot water!
And a good beating besides! When he will let him come!

DICCON [chucking DAME CHAT under the chin]. I've told you as my sister. And you know the meaning of "mum."

DAME CHAT. Never a word will I breathe.

DICCON. Go in then, and wait.
[She goes out right. RAT enters from GAMMER GURTON's house].

DOCTOR RAT. What news, Diccon? Is Dame Chat at home?

DICCON. She is, sir!

DOCTOR RAT. You saw the needle?

DICCON. I have seen it, indeed, sir!

DOCTOR RAT. How, Diccon?

DICCON. Will you hear?

DOCTOR RAT. Marry, I will!

DICCON.
As she sat there sewing a halter or a band,
I saw it! Gammer Gurton's needle in her hand!
When there's a knock, if the filth is in doubt,
She blows but one puff and her candle is out.
Now I, sir, knowing of every door the pin,
Went quietly, saying no word till I was in,

And there saw the needle, with my own two
  eyes;
Whoever says the contrary, I'll swear he lies!
  DOCTOR RAT. Oh, I wish I'd been there!
  DICCON. I can bring you to the place where
you'll catch the drab with the needle in her
hand.
  DOCTOR RAT. Bring me to the place, Diccon.
  DICCON. Very well, sir.
  DOCTOR RAT. And I'll give you a quart of the
best ale in town.
  DICCON. You must lay aside your gown.
  DOCTOR RAT [hurriedly taking off his gown].
It's off!
  DICCON [he puts his arm around DOCTOR
RAT's shoulder and points off right].
See what is there? A hole wherein you can
  creep,
Into the house and suddenly, unawares, among
  them leap!
  DOCTOR RAT. I see!
  DICCON [walking to the right]. Follow me.
  DOCTOR RAT. Are you sure, Diccon, there are
no swill-tubs about?
  DICCON.
Come, give me your hand—have no doubt.
Do as I bid you. Come, we'll go together.
Crawl into that hole, and find the jade with
  the needle!
  [They go out right]
  DOCTOR RAT [from within]. Help! Help! I
shall be slain among them!
  DICCON. If they don't give up the needle tell
'em you'll hang 'em!
  DOCTOR RAT. Help! Help! Oh! Oh-o-o-o.
  DICCON [running in from the right].
Now, my wenches, you have caught the fox
Who wished to steal the hens and cocks!
  DOCTOR RAT. Help! Oh-o-o-o-o! Help! Let
me out!
  DICCON [looking up]. Hoho! So!
  DOCTOR RAT. Oh-o-o-o! Ho! Oh-o-o-o!
  DICCON [putting his thumb to his nose].
He's getting well paid for all his pains,
Lord, I hope they don't beat out his brains!
  [He hurries up the street and exits left.
  DOCTOR RAT, with his face well beaten
  and his clothes in rags, runs in from the
  right]
  DOCTOR RAT.
Woe! Curse the hour that I came here!
Master Baily, I vow, if he is worth his ears
Will hang these murderers amid rejoicing and
  cheers!
  [Nursing his wounds, he hurries up the
  street and off left]

CURTAIN

ACT THREE

SCENE: *The same early next morning. Stools
and a wooden bench have been placed before*
GAMMER GURTON's *house.* GAMMER, *with* TIB
near her, is seated facing DAME CHAT *and*
DOLL. DOCTOR RAT, *his head bound in bandages, and* HODGE *are seated on the bench near
the door.* BAILY, *who conducts the court, is
seated in the middle of the semi-circle.*

  BAILY. Dame Chat, Master Doctor has com-
plained that you and your maid—
  HODGE [he points to DOLL who sticks her
tongue out at him]. That's her!
  BAILY. Yes, complains that you meant to
do murder.
  DAME CHAT. That I meant to murder him?
Fie on him, wretch!
  BAILY. Quiet! Quiet! I beseech!
  DAME CHAT [pointing to HODGE].
There is the knave that got the blow;
It was Hodge, so far as I know.
  DOCTOR RAT [pointing to CHAT]. 'Twas she!
  DAME CHAT. What, man, you say I broke
your head?
  DOCTOR RAT. I'll swear to it—living or dead!
  DAME CHAT [to BAILY]. I've not seen him
this last fortnight.
  DOCTOR RAT. She saw me not because she
blew out the light!
  BAILY. For Gog's sake, explain this thing!
  DAME CHAT.
Good Baily, last night a kind friend gave me
  warning,
And bade me keep watch of my roost and my
  pens,
  [She looks over at HODGE, who winces un-
  der her gaze]
For a sly, silly knave was out after my hens
And I, to save my goods, quietly took my
  watch.
  [She crosses her arms]
You know, fortune served me well, I got my
  catch!
  BAILY. But you've not told me the name of
the thief!
  DAME CHAT [she rises and points to HODGE].
There's the bag of mischief!
  HODGE. Me!
  DAME CHAT. You.
  HODGE. Me?
  DAME CHAT. You!
  GAMMER. You false jade, shame!
  BAILY [covering his ears]. Stop! Stop! In
heaven's name!
  GAMMER [to DAME CHAT]. I'll punch your
head to jelly!
  BAILY.
You knave, I'll teach you to steal hens and
  cocks,
By Gog, you'll sure kiss the stocks!
  DOCTOR RAT. Why, he wasn't even there!

BAILY. Not there?

DAME CHAT. Look on his pate!

DOCTOR RAT. I wish my head were half so whole!

BAILY [to the nervous HODGE]. Answer me this, is your head whole or broken?

HODGE. Is my head whole? Look! Whole, by every good token!

BAILY. Come over here.

HODGE. Yes, that I dare.

[He rises from his end of the bench and DOCTOR RAT, with a yell, topples over. HODGE runs to BAILY and sticks his head up into BAILY's astonished face]

BAILY [examining HODGE's head]. By our Lady, the head's not harmed.

GAMMER. It was the jade Chat who stole from me!

DAME CHAT. What have I ever stolen of yours, you ill-tempered old trot?

GAMMER. My needle . . . my needle. Did you not?

HODGE. Give Gammer back her goods you stole.

GAMMER [to BAILY].
This drab she keeps my goods. May she step
    in the devil's snare!
I pray you that I have a right action on her!

BAILY. What can you charge her with? Tell me. Well—

GAMMER. Marry, a vengeance to her heart. The trot stole my needle!

DAME CHAT.
Your needle, old witch! How so? It were
    alms your soul to knock!
'Twas yesterday you said I stole your yellow-
    legged cock!
And roasted him for my breakfast—which shall
    not be forgotten,
The devil pull out your tongue, and the lies of
    it so begotten!

GAMMER. Give me my needle!

BAILY.
Silence! You must leave off being so bold!
Silence! Do you think court's a place to scold?
Do you know Dame Chat has your needle?
    Who told you so?

GAMMER. Diccon, Master, Diccon, I am very sure you know him.

BAILY.
A false knave. Gog's pity. You should not trust
    that fool!
Did he not also say she stole your rooster from
    his stool?

DAME CHAT.
It was that wench Tib who said the cock was
    stolen,
The lying cat, she also said that in my house
    'twas eaten!

GAMMER [shaking her finger].
Surely, there somebody lied
My cock is safe and sound inside.

BAILY. This is a case. You're sure you've lost your needle?

GAMMER [shaking her head vigorously]. Yes, kind sir, I'm sure it is!

BAILY. Dame Chat says she has no rooster of yours. Do you insist she has your cock?

GAMMER. No, Mr. Baily, for I know she's not!

BAILY [to DAME CHAT]. Will you confess to taking the needle?

DAME CHAT. No, sir, I will not!

BAILY.
I think the end will prove this brawl did first
    arise
Upon no other ground save only Diccon's dev-
    ilish lies.

DAME CHAT.
Though some are lies, as you, Baily, have
    spied them,
Yet others may be true, I have some proof, and
    I believe them,
For 'twas Diccon told me Hodge would come;
    he came indeed,
But, as it so happened, with greater haste than
    speed—
This truth was said, and true was found, and
    truly I report.

BAILY. If Doctor Rat was not deceived it was of another sort.

DAME CHAT. A pair of foxes!

BAILY [to DAME CHAT]. Didn't Diccon ap-point the place where you were to meet him?

DAME CHAT. Yes, by the mass, and if he came told me to beat him.

BAILY [he chuckles]. The villain has de-ceived you all, inside and out!

DOCTOR RAT.
He is the cause of all this brawl, the dirty, ly-
    ing lout!
He set me in the black hole creeping on my
    two knees,
    [Feeling his bruised head. He looks at
        DAME CHAT]
I know the weight of your door-bar, if you
    please!

HODGE.
Thank Gog my poor head was saved the bolt,
Had I not had the better wit, I'd have been
    made a dolt!

DAME CHAT. Fie on Diccon! Fie! Fie! You all agree, that's plain.

GAMMER. Fie on the knave! Fie and fie and fie again!

DOCTOR RAT. Fie! Fie on him may I best say whom he almost had slain!

[DICCON, a little tipsy, comes sauntering in from the left]

DICCON. God bless you, God bless you all! So many all at once!

DAME CHAT. Come, knave, it were best to beat you, by Gog's bones! D'you see . . . d'you see your handiwork?

DICCON [*pointing to* DOCTOR RAT]. Him?
Why, my hands came nowhere near him!

BAILY [*grabbing* DICCON]. Have you not
told a lie or two and set these folks by the ears?

DICCON [*laughing*].
They've been fighting! Oh, and I—and I
missed seeing the fight!
I haven't seen a good one these many years.
[*Doubling over with laughter*]
You make me laugh till my eyes are full of
tears!
Doctor Rat! Hasn't the old fool wit to save
his ears?

DOCTOR RAT. In Gog's name, Baily, I charge
you to hold him fast.

DICCON [*still laughing*]. What, fast at running or fast asleep? That's the thing I did last.

DOCTOR RAT. Do! Fast in chains, false varlet, according to your deeds.

BAILY. Master Doctor, that is no remedy!
For this one needs some other sort of punishment—

DOCTOR RAT.
Yes, by all Hallows!
His punishment, if I were judge, would be the
gallows.

BAILY. I'll give him good punishment, but
yours is far too great.

GAMMER.
It is a shame, I tell you plain, with such false
knaves to treat!
Why, he has almost killed us all, and that's
as true as steel.
Yet for all this great ado I'm never the nearer
my needle!

BAILY. Can you tell us anything of *that*,
Diccon?

DICCON. Yes, marry, sir, this much I can
say— [*They all sit on the edge of their stools
expectantly*] Well . . . well, the needle is lost!
[DOLL'S *stool slips from under her and
with a whoop she sits on the ground.*
DAME CHAT *takes her by the ear and
re-seats her*]

BAILY. And can you tell where that needle
will be found?

DICCON. Yes, marry, sir, I can.
[*They are on the edges of their stools
again*]

BAILY. Well, where can Gammer Gurton's
needle be found?

DICCON. It can be found, the needle can be
found—

GAMMER. Speak out, knave!

DICCON. Your needle can be found where it
is—lost! [TIB'S *stool goes out from under her.*
GAMMER *swings at her,* TIB *ducks and* HODGE
is struck full in the face] But I can't tell where
it is for an hundred pound!

HODGE [*holding his face*]. You liar! You
promised the needle would be found. It's not
been seen.

DICCON [*he winks*]. But you ran away from
the devil! You know what I mean!

BAILY.
Doctor Rat, you must both learn and teach
us, to forgive,
Since Diccon has confessed and is so cleanly
shrive
If you'll consent I'll try to amend the heavy
chance
And make him do some open penance—

DAME CHAT. Say yes, Master Vicar.

DOCTOR RAT.
My part was the worse, still, since you all agree,
I'm ready to forget, that goes from me!

BAILY. Well, Doctor, are you willing and
ready on me to depend?

DICCON. Of course, Master. Do what you
like. I know you for a friend.

BAILY.
Before them all you must kneel down and so
confess,
And take an oath upon poor Hodge's old torn
breeches,
[DICCON *kneels down and* BAILY *takes hold
of his hair. Pulling it vigorously*]
First, for Master Doctor, upon pain of his
curse—
Where he will pay for all, you must never draw
a purse.
To Dame Chat you must bow and swear, in
the likewise,
If she refuses your money once, never to offer
it twice;
For good Gammer Gurton's sake, sworn you
must be
To help her find her needle again, to this you
must agree.
Last of all, for Hodge, your given oath to scan,
You must never, never take him for a fine
gentleman.

HODGE. Come on, fellow Diccon, I shall be
even with you now!

BAILY. You will not do this, Diccon? You
promise and vow?

DICCON.
Yes, my father's skin, I promise and lay my
hand to it!
Look, as I have promised, I will not deny it
even now!
[*He gives* HODGE *a slap on his torn
breeches*]

HODGE [*grabbing his leg*]. Gog's bones!

BAILY. What! Is he beating you again?

HODGE. He thrust me in the leg with a bodkin or a pin!

DICCON. A bodkin?

GAMMER. A pin?

HODGE [*discovering the needle*]. I say, Gammer! Gammer!

GAMMER. How now, Hodge, how now?

HODGE [*dancing about*]. Gog's malt, Gammer Gurton!

GAMMER. You're mad!

HODGE. The devil, Gammer!

GAMMER. What is it?

HODGE [*hopping about with one leg in the air*]. I have it, by the mass, Gammer!

GAMMER. What, Hodge? What?

HODGE. Your needle!

DAME CHAT. Her needle!

TIB. Her needle!

GAMMER. No . . . fie, you joke!

HODGE. I can't pull it out, Gammer! But it's in my leg—I feel it!

GAMMER. For all the loves on earth, Hodge, let me see it!

HODGE [*bending over*]. Can you see it?

GAMMER [*trying to pull the needle out of his leg*]. My needle! My needle!

TIB. I see it!

DAME CHAT. The needle?

GAMMER. Gog's light on you! You have made me whole forever!

HODGE. I knew I must find it—if I wished peace ever.

DAME CHAT. By my troth, Gossip Gurton, I am as glad as though I had found it!

BAILY. And I! Come, we'll pull it forth!

DOCTOR RAT. I rejoice so much at it . . . three needles' worth!

DICCON. Gammer, say "Thank you, Diccon," for springing the game.

GAMMER. Thank you, Diccon, twenty times! Oh, how glad I am.

BAILY. Come, let us pull the needle out.

[HODGE *leans over,* BAILY *takes him about the waist. Tug-of-war fashion;* DICCON *takes* BAILY. *On the other end is* GAMMER GURTON, *grabbing the end of the needle with both hands,* DAME CHAT, TIB *and* DOLL. *They pull and pull—and pull. At last the needle comes out of* HODGE's *leg. With a wild yell everyone falls backward*]

CURTAIN

THE REHEARSAL

By GEORGE VILLIERS, Second Duke of Buckingham, and Others.

DRAMATIS PERSONÆ

MEN:
  BAYES
  JOHNSON
  SMITH
  TWO KINGS OF BRENTFORD
  PRINCE PRETTY-MAN
  PRINCE VOLSCIUS
  GENTLEMAN-USHER
  PHYSICIAN
  DRAWCANSIR
  GENERAL
  LIEUTENANT-GENERAL
  CORDELIO
  TOM THIMBLE
  FISHERMAN
  SUN
  THUNDER
  PLAYERS
  SOLDIERS
  TWO HERALDS
  FOUR CARDINALS
  MAYOR
  JUDGES
  SERGEANTS AT ARMS
WOMEN:
  AMARYLLIS
  CLORIS
  PARTHENOPE
  PALLAS
  LIGHTNING
  MOON
  EARTH
Attendants of Men and Women
SCENE: *Brentford.*
[TIME: *Contemporary, 1671.*]

THE REHEARSAL

PROLOGUE

We might well call this short mock-play of
    ours
A posy made of weeds instead of flowers;
Yet such have been presented to your noses,
And there are such, I fear, who thought 'em
    roses.
Would some of 'em were here, to see, this night,
What stuff it is in which they took delight.
Here, brisk, insipid blades, for wit, let fall
Sometimes dull sense; but oft'ner, none at all:
There, strutting heroes, with a grim-faced train,
Shall brave the gods, in King Cambyses' vein.
For (changing rules, of late, as if men writ
In spite of reason, nature, art, and wit),
Our poets make us laugh at tragedy,
And with their comedies they make us cry.
Now, critics, do your worst, that here are met;
For, like a rook, I have hedged in my bet.
If you approve, I shall assume the state
Of those high-flyers whom I imitate;
And justly too, for I will show you more
Than ever they vouchsafed to show before:
I will both represent the feats they do,
And give you all their reasons for 'em too.
Some honor to me will from this arise;
But if, by my endeavors, you grow wise,
And what was once so praised you now despise,
Then I'll cry out, swelled with poetic rage,
'Tis I, John Lacy, have reformed your stage.

ACT ONE

SCENE I

[*Enter* JOHNSON *and* SMITH]

JOHNSON. Honest Frank! I'm glad to see
thee with all my heart: how long hast thou
been in town?

SMITH. Faith, not above an hour: and, if
I had not met you here, I had gone to look
you out; for I long to talk with you freely, of
all the strange new things we have heard in the
country.

JOHNSON. And, by my troth, I have longed
as much to laugh with you, at all the impertinent, dull, fantastical things we are tired
out with here.

SMITH. Dull and fantastical! that's an excellent composition. Pray, what are our men
of business doing?

JOHNSON. I ne'er enquire after 'em. Thou

know'st my humor lies another way. I love
to please myself as much and to trouble others
as little as I can, and therefore do naturally
avoid the company of those solemn fops who,
being incapable of reason, and insensible of wit
and pleasure, are always looking grave and
troubling one another, in hopes to be thought
men of business.

SMITH. Indeed, I have ever observed that
your grave lookers are the dullest of men.

JOHNSON. Aye, and of birds, and beasts too;
your gravest bird is an owl, and your gravest
beast is an ass.

SMITH. Well, but how dost thou pass thy
time?

JOHNSON. Why, as I use to do—eat and
drink as well as I can, have a she-friend to be
private with in the afternoon, and sometimes
see a play; where there are such things, Frank,
—such hideous, monstrous things,—that it has
almost made me forswear the stage and resolve
to apply myself to the solid nonsense of your
pretenders to business, as the more ingenious
pastime.

SMITH. I have heard, indeed, you have had
lately many new plays, and our country wits
commend 'em.

JOHNSON. Aye, so do some of our City wits
too; but they are of the new kind of wits.

SMITH. New kind? what kind is that?

JOHNSON. Why, your blade, your frank persons, your drolls—fellows that scorn to imitate
nature, but are given altogether to elevate and
surprise.

SMITH. Elevate and surprise? Prithee, make
me understand the meaning of that.

JOHNSON. Nay, by my troth, that's a hard
matter; I don't understand that myself. 'Tis
a phrase they have got among them, to express
their no-meaning by. I'll tell you, as well as
I can, what it is. Let me see; 'tis fighting, loving, sleeping, rhyming, dying, dancing, singing,
crying; and everything but thinking and sense.

[MR. BAYES *passes o'er the stage*]

BAYES. Your most obsequious and most ob-
servant very servant, sir.

JOHNSON. Godso, this is an author! I'll fetch
him to you.

SMITH. Nay, prithee, let him alone.

JOHNSON. Nay, by the Lord, I'll have him.
[*Goes after him*] Here he is. I have caught
him.—Pray, sir, for my sake, will you do a
favor to this friend of mine?

BAYES. Sir, it is not within my small capacity

55

to do favors, but receive 'em, especially from a person that does wear the honorable title you are pleased to impose, sir, upon this. [*Bowing to* SMITH] Sweet sir, your servant.

SMITH. Your humble servant, sir.

JOHNSON. But wilt thou do me a favor, now?

BAYES. Aye, sir. What is't?

JOHNSON. Why, to tell him the meaning of thy last play.

BAYES. How, sir, the meaning!—do you mean the plot?

JOHNSON. Aye, aye—anything.

BAYES. Faith, sir, the intrigo's now quite out of my head: but I have a new one, in my pocket, that I may say is a virgin; 't has never yet been blown upon. I must tell you one thing, 'tis all new wit; and, though I say it, a better than my last—and you know well enough how that took. In fine, it shall read, and write, and act, and plot, and show—aye, and pit, box and gallery, I gad, with any play in Europe. This morning is its last rehearsal—in their habits and all that—as it is to be acted; and if you and your friend will do it but the honor to see it in its virgin attire—though, perhaps, it may blush—I shall not be ashamed to discover its nakedness unto you. [*Puts his hand in his pocket*] I think it is o' this side.

JOHNSON. Sir, I confess I am not able to answer you in this new way; but if you please to lead, I shall be glad to follow you; and I hope my friend will do so too.

SMITH. Aye, sir, I have no business so considerable as should keep me from your company.

BAYES. Yes, here it is.—No, cry you mercy! this is my book of drama commonplaces, the mother of many other plays.

JOHNSON. Drama commonplaces! pray what's that?

BAYES. Why, sir, some certain helps that we men of art have found it convenient to make use of.

SMITH. How, sir, help for wit?

BAYES. Aye, sir, that's my position. And I do here aver that no man yet the sun e'er shone upon has parts sufficient to furnish out a stage except it be with the help of these my rules.

JOHNSON. What are those rules, I pray?

BAYES. Why, sir, my first rule is the "rule of transversion," or *"regula duplex"*—changing verse into prose, or prose into verse, alternative as you please.

SMITH. How's that, sir, by a rule, I pray?

BAYES. Why, thus, sir—nothing more easy when understood. I take a book in my hand—either at home or elsewhere, for that's all one—if there be any wit in't, as there is no book but has some, I transverse it: that is, if it be prose, put it into verse (but that takes up some time); if it be verse, put it into prose.

JOHNSON. Methinks, Mr. Bayes, that putting verse into prose should be called transprosing.

BAYES. By my troth, a very good notion, and hereafter it shall be so.

SMITH. Well, sir, and what d'ye do with it then?

BAYES. Make it my own. 'Tis so altered that no man can know it. My next rule is the rule of record, and by way of table-book. Pray, observe.

JOHNSON. Well, we hear you: go on.

BAYES. As thus. I come into a coffee-house, or some other place where witty men resort. I make as if I minded nothing (do you mark?), but as soon as any one speaks, pop! I slap it down, and make that, too, my own.

JOHNSON. But, Mr. Bayes, are not you sometimes in danger of their making you restore, by force, what you have gotten thus by art?

BAYES. No, sir, the world's unmindful; they never take notice of these things.

SMITH. But pray, Mr. Bayes, among all your other rules, have you no one rule for invention?

BAYES. Yes, sir, that's my third rule that I have here in my pocket.

SMITH. What rule can that be?

BAYES. Why, sir, when I have anything to invent, I never trouble my head about it, as other men do; but presently turn o'er this book, and there I have, at one view, all that Perseus, Montaigne, Seneca's tragedies, Horace, Juvenal, Claudian, Pliny, Plutarch's Lives, and the rest, have ever thought upon this subject; and so, in a trice, by leaving out a few words or putting in others of my own, the business is done.

JOHNSON. Indeed, Mr. Bayes, this is as sure and compendious a way of wit as ever I heard of.

BAYES. Aye, sirs; when you come to write yourselves, o' my word you'll find it so. But, gentlemen, if you make the least scruple of the efficacy of these my rules, do but come to the playhouse and you shall judge of 'em by the effects.

SMITH. We'll follow you, sir. [*Exeunt*]

[*Enter three* PLAYERS *upon the stage*]

1ST PLAYER. Have you your part perfect?

2ND PLAYER. Yes, I have it without book, but I do not understand how it is to be spoken.

3RD. PLAYER. And mine is such a one as I can't guess for my life what humor I'm to be in—whether angry, melancholy, merry, or in love. I don't know what to make on't.

1ST PLAYER. Phoo! the author will be here presently and he'll tell us all. You must know, this is the new way of writing; and these hard things please forty times better than the old plain way. For, look you, sir, the grand design upon the stage is to keep the auditors in suspense; for to guess presently at the plot and the sense, tries 'em before the end of the first act. Now, here, every line surprises you and brings in new matter. And, then, for scenes, clothes, and dancing, we put 'em quite down, all that ever went before us—and these are the things, you know, that are essential to a play.

2ND PLAYER. Well, I am not of thy mind, but so it gets us money 'tis no great matter.

[*Enter* BAYES, JOHNSON, *and* SMITH]

BAYES. Come, come in, gentlemen. Y'are very welcome, Mr.—a—. Ha' you your part ready?

1ST. PLAYER. Yes, sir.

BAYES. But do you understand the true humor of it?

1ST. PLAYER. Aye, sir, pretty well.

BAYES. And Amaryllis, how does she do? Does not her armor become her?

3RD PLAYER. Oh, admirably!

BAYES. I'll tell you, now, a pretty conceit. What do you think I'll make 'em call her, anon, in this play?

SMITH. What, I pray?

BAYES. Why, I'll make 'em call her Armaryllis, because of her armor—ha, ha, ha!

JOHNSON. That will be very well, indeed.

BAYES. Aye, it's a pretty little rogue; she is my mistress. I knew her face would set off armor extremely, and, to tell you true, I writ that part only for her. Well, gentlemen, I dare be bold to say, without vanity, I'll show you something here that's very ridiculous, I gad.

[*Exeunt* PLAYERS]

JOHNSON. Sir, that we do not doubt of.

BAYES. Pray, sir, let's sit down.—Look you, sir, the chief hinge of this play, upon which the whole plot moves and turns, and that causes the variety of all the several accidents, which, you know, are the thing in nature that make up the grand refinement of a play, is, that I suppose two kings to be of the same place— as, for example, at Brentford, for I love to write familiarly. Now the people having the same relations to 'em both, the same affections, the same duty, the same obedience, and all that, are divided among themselves in point of *devoir* and interest, how to behave themselves equally between 'em—these kings differing sometimes in particular, though in the main they agree.—I know not whether I make myself well understood.

JOHNSON. I did not observe you, sir; pray, say that again.

BAYES. Why, look you, sir (nay, I beseech you, be a little careful in taking notice of this, or else you'll never understand my notion of the thing), the people being embarrassed by their equal ties to both, and the sovereigns concerned in a reciprocal regard, as well to their own interest as the good of the people, may make a certain kind of a—you understand me—upon which there does arise several disputes, turmoils, heart-burnings, and all that.—

In fine, you'll apprehend it better when you see it. [*Exit, to call the* PLAYERS]

SMITH. I find the author will be very much obliged to the players, if they can make any sense of this.

[*Enter* BAYES]

BAYES. Now, gentlemen, I would fain ask your opinion of one thing. I have made a prologue and an epilogue which may both serve for either—do you mark? Nay, they may both serve too, I gad, for any other play as well as this.

SMITH. Very well. That's, indeed, well contrived.

BAYES. And I would fain ask your judgments, now, which of them would do best for the prologue. For, you must know, there is, in nature, but two ways of making very good prologues. The one is by civility, by insinuation, good language, and all that, to—a—in a manner, steal your plaudit from the courtesy of the auditors; the other, by making use of some certain personal things, which may keep a hank upon such censuring persons as cannot otherways, a gad, in nature, be hindered from being too free with their tongues. To which end, my first prologue is, that I come out in a long black veil, and a great, huge hang-man behind me, with a furred cap and his sword drawn; and there tell 'em plainly that if, out of good nature, they will not like my play, why I gad, I'll e'en kneel down, and he shall cut my head off. Whereupon they all clapping —a—

SMITH. But suppose they do not.

BAYES. Suppose! Sir, you may suppose what you please, I have nothing to do with your suppose, sir, nor am not at all mortified at it— not at all, sir; I gad, not one jot. "Suppose," quoth a!— [*Walks away*]

JOHNSON. Phoo! prithee, Bayes, don't mind what he says. He's a fellow newly come out of the country; he knows nothing of what's the relish, here, of the town.

BAYES. If I writ, sir, to please the country, I should have followed the old, plain way: but I write for some persons of quality and peculiar friends of mine, that understand what flame and power in writing is; and they do me the right, sir, to approve of what I do.

JOHNSON. Aye, aye, they will clap, I warrant you; never fear it.

BAYES. I'm sure the design's good: that cannot be denied. And then, for language, I gad, I defy 'em all, in nature, to mend it. Besides, sir, I have printed above a hundred sheets of paper, to insinuate the plot into the boxes: and withal, have appointed two or three dozen of my friends to be ready in the pit, who, I'm sure, will clap, and so the rest, you know, must follow; and then pray, sir, what becomes of your suppose?—Ha, ha, ha!

JOHNSON. Nay, if the business be so well laid, it cannot miss.

BAYES. I think so, sir, and therefore would choose this for the prologue. For if I could engage 'em to clap before they see the play, you know 'twould be so much the better, because then they were engaged; for let a man write never so well, there are, now-a-days, a sort of persons they call critics, that, I gad, have no more wit in 'em than so many hobby-horses. But they'll laugh you, sir, and find fault, and censure things that, I gad, I'm sure they are not able to do themselves—a sort of envious persons that emulate the glories of persons of parts and think to build their fame by calumniating of persons that, I gad, to my knowledge, of all persons in the world are, in nature, the persons that do as much despise all that as—a— In fine, I'll say no more of 'em.

JOHNSON. Aye, aye, you have said enough of 'em, in conscience— I'm sure more than they'll ever be able to answer.

BAYES. Why, I'll tell you, sir, sincerely, and *bona fide;* were it not for the sake of some ingenious persons and choice female spirits that have a value for me, I would see 'em all hanged before I would e'er more set pen to paper; but let 'em live in ignorance like ingrates.

JOHNSON. Aye, marry! that were a way to be revenged of 'em, indeed; and, if I were in your place, now, I would do it.

BAYES. No, sir: there are certain ties upon me that I cannot be disengaged from; otherwise, I would. But pray, sir, how do you like my hangman?

SMITH. By my troth, sir, I should like him very well.

BAYES. Aye, but how do you like it?—for I see you can judge. Would you have it for the prologue, or the epilogue?

JOHNSON. Faith, sir, it's so good, let it e'en serve for both.

BAYES. No, no! that won't do. Besides, I have made another.

JOHNSON. What other, sir?

BAYES. Why, sir, my other is Thunder and Lightning.

JOHNSON. That's greater; I'd rather stick to that.

BAYES. Do you think so? I'll tell you then; though there have been many witty prologues written of late, yet I think you'll say this is a *non pareillo.* I'm sure nobody has hit upon it yet. For here, sir, I make my prologue to be dialogue: and as in my first you see I strive to oblige the auditors by civility, by good nature, and all that, so in this by the other way, *in terrorem,* I choose for the persons Thunder and Lightning. Do you apprehend the conceit?

JOHNSON. Phoo, pox! then you have it cock-sure. They'll be hanged before they'll dare affront an author that has 'em at that lock.

BAYES. I have made, too, one of the most delicate, dainty similes in the whole world, I gad, if I knew but how to apply it.

SMITH. Let's hear it, I pray you.

BAYES. 'Tis an allusion to love.

So boar and sow, when any storm is nigh,
Snuff up, and smell it gath'ring in the sky:
Boar beckons sow to trot in chestnut groves,
And there consummate their unfinished loves.
Pensive, in mud, they wallow all alone,
And snort and gruntle to each other's moan.

—How do you like it now, ha?

JOHNSON. Faith, 'tis extraordinary fine; and very applicable to Thunder and Lightning, methinks, because it speaks of a storm.

BAYES. I gad, and so it does, now I think on't. Mr. Johnson, I thank you, and I'll put it in *profecto.* Come out, Thunder and Lightning.

[*Enter* THUNDER *and* LIGHTNING]

THUNDER. I am the bold Thunder.

BAYES. Mr. Cartwright, prithee, speak a little louder, and with a hoarser voice. "I am the bold Thunder?" Pshaw! speak it me in a voice that thunders it out indeed: I am the bold Thunder!

THUNDER. I am the bold Thunder.
LIGHTNING. The brisk Lightning, I.

BAYES. Nay, you must be quick and nimble. —The brisk Lightning, I.—That's my meaning.

THUNDER. I am the bravest Hector of the sky.
LIGHTNING. And I, fair Helen, that made Hector die.
THUNDER. I strike men down.
LIGHTNING. I fire the town.
THUNDER. Let the critics take heed how they grumble,
For then begin I for to rumble.
LIGHTNING. Let the ladies allow us their graces,
Or I'll blast all the paint on their faces,
And dry up their peter to soot.
THUNDER. Let the critics look to't.
LIGHTNING. Let the ladies look to't.
THUNDER. For Thunder will do't.
LIGHTNING. For Lightning will shoot.
THUNDER. I'll give you dash for dash.
LIGHTNING. I'll give you flash for flash.
Gallants, I'll singe your feather.
THUNDER. I'll Thunder you together.
BOTH. Look to't, look to't; we'll do't, we'll do't; look to't, we'll do't.
[*Twice or thrice repeated*]
[*Exeunt Ambo*]

BAYES. That's all. 'Tis but a flash of a prologue—a droll.

SMITH. 'Tis short, indeed, but very terrible.

BAYES. Aye, when the simile is in, it will do to a miracle, I gad. Come, come, begin the play.

[*Enter* FIRST PLAYER]

1ST PLAYER. Sir, Mr. Ivory is not come yet, but he'll be here presently; he's but two doors off.

BAYES. Come then, gentlemen, let's go out and take a pipe of tobacco. [*Exeunt*]

ACT TWO

Scene I

[*Enter* Bayes. Johnson, *and* Smith]

Bayes. Now, sir, because I'll do nothing here that ever was done before— [*Spits*]

Smith. A very notable design for a play, indeed.

Bayes. Instead of beginning with a scene that discovers something of the plot, I begin this with a whisper.

Smith. That's very new.

Bayes. Come, take your seats, Begin, sirs. [*Enter* Gentleman-Usher *and* Physician]

Physician. Sir, by your habit, I should guess you to be the gentleman-usher of this sumptuous place.

Usher. And by your gait and fashion I should almost suspect you rule the healths of both our noble kings, under the notion of physician.

Physician. You hit my function right.

Usher. And you, mine.

Physician. Then let's embrace.

Usher. Come then.

Physician. Come. [*They embrace*]

Johnson. Pray, sir, who are those two so very civil persons?

Bayes. Why, sir, the gentleman-usher and physician of the two kings of Brentford.

Johnson. But how comes it to pass, then, that they know one another no better?

Bayes. Phoo! that's for the better carrying on of the intrigue.

Johnson. Very well.

Physician. Sir, to conclude,

Smith. What, before he begins?

Bayes. No, sir; you must know they had been talking of this a pretty while without.

Smith. Where? In the tiring-room?

Bayes. Why aye, sir.—He's so dull!—Come, speak again.

Physician. Sir, to conclude, the place you fill has more than amply exacted the talents of a wary pilot, and all these threat'ning storms which, like impregnant clouds, do hover o'er our heads, (when they once are grasped but by the eye of reason) melt into fruitful showers of blessings on the people.

Bayes. Pray, mark that allegory. Is not that good?

Johnson. Yes; that grasping of a storm with the eye is admirable.

Physician. But yet some rumors great are stirring; and if Lorenzo should prove false (as none but the great gods can tell), you then perhaps would find that— [*Whispers*]

Bayes. Now they whisper.

Usher. Alone, do you say?

Physician. No; attended with the noble— [*Whispers*]

Usher. Who—he in gray?

Physician. Yes; and at the head of— [*Whispers*]

Bayes.—Pray, mark.

Usher. Then, sir, most certain, 'twill in time appear These are the reasons that induced 'em to't. First, he— [*Whispers*]

Bayes. Now t'other whispers.

Usher. Secondly, they— [*Whispers*]

Bayes. He's at it still.

Usher. Thirdly and lastly, both he and they— [*Whispers*]

Bayes. There they both whisper. [*Exeunt whispering*]—Now, gentlemen, tell me true and without flattery, is not this a very odd beginning of a play?

Johnson. In troth, I think it is, sir. But why two kings of the same place?

Bayes. Why? because it's new, and that's it I aim at. I despise your Jonson and Beaumont, that borrowed all they writ from nature: I am for fetching it purely out of my own fancy, I.

Smith. But what think you of Sir John Suckling, sir?

Bayes. By gad, I am a better poet than he.

Smith. Well, sir; but pray, why all this whispering?

Bayes. Why, sir (besides that it is new, as I told you before), because they are supposed to be politicians, and matters of state ought not to be divulged.

Smith. But then, sir, why—

Bayes. Sir, if you'll but respite your curiosity till the end of the fifth act, you'll find it a piece of patience not ill recompensed. [*Goes to the door*]

Johnson. How dost thou like this, Frank? Is it not just as I told thee?

Smith. Why, I did never, before this, see anything in nature, and all that (as Mr. Bayes says), so foolish but I could give some guess at what moved the fop to do it; but this, I confess, does go beyond my reach.

Johnson. Why, 'tis all alike: Mr. Wintershall has informed me of this play before. And I'll tell thee, Frank, thou shalt not see one scene here that either properly ought to come in, or is like anything thou canst imagine has ever been the practice of the world. And then, when he comes to what he calls "good language," it is, as I told thee, very fantastical, most abominably dull, and not one word to the purpose.

Smith. It does surprise me, I am sure, very much.

Johnson. Aye, but it won't do so long; by

that time thou hast seen a play or two that I'll show thee, thou wilt be pretty well acquainted with this new kind of foppery.

Scene II

[*Enter the two* Kings, *hand in hand*]

Bayes. These are the two kings of Brentford. Take notice of their style: 'twas never yet upon the stage; but, if you like it, I could make a shift, perhaps, to show you a whole play, written all just so.

1st King. Did you observe their whisper, brother king?
2nd King. I did; and heard besides a grave bird sing
That they intend, sweetheart, to play us pranks.

Bayes. This, now, is familiar, because they are both persons of the same quality.

Smith. 'Sdeath, this would make a man spew.

1st King. If that design appears,
I'll lug 'em by the ears
Until I make 'em crack.
2nd King. And so will I, i'fack.
1st King. You must begin, *mon foy.*
2nd King. Sweet sir, *pardonnes moy.*

Bayes. Mark that: I makes 'em both speak French to show their breeding.

Johnson. Oh, 'tis extraordinary fine.

2nd King. Then, spite of Fate, we'll thus combinèd stand;
And, like true brothers, walk still hand in hand.
[*Exeunt*]

Johnson. This is a very majestic scene indeed.

Bayes. Aye, 'tis a crust, a lasting crust for your rogue critics, I gad. I would fain see the proudest of 'em all but dare to nibble at this; I gad, if they do, this shall rub their gums for 'em, I promise you. It was I, you must know, writ the play I told you of, in this very style. And shall I tell you a very good jest? I gad, the players would not act it. Ha, ha, ha!

Smith. That's impossible.

Bayes. I gad, they would not, sir—ha, ha, ha! They refused it, I gad, the silly rogues: ha, ha, ha.

Johnson. Fie, that was rude.

Bayes. Rude! I gad, they are the rudest, uncivilest persons, and all that, in the whole world: I gad, there's no living with 'em. I have written, Mr. Johnson, I do verily believe, a whole cart-load of things, every whit as good as this; and yet, I vow to gad, these insolent rascals have turned 'em all back upon my hands again.

Johnson. Strange fellows, indeed.

Smith. But pray, Mr. Bayes, how came these two kings to know of this whisper? for, as I remember, they were not present at it.

Bayes. No, but that's the actors' fault, and not mine; for the kings should (a pox take 'em) have popped both their heads in at the door just as the others went off.

Smith. That, indeed, would ha' done it.

Bayes. Done it! Aye, I gad, these fellows are able to spoil the best things in christendom. I'll tell you, Mr. Johnson, I vow to gad, I have been so highly disobliged by the peremptoriness of these fellows, that I am resolved hereafter to bend all my thoughts for the service of the Nursery, and mump your proud players, I gad.

Scene III

[*Enter* Prince Pretty-man]

Pretty-man. How strange a captive am I grown of late!
Shall I accuse my love, or blame my fate?
My love, I cannot; that is too divine:
And against Fate what mortal dares repine?

[*Enter* Cloris]

—But here she comes.
Sure 'tis some blazing comet, is it not?
[*Lies down*]

Bayes. Blazing comet! mark that. I gad, very fine!

Pretty-man. But I am so surprised with sleep I cannot speak the rest.   [*Sleeps*]

Bayes. Does not that, now, surprise you, to fall asleep just in the nick? His spirits exhale with the heat of his passion, and all that, and—swop! falls asleep, as you see. Now here she must make a simile.

Smith. Where's the necessity of that, Mr. Bayes?

Bayes. Because she's surprised. That's a general rule: you must ever make a simile when you are surprised; 'tis the new way of writing.

Cloris. As some tall Pine, which we, on Ætna, find
T'have stood the rage of many a boist'rous wind,
Feeling without, that flames within do play
Which would consume his root and sap away,
He spreads his worsted arms unto the skies,
Silently grieves, all pale, repines and dies:
So, shrouded up, your bright eye disappears;
Break forth, bright scorching Sun, and dry my tears.   [*Exit*]

Bayes. I am afraid, gentlemen, this scene has made you sad; for I must confess, when I writ it, I wept myself.

Smith. No, truly, sir, my spirits are almost exhaled too, and I am likelier to fall asleep.

[Prince Pretty-man *starts up, and says*]

Pretty-man. It is resolved.   [*Exit*]

Smith. Mr. Bayes, may one be so bold as to ask you a question now, and you not be angry?

Bayes. O Lord, sir, you may ask me what

you please. I vow to gad, you do me a great deal of honor: you do not know me if you say that, sir.

SMITH. Then, pray, sir, what is it that this prince here has resolved in his sleep?

BAYES. Why, I must confess, that question is well enough asked for one that is not acquainted with this new way of writing. But you know, sir, that, to outdo all my fellow-writers, whereas they keep their *intrigo* secret till the very last scene before the dance, I now, sir, do you mark me—a—

SMITH. Begin the play and end it, without ever opening the plot at all?

BAYES. I do so; that's the very plain truth on't. Ha, ha, ha! I do, I gad. If they cannot find it out themselves, e'en let 'em alone for Bayes, I warrant you.—But here, now, is a scene of business. Pray observe it, for I dare say you'll think it no unwise discourse this, nor ill argued. To tell you true, 'tis a debate I overheard once betwixt two grand, sober, governing persons.

SCENE IV

[*Enter* GENTLEMAN-USHER *and* PHYSICIAN]

USHER. Come, sir; let's state the matter of fact, and lay our heads together.

PHYSICIAN. Right! lay our heads together. I love to be merry sometimes; but when a knotty point comes, I lay my head close to it, with a pipe of tobacco in my mouth, and then I whew it away, i'faith.

BAYES. I do just so, I gad, always.

USHER. The grand question is, whether they heard us whisper; which I divide thus: into when they heard, what they heard, and whether they heard or no.

JOHNSON. Most admirably divided, I swear.

USHER. As to the when, you say just now; so that is answered. Then, for what. Why, what answers itself; for what could they hear but what we talked of? So that naturally and of necessity we come to the last question, *videlicet,* whether they heard or no.

SMITH. This is a very wise scene, Mr. Bayes.

BAYES. Yes, you have it right. They are both politicians. I writ this scene for a pattern, to show the world how men should talk of business.

JOHNSON. You have done it exceeding well, indeed.

BAYES. Yes, I think this will do.

PHYSICIAN. Well, if they heard us whisper, they'll turn us out, and nobody else will take us.

USHER. Nobody else will take us.

SMITH. Not for politicians, I dare answer for it.

PHYSICIAN. Let's then no more ourselves in vain bemoan;
We are not safe until we them unthrone.

USHER. 'Tis right.
And, since occasion now seems debonair,
I'll seize on this, and you shall take that chair.
[*They draw their swords, and sit down in the two great chairs upon the stage*]

BAYES. There's now an odd surprise; the whole state's turn'd quite topsy-turvy, without any puther or stir in the whole world, I gad.

JOHNSON. A very silent change of government, truly, as ever I heard of.

BAYES. It is so. And yet you shall see me bring 'em in again, by and by, in as odd a way every jot.
[*The* USURPERS *march out flourishing their swords*]
[*Enter* SHIRLEY]

SHIRLEY. Hey ho, hey ho! what a change is here! Hey day, hey day! I know not what to do, nor what to say. [*Exit*]

SMITH. But pray, sir, how came they to depose the kings so easily?

BAYES. Why, sir, you must know, they long had a design to do it before, but never could put it in practice till now; and, to tell you true, that's one reason why I made 'em whisper so at first.

SMITH. Oh, very well: now I'm fully satisfied.

BAYES. And then, to show you, sir, it was not done so very easily neither, in this next scene you shall see some fighting.

SMITH. Oh, ho! so then you make the struggle to be after the business is done?

BAYES. Aye.

SMITH. Oh, I conceive you. That is very natural.

SCENE V

[*Enter four men at one door, and four at another, with their swords drawn*]

1ST. SOLDIER. Stand! Who goes here?
2ND SOLDIER. A friend.
1ST SOLDIER. What friend?
2ND SOLDIER. A friend to the house.
1ST SOLDIER. Fall on!
[*They all kill one another. Music strikes*]

BAYES [*to the music*]. Hold, hold! [*It ceaseth*] Now, here's an odd surprise: all these dead men you shall see rise up presently, at a certain note that I have made, in F *flat,* and fall a-dancing. Do you hear, dead men? [*To the music*] Remember your note in F *flat.* Play on.—Now, now, now! [*The music plays his note, and the dead men rise but cannot get in order*]—O Lord, O Lord!—Out, out, out!— Did ever men spoil a good thing so? no figure, no ear, no time, nothing! You dance worse than the angels in *Harry the Eight,* or the fat spirits in *The Tempest,* I gad.

1ST SOLDIER. Why, sir, 'tis impossible to do anything in time, to this tune.

BAYES. O Lord, O Lord! Impossible? why, gentlemen, if there be any faith in a person that's a Christian, I sate up two whole nights in composing this air and apting it for the business. For, if you observe, there are two several designs in this tune; it begins swift, and ends slow. You talk of time, and time; you shall see me do't. Look you now. [*Lies down flat on his face*] Here I am dead. Now mark my note in F *flat.*—Strike up music. Now. [*As he rises up hastily, he tumbles and falls down again*]—Ah, gadsookers! I have broke my nose.

JOHNSON. By my troth, Mr. Bayes, this is a very unfortunate note of yours, in F *flat.*

BAYES. A plague of this damned stage, with your nails and your tenter-hooks, that a man cannot come to teach you to act but he must break his nose, and his face, and the divel and all. Pray, sir, can you help me to a wet piece of brown paper?

SMITH. No indeed, sir; I don't usually carry any about me.

2ND. SOLDIER. Sir, I'll go get you some within presently.

BAYES. Go, go then; I'll follow you. Pray, dance out the dance, and I'll be with you in a moment. Remember, you four, that you dance like horsemen. [*Exit* BAYES]

[*They dance the dance, but can make nothing of it*]

1ST SOLDIER. A devil! let's try this no more. Play my dance that Mr. Bayes found fault with.

[*Dance, and exeunt*]

SMITH. What can this fool be doing all this while about his nose?

JOHNSON. Prithee, let's go see. [*Exeunt*]

ACT THREE

SCENE I

[*Enter* BAYES *with a paper on his nose, and the two gentlemen*]

BAYES. Now, sir, this I do because my fancy in this play is to end every act with a dance.

SMITH. Faith, that fancy is very good, but I should hardly have broke my nose for it, though.

JOHNSON. That fancy, I suppose, is new too.

BAYES. Sir, all my fancies are so. I tread upon no man's heels, but make my flight upon my own wings, I assure you. As now, this next scene some perhaps will say,—it is not very necessary to the plot. I grant it; what then? I meant it so. But then, it's as full of drollery as ever it can hold: 'tis like an orange stuck with cloves as for conceit.—Come, where are you? This scene will make you die with laughing if it be well acted; it is a scene of sheer wit, without any mixture in the world, I gad. [*Reads*]

[*Enter* PRINCE PRETTY-MAN *and* TOM THIMBLE, *his tailor*]

This, sirs, might properly enough be called a prize of wit; for you shall see 'em come in upon one another snip snap, hit for hit, as fast as can be. First one speaks, then presently t'other's upon him—slap! with a repartee; then he at him again—dash! with a new conceit, and so eternally, eternally, I gad, till they go quite off the stage. [*Goes to call the* PLAYERS]

SMITH. What a plague does this fop mean by his snip snap, hit for hit, and dash?

JOHNSON. Mean? why, he never meant anything in's life. What dost talk of meaning for? [*Enter* BAYES]

BAYES. Why don't you come in? [*Enter* PRINCE PRETTY-MAN *and* TOM THIMBLE]

PRETTY-MAN. But prithee, Tom Thimble, why wilt thou needs marry? If nine tailors make but one man, and one woman cannot be satisfied with nine men, what work art thou cutting out here for thyself, trow we?

BAYES. Good!

THIMBLE. Why, an't please your Highness, if I can't make up all the work I cut out, I shan't want journeymen to help me, I warrant you.

BAYES. Good again.

PRETTY-MAN. I am afraid thy journeymen, though, Tom, won't work by the day, but by the night.

BAYES. Good still.

THIMBLE. However, if my wife sits but cross-legg'd, as I do, there will be no great danger—not half so much as when I trusted you for your Coronation suit.

BAYES. Very good, i'faith.

PRETTY-MAN. Why, the times then lived upon trust; it was the fashion. You would not be out of time, at such a time as that, sure. A tailor, you know, must never be out of fashion.

BAYES. Right.

THIMBLE. I'm sure, sir, I made your cloth in the Court fashion, for you never paid me yet.

BAYES. There's a bob for the Court.

PRETTY-MAN. Why, Tom, thou art a sharp rogue when thou art angry, I see: thou pay'st me now, methinks.

THIMBLE. Aye, sir, in your own coin; you give me nothing but words.

BAYES. Admirable, before gad.

PRETTY-MAN. Well, Tom, I hope shortly I shall have another coin for thee; for now the wars come on, I shall grow to be a man of mettle.

BAYES. Oh, you did not do that half enough.

JOHNSON. Methinks he does it admirably.

BAYES. Aye, pretty well, but he does not hit me in't. He does not top his part.

THIMBLE. That's the way to be stamped yourself, sir. I shall see you come home, like an angel for the king's evil, with a hole bored through you. *[Exeunt]*

BAYES. That's very good, i'faith; ha, ha, ha! Ha, there he has hit it up to the hilts, I gad. How do you like it now, gentlemen? is not this pure wit?

SMITH. 'Tis "snip snap," sir, as you say, but methinks not pleasant nor to the purpose, for the play does not go on.

BAYES. Play does not go on? I don't know what you mean; why, is not this part of the play?

SMITH. Yes, but the plot stands still.

BAYES. Plot stand still! why, what a devil is the plot good for but to bring in fine things?

SMITH. Oh, I did not know that before.

BAYES. No, I think you did not—nor many things more that I am master of. Now, sir, I gad, this is the bane of all us writers: let us soar never so little above the common pitch, I gad, all's spoiled; for the vulgar never understand us. They can never conceive you, sir, the excellency of these things.

JOHNSON. 'Tis a sad fate, I must confess. But you write on still?

BAYES. Write on? I gad, I warrant you. 'Tis not their talk shall stop me; if they catch me at that lock, I'll give 'em leave to hang me. As long as I know my things to be good, what care I what they say?—What, they are gone, and forgot the song!

SMITH. They have done very well, methinks; there's no need of one.

BAYES. Alack, sir, you know nothing. You must ever interlard your plays with songs, ghosts and idols if you mean to—a—

JOHNSON. Pit, box and gallery, Mr. Bayes.

BAYES. I gad, sir, and you have nicked it. Hark you, Mr. Johnson, you know I don't flatter; I gad, you have a great deal of wit.

JOHNSON. O Lord, sir, you do me too much honor.

BAYES. Nay, nay, come, come, Mr. Johnson, 'ifacks this must not be said amongst us that have it. I know you have wit by the judgment you make of this play—for that's the measure I go by; my play is my touchstone. When a man tells me such a one is a person of parts, "Is he so?" say I. What do I but bring him presently to see this play. If he likes it, I know what to think of him; if not, "your most humble servant, sir, I'll no more of him upon my word; I thank you." I am *clara voyant*, I gad. Now, here we go on to our business.

SCENE II

[Enter the two USURPERS, hand in hand]

USHER. But what's become of Volscius the great?
His presence has not graced our court of late.
PHYSICIAN. I fear some ill, from emulation sprung,
Has from us that illustrious hero wrung.

BAYES. Is not that majestical?

SMITH. Yes, but who a devil is that Volscius?

BAYES. Why, that's a prince I make in love with Parthenope.

SMITH. I thank you, sir.

[Enter CORDELIO]

CORDELIO. My lieges, news from Volscius the Prince.
USHER. His news is welcome, whatsoe'er it be.

SMITH. How, sir, do you mean that—whether it be good or bad?

BAYES. Nay, pray, sir, have a little patience! Gadsookers, you'll spoil all my play! Why, sir, 'tis impossible to answer every impertinent question you ask.

SMITH. Cry you mercy, sir.

CORDELIO. His highness, sirs, commanded me to tell you
That the fair person whom you both do know,
Despairing of forgiveness for her fault,
In a deep sorrow, twice she did attempt
Upon her precious life; but, by the care
Of standers-by, prevented was.

SMITH. 'Sheart, what stuff's here!

CORDELIO.   At last,
Volscius the great this dire resolve embraced:
His servants he into the country sent,
And he himself to Piccadillé went;
Where he's informed, by letters, that she's dead!
USHER. Dead! Is that possible? Dead!
PHYSICIAN.   O ye gods!   *[Exeunt]*

BAYES. There's a smart expression of a passion—O ye gods! That's one of my bold strokes, I gad.

SMITH. Yes, but who is the fair person that's dead?

BAYES. That you shall know anon.

SMITH. Nay, if we know it at all, 'tis well enough.

BAYES. Perhaps you may find too, by and by, for all this, that she's not dead neither.

SMITH. Marry, that's good news. I am glad of that with all my heart.

BAYES. Now, here's the man brought in that is supposed to have killed her.

[A great shout within. Enter AMARYLLIS with a book in her hand, and ATTENDANTS]

AMARYLLIS. What shout triumphant's that?

[*Enter a* SOLDIER]

SOLDIER. Shy maid, upon the river brink, near
Twick'nam Town, the assassinate is tane.
AMARYLLIS. Thanks to the powers above for
this deliverance!
I hope its slow beginning will portend
A forward exit to all future end.

BAYES. Pish, there you are out! To all
future end? No, no—to all future *end:* you
must lay the accent upon "end," or else you
lose the conceit.

JOHNSON. Indeed the alteration of that accent does a great deal, Mr. Bayes.

BAYES. Oh, all in all, sir; they are these little
things that mar or set you off a play.

SMITH. I see you are perfect in these matters.

BAYES. Aye, sir; I have been long enough at
it to know something.

[*Enter* SOLDIERS *dragging in an old* FISH-
ERMAN]

AMARYLLIS. Villain, what monster did cor-
rupt thy mind
T'attack the noblest soul of human kind?
Tell me who set thee on.
FISHERMAN. Prince Pretty-man.
AMARYLLIS. To kill whom?
FISHERMAN. Prince Pretty-man.
AMARYLLIS. What, did Prince Pretty-man hire
you to kill Prince Pretty-man?
FISHERMAN. No; Prince Volscius.
AMARYLLIS. To kill whom?
FISHERMAN. Prince Volscius.
AMARYLLIS. What, did Prince Volscius hire you
to kill Prince Volscius?
FISHERMAN. No; Prince Pretty-man.
AMARYLLIS. So!—drag him hence.
Till torture of the rack produce his sense.
[*Exeunt* SOLDIERS *and* CAPTIVE]

BAYES. Mark how I make the horror of his
guilt confound his intellects—for that's the design of this scene.

SMITH. I see, sir, you have a several design
for every scene.

BAYES. Aye: that's my way of writing, and
so I can dispatch you, sir, a whole play, before another man, I gad, can make an end of
his plot. So, now enter Prince Pretty-man in
a rage.—Where the devil is he? [*Calls*] Why
Pretty-man! why when, I say? Oh, fie, fie, fie,
fie! all's marred—I vow to gad, quite marred.

[*Enter* PRETTY-MAN]

—Phoo, pox! you are come too late, sir; now
you may go out again if you please. I vow to
gad Mr.—a—I would not give a button for
my play, now you have done this.

PRETTY-MAN. What, sir?

BAYES. What, sir? 'Slife, sir, you should
have come out in choler, with a bounce upon
the stage just as the other went off. Must a
man be eternally telling you of these things?

JOHNSON [*aside*]. Sure this must be some
very notable matter that he's so angry at.

SMITH. I am not of your opinion.

BAYES. Pish! come, let's hear your part, sir.

PRETTY-MAN. Bring in my father; why d'ye
keep him from me?
Although a fisherman, he is my father.
Was ever son yet brought to this distress,
To be, for being a son, made fatherless?
Oh, you just gods, rob me not of a father.
The being of a son take from me rather.
[*Exit*]

SMITH. Well, Ned, what think you now?

JOHNSON. A devil, this is worst of all.—
Pray, Mr. Bayes, what's the meaning of this
scene?

BAYES. Oh, cry you mercy, sir: I purtest I
had forgot to tell you. Why, sir, you must
know that long before the beginning of this
play, this prince was taken by a fisherman.

SMITH. How, sir—taken prisoner?

BAYES. Taken prisoner! O Lord, what a
question's there! did ever any man ask such
a question? Taken prisoner! Gadsookers, he
has put the plot quite out of my head, with
this damned question. What was I going to
say?

JOHNSON. Nay, the Lord knows; I cannot
imagine.

BAYES. Stay, let me see—taken. Oh, 'tis true.
Why, sir, as I was going to say, his Highness
here, the prince, was taken in a cradle by a
fisherman and brought up as his child.

SMITH. Indeed!

BAYES. Nay, prithee, hold thy peace.—And
so, sir, this murder being committed by the
riverside, the fisherman, upon suspicion, was
seized, and thereupon the prince grew angry.

SMITH. So, so! now 'tis very plain.

JOHNSON. But, Mr. Bayes, is not that some
disparagement to a prince, to pass for a fisherman's son? Have a care of that, I pray.

BAYES. No, no, no—not at all, for 'tis but
for a while. I shall fetch him off again presently,
you shall see.

[*Enter* PRETTY-MAN *and* THIMBLE]

PRETTY-MAN. By all the gods, I'll set the
world on fire
Rather than let 'em ravish hence my sire.
THIMBLE. Brave Pretty-man, it is at length
revealed
That he is not thy sire who thee concealed.

BAYES. Lo' you now! there he's off again.

JOHNSON. Admirably done, i'faith.

BAYES. Aye, now the plot thickens very
much upon us.

PRETTY-MAN. What oracle this darkness can
evince?
Sometimes a fisher's son, sometimes a prince.
It is a secret, great as is the world;
In which, I, like the soul, am tossed and hurled.
The blackest ink of Fate, sure, was my lot,
And when she writ my name she made a blot.
[*Exit*]

BAYES. There's a blust'ring verse for you
now.

SMITH. Yes, sir; but pray, why is he so

mightily troubled to find he is not a fisherman's son?

BAYES. Phoo! that is not because he has a mind to be his son, but for fear he should be thought to be nobody's son at all.

SMITH. Aye, that would trouble a man, indeed.

BAYES. So; let me see. [*Reading*] Enter Prince Volscius, going out of town.

SMITH. I thought he had been gone to Piccadillé.

BAYES. Yes, he gave out so; but that was only to cover his design.

JOHNSON. What design?

BAYES. Why, to head the army that lies concealed for him in Knightsbridge.

JOHNSON. I see here is a great deal of plot, Mr. Bayes.

BAYES. Yes, now it begins to break, but we shall have a world of more business anon.

[*Enter* PRINCE VOLSCIUS, CLORIS, AMARYLLIS, *and* HARRY *with a riding-cloak and boots*]

AMARYLLIS. Sir, you are cruel, thus to leave the town and to retire to country solitude.

CLORIS. We hoped this summer that we should at least have held the honor of your company.

BAYES. Held the honor of your company! prettily exprest!—Held the honor of your company! Gadsookers, these fellows will never take notice of anything.

JOHNSON. I assure you, sir, I admire it extremely; I don't know what he does.

BAYES. Aye, aye, he's a little envious, but 'tis no great matter.—Come!

AMARYLLIS. Pray, let us two this single boon obtain,
That you will here with poor us still remain.
Before your horses come, pronounce our fate;
For then, alas, I fear 'twill be too late.

BAYES. Sad!

VOLSCIUS. Harry, my boots; for I'll go rage among
My blades encamped, and quit this urban throng.

SMITH. But pray, Mr. Bayes, is not this a little difficult, that you were saying e'en now, to keep an army thus concealed in Knightsbridge?

BAYES. In Knightsbridge?—stay.

JOHNSON. No, not if the innkeepers be his friends.

BAYES. His friends! Aye, sir, his intimate acquaintance; or else, indeed, I grant it could not be.

SMITH. Yes, faith, so it might be very easily.

BAYES. Nay, if I do not make all things easy, I gad, I'll give you leave to hang me. Now you would think that he is going out of town, but you shall see how prettily I have contrived to stop him presently.

SMITH. By my troth, sir, you have so amazed me, I know not what to think.

[*Enter* PARTHENOPE]

VOLSCIUS. Bless me! how frail are all my best resolves!
How, in a moment, is my purpose changed!
Too soon I thought myself secure from love.
Fair madam, give me leave to ask her name
Who does so gently rob me of my fame:
For I should meet the army out of town,
And, if I fail, must hazard my renown.
PARTHENOPE. My mother, sir, sells ale by the town walls,
And me her "dear Parthenope" she calls.
VOLSCIUS. Can vulgar vestments high-born beauty shroud?
Thou bring'st the morning pictured in a cloud.

BAYES. The morning pictured in a cloud! A gadsookers, what a conceit is there!

PARTHENOPE. Give you good ev'n, sir. [*Exit*]
VOLSCIUS. O inauspicious stars! that I was born
To sudden love and to more sudden scorn!
AMARYLLIS. Cloris—How! Prince Volscius in love? Ha, ha, ha. [*Exeunt laughing*]

SMITH. Sure, Mr. Bayes, we have lost some jest here that they laugh at so.

BAYES. Why did you not observe? He first resolves to go out of town, and then, as he is pulling on his boots, falls in love.— Ha, ha, ha!

SMITH. Oh, I did not observe; that, indeed, is a very good jest.

BAYES. Here, now, you shall see a combat betwixt love and honor. An ancient author has made a whole play on't, but I have dispatched it all in this scene.

[VOLSCIUS *sits down*]
VOLSCIUS. How has my passion made me Cupid's scoff!
This hasty boot is on, the other off,
And sullen lies, with amorous design
To quit loud fame and make that beauty mine.
My legs, the emblem of my various thought,
Show to what sad distraction I am brought.
Sometimes with stubborn honor, like this boot,
My mind is guarded, and resolved to do't;
Sometimes again, that very mind, by love
Disarmèd, like this other leg does prove.

JOHNSON. What pains Mr. Bayes takes to act this speech himself!

SMITH. Aye, the fool, I see, is mightily transported with it.

VOLSCIUS. Shall I to Honor or to Love give way?
"Go on," cries Honor; tender Love says, "Nay."
Honor, aloud, commands, "Pluck both boots on";
But softer Love does whisper, "Put on none."
What shall I do? what conduct shall I find
To lead me through this twilight of my mind?
For as bright Day, with black approach of Night
Contending, makes a doubtful, puzzling light,
So does my Honor and my Love together
Puzzle me so, I can resolve for neither.
[*Exit with one boot on and the other off*]

JOHNSON. By my troth, sir, this is as difficult a combat as ever I saw, and as equal; for 'tis determined on neither side.

BAYES. Aye, is't not, I gad?—ha! For, to go off hip hop, hip hop, upon this occasion, is a thousand times better than any conclusion in the world, I gad. But, sirs, you cannot make any judgment of this play, because we are come but to the end of the second act.—Come, the dance.

[*Enter* DANCERS *and dance*]

Well, gentlemen, you'll see this dance, if I am not mistaken, take very well upon the stage when they are perfect in their motions and all that.

SMITH. I don't know 'twill take, sir, but I am sure you sweat hard for't.

BAYES. Aye, sir, it costs me more pains and trouble to do these things than almost the things are worth.

SMITH. By my troth, I think so, sir.

BAYES. Not for the things themselves, for I could write you, sir, forty of 'em in a day; but I gad, these players are such dull persons, that if a man be not by upon every point and at every turn, I gad, they'll mistake you, sir, and spoil all.

[*Enter a* PLAYER]

—What, is the funeral ready?

PLAYER. Yes, sir.

BAYES. And is the lance filled with wine?

PLAYER. Sir, 'tis just now a-doing.

BAYES. Stay, then; I'll do it myself.

SMITH. Come, let's go with him.

BAYES. A match. But Mr. Johnson, I gad, I am not like other persons; they care not what becomes of their things, so they can but get money for 'em: now, I gad, when I write, if if be not just as it should be, in every circumstance, to every particular, I gad, I am not able to endure it. I am not myself; I'm out of my wits, and all that: I'm the strangest person in the whole world. For what care I for my money? I gad, I write for fame and reputation. [*Exeunt*]

ACT FOUR

SCENE I

[*Enter* BAYES *and the two* GENTLEMEN]

BAYES. Gentlemen, because I would not have any two things alike in this play, the last act beginning with a witty scene of mirth, I make this to begin with a funeral.

SMITH. And is that all your reason for it, Mr. Bayes?

BAYES. No, sir; I have a precedent for it too. A person of honor, and a scholar, brought in his funeral just so: and he was one (let me tell you) that knew as well what belonged to a funeral as any man in England, I gad.

JOHNSON. Nay, if that be so, you are safe.

BAYES. I gad, but I have another device—

a frolic, which I think yet better than all this —not for the plot or characters (for in my heroic plays I make no difference as to those matters), but for another contrivance.

SMITH. What is that, I pray?

BAYES. Why, I have designed a conquest, that cannot possibly, I gad, be acted in less than a whole week: and I'll speak a bold word, it shall drum, trumpet, shout and battle, I gad, with any the most warlike tragedy we have, either ancient or modern.

JOHNSON. Aye, marry, sir; there you say something.

SMITH. And pray, sir, how have you ordered this same frolic of yours?

BAYES. Faith, sir, by the rule of romance. For example, they divide their things into three, four, five, six, seven, eight, or as many tomes as they please; now, I would very fain know what should hinder me from doing the same with my things if I please.

JOHNSON. Nay, if you should not be master of your own works, 'tis very hard.

BAYES. That is my sense. And therefore, sir, whereas every one makes five acts to one play, what do I but make five plays to one plot, by which means the auditors have every day a new thing.

JOHNSON. Most admirably good, i'faith! and must certainly take, because it is not tedious.

BAYES. Aye, sir, I know that; there's the main point. And then, upon Saturday, to make a close of all (for I ever begin upon a Monday), I make you, sir, a sixth play, that sums up the whole matter to 'em, and all that, for fear they should have forgot it.

JOHNSON. That consideration, Mr. Bayes, indeed, I think, will be very necessary.

SMITH. And when comes in your share, pray, sir?

BAYES. The third week.

JOHNSON. I vow, you'll get a world of money.

BAYES. Why, faith, a man must live; and if you don't thus pitch upon some new device, I gad, you'll never do it; for this age (take it o' my word) is somewhat hard to please. There is one pretty, odd passage in the last of these plays, which may be executed two several ways, wherein I'd have your opinion, gentlemen.

JOHNSON. Well, what is't?

BAYES. Why, sir, I make a male person to be in love with a female.

SMITH. Do you mean that, Mr. Bayes, for a new thing?

BAYES. Yes, sir, as I have ordered it. You shall hear. He having passionately loved her through my five whole plays, finding at last that she consents to his love, just after that his mother had appeared to him like a ghost, he kills himself. That's one way. The other is, that she coming at last to love him with as violent a passion as he loved her, she kills herself. Now my question is, Which of these two persons should suffer upon this occasion?

JOHNSON. By my troth, it is a very hard case to decide.

BAYES. The hardest in the world, I gad; and has puzzled this pate very much. What say you, Mr. Smith?

SMITH. Why, truly, Mr. Bayes, if it might stand with your justice, I should now spare 'em both.

BAYES. I gad, and I think—ha—why then, I'll make him hinder her from killing herself. Aye, it shall be so.—Come, come, bring in the funeral.

[*Enter a Funeral, with the two* USURPERS *and* ATTENDANTS]

Lay it down there—no, here, sir.—So; now speak.

KING USHER. Set down the funeral pile, and
    let our grief
Receive from its embraces some relief.
KING PHYSICIAN. Was't not unjust to ravish
    hence her breath,
And in life's stead to leave us nought but death?
The world discovers now its emptiness,
And by her loss demonstrates we have less.

BAYES. Is not that good language, now? is not that elevate? It's my *non ultra*, I gad. You must know they were both in love with her.

SMITH. With her?—with whom?

BAYES. Why, this is Lardella's Funeral.

SMITH. Lardella! Aye, who is she?

BAYES. Why, sir, the sister of Drawcansir. —A lady that was drowned at sea and had a wave for her winding-sheet.

KING USHER. Lardella, O Lardella, from above
Behold the tragic issue of our love.
Pity us sinking under grief and pain,
For thy being cast away upon the main.

BAYES. Look you now, you see I told you true.

SMITH. Aye, sir, and I thank you for it, very kindly.

BAYES. Aye, I gad, but you will not have patience; honest Mr.—a—you will not have patience.

JOHNSON. Pray, Mr. Bayes, who is that Drawcansir?

BAYES. Why, sir, a fierce hero that frights his mistress, snubs up kings, baffles armies, and does what he will, without regard to good manners, justice, or numbers.

JOHNSON. A very pretty character.

SMITH. But, Mr. Bayes, I thought your heroes had ever been men of great humanity and justice.

BAYES. Yes, they have been so; but, for my part, I prefer that one quality of singly beating of whole armies above all your moral virtues put together, I gad. You shall see him

come in presently. [*To the* PLAYERS]—Zookers, why don't you read the paper?

KING PHYSICIAN. Oh, cry you mercy.
    [*Goes to take the paper*]

BAYES. Pish!—nay, you are such a fumbler. Come, I'll read it myself. [*Takes a paper from off the coffin*]—Stay, it's an ill hand; I must use my spectacles. This, now, is a copy of verses which I make Lardella compose just as she is dying with design to have it pinned on her coffin, and so read by one of the ursurpers, who is her cousin.

SMITH. A very shrewd design that, upon my word, Mr. Bayes.

BAYES. And what do you think I fancy her to make love like here in the paper?

SMITH. Like a woman. What should she make love like?

BAYES. O' my word you are out though, sir; I gad, you are.

SMITH. What then—like a man?

BAYES. No, sir, like a humble bee.

SMITH. I confess, that I should not have fancied.

BAYES. It may be so, sir. But it is, though, in order to the opinion of some of your ancient philosophers who held the transmigration of the soul.

SMITH. Very fine.

BAYES. I'll read the title: "To my dear Couz, King Physician."

SMITH. That's a little too familiar with a king though, sir, by your favor, for a humble bee.

BAYES. Mr. Smith, for other things I grant your knowledge may be above me; but as for Poetry, give me leave to say, I understand that better. It has been longer my practice; it has indeed, sir.

SMITH. Your servant, sir.

BAYES. Pray, mark it. [*Reads*]

Since death my earthly part will thus remove,
I'll come a humble bee to your chaste love.
With silent wings I'll follow you, dear couz;
Or else, before you, in the sun-beams buzz.
And when to melancholy groves you come,
An airy ghost, you'll know me by my hum;
For sound, being air, a ghost does well become.

SMITH [*after a pause*]. Admirable!

BAYES. At night into your bosom I will creep,
And buzz but softly if you chance to sleep;
Yet in your dreams I will pass sweeping by,
And then both hum and buzz before your eye.

JOHNSON. By my troth, that's a very great promise.

SMITH. Yes, and a most extraordinary comfort to boot.

BAYES. Your bed of love, from dangers I will
    free,
But most, from love of any future bee.

And when with pity your heart-strings shall
crack,
With empty arms I'll bear you on my back.

SMITH. A pick-a-pack, a pick-a-pack.

BAYES. Aye, I gad, but is not that *tuant* now,
ha? is it not *tuant?* Here's the end:

Then, at your birth of immortality,
Like any wingèd archer, hence I'll fly,
And teach you your first flutt'ring in the sky.

JOHNSON. Oh, rare! it is the most natural,
refined fancy this, that ever I heard, I'll swear.

BAYES. Yes, I think for a dead person it is
a good enough way of making love; for being
divested of her terrestrial part, and all that,
she is only capable of these little, pretty,
amorous designs that are innocent, and yet
passionate.—Come, draw your swords.

KING PHYSICIAN. Come sword, come sheath
thyself within this breast,
That only in Lardella's tomb can rest.
KING USHER. Come, dagger, come, and pene-
trate this heart,
Which cannot from Lardella's love depart.

[*Enter* PALLAS]

PALLAS. Hold! stop your murd'ring hands
At Pallas's commands!
For the supposèd dead, O kings,
Forbear to act such deadly things.
Lardella lives: I did but try
If princes for their loves could die.
Such celestial constancy
Shall, by the gods, rewarded be;
And from these funeral obsequies
A nuptial banquet shall arise.
[*The coffin opens, and a banquet is discovered*]

BAYES. Now it's out. This is the very funeral
of the fair person which Volscius sent word
was dead, and Pallas, you see, has turned it
into a banquet.

JOHNSON. By my troth, now, that is new,
and more than I expected.

BAYES. Yes, I knew this would please you;
for the chief art in poetry is to elevate your
expectation and then bring you off some extraordinary way.

KING USHER. Resplendent Pallas, we in thee do
find
The fiercest beauty and a fiercer mind:
And since to thee Lardella's life we owe,
We'll supple statues in thy temple grow.
KING PHYSICIAN. Well, since alive Lardella's
found,
Let, in full bowls, her health go round.
[*The two* USURPERS *take each of them a
bowl in their hands*]
KING USHER. But where's the wine?
PALLAS. That shall be mine.
Lo, from this conquering lance,
Does flow the purest wine of France;
[*Fills the bowls out of her lance*]
And, to appease your hunger, I
Have, in my helmet, brought a pie;
Lastly, to bear a part with these,
Behold a buckler made of cheese.
[*Vanish* PALLAS]

[*Enter* DRAWCANSIR]

KING PHYSICIAN. What man is this that dares
disturb our feast?
DRAWCANSIR. He that dares drink, and for
that drink dares die;
And, knowing this, dares yet think on, am I.

JOHNSON. That is as much as to say that
though he would rather die than not drink, yet
he would fain drink for all that too.

BAYES. Right; that's the conceit on't.

JOHNSON. 'Tis a marvellous good one, I
swear.

KING USHER. Sir, if you please, we should be
glad to know
How long you here will stay, how soon you'll go.

BAYES. Is not that now like a well-bred person, I gad?—so modest, so gent!

SMITH. Oh, very like.

DRAWCANSIR. You shall not know how long
I here will stay;
But you shall know I'll take my bowls away.
[*Snatches the bowls out of the* KING's
hands and drinks 'em off]

SMITH. But, Mr. Bayes, is that, too, modest
and gent?

BAYES. No, I gad, sir, but it's great.

KING USHER. Though, brother, this grum
stranger be a clown,
He'll leave us, sure, a little to gulp down.
DRAWCANSIR. Whoe'er to gulp one drop of
this dares think,
I'll stare away his very pow'r to drink.
[*The two* KINGS *sneak off the stage, with
their* ATTENDANTS]
I drink, I huff, I strut, look big and stare;
And all this I can do, because I dare.
[*Exit*]

SMITH. I suppose, Mr. Bayes, this is the
fierce hero you spoke of.

BAYES. Yes, but this is nothing: you shall
see him, in the last act, win above a dozen
battles, one after another, I gad, as fast as
they can possibly be represented.

JOHNSON. That will be a fight worth seeing,
indeed.

SMITH. But pray, Mr. Bayes, why do you
make the kings let him use 'em so scurvily?

BAYES. Phoo! that is to raise the character of
Drawcansir.

JOHNSON. O' my word, that was well thought
on.

BAYES. Now, sir, I'll show you a scene indeed; or rather, indeed the scene of scenes. 'Tis
an heroic scene.

SMITH. And pray, sir, what is your design
in this scene?

BAYES. Why, sir, my design is Roman clothes,
gilded truncheons, forced conceit, smooth verse,
and a rant; in fine, if this scene does not take,
I gad, I'll write no more. Come, come in, Mr.
—a—nay, come in as many as you can. Gentlemen, I must desire you to remove a little, for
I must fill the stage.

SMITH. Why fill the stage?

BAYES. Oh, sir, because your heroic verse never sounds well but when the stage is full.

SCENE II

[*Enter* PRINCE PRETTY-MAN *and* PRINCE VOLSCIUS]

BAYES. Nay, hold, hold! pray, by your leave a little.—Look you, sir, the drift of this scene is somewhat more than ordinary, for I make 'em both fall out because they are not in love with the same woman.

SMITH. Not in love? you mean, I suppose, because they are in love, Mr. Bayes?

BAYES. No, sir; I say not in love. There's a new conceit for you. Now, speak.

PRETTY-MAN. Since fate, Prince Volscius, has found out the way
For our so longed-for meeting here this day,
Lend thy attention to my grand concern.
VOLSCIUS. I gladly would that story of thee learn;
But thou to love dost, Pretty-man, incline:
Yet love in thy breast is not love in mine.

BAYES. Antithesis!—thine and mine.

PRETTY-MAN. Since love itself's the same, why should it be
Diff'ring in you from what it is in me?

BAYES. Reasoning; I gad, I love reasoning in verse.

VOLSCIUS. Love takes, chameleon-like, a various dye
From every plant on which itself does lie.

BAYES. Simile!

PRETTY-MAN. Let not thy love the course of nature fright:
Nature does most in harmony delight.
VOLSCIUS. How weak a deity would nature prove
Contending with the pow'rful god of love?

BAYES. There's a great verse.

VOLSCIUS. If incense thou wilt offer at the shrine
Of mighty love, burn it to none but mine.
Her rosy lips external sweets exhale,
And her bright flames make all flames else look pale.

BAYES. I gad, that is right.

PRETTY-MAN. Perhaps dull incense may thy love suffice,
But mine must be adored with sacrifice.
All hearts turn ashes which her eyes control:
The body they consume as well as soul.
VOLSCIUS. My love has yet a power more divine;
Victims her altars burn not, but refine.
Amidst the flames they ne'er give up the ghost,
But with her looks revive still as they roast.
In spite of pain and death, they're kept alive;
Her fiery eyes makes 'em in fire survive.

BAYES. That is as well as I can do.

VOLSCIUS. Let my Parthenope at length prevail.
BAYES. Civil, I gad.

PRETTY-MAN. I'll sooner have a passion for a whale,
In whose vast bulk, though store of oil doth lie,
We find more shape, more beauty, in a fly.

SMITH. That's uncivil, I gad.
BAYES. Yes; but as far a fetched fancy though, I gad, as ever you saw.

VOLSCIUS. Soft! Pretty-man, let not thy vain pretence
Of perfect love defame love's excellence.
Parthenope is sure as far above
All other loves as above all is love.

BAYES. Ah! I gad, that strikes me.

PRETTY-MAN. To blame my Cloris, gods would not pretend.

BAYES. Now mark.

VOLSCIUS. Were all gods joined, they could not hope to mend
My better choice; for fair Parthenope
Gods would, themselves, un-god themselves to see.

BAYES. Now the rant's a-coming.

PRETTY-MAN. Durst any of the gods be so uncivil,
I'd make that god subscribe himself a devil.

BAYES. Ah, gadsookers, that's well writ!

VOLSCIUS. Couldst thou that god from heav'n to earth translate,
He could not fear to want a heav'nly state.
Parthenope, on earth, can heav'n create.
PRETTY-MAN. Cloris does heav'n itself so far excel,
She can transcend the joys of heav'n in hell.

BAYES. There's a bold fight for you now! —'Sdeath, I have lost my peruke!—Well, gentlemen, this is that I never yet saw anyone could write but myself. Here's true spirit and flame all through, I gad. So, so! pray, clear the stage. [*He puts 'em off the stage*]

JOHNSON. But, Mr. Bayes, pray why is this scene all in verse?

BAYES. O sir, the subject is too great for prose.

SMITH. Well said, i'faith. I'll give thee a pot of ale for that answer; 'tis well worth it.

BAYES. Come, with all my heart. "I'll make that god subscribe himself a devil." That single line, I gad, is worth all that my brother poets ever writ. So! now let down the curtain. [*Exeunt*]

ACT FIVE

SCENE I

[*Enter* BAYES *and the two* GENTLEMEN]

BAYES. Now, gentlemen, I will be bold to say, I'll show you the greatest scene that ever England saw—I mean not for words, for those

I do not value, but for state, show, and magnificence. In fine, I'll justify it to be as grand to the eye every whit, I gad, as that great scene in *Harry the Eight*—and grander too, I gad; for, instead of two bishops, I have brought in two other cardinals.

[*The Curtain is drawn up, and the two usurping* KINGS *appear in state, with the four Cardinals,* PRINCE PRETTY-MAN, PRINCE VOLSCIUS, AMARYLLIS, CLORIS, PARTHENOPE, *&c. Before them,* HERALDS *and* SERGEANTS AT ARMS *with maces*]

SMITH. Mr. Bayes, pray what is the reason that two of the cardinals are in hats and the other two in caps?

BAYES. Why, sir, because—by gad, I won't tell you.

SMITH. I ask your pardon, sir.

KING USHER. Now, sir, to the business of the day.

VOLSCIUS. Dread sovereign lords, my zeal to you must not invade my duty to your son. Let me entreat that great Prince Pretty-man first do speak, whose high preëminence, in all things that do bear the name of good, may justly claim that privilege.

PRETTY-MAN. Royal father, upon my knees I beg
That the illustrious Volscius first be heard.

BAYES. Here it begins to unfold. You may perceive, now, that he is his son.

JOHNSON. Yes, sir; and we are very much beholden to you for that discovery.

VOLSCIUS. That preference is only due to Amaryllis, sir.

BAYES. I'll make her speak very well, by and by; you shall see.

AMARYLLIS. Invincible sovereigns—
                [*Soft Music*]
KING USHER. But stay, what sound is this invades our ears?

KING PHYSICIAN. Sure 'tis the music of the moving spheres.

PRETTY-MAN. Behold, with wonder! yonder comes from far,
A god-like cloud and a triumphant car;
In which our two right kings sit one by one,
With virgin vests, and laurel garlands on.
KING USHER. Then, Brother Phys', 'tis time that we were gone.
        [*The two* USURPERS *steal out of the Throne and go away*]

BAYES. Look you now, did not I tell you that this would be as easy a turn as the other?

SMITH. Yes, faith, you did so—though I confess, I could not believe you; but you have brought it about, I see.

[*The two right* KINGS OF BRENTFORD *descend in the clouds, singing in white garments; and three fiddlers sitting before them, in green*]

BAYES. Now, because the two right kings descend from above, I make 'em sing to the tune and style of our modern spirits.

1ST KING. Haste, brother king, we are sent from above.
2ND KING. Let us move, let us move—
        Move to remove the fate
        Of Brentford's long united state.
1ST KING. Tara, tara, tara, full east and by south,
2ND KING. We sail with Thunder in our mouth;
In scorching noon-day, whilst the traveller stays,
Busy, busy, busy, busy, we bustle along,
Mounted upon warm Phœbus his rays,
        Through the heavenly throng,
        Haste to those
Who will feast us, at night, with a pig's pettitoes.
1ST KING. And we'll fall with our pate
        In an olio of hate.
2ND KING. But now supper's done, the servitors try,
Like soldiers, to storm a whole half-moon pie.
1ST KING. They gather, they gather hot custard in spoons;
Alas, I must leave these half-moons,
And repair to my trusty dragoons.
2ND KING. Oh, stay, for you need not as yet go astray;
The tide, like a friend, has brought ships in our way,
And on their high ropes we will play.
Like maggots in filberts, we'll snug in our shell,
        We'll frisk in our shell,
        We'll firk in our shell,
        And farewell.
1ST KING. But the ladies have all inclination to dance,
And the green frogs croak out a coranto of France.

BAYES. Is not that pretty, now? The fiddlers are all in green.

SMITH. Aye, but they play no coranto.

JOHNSON. No, but they play a tune; that's a great deal better.

BAYES. "No coranto," quoth a!—that's a good one, with all my heart!—Come, sing on.

2ND KING. Now mortals that hear
        How we tilt and career,
        With wonder will fear
The event of such things as shall never appear.
1ST KING. Stay you to fulfil what the gods have decreed.
2ND KING. Then call me to help you if there shall be need.
1ST KING. So firmly resolved is a true Brentford king
To save the distressed and help to 'em bring,
That ere a full pot of good ale you can swallow,
He's here with a whoop, and gone with a holla.

[BAYES *fillips his finger and sings after 'em*]

BAYES. He's here with a whoop, and gone with a holla. This, sir, you must know, I thought once to have brought in with a conjurer.

JOHNSON. Aye, that would have been better.

BAYES. No, faith, not when you consider it, for thus 'tis more compendious and does the thing every whit as well.

SMITH. Thing!—what thing?

BAYES. Why, bring 'em down again into

the throne, sir. What thing would you have?

SMITH. Well; but methinks the sense of this song is not very plain.

BAYES. Plain? why, did you ever hear any people in clouds speak plain? They must be all for flight of fancy, at its full range, without the least check or control upon it. When once you tie up spirits and people in clouds to speak plain, you spoil all.

SMITH. Bless me, what a monster's this!

[The two KINGS light out of the clouds and step into the throne]

1ST KING. Come, now to serious counsel we'll advance.

2ND KING. I do agree; but first let's have a dance.

BAYES. Right. You did that very well, Mr. Cartwright. [Repeating] But first let's have a dance. Pray, remember that; be sure you do it always just so, for it must be done as if it were the effect of thought and premeditation. —But first, let's have a dance. Pray, remember that.

SMITH [aside]. Well, I can hold no longer; I must gag this rogue. There's no enduring of him.

JOHNSON. No, prithee, make use of thy patience a little longer; let's see the end of him now.

[Dance a grand dance]

BAYES. This, now, is an ancient dance, of right belonging to the Kings of Brentford, and since derived, with a little alteration, to the Inns of Court.

[An Alarm. Enter two HERALDS]

1ST KING. What saucy groom molests our privacies?

1ST HERALD. The army's at the door and, in disguise,
Desires a word with both your Majesties:

2ND HERALD. Having, from Knightsbridge, hither marched by stealth.

2ND KING. Bid 'em attend a while and drink our health.

SMITH. How, Mr. Bayes—the army in disguise?

BAYES. Aye, sir, for fear the usurpers might discover them that went out but just now.

SMITH. Why, what if they had discovered them?

BAYES. Why, then they had broke this design.

SMITH. That's true, indeed. I did not think of that.

1ST KING. Here, take five guineas for those warlike men.

2ND KING. And here's five more; that makes the sum just ten.

1ST HERALD. We have not seen so much the Lord knows when. [Exeunt HERALDS]

1ST KING. Speak on, brave Amaryllis.

AMARYLLIS. Invincible sovereigns, blame not my modesty

If at this grand conjuncture —
[Drum beats behind the stage]

1ST KING. What dreadful noise is this that comes and goes?

[Enter a SOLDIER with his sword drawn]

SOLDIER. Haste hence, great sirs, your royal persons save,
For the event of war no mortal knows!
The army, wrangling for the gold you gave,
First fell to words, and then to handy-blows. [Exit]

2ND KING. Oh, dangerous estate of sovereign pow'r!
Obnoxious to the change of every hour.

1ST KING. Let us for shelter in our cabinet stay:
Perhaps these threat'ning storms may pass away. [Exeunt KINGS]

JOHNSON. But, Mr. Bayes, did not you promise us, just now, to make Amaryllis speak very well?

BAYES. Aye, and so she would have done but that they hindered her.

SMITH. How, sir?—whether you would or no?

BAYES. Aye, sir; the plot lay so that, I vow to gad, it was not to be avoided.

SMITH. Marry, that was hard.

JOHNSON. But, pray, who hindered her?

BAYES. Why, the battle, sir, that's just coming in at door. And I'll tell you now a strange thing; though I don't pretend to do more than other men, I gad, I'll give you both a whole week to guess how I'll represent this battle.

SMITH. I had rather be bound to fight your battle, sir, I assure you.

BAYES. Why, there's it now: Fight a battle? there's the common error. I knew presently where I should have you. Why, pray, sir, do but tell me this one thing: Can you think it a decent thing, in a battle before ladies, to have men run their swords through one another, and all that?

JOHNSON. No, faith, 'tis not civil.

BAYES. On the other side: To have a long relation of squadrons here, and squadrons there —what is that but a dull prolixity?

JOHNSON. Excellently reasoned, by my troth!

BAYES. Wherefore, sir, to avoid both those indecorums, I sum up my whole battle in the representation of two persons only—no more —and yet so lively that, I vow to gad, you would swear ten thousand men were at it, really engaged. Do you mark me?

SMITH. Yes, sir; but I think I should hardly swear, though, for all that.

BAYES. By my troth, sir, but you would, though, when you see it; for I make 'em both come out in armor, cap-a-pie, with their swords drawn and hung with a scarlet ribbon at their wrists (which, you know, represents fighting enough), each of 'em holding a lute in his hand.

SMITH. How, sir—instead of a buckler?

BAYES. O Lord, O Lord!—Instead of a buckler? Pray, sir, do you ask no more questions. I make 'em, sir, play the battle in *recitativo*. And here's the conceit; just at the very same instant that one sings, the other, sir, recovers you his sword and puts himself in a warlike posture, so that you have at once your ear entertained with music and good language, and your eye satisfied with the garb and accoutrements of war. Is not that well?

JOHNSON. Aye; what would you have more? He were a devil that would not be satisfied with that.

SMITH. I confess, sir, you stupefy me.

BAYES. You shall see.

JOHNSON. But, Mr. Bayes, might not we have a little fighting? For I love those plays where they cut and slash one another, upon the stage, for a whole hour together.

BAYES. Why, then, to tell you true, I have contrived it both ways. But you shall have my *recitativo* first.

[*Enter at several doors the* GENERAL *and* LIEUTENANT-GENERAL, *armed cap-a-pie, each of them with a lute in his hand, and his sword drawn and hung with a scarlet ribbon at his wrist*]

LIEUTENANT-GENERAL. Villain, thou liest!
GENERAL. Arm, arm, Gonsalvo, arm! What ho!
The lie no flesh can brook, I trow.
LIEUTENANT-GENERAL. Advance, from Acton,
with the musketeers.
GENERAL. Draw down the Chelsea cuirassiers.
LIEUTENANT-GENERAL. The Band you boast of,
Chelsea cuirassiers,
Shall, in my Putney pikes, now meet their peers.
GENERAL. Chiswickians agèd, and renowned in fight,
Join with the Hammersmith brigade.
LIEUTENANT-GENERAL. You'll find my Mortlake boys will do them right,
Unless by Fulham numbers overlaid.
GENERAL. Let the left wing of Twick'nam foot advance
And line that eastern hedge.
LIEUTENANT-GENERAL. The horse I raised in
Petty-France
Shall try their chance.
And scour the meadows, overgrown with sedge.
GENERAL. Stand! give the word.
LIEUTENANT-GENERAL. Bright sword.
GENERAL. That may be thine,
But 'tis not mine.
LIEUTENANT-GENERAL. Give fire, give fire—
at once give fire—
And let those recreant troops perceive mine ire.
GENERAL. Pursue, pursue! They fly
That first did give the lie.
[*Exeunt*]

BAYES. This, now, is not improper, I think, because the spectators know all these towns, and may easily conceive them to be within the dominions of the two kings of Brentford.

JOHNSON. Most exceeding well designed!

BAYES. How do you think I have contrived to give a stop to this battle?

SMITH. How?

BAYES. By an eclipse—which, let me tell you, is a kind of fancy that was yet never so much as thought of, but by myself and one person more that shall be nameless. Come, come in, Mr.—a—

[*Enter* LIEUTENANT-GENERAL]

LIEUTENANT-GENERAL. What midnight darkness does invade the day,
And snatch the victor from his conquered prey?
Is the Sun weary of his bloody fight,
And winks upon us with his eye of light?
'Tis an eclipse. This was unkind, O Moon,
To clap between me and the Sun so soon.
Foolish Eclipse! thou this in vain hast done;
My brighter honor had eclips'd the Sun.
But now behold eclipses two in one. [*Exit*]

JOHNSON. This is an admirable representation of a battle as ever I saw.

BAYES. Aye, sir. But how would you fancy now to represent an eclipse?

SMITH. Why, that's to be supposed.

BAYES. Supposed! Aye, you are ever at your "suppose"—ha, ha, ha! Why, you may as well suppose the whole play. No, it must come in upon the stage, that's certain—but in some odd way that may delight, amuse, and all that. I have a conceit for't that I am sure is new and, I believe, to the purpose.

JOHNSON. How's that?

BAYES. Why, the truth is, I took the first hint of this out of a dialogue between Phœbus and Aurora, in *The Slighted Maid*—which, by my troth, was very pretty, though I think you'll confess this is a little better.

JOHNSON. No doubt on't, Mr. Bayes.

BAYES. But, sir, you have heard, I suppose, that your eclipse of the moon is nothing else but an interposition of the earth between the sun and moon; as likewise your eclipse of the sun is caused by an interlocation of the moon betwixt the earth and sun?

SMITH. I have heard so, indeed.

BAYES. Well, sir, what do I but make the earth, sun, and moon come out upon the stage and dance the hey-hum? And of necessity by the very nature of this dance, the earth must be sometimes between the sun and the moon, and the moon between the earth and sun; and there you have both your eclipses. That is new, I gad—ha?

JOHNSON. That must needs be very fine, truly.

BAYES. Yes, there is some fancy in't. And then, sir, that there may be something in it of a joke, I make the moon sell the earth a bargain.—Come! come out eclipse, to the tune of *Tom Tyler*.

[*Enter* MOON]

MOON [*singing*]. Orbis, O Orbis!
Come to me, thou little rogue Orbis.

[*Enter the* EARTH]

EARTH. What calls Terra firma, pray?

MOON. Luna that ne'er shines by day.
EARTH. What means Luna in a veil?
MOON. Luna means to show her tail.

[*Enter* SUN]

SUN. Fie, sister, fie! thou mak'st me muse,
  Dery, dery down,
  To see thee Orb abuse.
MOON. I hope his anger 'twill not move,
  Since I did it out of love.
  Hey down, dery down.
EARTH. Where shall I thy true love know,
  Thou pretty, pretty Moon?
MOON. To-morrow soon, ere it be noon—
        [*Together*]
  On Mount Vesuvio.
SUN. Then I will shine.
EARTH. And I will be fine.
MOON. And we will drink nothing but Lipari
 wine.
ALL. And we, etc.

BAYES. So, now, vanish Eclipse, and enter
t'other battle, and fight. Here now, if I am not
mistaken, you will see fighting enough.
 [*A battle is fought between foot- and great-
 hobby-horses. At last,* DRAWCANSIR
 *comes in, and kills 'em all on both sides.
 All this while the battle is fighting,* BAYES
 *is telling them when to shout, and shouts
 with 'em*]

DRAWCANSIR. Others may boast a single man
 to kill,
But I the blood of thousands daily spill.
Let petty kings the names of parties know;
Where'er I come, I slay both friend and foe.
The swiftest horsemen my swift rage controls,
And from their bodies drives their trembling souls.
If they had wings and to the gods could fly,
I would pursue, and beat 'em, through the sky;
And make proud Jove, with all his thunder, see
This single arm more dreadful is than he.
        [*Exit*]

BAYES. There's a brave fellow for you now,
sirs. I have read of your Hector, your Achilles,
and a hundred more; but I defy all your his-
tories, and your romances too, I gad, to show
me one such conqueror as this Drawcansir.
JOHNSON. I swear, I think you may.
SMITH. But, Mr. Bayes, how shall all these
dead men go off? for I see none alive to help
'em.
BAYES. Go off! why, as they came on—upon
their legs. How should they go off? Why, do
you think the people do not know they are
not dead? He is mighty ignorant, poor man;
your friend here is very silly, Mr. Johnson, I
gad, he is. Come, sir, I'll show you "go off."—
Rise, sirs, and go about your business. There's
"go off" for you.—Hark you, Mr. Ivory.—
Gentlemen, I'll be with you presently. [*Exit*]
JOHNSON. Will you so? then we'll be gone.
SMITH. Aye, prithee, let's go, that we may
preserve our hearing. One battle more would
take mine quite away. [*Exeunt*]
 [*Enter* BAYES *and* PLAYERS]
BAYES. Where are the gentlemen?
1ST PLAYER. They are gone, sir.

BAYES. Gone! 'Sdeath, this last act is best
of all. I'll go fetch 'em again. [*Exit*]
3RD PLAYER. Stay, here's a foul piece of paper
of his. Let's see what 'tis. [*Reads: The Argument of the Fifth Act*]

Cloris, at length, being sensible of Prince
Pretty-man's passion, consents to marry him; but
just as they are going to church, Prince Pretty-
man meeting, by chance, with old Joan the
chandler's widow, and rememb'ring it was she that
brought him acquainted with Cloris, out of a high
point of honor breaks off his match with Cloris
and marries old Joan. Upon which, Cloris in despair drowns herself, and Prince Pretty-man dis-
contentedly walks by the river side.

1ST PLAYER. Pox on't, this will never do; 'tis
just like the rest. Come, let's be gone. [*Exeunt*]
 [*Enter* BAYES]
BAYES. A plague on 'em both for me! they
have made me sweat to run after 'em. A couple
of senseless rascals that had rather go to dinner
than see this play out, with a pox to 'em! What
comfort has a man to write for such dull
rogues?— [*Calls*] Come Mr.—a—Where are
you, sir? come away quick—quick!
 [*Enter* PLAYERS *again*]
PLAYER. Sir, they are gone to dinner.
BAYES. Yes, I know the gentlemen are gone,
but I ask for the players.
PLAYER. Why, an't please your worship, sir,
the players are gone to dinner too.
BAYES. How! are the players gone to dinner?
'Tis impossible: the players gone to dinner! I
gad, if they are, I'll make 'em know what it is
to injure a person that does 'em the honor to
write for 'em, and all that. A company of
proud, conceited, humorous, cross-grained persons, and all that. I gad, I'll make 'em the most
contemptible, despicable, inconsiderable persons, and all that, in the whole world, for this
trick. I gad, I'll be revenged on 'em; I'll sell
this play to the other house.
PLAYER. Nay, good sir, don't take away the
book; you'll disappoint the town, that comes
to see it acted here this afternoon.
BAYES. That's all one. I must reserve this
comfort to myself. My book and I will go together; we will not part, indeed, sir. The town!
why, what care I for the town? I gad, the town
has used me as scurvily as the players have
done. But I'll be revenged on them too; I will
both lampoon and print 'em too, I gad. Since
they will not admit of my plays, they shall
know what a satirist I am. And so farewell to
this stage forever, I gad. [*Exit*]
1ST PLAYER. What shall we do now?
2ND PLAYER. Come, then, let's set up bills for
another play. We shall lose nothing by this, I
warrant you.
1ST PLAYER. I am of your opinion. But before we go let's see Haynes and Shirley practise
the last dance, for that may serve for another
play.

2ND PLAYER. I'll call 'em; I think they are in the tiring-room.

[*Enter* DANCERS: *they dance. The Dance done*]

1ST PLAYER. Come, come; let's go away to dinner. [*Exeunt Omnes*]

EPILOGUE

The play is at an end, but where's the plot?
That circumstance our poet Bayes forgot,
And we can boast, though 'tis a plotting age,
No place is freer from it than the stage.
The ancients plotted though, and strove to please
With sense that might be understood with ease;
They every scene with so much wit did store
That who brought any in, went out with more.
But this new way of wit does so surprise,
Men lose their wits in wond'ring where it lies.
If it be true that monstrous births presage
The following mischiefs that afflict the age.
And sad disasters to the state proclaim,
Plays without head or tail may do the same.
Wherefore, for ours, and for the kingdom's peace,
May this prodigious way of writing cease.
Let's have at least once in our lives a time
When we may hear some reason, not all rhyme:
We have these ten years felt its influence;
Pray, let this prove a year of prose and sense.

THE DOCTOR IN SPITE OF HIMSELF

A Farce in Two Acts

By MOLIERE

ACTING VERSION BY BARRETT H. CLARK

PERSONS IN THE PLAY

SGANARELLE, *a woodcutter*
MARTINE, *Sganarelle's wife*
ROBERT, *Sganarelle's neighbor*
VALÈRE, *Géronte's servant*
LUCAS, *Jacqueline's husband*
JACQUELINE, *Lucas' wife, and nurse in Géronte's home*
LUCINDE, *Géronte's daughter*
GÉRONTE, *a country gentleman*
LÉANDRE, *in love with Lucinde*
SCENE: *A clearing in a wood, and before Géronte's house.*
TIME: *Late seventeenth century.*

THE DOCTOR IN SPITE OF HIMSELF

ACT ONE

SCENE: *A wood.*

[*Enter* SGANARELLE *and* MARTINE, *quarrelling*]

SGANARELLE. No, I tell you, I will do nothing of the kind: I am master here.

MARTINE. And I tell you you shall live as I want you to. I didn't marry you to put up with your nonsense.

SGANARELLE. Oh, what a plague it is to have a wife!

MARTINE. Cursed be the day when I took it into my head to say Yes.

SGANARELLE. Cursed be the notary who made me sign my own ruination!

MARTINE. What right have you to complain of that? Oughtn't you rather to be thanking heaven that you have me for a wife?

SGANARELLE. It's true you honored me too greatly. Good Lord, don't provoke me: I might tell you something—

MARTINE. Come, now, what could you tell me?

SGANARELLE. Enough; let us stop right here. It's enough that I know what I know; and I repeat you were very lucky to get me.

MARTINE. What do you mean by your "very lucky to get you?" A man who will drive me into the gutter, a drunkard who eats up all I have!

SGANARELLE. Now, that's a lie: I drink part of it.

MARTINE. Who sells everything in the house.

SGANARELLE. That's what I call living within one's income.

MARTINE. Who has taken away my very bed from under me!

SGANARELLE. You will get up all the earlier.

MARTINE. Who leaves me nothing in the whole house.

SGANARELLE. There won't be so much bother when we move.

MARTINE. Who from morning to night does nothing but eat and drink.

SGANARELLE. That's to keep me occupied.

MARTINE. And what do you think I shall do with my family meanwhile?

SGANARELLE. Whatever you please.

MARTINE. I have four poor little children on my hands.

SGANARELLE. Put them on the ground.

MARTINE. Who are continually begging me for bread.

SGANARELLE. Give them the rod. When I have enough to eat and drink, the family ought to be satisfied.

MARTINE. And do you mean to say, you drunkard, that—?

SGANARELLE. Gently, please.

MARTINE. I am forever to put up with your insolence and—?

SGANARELLE. Let's keep calm, wife.

MARTINE. Who could possibly keep calm, with you for a husband!

SGANARELLE. My dear; you know my patience is very short-lived, and my arm knows how to wield a club.

MARTINE. I laugh at your silly threats. See, I'm not in the least afraid of you.

SGANARELLE. My better half, you desire a beating, I see.

MARTINE. You think I'm frightened at your talk!

SGANARELLE. Sweet object of my love, I shall box your ears.

MARTINE. Drunkard!

SGANARELLE [*He beats her; she screams*]. That is the best way to make you keep still.

[*Enter* M. ROBERT]

M. ROBERT. Here, here, here! What's this? What a disgraceful affair!

[MARTINE *comes up to him, looks him in the face, and after a short pause, deliberately slaps him*]

MARTINE. I like to have him beat me.

M. ROBERT. Very well, then; I don't object.

MARTINE. What business is it of yours?

M. ROBERT. None whatsoever.

MARTINE. Impertinent fellow, to interfere with a husband who is beating his wife!

M. ROBERT. I am very sorry, indeed.

MARTINE. Mind your own business.

M. ROBERT. I shall say nothing more.

MARTINE. I tell you, I wish to be beaten.

M. ROBERT. Very well, then.

MARTINE. You are a fool to interfere with other people's business.

[M. ROBERT *goes to* SGANARELLE, *who hits him and drives him off*]

M. ROBERT. Neighbor, I beg your pardon. Go on, whack your wife as much as you please; I'll help you if you like.

SGANARELLE. I do not like.

M. ROBERT. That's a different matter.

SGANARELLE. I'll beat her if I like; and I shan't beat her if I don't like.

M. ROBERT. Very well, it's not my fault.

SGANARELLE. She is my wife, and not yours.

M. ROBERT. I don't doubt it in the least, Monsieur.

SGANARELLE. You are exceedingly impudent to meddle in other people's concerns. [M. ROBERT *goes out.* SGANARELLE *goes to his wife and takes her hand*] Come, now, let's make up and be happy.

MARTINE. I won't.

SGANARELLE. What!

MARTINE. No, I won't.

SGANARELLE. Now, now.

MARTINE. I shan't do anything of the kind.

SGANARELLE. Come, come, come.

MARTINE. No, I *will* be angry.

SGANARELLE. Come, now; it's only a trifle.

MARTINE. Let me be, I tell you.

SGANARELLE. I ask your forgiveness.

MARTINE. Well, I forgive you this time. [*Aside*] But you will pay for it!

SGANARELLE. A little tiff now and then between those who truly love only increases their affections. There now, I'm going to the wood, and I promise you more than a hundred faggots to-day. [*He goes out*]

MARTINE. I shan't forget what I owe him for that beating. I'll get him a trouncing he won't soon forget. [*She retires to the rear of the stage, apparently planning*]

[*Enter* VALÈRE *and* LUCAS]

LUCAS. I'll be cursed if we haven't the devil of an errand; I don't know neither, what I'll get out of it.

VALÈRE. What can we do? We must obey our master; besides, our mistress' health seriously affects us; because her wedding, which is delayed because of her strange malady, may prove a windfall for us. Cléante, who wishes to marry her, seems likely to get her, though I've noticed she has some inclination for Léandre. Of course, her father would never have *him* for a son-in-law.

LUCAS. What has he got into his head, I wonder? How do we know where to find a doctor for our mistress?

VALÈRE. We have only to look, and I feel sure our efforts will be rewarded.

[MARTINE, *who has been talking to herself at the back of the stage, is heard saying:*]

MARTINE. Yes, I must give it to him. I can't get over that beating he gave me. [*She inadvertently bumps into* LUCAS *and* VALÈRE] Ah, Messieurs, I beg your pardon. I didn't see you, as I was racking my brains over something that bothers me.

VALÈRE. Everyone has his troubles on this earth of ours. We too are looking for something.

MARTINE. Possibly I could help you?

VALÈRE. Possibly. We are looking for a skilful physician, to cure our master's daughter. She was stricken dumb a short while ago. Several doctors have employed their utmost knowledge and profoundest skill, but in vain.

MARTINE. Ah, Messieurs, you could not possibly have found one better able to help you than your humble servant: I know of a wonderful man, exactly the one you are looking for.

VALÈRE. Good! Where is he?

MARTINE. You will find him there, chopping wood and making faggots. He does it for his amusement.

LUCAS. A physician chopping wood!

VALÈRE. Impossible!

MARTINE. Nothing's impossible. He is an odd fellow who takes his amusement that way—a peculiar, eccentric man. You would never in the world take him for a doctor. He goes about dressed like a woodsman, pretends to be ignorant, and heartily dislikes making use of his wonderful skill.

VALÈRE. It's strange how all men of genius are slightly off in the head, so to speak.

MARTINE. Oh, he's madder than you'd think; sometimes he has to be beaten before he will admit he's a doctor at all. We have to beat him whenever anyone's sick.

LUCAS. Incredible.

MARTINE. Quite true, but when he has finally confessed, he does wonderful things.

VALÈRE. What's his name?

MARTINE. Sganarelle. He's a man with a long black beard, wearing a ruff, and a yellow and green coat.

LUCAS. A yellow and green coat?

VALÈRE. But can he really work such wonders as you say?

MARTINE. Miracles! Six months ago, a woman was given up for dead and was about to be buried. This Sganarelle was brought and, after a severe beating, put a drop of some magical liquid into the poor woman's mouth, after which she rose and walked about as if nothing had happened.

LUCAS. Wonderful! He must have some magic cure.

MARTINE. I shouldn't wonder.

LUCAS. Well, he's the very man we want. We'll find him at once.

VALÈRE. We are deeply obliged to you, Madame.

MARTINE. Pray, don't mention it. And don't forget what I said about that beating, for I am very anxious to have you succeed.

LUCAS. Never fear, my fine lady. If it's only a beatin' he wants, I'll satisfy him!

VALÈRE. Ah, Lucas, we are very lucky indeed. This *is* a find. [VALÈRE *and* LUCAS *retire to the back of the stage, and converse in whispers*]

[*Enter* SGANARELLE, *with a bottle, singing*]

VALÈRE. Hush-sh-sh. I hear someone singing, and I just heard someone chopping wood.

SGANARELLE [*laying down his bottle, and stretching out his arms, after yawning*]. Well, this *is* hard work! Time for some comforting spirits. [*He drinks from the bottle, and then sings*]

"What comfort is there more on earth
　　Than thou, Oh bottle brown?
Thou rousest all mankind to mirth,
　　And dost dispel the frown."

Ah, a little of the bottle now and then, to chase away black melancholy.

VALÈRE. That's the fellow, I do believe.

LUCAS. I think you're right, Valère.

VALÈRE. Let's come nearer.

SGANARELLE [*aside*]. What the devil do these people want?

VALÈRE. I'm sure he's the one.

SGANARELLE [*He puts the bottle on the ground, but seeing* VALÈRE *approach, picks it up and puts it on the opposite side; then, seeing* LUCAS *approach from the other, he takes it up and hugs it*]. What in the world do they want?

VALÈRE. Monsieur, isn't your name Sganarelle?

SGANARELLE [*to* VALÈRE]. Yes— [*To* LUCAS] and No. It depends on what you want with Sganarelle.

VALÈRE. We don't want anything except to offer him our profound respects.

SGANARELLE. Well, then—my name *is* Sganarelle.

VALÈRE. Honored to meet you, Monsieur. We have been recommended to you for a service we are in great need of. We have come to ask your help.

SGANARELLE. Messieurs, if it is anything in my power, to grant, I am entirely at your service.

VALÈRE. You are too kind, Monsieur. Skilful people are much in demand, and we have been told of your wonderful cures.

SGANARELLE. Ah, you flatter me, though, without bragging, I must confess I'm the best in the world at faggot-making.

VALÈRE. No doubt, Monsieur.

SGANARELLE. I never give short measure—I do my work in a—

VALÈRE. That is not the reason we came to see you. We have—

SGANARELLE. And I sell them at ten sous the hundred.

VALÈRE. Let's drop that subject, if you please.

SGANARELLE. I declare, I can't afford to sell them cheaper. As it is, I only—

VALÈRE. We know that, Monsieur, but we—

SGANARELLE. If you know that, then you know I am honest and upright in my dealings.

VALÈRE. You are joking, Monsieur.

SGANARELLE. I am not joking: I can't make them for less.

VALÈRE. Pray, Monsieur, let's change the subject.

SGANARELLE. You can get someone else to make your faggots for you. I tell you I can't—

VALÈRE. Ah, Monsieur, let's not go on in this fashion.

SGANARELLE. I swear I can't make them for a sou less.

VALÈRE. Come, come.

SGANARELLE. It's impossible to get them for less. And I don't overcharge, either.

VALÈRE. Ought so great a doctor as you to hide his ability from the world?

SGANARELLE [*aside*]. He's cracked.

VALÈRE. Now, now, don't try to make me believe—

SGANARELLE. What do you mean, Monsieur?

LUCAS. Come, this is all nonsense. I know what I know.

SGANARELLE. What is it, then? Who do you think I am?

VALÈRE. Exactly who you are: a great doctor.

SGANARELLE. Doctor yourself! I'm not one, I never was, and I never will be a doctor.

VALÈRE [*aside*]. Now he's having his fit. [*To* SGANARELLE] Don't pretend any longer, Monsieur, and please don't force us to extreme measures.

SGANARELLE. What's that?

VALÈRE. To something we should not like to do.

SGANARELLE. Lord! Do whatever you like. I'm no doctor and I don't understand a word you are saying.

VALÈRE. Once more, Monsieur, I beg you to confess that you are a doctor.

SGANARELLE. Why, I'm only a common wood-cutter. Do you want to drive me distracted?

VALÈRE. Why do you persist in lying?

SGANARELLE. What's the use of my telling you a thousand times I am no doctor?

VALÈRE. You are not a doctor?

SGANARELLE. No, I tell you.

VALÈRE. So be it, then.

[*They beat him severely*]

SGANARELLE. Stop, stop! Messieurs, I'll be anything you like.

VALÈRE. That's better, now. But why did you force us to do this, Monsieur? I assure you I regret it infinitely.

SGANARELLE. What the devil? For Heaven's sake, are you joking, or are you both out of your heads? Do you say I am a—you're mad —a doctor?

VALÈRE. You don't admit it yet? You still deny that you're a doctor?

SGANARELLE. Plague take me if I am!

LUCAS. Ain't you a doctor?

SGANARELLE. No, I tell you. [*They beat him again*] Oh, oh! Well, since you *will* have it so,

I *am* a doctor—an apothecary, too, if you like. I'll agree to anything rather than be beaten again.

VALÈRE. Very well, Monsieur, I'm pleased to see you so reasonable. I ask your pardon with all my heart and soul, Monsieur.

SGANARELLE [*aside*]. Bless me, have I really become a doctor without knowing it?

VALÈRE. You shall have no cause to regret anything, Monsieur. You shall be satisfied.

SGANARELLE. But, tell me, are you quite sure you're not mistaken? Are you sure I'm a real doctor?

LUCAS. Undoubtedly.

SGANARELLE. Really?

VALÈRE. Assuredly.

SGANARELLE. Devil take me if I knew it!

VALÈRE. Why, you are the greatest doctor in the world.

SGANARELLE. Indeed!

LUCAS. A doctor who has made innumerable cures.

SGANARELLE. The devil!

VALÈRE. In short, Monsieur, you will be satisfied, and be paid any fee you care to name, if you will let us take you with us.

SGANARELLE. Any fee I care to name?

VALÈRE. Yes.

SGANARELLE. In that case, I assuredly am a doctor. I must have forgotten it; but now I remember. Where do I go?

VALÈRE. We shall take you; it is to see a young girl who has lost her speech.

SGANARELLE. I haven't found it.

VALÈRE. Come, Monsieur.

SGANARELLE. Here, Monsieur, you carry this bottle. I—I—a—a—keep my medicine in it. [*They go out*]

CURTAIN

ACT TWO

SCENE: *Before* GÉRONTE's *house.*

[*Enter* GÉRONTE, VALÈRE, LUCAS *and* JACQUELINE]

VALÈRE. Yes, Monsieur, I'm sure you will be satisfied; we have brought you the most illustrious doctor in the world.

LUCAS. He has mended folks that's dead; that's what he's done.

VALÈRE. He is rather peculiar, as I said. Lucas declares he is a little mad.

LUCAS. That's what I said.

VALÈRE. But in reality, this is only a pretence to conceal his great learning.

GÉRONTE. I should like very much to see him; send for him at once.

VALÈRE. Very well. [*He goes out*]

JACQUELINE. You can take my word for it,

Monsieur, this doctor'll be just like all the rest of them. I tell you, a husband to her liking is the only cure for her.

GÉRONTE. Come, now, you do a lot of meddling, nurse.

JACQUELINE. All the same, it's a husband she wants, it is.

GÉRONTE. Who would take her as she is now? I offered to let her marry Cléante, but she refused.

JACQUELINE. And no wonder; you wanted to give her to a man she didn't like. Why don't you give her to Léandre? She likes him.

GÉRONTE. I don't like Léandre; he has no money and Cléante has.

JACQUELINE. Ah, parents nowadays always ask: "How much has he?" What's the use of anything, if you can't be happy, I say?

GÉRONTE. Will you keep still.

[*Enter* VALÈRE *and* SGANARELLE]

VALÈRE. Here comes the doctor, Monsieur.

GÉRONTE. I am delighted to see you, Monsieur. We have great need of you.

SGANARELLE [*in a black gown and high hat*]. Hippocrates says that both of us should put on our hats.

GÉRONTE. Hippocrates says that?

SGANARELLE. Yes.

GÉRONTE. In what chapter does he say that?

SGANARELLE. In his chapter—on hats.

GÉRONTE. Well, if Hippocrates says so it must be done.

SGANARELLE. Now, doctor, since I have—

GÉRONTE. Whom are you addressing, Monsieur?

SGANARELLE. You.

GÉRONTE. I am not a doctor.

SGANARELLE. You are not a doctor?

GÉRONTE. Certainly not.

SGANARELLE [*beating him*]. Really?

GÉRONTE. Oh, oh,—really! I tell you I am no doctor.

SGANARELLE. *Now* you are a doctor. I have received no other degree than you.

GÉRONTE. What sort of fellow is this you have brought me?

VALÈRE. Didn't I tell you he was rather eccentric?

GÉRONTE. I don't like his eccentricities.

VALÈRE. Never mind, Monsieur, he was only joking.

GÉRONTE. I dislike his kind of joking.

SGANARELLE. Pardon the liberty I have taken. I am very sorry.

GÉRONTE. Say no more about it. I have a daughter who was stricken with a strange disease.

SGANARELLE. I am delighted to hear it, I assure you.

GÉRONTE. Many thanks.

SGANARELLE. What is your daughter's name?

GÉRONTE. Lucinde.

SGANARELLE. Lucinde? A charming name!

GÉRONTE. I shall go and see what she is doing. [*He goes out*]

SGANARELLE. An interesting case, upon my word.—Ha! someone is coming. [*Walks up and down a moment, then*]

[*Re-enter* GÉRONTE, *leading* LUCINDE *by the hand*]

GÉRONTE. Here is my daughter.

SGANARELLE. Is this the patient?

GÉRONTE. Yes: my only child. I should never get over it if anything were to happen to her. If she should die—

SGANARELLE. Impossible, Monsieur. She cannot die without a regular prescription from the Academy.

GÉRONTE. Bring a chair, there. [*A chair is brought*]

SGANARELLE. By no means unattractive, this patient!

GÉRONTE. She smiles, Monsieur; you have made her smile.

SGANARELLE. Naturally, Monsieur, it's my business. This is splendid. A very good symptom. Well, Mademoiselle, what ails you? What pains do you feel?

LUCINDE [*making gesticulations*]. Ow! Ooh! Oi!

SGANARELLE. What's that?

LUCINDE. Oi, oi.

SGANARELLE. Ouh, ouh, oi, oi. I don't understand such gibberish.

GÉRONTE. That's just what's the matter, Monsieur. She is dumb, and I have been compelled to put off the marriage.

SGANARELLE. Why was that?

GÉRONTE. The man she is to marry wants to wait for her recovery.

SGANARELLE. What! Show me the man who doesn't want his wife dumb! I only wish mine had that disease! I should see that she wasn't soon cured!

GÉRONTE. I should like you to cure this case, at any rate.

SGANARELLE. Don't worry, Monsieur. Is her pain very acute?

GÉRONTE. Yes—very.

SGANARELLE. Excellent. [*To* LUCINDE] Let me feel your pulse. [*To* GÉRONTE] Monsieur, I am enlightened as to your daughter's condition: she is dumb!

GÉRONTE. Yes; that's just it. You found it out immediately.

SGANARELLE. Of course! We great doctors know things at once. A fool would have been disturbed and puzzled, and would have beat about the bush. But I tell you plainly: your daughter is dumb.

GÉRONTE. Yes; but how did it happen?

SGANARELLE. Very simply: she lost her speech.

GÉRONTE. Very good; but why?

SGANARELLE. Our best authorities seem to agree that it arises from an impediment of the tongue.

GÉRONTE. Yes, but tell me the causes. The authorities must surely—

SGANARELLE. Well, Aristotle says—many fine things.

GÉRONTE. I can readily believe it.

SGANARELLE. He was a great man.

GÉRONTE. No doubt of it.

SGANARELLE. A *very* great man; a man who was far greater than I am. But to return to the question: I am of the opinion that this impediment arises from some certain peccant humors. Peccant—that is to say—a—a—peccant. For, as the vapors exhumed are formed by a certain exhalation of circuitous—a—you understand Latin?

GÉRONTE. No.

SGANARELLE. What, you don't understand Latin?

GÉRONTE. No Sir.

SGANARELLE. Carborias influxorioum arci thrumbi thantrat—

GÉRONTE. Ah, why didn't I study and learn things when I was young?

SGANARELLE. So these vapors, passing from the left to the right side, come into contact with the lungs—Latin armyan—Hebrew polyglum—and from there they proceed immediately to the—please follow me more attentively.

GÉRONTE. I am.

SGANARELLE. And have a certain malignity by a—pay attention to me now.

GÉRONTE. I am paying attention, Monsieur.

SGANARELLE. Which is always caused by a sharpness of these, and the concavity of the diaphragm—nequaquam in uterque imibus. And for these reasons your daughter is dumb.

GÉRONTE. No one could possibly argue better. But, Monsieur, what do you think should be done?

SGANARELLE. What do I think should be done?

GÉRONTE. Yes.

SGANARELLE. I suggest that she be put immediately to bed, and take plenty of bread and wine.

GÉRONTE. Why, if you please?

SGANARELLE. Because this wonderful combination often produces speech.

GÉRONTE. What a great man you are! Quick, bring bread and wine!

SGANARELLE. I shall return soon to see how the patient is getting on. I wish you good-day.

GÉRONTE. One moment, please.

SGANARELLE. What do you want?

GÉRONTE. To give you your fee.

SGANARELLE [*holding out his hand*]. I shall not take it.

GÉRONTE. Ah, Monsieur!

SGANARELLE. I refuse.

GÉRONTE. I beg of you—

SGANARELLE. I do not practise for money.

GÉRONTE. I'm quite sure of *that*.

SGANARELLE [*taking the money*]. Is it full weight?

GÉRONTE. Certainly.

SGANARELLE. I am not a mercenary doctor.

GÉRONTE. I can readily believe it.

SGANARELLE. I am not inspired by any base desire for gold.

GÉRONTE. I don't doubt it in the least. Well, I bid you good-day.

SGANARELLE. Good-day, Monsieur. Don't forget: I never practise for money.

[GÉRONTE *goes out. Enter* LÉANDRE]

SGANARELLE. Well, this isn't so bad after all.

LÉANDRE. I beg your pardon, Monsieur—I wish help: I am—

SGANARELLE [*Goes up to him and feels his pulse*]. Your pulse is very bad. You have a severe case of—

LÉANDRE. I'm not sick, Monsieur; it isn't *that* I came to see you about.

SGANARELLE. If you are not sick, why the devil don't you say so? How am I to know?

LÉANDRE. My name is Léandre. I am in love with Lucinde, and want you to help me to see her, as I am forbidden to enter her home. I have a little plan in which you can help me, and upon which my life and happiness depend.

SGANARELLE. Why, what do you think I am? Do you believe doctors can afford to lower their dignity by dabbling in others' love affairs?

LÉANDRE. You needn't make such a racket!

SGANARELLE. I shall make as much noise as I please, you impudent scoundrel!

LÉANDRE. Gently, gently, Monsieur!

SGANARELLE. Puppy!

LÉANDRE. Oh, I beseech you!

SGANARELLE. I'll teach you to insult one of my rank and—

LÉANDRE [*giving him a purse*]. Please, Monsieur, accept—

SGANARELLE. Well, this is—I was not speaking of you—of course not—the idea! You are a gentleman, and I am your most obedient servant. I was saying that there are *some* impudent puppies in the world who think they can insult me with impunity; and I can't help getting angry at them.

LÉANDRE. I beg your pardon, Monsieur, for the liberty—

SGANARELLE. Don't say another word. What is the business in hand, now?

LÉANDRE. I must tell you, Monsieur, that Lucinde's malady is a mere pretence. The doctors know nothing at all about it. I tell you, love's the cause. She has pretended this illness in order to escape that odious marriage with Cléante. Come with me, please, and let me tell you all about it on the way.

SGANARELLE. Very well, Monsieur. You have interested me so much in your affair that I promise you the patient shall either be yours or die.

[*They go out and return a moment later,* LÉANDRE *disguised as an apothecary*]

LÉANDRE. I don't think I make a bad apothecary! I shall deceive her father without the least trouble.

SGANARELLE. No doubt of it.

LÉANDRE. I wish I knew five or six long Latin words to mix into my conversation. Then I should be a learned man.

SGANARELLE. Nonsense; it's not necessary. The dress is sufficient. I don't know any more about medicine than you do.

LÉANDRE. How's that?

SGANARELLE. Devil take me if I know a thing about it. I confide in you, Monsieur.

LÉANDRE. What! you're not really—?

SGANARELLE. Of course not. They made me a doctor. I don't know anything, I tell you. I left school at the end of the sixth form. But now I'm a doctor. A shoemaker who spoils a pair of shoes is blamed for it, but when we doctors make a slip, our dead patients cannot blame us. They can never tell what medicine killed them. Here come some people who want to be cured. Let's get out of their way. Go and wait for me near Lucinde's home. [LÉANDRE *goes out. Enter* JACQUELINE *and* LUCAS] Here is a monstrous fine nurse! Ah, nurse of my heart, I am charmed to meet you; the sight of you is like cassia, rhubarb and senna to me, and when you—

JACQUELINE. Gracious me, Mr. Doctor, it's no use talkin' to me that way. I don't understand a single word of your Latin.

SGANARELLE. It is not necessary for one to know Latin nowadays. Who's this? [*Hides*]

[*Enter* GÉRONTE]

GÉRONTE. Lucas, have you seen our doctor lately?

LUCAS. Yes, Monsieur, I've seen him.

GÉRONTE. Where is he?

LUCAS. I don't know.

GÉRONTE. Go and see what my daughter is doing. [LUCAS *goes out. Enter* SGANARELLE *and* LÉANDRE] Ah, Monsieur, I was looking for you.

SGANARELLE. I was coming. How is our patient?

GÉRONTE. She is somewhat worse since taking your remedy.

SGANARELLE. So much the better: she is going to be cured.

GÉRONTE. Possibly, but I think she will choke to death before then.

SGANARELLE. Don't be anxious about her. I have some further remedies in case all the others fail.

GÉRONTE. Who is that man with you?

SGANARELLE. He is an apothecary.

GÉRONTE. Ah, I see.

SGANARELLE. Your daughter will need him, I feel sure.

[Enter JACQUELINE and LUCINDE]

JACQUELINE. Here is your daughter, master; she wished to walk about a little.

SGANARELLE. That is the best thing for her. Feel her pulse, apothecary, I shall consult about further measures. [He draws GÉRONTE over to the opposite side of the stage and turns him away from LUCINDE and LÉANDRE. Each time GÉRONTE starts to turn round, SGANARELLE prevents him] Monsieur, this is a grave question among us doctors. For, Monsieur, as I said before, I think it highly probable that—with the inequality of such peccant—

[LUCINDE is heard muttering]

GÉRONTE. Listen! My daughter speaks! Oh, great doctor, excellent doctor! What miracles you perform! How can I ever repay you for the great service you have done me!

SGANARELLE [strutting about and stroking his beard] Hem! hem! This has been a very troublesome case indeed.

LUCINDE. Yes, father, I have recovered my speech, but only to tell you that I will marry no one but Léandre, and that it is useless for you to try to force me to accept Cléante.

GÉRONTE. But I shall—

LUCINDE. Nothing can shake my resolution.

GÉRONTE. What is this? Am I to—?

LUCINDE. All your arguments are useless.

GÉRONTE. But I will force you to marry him, and if you don't—

LUCINDE. I will not submit to such tyranny. No, no, no! [She says this last in a shrill and piercing voice]

GÉRONTE. My, oh, my! Doctor, I beseech you to make her dumb again! My fortune will be yours if you can do it.

SGANARELLE. My utmost skill can but make you deaf, which is some consolation.

GÉRONTE. Many thanks! [To LUCINDE] And as for you, you will marry Cléante this very evening.

LUCINDE. I would sooner die!

SGANARELLE. Stop this wrangling at once. I know a remedy that will cure her.

GÉRONTE. Is it possible?

SGANARELLE. Just let me arrange it. I shall need the apothecary for this. [To LÉANDRE, aside] One word, Monsieur. The only remedy I know of in this case is one matrimonium pill. You must persuade her to take the medicine immediately. Give her also a dose of elopement. Go into the garden now and persuade her to take these medicines. I shall speak with her father meanwhile.

[LUCINDE and LÉANDRE go out]

GÉRONTE. What are those drugs you just mentioned, Monsieur? I don't think I ever heard of them before.

SGANARELLE. They are used in extreme cases.

GÉRONTE. Did you ever see such impudence?

SGANARELLE. Indeed, never.

GÉRONTE. I think she is just the kind of girl who would elope with him.

SGANARELLE. You don't believe that?

GÉRONTE. I shall take good care that they don't see each other again.

SGANARELLE. Believe me, that is a very prudent resolution.

[Enter LUCAS]

LUCAS. Oh, master, here's a pretty mess! Your daughter's run away with her Léandre! It was him as played the 'pothecary, and this is the doctor that gave the remedy.

GÉRONTE. What! Abuse me in this shameful manner! Quick! fetch the police. Here, you hold the rascal! [GÉRONTE goes out]

LUCAS [collaring SGANARELLE]. Take my word for it, you'll hang for this!

[Enter MARTINE]

MARTINE. Goodness me! What's become of that doctor I recommended to you?

LUCAS. Here he is. He's just going to be hanged.

MARTINE. My husband hanged! Why?

LUCAS. He helped someone elope with the master's daughter.

MARTINE. Alas, my dear husband, are you going to be hanged?

SGANARELLE. You see! What can I do now?

MARTINE. Unhappy me! If you had only finished chopping the wood, there might have been some consolation.

SGANARELLE. Go away, you grieve me.

MARTINE. No, no, I shall stay and encourage you to die; I'll not leave you until I see you hanged.

SGANARELLE. Ah, thanks, my dear wife.

[Enter GÉRONTE]

GÉRONTE. The police officer will soon be here and you will be sent to prison!

SGANARELLE. Ah, my dear Monsieur, [Bowing and taking off his hat] wouldn't a few blows from that stick be sufficient to allay your wrath?

GÉRONTE. No, it is a matter of law.—But what's this?

[Enter LÉANDRE, LUCINDE, JACQUELINE and LUCAS]

LÉANDRE. I appear now as Léandre, and bring you back your daughter. We intended to elope and marry, but I refuse to steal your daughter from you; I shall only receive her from your own hands. I also wish to let you know that I have just received word of the death of my uncle, who has made me heir to a large fortune and—

GÉRONTE. A large—? Ah, my son, your many sterling qualities appeal to me with a peculiar attraction, and I hereby give you my daughter with the greatest of pleasure.

MARTINE. Since you are not going to be hanged, thank me for making you a doctor; I gained you that honor.

SGANARELLE. And also the honor of a severe thrashing. But come, this time I forgive you.

CURTAIN

PATRIE!

An Historical Drama in Five Acts (Eight Scenes)

By VICTORIEN SARDOU

TRANSLATED FROM THE FRENCH BY
BARRETT H. CLARK

TRANSLATOR'S NOTE

I have tried to preserve so far as possible the spirit of the original text; to that end I have left the names, titles, and occasional expressions (such as the Duke's "Vive-Dieu!") unchanged. The style of the dialogue is at times rhetorical and somewhat stilted, but I have preserved this so far as I was able, believing that any sort of paraphrase would tend to throw the whole out of key. The stage-directions are complete and, even if they are found at times to be unnecessarily so for the reader, I have considered it better to present a Sardou play to the English reading public for the first time as it came from the dramatist.

PERSONS IN THE PLAY

COUNT DE RYSOOR, *a Flemish nobleman*
MARQUIS DE LA TRÉMOÏLLE, *a French nobleman*
JONAS THE BELLRINGER
KARLOO VAN DER NOOT, *a Flemish nobleman*
DUKE OF ALBA
NOIRCARMES, *Grand Provost*
VARGAS, *of the Spanish court*
MAÎTRE ALBERTI, *Doña Rafaële's physician*
DELRIO, *of the Spanish court*
FIRST OFFICER OF THE PRINCE OF ORANGE
GALÈNA, *a Flemish citizen*
SECOND OFFICER OF THE PRINCE OF ORANGE
WILLIAM OF ORANGE
A BREWER
RINCON, *a Spanish captain*
NAVARRA, *a Spanish officer*
GOBERSTRAET, *a Flemish citizen*
A PASTOR
MIGUEL, *of the Spanish court*
MAÎTRE CHARLES, *the executioner*
CORTADILLA, *of the Spanish court*
BAKKERZEEL, *a Flemish citizen*
CORNÉLIS, *a Flemish citizen*
AN ENSIGN (*Spanish*)
A SPY
THE HERALD
DOMINGO, *servant of Alba*
A MAJORDOMO
A COURIER
A SOLDIER
DOÑA DOLORÈS, *wife of Rysoor*
DOÑA RAFAËLE, *Alba's daughter*
SARAH MATHISOON, *a Flemish woman*
THE WOMAN SHOPKEEPER
GUDULE, *servant of Dolorès*
A WOMAN OF THE STREETS
JOSUAH KOPPESTOCK, *a Fleming*

The scene is Brussels, in 1568.

PATRIE!

ACT ONE

SCENE I

*The market-place of the Vieille Boucherie at
Brussels. Large pillars and cross-beams with
iron hooks on them. This market-place, abandoned by the merchants, has been occupied by
the Spanish troops, who have turned it into a
camp. Up-stage the end of a street is seen, and
some gables of houses covered with snow. Under the pillars are three huge fires: up-stage
right and down-stage left. Here and there
among the pillars, cuirasses, flags, arms, and
rugs of various sorts are strewn about. There
is a group of officers gathered round the fire to
the left, and groups of soldiers round the other
two, lying on straw or seated on old rugs, playing dice, drinking, polishing their weapons,
cooking. Soldiers' children and women of the
streets come and go, and from time to time
pour out drinks for soldiers or officers. Scattered about are heaps of broken furniture, objects of all sorts, indications of the pillage.
Halfway up-stage left is a cart full of linens,
vases, etc. Disorder incident to the military occupation of a city is everywhere visible. Patrols
come and go. The beat of drums and distant
fusillades are occasionally heard. Here and
there are benches and casks. Down-stage left
is a table with tankards of beer and goblets;
right, in front of a pillar, are two stools.*

*As the curtain rises, the following are dis-
covered:* RINCON, NAVARRA, MIGUEL, *an Ensign, soldiers, lancers, pikemen, artillerymen,
women of the streets, and children. A loud roll
of drums in the street.*

RINCON [*seated, left, at the table, with the*
ENSIGN *and* NAVARRA, *with whom he is throwing dice*]. What's that?

MIGUEL [*looking up-stage*]. Another con-
signment of prisoners.

RINCON. The devil! That makes the twentieth that's entered Brussels since morning.
Why are they brought here? Put them in
the Jacobins'!

MIGUEL. But, Captain, the Jacobins', the
wood market, the Egmont palace, are all full
to overflowing.

RINCON. And so is the Boucherie. Where the
devil can we put them?

ENSIGN. Well, Señor Rincon, over there is a
sort of stable, by the old pig-pen. Throw them
in there—it's good enough for them.

RINCON [*rising*]. I'll look at it. [*To the soldiers*] Throw some wood on the fire. Hell and
damnation, we're freezing! [*He goes out, left*]

MIGUEL [*to the soldiers*]. Hey! Wood, you
there!

SOLDIERS. No more left.

MIGUEL [*taking* RINCON'S *place*]. Well, chop
some.

SOLDIERS. Very well, Lieutenant. [*They break
up a cask with a hatchet*]

NAVARRA [*playing*]. Ten! Nine— [*Gunshots
in the distance*]. Hello, what's that?

MIGUEL. Rebels—they've been dispatched on
short notice.

NAVARRA. Idiotic to waste good powder that
way! Too good for these heretic dogs!

[CORTADILLA *appears up-stage. He is
greeted with laughter, as he gives some
geese which he has stolen to some of the
women to pluck. He then draws forth a
rabbit from his voluminous breeches;
the soldiers immediately snatch it from
him. Laughing, noise of arguments, cries,
etc.*]

Hey there! Silence! *Mille diables!*

ENSIGN. They're drunk!

MIGUEL [*playing*]. Bah! let them be! This
is carnival season.

ENSIGN. That's so—*Mardi-gras.*

NAVARRA. And to think we're here, freezing
to death because of these damned Flemings!

A SOLDIER [*who has entered from the rear*].
Captain Rincon's presence is requested at the
Town Hall.

MIGUEL. He isn't here.

NAVARRA [*to the* ENSIGN, *who holds a tankard*]. Pour!

ENSIGN. Empty! [*To one of the women*]
Hey, Carmelita!

CARMELITA [*coming forward*]. Do the señors
wish something to drink?

ENSIGN. Yes, fair child! [*She pours beer for
them*]

RINCON [*reëntering*]. Upon my faith! I
don't know what to do: here comes the whole
town!

MIGUEL. Captain, you are wanted at the
Town Hall.

RINCON. I know it—it is about the Civil
Guard.

ENSIGN. Are they being disarmed?

RINCON. Yes, it is much safer! [*To the soldier at the right who is polishing his sword*]
Hand me your sword and a glass of beer. [*To

CARMELITA, *who runs to him*] Ah, it's you, Carmelita?

CARMELITA [*pouring beer for him*]. Yes, Captain.

RINCON [*as he drinks, he notices a gold chain she wears round her neck*]. You have a pretty chain—who gave it to you, child?

[*Other women about look at the chain*]
CARMELITA. Pacheco gave it to me.

RINCON [*kissing her*]. Pacheco is a happy mortal! Good-bye!

A SOLDIER [*at the left*]. Captain, here are a dozen more who've been arrested.

RINCON. A dozen? Ten thousand devils!

MIGUEL. Put them under these pillars.

RINCON. Wherever you like, so far as I am concerned! I give it up, Miguel! [*He goes out, up-stage to the right*]

MIGUEL [*to the soldiers*]. Bring in the prisoners!

[*La Trémoïlle and Rysoor are brought in at the back, left, guarded by two files of soldiers, with an officer at the head*]

OFFICER [*to La Trémoïlle, who halts, showing surprise at being conducted to such a place. The Officer urges him forward, pushing his shoulder*]. March, you!

LA TRÉMOÏLLE [*with dignity*]. Your pardon, friend! My sword has been taken from me, but I still have my cane, and I warn you if you touch me again as you did a moment ago I shall break it over your shoulders.

OFFICER [*raising his sword*]. What's that, rascal?

LA TRÉMOÏLLE [*disarming him by a stroke of the cane, and beating him over the shoulders*]. Take that, you scoundrel!

[*A menacing movement among the soldiers. The Officer picks up his sword and is about to rush at La Trémoïlle, when Navarra and Miguel interpose*]

MIGUEL [*to La Trémoïlle*]. You'll get cut to pieces!

LA TRÉMOÏLLE [*eying him*]. I beg your pardon, you are—?

MIGUEL. Lieutenant—

LA TRÉMOÏLLE. And I—Marquis de la Trémoïlle, faithful subject and friend of his Majesty Charles King of France; though I am a prisoner, I shall allow no subaltern to raise his hand against me! You may tell that to your Government. Is there no place to sit down here?

MIGUEL [*who, together with Navarra and the Ensign, has taken off his hat politely at mention of La Trémoïlle's name*]. Monsieur le Marquis—that is different! Here are seats, over against the pillar.

LA TRÉMOÏLLE. I trust they are clean? [*He goes to the right and notices Rysoor, who is about to sit down on one of the stools*] Monsieur, I beg your pardon!

RYSOOR [*bowing*]. After you, Monsieur!

LA TRÉMOÏLLE [*bowing likewise*]. I beg you, Monsieur!

[*The officers return, left, to warm themselves by the fire*]

RYSOOR. You are French, Monsieur, while I am a citizen of this city: I am the host!

LA TRÉMOÏLLE. Monsieur, I need not inquire whether you are a gentleman!

RYSOOR [*bowing*]. Count de Rysoor, Monsieur, at your service.

LA TRÉMOÏLLE [*bowing*]. Marquis de la Trémoïlle, Monsieur—at yours! [*They put on their hats again*] Since you belong to this city, perhaps you will be good enough to inform me where we are?

RYSOOR. Monsieur le Marquis, this building is the former slaughter-house. The Spaniards have used it for a camp, as you see.

LA TRÉMOÏLLE [*looking up-stage*]. What a camp!

RYSOOR. And what soldiers! The scum of the earth! Neapolitans, Swiss, Portuguese, all of them adventurers, highway robbers, cutthroats, and pillagers; they've gathered here with their women and their bastards, under a flag that permits them to commit with impunity the vilest outrages! This is our shameful yoke—it is killing us: this armed rabble calling itself Spanish troops!

LA TRÉMOÏLLE. Then this, Monsieur, is where they pack those who are arrested—people like you and me?

RYSOOR. And who are executed, if need be.

LA TRÉMOÏLLE. Butchery?

RYSOOR. Always!

LA TRÉMOÏLLE. I beg your pardon, Monsieur le Comte, but I have just arrived. This is my first visit to Brussels.

RYSOOR. A disagreeable beginning, Monsieur le Marquis!

LA TRÉMOÏLLE. Especially for a pleasure journey!

RYSOOR. Pleasure?

LA TRÉMOÏLLE. Exactly. I don't bore you, I hope?

RYSOOR. On the contrary! We could not spend our time to better advantage waiting for the Grand Provost, who is to decide our fate.

LA TRÉMOÏLLE [*about to sit down*]. Let us gossip, then. But one thing more: I must tell you I am a Calvinist.

RYSOOR. I am delighted to hear it, Monsieur.

LA TRÉMOÏLLE. Are you perhaps of the same faith?

RYSOOR. I am proud to admit it!

LA TRÉMOÏLLE [*offering his hand*]. Well, well, Monsieur le Comte, let me shake your hand. It is a distinct pleasure to do so.

RYSOOR [*shaking hands*]. Monsieur!

[*Shots are heard in the distance*]

LA TRÉMOÏLLE. What is that?

Rysoor [*taking off his hat*]. Heretics, like you and me—they are being shot!

La Trémoïlle. [*taking off his hat*]. God receive their souls! [*He sits*] I was saying that His Majesty, in whose favor I am so fortunate as to find myself on account of my tennis—I am a champion—His Majesty summoned me to him, and said: "La Trémoïlle, it is too warm for you here, my friend. Go and visit Italy or the Netherlands!" I came to the Netherlands. At the frontier, exactly in the middle of the river, whom do I see surrounded by a company of cavaliers, but M. Louis de Nassau, who shouts: "Hola, La Trémoïlle!" I used to know him at the Louvre, when he came there in company with his brother, the Prince of Orange, an excellent gentleman!

Rysoor. The Prince of Orange? Ah, Monsieur le Marquis, there is the loyalest, wisest, and bravest citizen of this land! The pride of the Netherlands—perhaps its savior! So his brother, Monsieur de Nassau, hailed you?

La Trémoïlle. And I cried out to him: "Monsieur, what the devil are you doing in the water there?" Then he answered: "I'm looking for a ford for my men! Will you join us?" "What are you doing?" "We're going to break a lance with the Spanish señors!" I was delighted. As a Protestant, you understand, I have no love for His Catholic Majesty King Philip.

Rysoor. And as for me, I hate him cordially!

La Trémoïlle. He's a melancholiac: I dislike him, too. Then I said to Monsieur de Nassau: "Indeed I will join you, and gladly!" We went on all day, and our band increased every mile we rode. By night, we were a veritable little army. Next day we encountered the Spaniards at Jemmingen! We fought, or rather, *they* fought us—a total defeat. My horse was wounded, shot under me; then the horse fell on top me! A Spaniard disarmed me and sold me to his captain for a hundred pistoles—harness included. The captain sold me in turn to the colonel for a thousand ducats, who resold me for three times that amount to the Duke of Alba, who fixes my ransom at a hundred thousand French crowns.

Rysoor. And the Duke sold you for—?

La Trémoïlle. It stopped there, luckily. The price might grow to more than I am worth!

Rysoor. Well, a hundred thousand crowns is very—

La Trémoïlle. It *is* considerable! I wrote to my brother and asked him to raise the sum. It will cost me two or three castles, but from among the forty districts I shall still have a few left.

Rysoor. And in the meantime?

La Trémoïlle. Meantime I've been bored, as you may easily imagine! To come to the Netherlands on a pleasure trip, and then find myself penned up at Jemmingen between two guards! Well, I said to myself: "I gave my word not to cross the frontier; therefore I shall not cross the frontier, but—I *must* see Brussels! Ventre-Mahon! Never may it be said that I made a pleasure journey to the Netherlands without seeing Brussels in carnival time!"

Rysoor. And here we are!

La Trémoïlle. Yes, here I am, arrested the moment I set foot in the land. It *is* rather unfortunate, on *Mardi-gras*.

[*Sounds of a dispute between two women up-stage. They enter, surrounded by soldiers, who encourage them. Miguel and some officers separate the combatants*]

Rysoor [*carefully watching the group at the back, which gradually disperses among the pillars*]. Yes, to-day is *Mardi-gras!* Ah, Monsieur le Marquis, this day three years ago, under Cardinal Granville and Madame la Gouvernante, you would have seen nothing but continual feasting and merrymaking—masks, dancing, and jousts! The entire week there was dancing, night and day, at the Egmont palace, while for a whole month the Prince of Orange held open house. To-day Egmont is dead: he died on the scaffold, and his wife goes from door to door begging bread for her little ones; the Prince of Orange has no longer a roof over his head: he who once had a king's fortune is reduced to the necessity of selling his gold-plate to the Jews of Strassburg to supply ammunition for his followers. And this city! This once flourishing city, rich beyond her rivals—this unfortunate city is nothing more than a bivouac where the Spaniards and their horses wallow in the straw at every street corner. Everywhere streets are hushed in silence and sorrow, streets through which an occasional passer-by skulks, clinging close to the walls for fear of jostling drunken soldiers! Everywhere the shops are closed, workshops stand empty! From every belfry floats the black flag! On every door hangs mourning! [*Gunshots in the distance*] Every instant that rattle of musketry telling the tale of death—a ghastly knell reminding us that more poor devils are seeing the last of life.

La Trémoïlle. Monsieur le Comte, this is a hideous carnival!

Rysoor. You have already seen how it is celebrated in the country. There it is different: they don't even take the trouble to bury the dead! The course of the Royal Army can be traced by the flight of vultures—entire villages without a soul in them! Smoking ruins everywhere you look. Ruined walls! Before every door a pool of blood, where bodies fester, lying about at the mercy of wolves! Herds of women and children, dying of hunger, snatching food from the very beasts of the field. And everywhere, everywhere the eternal gibbet! When the gallows are too heavy to bear an extra burden they use trees; when the trees are overweighted, then gates, sheds, gable-ends, sign-posts! Every overhanging projection is a gallows. And when these leave no room—a wheel on a pole, each spoke displaying its victim. These objects line every approach to the gates of Brussels: avenues of human flesh! When rope is lacking and they cannot steal more, they try grapeshot; when powder is scarce, they resort to drowning! When the rivers choke, they burn their victims! This is winter—they must make use of their opportunities: the garrison must be kept warm!

La Trémoïlle. Horrible!

Rysoor. And all this because we, citizens of Flanders, are unwilling to be subjects of the King of Spain, who is for us nothing but the Duc de Brabant. Nor do we wish to be judged by the frightful Inquisition! Because we, the rightful heirs of those franchises and privileges which our forefathers won at the price of their life's blood, will not allow ourselves to be outraged by this double-faced and perjured king, who with his hand on the Holy Scripture swore, before God and man, to protect these rights and privileges! Because we want no other faith than that which is right according to our consciences, nor other soldiers than our own! Because, in short, we are a free-born people who refuse, so long as there remains a single drop of Flemish blood in our Flemish veins, to remain the slaves of a despot, an inhuman butcher, and an ambitious monk!

La Trémoïlle. Spoken like a gentleman! You are right. I have no idea what fate has in store for us, you and me, but if we escape alive here are two strong arms and a loyal heart at your service.

Rysoor. My thanks, Monsieur le Marquis! But there is no doubt as to what will happen to us: you will be freed, I put to death.

La Trémoïlle. Why?

Rysoor. I do not know the reason. I may perhaps be accused of having left the city in defiance of the edict forbidding us to pass the gates without official permission of the Duke of Alba.

La Trémoïlle. There is an edict—forbidding that?

Rysoor. And seventeen others, each with the simplest penalty for infringement: death.

La Trémoïlle. For this, too?

Rysoor. For this.

La Trémoïlle. Terrible!

Rysoor. This is the government under which we exist, Monsieur le Marquis, and have existed since the Duke of Alba annulled all our laws and imposed on their ruin his infamous court. He calls it the Court of Troubles; we call it the Court of Blood. And worse—do you see that placard, the brown and yellow one over there, on the pillar? [*He points to the first pillar to the left*]

La Trémoïlle. Yes.

Rysoor. These are the words: (I had to read it three times in order to believe my eyes): "In the name of the Holy Church and of the King, the Duke of Alba, the commander-general, it is decreed: All the inhabitants"—(*all*, mark you, all the inhabitants of the Netherlands)—"without distinction of rank, age, or sex, are condemned to death as heretics!"

La Trémoïlle. *All* the inhabitants?

Rysoor. *All,* three millions of men condemned with one scratch of the pen!

La Trémoïlle [*going to the left to read the placard*]. This is madness!

Rysoor. Yes, but how expeditious. No more cross-questioning, no witnesses! Every man who is arrested may be executed on a moment's notice: he is condemned in advance.

La Trémoïlle. Monsieur le Comte, are we in the Netherlands, or is this hell?

Rysoor. Ah, King Philip has chosen the right man! This insane monarch needed a fanatical and bloodthirsty servant, a man whose face is the only human thing about him. Yet, he is a father, a good father. He has a daughter whom he idolizes. She is ill and slowly dying—*he* is desperate. The air even of her native Spain could not prolong the days of the poor child, and that of Brussels, so dark and humid, hastens her end. And this father—how sure is God's vengeance!—this father in despair only aggravates his daughter's malady. These massacres, these unspeakable horrors, are breaking the girl's heart. She is good and charitable, but her despair is killing her! What a heavenly chastisement, striking the father through his child! Each stroke he deals is a deathblow at his daughter's heart; the more he kills—the monster—the nearer she approaches to her death.

La Trémoïlle. And this nation allows itself to perish as that girl is perishing, through laziness and torpor! Why have not these three million men, condemned as one, thrown themselves on this madman and torn him to pieces?

Rysoor. Patience. The time is near: revolution is growing in the upper provinces—we have command of nearly all the coast. William de la Marck has entered the harbor of La Brielle; the province of Utrecht refused to pay its taxes and is now secretly arming. Overburdened with debts, at the end of his resources, stripped of the subsidies he expected from Spain by the English pirates, the Duke has just raised the taxes again and a wave of horror and hatred runs through the Netherlands: it means ruin to the entire nation. Let the Prince of Orange, our savior, our God, once make up for his setback at Jemmingen and gain one victory over the Spaniards—behold, the rebellion breaks forth, enveloping and devouring the oppressors!

LA TRÉMOÏLLE. Monsieur le Comte, I shall be ready to take any part!

RYSOOR. Ah! Monsieur, shall *I* live that long? [*Roll of drums in the distance*] The drums we hear may be those of the Grand Provost and his worthy acolytes! [*He goes to the right*]

LA TRÉMOÏLLE [*following*]. Is it the Grand Provost who will decide our fate?

RYSOOR. Yes—Noircarmes, a vile brute, who has well deserved by his exploits the nickname of Butcher! Delrio, an insane fanatic, more stupid than wicked, is with him; and Vargas, secretary of the council, a nasty fellow who was forced to leave Spain after violating a young girl whose tutor he was; he is acquiring a fortune here by confiscation and robbery.

LA TRÉMOÏLLE. And of these three scoundrels not one, I dare say, is a gentleman?

RYSOOR. No.

LA TRÉMOÏLLE. Good! I shall use language fitting to their station!

[*The noise of the drums sounds nearer*]

RYSOOR. Here they come, Monsieur le Marquis. This may be our last hour. May I offer you some advice?

LA TRÉMOÏLLE. I beg you.

RYSOOR. If you are questioned about your religious beliefs, conceal the fact that you are a Calvinist! If that were discovered it might mean the forfeiture of your life.

LA TRÉMOÏLLE. Monsieur le Comte, if I gave you the same advice, would you act on it?

RYSOOR. No.

LA TRÉMOÏLLE. Then allow me to imitate you in one respect: that is the only way I can accomplish my duty.

RYSOOR [*grasping* LA TRÉMOÏLLE'S *hands*]. You are right, Monsieur. God save you!

[*The beat of drums is heard in the street. All the soldiers, women, etc., reënter, station themselves about, awaiting the arrival of the court; some crowd the benches, other various articles of furniture, carts, etc. The stage, all except the center, is filled with soldiers, who have run in from all sides. Four of the Provost's Guards, two of them carrying torches, precede* NOIRCARMES; *the torch-bearers go to the left and station themselves around the fire. The other two, sword in hand, put the crowd into place. Enter* NOIRCARMES, VARGAS, *and* DELRIO, *followed by two clerks of the court and more soldiers, who carry drawn swords*]

NOIRCARMES [*brutally, as he enters*]. It's cold as the devil here. Wood! [*He approaches the fire, left*]

SOLDIERS [*up-stage*]. Wood!

VARGAS [*also going to the fire*]. Light torches, too. We shan't be able to see a thing in a few minutes.

MIGUEL. Torches!

SOLDIERS [*outside*]. Torches!

DELRIO [*going to the table*]. Come, let's waste no time! We almost froze at the Jacobins'!

NOIRCARMES. Where is Captain Rincon?

MIGUEL. At the Town Hall, my lord, in order to disarm the Civil Guard.

NOIRCARMES. Good! And, by the way, has this Karloo van der Noot been found?

RYSOOR [*quivering, aside*]. Karloo! Good God, what do these wretches want with him? [*He listens with an air of anxiety*]

MIGUEL. Monseigneur, Karloo was not at home.

VARGAS [*warming his feet*]. Who is this Karloo?

NOIRCARMES [*going to the right of the table in order to sit in the place first occupied by* RINCON]. Former trumpeter of Monsieur d' Egmont, at the battle of Gravelines—very suspicious character!

DELRIO. Calvinist?

NOIRCARMES. No, a Catholic, but no better than a Calvinist. When he was captain of the Civil Guard he received an order to disarm his whole company within twenty-four hours; he did nothing whatsoever about it! [*He sits down*]

DELRIO [*above the table*]. That looks very suspicious.

VARGAS. Miguel, send a soldier at once to the captain with this order: "Karloo is granted the right to take the weapons from his company to the Town Hall. If, however, at seven o'clock in the morning we lack a single musket, at a quarter-past he will have an opportunity at a distance of ten feet from the ground of meditating on the advantages of exactitude."

[*The soldiers laugh*]

NOIRCARMES [*in an undertone*]. It might be wise to begin at that point.

VARGAS [*in an undertone, sitting down, left*]. Yes, but we should not then have the muskets. There is always time later on.

RYSOOR [*drawing a free breath*]. He is saved!

LA TRÉMOÏLLE [*in a whisper*]. Until to-morrow.

RYSOOR [*likewise in a whisper, hopefully*]. Oh, to-morrow!

LA TRÉMOÏLLE. Really, Monsieur, you trembled much more for him than for yourself.

RYSOOR. I did, for I love him as a brother— I might say like a child!

NOIRCARMES. Let us begin now, Miguel. [*At a signal from* DELRIO, *the clerks lay the registers on the table, where they have already placed inkstands and pens*] How many prisoners are here?

MIGUEL. Excellency, a hundred and fifty—and close-packed!

NOIRCARMES. Let us enlighten them! [*The soldiers laugh. To* DELRIO] Has Your Grace the papers?

DELRIO. Here.

NOIRCARMES [*to* MIGUEL]. Proceed—and quickly.

[*The soldiers have filled the benches; others sit round the bases of the pillars and on the tables. The stage is so crowded that scarcely anything of the men can be seen but their heads. Night falls; the place is lighted only by the flickering torches and the reflections from many hearths. A prisoner, dressed in black, is brought forward from the back, right*]

VARGAS [*looking over the documents which he and* DELRIO *have received from the clerks*]. Who is this fellow?

MIGUEL [*to the prisoner*]. What's your name?

PRISONER. Balthazar Cuyp.

NOIRCARMES. Profession?

PRISONER [*simply*]. Pastor.

[*Murmurs from the soldiers*]

DELRIO. Very well. This simplifies matters.

NOIRCARMES. Good. [*To* MIGUEL] Take him away.

SOLDIERS. Death! Death!

MIGUEL. Hang him!

NOIRCARMES. Yes.

MIGUEL. Monseigneur, we have no more rope!

DELRIO. Shoot him.

VARGAS [*his nose buried among the documents*]. Don't waste powder. Burn him with the others—that's the simplest way. Wood costs nothing.

NOIRCARMES. You are right. Away with him to the Jacobins'!

MIGUEL. To the Jacobins'! [*The soldiers open their ranks and allow* CUYP *to pass; then close them at once, left, as they shout: "Death! Death!"*] Next!

[*The soldiers bring forward an old man*]

NOIRCARMES. Who is this?

DELRIO [*looking at a document*]. Goberstraet from Naerden.

OLD MAN [*trembling*]. Pity me, Monseigneur. I'm a poor, harmless old man. I'm a father—I have a family. Pity me!

NOIRCARMES [*to* DELRIO]. What is the charge?

DELRIO. Protested against the latest tax.

OLD MAN. I meant no harm, Monseigneur. Pity me!

NOIRCARMES [*pointing to the placard on the pillar*]. Haven't you read the edict—article nine?

OLD MAN. Have mercy! [*He disappears as the first prisoner did, amid the derision of the soldiers*]

NOIRCARMES. Next!

[*A youth of fourteen, who struggles with his guards, is brought forward. The soldiers have to drag him along on his knees*]

DELRIO. A child?

MIGUEL. Josuah Koppestock.

VARGAS. Refused to take off his cap as the procession passed.

[*Murmurs in the crowd*]

CHILD [*terror-stricken*]. Have pity, Monseigneur, I'm so young!

NOIRCARMES. All the more reason—if we allowed these children to grow up as rebels! [*To the soldiers*] Take him away.

CHILD [*breaking loose from his two guards and clasping* NOIRCARMES'S *knee, then his arm*] Monseigneur, have pity on me—pardon me!

NOIRCARMES [*casting him off*]. Take him away. If we listened to them they would all be innocent! Take him off at once.

CHILD [*still struggling with the guards, who finally take him off*] Pity me! Help! Let me be! Help! Mother! Mamma! [*He disappears as the others have done, crying out as he goes*]

LA TRÉMOÏLLE [*aside to* RYSOOR]. This waiting tears my heart!

RYSOOR [*also aside*]. Poor child—and his mother!

LA TRÉMOÏLLE. Are you married, Monsieur le Comte?

RYSOOR. Alas, Monsieur: to a wife whom I adore.

LA TRÉMOÏLLE. Courage, Monsieur.

VARGAS. Now, the next? Hurry up! We're freezing.

[*The soldiers laugh brutally as* JONAS *is brought forward*]

RYSOOR [*nervously*]. Ah, the bellringer! Poor devil! How does he happen to be here?

NOIRCARMES. Come forward. [*He takes the documents from* VARGAS]

VARGAS. Battery and assault against a soldier.

NOIRCARMES [*to* JONAS]. Your name is Jonas?

JONAS. Yes, Monseigneur. I'm also called "Blockhead," but I don't insist on that!

[*The soldiers laugh*]

DELRIO [*smiling*]. Fine face! Ha!

NOIRCARMES [*also smiling*]. Yes. What do you do, my friend?

JONAS [*confidently*]. Just now, Monseigneur, I spend my time objecting to things as they are, but a year ago, before the Duke of Alba came, I was bellringer of the Town Hall.

NOIRCARMES. Ah, you're the bellringer? You live in the belfry?

JONAS. Yes, Monseigneur, with my wife and little ones. They left me my lodgings on the main floor, after they'd stopped the ringing of the bells for service!

VARGAS. Yes—and you are now lodging Cortadilla the trumpeter at your place, are you not?

[CORTADILLA *advances and makes a military salute*]

JONAS. Yes, Monseigneur—unfortunately.

VARGAS. Well, the trumpeter Cortadilla, who is present, complains that he has suffered many humiliations at your hands.

JONAS. He *is* deprived of some things, Monseigneur—my wine! He drank the whole cellar dry.

[*The soldiers laugh*]

NOIRCARMES. You should count yourself lucky, Maître Jonas, to be allowed to quench the thirst of one of His Catholic Majesty's servants! Especially when he is the victim of such an infirmity: for he is dumb, you know—ever since the battle of Saint-Quentin.

JONAS. Yes, Monseigneur, he told me about that—a bullet that cut off half his tongue.

NOIRCARMES. Well, then—

JONAS. A very unfortunate accident. An awful tragedy! What a talker he must have been *before* the battle! But now it's much worse—you can't understand a damned word he says: he explains himself with his trumpet! One tune announces that he is ready for meals; one means he wants soup; one for more wine, and I know *that* one. We lead a dog's life, Monseigneur! He comes home at one in the morning. [*He imitates the call of a trumpet*] Ta ra ta ta ta! That means: "Open the door!" I get up—he goes to bed; no sooner do I drop off to sleep than— [*He again imitates the call, sadly*]— Ta ra ta ta ta! He's sick! Again I get up and help him. No more sleep that night. But that's not so bad, but this morning he took it into his head to invent a new call! [*Once more he imitates a call, this time allegro*] Ta ra ta ta ta! D'you know what that means?

NOIRCARMES. No—what?

JONAS. "Have Madame Jonas come up to my room at once. I must speak to her." [*The soldiers laugh*] I pretended not to hear. Then a louder call. I got angry—we quarrelled; but, what the devil, he always has the last word with his trumpet. I'm damned if I take the rascal back!

VARGAS. By the way, Maître Jonas, I notice here that there are serious charges against you.

JONAS. Lord in Heaven! About me?

VARGAS. Yes, about your opinions.

JONAS. My belfry gives me the only opinions I ever have.

VARGAS. Your belfry is under suspicion!

JONAS. My belfry?

VARGAS. It is suspected of belonging to the rebels.

JONAS. It never says anything.

VARGAS. Because it cannot; but everyone knows that, if it weren't muffled, it would play only Flemish airs—music hostile to the King!

JONAS. But—

NOIRCARMES. Enough! How many bells are there in your belfry?

JONAS [*intimidated*]. Three, Monseigneur: the big one, called Roland; then there's Jacqueline, and Jeanneton. They're for holidays, when the people used to have good times.

DELRIO. You have been ordered to cut all the ropes from these bells.

JONAS. That's been done; even the stairs leading up to the first landing have been smashed.

NOIRCARMES. That is not enough. You were also ordered to play Spanish instead of Flemish melodies. Have you done that?

JONAS. I've tried to, Monseigneur, but my bells can't change so easily; they're terribly stubborn.

VARGAS. The clown is making game of us!

DELRIO [*aside*]. Yes; but, you see, he's the only man in the city who can ring the bells. We'll hang him later.

NOIRCARMES. Master bellringer, we give you exactly forty-eight hours in which to transform your Flemish belfry into a good Spanish one, faithful to the King and the Church. Don't forget it. Now go.

[JONAS *is about to leave*]

VARGAS. One more word: you referred a moment ago to the days when people had a good time. This is *Mardi-gras,* the time when people should be gay—

JONAS. Well, you see—

VARGAS. You clown, in the days when you lived in disorder and anarchy your life was one series of festivals and debauchery; now that the city is filled with soldiers who are maintaining discipline, you pretend to be downcast. There's not a mask in the streets; and on a holiday of this sort, too—not even a drunken reveller.

JONAS [*pointing to* CORTADILLA]. I beg your pardon—there's the trumpeter!

[*Laughs in the crowd*]

NOIRCARMES. Ah, I had forgotten! Trumpeter Cortadilla, give your arm to this ape; then decorate his head with feathers, or give him a mask—do anything you like—then walk around with him, from wine shop to wine shop, and gather as many comrades as you can. He will bear all expenses—and set an example. Go now, and enjoy yourselves.

JONAS [*as* CORTADILLA *takes his arm*]. Only too happy, Monseigneur—too happy. At least don't let him play his old trumpet!

SOLDIERS [*laughing*]. Yes! Yes! Yes!

NOIRCARMES. You're mistaken—that will add to the festivities. [*As* JONAS *is being taken off*]

JONAS. That is too much pleasure at one time.

[*They go out arm in arm, while the soldiers laugh*]

RYSOOR [*to* LA TRÉMOÏLLE]. Well, the poor man got off easily.

NOIRCARMES. Next!

MIGUEL. It's a woman.

[*There is a movement in the crowd. A woman is brought in*]

NOIRCARMES. Name?

DELRIO [*reading a document which is handed to him*]. Sarah Mathisoon—killed Spanish soldiers.

[*Threatening murmurs among the soldiers*]

NOIRCARMES [*to the woman*]. Have you killed soldiers?

WOMAN. I've killed ten!

SOLDIERS. Death! She's a sorceress. Kill her. Death!

NOIRCARMES. Silence! What the devil!

WOMAN. Bellow, you beasts!

NOIRCARMES. Why did you kill them?

WOMAN. Do *you* ask me why? I'll tell you: I'm a country woman—your soldiers broke into our house—they pillaged, stole, got drunk! When they drank all they could they beat my husband to death. They roasted my son alive to make him confess where we'd hidden our gold! Drunk with blood, they took my pure and innocent daughter, a girl of sixteen, threw and innocent daughter, a girl of sixteen, threw her about from one to the other—for fun, they said—until she died of shame and anger! And I was praying, calling to God, who is deaf! He didn't do a thing. There *is no* God!

ALL [*revolted at the idea*]. Oh! Oh!

WOMAN [*turning to the soldiers*]. No, there *is no* God! You are highway robbers and brutes! Why does He let you behave as you do? He doesn't avenge our wrongs: *I* had to do it! I myself! I made them all drink; and at last they fell down dead drunk. I locked every door and window of the house and set it on fire, and burned them all! Burned them alive, and heard them howl inside! I regret only one thing: that they died too soon, and that all of you were not with them, so that I could tear your hearts to pieces with my finger-nails, and gnaw them with my teeth—you devils!

SOLDIERS [*furiously*]. She's blaspheming! Death! Drown the sorceress!

NOIRCARMES [*to* VARGAS *and* DELRIO]. Suppose we give her over to them?

VARGAS. Good!

NOIRCARMES. We'll give her to you. Take her away.

[*The soldiers, with joyful cries, seize her. A bell rings, and the drums beat*]

VARGAS [*standing up with* NOIRCARMES *and* DELRIO]. The Angelus!

[*The soldiers fall to their knees. There is silence as the bell continues striking*]

RYSOOR [*who stands without taking his hat off; to* LA TRÉMOÏLLE *in an undertone*]. Please, please, Marquis, take off your hat!

LA TRÉMOÏLLE [*aside to* RYSOOR]. Will you take off yours, Monsieur le Comte?

RYSOOR. No!

LA TRÉMOÏLLE. Then I shall keep on mine.

[*The Angelus ceases striking. The soldiers rise as the drum beats, and take the shrieking woman away*]

SOLDIERS. Drown her! Drown her!

WOMAN [*as she is carried out*]. Cut-throats! Kill me, torture me! You can't have back the lives of the men I killed!

RYSOOR [*aside*]. Will this torture never end? My God!

NOIRCARMES [*who, together with* DELRIO *has reseated himself*]. Let us make haste; it is nearly night. [*Catching sight of* RYSOOR] Who is that over there?

MIGUEL. Monseigneur, a citizen who has just been arrested. A spy has reported him.

NOIRCARMES. His name?

RYSOOR [*advancing toward* NOIRCARMES]. I am the Count de Rysoor!

VARGAS [*who has been standing in order to warm his feet, suddenly turning round*]. Count de Rysoor? [*To* NOIRCARMES] I have certain notes regarding this prisoner, who deserves particular attention. [*To* RYSOOR] Was not Your Grace one of the chief officers of the city under the Queen Regent?

RYSOOR. I was so honored, and Madame la Régente deigned to receive me at her councils.

DELRIO. Then we should have no reason to wonder that matters turned out so badly in her time.

VARGAS [*at the table, about to sit down*]. You are charged with having attended the celebrated banquet at the Hôtel de Culembourg!

RYSOOR. Yes, Monsieur.

VARGAS. You confess to having worn the costume of the Queen's family—the Wallet and Shield—insignia of the revolt against royal authority?

RYSOOR. I beg to differ: I am emphatically opposed to senseless buffoonery, and have given my opinion to Monsieur de Bréderode, who agrees with the Prince of Orange.

VARGAS [*sitting down*]. Good! Let us speak of the Prince of Orange. You are accused of being a friend of his.

RYSOOR. I am his childhood friend, Monsieur—one of his most faithful friends.

NOIRCARMES. Of that rebel?

DELRIO. Heretic?

RYSOOR. He lives according to the dictates of his conscience. Happy the man who can lay his head on the pillow without having obeyed another master!

VARGAS. Your being simply a friend is not so important; you are cited as his accomplice. You are here to clear yourself of that suspicion.

RYSOOR. If your Excellencies will be good enough to let me hear the charge, I shall answer.

VARGAS [*to whom* MIGUEL *has given a note*]. You are charged, Monsieur le Comte, with having been absent from this city for a period of four days. The object of this sojourn was an interview with William the Silent.

RYSOOR. Who makes that charge?

VARGAS [*pointing to a spy, who comes forward to the right*]. This man. Tell him what you know.

SPY. I know that Monsieur le Comte left his home Saturday at noon, and only returned to-day, Tuesday, after Vespers.

RYSOOR. That fellow is a groom who was discharged from my service for theft. For the accomplishment of his base profession he gets six sous a day from headquarters. If I were to ask him to lay his hand on the Holy Scriptures and swear I had never left my door, he would do so, but I should have to offer him twelve sous.

[*The soldiers laugh; their jeers serve as accompaniment to the spy's exit*]

NOIRCARMES. Silence! [*The spy disappears*] Here is another proof: the clerk of the court presented himself at your home yesterday, Monday, during the afternoon: you were not there.

RYSOOR. How was I to know he was coming?

VARGAS. When your wife was questioned she was seriously embarrassed, and answered that you had gone out!

RYSOOR. So I had.

VARGAS. Very good; but you must prove that you were at home when the curfew rang.

RYSOOR. Let your Excellencies ask me to give you proof of that by a witness.

NOIRCARMES. You will have a chance of doing that, and easily. You are, as a rich merchant, lodging a Spanish officer at your home.

RYSOOR. Captain Rincon and three soldiers.

NOIRCARMES [*to* MIGUEL]. Have Captain Rincon brought at once. [*Soldiers run out*] Your Grace may be seated. If the captain's statement does not constitute sure proof that you were at home last night, then your absence is a certainty, and you may as well confess to the other charges.

[*During the following* NOIRCARMES, VARGAS, *and* DELRIO *sign documents*]

RYSOOR. God's will be done! [*He returns to his place*]

LA TRÉMOÏLLE [*in an undertone*]. Well, that's over. Let us not lose hope.

RYSOOR [*aside, quickly*]. Monsieur le Marquis, I am lost.

LA TRÉMOÏLLE. Good God! Did you leave the city?

RYSOOR. For four days. The captain will swear I was away. I haven't a quarter of an hour to live!

LA TRÉMOÏLLE. Ah, Monsieur le Comte!

RYSOOR. Every minute is numbered. I have a cruel favor to ask of you.

LA TRÉMOÏLLE. At your service.

RYSOOR. If you ever escape from this hell, as I sincerely hope you will, go to the Place du Grand-Marché, where I live, see the Countess de Rysoor and tell her what they have done to me.

LA TRÉMOÏLLE. I give you my word of honor, I will do it.

RYSOOR. Break the news gently, you understand? Do not tell it bluntly, but come gradually to the point. Though I may appear ridiculous to you, Monsieur le Comte, with my gray hair, I love my wife with the passion of a youth of twenty; and if I show any weakness now it is not the soldier who trembles, but the husband who fears the separation to come, and who does not consider it cowardly to shed a tear at the thought of lost happiness

LA TRÉMOÏLLE. You may rely on me, Monsieur. But doubtless your errand from the city was for a purpose—there was some secret plan?

RYSOOR. Yes.

LA TRÉMOÏLLE. Please treat me as a friend; I beg you, and if I can help—

RYSOOR. Many thanks. But before I was arrested, thank God, I had taken the necessary precautions!

LA TRÉMOÏLLE. Good!

RYSOOR. I shall not be saved, but I shall be avenged.

MIGUEL. Captain Rincon!

[*Enter* CAPTAIN RINCON]

NOIRCARMES. Step forward, Captain Rincon. Do you live with the Count de Rysoor? With that person?

RINCON. Yes, Monseigneur, together with three of my men.

NOIRCARMES. Since when?

RINCON. Since the Sunday of the Purification—last week.

VARGAS. Have you noticed during these past four days that Monsieur de Rysoor was at home?

RINCON. Yesterday, during the day, Monseigneur—he was not.

[*The soldiers show interest*]

VARGAS, DELRIO, *and* NOIRCARMES [*triumphantly*]. Last night?

[RYSOOR *moves about*]

Rincon. Yes, Monsieur le Prévôt—last night he was home!

Vargas. Think well, Rincon—are you positive? Last night, you say, you saw Monsieur de Rysoor—the man who sits over there?

Rincon. I am positive. I fought with him!

[General excitement]

Rysoor [aside]. With me?

Noircarmes. Explain.

Rincon. Last night I had dined extremely well, and when I came home my head was heavy! Not a light to be seen. I went upstairs, striking each stair with the end of my sword. All of a sudden someone comes running out of Monsieur le Comte's room. A lady is holding a light for him—he pushes against me. "Who's there?" I shout. "Who's there yourself? Can't I leave my own room?" I draw my sword; Monsieur le Comte snatches it from me, throws it downstairs, and shouts to me: "Drunkard!", and then he disappears. "Drunkard" I couldn't swallow, you know, though I was drunk; and then I saw I was in the wrong to insult the head of the house, so I went calmly to sleep on the stairs.

Vargas. Have you heard, Monsieur le Comte?

La Trémoïlle [to Rysoor]. Monsieur, you are being spoken to.

Rysoor [making an effort]. Yes, Monsieur, I hear.

Noircarmes. Is the story true?

Rysoor [making an effort to appear calm]. In every detail.

Vargas. Then you were the man?

Rysoor [standing up, very pale]. Who could have been coming from my room at such a time if not myself? Did the captain doubt it for an instant?

Rincon. Not for a second.

Rysoor. Your Excellencies now see that I was at home last night.

Delrio. We must believe it.

Noircarmes [to Vargas]. What do you think?

Vargas [in an undertone]. Let us close the case. We shall be able to get him again.

Delrio. Let us have supper.

Noircarmes. We've done enough to-day. [The soldiers move about] Monsieur le Comte, you are free.

[Noircarmes, Delrio, and Vargas rise, and the soldiers prepare to escort them]

La Trémoïlle [to Rysoor, aloud and joyfully]. Saved, Monsieur!

Noircarmes [noticing La Trémoïlle]. Wait. Who is that?

La Trémoïlle [nonchalantly]. I beg you not to trouble about me.

Noircarmes. I beg your pardon?

La Trémoïlle. Nothing. I am not worth it. Good heavens, let us have supper.

Noircarmes. Well, well, who are you?

La Trémoïlle. Less than nothing: Marquis de la Trémoïlle.

Vargas. Monsieur de la Trémoïlle!

[All take off their hats]

Noircarmes. Taken prisoner at Jemmingen.

La Trémoïlle. Of course.

Vargas. And here?

La Trémoïlle [jokingly]. As you see.

Noircarmes. Monsieur le Marquis, I might have you executed this moment.

La Trémoïlle [gayly]. Oh, you wouldn't think of doing that!

Noircarmes. I beg your pardon?

La Trémoïlle. I say no! Come, let us reason: at this precise moment I am worth a hundred thousand crowns—the price of my ransom! Dead, I should not be worth a sou. The Duke of Alba knows more than to kill a hundred thousand good crowns in flesh and blood, belonging to him!

Delrio. That is true, yet—

La Trémoïlle [lowering his voice]. Especially as you have no money.

Vargas. But—

La Trémoïlle. You haven't, have you? I know the state of your finances!

Delrio. Monsieur!

La Trémoïlle [as before, but speaking naturally]. One word more, Monsieur: if I shout to your soldiers that you have no money to pay them their next month's wages—

Noircarmes [quickly]. Monsieur le Marquis—

La Trémoïlle [as before]. You see? Go and have your supper, Messieurs; go, I beg you. Give my compliments to the Duke of Alba.

Noircarmes. Monsieur le Marquis will present them in person, for he will kindly follow me to the Palace.

La Trémoïlle. Ha! Ha!

Noircarmes. Whether Monsieur le Marquis is willing or not.

La Trémoïlle. Very well, Messieurs, but on one condition: that you follow me, for I will march ahead.

Noircarmes. Monsieur le Marquis—

La Trémoïlle [with dignity and determination]. Monsieur! At the Court of France the family of La Trémoïlle walks directly after the King. I did not come to Brussels to do honor to the Grand Provost of Brabant.

Vargas [impatiently]. As you please, Monsieur le Marquis, only let us go.

La Trémoïlle. Very well. [He turns round and sees soldiers barring his way] Have these fellows make way for us—I dislike the rabble. [He comes to Rysoor] Monsieur le Comte, my heartiest regards. I shall look forward with extreme impatience to seeing you again. [To Noircarmes, Delrio, and Vargas, as he puts on his hat] Messieurs, you may follow me. [He precedes them out, to the beat of drums]

[*The soldiers take up their torches again. The crowd gradually disperses until scarcely anyone but the sentinels at the back is to be seen. The stage is in partial darkness*]

RYSOOR [*recovering from the shock he has suffered, and crossing the stage. To* RINCON, *who looks after the departing soldiers*]. Captain! Captain! One word, if you please.

RINCON [*coming toward* RYSOOR]. At Your Grace's service.

RYSOOR [*scanning* RINCON *anxiously*]. You have just saved my life, Monsieur, but you must admit that your generosity led you to—to modify the facts a little?

RINCON. I told only the truth: Your Grace knows that.

RYSOOR [*still nervous*]. No, I do not know that. [RINCON *shows surprise*] I beg your pardon, Captain, I've been so disturbed since my arrest. Now, let me see. Remember, you were drunk—you admitted that—it was night, and very dark! You might imagine a thousand things under those circumstances.

RINCON. Now, now, I think I'm able to—

RYSOOR. Even I myself am not sure that it was I who left that room.

RINCON. *Your* room it was, by God! You sent me down those stairs quick enough. My sore shoulder would remind me even if my memory failed.

RYSOOR. But that woman who held the light—are you sure?

RINCON. Now you are making fun of me, Monsieur le Marquis. I saw Madame la Comtesse as plainly as I see you at this moment. I can still hear you saying: "Come back, Madame. Come back at once and be careful."

RYSOOR. I said that?

RINCON. Your very words.

RYSOOR. And then the door closed?

RINCON. At once. Now do you understand?

RYSOOR. Thank you, Monsieur, thank you!

RINCON. No ill-feeling? Shake hands!

RYSOOR. Shake hands.

RINCON. Yes. That was an awful cut you got from the sword you took from me.

RYSOOR. Oh, yes, I—

RINCON. And how you shrieked! When I picked up my sword it was covered with blood.

RYSOOR. Indeed.

RINCON. The right hand. [*He points to* RYSOOR's *right hand, which is gloved*]

RYSOOR. Yes.

RINCON. It will trouble you for two or three days.

RYSOOR. Possibly.

RINCON. As a matter of fact, we should have shown it as additional proof to their Excellencies.

RYSOOR. It's only a trifle.

RINCON. But an indisputable proof! [*He goes up-stage*]

RYSOOR [*quickly*]. Yes!

RINCON [*returning to* RYSOOR]. I beg your pardon?

[*The night patrol is heard outside*]

RYSOOR. Nothing. Good-bye, Captain.

RINCON. Ah, here is the patrol! [*Turning to the right as he cries out*] Close your gates!

VOICE OF MIGUEL [*in the distance*]. Close your gates!

DISTANT VOICES. Close your gates!

RINCON. Monsieur le Comte, it is time to close for the night. Go home, and do not stay around the streets. You are now out of trouble. [*He goes up-stage*]

RYSOOR [*aside, greatly distressed*]. Out of trouble! There is no end to my trouble—it is only beginning now. [*He makes his way slowly up-stage*]

RINCON [*at the back*]. Put up the chains.

VOICES OF SOLDIERS [*in the distance*]. Put up the chains!

VOICES [*at a greater distance*]. Put up the chains!

CURTAIN

ACT TWO

SCENE I

In RYSOOR's *home: a Flemish interior; it is a large room, richly but severely decorated. Everywhere are life-sized wood carvings; the walls are hung with tapestries. The ceiling is wainscoted. Down-stage left is a small door; halfway up-stage on the same side is the principal entrance to the room; at the back, a little to the left of center, is a huge fireplace in which a fire is burning. Up-stage right is an arched Renaissance window, obliquely situated, and of stained glass; this opens upon the Place de l'Hôtel-de-Ville, which can be seen outside by the light of the moon. Down-stage right is a Flemish chest loaded with rich plate and jewels. Left is a table, with chairs on either side, and a high tabouret in front of it. Right is a Flemish bench with room for two persons. As the curtain rises* GUDULE *and the* MAJORDOMO *are present.*

MAJORDOMO [*standing on the threshold of the dining-room*]. Has not Madame la Comtesse returned from service this evening?

GUDULE [*engaged in arranging things at the right*]. I think this is she.

[*The door opens and* DOLORÈS *enters, crosses, takes off her mantle and lays down her Book of Hours. After a pause, during which* GUDULE *lays the mantle*

aside on a chair right of the fireplace,
Dolorès *speaks*]

Dolorès. Has Monsieur Karloo come yet?

Gudule. No, Madame.

Majordomo. Has Madame la Comtesse any orders to give for supper?

Dolorès. What time is it?

Majordomo. Just eight, Madame.

Dolorès. No. Serve it later. Leave me now.

Gudule. Madame—Monsieur Karloo!

Dolorès [*joyfully*]. At last!

[*Enter* Karloo]

Karloo [*pale and nervous, crosses the stage and kisses* Dolorès' *hand. In an undertone*]. Send away the servants.

Dolorès. What has happened? Why are you so pale?

Karloo [*in a whisper*]. I must see you alone for an instant. For God's sake, only an instant!

Dolorès. I can't—at this time. They would suspect.

Karloo [*as before*]. *Do* send them away.

Dolorès. Gudule.

Gudule. Madame?

Dolorès. Lay the cloth.

[Gudule *and the* Majordomo *go out, leaving open one side of the double-door, while* Karloo *lays his cape and hat on the bench under the window*]

Dolorès [*showing anxiety ** *]. Are you hurt? What is that wound? Your hand? †

Karloo. Nothing at all.

Dolorès. May I see it? Show me.

Karloo [*showing his hand, which is gloved*]. Yes, you *can* see it—but who would guess?

Dolorès. That soldier?

Karloo. The drunkard. *He* doesn't remember. No, that is not what troubles me.

Dolorès [*nervously*]. What then?

Karloo [*with an effort*]. *He* is back.

Dolorès [*quickly*]. No!

Karloo. Yes: Galèna has seen him.

Dolorès. He has not come home yet.

Karloo. No, but he is in the city—I know that.

Dolorès [*sitting down, after a pause*]. Well, we might have expected that, might we not?

Karloo [*looking at her with a kind of terror*]. Dolorès, you say that as if you had hoped that he would never return.

Dolorès. Don't you wish—?

Karloo [*quickly*]. May God strike me if I ever harbored so horrible a thought!

Dolorès. To tell you the truth, I'm in despair—I'm disgusted—at the idea of his return. God should never have allowed it.

* There is an author's note here to the effect that "this part of the scene is played in an undertone, while each of the speakers appears to be on his guard."—Translator.

† She uses the familiar—"tu"—form; they employ this throughout the play.

Karloo [*sitting down near her*]. God?

Dolorès. Yes, God! That man is a traitor.

Karloo. How do you know that?

Dolorès. Ah, what I know! Do you think he can deceive me by telling me he is going away on business? And when he goes out at night, or to the Porte de Louvain, to attend Protestant service?

Karloo. He?

Dolorès. I am telling you what he says. You know nothing of it, of course! You are a Catholic, like me. And he would not be likely to choose you for a confidant, and tell you of his apostasy. But I tell you he goes every other day to the place I mentioned. For three months this has been going on. Once I followed him without his knowing it.

Karloo [*nervously*]. Did you do that?

Dolorès. I did.

Karloo. And why do you imagine that this latest journey of his—?

Dolorès [*interrupting him*]. These people, for instance, who keep coming all the time to inquire about his return. And see how careful he is to keep secret the fact that he is away. And the fact that he *has* gone away, at the risk of his life. And his beliefs, finally, which perhaps he doesn't confide to you, who are not a rebel. But *I* see. I can penetrate even his silences. For instance, the other week, when you saved Doña Rafaële from the howling mob that tried to avenge itself on the Duke of Alba through his daughter—how did he receive the news of that? He merely said: "You did your duty." A true brother in the cause would have taken you in his arms. I assure you, my woman's instinct is not mistaken. And how could he do anything but hate the Duke of Alba? A Calvinist! Traitor to his God, traitor to his King. Ha! And I am also positive that that man is conspiring—

Karloo [*suddenly springing up*]. Not another word, you— What if we should be overheard? [*As he looks toward the door, he goes behind the back of the chair*]

Dolorès [*oblivious of* Karloo's *demand*]. It makes little difference.

Karloo. It would mean death to him—and others, too.

Dolorès. What others? You are not one of his band, are you?

Karloo [*quickly*]. What an idea!

Dolorès. Then what do I care for the others? And for him, either? Then we could love one another. It would be no crime *then!*

Karloo. That wish is another crime.

Dolorès. Isn't living as we live worse than anything else? And, more, a horrible torture?

Karloo. My God, yes.

Dolorès. Well, then? [*A pause.* Karloo *is standing with his elbows on the back of the chair, his head resting on his hands*] Well, we must decide, must we not? This cannot go on. What shall we do?

KARLOO. What we have been doing: lie, lie, and then lie!

DOLORÈS. Don't you find that horrible? Is it not hateful that we dare not talk during the day with that door standing open, for fear of being spied upon? Even the night brings its dangers—last night, for instance.

KARLOO. Oh, the thought is always with me.

DOLORÈS. What an awful ordeal is the return of this man! Think of it. Oh, I love you! I am yours. [*She rises and goes left*]

KARLOO. Dolorès!

DOLORÈS. You don't care whether he comes back or not! What harm can it do you, after all? The lie of a friendly handshake and a kind word—that is all. But I?

KARLOO. Be careful, the servants are near.

DOLORÈS. Then try to close the door.

KARLOO. How?

DOLORÈS. Oh, casually.

KARLOO. I can't.

DOLORÈS. Let me do it. [*In a rather high-pitched, affected voice*] Won't the fire burn, Karloo? I'm frozen to death.

KARLOO [*near the fireplace*]. Indeed, Madame, it *is* cold.

DOLORÈS [*calmly*]. It must be the open door. [*Calling*] Gudule! *Gudule!*

GUDULE [*appearing*]. Madame?

DOLORÈS. Close the door.

GUDULE. Very well, Madame. [*She closes the door and disappears*]

DOLORÈS. That is done. Now let me tell you the truth, Karloo. I cannot stand this life any longer. If you were as weary as I am— [*She sits on a chair to the right of the table*]

KARLOO. Am I weary of it? Thanks be to God, at last I can talk freely. Don't you think I, too, am tortured every instant by these lies I am forced to tell? My eyes lie, my mouth, this very hand of mine lies! It's so utterly unworthy. It is infamous. If *that* is what you mean—yes, *I am* weary of it all—terribly weary—unspeakably.

DOLORÈS [*nervously*]. So much?

KARLOO. Yes, yes—*so* much!

DOLORÈS. And why? After all, what do you suffer? For your love I live in agony in this world and am damned in the next. What are you sacrificing for me?

KARLOO [*coming down to the left of the table*]. What am I sacrificing for you? My most sacred possessions: my honor and my loyalty, my conscience, my self-respect, the unparalleled joy of being able to say: "I am an honest man—I am doing my duty." You sacrifice your future life, I am sacrificing this one,

and I carry my damnation about with me all the time. Here is *my* hell; it follows me everywhere: contempt for myself. [*He goes up-stage again*]

DOLORÈS [*looking at him uneasily*]. Karloo!

KARLOO [*returning to her, and standing above the table*]. Think of it: the part I play in your house is hateful, revolting. This man calls me friend, receives me with open arms and in full confidence—a generous and devoted man. I deceive him, like the lowest of blackguards. His friendship, so freely offered, I use as a dagger to cut his throat. Nor is that all: this man of all men is the most virtuous— I worship his goodness—yes, it is an awful thing to say, it seems like the worst of follies: I would strangle the person who dared deceive him, even as *I* am deceiving him. *I* am your lover, and I lack the courage to stop. God knows I hated him as you hate him, but remorse—. You are fortunate because you hate him. I worship him. Yes, I love him. That is the most infamous of all. I love him and I lie to him, deceive him, rob him!

DOLORÈS [*terror-stricken*]. Don't you love me any more?

KARLOO [*with a gesture of despair*]. Ah!

DOLORÈS [*quickly*]. No! You used not to have those scruples.

KARLOO. Remorse, rather. And you blamed me just now for having none.

DOLORÈS [*as before, with anxiety*]. Now you have too many. Tell me the truth—tell it— don't you love me any more?

KARLOO. Oh, if I could!

DOLORÈS. You see.

KARLOO [*approaching but not looking at her*]. Yes, I see that I am as powerless to snatch from my heart this fatal poison as I was to prevent its taking root there. You have so caught me by your spells and magic, you love-sorceress, that in spite of myself I loved you, desired you with my whole being, and now even as I curse you I love you, and desire you more than ever before!

DOLORÈS [*standing up*]. Tell me, then, do you want me to have courage for us both? Shall I give you your liberty?

KARLOO. Dolorès!

DOLORÈS. Then—adieu! Go away: I don't want to see you again!

KARLOO [*drawing her passionately to him*]. Ah, do that—and I will kill you!

DOLORÈS [*throwing herself into his arms*]. Yes, yes, you love me! Take me away from that man—take me away.

KARLOO. Take you away?

DOLORÈS. To the end of the world—we two together! Let us be free. To-night let us go.

KARLOO. Good God! that's not possible!

DOLORÈS. Why?

KARLOO. No one is allowed to leave the city.

DOLORÈS. But to-morrow?

KARLOO. Sh! Some one is coming! [*They separate quickly*]

[*Enter* GUDULE *suddenly*]

GUDULE [*nervously*]. Madame la Comtesse, it's Jonas the bellringer; he brings bad news.

KARLOO. Bad news?

JONAS [*as he enters, nervously*]. Madame, has Monsieur le Comte come in yet?

DOLORÈS. No.

JONAS. Then an accident's happened. He was arrested this afternoon.

KARLOO. Arrested?

JONAS. Yes, Captain.

KARLOO [*going quickly toward the window to get his cape and hat, while* JONAS *and* GU- DULE *are speaking in the doorway*]. I'll go at once.

DOLORÈS [*in an undertone*]. What are you going to do?

KARLOO. Save him, if I can.

DOLORÈS. You?

KARLOO. Yes, I. [*Aloud*] Jonas, torches! There, let us start. [JONAS *goes out quickly with* GUDULE]

DOLORÈS. You are not going!

KARLOO. This may mean his death.

DOLORÈS. Well?

KARLOO [*coming down-stage right; nerv- ously*]. Ah, Dolorès, you make me afraid.

DOLORÈS. You make me pity you. Save him, then! My husband. My master. Too bad I can- not deceive him to-morrow for you. Nor you this evening for him.

KARLOO [*shocked*]. Devil!

DOLORÈS [*passionately*]. I love you!

JONAS [*joyfully announces in the doorway*]. Monsieur le Comte.

[*Enter* RYSOOR]

KARLOO [*running to him and taking his hands effusively*]. Thank God, you've returned alive from those hangmen!

RYSOOR [*shaking his hand, but keeping an eye on* DOLORÈS]. You knew I was arrested?

DOLORÈS [*going to him and offering her fore- head to be kissed*]. Jonas just brought us the news, my dear master. We were both in mor- tal terror.

RYSOOR [*taking her hands in his and kissing her forehead. He looks at her with infinite ten- derness*]. You are trembling, Dolorès?

DOLORÈS. Yes, this sudden news—and then your arrival an instant later.

RYSOOR. Dolorès, there's nothing to fear now. I am at home once more, in the midst of my loved ones. How pale you are!

DOLORÈS [*trying to smile*]. It's nothing.

KARLOO [*after laying his cape and hat on the table*]. Natural—emotions!

DOLORÈS. Yes.

[RYSOOR *goes up to the window and lays his sword on the bench*]

KARLOO [*aside to* DOLORÈS]. How infamous of us!

DOLORÈS [*aside to* KARLOO]. There is some- thing worse. [*To* RYSOOR, *who returns down- stage*] I shall have your supper served, master. You must be faint with hunger.

RYSOOR. No, I have some business affairs to discuss first with Karloo. The supper may wait. And let the servants retire.

DOLORÈS. I shall see to it at once. [*She goes out*]

RYSOOR [*following* DOLORÈS *with his eyes until she disappears*]. Jonas, close the door and keep watch.

JONAS. Very well, master. [*He takes his place by the door*]

RYSOOR [*to* KARLOO]. Quick now! Have you just seen Galèna?

KARLOO. As soon as you arrived, Jonas came himself to tell us: Bakkerzeel, Cornélis, and me. *There* I learned of your arrival.

RYSOOR. And the results accomplished?

KARLOO. Everything. The Prince of Orange is coming to help us with his most powerful supporters; he made an advance under cover of night, through the Forest de Soignes.

RYSOOR. And at this moment, my dear Kar- loo, he is hidden in the wood of La Cambre, one quarter of a league's distance from the city.

KARLOO. At last! And to-night?

RYSOOR [*taking* KARLOO's *hands in his*]. To- night!

KARLOO. May the hour of battle, of libera- tion, be blessed!

RYSOOR. My good, my brave Karloo!

KARLOO. You can never know how I thirst for the sacrifice. I feel capable of the most ex- alted deeds.

RYSOOR. We are on the eve of great things. Is everything prepared?

KARLOO. Everything. The Weavers' Guild marches under Bakkerzeel; the Tanners' and the Brewers' under Cornélis; the Civil Guard under me.

RYSOOR. By the way, the bailiff has gone.

KARLOO. To my home—to order disarma- ment. You can imagine how I followed his or- ders! This command, too, will serve our cause.

RYSOOR. How?

KARLOO [*pointing outside to the Place*]. Those chains around the Grande-Place would stop the Prince's cavalry. I hope to get per- mission this evening to unhook them, on the pretext that I must send away my muskets.

RYSOOR. Then you will not be with us at ten o'clock, in the trench by the Porte de Louvain?

KARLOO. What difference will that make? I am not greatly needed there. Here, on the other hand, I can have all my men ready at a moment's notice—weapons ready, and the passage free.

RYSOOR. Then we shall meet at the Town Hall.

KARLOO. At eleven, by Jonas' door.

RYSOOR [*going to the table, as* KARLOO *goes up-stage to get his cape and hat*]. Jonas!

JONAS [*coming down-stage to* RYSOOR]. Your Honor?

RYSOOR. Has Galèna given you your instructions?

JONAS. All.

RYSOOR. How about the soldier who was forced on you as a comrade?

JONAS. The trumpeter? He's there in the middle of the Grande-Place, asleep in the snow.

RYSOOR. Drunk?

JONAS. Dead drunk!

RYSOOR. Good. Now, go away, and not a word, above all, to your wife.

JONAS [*at the small door, down-stage*]. A bellringer's wife! Lord! [*Showing his tongue*] A bell-clapper. [*He goes out, leaving the door open*]

RYSOOR [*to* KARLOO]. Are you going?

KARLOO. Yes, with Jonas, through the garden.

RYSOOR. Go, then, my dear Karloo. This evening, as never before, I feel the need of pressing a loyal heart to my heart, a faithful and devoted one like yours.

KARLOO [*troubled*]. Until to-night, then.

RYSOOR [*going to the window again*]. Until to-night.

KARLOO [*about to leave; aside*]. This agony! I can escape *him* still, but can I escape from myself? [*He goes out*]

RYSOOR [*to himself*]. *Patrie,* you can have no doubt of my devotion: I have set your affairs in order before my own!

[*Enter* DOLORÈS *through the large door*]

DOLORÈS. Now! [*Stopping*] Isn't Karloo here?

RYSOOR. No, Dolorès, he has gone. The servants have retired?

DOLORÈS [*going to a position above the table, to the right*]. You asked to have them out of the way.

RYSOOR. Yes, I wanted to be alone with you—I have something very important to say. [*He goes up-stage above her, to the left, closes the door, then returns*]

DOLORÈS [*anxiously*]. To me?

RYSOOR. Yes.

DOLORÈS. What is it? You seem disturbed.

RYSOOR [*looking attentively at her*]. Dolorès, something has happened in this house since I went away. What do you know about a man who was seen leaving your room last night?

DOLORÈS [*quickly*]. My room?

RYSOOR. Yes.

DOLORÈS. It is a lie!

RYSOOR. No, there is not the shadow of a doubt! For the sake of your honor and mine, only one thing remains to be known: why was that man there?

DOLORÈS. What do I know?

RYSOOR. Let us try to learn who—

DOLORÈS. Perhaps one of the maids—

RYSOOR. Then how did it happen that the man said, addressing the maid: "It's nothing —go back—*Madame!*" [*A gesture of surprise from* DOLORÈS] *Madame* was the word.

DOLORÈS [*terrified*]. It's a lie!

RYSOOR. These words were spoken and heard.

DOLORÈS [*losing her presence of mind*]. Never. That Spaniard lied!

RYSOOR [*bursting forth*]. How do you know he was a Spaniard?

DOLORÈS [*panic-stricken*]. Oh!

RYSOOR [*beside himself with anger*]. Then it was true! Miserable woman! Your lover?

DOLORÈS. Monsieur!

RYSOOR. Dare to deny it! He was your lover.

DOLORÈS [*resolutely*]. Yes!

RYSOOR. Ah!

DOLORÈS. You force me to admit it, and I *do* admit it.

RYSOOR. And you don't regret it. You are treacherous, disloyal. You are not even afraid. You have no particle of shame. Haven't you even the modesty to defend yourself?

DOLORÈS. Say rather, Monsieur, that I have not sunk so low: do not blame me for the little decency I still have, the decency to confess. Yes, it is true: I am guilty. I have no excuse to offer you, either; I have no pity for myself. Kill me! You have the right. I am ready to die. No, I shan't try to save myself by further lies. I have no more lies, no more hypocrisy, thank God! Now you know everything. Kill me, strike me, and let us make an end of it.

RYSOOR [*confused*]. You say that to me!

DOLORÈS. Monsieur, you don't know what I feel. I swear there is a time when death itself seems a deliverance. At least I shan't be forced to mask my troubles under an everlasting smile, and sympathize with your enthusiasm, which I detest—to smile that hideous smile of love, when I feel only hatred.

RYSOOR. Hatred!

DOLORÈS. How sweet it is to be able to tell you that.

[*He totters into one of the chairs to the right*]

RYSOOR. Do you hate me? What an unworthy, ungrateful coward you are! Then when I spoke to you, an orphan without a sou, when I offered you my love, and said: "Here is my fortune, my position, my name—take them, they are all yours," I was to blame that day

—in the darkest street of the poorest quarter of this city, when I took you from your miserable room, your hearth without a fire, your table without bread, from that bed where your mother agonized in the midst of poverty! And since then, have you found me a suspicious husband, or jealous, or tyrannical? Have I deserved your hatred?

DOLORÈS. Ah, Monsieur.

RYSOOR. My God! Do your duty as an upright husband, have only one thought: your wife's happiness. In exchange for satisfying every whim, every wish of yours, I ask only a little affection. Then I come home—and this greets me. A crime so brazen, so open, so shameless, and you say: "Well, yes—that's the way it is! And then—" I presume you will now prove with a word that *I* am to blame?

DOLORÈS. Oh, God! Yes, you *are* to blame!

RYSOOR. Ha!

DOLORÈS. You.

RYSOOR. I?

DOLORÈS. You have been too good to me, Monsieur. I realize that—I confess it. For ten years I have been thankful to you. God knows I came to you an honest woman, with every intention of remaining so. Have you helped me? Never. You killed my gratitude by boring me; my tenderness you repaid with indifference.

RYSOOR. But my love!

DOLORÈS [*rising and going to the left*]. Your love! You talk of your love. I know who your first love is! I know my rival: your beloved Flanders! Your Fatherland, your *Patrie*, as you call it. She is your real wife—your mistress. She is your only love, and I—ha!

RYSOOR. Now you insult the only faith I have left.

DOLORÈS. Really, Monsieur, the life I have led—you with your insane passion for that something that you call "Liberty!" What is my life, with you going off eternally on these suspicious journeys, your comings and goings at night? Then you sit so silent at meals, and look at nothing, or something mysterious that lies beyond me. Yet I am there all the time, and I say to myself: "He is thinking of her!" Ah, Monsieur, you have not counted the days I have suffered nor the nights when I cried myself to sleep. You never even suspected my frightful loneliness, you never understood how my heart was burning with tenderness! To that heart crying out the only answer that came was "Patriotism!" What difference does it make to me whether or not the Netherlands are free? I am a woman, and my *Patrie* is love! If you had paid one quarter the attention to it that you have to your *Patrie,* you and I would not be in this situation.

RYSOOR. I am not trying to make you see that both are the same.

DOLORÈS. I admit, you couldn't make me understand that!

RYSOOR. You are a true daughter of that wretched race that is crushing us. Oh, thrice-cursed Spain, selfish, cruel, here is your blood!

DOLORÈS. You are right, our races cannot be mixed; we must rend one another to pieces. You had no business marrying me. I should never have thought of it, I, a Spaniard and a Catholic. I am proud of that. A Flemish husband—and a rebel! An apostate, a coward, and a perjurer!

RYSOOR. What do you know of that?

DOLORÈS. It makes no difference now. Let's make an end to this. [*She sits on the small chair before the table*] You are the master and I am your slave! Kill me! I have told you to, and I am ready to die.

RYSOOR. It seems to agree with you Spaniards, this spilling the blood of women. But that will not be my method of punishment.

DOLORÈS. Then, Monsieur, what have you decided to do with me?

RYSOOR. I shall tell you that when I know the name of your lover, which you are going to tell me.

DOLORÈS [*ironically*]. Ah, if you hope to learn that—

RYSOOR. Who is he?

DOLORÈS. You will never know.

RYSOOR. Who is the man? Tell me?

DOLORÈS. No!

RYSOOR [*taking her violently by the wrist, and bringing her to a standing position*]. Tell me!

DOLORÈS [*crying from the pain, as she disengages herself and goes toward the right*]. I see it is not necessary to be Spanish in order to know how to torture a woman!

RYSOOR [*as he looses her hand*]. True. [*Controlling himself*] It was unworthy! Well, I don't need you. I have a way of knowing: by the wound.

DOLORÈS [*in an undertone, frightened*]. The hand.

RYSOOR. Yes, you have said it: the hand!

DOLORÈS [*terrified*]. Oh, he knows! He will find out who—he will kill him!

RYSOOR. Yes, I swear to you I will kill him!

DOLORÈS [*aside*]. Kill me, yes! But him—I know a way to prevent that.

[*A distant clock strikes nine*]

RYSOOR [*trembling*]. The hour is striking. [*He goes to the window*]

DOLORÈS [*to herself, as she looks at* RYSOOR]. It is the hour for his church service—he is going.

RYSOOR [*to himself, as he takes his sword*]. Duty first, then revenge. [*He goes to the door at the left and, as he is about to leave:*] To-morrow, Madame, to-morrow, when your lover will be dead! [*He goes out*]

Dolorès. Dead! My Karloo! Yes, if I allow you the time to kill him. [*She goes up-stage quickly, and takes her mantle, which lies on the chair*]

CURTAIN

ACT TWO

Scene II

A trench not far from the Porte de Louvain. Right, at the back, seen from an oblique angle, is the Porte de Louvain and the profile of the rampart, above which are the steeples and houses of the higher part of the city. Stretching from the back of the stage, left, to the front, is the counterscarp of the trench, which is very deep. The trench is "practicable" and entirely on the stage, the right side extending between the rampart and the counterscarp, which runs crosswise. To the left is a patrol path, easily visible to the audience. It leads from the top of the counterscarp down into the trench. Down-stage, on the same side, is a ruined windmill, among shrubs of various sorts. To the right rises a tower, the top of which is invisible. At the back a country landscape can be seen, with windmills covered with snow and glistening in the moonlight. To the right, in front of the counterscarp, a large hole has been dug through the ice in the trench.

As the curtain rises, the First and Second Officers of the Prince of Orange and a soldier are seen coming cautiously down the path on the left, crouching for fear of being seen from the rampart. The soldier follows the officers.

Second Officer [*who walks behind the First*]. Gérard, do you see anything?

First Officer [*going to the right*]. Nothing. The water in the trench is frozen solid, but I see no one.

Second Officer [*pointing to a sentinel unseen by the audience, as he is supposed to be standing behind the tower*]. Look out for that sentinel.

First Officer. And you look out for that big hole in the ice.

Second Officer. This bright moonlight is bad for us.

First Officer. Be patient, it's beginning to cloud over. [*To the soldier*] Keep careful watch at the counterscarp.

[*The soldier begins to climb the path. A bell in the city rings*]

Second Officer. Quarter to ten.

First Officer. It's time—and no one here.

Second Officer. There is something mysterious about this. Sh! Don't move! Some one's coming. Here they are.

First Officer. Probably. But stand aside, comrade. [*To the soldier*] Run to the Prince!

[*They crouch behind the bushes to the left. Rysoor appears on the right. With Rysoor are Galèna, Jonas, Bakkerzeel, and Cornélis. Rysoor leads the party. He comes down to the middle of the stage, beckoning to the rest to follow him. They do so and come down the path*]

Rysoor [*going unaccompanied toward the left and looking at the snow in the trench*]. Here are footsteps in the snow. They are here, Galèna.

First Officer [*to the other*]. Yes, it is they.

Rysoor [*seeing the officers, who come forth from their place of hiding*]. Who goes there?

Second Officer. Orange.

Rysoor. Brabant. God be with you, comrades!

[*He and his companions salute the officers*]

First and Second Officers [*saluting as they advance*]. And with you, Messieurs.

Rysoor. Is the Prince there?

First Officer. Here he is.

[*The Prince of Orange, followed by two soldiers, appears on the path at the left*]

Rysoor. Yes, it's he. Galèna, keep strict watch over there—we may be surprised.

The Prince. Rysoor, my friend, I was beginning to think that something had happened to you.

Rysoor. Thank God, no! Monseigneur, here are the leaders of our enterprise—all except one—but he is helping us to his utmost.

The Prince. Messieurs, I grasp all your loyal hands in that of the Count. God protect our cause!

The Conspirators [*saluting*]. And your Excellency!

The Prince. And now to work. We have little time. But first—those sentinels up there?

Rysoor. Safe and tried. Bound to our cause.

The Prince. There's nothing to fear, then?

Rysoor. Nothing, Monseigneur.

The Prince. What is this hole?

Rysoor. It has been cut in the ice for victims: the cemeteries are full to overflowing.

The Prince. Poor city! Are we not halfway between the Porte de Cologne and the Porte de Louvain?

Cornélis. Yes, Monseigneur: there is the Porte de Louvain over there.

The Prince. Good.

Bakkerzeel. How many men has your Excellency hidden in the wood of La Cambre?

The Prince. Three thousand picked cavalry, each one with a foot-soldier whom he can carry on the croup with him. In all, six thousand of the best men.

Rysoor. The city can muster twelve thousand. We are numerous.

THE PRINCE. Yes, but we must effect an entrance first.

RYSOOR. We will, Monseigneur. All the guards at the Porte de Louvain are our men, like these sentinels on the rampart.

THE PRINCE [*joyfully*]. Is that your work, Rysoor?

RYSOOR. No, not mine, but Bakkerzeel's and Galèna's. They did that when I was away.

THE PRINCE. Thanks be to God! Messieurs, a master-stroke.

RYSOOR. They are German lancers, Lutherans and Calvinists, threatened by the Duke of Alba. Their fear has brought them over to our side.

THE PRINCE. So they will open the gate?

CORNÉLIS. At a signal from the belfry.

THE PRINCE. Which will be given by—?

JONAS. By me, Monseigneur.

THE PRINCE. Jonas?

JONAS. Does Monseigneur recognize me?

THE PRINCE. Why, our dear old bellringer.

RYSOOR. At midnight Jonas will ring the big bell as hard as he can, the portcullis drops, and your six thousand men are inside! All our friends rush into the streets, crying: "To arms!" Galèna runs to the Palace, Bakkerzeel occupies the Jacobins', I the Town Hall. Ten thousand men coming forth from the shadows throw themselves on the Spaniards. The Duke of Alba is cut to pieces before he has time to put on his spurs.

THE PRINCE. Good. But we must prepare for every emergency: the most unexpected turn of affairs has often destroyed the best-laid plans! In an hour's time we may be still unprepared.

RYSOOR. In that case, Monseigneur, instead of giving the signal to come forth, Jonas will give one meaning, "Save yourselves!"

THE PRINCE. Another signal?

RYSOOR. Yes. If all goes well, then the big bell—

JONAS. Roland!

RYSOOR. Yes, Roland will then ring as loud as possible, as on the great festival days.

THE PRINCE. And in case of disaster?

RYSOOR. The death-knell. In this city of death that is always appropriate.

THE PRINCE. So then: the call to arms, and the call for retreat. Good.

[*The hour strikes in the distance, and is repeated by many other bells*]

RYSOOR. Sainte-Gudule is striking ten. If your men start at eleven, they will be able to advance without being heard to within a thousand steps of the ramparts, and be ready for the signal.

THE PRINCE. One thing more: how shall we be able to recognize our allies in the city streets?

RYSOOR [*showing a white neck-cloth attached to the hilt of his sword*]. This white neck-cloth, Monseigneur, attached either to the sword or on the hat.

THE PRINCE. Everything seems wisely planned, Rysoor. Messieurs, I am not a man of many words: I shall not speak of the lamentable condition of our *Patrie*. You know it, alas! only too well. We are engaged in a desperate enterprise; one false step may ruin everything. In the name of all that you hold sacred, my friends, do not for an instant forget yourselves. No frivolity—not a useless word —especially to the women! Return to your homes, put out the lights, hide your weapons. Let the city sleep more soundly to-night than usual. Now, let us separate—until later. May God give us only a little help and—you and I will take care of the rest.

RYSOOR. Until later, Monseigneur.

GALÈNA [*pointing to the left*]. Silence. A patrol.

RYSOOR. Which direction?

GALÈNA. On the counterscarp.

RYSOOR [*uneasily*]. How does it happen to be there?

[JONAS *climbs up the embankment*]

BAKKERZEEL. That's the guard from the Porte de Cologne. It comes this far.

THE PRINCE. Bend down, Messieurs. Not a word! [*To* JONAS] Is it coming?

JONAS [*lying down on the rampart*]. Yes, Monseigneur.

CORNÉLIS [*who is looking toward the right, quickly*]. There's another, coming toward us, following the walls.

GALÈNA. Caught between two fires!

RYSOOR [*pointing to the left*]. Your swords, Messieurs! Let us charge on this side.

[*He draws his sword, while the other conspirators do likewise, and stand ready to fall upon the patrol*]

THE PRINCE [*quickly*]. This is madness. We shall spoil everything!

RYSOOR. But we are trapped in this trench!

THE PRINCE. Keep cool, Rysoor, keep cool. [*To the* FIRST OFFICER] Gérard! Quick, my Icelanders, quick! Behind these walls, Messieurs! Then let the sea-dogs loose. They are used to this sort of thing.

[*Together with the officers, he hides behind the mill, while* RYSOOR *and the conspirators seek the shadow of the town, on the right. The sea-dogs, coming out of the underbrush at the left, come on to the stage, then conceal themselves by the side of the rampart. At the top of the path a patrol of six men is seen, one of them an officer. The Spaniards descend the path to the stage and turn toward the trench, when they find their way barred. At a signal, which sounds like the cry of an owl, all the sea-dogs* attack the patrol simultaneously: two to each Spaniard. One throws a lasso over the Spaniard's neck, while the other disarms him instantaneously. The surprised soldiers, finding themselves gagged, struggle. There is a fierce conflict, during which choked cries of rage are heard. The conspirators come from their hiding-places to help the Icelanders who, having strangled all the soldiers, throw their bodies into the open pit. Some of the conspirators scale the counterscarp, thus precipitating a great mass of snow down into the trench; others stamp on the snow over the pit, while two soldiers gather up the weapons that have fallen during the struggle]

RYSOOR. That is over with!

[The sea-dogs run out. There is no trace of the buried patrol]

THE PRINCE [walking up the path]. Until midnight, Messieurs. And—courage!

RYSOOR. Quick, Monseigneur! Here comes the other patrol.

[THE PRINCE and his officers quickly disappear along the path. RYSOOR and his companions hide behind the wall. The patrol appears toward the right, crosses the stage, where it is plainly seen in the bright moonlight, marching over the very spot where their dead comrades lie buried, and then goes up the other side. The moment it reaches the top of the counterscarp RYSOOR and his friends come cautiously from their places, crouching and looking after the disappearing soldiers as the bells of the city are heard ringing]

JONAS [standing by the pit]. My bell is not heard!

[They all disappear behind the tower.]

CURTAIN

ACT THREE

SCENE I

The DUKE OF ALBA'S private room in the palace of the government. The room has a high, vaulted ceiling; the general effect is rich but sombre. Down-stage right is a door leading to the interior apartments; before it is a large armchair. Halfway up-stage on the same side is a huge Flemish fireplace, above which hangs a portrait of King Philip II. The room narrows toward the back of the stage. There are doors right and a window at the back giving a view of the city. Halfway up-stage left is an entrance. There are two tables covered with velvet tapestries bearing the arms of the House of

Austria: one left, down-stage, the other facing obliquely, at the right, opposite the fireplace. The Duke of Alba, seated by the fireplace in a large armchair, his features outlined by the light of the fire, is buried in thought, his elbow resting on the table, as he looks into the burning embers. VARGAS and DELRIO, sitting at the table left, are busied with their correspondence. At the back of the stage is MAÎTRE CHARLES, the city executioner. LA TRÉMOÏLLE is sitting at a small table reading by the light of a double-branched candelabrum. The room is lighted with candelabra decorated with the Austrian arms, and bearing large candles of yellow wax. Left of the Duke's table is a seat without a back.

LA TRÉMOÏLLE [rising, book in hand, and coming down-stage to the left]. Charming room! [To VARGAS, in an undertone] Messieurs.

VARGAS. Monsieur le Marquis?

LA TRÉMOÏLLE. Is Monsieur le Duc always in this peculiar humor?

DELRIO [aside to LA TRÉMOÏLLE]. No, Monsieur le Marquis, he is troubled about Doña Rafaële's health.

VARGAS [also under his breath]. Doña Rafaële left the table this evening after a frightful coughing fit, and her physician, Maître Alberti, has just had what I imagine was a serious conference with the Duke.

LA TRÉMOÏLLE. Poor child.

DELRIO. It will doubtless be necessary to send the Señora to Spain, for Maître Alberti declares that the climate of Flanders is killing her. She needs, he says, the warm and perfumed air of Andalusia; she cannot hope to last in this damp climate until even early April.

VARGAS. This separation will be a terrible blow to Monsieur le Duc. He loves his daughter more than anything else in the world.

DELRIO. A city in war-time is no place for a young girl.

[A guard enters, and goes tiptoe to DELRIO and VARGAS, speaking to them, as LA TRÉMOÏLLE resumes his place and continues reading]

DELRIO [rises quietly, crosses the stage, and says to the Duke in an undertone]. Monseigneur, the messenger from Spain has arrived.

ALBA. Ah, news from the King. Let him come in.

[The messenger quietly enters, makes a low bow, then draws forth the dispatches from a small leather sack, laying them on a silver tray which is on the table] You have been quick, Perez.

MESSENGER. Only fifteen days, Monseigneur, and in this snow. I have had to look out for these rebel bands which overrun the country.

ALBA. Rest yourself—you must return tomorrow. [The messenger goes out with the guard. ALBA opens the packet of dispatches]

A letter for you, Vargas, in His Majesty's own hand!

VARGAS [*going to the Duke and taking the letter very respectfully*]. I am truly honored by the King.

ALBA. And one for you, too, Delrio.

DELRIO [*following* VARGAS's *example, and kissing the seal obsequiously*]. God save the King!

[VARGAS *goes to the table, takes a pair of scissors, with which he severs the silk cord holding the seal, then reads the letter down-stage, while* DELRIO *goes to the small table up-stage, and opens his letter in the same manner as* VARGAS]

VARGAS [*reading in an undertone*]. "Señor Vargas: Your reports I treasure highly. Continue to keep me secretly informed of all you know about Monsieur le Duc. Burn this letter carefully. God be with you, Philip. I mistrust Delrio. Keep strict watch over him—" [*He goes toward the left, reading all the while, then returns, passing the table*]

DELRIO [*coming down to the center of the stage, as he reads his letter*]. "Señor Delrio: Many thanks for your excellent information. Continue to send me these secret reports as to what you learn of Monsieur le Duc. Burn this letter. God be with you, Philip. I have small confidence in Vargas: never allow him out of your sight." [*He returns to his place in the same manner as* VARGAS]

VARGAS [*bowing to* DELRIO *before seating himself*]. My compliments!

DELRIO [*bowing to* VARGAS]. And mine to you.

ALBA. Messieurs, here is a post-script from the King for you: "My son Don Carlos died suddenly on Christmas Eve!"

VARGAS *and* DELRIO. The Infante?

ALBA [*continuing*]. "I had forgotten to tell you before—"

LA TRÉMOÏLLE [*who is still reading, aside*]. Three months ago: a model father!

ALBA [*continuing*]. "This wretched son of mine has been the occasion of so much trouble that I am not sure whether we ought to mourn his death or congratulate ourselves." Messieurs, we shall participate in His Majesty's grief by adopting mourning.

DELRIO. Of course, Monseigneur.

[*He and* VARGAS *seat themselves*]

LA TRÉMOÏLLE [*to himself*]. With pleasure.

ALBA. Ah, you are still here, Monsieur le Marquis?

LA TRÉMOÏLLE. Your Excellency having afforded me the hospitality of your palace for a prison, while I await your pleasure to release me, I distract myself by reading of the campaigns of the Emperor Charles the Fifth.

ALBA [*sarcastically*]. A great king, Monsieur le Marquis. You French know something of *that*.

LA TRÉMOÏLLE. He was indeed a great king, Monsieur le Duc. I once had the honor of dining with His Majesty at the convent of Saint-Just, and I still marvel at the vast amount of victuals His Majesty was able to consume. Great God, what an appetite!

ALBA. Imperative!

LA TRÉMOÏLLE. Imperial!

ALBA. Great monarchs are great in all ways.

LA TRÉMOÏLLE. Ah, King Philip has not the capacity of his worthy father.

ALBA [*biting his lip*]. We have fixed your ransom, Monsieur le Marquis, at—

LA TRÉMOÏLLE. A hundred thousand crowns, Monsieur le Duc.

ALBA. A trifle. The French are so clever, they should be taxed double.

LA TRÉMOÏLLE [*unruffled*]. Then, Monsieur le Duc, I should pay three hundred thousand crowns, and you Spaniards would be none the richer.

ALBA [*violently*]. Maître Charles!

[*Everyone's attention is riveted on the Duke. The executioner steps forward.* DELRIO *and* VARGAS *raise their heads and* LA TRÉMOÏLLE *quietly scans the Duke, who is scarcely able to overcome his wrath*]

ALBA [*to the executioner*]. What were you telling me just now?

CHARLES. I took the liberty to remark that my assistants are asking for double pay, because of the nasty jobs they have to perform.

ALBA. Very well. And then?

CHARLES. We're out of rope!

ALBA. Vargas, ask Rincon to have twenty of his men spend the night weaving hemp. Then?

CHARLES. Then, Monsieur le Duc, when *that* job's over—well, we don't know where to bury them—all those—

ALBA. I gave an order that holes were to be cut in the ice at each of the city gates.

VARGAS. That has been done, Monseigneur, at the Porte d'Anderleke and the Porte de Louvain.

ALBA. Do you hear, Maître Charles?

CHARLES. Yes, Monseigneur.

ALBA. Anything else?

CHARLES. That's all. [ALBA *strikes a bell*] That is, unless Monseigneur has some commission for me to-night.

ALBA. I may have—wait! [*He rises. A valet appears at the right*] Domingo, see whether Doña Rafaële is resting. [DOMINGO *goes out through the same door by which he entered*] Well, how is the city this evening, Delrio?

[DELRIO *and* VARGAS, *seeing the Duke standing, rise, but he motions them to be seated*]

DELRIO. Splendid, Monseigneur—capital *Mar-*

di-gras: life, gaiety, yet all in good order—
everything is satisfactory.

ALBA [*coming down-stage, in front of the
table*]. I went out for a moment after the
Angelus, and the lower part of the city seemed
very quiet.

DELRIO. Monseigneur knows that the Flemish
lack gaiety. There lacks the Spanish spontaneity.
No, the Fleming takes his pleasure internally.
There is nothing on the surface.

ALBA. I did not see a single mask during my
walk. [*He goes to the window at the back*]

LA TRÉMOÏLLE. Ah, these gentlemen! I saw
one not long ago, arm in arm with the bellringer. The rascal! *He* was enjoying himself.

ALBA [*opening the window*]. See how the
city sleeps. There's not a light—in the whole
Place there's not a sound.

VARGAS. That shows how tranquil the city is.

ALBA. Too much so. Still waters. How is it
that that tavern is not lighted up as usual?

DELRIO. Ah, the tavern, Monseigneur: we
have reason to be dissatisfied with the innkeepers.

VARGAS. And the bakers.

DELRIO. And the butchers, too.

ALBA. What do you mean?

VARGAS. We should tell your Excellency that
only this morning eighteen innkeepers, bakers,
and butchers, among the most influential in the
city, refused to open their shops and make
their display.

ALBA. Eighteen?

VARGAS. No less.

ALBA. And you did not force them?

DELRIO. Your pardon, Monseigneur. We gave
them until noon to reconsider; as they still remained obdurate, we shut them up in the
Jacobins'.

LA TRÉMOÏLLE [*to himself*]. That will
scarcely improve business.

ALBA [*coming down-stage*]. Indeed? rebellion among the merchants.

DELRIO. Ah, Monseigneur, it is all because
of this latest tax.

VARGAS. Since your Excellency has imposed
a tax of ten per cent. on all provisions, mer-
chandise and personal property—

DELRIO. What, opposition from the trades-
people?

VARGAS. They are fearfully wrought up.

ALBA. Really.

DELRIO. This nation of shopkeepers is so
sensitive about material advantages.

ALBA. Well, by Saint-Jacques, its neck will
have a chance to feel sensitive! Maître Charles,
have eighteen new ropes prepared. At sunrise
to-morrow I want to see these eighteen rascals
dangling above their own doorsteps. Understand? From their own sign-posts! You may
go. Now you have something to busy you with
to-night.

LA TRÉMOÏLLE [*to himself*]. That won't settle
matters.

ALBA [*to* DOMINGO, *who reappears*]. Well?

DOMINGO. Doña Rafaële thanks your Excellency, and begs to wish you good-night before
she retires.

ALBA. Dear child! I shall go to her at once.
The news from Holland, Messieurs, in three
words?

DELRIO [*holding some letters*]. Wholly favor-
able, Monseigneur. Amsterdam is quiet—the
whole of the low country inundated—but that
makes no difference to us.

ALBA. And the Prince of Orange?

DELRIO. According to the spies' reports, from
the fifteenth of the present month, the Prince
was in the neighborhood of Leyden.

ALBA. That is very well. [*He walks toward
the right*]

VARGAS [*looking through his notes*]. No. I
beg your pardon—Mons—

[*The Duke stops short*]

DELRIO [*showing him the report*]. No—Leyden. [*Also rising*] Here is mine.

ALBA [*angrily*]. By Saint-Jacques, we have
treacherous spies! Are they making game of
me?

VARGAS [*showing a letter*]. Monsieur le
Comte de Nassau—

ALBA [*violently snatching the letter from him,
crumpling and throwing it across the room*].
I care nothing about the Comte de Nassau!
He will make no more than a mouthful. Good
God! Messieurs, I give you exactly an hour in
which to find the whereabouts of Orange! He
is the only one I fear.

[NOIRCARMES *enters, left, during the last
part of this speech*]

NOIRCARMES. Then let your Excellency rest
assured; you need have no further fear of him.

ALBA. How is that?

NOIRCARMES. Recent and authentic reports
have arrived: he crossed back over the Rhine
at Strassburg last Sunday with three hundred
men. All his troops had revolted because there
was no pay for them—they have scattered, disappeared.

ALBA. Where did you get your information?

NOIRCARMES. From the French Ambassador,
who wishes your Excellency a good-night.

ALBA. Splendid, Vive-Dieu! This is news; it
puts new blood into my veins. Messieurs, let
me sign your papers. [VARGAS *pushes forward
his chair upon which the Duke sits to sign the
papers which are given to him*] Nothing suspicious this evening?

NOIRCARMES. Absolutely nothing, Monseigneur; the city sleeps.

ALBA [*rising*]. Then, Messieurs, I think we
might well follow its example. Let us arrange
these papers first and then retire. [*To* LA

TRÉMOÏLLE] Monsieur le Marquis, your room is next to mine, and—

[*Enter* RAFAËLE, *a nun, and a maid*]

ALBA [*going to* RAFAËLE *and taking her tenderly in his arms*]. My dear child. Well?

RAFAËLE [*supported by the two women*]. Better.

ALBA [*to the women*]. That chair! How is the cough?

RAFAËLE. Cough? [LA TRÉMOÏLLE *goes ahead of the women and places the chair for* RAFAËLE] Not so bad. [*She coughs*]

ALBA. Sit down. [*He makes her sit in the chair*] And your pains?

RAFAËLE [*smiling sadly*]. The same as always.

ALBA. But Maître Alberti promised me to make you sleep.

RAFAËLE. Oh, I shall.

ALBA. Noircarmes, the window. The air is icy cold. [*He goes up toward the window, which* NOIRCARMES *closes. During this time* LA TRÉMOÏLLE *has placed a cushion under* RAFAËLE's *feet*]

RAFAËLE. Thank you, Monsieur.

ALBA [*coming down-stage again*]. Thank you, Marquis. [*He takes his daughter's hand*] Always that same fever! Your hands are burning!

[RINCON *enters on tiptoe and speaks with* NOIRCARMES]

RAFAËLE. I have just suffered such agonies; but now, truly, I am better.

ALBA [*kissing her hands affectionately*]. Dear, sweet child! Sweet, tender little one!

[NOIRCARMES, VARGAS, *and* DELRIO, *to whom* RINCON *has just been speaking, hesitate, then* NOIRCARMES *decides*]

NOIRCARMES [*timidly*]. Monseigneur.

ALBA. What is it? I shall not need you further—you may go.

NOIRCARMES. I beg your Excellency's pardon, but there is something important.

ALBA [*impatiently*]. Must there always be something? I seem never to have the time or the right to be a father. Well, what is it?

NOIRCARMES. The captain of the militia—

ALBA. There is no longer any militia.

NOIRCARMES. Exactly, Monseigneur. This young man used to command the Civil Guard; we gave him an order just now which he cannot execute without your Excellency's permission.

ALBA. Let him come in—and now, for God's sake, let us get things finished!

RINCON. Come in, Captain.

[*Enter* KARLOO]

RAFAËLE [*aside*]. He?

ALBA. Let me tell you at once, Monsieur, it is most daring of you to appear in my presence with your sword hanging at your side.

KARLOO. Monsieur le Duc, I am a captain.

[RINCON *stands at the back of the stage, near the door;* NOIRCARMES *near the Duke's table;* LA TRÉMOÏLLE *in front of the fireplace, the nun and the maid before the door*]

ALBA. No longer. The Civil Guard has been abolished. Your sword, Monsieur.

[*Without saying a word* KARLOO *gives his sword to* NOIRCARMES, *who hands it to* RINCON, *who lays it on the table to the left*]

RAFAËLE [*to the Duke as she takes his hands in hers*]. Father, I beg you, don't be angry. It makes me ill to hear you.

ALBA. Very well, child. [*More softly to* KARLOO] Monsieur, what do you wish?

KARLOO. Monsieur le Duc, Monsieur le Grand Prévôt ordered me this afternoon to gather together all the weapons of my company to-night and take them to the Town Hall—on pain of death.

[RAFAËLE *starts. She still holds her father's hand, trembling*]

ALBA. Well?

KARLOO. Well, Monsieur le Duc, I am ready to obey the moment I have the means of doing so; it is quite impossible to transport eight hundred cuirasses, muskets, and helmets, on account of the chains that block the way into the Grand-Marché.

ALBA. Nonsense!

RAFAËLE. But that is only reasonable, Father.

ALBA [*softening*]. Hush, child. [*To* KARLOO] And you ask—?

KARLOO. To have the chains removed to-night, Monsieur le Duc, in the vicinity of the Town Hall.

ALBA. And if I refuse?

KARLOO. Then your Excellency need not ask for the weapons—only my head. That is simpler.

RAFAËLE [*to her father*]. He is right, Father.

ALBA. Noircarmes, do you see any objection?

NOIRCARMES. None whatsoever, Monseigneur —only for one night.

ALBA. Very well. Now leave me.

[KARLOO *salutes, and turns to go*]

RAFAËLE [*quickly, in an undertone*]. Father, don't let him go yet.

ALBA [*to* KARLOO]. Wait. [*To* RAFAËLE] What is it?

RAFAËLE. Please give him back his sword. There is nothing so humiliating for a soldier as to be weaponless.

ALBA. Little silly! Why, a Civil Guard would not know how to use a sword.

RAFAËLE. Oh, yes, he would.

ALBA. How do you know?

RAFAËLE. I have seen them in action.

ALBA. Where?

RAFAËLE. The day I went to the Convent of Groenendaal. You remember, Father? Where I was insulted—the people threw stones at me.

ALBA. Vermin!

RAFAËLE. Well, the man who defended me so splendidly—

ALBA. Is this the man?

RAFAËLE. Yes.

ALBA. Vive-Dieu! Why not say so at once? [*Graciously, to* KARLOO] Captain, will you please come here? [KARLOO *comes down-stage*] Here is a lady, I understand, who is under obligations to you.

KARLOO. Monsieur le Duc, I only did my duty toward a woman; I simply protected her against insult.

RAFAËLE. And I, Seigneur Karloo, do my duty by remembering what you did.

ALBA. Karloo. I seem to know that name. Captain, were you not at Gravelines?

KARLOO. Yes, Monsieur le Duc, and at Saint-Quentin; I was standard-bearer of Monsieur le Comte d'Egmont.

ALBA. Well, Seigneur Karloo, a man who has made such good use of his sword shall not be deprived of it. You may have your weapon.

RAFAËLE [*joyfully pressing her father's hand*]. I am so happy.

KARLOO. Your pardon, Monsieur le Duc. I may have my sword, you say, but in what capacity?

ALBA. As lieutenant of my guards. Noircarmes will send you your papers to-morrow.

RAFAËLE [*delighted*]. I am so glad!

ALBA [*To* RAFAËLE]. Are you happy?

RAFAËLE [*as before*]. Oh, yes!

KARLOO. Monsieur le Duc, I cannot take the sword.

ALBA [*surprised*]. Pardon, Monsieur?

KARLOO. I am a Fleming, and as such I cannot serve in the King's army.

ALBA. Yet you served him under Monsieur d'Egmont?

KARLOO. Against the French, Monseigneur; but when it is a question of serving against my own people—never!

ALBA. By God! the audacity!

RAFAËLE [*trying to restrain her father during the following*]. Father!

KARLOO [*taking his sword from the table*]. Your Excellency has not noticed this blade: it is a simple, rustic piece of work, intended to guard over the sleeping city, or the *Patrie* when it is threatened; protect old men, women, children. Then it leaps forth joyfully from its sheath into the sunlight, ready for its duty! But when there is a question of matching it with the executioner's blade or using it as a signal for massacre in burning towns, I know well, Monsieur le Duc, it would turn its point to my own breast. We are far too Flemish, it and I. We understand nothing of Spanish ways. [*He lays his sword on the table. All are surprised*]

ALBA [*jumping up from his chair in fury*]. Noircarmes!

RAFAËLE [*also quickly rising, then throwing herself into his arms*]. Father!

[*Everyone stands still*].

ALBA [*restraining himself, after a pause*]. Monsieur, I can at least be grateful for a service rendered. You may thank your destiny, for no one else would have escaped in this way. Now go.

[KARLOO *bows to* DOÑA RAFAËLE *and is again about to leave*]

NOIRCARMES. But the chains, Monseigneur?

ALBA. I have already given the order—let them down.

[KARLOO *goes out*]

RAFAËLE [*exhausted*]. How terrible!

ALBA [*to his daughter, who is still in his arms, crying*]. See what you make me do, you whimsical, spoiled child!

RAFAËLE. Oh, I should so like to have seen at least *one* man on our side—*him* especially.

ALBA. My dear.

RAFAËLE [*sobbing desperately*]. Now it's over. No one will ever care for us!

ALBA. Rafaële, my dearest, come, rest yourself—you must not get so excited.

RAFAËLE [*to the nun and the maid*]. Take me now—take me away.

ALBA [*alarmed*]. The doctor—quick! [*The women run to her.* LA TRÉMOÏLLE *opens the door and goes out with them and* RAFAËLE, *at the moment when* MIGUEL *appears at the back, having entered by the side door, which he leaves open*] You may retire, Messieurs—go! I shall keep watch. Good-night. [*About to follow his daughter*]

NOIRCARMES [*to whom* MIGUEL *has been speaking in an undertone*]. Monseigneur, one thing more.

ALBA. I want to hear nothing. Leave me in peace.

VARGAS. This is most important!

ALBA. Not more so than my daughter's health.

NOIRCARMES. Monseigneur, I beg you!

VARGAS. There is a woman here who insists on speaking to your Excellency.

ALBA. Why?

NOIRCARMES. From what I can gather, the matter is of pressing importance.

ALBA. Some maniac. To-morrow.

ALL THREE [*insistently*]. Monseigneur.

ALBA [*losing his self-control*]. To-morrow, I say! To-morrow. [*He turns to leave*]

[DOLORÈS *has entered during these last words*]

DOLORÈS. To-morrow, Monseigneur? Are you sure you will see to-morrow?

[ALBA *comes down-stage and looks at her*]

ALBA. That woman?

DOLORÈS. Yes, that woman, who implores you, Monsieur le Duc, who prays to you to listen to her.

ALBA. Take care, Madame; if I find I am

dealing with some fanatic you had better go, for, by the living God your head won't be worth a sou!

DOLORÈS. And you, Monseigneur, had better listen to what I have to say! And, by the same God, your head won't be worth a sou!

ALBA [coldly]. Very well. Messieurs, stand apart and be ready to come at the first signal.

[VARGAS, NOIRCARMES, and DELRIO go out left; MIGUEL through the large door at the back, while ALBA closes that on the right]

ALBA. Now, Madame, in a word, what brings you here?

DOLORÈS [pale and distracted]. In a word, Monseigneur, there is a man in this city whom I hate. That man threatened to kill me this evening and, worse still, to kill another man whom I love—he is my lover. That, in a word, is what brings me.

ALBA. And what is this to me?

DOLORÈS. It is a great deal to me! Yet it is strange what I am going to do. Let me speak.

ALBA. But—

DOLORÈS [as before]. For God's sake, let me speak! I know what I am saying. Don't you see, too, that if my reason returns to me, granted I am out of my mind, I shan't say a word? You don't know. Take advantage of my madness; it will save you!

ALBA [surprised and interested, as he sits on the tabouret]. Continue, Madame.

DOLORÈS. Where was I? I can't remember. Oh, yes; he threatened me, that man, and left me after saying that "he must go to the Protestant service."

ALBA. In this city?

DOLORÈS Yes, in this city! Do you imagine that because your soldiers fill the streets people don't defy your edicts—in secret? I swear to you there are ten thousand heretics here, who gather together at night in cellars, in attics, behind walls, to praise God, and curse you in their own way! Then I say to myself: "You are going to your service, are you? And you want to kill him? Well, you will not kill him, because I can act sooner than you; I can strike before you can!"

ALBA. Good.

DOLORÈS. No, it is not good! I tell you it is infamous! This is between me and God. I must save my lover first of all. I will settle accounts with God later.

ALBA. Did you follow this man through the streets?

DOLORÈS. The black streets! It is a dead city except for the patrols and your drunken soldiers. He goes on and on, and I follow; he runs, then I run. We arrive finally at the Porte de Louvain. Shadows come and go, talk together and separate. Then everything is swallowed up,

disappears into a dark, narrow passage, that leads underground—

ALBA. And then?

DOLORÈS. It all passes from my sight; I want to go down there, too, but I hear a voice from below: "Who goes there?" I am fearfully frightened, and I go back. Then the moon comes out—no one! All this confusion, the cry of the sentinels in the distance, the clocks striking the hour. I look about me, I turn round, for I want to know, I want to see. It is a matter of life and death! In the midst of the rubbish I see a deep trench that sheds the rain-water off into the ditches. I put one foot into it—cold as ice! Then I go down. It is a vault. Yes, I will chance it. I go straight on, and see a bluish light; I hear confused sounds. At last I come to an iron grate. I draw a free breath, for I can see; finally, I can hear.

ALBA. And then what?

DOLORÈS. In this pit ten men are collected, under shelter of the counterscarp. The sound of their talking comes to me in gusts; they speak louder than usual. They take no notice of the sentinels on the rampart, or the postern guards; these are accomplices. [The Duke starts] Yes! Yes! that is what is happening on your ramparts. I listen closely, and at the very first words I learn that they are not heretics, worshipping God in their own way: they are rebels in council! This is no Protestant service; it is a conspiracy. The man they gather round, standing, with uncovered heads, is in command. He is no pastor, he is their chief: the Liberator, as they call him. Your most dangerous enemy —the Prince of Orange!

ALBA [quickly springing up]. The Prince? Ridiculous, Madame. Impossible!

DOLORÈS. Impossible? I saw him as plainly as I see you.

ALBA. Hallucination. According to the latest news he was fifty leagues away at the gates of Strassburg!

DOLORÈS. Well, according to the latest I heard he was fifty steps away at the gates of Brussels!

ALBA. Good God, if this is true! I can't listen to this alone. [He goes to the door at the left, opens it, and calls] Vargas! Noircarmes! The die is cast! Madame, so much the worse for you if this is false! I have called my men.

DOLORÈS [coming down-stage]. Call them! It makes no difference to me now. I have done what I had to do.

[Enter VARGAS, DELRIO, and NOIRCARMES]

ALBA. Messieurs, do you know what I have been told? The Prince of Orange—at the gates of Brussels!

VARGAS. The Prince?

DELRIO. Nonsense!

NOIRCARMES. Impossible. Who saw him?

ALBA. Madame.

Simultaneously ⎰ VARGAS. Absurd!
DELRIO. How can that be?
⎱ NOIRCARMES. All our reports—

ALBA [*motioning them to silence, and coming down to* DOLORÈS, *passing behind her*]. Now, now, let us keep cool. You have seen him, Madame? Good! And heard him, too. Did these men say anything?

DOLORÈS. Yes.

ALBA. What?

DOLORÈS. I could see quite plainly, because of the snow, but it was hard to hear—certain sentences—a word here and there.

ALBA. What sentences? What words? Try to recall.

DOLORÈS. The Town Hall first. They spoke all the time about the Town Hall.

NOIRCARMES. Then, perhaps, a signal?

DOLORÈS. Yes, the signal. At midnight—a signal—from the belfry!

VARGAS. What was it to be?

DOLORÈS. Oh, I don't know—that. I did not hear!

ALBA. That makes little difference. What next?

DOLORÈS. At that signal the whole city is to rise up.

VARGAS. But—weapons?

DOLORÈS. They are armed.

DELRIO. And the Prince?

DOLORÈS. After the signal he is to enter the city, filling the streets with his men.

ALBA. Are there many?

DOLORÈS. Six thousand.

ALL [*in terror*]. Six thousand?

DOLORÈS. I heard that perfectly. He is to come to the Grande-Place—the chains will be let down. One of them was to see to that: he will come here—or—he has come, has he not?

VARGAS. Indeed, he—

DOLORÈS. [*triumphantly*]. You see?

NOIRCARMES. Yes, a short time ago.

DELRIO. That captain?

DOLORÈS [*excitedly*]. He is a conspirator, a traitor. Didn't you suspect that—didn't you understand? The way he talked? His— [*Seeing the sword on the table*] Why, this sword! [*She goes rapidly to the table and takes the sword; the others follow and crowd round her*] This sword! This is his.

ALBA. Yes. How did you know?

DOLORÈS [*first showing, then handing him the sword*]. Why, this neck-cloth—that is the sign by which they are to recognize one another. Have that man followed, Monseigneur: he is a conspirator; he is one of their chiefs— the boldest of them all; he even dared to come to you in person! [*She crosses back to the right*]

ALBA. He will be found again, Madame.

[*He hands the sword to* NOIRCARMES, *who lays it on the table.* DELRIO *motions to* MAÎTRE CHARLES, *who enters*]

NOIRCARMES. Yes, *he* is known.

ALBA. Quick, now. Tell us about the others. You saw them, did you not?

[*Again they gather about* DOLORÈS]

DOLORÈS. Yes.

VARGAS. Do you know them?

DOLORÈS. All!

ALBA [*making a sign to* DELRIO]. Delrio. [*To* DOLORÈS] Their names—quickly!

[DELRIO *seats himself at the table, and prepares to write*]

DOLORÈS [*alarmed*]. Their names?

ALBA. Yes.

DOLORÈS. Must I also give you—?

ALBA. The name of the chief first—this man you hate!

DOLORÈS. He—he is—

ALL. He is?

DOLORÈS [*suddenly becoming panic-stricken*]. Oh, this is horrible!

VARGAS. Tell us.

DOLORÈS. I don't want to. Leave me. I am afraid.

ALBA. You are afraid for the man you love?

DOLORÈS. Monseigneur!

ALBA. But he will kill this man—remember, now.

DOLORÈS. Yes.

ALBA. He is a heretic.

NOIRCARMES. A rebel.

VARGAS. A traitor.

DOLORÈS. Yes.

ALBA [*quickly*]. Your husband?

VARGAS. Rysoor?

DOLORÈS [*terror-stricken, as she falls back toward the table*]. I—didn't say that!

ALBA. No, but I suspect it. So, he is your husband? [*To* DELRIO] Write "Rysoor."

DOLORÈS. Monseigneur, this is terrible—you are making me sell my soul.

ALBA. On the contrary, I am saving it; you are doing this for your King and your God. Now, the others?

DOLORÈS. What others?

VARGAS. The other conspirators?

ALBA. Their names—come, now.

DOLORÈS. But I have nothing against them. I don't want to tell their names.

ALBA. You will please let us have all the names.

DOLORÈS. But I don't want to—that would be too infamous—they are all innocent! To begin with, I don't know them.

ALBA [*calmly*]. You know them—you have just told us that. What are their names?

DOLORÈS [*coming down-stage*]. Let me go! I want to leave here—now. Let me go!

ALBA [*violently retaining her, and forcing her*

to her knees]. You are not going. You are to stay here. Now, tell us.

DOLORÈS [*distracted*]. Monseigneur, pity me!

ALBA. The names.

DOLORÈS. Never!

ALBA [*taking hold of her arms, he raises her so that she catches sight of* MAÎTRE CHARLES, *who has come down-stage left*]. Their names! Their names! You poor God-forsaken woman, speak or we shall have the executioner make you.

DOLORÈS [*faint with fear at seeing the executioner*]. O God! My God! Why did I come?

ALBA [*twisting her wrists as she hesitates*]. You were saying—?

DOLORÈS [*murmurs in an undertone*]. Galèna.

ALBA [*to* NOIRCARMES]. Galèna.

NOIRCARMES [*to* DELRIO]. Galèna.

ALBA. Then?

DOLORÈS. Bakkerzeel—I think—I think—I am not sure.

ALBA [*to* NOIRCARMES]. Bakkerzeel.

NOIRCARMES [*to* DELRIO]. Bakkerzeel.

VARGAS. And—?

DOLORÈS [*nearly exhausted*]. I don't know.

ALBA. Maître Charles!

DOLORÈS [*sobbing in desperation*]. My God! forgive me! forgive me!

ALBA. One more—and I will release you.

DOLORÈS. The bellringer, Jonas.

[DELRIO *inscribes the name*]

ALBA. And Cornélis, too, eh?

DOLORÈS. Yes—I believe so. Oh, I'm dying! [*She falls down, utterly worn out*]

ALBA [*letting her hand drop, as he says cold-bloodedly*]. These will be sufficient. [*He goes up-stage and writes. To* VARGAS] Send this to Navarra. [*To* NOIRCARMES] Send this to Francisco Vegas.

NOIRCARMES [*in an undertone*]. Very well, Monseigneur. I shall have someone run off immediately.

[*They all start to go*]

ALBA [*stopping them with a gesture*]. In the name of heaven, no! Not a word—and the calm of death.

NOIRCARMES. Good, Monseigneur. But how about the chains?

ALBA. Down—as ordered!

NOIRCARMES. But the captain?

ALBA. That is another matter. Get this Karloo, alive or dead.

DOLORÈS [*rising*]. Karloo?

NOIRCARMES. And hang him?

ALBA. No, save him for the scaffold!

DOLORÈS [*on her knees, deadly pale*]. The scaffold! Karloo?

NOIRCARMES [*ready, together with* DELRIO *and* MAÎTRE CHARLES, *at the left*]. Van der Noot.

VARGAS [*pointing to the sword on the table*]. The man with the sword.

DOLORÈS. It's he! It is— Oh, God in heaven! *He* is in it! My Karloo. And I have— No, no, no, not that! [*She attempts to get to the door*]

ALBA [*barring her way and retaining her by force*]. I beg your pardon. You are not to leave until you have orders to do so.

DOLORÈS [*struggling to free herself*]. Let me go—you! Let me go! I want to go!

ALBA. Go, Messieurs, and have guards stationed at every gate.

[*They go out.* VARGAS *leaves by the side-door on the left*]

DOLORÈS. Butchers! Wretches! Hangdogs!

ALBA [*throwing her aside, toward the left*]. It is eleven o'clock, Madame; you may leave at daybreak.

DOLORÈS. After you have arrested him, you— [*The Duke stops and looks at her with a threatening glance*] No, forgive me, Monseigneur! [*She clings to him*] Have pity on him! Pity him! Take them all, but not him. Not my Karloo!

ALBA [*disengaging himself and pushing her aside*]. Pray for him—that is the best thing for you to do. [*He goes out right, closing the door. The door is double-locked; the sound of the turning key is heard*]

DOLORÈS [*she throws herself against the door*]. No, wait! Monseigneur! [*She beats on the door, trying to break through it*] Open the door. Help! Help! Now it's all over. I have killed him. [*Sobbing*] How wretched I am—and I have killed him. I have killed him! [*She falls down, exhausted*]

CURTAIN

ACT THREE

SCENE II

Interior of the Brussels Town Hall. At the back above the level of the stage is the Great Hall, the windows of which shine in the moonlight. Down-stage is a tower room, under the belfry. These two sections of the stage are connected by two staircases, right and left. Between these staircases, in the middle of the stage, is an archway which leads from the upper room to the floor. Down-stage to the right is a large door giving access to another part of the building by means of a staircase of five steps. This staircase is open on three sides. To the left is a door opening upon the stairs to the belfry. Here and there are mutilated statues and débris, indicating that the Hall has been pillaged. Left is a stone table. It is night, but the stage is illuminated by reflected moonlight. JONAS *and* GALÈNA *appear under the archway at the back;* JONAS *is ahead, and carries a lantern, also two swords and a hatchet under his arm.*

JONAS [*lighting the way for* GALÈNA]. This way, Seigneur Galèna.

GALÈNA. Where are you taking me?

JONAS. Under the belfry, your honor. Here is the staircase leading to the bells.

GALÈNA. Oh, yes, now I know where I am.

JONAS. Up there is the Great Hall, where our masters of the Commune used to deliberate.

GALÈNA. And now—what neglect and ruin!

JONAS. It's easy to see that the Spanish señors have passed this way! [*Turning his lantern toward the damaged statues*] See—our poor burgomasters.

GALÈNA. Patience. Those dead will resume their places again—and the living, too. Are you sure no one ever comes here?

JONAS. No one but myself. [*He lays the swords on the table*] At any rate here are weapons for us. I cleaned them purposely for carnival time.

GALÈNA. Will you fight, too?

JONAS. To protect my bells! Indeed I will. [*He lays the lantern on the table*]

GALÈNA. Sh! Did you hear?

JONAS [*pointing right*]. There?

GALÈNA. Yes.

[*Enter* RYSOOR, *right*]

RYSOOR. Is that you, Galèna?

GALÈNA. Yes.

RYSOOR. Is Karloo here?

[KARLOO *appears at the back*]

KARLOO. Patience, friends. Here he is.

RYSOOR. Welcome!

GALÈNA. What news?

KARLOO. The best.

GALÈNA. The Spaniards?

KARLOO. Safe. I have just come from the Duke's.

RYSOOR. And the chains?

KARLOO. Let down with my own hands.

RYSOOR *and* GALÈNA [*joyfully*]. Good.

RYSOOR. Then nothing is suspected at the Palace? How about the road?

KARLOO. No danger. The usual sentinels and patrols. On the Place there is a guard of only fifty men, half of them asleep round the fire, while the other half are trying to sober down after their *Mardi-gras* debauch.

RYSOOR. Your musketeers?

KARLOO. All ready. From the Hôtel de Nassau as far as the Grand-Marché I gave the signal agreed on at more than fifty doors, and everyone gave back the answer: "We are ready." Bakkerzeel, who is on guard below, has left all his weavers at the Porte de Flandre, hiding in their cellars. Lalos stationed his brewers on the lookout under some sheds. Throughout this sad and silent city where not a ray of light shines from a window, where the snow deadens the sound of everything, even our footsteps, there is no house but has its eyes peering in the black of the night, its ears pricked up— fully armed—impatient for battle.

RYSOOR. Let us make ready, friends; the hour is near. Galèna, warn Cornélis and our friends waiting under the arcades. Let them all join us, and then—forward!

GALÈNA. I shall go at once. [*To* JONAS] Come, Jonas.

[*They go out at the back*]

RYSOOR [*after laying his cape and hat on the table*]. And now, Karloo, let me tell you what I expect of you.

KARLOO. Tell me.

RYSOOR. I have named this place for all our leaders, because it is the Town Hall, the communal meeting-place of the people.

KARLOO. I understand.

RYSOOR. Here, Karloo, our fathers framed the laws we are about to defend. From these windows they proclaimed those rights which we are about to assert once more. This is the very heart of the city, of which the Spaniards have made a corpse. Now let this corpse live again. May it rise up in the night, magnificent with the flare of our torches and our bare swords and cry "To arms!" at the call from every bell! Then will this disheartened people know that Flemish liberty still exists—its great soul stirs again—beneath our roofs. The people know what they are struggling for: for our flag—for the ringing bells. They are the spirit of the city. Better still, the nation; best of all, the *Patrie!* And they will fight and die for Her, for She says to them: "Defend me, oh my sons, and save me, for I am being crushed—and I am your mother!"

KARLOO. She is.

RYSOOR. Here, then, Karloo, is the center of the struggle; here must we take our stand at any cost, until the Liberator arrives. I leave this sacred building in your care. Command it, defend it.

KARLOO. In yours, rather.

RYSOOR. No, no. I have not yet won the right, as you have at Saint-Quentin and Gravelines, to lead these brave men to battle. Karloo, I shall follow you; you must march at their head. You are the only one who can teach them to conquer; *I* can but teach them to die.

KARLOO. Very well, since you wish it; but if I consent the honor will be yours as well as mine, while for me the danger is merely greater.

RYSOOR. Your sword?

KARLOO. It was taken from me at the Palace.

RYSOOR. Then take this. [*He takes the sword lying on the table, and is about to give it to* KARLOO, *who extends his ungloved hand to receive it.* RYSOOR *takes the hand and utters a cry*]

KARLOO [*surprised*]. What is it?

RYSOOR [*looking at him, very pale*]. That hand!

KARLOO. Yes?

RYSOOR [*leading* KARLOO *to the table, and*

examining the palm of his hand by lantern light]. This wound?

KARLOO. A trifle; my arm can still do its duty.

RYSOOR. And you? Have you done yours?

KARLOO [*uneasily*]. Rysoor, what do you mean?

RYSOOR. This wound? How did you get it?

KARLOO [*hesitating*]. I was careless with a sword.

RYSOOR. A Spanish soldier, was he not?

KARLOO. Why?

RYSOOR. At night—at my home?

KARLOO [*terrified*]. Oh!

RYSOOR [*bursting forth*]. You miserable—! It is you!

KARLOO. Rysoor!

RYSOOR [*raising the sword*]. You thief of love! Destroyer of my honor! I have a right to kill you!

KARLOO [*desperately, as he falls to his knees*]. Kill me, then. Death at your hands would be the sweetest of tortures. Kill me! You have every right. Kill me!

RYSOOR. Blackguard, you think you can soften me!

KARLOO. For God's sake, kill me, Rysoor; only kill me at once. Your words wound me far more than the cold steel of your sword could possibly do. Yes, I am a blackguard and a coward! I have deceived you—it was infamous; I confess, and I now weep tears of blood. Death! I ask you for it on bended knees—death!

RYSOOR [*letting his sword fall and looking down, as he sobs in desperation*]. I am desperately unhappy. I loved you too much—and for this woman. That was horrible enough, but that of all men it should be *you* who—. You, Karloo—Karloo, to whom I have unburdened my whole heart. And loved you as a son. What poison is there in your love for this woman that turns a loyal and generous soul like yours to a festering mass of treason and ingratitude? I had faith in but three things: the *Patrie*, her, and you. You see what remains —and it is your fault. Only tell me—tell me what I have done to you, that you should make me suffer thus?

KARLOO. You are torturing me. This is frightful. Stop. Don't reproach me this way.

RYSOOR. What if I do kill you? Will your death give me back my honor? My peace that has been destroyed? Will it heal the wound which is now sapping my life's blood?

KARLOO. My God! You still insist—?

RYSOOR. What good will your death do me? Satisfy my desire for revenge? Will it serve the cause we are now defending?

KARLOO. Do you want—?

RYSOOR. Will your dead body lead these men into battle?

KARLOO. I am no longer worthy.

RYSOOR. Worthy or not, does your blood belong to me? When the whole city has scarcely enough in its veins for to-night's struggle! Should it waste these precious drops, should I strike low this arm of yours which must defend us all? Great God, no! If I did that, I should be guilty of treason as great against Her as yours is against me. I have no more right to rob Her of your courage than you have to deprive me of my happiness.

KARLOO. Then you refuse?

RYSOOR. Make ready, and take that sword.

KARLOO. I?

RYSOOR. Take that sword, I tell you, and go battle. Go where your duty calls, where my duty sends you. If God wills that you die, do not die like a criminal, but like a martyr, a soldier. Then at least your death will have served some cause.

KARLOO [*dejectedly taking the sword*]. You will never again see me alive: that I swear to you.

RYSOOR [*quickly*]. Living? It makes no difference, so long as you conquer.

KARLOO [*standing up, warmly*]. That gives me some hope of forgiveness, Rysoor.

RYSOOR. Go, now—and take revenge on yourself. You have robbed me of my honor; give me my liberty. A woman, ha! Give me back my *Patrie*. We shall see later whether your bravery has washed clean your crime, and whether I ought to be grateful to you or hate you.

KARLOO. You will forgive me, Rysoor. I will make you. [*To his sword*] Ready, now, and help me win my cause!

[*Enter* GALÈNA, BAKKERZEEL, CORNÉLIS, JONAS, *and other conspirators, armed*]

GALÈNA. Rysoor, all the men are below waiting for the signal. It is time now.

RYSOOR [*pointing to* KARLOO]. Karloo is to command you.

BAKKERZEEL. Karloo, here we are.

KARLOO. Are you all armed and ready?

ALL. All.

KARLOO. Ready to brave the stake, to face torture and death?

ALL. All of us!

KARLOO. To work, then. Now if the heart of one of you fail in the thick of the fight, remember that your defeat delivers your wives and children to the fury of the Spaniards. Think of your city being pillaged, your homes in ashes—and blame this infamous Spain.

ALL [*together in confused uproar*]. Yes, yes! To arms. Forward! Let us attack!

RYSOOR. Silence! Listen.

[*A pause; the beat of Spanish drums is heard in the far distance*]

KARLOO. The drum!

RYSOOR. Beating the charge!

JONAS [*running down from the back of the stage*]. The Spaniards!

[*Gunshots are heard*]

ALL. Treason!

KARLOO. Let us lose no time! Cry out in the Place: "To arms!", my friends! Ten thousand fighters will come forth out of the night in answer. [*More gunshots; trumpets sound, and the beat of drums approaches, on the charge*] Guard the archway. Cornélis! Bakkerzeel, you the stairway!

GALÈNA [*from above*]. There they are on the Place!

KARLOO. Rysoor, watch this door. [*He points to the door right, to which* RYSOOR *quickly goes*] And the signal. For God's sake, Jonas, the signal, or we are lost! [*To the others*] You there, guard the windows!

[*He rushes to the left stairway at the moment when* JONAS *disappears up the stairs leading to the belfry. Again the reports of muskets. Just after* KARLOO *reaches the stairs with the conspirators, a troop of Spaniards under the leadership of* NOIRCARMES *appears in the large hall above, flags flying, drums and trumpets sounding the charge. The conspirators, who number more than a dozen, return from the stairs and make their way headlong to the archway, whence* CORNÉLIS *and his men are flung, while* BAKKERZEEL *and his companions defend the stairway on the right. More shots are heard*]

KARLOO. To the Great Gate!

[*He springs forward with his men to the principal doorway, right; this he tries to open, but cannot. At the same time the door leading to the belfry opens, and a company of Spaniards, led by* MIGUEL, *comes forth, with* JONAS *in their midst, his hands bound. This company fires on the conspirators, who are forced back to the stairs leading to the principal entrance, leaving their dead where they fell*]

RYSOOR [*showering blows on the closed door*]. This door!

KARLOO. Break it in! [*He takes a hatchet and beats furiously on the door*]

NOIRCARMES [*from above*]. Surrender!

KARLOO [*who continues his task*]. Never! Long live Flanders!

ALL THE CONSPIRATORS. Long live Flanders!

NOIRCARMES [*to his men*]. Fire!

[*The Spaniards fire. Seven or eight conspirators fall dead or wounded on the steps*]

KARLOO. Fire!

[*The conspirators return the volley. The Spaniards, who were advancing, now retreat. On the side of the conspirators only* RYSOOR, KARLOO, GALÈNA, BAKKERZEEL, *and five others remain standing*]

RYSOOR. Courage, Karloo!

KARLOO [*finally breaking the lock*]. The door is giving!

[*The door falls outward, causing considerable uproar. They rush forward, but fall back a moment later before other soldiers who advance against them.* KARLOO *is armed only with the hatchet;* RYSOOR *and the others retreat toward the center of the stage, forming a little group. They have only swords with which to defend themselves*]

NOIRCARMES [*raising his staff*]. Forward!

[*They charge again. All the Spaniards descend the great stairs at the back in a body, and surround the conspirators with a circle of steel and muskets*]

RYSOOR. Now we have only to die!

KARLOO. Fire, you cowards—fire! You see, we will not surrender!

[*They throw down their weapons.* NOIRCARMES *raises his sword to give the signal to fire as* ALBA *appears at the head of the stairway, in full battle array, his commanding staff in hand. Behind him are his officers.* LA TRÉMOÏLLE *is among these.* ALBA *stretches forth his staff; the drums cease beating, the trumpets are silent, every musket is lowered*]

ALBA [*to the conspirators, after a pause*]. Which of you, Messieurs, do you consider your leader?

KARLOO. I!

RYSOOR [*interrupting him*]. In battle, yes, but here—it is I. Comte de Rysoor.

ALBA. Very well, Monsieur le Comte. Now that we are in a position to receive William of Orange we shall ask him to enter the city—[*consternation among the conspirators*]—and then make an end to the rebellion by depriving him of his head.

RYSOOR [*anxiously, to* KARLOO]. If he enters he is lost.

ALBA. What signal have you agreed on?

RYSOOR [*hopefully*]. Thank God, you don't know that!

ALBA. Rincon, bring me the bellringer Jonas. [*JONAS is brought forth from the foot of the stairs, bound*] Do you know the signal?

JONAS [*trembling*]. Yes, Monseigneur.

ALBA. Loose his hands, and let him sound it.

[*A soldier unties* JONAS's *hands*]

KARLOO [*quickly*]. Jonas, don't do it.

RYSOOR. Don't!

JONAS [*terror-stricken*]. I'm only a poor man, Messieurs. They'll kill me, and I have a wife and children.

KARLOO [*supplicating him*]. There are three

millions souls to save! Your children are among them.

RYSOOR. Save the Prince!

KARLOO. Save Flanders!

RYSOOR. On my bended knees, Jonas. I beg you on bended knees—

JONAS [*who, after being free, has been taken to the left by* RINCON]. My God! My God!

ALBA [*furiously*]. Put an end to this!

THE CONSPIRATORS [*intercepting* JONAS, *clinging to him as he is being taken out into the passage*]. Jonas—don't ring!

ALBA [*to* RINCON]. Put a pistol to his throat; if he winces, kill him.

[JONAS *is dragged to the staircase leading to the belfry. The conspirators hang back, and appear desperate*]

ALBA. Has everything been made ready, Noircarmes?

NOIRCARMES. Oh, Monseigneur, the moment the Prince enters the city he will find himself between two fires: not a man will get as far as the Place.

ALBA [*triumphantly*]. At last I have him between my fingers.

RYSOOR. Good God, merciful Savior, do not allow this iniquity! Save the Prince, save him! Thou owest us at least that much.

[*A pause, then the bell rings. Everyone listens anxiously. The death-knell strikes. The conspirators cannot restrain a movement of joy*]

ALBA [*nervously, as he looks at the conspirators*]. The death-knell!

NOIRCARMES. Yes, Monseigneur.

ALBA. Is *that* the signal?

KARLOO [*radiantly*]. Yes, Monsieur le Duc, that is the signal, but it says to the Prince: "Do not enter—go away!" It is the signal that saves him, and with him the liberty of Flanders!

ALBA [*furiously*]. By the fires of hell, stop that man! Kill him, kill him! Kill him, I say!

[*A gunshot is heard in the belfry. The bell stops ringing*]

NOIRCARMES. It is done.

ALBA. But too late—*he* will escape. I must wait for another chance.

[*Four soldiers enter from the staircase leading to the belfry, carrying the body of* JONAS *on their muskets*]

RINCON [*stopping the soldiers, and raising the mantle which covers* JONAS, *to see whether the man is dead*]. He is dead, Monsieur le Duc.

RYSOOR [*taking off his hat before the body, as do all the conspirators*]. Poor obscure martyr, we honor you. One second's deed has made a martyr of you. May our children revere your memory and when they are free take thought of the humble bellringer to whom they will owe their freedom. [JONAS's *body is carried under the archway*] Come, Messieurs, on this

beautiful night only *we* are lost. Long live Flanders!

THE CONSPIRATORS. Long live Flanders!

ALBA. Take away these men, Noircarmes—the scaffold on the Place, there—to-night, and every night hereafter!

[*The conspirators are surrounded and conducted up the large staircase to the left*]

LA TRÉMOÏLLE [*as they mount the first steps*]. Messieurs—[*they stop and turn around*] —I salute you—and I have but one regret: to be deprived of the honor of being one of your number.

ALBA. Marquis!

LA TRÉMOÏLLE [*putting on his hat again and looking straight at the Duke*]. For all the gold of my ransom, Monsieur le Duc, I would not say the same to *you!*

[*The conspirators ascend the staircase between two files of soldiers. Drums beat, and trumpets sound, as the curtain falls*]

CURTAIN

ACT FOUR

SCENE I

A room in the Palace contiguous to the Court of Blood. Down-stage right, opening upon a small platform leading to the stage by two steps, is the entrance to the Court. Left is a door leading to the apartments of the Duke of Alba. Halfway up-stage, right, is an alcove; left is another, similar to that opposite. Center is a large table covered with a black cloth; there is a chair to the right and one to the left of this table. At the back of the stage is a large fireplace, above which hang the arms of the House of Austria. Mural paintings adorn the walls, representing martyrs and saints. There is a somber, sinister air about the whole room. It is daytime. ALBA, NOIRCARMES, VARGAS, *and* RINCON *are present as the curtain rises. There is also a soldier at the door of the left alcove.*

ALBA. Noircarmes.

NOIRCARMES. Monseigneur?

ALBA [*who has just come from the chamber of torture and walked in silence to a position in front of the table*]. What is the time?

NOIRCARMES. Seven o'clock, Monsieur le Duc.

ALBA. Is everything ready on the Place?

NOIRCARMES. Yes, Monseigneur.

ALBA. The scaffold? The faggots?

NOIRCARMES. The scaffold is just being erected.

ALBA. Rincon, the Lombard regiment on the Place, as when Egmont and Horn were disposed of.

RINCON. Very well, Monsieur le Duc.

ALBA. The Sardinian regiment will guard all

the city gates, which are now being closed, and which will not be opened again until after the execution. The Sicilian and Neapolitan regiments will perform their usual duties. Serbelloni will place cannons loaded with grapeshot at every entrance to the Grande-Place. That will do.

[RINCON *goes out through alcove right*]

VARGAS. Monseigneur, the Ambassador from France has received the ransom for Monsieur de la Trémoïlle on a bill through the House of Fugger at Augsburg.

ALBA [*signing a passport which lies on the table*]. A passport to Lille for this Frenchman. Let him leave the place immediately. [*He gives* VARGAS *the passport*]

VARGAS. Very well, Monseigneur. [*He goes to the soldier, hands him the passport, and returns down-stage, as the soldier goes out*]

ALBA [*seated right of the table*]. Noircarmes, we must know more about this matter; here is an entire city in revolt—we have only this handful of men; the rest are at large. I must have their names. Their names, I say! if we have to execute half the citizens.

NOIRCARMES. We shall see to that, Monseigneur.

ALBA. I count on your doing so. This Rysoor, for instance, the soul of the conspiracy—tell Maître Charles that *he* must be questioned in an exquisite manner—even if he dies on the rack. If our old methods of inquisition fail to produce results, let him invent new ones.

NOIRCARMES. Maître Charles shall be informed, Monseiur le Duc. [*He goes out into the inquisition chamber*]

ALBA. By the way, is that woman—his wife—?

VARGAS. We found her in your Excellency's room—she had fainted—she looked as if she were dead. We tried to prevent her leaving the Palace, but her cries were so horrible that we were afraid Doña Rafaële—

ALBA [*rising and speaking quickly*]. Good God! my daughter must know nothing of all this.

VARGAS. That goes without saying, Monseigneur.

ALBA. Are you sure she heard nothing this evening?

VARGAS. I believe so, Monseigneur. In any event, Maître Alberti can tell her—

ALBA. Yes, yes, tell the doctor to come here—at once. And that woman, too. Bring her. I want to have done with her once for all.

VARGAS. Very well, Monseigneur. [*He goes out through the alcove left*]

[*Enter* ALBERTI *through the door downstage left*]

ALBA [*going quickly to the doctor; quietly and anxiously*]. Maître Alberti, how is our patient?

ALBERTI. Passing a better night than I had expected, Monseigneur.

ALBA [*pressing* ALBERTI's *hands*]. Thank you, Alberti, for this good news. She heard nothing of the drums, or the fusillades?

ALBERTI. Nothing, Monsieur le Duc—fortunately. But I cannot conceal from your Excellency that the preparations now under way make me very apprehensive for Doña Rafaële.

ALBA. Indeed.

[DOLORÈS *enters through the alcove left, followed by* VARGAS. *She crosses the stage between the fireplace and the table. She has heard the last words of* ALBERTI. *The Duke does not notice her presence*]

ALBERTI. In her present condition the slightest emotional strain might prove fatal. Your Excellency was able to calm her only by promising to sacrifice no more victims, and if she were to learn that this morning five men were burned on the Place—

DOLORÈS [*aside, terror-stricken*]. This morning?

ALBA [*quickly*]. She need not know.

ALBERTI. That would kill her!

ALBA. She shall not know! Alberti, have her wakened.

ALBERTI. She is already awake, Monseigneur.

ALBA. Then let her women dress her, at once. Order a chair and have her taken to the Convent of Groenendaal, where she shall remain until to-night.

ALBERTI. Very well, Monseigneur—at once.

ALBA [*intercepting him as he turns to go*]. You will save her for me, Alberti—promise me you will save her?

ALBERTI. With the help of God, Monseigneur!

ALBA [*accompanying him to the door*]. Yes, yes, you will save her. I will cover you with medals and honors. I will make you the greatest doctor in Christendom. Now go, dear Alberti, go. You know how much I think of you—quickly, now.

[ALBERTI *goes out through the same door by which he entered.* ALBA *turns round and sees* DOLORÈS. *He makes a sign to* VARGAS, *who goes out through the alcove left, and then addresses* DOLORÈS *in a brusque and harsh manner*]

ALBA. Now, Madame, your case! You want to save Karloo's life, do you not? Well, you cannot.

DOLORÈS. Monseigneur.

ALBA. You cannot. The man is a traitor—he has been caught red-handed, sword in hand. He deserves to die, and he shall die. Spare me your tears and entreaties.

DOLORÈS. My tears! I have no more. I have been crying all night.

ALBA. Well?

DOLORÈS. Monsieur le Duc, this is infamous!

ALBA. Madame.

DOLORÈS. Infamous! I came to you this evening, and made a bargain with you. Deny it! I said to you: "There is a man I love; some one wants to kill him, and you, too! Give me his life for yours. Save his life, and I will save yours!" Did I say that, did I?

ALBA. If heaven has seen fit—

DOLORÈS. Heaven has nothing to do with this. Let us stay in this hell where we are, you and I. I have kept my promise, I, a woman. You are the Duke of Alba, a nobleman of Spain, commander-in-chief of the Netherlands. If you fail to keep your promise with me you are not even a gentleman. I implore you to keep your word as a man of honor.

ALBA. Listen to me, Madame. If any one but you had dared address me in this way, he would never have left this place alive! As a matter of fact, you have rendered a service to His Majesty.

DOLORÈS. To you!

ALBA. To me? Very well—and to prove that I realize it—you are still here.

DOLORÈS. Ah, why not arrest me, and make your infamy complete?

ALBA. And why not?

DOLORÈS. You dare a great deal, Monsieur le Duc, but you would not do that.

ALBA. Perhaps I would. Now, since we are on the subject of honor, where I allow no one to instruct me, let me tell you that I never, never promised you the life of this man—never!

DOLORÈS. When you encouraged me to betray all the others for his sake, wasn't that a promise? And the leader of them all—do you know who he was?

ALBA. You have just condemned him. You were pleading here for your lover when you should have thrown yourself at my feet for your husband.

DOLORÈS. I know it better than you—but that you should blame me! By now you would have been dragged through the gutters of the city, with a rope round your neck. [The Duke starts] Come now, you know that would have happened unless I had been a faithless wife, a woman mad with love. You are an accomplice in my crime, you who reap the benefit!

ALBA. Ah!

DOLORÈS. You alone! Yes, you. Now, Monsieur le Duc, let us not play the hypocrite, you and I; you are as bad as I am. I have done something awful—revealing the secret of these poor men and selling it to you; but you must admit that it is atrocious for you to catch them in your net and then shed their blood in the public square. That is your passion: despotism. Mine was adultery. We are equally guilty; both are implicated in the same murder. Only I denounce while you execute; I am the greater coward of the two, you the more ferocious. That is the only difference.

ALBA. Madame, take care.

DOLORÈS. No, I am mistaken: you are the cleverer, for you get all the spoils. Well, I want my share. If you don't give it to me I will cry from the housetop that the Duke of Alba is a coward, he puts the dagger in your hand, and when the deed is done refuses to pay you!

ALBA [enraged]. Then you will—

DOLORÈS [losing her self-control]. I want my share! I want it! I have saved you, you and your army. I have delivered three million souls into your hands, bound hand and foot, and you refuse me the life of a single man. Monseigneur, you must be mad! Give him to me—pay me. Then we shall be even!

ALBA. We are now. I am not condemning him, but you, for as I have been listening to you I have condemned you to death three times!

DOLORÈS. Me?

ALBA [bursting forth]. Leave this room—leave it! I say. The man is going to die. And if you say another word—[He points to the torture chamber]—I will torture you.

DOLORÈS [terror-stricken]. Oh, Monseigneur! Pity me. It was wrong to threaten, I haven't the right. I don't ask it—I beg you—I implore—

[The Duke goes to the table and rings a bell]

Monseigneur, God doesn't pardon those who have no pity. For your daughter's sake, have pity on the woman who saved your life.

ALBA [calling]. Vargas.

DOLORÈS [desperately]. Devil! I dug down to his heart—but has he a heart?

[Enter VARGAS and ALBERTI]

ALBA [to ALBERTI]. Well?

ALBERTI. Monsieur le Duc, Doña Rafaële is ready. She is now coming—here she is.

DOLORÈS [hopefully]. Ah!

ALBA [going quickly to meet his daughter]. Not here! Take that woman out.

DOLORÈS. No, I will not go!

ALBA [angrily]. Vargas!

DOLORÈS [pushing VARGAS away]. I will not go. Don't touch me! I will tell her everything if you do.

ALBA [terrible in his fury]. One word and you die.

[At the moment VARGAS tries to drag DOLORÈS from the room, DOÑA RAFAËLE enters from the apartment left, with a nun and a maidservant. VARGAS falls back, and DOLORÈS remains standing where she was]

ALBA [turning around. To his daughter, who comes in smiling, as he takes her in his arms]. Ah, Rafaële, my darling girl—and all alone?

RAFAËLE [gayly]. You see? I feel especially well this morning. [She coughs. MAÎTRE ALBERTI takes the chair away from the left of the table, and places it for her]

ALBA [*anxiously*]. But—

RAFAËLE. Oh, that is nothing. Is it, Maître Alberti?

ALBA. Did he tell you—?

RAFAËLE. Yes; you want me to go to Groenendaal?

ALBA. You have not been out for so long!

RAFAËLE. It will be good for me.

ALBA. And you will come back to me in time for supper. Alberti, have the shawls and blankets been attended to?

ALBERTI [*pointing to the wraps which the women are carrying*]. Yes, Monsieur le Duc.

ALBA. Well, go then, dearest.

[DOLORÈS *moves about, calling attention to herself*]

RAFAËLE. This evening, then. [*Seeing* DOLORÈS—*in an undertone*] Oh, I had not seen this lady.

ALBA [*trying to usher his daughter out of the door*]. She—she is just a—a person of the town.

RAFAËLE [*standing her ground*]. She seems so sad—has she been crying?

ALBA [*again trying to urge her out*]. Possibly.

RAFAËLE [*aside to her father*]. Some poor woman who has asked you a favor?

ALBA. Yes—and now, good-bye.

RAFAËLE. See, I guessed. [*To her father, coquettishly*] Don't you want to grant it?

ALBA. No, indeed.

RAFAËLE. But mine? Won't you grant mine?

ALBA. Yours?

RAFAËLE. I feel so well this morning—see how easily I breathe. I have not felt so well for many a day.

ALBA [*joyfully*]. How glad I am. How profoundly happy.

RAFAËLE. You are happy, are you not?

ALBA. My God, yes!

RAFAËLE. Well, this happiness must not be for us alone, then; and to thank God for what we have received, please let this poor lady have what she asks for.

ALBA [*impatiently*]. I cannot. Now go.

RAFAËLE. Then it is something serious?

ALBA [*forgetting himself*]. Very.

RAFAËLE [*suddenly, and alarmed*]. Ah, something I know nothing about—something you are hiding from me?

ALBA [*quickly*]. No, no.

RAFAËLE. But those drums last night? Those shots?

ALBA. Nothing!

RAFAËLE [*casting a look of interrogation toward the two women*]. My God, and you promised me! If there were to be more killing—

ALBA [*quickly*]. I tell you there is nothing. Absolutely nothing. [*Looking at* DOLORÈS *angrily, and in an undertone*] That damned woman!

RAFAËLE [*going quickly past her father*]. If there is nothing, then you can grant it. I shall speak to her. I—

ALBA. Rafaële!

RAFAËLE [*to her father*]. Let me be—I will! [*To* DOLORÈS, *as she sits on the chair left of the table*] Will you tell me your trouble, Madame?

[ALBA *stands behind his daughter's chair, threatening* DOLORÈS *with a look*]

DOLORÈS [*standing in front of the table—softly*]. Oh, Madame, it is simple enough. It is about a person who is known to your Grace: Captain Karloo.

RAFAËLE. Surely I know him! Well?

DOLORÈS. Señora, he was arrested last night— [*The Duke starts*]

RAFAËLE. Arrested?

DOLORÈS [*looking defiantly at the Duke*]. And on the slightest suspicion! Monsieur le Duc will tell you how unimportant it was.

RAFAËLE. Possibly that was what happened yesterday evening?

DOLORÈS. Probably—yes.

RAFAËLE [*reproachfully*]. Oh, Father, you are too severe.

DOLORÈS. Is he not?

RAFAËLE. Well, if this is all—

[ALBA *goes behind his daughter, keeping his eyes fixed on* DOLORÈS *all the time*]

DOLORÈS. That is all; his Excellency himself cannot tell you of a single other thing.

RAFAËLE. And, of course, you ask—?

DOLORÈS. Madame, I ask that he be released from prison and given a passport from his Excellency. That is all.

RAFAËLE. You are right. [*The Duke starts*] Father, Madame is just and reasonable. It is very kind of you, Madame, to do that for him. Are you a friend of his?

DOLORÈS. Yes, Señora, he is my lover.

RAFAËLE. He deserves to be loved. I think a great deal of him, too. Now, Madame, that two of us are on his side we shall be stronger.

DOLORÈS. My God! I hope your father will listen.

RAFAËLE [*rising*]. See how easily he will be influenced. Father, Monsieur de Vargas will release our Captain, will he not? This is a small matter to you.

ALBA [*ironically*]. Indeed!

RAFAËLE [*quickly*]. Did you say yes?

ALBA. No, I say—no!

RAFAËLE [*anxiously*]. Then I have not been told the truth. Madame, tell me the whole truth.

ALBA [*quickly coming between the two women*]. She shall say nothing more, as there *is* nothing more to say.

DOLORÈS. Nothing, indeed!

RAFAËLE [*wrought up*]. Then you refuse? Father, you are very cruel.

ALBA. Rafaële.

RAFAËLE. I was so happy. And now—oh, the day began so beautifully. [*She falls into a chair.* ALBERTI *goes to her*]

ALBA [*in depression, as he kneels at his daughter's feet*]. My dear girl. Maître Alberti! [*To* DOLORÈS, *his voice choked*] You fiend!

DOLORÈS [*braving him, as she leans over him, in an undertone*]. I use what weapons I can find.

ALBA [*to his daughter*]. Rafaële, my dearest!

RAFAËLE [*coughing*]. I was so well. My God!

ALBA. You will feel better at once, my treasure.

RAFAËLE [*with tenderness*]. If you will only do what I asked.

ALBA. Anything!

RAFAËLE [*half rising*]. Do you mean it this time?

ALBA. Yes.

RAFAËLE. Is he free?

ALBA. Yes.

RAFAËLE. Will you swear it?

ALBA. On your life!

RAFAËLE [*she rises, goes to the table, takes a pen and offers it to the Duke*]. Write it at once. Here. At once.

[ALBA *rises, takes the pen and writes as he stands*]

DOLORÈS [*falling on her knees before* RAFAËLE]. Ah, Señora, may God recompense you! Thank you with all my heart.

RAFAËLE. Are you crying for so small a matter?

DOLORÈS [*quickly*]. You seem to be suffering so.

RAFAËLE [*whispering in her ear*]. I made it seem a little worse than I was.

DOLORÈS [*kissing her hands*]. You angel!

RAFAËLE. Shh! [RAFAËLE *returns to the left where, during the following, the women give her her mantle*]

ALBA [*to* VARGAS]. Vargas, here is an order releasing Captain Karloo. Give him a passport to Lille.

DOLORÈS. Oh, Monseigneur!

ALBA [*going to* DOLORÈS, *above the table, and saying in an undertone*]. Do not thank me, Madame, for a favor which you have forced from me, but thank heaven for it! You have until this evening, you and he, to leave the city. [*Indicating the table*] Your passport is there. [*He returns to his daughter*] Now, Rafaële, come while I put you in your carriage myself.

RAFAËLE [*to* DOLORÈS]. Adieu, Madame. [*To the Duke*] See how easy it is to be good? Ah, if you would only listen to me. If I were always with you!

[*They go out, left*]

DOLORÈS [*taking her passport from the table*]. Now threaten if you like—he is saved! [*To* VARGAS] Monsieur, may I see—?

VARGAS. Captain Karloo? No, Madame; you will find him at the gates.

DOLORÈS. Very well. [*As she is about to leave by the alcove at the left, she stops*] Who are those men passing by over there?

VARGAS [*looking*]. The prisoners coming from the court. They are being taken back to their prison.

DOLORÈS. [*with an exclamation of terror*]. I don't want to see them. [*She comes downstage and crosses toward the door at the right*]

VARGAS. Not that way, Madame; that is the torture chamber.

DOLORÈS [*stepping back in terror*]. Oh!

VARGAS [*pointing to the alcove to the right*]. This side, please.

DOLORÈS. Oh, yes—I want to go. [*She stops short and looks at* VARGAS] Who is that man coming in?

VARGAS. The Comte de Rysoor.

DOLORÈS [*terrified, she comes down and crosses left*]. I don't want to see him, Monsieur. Monsieur, I am so afraid—let me go. Monsieur, I *must* not see that man! I shall always see him in my dreams. He's coming. [*Desperately*] Can't I leave this horrible house?

VARGAS [*indicating the door to the right*]. That way, Madame; only do not cross the Duke's path.

DOLORÈS. The Duke—hangdog—devil! I am willing to meet him, to pass through hell—everything—only I must not meet *that* man. My God, not him!

[*She goes out left, as* RINCON *enters. He is followed by soldiers, who stand back in the alcove, and* RYSOOR, *to whom he first beckons*]

RYSOOR. Where are you leading me, Captain, and why am I separated from the others?

RINCON. Because they are already disposed of, Monsieur, and—I am really sorry to say—you are not.

RYSOOR. And what can possibly await me between the court and the stake?

RINCON. Alas, Monsieur le Comte, that room over there: the examination chamber.

RYSOOR. Torture—ah, yes, I had forgotten: the Duke of Alba—

RINCON. If what I have been told is true, I advise you to summon up all your courage.

RYSOOR. Do they think they can force me to speak?

RINCON. They are sure.

RYSOOR [*after a pause*]. God knows I am not afraid to suffer. Pain and I are too good friends! But who can be sure that his body will not be weaker than his spirit? Possibly these tortures will wrest some cry, some confession, from me. Some name? Ah, Monsieur, the thought that suffering might make me betray a friend—*that* is *my* torture!

RINCON [*in an undertone*]. Then you would prefer of your own free will?

RYSOOR. God! if I could kill myself.

RINCON. Then follow my advice: your lordship must not utter a sound nor move a single hair—we are being watched. Monsieur le Marquis de la Trémoïlle has arranged for this contingency.

RYSOOR [*hopefully*]. Ah!

RINCON. I shall escort you to the examination chamber. Now in the hallway, which is rather dark, extend your hand in my direction.

RYSOOR [*suddenly grasping his hand*]. Ah! Captain—thanks. For you and for him.

RINCON [*aloud*]. Perhaps your lordship would like a priest?

RYSOOR. No, Captain, no. God alone is sufficient.

[KARLOO *enters through the alcove to the left, followed by* MIGUEL *and two soldiers.* NAVARRA *also comes in*]

RYSOOR [*seeing* KARLOO]. Karloo! [*Aside to* RINCON, *as he says, terrified, pointing to the chamber of torture*] He, too?

[VARGAS *enters from the Duke's apartments*]

VARGAS [*to the officers*]. Messieurs, Captain Karloo is free.

RYSOOR [*joyfully*]. Free?

KARLOO. I? [*To* VARGAS, *as he comes quickly down-stage*] Why am *I* free, and not Monsieur?

VARGAS. His Excellency, Monsieur, has deigned to grant you a pardon.

KARLOO. But I do not deign to accept it.

VARGAS. Monsieur!

KARLOO. By what right am I offered the insult of his mercy—mercy which I have not asked for?

VARGAS. It was a request of Doña Rafaële.

KARLOO. Not mine.

VARGAS. It is the Duke's pleasure.

KARLOO. But not my pleasure. I conspired, I fought, I struggled with all my friends. The same conspiracy should lead to the same punishment: the scaffold. It is my right and I demand it. I deny the Duke the right to impose upon me the torture of his pity.

VARGAS. Ah, Monsieur!

KARLOO. I demand my scaffold, my stake, of which I am proud. I want no pity from you: it is an insult. Go to your Duke, Monsieur, and tell him that I wish to have nothing to do with his pardon.

VARGAS [*giving the passport to* MIGUEL]. You will tell him in person, Monsieur; I can only execute the orders which are given me. [*He goes out, left*]

[MIGUEL *joins* RINCON *at the back, by the entrance of the alcove at the right.* RYSOOR *and* KARLOO *stand alone before the table*]

KARLOO. Very well, where is he?

RYSOOR [*intercepting* KARLOO]. Are you going to do that?

KARLOO. Without the shadow of a doubt.

RYSOOR [*retaining him*]. Karloo.

KARLOO. Would *you* prevent me?

RYSOOR. Great God, yes, I!

KARLOO. Rysoor, let me go.

RYSOOR. Stay here, I say!

KARLOO. In the name of heaven, let me die! Let the executioner avenge you!

RYSOOR. But what if I do not wish to be avenged by the executioner? [*Good-humoredly*] How unfortunate for you, poor man, if I do not.

KARLOO. Can I accept your forgiveness without having deserved it? No, I say.

RYSOOR. You will, I am sure, give me the right to administer forgiveness, and if, as you say, your crime has given me the right to dispose of your life—

KARLOO. Of course it has.

RYSOOR. Very well, I am now disposing of it. I am not asking you to live: I command you.

KARLOO. Ah, Rysoor, I prefer your anger to this goodness, which is too much for me.

RYSOOR. Karloo, I shall die soon. The miseries and mad passions of this earth seem like floating mists about to vanish as in a dream. Allow me this last happiness: to forget and forgive. Allow me to die without having lost faith in everything. Let the last hand I grasp be that of a friend—a hand that is dearest to me because I had thought it the hand of a lost friend. Let me find that friend again—cleansed and purified by tears and repentence.

KARLOO [*pressing and kissing* RYSOOR'S *hands*]. Then let it be so.

RYSOOR. Live, Karloo, live—obey me! But above all, live in order to serve our sacred cause. Now, more than ever before, it has need of your devotion. Let your *Patrie* henceforward be your only love. She, Karloo, knows no deceits. She is an idol who will always be great and inspiring. Her cult is so pure that it can reconcile to a single faith two men so different as you and I, separated by a mortal hatred. You are still young and will see our beloved Flanders a free land! Karloo, the day the flag of independence floats above our ramparts, remember the old friend who fought at your side and my spirit will bless you as joyfully as it now forgives you.

KARLOO. Oh, Rysoor, your forgiveness must not end with me; forgive her, too.

RYSOOR. No! I cannot do that. [*Forcefully*] No, I cannot forgive her. I am not so far detached from humanity that I can smother an irresistible desire for revenge.

KARLOO. You!

RYSOOR. It does not concern me alone. This time not I alone have been injured; but the whole people. She—no, I hardly believe God Himself would ask me to forget that.

KARLOO. Tell me!

RYSOOR [*lowering his voice in order not to be overheard by the soldiers*]. Karloo, we have been betrayed. There is one who is accursed among us, one who surprised our secrets and sold us!

KARLOO. Ah, otherwise—

RYSOOR. We do not know who it is. Ignorant as we are, to-morrow perhaps he will renew his work; our most carefully thought-out plans may be in vain, and our best blood be shed, a whole people die in agony and terror because there is one fiend in our midst unpunished.

KARLOO. And you wish—?

RYSOOR. I wish—. Listen: this is my last will, Karloo, I bequeath to you a sacred duty.

KARLOO. Yes?

RYSOOR. This traitor to his country, this dealer in our blood—find him, Karloo, find him. When you have him—no matter what his name or rank—crush him, have no pity for him. It will not be murder, but legitimate defence. Common justice. You will be defending not only your *Patrie*, which has been sold and crucified by him: you will be saving Her. So strike hard, my son, strike!

KARLOO. On my soul, I swear it.

RYSOOR. Take care: it is a sacred oath.

KARLOO. I swear.

RYSOOR. No matter who the person may be?

KARLOO. On my hope of salvation—if I had to strike at my own fireside, at the foot of the altar! I have sworn to pierce his traitorous heart—with this hand.

RYSOOR. Then you see how wise I was to save your life. It is saved for a purpose!

[*The door at the right opens and* NOIR-CARMES *appears on the threshold, with the clerk and the court*]

KARLOO [*nervously*]. Are they coming?

RYSOOR [*seeing* RINCON, *who is coming down-stage*]. Yes, I know what they want.

KARLOO. What?

RYSOOR [*smiling to reassure* KARLOO]. It appears that Monsieur le Duc wishes to—question me.

KARLOO. You will return this way. I shall see you later.

RYSOOR [*his voice choked with emotion as he takes* KARLOO's *hand*]. Surely. Now, Karloo, my son, let us separate.

KARLOO [*apprehensively*]. I want to wait for you.

RYSOOR. Don't stay here—it might be dangerous. Remember, your life does not belong to you: think of your promise!

KARLOO. It seems as if you were saying good-bye for the last time.

RYSOOR [*smiling*]. Oh, no. I firmly hope to see you again.

RINCON [*coming down-stage*]. Ready, Monsieur!

RYSOOR. Ready, Captain. [*To* KARLOO, *from the top of the steps*] Remember your oath, Karloo. Remember!

[NOIRCARMES *reënters.* RYSOOR *and* RINCON *disappear from the same side. The door is closed after them. The Ensign appears*]

KARLOO [*following them with his eyes*]. The way he spoke to me! What can the Duke want with him? Where are they taking him? [*He starts to mount the staircase*]

MIGUEL [*stopping him*]. Careful, Monsieur, you must not go that way!

KARLOO. Very well, Monsieur, I shall wait.

MIGUEL. You may not wait here, either, Monsieur; you must go at once, please. Here is your passport.

KARLOO [*taking the passport*]. Please, Monsieur, I wish to wait until he comes out.

MIGUEL. Your friend? That may be a long time.

KARLOO [*uneasily*]. You think so?

MIGUEL. Surely—he is being questioned.

KARLOO [*in terror*]. Questioned? Saints of heaven! He lied to me, and I did not understand. What a fool I was! I must see him! [*He dashes forward, but officers bar his way*]

MIGUEL. You are mad, Monsieur; you cannot go in there.

KARLOO [*desperate, as he struggles with the soldiers, who thrust him down-stage, left, behind the table just beyond the fireplace*]. Let me go! I must see him once more!

MIGUEL [*who, together with the others, holds* KARLOO *fast*]. I tell you, Monsieur, you cannot go there.

[*The door of the torture chamber opens, and* NOIRCARMES *appears*]

KARLOO [*hopefully*]. They are coming back!

VARGAS [*reëntering from the Duke's apartments*]. Well, Noircarmes?

NOIRCARMES. It is over.

KARLOO [*joyfully*]. Already?

VARGAS. Did he confess?

NOIRCARMES [*shrugging his shoulders*]. He said one word: "*Patrie!*", then he died!

KARLOO. Dead!

VARGAS [*to* NOIRCARMES]. Dead?

NOIRCARMES. On the threshold—he killed himself with this dagger. [*He throws a dagger on to the table*]

KARLOO [*sobbing brokenly*]. My God! My God!

NOIRCARMES [*to the officers*]. Really, Messieurs, you should search your prisoners with greater care!

VARGAS. Come to his Excellency.

KARLOO [*pale and calm, going to the table*]. Messieurs, do you wish to keep this dagger?

NOIRCARMES [*surprised, as he looks at* KARLOO]. No, Monsieur, no.

KARLOO. Then will you allow me to keep it?

NOIRCARMES. As you like.

[*They go out left*]

KARLOO. Thank you. [*He takes the dagger and goes out quickly, right*]

[*The soldiers look at him wonderingly*]

CURTAIN

ACT FOUR

SCENE II

A square in the city. At the back, a flight of stairs with a railing rises at an oblique angle to the left, toward the higher part of the city, the roofs of which are seen, covered with half-melted snow, rising one above the other. This flight of stairs passes under the fortified gate, then turns and loses itself from view toward the right, in the direction of the church of Sainte-Gudule, the two towers of which can be seen above the roofs. To the right and left is a street; down-stage left is a small shop facing the stage. The interior can be seen only from the stage boxes. It is daytime. Drums are heard in the distance, beating a call to arms. Merchants, burghers, workmen, women, and children are conversing in undertones, as they walk back and forth down-stage; they accost one another as if in mortal terror of something. Soldiers come and go, singly and in patrols. A brewer, an innkeeper and several women of the street may be distinguished, then MIGUEL *and* RINCON.

A WOMAN [*to another woman, in an undertone*]. The call to arms!

INNKEEPER [*also in an undertone*]. Yes, they will come this way.

A WOMAN SHOPKEEPER [*who is sitting on a chair down-stage to the left, in front of her shop*]. Have you been to see the Place du Marché?

A VOICE. No.

WOMAN SHOPKEEPER. A great heap of faggots, covered with black—it gives you goose-flesh to look at it!

BREWER. And those cannons all around, blocking every street.

A WORKMAN [*coming forward*]. Every gate of the city is closed, you know, till after the execution.

BREWER. They had to do that, to raise the prices—with this new tax of theirs.

WOMAN SHOPKEEPER. You'll see how bad business will be—worse, if possible, than before.

BREWER. You see the result of all these at-tempts. Have to pull our belts tighter. We ought to turn our backs until it's all over.

[*Enter* KARLOO *alone, quickly, at the right. Everyone stops as he appears, and those who were speaking point at him.* LA TRÉMOÏLLE *enters behind* KARLOO, *booted and spurred, ready to leave the city. He plants himself in front of* KARLOO, *then stops him as he is about to make his way toward the left*]

LA TRÉMOÏLLE. Captain, I have followed you from the Palace; forgive me if I speak to you as if I were a friend. Where are you going? You look pale, and in a hurry. Take my advice, and do not go in that direction.

KARLOO. Thank you, Monsieur, but this way I must go: to the Grande-Place, where I have someone to see.

LA TRÉMOÏLLE [*quickly*]. You will see only a hideous spectacle. Please, Captain, let us wait in this deserted street until the gates are opened again! I have two good horses at the Porte de Flandre.

KARLOO. You speak as if you were a friend of twenty years standing, Monsieur, and I am heartily thankful for your kindness. But I really cannot accept your offer. The Comte de Rysoor is dead.

LA TRÉMOÏLLE. I know.

KARLOO. But his widow does not. I must tell her. After that I have a number of errands to do in the city.

LA TRÉMOÏLLE. Captain, I am very sorry. Adieu, then.

KARLOO. Adieu. [*He starts to go out left.* LA TRÉMOÏLLE *keeps his eyes on him*]

MIGUEL [*stopping* KARLOO]. Where are you going, Monsieur?

KARLOO. To the Grande-Place.

MIGUEL. Don't go there.

KARLOO. Why not?

MIGUEL. Not until the prisoners pass.

LA TRÉMOÏLLE [*to* KARLOO, *who returns*]. Now you must stay with me.

KARLOO. Yes, I must.

[*Excitement and cries are heard to the right. Enter* ALBERTI]

A VOICE [*off-stage*]. This way. This way.

ALBERTI [*who has entered left, goes to* RINCON *and* MIGUEL, *who stand in the middle of the square very much wrought up*]. Messieurs —Captain—come and help me. As I was taking his Excellency's daughter to the Convent of Groenendaal, we passed the city gates; when Doña Rafaële saw the men who had been hanged she was so terrified that she would walk back, in spite of all I could do. Here she is—in this street. She insists on returning to the Palace. I beg you, Captain, conduct us there by a roundabout route.

[*Drums are heard in the distance*]

RINCON. Very well, Monsieur. Bring your

chair here at once. The procession has already left the Palace.

ALBERTI. This way, Señora, this way.

[RAFAËLE *enters in her chair; the nun sits facing her. She is followed by women attendants and two pages*]

ALBERTI. Straight ahead?

RINCON. Straight ahead, but quickly.

RAFAËLE. Wait. [*They all stop*]

ALBERTI. Why are you stopping, Señora? Let us go on.

RAFAËLE. Not yet. First I want to know the meaning of all these crowds and soldiers and drums. What is happening here, Messieurs?

RINCON [*at a sign from* ALBERTI]. Nothing at all, Señora—the troops are being reviewed.

RAFAËLE. Ah!

[*Trumpets are heard in the gateway*]

THE HERALD [*appearing*]. By order of the King our master and his Excellency the Duke of Alba, be it known to the people of this city: it is commanded that you all kneel in silence as the rebels pass this way— [*Murmurs from the crowd*]—on pain of death. Glory be to God and to the King!

[*The Herald retires and a moment later is heard making the same proclamation in the distance*]

RAFAËLE [*nervously*]. What does that man say?

ALBERTI. He says, Madame, that the people should make way for the troops here.

RAFAËLE. But he spoke of rebels?

ALBERTI. A mistake—he said nothing of the sort! Did he, Messieurs?

LA TRÉMOÏLLE. Nothing at all, Señora.

ALBERTI. Now let us proceed.

RAFAËLE. I must get out.

ALBERTI. Madame.

RAFAËLE. I want to walk.

ALBERTI. I have orders.

RAFAËLE. To take orders from me, Monsieur! I wish it, do you understand? [*She gets out of her chair with considerable effort, aided by her servants*]

LA TRÉMOÏLLE. Then on foot—if your Grace so wishes—will you honor me by accepting my hand?

[*The chair is taken off right by servants. LA TRÉMOÏLLE offers RAFAËLE his hand. The city bells ring the death-knell in the distance*]

RAFAËLE. Yes, on foot. [*Catching sight of KARLOO*] Oh, Captain. It is you? You surely will tell me what is happening?

KARLOO. Only what has been told you, Madame: it is a review.

RAFAËLE. But those bells?

KARLOO. They ring on all occasions presided over by Monseigneur le Duc.

RAFAËLE. But these terrified faces I see around me? You yourself? You are pale.

KARLOO. Oh, I have been freed from prison, thanks to you. And I am like the rest of the inhabitants of this city: not a whit too gay.

RAFAËLE [*very anxious and nervous*]. They are hiding something from me.

ALBERTI. Madame, in the name of heaven, let us go. In a few moments we shall be unable to get through this crowd.

ALL [*supplicating her*]. Señora!

RAFAËLE. Yes, yes. [*Aside*] They are all lying! [*Taking a little child by the hand and drawing it to her*] Come here, my dear child. Are you here to see the soldiers, too?

CHILD. Yes, Madame, and the condemned prisoners. They're going to burn them in the Place.

RAFAËLE [*with a piercing cry*]. Oh! [*She falls into the arms of her attendants. The child is taken from her*]

ALBERTI. That wretched child!

RAFAËLE [*her hand on her breast*]. How horrible! This everlasting slaughter! My God, what I am suffering! Take me away. My God.

KARLOO [*rushing forward and supporting her*]. Madame.

[*The chair is quickly brought to her*]

RAFAËLE. My God! Give me air! Air! I'm choking! Blood! I'm choking! [*She is made to sit down*]

KARLOO [*in despair*]. Madame, in the name of heaven— My dear, dear child.

WOMAN SHOPKEEPER [*crying*]. Dear angel.

[DOÑA RAFAËLE *is surrounded. The women are especially attentive*]

ALBERTI [*bent over her*]. My God, she's dying!

[DOÑA RAFAËLE *rises, supporting herself on the two women, trying to breathe; then she falls back heavily into the chair*]

KARLOO. Dead!

[*The word is repeated in whispers and undertones by those immediately about her. The men take off their hats*]

ALBERTI. Messieurs, Messieurs, not a word to Monseigneur. Let me have time to prepare him for this awful news.

[RAFAËLE *is carried into the shop, where the women crowd round her body, crying. They screen her from the audience during the following. The drums, which have not ceased to beat, sound closer; the bells ring as before*]

LA TRÉMOÏLLE. Divine vengeance!

KARLOO. And that angel will pray for him!

[*A company of halberdiers appears in the gateway and clears the way of people, who scatter right and left, standing behind the ranks of soldiers. After the halberdiers comes the procession, which marches slowly as at a funeral. At the head are three drummers assiduously beating the funeral roll. The whole pro-*]

cession descends the stairs, then turns to
the left, reaching the stage, and finally
disappears into the street on the same
side]

[After the drummers come the Spanish
musketeers and pikemen in armor. Then
trumpeters, the herald, mace-bearers,
standard-bearers of the Swiss regiments,
Lombards, Portuguese, Neapolitans, Ger-
mans, etc. Then three drummers precede
the lancemen, who enter, followed by the
clerks of the Court of Blood, judges, and
provosts' guards. NOIRCARMES appears,
then VARGAS and DELRIO. Finally, beneath a dais carried by lackeys bearing his
arms, comes the Duke, accompanied by
his pages and the attendants of his house.
As he arrives under the gateway all save
KARLOO and LA TRÉMOÏLLE kneel; they
stand with their backs to the wall at the
right. After the Duke appears, the chanting of the penitents (their heads in cowls,
and wax candles in hand, marching in
two lines, at some distance apart) is
heard above the sound of the drums and
ringing of the bells. These are under the
gate when the Duke arrives at the center
of the stage. As this chant increases,
DOÑA RAFAËLE'S attendants give way to
their grief; they sob, kneeling. The Duke,
who cannot see RAFAËLE'S body, stops
and speaks to VARGAS, who is ahead of
him]

ALBA. Vargas, why are those women crying?
I have forbidden that.

[VARGAS bows and goes to the women.
ALBERTI shows him RAFAËLE'S body,
stretched out on the chair, a crucifix on
her breast. VARGAS, deeply moved, stands
stockstill, and takes off his hat]

VARGAS. Monseigneur, there is someone dead
in this house: a young girl.

[They all take off their hats]

ALBA [the thought of his own daughter occurs
to him, and he takes off his hat]. A young girl!
God is terrible in His vengeance!

KARLOO [aside]. He is, tyrant!

ALBA. Let them weep, Vargas, let them mourn
for the young girl.

[He makes a sign for the procession to advance. It continues as before. The Swiss
Guards follow the Duke, then come
monks wearing cowls, and chanting the
"Dies Iræ." The gray monks walk slowly.
Then comes a monk dressed in white,
bearing the Spanish crucifix. Black monks
appear carrying candles. GALÈNA, BAK-
KERZEEL, and CORNÉLIS enter, hands
bound, each escorted by a soldier, who
walks at his right. Then comes MAÎTRE
CHARLES with his assistants. When the
prisoners arrive upon the stage, left, and

pass near KARLOO, they see him weeping]

GALÈNA [in an undertone, as he advances
toward him]. Coward, you are free! We are
about to die!

CORNÉLIS [following GALÈNA]. How much
did you get for betraying us, traitor?

KARLOO. Traitor? I?

BAKKERZEEL. Accursed Judas!

ALL THE PRISONERS. Judas! Judas!

KARLOO. This is frightful! You accuse me?
Me? Me?

[The procession continues during the following. Next come the Italian musketeers
and arquebusiers, then the regular infantry, under MIGUEL and RINCON; these
close the column]

LA TRÉMOÏLLE [controlling KARLOO]. Monsieur, I beg you—

KARLOO [to LA TRÉMOÏLLE]. But this is horrible! It's a lie! It was not I, Monsieur! I swear
it was not I!

LA TRÉMOÏLLE [quickly]. I know that—it
was a woman.

KARLOO. A woman? What is her name? Monsieur, tell me her name!

LA TRÉMOÏLLE. I do not know that; I know
only that she came to Monsieur le Duc last
night, and that she left the Palace this morning with a passport to Lille.

KARLOO. That is at least a clue—a passport
for Lille.

LA TRÉMOÏLLE. Like yours and mine.

KARLOO. I have only time enough to run to
the Grande-Place, through the by-streets. I
shall meet you at the Porte de Flandre—she
must have gone that way. Wait for me, Monsieur, wait for me.

LA TRÉMOÏLLE. Very well, Captain.

KARLOO. Ah, these insults! The dead man reminds me of my oath. Sleep in peace, your revenge is about to be accomplished! [He goes
up-stage left, and disappears in the direction
taken by the procession]

[The crowd covers the stage again. In its
endeavor to follow the procession it
rushes to the stairway, knocking aside
the bystanders and finally disappears
under the gateway, while LA TRÉMOÏLLE
gives a last look at the dead girl]

CURTAIN

ACT FIVE

SCENE I

RYSOOR'S home; the same scene as in ACT II.
The tabouret is no longer before the table, and
the chair which was right of the table is now
at the back, near the fireplace. DOLORÈS and
GUDULE are present.

GUDULE [*standing at the window, which she closes, frightened*]. Oh, Madame, the crowd is overflowing the Place. The soldiers are forming ranks. The church is wide open; all the priests are standing at the doors to give absolution to the prisoners who are coming.

DOLORÈS [*who is watching for* KARLOO, *standing at the entrance of the room*]. Yes, but *he* doesn't come!

GUDULE. Madame, dear Madame, we can't remain here. Even the servants have left the house. Let us go away! Don't look at the horrible scene!

DOLORÈS [*she now looks for* KARLOO *out of the door down-stage*]. Run away if you like, I—well, if I don't watch for him here, where else can I?

GUDULE. Oh, Madame!

DOLORÈS [*bitterly, as she goes toward the right*]. He is not coming. He has been free for an hour. He should have come to me first, but —no! God knows what he is doing. Where can he be? Does he think of *me?*

[KARLOO *enters precipitately through the garden door. The moment* GUDULE *sees him she goes out through the main door, which she closes behind her*]

DOLORÈS [*seeing* KARLOO]. It's he at last! [*She runs to him*] My God! it's you! At last! [KARLOO, *without answering her, lays his cape and hat on the table*] My Karloo, you are free —free and safe!

KARLOO [*standing with the table between them, and not looking at her*]. Dolorès.

DOLORÈS. What if they were bringing you with them, *there!* I should have thrown myself from this window!

KARLOO [*disturbed*]. Dolorés, what are you saying? And at this time!

DOLORÈS. Let me tell you how much I love you. I have suffered so much, I have the right to be mad with joy.

KARLOO. No, Dolorès, I swear you haven't that right.

DOLORÈS. But if I have you again—

KARLOO. Your husband is dead.

DOLORÈS. Ah!

KARLOO. He killed himself.

DOLORÈS [*sorrowfully*]. Ah—God!

KARLOO. Dead, Dolorès—that is what I had to tell you—[*His voice trembling*]—dead. He forgave us, you and me.

DOLORÈS [*at first she sobs, then says joyfully*]. Pardoned, both of us? Then you have no more regret? Why do you look at me that way?

KARLOO. Are you sure that he understood this pardon as you do? He said that we must separate—forever.

DOLORÈS. Separate? Then do I want his forgiveness? This is not forgiveness; it is chastisement.

KARLOO. Dolorès, this is blasphemy—he is now dead—your husband! Take care.

DOLORÈS [*with tenderness*]. Did you accept this pardon on those conditions?

KARLOO. I don't know.

DOLORÈS. You don't know?

KARLOO. No; I came here with a fixed determination; ready to leave you—but the moment I see you my head is turned—love, duty, crime, virtue—everything is confused! I am not sure what I want—I don't know. [*He falls into a chair*]

DOLORÈS [*going to him, tenderly*]. I know; you love me—we are everything to each other —that is the truth. [KARLOO *tries to close her lips*] Karloo, our awful nightmare is now at an end. Let us leave this house, which is not ours; let us escape from this past where we were not alone. Let us go and be happy and free, both of us. Let us love somewhere else.

[*The drums beat the funeral march in the distance, which sounds nearer and nearer*]

KARLOO [*trembling*]. Listen!

DOLORÈS. What?

KARLOO [*standing*]. They are coming. [*He goes quickly to the window and opens it*]

DOLORÈS. Poor wretches—that is one more reason—let us go.

KARLOO [*springing back in horror*]. The scaffold! There it is—and the faggots.

DOLORÈS [*runs forward and stands between* KARLOO *and the window, which she closes*]. What difference does that make? They are not prepared for you.

KARLOO. No, no—I want to wait for them— see them.

DOLORÈS [*forcing him to come down-stage right*]. See them? Why?

KARLOO. Do you know what they shouted at me, just now, as they were passing through the streets? They called me coward, traitor, Judas! They accused me of betraying them—me— think of it! Me, Karloo! [*He goes up-stage, left, above the sofa*]

DOLORÈS. What of it?

KARLOO. Horrible! To be accused of treason —and by them. Now they are about to die, there, at the stake. Their last words will be to curse me. [*He again goes up to the window*]

DOLORÈS [*intercepting him, then taking him to the left*]. Let them curse you, what of it? Let them cry out at you—now come!

KARLOO [*with his eyes on the Place, in spite of* DOLORÈS]. But not to know that wretch who has betrayed us, be unable to carry out my oath!

DOLORÈS. My God! Not go away? Did you make an oath?

KARLOO. On my life!

DOLORÈS. Leave the dead in peace, and remember only the oaths you made to me. They are the only good ones.

KARLOO. I have sworn, do you hear? On my hope of a future life.

DOLORÈS. What did you swear?

KARLOO [*disengaging himself and running to the window, which he opens*]. To put a dagger in the person who betrayed us.

DOLORÈS [*speechless with terror at first, she staggers back to the table, where she supports herself for an instant*]. A fine promise—really!

KARLOO [*standing between DOLORÈS and the window*]. I swore!

DOLORÈS. To be an assassin, in order to please that dead man? And you dare admit it—that is horrible! [*She rushes to him and forces him to come down-stage left*]

KARLOO. I made an oath.

DOLORÈS. You, my Karloo, put a dagger into someone—nonsense! That would be sheer madness. Poor Karloo, don't do that. You have been betrayed—very well, what is done is done! Let us go away—I won't betray *you*. [*She has gradually pushed him in front of the table*]

KARLOO. And then have all Brussels say, as those poor prisoners did: "There is the man who betrayed us!" Drag out a life of dishonor —no. I must prove my innocence, and I will write it with the blood of the guilty one on the flagstones of this city.

DOLORÈS [*standing at the other side of the table*]. You are out of your mind. Where is the guilty one? Who will tell you who he is? Who?

KARLOO. I have already been told that it is a woman.

DOLORÈS. A woman? You say a woman? My God, that is absurd—a woman! Do women meddle with such things? Do you believe that? Can you really think?

KARLOO [*again going up-stage*]. I am sure— the person who told me—

DOLORÈS [*again barring his passage*]. A poor wretch and a coward! He knows nothing about it. So you believe everything that is told you now?

[*The drums are heard approaching*]

KARLOO. There they are. [*He clings trembling to the table*]

DOLORÈS. No, not yet. Karloo, Karloo whom I adore! Don't stay here. Don't! You cannot stand it—only listen to me—do this for my sake; I have been willing to sacrifice my life for you—and I love you. Do you love me? Tell me—yes or no?

KARLOO [*still looking out the window*]. O God, yes! And I have promised not to.

DOLORÈS. Then come, Karloo. Don't look! Think of it: we have a whole lifetime of love and happiness before us—[*the drums sound still nearer*] there is no one to stand between us now. [*She cries out against the drums, which are now beating very loudly*] Stop it, you

cursèd—! [*The drums cease beating*] It's nothing, you see? They are far away now. Don't listen! Come with me—just a step. It's all over now. Now we are free!

[*The drums beat louder than before. There is the noise of great excitement on the Place. The music from an organ is heard playing until the end of the scene*]

KARLOO. Ah! [*He leaves DOLORÈS side, and goes to the arched window*]

DOLORÈS [*in despair, as she comes down to the left of the table*]. This is how men love! While we sacrifice ourselves.

KARLOO [*sobbing, as he steps back from the window*]. You are right, Dolorès, this is ghastly. They are now standing on the faggot heap! Bakkerzeel—and poor Galèna! My friends. Oh, I can't look! I can't. Take me away! [*He staggers down as far as the table*]

DOLORÈS [*triumphantly, as she runs to open the garden door*]. At last!

KARLOO [*worn out, leans upon the table, and says in a whisper, his eyes always turned toward the Place*]. Let us leave this house—this city.

DOLORÈS [*returning to him—also in a whisper*]. Yes—both of us!

KARLOO [*with the table still between them*]. Together.

DOLORÈS. Together—yes—now, come.

KARLOO. But can we leave the city?

DOLORÈS. You have your passport?

KARLOO. Yes, but you?

DOLORÈS. I have mine.

KARLOO [*trembling, as he still clutches the edge of the table. He turns suddenly toward her*]. Yours?

DOLORÈS. Like yours—to Lille.

KARLOO. To Lille?

DOLORÈS. Yes.

KARLOO. You?

DOLORÈS. I am telling you! Come, now.

KARLOO [*looking wildly at her*]. How did you get it?

DOLORÈS. I went to the Palace for it.

KARLOO. This morning?

DOLORÈS. Yes.

KARLOO [*stepping back, thunderstruck*]. Great God! how horrible!

DOLORÈS. What *is* the matter?

KARLOO. That woman—at the Duke's—this morning! That woman—at the Duke's—last night!

DOLORÈS. Last night?

KARLOO. It is she.

DOLORÈS. No!

KARLOO. It's you. It's you! You have betrayed us! You miserable—! Dare you deny that you are the one?

DOLORÈS. Ah, Karloo!

KARLOO. Leave me—don't touch me! [*He disengages himself and darts toward the right, where he falls into a chair*]

DOLORÈS. Pity me.

KARLOO. God's vengeance! And I have been looking for her! And here she is. Who else?

DOLORÈS [*who has fallen to the floor*]. Ah, Karloo! Don't curse me! Let the others do that —not you.

KARLOO. Fiend—traitress—coward—coward!

DOLORÈS [*on her knees, making her way toward him*]. You don't know all, my Karloo. He wanted to kill you. When he left me he said: "I am going to kill him!" I was mad with terror—stark mad—Karloo! I swear I was raving mad! I only tried to save you—I loved you so much! It was for your sake, for you!

KARLOO [*taking her hands in his*]. Your love. Your love has made me a perjurer and a traitor! Your fatal love has brought these poor wretches to the scaffold, and a whole nation to its ruin. Your love is hellish, deadly! I *do* curse you! I execrate, I hate you! [*He casts her to the floor*]

DOLORÈS. Ah, Karloo, you are killing me!

KARLOO. No, not yet!

DOLORÈS. What are you going to do?

KARLOO [*dragging her to the window*]. Come here, Madame! First, look at your work.

DOLORÈS. Pity me!

[*The windows are red with the reflected light of the faggots. Screams and murmurs of horror are heard from the Place*]

KARLOO. Look at it! Look at your faggot heap—it's burning!

DOLORÈS. Pity me!

KARLOO. Look—count your victims!

DOLORÈS. Karloo—ungrateful—

KARLOO [*raising her and forcing her to look*]. You must accustom yourself to flames—you must have some notion of what hell is like— hell, where your love is dragging us!

DOLORÈS. Mercy!

KARLOO. Listen! They have caught sight of me! Listen now, listen!

THE PRISONERS. Karloo—traitor! Traitor!

KARLOO. Do you hear?

DOLORÈS. My God!

KARLOO. And do you not also hear the dead man crying out: "Remember your oath"?

DOLORÈS [*rising in terror*]. No. No.

KARLOO. "No matter who the guilty one may be, strike, have no mercy!"

DOLORÈS. Karloo, would you strike me?

KARLOO [*drawing the dagger*]. My oath!

DOLORÈS [*wild with terror, as she struggles to free herself*]. With your own hand—no! You wouldn't do that! Pity me—I'm afraid!

KARLOO [*losing his self-control*]. I have sworn!

DOLORÈS. No, no—don't—leave me!

KARLOO. I have sworn, I have sworn! [*He plunges the dagger into her*]

DOLORÈS [*falling to the floor*]. Now go—you have killed me. And I loved you so! I loved you so—

[KARLOO *throws his dagger down*]

KARLOO [*nearly out of his mind*]. I have killed you! I! I!

DOLORÈS. At least you can join me, now! Come.

KARLOO [*falling to his knees before her, an inanimate mass, and covering her with kisses, while he sobs*]. I will come with you—I am so miserable! Dolorès, my sweetest love! O God! O God!

DOLORÈS. Come, then.

KARLOO [*standing*]. Wait! I am coming. [*He runs to the window, stands in it, and cries out*] Executioner— [*Excitement in the Place*]—you lack one man! Make way for me on your faggot heap!

DOLORÈS [*rising in order to see him*]. Ah!

KARLOO [*to* DOLORÈS, *his voice full of loving tenderness*]. You see? I am coming, I am coming! [*He goes swiftly from the room.* DOLORÈS *dies*]

CURTAIN

BELLE LAMAR

An Episode of the Civil War

By DION BOUCICAULT

The acting rights of this play are fully protected by law. For permission to perform, either by professionals or amateurs; to read in public, to broadcast by radio, or in any way reproduce them, application must be made to Samuel French, at 25 West 45th St., New York, N. Y., or at 811 West 7th St., Los Angeles, Calif.
Printed through the courtesy of Commander Fitzhugh Green.

CHARACTERS

PHILIP BLIGH, *Colonel in the United States Army, commanding at Whitestone Gap*

MARSTON PIKE
GIRARD } *officers of the United States Army*
GETZ

GENERAL THOMAS J. JACKSON, *commanding the Confederate troops, known as "Stonewall"*
Jackson

PATRICK STUART
CLARBORNE RHETT } *officers in Jackson's Army*

REMMY SHEA
PAT DWYER } *soldiers in Marston Pike's command*

UNCLE DAN, *an old negro slave*
ISABEL LAMAR, *a Virginian Lady*
HONOR McQUADE, *attached to Bligh's service and following his regiment*

SYNOPSIS

The scene is laid at and in the vicinity of Mount Lamar, an estate in the Shenandoah Valley. Time—The Spring of 1862.

ACT I.—SCENE 1. *The Banks of the Blackadder—Night. The Outpost.—The Irish Sentinel.*

> *Oh! why did I lave the County Clare*
> *To sail across the sea?*
> *Oh! why did I lave you, Mary Meagher.*
> *Alone to pine for me*
> *In far Kilkee?*
>
> *The sky is blue, the land is fair,*
> *And goold, they say is plenty here;*
> *But oh! the blue of Mary's eye*
> *Is bluer than your southern sky,*
> *And the goold I love is the goolden hair*
> *Of the fairest girl in the County Clare.*

The Reply of the Rebel Outpost. The Relief Guard. The Watchword. Remmy puts Pat Dwyer through his facings, and has a narrow escape. The Signal. The Tryst. Marston meets Belle. The Price of Treason. Uncle Dan. The Confederate plot to waylay bearer of despatches.
SCENE 2. *A room in Mount Lamar. The old Virginian Home. The arrival of Bligh's Regiment. Two schoolfellows meet and compare lives. The Vipers on the Hearth. Bad news. The Confederate Spy. Bligh's appeal to Headquarters. The confession. The Rivals. The Captive.*
ACT II—*Mount Lamar. Love and duty. Philip's dilemma. "Dare you kneel to me for your lover's life?" Philip and Belle. The Court-martial. The Bribe. Life for Life. The fellow-students. The Defiance. The Avowal. The Verdict. The Flag of Truce. The Pass. The Escape. Stonewall Jackson moves across the Blackadder.*
ACT III—*Whitestone Gap. The forlorn redoubt. Hemmed in. Bligh holds his own. The piney patch. Remmy gets a fright at last and takes a header. A message. Terms of surrender. Honor wants to know how to "die dacent." The soul of a Cæsar in the Irish peasant girl. The living curse. Nailing the colors to the mast. The lone horseman. "Nations have been lost or saved in thirty minutes."*

BELLE LAMAR

ACT ONE

SCENE I. *Night.*

The banks of the Blackadder, a small river in the Shenandoah Valley, Virginia, densely wooded. A sentinel in the uniform of the Northern troops is seen posted L.C. *Music. Pause. Drum* R. *Distant bugle* L. *Sentinel's song (Irish).*

Why did I lave the County Clare
    To sail across the sea?
Why did I lave you? Mary Meagher,
    Alone to pine for me,
              In far Kilkee?

The sky is blue, the land is fair,
And goold they say is plenty here.
But oh! the blue of Mary's eye
Is bluer than the Southern sky—
And the goold I love is the goolden hair,
Of the fairest girl in the County Clare.

[After singing his two verses, his head falls in reverie on his rifle. A pause. From the other side of the river is heard a distant voice replying. It is a sentinel on the Confederate outpost singing to himself]

Toward my home the wind doth blow,
              Maryland.
To thee my loving words will go,
              Maryland.
I'm thine whatever fate bestow
Through life to death, for weal, for woe;
For thee my heart's best blood shall flow,
              Maryland.

[These two songs, sung on opposite sides of the river by the two, should be sung tenderly and not intended as defiances]
[Enter REMMY *with four soldiers.* R.H.]
REMMY. Halt!
SENTINEL. Who goes there?
REMMY. Relief guard.
SENTINEL. Advance relief guard, and give the word.
REMMY *[advances]*. Choctaw.
SENTINEL. Pass relief guard.
REMMY. Stand out, Pat Dwyer! *[*PAT *advances* L.] You are to mount guard here in Tom Mulligan's place. D'ye know how to do that? Eh? I'll go bail you don't. Kape your hand down from scratchin' your head! Attintion, and

I'll tell you, Pat: you are goin' to be an outpost. Oh! whin you left the County Tyrone nine weeks ago you little thought you'd get a fine post like this undher Government in the Shanandoah Valley, State of Virginia, in South America, before you had been tin days in the counthry! You have the divil's own luck, Pat! D'ye see that stump beyant? *[Points out* L.] Well, you will walk betune this place and that stump! That's your ground. The enemy is on the other side of the river. *[Points out back]* Attintion now, and listen to the pass-word. *[Whispers in his ear]* "Choctaw," don't forget it—reharse it now. What's the word?
PAT. Shaughrawn.
REMMY. Shaughrawn. Well that's Irish for it, anyway! Mind if ye see any livin' mortial thing stirring out there, you'll cry, "Stand, who goes there?" and manewhile cover the crapin' blackguard wid your gun. If he doesn't say "Choctaw," before you count three, shoot and retire on Jemmy Doolan, that I'm going to post beyant. Wait now till I thry if you know your jooty. Attintion! I'll be the inemy crapin' opon yez onbeknownst. *[Exit* R.1.E.]
    *[*PAT *walks up and down* L.H., REMMY *comes on stealthily]*
PAT. Stand, who goes there! *[Points his gun at him]*
REMMY. That's elegant!
PAT. One—two—three. *[He fires and retreats]*
REMMY. Tare alive—what did you do that for?
PAT. Ye didn't say, 'Shaughrawn'!
REMMY *[taking off his hat and examining it]*. I believe you are right; but bad luck to you for spoiling my hat!
PAT. Didn't I do my jooty well?
REMMY. No you didn't—you missed me.
    [Enter MARSTON PIKE]
MARSTON. The general orders forbid outposts exchanging shots with the enemy: your men are too exposed here on the river bank. They invite this useless duelling. Corporal Remmy, you will retire your line of sentries to the pine wood, yonder.
REMMY. All right, sir—fall in boys. *[The men fall in]*
MARSTON. They will find better cover in the oak scrub.
REMMY. Egorra, Captain, the most of us would rather be batin' a cover for the grey game beyant than hidin' in it! Will we niver get a fight

again, sir? Sure, we are gettin' blue mouldey from lyin' by this way in this same Shannondoo Valley. Left face—boys! What have we done that we should be put in the corner while the finest of fightin' is going on all round Richmond below there? It is mighty hard, so it is. Quick march! [*Exit with his men* L.H.1.E.]

MARSTON. They are gone. I may show the signal.

[*Draws a lantern from under his cloak. Lights it and places it on the limb of a tree.* L.H. *The light away from the audience, directed to back of stage*]

I was seeking for a pretext to draw back the line of posts and leave the bank unguarded: the blunders of these Irish recruits came happily to my assistance— [*A pause*] There is a dark shadow on the water. It is the canoe crossing the stream. How my heart beats. If any sentinels should have lingered behind, the reckless girl is lost. [*Looks off to left*]

[*Enter* BELLE LAMAR, R.2.E.]

BELLE. Marston!

MARSTON. Dear Miss Lamar. You cannot understand the danger you affront in thus crossing between our outposts and those of the enemy.

BELLE. I am a soldier's daughter, and danger is my element! How you tremble!

MARSTON. Because you expose a life dearer to me than my own.

BELLE. What news?

MARSTON. The worst. I am ordered to get my men under arms to-night in readiness to march an hour before daylight.

BELLE. So you leave Mount Lamar to-morrow—who takes your place?

MARSTON. Bligh's regiment of cavalry.

BELLE. Philip Bligh is coming to my house!

MARSTON. Do you know him? He is my oldest friend; a man made of one perfect piece, without a flaw or speck. We roomed together at West Point, where we were fellow students. He was my senior by some years; but such a nature that, living by his side, I seemed to breathe a purer air and felt a better self within me that came forth to keep him company.

BELLE. Philip Bligh at Mount Lamar!

MARSTON. You know him?

BELLE. As the most unrelenting foe to the South! and this man is coming to my house.

MARSTON. Dearest Belle, why do you not return there? It is your home. Your presence will restrain the license of his troops.

BELLE. Return to my home! play hostess to his comrades in my hall—and cater for his mercenaries in my kitchen—with a smile on my lips and hate in my heart? [*Cross* L.] No, Marston; I have no home but my father's tent in Stonewall Jackson's camp. Every night I creep down like a wild beast to the river bank below, and gaze upon the lights that shine from every window in Mount Lamar, the home of my childhood. Yonder is the window of my mother's room where I was born; it has never been occupied since she died, fifteen years ago. A corporal's guard is lodged there now; instead I hear their drunken songs borne across the fields. There is the nursery where she taught me my childish prayers. At that familiar window, wreathed with the flowers I planted, two troopers curse over a game of cards.

MARSTON. At least you will be safe there; it is very unlikely the coming struggle will take place in this part of the Valley.

BELLE. What struggle?

MARSTON. General McDowell is in force at Front Royal. Colonel Philip Bligh comes to meet despatches which should arrive at Mount Lamar to-night.

BELLE. Frémont at Franklin! McDowell at Front Royal!

MARSTON. And Banks at Strasbourg—Right, left, and centre. Three Northern armies are advancing to crush rebellion and make short work of war. You see how hopeless is resistance.

BELLE. Hopeless!

MARSTON. Believe me, the end has come. In a week or two all will be over, and peace restored. Meanwhile this valley is no place for you, dear one. Go seek my home in the North, where my mother awaits your arrival, for you have promised to become my wife; and you will keep your promise, will you not?

BELLE. Yes, I have promised to be your wife when the war is over. It matters little then what becomes of me. You may take my life! do with it what you will! I'll have no further use for it.

MARSTON. I know the Southern cause fills your heart, so that you have no room in your breast for me, but I am not jealous of that rival, nor do I despair of expelling the foe, and conquering this fair country. Time and my love, will work wonders, for true love is patience, and I will be patient.

BELLE. Poor Marston; you will find the conquest not worth the struggle.

MARSTON. Here is a pass which will enable you and your attendant to cross our lines to-night. [*He gives her a paper*]

BELLE. To-night!

MARSTON. You forget that to-morrow another officer will supersede me in command of this post.

BELLE. Yes! Philip Bligh.

MARSTON. My signature will no longer serve you.

BELLE. True,—but my name upon this paper may excite suspicion.

MARSTON. I have called you by mine.—You appear there as Isabel Marston—will it not be yours in a few weeks—when the rebels are defeated? Pardon my selfish love, its hopes are built on your despair. Oh, Belle, have you not one loving word to give me at this moment? —not one?

BELLE. Nay! forgive me, Marston, if my heart lags behind your rapture. It is not so I should return your love. But when you speak of Northern triumphs do not forget I stood by my father's side at Falling Waters, when your bullets struck him down. Those bullets are here now—here in my breast—they have never been extracted! And if I shrink from your embrace, remember my wounds are tender still. Good-night.

MARSTON. Good-night. [*Going* L., *returns. Kisses her hand*]

BELLE [*extending her hand to him*]. Good night. [*Exit* MARSTON L.] He is gone. Hist! Dan, Uncle Dan!

[*Enter* UNCLE DAN. R.2.E.]

UNCLE DAN. Dass me. Is de road clar? You kin walk in genelums. Dar's nobody to hum 'cept de muskitos.

[*Enter* STONEWALL JACKSON R.3, *followed by* MAJOR RHETT R.1 *and* STUART R.2]

BELLE. Did you hear what passed?

STONEWALL. The intelligence you have obtained is of vital value and saves our army from impending disaster. The presence of McDowell at Front Royal betrays a design to overwhelm us by the concert of these three advancing forces; if they unite we must be annihilated. Rhett, you will ride to-night for Gordonsville: beg General Ewell to join me and put heart into his speed. Combined we can fall on McDowell's division: that broken, Banks at Strasbourg will find himself outflanked and must fall back. Do not lose an hour. [*Exit* RHETT. R.2.E.] Stuart, these despatches from Front Royal should contain important matter. They must be intercepted at any cost. By what road do they come?

BELLE. There is but one—across the mountain.

STUART. I shall need a guide. This part of the country is strange to me. The night is dark: I may fail to find my way: it will be dangerous to ask it.

UNCLE DAN [L.C.]. I know every stump in de country. I'll go along too. You stick by Uncle Dan, he'll put you through, Major.

STONEWALL. Can you ride?

UNCLE DAN. Ride! certainly I kin—in a waggin.

BELLE [*going* C.] I will go. We must use this pass to effect your object, and it enables Isabel Marston and her attendant to cross the lines.

STONEWALL. I cannot permit you to affront so great a peril; the debt our cause owes to you for service is already incalculable. The news you have obtained from day to day of the movements of the Northern troops enabled us to defeat their armies and to distract their operations, but this adventure to-night is too desperate a business.

BELLE [L.C.]. I am a desperate woman, sir.

STONEWALL [R.C.]. If you fail and are taken prisoners, you will be subject to the treatment of spies.

UNCLE DAN [*down* C.]. Oh, Missee, let ole Uncle Dan go. If he's cotch an' hung he aint wort much—nobody aint a waitin' for him when de war's over.

BELLE [*to* STUART]. Are you ready, sir? Look to your arms; we waste time. [*Exit* STUART L.] Good-night, General.

STONEWALL. You are a brave woman, Miss Lamar.

BELLE. Oh, sir, this is not courage.

STONEWALL. What is it, then?

BELLE. Despair. [*Exit.* R.2.E.]

STONEWALL. Strange girl! What is the matter with her?

UNCLE DAN [L.]. I'll tell you, General. She have been an sold herself to dis yar young Captin. She ses to him, you gib me news of wass is gwine on round your side and I'll gib myself to you when dis yar war is ober. Well, sah, now she's afeard it *is* putty nigh ober and pay day is comin' round: so she cal'lates, if she can get killed right off she had rudder close de' count dat way. Dass wass de matter wid dat gal, sah—sure! [*Exeunt.* R.2.E.]

CURTAIN

SCENE II. *A Room in Mount Lamar.*

REMMY [*outside*]. Guard! turn out! [*Roll of drum* L.U.E. *Enter six Soldiers,* L., *and* REMMY] Fall in, boys. Here's a whole regiment of horse riding up the hill—fall in: dhress up. It's the Colorado Rangers themselves, divil a less; wid Colonel Philip Bligh himself at their head. [*A bugle sounds outside*] There they are—steady now—shoulder arrums! [*Enter* PHILIP BLIGH, *followed by* GIRARD *and* GETZ. L.U.E.] Carry arrums!

PHILIP. Where is the officer commanding this post?

REMMY. Is it the Captin, sir? Captin Pike!

[*Enter* MARSTON PIKE. L.U.E.]

MARSTON. Philip!

PHILIP. Marston! [*They embrace*] We have ridden thirty miles since sundown. Have the despatches we expect from Front Royal arrived?

MARSTON. Not yet.

PHILIP [*looking at his watch*]. They are due. Let your guard turn in. [*Men go off* R.U.E.] And while my men rub down and feed their cattle, let yours get ready a hearty meal, for my lads have earned their supper and a good night's rest. [*To* REMMY] I should know your face; where have I seen it?

REMMY. At Romney and Carrick's Ford. And it was not much of my face you saw, for I had you on my back.

PHILIP. You were the fellow that, when I fell, carried me out of the fire.

REMMY. One good turn, colonel, desarves another. Your honour carried me into it.

PHILIP. And as soon as you dumped me behind a ditch you scrambled—

REMMY. Back, for fear I'd lose my place in it, sir.

PHILIP. Are you as fond of a fight as ever?

REMMY. I don't know. It's so long since I had a taste of one, sir! But now your honour is come, plaze God, there will be sticks out and wigs on the green.

PHILIP. Bring lights and set me a table there. [REMMY *and two men go off* L.H. *door*] Girard, spread out my maps.

[*Enter* HONOR MCQUADE, R.H.3.E., *with a brown jug in one hand, a roast turkey under one arm, and under the other a table-cloth and a bottle, a basket of knives and forks in the other hand, with long loaf of bread, also in the basket. She is followed by a coloured girl with a table*]

HONOR [R.]. Put it down there!

PHILIP [L.]. Why, Honor, you have not been five minutes in Mount Lamar, and already you have pillaged the larder and carried the cellar by assault. Stop! I want that table to hold my maps.

[GIRARD *advances* L.]

HONOR. Then ye won't get an inch of it. [*Standing on the defense*] Since midday not a bit of sup has crossed your lips—barrin' a dhrink of cowld water you tuk at Cross Keys. You thought I wasn't watching ye—go on now —you'll get no maps on this table till you clear that turkey off of it. [*During the above, aided by the girl, she has put the food on the table* L.H. PHILIP *listens to her with a grim smile*]

PHILIP. Well. [*Points to bureau,* L.H.] Place them there awhile. [*He and* MARSTON *speak apart with* GIRARD *and* GETZ, *while* PHILIP *unbuckles his sword. Sits*] See here. I am commanded to vacate this post at once and occupy a gorge upon our right called the Whitestone Gap. The mountain road by which Frémont is now advancing over the Shenandoah range lies through this gorge. A bridge spans the river at this spot. If the enemy get possession of that bridge they can lock up Frémont and 20,000 men in the mountains beyond, and leave themselves free to deal with McDowell and with Banks.

GIRARD. I know the bridge well: it is commanded by a spur in the hillside above. An old log cabin marks the spot. A few hours'

work will plant a battery there. Whoever holds the cabin holds the bridge.

MARSTON. My Company are ready to march.

PHILIP. How far is it from this place?

MARSTON. About twelve miles by the road— but there is a shorter path through the woods, if we can find a guide.

PHILIP. I will ride over there to-morrow, and inspect the position.

[*Enter* REMMY *with candles. Places on table* R., *meets* HONOR]

REMMY. Honor! Honor McQuade!

HONOR [*dropping the turkey*]. Remmy!—bad cess to you for making me dhrop the bird—if it had been the bottle I'd never have forgiven you.

PHILIP. What! Remmy! have you found an old friend in my sturdy henchwoman?

REMMY. Two years ago I left her in Belfast, when I came across the sea to make my fortune. We broke a sixpence betune us. Where's your pledge, Honor?—have you got it still— here is mine?

HONOR. D'ye think I could go through the world wid thruppence?

REMMY. Is that all you have to say to me after two years' separation? Haven't you a dacent word to fling me?

HONOR. Go down to my wagon that's hitched up to the kitchen dure, and wather the mule.

REMMY. Well, that same mule and meself will make a pair for you to dhrive, for if he's only half an ass—sure I'm the other half. [*Exit.* L.U.E.]

PHILIP [*rising*]. Getz, you will see the men well housed. You, Girard, take a guide, and with a dozen scouts ride for the mountain road by which this officer with despatches from McDowell is expected. [*Exeunt* GETZ *and* GIRARD R.U.E.] Honor, you can leave us now. Remmy is waiting for you outside. Go—say a kind word to him.

HONOR. Is it to the likes of that fellow! Sure I'm a County Down girl, an' I'd never bemane the North by takin' up with a poor scrap o' the County Cork like him.

PHILIP. Well, go; tell him so.

HONOR. 'Deed an' I will. [*Exit* L.H.U.E.]

PHILIP. Every country has its North and South you see. Come, Marston, 'tis seven years since we parted at West Point. [*They sit at table*] Where have you been quartered during that time?

MARSTON. In Florida and on the Gulf Coast chiefly.

PHILIP. I in the West. A glorious school for cavalry! Would you had been with me! Seven years; they seem like seven days. You recollect Sam Noyes?

MARSTON. Well.

PHILIP. He graduated in my year. And Claiborne, and young Goss?

MARSTON. Yes. Very well.

PHILIP. They all went South to join the rebel ranks. Goss fell at Shiloh. A letter from his wife was found upon him, which proved her to be a Southern spy living at Washington on Confederate pay.

MARSTON. What was her fate?

PHILIP. Fort Lafayette. She was a woman, and they spared her the penalty of death. False clemency, Marston. When the serpent coils to take its spring, do we regard its sex ere we set a heel upon its venomous fangs? By these Dalilahs our Samson of the North is shorn of half his might. There is not a plan resolved in Washington—there's not a movement of our armies discussed there in secret, but it is betrayed to one of them and transmitted straight to Richmond. These women have placed their beauty at the service of the South. General Crinoline at the Capitol defeats the operations of General McClellan in the peninsula. There is more than one Judas amongst our statesmen at the Council board who betray their country with a kiss.

MARSTON. And thus betrayed, how can it prosper and prevail?

PHILIP. A Christian cause will prosper and prevail above all treachery. Judas went and hanged himself, but the cause he betrayed survives for ever.

[*Re-enter* GIRARD. L.U.E.]

GIRARD. The bearer of despatches from Front Royal has been waylaid in the mountains in our rear, close to our lines. His papers have been taken by the enemy.

MARSTON. It is impossible. No one could pass our outposts without detection.

GIRARD. 'Tis positive. The wounded man is here. It happened scarce three miles from this place, and not half an hour ago. A shot from the roadside brought our man and horse to the ground, where he lay stunned awhile. On recovering his senses he found a fellow bending over him and searching for the despatches in his breast. Though badly hurt, he drew his pistol and shot the rebel down. A woman who stood by caught up the papers, and flying through the woods made for the river.

[*Enter* REMMY, L.U.E.]

REMMY. She's caught, never fear, yer honor, she's caught.—Thanks to yourself, Captain, that posted our boys under cover. She thought the river bank was clear and free o' them an' she was within two hundred yards of it when up jumped a blue fringe of our chaps and cut her off; but she doubled like a hare back again into the woods, and the boys afther her like a pack o' dogs.

PHILIP. You said she was taken.

REMMY. Well, it is all one, colonel. She is in the trap. There's no escape for her, barrin' she's a bird. [*Exit.* L.U.E.]

PHILIP [*cross to* L.]. Is the man, her companion, dead?

GIRARD. No, he will recover; he is here.

PHILIP. Bring him in. [*Enter* MAJOR STUART, L.U.E. *guarded;* GETZ *with him;* STUART *is wounded*] Your name?

STUART. Patrick Henry Stuart.

PHILIP. A rebel spy, ha!

STUART. A major in the Confederate Army.

PHILIP. Is that your uniform?

STUART. No, sir; it is a disguise. I knew the penalty of failure when I assumed it, and I am ready to meet my fate.

PHILIP. You know then—Major Stuart, you have six hours to live.

STUART. Six hours! You are liberal! When we take one of your spies he is tried, condemned, and executed within thirty minutes.

PHILIP. Our justice proceeds with more deliberation and in this case we employ more ceremony; for you will have a companion; and that she may share your fate requires approval from headquarters.

STUART. You will not dare to—execute—a woman!

PHILIP [*rising*]. Spies and assassins have no sex, sir. By the blood of my comrades shed by these vipers on our hearths, you shall share her fate—and she yours.

STUART. I shall recall that oath to your memory, Philip Bligh.

PHILIP. Take him away. [*Exit* STUART *guarded, with* GIRARD. L.U.E.] See to his wound Getz, let him be well cared for; he is a brave fellow. [*Exit* GETZ R.D.] Marston, you recollect that man at college?

MARSTON [c.]. Very well. He was a slim and sickly boy ten years ago. You nursed him through a fever.

PHILIP [*at desk* L.]. And you also, Marston. I recollect the night his mother came from Alabama. She was a widow and he her only son. We were watching by his bedside when she entered his room. The doctor told her we had saved his life. She said nothing, but after bending over his pillow, she raised her eyes full of tears and turned them on us—from one to the other—with a speechless blessing in them I have never forgotten. Oh God—if she could see us now! Sit there, and write, my hand is not steady to-night. [MARSTON *sits* L.H. PHILIP *dictates, while* MARSTON *writes at desk* L.]

"General, your despatches have not arrived. The bearer was intercepted on his road hither, and robbed by two rebel spies. They have been captured. I await your orders, to bring them before a court martial. One of them is a woman. The clemency heretofore extended to assassins of her sex encourages their trade of murder. The North continues to pour out its blood like water, the widows and orphans of our dead, pleading for the wives and children of our soldiers, claim a stern and prompt application of the extreme penalty of death to this person, in accordance with the articles of war." [*Enter* GIRARD R.U.E.] Well?

GIRARD. The woman has been taken.

PHILIP. I will see her presently.

MARSTON. This is done.

PHILIP [*crossing to and fro*]. Have you recovered the despatches?

GIRARD [*while* PHILIP *reads silently the letter* MARSTON *has written*]. No. Either she destroyed them during her flight, or she passed them to some companion whom we have failed to discover. Our lads beat the woods thoroughly, but found nothing there but an old negro and a blind dog.

PHILIP. Good! That is well. [*Writes*] There—. Girard, you will ride with this letter to headquarters; and bring his answer. Take my spare charger; he is fresh. I expect you back by daylight.

GIRARD. We have discovered the means whereby this woman and her companion succeeded in their attempt. They were furnished with a forged pass—here it is—it was the only paper found upon her.

PHILIP. This is a common trick. [*Takes the pass from* GIRARD]

GIRARD. Farewell—Colonel! [*Exit* GIRARD L.U.E.]

PHILIP. Farewell.

MARSTON [*aside*]. A forged pass! a shapeless terror seizes me—it cannot be that—

PHILIP. Why—it is in your name! Your handwriting too is closely imitated—see—it would have deceived anyone; and this woman calls herself by your name—Isabel Marston—what impudence! Why do you look so white? What shakes you thus? Speak, man!

MARSTON. Philip!

PHILIP. Ay.

MARSTON. This is no forgery.

PHILIP. No forgery! what is it then?

MARSTON. I wrote it.

PHILIP. You! Why then it was stolen from the person to whom you gave it!

MARSTON. No, I fear—I—I—I cannot tell.

PHILIP. Why, Marston, what is this? Stand fast, man: look straight and speak. What have you done?

MARSTON. I gave that pass to the woman I love, that she might escape.

PHILIP. Escape! from whence?

MARSTON. From Stonewall Jackson's camp.

PHILIP. You have maintained relations with the enemy?

MARSTON. No—I—she—met me—sometimes—

PHILIP. Where?

MARSTON. Below, by the river bank—at our outpost.

PHILIP. To which vile tryst you stole down to betray your country. Leagued with our deadliest foes, you gave them notice of our movements; told them the strength of each division, the number of our guns.

MARSTON. No, Philip. She accepted that pass that she might seek my mother's house in the North.

PHILIP. In company with Major Stuart? And this enterprise to waylay and secure these papers, all were accidents upon the road to where your mother lives? How came they by the knowledge these despatches were expected? From you! was it not so? How did they know the time and place to execute their purpose? Ha! only your silence answers me! Fool, dupe, and traitor!

MARSTON. Spare me, Philip.

PHILIP. I would sooner spare this rebel officer, for he but did his duty. You betrayed yours. He staked his life—'twas his to stake. You staked the lives of your comrades. You staked the fortunes of your cause and country against the kisses of a wanton—betrayed a nation's trust for her lies—exchanged your honour for her infamy. Sentry! [*Sentry comes on* R.U.E., *receives orders and off* R.U.E.] Pass the word to send a guard here. You are a prisoner, sir. Give up your sword. You must take your place beside your accomplice.

MARSTON [*drawing his sword*]. If she is captured, do you think I would take any other?

PHILIP [*contemplating him sternly*]. He has no conscience of his crime.

MARSTON. 'Tis you have no humanity. Cold, stern, unfeeling: because you have never loved. Ah! you have no heart, or you would pity me.

PHILIP. I have never loved!! There is not in the sum of all your sighs enough to fill my bosom with one breath. Women to you are toys, and as a child you cry for them: such is the measure of your puny sorrow. Would you know how men do love—can suffer? Listen. Not long ago, I met one to whom all that was good and noble within me went forth at once to know if her virtue could equal her beauty. And as my soul stood beside hers, I thanked God that he had made a woman so perfect, and had given her to me: for she loved me and became my wife—not my companion—but my happier, better self, my pride, the casket where I stored my best-loved follies, my secret hopes, my jewelled dreams. Brief ecstasy! This war broke out and I was summoned to my duty. She was of Southern family; they had espoused the cause of Secession with vehemence, and their blood ran hotly in her veins. Pointing to many officers who deserted their flag, she urged me to follow their example. I refused. She left me: fled to her family in the South, and waited for me to join her there. What I suffered, God and I alone know; but He led me to the altar of my country, and, standing beside it, I plucked out my heart, and offered up a human sacrifice. That is why I have none now to pity you. [*Going* L.H. *He takes the sword*]

MARSTON. Then let me suffer, but spare her I love. Not for my sake, but for the sake of her who wears your name.

PHILIP. She wears my name no longer. Her family obtained a divorce and she resumed her own. Her name is Isabel Lamar.

MARSTON. Lamar!

PHILIP. She's the mistress of this house.

[*Enter* HONOR *very pale.* R.U.E.]

HONOR. Master, oh, Master Philip.

PHILIP. What ails the girl? why, Honor, have you seen a ghost?

HONOR. I wish it was a ghost I saw; they brought her in amongst them, torn, bleeding at every limb, her long hair wild about her shoulders; and her face as white as mine is now, but not from fear.

PHILIP. Are you mad?

[*Enter* REMMY. L.U.E.]

REMMY. Hurroo! I tould ye she'd be caught. Bring her along. 'Twas my boys did it.

HONOR. Then my bitter curse on them that laid a finger on her.

PHILIP. On whom?

HONOR. Look there!

[*Enter* BELLE LAMAR *followed by a crowd of soldiers*]

PHILIP. Isabel! my wife!

[*Her coat is torn off, her hair dishevelled, her limbs bleeding. She stands at bay, the soldiers guarding her.* HONOR *runs to her and, falling at her feet, clasps her dress.* PHILIP *aghast, stands gazing at her, she at him.* MARSTON *has fallen into a chair, with his head buried in his hands, when* BELLE *faces* PHILIP—]

TABLEAU AND QUICK CURTAIN

ACT TWO

Music to rise.
Scene—the same as Act I. *Scene* 2.

HONOR, *seated near the door,* R. REMMY *is walking before it.* GIRARD *stands* C. *dusty and travel-stained.* PHILIP *at table,* L.H., *on which papers, maps, &c. are spread. He is reading a despatch. Sentry at the back.*

PHILIP [*at table*]. You have made good speed. So; as you were saying—

GIRARD. When I arrived the generals of the division were holding a council of war. The camp was in confusion—the enemy had by some means obtained timely information of our flank movement, and our plans were all disordered.

PHILIP [*reading*]. "This fresh disaster is the fruit of treachery. The article of war concerning spies and traitors makes no exceptions as to sex. Let its penalty be sternly applied to those prisoners in your hands, and let your execution be prompt. We rely on you. There is no citizen in whom the Government of the United States reposes more faith, no officer in whom the army places more confidence. Your mother country will never forget the services her noblest sons have rendered in her hour of need."

GIRARD. Shall I get the men under arms at once? The court may meet here for the despatch of these prisoners. Getz, Marston, and myself will serve. Shall it be so.

PHILIP. Yes. [*Exit* GIRARD. R.U.E.]

[HONOR *rises and crosses to* PHILIP]

HONOR [*pointing to sentry*]. Send that man away.

PHILIP. No.

HONOR. I want to spake to you.

PHILIP. Well, speak.

HONOR. Not while he is by.

PHILIP. I dare not listen when he is gone.

HONOR. If he is here to guard the prisoners let him go inside; they will be better watched under his eye.

PHILIP. My fear is not for their safekeeping, but for my own.

HONOR. You will not let her come to this?

PHILIP. I am powerless. Bound by these fetters I have forged for myself, I await, my own victim—the executioner of the justice I have invoked. [*A pause*] You have spoken with her. What does she say?

HONOR. Nothin'. She holds her head betune her hands. I cannot get a word out of her good or bad, only broken sobs an' bitter taunts.

PHILIP. Against me?

HONOR. No. Agin herself. Your name never crossed her lips—but once—and then she axed if you would see her.

PHILIP. To what end? She has made us strangers.

HONOR. Strangers! Oh, Master Philip—is it the girl that gave you her pure troth? the wife that laid her head upon your breast? A man and woman that have truly loved each other never can be strangers, God forbid. [*His head falls between his hands. She goes to door* L.H., *pushes it open*] Come in.

[*Enter* BELLE LAMAR. *The Sentinel opposes his rifle to stay her*]

PHILIP [*to the sentinel*]. Stand within the room. [*Exit the sentinel.* R.D.3. E.]

HONOR. That is what I wanted. [*Exit, taking* REMMY *with her.* L.U.E.]

PHILIP. You wish to speak to me?

BELLE. I come to plead for mercy. I have no other claim upon your pity than what a very miserable and prostrate creature can prefer; but you may know what torture she suffers at

this moment when it wrings from her a supplication to you.

PHILIP [*aside*]. More miserable and more
prostrate is the wretch whose heart crouches
like a dog at her voice, and trembles before
her penitence.

BELLE. Your pride can measure how low
mine has fallen when I stoop as I do now to
ask your pity. And you should know what torture I suffer at this moment, when it wrings
from me a supplication to you. I dare not in-
voke our past, and yet I build my hopes of
clemency out of the wreck I have made there.
Oh save me, Philip! from the rising tide of
terror gathering round me—save one who never
felt shame or remorse till now.

PHILIP. If you could recall that past—if you
could undo the wrongs you have inflicted on
one who has loved you.

BELLE. With all my heart I would. I look
back with horror on what I have done. Help
me to repair it. One word of yours can do it.
Remember your own struggle between love and
duty [*She kneels beside him*]; do not judge a
weaker soul by the strength of yours.

PHILIP. What would you have me do?

BELLE. To you alone he confessed how sorely
I had tempted him—but not how basely he had
been deceived. You alone can prove his guilt.
Do not be his accuser.

PHILIP. But sparing him will not save you!

BELLE. I do not ask for that, but do not let
him suffer for my wrong: do not make me utterly base by rendering me his executioner.

PHILIP. What! do you dare to kneel to me
for your lover's life?

BELLE [*starting up and gazing at him*]. My
God! he thought I was pleading for my own.

PHILIP [*rising*]. Before you speak, before
you avow to me your love for him—hear me—
they tell me that you have the right to give
yourself to another without shame or sin, because the law has made you free. A few words
were spoken over us two years ago. We signed
a page, and were told that we were man and
wife. Time passed, you left me, and then some
other words were spoken; the page was torn
and we were told that we were strangers,—
your life that had grown part of me was
wrenched away; but hearts are not divorced by
forms of law, and mine has followed you—too
honest, now to deny its worship, too proud to
deny its suffering. Let this confession protect
me against yours. Now speak Isabel—you come
to plead for mercy—show it.

BELLE. If I loved this man, do you think I
would descend to beg his life of you?

PHILIP. And yet you promised to become
his wife?

BELLE. Yes.

PHILIP. You were to be the price paid for
his treachery?

BELLE. Yes. He accepted the bribe you refused.

PHILIP. And in him you may see what a
crawling thing you would have made of me.
For he is appointed one of the court martial,
charged to pass judgment on you, and on
your companion.

BELLE. He will not discharge the office.

PHILIP. He must. Here is the commission in
which the members of the Court are named.

BELLE. Then he will escape to the Southern
lines.

PHILIP. And leave you to your fate. So!
They will gain a renegade and a coward. We
shall be quit of a traitor and for the sake of
such a man, you ask me to become his accomplice, and yours, by conniving at his evasion.

BELLE. I ask you not to betray a confession
confided to you by a dear friend. I know you
have invoked the stern penalty the laws of war
apply to my case, and a just Providence elects
the judge to be the lover I betrayed and the
executioner to be the husband I deserted.

PHILIP. Oh, cruel and unnatural conflict—
where right is wrong, virtue is crime, love is
hate; where noble natures that God made dear
companions must meet in deadly feud midst
havoc and confusion. Oh, we are drunk on
venom whose mortal poison permeates the
world and drives us mad. [*Crosses* R.H.]

[*Enter* UNCLE DAN. R.U.E.]

Ay! There it is. Where do you come from?

UNCLE DAN. Out yander.

PHILIP. The Rebel Camp?

UNCLE DAN. Round 'bout dar.

PHILIP. And you deserted those who come to
shed their blood for your sake, and consorted
with your bitterest foes and ours.

UNCLE DAN. Dunno 'zackly—wot all dat
is Curnel, an' I guess Uncle Dan is too old to
larn.

PHILIP. What brings you back?

UNCLE DAN. Ole blind Sal. You rec'lect de
pinter dog—not good for much—like me? Wall,
when your folks come along up de Valley last
fall time—the missus dere she would not stop
in Mount Lamar and all de slaves was tole to
go—for dey was free. Yes, Curnel, jest so.
T'odders dey went—dey clar'd right out—all
but me. Dar was no Christians left in dis old
Virginny home cept Uncle Dan, dat pinter dog,
and de picturs agin de wall! Den I ses to Sal;
we've got our freedom—dars whats de matter,
wot am you gwine to do wi' your'n. De blind
dog licked de tears off my face, and den sniffen
round until she struck a track her ole heart
knew so well; she whined me on to follow—so
I did ober many a mile until we found Miss
Belle. Wha' she is, Sal and me's to hum, so
we're come 'long here, Curnel—dass wass de
matter. Glad to see you lookin' well, sah.

PHILIP [*aside*]. How can I blame him—for

even so, my heart has followed her in love, with slavery. [*To* UNCLE DAN] Last night you were in the woods when she was hunted down by my men. It was to you she gave the lost despatch. [UNCLE DAN *looks amazed from* BELLE *to* PHILIP] It was through your hands it passed to the enemy. You are the traitor! You!

DAN [*a light breaking in on him*]. Eh! oh! Dar's a fact!—golly—yack—I see you two ha' been callatin' togeder dat she kin get off, ef you put de scratch on somebody else.—I'm de feller— You got him now Curnel sure— Ole Dan's to blame. I'll bar it—let her stan' from under. Oh laws, massy, bless you bot' for tinkin o' me.

[*Enter* GIRARD. R.U.E. *down* R.C.]

GIRARD. The men are under arms—we wait your orders.

PHILIP. Let the officers be summoned [GIRARD *goes up and off* R.U.E. *To* BELLE] You may buy my silence as to Marston's share in it on one condition.

BELLE [L.]. Name it.

PHILIP [R.]. Save yourself. The officers, my comrades who will be your judges, are ignorant of the relations you have borne to me. Tell them you are my wife.

BELLE. Your wife! But I am not so now.

PHILIP. I shall not deny the claim [*Cross to* L.H.]

BELLE. What then?

PHILIP. What then? Then you are free to go.

BELLE. And Marston?

PHILIP. He—is free to follow you.

BELLE. Is that all you had to say? [*Going* R.H.]

PHILIP. That is all.

[*Exit* BELLE R.3.E.]

She loves him, and is ashamed to say so.

[*Enter* GETZ, GIRARD, *two Officers, soldiers,* REMMY, R.U.E. *As soldiers come on,* DAN *assumes attitude of dignified resolution and resignation*]

DAN. Dem sogers is for me. I'm gwine to be a prisoner.

GIRARD [*pointing to* DAN]. Clear that man out.

DAN. Me? Clar me out?

REMMY [*throwing him out*]. Now then, ould Tarbox, there's room for you outside.

DAN. Dere's a mistake. I'm a prisoner—ax de Curnel whar I'm to go.

REMMY. To the divil if you like!

DAN [*as he is going out*]. Curnel, when I'm wanted, I'll be dar—down below.

REMMY. No doubt of it. [*Turns him out* R.U.E.]

GIRARD. Where's Marston?

[*Enter* MARSTON L.2.E.]

MARSTON. Here!

[PHILIP *turns at his voice.* MARSTON *is very pale*]

PHILIP [*sitting at desk*]. Proceed. I will sit here. Captain Girard you will act as Judge Advocate. [*He writes.* GIRARD, GETZ, *and* MARSTON *sit*]

GIRARD. Bring in the prisoners.

[*Enter* REMMY, *then enter* MAJOR STUART *and two guards, then* BELLE *followed by two guards.* GETZ *writes at table,* L. *Enter* HONOR]

HONOR [*aside to* BELLE]. He is not wid the rest of 'em! What does that mane?

BELLE [*aside to her*]. Be silent, whatever happens.

GIRARD. Your name is Patrick Stuart?

STUART. Patrick Henry Stuart.

GETZ. You are charged—

STUART. Pardon me if I delay this investigation for one moment. The gentlemen yonder [*Points to the soldiers*] who searched me dutifully last night to see I had no arms concealed about my person, relieved me of my watch and my cigar case. The watch they are welcome to —as I shall not need it to count many hours— but the cigars I do regret.

GETZ. Accept mine. [*Offers his case*]

STUART. You are very kind. I'll take one only. It will last my time. [*Takes a cigar, then turning to* BELLE] —Will you permit me to smoke? [BELLE *bows*] Thank you. Now gentlemen, I am yours. [GETZ *gives him a light*]

GETZ. We desire to ascertain from whom you received the intelligence by which you were enabled to make this attempt upon our communications.

STUART. I do not quite see the drift of that question.

GETZ. The drift, sir, is this. We had rather detect a traitor in our camp than punish a spy in yours.

GIRARD. Come, Major. My office enables me to tender you a friendly counsel. Confess the source from which you obtained this information. We are satisfied that you have some correspondent in our ranks. Let that person take the place where you and that lady stand. Weigh the matter well—we offer you life for life!

STUART. We were fellow students, gentlemen —[GIRARD *and* GETZ *bow in assent*]—and side by side we learned out of the same book the duty of a soldier: there must have been one lesson I overlooked or skipped—I never learned how to turn informer. [*Bows and returns to his place,* R.]

GIRARD. Remember, Stuart, it is life for life.

STUART. No, Girard, it is life for infamy.

PHILIP [*aside*]. And—he—Marston is silent. Coward! Coward!

GIRARD [*to* BELLE]. Madam, upon this pass found in your possession, you are called Isabel Marston. Is that your name?

BELLE. No.

GIRARD. What is your name then?

BELLE. I refuse to answer.

GIRARD. How came you by this paper?

BELLE. I forged it.

GETZ. You presume upon the tenderness with which your sex is regarded by ours. Dismiss all such delusion. It will not save you from sharing the fate that awaits your companion. The Council of War has resolved upon applying to your crime the extreme penalty of death.

PHILIP [aside]. How she must despise him!

GIRARD. You heard the offer we made to Major Stuart?

BELLE. Yes! You heard his answer.

GIRARD. It was the answer of a soldier! but you, a woman, have not a soldier's honour to vindicate. We implore you to spare us the performance of a cruel but inevitable duty; spare us by saving yourself. We offer you your life in exchange for the name of your accomplice.

BELLE. My life, sir, is the most worthless thing about me. Take it! I had no accomplice.

MARSTON. 'Tis false!—I am he!

GETZ } [together]. Marston!
GIRARD }

MARSTON. I accept your offer—life for life. I am the traitor you are in search of.

PHILIP [to GIRARD, GETZ, and OFFICERS, who have risen in amazement and confusion]. Be seated, gentlemen. [MARSTON draws his sword and placing it on the table, L.H., crosses to the side of STUART, constituting himself a prisoner] Sergeant of the guard, Captain Marston Pike is your prisoner. Your avowal, sir, will fail to serve its purpose. It is not her act but yours, and we cannot attribute to her the benefit of your confession.

MARSTON. For myself, gentlemen, I ask neither your pity nor your favour, for were I still sitting there beside you, I should show myself no mercy; but here is one who disdains to seek the shelter one word from her proud lips would secure. Her name is Isabel Lamar, and she is your Colonel's wife. [GETZ, GIRARD, and the OFFICERS rise, bow and turn towards PHILIP, whose head has fallen between his hands] She refused to shield her treason behind his loyalty, or to purchase your mercy with his shame.

PHILIP [raising his head]. I ask your pardon, Marston Pike. I did you wrong just now. Gentlemen, the evidence is complete. Sergeant of the guard, re-conduct your prisoners.

[Exeunt MARSTON, BELLE, and STUART. HONOR and the guards withdraw. REMMY remains on guard at door R.H.]

Well, sirs, it is my duty to ask you,—Is Major Stuart guilty?

ALL [bowing]. Guilty.

PHILIP. Is Captain Marston Pike guilty?

ALL [bowing]. Guilty.

PHILIP. Isabel Lamar—is—she— [He hesitates: they look at each other] Speak, men—is she guilty or not guilty?

GIRARD. Colonel Bligh, we respectfully decline to answer that question.

PHILIP. It is your—duty—gentlemen, to bring in a verdict. [He falls in a chair]

GETZ. Then we fail in our duty, and we are prepared to suffer the consequences. [They salute PHILIP, and are going out R.U.E.]

PHILIP. Getz—Girard! [He holds out one hand to them, they advance, clasp it silently and then go out] Brave hearts! their gentleness unmans mine. And Marston, too, no craven: he proved a noble match for young Stuart. Then, above all, my lion-hearted love, my own brave Belle!—Must all this wealth of human nature be squandered?

[Enter a sentinel, who speaks to REMMY in dumb show]

REMMY. Plaze your honour, there's two officers wid a flag of truce outside.

BLIGH. Pass the flag. I will see them here.

REMMY. Guard, turn out.

[Voices are heard outside, crying, "Guard, turn out." A sharp, short roll of the drum. Enter STONEWALL JACKSON and RHETT R.U.E.]

BLIGH. You are welcome, sir.

STONEWALL. If my eye has not lost its measure of a soldier, you are known to us in the South as gallant Bligh.

PHILIP. If I mistake not, sir, you bear a name enshrined with mournful pride in the heart of the North. Are you not known to us as the General Stonewall Jackson?

REMMY [starting]. Oh, murther! [Nearly drops his rifle, then recovering it, presents arms]

[Enter HONOR with a tray, door L.3.E., on which are glasses and bottles of liquor. She places them on the table]

PHILIP. Be seated, General. [At table]

STONEWALL. This is Major Rhett. [They bow]

PHILIP. Gentlemen, in what can I serve you?

HONOR. There's Irish and Monongahela.

STONEWALL. The major will represent me, and give my regards to both. If you will permit me, I prefer a glass of water. [RHETT fills]

PHILIP. I pledge you a speedy end to the war.

STONEWALL. May it end with honour to both sides. [HONOR, who has concealed a glass of spirits, stands with her back to REMMY, who drinks it] I have learned the capture you made last night. Here is the intercepted despatch you see its seal is unbroken. In exchange for Major Stuart and Miss Lamar we offer to restore this paper and two of your field-officers now on parole in my camp.

PHILIP. Prisoners under sentence of death are not subject to exchange.

STONEWALL. Has the lady been placed upon her trial?

PHILIP. She stands accused; but she is not condemned. My comrades refused to utter any verdict.

STONEWALL. You will treat for her release then?

PHILIP. Can I do so?

STONEWALL. It is an honorable weakness that prompts your doubt.

PHILIP. It is no weakness, sir.

STONEWALL. If she were not your wife, would you hesitate? Your professional honour opposes her claim upon your human nature. Fear makes you cruel! Your comrades, showing more tenderness for you than you dare to show for yourself, convict you of that kind of hypocrisy called the vanity of virtue.

REMMY [aside]. Honor!

HONOR [aside]. Well!

REMMY [aside]. Father Maguire never spoke finer.

HONOR [aside]. Whisht.

PHILIP [after reflection]. If she will give her word to withdraw to some Northern City, there to abide until the end of the war— I will beg my General to accept the terms you propose.

STONEWALL. Will you allow me to see her?

PHILIP. Yes. Honor, request her to come. [Exit HONOR R.D.3.E.] I will write the pass [Goes to desk L.H.] which will convey her in safety to headquarters. [Writes at desk]

REMMY [aside]. Well to be sure. I can't get over it! And that is the man that gave us such a fine batin' a while ago. I've got a bullet belonging to him in the small o' me back; and he lookin' so paceable there! It is them quiet ones is the divil.

[Enter BELLE. R.3.E. HONOR follows her]

BELLE. Ah! [She runs to JACKSON]

STONEWALL. My poor child, you are pale.

BELLE. I knew you would not forsake me.

STONEWALL. Why do you weep?

BELLE [kneeling]. I am so glad to see you. It is your kindness moves my heart, and overcomes me! Don't mind these tears, I'm not in the habit of crying—like this.

[RHETT exits up L.U.E.]

BELLE [after looking eagerly and furtively around to be assured she is not overheard].— The despatch reached you safely.

STONEWALL. Safely, yes. Here it is, untouched. I bring it back.

BELLE. It cost us dearly, sir.

STONEWALL. Too dearly, child. I cannot pay the price—your life—and so I have brought it here to ransom you.

BELLE. And Stuart—and—Marston—

STONEWALL. One at a time.

BELLE. They are condemned to death.

STONEWALL. Every soldier is—he survives only by the reprieve of the All Merciful. Lis-

ten, my dear child, I have obtained your release. Bligh will petition his superior officer to grant you a parole and a safe conduct to the North where you must remain, until the unhappy struggle is over.

BELLE. The North! and you would counsel me to desert my country?

STONEWALL. I am not unmindful of the service you have rendered it. But such service is not a woman's business. The field of battle is not her place. There are some weapons we soldiers consider to be too inhuman for civilized warfare—such appear to me the use of agents like you, my child! Do not think me ungrateful or unkind to speak thus! What is your position at this moment? You have been capable of inflicting on the North many mortal injuries, and you see they shrink from inflicting on you the penalty. This is not honorable strife! A woman's country is her husband's home— her cause, his happiness—her only place in the world, his side; and death alone should part them.

BELLE. Right or wrong?

STONEWALL. A husband is a king in a wife's eyes, and a king can do no wrong.

BELLE. I will do as you direct.

STONEWALL. No—as your heart directs—it is a noble, pure, and loving one.

[Re-enter GIRARD, who speaks aside to PHILIP. L.U.E.]

GIRARD. The men are under arms—the firing party is told off—all is ready.

REMMY [to HONOR]. Murther alive—did ye hear?

HONOR. What?

REMMY. Whisht!

[PHILIP advances]

STONEWALL. She consents to accept your terms—she is ready to depart.

PHILIP. There is the pass. Remmy, this lady is in your charge,—you will be her escort. See the horses are saddled and ready within an hour.

STONEWALL [to PHILIP]. There, Colonel, is the despatch. [Hands him the paper] Farewell, my dear child. Heaven bless and keep you! Farewell, sir, I thank you for your courtesy!

PHILIP. I am sorry, General, to refuse you anything. Farewell. [JACKSON and RHETT go out. R.U.E., also GIRARD] Remmy!

REMMY. Sir.

PHILIP. I will order two horses to be saddled at once,—my grey charger, Lexington, will carry the lady. Proceed directly to headquarters at Strasbourg; there she will receive a safe conduct to carry her northward. Here is the pass. Can you read?

REMMY. Not a word.

PHILIP. Can you ride?

REMMY. Can a duck swim? [He gives him the pass]

BELLE. And these young men who share my prison yonder—Marston and Stuart. What is to be done with them?

PHILIP [*turning away to the table and taking up the despatch and opening it*]. Let your own fate concern you. Leave theirs to me. Farewell. [*Exit* L.U.E.]

REMMY. They are to be shot—and you are not to know it.

BELLE. You are sure of this?

REMMY. Is not the firing party tould off and ready for the bloody work?

BELLE. I cannot leave him.

HONOR. Yet, what can your presence do? you cannot save the lad: you can only stay to witness what you cannot prevent.

REMMY. Oh, Honor! by the piper, I believe I've got it. Read that paper, Miss, and tell me what is on it. [*Hands to* BELLE *the pass given to him by* PHILIP]

BELLE [*reads*]. Pass the bearer, belonging to my command, going in charge of a prisoner from Mount Lamar to Strasbourg. Signed, Philip Bligh.

REMMY. Give that to my captin inside, and let him go well yourself in my place.

BELLE. In your place?

HONOR [*throwing her arms around* REMMY's *neck*]. Oh, Remmy, kiss me!

BELLE. But if he takes your place, you will suffer death for this act.

REMMY. Ah, Miss, I'd be hung every morning if I could go through this on my way to the gallows.

BELLE [*aside*]. Is there no escape without accepting the sacrifice of this poor fellow's life? Ah! Yes! [*Goes to desk* L.H. *and writes*]

HONOR. Remmy, dear.

REMMY. That's me—say it again, dear.

HONOR. Remmy, darlin'!

REMMY. Don't say it anymore—it will make me too fond of the blackguard.

HONOR. I don't want you to die, Remmy.

REMMY. I'm that way of thinkin' myself, Honor.

HONOR. Is there no chance of escape?

REMMY. The rope might break, dear.

HONOR. Oh!

[BELLE *having written a paper similar to that on which* PHILIP *has written the pass, is seen to compare the two, while she approaches* REMMY *and* HONOR *with the other paper.* HONOR *starts and turns, standing between* BELLE *and* REMMY, *breathless and panting*]

No! I—I—can't—Miss—I can't spare him— oh forgive me. I couldn't let him do it.

BELLE. I do not mean that he should. Take back the paper. Heaven bless your brave and honest heart. [*Gives him the paper*]

[*Enter* UNCLE DAN R.U.E.]

DAN. De horses is all ready.

BELLE. Where are they?

DAN. Hitched afore the door.

BELLE. Take them round to the back of the house. I do not wish to parade my departure. Go! At once! [*Exit* DAN R.U.E.] And you will wait here while I take leave of my fellow prisoners. [*Exit* R.D.1.]

[*Dead March and muffled drums are heard in the orchestra*]

HONOR. What's the matter, Remmy? There is somethin' quare goin' on outside.

REMMY. Yes, dear.

HONOR. What is it? Why do you look so wild?

REMMY. Its nothin at all—only— oh, Honor, tell the Mistress to hurry. Let her get away out o' this—quick—before—

HONOR. Before what?

REMMY. It's the muffled drums you hear! It's the Dead March!

HONOR [*looking off at back* R.U.E.]. No! not yet! not yet! Oh, you are wrong, Remmy, see,— the regiment are all standing in the ranks so paceable.

REMMY. Do you see them twelve men yonder? [*Looking* R.U.E.] They stand apart from the rest, and there in front o' them are two long wooden boxes. In a few minutes my captain, and a rebel officer will fill them. See! Here comes the guard to fetch them. Go, Honor, quick! Tell the Mistress to come here. Let us be gone before she can see it done.

[*Enter* GIRARD *and six men* R.U.E. *Enter* BLIGH L.U.E.]

GIRARD. We come for the prisoners.

PHILIP [L.C.]. I have sent the lady under escort to headquarters. [*Seeing* REMMY] Are you not gone yet?

REMMY. Plase your honour, she axed me to stop here while she got ready.

[*Enter* DAN R.U.E.]

DAN. Dey's gone—dey's off—I knew Missee Belle would save de Captain after all.

[*Enter* GETZ *and six soldiers* R.U.E.]

PHILIP. Gone! Marston escaped! How is this? Was the guard withdrawn?

GETZ. No sir: here is the man—he says the lady showed him your pass—and the horses were provided by your orders.

PHILIP [*to* REMMY]. Traitor! What have you done?

REMMY. The divil a know I know. I'm bothered intirely!

PHILIP. You have parted with the pass I gave you to enable these prisoners to escape.

REMMY. No,—here it is. I let the lady have it to rade over—but she gave it back to me.

[*Music until curtain*]

PHILIP. "Do not blame the poor fellow who is unable to detect the fraud by which I substitute this pass for the safe conduct"—Gone! Escaped with her lover!

[*Enter* BELLE. R.D.3.E.]

BELLE. No, I have remained to exchange my liberty for the liberty of those I have betrayed, and take their place.

PHILIP. They have escaped by my pass—by the means I provided. You have made me appear guilty of a crime for which your lover was condemned to death.

GIRARD. The enemy is crossing the river in force. They have driven back our outposts. [*Guns sound outside*] There go their guns. Mount Lamar is under fire!

GETZ. The road to Whitestone Gap is occupied in force.

PHILIP. There is another through the wood. This negro knows the way.

BELLE. He will betray you. I'll be your guide. Will you trust me? But you cannot hold this place against the odds he brings. He has twelve thousand men; you, but a single regiment.

PHILIP. Had I but one troop, and that troop reduced to a single man, I'd fight him while there was enough of Philip Bligh to hold his heart!

QUICK CURTAIN

ACT THREE

The White Stone Gap. A gorge in the Shenandoah Mountains. An hour before daylight. At the back, in the distance, is seen the range of mountain-tops, and in the half-distance a plateau, cut by a chasm in which a river flows across the picture. The river is visible only L.H., *where it bends towards the spectator—here it is spanned by a bridge. In front, a rocky ledge, with a rude log cabin. Military works have been thrown up, to turn the place into a redoubt, furnished with pieces of artillery, commanding the bridge below it. The United States flag, in a tattered state, as if it had been riddled by bullets, is seen over the log cabin. Sentinels on guard. Northern soldiers lying about, or standing in groups—some playing cards. Chorus of Soldiers round the fire singing "Tenting on the Old Camp Ground"*
Slow curtain after first eight bars—Quartette. Two verses—two for encore—Count five.— PHILIP and GIRARD *discovered.* PHILIP *smoking. They stroll off* R.1.E. *after first verse. Low roll of drum* L.H. *Then when chorus is over—*

ALL. Bravo! Hurroo! Now, Remmy, it's your turn!

REMMY. Gentlemen, the country I came from is where music was born, bred, and from which it emigrated all over the world. Divil a tune there is alive that's worth a cint, but it was begged, borryed, or stolen from the melodies of my native land, and spoiled to make it pass for your own.

ALL. Bravo! Remmy!

REMMY. Music is the food of the heart, and sure if you could feel over the world to find where its heart lies, you would feel it batin undher your hand when it was over ould Ireland. It was there every musical instrument was invented.

HONOR [*lifting her head*]. Especially thrumpets—go on, Remmy, and don't be making an omadhaun of yourself.

ALL. Silence, boys, for a song from Remmy.

[*Enter* PHILIP *and* GIRARD R.1.E.]

REMMY. Whisht, boys, here's the Colonel.

PHILIP. Do not let my presence stop you. I did not know that singing was one of your accomplishments, Remmy.

HONOR. He larned it of a cart-wheel, your honour.

REMMY. Ah, thin, it is mighty little grease I get from the likes of you, Honor, to encourage me.

PHILIP. Never mind her, Remmy.

REMMY. Isn't this purty thratment of a poor boy, that is over head and ears in love wid her?

HONOR. Over your head you may be; over your ears you can't.

PHILIP. Getz has not returned yet. I sent him out to reconnoitre the position of the enemy.

REMMY. There's the way of it. As soon as them grey divils crossed the river, we started at a run that never stopped until we rached this, and divil a blow sthruck. Afther all! Bad luck to that ould nigger, Dan, that tuk us by a road through the woods—where we never met the size of a head to crack. When I went to the wars I thought I was goin' to get a fight every day—but, baithershin! I done little else than walk in the mud, dig ditches, and make baskets to hould dirt like a paceable workin' man at nine shillings a week in the County Cork!

GIRARD. I hope no harm has befallen Getz. Ha! No. Here he comes!

[*Enter* GETZ R.1.E.]

PHILIP. Welcome back. Well? What news?

GETZ. The enemy have crept round to our rear during the night.

PHILIP [*looking at his watch*]. It will be daylight in an hour. No signs of McDowell from the North. If we could send him news of our position, he would come at the double to our rescue.

GIRARD. We can hold this place against an army while our ammunition lasts. Our guns command the bridge below. Frémont is approaching by that road. He cannot be far.

PHILIP. Ay! So long as we can secure the bridge, we may defy— What is that moving on the mountain ridge yonder?

GETZ. Where?

PHILIP. On that shelf of rocks above us,

where the dark trees cling to the hill-side. I saw two shadows cross the boulders.

GIRARD. Some stray goats, perhaps!

GETZ. Nothing else would dare to make an attempt to scale that precipice.

PHILIP. Yes; I would, if I were Jackson. He has the eye of a hawk.

REMMY. He'd want the wings as well as the eyes to get up there.

PHILIP. Getz, take a company and search that patch of wood. My mind misgives me strangely. If Jackson gained a footing there, he could make this spot too hot to hold us.

GETZ. Fall in there, Company D.

[*Eight men fall in*]

REMMY. Long life t'ye, Colonel, let me go, too.

PHILIP. Very well! [*To* GETZ] Leave a guard up there.

[*The men have fallen into line,* REMMY *with them—the last man*]

GETZ. Right face; quick march!

PHILIP. It was an oversight to leave the place uncared for.

[*Exeunt* GETZ *and the men with* REMMY, *one of the men carrying a flag. He looks at* BELLE, *sleeping.* L.H.]

How soundly she sleeps.

BELLE. I am not asleep. Sleep is rest; and rest and I are strangers.

PHILIP. You must be gone before daylight.

BELLE [*rising*]. Why should I go?

PHILIP. You ask me why you should go: because within a few days, at furthest, the Northern armies will be here.

BELLE. Well, what then?

PHILIP. You will be brought to trial before those who will show you no favour.

BELLE. I shall not ask it.

PHILIP. You misunderstand your position. Yesterday our cause had suffered but little by your act: we had defeated an attempt, the spy was captured, and a traitor discovered and convicted. Their deaths would have satisfied military justice and lightened your penalty. But to-day, your position is changed. These prisoners escaped by your connivance—escaped to the enemy, to bring his whole force down upon us. Driven before him, my command is cornered here, cut off from help, supplies, and communication. The plans by which three armies are operating are disconcerted. The fortune of the campaign is imperilled, and the lives of eighty thousand men are compromised.

BELLE. What you order, I shall do.

PHILIP. There is but one road open to you now, and that leads to Jackson's lines. Go there —follow your heart—rejoin him, who gave you the only proof of love a woman will believe in—the sacrifice of a man's honour. When he became criminal for your sake, then he was irresistible—then he was base enough

to be worthy—vile enough to be adored.

BELLE. I do not love him. I never professed to.

PHILIP. He paid for you the price you set upon yourself. Are you as false to him now as you were to me?

BELLE. If the biting lash of your words could kill me, I would rather die under the sweet torture of your jealousy, than live the victim of his passion. Nay, Philip, I listened to your confession—hear mine! The Demon Pride prompted me to challenge your love to a supreme sacrifice for my sake. You resisted, and I left you. I never knew the depth of my heart until I found myself alone, and measured my love by the depth of my despair. Lifeless, hopeless, worthless—for all my life had deserted me to dwell by your side. I would have returned to ask your pardon but the same fiend who had betrayed me—Pride—stood in the path of my repentance, and scorned me back.

PHILIP. Isabel, yonder in the rebel camp, Marston awaits you.

BELLE. No. You wrong him. He learned from Stuart the confederate plan to surround you at Mount Lamar, and he used his liberty to reach the Northern lines and bring you help.

PHILIP. When I look into your eyes, I cannot blame him. Call *him* weak while *I* yield?— or refuse him pardon when I wrong him thus?

[*Roll of drum. Tumult outside. Enter* UNCLE DAN. R.2.E.]

UNCLE DAN. Oh, mussy on us all—dar's a heap o' trouble gwine on up dar.

PHILIP. Where?

UNCLE DAN. On top, where de soldiers go jest now. I watch 'em—climbin' up de cliff—till dey get into de scrub—den dar rise up out o' dat wood sech a hally loogerum as if a hull congregation o' catamounts broke loose from below. [*Tumult*] Dar dey is—at it agin'!

[*Enter* GIRARD *hastily*]

GIRARD. Our boys found the wood in possession of the enemy. A hand-to-hand fight ensued. We are unable to assist them without bringing our own men under fire.

[*Enter* HONOR]

HONOR. He is amongst them! He is in the thick of it! They are murtherin' the boy, I tell you. Is there never a man among you to lend a helpin' hand?

[*Shots*]

PHILIP. Our men are driven from the wood! See—ha! our flag is down!

[*Shots*]

GIRARD. No, 'tis up again! See, one of our boys wraps it round his rifle!

PHILIP. 'Tis Remmy!

HONOR. Remmy! Where is he—where is he?

PHILIP. Yonder! He stands on the very verge of the cliff. [*Shots*] Throw your rifle over, man, and surrender! Send us the colours and save yourself! [*Shots*] The fool still fights against three to one. He's down; but in his grip he holds a foe. [*Shots*] Yield, Remmy, yield! By Heaven he is trying to roll with his antagonist over the cliff into the abyss!

[HONOR *utters a yell of fright, and throws her apron over her head, falling on her knees*]

[*During the preceding speeches the Soldiers, one by one, enter and form groups, directing their faces upwards and off to* R., *where the action described is supposed to be taking place*]

ALL. Hurrah!

[GIRARD *and several of the men rush out,* R.2.E., *as if to pick up the fallen man*]

PHILIP. Do not weep, Honor, he has fallen like a man—he was worthy of any woman's love. You may be proud of him.

HONOR. Proud! Oh, that's what I've been too much! It was the pride in me that made me spake so hardly to him. Oh! Remmy! Remmy! Will I never spake an unkind word to you again?

[*Enter* GIRARD *and three men carrying* REMMY, *his uniform torn. He is pale and bleeding. He grasps the barrel of his broken rifle—the rescued flag is twisted round it*]

GIRARD. He breathes. He is not dead yet.

HONOR [*running to him*]. Not dead—no—his heart beats—and his eyes open. There's life in him. [REMMY *struggles and begins to renew the contest*] Remmy, dear—don't! don't! It is all over, I tell you—don't you know me?

REMMY [*after looking around, breaks into a grim smile*]. Oh!

HONOR. What's the matther, dear?

REMMY. I've had a fight.

HONOR. Bad cess to ye—is that all you have to say to me after the fright I've had? Where are ye hurt? Spake boy—have you anything broken?

REMMY. Yes! I've broke my gun. [*Looks at the rifle in distress*]

PHILIP. See him well cared for.

[*He is taken to* L.H. *where* HONOR *wipes the blood from his face with a handkerchief she tears from his neck. Looking to find something to bind his arm, snatches the flag from a soldier, who has taken it and the rifle, and binds* REMMY's *wounded limb with it, while* BELLE *gives him drink*]

GIRARD. Getz is a prisoner or killed—the wood above is in their possession—there goes their flag over the trees.

PHILIP. Ay, Jackson has give me checkmate. His artillery will soon be slung into position there; and when his guns are brought to bear upon this spot, we cannot hold it for an hour. Then the bridge will fall, and ruin—

utter ruin will ensue. [*A bugle call is heard outside*] That comes from the enemy. Go see what he wants. [*Exit* GIRARD. R.2.E.] Uncle Dan.

UNCLE DAN. Dass me, sah.

PHILIP. Come here. I shall commit your mistress and Honor to your charge. That bugle announces some message from the Confederates, and you will avail yourself of the parley to conduct them out of danger.

[*Re-enter* GIRARD, *followed by* JACKSON, RHETT, *and another officer, and a bugler carrying a white flag on his trumpet*]

PHILIP. You are welcome, General.

STONEWALL. I come in person, Colonel Bligh, to ask you to arrest a useless effusion of blood and waste of life. You know your position is hopeless. Within half-an-hour my guns will render this place untenable—resistance will not be bravery; it will simply be submission to slaughter.

PHILIP. My orders, General, are to occupy this post, and to hold it. It may so happen that within the very half-hour you give us, the columns of Frémont will pour across yonder bridge—or, McDowell, falling on your rear and flank, may turn the scale of victory. Nations have been saved and lost in thirty minutes!

STONEWALL. It is bravely resolved, sir; but your hopes are vain. Even were those armies as near us as you hope, it would not save you from destruction.

PHILIP. Well, sir, the fate you offer me is preferable to that awaiting me if I survive. My military offences—the crimes and blunders which enable you to dictate terms to me, will subject me to disgrace and death. I had rather fall under your bullets than under those of my own comrades.

STONEWALL. We are soldiers, Colonel Bligh. Do not oblige us to be executioners. Accept my offer. Your men shall march out with their colours flying, the officers with their side arms. Surely you can accept such terms with dignity.

PHILIP. A commander who capitulates must show an unstained record. Mine is not so. My men, you hear the offer made you, and you have heard how hopeless is our position. Let those who accept the offer, step out. [*A pause*] You see, General, not a man stirs. Their silence is my answer.

STONEWALL. You will not detain Miss Lamar?

PHILIP. No, she is at liberty to accompany you; and I have prayed her to do so. Will you extend the like protection to this girl? I accept your offer.

BELLE [*advancing*]. And I refuse it.

STONEWALL. Why?

BELLE. Because a woman's country is her husband's home; her cause, his happiness. Her only place, his side, and death alone should part them. Oh, Philip, Philip, do not send me from you! This wilful, proud, but loving heart has never wandered from you as I have done: never had any cause but one—its faithful love. Let me stay and die—if die you must—by your side.

STONEWALL. Farewell, Colonel Bligh. When the time I have given you expires, my trumpets will announce to you that I must open fire. They will sound three times. If you revise your decision and accept my terms, you will haul down that flag [*Points to the flag over the cabin*] as a signal of your surrender. And you, noble girl—whose devotion I cannot blame, however I may regret it—we meet for the last time. I cannot blame your choice. [BELLE *runs to him. He takes her head between his hands, and kisses her forehead*] Heaven bless you! [*Exit with* GIRARD. R.2.E.]

RHETT. Does the girl yonder accompany us?

HONOR. Ah! Go on!

[*Exit* RHETT, *Officer and Bugler. And Soldiers* R.2.E.]

PHILIP. I would not exchange this supreme moment of my expiring life for all the barren years I have to come. All my happiness is gathered into this one hour and fills my joy full to the brim. Such an end I would have asked for. But can you look death in the face?

BELLE. Let me look into yours. I shall heed nothing else. Let it find me in your arms. I shall never know when life ends, and Heaven begins.

PHILIP. I cannot believe those eyes will soon be quenched; those trembling lips grow livid; this beating heart be stilled. A coward hope overcomes me,—that all may not be lost. And yet I know how vain such hope must be.

BELLE. I do not care where our love may spend its life, here or hereafter.

PHILIP. Oh! but to regain that love only to lose it.

BELLE. Not to lose it, Philip; but to meet again where there is no strife—no pride—no sorrow—in the life where there is no death.

[*Bugle* R.1.E. *No. 1*]

PHILIP. One. There is the signal. [*He looks up to the flag*] Pat Dwyer, take a hammer, go up there and nail those colours fast; a shot might cut the lines and the enemy mistake an accident for a surrender.

[DWYER *climbs to the flag and nails it to the pole*]

HONOR. Remmy, dear. How do you feel?

REMMY. I'm beautiful.

HONOR. Did ye hear what is goin' to become of us?

REMMY. I did.

HONOR. Is it hard to die, Remmy?

REMMY. I don't know, Honor, I never tried.

HONOR. But you have seen them as did.

REMMY. And helped them to it.

HONOR. I'd like to die dacent, Remmy—if—

REMMY. If what, Honor?

HONOR. If I knew how. I'd not like to disgrace meself, nor you, dear. Whisper, darlin'! How do they do it? What'll I do? I never saw death in all my life. I'm new to it—an—an—oh, Remmy—stand by me—close—and may be I'll not be afeard.

UNCLE DAN. Stan' close by de side of Him dat died for you and all ob us, and you'll not be skeered.

HONOR. What brings you here? Begone, I tell you—go! You, and the likes of you, brought us all to this. You are the living curse that dhrives us—

REMMY. Whisht, Honor, don't go out o' the world wid a curse in your mouth.

HONOR. Oh, Remmy! is it come to that?

[*A distant bugle sounds*]

PHILIP. Two! In a few moments our fate will be decided.

[*Enter* GIRARD. R.2.E.]

GIRARD. A single horseman is riding from the west,—in another moment he will be within the line of Confederate fire. See, yonder he comes over the hill beyond the bridge.

PHILIP. By heaven! I should know that horse—it is my own grey charger, Lexington.

BELLE. 'Tis he. 'Tis Marston. That was the horse on which he escaped.

GIRARD. Now he gains the river.

[*The horse and man are seen to cross the distant bridge. Scattering distant shots are heard*]

PHILIP. They see him—he is coming here. Out! men, quick—line the hill-side—and protect his flight. [GIRARD *and men leap over bastions and disappear*] What does this mean? It cannot be he!

[*A bugle sounds in the distance. Shouts* L.U.E. *Enter* MARSTON *and Soldiers*]

MARSTON. Fight to your last drop of blood, Bligh. Help is at hand. Stuart, my fellow prisoner, told me Jackson's plan to rescue him, and I used my freedom to reach Frémont.

PHILIP. Stand to your guns, men. See the cloud of dust rising from the road between the hills. [*A distant military band is heard. March:* "Johnny comes marching home." *Increase it forte—Shots—Drums—Bugles—*"Johnny comes marching home." *A bugle sounds*] Ah, Jackson! I told you that a nation was saved or lost in thirty minutes.

[*The head of a column of National troops is seen coming rapidly across the distant bridge. It disappears for a moment behind a grove of trees; then spreads out, and lines of troops appear.*

[*At the same moment at the plateau in the center above, from the line of woods, other columns appear moving down and forward.*

[*Distant file firing is heard in the valley. Guns appear on salient points, and*

their rapid flash and report is mingled with the drums, bugle calls, and regimental music, distant cheers—which grow louder.
[*Several field officers and men mount the bastions, leap over, and greet* PHILIP.

The men wave their hats on their rifles]

TABLEAU.

[*Guns—Music—Shouts*]

QUICK CURTAIN

THE WILD DUCK

A Play in Five Acts

By HENRIK IBSEN

CHARACTERS

WERLE, *a merchant, manufacturer, etc.*
GREGERS WERLE, *his son*
OLD EKDAL
HIALMAR EKDAL, *his son, a photographer*
GINA EKDAL, *Hialmar's wife*
HEDVIG, *their daughter, a girl of fourteen*
MRS. SÖRBY, *Werle's housekeeper*
RELLING, *a doctor*
MOLVIK, *a student of theology*
GRÅBERG, *Werle's bookkeeper*
PETTERSEN, *Werle's servant*
JENSEN, *a hired waiter*
A FLABBY GENTLEMAN
A THIN-HAIRED GENTLEMAN
A SHORT-SIGHTED GENTLEMAN
Six other gentlemen, guests at Werle's dinner-party
Several hired waiters

The first act passes in Werle's house, the remaining acts at Hialmar Ekdal's

PRONUNCIATION OF NAMES

Gregers Werle = Grayghers Verlë
Hialmar Ekdal = Yalmar Aykdal
Gina = Gheena
Gråberg = Groberg
Jensen = Yensen

THE WILD DUCK

ACT FIRST

At WERLE'S *house. A richly and comfortably furnished study; bookcases and upholstered furniture; a writing-table, with papers and documents, in the centre of the room; lighted lamps with green shades, giving a subdued light. At the back, open folding-doors with curtains drawn back. Within is seen a large and handsome room, brilliantly lighted with lamps and branching candlesticks. In front, on the right (in the study), a small baize door leads into* WERLE'S *office. On the left, in front, a fireplace with a glowing coal fire, and farther back a double door leading into the dining-room.*

WERLE'S *servant,* PETTERSEN, *in livery, and* JENSEN, *the hired waiter, in black, are putting the study in order. In the large room, two or three other hired waiters are moving about, arranging things and lighting more candles. From the dining-room, the hum of conversation and laughter of many voices is heard; a glass is tapped with a knife; silence follows, and a toast is proposed; shouts of "Bravo!" and then again a buzz of conversation.*

PETTERSEN [*lights a lamp on the chimney-place and places a shade over it*]. Hark to them, Jensen! now the old man's on his legs holding a long palaver about Mrs. Sörby.

JENSEN [*pushing forward an arm-chair*]. Is it true, what folks say, that they're—very good friends, eh?

PETTERSEN. Lord knows.

JENSEN. I've heard tell as he's been a lively customer in his day.

PETTERSEN. May be.

JENSEN. And he's giving this spread in honour of his son, they say.

PETTERSEN. Yes. His son came home yesterday.

JENSEN. This is the first time I ever heard as Mr. Werle had a son.

PETTERSEN. Oh yes, he has a son, right enough. But he's a fixture, as you might say, up at the Höidal works. He's never once come to town all the years I've been in service here.

A WAITER [*in the doorway of the other room*]. Pettersen, here's an old fellow wanting—

PETTERSEN [*mutters*]. The devil—who's this now?

[OLD EKDAL *appears from the right, in the inner room. He is dressed in a thread-*

bare overcoat with a high collar; he wears woolen mittens, and carries in his hand a stick and a fur cap. Under his arm, a brown paper parcel. Dirty red-brown wig and small grey moustache]

PETTERSEN [*goes towards him*]. Good Lord —what do you want here?

EKDAL [*in the doorway*]. Must get into the office, Pettersen.

PETTERSEN. The office was closed an hour ago, and—

EKDAL. So they told me at the front door. But Gråberg's in there still. Let me slip in this way, Pettersen; there's a good fellow. [*Points towards the baize door*] It's not the first time I've come this way.

PETTERSEN. Well, you may pass. [*Opens the door*] But mind you go out again the proper way, for we've got company.

EKDAL. I know, I know—h'm! Thanks, Pettersen, good old friend! Thanks! [*Mutters softly*] Ass! [*He goes into the office*]

[PETTERSEN *shuts the door after him*]

JENSEN. Is he one of the office people?

PETTERSEN. No, he's only an outside hand that does odd jobs of copying. But he's been a tip-topper in his day, has old Ekdal.

JENSEN. You can see he's been through a lot.

PETTERSEN. Yes; he was an army officer, you know.

JENSEN. You don't say so?

PETTERSEN. No mistake about it. But then he went into the timber trade or something of the sort. They say he once played Mr. Werle a very nasty trick. They were partners in the Höidal works at the time. Oh, I know old Ekdal well, I do. Many a nip of bitters and bottle of ale we two have drunk at Madam Eriksen's.

JENSEN. He don't look as if he'd much to stand treat with.

PETTERSEN. Why, bless you, Jensen, it's me that stands treat. I always think there's no harm in being a bit civil to folks that have seen better days.

JENSEN. Did he go bankrupt then?

PETTERSEN. Worse than that. He went to prison.

JENSEN. To prison!

PETTERSEN. Or perhaps it was the Penitentiary. [*Listens*] Sh! They're leaving the table.

[*The dining-room door is thrown open from within, by a couple of waiters.*

MRS. SÖRBY *comes out conversing with two gentlemen. Gradually the whole company follows, amongst them* WERLE. *Last come* HIALMAR EKDAL *and* GREGERS WERLE]

MRS. SÖRBY [*in passing, to the servant*]. Tell them to serve the coffee in the music-room, Pettersen.

PETTERSEN. Very well, Madam.

[*She goes with the two Gentlemen into the inner room, and thence out to the right.* PETTERSEN *and* JENSEN *go out the same way*]

A FLABBY GENTLEMAN [*to a* THIN-HAIRED GENTLEMAN]. Whew! What a dinner!—It was no joke to do it justice!

THE THIN-HAIRED GENTLEMAN. Oh, with a little good-will one can get through a lot in three hours.

THE FLABBY GENTLEMAN. Yes, but afterwards, afterwards, my dear Chamberlain!

A THIRD GENTLEMAN. I hear the coffee and maraschino are to be served in the music-room.

THE FLABBY GENTLEMAN. Bravo! Then perhaps Mrs. Sörby will play us something.

THE THIN-HAIRED GENTLEMAN. [*in a low voice*]. I hope Mrs. Sörby mayn't play us a tune we don't like, one of these days!

THE FLABBY GENTLEMAN. Oh no, not she! Bertha will never turn against her old friends.

[*They laugh and pass into the inner room*]

WERLE [*in a low voice, dejectedly*]. I don't think anybody noticed it, Gregers.

GREGERS [*looks at him*]. Noticed what?

WERLE. Did you not notice it either?

GREGERS. What do you mean?

WERLE. We were thirteen at table.

GREGERS. Indeed? Were there thirteen of us?

WERLE [*glances towards* HIALMAR EKDAL]. Our usual party is twelve. [*To the others*] This way, gentlemen!

[WERLE *and the others, all except* HIALMAR *and* GREGERS, *go out by the back, to the right*]

HIALMAR [*who has overheard the conversation*]. You ought not to have invited me, Gregers.

GREGERS. What! Not ask my best and only friend to a party supposed to be in my honour—?

HIALMAR. But I don't think your father likes it. You see I am quite outside his circle.

GREGERS. So I hear. But I wanted to see you and have a talk with you, and I certainly shan't be staying long.—Ah, we two old school-fellows have drifted far apart from each other. It must be sixteen or seventeen years since we met.

HIALMAR. Is it so long?

GREGERS. It is indeed. Well, how goes it with you? You look well. You have put on flesh, and grown almost stout.

HIALMAR. Well, "stout" is scarcely the word; but I daresay I look a little more of a man than I used to.

GREGERS. Yes, you do; your outer man is in first-rate condition.

HIALMAR [*in a tone of gloom*]. Ah, but the inner man! That is a very different matter, I can tell you! Of course you know of the terrible catastrophe that has befallen me and mine since last we met.

GREGERS [*more softly*]. How are things going with your father now?

HIALMAR. Don't let us talk of it, old fellow. Of course my poor unhappy father lives with me. He hasn't another soul in the world to care for him. But you can understand that this is a miserable subject for me.—Tell me, rather, how you have been getting on up at the works.

GREGERS. I have had a delightfully lonely time of it—plenty of leisure to think and think about things. Come over here; we may as well make ourselves comfortable. [*He seats himself in an arm-chair by the fire and draws* HIALMAR *down into another alongside of it*]

HIALMAR [*sentimentally*]. After all, Gregers, I thank you for inviting me to your father's table; for I take it as a sign that you have got over your feeling against me.

GREGERS [*surprised*]. How could you imagine I had any feeling against you?

HIALMAR. You had at first, you know.

GREGERS. How at first?

HIALMAR. After the great misfortune. It was natural enough that you should. Your father was within an ace of being drawn into that—well, that terrible business.

GREGERS. Why should that give me any feeling against you? Who can have put that into your head?

HIALMAR. I know it did, Gregers; your father told me so himself.

GREGERS [*starts*]. My father! Oh indeed. H'm.—Was that why you never let me hear from you?—not a single word.

HIALMAR. Yes.

GREGERS. Not even when you made up your mind to become a photographer?

HIALMAR. Your father said I had better not write to you at all, about anything.

GREGERS [*looking straight before him*]. Well well, perhaps he was right.—But tell me now, Hialmar: are you pretty well satisfied with your present position?

HIALMAR [*with a little sigh*]. Oh yes, I am; I have really no cause to complain. At first, as you may guess, I felt it a little strange. It was such a totally new state of things for me. But of course my whole circumstances were totally changed. Father's utter, irretrievable ruin,—the shame and disgrace of it, Gregers—

GREGERS [*affected*]. Yes, yes; I understand.

HIALMAR. I couldn't think of remaining at college; there wasn't a shilling to spare; on the contrary, there were debts—mainly to your father I believe—

GREGERS. H'm—

HIALMAR. In short, I thought it best to break, once for all, with my old surroundings and associations. It was your father that specially urged me to it; and since he interested himself so much in me—

GREGERS. My father did?

HIALMAR. Yes, you surely knew that, didn't you? Where do you suppose I found the money to learn photography, and to furnish a studio and make a start? All that costs a pretty penny, I can tell you.

GREGERS. And my father provided the money?

HIALMAR. Yes, my dear fellow, didn't you know? I understood him to say he had written to you about it.

GREGERS. Not a word about his part in the business. He must have forgotten it. Our correspondence has always been purely a business one. So it was my father that—!

HIALMAR. Yes, certainly. He didn't wish it to be generally known; but he it was. And of course it was he, too, that put me in a position to marry. Don't you—don't you know about that either?

GREGERS. No, I haven't heard a word of it. [*Shakes him by the arm*] But, my dear Hialmar, I can't tell you what pleasure all this gives me—pleasure, and self-reproach. I have perhaps done my father injustice after all—in some things. This proves that he has a heart. It shows a sort of compunction—

HIALMAR. Compunction—?

GREGERS. Yes, yes—whatever you like to call it. Oh, I can't tell you how glad I am to hear this of father.—So you are a married man, Hialmar! That is further than I shall ever get. Well, I hope you are happy in your married life?

HIALMAR. Yes, thoroughly happy. She is as good and capable a wife as any man could wish for. And she is by no means without culture.

GREGERS [*rather surprised*]. No, of course not.

HIALMAR. You see, life is itself an education. Her daily intercourse with me— And then we know one or two rather remarkable men, who come a good deal about us. I assure you, you would hardly know Gina again.

GREGERS. Gina?

HIALMAR. Yes; had you forgotten that her name was Gina?

GREGERS. Whose name? I haven't the slightest idea—

HIALMAR. Don't you remember that she used to be in service here?

GREGERS [*looks at him*]. Is it Gina Hansen—?

HIALMAR. Yes, of course it is Gina Hansen.

GREGER. —who kept house for us during the last year of my mother's illness?

HIALMAR. Yes, exactly. But, my dear friend, I'm quite sure your father told you that I was married.

GREGERS [*who has risen*]. Oh yes, he mentioned it; but not that— [*Walking about the room*] Stay—perhaps he did—now that I think of it. My father always writes such short letters. [*Half seats himself on the arm of the chair*] Now, tell me, Hialmar—this is interesting—how did you come to know Gina—your wife?

HIALMAR. The simplest thing in the world. You know Gina did not stay here long; everything was so much upset at that time, owing to your mother's illness and so forth, that Gina was not equal to it all; so she gave notice and left. That was the year before your mother died—or it may have been the same year.

GREGERS. It was the same year. I was up at the works then. But afterwards—?

HIALMAR. Well, Gina lived at home with her mother, Madam Hansen, an excellent hard-working woman, who kept a little eating-house. She had a room to let too; a very nice comfortable room.

GREGERS. And I suppose you were lucky enough to secure it?

HIALMAR. Yes; in fact, it was your father that recommended it to me. So it was there, you see, that I really came to know Gina.

GREGERS. And then you got engaged?

HIALMAR. Yes. It doesn't take young people long to fall in love—; h'm—

GREGERS [*rises and moves about a little*]. Tell me: was it after your engagement—was it then that my father—I mean was it then that you began to take up photography?

HIALMAR. Yes, precisely. I wanted to make a start, and to set up house as soon as possible; and your father and I agreed that this photography business was the readiest way. Gina thought so too. Oh, and there was another thing in its favour, by-the-bye: it happened, luckily, that Gina had learnt to retouch.

GREGERS. That chimed in marvellously.

HIALMAR [*pleased, rises*]. Yes, didn't it? Don't you think it was a marvellous piece of luck?

GREGERS. Oh, unquestionably. My father seems to have been almost a kind of providence for you.

HIALMAR [*with emotion*]. He did not forsake his old friend's son in the hour of his need. For he has a heart, you see.

MRS. SÖRBY [*enters, arm-in-arm with*

WERLE]. Nonsense, my dear Mr. Werle; you mustn't stop there any longer staring at all the lights. It's very bad for you.

WERLE [*lets go her arm and passes his hand over his eyes*]. I daresay you are right.

[PETTERSEN *and* JENSEN *carry round refreshment trays*]

MRS. SÖRBY [*to the Guests in the other room*]. This way, if you please, gentlemen. Whoever wants a glass of punch must be so good as to come in here.

THE FLABBY GENTLEMAN [*comes up to* MRS. SÖRBY]. Surely, it isn't possible that you have suspended our cherished right to smoke?

MRS. SÖRBY. Yes. No smoking here, in Mr. Werle's sanctum, Chamberlain.

THE THIN-HAIRED GENTLEMAN. When did you enact these stringent amendments on the cigar law, Mrs. Sörby?

MRS. SÖRBY. After the last dinner, Chamberlain, when certain persons permitted themselves to overstep the mark.

THE THIN-HAIRED GENTLEMAN. And may one never overstep the mark a little bit, Madame Bertha? Not the least little bit?

MRS. SÖRBY. Not in any respect whatsoever, Mr. Balle.

[*Most of the Guests have assembled in the study; servants hand round glasses of punch*]

WERLE [*to* HIALMAR, *who is standing beside a table*]. What are you studying so intently, Ekdal?

HIALMAR. Only an album, Mr. Werle.

THE THIN-HAIRED GENTLEMAN [*who is wandering about*]. Ah, photographs! They are quite in your line of course.

THE FLABBY GENTLEMAN [*in an arm-chair*]. Haven't you brought any of your own with you?

HIALMAR. No, I haven't.

THE FLABBY GENTLEMAN. You ought to have; it's very good for the digestion to sit and look at pictures.

THE THIN-HAIRED GENTLEMAN. And it contributes to the entertainment, you know.

THE SHORT-SIGHTED GENTLEMAN. And all contributions are thankfully received.

MRS. SÖRBY. The Chamberlains think that when one is invited out to dinner, one ought to exert oneself a little in return, Mr. Ekdal.

THE FLABBY GENTLEMAN. Where one dines so well, that duty becomes a pleasure.

THE THIN-HAIRED GENTLEMAN. And when it's a case of the struggle for existence, you know—

MRS. SÖRBY. I quite agree with you!

[*They continue the conversation, with laughter and joking*]

GREGERS [*softly*]. You must join in, Hialmar.

HIALMAR [*writhing*]. What am I to talk about?

THE FLABBY GENTLEMAN. Don't you think, Mr. Werle, that Tokay may be considered one of the more wholesome sorts of wine?

WERLE [*by the fire*]. I can answer for the Tokay you had to-day, at any rate; it's of one of the very finest seasons. Of course you would notice that.

THE FLABBY GENTLEMAN. Yes, it had a remarkably delicate flavour.

HIALMAR [*shyly*]. Is there any difference between the seasons?

THE FLABBY GENTLEMAN [*laughs*]. Come! That's good!

WERLE [*smiles*]. It really doesn't pay to set fine wine before you.

THE THIN-HAIRED GENTLEMAN. Tokay is like photographs, Mr. Ekdal: they both need sunshine. Am I not right?

HIALMAR. Yes, light is important no doubt.

MRS. SÖRBY. And it's exactly the same with Chamberlains—they, too, depend very much on sunshine,* as the saying is.

THE THIN-HAIRED GENTLEMAN. Oh fie! That's a very threadbare sarcasm!

THE SHORT-SIGHTED GENTLEMAN. Mrs. Sörby is coming out—

THE FLABBY GENTLEMAN. —and at our expense, too. [*Holds up his finger reprovingly*] Oh, Madame Bertha, Madame Bertha!

MRS. SÖRBY. Yes, and there's not the least doubt that the seasons differ greatly. The old vintages are the finest.

THE SHORT-SIGHTED GENTLEMAN. Do you reckon me among the old vintages?

MRS. SÖRBY. Oh, far from it.

THE THIN-HAIRED GENTLEMAN. There now! But me, dear Mrs. Sörby—?

THE FLABBY GENTLEMAN. Yes, and me? What vintage should you say that we belong to?

MRS. SÖRBY. Why, to the sweet vintages, gentlemen.

[*She sips a glass of punch. The Gentlemen laugh and flirt with her*]

WERLE. Mrs. Sörby can always find a loophole—when she wants to. Fill your glasses, gentlemen! Pettersen, will you see to it—! Gregers, suppose we have a glass together. [GREGERS *does not move*] Won't you join us, Ekdal? I found no opportunity of drinking with you at table.

[GRÅBERG, *the Bookkeeper, looks in at the baize door*]

GRÅBERG. Excuse me, sir, but I can't get out.

WERLE. Have you been locked in again?

GRÅBERG. Yes, and Flakstad has carried off the keys.

WERLE. Well, you can pass out this way.

* The "sunshine" of Court favour.

GRÅBERG. But there's some one else—

WERLE. All right; come through, both of you. Don't be afraid.

[GRÅBERG *and* OLD EKDAL *come out of the office*]

WERLE [*involuntarily*]. Ugh!

[*The laughter and talk among the Guests cease.* HIALMAR *starts at the sight of his father, puts down his glass, and turns towards the fireplace*]

EKDAL [*does not look up, but makes little bows to both sides as he passes, murmuring*]. Beg pardon, come the wrong way. Door locked —door locked. Beg pardon.

[*He and* GRÅBERG *go out by the back, to the right*]

WERLE [*between his teeth*]. That idiot Gråberg!

GREGERS [*open-mouthed and staring, to* HIALMAR]. Why surely that wasn't—!

THE FLABBY GENTLEMAN. What's the matter? Who was it?

GREGERS. Oh, nobody, only the bookkeeper and some one with him.

THE SHORT-SIGHTED GENTLEMAN [*to* HIALMAR]. Did you know that man?

HIALMAR. I don't know—I didn't notice—

THE FLABBY GENTLEMAN. What the deuce has come over every one? [*He joins another group who are talking softly*]

MRS. SÖRBY [*whispers to the Servant*]. Give him something to take with him;—something good, mind.

PETTERSEN [*nods*]. I'll see to it. [*Goes out*]

GREGERS [*softly and with emotion, to* HIALMAR]. So that was really he!

HIALMAR. Yes.

GREGERS. And you could stand there and deny that you knew him!

HIALMAR [*whispers vehemently*]. But how could I—?

GREGERS. —acknowledge your own father?

HIALMAR [*with pain*]. Oh, if you were in my place—

[*The conversation amongst the Guests, which has been carried on in a low tone, now swells into constrained joviality*]

THE THIN-HAIRED GENTLEMAN [*approaching* HIALMAR *and* GREGERS *in a friendly manner*]. Aha! Reviving old college memories, eh? Don't you smoke, Mr. Ekdal? May I give you a light? Oh, by-the-bye, we mustn't—

HIALMAR. No, thank you, I won't—

THE FLABBY GENTLEMAN. Haven't you a nice little poem you could recite to us, Mr. Ekdal? You used to recite so charmingly.

HIALMAR. I am sorry I can't remember anything.

THE FLABBY GENTLEMAN. Oh, that's a pity. Well, what shall we do, Balle?

[*Both Gentlemen move away and pass into the other room*]

HIALMAR [*gloomily*]. Gregers—I am going! When a man has felt the crushing hand of Fate, you see— Say good-bye to your father for me.

GREGERS. Yes, yes. Are you going straight home?

HIALMAR. Yes. Why?

GREGERS. Oh, because I may perhaps look in on you later.

HIALMAR. No, you mustn't do that. You must not come to my home. Mine is a melancholy abode, Gregers; especially after a splendid banquet like this. We can always arrange to meet somewhere in the town.

MRS. SÖRBY [*who has quietly approached*]. Are you going, Ekdal?

HIALMAR. Yes.

MRS. SÖRBY. Remember me to Gina.

HIALMAR. Thanks.

MRS. SÖRBY. And say I am coming up to see her one of these days.

HIALMAR. Yes, thank you. [*To* GREGERS] Stay here; I will slip out unobserved. [*He saunters away, then into the other room, and so out to the right*]

MRS. SÖRBY [*softly to the Servant, who has come back*]. Well, did you give the old man something?

PETTERSEN. Yes; I sent him off with a bottle of cognac.

MRS. SÖRBY. Oh, you might have thought of something better than that.

PETTERSEN. Oh no, Mrs. Sörby; cognac is what he likes best in the world.

THE FLABBY GENTLEMAN [*in the doorway with a sheet of music in his hand*]. Shall we play a duet, Mrs. Sörby?

MRS. SÖRBY. Yes, suppose we do.

THE GUESTS. Bravo, bravo!

[*She goes with all the Guests through the back room, out to the right.* GREGERS *remains standing by the fire.* WERLE *is looking for something on the writing-table, and appears to wish that* GREGERS *would go; as* GREGERS *does not move,* WERLE *goes towards the door*]

GREGERS. Father, won't you stay a moment?

WERLE [*stops*]. What is it?

GREGERS. I must have a word with you.

WERLE. Can it not wait till we are alone?

GREGERS. No, it cannot; for perhaps we shall never be alone together.

WERLE [*drawing nearer*]. What do you mean by that?

[*During what follows, the pianoforte is faintly heard from the distant music-room*]

GREGERS. How has that family been allowed to go so miserably to the wall?

WERLE. You mean the Ekdals, I suppose.

GREGERS. Yes, I mean the Ekdals. Lieutenant Ekdal was once so closely associated with you.

WERLE. Much too closely; I have felt that to my cost for many a year. It is thanks to him that I—yes *I*—have had a kind of slur cast upon my reputation.

GREGERS [*softly*]. Are you sure that he alone was to blame?

WERLE. Who else do you suppose—?

GREGERS. You and he acted together in that affair of the forests—

WERLE. But was it not Ekdal that drew the map of the tracts we had bought—that fraudulent map! It was he who felled all that timber illegally on Government ground. In fact, the whole management was in his hands. I was quite in the dark as to what Lieutenant Ekdal was doing.

GREGERS. Lieutenant Ekdal himself seems to have been very much in the dark as to what he was doing.

WERLE. That may be. But the fact remains that he was found guilty and I acquitted.

GREGERS. Yes, I know that nothing was proved against you.

WERLE. Acquittal is acquittal. Why do you rake up these old miseries that turned my hair grey before its time? Is that the sort of thing you have been brooding over up there, all these years? I can assure you, Gregers, here in the town the whole story has been forgotten long ago—so far as *I* am concerned.

GREGERS. But that unhappy Ekdal family.

WERLE. What would you have had me do for the people? When Ekdal came out of prison he was a broken-down being, past all help. There are people in the world who dive to the bottom the moment they get a couple of slugs in their body, and never come to the surface again. You may take my word for it, Gregers, I have done all I could without positively laying myself open to all sorts of suspicion and gossip—

GREGERS. Suspicion—? Oh, I see.

WERLE. I have given Ekdal copying to do for the office, and I pay him far, far more for it than his work is worth—

GREGERS [*without looking at him*]. H'm; that I don't doubt.

WERLE. You laugh? Do you think I am not telling you the truth? Well, I certainly can't refer you to my books, for I never enter payments of that sort.

GREGERS [*smiles coldly*]. No, there are certain payments it is best to keep no account of.

WERLE [*taken aback*]. What do you mean by that?

GREGERS [*mustering up courage*]. Have you entered what it cost you to have Hialmar Ekdal taught photography?

WERLE. I? How "entered" it?

GREGERS. I have learnt that it was you who

paid for his training. And I have learnt, too, that it was you who enabled him to set up house so comfortably.

WERLE. Well, and yet you talk as though I had done nothing for the Ekdals! I can assure you these people have cost me enough in all conscience.

GREGERS. Have you entered any of these expenses in your books?

WERLE. Why do you ask?

GREGERS. Oh, I have my reasons. Now tell me: when you interested yourself so warmly in your old friend's son—it was just before his marriage, was it not?

WERLE. Why, deuce take it—after all these years, how can I—?

GREGERS. You wrote me a letter about that time—a business letter, of course; and in a postscript you mentioned—quite briefly—that Hialmar Ekdal had married a Miss Hansen.

WERLE. Yes, that was quite right. That was her name.

GREGERS. But you did not mention that this Miss Hansen was Gina Hansen—our former housekeeper.

WERLE [*with a forced laugh of derision*]. No; to tell the truth, it didn't occur to me that you were so particularly interested in our former housekeeper.

GREGERS. No more I was. But [*Lowers his voice*] there were others in this house who were particularly interested in her.

WERLE. What do you mean by that? [*Flaring up*] You are not alluding to me, I hope?

GREGERS [*softly but firmly*]. Yes, I am alluding to you.

WERLE. And you dare—! You presume to—! How can that ungrateful hound—that photographer fellow—how dare he go making such insinuations!

GREGERS. Hialmar has never breathed a word about this. I don't believe he has the faintest suspicion of such a thing.

WERLE. Then where have you got it from? Who can have put such notions in your head?

GREGERS. My poor unhappy mother told me; and that the very last time I saw her.

WERLE. Your mother! I might have known as much! You and she—you always held together. It was she who turned you against me, from the first.

GREGERS. No, it was all that she had to suffer and submit to, until she broke down and came to such a pitiful end.

WERLE. Oh, she had nothing to suffer or submit to; not more than most people, at all events. But there's no getting on with morbid, overstrained creatures—that I have learnt to my cost.—And you could go on nursing such a suspicion—burrowing into all sorts of old rumours and slanders against your own father! I must say, Gregers, I really think that at your age you might find something more useful to do.

GREGERS. Yes, it is high time.

WERLE. Then perhaps your mind would be easier than it seems to be now. What can be your object in remaining up at the works, year out and year in, drudging away like a common clerk, and not drawing a farthing more than the ordinary monthly wage? It is downright folly.

GREGERS. Ah, if I were only sure of that.

WERLE. I understand you well enough. You want to be independent; you won't be beholden to me for anything. Well, now there happens to be an opportunity for you to become independent, your own master in everything.

GREGERS. Indeed? In what way—?

WERLE. When I wrote you insisting on your coming to town at once—h'm—

GREGERS. Yes, what is it you really want of me? I have been waiting all day to know.

WERLE. I want to propose that you should enter the firm, as partner.

GREGERS. I! Join your firm? As partner?

WERLE. Yes. It would not involve our being constantly together. You could take over the business here in town, and I should move up to the works.

GREGERS. You would?

WERLE. The fact is, I am not so fit for work as I once was. I am obliged to spare my eyes, Gregers; they have begun to trouble me.

GREGERS. They have always been weak.

WERLE. Not as they are now. And besides, circumstances might possibly make it desirable for me to live up there—for a time, at any rate.

GREGERS. That is certainly quite a new idea to me.

WERLE. Listen, Gregers: there are many things that stand between us; but we are father and son after all. We ought surely to be able to come to some sort of understanding with each other.

GREGERS. Outwardly, you mean, of course?

WERLE. Well, even that would be something. Think it over, Gregers. Don't you think it ought to be possible? Eh?

GREGERS [looking at him coldly]. There is something behind all this.

WERLE. How so?

GREGERS. You want to make use of me in some way.

WERLE. In such a close relationship as ours, the one can always be useful to the other.

GREGERS. Yes, so people say.

WERLE. I want very much to have you at home with me for a time. I am a lonely man Gregers; I have always felt lonely, all my life through; but most of all now that I am getting up in years. I feel the need of some one about me—

GREGERS. You have Mrs. Sörby.

WERLE. Yes, I have her; and she has become, I may say, almost indispensable to me. She is lively and even-tempered; she brightens up the house; and that is a very great thing for me.

GREGERS. Well then, you have everything just as you wish it.

WERLE. Yes, but I am afraid it can't last. A woman so situated may easily find herself in a false position, in the eyes of the world. For that matter it does a man no good, either.

GREGERS. Oh, when a man gives such dinners as you give, he can risk a great deal.

WERLE. Yes, but how about the woman, Gregers? I fear she won't accept the situation much longer; and even if she did—even if, out of attachment to me, she were to take her chance of gossip and scandal and all that—? Do you think, Gregers—you with your strong sense of justice—

GREGERS [interrupts him]. Tell me in one word: are you thinking of marrying her?

WERLE. Suppose I were thinking of it? What then?

GREGERS. That's what I say: what then?

WERLE. Should you be inflexibly opposed to it!

GREGERS. Not at all. Not by any means.

WERLE. I was not sure whether your devotion to your mother's memory—

GREGERS. I am not overstrained.

WERLE. Well, whatever you may or may not be, at all events you have lifted a great weight from my mind. I am extremely pleased that I can reckon on your concurrence in this matter.

GREGERS [looking intently at him]. Now I see the use you want to put me to.

WERLE. Use to put you to? What an expression!

GREGERS. Oh, don't let us be nice in our choice of words—not when we are alone together, at any rate. [With a short laugh] Well well! So this is what made it absolutely essential that I should come to town in person. For the sake of Mrs. Sörby, we are to get up a pretence at family life in the house—a tableau of filial affection! That will be something new indeed.

WERLE. How dare you speak in that tone!

GREGERS. Was there ever any family life here? Never since I can remember. But now, forsooth, your plans demand something of the sort. No doubt it will have an excellent effect when it is reported that the son has hastened home, on the wings of filial piety, to the grey-haired father's wedding-feast. What will then remain of all the rumours as to the wrongs the poor dead mother had to submit to? Not a vestige. Her son annihilates them at one stroke.

WERLE. Gregers—I believe there is no one in the world you detest as you do me.

GREGERS [softly]. I have seen you at too close quarters.

WERLE. You have seen me with your mother's eyes. [Lowers his voice a little] But you should remember that her eyes were—clouded now and then.

GREGERS [quivering]. I see what you are hinting at. But who was to blame for mother's unfortunate weakness? Why you, and all those—! The last of them was this woman that you palmed off upon Hialmar Ekdal, when you were— Ugh!

WERLE [shrugs his shoulders]. Word for word as if it were your mother speaking!

GREGERS [without heeding]. And there he is now with his great, confiding, childlike mind, compassed about with all this treachery—living under the same roof with such a creature, and never dreaming that what he calls his home is built upon a lie! [Comes a step nearer] When I look back upon your past, I seem to see a battle-field with shattered lives on every hand.

WERLE. I begin to think the chasm that divides us is too wide.

GREGERS [bowing, with self-command]. So I have observed; and therefore I take my hat and go.

WERLE. You are going! Out of the house?

GREGERS. Yes. For at last I see my mission in life.

WERLE. What mission?

GREGERS. You would only laugh if I told you.

WERLE. A lonely man doesn't laugh so easily, Gregers.

GREGERS [pointing towards the background]. Look, father,—the Chamberlains are playing blind-man's-bluff with Mrs. Sörby.—Goodnight and good-bye. [He goes out by the back to the right]

[Sounds of laughter and merriment from the Company, who are now visible in the outer room]

WERLE [muttering contemptuously after GREGERS]. Ha—! Poor wretch—and he says he is not overstrained!

ACT SECOND

HIALMAR EKDAL'S studio, a good-sized room, evidently in the top storey of the building. On the right, a sloping roof of large panes of glass, half-covered by a blue curtain. In the right-hand corner, at the back, the entrance door; farther forward, on the same side, a door leading to the sitting-room. Two doors on the opposite side, and between them an iron stove. At the back, a wide double sliding-door. The studio is plainly but comfortably fitted up and furnished. Between the doors on the right, standing out a little from the wall, a sofa with a table and some chairs; on the table a lighted lamp with a shade; beside the stove an old armchair. Photographic instruments and apparatus of different kinds lying about the room. Against the back wall, to the left of the double door, stands a bookcase containing a few books, boxes, and bottles of chemicals, instruments, tools, and other objects. Photographs and small articles, such as camel's-hair pencils, paper, and so forth, lie on the table.

GINA EKDAL sits on a chair by the table, sewing. HEDVIG is sitting on the sofa, with her hands shading her eyes and her thumbs in her ears, reading a book.

GINA [glances once or twice at HEDVIG, as if with secret anxiety; then says:] Hedvig!

HEDVIG [does not hear].

GINA [repeats more loudly]. Hedvig!

HEDVIG [takes away her hands and looks up]. Yes, mother?

GINA. Hedvig dear, you mustn't sit reading any longer now.

HEDVIG. Oh mother, mayn't I read a little more? Just a little bit?

GINA. No no, you must put away your book now. Father doesn't like it; he never reads hisself in the evening.

HEDVIG [shuts the book]. No, father doesn't care much about reading.

GINA [puts aside her sewing and takes up a lead pencil and a little account-book from the table]. Can you remember how much we paid for the butter to-day?

HEDVIG. It was one crown sixty-five.

GINA. That's right. [Puts it down] It's terrible what a lot of butter we get through in this house. Then there was the smoked sausage, and the cheese—let me see— [Writes]—and the ham— [Adds up] Yes, that makes just—

HEDVIG. And then the beer.

GINA. Yes, to be sure. [Writes] How it do mount up! But we can't manage with no less.

HEDVIG. And then you and I didn't need anything hot for dinner, as father was out.

GINA. No; that was so much to the good. And then I took eight crowns fifty for the photographs.

HEDVIG. Really! So much as that?

GINA. Exactly eight crowns fifty.

[Silence. GINA takes up her sewing again, HEDVIG takes paper and pencil and begins to draw, shading her eyes with her left hand]

HEDVIG. Isn't it jolly to think that father is at Mr. Werle's big dinner-party?

GINA. You know he's not really Mr. Werle's guest. It was the son invited him. [After a pause] We have nothing to do with that Mr. Werle.

HEDVIG. I'm longing for father to come

home. He promised to ask Mrs. Sörby for something nice for me.

GINA. Yes, there's plenty of good things going in that house, I can tell you.

HEDVIG [goes on drawing]. And I believe I'm a little hungry too.

[OLD EKDAL, with the paper parcel under his arm and another parcel in his coat pocket, comes in by the entrance door]

GINA. How late you are to-day, grandfather!

EKDAL. They had locked the office door. Had to wait in Gråberg's room. And then they let me through—h'm.

HEDVIG. Did you get some more copying to do, grandfather?

EKDAL. This whole packet. Just look.

GINA. That's capital.

HEDVIG. And you have another parcel in your pocket.

EKDAL. Eh? Oh never mind, that's nothing. [Puts his stick away in a corner] This work will keep me going a long time, Gina. [Opens one of the sliding-doors in the back wall a little] Hush! [Peeps into the room for a moment, then pushes the door carefully to again] Hee-hee! They're fast asleep, all the lot of them. And she's gone into the basket herself. Hee-hee!

HEDVIG. Are you sure she isn't cold in that basket, grandfather?

EKDAL. Not a bit of it! Cold? With all that straw? [Goes towards the farther door on the left] There are matches in here, I suppose.

GINA. The matches is on the drawers.

[EKDAL goes into his room]

HEDVIG. It's nice that grandfather has got all that copying.

GINA. Yes, poor old father; it means a bit of pocket-money for him.

HEDVIG. And he won't be able to sit the whole forenoon down at that horrid Madam Eriksen's.

GINA. No more he won't.

[Short silence]

HEDVIG. Do you suppose they are still at the dinner-table?

GINA. Goodness knows; as like as not.

HEDVIG. Think of all the delicious things father is having to eat! I'm certain he'll be in splendid spirits when he comes. Don't you think so, mother?

GINA. Yes; and if only we could tell him that we'd got the room let—

HEDVIG. But we don't need that this evening.

GINA. Oh, we'd be none the worse of it, I can tell you. It's no use to us as it is.

HEDVIG. I mean we don't need it this evening, for father will be in a good humour at any rate. It is best to keep the letting of the room for another time.

GINA [looks across at her]. You like having

some good news to tell father when he comes home in the evening?

HEDVIG. Yes; for then things are pleasanter somehow.

GINA [thinking to herself]. Yes, yes, there's something in that.

[OLD EKDAL comes in again and is going out by the foremost door to the left]

GINA [half turning in her chair]. Do you want something out of the kitchen, grandfather?

EKDAL. Yes, yes, I do. Don't you trouble. [Goes out]

GINA. He's not poking away at the fire, is he? [Waits a moment] Hedvig, go and see what he's about.

[EKDAL comes in again with a small jug of steaming hot water]

HEDVIG. Have you been getting some hot water, grandfather?

EKDAL. Yes, hot water. Want it for something. Want to write, and the ink has got as thick as porridge.—h'm.

GINA. But you'd best have your supper, first, grandfather. It's laid in there.

EKDAL. Can't be bothered with supper, Gina. Very busy, I tell you. No one's to come to my room. No one—h'm. [He goes into his room]

[GINA and HEDVIG look at each other]

GINA [softly]. Can you imagine where he's got money from?

HEDVIG. From Gråberg, perhaps.

GINA. Not a bit of it. Gråberg always sends the money to me.

HEDVIG. Then he must have got a bottle on credit somewhere.

GINA. Poor grandfather, who'd give him credit?

[HIALMAR EKDAL, in an overcoat and grey felt hat, comes in from the right]

GINA [throws down her sewing and rises]. Why, Ekdal. Is that you already?

HEDVIG [at the same time jumping up]. Fancy your coming so soon, father!

HIALMAR [taking off his hat]. Yes, most of the people were coming away.

HEDVIG. So early?

HIALMAR. Yes, it was a dinner-party, you know. [Is taking off his overcoat]

GINA. Let me help you.

HEDVIG. Me too.

[They draw off his coat; GINA hangs it up on the back wall]

HEDVIG. Were there many people there, father?

HIALMAR. Oh no, not many. We were about twelve or fourteen at table.

GINA. And you had some talk with them all?

HIALMAR. Oh yes, a little; but Gregers took me up most of the time.

GINA. Is Gregers as ugly as ever?

HIALMAR. Well, he's not very much to look at. Hasn't the old man come home?

HEDVIG. Yes, grandfather is in his room, writing.

HIALMAR. Did he say anything?

GINA. No, what should he say?

HIALMAR. Didn't he say anything about—? I heard something about his having been with Gråberg. I'll go in and see him for a moment.

GINA. No, no, better not.

HIALMAR. Why not? Did he say he didn't want me to go in?

GINA. I don't think he wants to see nobody this evening—

HEDVIG [making signs]. H'm—h'm!

GINA [not noticing]. —he has been in to fetch hot water—

HIALMAR. Aha! Then he's—

GINA. Yes, I suppose so.

HIALMAR. Oh God! my poor old white-haired father!— Well, well; there let him sit and get all the enjoyment he can.

[OLD EKDAL, in an indoor coat and with a lighted pipe, comes from his room]

EKDAL. Got home? Thought it was you I heard talking.

HIALMAR. Yes, I have just come.

EKDAL. You didn't see me, did you?

HIALMAR. No; but they told me you had passed through—so I thought I would follow you.

EKDAL. H'm, good of you, Hialmar.—Who were they, all those fellows?

HIALMAR. Oh, all sorts of people. There was Chamberlain Flor, and Chamberlain Balle, and Chamberlain Kaspersen, and Chamberlain—this, that, and the other—I don't know who all—

EKDAL [nodding]. Hear that, Gina! Chamberlains every one of them!

GINA. Yes, I hear as they're terrible genteel in that house nowadays.

HEDVIG. Did the Chamberlains sing, father? Or did they read aloud?

HIALMAR. No, they only talked nonsense. They wanted me to recite something for them; but I knew better than that.

EKDAL. You weren't to be persuaded, eh?

GINA. Oh, you might have done it.

HIALMAR. No; one mustn't be at everybody's beck and call. [Walks about the room] That's not my way, at any rate.

EKDAL. No no; Hialmar's not to be had for the asking, he isn't.

HIALMAR. I don't see why I should bother myself to entertain people on the rare occasions when I go into society. Let the others exert themselves. These fellows go from one great dinner-table to the next and gorge and guzzle day out and day in. It's for them to bestir themselves and do something in return for all the good feeding they get.

GINA. But you didn't say that?

HIALMAR [humming]. Ho-ho-ho—; faith, I gave them a bit of my mind.

EKDAL. Not the Chamberlains?

HIALMAR. Oh, why not? [Lightly] After that, we had a little discussion about Tokay.

EKDAL. Tokay! There's a fine wine for you!

HIALMAR [comes to a standstill]. It may be a fine wine. But of course you know the vintages differ; it all depends on how much sunshine the grapes have had.

GINA. Why, you know everything, Ekdal.

EKDAL. And did they dispute that?

HIALMAR. They tried to; but they were requested to observe that it was just the same with Chamberlains—that with them, too, different batches were of different qualities.

GINA. What things you do think of!

EKDAL. Hee-hee! So they got that in their pipes too?

HIALMAR. Right in their teeth.

EKDAL. Do you hear that, Gina? He said it right in the very teeth of all the Chamberlains.

GINA. Fancy—! Right in their teeth!

HIALMAR. Yes, but I don't want it talked about. One doesn't speak of such things. The whole affair passed off quite amicably of course. They were nice, genial fellows; I didn't want to wound them—not I!

EKDAL. Right in their teeth, though—!

HEDVIG [caressingly]. How nice it is to see you in a dress-coat! It suits you so well, father.

HIALMAR. Yes, don't you think so? And this one really sits to perfection. It fits almost as if it had been made for me;—a little tight in the arm-holes perhaps;—help me, Hedvig. [Takes off the coat] I think I'll put on my jacket. Where is my jacket, Gina?

GINA. Here it is. [Brings the jacket and helps him]

HIALMAR. That's it! Don't forget to send the coat back to Molvik first thing to-morrow morning.

GINA [laying it away]. I'll be sure and see to it.

HIALMAR [stretching himself]. After all, there's a more homely feeling about this. A free-and-easy indoor costume suits my whole personality better. Don't you think so, Hedvig?

HEDVIG. Yes, father.

HIALMAR. When I loosen my necktie into a pair of flowing ends—like this—eh?

HEDVIG. Yes, that goes so well with your moustache and the sweep of your curls.

HIALMAR. I should not call them curls exactly; I should rather say locks.

HEDVIG. Yes, they are too big for curls.

HIALMAR. Locks describe them better.

HEDVIG [*after a pause, twitching his jacket*]. Father.

HIALMAR. Well, what is it?

HEDVIG. Oh, you know very well.

HIALMAR. No, really I don't—

HEDVIG [*half laughing, half whimpering*]. Oh yes, father; now don't tease me any longer!

HIALMAR. Why, what do you mean?

HEDVIG [*shaking him*]. Oh what nonsense; come, where are they, father? All the good things you promised me, you know?

HIALMAR. Oh—if I haven't forgotten all about them!

HEDVIG. Now you're only teasing me, father! Oh, it's too bad of you! Where have you put them?

HIALMAR. No, I positively forgot to get anything. But wait a little! I have something else for you, Hedvig. [*Goes and searches in the pockets of the coat*]

HEDVIG [*skipping and clapping her hands*]. Oh mother, mother!

GINA. There, you see: if you only give him time—

HIALMAR. [*with a paper*]. Look, here it is.

HEDVIG. That? Why, that's only a paper.

HIALMAR. That is the bill of fare, my dear; the whole bill of fare. Here you see: "Menu"—that means bill of fare.

HEDVIG. Haven't you anything else?

HIALMAR. I forgot the other things, I tell you. But you may take my word for it, these dainties are very unsatisfying. Sit down at the table and read the bill of fare, and then I'll describe to you how the dishes taste. Here you are, Hedvig.

HEDVIG [*gulping down her tears*]. Thank you. [*She seats herself, but does not read*]

[*GINA makes signs to her; HIALMAR notices it*]

HIALMAR [*pacing up and down the room*]. It's monstrous what absurd things the father of a family is expected to think of; and if he forgets the smallest trifle, he is treated to sour faces at once. Well, well, one gets used to that too. [*Stops near the stove, by the old man's chair*] Have you peeped in there this evening, father?

EKDAL. Yes, to be sure I have. She's gone into the basket.

HIALMAR. Ah, she has gone into the basket. Then she's beginning to get used to it.

EKDAL. Yes; just as I prophesied. But you know there are still a few little things—

HIALMAR. A few improvements, yes.

EKDAL. They've got to be made, you know.

HIALMAR. Yes, let us have a talk about the improvements, father. Come, let us sit on the sofa.

EKDAL. All right. H'm—think I'll just fill my pipe first. Must clean it out, too. H'm. [*He goes into his room*]

GINA [*smiling to* HIALMAR]. His pipe!

HIALMAR. Oh yes, yes, Gina; let him alone—the poor shipwrecked old man.—Yes, these improvements—we had better get them out of hand to-morrow.

GINA. You'll hardly have time to-morrow, Ekdal.

HEDVIG [*interposing*]. Oh yes he will, mother!

GINA. —for remember them prints that has to be retouched; they've sent for them time after time.

HIALMAR. There now! those prints again! I shall get them finished all right! Have any new orders come in?

GINA. No, worse luck; to-morrow I have nothing but those two sittings, you know.

HIALMAR. Nothing else? Oh no, if people won't set about things with a will—

GINA. But what more can I do? Don't I advertise in the papers as much as we can afford?

HIALMAR. Yes, the papers, the papers; you see how much good they do. And I suppose no one has been to look at the room either?

GINA. No, not yet.

HIALMAR. That was only to be expected. If people won't keep their eyes open—. Nothing can be done without a real effort, Gina!

HEDVIG [*going towards him*]. Shall I fetch you the flute, father?

HIALMAR. No; no flute for me; I want no pleasures in this world. [*Pacing about*] Yes, indeed I will work to-morrow; you shall see if I don't. You may be sure I shall work as long as my strength holds out.

GINA. But my dear good Ekdal, I didn't mean it in that way.

HEDVIG. Father, mayn't I bring in a bottle of beer?

HIALMAR. No, certainly not. I require nothing, nothing— [*Comes to a standstill*] Beer? Was it beer you were talking about?

HEDVIG [*cheerfully*]. Yes, father; beautiful fresh beer.

HIALMAR. Well—since you insist upon it, you may bring in a bottle.

GINA. Yes. Yes, do; and we'll be nice and cosy.

[*HEDVIG runs towards the kitchen door*]

HIALMAR [*by the stove, stops her, looks at her, puts his arm round her neck and presses her to him*]. Hedvig, Hedvig!

HEDVIG [*with tears of joy*]. My dear, kind father.

HIALMAR. No, don't call me that. Here have I been feasting at the rich man's table,—battening at the groaning board—! And I couldn't even—!

GINA [*sitting at the tabe*]. Oh nonsense, nonsense, Ekdal.

HIALMAR. It's not nonsense! And yet you mustn't be too hard upon me. You know that I love you for all that.

HEDVIG [*throwing her arms round him*]. And we love you, oh so dearly, father!

HIALMAR. And if I am unreasonable once in a while,—why then—you must remember that I am a man beset by a host of cares. There, there! [*Dries his eyes*] No beer at such a moment as this. Give me the flute.

[HEDVIG *runs to the bookcase and fetches it*]

HIALMAR. Thanks! That's right. With my flute in my hand and you two at my side—ah—!

[HEDVIG *seats herself at the table near* GINA; HIALMAR *paces backwards and forwards, pipes up vigorously, and plays a Bohemian peasant dance, but in a slow plaintive tempo, and with sentimental expression*]

HIALMAR [*breaking off the melody, holds out his left hand to* GINA, *and says with emotion:*]. Our roof may be poor and humble, Gina! but it is home. And with all my heart I say: here dwells my happiness. [*He begins to play again*]

[*Almost immediately after, a knocking is heard at the entrance door*]

GINA [*rising*]. Hush, Ekdal,—I think there's some one at the door.

HIALMAR [*laying the flute on the bookcase*]. There! Again!

[GINA *goes and opens the door*]

GREGERS WERLE [*in the passage*]. Excuse me—

GINA [*starting back slightly*]. Oh!

GREGERS. —does not Mr. Ekdal, the photographer, live here?

GINA. Yes, he does.

HIALMAR [*going towards the door*]. Gregers? You here after all? Well, come in then.

GREGERS [*coming in*]. I told you I would come and look you up.

HIALMAR. But this evening—? Have you left the party?

GREGERS. I have left both the party and my father's house.—Good evening, Mrs. Ekdal. I don't know whether you recognise me?

GINA. Oh yes; it's not difficult to know young Mr. Werle again.

GREGERS. No, I am like my mother; and no doubt you remember her.

HIALMAR. Left your father's house, did you say?

GREGERS. Yes, I have gone to a hotel.

HIALMAR. Indeed. Well, since you're here, take off your coat and sit down.

GREGERS. Thanks. [*He takes off his overcoat. He is now dressed in a plain grey suit of a countrified cut*]

HIALMAR. Here, on the sofa. Make yourself comfortable.

[GREGERS *seats himself on the sofa;* HIALMAR *takes a chair at the table*]

GREGERS [*looking around him*]. So these are your quarters, Hialmar—this is your home.

HIALMAR. This is the studio, as you see—

GINA. But it's the largest of our rooms, so we generally sit here.

HIALMAR. We used to live in a better place; but this flat has one great advantage: there are such capital outer rooms—

GINA. And we have a room on the other side of the passage that we can let.

GREGERS [*to* HIALMAR]. Ah—so you have lodgers too?

HIALMAR. No, not yet. They're not so easy to find, you see; you have to keep your eyes open. [*To* HEDVIG] What about that beer, eh?

[HEDVIG *nods and goes out into the kitchen*]

GREGERS. So that is your daughter?

HIALMAR. Yes, that is Hedvig.

GREGERS. And she is your only child?

HIALMAR. Yes, the only one. She is the joy of our lives, and— [*Lowering his voice*]—at the same time our deepest sorrow, Gregers.

GREGERS. What do you mean?

HIALMAR. She is in serious danger of losing her eyesight.

GREGERS. Becoming blind?

HIALMAR. Yes. Only the first symptoms have appeared as yet, and she may not feel it much for some time. But the doctor has warned us. It is coming, inexorably.

GREGERS. What a terrible misfortune! How do you account for it?

HIALMAR [*sighs*]. Hereditary, no doubt.

GREGERS [*starting*]. Hereditary?

GINA. Ekdal's mother had weak eyes.

HIALMAR. Yes, so my father says; I can't remember her.

GREGERS. Poor child! And how does she take it?

HIALMAR. Oh, you can imagine we haven't the heart to tell her of it. She dreams of no danger. Gay and careless and chirping like a little bird, she flutters onward into a life of endless night. [*Overcome*] Oh, it is cruelly hard on me, Gregers.

[HEDVIG *brings a tray with beer and glasses, which she sets upon the table*]

HIALMAR [*stroking her hair*]. Thanks, thanks, Hedvig.

[HEDVIG *puts her arm round his neck and whispers in his ear*]

HIALMAR. No, no bread and butter just now. [*Looks up*] But perhaps you would like some, Gregers.

GREGERS [*with a gesture of refusal*]. No, no thank you.

HIALMAR [*still melancholy*]. Well, you can bring in a little all the same. If you have a crust, that is all I want. And plenty of butter on it, mind.

[HEDVIG *nods gaily and goes out into the kitchen again*]

GREGERS [*who has been following her with his eyes*]. She seems quite strong and healthy otherwise.

GINA. Yes. In other ways there's nothing amiss with her, thank goodness.

GREGERS. She promises to be very like you, Mrs. Ekdal. How old is she now?

GINA. Hedvig is close on fourteen; her birthday is the day after to-morrow.

GREGERS. She is pretty tall for her age, then.

GINA. Yes, she's shot up wonderful this last year.

GREGERS. It makes one realise one's own age to see these young people growing up.—How long is it now since you were married?

GINA. We've been married—let me see—just on fifteen years.

GREGERS. Is it so long as that?

GINA [*becomes attentive; looks at him*]. Yes, it is indeed.

HIALMAR. Yes, so it is. Fifteen years all but a few months. [*Changing his tone*] They must have been long years for you, up at the works, Gregers.

GREGERS. They seemed long while I was living them; now they are over, I hardly know how the time has gone.

[OLD EKDAL *comes from his room without his pipe, but with his old-fashioned uniform cap on his head; his gait is somewhat unsteady*]

EKDAL. Come now, Hialmar, let's sit down and have a good talk about this—h'm—what was it again?

HIALMAR [*going towards him*]. Father, we have a visitor here—Gregers Werle.—I don't know if you remember him.

EKDAL [*looking at* GREGERS, *who has risen*]. Werle? Is that the son? What does he want with me?

HIALMAR. Nothing; it's me he has come to see.

EKDAL. Oh! Then there's nothing wrong?

HIALMAR. No, no, of course not.

EKDAL [*with a large gesture*]. Not that I'm afraid, you know; but—

GREGERS [*goes over to him*]. I bring you a greeting from your old hunting-grounds, Lieutenant Ekdal.

EKDAL. Hunting-grounds?

GREGERS. Yes, up in Höidal, about the works, you know.

EKDAL. Oh, up there. Yes, I knew all those places well in the old days.

GREGERS. You were a great sportsman then.

EKDAL. So I was, I don't deny it. You're looking at my uniform cap. I don't ask anybody's leave to wear it in the house. So long as I don't go out in the streets with it—

[HEDVIG *brings a plate of bread and butter, which she puts upon the table*]

HIALMAR. Sit down, father, and have a glass of beer. Help yourself, Gregers.

[EKDAL *mutters and stumbles over to the sofa.* GREGERS *seats himself on the chair nearest to him,* HIALMAR *on the other side of* GREGERS. GINA *sits a little way from the table, sewing;* HEDVIG *stands beside her father*]

GREGERS. Can you remember, Lieutenant Ekdal, how Hialmar and I used to come up and visit you in the summer and at Christmas?

EKDAL. Did you? No, no, no; I don't remember it. But sure enough I've been a tidy bit of a sportsman in my day. I've shot bears too. I've shot nine of 'em, no less.

GREGERS [*looking sympathetically at him*]. And now you never get any shooting?

EKDAL. Can't just say that, sir. Get a shot now and then perhaps. Of course not in the old way. For the woods you see—the woods, the woods—! [*Drinks*] Are the woods fine up there now?

GREGERS. Not so fine as in your time. They have been thinned a good deal.

EKDAL. Thinned? [*More softly, and as if afraid*] It's dangerous work that. Bad things come of it. The woods revenge themselves.

HIALMAR [*filling up his glass*]. Come—a little more, father.

GREGERS. How can a man like you—such a man for the open air—live in the midst of a stuffy town, boxed within four walls?

EKDAL [*laughs quietly and glances at* HIALMAR]. Oh, it's not so bad here. Not at all so bad.

GREGERS. But don't you miss all the things that used to be a part of your very being—the cool sweeping breezes, the free life in the woods and on the uplands, among beasts and birds—?

EKDAL [*smiling*]. Hialmar, shall we let him see it?

HIALMAR [*hastily and a little embarrassed*]. Oh no no, father; not this evening.

GREGERS. What does he want to show me?

HIALMAR. Oh, it's only something—you can see it another time.

GREGERS [*continues, to the old man*]. You see I have been thinking, Lieutenant Ekdal, that you should come up with me to the works; I am sure to be going back soon. No doubt you could get some copying there too. And here, you have nothing on earth to interest you—nothing to liven you up.

EKDAL [*stares in astonishment at him*]. Have *I* nothing on earth to—!

GREGERS. Of course you have Hialmar; but then he has his own family. And a man like you, who has always had such a passion for what is free and wild—

EKDAL [*thumps the table*]. Hialmar, he shall see it!

HIALMAR. Oh, do you think it's worth while, father? It's all dark.

EKDAL. Nonsense; it's moonlight. [*Rises*] He shall see it, I tell you. Let me pass! Come and help me, Hialmar.

HEDVIG. Oh yes, do, father!

HIALMAR [*rising*]. Very well then.

GREGERS [*to* GINA]. What is it?

GINA. Oh, nothing so very wonderful, after all.

[EKDAL *and* HIALMAR *have gone to the back wall and are each pushing back a side of the sliding door;* HEDVIG *helps the old man;* GREGERS *remains standing by the sofa;* GINA *sits still and sews. Through the open doorway a large, deep irregular garret is seen with odd nooks and corners; a couple of stove-pipes running through it, from rooms below. There are skylights through which clear moonbeams shine in on some parts of the great room; others lie in deep shadow*]

EKDAL [*to* GREGERS]. You may come close up if you like.

GREGERS [*going over to them*]. Why, what is it?

EKDAL. Look for yourself. H'm.

HIALMAR [*somewhat embarrassed*]. This belongs to father, you understand.

GREGERS [*at the door, looks into the garret*]. Why, you keep poultry, Lieutenant Ekdal.

EKDAL. Should think we did keep poultry. They've gone to roost now. But you should just see our fowls by daylight, sir!

HEDVIG. And there's a—

EKDAL. Sh—sh! don't say anything about it yet.

GREGERS. And you have pigeons too, I see.

EKDAL. Oh yes, haven't we just got pigeons! They have their nest-boxes up there under the roof-tree; for pigeons like to roost high, you see.

HIALMAR. They aren't all common pigeons.

EKDAL. Common! Should think not indeed! We have tumblers, and a pair of pouters, too. But come here! Can you see that hutch down there by the wall?

GREGERS. Yes; what do you use it for?

EKDAL. That's where the rabbits sleep, sir.

GREGERS. Dear me; so you have rabbits too?

EKDAL. Yes, you may take my word for it, we have rabbits! He wants to know if we have rabbits, Hialmar! H'm! But now comes the thing, let me tell you! Here we have it! Move away, Hedvig. Stand here; that's right, —and now look down there.—Don't you see a basket with straw in it?

GREGERS. Yes. And I can see a fowl lying in the basket.

EKDAL. H'm—"a fowl"—

GREGERS. Isn't it a duck?

EKDAL [*hurt*]. Why, of course it's a duck.

HIALMAR. But what kind of duck, do you think?

HEDVIG. It's not just a common duck—

EKDAL. Sh!

GREGERS. And it's not a Muscovy duck either.

EKDAL. No, Mr.—Werle; it's not a Muscovy duck; for it's a wild duck!

GREGERS. Is it really? A wild duck?

EKDAL. Yes, that's what it is. That "fowl" as you call it—is the wild duck. It's our wild duck, sir.

HEDVIG. My wild duck. It belongs to me.

GREGERS. And can it live up here in the garret? Does it thrive?

EKDAL. Of course it has a trough of water to splash about in, you know.

HIALMAR. Fresh water every other day.

GINA [*turning towards* HIALMAR]. But my dear Ekdal, it's getting icy cold here.

EKDAL. H'm, we had better shut up then. It's as well not to disturb their night's rest, too. Close up, Hedvig.

[HIALMAR *and* HEDVIG *push the garret doors together*]

EKDAL. Another time you shall see her properly. [*Seats himself in the arm-chair by the stove*] Oh, they're curious things, these wild ducks, I can tell you.

GREGERS. How did you manage to catch it, Lieutenant Ekdal?

EKDAL. *I* didn't catch it. There's a certain man in this town whom we have to thank for it.

GREGERS [*starts slightly*]. That man was not my father, was he?

EKDAL. You've hit it. Your father and no one else. H'm.

HIALMAR. Strange that you should guess that, Gregers.

GREGERS. You were telling me that you owed so many things to my father; and so I thought perhaps—

GINA. But we didn't get the duck from Mr. Werle himself—

EKDAL. It's Håkon Werle we have to thank for her, all the same, Gina. [*To* GREGERS] He was shooting from a boat, you see, and he brought her down. But your father's sight is not very good now. H'm; she was only wounded.

GREGERS. Ah! She got a couple of slugs in her body, I suppose.

HIALMAR. Yes, two or three.

HEDVIG. She was hit under the wing, so that she couldn't fly.

GREGERS. And I suppose she dived to the bottom, eh?

EKDAL [*sleepily, in a thick voice*]. Of course. Always do that, wild ducks do. They shoot to the bottom as deep as they can get, sir—and bite themselves fast in the tangle and sea-weed—and all the devil's own mess that grows down there. And they never come up again.

GREGERS. But your wild duck came up again, Lieutenant Ekdal.

EKDAL. He had such an amazingly clever dog, your father had. And that dog—he dived in after the duck and fetched her up again.

GREGERS [*who has turned to* HIALMAR]. And then she was sent to you here?

HIALMAR. Not at once; at first your father took her home. But she wouldn't thrive there; so Pettersen was told to put an end to her—

EKDAL [*half asleep*]. H'm—yes—Pettersen —that ass—

HIALMAR [*speaking more softly*]. That was how we got her, you see; for father knows Pettersen a little; and when he heard about the wild duck he got him to hand her over to us.

GREGERS. And now she thrives as well as possible in the garret there?

HIALMAR. Yes, wonderfully well. She has got fat. You see, she has lived in there so long now that she has forgotten her natural wild life; and it all depends on that.

GREGERS. You are right there, Hialmar. Be sure you never let her get a glimpse of the sky and the sea—. But I mustn't stay any longer; I think your father is asleep.

HIALMAR. Oh, as for that—

GREGERS. But, by-the-bye—you said you had a room to let—a spare room?

HIALMAR. Yes; what then? Do you know of anybody—?

GREGERS. Can *I* have that room?

HIALMAR. You?

GINA. Oh no, Mr. Werle, you—

GREGERS. May I have the room? If so, I'll take possession first thing to-morrow morning.

HIALMAR. Yes, with the greatest pleasure—

GINA. But, Mr. Werle, I'm sure it's not at all the sort of room for you.

HIALMAR. Why, Gina! how can you say that?

GINA. Why, because the room's neither large enough nor light enough, and—

GREGERS. That really doesn't matter, Mrs. Ekdal.

HIALMAR. I call it quite a nice room, and not at all badly furnished either.

GINA. But remember the pair of them underneath.

GREGERS. What pair?

GINA. Well, there's one as has been a tutor—

HIALMAR. That's Molvik—Mr. Molvik, B.A.

GINA. And then there's a doctor, by the name of Relling.

GREGERS. Relling? I know him a little; he practised for a time up in Höidal.

GINA. They're a regular rackety pair, they are. As often as not, they're out on the loose in the evenings; and then they come home at all hours, and they're not always just—

GREGERS. One soon gets used to that sort of thing. I daresay I shall be like the wild duck—

GINA. H'm; I think you ought to sleep upon it first, anyway.

GREGERS. You seem very unwilling to have me in the house, Mrs. Ekdal.

GINA. Oh no! What makes you think that?

HIALMAR. Well, you really behave strangely about it, Gina. [*To* GREGERS] Then I suppose you intend to remain in the town for the present?

GREGERS [*putting on his overcoat*]. Yes, now I intend to remain here.

HIALMAR. And yet not at your father's? What do you propose to do, then?

GREGERS. Ah, if I only knew that, Hialmar, I shouldn't be so badly off! But when one has the misfortune to be called Gregers—! "Gregers"— and then "Werle" after it; did you ever hear anything so hideous?

HIALMAR. Oh, I don't think so at all.

GREGERS. Ugh! Bah! I feel I should like to spit upon the fellow that answers to such a name. But when a man is once for all doomed to be Gregers—Werle in this world, as I am—

HIALMAR [*laughs*]. Ha ha! If you weren't Gregers Werle, what would you like to be?

GREGERS. If I could choose, I should like best to be a clever dog.

GINA. A dog!

HEDVIG [*involuntarily*]. Oh no!

GREGERS. Yes, an amazingly clever dog; one that goes to the bottom after wild ducks when they dive and bite themselves fast in tangle and sea-weed, down among the ooze.

HIALMAR. Upon my word now, Gregers—I don't in the least know what you're driving at.

GREGERS. Oh well, you might not be much the wiser if you did. It's understood, then, that I move in early to-morrow morning. [*To* GINA] I won't give you any trouble; I do everything for myself. [*To* HIALMAR] We can talk about the rest to-morrow.—Good-night, Mrs. Ekdal. [*Nods to* HEDVIG] Good-night.

GINA. Good-night, Mr. Werle.

HEDVIG. Good-night.

HIALMAR [*who has lighted a candle*]. Wait a moment; I must show you a light; the stairs are sure to be dark.

[GREGERS *and* HIALMAR *go out by the passage door*]

GINA [*looking straight before her, with her sewing in her lap*]. Wasn't that queer-like talk about wanting to be a dog?

HEDVIG. Do you know, mother—I believe he meant something quite different by that.

GINA. Why, what should he mean?

HEDVIG. Oh, I don't know; but it seemed to me he meant something different from what he said—all the time.

GINA. Do you think so? Yes, it was sort of queer.

HIALMAR [*comes back*]. The lamp was still burning. [*Puts out the candle and sets it down*] Ah, now one can get a mouthful of food at last. [*Begins to eat the bread and butter*] Well, you see, Gina—if only you keep your eyes open—

GINA. How, keep your eyes open—?

HIALMAR. Why, haven't we at last had the luck to get the room let? And just think— to a person like Gregers—a good old friend.

GINA. Well, I don't know what to say about it.

HEDVIG. Oh mother, you'll see; it'll be such fun!

HIALMAR. You're very strange. You were so bent upon getting the room let before; and now you don't like it.

GINA. Yes I do, Ekdal; if it had only been to some one else— But what do you suppose Mr. Werle will say?

HIALMAR. Old Werle? It doesn't concern him.

GINA. But surely you can see that there's something amiss between them again, or the young man wouldn't be leaving home. You know very well those two can't get on with each other.

HIALMAR. Very likely not, but—

GINA. And now Mr. Werle may fancy it's you that has egged him on—

HIALMAR. Let him fancy so, then! Mr. Werle has done a great deal for me; far be it from me to deny it. But that doesn't make me everlastingly dependent upon him.

GINA. But, my dear Ekdal, maybe grandfather 'll suffer for it. He may lose the little bit of work he gets from Gråberg.

HIALMAR. I could almost say: so much the better! Is it not humiliating for a man like me to see his grey-haired father treated as a pariah? But now I believe the fulness of time is at hand. [*Takes a fresh piece of bread and butter*] As sure as I have a mission in life, I mean to fulfil it now!

HEDVIG. Oh yes, father, do!

GINA. Hush! Don't wake him!

HIALMAR [*more softly*]. I will fulfil it, I say. The day shall come when— And that is why I say it's a good thing we have let the room; for that makes me more independent. The man who has a mission in life must be independent. [*By the arm-chair, with emotion*] Poor old white-haired father! Rely on your Hialmar. He has broad shoulders—strong shoulders, at any rate. You shall yet wake up some fine day and— [*To* GINA] Do you not believe it?

GINA [*rising*]. Yes, of course I do; but in the meantime suppose we see about getting him to bed.

HIALMAR. Yes, come.

[*They take hold of the old man carefully*]

ACT THIRD

HIALMAR EKDAL'S *studio. It is morning: the daylight shines through the large window in the slanting roof; the curtain is drawn back.*

HIALMAR *is sitting at the table, busy retouching a photograph; several others lie before him. Presently* GINA, *wearing her hat and cloak, enters by the passage door; she has a covered basket on her arm.*

HIALMAR. Back already, Gina?

GINA. Oh yes, one can't let the grass grow under one's feet. [*Sets her basket on a chair, and takes off her things*]

HIALMAR. Did you look in at Gregers' room?

GINA. Yes, that I did. It's a rare sight, I can tell you; he's made a pretty mess to start off with.

HIALMAR. How so?

GINA. He was determined to do everything for himself, he said; so he sets to work to light the stove, and what must he do but screw down the damper till the whole room is full of smoke. Ugh! There was a smell fit to—

HIALMAR. Well, really!

GINA. But that's not the worst of it; for then he thinks he'll put out the fire, and goes and empties his water-jug into the stove, and so makes the whole floor one filthy puddle.

HIALMAR. How annoying!

GINA. I've got the porter's wife to clean up after him, pig that he is! But the room won't be fit to live in till the afternoon.

HIALMAR. What's he doing with himself in the meantime?

GINA. He said he was going out for a little while.

HIALMAR. I looked in upon him too, for a moment—after you had gone.

GINA. So I heard. You've asked him to lunch.

HIALMAR. Just to a little bit of early lunch, you know. It's his first day—we can hardly do less. You've got something in the house, I suppose?

GINA. I shall have to find something or other.

HIALMAR. And don't cut it too fine, for I fancy Relling and Molvik are coming up too. I just happened to meet Relling on the stairs, you see; so I had to—

GINA. Oh, are we to have those two as well?

HIALMAR. Good Lord—a couple more or less can't make any difference.

OLD EKDAL [*opens his door and looks in*]. I say, Hialmar— [*Sees* GINA] Oh!

GINA. Do you want anything, grandfather?

EKDAL. Oh no, it doesn't matter. H'm! [*Retires again*]

GINA [*takes up the basket*]. Be sure you see that he doesn't go out.

HIALMAR. All right, all right. And, Gina, a little herring-salad wouldn't be a bad idea; Relling and Molvik were out on the loose again last night.

GINA. If only they don't come before I'm ready for them—

HIALMAR. No, of course they won't; take your own time.

GINA. Very well; and meanwhile you can be working a bit.

HIALMAR. Well, I am working! I am working as hard as I can!

GINA. Then you'll have that job off your hands, you see. [*She goes out to the kitchen with her basket*]

[*HIALMAR sits for a time pencilling away at the photograph, in an indolent and listless manner*]

EKDAL [*peeps in, looks round the studio, and says softly:*] Are you busy?

HIALMAR. Yes, I'm toiling at these wretched pictures—

EKDAL. Well, well, never mind,—since you're so busy—h'm! [*He goes out again; the door stands open*]

HIALMAR [*continues for some time in silence; then he lays down his brush and goes over to the door*]. Are you busy, father?

EKDAL [*in a grumbling tone, within*]. If you're busy, I'm busy too. H'm!

HIALMAR. Oh, very well, then. [*Goes to his work again*]

EKDAL [*presently, coming to the door again*]. H'm; I say, Hialmar, I'm not so very busy, you know.

HIALMAR. I thought you were writing.

EKDAL. Oh, devil take it! can't Gråberg wait a day or two? After all, it's not a matter of life and death.

HIALMAR. No; and you're not his slave either.

EKDAL. And about that other business in there—

HIALMAR. Just what I was thinking of. Do you want to go in? Shall I open the door for you?

EKDAL. Well, it wouldn't be a bad notion.

HIALMAR [*rises*]. Then we'd have that off our hands.

EKDAL. Yes, exactly. It's got to be ready first thing to-morrow. It is to-morrow, isn't it? H'm?

HIALMAR. Yes, of course it's to-morrow.

[*HIALMAR and EKDAL push aside each his half of the sliding door. The morning sun is shining in through the skylights; some doves are flying about; others sit cooing, upon the perches; the hens are heard clucking now and then, further back in the garret.*]

HIALMAR. There; now you can get to work, father.

EKDAL [*goes in*]. Aren't you coming too?

HIALMAR. Well really, do you know—; I almost think— [*Sees GINA at the kitchen door*] I? No; I haven't time; I must work.— But now for our new contrivance—

[*He pulls a cord, a curtain slips down inside, the lower part consisting of a piece of old sailcloth, the upper part of a stretched fishing net. The floor of the garret is thus no longer visible*]

HIALMAR [*goes to the table*]. So! Now, perhaps I can sit in peace for a little while.

GINA. Is he rampaging in there again?

HIALMAR. Would you rather have had him slip down to Madam Eriksen's. [*Seats himself*] Do you want anything? You know you said—

GINA. I only wanted to ask if you think we can lay the table for lunch here?

HIALMAR. Yes; we have no early appointment, I suppose.

GINA. No, I expect no one to-day except those two sweethearts that are to be taken together.

HIALMAR. Why the deuce couldn't they be taken together another day!

GINA. Don't you know, I told them to come in the afternoon, when you are having your nap.

HIALMAR. Oh, that's capital. Very well, let us have lunch here then.

GINA. All right; but there's no hurry about laying the cloth; you can have the table for a good while yet.

HIALMAR. Do you think I am not sticking at my work? I'm at it as hard as I can!

GINA. Then you'll be free later on, you know. [*Goes out into the kitchen again*]

[*Short pause*]

EKDAL [*in the garret doorway, behind the net*]. Hialmar!

HIALMAR. Well?

EKDAL. Afraid we shall have to move the water-trough, after all.

HIALMAR. What else have I been saying all along?

EKDAL. H'm—h'm—h'm. [*Goes away from the door again*]

[*HIALMAR goes on working a little; glances towards the garret and half rises. HEDVIG comes in from the kitchen*]

HIALMAR [*sits down again hurriedly*]. What do you want?

HEDVIG. I only wanted to come in beside you, father.

HIALMAR [*after a pause*]. What makes you go prying around like that? Perhaps you are told off to watch me?

HEDVIG. No, no.

HIALMAR. What is your mother doing out there?

HEDVIG. Oh, mother's in the middle of making the herring-salad. [*Goes to the table*] Isn't there any little thing I could help you with, father?

HIALMAR. Oh no. It is right that I should bear the whole burden—so long as my strength holds out. Set your mind at rest, Hedvig; if only your father keeps his health—

HEDVIG. Oh no, father! You mustn't talk in that horrid way. [*She wanders about a little, stops by the doorway and looks into the garret*]

HIALMAR. Tell me, what is he doing?

HEDVIG. I think he's making a new path to the water-trough.

HIALMAR. He can never manage that by himself! And here am I doomed to sit—!

HEDVIG [*goes to him*]. Let me take the brush, father; I can do it, quite well.

HIALMAR. Oh nonsense; you will only hurt your eyes.

HEDVIG. Not a bit. Give me the brush.

HIALMAR [*rising*]. Well, it won't take more than a minute or two.

HEDVIG. Pooh, what harm can it do then? [*Takes the brush*] There! [*Seats herself*] I can begin upon this one.

HIALMAR. But mind you don't hurt your eyes! Do you hear? *I* won't be answerable; you do it on your own responsibility—understand that.

HEDVIG [*retouching*]. Yes yes, I understand.

HIALMAR. You are quite clever at it, Hedvig. Only a minute or two, you know. [*He slips through by the edge of the curtain into the garret*]

[HEDVIG *sits at her work.* HIALMAR *and* EKDAL *are heard disputing inside*]

HIALMAR [*appears behind the net*]. I say, Hedvig—give me those pincers that are lying on the shelf. And the chisel. [*Turns away inside*] Now you shall see, father. Just let me show you first what I mean!

[HEDVIG *has fetched the required tools from the shelf, and hands them to him through the net*]

HIALMAR. Ah, thanks. I didn't come a moment too soon. [*Goes back from the curtain again*]

[*They are heard carpentering and talking inside.* HEDVIG *stands looking in at them. A moment later there is a knock at the passage door; she does not notice it*]

GREGERS WERLE [*bareheaded, in indoor dress, enters and stops near the door*] H'm—!

HEDVIG [*turns and goes towards him*]. Good morning. Please come in.

GREGERS. Thank you. [*Looking towards the garret*] You seem to have workpeople in the house.

HEDVIG. No, it is only father and grandfather. I'll tell them you are here.

GREGERS. No no, don't do that; I would rather wait a little. [*Seats himself on the sofa*]

HEDVIG. It looks so untidy here— [*Begins to clear away the photographs*]

GREGERS. Oh, don't take them away. Are those prints that have to be finished off?

HEDVIG. Yes, they are a few I was helping father with.

GREGERS. Please don't let me disturb you.

HEDVIG. Oh no. [*She gathers the things to her and sits down to work*]

[GREGERS *looks at her, meanwhile, in silence*]

GREGERS. Did the wild duck sleep well last night?

HEDVIG. Yes, I think so, thanks.

GREGERS [*turning towards the garret*]. It looks quite different by day from what it did last night in the moonlight.

HEDVIG. Yes, it changes ever so much. It looks different in the morning and in the afternoon; and it's different on rainy days from what it is in fine weather.

GREGERS. Have you noticed that?

HEDVIG. Yes, how could I help it?

GREGERS. Are you, too, fond of being in there with the wild duck?

HEDVIG. Yes, when I can manage it—

GREGERS. But I suppose you haven't much spare time; you go to school, no doubt.

HEDVIG. No, not now; father is afraid of my hurting my eyes.

GREGERS. Oh; then he reads with you himself?

HEDVIG. Father has promised to read with me; but he has never had time yet.

GREGERS. Then is there nobody else to give you a little help?

HEDVIG. Yes, there is Mr. Molvik; but he is not always exactly—quite—

GREGERS. Sober?

HEDVIG. Yes, I suppose that's it!

GREGERS. Why, then you must have any amount of time on your hands. And in there I suppose it is a sort of world by itself?

HEDVIG. Oh yes, quite. And there are such lots of wonderful things.

GREGERS. Indeed?

HEDVIG. Yes, there are big cupboards full of books; and a great many of the books have pictures in them.

GREGERS. Aha!

HEDVIG. And there's an old bureau with drawers and flaps, and a big clock with figures that go out and in. But the clock isn't going now.

GREGERS. So time has come to a standstill in there—in the wild duck's domain.

HEDVIG. Yes. And then there's an old paint-box and things of that sort; and all the books.

GREGERS. And you read the books, I suppose?

HEDVIG. Oh yes, when I get the chance. Most of them are English though, and I don't understand English. But then I look at the pictures.—There is one great big book called "Harrison's History of London." It must be a hundred years old; and there are such heaps of pictures in it. At the beginning there is Death with an hour-glass and a woman. I think that is horrid. But then there are all the other pictures of churches, and castles, and streets, and great ships sailing on the sea.

GREGERS. But tell me, where did all those wonderful things come from?

HEDVIG. Oh, an old sea captain once lived here, and he brought them home with him. They used to call him "The Flying Dutchman." That was curious, because he wasn't a Dutchman at all.

GREGERS. Was he not?

HEDVIG. No. But at last he was drowned at sea; and so he left all those things behind him.

GREGERS. Tell me now—when you are sitting in there looking at the pictures, don't you wish you could travel and see the real world for yourself?

HEDVIG. Oh no! I mean always to stay at home and help father and mother.

GREGERS. To retouch photographs?

HEDVIG. No, not only that. I should love above everything to learn to engrave pictures like those in the English books.

GREGERS. H'm. What does your father say to that?

HEDVIG. I don't think father likes it; father is strange about such things. Only think, he talks of my learning basket-making, and straw-plaiting! But I don't think that would be much good.

GREGERS. Oh no, I don't think so either.

HEDVIG. But father was right in saying that if I had learnt basket-making I could have made the new basket for the wild duck.

GREGERS. So you could; and it was you that ought to have done it, wasn't it?

HEDVIG. Yes, for it's my wild duck.

GREGERS. Of course it is.

HEDVIG. Yes, it belongs to me. But I lend it to father and grandfather as often as they please.

GREGERS. Indeed? What do they do with it?

HEDVIG. Oh, they look after it, and build places for it, and so on.

GREGERS. I see; for no doubt the wild duck is by far the most distinguished inhabitant of the garret?

HEDVIG. Yes, indeed she is; for she is a real wild fowl, you know. And then she is so much

to be pitied; she has no one to care for, poor thing.

GREGERS. She has no family, as the rabbits have—

HEDVIG. No. The hens too, many of them, were chickens together; but she has been taken right away from all her friends. And then there is so much that is strange about the wild duck. Nobody knows her, and nobody knows where she came from either.

GREGERS. And she has been down in the depths of the sea.

HEDVIG [with a quick glance at him, represses a smile and asks:] Why do you say "the depths of the sea"?

GREGERS. What else should I say?

HEDVIG. You could say "the bottom of the sea."

GREGERS. Oh, mayn't I just as well say the depths of the sea?

HEDVIG. Yes; but it sounds so strange to me when other people speak of the depths of the sea.

GREGERS. Why so? Tell me why?

HEDVIG. No, I won't; it's so stupid.

GREGERS. Oh no, I am sure it's not. Do tell me why you smiled.

HEDVIG. Well, this is the reason: whenever I come to realise suddenly—in a flash—what is in there, it always seems to me that the whole room and everything in it should be called "the depths of the sea."—But that is so stupid.

GREGERS. You mustn't say that.

HEDVIG. Oh yes, for you know it is only a garret.

GREGERS [looks fixedly at her]. Are you so sure of that?

HEDVIG [astonished]. That it's a garret?

GREGERS. Are you quite certain of it?

[HEDVIG is silent, and looks at him open-mouthed. GINA comes in from the kitchen with the table things]

GREGERS [rising]. I have come in upon you too early.

GINA. Oh, you must be somewhere; and we're nearly ready now, any way. Clear the table, Hedvig.

[HEDVIG clears away her things; she and GINA lay the cloth during what follows. GREGERS seats himself in the arm-chair, and turns over an album]

GREGERS. I hear you can retouch, Mrs. Ekdal.

GINA [with a side glance]. Yes, I can.

GREGERS. That was exceedingly lucky.

GINA. How—lucky?

GREGERS. Since Ekdal took to photography, I mean.

HEDVIG. Mother can take photographs too.

GINA. Oh, yes; I was bound to learn that.

GREGERS. So it is really you that carry on the business, I suppose?

GINA. Yes, when Ekdal hasn't time himself—

GREGERS. He is a great deal taken up with his old father, I daresay.

GINA. Yes; and then you can't expect a man like Ekdal to do nothing but take car-de-visits of Dick, Tom and Harry.

GREGERS. I quite agree with you; but having once gone in for the thing—

GINA. You can surely understand, Mr. Werle, that Ekdal's not like one of your common photographers.

GREGERS. Of course not; but still—

[*A shot is fired within the garret*]

GREGERS [*starting up*]. What's that?

GINA. Ugh! now they're firing again!

GREGERS. Have they firearms in there?

HEDVIG. They are out shooting.

GREGERS. What! [*At the door of the garret*] Are you shooting, Hialmar?

HIALMAR [*inside the net*]. Are you there? I didn't know; I was so taken up— [*To HEDVIG*] Why did you not let us know? [*Comes into the studio*]

GREGERS. Do you go shooting in the garret?

HIALMAR [*showing a double-barrelled pistol*]. Oh, only with this thing.

GINA. Yes, you and grandfather will do yourselves a mischief some day with that there pigstol.

HIALMAR [*with irritation*]. I believe I have told you that this kind of firearm is called a pistol.

GINA. Oh, that doesn't make it much better, that I can see.

GREGERS. So you have become a sportsman too, Hialmar.

HIALMAR. Only a little rabbit-shooting now and then. Mostly to please father, you understand.

GINA. Men are strange beings; they must always have something to pervert theirselves with.

HIALMAR [*snappishly*]. Just so; we must always have something to divert ourselves with.

GINA. Yes, that's just what I say.

HIALMAR. H'm. [*To GREGERS*] You see the garret is fortunately so situated that no one can hear us shooting. [*Lays the pistol on the top shelf of the bookcase*] Don't touch the pistol, Hedvig! One of the barrels is loaded; remember that.

GREGERS [*looking through the net*]. You have a fowling-piece too, I see.

HIALMAR. That is father's old gun. It's of no use now; something has gone wrong with the lock. But it's fun to have it all the same; for we can take it to pieces now and then, and clean and grease it, and screw it together again.—Of course, it's mostly father that fiddle-faddles with all that sort of thing.

HEDVIG [*beside GREGERS*]. Now you can see the wild duck properly.

GREGERS. I was just looking at her. One of her wings seems to me to droop a bit.

HEDVIG. Well, no wonder; her wing was broken, you know.

GREGERS. And she trails one foot a little. Isn't that so?

HIALMAR. Perhaps a very little bit.

HEDVIG. Yes, it was by that foot the dog took hold of her.

HIALMAR. But otherwise she hasn't the least thing the matter with her; and that is simply marvellous for a creature that has a charge of shot in her body, and has been between a dog's teeth—

GREGERS [*with a glance at HEDVIG*]. —and that has lain in the depths of the sea—so long.

HEDVIG [*smiling*]. Yes.

GINA [*laying the table*]. That blessèd wild duck! What a lot of fuss you do make over her.

HIALMAR. H'm;—will lunch soon be ready?

GINA. Yes, directly. Hedvig, you must come and help me now.

[*GINA and HEDVIG go out into the kitchen*]

HIALMAR [*in a low voice*]. I think you had better not stand there looking in at father; he doesn't like it. [*GREGERS moves away from the garret door*] Besides I may as well shut up before the others come. [*Claps his hands to drive the fowls back*] Shh—shh, in with you! [*Draws up the curtain and pulls the doors together*] All the contrivances are my own invention. It's really quite amusing to have things of this sort to potter with, and to put to rights when they get out of order. And it's absolutely necessary, too; for Gina objects to having rabbits and fowls in the studio.

GREGERS. To be sure; and I suppose the studio is your wife's special department?

HIALMAR. As a rule, I leave the everyday details of business to her; for then I can take refuge in the parlour and give my mind to more important things.

GREGERS. What things may they be, Hialmar?

HIALMAR. I wonder you have not asked that question sooner. But perhaps you haven't heard of the invention?

GREGERS. The invention? No.

HIALMAR. Really? Have you not? Oh no, out there in the wilds—

GREGERS. So you have invented something, have you?

HIALMAR. It is not quite completed yet; but I am working at it. You can easily imagine that when I resolved to devote myself to photography, it wasn't simply with the idea of taking likenesses of all sorts of commonplace people.

GREGERS. No; your wife was saying the same thing just now.

HIALMAR. I swore that if I consecrated my powers to this handicraft, I would so exalt it that it should become both an art and a science. And to that end I determined to make this great invention.

GREGERS. And what is the nature of the invention? What purpose does it serve?

HIALMAR. Oh, my dear fellow, you mustn't ask for details yet. It takes time, you see. And you must not think that my motive is vanity. It is not for my own sake that I am working. Oh no; it is my life's mission that stands before me night and day.

GREGERS. What is your life's mission?

HIALMAR. Do you forget the old man with the silver hair?

GREGERS. Your poor father? Well, but what can you do for him?

HIALMAR. I can raise up his self-respect from the dead, by restoring the name of Ekdal to honour and dignity.

GREGERS. Then that is your life's mission?

HIALMAR. Yes. I will rescue the shipwrecked man. For shipwrecked he was, by the very first blast of the storm. Even while those terrible investigations were going on, he was no longer himself. That pistol there—the one we use to shoot rabbits with—has played its part in the tragedy of the house of Ekdal.

GREGERS. The pistol? Indeed?

HIALMAR. When the sentence of imprisonment was passed—he had the pistol in his hand—

GREGERS. Had he—?

HIALMAR. Yes; but he dared not use it. His courage failed him. So broken, so demoralised was he even then! Oh, can you understand it? He, a soldier; he, who had shot nine bears, and who was descended from two lieutenant-colonels—one after the other of course. Can you understand it, Gregers?

GREGERS. Yes. I understand it well enough.

HIALMAR. I cannot. And once more the pistol played a part in the history of our house. When he had put on the grey clothes and was under lock and key—oh, that was a terrible time for me, I can tell you. I kept the blinds drawn down over both my windows. When I peeped out, I saw the sun shining as if nothing had happened. I could not understand it. I saw people going along the street, laughing and talking about indifferent things. I could not understand it. It seemed to me that the whole of existence must be at a standstill—as if under an eclipse.

GREGERS. I felt like that too, when my mother died.

HIALMAR. It was in such an hour that Hialmar Ekdal pointed the pistol at his own breast.

GREGERS. You too thought of—!

HIALMAR. Yes.

GREGERS. But you did not fire?

HIALMAR. No. At the decisive moment I won the victory over myself. I remained in life. But I can assure you it takes some courage to choose life under circumstances like those.

GREGERS. Well, that depends on how you look at it.

HIALMAR. Yes, indeed, it takes courage. But I am glad I was firm: for now I shall soon perfect my invention; and Dr. Relling thinks, as I do myself, that father may be allowed to wear his uniform again. I will demand that as my sole reward.

GREGERS. So that is what he meant about his uniform—?

HIALMAR. Yes, that is what he most yearns for. You can't think how my heart bleeds for him. Every time we celebrate any little family festival—Gina's and my wedding-day, or whatever it may be—in comes the old man in the lieutenant's uniform of happier days. But if he only hears a knock at the door—for he daren't show himself to strangers, you know—he hurries back to his room again as fast as his old legs can carry him. Oh, it's heart-rending for a son to see such things!

GREGERS. How long do you think it will take you to finish your invention?

HIALMAR. Come now, you mustn't expect me to enter into particulars like that. An invention is not a thing completely under one's own control. It depends largely on inspiration—on intuition—and it is almost impossible to predict when the inspiration may come.

GREGERS. But it's advancing?

HIALMAR. Yes, certainly, it is advancing. I turn it over in my mind every day; I am full of it. Every afternoon, when I have had my dinner, I shut myself up in the parlour, where I can ponder undisturbed. But I can't be goaded to it; it's not a bit of good; Relling says so too.

GREGERS. And you don't think that all that business in the garret draws you off and distracts you too much?

HIALMAR. No, no, no; quite the contrary. You mustn't say that. I cannot be everlastingly absorbed in the same laborious train of thought. I must have something alongside of it to fill up the time of waiting. The inspiration, the intuition, you see—when it comes, it comes, and there's an end of it.

GREGERS. My dear Hialmar, I almost think you have something of the wild duck in you.

HIALMAR. Something of the wild duck? How do you mean?

GREGERS. You have dived down and bitten yourself fast in the undergrowth.

HIALMAR. Are you alluding to the well-nigh

fatal shot that has broken my father's wing
—and mine too?

GREGERS. Not exactly to that. I don't say
that your wing has been broken; but you
have strayed into a poisonous marsh, Hialmar; an insidious disease has taken hold of
you, and you have sunk down to die in the
dark.

HIALMAR. I? To die in the dark? Look here,
Gregers, you must really leave off talking such
nonsense.

GREGERS. Don't be afraid; I shall find a way
to help you up again. I too have a mission in
life now; I found it yesterday.

HIALMAR. That's all very well; but you will
please leave me out of it. I can assure you
that—apart from my very natural melancholy,
of course—I am as contented as any one can
wish to be.

GREGERS. Your contentment is an effect of
the marsh poison.

HIALMAR. Now, my dear Gregers, pray do
not go on about disease and poison; I am not
used to that sort of talk. In my house nobody ever speaks to me about unpleasant
things.

GREGERS. Ah, that I can easily believe.

HIALMAR. It's not good for me, you see.
And there are no marsh poisons here, as you
express it. The poor photographer's roof is
lowly, I know—and my circumstances are
narrow. But I am an inventor, and I am the
breadwinner of a family. That exalts me above
my mean surroundings.—Ah, here comes lunch!

[GINA and HEDVIG bring bottles of ale,
   a decanter of brandy, glasses, etc. At
   the same time, RELLING and MOLVIK
   enter from the passage; they are both
   without hat or overcoat. MOLVIK is
   dressed in black]

GINA [placing the things upon the table].
Ah, you two have come in the nick of time.

RELLING. Molvik got it into his head that
he could smell herring-salad, and then there
was no holding him.—Good morning again,
Ekdal.

HIALMAR. Gregers, let me introduce you to
Mr. Molvik. Doctor— Oh, you know Relling,
don't you?

GREGERS. Yes, slightly.

RELLING. Oh, Mr. Werle, junior! Yes, we
two have had one or two little skirmishes up
at the Höidal works. You've just moved in?

GREGERS. I moved in this morning.

RELLING. Molvik and I live right under you;
so you haven't far to go for the doctor and
the clergyman, if you should need anything
in that line.

GREGERS. Thanks, it's not quite unlikely; for
yesterday we were thirteen at table.

HIALMAR. Oh, come now, don't let us get
upon unpleasant subjects again!

RELLING. You may make your mind easy,
Ekdal; I'll be hanged if the finger of fate
points to you.

HIALMAR. I should hope not, for the sake
of my family. But let us sit down now, and
eat and drink and be merry.

GREGERS. Shall we not wait for your father?

HIALMAR. No, his lunch will be taken in to
him later. Come along!

[The men seat themselves at table, and
   eat and drink. GINA and HEDVIG go in
   and out and wait upon them]

RELLING. Molvik was frightfully screwed
yesterday, Mrs. Ekdal.

GINA. Really? Yesterday again?

RELLING. Didn't you hear him when I
brought him home last night.

GINA. No, I can't say I did.

RELLING. That was a good thing, for Molvik was disgusting last night.

GINA. Is that true, Molvik?

MOLVIK. Let us draw a veil over last night's
proceedings. That sort of thing is totally foreign to my better self.

RELLING [to GREGERS]. It comes over him
like a sort of possession, and then I have to
go out on the loose with him. Mr. Molvik is
dæmonic, you see.

GREGERS. Dæmonic?

RELLING. Molvik is dæmonic, yes.

GREGERS. H'm.

RELLING. And dæmonic natures are not
made to walk straight through the world; they
must meander a little now and then.—Well, so
you still stick up there at those horrible grimy
works?

GREGERS. I have stuck there until now.

RELLING. And did you ever manage to
collect that claim you went about presenting?

GREGERS. Claim? [Understands him] Ah, I
see.

HIALMAR. Have you been presenting claims,
Gregers?

GREGERS. Oh, nonsense.

RELLING. Faith, but he has, though! He went
round to all the cottars' cabins presenting
something he called "the claim of the ideal."

GREGERS. I was young then.

RELLING. You're right; you were very
young. And as for the claim of the ideal—
you never got it honoured while I was up
there.

GREGERS. Nor since either.

RELLING. Ah, then you've learnt to knock
a little discount off, I expect.

GREGERS. Never, when I have a true man to
deal with.

HIALMAR. No, I should think not, indeed.
A little butter, Gina.

RELLING. And a slice of bacon for Molvik.

MOLVIK. Ugh! not bacon!

[*A knock at the garret door*]

HIALMAR. Open the door, Hedvig; father wants to come out.

[HEDVIG *goes over and opens the door a little way;* EKDAL *enters with a fresh rabbit-skin; she closes the door after him*]

EKDAL. Good morning, gentlemen! Good sport to-day. Shot a big one.

HIALMAR. And you've gone and skinned it without waiting for me—!

EKDAL. Salted it too. It's good tender meat, is rabbit; it's sweet; it tastes like sugar. Good appetite to you, gentlemen! [*Goes into his room*]

MOLVIK [*rising*]. Excuse me—; I can't—; I must get downstairs immediately—

RELLING. Drink some soda water, man!

MOLVIK [*hurrying away*]. Ugh—ugh! [*Goes out by the passage door*]

RELLING [*to* HIALMAR]. Let us drain a glass to the old hunter.

HIALMAR [*clinks glasses with him*]. To the undaunted sportsman who has looked death in the face!

RELLING. To the grey-haired— [*Drinks*] By-the-bye, is his hair grey or white?

HIALMAR. Something between the two, I fancy; for that matter, he has very few hairs left of any colour.

RELLING. Well well, one can get through the world with a wig. After all, you are a happy man, Ekdal; you have your noble mission to labour for—

HIALMAR. And I do labour, I can tell you.

RELLING. And then you have your excellent wife, shuffling quietly in and out in her felt slippers, with that see-saw walk of hers, and making everything cosy and comfortable about you.

HIALMAR. Yes, Gina— [*Nods to her*]—you are a good helpmate on the path of life.

GINA. Oh, don't sit there cricketizing me.

RELLING. And your Hedvig too, Ekdal!

HIALMAR [*affected*]. The child, yes! The child before everything! Hedvig, come here to me. [*Strokes her hair*] What day is it to-morrow, eh?

HEDVIG [*shaking him*]. Oh no, you're not to say anything, father.

HIALMAR. It cuts me to the heart when I think what a poor affair it will be; only a little festivity in the garret—

HEDVIG. Oh, but that's just what I like!

RELLING. Just you wait till the wonderful invention sees the light, Hedvig!

HIALMAR. Yes indeed—then you shall see—! Hedvig, I have resolved to make your future secure. You shall live in comfort all your days. I will demand—something or other—on your behalf. That shall be the poor inventor's sole reward.

HEDVIG [*whispering, with her arms round his neck*]. Oh you dear, kind father!

RELLING [*to* GREGERS]. Come now, don't you find it pleasant, for once in a way, to sit at a well-spread table in a happy family circle?

HIALMAR. Ah yes, I really prize these social hours.

GREGERS. For my part, I don't thrive in marsh vapours.

RELLING. Marsh vapours?

HIALMAR. Oh, don't begin with that stuff again!

GINA. Goodness knows there's no vapours in this house, Mr. Werle; I give the place a good airing every blessed day.

GREGERS [*leaves the table*]. No airing you can give will drive out the taint I mean.

HIALMAR. Taint!

GINA. Yes, what do you say to that, Ekdal!

RELLING. Excuse me—may it not be you yourself that have brought the taint from those mines up there?

GREGERS. It is like you to call what I bring into this house a taint.

RELLING [*Goes up to him*]. Look here, Mr. Werle, junior: I have a strong suspicion that you are still carrying about that "claim of the ideal" large as life, in your coat-tail pocket.

GREGERS. I carry it in my breast.

RELLING. Well, wherever you carry it, I advise you not to come dunning us with it here, so long as *I* am on the premises.

GREGERS. And if I do so none the less?

RELLING. Then you'll go head-foremost down the stairs; now I've warned you.

HIALMAR [*rising*]. Oh, but Relling—!

GREGERS. Yes, you may turn me out—

GINA [*interposing between them*]. We can't have that, Relling. But I must say, Mr. Werle, it ill becomes you to talk about vapours and taints, after all the mess you made with your stove.

[*A knock at the passage door*]

HEDVIG. Mother, there's somebody knocking.

HIALMAR. There now, we're going to have a whole lot of people!

GINA. I'll go— [*Goes over and opens the door, starts, and draws back*] Oh—oh dear!

[WERLE, *in a fur coat, advances one step into the room*]

WERLE. Excuse me; but I think my son is staying here.

GINA [*with a gulp*]. Yes.

HIALMAR [*approaching him*]. Won't you do us the honour to—?

WERLE. Thank you, I merely wish to speak to my son.

GREGERS. What is it? Here I am.

WERLE. I want a few words with you, in your room.

GREGERS. In my room? Very well— [*About to go*]

GINA. No, no, your room's not in a fit state—

WERLE. Well then, out in the passage here; I want to have a few words with you alone.

HIALMAR. You can have them here, sir. Come into the parlour, Relling.

[HIALMAR *and* RELLING *go off to the right.* GINA *takes* HEDVIG *with her into the kitchen*]

GREGERS [*after a short pause*]. Well, now we are alone.

WERLE. From something you let fall last evening, and from your coming to lodge with the Ekdals, I can't help inferring that you intend to make yourself unpleasant to me, in one way or another.

GREGERS. I intend to open Hialmar Ekdal's eyes. He shall see his position as it really is— that is all.

WERLE. Is that the mission in life you spoke of yesterday?

GREGERS. Yes. You have left me no other.

WERLE. Is it I, then, that have crippled your mind, Gregers?

GREGERS. You have crippled my whole life. I am not thinking of all that about mother— But it's thanks to you that I am continually haunted and harassed by a guilty conscience.

WERLE. Indeed! It is your conscience that troubles you, is it?

GREGERS. I ought to have taken a stand against you when the trap was set for Lieutenant Ekdal. I ought to have cautioned him; for I had a misgiving as to what was in the wind.

WERLE. Yes, that was the time to have spoken.

GREGERS. I did not dare to, I was so cowed and spiritless. I was mortally afraid of you— not only then, but long afterwards.

WERLE. You have got over that fear now, it appears.

GREGERS. Yes, fortunately. The wrong done to old Ekdal, both by me and by—others, can never be undone; but Hialmar I can rescue from all the falsehood and deception that are bringing him to ruin.

WERLE. Do you think that will be doing him a kindness?

GREGERS. I have not the least doubt of it.

WERLE. You think our worthy photographer is the sort of man to appreciate such friendly offices?

GREGERS. Yes, I do.

WERLE. H'm—we shall see.

GREGERS. Besides, if I am to go on living, I must try to find some cure for my sick conscience.

WERLE. It will never be sound. Your conscience has been sickly from childhood. That is a legacy from your mother, Gregers—the only one she left you.

GREGERS [*with a scornful half-smile*]. Have you not yet forgiven her for the mistake you made in supposing she would bring you a fortune?

WERLE. Don't let us wander from the point. —Then you hold to your purpose of setting young Ekdal upon what you imagine to be the right scent?

GREGERS. Yes, that is my fixed resolve.

WERLE. Well, in that case I might have spared myself this visit; for of course it is useless to ask whether you will return home with me?

GREGERS. Quite useless.

WERLE. And I suppose you won't enter the firm either?

GREGERS. No.

WERLE. Very good. But as I am thinking of marrying again, your share in the property will fall to you at once.

GREGERS [*quickly*]. No, I do not want that.

WERLE. You don't want it?

GREGERS. No, I dare not take it, for conscience' sake.

WERLE [*after a pause*]. Are you going up to the works again?

GREGERS. No; I consider myself released from your service.

WERLE. But what are you going to do?

GREGERS. Only to fulfil my mission; nothing more.

WERLE. Well, but afterwards? What are you going to live upon?

GREGERS. I have laid by a little out of my salary.

WERLE. How long will that last?

GREGERS. I think it will last my time.

WERLE. What do you mean?

GREGERS. I shall answer no more questions.

WERLE. Good-bye then, Gregers.

GREGERS. Good-bye.

[WERLE *goes*]

HIALMAR [*peeping in*]. He's gone, isn't he?

GREGERS. Yes.

[HIALMAR *and* RELLING *enter; also* GINA *and* HEDVIG *from the kitchen*]

RELLING. That luncheon-party was a failure.

GREGERS. Put on your coat, Hialmar; I want you to come for a long walk with me.

HIALMAR. With pleasure. What was it your father wanted? Had it anything to do with me?

GREGERS. Come along. We must have a talk. I'll go and put on my overcoat. [*Goes out by the passage door*]

GINA. You shouldn't go out with him, Ekdal.

RELLING. No, don't you do it. Stay where you are.

HIALMAR [*gets his hat and overcoat*]. Oh, nonsense! When a friend of my youth feels impelled to open his mind to me in private—

RELLING. But devil take it—don't you see that the fellow's mad, cracked, demented!

GINA. There, what did I tell you! His mother before him had crazy fits like that sometimes.

HIALMAR. The more need for a friend's

watchful eye. [*To* GINA] Be sure you have dinner ready in good time. Good-bye for the present. [*Goes out by the passage door*]

RELLING. It's a thousand pities the fellow didn't go to hell through one of the Höidal mines.

GINA. Good Lord! what makes you say that?

RELLING [*muttering*]. Oh, I have my own reasons.

GINA. Do you think young Werle is really mad?

RELLING. No, worse luck; he's no madder than most other people. But one disease he has certainly got in his system.

GINA. What is it that's the matter with him?

RELLING. Well, I'll tell you, Mrs. Ekdal. He is suffering from an acute attack of integrity.

GINA. Integrity?

HEDVIG. Is that a kind of disease?

RELLING. Yes, it's a national disease; but it only appears sporadically. [*Nods to* GINA] Thanks for your hospitality. [*He goes out by the passage door*]

GINA [*moving restlessly to and fro*]. Ugh, that Gregers Werle—he was always a wretched creature.

HEDVIG [*standing by the table, and looking searchingly at her*]. I think all this is very strange.

ACT FOURTH

HIALMAR EKDAL'S *studio. A photograph has just been taken; a camera with the cloth over it, a pedestal, two chairs, a folding table, etc., are standing out in the room. Afternoon light; the sun is going down; a little later it begins to grow dusk.*

GINA *stands in the passage doorway, with a little box and a wet glass plate in her hand, and is speaking to somebody outside.*

GINA. Yes, certainly. When I make a promise I keep it. The first dozen shall be ready on Monday. Good afternoon.

[*Some one is heard going downstairs.* GINA *shuts the door, slips the plate into the box, and puts it into the covered camera*]

HEDVIG [*comes in from the kitchen*]. Are they gone?

GINA [*tidying up*]. Yes, thank goodness, I've got rid of them at last.

HEDVIG. But can you imagine why father hasn't come home yet?

GINA. Are you sure he's not down in Relling's room?

HEDVIG. No, he's not; I ran down the kitchen stairs just now and asked.

GINA. And his dinner standing and getting cold, too.

HEDVIG. Yes, I can't understand it. Father's always so careful to be home to dinner!

GINA. Oh, he'll be here directly, you'll see.

HEDVIG. I wish he would come; everything seems so queer to-day.

GINA [*calls out*]. There he is!

[HIALMAR EKDAL *comes in at the passage door*]

HEDVIG [*going to him*]. Father! Oh what a time we've been waiting for you!

GINA [*glancing sidelong at him*]. You've been out a long time, Ekdal.

HIALMAR [*without looking at her*]. Rather long, yes. [*He takes off his overcoat*]

[GINA *and* HEDVIG *go to help him; he motions them away*]

GINA. Perhaps you've had dinner with Werle?

HIALMAR [*hanging up his coat*]. No.

GINA [*going towards the kitchen door*]. Then I'll bring some in for you.

HIALMAR. No; let the dinner alone. I want nothing to eat.

HEDVIG [*going nearer to him*]. Are you not well, father?

HIALMAR. Well? Oh yes, well enough. We have had a tiring walk, Gregers and I.

GINA. You didn't ought to have gone so far, Ekdal, you're not used to it.

HIALMAR. H'm; there's many a thing a man must get used to in this world. [*Wanders about the room*] Has any one been here whilst I was out?

GINA. Nobody but the two sweethearts.

HIALMAR. No new orders?

GINA. No, not to-day.

HEDVIG. There will be some to-morrow, father, you'll see.

HIALMAR. I hope there will; for to-morrow I am going to set to work in real earnest.

HEDVIG. To-morrow! Don't you remember what day it is to-morrow?

HIALMAR. Oh yes, by-the-bye—. Well, the day after, then. Henceforth I mean to do everything myself; I shall take all the work into my own hands.

GINA. Why, what can be the good of that, Ekdal? It'll only make your life a burden to you. I can manage the photography all right; and you can go on working at your invention.

HEDVIG. And think of the wild duck, father, —and all the hens and rabbits and—!

HIALMAR. Don't talk to me of all that trash! From to-morrow I will never set foot in the garret again.

HEDVIG. Oh but, father, you promised that we should have a little party—

HIALMAR. H'm, true. Well then, from the day after to-morrow. I should almost like to wring that cursèd wild duck's neck!

HEDVIG [*shrieks*]. The wild duck!

GINA. Well I never!

HEDVIG [*shaking him*]. Oh no, father; you know it's my wild duck!

HIALMAR. That is why I don't do it. I haven't the heart to—for your sake, Hedvig. But in my inmost soul I feel that I ought to do it. I ought not to tolerate under my roof a creature that has been through those hands.

GINA. Why, good gracious, even if grandfather did get it from that poor creature, Pettersen—

HIALMAR [*wandering about*]. There are certain claims—what shall I call them?—let me say claims of the ideal—certain obligations, which a man cannot disregard without injury to his soul.

HEDVIG [*going after him*]. But think of the wild duck,—the poor wild duck!

HIALMAR [*stops*]. I tell you I will spare it—for your sake. Not a hair of its head shall be —I mean, it shall be spared. There are greater problems than that to be dealt with. But you should go out a little now, Hedvig, as usual; it is getting dusk enough for you now.

HEDVIG. No, I don't care about going out now.

HIALMAR. Yes do; it seems to me your eyes are blinking a great deal; all these vapours in here are bad for you. The air is heavy under this roof.

HEDVIG. Very well then, I'll run down the kitchen stair and go for a little walk. My cloak and hat?—oh, they're in my own room. Father —be sure you don't do the wild duck any harm whilst I'm out.

HIALMAR. Not a feather of its head shall be touched. [*Draws her to him*] You and I, Hedvig—we two—! Well, go along.

[HEDVIG *nods to her parents and goes out through the kitchen*]

HIALMAR [*walks about without looking up*]. Gina.

GINA. Yes?

HIALMAR. From to-morrow—or, say, from the day after to-morrow—I should like to keep the household account-book myself.

GINA. Do you want to keep the accounts too, now?

HIALMAR. Yes; or to check the receipts at any rate.

GINA. Lord help us! that's soon done.

HIALMAR. One would hardly think so; at any rate you seem to make the money go a very long way. [*Stops and looks at her*]. How do you manage it?

GINA. It's because me and Hedvig, we need so little.

HIALMAR. Is it the case that father is very liberally paid for the copying he does for Mr. Werle?

GINA. I don't know as he gets anything out of the way. I don't know the rates for that sort of work.

HIALMAR. Well, what does he get, about? Let me hear!

GINA. Oh, it varies; I daresay it'll come to about as much as he costs us, with a little pocket-money over.

HIALMAR. As much as he costs us! And you have never told me this before!

GINA. No, how could I tell you? It pleased you so much to think he got everything from you.

HIALMAR. And he gets it from Mr. Werle.

GINA. Oh well, he has plenty and to spare, he has.

HIALMAR. Light the lamp for me, please!

GINA [*lighting the lamp*] And of course we don't know as it's Mr. Werle himself; it may be Gråberg—

HIALMAR. Why attempt such an evasion?

GINA. I don't know; I only thought—

HIALMAR. H'm!

GINA. It wasn't me that got grandfather that copying. It was Bertha, when she used to come about us.

HIALMAR. It seems to me your voice is trembling.

GINA [*putting the lamp-shade on*]. Is it?

HIALMAR. And your hands are shaking, are they not?

GINA [*firmly*]. Come right out with it, Ekdal. What has he been saying about me?

HIALMAR. Is it true—can it be true that— that there was an—an understanding between you and Mr. Werle, while you were in service there?

GINA. That's not true. Not at that time. Mr. Werle did come after me, that's a fact. And his wife thought there was something in it, and then she made such a hocus-pocus and hurly-burly, and she hustled me and bustled me about so, that I left her service.

HIALMAR. But afterwards, then?

GINA. Well, then I went home. And mother— well, she wasn't the woman you took her for Ekdal; she kept on worrying and worrying at me about one thing and another—for Mr Werle was a widower by that time.

HIALMAR. Well, and then?

GINA. I suppose you've got to know it. He gave me no peace until he'd had his way.

HIALMAR [*striking his hands together*]. And this is the mother of my child! How could you hide this from me?

GINA. Yes, it was wrong of me; I ought certainly to have told you long ago.

HIALMAR. You should have told me at the very first;—then I should have known the sort of woman you were.

GINA. But would you have married me all the same?

HIALMAR. How can you dream that I would—

GINA. That's just why I didn't dare tell you anything, then. For I'd come to care for you so much, you see; and I couldn't go and make myself utterly miserable—

HIALMAR [*walks about*]. And this is my Hedvig's mother. And to know that all I see before me— [*Kicks at a chair*]—all that I call my home—I owe to a favoured predecessor! Oh that scoundrel Werle!

GINA. Do you repent of the fourteen—the fifteen years as we've lived together?

HIALMAR [*placing himself in front of her*]. Have you not every day, every hour, repented of the spider's-web of deceit you have spun around me? Answer me that! How could you help writhing with penitence and remorse?

GINA. Oh, my dear Ekdal, I've had all I could do to look after the house and get through the day's work—

HIALMAR. Then you never think of reviewing your past?

GINA. No; Heaven knows I'd almost forgotten those old stories.

HIALMAR. Oh, this dull, callous contentment! To me there is something revolting about it. Think of it—never so much as a twinge of remorse!

GINA. But tell me, Ekdal—what would have become of you if you hadn't had a wife like me?

HIALMAR. Like you—!

GINA. Yes; for you know I've always been a bit more practical and wide-awake than you. Of course I'm a year or two older.

HIALMAR. What would have become of me!

GINA. You'd got into all sorts of bad ways when first you met me; that you can't deny.

HIALMAR. "Bad ways" do you call them? Little do you know what a man goes through when he is in grief and despair—especially a man of my fiery temperament.

GINA. Well, well, that may be so. And I've no reason to crow over you, neither; for you turned a moral of a husband, that you did, as soon as ever you had a house and home of your own.—And now we'd got everything so nice and cosy about us; and me and Hedvig was just thinking we'd soon be able to let ourselves go a bit, in the way of both food and clothes.

HIALMAR. In the swamp of deceit, yes.

GINA. I wish to goodness that detestable being had never set his foot inside our doors!

HIALMAR. And I, too, thought my home such pleasant one. That was a delusion. Where shall I now find the elasticity of spirit to bring my invention into the world of reality? Perhaps it will die with me; and then it will be your past, Gina, that will have killed it.

GINA [*nearly crying*]. You mustn't say such things, Ekdal. Me, that has only wanted to do the best I could for you, all my days!

HIALMAR. I ask you, what becomes of the breadwinner's dream? When I used to lie in there on the sofa and brood over my invention, I had a clear enough presentiment that it would sap my vitality to the last drop. I felt even then that the day when I held the patent in my hand—that day—would bring my—release. And then it was my dream that you should live on after me, the dead inventor's well-to-do widow.

GINA [*drying her tears*]. No, you mustn't talk like that, Ekdal. May the Lord never let me see the day I am left a widow!

HIALMAR. Oh, the whole dream has vanished. It is all over now. All over!

[GREGERS WERLE *opens the passage door cautiously and looks in*]

GREGERS. May I come in?

HIALMAR. Yes, come in.

GREGERS [*comes forward, his face beaming with satisfaction, and holds out both his hands to them*]. Well, dear friends—! [*Looks from one to the other, and whispers to* HIALMAR] Have you not done it yet?

HIALMAR [*aloud*]. It is done.

GREGERS. It is?

HIALMAR. I have passed through the bitterest moments of my life.

GREGERS. But also, I trust, the most ennobling.

HIALMAR. Well, at any rate, we have got through it for the present.

GINA. God forgive you, Mr. Werle.

GREGERS [*in great surprise*]. But I don't understand this.

HIALMAR. What don't you understand?

GREGERS. After so great a crisis—a crisis that is to be the starting-point of an entirely new life—of a communion founded on truth, and free from all taint of deception—

HIALMAR. Yes yes, I know; I know that quite well.

GREGERS. I confidently expected, when I entered the room, to find the light of transfiguration shining upon me from both husband and wife. And now I see nothing but dulness, oppression, gloom—

GINA. Oh, is that it? [*Takes off the lampshade*]

GREGERS. You will not understand me, Mrs. Ekdal. Ah well, you, I suppose, need time to—. But you, Hialmar? Surely you feel a new consecration after the great crisis.

HIALMAR. Yes, of course I do. That is—in a sort of way.

GREGERS. For surely nothing in the world can compare with the joy of forgiving one who has erred, and raising her up to oneself in love.

HIALMAR. Do you think a man can so easily throw off the effects of the bitter cup I have drained?

GREGERS. No, not a common man, perhaps. But a man like you—!

HIALMAR. Good God! I know that well enough. But you must keep me up to it, Gregers. It takes time, you know.

GREGERS. You have much of the wild duck in you, Hialmar.

[RELLING *has come in at the passage door*]

RELLING. Oho! is the wild duck to the fore again?

HIALMAR. Yes; Mr. Werle's wing-broken victim.

RELLING. Mr. Werle's—? So it's him you are talking about?

HIALMAR. Him and—ourselves.

RELLING [*in an undertone to* GREGERS]. May the devil fly away with you!

HIALMAR. What is that you are saying?

RELLING. Only uttering a heartfelt wish that this quacksalver would take himself off. If he stays here, he is quite equal to making an utter mess of life, for both of you.

GREGERS. These two will not make a mess of life, Mr. Relling. Of course I won't speak of Hialmar—him we know. But she, too, in her innermost heart, has certainly something loyal and sincere—

GINA [*almost crying*]. You might have let me alone for what I was, then.

RELLING [*to* GREGERS]. Is it rude to ask what you really want in this house?

GREGERS. To lay the foundations of a true marriage.

RELLING. So you don't think Ekdal's marriage is good enough as it is?

GREGERS. No doubt it is as good a marriage as most others, worse luck. But a true marriage it has yet to become.

HIALMAR. You have never had eyes for the claims of the ideal, Relling.

RELLING. Rubbish, my boy!—But excuse me, Mr. Werle: how many—in round numbers—how many true marriages have you seen in the course of your life?

GREGERS. Scarcely a single one.

RELLING. Nor I either.

GREGERS. But I have seen innumerable marriages of the opposite kind. And it has been my fate to see at close quarters what ruin such a marriage can work in two human souls.

HIALMAR. A man's whole moral basis may give away beneath his feet; that is the terrible part of it.

RELLING. Well, I can't say I've ever been exactly married, so I don't pretend to speak with authority. But this I know, that the child enters into the marriage problem. And you must leave the child in peace.

HIALMAR. Oh—Hedvig! my poor Hedvig!

RELLING. Yes, you must be good enough to keep Hedvig outside of all this. You two are grown-up people; you are free, in God's name, to make what mess and muddle you please of your life. But you must deal cautiously with Hedvig, I tell you; else you may do her a grea injury.

HIALMAR. An injury!

RELLING. Yes, or she may do herself an injury —and perhaps others too.

GINA. How can you know that, Relling?

HIALMAR. Her sight is in no immediat danger, is it?

RELLING. I am not talking about her sight Hedvig is at a critical age. She may be gettin, all sorts of mischief into her head.

GINA. That's true—I've noticed it already She's taken to carrying on with the fire, out i the kitchen. She calls it playing at house-on-fire I'm often scared for fear she really sets fire t the house.

RELLING. You see; I thought as much.

GREGERS [*to* RELLING] But how do you ac count for that?

RELLING [*sullenly*]. Her constitution's chang ing, sir.

HIALMAR. So long as the child has me—! S long as *I* am above ground—!

[*A knock at the door*]

GINA. Hush, Ekdal; there's some one in th passage. [*Calls out*] Come in!

[MRS SÖRBY, *in walking dress, comes in*

MRS. SÖRBY. Good evening.

GINA [*going towards her*]. Is it really you Bertha?

MRS. SÖRBY. Yes, of course it is. But I'm dis turbing you, I'm afraid?

HIALMAR. No, not at all; an emissary fron that house—

MRS. SÖRBY [*to* GINA]. To tell the truth, hoped your men-folk would be out at this tim I just ran up to have a little chat with you and to say good-bye.

GINA. Good-bye? Are you going away, then

MRS. SÖRBY. Yes, to-morrow morning,—u to Höidal. Mr. Werle started this afternoo [*Lightly to* GREGERS] He asked me to say good bye for him.

GINA. Only fancy—!

HIALMAR. So Mr. Werle has gone? And no you are going after him?

MRS. SÖRBY. Yes, what do you say to tha Ekdal?

HIALMAR. I say: beware!

GREGERS. I must explain the situation. M father and Mrs. Sörby are going to be marriec

HIALMAR. Going to be married!

GINA. Oh Bertha! So it's come to that a last!

RELLING [*his voice quivering a little*]. This surely not true?

MRS. SÖRBY. Yes, my dear Relling, it's tru enough.

RELLING. You are going to marry again?

MRS. SÖRBY. Yes, it looks like it. Werle ha got a special licence, and we are going to b married quite quietly, up at the works.

GREGERS. Then I must wish you all happiness, like a dutiful stepson.

MRS. SÖRBY. Thank you very much—if you mean what you say. I certainly hope it will lead to happiness, both for Werle and for me.

RELLING. You have every reason to hope that. Mr. Werle never gets drunk—so far as I know; and I don't suppose he's in the habit of thrashing his wives, like the late lamented horse-doctor.

MRS. SÖRBY. Come now, let Sörby rest in peace. He had his good points too.

RELLING. Mr. Werle has better ones, I have no doubt.

MRS. SÖRBY. He hasn't frittered away all that was good in him, at any rate. The man who does that must take the consequences.

RELLING. I shall go out with Molvik this evening.

MRS. SÖRBY. You mustn't do that, Relling. Don't do it—for my sake.

RELLING. There's nothing else for it. [*To* HIALMAR] If you're going with us, come along.

GINA. No, thank you. Ekdal doesn't go in for that sort of dissertation.

HIALMAR [*half aloud, in vexation*]. Oh, do hold your tongue!

RELLING. Good-bye, Mrs.—Werle. [*Goes out through the passage door*]

GREGERS [*to* MRS. SÖRBY]. You seem to know Dr. Relling pretty intimately.

MRS. SÖRBY. Yes, we have known each other for many years. At one time it seemed as if things might have gone further between us.

GREGERS. It was surely lucky for you that they did not.

MRS. SÖRBY. You may well say that. But I have always been wary of acting on impulse. A woman can't afford absolutely to throw herself away.

GREGERS. Are you not in the least afraid that I may let my father know about this old friendship?

MRS. SÖRBY. Why, of course I have told him all about it myself.

GREGERS. Indeed?

MRS. SÖRBY. Your father knows every single thing that can, with any truth, be said about me. I have told him all; it was the first thing I did when I saw what was in his mind.

GREGERS. Then you have been franker than most people, I think.

MRS. SÖRBY. I have always been frank. We women find that the best policy.

HIALMAR. What do you say to that, Gina?

GINA. Oh, we're not all alike, us women aren't. Some are made one way, some another.

MRS. SÖRBY. Well, for my part, Gina, I believe it's wisest to do as I've done. And Werle has no secrets either, on his side. That's really the great bond between us, you see. Now he can talk to me as openly as a child. He has never

had the chance to do that before. Fancy a man like him, full of health and vigour, passing his whole youth and the best years of his life in listening to nothing but penitential sermons! And very often the sermons had for their text the most imaginary offences—at least so I understand.

GINA. That's true enough.

GREGERS. If you ladies are going to follow up this topic, I had better withdraw.

MRS. SÖRBY. You can stay so far as that's concerned. I shan't say a word more. But I wanted you to know that I had done nothing secretly or in an underhand way. I may seem to have come in for a great piece of luck; and so I have, in a sense. But after all, I don't think I am getting any more than I am giving. I shall stand by him always, and I can tend and care for him as no one else can, now that he is getting helpless.

HIALMAR. Getting helpless?

GREGERS [*to* MRS. SÖRBY]. Hush, don't speak of that here.

MRS. SÖRBY. There is no disguising it any longer, however much he would like to. He is going blind.

HIALMAR [*starts*]. Going blind? That's strange. He too going blind!

GINA. Lots of people do.

MRS. SÖRBY. And you can imagine what that means to a business man. Well, I shall try as well as I can to make my eyes take the place of his. But I musn't stay any longer; I have such heaps of things to do.—Oh, by-the-bye, Ekdal, I was to tell you that if there is anything Werle can do for you, you must just apply to Gråberg.

GREGERS. That offer I am sure Hialmar Ekdal will decline with thanks.

MRS. SÖRBY. Indeed? I don't think he used to be so—

GINA. No, Bertha, Ekdal doesn't need anything from Mr. Werle now.

HIALMAR [*slowly and with emphasis*]. Will you present my compliments to your future husband, and say that I intend very shortly to call upon Mr. Gråberg—

GREGERS. What! You don't really mean that?

HIALMAR. To call upon Mr. Gråberg, I say, and obtain an account of the sum I owe his principal. I will pay that debt of honour—ha ha ha! a debt of honour, let us call it! In any case, I will pay the whole, with five per cent. interest.

GINA. But, my dear Ekdal, God knows we haven't got the money to do it.

HIALMAR. Be good enough to tell your future husband that I am working assiduously at my invention. Please tell him that what sustains me in this laborious task is the wish to free myself from a torturing burden of debt. That is my reason for proceeding with the invention.

The entire profits shall be devoted to releasing me from my pecuniary obligations to your future husband.

MRS. SÖRBY. Something has happened here.

HIALMAR. Yes, you are right.

MRS. SÖRBY. Well, good-bye. I had something else to speak to you about, Gina; but it must keep till another time. Good-bye.

[HIALMAR and GREGERS bow silently. GINA follows MRS. SÖRBY to the door]

HIALMAR. Not beyond the threshold, Gina!

[MRS. SÖRBY goes; GINA shuts the door after her]

HIALMAR. There now, Gregers; I have got that burden of debt off my mind.

GREGERS. You soon will, at all events.

HIALMAR. I think my attitude may be called correct.

GREGERS. You are the man I have always taken you for.

HIALMAR. In certain cases, it is impossible to disregard the claim of the ideal. Yet, as the breadwinner of a family, I cannot but writhe and groan under it. I can tell you it is no joke for a man without capital to attempt the repayment of a long-standing obligation, over which, so to speak, the dust of oblivion had gathered. But it cannot be helped: the Man in me demands his rights.

GREGERS [laying his hand on HIALMAR's shoulder]. My dear Hialmar—was it not a good thing I came?

HIALMAR. Yes.

GREGERS. Are you not glad to have had your true position made clear to you?

HIALMAR [somewhat impatiently]. Yes, of course I am. But there is one thing that is revolting to my sense of justice.

GREGERS. And what is that?

HIALMAR. It is that—but I don't know whether I ought to express myself so unreservedly about your father.

GREGERS. Say what you please, so far as I am concerned.

HIALMAR. Well then, is it not exasperating to think that it is not I, but he, who will realise the true marriage?

GREGERS. How can you say such a thing?

HIALMAR. Because it is clearly the case. Isn't the marriage between your father and Mrs. Sörby founded upon complete confidence, upon entire and unreserved candour on both sides? They hide nothing from each other, they keep no secrets in the background; their relation is based, if I may put it so, on mutual confession and absolution.

GREGERS. Well, what then?

HIALMAR. Well, is not that the whole thing? Did you not yourself say that this was precisely the difficulty that had to be overcome in order to found a true marriage?

GREGERS. But this is a totally different matter,

HIALMAR. You surely don't compare either yourself or your wife with those two—? Oh, you understand me well enough.

HIALMAR. Say what you like, there is something in all this that hurts and offends my sense of justice. It really looks as if there were no just Providence to rule the world.

GINA. Oh no, Ekdal; for God's sake don't say such things.

GREGERS. H'm; don't let us get upon those questions.

HIALMAR. And yet, after all, I cannot but recognise the guiding finger of Fate. He is going blind.

GINA. Oh, you can't be sure of that.

HIALMAR. There is no doubt about it. At all events there ought not to be; for in that very fact lies the righteous retribution. He has hoodwinked a confiding fellow creature in days gone by—

GREGERS. I fear he has hoodwinked many.

HIALMAR. And now comes inexorable, mysterious Fate, and demands Werle's own eyes.

GINA. Oh, how dare you say such dreadful things! You make me quite scared.

HIALMAR. It is profitable, now and then, to plunge deep into the night side of existence.

[HEDVIG, in her hat and cloak, comes in by the passage door. She is pleasurably excited, and out of breath]

GINA. Are you back already?

HEDVIG. Yes, I didn't care to go any farther. It was a good thing, too; for I've just met some one at the door.

HIALMAR. It must have been that Mrs. Sörby.

HEDVIG. Yes.

HIALMAR [walks up and down]. I hope you have seen her for the last time.

[Silence. HEDVIG, discouraged, looks first at one and then at the other, trying to divine their frame of mind]

HEDVIG [approaching, coaxingly]. Father.

HIALMAR. Well—what is it, Hedvig?

HEDVIG. Mrs. Sörby had something with her for me.

HIALMAR [stops]. For you?

HEDVIG. Yes. Something for to-morrow.

GINA. Bertha has always given you some little thing on your birthday.

HIALMAR. What is it?

HEDVIG. Oh, you mustn't see it now. Mother is to give it to me to-morrow morning before I'm up.

HIALMAR. What is all this hocus-pocus that I am to be kept in the dark about!

HEDVIG [quickly]. Oh no, you may see it if you like. It's a big letter. [Takes the letter out of her cloak pocket]

HIALMAR. A letter too?

HEDVIG. Yes, it is only a letter. The rest will come afterwards, I suppose. But fancy—

etter! I've never had a letter before. And
here's "Miss" written upon it. [*Reads*] "Miss
Hedvig Ekdal." Only fancy—that's me!

HIALMAR. Let me see that letter.

HEDVIG [*hands it to him*]. There it is.

HIALMAR. That is Mr. Werle's hand.

GINA. Are you sure of that, Ekdal?

HIALMAR. Look for yourself.

GINA. Oh, what do *I* know about such-like
things?

HIALMAR. Hedvig, may I open the letter—
and read it?

HEDVIG. Yes, of course you may, if you want
to.

GINA. No, not to-night, Ekdal; it's to be kept
till to-morrow.

HEDVIG [*softly*]. Oh, can't you let him read
it! It's sure to be something good; and then
father will be glad, and everything will be nice
again.

HIALMAR. I may open it then?

HEDVIG. Yes do, father. I'm so anxious to
know what it is.

HIALMAR. Well and good. [*Opens the letter,
takes out a paper, reads it through, and appears
bewildered*] What is this—!

GINA. What does it say?

HEDVIG. Oh yes, father—tell us!

HIALMAR. Be quiet. [*Reads it through again;
he has turned pale, but says with self-control:*]
It is a deed of gift, Hedvig.

HEDVIG. Is it? What sort of gift am I to have?

HIALMAR. Read for yourself.

[HEDVIG *goes over and reads for a time
by the lamp*]

HIALMAR [*half-aloud, clenching his hands*].
The eyes! The eyes—and then that letter!

HEDVIG [*leaves off reading*]. Yes, but it seems
to me that it's grandfather that's to have

HIALMAR [*takes the letter from her*]. Gina—
can you understand this?

GINA. I know nothing whatever about it;
tell me what's the matter.

HIALMAR. Mr. Werle writes to Hedvig that
her old grandfather need not trouble himself
any longer with the copying, but that he can
henceforth draw on the office for a hundred
crowns a month—

GREGERS. Aha!

HEDVIG. A hundred crowns, mother! I read
that.

GINA. What a good thing for grandfather!

HIALMAR. —a hundred crowns a month so
long as he needs it—that means, of course, so
long as he lives.

GINA. Well, so he's provided for, poor dear.

HIALMAR. But there is more to come. You
didn't read that, Hedvig. Afterwards this gift
is to pass on to you.

HEDVIG. To me! The whole of it?

HIALMAR. He says that the same amount is

assured to you for the whole of your life. Do
you hear that, Gina?

GINA. Yes, I hear.

HEDVIG. Fancy—all that money for me!
[*Shakes him*] Father, father, aren't you glad—?

HIALMAR [*eluding her*]. Glad! [*Walks about*]
Oh, what vistas—what perspectives open up
before me! It is Hedvig, Hedvig that he showers these benefactions upon!

GINA. Yes, because it's Hedvig's birthday—

HEDVIG. And you'll get it all the same, father!
You know quite well I shall give all the money
to you and mother.

HIALMAR. To mother, yes! There we have it.

GREGERS. Hialmar, this is a trap he is setting
for you.

HIALMAR. Do you think it's another trap?

GREGERS. When he was here this morning he
said: Hialmar Ekdal is not the man you imagine
him to be.

HIALMAR. Not the man—!

GREGERS. That you shall see, he said.

HIALMAR. He meant you should see that I
would let myself be bought off—!

HEDVIG. Oh mother, what does all this mean?

GINA. Go and take off your things.

[HEDVIG *goes out by the kitchen door, half-
crying*]

GREGERS. Yes, Hialmar—now is the time to
show who was right, he or I.

HIALMAR [*slowly tears the paper across, lays
both pieces on the table, and says:*] Here is my
answer.

GREGERS. Just what I expected.

HIALMAR [*goes over to* GINA, *who stands by
the stove, and says in a low voice:*] Now please
make a clean breast of it. If the connection between you and him was quite over when you
—came to care for me, as you call it—why did
he place us in a position to marry?

GINA. I suppose he thought as he could come
and go in our house.

HIALMAR. Only that? Was not he afraid of a
possible contingency?

GINA. I don't know what you mean.

HIALMAR. I want to know whether—your
child has the right to live under my roof.

GINA [*draws herself up; her eyes flash*]. You
ask that!

HIALMAR. You shall answer me this one question: Does Hedvig belong to me—or—? Well!

GINA [*looking at him with cold defiance*]. I
don't know.

HIALMAR [*quivering a little*]. You don't
know!

GINA. How should *I* know? A creature like
me—

HIALMAR [*quietly turning away from her*].
Then I have nothing more to do in this house.

GREGERS. Take care, Hialmar! Think what
you are doing!

HIALMAR [*puts on his overcoat*]. In this case,

there is nothing for a man like me to think twice about.

GREGERS. Yes indeed, there are endless things to be considered. You three must be together if you are to attain the true frame of mind for self-sacrifice and forgiveness.

HIALMAR. I don't want to attain it. Never, never! My hat! [*Takes his hat*] My home has fallen in ruins about me. [*Bursts into tears*] Gregers, I have no child!

HEDVIG [*who has opened the kitchen door*]. What is that you're saying? [*Coming to him*] Father, father!

GINA. There, you see!

HIALMAR. Don't come near me, Hedvig! Keep far away. I cannot bear to see you. Oh! those eyes—! Good-bye. [*Makes for the door*]

HEDVIG [*clinging close to him and screaming loudly*]. No! no! Don't leave me!

GINA [*cries out*]. Look at the child, Ekdal! Look at the child!

HIALMAR. I will not! I cannot! I must get out—away from all this! [*He tears himself away from* HEDVIG, *and goes out by the passage door*]

HEDVIG [*with despairing eyes*]. He is going away from us, mother! He is going away from us! He will never come back again!

GINA. Don't cry, Hedvig. Father's sure to come back again.

HEDVIG [*throws herself sobbing on the sofa*]. No, no, he'll never come home to us any more.

GREGERS. Do you believe I meant all for the best, Mrs. Ekdal?

GINA. Yes, I daresay you did; but God forgive you, all the same.

HEDVIG [*lying on the sofa*]. Oh, this will kill me! What have I done to him? Mother, you must fetch him home again!

GINA. Yes, yes, yes; only be quiet, and I'll go out and look for him. [*Puts on her outdoor things*] Perhaps he's gone in to Relling's. But you mustn't lie there and cry. Promise me!

HEDVIG [*weeping convulsively*]. Yes, I'll stop, I'll stop; if only father comes back!

GREGERS [*to* GINA, *who is going*]. After all, had you not better leave him to fight out his bitter fight to the end?

GINA. Oh, he can do that afterwards. First of all, we must get the child quieted. [*Goes out by the passage door*]

HEDVIG [*sits up and dries her tears*]. Now you must tell me what all this means. Why doesn't father want me any more?

GREGERS. You mustn't ask that till you are a big girl—quite grown-up.

HEDVIG [*sobs*]. But I can't go on being as miserable as this till I'm grown-up.—I think I know what it is.—Perhaps I'm not really father's child.

GREGERS [*uneasily*]. How could that be?

HEDVIG. Mother might have found me. And perhaps father has just got to know it; I've read of such things.

GREGERS. Well, but if it were so—

HEDVIG. I think he might be just as fond of me for all that. Yes, fonder almost. We got the wild duck as a present, you know, and I love it so dearly all the same.

GREGERS [*turning the conversation*]. Ah, the wild duck, by-the-bye! Let us talk about the wild duck a little, Hedvig.

HEDVIG. The poor wild duck! He doesn't want to see it any more either. Only think, he wanted to wring its neck!

GREGERS. Oh, he won't do that.

HEDVIG. No; but he said he would like to. And I think it was horrid of father to say it; for I pray for the wild duck every night, and ask that it may be preserved from death and all that is evil.

GREGERS [*looking at her*]. Do you say your prayers every night?

HEDVIG. Yes.

GREGERS. Who taught you to do that?

HEDVIG. I myself; one time when father was very ill, and had leeches on his neck, and said that death was staring him in the face.

GREGERS. Well?

HEDVIG. Then I prayed for him as I lay in bed; and since then I have always kept it up.

GREGERS. And now you pray for the wild duck too?

HEDVIG. I thought it was best to bring in the wild duck; for she was so weakly at first.

GREGERS. Do you pray in the morning, too?

HEDVIG. No, of course not.

GREGERS. Why not in the morning as well?

HEDVIG. In the morning it's light, you know, and there's nothing in particular to be afraid of.

GREGERS. And your father was going to wring the neck of the wild duck that you love so dearly?

HEDVIG. No; he said he ought to wring its neck, but he would spare it for my sake; and that was kind of father.

GREGERS [*coming a little nearer*]. But suppose you were to sacrifice the wild duck of your own free will for his sake.

HEDVIG [*rising*]. The wild duck!

GREGERS. Suppose you were to make a free-will offering, for his sake, of the dearest treasure you have in the world!

HEDVIG. Do you think that would do any good?

GREGERS. Try it, Hedvig.

HEDVIG [*softly, with flashing eyes*]. Yes, I will try it.

GREGERS. Have you really the courage for it, do you think?

HEDVIG. I'll ask grandfather to shoot the wild duck for me.

GREGERS. Yes, do. But not a word to your mother about it.

HEDVIG. Why not?

GREGERS. She doesn't understand us.

HEDVIG. The wild duck! I'll try it to-morrow morning.

[GINA *comes in by the passage door*]

HEDVIG [*going towards her*]. Did you find him, mother?

GINA. No, but I heard as he had called and taken Relling with him.

GREGERS. Are you sure of that?

GINA. Yes, the porter's wife said so. Molvik went with them too, she said.

GREGERS. This evening, when his mind so sorely needs to wrestle in solitude—!

GINA [*takes off her things*]. Yes, men are strange creatures, so they are. The Lord only knows where Relling has dragged him to! I ran over to Madam Eriksen's, but they weren't there.

HEDVIG [*struggling to keep back her tears*]. Oh, if he should never come home any more!

GREGERS. He will come again. I shall have news to give him to-morrow; and then you shall see how he comes home. You may rely upon that, Hedvig, and sleep in peace. Good-night. [*He goes out by the passage door*]

HEDVIG [*throws herself sobbing on* GINA'S *neck*]. Mother, mother!

GINA [*pats her shoulder and sighs*]. Ah yes; Relling was right, he was. That's what comes of it when crazy creatures go about presenting the claims of the—what-you-may-call-it.

ACT FIFTH

HIALMAR EKDAL'S *studio. Cold, grey, morning light. Wet snow lies upon the large panes of the sloping roof-window.*

GINA *comes from the kitchen with an apron and bib on, and carrying a dusting-brush and a duster; she goes towards the sitting-room door. At the same moment* HEDVIG *comes hurriedly in from the passage*]

GINA [*stops*]. Well?

HEDVIG. Oh, mother, I almost think he's down at Relling's—

GINA. There, you see!

HEDVIG.—because the porter's wife says she could hear that Relling had two people with him when he came home last night.

GINA. That's just what I thought.

HEDVIG. But it's no use his being there, if he won't come up to us.

GINA. I'll go down and speak to him at all events.

[OLD EKDAL, *in dressing-gown and slippers, and with a lighted pipe, appears at the door of his room*]

EKDAL. Hialmar— Isn't Hialmar at home?

GINA. No, he's gone out.

EKDAL. So early? And in such a tearing snow-storm? Well, well; just as he pleases; I can take my morning walk alone.

[*He slides the garret door aside;* HEDVIG *helps him; he goes in; she closes it after him*]

HEDVIG [*in an undertone*]. Only think, mother, when poor grandfather hears that father is going to leave us.

GINA. Oh, nonsense; grandfather mustn't hear anything about it. It was a heaven's mercy he wasn't at home yesterday in all that hurly-burly.

HEDVIG. Yes, but—

[GREGERS *comes in by the passage door*]

GREGERS. Well, have you any news of him?

GINA. They say he's down at Relling's.

GREGERS. At Relling's! Has he really been out with those creatures?

GINA. Yes, like enough.

GREGERS. When he ought to have been yearning for solitude, to collect and clear his thoughts—

GINA. Yes, you may well say so.

[RELLING *enters from the passage*]

HEDVIG [*going to him*]. Is father in your room?

GINA [*at the same time*]. Is he there?

RELLING. Yes, to be sure he is.

HEDVIG. And you never let us know!

RELLING. Yes; I'm a brute. But in the first place I had to look after the other brute; I mean our dæmonic friend, of course; and then I fell so dead asleep that—

GINA. What does Ekdal say to-day?

RELLING. He says nothing whatever.

HEDVIG. Doesn't he speak?

RELLING. Not a blessed word.

GREGERS. No, no; I can understand that very well.

GINA. But what's he doing then?

RELLING. He's lying on the sofa, snoring.

GINA. Oh is he? Yes, Ekdal's a rare one to snore.

HEDVIG. Asleep? Can he sleep?

RELLING. Well, it certainly looks like it.

GREGERS. No wonder, after the spiritual conflict that has rent him—

GINA. And then he's never been used to gadding about out of doors at night.

HEDVIG. Perhaps it's a good thing that he's getting sleep, mother.

GINA. Of course it is; and we must take care we don't wake him up too early. Thank you, Relling. I must get the house cleaned up a bit now, and then— Come and help me, Hedvig.

[GINA *and* HEDVIG *go into the sitting-room*]

GREGORS [*turning to* RELLING]. What is your explanation of the spiritual tumult that is now going on in Hialmar Ekdal?

RELLING. Devil a bit of a spiritual tumult have *I* noticed in him.

GREGERS. What! Not at such a crisis, when his whole life has been placed on a new foundation—? How can you think that such an individuality as Hialmar's—?

RELLING. Oh, individuality—he! If he ever had any tendency to the abnormal developments you call individuality, I can assure you it was rooted out of him while he was still in his teens.

GREGERS. That would be strange indeed,—considering the loving care with which he was brought up.

RELLING. By those two high-flown, hysterical maiden aunts, you mean?

GREGERS. Let me tell you that they were women who never forgot the claim of the ideal —but of course you will only jeer at me again.

RELLING. No, I'm in no humour for that. I know all about those ladies; for he has ladled out no end of rhetoric on the subject of his "two soul-mothers." But I don't think he has much to thank them for. Ekdal's misfortune is that in his own circle he has always been looked upon as a shining light—

GREGERS. Not without reason, surely. Look at the depth of his mind!

RELLING. *I* have never discovered it. That his father believed in it I don't so much wonder; the old lieutenant has been an ass all his days.

GREGERS. He has had a child-like mind all his days; that is what you cannot understand.

RELLING. Well, so be it. But then, when our dear, sweet Hialmar went to college, he at once passed for the great light of the future amongst his comrades too! He was handsome, the rascal —red and white—a shop-girl's dream of manly beauty; and with his superficially emotional temperament, and his sympathetic voice, and his talent for declaiming other people's verses and other people's thoughts—

GREGERS [*indignantly*]. Is it Hialmar Ekdal you are talking about in this strain?

RELLING. Yes, with your permission; I am simply giving you an inside view of the idol you are grovelling before.

GREGERS. I should hardly have thought I was quite stone blind.

RELLING. Yes you are—or not far from it. You are a sick man, too, you see.

GREGERS. You are right there.

RELLING. Yes. Yours is a complicated case. First of all there is that plaguey integrity-fever; and then—what's worse—you are always in a delirium of hero-worship; you must always have something to adore, outside yourself.

GREGERS. Yes, I must certainly seek it outside myself.

RELLING. But you make such shocking mistakes about every new phœnix you think you have discovered. Here again you have come to a cottar's cabin with your claim of the ideal; and the people of the house are insolvent.

GREGERS. If you don't think better than that of Hialmar Ekdal, what pleasure can you find in being everlastingly with him?

RELLING. Well, you see, I'm supposed to be a sort of a doctor—save the mark! I can't but give a hand to the poor sick folk who live under the same roof with me.

GREGERS. Oh, indeed! Hialmar Ekdal is sick too, is he!

RELLING. Most people are, worse luck.

GREGORS. And what remedy are you applying in Hialmar's case?

RELLING. My usual one. I am cultivating the life-illusion in him.

GREGERS. Life—illusion? I didn't catch what you said.

RELLING. Yes, I said illusion. For illusion, you know, is the stimulating principle.

GREGERS. May I ask with what illusion Hialmar is inoculated?

RELLING. No, thank you; I don't betray professional secrets to quacksalvers. You would probably go and muddle his case still more than you have already. But my method is infallible. I have applied it to Molvik as well. I have made him "dæmonic." That's the blister I have to put on his neck.

GREGERS. Is he not really dæmonic then?

RELLING. What the devil do you mean by dæmonic! It's only a piece of gibberish I've invented to keep up a spark of life in him. But for that, the poor harmless creature would have succumbed to self-contempt and despair many a long year ago. And then the old lieutenant! But he has hit upon his own cure, you see.

GREGERS. Lieutenant Ekdal? What of him?

RELLING. Just think of the old bear-hunter shutting himself up in that dark garret to shoot rabbits! I tell you there is not a happier sportsman in the world than that old man pottering about in there among all that rubbish. The four or five withered Christmas-trees he has saved up are the same to him as the whole great fresh Höidal forest; the cock and the hens are the game-birds in the fir-tops; and the rabbits that flop about the garret floor are the bears he has to battle with—the mighty hunter of the mountains!

GREGERS. Poor unfortunate old man! Yes; he has indeed had to narrow the ideals of his youth.

RELLING. While I think of it, Mr. Werle, junior—don't use that foreign word: ideals. We have the excellent native word: lies.

GREGERS. Do you think the two things are related?

RELLING. Yes, just about as closely as typhus and putrid fever.

GREGERS. Dr. Relling, I shall not give up the

struggle until I have rescued Hialmar from your clutches!

RELLING. So much the worse for him. Rob the average man of his life-illusion, and you rob him of his happiness at the same stroke. [*To* HEDVIG, *who comes in from the sitting-room*] Well, little wild-duck-mother, I'm just going down to see whether papa is still lying meditating upon that wonderful invention of his. [*Goes out by the passage door*]

GREGERS [*approaches* HEDVIG]. I can see by your face that you have not yet done it.

HEDVIG. What? Oh, that about the wild duck! No.

GREGERS. I suppose your courage failed when the time came.

HEDVIG. No, that wasn't it. But when I awoke this morning and remembered what we had been talking about, it seemed so strange.

GREGERS. Strange?

HEDVIG. Yes, I don't know—. Yesterday evening, at the moment, I thought there was something so delightful about it; but since I have slept and thought of it again, it somehow doesn't seem worth while.

GREGERS. Ah, I thought you could not have grown up quite unharmed in this house.

HEDVIG. I don't care about that, if only father would come up—

GREGERS. Oh, if only your eyes had been opened to that which gives life its value—if you possessed the true, joyous, fearless spirit of sacrifice, you would soon see how he would come up to you.—But I believe in you still, Hedvig. [*He goes out by the passage door*]

[HEDVIG *wanders about the room for a time; she is on the point of going into the kitchen when a knock is heard at the garret door.* HEDVIG *goes over and opens it a little; old* EKDAL *comes out; she pushes the door to again*]

EKDAL. H'm, it's not much fun to take one's morning walk alone.

HEDVIG. Wouldn't you like to go shooting, grandfather?

EKDAL. It's not the weather for it to-day. It's so dark there, you can scarcely see where you're going.

HEDVIG. Do you never want to shoot anything besides the rabbits?

EKDAL. Do you think the rabbits aren't good enough?

HEDVIG. Yes, but what about the wild duck?

EKDAL. Ho-ho! are you afraid I shall shoot your wild duck? Never in the world. Never.

HEDVIG. No, I suppose you couldn't; they say it's very difficult to shoot wild ducks.

EKDAL. Couldn't! Should rather think I could.

HEDVIG. How would you set about it, grand-father?—I don't mean with my wild duck, but with others?

EKDAL. I should take care to shoot them in the breast, you know; that's the surest place. And then you must shoot against the feathers, you see—not the way of the feathers.

HEDVIG. Do they die then, grandfather?

EKDAL. Yes, they die right enough—when you shoot properly. Well, I must go and brush up a bit. H'm—understand—h'm. [*Goes into his room*]

[HEDVIG *waits a little, glances towards the sitting-room door, goes over to the book-case, stands on tip-toe, takes the double-barrelled pistol down from the shelf, and looks at it.* GINA, *with brush and duster, comes from the sitting-room.* HEDVIG *hastily lays down the pistol, un-observed*]

GINA. Don't stand raking amongst father's things, Hedvig.

HEDVIG [*goes away from the bookcase*]. I was only going to tidy up a little.

GINA. You'd better go into the kitchen, and see if the coffee's keeping hot; I'll take his breakfast on a tray, when I go down to him.

[HEDVIG *goes out.* GINA *begins to sweep and clean up the studio. Presently the passage door is opened with hesitation, and* HIALMAR EKDAL *looks in. He has on his overcoat, but not his hat; he is unwashed, and his hair is dishevelled and unkempt. His eyes are dull and heavy*]

GINA [*standing with the brush in her hand, and looking at him*]. Oh, there now, Ekdal—so you've come after all?

HIALMAR [*comes in and answers in a tone-less voice*]. I come—only to depart again immediately.

GINA. Yes, yes, I suppose so. But, Lord help us! what a sight you are!

HIALMAR. A sight?

GINA. And your nice winter coat too! Well, that's done for.

HEDVIG [*at the kitchen door*]. Mother, hadn't I better—? [*Sees* HIALMAR, *gives a loud scream of joy, and runs to him*] Oh, father, father!

HIALMAR [*turns away and makes a gesture of repulsion*]. Away, away, away! [*To* GINA] Keep her away from me, I say!

GINA [*in a low tone*]. Go into the sitting-room, Hedvig.

[HEDVIG *does so without a word*]

HIALMAR [*fussily pulls out the table-drawer*]. I must have my books with me. Where are my books?

GINA. Which books?

HIALMAR. My scientific books, of course; the technical magazines I require for my invention.

GINA [*searches in the bookcase*]. Is it these here paper-covered ones?

HIALMAR. Yes, of course.

GINA [*lays a heap of magazines on the table*]. Shan't I get Hedvig to cut them for you?

HIALMAR. I don't require to have them cut for me.

[*Short silence*]

GINA. Then you're still set on leaving us, Ekdal?

HIALMAR [*rummaging amongst the books*]. Yes, that is a matter of course, I should think.

GINA. Well, well.

HIALMAR [*vehemently*]. How can I live here, to be stabbed to the heart every hour of the day?

GINA. God forgive you for thinking such vile things of me.

HIALMAR. Prove—!

GINA. I think it's you as has got to prove.

HIALMAR. After a past like yours? There are certain claims—I may almost call them claims of the ideal—.

GINA. But what about grandfather? What's to become of him, poor dear?

HIALMAR. I know my duty; my helpless father will come with me. I am going out into the town to make arrangements—. H'm— [*hesitatingly*] has any one found my hat on the stairs?

GINA. No. Have you lost your hat?

HIALMAR. Of course I had it on when I came in last night; there's no doubt about that; but I couldn't find it this morning.

GINA. Lord help us! where have you been to with those two ne'er-do-weels?

HIALMAR. Oh, don't bother me about trifles. Do you suppose I am in the mood to remember details?

GINA. If only you haven't caught cold, Ekdal. [*Goes out into the kitchen*]

HIALMAR [*talks to himself in a low tone of irritation, whilst he empties the table-drawer*]. You're a scoundrel, Relling!—You're a low fellow!—Ah, you shameless tempter!—I wish I could get some one to stick a knife into you!

[*He lays some old letters on one side, finds the torn document of yesterday, takes it up and looks at the pieces; puts it down hurriedly as GINA enters*]

GINA [*sets a tray with coffee, etc., on the table*]. Here's a drop of something hot, if you'd fancy it. And there's some bread and butter and a snack of salt meat.

HIALMAR [*glancing at the tray*]. Salt meat? Never under this roof! It's true I have not had a mouthful of solid food for nearly twenty-four hours; but no matter.—My memoranda! The commencement of my autobiography! What has become of my diary, and all my important papers? [*Opens the sitting-room door but draws back*] She is there too!

GINA. Good Lord! the child must be somewhere!

HIALMAR. Come out. [*He makes room*]

[HEDVIG *comes, scared, into the studio*]

HIALMAR [*with his hand upon the door-handle, says to* GINA:] In these, the last moments I spend in my former home, I wish to be spared from interlopers— [*Goes into the room*]

HEDVIG [*with a bound towards her mother, asks softly, trembling*]. Does that mean me?

GINA. Stay out in the kitchen, Hedvig; or, no—you'd best go into your own room. [*Speaks to* HIALMAR *as she goes in to him*] Wait a bit, Ekdal; don't rummage so in the drawers; I know where everything is.

HEDVIG [*stands a moment immovable, in terror and perplexity, biting her lips to keep back the tears; then she clenches her hands convulsively, and says softly:*] The wild duck. [*She steals over and takes the pistol from the shelf, opens the garret door a little way, creeps in, and draws the door to after her*]

[HIALMAR *and* GINA *can be heard disputing in the sitting-room*]

HIALMAR [*comes in with some manuscript books and old loose papers, which he lays upon the table*]. That portmanteau is of no use! There are a thousand and one things I must drag with me.

GINA [*following with the portmanteau*]. Why not leave all the rest for the present, and only take a shirt and a pair of woolen drawers with you?

HIALMAR. Whew!—all these exhausting preparations—! [*Pulls off his overcoat and throws it upon the sofa*]

GINA. And there's the coffee getting cold.

HIALMAR. H'm. [*Drinks a mouthful without thinking of it, and then another*]

GINA [*dusting the backs of the chairs*]. A nice job you'll have to find such another big garret for the rabbits.

HIALMAR. What! Am I to drag all those rabbits with me too?

GINA. You don't suppose grandfather can get on without his rabbits.

HIALMAR. He must just get used to doing without them. Have not I to sacrifice very much greater things than rabbits!

GINA [*dusting the bookcase*]. Shall I put the flute in the portmanteau for you?

HIALMAR. No. No flute for me. But give me the pistol!

GINA. Do you want to take the pigstol with you?

HIALMAR. Yes. My loaded pistol.

GINA [*searching for it*]. It's gone. He must have taken it in with him.

HIALMAR. Is he in the garret?

GINA. Yes, of course he's in the garret.

HIALMAR. H'm—poor lonely old man. [*He takes a piece of bread and butter, eats it, and finishes his cup of coffee*]

GINA. If we hadn't have let that room, you could have moved in there.

HIALMAR. And continued to live under the same roof with—! Never,—never!

GINA. But couldn't you put up with the sitting-room for a day or two? You could have it all to yourself.

HIALMAR. Never within these walls!

GINA. Well then, down with Relling and Molvik.

HIALMAR. Don't mention those wretches' names to me! The very thought of them almost takes away my appetite.—Oh no, I must go out into the storm and the snow-drift,—go from house to house and seek shelter for my father and myself.

GINA. But you've got no hat, Ekdal! You've been and lost your hat, you know.

HIALMAR. Oh those two brutes, those slaves of all the vices! A hat must be procured. [*Takes another piece of bread and butter*] Some arrangement must be made. For I have no mind to throw away my life, either. [*Looks for something on the tray*]

GINA. What are you looking for?

HIALMAR. Butter.

GINA. I'll get some at once. [*Goes out into the kitchen*]

HIALMAR [*calls after her*]. Oh it doesn't matter; dry bread is good enough for me.

GINA [*brings a dish of butter*]. Look here; this is fresh churned. [*She pours out another cup of coffee for him*]

[*He seats himself on the sofa, spreads more butter on the already buttered bread, and eats and drinks a while in silence*]

HIALMAR. Could I, without being subject to intrusion—intrusion of any sort—could I live in the sitting-room there for a day or two?

GINA. Yes, to be sure you could, if you only would.

HIALMAR. For I see no possibility of getting all father's things out in such a hurry.

GINA. And besides, you've surely got to tell him first as you don't mean to live with us others no more.

HIALMAR [*pushes away his coffee cup*]. Yes, there is that too; I shall have to lay bare the whole tangled story to him—. I must turn matters over; I must have breathing-time; I cannot take all these burdens on my shoulders in a single day.

GINA. No, especially in such horrible weather as it is outside.

HIALMAR [*touching WERLE's letter*]. I see that paper is still lying about here.

GINA. Yes, I haven't touched it.

HIALMAR. So far as I am concerned it is mere waste paper—

GINA. Well, I have certainly no notion of making any use of it.

HIALMAR. —but we had better not let it get lost all the same;—in all the upset when I move, it might easily—

GINA. I'll take good care of it, Ekdal.

HIALMAR. The donation is in the first instance made to father, and it rests with him to accept or decline it.

GINA [*sighs*]. Yes, poor old father—

HIALMAR. To make quite safe— Where shall I find some gum?

GINA [*goes to the bookcase*]. Here's the gum-pot.

HIALMAR. And a brush?

GINA. The brush is here too. [*Brings him the things*]

HIALMAR [*takes a pair of scissors*]. Just a strip of paper at the back— [*Clips and gums*] Far be it from me to lay hands upon what is not my own—and least of all upon what belongs to a destitute old man—and to—the other as well.—There now. Let it lie there for a time; and when it is dry, take it away. I wish never to see that document again. Never!

[*GREGERS WERLE enters from the passage*]

GREGERS [*somewhat surprised*]. What,—are you sitting here, Hialmar?

HIALMAR [*rises hurriedly*]. I had sunk down from fatigue.

GREGERS. You have been having breakfast, I see.

HIALMAR. The body sometimes makes its claims felt too.

GREGERS. What have you decided to do?

HIALMAR. For a man like me, there is only one course possible. I am just putting my most important things together. But it takes time, you know.

GINA [*with a touch of impatience*]. Am I to get the room ready for you, or am I to pack your portmanteau?

HIALMAR [*after a glance of annoyance at GREGERS*] Pack—and get the room ready!

GINA [*takes the portmanteau*]. Very well; then I'll put in the shirt and the other things. [*Goes into the sitting-room and draws the door to after her*]

GREGERS [*after a short silence*]. I never dreamed that this would be the end of it. Do you really feel it a necessity to leave house and home?

HIALMAR [*wanders about restlessly*]. What would you have me do?—I am not fitted to bear unhappiness, Gregers. I must feel secure and at peace in my surroundings.

GREGERS. But can you not feel that here? Just try it. I should have thought you had firm ground to build upon now—if only you start afresh. And remember, you have your invention to live for.

HIALMAR. Oh don't talk about my invention. It's perhaps still in the dim distance.

GREGERS. Indeed!

HIALMAR. Why, great heavens, what would

you have me invent? Other people have invented almost everything already. It becomes more and more difficult every day—

GREGERS. And you have devoted so much labour to it.

HIALMAR. It was that blackguard Relling that urged me to it.

GREGERS. Relling?

HIALMAR. Yes, it was he that first made me realise my aptitude for making some notable discovery in photography.

GREGERS. Aha—it was Relling!

HIALMAR. Oh, I have been so truly happy over it! Not so much for the sake of the invention itself, as because Hedvig believed in it—believed in it with a child's whole eagerness of faith.—At least, I have been fool enough to go and imagine that she believed in it.

GREGERS. Can you really think that Hedvig has been false towards you?

HIALMAR. I can think anything now. It is Hedvig that stands in my way. She will blot out the sunlight from my whole life.

GREGERS. Hedvig! Is it Hedvig you are talking of? How should she blot out your sunlight?

HIALMAR [without answering]. How unutterably I have loved that child! How unutterably happy I have felt every time I came home to my humble room, and she flew to meet me, with her sweet little blinking eyes. Oh, confiding fool that I have been! I loved her unutterably;—and I yielded myself up to the dream, the delusion, that she loved me unutterably in return.

GREGERS. Do you call that a delusion?

HIALMAR. How should I know? I can get nothing out of Gina; and besides, she is totally blind to the ideal side of these complications. But to you I feel impelled to open my mind, Gregers. I cannot shake off this frightful doubt—perhaps Hedvig has never really and honestly loved me.

GREGERS. What would you say if she were to give you a proof of her love? [Listens] What's that? I thought I heard the wild duck—?

HIALMAR. It's the wild duck quacking. Father's in the garret.

GREGERS. Is he? [His face lights up with joy] I say you may yet have proof that your poor misunderstood Hedvig loves you!

HIALMAR. Oh, what proof can she give me? I dare not believe in any assurances from that quarter.

GREGERS. Hedvig does not know what deceit means.

HIALMAR. Oh Gregers, that is just what I cannot be sure of. Who knows what Gina and that Mrs. Sörby may many a time have sat here whispering and tattling about? And Hedvig usually has her ears open, I can tell you. Perhaps the deed of gift was not such a surprise

to her, after all. In fact, I'm not sure but that I noticed something of the sort.

GREGERS. What spirit is this that has taken possession of you?

HIALMAR. I have had my eyes opened. Just you notice;—you'll see, the deed of gift is only a beginning. Mrs. Sörby has always been a good deal taken up with Hedvig; and now she has the power to do whatever she likes for the child. They can take her from me whenever they please.

GREGERS. Hedvig will never, never leave you.

HIALMAR. Don't be so sure of that. If only they beckon to her and throw out a golden bait—! And oh! I have loved her so unspeakably! I would have counted it my highest happiness to take her tenderly by the hand and lead her, as one leads a timid child through a great dark empty room!—I am cruelly certain now that the poor photographer in his humble attic has never really and truly been anything to her. She has only cunningly contrived to keep on a good footing with him until the time came.

GREGERS. You don't believe that yourself, Hialmar.

HIALMAR. That is just the terrible part of it—I don't know what to believe,—I never can know it. But can you really doubt that it must be as I say? Ho-ho, you have far too much faith in the claim of the ideal, my good Gregers! If those others came, with the glamour of wealth about them, and called to the child:— "Leave him: come to us: here life awaits you—!"

GREGERS [quickly]. Well, what then?

HIALMAR. If I then asked her: Hedvig, are you willing to renounce that life for me? [Laughs scornfully] No thank you! You would soon hear what answer I should get.

[A pistol shot is heard from within the garret]

GREGERS [loudly and joyfully]. Hialmar!

HIALMAR. There now; he must needs go shooting too.

GINA [comes in]. Oh Ekdal, I can hear grandfather blazing away in the garret by hisself.

HIALMAR. I'll look in—

GREGERS [eagerly, with emotion]. Wait a moment! Do you know what that was?

HIALMAR. Yes, of course I know.

GREGERS. No you don't know. But I do. That was the proof!

HIALMAR. What proof?

GREGERS. It was a child's free-will offering. She has got your father to shoot the wild duck.

HIALMAR. To shoot the wild duck!

GINA. Oh, think of that—!

HIALMAR. What was that for?

GREGERS. She wanted to sacrifice to you her most cherished possession; for then she thought you would surely come to love her again.

HIALMAR [*tenderly, with emotion*]. Oh, poor child!

GINA. What things she does think of!

GREGERS. She only wanted your love again, Hialmar. She could not live without it.

GINA [*struggling with her tears*]. There, you can see for yourself, Ekdal.

HIALMAR. Gina, where is she?

GINA [*sniffs*]. Poor dear, she's sitting out in the kitchen, I daresay.

HIALMAR [*goes over, tears open the kitchen door, and says:*]. Hedvig, come, come in to me! [*Looks round*] No, she's not here.

GINA. Then she must be in her own little room.

HIALMAR [*without*]. No, she's not here either. [*Comes in*] She must have gone out.

GINA. Yes, you wouldn't have her anywheres in the house.

HIALMAR. Oh, if she would only come home quickly, so that I can tell her— Everything will come right now, Gregers; now I believe we can begin life afresh.

GREGERS [*quietly*]. I knew it; I knew the child would make amends.

[*Old EKDAL appears at the door of his room; he is in full uniform, and is busy buckling on his sword*]

HIALMAR [*astonished*]. Father! Are you there?

GINA. Have you been firing in your room?

EKDAL [*resentfully, approaching*]. So you go shooting alone, do you, Hialmar?

HIALMAR [*excited and confused*]. Then it wasn't you that fired that shot in the garret?

EKDAL. Me that fired? H'm.

GREGERS [*calls out to HIALMAR*]. She has shot the wild duck herself.

HIALMAR. What can it mean? [*Hastens to the garret door, tears it aside, looks in and calls loudly:*] Hedvig!

GINA [*runs to the door*]. Good God, what's that!

HIALMAR [*goes in*]. She's lying on the floor!

GREGERS. Hedvig! lying on the floor! [*Goes in to HIALMAR*]

GINA [*at the same time*]. Hedvig! [*Inside the garret*] No, no, no!

EKDAL. Ho-ho! does she go shooting too, now?

[*HIALMAR, GINA, and GREGERS carry HEDVIG into the studio; in her dangling right hand she holds the pistol fast clasped in her fingers*]

HIALMAR [*distracted*]. The pistol has gone off. She has wounded herself. Call for help! Help!

GINA [*runs into the passage and calls down*]. Relling! Relling! Doctor Relling; come up as quick as you can!

[*HIALMAR and GREGERS lay HEDVIG down on the sofa*]

EKDAL [*quietly*]. The woods avenge themselves.

HIALMAR [*on his knees beside HEDVIG*]. She'll soon come to now. She's coming to—; yes, yes, yes.

GINA [*who has come in again*]. Where has she hurt herself? I can't see anything—

[*RELLING comes hurriedly, and immediately after him MOLVIK; the latter without his waistcoat and necktie, and with his coat open*]

RELLING. What's the matter here?

GINA. They say Hedvig has shot herself.

HIALMAR. Come and help us!

RELLING. Shot herself! [*He pushes the table aside and begins to examine her*]

HIALMAR [*kneeling and looking anxiously up at him*]. It can't be dangerous? Speak, Relling! She is scarcely bleeding at all. It can't be dangerous?

RELLING. How did it happen?

HIALMAR. Oh, we don't know—!

GINA. She wanted to shoot the wild duck.

RELLING. The wild duck?

HIALMAR. The pistol must have gone off.

RELLING. H'm. Indeed.

EKDAL. The woods avenge themselves. But I'm not afraid, all the same. [*Goes into the garret and closes the door after him*]

HIALMAR. Well, Relling,—why don't you say something?

RELLING. The ball has entered the breast.

HIALMAR. Yes, but she's coming to!

RELLING. Surely you can see that Hedvig is dead.

GINA [*bursts into tears*]. Oh my child, my child.

GREGERS [*huskily*]. In the depths of the sea—

HIALMAR [*jumps up*]. No, no, she must live! Oh, for God's sake, Relling—only a moment— only just till I can tell her how unspeakably I loved her all the time!

RELLING. The bullet has gone through her heart. Internal hemorrhage. Death must have been instantaneous.

HIALMAR. And I! I hunted her from me like an animal! And she crept terrified into the garret and died for love of me! [*Sobbing*] I can never atone to her! I can never tell her—! [*Clenches his hands and cries, upwards*] O Thou above—! If Thou be indeed! Why hast Thou done this thing to me?

GINA. Hush, hush, you mustn't go on that awful way. We had no right to keep her, I suppose.

MOLVIK. The child is not dead, but sleepeth.

RELLING. Bosh!

HIALMAR [*becomes calm, goes over to the sofa, folds his arms, and looks at HEDVIG*]. There she lies so stiff and still.

RELLING [*tries to loosen the pistol*]. She's holding it so tight, so tight.

GINA. No, no, Relling, don't break her fingers!
let the pigstol be.

HIALMAR. She shall take it with her.

GINA. Yes, let her. But the child mustn't lie
here for a show. She shall go to her own room,
so she shall. Help me, Ekdal.

[HIALMAR and GINA take HEDVIG between
them]

HIALMAR [as they are carrying her]. Oh Gina,
Gina, can you survive this!

GINA. We must help each other to bear it.
For now at least she belongs to both of us.

MOLVIK [stretches out his arms and mum-
bles]. Blessed be the Lord; to earth thou shalt
return; to earth thou shalt return—

RELLING [whispers]. Hold your tongue, you
fool; you're drunk.

[HIALMAR and GINA carry the body out
through the kitchen door. RELLING shuts
it after them. MOLVIK slinks out into the
passage]

RELLING [goes over to GREGERS and says:]
No one shall ever convince me that the pistol
went off by accident.

GREGERS [who has stood terrified, with convulsive twitchings]. Who can say how the
dreadful thing happened?

RELLING. The powder has burnt the body
of her dress. She must have pressed the pistol
right against her breast and fired.

GREGERS. Hedvig has not died in vain. Did
you not see how sorrow set free what is noble
in him?

RELLING. Most people are ennobled by the
actual presence of death. But how long do you
suppose this nobility will last in him?

GREGERS. Why should it not endure and increase throughout his life?

RELLING. Before a year is over, little Hedvig
will be nothing to him but a pretty theme for
declamation.

GREGERS. How dare you say that of Hialmar
Ekdal?

RELLING. We will talk of this again, when the
grass has first withered on her grave. Then
you'll hear him spouting about "the child too
early torn from her father's heart;" then you'll
see him steep himself in a syrup of sentiment
and self-admiration and self-pity. Just you
wait!

GREGERS. If you are right and I am wrong,
then life is not worth living.

RELLING. Oh, life would be quite tolerable,
after all, if only we could be rid of the confounded duns that keep on pestering us, in our
poverty, with the claim of the ideal.

GREGERS [looking straight before him]. In
that case, I am glad that my destiny is what
it is.

RELLING. May I inquire,—what is your
destiny?

GREGERS [going]. To be the thirteenth at
table.

RELLING. The devil it is.

THE END

CYRANO DE BERGERAC

TRANSLATED FROM THE FRENCH OF EDMOND ROSTAND
INTO ENGLISH VERSE

By HOWARD THAYER KINGSBURY

This version is from the original prompt book of Richard Mansfield through the courtesy of Mrs. Mansfield and the Smithsonian Institute.

Reprinted by permission of Howard Thayer Kingsbury, and by the courtesy of Mrs. Richard Mansfield.

DRAMATIS PERSONÆ

CYRANO DE BERGERAC,
CHRISTIAN DE NEUVILLETTE,
THE COMTE DE GUICHE,
RAGUENEAU,
LE BRET,
CAPTAIN CARBON DE CASTEL-JALOUX,
THE CADETS,
LIGNIÈRE,
DE VALVERT,
A MARQUIS,
SECOND MARQUIS,
THIRD MARQUIS,
MONTFLEURY,
BELLEROSE,
JODELET,
CUIGY,
BRISSAILLE,
A BUSYBODY,
A MUSKETEER,
ANOTHER,
A SPANISH OFFICER,
A LIGHT GUARDSMAN,
CHAMPAGNE,
FLANQUIN,
THE DOORKEEPER,
A TRADESMAN,
HIS SON,
A PICKPOCKET,
A SPECTATOR,
A GUARD,
BERTRANDOU, THE FIFER,
THE CAPUCHIN,
TWO MUSICIANS,
THE POETS,
THE PASTRY-COOKS,

———

ROXANE,
SISTER MARTHA,
LISE,
MOTHER MARGARET DE JÉSUS,
SISTER CLAIRE,
THE ORANGE-GIRL,
THE DUENNA,
AN ACTRESS,
THE SOUBRETTE,
THE PAGES,
THE FLOWER-GIRL.

The Crowd, Tradesmen, Marquises, Musketeers, Pickpockets, Pastry-cooks, Poets, Gascon Cadets, Actors, Violinists, Pages, Children, Spanish Soldiers, Spectators, Blue-stockings, Actresses, Nuns, Lackeys, etc.

THE SCENES

FIRST ACT.—*The Hall of the Hôtel de Bourgogne.*
SECOND ACT.—*The Poet's Cookshop.*
THIRD ACT.—*A Small Square in the Old Marais. Roxane's Kiss.*
FOURTH ACT.— *The Station occupied by Carbon de Castle. The Gascon Cadets.*
FIFTH ACT.—*The Park of the Convent. Cyrano's Gazette.*
          (*The first Four Acts in 1640; the Fifth in 1655.*)

CYRANO DE BERGERAC

FIRST ACT

A PERFORMANCE AT THE HÔTEL DE BOURGOGNE

The hall of the Hôtel de Bourgogne in 1640. A sort of tennis court arranged and decorated for performances. The hall is oblong, seen diagonally, so that one of its sides forms the background, which runs from the first entrance on the right to the last entrance on the left, where it meets the stage, which is seen obliquely. This stage is provided with benches on each side, along the wings. The curtain is composed of two pieces of tapestry which can be separated. Above Harlequin's cloak are the royal arms. High steps lead down from the platform to the floor. On each side of these steps is the orchestra. Candles serve as footlights. Two galleries along the side, one above the other; the upper gallery is divided into boxes. No seats in the parterre, which is the actual stage of the theatre; in the rear of this parterre, that is to say, to the right, first entrance, are benches rising in tiers; and under a staircase which leads to the upper seats, and of which only the beginning is visible, a sort of sideboard provided with little candelabra, vases of flowers, glasses, plates of cake, bottles, etc. In the middle of the background, under the tier of boxes, the entrance of the theatre. A large door, which partly opens to let in the audience. On the leaves of the door, as well as in several other places, and above the sideboard, red posters on which are the words "La Clorise." When the curtain rises the hall is half lighted and still empty, the chandeliers are lowered in the middle of the parterre, waiting to be lighted.

The Public, arriving little by little. GENTLEMEN, TRADESMEN, LACKEYS, PAGES, PICK-POCKETS, *the* DOORKEEPER, *etc; then the* MARQUISES, CUIGY, BRISSAILLE, *the* ORANGE-GIRL, THE VIOLINS, *etc.*

    [*A sound of voices is heard behind the door; then a* GENTLEMAN *enters suddenly*]

THE DOORKEEPER [*following him*].
Holloa! Your fifteen pence!
THE GENTLEMAN.   I come in free.
THE DOORKEEPER. Why?
THE GENTLEMAN.   I'm a guardsman
     of the Royal Household.
THE DOORKEEPER [*to another* GENTLEMAN *who has just come in*].
And you?

SECOND GENTLEMAN. Oh, no!
THE DOORKEEPER.   But—
SECOND GENTLEMAN.   I'm a musketeer!
FIRST GENTLEMAN [*to the second*].
The play does not begin till two o'clock;
The house is empty, let us try our foils.
    [*They fence with the foils which they have brought*]
CHAMPAGNE [*entering*].
Pst—Flanquin!—
FLANQUIN [*already in*].
     Champagne?—
CHAMPAGNE [*showing him games which he takes out of his doublet*]. Cards, dice.
    [*Sits down on the ground*]   Let us play.
FLANQUIN [*same action*].
Why, yes, my boy!
CHAMPAGNE [*taking from his pocket a candle end, which he lights and sets on the floor*].   I've taken from my master
A bit of candle.
A GUARD [*to a* FLOWER-GIRL *who comes forward*].   It is fine to come
Before the lights are lit.
ONE OF THE FENCERS [*getting a stroke of the foil*].   Touched!
ONE OF THE GAMESTERS [*enter A* MAN *paying* DOORKEEPER].   Clubs!
THE GUARD [*pursuing the girl*]. A kiss!
THE FLOWER-GIRL [*breaking away*].
We shall be seen.
THE GUARD [*dragging her into a dark corner*].   No danger!
A MAN [*sitting on the floor, together with others who have brought eatables. First and second* GENTLEMEN *resume fencing*].
     When one comes
Before the play, one has a chance to eat.
A TRADESMAN [*up right center, escorting his son*].
Let us wait here, my son.
A GAMBLER [*down right*]. Aces!
A MAN [*up left, taking a bottle of wine from under his cloak, and sitting down*].
     A drinker
Should drink his Burgundy
[*drinks*]   at the Hôtel de Bourgogne.
THE TRADESMAN [*enter four* PAGES, *fuss with* DOORKEEPER, *trying to enter without paying. Up right center* GAMBLERS *down right rise and join crowd upstage. To his son*].
Would you not think it was some evil place?
    [*Points out the drinker with the end of his cane*]

Drinkers!

[*As they separate, one of the fencers pushes him over*]

Fighters!

[*Falls among the card-players*]

Gamblers!

THE GUARD [*left, behind him, still struggling with the girl*]. A kiss!

THE TRADESMAN [*drawing his son away quickly*]. Good heavens!

And just to think that in a hall like this
They played Rotrou, my son!

THE YOUNG MAN. And Corneille too!

FOUR PAGES [*holding one another's hands, enter, singing and dancing*].

Tra la la la la la la la la la-lère.

THE DOORKEEPER [A YOUNG MAN *watching* GAMBLERS *and* TRADESMAN *pulling him away. Severely, to the pages*].

No nonsense, boys!

FIRST PAGE [*with wounded dignity*]. Oh, sir, what a suspicion!

[*Quickly to the second, as soon as the* DOORKEEPER *has turned his back*]

Have you some string?

THE SECOND. Yes, and a hook as well.

FIRST PAGE. From up above there we can fish for wigs.

[FIRST, THIRD, *and* FOURTH PAGES *run up stairs*]

A PICKPOCKET [*gathering several evil-looking men about him*].

And now, young rascals, come and take your lesson,

Since this will be your first attempt at thieving.

SECOND PAGE [*calling to other pages already in position in the upper galleries*].

Holloa! Have you your blow-guns?

THIRD PAGE [*from up above*]. Yes, and peas!

[*Blows, and showers them with peas*]

THE YOUNG MAN [*to his father*].

What is the play?

THE TRADESMAN. "Clorise."

THE YOUNG MAN. Whose work is it?

THE TRADESMAN. Monsieur Balthazar Baro's.

'Tis a piece!

[*Taking his son's arm, he joins crowd*]

THE PICKPOCKET [*to his pupils*].

Cut off the lace from the embroidered sleeve!

ONE OF THE AUDIENCE [*to another, pointing out one of the upper seats*].

I sat there on the first night of "The Cid"!

THE PICKPOCKET [*making the gesture of snatching*].

Watches—

THE TRADESMAN [*returning, to his son*].

You'll see the most distinguished actors—

THE PICKPOCKET [*making the gesture of pulling out with little stealthy jerks*].

Handkerchiefs—

THE TRADESMAN. Montfleury—

A MAN [*calling from the upper gallery*].

Light up the candles!

THE TRADESMAN. Bellerose, L'Épy, Beaupré, and Jodelet!

A PAGE [*in the parterre*].

Ah, here's the Orange-girl!

THE ORANGE-GIRL. Oranges, milk,

Raspberry syrup, lemonade! [*She is afterwards seen in the different boxes*]

[*A noise at the door*]

A FALSETTO VOICE. Room, beasts!

A LACKEY [*in surprise*].

Marquises—in the pit?

ANOTHER LACKEY. Oh, for a moment!

[*Enter a little band of* MARQUISES]

A MARQUIS [*seeing the hall empty*].

How's this? Do we arrive like simple shopmen,

Disturbing no one, treading on no toes?

Ah, fie for shame!

[*Finds himself facing some other gentlemen who have come in a few moments before*]

Cuigy, Brissaille!

[*Great embracings*]

CUIGY. The faithful!

Yes, we arrive even before the candles.

THE MARQUIS. Tell me not of it. I'm in such a humor—

ANOTHER. Cheer up, Marquis! [*Enter* TWO LAMPLIGHTERS *with lighted tapers*]

Here the lamplighters come!

THE HALL [*greeting the entrance of the* LAMPLIGHTERS]. Ah!

[*Groups are formed around the candelabra, which he lights. A few people have taken their places in the galleries.* LIGNIÈRE *enters the parterre, giving his arm to* CHRISTIAN DE NEUVILLETTE. LIGNIÈRE *is somewhat dishevelled, and looks dissipated, but distinguished.* CHRISTIAN *is handsomely dressed, but rather behind the fashion, appears preoccupied, and looks at the boxes*]

CUIGY. Lignière!

BRISSAILLE [*smiling*]. Not drunk yet?

LIGNIÈRE [*aside to* CHRISTIAN]. Shall I introduce you?

[*Sign of assent from* CHRISTIAN].

Baron de Neuvillette.

[*Bows*]

THE HALL [*hailing the ascent of the first lighted chandelier*]. Ah!

CUIGY [*to* BRISSAILLE, *looking at* CHRISTIAN]. Charming head!

[*People enter boxes ushered in by* LACKEY]

FIRST MARQUIS [*who has heard*].

Pooh!

LIGNIÈRE [*introducing them to* CHRISTIAN]. Messieurs de Cuigy, de Brissaille—

CHRISTIAN [*bowing*]. Delighted!

FIRST MARQUIS [*to the second*].
He's well enough, but not quite in the style.
LIGNIÈRE [*to* CUIGY].
He's just from the Touraine.
CHRISTIAN. Yes, I have been
Scarce twenty days in Paris. But to-morrow
I join the guards, to serve with the Cadets.
FIRST MARQUIS [*looking at the people as they come into the boxes*].
There's Madame Aubry.
THE ORANGE-GIRL. Oranges, grapes—!
THE VIOLINS [*tuning up*]. La, la!
CUIGY [*to* CHRISTIAN, *indicating the hall, which is filling up*]. A crowd!
CHRISTIAN. Yes, quite.
FIRST MARQUIS. All the fine people.
[*They name the women as they enter the boxes arrayed in all their finery. Exchange of bows and smiles*]
SECOND MARQUIS. Mesdames
De Guémenée—
CUIGY. Bois Dauphin—
FIRST MARQUIS. Whom we loved—
BRISSAILLE. De Chavigny—
SECOND MARQUIS. Who plays with all our hearts.
LIGNIÈRE. Monsieur de Corneille has come back from Rouen.
THE YOUNG MAN [*to his father*].
The Academy is there?
THE TRADESMAN. Oh, yes! I see
More than a few—Boudu, Boissat, Cureau,
Porchères, Colomby, Bourzeys, and Bourdon:
All names that will not die; how fine it is!
FIRST MARQUIS. Attention! Our blue-stockings take their places!
Barthénoïde, Urimédonte, Félixe.
Cassandacé.
SECOND MARQUIS. Heavens, what charming names!
You know them all, Marquis?
FIRST MARQUIS. I know them all.
LIGNIÈRE [*taking* CHRISTIAN *aside*].
My friend, I came to-night to lend you aid;
The lady comes not. Back to drink I go.
CHRISTIAN [*entreating*].
No! You, who tell me tales of town and court,
Stay; you will know for whom I die of love!
THE FIRST VIOLIN [*rapping on his desk with his bow*]. Attention, sirs!
[*Raises his bow*]
THE ORANGE-GIRL. Macaroons, lemonade!
CHRISTIAN. I fear lest she be a coquette and witty.
I dare not talk to her; I have no brains.
The language that folk write and speak to-day
Troubles me much. I'm but a timid soldier.
She's always there—to the right, the empty box.
LIGNIÈRE [*moving as if to start*]. I go.
CHRISTIAN [*still holding him back*]. No, stay!

LIGNIÈRE. I cannot. D'Assoucy
Waits for me at the tavern. Here 'tis thirsty.
THE ORANGE-GIRL [*passing him with a tray*]. Orange juice?
LIGNIÈRE. No!
THE ORANGE-GIRL. Milk?
LIGNIÈRE. Pooh.
THE ORANGE-GIRL. Muscatel?
LIGNIÈRE. Stop!
[*to* CHRISTIAN] I'll stay a bit. Let's try your muscatel.
[*Sits down by the sideboard. The girl pours out his muscatel*]
CRIES IN THE CROWD [*on the entrance of a little man, rather fat and very beaming*].
Ah, Ragueneau!
LIGNIÈRE [*to* CHRISTIAN]. Ragueneau, the pastry-cook.
RAGUENEAU [*dressed in the Sunday costume of a pastry-cook, quickly advancing towards* LIGNIÈRE].
Sir, have you seen Monsieur de Cyrano?
LIGNIÈRE [*introducing* RAGUENEAU *to* CHRISTIAN].
The pastry-cook of actors and of poets!
RAGUENEAU [*in confusion*].
You honor me too much—
LIGNIÈRE. Be still, Mæcenas!
RAGUENEAU. These gentlemen are served by me—
LIGNIÈRE. On credit.
He is himself a poet—
RAGUENEAU. So they say.
LIGNIÈRE. Crazy on verse.
RAGUENEAU. 'Tis true that for an ode—
LIGNIÈRE. You'd give a tart.
RAGUENEAU. Oh, just a little one!
LIGNIÈRE. He would disclaim it.—And for a triolet
Would you not give—
RAGUENEAU. Some rolls!
LIGNIÈRE [*severely*]. Milk-rolls, of course.
You like the theatre, then?
RAGUENEAU. I idolize it!
LIGNIÈRE. You buy your theatre-tickets with your cakes.
Your place to-day among us cost how much?
RAGUENEAU. Four cream-puffs, fifteen patties [*looks around on every side*] —I'm astonished!
Monsieur de Cyrano has not arrived?
LIGNIÈRE. But why?
RAGUENEAU. Montfleury plays!
LIGNIÈRE. 'T is true, this barrel
Will play for us to-night the role of Phédon.
But what cares Cyrano?
RAGUENEAU. You do not know?
Montfleury, whom he hates, sirs, he forbade
To appear upon the stage for a whole month.
LIGNIÈRE [*who has reached his fourth glass*].
Well, then?
RAGUENEAU. Montfleury plays.

CUIGY [*who has approached with his group
    of friends*].   He cannot stop him.
RAGUENEAU. Oh! Oh! I've come to see.
FIRST MARQUIS.   Who is this man,
This Cyrano?
CUIGY. A lad well skilled in sword-play.
SECOND MARQUIS. Noble?
CUIGY. Enough. In the Guards; a Cadet.
    [*Pointing out a gentleman going to and
    fro in the hall, as if looking for
    some one*]
His friend Le Bret can tell you.
    Calls].   Oh, Le Bret!
    [LE BRET *comes toward them*]
You look for Bergerac?
LE BRET.   Yes, I am anxious—
CUIGY. He is a man who's quite out of the
    common?
LE BRET [*affectionately*].
He is the choicest soul of mortal men.
RAGUENEAU. A poet!
CUIGY.   Swordsman!
BRISSAILLE.   Doctor!
LE BRET.   And musician!
LIGNIÈRE. And what a strange appearance
    he presents!
RAGUENEAU. In truth, I think that Philippe
    de Champaigne,
Solemn and grave, will never paint him for
    us;
But with his strange, grotesque extrava-
    gances
He would have lent to Jacques Callot, now
    dead,
A swashbuckler, to place among his masks.
His hat is triply plumed, his doublet puffed,
His sword-point holds his cloak far out
    behind,
Like the tail feathers of a strutting cock;
Prouder than all the braves that Gascony
Has borne and e'er will cherish like a mother;
He bears, projecting from his spreading ruff,
A nose—ah, what a nose it is, my lords!
To see one pass with such a nose as that
You could but cry, "Oh, no! 'Tis magnified!"
And then you smile and say, "He'll take it off,"
But this Monsieur de Bergerac never does.
    [*Low laugh from all*]
LE BRET [*shaking his head*].
Let him that would remark on it beware!
RAGUENEAU [*proudly*].
His blade's the half of the dread shears of
    Fate!
FIRST MARQUIS [*shrugging his shoulders*].
He will not come.
RAGUENEAU. He will—I bet a chicken
Cooked à la Ragueneau!
THE MARQUIS [*smiling*]. Done!
    [*Noises of admiration in the hall.* ROXANE
    *has just appeared in her box. She sits
    down in front, and her duenna takes her
    place in the rear.* CHRISTIAN, *busy pay-*

ing the ORANGE-GIRL, *does not see her*]
SECOND MARQUIS [*with little exclamations*].
                        Ah, sirs, she is
Terribly ravishing!
FIRST MARQUIS. A blushing peach
Smiling with strawberry lips!
SECOND MARQUIS.   And so refreshing,
If you come near you catch cold in your heart.
CHRISTIAN [*raises his head, sees* ROXANE,
    and quickly grasping LIGNIÈRE *by the arm*].
'T is she!
LIGNIÈRE [*looking*]. Ah?
CHRISTIAN. Yes, speak quick. I am afraid!
LIGNIÈRE [*swallowing his muscatel in little
    sips*].
Madeleine Robin, called Roxane,—a wit
And learned.
CHRISTIAN. Alas!
LIGNIÈRE.   Free, orphan, and a cousin
Of Cyrano—of whom we spoke.
    [*At this instant a very distinguished-looking
    nobleman, with the blue ribbon around
    his neck, enters the box, and stands
    talking for a moment with* ROXANE]
CHRISTIAN [*starting*].   This man?—
LIGNIÈRE [*beginning to show the effect of
    drink, winking*].
Ha! ha! The Comte de Guiche, in love with
    her,—
Married to Richelieu's niece,—would marry
    Roxane
To a Monsieur de Valvert, old and dull,
A vicomte, and obliging,—you know the way!
She's not consented, but De Guiche has power;
He well can persecute a simple girl.
Besides, I have exposed his evil plan
In a song,— Ho, he should bear me a grudge!
The end was biting,— Listen,—
    [*Gets up, staggering, and holding his glass
    aloft ready to sing*]
CHRISTIAN.   No, good night.
LIGNIÈRE. You go?
CHRISTIAN. To seek De Valvert.
LIGNIÈRE.   Have a care.
'T is he will kill you!
    [*Indicating* ROXANE *with the corner of his
    eye*]
                    Stay, they're looking at you.
CHRISTIAN. 'Tis true.
    [*He remains lost in thought. The group of
    pickpockets at this moment, seeing him
    with head in air and mouth open, draws
    near him*]
LIGNIÈRE. I go; I'm thirsty. I'm expected
In the wine shops!
    [*Goes out in a zigzag course*]
LE BRET [*who has made the tour of the
    hall, returning towards* RAGUENEAU, *with
    reassured voice*]. No Cyrano.
RAGUENEAU [*incredulously*].   And yet—
LE BRET. I still have hopes he has not seen
    the poster.

THE HALL. Begin! Begin!

A MARQUIS [*seeing* DE GUICHE *coming out of* ROXANE'S *box and crossing the parterre surrounded by obsequious gentlemen, the* VICOMTE DE VALVERT *among them*].
De Guiche has quite a court!

ANOTHER. Pf!— Still a Gascon.

THE FIRST.   A Gascon keen and cool.
That kind succeeds! Let us pay our respects.
[*They go towards* DE GUICHE]

SECOND MARQUIS. Beautiful ribbons! What color, Comte de Guiche?
"Kiss-me-my-darling," or "Breast-of-the doe"?

DE GUICHE. The color's called "Sick Spaniard."

FIRST MARQUIS.   Then the color
Tells but the truth, for soon, thanks to your valor,
The Spaniard will fare very ill in Flanders.

DE GUICHE. I go upon the stage. You come?
[*He turns toward the stage, followed by all the* MARQUISES *and gentlemen. He turns back and calls*]
Valvert!

CHRISTIAN [*watching and listening to them, starts when he hears this name*].
The Vicomte! Ah, let me throw in his face—
[*Puts his hand in his pocket and finds the hand of a thief about to rob him. Turns around*]
What?

THE PICKPOCKET. Oh!

CHRISTIAN.   I want a glove!

THE PICKPOCKET [*with a piteous smile*].
You find a hand.
[*Changing his tone, quickly, and aside*]
Let go! I'll tell a secret—

CHRISTIAN [*still holding fast*]. What?

THE PICKPOCKET.   Lignière,
Who just left—

CHRISTIAN [*same action*]. Well?

THE PICKPOCKET. —is near to his last hour.
A song of his cut deep one of the great—
A hundred men—I'm one—to-night are posted—

CHRISTIAN. A hundred? And by whom?

THE PICKPOCKET.   A secret.

CHRISTIAN [*shrugging his shoulders*]. Oh!

THE PICKPOCKET [*with great dignity*].
Professional confidence!

CHRISTIAN.   Where will they be?

THE PICKPOCKET. Hard by the Porte de Nesle, upon his way.
Warn him!

CHRISTIAN [*at last letting go of the man's hand*]. But where to find him?

THE PICKPOCKET.   Go the rounds

Of all the wine shops. Try the Golden Winepress,
The Pine Cone, or the Sign o' the Broken Belt,
The Double Torch, the Funnels,—and in each
Leave him a little note to give him warning.

CHRISTIAN. I run. The scoundrels! 'Gainst one man a hundred!
[*Looking at* ROXANE *with love*]
Leave her!
[*At Valvert, with fury*]
And him! But Lignière I must save.
[*Goes out on a run.* DE GUICHE, *the* VICOMTE, *the* MARQUISES, *and all the gentlemen have disappeared behind the curtain to take their places on the stage benches. The parterre is entirely filled. Not an empty place in the galleries or the boxes*]

THE HALL. Begin!

A TRADESMAN [*whose wig flies away at the end of a string, fished up by a page in the upper gallery*]. My wig!

CRIES OF JOY. He's bald. Cheer for the pages!
Ha! ha! ha!

THE TRADESMAN [*furious and shaking his fist*].   Little rascal!

LAUGHTER AND SHOUTS [*beginning very loud and diminishing*].   Ha! ha! ha!
[*Total silence*]

LE BRET [*astonished*].
This sudden silence?
[*A spectator speaks to him aside*]
Ah?

A SPECTATOR.   They say 'tis certain!

SCATTERING MURMURS. Hush! He appears?
No! Yes! In the latticed box.
The Cardinal! The Cardinal? 'Tis he!

A PAGE. The devil! Now we must behave ourselves.
[*A rapping on the stage. Every one becomes motionless. A pause*]

THE VOICE OF A MARQUIS [*in the silence, behind the curtain*].
That candle should be snuffed!

ANOTHER MARQUIS [*thrusting his head out between the curtains*].   A chair!
[*A chair is passed up over the heads of the crowd, from hand to hand. The* MARQUIS *takes it and disappears, after having thrown several kisses to the boxes*]

A SPECTATOR.   Be still!
[*The three raps are heard. The curtain opens. Tableau. The* MARQUISES *are seated at the sides in careless attitudes. The background represents a pastoral scene, painted in light colors. Four little crystal chandeliers light the stage. The Violins play softly*]

LE BRET [*to* RAGUENEAU, *aside*].
Montfleury will appear?

RAGUENEAU [*also aside*]. Yes, he begins.

LE BRET. Cyrano is not there?

RAGUENEAU. I've lost my bet.

LE BRET. So much the better!

[*The music of a shepherd's pipe is heard, and* MONTIFLEURY *appears, very fat, in a shepherd's costume, his hat decorated with roses and cocked over one ear. He is blowing on a pipe ornamented with ribbons*]

THE PARTERRE [*applauding*]. Bravo, Montfleury!

MONTFLEURY [*after bowing, playing the role of* PHÉDON].

"Oh, happy he, who in sweet solitude
Becomes a willing exile from the Court;
And who, when Zephyrus has gently breathed"—

A VOICE [*in the middle of the parterre*].

Rascal, was't not for a month I warned you off?

[*Amazement. Every one turns around, murmers*]

VARIOUS VOICES. What is't?

[*People stand up in the boxes to look*]

CUIGY. 'Tis he!

LE BRET [*in alarm*]. Cyrano!

THE VOICE. King of gluttons, Off from the stage at once!

ALL THE HALL [*in indignation*]. Oh!

MONTFLEURY. But—

THE VOICE. You balk?

VARIOUS VOICES [*from the parterre and the boxes*].

Enough! Hush! Play, Montfleury,—do not fear!

MONTFLEURY [*in a voice ill at ease*].

"Oh, happy he who in sweet solitude"—

THE VOICE [*more threateningly*].

Well, must I plant a forest on your shoulders, Monarch of scoundrels?

[*A cane at the end of an arm springs out above the heads of the crowd*]

MONTFLEURY [*his voice growing weaker and weaker*]. "Happy he"—

[*The cane is shaken*]

THE VOICE. Go!

THE PARTERRE. Oh!

MONTFLEURY [*choking*].

"Oh, happy he who"—

CYRANO [*rising from the parterre, standing on a chair, his arms crossed, his hat cocked, his moustache bristling, his nose terrible*]. Ah, I shall grow angry!

[*Sensation at his appearance*]

MONTFLEURY [*to the* MARQUISES].

Come to my aid, sirs!

A MARQUIS [*indifferently*]. Well, go on and act.

CYRANO. Lump, if you act, I needs must punish you!

THE MARQUIS. Hold!

CYRANO. Let the Marquises sit quietly;

Or else my cane may trifle with their ribbons!

ALL THE MARQUISES [*standing*].

This is too much! Montfleury—

CYRANO. Let him go;

Or I shall clip his ears, and rip him up!

A VOICE. But—

CYRANO. Let him go!

ANOTHER VOICE. And yet—

CYRANO. 'Tis not yet done?

[*Going through the motion of rolling up his sleeves*]

Good! I approach the stage as 'twere a sideboard,

To carve in slices this Italian sausage.

MONTFLEURY [*collecting all his dignity*].

Your words to me insult the Comic Muse!

CYRANO [*very politely*].

If this Muse, sir, to whom you are as naught,

To meet you had the honor, mark my words,

When she saw all your fat stupidity

She'd use her sandals on you with a will!

THE PARTERRE. Montfleury! Montfleury!

Give Baro's play!

CYRANO [*to those who are shouting around him*].

I beg of you, have pity on my scabbard;

If you keep on it will yield up its blade!

[*The circle grows larger*]

THE CROWD [*drawing back*]. Holloa!

CYRANO [*to* MONTFLEURY]. Get off the stage!

THE CROWD [*drawing nearer and grumbling*]. Oh!

CYRANO [*turning around quickly*]. Who objects?

[*They draw back again*]

A VOICE [*singing in the background*].

Monsieur de Cyrano
Rules us with iron sway;
But, though he says us no,
Still "Clorise" they will play.

ALL THE HALL [*singing*].

—Still "Clorise" they will play.

CYRANO. If once again I hear you sing this song,

I'll slay you all.

A TRADESMAN. You are not Samson yet!

CYRANO. Will you, sir, kindly lend to me your jawbone?

A LADY [*in one of the boxes*].

This is unheard of!

A NOBLEMAN. It is scandalous!

A TRADESMAN. It is vexatious!

A PAGE. And this is amusement!

THE PARTERRE. Ksss— Cyrano!— Montfleury!

CYRANO. Silence, all!

[*Shows and cat-calls from the parterre*]

CYRANO. I order you straightway to hold your tongues;

I send a general challenge to you all!

Come on, young heroes, I will take your names,

Each in his turn; I'll give to each his number!
Come, who's the man who bravely heads the
     list?
You, sir? No! You? No! Who is for a
     duel?
I'll speed him with the honors which are due.
Let all who wish to die now raise their hands.
     [*Silence*]
Shame will not let you see my naked blade?
No name? No hand?— 'Tis well. I shall
     go on.
     [*Turning back towards the stage, where*
     MONTFLEURY *waits in despair*]
Now! I desire to see the theatre healed
Of this foul sore. If not—
[*his hand on his sword*]   —the lancet, then.
MONTFLEURY. I—
     CYRANO [*descends from his chair, sits down
     in the middle of a circle which is formed
     around him, and settles himself as if at
     home*].
I shall clap my hands three times, like this!
You'll vanish at the third.
THE PARTERRE [*amused*]. Ah!
CYRANO [*clapping his hands*]. One!
MONTFLEURY.   I—
A VOICE [*from the boxes*].   Stay!
THE PARTERRE. He'll stay—he will not—
MONTFLEURY.   I think, gentlemen—
CYRANO. Two!
MONTFLEURY. I am sure it would be bet-
ter—
CYRANO.   Three!
     [MONTFLEURY *disappears as if through a
     trap door. A burst of laughter, hisses,
     and hoots*]
THE HALL. Coward! Come back!
CYRANO [*beaming, drops back in his chair and
     crosses his legs*].
Let him come, if he dare!
A TRADESMAN. The spokesman of the troupe!
     [BELLEROSE *advances and bows*]
THE BOXES. Ah!—there's Bellerose!
BELLEROSE [*with elegance*].
Most noble lords—
THE PARTERRE. No! Jodelet!
JODELET [*comes forward, talking through his
     nose*].   Pack of curs!
THE PARTERRE. Oh! Bravo! Good enough!
     Bravo!
JODELET. No bravos!
The fat tragedian whose girth you love
Felt—
THE PARTERRE. He's a coward.
JODELET.   —that he should go out!
THE PARTERRE. Let him come back!
SOME OF THE CROWD.   No!
OTHERS.   Yes!
A YOUNG MAN [*to* CYRANO]. But, sir, in
     short,
What reason have you to hate Montfleury?
CYRANO [*graciously, still seated*].

Young bantling, I have two, and each alone
Is quite enough: First, he's a wretched actor,
Who mouths, and utters with a porter's grunts
The lines which ought to fly away like birds;
The second—is my secret.
     THE OLD TRADESMAN [*behind him*]. But you
     rob us
Of "Clorise," without scruples,—I object—
CYRANO [*turning his chair towards the*
     TRADESMAN, *respectfully*].
Old mule, since Baro's verse is less than nothing
I interrupt without regret!
     THE BLUE-STOCKINGS [*in the boxes*]. Our
     Baro!
My dear! How can he say it? Ah! Good
     heavens!
CYRANO [*turning his chair towards the boxes,
     gallantly*].
Fair creatures, beam and blossom; be senes-
     chals
Of dreams, and with a smile charm us to death.
Inspire poetry—but judge it not!
BELLEROSE. The money that must be re-
     turned?
CYRANO [*turning his chair towards the stage*].
     Bellerose,
You have just spoken the first word of sense!
I make no holes in Thespis' honored cloak.
     [*Gets up and tosses a bag on the stage*]
Catch this purse on the fly and hold your
     tongue!
     THE HALL [*dazed*]. Ah! Oh!
JODELET [*deftly catching the purse and try-
     ing its weight*]. For this price, sir, I give you
     leave
To come each night to stop "Clorise."
THE HALL.   Hoo! hoo!
JODELET. We should be hissed together—
BELLEROSE.   Clear the hall!
     [*They begin to go out, while* CYRANO *looks
     on with a satisfied air. But the crowd
     soon stops to listen to the scene which
     ensues, and the exit ceases. The women
     in the boxes, who were already standing
     with their cloaks on, stop to listen and
     end by sitting down again*]
LE BRET [*to* CYRANO]. 'Tis mad!
A BUSYBODY [*who has approached* CYRANO].
          Montfleury! It is scandalous!
He is protected by the Duc de Candale.
Have you a patron?
CYRANO.   No!
THE BUSYBODY.   You have not?
CYRANO.   No!
THE BUSYBODY. What, no great lord to shield
     you with his name?
CYRANO [*with visible annoyance*].
I said no twice. Must I then make it three?
No; no protector—
[*his hand on his sword*]—but a good protec-
     tress!
     THE BUSYBODY. But you will leave the town?

CYRANO. That all depends.

THE BUSYBODY. The Duc de Candale's arm is long.

CYRANO.   Less long
Than mine is—
[showing his sword]—when I give it this extension.

THE BUSYBODY. You do not dream of trying—

CYRANO. Yes, I do!

THE BUSYBODY. But—

CYRANO.   Right about face, now!

THE BUSYBODY.   But—

CYRANO.   Right about!
Or tell me why you are looking at my nose.

THE BUSYBODY [in confusion]. I—

CYRANO [stepping up to him]. What is strange about it?

THE BUSYBODY [drawing back]. You mistake—

CYRANO. Is it, sir, soft and swinging, like a trunk?

THE BUSYBODY [same action]. I did not—

CYRANO. Or hooked, like an owl's beak?

THE BUSYBODY. I—

CYRANO.   There's a wart upon it?

THE BUSYBODY.   But—

CYRANO.   Or a fly
Walking along it slowly? What's so strange?

THE BUSYBODY. Oh—

CYRANO. Is't a freak of nature?

THE BUSYBODY.   But I knew
Enough to keep my eyes from glancing at it.

CYRANO. And, if you please, why should you not look at it?

THE BUSYBODY. I—

CYRANO.   It disgusts you, then?

THE BUSYBODY.   Sir—

CYRANO.   Seems its color
Unwholesome to you?

THE BUSYBODY.   Sir!

CYRANO.   Does its shape shock you?

THE BUSYBODY. No, not at all!

CYRANO.   Why so disparaging?
Perhaps you think it is a trifle large.

THE BUSYBODY [stammering].
I think it small, quite small, a tiny one!

CYRANO. What? Call it so absurd a name as that?
Call my nose little?

THE BUSYBODY. Heavens!

CYRANO.   My nose is huge!
Poor flat-nose, stupid snub-nose, flat-head, learn
'Tis an appendage I am proud to bear,
Because a large nose is the unfailing sign
Of a good man and kindly, generous,
Courteous, full of courage and of wit;
Such as I am, and such as you're forbidden
Ever to dream yourself, poor good-for-naught!
For the inglorious face above your collar,

Which my hand now will find, is full as bare—
[Boxes his ears]

THE BUSYBODY. Oh!

CYRANO. —Of pride, of wit, of poetry, of art,
Of all adornment, and in fine of nose—
[Turns him about by the shoulders, suiting the action to the word]
—As that my boot shall find below your backbone!

THE BUSYBODY [escaping].
The Guard! Help! Help!

CYRANO.   My warning to the idlers
Who find the middle of my face amusing;—
And if the joker's noble, 'tis my custom
To give to him before I let him go
Steel and not leather, in front, and higher up.

DE GUICHE [who has come down from the stage, with the MARQUISES].
He becomes tiresome!

THE VICOMTE DE VALVERT [shrugging his shoulders].   He blows his trumpet!

DE GUICHE. Will no one answer him?

THE VICOMTE.   No one? But wait!
I shall fling at him now some of my wit!
[Advances towards CYRANO, who is watching him, and takes his place in front of him with a silly air]
You—your nose is—nose is—very large.

CYRANO [gravely]. Very!

THE VICOMTE [smiling]. Ha!

CYRANO [imperturbable]. That is all?

THE VICOMTE.   But—

CYRANO.   No, young man.
That is somewhat too brief. You might say—
Lord!—
Many and many a thing, changing your tone,
As for example these;—Aggressively:
"Sir, had I such a nose I'd cut it off!"
Friendly: "But it must dip into your cup.
You should have made a goblet tall to drink from."
Descriptive: " 'Tis a crag—a peak—a cape!
I said a cape?—'tis a peninsula."
Inquisitive: "To what use do you put
This oblong sheath; is it a writing-case
Or scissors-box?" Or, in a gracious tone:
"Are you so fond of birds, that like a father
You spend your time and thought to offer them
This roosting-place to rest their little feet?"
Quarrelsome: "Well, sir, when you smoke your pipe
Can the smoke issue from your nose, without
Some neighbor crying, 'the chimney is a-fire'?"
Warning: "Be careful, lest this weight drag down
Your head, and stretch you prostrate on the ground."
Tenderly: "Have a small umbrella made,
For fear its color fade out in the sun."
Pedantic: "Sir, only the animal
Called by the poet Aristophanes

'Hippocampelephantocámelos'
Should carry so much flesh and bone upon
    him!"
Cavalier: "Friend, is this peg in the fashion?
To hang one's hat on, it must be convenient."
Emphatic: "Magisterial nose, no wind
Could give thee all a cold, except the mistral."
Dramatic: " 'Tis the Red Sea when it bleeds!"
Admiring: "What a sign for a perfumer!"
Poetic: "Is't a conch; are you a Triton?"
Naïve: "When does one visit this great sight?"
Respectful: "Let me, sir, pay my respects.
This might be called fronting upon the street."
Countrified: "That's a nose that is a nose!
A giant turnip or a baby melon!"
Or military: "Guard against cavalry!"
Practical: "Will you put it in a raffle?
It surely, sir, would be the winning number!"
Or parodying Pyramus, with a sob:
"There is the nose that ruins the symmetry
Of its master's features; the traitor blushes
    for it."
My friend, that is about what you'd have said
If you had had some learning or some wit;
But wit, oh! most forlorn of human creatures,
You never had a bit of; as for letters
You only have the four that spell out "Fool"!
Moreover, had you owned the imagination
Needed to give you power, before this hall,
To offer me these mad jests—all of them—
You would not even have pronounced the
    quarter
O' the half of one's beginning, for I myself
Offer them to myself with dash enough,
But suffer no one else to say them to me.
  DE GUICHE [trying to lead away the dazed
    VICOMTE]. Vicomte, leave off!
  THE VICOMTE [choking]. These great and
    lofty airs!
A rustic, who—who—even wears no gloves,
And goes about without a single ribbon.
  CYRANO. It is my character that I adorn.
I do not deck me like a popinjay;
But though less foppish, I am better dressed:
I would not sally forth, through carelessness,
With an insult ill wiped out, or with my con-
    science
Sallow with sleep still lingering in its eyes,
Honor in rags, or scruples dressed in mourn-
    ing.
But I go out with all upon me shining,
With liberty and freedom for my plume,
Not a mere upright figure;—'tis my soul
That I thus hold erect as if with stays,
And decked with daring deeds instead of
    ribbons,
Twirling my wit as it were my moustache,
The while I pass among the crowd, I make
Bold truths ring out like spurs.
  THE VICOMTE.   But, sir—
  CYRANO.   I have
No gloves?—A pity!—I had just one left,

One of a worn-out pair!—which troubled
    me!
I left it recently in some one's face.
  THE VICOMTE. Knave, rascal, booby, flat-
    foot, scum o' the earth!
  CYRANO [taking off his hat and bowing as if
    the VICOMTE had just introduced himself].
Ah? And I—Cyrano-Savinien-Hercule de Ber-
    gerac.
  [Laughter]
  THE VICOMTE [in a temper]. Buffoon!
  CYRANO [giving a cry like one who feels a
    sudden pain]. Oh!
  THE VICOMTE [who was going off, turning
    about].   What's he saying now?
  CYRANO [with grimaces of pain].   I must
Shake it, because it falls asleep—the fault
Of leaving it long idle—
  THE VICOMTE.   What's the matter?
  CYRANO. My sword-blade tingles!
  THE VICOMTE [drawing his own sword].
                        Very well, come on!
  CYRANO. I shall give you a charming little
    stroke.
  THE VICOMTE [with disdain]. Poet!—
  CYRANO.   A poet, yes! and such a one,
That, while I fence with you, I'll improvise
A ballade for you.
  THE VICOMTE.   A ballade?
  CYRANO.   I suppose
You do not e'en imagine what that is?
  THE VICOMTE. But—
  CYRANO [as if reciting a lesson].
The ballade, then, is made up of three stanzas,
Of eight lines—
  THE VICOMTE [shuffling his feet]. Oh!
  CYRANO [continuing]. And a refrain of four.
  THE VICOMTE. You—
  CYRANO. I'll make one and fight you, both at
    once.
And at the last verse touch you, sir.
  THE VICOMTE.   No!
  CYRANO.   No?
The ballade of Monsieur de Bergerac's duel
At the Hôtel de Bourgogne with a booby.
  THE VICOMTE. What is that, if you please?
  CYRANO.   That is the title.
  THE HALL [excited to the highest pitch].
In place!— No noise!— In line!— This is
    amusing.
  [Tableau. A circle of curious onlookers in
    the parterre, the MARQUISES and the
    OFFICERS mixed in with the TRADESMEN
    and common people. The PAGES climb on
    people's shoulders to see better. All the
    women stand up in the boxes. To the
    right DE GUICHE and his gentlemen. To
    the left LE BRET, RAGUENEAU, CUIGY,
    etc.]
  CYRANO [closing his eyes for a moment].
Wait, let me choose my rhymes—I have them
    now:

My hat I toss lightly away;
From my shoulders I slowly let fall
The cloak which conceals my array,
And my sword from my scabbard I call,
Like Céladon, graceful and tall,
Like Scaramouche, quick hand and brain,—
And I warn you, my friend, once for all,
I shall thrust when I end the refrain.

[*The swords meet*]

You were rash thus to join in the fray;
Like a fowl I shall carve you up small,
Your ribs, 'neath your doublet so gay,
Your breast, where the blue ribbons fall,
Ding dong! ring your bright trappings all;
My point flits like a fly on the pane,
As I clearly announce to the hall
I shall thrust when I end the refrain.

I need one more rhyme for "array"—
You give ground, you turn white as the wall,—
And so lend me the word "runaway."
There! you have let your point fall
As I parry your best lunge of all;
I begin a new line, the end's plain,
Your skewer hold tight, lest it fall.
I shall thrust when I end the refrain.

[*Announces solemnly*]

REFRAIN.

Prince, on the Lord you must call!
I gain ground, I advance once again,
I feint, I lunge. [*Lunging*] There! that is all!

[*The* VICOMTE *staggers.* CYRANO *salutes*]
For I thrust as I end the refrain.
[*Shouts. Applause in the boxes. Flowers
and handkerchiefs are thrown. The
OFFICERS surround CYRANO and congrat-
ulate him.* RAGUENEAU *dances with en-
thusiasm.* LE BRET *is dizzy with joy.
The* VICOMTE's *friends hold him up and
lead him away*]
THE CROWD [*in one long cry*]. Ah!
A LIGHT GUARDSMAN.   Superb!
A WOMAN.   A pretty stroke!
RAGUENEAU.   Magnificent!
A MARQUIS. Something quite new!
LE BRET.   Mad folly!
VOICES [*in the confusion about* CYRANO].
                        Compliments,
Congratulations, bravo!
VOICE OF A WOMAN.   He's a hero!
A MUSKETEER [*advancing quickly toward*
CYRANO *with outstretched hands*].
Will you allow me, sir?—'Twas right well
done,
And these are things I think I understand;
Besides, I have expressed my joy by stamping!
[*Withdraws*]

CYRANO [*to* CUIGY]. Who is this gentleman?
CUIGY.   He's D'Artagnan!
LE BRET [*to* CYRANO, *taking him by the
arm*].
Come, let us talk—
CYRANO.   Let the crowd go out first.
[*To* BELLEROSE] May I wait?
BELLEROSE [*respectfully*]. Certainly!
[*Shouts are heard without*]
JODELET [*after looking out*]. They hiss
Montfleury!
BELLEROSE [*solemnly*]. "Sic transit"—
[*Changing his tone, to the* DOORKEEPER
and the candle-snuffer] Sweep. Close up.
But leave the lights.
We shall return when we have had our sup-
per,
For a rehearsal of to-morrow's farce.
[*JODELET and* BELLEROSE *go out, after low
bows to* CYRANO]
THE DOORKEEPER [*to* CYRANO]. You do not
dine?
CYRANO. I?—No!
LE BRET [*to* CYRANO]. Because?
CYRANO [*proudly*].   Because—
[*Changing his tone when he sees that the*
DOORKEEPER *has gone*]
I have no money!
LE BRET [*making the gesture of throwing a
bag*].   What! the bag of crowns?
CYRANO. Inheritance, in one day thou art
spent!
LE BRET. How will you live this month, then?
CYRANO [*tightening his belt*].
Naught is left.
LE BRET. What folly 'twas to throw away
the bag!
CYRANO.   But what a gesture!
THE ORANGE-GIRL [*coughing behind her little
counter*]. Hum! hum!
[*CYRANO and* LE BRET *turn about. She
advances timidly*]
                        To see you fasting—
It breaks my heart.
[*Showing the sideboard*] I have all that is
needed.
[*With enthusiasm*] Take what you wish!
CYRANO [*taking off his hat*]. My Gascon
pride forbids me,
My child, to take one dainty from your hands,
And yet I fear that this may cause you pain,
And so I shall accept—
[*goes to the sideboard and chooses*]—oh, noth-
ing much!
A grape—
[*She starts to give him the bunch; he picks one
grape*] But one! This glass of water!
[*She starts to pour in some wine; he stops her*]
                        Clear!
And half a macaroon!
[*He returns the other half*]
LE BRET.   But this is foolish!

THE ORANGE-GIRL. Oh, something more!

CYRANO. Why, yes, your hand to kiss!

[*He kisses the hand which she holds out,
as he would the hand of a princess*]

THE ORANGE-GIRL. I thank you, sir.

[*She courtesies*] Good night!

[*She goes out*]

CYRANO [*to* LE BRET]. Talk, I will listen.

[*He takes his place before the sideboard,
arranging before him the macaroon*]

Dinner!

[*the glass of water,*] Drink!

[*the grape*] Sweets!

[*He sits down*] There, I sit down at table!

Ah, friend, I was unconscionably hungry!

[*Eating*] You said?

LE BRET. That these fools, with their warlike airs,

Will spoil your wit if you consort with them;

Consult men of good sense, and so find out

The effect of your mad sally.

CYRANO [*finishing his macaroon*]. It was
huge.

LE BRET. The Cardinal—

CYRANO [*beaming*]. So the Cardinal was
there?

LE BRET.—Must have esteemed it—

CYRANO. Quite original!

LE BRET. Yet—

CYRANO. He's an author. It cannot displease
him

If some one come to spoil a rival's work.

LE BRET. You'll have too many enemies
against you!

CYRANO [*attacking the grape*].

About how many have I made to-night?

LE BRET. Without the women, forty-eight.

CYRANO. Come, count!

LE BRET. De Guiche, Montfleury, Valvert,
and the Tradesman;

The Academy and Baro—

CYRANO. That's enough.

You greatly please me!

LE BRET. But this mode of life

Where will it lead you? And what is your plan?

CYRANO. I wandered in a maze; too many
courses,

And too bewildering, there were to choose.

I've chosen—

LE BRET. What?

CYRANO. Oh, far the simplest one:

I have resolved in all things to excel!

LE BRET [*shrugging his shoulders*].

So be it. But the reason of your hatred

For Montfleury, the real one!

CYRANO [*getting up*]. This Silenus,

Who cannot reach the centre of his paunch,

Thinks himself still a charmer of the women;

And while he plays his part and mouths his
words

Casts glances at them with his fishy eyes!

Him have I hated since one night he let

His gaze rest on her— Oh, I seemed to see

Upon a flower fair a great slug crawling.

LE BRET [*amazed*].

What? What? And can it be—

CYRANO [*with a bitter smile*]. That I should
love?—

[*Changing his tone and seriously*]

I love.

LE BRET. And may I know? You never told
me

CYRANO. Whom I love? Think, it is forbidden me

To dream of love from e'en the most ill-
favored—

This nose, which goes before me half a mile!—

And so whom do I love?—the answer's plain!

I love—it is absurd—the very fairest!

LE BRET. The fairest?

CYRANO. Yes. In short, in the whole world;

The most consummate charms,—

[*with great dejection*] —the fairest hair!

LE BRET. Heavens, who is this woman?

CYRANO. A mortal danger,

Without intention; charming, without thought;

A trap by nature set, a damask rose

In which, close hid in ambush, Love is lurking!

He who has known her smile has known perfection.

Her grace is all unconscious; she sums up

The whole of heaven in a single movement;

And, Venus, thou couldst never mount thy
shell,

Nor thou, Diana, walk the leafy forests,

As she mounts in her chair and walks these
streets!

LE BRET. I understand. 'Tis clear!

CYRANO. 'Tis quite transparent!

LE BRET. Your cousin Magdeleine Robin?

CYRANO. Yes, Roxane.

LE BRET. Well, that is for the best. You love
her? Tell her!

You won great glory in her eyes to-day!

CYRANO. Look at me, friend, and tell me
what fond hopes

This great protuberance could ever leave me?

Oh! I have no illusions!—By the gods,

Sometimes I soften, on an evening clear;

I seek some green spot, when the hour is sweet,

I scent the Spring with my poor monstrous
nose.

'Neath the moon's silver beams my gaze will
follow

Some woman passing on her lover's arm,

And then I think I too should like to walk,

With sweetheart on my arm, in the fair moonlight.

My fancy rises, I forget,—and then

I see my profile's shadow on the wall!

LE BRET [*with emotion*]. My friend!—

CYRANO. My friend, I have my gloomy hours,

Knowing myself so ugly, and sometimes,

When quite alone—
  LE BRET [*quickly taking his hand*]. You
    weep?
  CYRANO. Ah, never that!
No, that would be too ugly, if along
This monstrous nose a tear should trickle down!
I'll not permit, so long as I am master,
That such gross ugliness contaminate
The grace divine of tears! For, mark you well,
There's nothing more sublime on earth than
    tears;
I would not have one put to ridicule
By me, the while my plight should raise a
    laugh.
  LE BRET. Be not so mad! For love is naught
    but luck!
  CYRANO [*shaking his head*].
No, I love Cleopatra. Am I Cæsar?
I worship Berenice. Am I Titus?
  LE BRET. But your wit! Your courage!—
    This poor child,
Who offered you just now this modest meal,—
Her eyes, you plainly saw, misliked you not!
  CYRANO [*struck by the idea*]. That is the
    truth!
  LE BRET. Well, then; Roxane herself
Grew pale watching your duel.
  CYRANO.   She grew pale?
  LE BRET. Her heart and mind already are
    much moved.
Dare, tell her, so that—
  CYRANO.   She'll laugh in my face!
No! 'Tis the one thing in the world I fear.
  THE DOORKEEPER [*introducing some one to
    CYRANO*]. Sir, you are asked for.
  CYRANO [*seeing the* DUENNA]. Heavens! her
    duenna!

  THE DUENNA [*with a profound bow*].
Some one would be informed by her brave
    cousin
Where one can see him secretly.
  CYRANO [*in amazement*].   See me?
  THE DUENNA [*with a courtesy*].
See you. Some one has things to tell you.
  CYRANO.   Things?
  THE DUENNA [*with another courtesy*]. Yes.
  CYRANO [*staggering*].   Heavens!
  THE DUENNA. To-morrow, at the blush of
    dawn,
Some one will go to hear mass at Saint Rock.
  CYRANO [*leaning on* LE BRET]. Heavens!
  THE DUENNA. And after, where can some
    one stop
For a short talk?
  CYRANO [*delighted*]. Where—I—but—Lord—
  THE DUENNA. Speak quick.
  CYRANO. I'm thinking—
  THE DUENNA. Where?
  CYRANO. Ragueneau's, the pastry-cook's.
  THE DUENNA. Where?
  CYRANO. On the Rue— Ah, God! St. Honoré.

  THE DUENNA [*retiring*]. She'll go, be there,
at seven o'clock.
  CYRANO.   I shall!
    [*Enter* ACTORS *and* ACTRESSES *who begin
      rehearsing*]
  CYRANO [*falling into* LE BRET'S *arms*].
From her—for me—a meeting.
  LE BRET.   You are sad
No more?
  CYRANO. At least, she knows that I exist.
  LE BRET. And now you will be calm?
  CYRANO [*beside himself*]. And now—and
    now—
I shall be full of frenzy and of thunders!
I want a regiment to put to rout!
I've ten hearts; twenty arms; 'tis not enough
To hew down dwarfs,—
  [*Shouts at the top of his voice*]—giants are
    what I want!
    [*For the past moment, shadows of* ACTORS
      and ACTRESSES *have been moving about
      on the stage in the background and
      whispering; the rehearsal begins. The
      Violins have resumed their places*]
  A VOICE [*from the stage*].
Eh! down there! quiet! this is a rehearsal!
  CYRANO [*smiling*]. We go!
    [*He starts to withdraw; by the great door
      in the background enter* CUIGY, BRIS-
      SAILLE, *and several* OFFICERS, *who are
      holding up* LIGNIÈRE, *now very drunk*]
  CUIGY.   Cyrano!
  CYRANO.   What?
  CUIGY.   A heavy load
We bring you.
  CYRANO [*recognizing him*]. Lignière—what
    has happened to you?
  CUIGY. He's looking for you!
  BRISSAILLE.   He cannot go home!
  CYRANO. Why?
  LIGNIÈRE [*with a thick voice, showing him
    a crumpled note*].
This letter warns me—a hundred men against
    me—
Because—my song—great danger threatens
    me—
The Porte de Nesle—I pass it on my way—
Let me go with you—sleep under your roof!
  CYRANO. You said a hundred. You shall
    sleep at home!
  LIGNIÈRE [*alarmed*]. But—
  CYRANO [*with a terrible voice, showing him
    the lighted lantern, which the* DOORKEEPER
    *swings, while he listens with curiosity to
    the conversation*]. Take this lantern!—
    [LIGNIÈRE *hurriedly seizes the lantern*]
                          March! I swear to you
That it is I shall shelter you to-night!—
  [*To the* OFFICERS] Follow, but hold your dis-
    tance,—be my seconds!
  CUIGY. A hundred men—
  CYRANO.   To-night I want no less!

[The ACTORS *and* ACTRESSES *who have come down from the stage approach in their various costumes]*

LE BRET. But why should you protect—

CYRANO. Hear Le Bret scold!

LE BRET.—This common drunkard?

CYRANO *[tapping* LIGNIÈRE *on the shoulder].*

Just because this drunkard,
This tun of muscatel, this cask of brandy,
One day performed a wholly charming deed;
For as he left the mass, seeing his sweetheart,
After the custom, take the holy water,—
Though he flees water,—hastened to the font,
Leaned over it, and straightway drank it all!

AN ACTRESS *[in soubrette costume].*

Now that was fine!

CYRANO. And was it not, my dear?

THE ACTRESS *[to the others].*

But why are there a hundred 'gainst one poet?

CYRANO. Forward!—

[To the OFFICERS*]* And you, sirs, when you
see me charge,
Give me no help, whatever be the danger.

ANOTHER ACTRESS *[jumping down from the stage].*

Oh, I am coming!—

CYRANO. Come—

ANOTHER *[also jumping down, to an old* ACTOR*].* And you, Cassandra?

CYRANO. Come all, Leander, Isabelle, the Doctor,—

All! You shall join, oh, pleasant madcap throng,
Italian farce unto this Spanish drama,
And o'er its thunder jingling antic noise
Hang bells around it, like a tambourine!

ALL THE WOMEN *[jumping with joy].*

Bravo! A cape! A cloak, quick!

JODELET. Come along!

CYRANO *[to the* VIOLINS*].*

Now, Violins, you'll play a tune for us!

[The VIOLINS *join the parade which is forming. Lighted candles are taken from the footlights and distributed. It becomes a torchlight procession]*

Bravo! Women in costume, officers,
And twenty paces to the front—

[Takes his place as he speaks] —myself
Alone, beneath the plume by glory placed,
Full proud as Scipio three times Nasica!
'Tis understood? No one to lend a hand!
Ready? One, two, three! Porter, clear the way!

[The DOORKEEPER *opens both leaves of the door. A picturesque moonlit corner of old Paris appears]*

Ah! Paris seems almost dissolved in haze:
The moonlight falls over the slanting roofs;
A charming frame makes ready for the scene.
There, 'neath its wreathing mists, the river
Seine,
Like a mysterious and magic mirror,
Shimmers,—and you shall see what you shall
see.

ALL. On to the Porte de Nesle!

CYRANO *[standing on the threshold].* The
Porte de Nesle!

[Turning, before going out, to the Soubrette]

Did you not ask me why, mademoiselle,
Against one poet five-score men are set?

[Draws his sword and concludes placidly]

Because 'tis known he is a friend of mine.

*[He goes out. The procession—*LIGNIÈRE *zigzagging at the head, then the* ACTRESSES, *taking the* OFFICERS' *arms, then the* ACTORS *frolicking—starts on its midnight march to the music of the Violins, and the flaming light of the candles,—all shouting, "On to the Porte de Nesle"]*

CURTAIN

SECOND ACT

THE POET'S COOK-SHOP

The shop of RAGUENEAU, *baker and pastry-cook, a large establishment at the corner of the Rue Saint-Honoré and the Rue de l'Arbre Sec, a general view of which, gray in the first light of dawn, is seen in the background through the glass panels of the door. To the left, first entrance, there is a counter, and over it a wrought-iron canopy, to which are hung white peacocks, ducks, and geese. In great china vases there are tall bouquets of common flowers, principally yellow sun-flowers. On the same side, second entrance, there is a huge fireplace, in front of which, between large andirons, each of which supports a little saucepan, the roasts are dripping into pans. To the right, at the first entrance, a door. At the second entrance a staircase leading to a small room in a sort of loft, the interior of the room being visible through open blinds; a table is set there, lit by a little Flemish candlestick; it is a kind of private dining-room. A wooden gallery, extending from the head of the stairs, seems to lead to other similar small rooms. In the middle of the cook-shop an iron ring, which may be lowered by means of a cord, and upon which heads of large game are hanging, makes a sort of chandelier. The ovens, in the shadow under the staircase, are glowing. The coppers glisten. The spits are turning. There are great piles of fancy dishes all around. Hams hang from their hooks. It is the morning baking. There is a bustle of frightened scullions, tall cooks, and little knife-boys. Their caps bristle with chicken feathers or guinea fowls' wings. Rows of cream puffs and collections of fancy cakes are brought in on iron trays and wicker stands. Some of the tables are covered with cakes and other dishes. Others are surrounded with chairs, waiting for customers. A smaller table, in one corner, is hidden under a mass of papers. When the curtain rises* RAGUENEAU *is seated there, writing with an inspired air, and counting on his fingers.*

FIRST PASTRY-COOK [*with a plate*].
Puff paste!

SECOND PASTRY-COOK [*with a dish*]. And candied fruits!

THIRD PASTRY-COOK [*with a roast decorated with feathers*]. A peacock!

FOURTH PASTRY-COOK [*with a plate of cakes*]. Sweetmeats!

FIFTH PASTRY-COOK [*with a sort of pan*].
Fillet of beef with sauce!

RAGUENEAU [*stopping his writing and raising his head*]. The silver light
Of dawn already glistens on the coppers!
Smother the god that sings in thee, Ragueneau!
The lute's hour comes—this is the hour of ovens!
[*Gets up,—to a cook*]
Lengthen this sauce for me, it is too short.

THE COOK. How much?

RAGUENEAU. Three feet.
[*Passes on*]

FIRST PASTRY-COOK. The patty!

SECOND PASTRY-COOK. And the tart!

RAGUENEAU [*in front of the fireplace*].
Depart, my muse, for fear thy charming eyes
Should be made red by all this faggot smoke!
[*To a* PASTRY-COOK, *showing him some loaves of bread*]
You've split these loaves quite wrong, for in the middle
Goes the cæsura—between the hemistiches!
[*To another, showing him an unfinished pasty*]
You need a roof upon this pie-crust palace—
[*To a young apprentice seated on the ground, who is putting fowls on a spit*]
And you upon this endless spit should put
The modest chicken, and the turkey proud,
Alternately, my son, as old Malherbe
Arranged the long lines with the shorter ones;
And turn the roasts before the fire in strophes.

ANOTHER APPRENTICE [*coming forward with a platter covered with a napkin*].
Master, with thought of you I have prepared
This, which I hope will please you.
[*Uncovers the platter, and shows a great lyre of pastry*]

RAGUENEAU [*dazzled*]. Ah! A lyre!

THE APPRENTICE. 'Tis made of puff paste.

RAGUENEAU [*with emotion*]. And with candied fruits!

THE APPRENTICE. And look! the strings are made all of spun sugar.

RAGUENEAU [*giving him money*].
Go, drink my health!
[*Seeing* LISE *coming in*] Hush, there's my wife! Make off!

And hide this money!
[*To* LISE, *with an air of annoyance, showing her the lyre*] Is't not fine?

LISE. Absurd!
[*Puts a pile of paper bags on the counter*]

RAGUENEAU. Bags? Good—I thank you.
[*Looks at them*] Heavens! My honored books—
The verses of my friends! Torn! Cut to pieces!
To make up bags wherein to carry biscuits—
Ah! Orpheus and the Mænads you repeat!

LISE [*drily*]. And have I not the right to use
The only thing they ever leave for payment—
Your wretched scribblers of uneven lines?

RAGUENEAU. Ant!—do not thus insult divine grasshoppers.

LISE. My dear, before these folk became your friends
You did not call me Mænad—nor yet ant!

RAGUENEAU. To do such things to poetry!

LISE. Naught else!

RAGUENEAU. What would you then have done had it been prose?
[*Two* CHILDREN *have just come into the shop*]

RAGUENEAU. What do you wish, my dears?

FIRST CHILD. Three patties, please.

RAGUENEAU [*waiting on them*].
There, nicely done,—and hot.

SECOND CHILD. And, if you please,
Wrap them up for us.

RAGUENEAU [*aside*]. Ah! One of my bags!
[*To the* CHILDREN] Wrap them up for you?
Certainly, my dears.
[*Takes a bag, and just as he is putting the patties into it, reads:*]
"Ulysses, when he left Penelope"—
Not that one!
[*Puts it aside and takes another. Just as he is putting the patties in, reads:*]
"Bright-haired Phœbus"— Nor yet that!
[*Same action*]

LISE [*with impatience*].
Well? What is keeping you?

RAGUENEAU. There! There you are!
[*Takes a third, and resigns himself to his fate*]
The sonnet unto Phyllis! It is hard!

LISE. I'm glad he has decided.
[*Shrugging her shoulders*] Nicodemus!
[*Stands on a chair and sets about arranging dishes on a high sideboard*]

RAGUENEAU [*taking advantage of the fact that she has turned her back, calls back the* CHILDREN, *already at the door*].
Pst, children! Give me back the lines to Phyllis
And I will give six patties for your three.
[*The* CHILDREN *give the bag back to him, snatch the cakes, and run off.* RAGUENEAU, *smoothing out the paper, begins to declaim as he reads*]

"Phyllis!" On this sweet name a spot of butter—
"Phyllis!"
[CYRANO *enters hurriedly*]
CYRANO. What time is it?
RAGUENEAU [*bowing to him ceremoniously*].
Six.
CYRANO [*with emotion*]. In an hour!
[*Walks to and fro in the shop*]
RAGUENEAU [*following him*].
Bravo! I saw—
CYRANO. Well, what?
RAGUENEAU. Your fight!
CYRANO. Which one?
RAGUENEAU. At the Hôtel de Bourgogne!
CYRANO [*disdainfully*]. Oh, the duel!
RAGUENEAU [*admiringly*].
The duel fought in verse!
LISE. He's full of it!
CYRANO. I'm glad to hear it.
RAGUENEAU [*fencing with a spit he has caught up*].
"I shall thrust when I end the refrain!"
Ah, how fine it was!
"I shall thrust when I end the refrain."
[*With growing enthusiasm*]
"I shall thrust when I end"—
CYRANO. What time is it?
RAGUENEAU [*stopping his fencing while he looks at the clock*].
Five minutes after!—*"the refrain."*
[*Straightens up*] A ballade!
To think of writing one!
LISE [*to* CYRANO *who has absent-mindedly shaken her hand as he passed her desk*].
You've hurt your hand?
CYRANO. Nothing. A little cut.
RAGUENEAU. You were in danger?
CYRANO. No, none at all.
LISE [*shaking her finger at him*]. I think that you are lying!
CYRANO. And think you that would set my nose a-tremble?
'Twould have to be a most tremendous lie!
[*Changing his tone*]
I wait for some one here. If not in vain,
You will leave us alone.
RAGUENEAU. But that I cannot.
My poets soon will come—
LISE [*ironically*]. For their first meal.
CYRANO. You'll get them hence when I shall give the signal.
The time?
RAGUENEAU. Ten minutes past.
CYRANO [*nervously sitting down at* RAGUE-NEAU'S *table, and taking a sheet of paper*].
A pen?
RAGUENEAU [*offering him the one at his ear*].
A swan's quill!
A MUSKETEER [*with tremendous moustache, and speaking in stentorian tones, enters*].
Greeting!

[LISE *goes quickly to meet him*]
CYRANO [*turning*]. Who's that?
RAGUENEAU. A great friend of my wife's.
A terrible warrior,—by what he says!
CYRANO [*taking the pen again and motioning to* RAGUENEAU *to withdraw*].
Hush! Write,—seal—
[*aside*] —give it to her—and escape.
[*Throwing away the pen*]
Coward! May I be hanged if I have courage
To speak to her a single word,—
[*To* RAGUENEAU] The time?
RAGUENEAU. A quarter past.
CYRANO [*tapping his chest*]. Of those that I have here!
While if I write—
[*Takes up the pen*] Oh! well, then! let us write it!
The letter I have thought out to myself
A hundred times, so that it now is ready;
And if I put my soul beside the paper
I shall need only to recopy it.
[*Writes. Behind the glass doors, thin and hesitating figures are seen moving. The* POETS, *dressed in black, with stockings slipping down and covered with mud*]
LISE [*entering, to* RAGUENEAU].
Here are your scarecrows!
FIRST POET [*entering, to* RAGUENEAU]. Colleague!
SECOND POET [*same action, shaking his hand*].
Honored colleague!
THIRD POET. Eagle of pastry-cooks!
[*sniffs*] It smells good here.
FOURTH POET. Phœbus of bakers!
FIFTH POET. Apollo of the oven!
RAGUENEAU [*surrounded, embraced, shaken by the hand*].
How speedily one feels at ease with them!
FIRST POET. The crowd, collected at the Porte de Nesle,
Delayed us.
SECOND POET. Eight cut-purses, all a-bleeding
With gaping sword-wounds, lay about the pavement!
CYRANO [*lifting his head a moment*].
Eight? It was seven, I thought.
[*Returns to his letter*]
RAGUENEAU [*to* CYRANO]. Do you then know
The hero of the battle?
CYRANO [*carelessly*]. I? No!
LISE [*to the* MUSKETEER]. And you?
THE MUSKETEER [*twisting his moustache*].
Perhaps!
CYRANO [*still writing, is heard from time to time to murmur a word aside*]. *I love you!*
FIRST POET. They say one man alone
Put a whole band to rout!
SECOND POET. A curious sight!

The ground was strewn with cudgels and with pikes!

CYRANO [*writing*]. Your eyes—

THIRD POET. To the Goldsmith's Quay the hats were strewn!

FIRST POET. He must have been a savage one!

CYRANO [*same action*]. *Your lips—*

FIRST POET. A giant terrible, who wrought these deeds!

CYRANO [*same action*]. *And yet I faint with fear when I perceive you.*

SECOND POET [*snatching a cake*]. What verses have you written, Ragueneau, lately?

CYRANO [*same action*]. *Who love you—*

[*Stops just as he is about to sign the letter, and gets up, putting it in his doublet*]

Signing's needless, I shall give it To her myself.

RAGUENEAU [*to the* SECOND POET]. A recipe in verse.

THIRD POET [*taking his place near a platter of puffs*]. Give us the poem!

FOURTH POET [*looking at a cake he has taken*]. This cake has put on Its cap wrong-side before.

[*Bites off the top*]

FIRST POET. This spice cake follows The starveling rhymester, with its almond eyes, And candy eyebrows!

[*Takes the piece of spice-cake*]

SECOND POET. We are listening.

THIRD POET [*squeezing a cream-puff softly between his fingers*]. This cream puff's running over. It is laughing.

SECOND POET [*biting at the great lyre of pastry itself*]. For the first time the Lyre gives me food!

RAGUENEAU [*after getting ready to recite, coughing, settling his cap, and striking an attitude*]. A recipe in verse—

SECOND POET [*to the first, nudging him*]. Breakfast?

FIRST POET [*to the* SECOND]. No, dinner!

RAGUENEAU. *How to make almond cream tarts:*

Beat some eggs till they be light,
And frothy quite;
Then, when light enough they seem,
From a lemon squeeze the juice
For your use,
Then mix in sweet almond cream.

Next with puff-paste, light as air,
With great care
Line your moulds up to the top;
With skilled fingers shape the paste
To your taste,
Pour the cream in drop by drop.

When filled with this frothy mass,
Let them pass
To the oven, till they seem
Brown enough, and you will see
Merrily
Emerge the tarts of almond cream.

THE POETS [*their mouths full*].
Charming! Delicious!

A POET [*choking*]. Humph!

[*They retire into the background, still eating*]

CYRANO [*who has watched them, goes toward* RAGUENEAU]. Soothed by your voice, Do you not see the way they stuff themselves?

RAGUENEAU [*smiling, in a lower voice*]. I see—but do not look, lest it should pain them; And, so to speak, my verses give to me A double pleasure, since I satisfy An amiable weakness of my own, The while I feed those who might hungry go!

CYRANO [*tapping him on the shoulder*]. I like you.

[RAGUENEAU *rejoins his friends,* CYRANO *follows him with his eyes, and then speaking rather sharply*]

Lise, come here!

[LISE *in tender discourse with the* MUSKETEER, *gives a start, and comes towards* CYRANO]

This warrior bold Besieges you?

LISE [*offended*]. My eyes, with haughty glance, Know how to conquer any lover rash Who would assail my virtue.

CYRANO. Eugh! your eyes, For conquerors, seem of a yielding spirit.

LISE [*choking*]. But—

CYRANO [*sharply*]. Ragueneau's my friend, Dame Lise, and so I will not see him made a laughing-stock.

LISE. But—

CYRANO [*raising his voice so that the* MUSKETEER *may hear him*]. To the wise a word—

[*Bows to the* MUSKETEER, *and takes a post of observation at the door in the background, after having looked at the clock*]

LISE [*to the* MUSKETEER, *who has merely returned* CYRANO'S *bow*]. I wonder at you! Answer him—on his nose—

THE MUSKETEER. On his nose, no!

[*Withdraws quickly.* LISE *follows him*]

CYRANO [*from the door in the background, motioning to* RAGUENEAU *to get the poets out of the way*]. Pst!—

RAGUENEAU [*showing the* POETS *the door on the right*]. We shall find it better—

CYRANO [*growing impatient*]. Pst!—

RAGUENEAU [*pulling them along*]. To read Poetry—

FIRST POET [*in despair, with his mouth full*]. But the cakes!

SECOND POET.   Take them along.

[*They all follow* RAGUENEAU *out in a procession, after a clean sweep of all the cakes*]

CYRANO. I'll use the letter if I think there be The smallest hope—

[ROXANE *appears behind the glass door, masked and followed by* THE DUENNA. CYRANO *opens the door quickly*]

Come in!

[*Walking up to* THE DUENNA] A word with you!

THE DUENNA. Two.

CYRANO.   Are you fond of sweets?

THE DUENNA.   To make me sick.

CYRANO [*quickly taking some of the paper bags from the counter*].

Here are two sonnets Benserade has written—

THE DUENNA. Pooh!

CYRANO. Which I'll fill with wine-cakes.

THE DUENNA [*changing her expression*].

Oh!

CYRANO.   You like These cream puffs also?

THE DUENNA.   Oh, I dote upon them!

CYRANO. Six of them I will put within the bosom

Of a poem by Saint-Amant! In these verses Of Chapelain, I'll put a piece of sponge cake,— You like fresh cakes, then?

THE DUENNA.   Oh! I love them madly!

CYRANO [*filling her arms with the bags of cakes*].

Be kind enough to eat all these outside.

THE DUENNA. But—

CYRANO [*pushing her out*]. Come not back till you have finished them!

[*Closes the door, comes back to* ROXANE, *and stops, uncovered, at a respectful distance*]

CYRANO. Now let this moment be most blest of all,

When, ceasing to forget I humbly breathe, You come to say to me—to say to me—

ROXANE [*after having unmasked*].

To thank you first, because the knavish dolt Whom you put to the laugh, with your good sword,

Is he whom a great lord—in love with me—

CYRANO. De Guiche!

ROXANE [*lowering her eyes*].—has tried to give me—for a husband.

CYRANO. So-called?

[*Bowing*] Then I have fought, and better so, For your bright eyes, not for my ugly nose.

ROXANE. And then—I wished—but to make this avowal

I needs must see in you the—almost brother,

With whom I played, in the park, by the lake!

CYRANO. Yes; you came every year to Bergerac.

ROXANE. The reeds then furnished you with wood for swords.

CYRANO. And the corn, yellow hair to deck your dolls.

ROXANE. Those were the days of games—

CYRANO.   —of berry-picking—

ROXANE. The days when you did all things that I wished!

CYRANO. Roxane, in dresses short, was called Madeleine.

ROXANE. And I was pretty then?

CYRANO.   You were not ugly.

ROXANE. Sometimes, when you had cut your hand in climbing

You ran to me; then I would play the mother, And say with voice that tried hard to be stern

[*Takes his hand*]

"What is this scratch now?"

[*Stops in amazement*] Ah, too bad! And this?

[CYRANO *tries to draw back his hand*]

No! Show it to me! What? At your age, still? How came it?

CYRANO.   Playing, at the Porte de Nesle.

ROXANE [*sitting at a table and dipping her handkerchief in a glass of water*].

Come!

CYRANO [*also sitting down*]. Like a fond and happy little mother!

ROXANE. And tell me, while I wipe away the blood,

How many were there?

CYRANO.   Oh! Not quite a hundred.

ROXANE. Tell me!

CYRANO. No, let it go! But you tell me That which just now you dared not—

ROXANE [*without letting go of his hand*].

Now I dare.

The past's sweet odor gives me courage new. Yes, now I dare. Listen, I love someone.

CYRANO. Ah!

ROXANE. Who has not guessed it!

CYRANO.   Ah!

ROXANE.   At least, not yet.

CYRANO. Ah!

ROXANE. But who soon will know, if he knows it not.

CYRANO. Ah!

ROXANE. A poor lad, who has loved me until now

Timidly, from afar, nor dared to speak.

CYRANO. Ah!

ROXANE. Leave me your hand, it is all feverish!—

But I have seen love trembling on his lips.

CYRANO. Ah!

ROXANE [*finishing a little bandage for him made of her handkerchief*].

And do you know, my cousin, that in fact He now is serving in your regiment!

CYRANO. Ah!

ROXANE [*smiling*].
In your own company he's a cadet!

CYRANO. Ah!

ROXANE. His forehead shows his genius and
his wit,
He's young, proud, noble, brave, and fair—

CYRANO [*getting up, very pale*]. What, fair?

ROXANE. Why, what's the matter?

CYRANO.   Nothing—'tis—
[*With a smile, showing his hand*]—this wound.

ROXANE. In fine, I love him. I must tell you,
too,
That I have seen him only at the play—

CYRANO. You have not spoken?

ROXANE.   Only with our eyes.

CYRANO. How do you know him then?

ROXANE.   Under the lindens,
In the Place Royale, there is talk; and gossip
Has told me—

CYRANO.   He is a cadet?

ROXANE.   He is.
He's in the Guards.

CYRANO.   His name?

ROXANE.   The Baron Christian
De Neuvillette—

CYRANO. What? He's not in the Guards.

ROXANE. Yes, since this morning, under
Captain Carbon
De Castel-Jaloux.

CYRANO.   Ah! how quick is love!
But my poor child—

THE DUENNA [*opening the door in the background*].   Monsieur de Bergerac,
I've finished all the cakes.

CYRANO.   Well, read the verses
Upon the bags. [THE DUENNA *disappears*]
               My poor child, you who love
Keen wit and courtly speech, if he should be
A man unlearned, unpolished, in the rough!

ROXANE. No, he has hair like one of d'Urfé's
heros!

CYRANO. His speech may lack the grace his
hair displays!

ROXANE. No, every word he speaks I know
is brilliant.

CYRANO. Yes, words are brilliant from a fair
moustache;
But if he were a dolt!—

ROXANE [*tapping with her foot*]. Then I
should die!

CYRANO [*after pause*].
So you have brought me here to tell me that.
I cannot see the good of it, Madame!

ROXANE. Ah! yesterday I had a deadly
shock,—
I heard that you are Gascons, every one,
All of your company—

CYRANO.   And that we pick
Quarrels with all recruits, who by mere favor
Gain entrance to our ranks of Gascon blood,
And are not Gascons? That is what you heard?

ROXANE. Think how I trembled for him!

CYRANO [*between his teeth*].   With good
reason!

ROXANE. But yesterday when you appeared
to us
So mighty and so brave, holding your own
Against the rabble, punishing that knave,
I thought—if he but would, whom all men
fear—

CYRANO. 'Tis well, I will protect your little
baron.

ROXANE. Ah, then you will protect him well
for me?
I've always had so warm a friendship for you!

CYRANO. Yes, yes.

ROXANE.   You'll be his friend?

CYRANO.   I'll be his friend.

ROXANE. And he shall fight no duels?

CYRANO.   On my oath!

ROXANE. I am so fond of you! Now I
must go.
[*Quickly puts on her mask, and a bit of
lace over her head, and absent-mindedly*]
But you have not yet told me of the battle
Last night. It must have been a mighty feat—
Tell him to write.
[*Throws him a little kiss with her fingers*]
               I am so fond of you!

CYRANO. Yes, yes.

ROXANE.   Five score against you?
Well, good-by,
We are great friends?

CYRANO.   Yes, yes.

ROXANE   Tell him to write.
A hundred! You will tell me later. Now
I cannot stay. A hundred! Oh! what courage!

CYRANO [*bowing to her*]. I have done better
since.
[*Exit* ROXANE. CYRANO *remains motionless, his eyes fixed on the ground. Silence
for a time. The door on the right opens
and* RAGUENEAU'S *head appears*]

RAGUENEAU.   May we come back?

CYRANO [*without moving*]. Yes.
[RAGUENEAU *gives the signal and his friends
come back. At the same time, at the door
in the background,* CARBON DE CASTEL-
JALOUX *appears, in his uniform as Captain of the Guards, making sweeping
gestures as he perceives* CYRANO]

CARBON DE CASTEL-JALOUX. There he is now!

CYRANO [*raising his head*]. Captain!

CARBON [*in exultation*].   Our hero!
We know the story! Thirty of my men
Are waiting—

CYRANO [*drawing back*]. But—

CARBON [*trying to draw him along*]. Come
now! They wish to see you.

CYRANO. No!

CARBON. They're drinking at the tavern opposite.

CYRANO. I—

CARBON [*going back to the door, and calling behind the scenes in a thundering voice*]. He refuses. He's in an ill humor!

A VOICE [*without*]. Ah, by the Lord!

[*A tumult without, noise of swords and spurs approaching*]

CARBON. You hear them cross the street!

[*The* CADETS *enter the cook-shop with a chorus of Gascon oaths and exclamations*]

RAGUENEAU [*drawing back in alarm*]. Gentlemen, are you all from Gascony?

THE CADETS. All!

A CADET [*to* CYRANO]. Bravo!

CYRANO. Baron!

ANOTHER [*shaking his hands*]. Hurrah!

CYRANO. Baron!

THIRD CADET [*embracing him*]. Greeting!

CYRANO. Baron!

SEVERAL CADETS. Embrace him!

CYRANO [*not knowing whom to answer*]. Baron! baron! spare me!

RAGUENEAU. Gentlemen, is each one of you a baron?

THE CADETS. All!

RAGUENEAU. Are they?

FIRST CADET. Just our crests would build a tower!

LE BRET [*entering and running towards Cyrano*] A crowd, led by your escort of last night, Is looking for you madly everywhere!

CYRANO [*in alarm*]. You did not tell them where I am?

LE BRET [*rubbing his hands*]. I did!

A TRADESMAN [*entering, followed by a crowd*]. Monsieur, the whole Marais is coming hither!

[*The street outside is full of people. Carriages and sedan chairs block the way*]

LE BRET [*aside, with a smile, to* CYRANO]. And Roxane?

CYRANO [*brusquely*]. Hush!

THE CROWD [*shouting without*]. Cyrano!

[*A mob bursts into the cook-shop. Confusion and shouting*]

RAGUENEAU [*standing on a table*]. In they swarm! They're breaking everything! 'Tis glorious!

PEOPLE [*surrounding* CYRANO]. My friend! My friend!

CYRANO. I had not yesterday So many friends!

LE BRET [*delighted*]. Success!

A LITTLE MARQUIS [*running up with outstretched hands*]. If thou didst know—

CYRANO. If thou?—if thou?—Now what have we in common?

ANOTHER MARQUIS. Monsieur, may I present you to some ladies Who are waiting in my carriage?

CYRANO [*coldly*]. Who will first

Present you to me.

LE BRET [*in amazement*]. What's the matter?

CYRANO. Hush!

A MAN OF LETTERS [*with a writing-case*]. May I have the details?—

CYRANO. No!

LE BRET [*nudging him*]. The inventor Of the "Gazette"—Théophraste Renaudot!

CYRANO. No matter!

LE BRET. 'Tis the sheet that tells so much. They say this new idea has a great future.

A POET [*coming forward*]. Monsieur—

CYRANO. Another!

THE POET. I should like to make A pentacrostic on your name—

A MAN [*also advancing*]. Monsieur—

CYRANO. Enough!

[*A movement in the crowd. People take their places.* DE GUICHE *appears, escorted by* OFFICERS. *Enter* CUIGY, BRISSAILLE, *and the other* OFFICERS *who started with* CYRANO *at the end of the First Act.* CUIGY *approaches* CYRANO *rapidly*]

CUIGY [*to* CYRANO]. Monsieur de Guiche!

[*Murmuring. All take position*] He represents Marshal de Gassion!

DE GUICHE [*bowing to* CYRANO]. Who sends to you His compliments upon your latest feat, The news of which has reached him.

THE CROWD. Bravo! Bravo!

CYRANO [*with a bow*]. The Marshal is expert in daring deeds.

DE GUICHE. He would have disbelieved, save on the oath Of these who saw it.

CUIGY. With our very eyes!

LE BRET [*aside, to* CYRANO, *who seems absent-minded*]. But—

CYRANO. Hush!

LE BRET. You seem in pain!

CYRANO [*with a start, and quickly drawing himself up*]. Before this crowd?

[*His moustache bristles; he throws out his chest*] I seem in pain?—You'll see!

DE GUICHE [*to whom* CUIGY *has been whispering*]. Your life already Is full of doughty deeds. With these mad Gascons You're serving, are you not?

CYRANO. With the Cadets.

A CADET [*with stentorian voice*]. With us!

DE GUICHE [*looking at the* GASCONS, *standing in line behind* CYRANO]. Ah! Ah! All these, of lordly mien, Are then the famous—

CARBON DE CASTEL—JALOUX. Cyrano!

CYRANO. What, captain?

CARBON. Since now my company has filled its roster, Present it to the Count in all due form.

CYRANO [*advancing two paces towards* DE
  GUICHE *and indicating the* CADETS].
These be cadets of Gascony,
Carbon de Castel-Jaloux's men:
They fight, they lie full shamelessly,
These be cadets of Gascony!
Their talk is all of heraldry—
Nobler are they than highwaymen;
These be cadets of Gascony,
Carbon de Castel-Jaloux's men.

With stork's long leg and eagle's eye,
And cat's moustache and wolf's keen fangs,
Thrusting the growling rabble by,
With stork's long leg and eagle's eye,
They march, hats cocked on heads held high,—
The holes hid, where the feather hangs,—
With stork's long leg and eagle's eye,
And cat's moustache and wolf's keen fangs!

Friends Belly-thrust and Break-your-pate,
Such are their nicknames soft and sweet;
On glory they're intoxicate!
Friends Belly-thrust and Break-your-pate.
Where quarrels start at fastest rate,
These are the places where they meet.
Friends Belly-thrust and Break-your-pate.
Such are their nicknames soft and sweet!

See the cadets of Gascony,
Who plant horns on the husband's brow!
Oh, woman, loved so tenderly,
See the cadets of Gascony!
Let husbands old frown angrily,
Let cuckoos sing from every bough!
See the cadets of Gascony,
Who plant horns on the husband's brow!

  DE GUICHE [*carelessly seated in an arm-
    chair which* RAGUENEAU *has quickly
    brought him*].
A poet is a modern luxury,
Will you belong to me?
  CYRANO.   No, sir, to no one.
  DE GUICHE. Your dash amused my uncle
    Richelieu
Yesterday. I would help you with him.
  LE BRET [*dazzled*].   Lord!
  DE GUICHE. I take it you have done a play
    in verse!
  LE BRET [*whispering to* CYRANO].
You'll get your "Agrippina" played, my
    friend.
  DE GUICHE. Take it to him.
  CYRANO [*tempted and rather pleased*].
Well—
  DE GUICHE.   He is most expert.
He'll only change a line or two of yours!
  CYRANO [*whose face has immediately
    flushed*].
Impossible, Monsieur; my blood runs cold,
To think of changing even one small comma.
  DE GUICHE. But when he likes a verse, my
    friend, he pays,

And pays right dear.
  CYRANO.   He pays for it less dear
Than I do, when I've made a verse I like;
I pay for it, singing it to myself.
  DE GUICHE. You're proud.
  CYRANO. Ah! really, you have noticed it?
  A CADET [*entering with a collection of shabby
    hats spitted on his sword, their plumes be-
    draggled and holes through the brims*].
Look, Cyrano! this morning on the quay,
What strangely feathered game we gathered in;
The hats left in the rout—
  CARBON.   The spoils of war!
  EVERY ONE [*laughing*]. Ha! ha!
  CUIGY. Whoever set this band of cut-throats
Is in a rage to-day.
  BRISSAILLE.   Is it known who?
  DE GUICHE. 'Twas I! [*The laughter ceases*]
    I charged them to chastise—a task
One does not do one's self—a drunken rhyme-
    ster.
    [*A constrained silence*]
  THE CADET [*in an undertone to* CYRANO,
    showing him the hats]
What shall we make of them? A stew? They're
    greasy.
  CYRANO [*taking the sword upon which they
    are impaled, salutes, and lets them all slip
    off at* DE GUICHE'S *feet*]
Monsieur, will you return them to your friends?
  DE GUICHE [*rising, in a peremptory tone*].
My bearers and my chair, at once,—I go.
    [*To* CYRANO *angrily*]
You, sir!—
  A VOICE [*in the street, shouting*].
            The bearers of my lord the Comte
de Guiche!
  DE GUICHE [*regaining his self-control, with
    a smile*]. Have you read "Don Quixote"?
  CYRANO.   Yes,
And at this crack-brain's name I doff my hat.
  DE GUICHE. Bethink yourself upon—
  A BEARER [*appearing in the background*].
                          The chair is here.
  DE GUICHE. The chapter of the windmills!
  CYRANO [*bowing*].   The thirteenth.
  DE GUICHE. When one attacks them, it will
    oft befall—
  CYRANO. Then I attack folk turned by every
    wind?
  DE GUICHE. That while their sails in circles
    sweep about
They'll land you in the mud!
  CYRANO.   Or in the stars!
    [*Exit* DE GUICHE. *He is seen getting into
    his chair. The gentlemen of his escort
    withdraw whispering together.* LE BRET
    *accompanies them to the door. The
    crowd departs*]
  CYRANO [*bowing to them mockingly as they
    go out without daring to bow to him*].
Gentlemen! Gentlemen—

Le Bret [*returning in despair, throwing up his arms*]. What a misfortune!

Cyrano. Oh, you! you'll scold!

Le Bret. You surely must admit
Murdering every passing chance becomes
Exaggerated.

Cyrano. Well, I exaggerate.

Le Bret [*in triumph*]. Ah!

Cyrano. But upon principle, and as a practice,
I find it well thus to exaggerate.

Le Bret. If you would lay aside your guardsman's spirit,
Fortune and glory—

Cyrano. And what must I do?
Seek some protector strong, get me a patron,
And like some humble vine, that twines a trunk,
Upheld by it, the while it strips its bark,
Climb by mere artifice, not rise by strength?
No, thank you. Dedicate, as others do,
Verses to bankers? Make myself a clown
In hopes of seeing on a statesman's lips
A friendly smile appear? I thank you, no!
Shall I be a toad-eater all my days?
My waist worn out by bending, and my skin
Grown quickly soiled in the region of my knees?
Or shall I show how limber is my back?—
No, thank you! On both shoulders carry water,
And sit the fence a-straddle, while I flatter
Each to his face, and feather my own nest?
No, thank you! Raise myself from step to step,
Become the little great man of a clique,
And steer my boat, with madrigals for oars,
And sighs of ancient dames to fill my sails?
No, thank you! Pay the editor De Sercy,
For publishing my poems? No, I thank you!
Or shall I have myself proclaimed as pope
By councils held in drinking-shops by fools?
No, thank you! Shall I make a reputation
Upon one sonnet, rather than write others?
Find talent only in the commonplace?
Be constantly in fear of errant sheets,
And always say: "Oh, let my name be seen
Upon the pages of the 'Mercure François'?"
No, thank you! Plan, be pale, and be afraid,
And make a call rather than write a poem,
Prepare petitions, have myself presented?
No, thank you! No, I thank you! No! But—
sing,
Dream, laugh, and go about, alone and free,
Have eyes that see things clear, and voice that rings,
And, if you like, wear your hat wrong side front;
Fight for a yes or no—or make a poem;
Work without thought of fortune or of glory;
Fly to the moon in fancy, if you wish!
Write not a word that comes not from your heart,
And still be modest; tell yourself, "My child,
Content yourself with flowers and fruits,—with leaves,—
If you have gathered them in your own garden!"
Then, if by chance you gain some small success,
No tribute money need you pay to Cæsar,
And all the honor is your very own.
In short, scorning to be the clinging vine,
When you are neither oak nor linden tree,
Mount not so high perhaps, but all alone!

Le Bret. Alone, so be it! But not one against all!
How did you get this mad idea of yours
Of making enemies where'er you go?

Cyrano. From seeing you making so many friends,
And smiling at these crowds of friends you make
With lips pursed up and wrinkled! I prefer
To have few bows to make when I go forth,
And gladly shout, "Another enemy!"

Le Bret. But this is madness!

Cyrano. Well, yes, 'tis my weakness.
To displease is my pleasure. Hate I love.
My friend, if you but knew how light one walks
Under the fusillade of hostile eyes;
What pleasant little spots upon one's doublet
Are made by envy's gall and cowards' spittle!—
But the soft friendship you wrap round yourself
Is like those great Italian collars, floating,
And made of openwork, in which one's neck
Grows soft like to a woman's: wearing them
One feels at ease—but holds his head less high;
For, having neither order nor support,
It weakly rolls about on every side.
While, as for me, Hate sheathes me every day,
Gives me a ruff that holds my head erect.
Every new enemy is another pleat,
A new constraint, and one more ray of glory,
For, like in all points to the Spanish ruff,
Hate is at once a collar and a halo!

Le Bret [*after a pause, putting his arm through* Cyrano's].
Be proud and bitter to the world, but softly
Tell me quite simply that she loves thee not.

Cyrano [*sharply*]. Hush!

[*After a moment* Christian *enters and joins the* Cadets. *They do not speak to him; at last he sits down at a small table, where* Lise *waits on him*]

A Cadet [*seated at a table in the background, glass in hand*]. Cyrano!

[Cyrano *turns*] The story?

Cyrano. In a moment.
[*Withdraws on* Le Bret's *arm. They talk in undertones*]

The Cadet [*rising and coming forward*].
The story of the fight! 'Twill be a lesson—

[*Stops before the table where* CHRISTIAN *is seated*]

—For this untried recruit.

CHRISTIAN [*raising his head*]. Untried recruit?

ANOTHER CADET. Yes, northern weakling!

CHRISTIAN.   Weakling, did you say?

FIRST CADET [*mockingly*].

Monsieur de Neuvillette, learn this one thing:
There is one object which we do not mention
More than the rope in the household of one
hanged.

CHRISTIAN. And what is that?

ANOTHER CADET [*in an impressive voice*].
       Behold me!

[*Mysteriously touches his finger to his nose
three times*]   Understand?

CHRISTIAN. Ah! 'tis the—

ANOTHER. Hush—that word is never uttered!

[*Indicates* CYRANO, *who is talking with*
LE BRET *in the background*]

Or 'tis with him there you will have to do.

ANOTHER [*who has silently sat down on the
table behind him, while he has been turning to face the others*]

Two men he slew because he liked it not
That they talked through their noses.

ANOTHER [*rising from under the table where
he has crawled on all fours, in a hollow
voice*].   And one cannot

Without departing, cut off in his youth,
Make one allusion to the fatal feature!

ANOTHER [*laying his hand on his shoulder*].
One word's enough! I said a word?—a gesture!

To draw one's kerchief is to draw one's shroud.

[*Silence. All around him fold their arms
and watch him. He rises and walks
towards* CARBON DE CASTEL-JALOUX, *who
is talking with an officer and seems to see
nothing*]

CHRISTIAN. Captain!

CARBON [*turning and looking him over*].
       Monsieur?

CHRISTIAN.   What is the thing to do,
When Southrons are too boastful?

CARBON.   Prove to them
One can be from the North, and brave.

[*Turns his back on him*]

CHRISTIAN.   I thank you.

FIRST CADET [*to* CYRANO]. Your story now!

ALL.   His story!

CYRANO [*coming forward towards them*].
       What, my story?

[*All draw their benches towards him, and
form a group, craning their necks.*
CHRISTIAN *straddles a chair*]

Well: I was marching all alone, to meet them,
The moon shone in the sky like a great watch,
When suddenly some watchmaker, with care,
Starting to draw a piece of cloudy cotton
Across the silver case of this round watch,

The night became the blackest ever seen;
And as there are no lights upon the quays,
Good Lord! you could not see beyond—

CHRISTIAN.   Your nose?

[*Silence. Every one rises slowly. They look
at* CYRANO *in terror. He breaks off in
amazement. A pause*]

CYRANO. Who is that man there?

A CADET [*in an undertone*]. He's a man who
came
This morning.

CYRANO [*taking a step towards* CHRISTIAN].
      Did you say this morning?

CARBON [*in an undertone*].   Named
Baron de Neuvil—

CYRANO [*quickly stopping*]. Ah, 'tis well—

[*Turns pale, then red, and makes another
movement as if to fling himself upon*
CHRISTIAN]   —I

[*Then regains his composure and says in a
quiet voice*]   Well—

[*Begins again*]

As I was saying—

[*With a burst of anger in his voice*] God—

[*Continues in a natural tone*] —you could
not see.

[*Amazement. They take their seats, watching him*]

And so I went, thinking that for a beggar
I was about to offend some mighty prince,
Who surely would bear me a bitter grudge;
In short, that rashly and without concern,
I was about to thrust—

CHRISTIAN.   Your nose?

CYRANO.   —my finger
Between the bark and tree, since this great man
Might well be strong enough to deal a blow
Upon—

CHRISTIAN. Your nose?

CYRANO [*wiping the sweat from his face*].
    —upon my meddling fingers
But then I added: "Gascon, do your duty!
Cyrano, march!" Then, onward in the dark,
I go and feel—

CHRISTIAN. A fillip on the nose?

CYRANO. I parry. Suddenly I find myself—

CHRISTIAN. Nose against nose—

CYRANO [*leaping at him*]. Damnation!

[*All the* GASCONS *rush forward to see
when* CYRANO *reaches* CHRISTIAN *he regains his self-control and continues*]
       With a hundred

Roistering ruffians, stinking—

CHRISTIAN.   'Neath your nose—

CYRANO [*pale and smiling*].

—With sour wine and onions! Then I rush
Head down—

CHRISTIAN. Nose on the scent—

CYRANO.   And so I charge
Two I rip up! I run another through!
The some one lunges—Paf! I answer—

CHRISTIAN.   Pif!

CYRANO [*exploding*].
The devil! Out with you!
[*All the* CADETS *rush towards the doors*]
FIRST CADET. The tiger wakes!
CYRANO. Every one! With this man leave me
alone!
SECOND CADET. We'll find him cut in mince-
meat!
RAGUENEAU. What, in mincemeat?
ANOTHER CADET. Filling one of your patties!
RAGUENEAU. I grow pale
And limp as any napkin.
CARBON. Let us go!
ANOTHER. He will not leave a single morsel
of him!
ANOTHER. I die of fright thinking what will
befall!
ANOTHER [*closing the door on the right*].
Something most terrible!
[*They all go out, some by the rear, some
by the sides, some by the stairway.
CYRANO and CHRISTIAN remain face to
face, and look at each other for a mo-
ment*]
CYRANO. Give me your hand!
CHRISTIAN. Monsieur—
CYRANO. Brave man!
CHRISTIAN. But—
CYRANO. Very brave; I like it!
CHRISTIAN. But tell me?—
CYRANO. Come, your hand, I am her
brother.
CHRISTIAN. Whose?
CYRANO. Hers!
CHRISTIAN. What?
CYRANO. Roxane's!
CHRISTIAN [*rushing to him*]. Heavens!
You? Her brother?
CYRANO. Yes; or almost: a cousin like a
brother.
CHRISTIAN. She's told you?—
CYRANO. All!
CHRISTIAN. She loves me?
CYRANO. That may be.
CHRISTIAN [*taking his hand*].
Monsieur, I am so happy to have met you?
CYRANO. This is what might be called a
sudden friendship.
CHRISTIAN. Forgive me—
CYRANO [*looking at him and laying his hand
on his shoulder*]. True, he is a handsome
rascal!
CHRISTIAN. If you knew, sir, how I admire
you.
CYRANO. But all these "noses" which—
CHRISTIAN. I take them back.
CYRANO. Roxane to-night expects a letter—
CHRISTIAN. Ah!
CYRANO. What?
CHRISTIAN. I shall spoil my chances if I
speak!
CYRANO. Why?

CHRISTIAN. I'm so stupid that I die of shame!
CYRANO. No, you are not, since you take
count of it,
And your attack on me was not so stupid.
CHRISTIAN. Bah! Words come quickly when
one starts to fight.
Yes, I may have a ready soldier's wit,
But before women I must hold my tongue.
Their eyes smile kindly on me as I pass—
CYRANO. And when you stop, do not their
hearts the like?
CHRISTIAN. No; for I am—I know it, and
I tremble—
A man who cannot talk of love.
CYRANO. I think,
Had I been one fashioned more carefully
I could have talked of it among the best.
CHRISTIAN. Oh, for the power to speak one's
thoughts with grace!
CYRANO. To walk about, a handsome muske-
teer!
CHRISTIAN. Roxane is learnèd, I shall surely
kill
All her illusions!
CYRANO. If I only had
Such an interpreter to speak my soul!
CHRISTIAN [*in despair*].
I need fair words.
CYRANO [*abruptly*]. And I will lend them to
you!
And you lend me your conquering comeliness;
And so combined together let us make
A hero of romance!
CHRISTIAN. What?
CYRANO. You could learn
To speak the words I'll teach you—
CHRISTIAN. You suggest?—
CYRANO. Roxane shall never lose her fond
illusions!
Together let us win her, say you so?
And shall I breathe in you my very soul,
From my buff jerkin to your broidered
doublet?—
CHRISTIAN. But, Cyrano!—
CYRANO. You will?
CHRISTIAN. You frighten me!
CYRANO. You fear lest by yourself you chill
her heart?
Shall we not join your lips and my fine words?
And very soon you'll fold her in your arms.
CHRISTIAN. Your eyes are gleaming!
CYRANO. Will you?
CHRISTIAN. What! Will that
Give you such pleasure?
CYRANO [*with elation*]. That—
[*Stopping himself, and in the tone of an
artist pleased with his work*]
—that will amuse me.
'Tis an experiment to tempt a poet.
Shall we be each the other's complement?
I shall walk in the shadow by your side,
You will be my good looks and I your wit.

CHRISTIAN. But I can never write the needed letter
Which must be sent forthwith—

CYRANO [*taking from his doublet the letter he had written*].   There is your letter!

CHRISTIAN. What?

CYRANO. There is nothing lacking but the name.

CHRISTIAN. I—

CYRANO. You can send it. Reassure yourself. It is a good one.

CHRISTIAN. You—

CYRANO.   We always have them
With us: letters to Chloris—in our minds;
For we are such as have for sweethearts only
Dreams breathed into the bubble of a name.
Take it, and change these fancies into facts,—
I shot at random these pleas, these avowals,—
And all these flitting birds you'll bring to perch!
You'll see that in this letter I was—take it!—
As eloquent as I was insincere!
Take it, and end the talk!

CHRISTIAN.   Will not some words
Need to be changed. Written thus at a venture,
Will it fit Roxane?

CYRANO.   'Twill fit her like a glove.

CHRISTIAN. But—

CYRANO. Self-conceit so well deceives itself,
Roxane will think 'twas written all for her!

CHRISTIAN. My friend!
[*Throws himself into* CYRANO'S *arms. They stand embracing each other*]

A CADET [*partly opening the door*].
No word. The silence of the grave.
I dare not look—
[*Puts his head in*] What?

ALL THE CADETS [*entering and seeing* Cyrano *and* CHRISTIAN *embracing*]
Ah! Oh!

A CADET.   What is this?
[*General surprise*]

THE MUSKETEER [*mockingly*]. Well?

CARBON. Mild as a saint our demon has become?
Smitten upon one cheek he turns the other?

THE MUSKETEER. Now you may speak to him about his nose.
[*Triumphantly calling* LISE]
Oh! Lise. You'll see!
[*Pretending to be smelling the air*]
Oh! Oh! It is surprising!
This odor!
[*Approaching* CYRANO] Sir, have you not noticed it?
What does it smell of here?

CYRANO [*boxing his ears*]. I think a nosegay!
[*Rejoicing. The* CADETS *find that* CYRANO *is unchanged. They turn somersaults*]

CURTAIN

THIRD ACT

ROXANE'S KISS

A small square in the old Marais, with ancient houses, and a perspective of narrow streets. To the right, ROXANE'S *house, and the wall of its garden, bordered with abundant foliage. Above the door, a window and balcony. A bench before the threshold. Vines climb the wall; jasmine wreathes the balcony and hangs quivering. By means of the bench and stones jutting out from the wall it is easy to climb to the balcony. Opposite, an old house of the same style, of brick and stone, with a door of entrance. The knocker of this door is wrapped with linen like an injured thumb. When the curtain rises* THE DUENNA *is seated on the bench. The window is wide open on* ROXANE'S *balcony.* RAGUENEAU, *dressed in a sort of livery, is standing by* THE DUENNA. *He is finishing a narrative, and wiping his eyes.*

RAGUENEAU. And then she left me for a musketeer!
I was alone and ruined—I hanged myself,
Monsieur de Bergerac came and cut me down,
And offers me to his cousin as a steward.

THE DUENNA. But how do you explain this plight of yours?

RAGUENEAU. Lise loved the soldiers; I was fond of poets!
And Mars ate all the cakes Apollo left;
And so—you understand—the end soon came.

THE DUENNA [*rising and calling towards the open window*].
Roxane, they're waiting for us,—are you ready?

ROXANE. I'm putting on my cloak.

THE DUENNA [*to* CYRANO, *pointing to the door opposite*].   They wait for us
Opposite, at Clomire's. In her retreat
She keeps an exchange for wits. This afternoon
There'll be a discourse on the Tender Passion.

RAGUENEAU. The Tender Passion?

THE DUENNA [*simpering*]. Certainly.
[*Calling towards the window*]   Roxane
You must come down, or we shall miss the discourse
Upon the Tender Passion!

ROXANE'S VOICE.   I am coming.
[*A sound of stringed instruments is heard approaching*]

CYRANO'S VOICE [*singing in the wings*].
La, la! la, la!

THE DUENNA [*surprised*]. They're playing piece for us!

CYRANO [*followed by two* PAGES *carrying lutes*].
That note's a demi-semi-quaver, fool!

FIRST PAGE [*ironically*].
You know what is a demi-semi-quaver?

CYRANO. I'm a musician, like all Gassendi's pupils!

THE PAGE [*playing and singing*].
La, la!

CYRANO [*snatching away the lute and continuing the bar*]. I can go on— La, la! La, la!

ROXANE [*appearing on the balcony*].
'Tis you.

CYRANO [*going on with the air, and singing*].
'Tis I—come to salute your lilies,
And to pay my respects unto your roses!

ROXANE. I'm coming down [*leaves the balcony*]

THE DUENNA [*indicating the* PAGES].
Who are these *virtuosi?*

CYRANO. It is a bet I won from D'Assoucy.
We argued warmly on a point of grammar,
When suddenly he pointed to these giants
Who strike the strings with such a skilful hand,
And always from his escort; saying to me,
"I lay you a day of music"—and he lost!
And now, till Phœbus starts another round,
I have these lutists at my heels all day,
Musical witnesses of all I do.
At first 'twas charming, now I find it palls.
[*To the musicians*]
Go—play a minuet to Montfleury.
[*The* PAGES *start to go out. To* THE DUENNA]
I came to ask Roxane, as every night—
[*To the* PAGES *as they go out*]
Play on—and off the key!
[*To* THE DUENNA]   —Whether her friend
Is still perfection?

ROXANE [*coming out of the house*].
Ah! how fair he is,
And what a mind he has, and how I love him!

CYRANO [*smiling*].
Christian has such a mind?

ROXANE.   Yes, more than you!

CYRANO. That I admit.

ROXANE.   I think there could not be
A better framer of those pretty phrases
Which may be naught, and yet are everything.
Sometimes he seems distraught,—his Muse is gone;
Then, all at once, he says such charming things!

CYRANO [*skeptically*]. Really?

ROXANE.   This is too much.
See what men are!
Because a man has looks, he has no brains!

CYRANO. Can he talk of the heart in clever fashion?

ROXANE. He more than talks, he teaches!

CYRANO.   Does he write?

ROXANE. Yes, even better! Listen to a bit.
[*Declaiming*]
The more you steal my heart, the more I have."
Triumphantly to CYRANO] Well?

CYRANO.   Pooh!

ROXANE.   And this:
"But since I need another
To suffer with, if you keep mine yourself,
Send me your own."

CYRANO. Sometimes he has too much;
And sometimes not enough. What does he want?

ROXANE. You grate on me! It is the jealousy—

CYRANO [*giving a start*]. What!

ROXANE.   —of an author that quite eats you up!
And this, the very tenderest of them all:
"Believe me that my heart makes but one cry
To you; and that if kisses could be written,
Madame, you'd read my letter with your lips."

CYRANO [*smiling with satisfaction in spite of himself*]
Ha, ha! those lines are,—eh, eh!
[*Stopping himself, and with disdain*]
    —pretty weak!

ROXANE. And this—

CYRANO [*delighted*]. You know his letters, then, by heart?

ROXANE. All!

CYRANO.   There's naught else to say; 'tis flattering!

ROXANE. He is a master.

CYRANO [*modestly*]. Oh!—a master!—

ROXANE [*peremptorily*].   Yes!
A master.

CYRANO. So be it then—a master!

THE DUENNA [*who had withdrawn, coming back quickly*]. Monsieur de Guiche. [*To* CYRANO, *pushing him towards the house*]
Go in—perhaps 'twere better
He should not find you here; because it might
Put him upon the scent—

ROXANE [*to* CYRANO]. Of my dear secret!
He loves me; he has power; he must not know!
For he might deal my love a cruel stroke.

CYRANO [*going into the house*].
Well, very well!
[*DE GUICHE appears*]

ROXANE [*to* DE GUICHE, *making him a courtesy*]. I'm going out.

DE GUICHE.   I come to take my leave.

ROXANE. You go away?

DE GUICHE.   To the war!

ROXANE.   Ah?

DE GUICHE.   Yes, to-night.

ROXANE. Ah!

DE GUICHE. I am under orders. We besiege
Arras—

ROXANE. A siege?

DE GUICHE.   Yes, but my departure
Seems to leave you indifferent.

ROXANE.   Oh!

DE GUICHE.   As for me,
I'm in despair! When shall we meet again?
You know that I am to command the force?

ROXANE [*indifferently*]. Bravo!

DE GUICHE. The regiment of the Guards—

ROXANE [*interested at once*]. The Guards?

DE GUICHE. In which your cousin serves, that braggart bold;

I shall have my revenge on him down there.

ROXANE [*choking with emotion*].
The Guards are going?

DE GUICHE [*smiling*]. 'Tis my regiment.

ROXANE [*falling back on the bench, aside*].
Christian!

DE GUICHE. What is the matter?

ROXANE [*much moved*]. This—departure—
Will break my heart! To care for any one
And know him at the war!

DE GUICHE [*surprised and charmed*]. For the first time
To speak me kindly, the day I go away!

ROXANE [*changing her tone, and fanning herself*].
Then—you would take revenge upon my cousin?

DE GUICHE. You're on his side?

ROXANE.   Oh, no! against!

DE GUICHE.   You see him?

ROXANE. Seldom.

DE GUICHE. One meets him everywhere with one
Of the Cadets.
[*Trying to think of the name*] This Neuvillen
—viller—

ROXANE. A tall man?

DE GUICHE.   Blond.

ROXANE.   Flaxen-haired—

DE GUICHE.   Handsome!—

ROXANE.   Pooh!—

DE GUICHE. But somewhat stupid.

ROXANE.   Yes, he seems to be!
[*Changing her tone*]
But your revenge on Cyrano— Perhaps
'Tis to put him under fire, which he loves?—
That were small comfort. As for me, I know
The way to break his heart!

DE GUICHE.   And how is that?

ROXANE. But let the regiment depart, and leave him,
With folded arms, in Paris, through the war,
With his beloved Cadets. That is the way
To rouse a man like him to bitter wrath,
'Twill punish him to keep him out of danger.

DE GUICHE. A woman's wit!—and no one but a woman
Would think of such a trick!

ROXANE.   He'll eat his heart out;
His friends will gnaw their fists, thus left behind;
And you will be revenged.

DE GUICHE [*drawing nearer*]. You love me then
A little?

[*She smiles*] In thus taking up my grudge
I fain would see a proof of love, Roxane!

ROXANE. A proof of love it is.

DE GUICHE [*showing several sealed packets*].
Here are the orders,
Which will be sent this moment to each troop,
Except—
[*detaches one*]—this one, for the Cadets.
[*Puts it in his pocket*]   I keep it!
[*Smiling*]
Ah! Ah! Ah! Cyrano!—his thirst for battle!
You play these tricks on people then?

ROXANE.   Sometimes.

DE GUICHE [*very close to her*].
You fill me with delight! Listen: to-night
I should be gone—but—go, when you are moved?
Listen: hard by, in the Rue d'Orléans,
There stands a convent, founded by the head
Of the Capuchins—Father Athanasius.
A layman cannot enter; but the fathers
May stretch a point for me; their sleeves are large,
They'll cover me with ease. These are the monks
Who wait on Richelieu in his own household;
Dreading the uncle, they will fear the nephew.
People will think me gone; I'll come in mask.
Let me wait but one day, capricious love!

ROXANE. But if 'tis known, your glory—

DE GUICHE.   Bah!

ROXANE.   The siege—
Arras—

DE GUICHE. So much the worse. Pray let me!

ROXANE. No!

DE GUICHE. Yes!

ROXANE [*tenderly*]. I should forbid you!

DE GUICHE.   Ah!

ROXANE.   Go!
[*Aside*]   Christian stays.
[*Aloud*]
I would have you a hero—Antony!

DE GUICHE. Heavenly word! So you admire him?

ROXANE. For him my heart has thrilled.

DE GUICHE.   Ah, well, I go!
[*Kisses her hand*] Are you content?

ROXANE.   Yes, my friend!
[*He goes out*]

THE DUENNA [*making him a mock courtesy behind his back*]   Yes, my friend!

ROXANE [*to the* DUENNA].
Let us be silent over what I've done.
Cyrano'ld take it ill to think I'd robbed him
Of going to the war.
[*Calls towards the house*] Cousin! We're going
To Clomire's.
[*Points to the door opposite*]
There'll be speeches by Alcandre
And Lysimon!

THE DUENNA [*putting her little finger in her ear*].   Yes! But my little finger
Says we shall miss them!

CYRANO [*to* ROXANE]. Do not miss these wonders!

[They arrive in front of CLOMIRE'S *door]*
THE DUENNA *[with rapture].*
Oh, see! The knocker's wrapped with linen
cloths.
[To the knocker]
So you are muffled, that your iron clang
May not disturb their discourse—wicked child!
*[Raises it with infinite care and raps
softly]*
ROXANE *[seeing the door open].*
Let us go in!
[From the threshold, to CYRANO] Let Christian
wait for me,
If he comes here, as I suppose he will.
CYRANO *[quickly, as she is about to disap-
pear].* Ah!
[She turns back] On what do you intend to
question him,
To-day, after your habit?
ROXANE.   On—
CYRANO *[quickly].*   On what?
ROXANE. But you'll be silent on it!
CYRANO.   Like a wall.
ROXANE. Oh nothing!—I shall tell him,
"Loose the reins!
Improvise; talk of love. Be glorious!"
CYRANO *[smiling].* Good!
ROXANE.   Hush!
CYRANO.   Hush!
ROXANE.   Not a word!
[Goes in and shuts the door]
CYRANO *[bowing to her, after the door is
shut].*   Accept my thanks!
[The door opens again and ROXANE *puts
out her head]*
ROXANE. He would prepare himself—
CYRANO.   Oh, no!
BOTH TOGETHER.   Hush!—
[The door closes]
CYRANO *[calling].*   Christian!
I know just what is needed. Give good heed,
This is your chance for glory. Lose no time,
Make no objections. Quickly let us go
To where you lodge. And I will teach you—
CHRISTIAN.   No!
CYRANO. What?
CHRISTIAN. No, I wait for Roxane here.
CYRANO.   What madness
Has seized upon you? Come and quickly
learn—
CHRISTIAN. I tell you no! I'm sick of bor-
rowing
Letters and speeches, playing this timid part.
Twas good at first! But now I feel she loves
me!
Thanks, I am not afraid, I'll speak myself.
CYRANO. Ah!
CHRISTIAN. And who will say that I shall not
know how?
'm not so stupid after all. You'll see!
Besides, my friend, I've learned a deal from
you.

I can speak quite alone! And by the gods,
One thing I can do, take her in my arms!—
[Seeing ROXANE *as she comes out of*
CLOMIRE'S *house]*
'Tis she! No, do not leave me, Cyrano!
CYRANO *[bowing to him].* Speak quite alone,
sir.
[Disappears behind the garden wall]
ROXANE *[coming out of* CLOMIRE'S *house,
with a number of people of whom she
takes her leave, courtesies and bows].*
Barthénoïde! Alcandre!
THE DUENNA *[in distress].* We missed the
discourse on the Tender Passion!
[Returns to ROXANE'S *house]*
ROXANE *[still bowing].*
Grémionë! Urimédonte! Adieu!
[All bow to ROXANE, *and to each other,
separate, and depart by different streets.*
ROXANE *sees* CHRISTIAN]
'Tis you!
[Goes to him]
The evening falls. Wait. They are gone.
The air is soft. No one is near. Sit down.
Speak. I am listening.
CHRISTIAN *[sits by her on the bench. A
pause].*   I love you.
ROXANE *[closing her eyes].*   Yes,
Talk about love.
CHRISTIAN.   I love thee!
ROXANE.   'Tis the theme,
Embroider it.
CHRISTIAN. I love thee!
ROXANE.   Yes!
CHRISTIAN.   So much!
ROXANE. Of course, and then—
CHRISTIAN.   And then—I'd be so glad
If you loved me!—Tell me, Roxane, you do!
ROXANE *[with a little grimace].*
You offer gruel when I hoped for sweets!
Explain a little how you love!
CHRISTIAN.   But—much!
ROXANE. Untwine your feelings from this
single string!
CHRISTIAN. Your neck!—I should so like to
kiss it!
ROXANE.   Christian!
CHRISTIAN. I love you.
ROXANE *[starting to get up].* Once again!
CHRISTIAN *[quickly, holding her back].* I
love you not!
ROXANE *[sitting down again].*
'Tis fortunate!
CHRISTIAN.   I worship you!
ROXANE *[getting up and going away].* Oh.
CHRISTIAN.   Yes!
I grow a fool.
ROXANE *[drily].* And that displeases me,
Just as it would if you should ugly grow.
CHRISTIAN. But—
ROXANE.   Gather up your scattered
eloquence.

CHRISTIAN.   I—
ROXANE. I know; you love me. Good-bye.
CHRISTIAN.   Not at once!
I'll tell you—
  ROXANE [*opening the door to go in*]. That
      you worship me—I know.
No! go away!
  CHRISTIAN. But I—
      [*She shuts the door in his face*]
  CYRANO [*who has come in unperceived a
      moment before*].   'Tis a success!
  CHRISTIAN.   Help!
  CYRANO.   No, Sir!
  CHRISTIAN.   I shall die unless at once
I win her smiles again—
  CYRANO.   And how the devil
Can I teach you to do it on the spot?
  CHRISTIAN [*seizing his arm*].
Oh! come now, see!
      [*The window of the balcony is lighted up*]
  CYRANO [*with emotion*]. Her window!
  CHRISTIAN.   I shall die!
  CYRANO. Lower your voice.
  CHRISTIAN [*in very low voice*]. Shall die—
  CYRANO.   The night is dark—
  CHRISTIAN. Well?
  CYRANO. It may be helped, though you do
      not deserve it.
Take your position there, unhappy wight!
Before the balcony! I shall stand beneath
And prompt you with your words.
  CHRISTIAN.   But—
  CYRANO.   Hold your tongue.
  THE PAGES [*reappearing in the background,
      to* CYRANO]. Holloa!
  CYRANO.   Hush!—
      [*Signals to them to speak low*]
  FIRST PAGE [*in a low voice*]. We've just given
      Montfleury
His serenade—
  CYRANO [*aside, quickly*]. Go, put yourselves
      in ambush.
One at this end the street, the other there,
And if some inconvenient passer comes
Then play a tune.
  SECOND PAGE. What tune, Gassendi's pupil?
  CYRANO. Gay for a woman, mournful for a
      man.
      [*The* PAGES *disappear, one at each end of
      the street. To* CHRISTIAN]
Call her!
  CHRISTIAN. Roxane!
  CYRANO [*picking up some pebbles and throw-
      ing them at the panes*].
                Wait till I throw a pebble.
  ROXANE [*half opening the window*].
Who calls me?
  CHRISTIAN.   I.
  ROXANE.   Who?
  CHRISTIAN.   Christian.
  ROXANE [*with disdain*].   Is it you?
  CHRISTIAN. I would speak with you.

  CYRANO [*under the balcony*]. Good! Good!
      Almost whisper.
  ROXANE. Oh, no! You speak too ill. Begone!
  CHRISTIAN.   I beg you!
  ROXANE. No, you love me no longer.
  CHRISTIAN [CYRANO *prompting him*]. What
      a charge!—Ye gods!—to love no more—
      when—I love most!
  ROXANE [*stopping, as she was about to close
      the window*]. That's better!
  CHRISTIAN [*same action*]. Love grows—
      cradled in my soul—
My troubled soul—the which this cruel babe
Has taken for his cot.
  ROXANE [*coming out on the balcony*]. That's
      better now!
But since this love is cruel, you were foolish
That in his cot you did not smother him.
  CHRISTIAN [*same action*].
That did I try—but the attempt was vain;
This new-born babe—is a little—Hercules.
  ROXANE. That's better!
  CHRISTIAN [*same action*]. So that in a trice
      —he strangled
The serpents—Pride and—Doubt.
  ROXANE [*leaning on the balcony rail*]. That's
      very good.
But why with halting accents do you speak?
Your fancy's lame?
  CYRANO [*pulling* CHRISTIAN *under the bal-
      cony and gliding into his place*]. Hush!
      This becomes too hard.
  ROXANE. To-day your words are faltering.
      Why is this?
  CYRANO [*talking in an undertone, like* CHRIS-
      TIAN].
Because it now is night; and in the dark
They grope about, striving to find your ear.
  ROXANE. But mine encounter no such ob-
      stacles.
  CYRANO. They find their way at once? That
      is not strange,
Because 'tis in my heart that I receive them—
My heart is large—your ear is wondrous small.
Besides, your words descend; their pace is
      swift,
While mine must climb, Madame, a longer task.
  ROXANE. But they climb better in these last
      few moments.
  CYRANO. As they have practised, they have
      learned the way.
  ROXANE. Truly, 'tis from a height I speak
      to you.
  CYRANO. And you would kill me, if you
      should let fall
From such a height, a hard word on my heart
  ROXANE [*with a motion*]. I'm coming down
  CYRANO [*quickly*].   No!
  ROXANE [*showing him the bench which i
      under the balcony*].
                Climb upon the bench
Quickly!

CYRANO [*drawing back with alarm into the darkness*]. No!

ROXANE. What?—No?

CYRANO [*his feelings gaining on him more and more*].

For a moment let me
Improve this chance which offers—to be able
To talk in accents soft, but not to see.

ROXANE. But not to see?

CYRANO. Yes, 'tis a sheer delight;
We guess at one another in the dark,
You see the blackness of a trailing cloak,
I see the whiteness of a summer robe,
And I am but a shadow, you a radiance.
You know not what these moments mean for me!
If ever I was eloquent—

ROXANE. You were!

CYRANO. Until this hour my words have never come
From my own heart—

ROXANE. Why?

CYRANO. Because, until now
I spoke through—

ROXANE. What?

CYRANO. —the dizziness where swims
Whome'er you look on— But to-night it seems
That for the first time I shall speak to you.

ROXANE. 'T is true that you have quite another voice.

CYRANO [*drawing near, feverishly*].
Yes, quite another, for in the sheltering night
I dare at last to be myself—I dare—
[*Stops, and in bewilderment*]
What was I saying—I know not— All of this—
Forgive my mounting passion—is so sweet—
And is so new for me.

ROXANE. So new?

CYRANO [*distracted and still trying to take back his words*]. So new—
—Why, yes!—to be sincere—without constraint,
The fear of being mocked has wrung my heart.

ROXANE. Mocked about what?

CYRANO. Oh—but—about my ardor—
My heart for shame has ever clothed itself
With wit as with a garment. I start forth
To snatch a star from out the sky,—I stop
In fear of ridicule,—and pluck a flower.

ROXANE. The flower has charms.

CYRANO. This evening let us scorn it.

ROXANE. You never yet have talked to me like this!

CYRANO. Oh! far removed from Cupid's enginery
'T is pleasant to escape to greener things.
Instead of drinking from a golden thimble
Insipid syrups, slowly, drop by drop,
Shall we not let the soul allay its thirst
By drinking freely from the river's flood?

ROXANE. But your wit?

CYRANO. I used to make you stay.
But now to speak with a court poet's phrases
Would be to affront this night, these odors sweet,
This magic hour, and even Nature's self.
Let Heaven, with one glance of her gleaming stars,
Take away all our wonted artifice;
I fear, lest in our subtle alchemy
The heart's true feeling may go up in smoke,
The soul may spend itself in empty play,
And e'en refinement be refined to naught.

ROXANE. But your wit?

CYRANO. I hate, when it plays with love.
For when one truly loves, it is a crime
Too long to thrust and parry. The moment comes—
And those to whom it never comes I pity—
When in our hearts we feel a noble passion
Saddened by every clever phrase we turn.

ROXANE. If to us two this moment now has come,
What words will you speak to me?

CYRANO. Every word
That rises to my lips. I'll cast them all
Before you in a heap, with no arrangement—
I love you—I am smothered—I am mad—
I love you—I am faint—it is too much;
Your name hangs in my heart like a bell's tongue,
And evermore, Roxane, with love I tremble,
And the bell swings, and then your name rings out.
And everything you do lives in my heart;
Last year there was one day I well remember,
The tenth of May, one morn you dressed your hair
So that its radiance burnt into my soul;
And just as he, who at the sun too long
Has gazed, sees circles red where'er he looks;
So when I left the flames in which I swam
My eyes saw blots of gold on everything.

ROXANE. Yes, this indeed is love—

CYRANO. Truly, this passion
Jealous and terrible, which sweeps me on,
Is love indeed, with all its mournful madness!
Is love indeed, and yet it is not selfish!
Ah! for your joy I'd gladly give my own,
Even if you should never know; if I
Might sometimes from afar hear the soft laugh
Of happiness born from my sacrifice,—
Your very look rouses new worth in me,
Do you begin to understand it now?
And feel my soul climb slowly through the dark?
Ah! but this night is all too fair, too sweet!
I say all this to you; and you, you listen;
It is too much. E'en in my maddest hopes
I never hoped so much. There's nothing left,
Except for me to die at once. She trembles,
There through the branches dark, and for my words,

For you are trembling, a leaf among the leaves,
For thou art trembling, and I plainly felt
Whether thou wouldst or no, the trembling dear
Of thy sweet hand descend the jasmine branch.
[*Madly kisses the end of a hanging branch*]
ROXANE. I tremble, I weep, I love thee, I am thine—
Aye, drunk with love!
    CYRANO.   Then let death come at once.
Since it is I who mixed the cup for thee!
I ask but one thing more—
    CHRISTIAN [*under the balcony*]. A kiss!
    ROXANE [*drawing back*].   What?
    CYRANO.   Oh!
    ROXANE. You're asking?
    CYRANO.   Yes—I—
[*To* CHRISTIAN, *aside*] You go far too fast!
    CHRISTIAN. Since she is moved, I must improve my chance!
    CYRANO [*to* ROXANE].
Yes, I—I asked, 'tis true, but, gracious heavens!
I understand, I was too bold by far.
    ROXANE [*somewhat disappointed*].
You insist no more than that?
    CYRANO.   Yes, I insist—
Without insisting. Yes! Your modesty
Is saddened— Well, this kiss—grant me it not.
    CHRISTIAN [*to* CYRANO, *pulling his cloak*].
Why?
    CYRANO. Hush, Christian.
    ROXANE [*leaning over*]. What do you say so low?
    CYRANO. I scold myself for having gone too far,
And to myself I said, "Hush, Christian."
[*The lutes begin to play*]   Wait!
Some one is coming.
    [ROXANE *closes the window.* CYRANO *listens
    to the lutes, one of which plays a lively
    air, the other a mournful one*]
    Sad? Gay? What's their plan?
Is it a man, or woman?—'tis a monk!
    [*A* CAPUCHIN *enters, going from house to
    house, lantern in hand, looking at the
    doors*]
    CYRANO [*to the* CAPUCHIN].
Who's this new follower of Diogenes?
    THE CAPUCHIN. I'm looking for the house—
    CHRISTIAN.   He's in our way!
    THE CAPUCHIN. Of Madame Magdeleine Robin.
    CHRISTIAN.   What's he after?
    CYRANO [*showing him a street leading away*].
This way, keep to the right,—still to the right.
    THE CAPUCHIN. Thank you! I'll say for you
a *pater noster*.
    [*Goes out*]
    CYRANO. Good luck. My prayers accompany
your cowl!
    [*Comes back to* CHRISTIAN]
    CHRISTIAN. Get me this kiss!—

    CYRANO.   No!
    CHRISTIAN.   Soon or late—
    CYRANO.   'Tis true!
'T will come; this moment of supreme delight
When your two mouths together shall be drawn
Because of her red lips, and your moustache.
    [*To himself*]
I'd rather that it were because—
    [*Noise of shutters reopening.* CHRISTIAN
    hides under the balcony*]
    ROXANE [*coming forward on the balcony*].
    'T is you?
We were speaking of—of—of a—
    CYRANO.   Of a kiss.
The word is sweet, I see not why your lips
So fear to speak it; if it burns them now
What will it be itself? Be not afraid.
Make not a terror of it. Did you not,
Just now, unknowingly, without alarm,
Leave off your mockery, and softly pass
From sigh to sigh, and from a sigh to tears?
Pass on yet further by the easy path—
'Twixt tears and kiss there's but a moment's tremble.
    ROXANE. Be still!
    CYRANO. A kiss, when all is said, what is it?
An oath sworn nearer by; a promise made
With greater certainty; a vow which seeks
To make itself more binding; a rosy dot
Placed on the "i" in loving; 'tis a secret
Told to the mouth instead of to the ear;
A moment of the infinite, which makes
A sound like to the humming of bees' wings;
A greeting like the sweet breath of a flower;
A way to feel the heart beat for a space,
And taste the soul a moment on the lips.
    ROXANE. Be still!
    CYRANO. A kiss, Madame, it is so noble
That e'en the Queen of France, the Queen herself,
Let her most happy courtier take one!
    ROXANE.   Well!
    CYRANO [*growing more impassioned*].
Like Buckingham, I've suffered silent pangs;
Like him, a Queen I worship—you, my Queen.
Like him, I'm sad and faithful.
    ROXANE.   And like him
You're fair.
    CYRANO [*aside, sobered*]. True, I am fair, I
quite forgot.
    ROXANE. Well, climb and pluck this flower
without a peer!
    CYRANO [*pushing* CHRISTIAN *toward the balcony*]. Climb!
    ROXANE. This heart beat.
    CYRANO.   Climb!
    ROXANE.   This humming of bees' wings.
    CYRANO. Climb!
    CHRISTIAN [*hesitating*]. But now it seems
perhaps I'd better not!
    ROXANE. This moment of the infinite.
    CYRANO [*pushing him*].   Climb, fool!

[CHRISTIAN *plunges forward, and by means of the bench, the branches, and the pillars reaches the balustrade, which he vaults*]

CHRISTIAN. Ah! Roxane!

[*Embraces her and bends over her lips*]

CYRANO. Ah! My heart, what torture strange!
Kiss, feast of love where I am Lazarus,
There reach me in the dark some crumbs from thee;
But still I feel my heart has something gained
Since on these lips where Roxane now is caught
It is the words I spoke just now she kisses.

[*The lutes are heard*]

Now sad, now gay, the Capuchin!

[*Pretends to run as if he were arriving from a distance, and calls in a loud voice*]
Holloa!

ROXANE. What is it?

CYRANO. It is I, I was just passing—
Christian's still there?

CHRISTIAN [*greatly astonished*]. What, Cyrano?

ROXANE. Good evening, Cousin!

CYRANO. Good evening, cousin!

ROXANE. I'm coming down.

[*Disappears in the house. The CAPUCHIN re-enters in the background*]

CHRISTIAN [*seeing him*]. Again!

THE CAPUCHIN. 'T is here—I'm sure— Magdeleine Robin!

CYRANO. You said Ro-*lin*.

THE CAPUCHIN. No, *Bin:* B, i, n, *bin!*

ROXANE [*appearing on the threshold of the house, followed by RAGUENEAU carrying a lantern, and by CHRISTIAN*]. What is it?

THE CAPUCHIN. A letter.

CHRISTIAN. What?

THE CAPUCHIN [*to ROXANE*]. Oh! It must be About some holy matter. It was a lord, A worthy lord who—

ROXANE. 'T is De Guiche!

CHRISTIAN. He dares?—

ROXANE. Oh, but he will not trouble me forever.

[*Unsealing the letter*]
I love you, and if—
[*She reads by the light of RAGUENEAU's lantern, aside in a low voice*] "Mademoiselle—
[*Aside, and apart from the others*] The drums Beat loud, my soldiers buckle on their tunics; They go, 'tis thought that I am gone; I stay, I disobey you. I am in this convent. I am coming and I warn you of it first, By a monk who is as simple as a lamb, And who knows naught of this. Your lips have smiled Just now too kindly on me; I have wished To see them once again. Bid all begone,

And graciously receive a man too bold, And yet already pardoned, may I hope? Who signs himself your very humble—"
[*To the CAPUCHIN*] Father, Here's what this letter tells me, listen to it:
[*All draw near, she reads aloud*] "Mademoiselle,
We must submit ourselves To the Cardinal's will, hard though it be for you; And that is why I've chosen a Capuchin, Very discreet, intelligent, and holy, To send this letter unto your fair hands. We wish that he should give you, at your dwelling, At once, the Church's blessing—
[*turns the page*] —on your marriage. Christian must secretly become your husband. I send him. You dislike him. Be resigned. Bethink yourself that heaven will bless your zeal, And be assured again, Mademoiselle, Of his respect who is, and ever will be, Your very humble, very—*et cœtera.*"

THE CAPUCHIN. The worthy lord! I had no fear; I said so. It could be only on some holy errand.

ROXANE [*aside to CHRISTIAN*]. Do I read letters well?

CHRISTIAN. Hum!

ROXANE [*aloud, in despair*]. Ah! 'T is frightful.

THE CAPUCHIN [*turning the light of his lantern on CYRANO*]. Is it you?

CHRISTIAN. It is I!

THE CAPUCHIN [*turning the light towards him and apparently seized with doubts, when he sees his good looks*]. But why—

ROXANE [*quickly*]. Post scriptum. "Give for the convent six score gold pistoles."

THE CAPUCHIN. A worthy, worthy lord!
[*To ROXANE*] Resign yourself.

ROXANE [*like a martyr*]. I am resigned.

[*While RAGUENEAU opens the doors to the CAPUCHIN, whom CHRISTIAN invites to enter, she says aside to CYRANO*] You make De Guiche wait here. He's coming—let him not come in before—

CYRANO. I understand.
[*To the CAPUCHIN*] To bless them takes how long?

THE CAPUCHIN. A quarter of an hour.

CYRANO [*pushing them all towards the house*]. Go, I stay.

ROXANE [*to CHRISTIAN*]. Come.

[*They go in*]

CYRANO. How to make De Guiche lose fifteen minutes?

[*Rushes to the bench and climbs up the wall towards the balcony*]

There! Let us climb—my plan is made—
[*The lutes begin to play a doleful bar*] Holloa!
It is a man!
[*The tremolo becomes mournful*]
        Ho! ho. This time it is one!
[*He is on the balcony, pulls his hat over his eyes, takes off his sword, then leans forward and looks out*]

No, it is not too high.
[*He vaults the balustrade, and drawing towards him the long branch of one of the trees which border the wall of the garden, he grasps it with both hands, ready to let himself fall*]
        This atmosphere
I am about to trouble.

DE GUICHE [*entering, masked, feeling his way in the night*].
What is this cursèd Capuchin about?

CYRANO. The deuce, my voice?—If he should recognize it?
[*Letting go with one hand, he pretends to turn an invisible key*]

Cric, crac!
[*Solemnly*] Speak like a Gascon, Cyrano.

DE GUICHE [*looking at the house*].
'Tis there! I cannot see. This mask annoys me.
[*Starts to go in.* CYRANO *leaps from the balcony, holding on to the branch, which bends, and lands him between* DE GUICHE *and the door; he pretends to fall heavily, as if from a great distance, and flattens out on the ground, where he remains motionless, as if stunned.* DE GUICHE *jumps backward*]

Hah! What!
[*When he lifts his eyes, the branch has swung back; he sees only the sky; he does not understand*]
        Whence falls this man here?

CYRANO [*sitting up, and speaking with a Gascon accent*].
        From the moon.

DE GUICHE. From the—?

CYRANO [*in a dreamy voice*]. What time is it?

DE GUICHE.   He's lost his mind.

CYRANO. What country? What o'clock? What day? What season?

DE GUICHE. But—

CYRANO. I am dazed.

DE GUICHE.   Monsieur—

CYRANO.   For like a bomb
I've fallen from the moon!

DE GUICHE [*impatient*]. Yes, but Monsieur!—

CYRANO [*getting up, with a terrible voice*].
Thence have I fallen!

DE GUICHE [*drawing back*]. Yes, yes, thence you fell!

—Perhaps he is a madman.

CYRANO [*advancing towards him*]. And my fall,—
It is no metaphor!

DE GUICHE.   But—

CYRANO.   A century since.
Or else a moment—in my fall I lost
All track of time,—I was in that yellow ball!

DE GUICHE [*shrugging his shoulders*].
Yes, let me pass.

CYRANO [*standing in his way*]. Where am I?
Tell me frankly,
Keep nothing hid! In what place, in what spot,
Monsieur, have I just fallen like a meteor?

DE GUICHE. The devil!

CYRANO.   As I fell I could not choose
My landing-place—I know not where I fell!—
And is it to a moon or to a world,
Whither my weight has just now drawn me down?

DE GUICHE. But sir, I tell you—

CYRANO [*with a cry of terror which makes* DE GUICHE *draw back*]. Ha! Ye gods! Meseems
That in this country folk have faces black!

DE GUICHE [*raising his hand to his face*].
What?

CYRANO [*with a distinct show of fear*]. Am I in Algiers? Are you a native?

DE GUICHE [*who has felt his mask*].
This mask—

CYRANO [*pretending to be somewhat reassured*].
I'm then in Genoa or Venice?

DE GUICHE [*trying to pass*].
A lady waits me—

CYRANO [*wholly reassured*]. Then I am in Paris!

DE GUICHE [*smiling in spite of himself*].
He's an amusing fellow.

CYRANO.   Ah! You laugh?

DE GUICHE. I laugh, but wish to pass.

CYRANO [*beaming*].   Indeed, 'tis Paris
[*Entirely at his ease, smiling, brushing himself, and bowing*]
I came—excuse me—by the latest whirl-wind
The ether clings to me. I've travelled far!
My eyes are filled with star-dust. On my spur
I still have shreds torn from a planet's hide!
[*Picking something from his sleeve*]
See, on my doublet, there's a comet's hair!
[*Puffs as if to blow it away*]

DE GUICHE [*beside himself*].
Monsieur!—

CYRANO [*just as he starts to pass, holds out his leg as if to show him something, and stops him*]
        And in my leg I bring a toot
From the Great Bear,—and as I passed the Trident
Trying to dodge one of its three sharp prongs,
I fell, and landed seated on the Scales,
Whose needle at this moment marks my weight

[*Quickly preventing* DE GUICHE *from passing, and taking him by the button of his doublet*]

If you should press my nose between your fingers,

It would spurt milk!—

DE GUICHE.   What? Milk?

CYRANO.   From the Milky Way!

DE GUICHE. Oh, by the lords of Hell!—

CYRANO.   'T is Heaven that sends me!

[*Folding his arms*] Now, would you think, I saw it as I fell,—

That Sirius, at night, puts on a cap?

[*Confidentially*] The other Bear is still too small to bite.

[*Smiling*] And as I crossed the Lyre, I broke a string.

[*Proudly*] But I shall write a book about it all,

And the golden stars, that in my scorchèd cloak

I brought away at my own risk and peril,

Will serve as asterisks when it is printed.

DE GUICHE. Finally, I insist—

CYRANO.   I catch your meaning!

DE GUICHE. Monsieur!

CYRANO. You wish to hear from my own mouth

Of what the moon is made, and if folk dwell

Within the roundness of this strange alembic?

DE GUICHE. No! No! I wish—

CYRANO.   To know how I ascended?

'Twas by a means that I devised myself.

DE GUICHE [*discouraged*]. He's mad!

CYRANO [*scornfully*]. I did not use the stupid eagle

Of Regiomontanus, nor the pigeon

Archytas used—

DE GUICHE. Mad! but a learnèd madman!

CYRANO. I followed naught that had been done before.

[DE GUICHE *has succeeded in passing, and is striding towards* ROXANE's *door.* CYRANO *follows him, ready to lay hold of him*]

Six ways did I devise to violate

The virgin Azure!

DE GUICHE [*turning*]. Six?

CYRANO [*volubly*].   I deck my body,

Naked as on the day that I was born,

With crystal phials filled up to the brim,

With tears dropped from the morning sky, and then

Expose me to the full blaze of the sun,

Which draws me up the while it drinks the dew,

DE GUICHE [*surprised and taking a step towards* CYRANO]. Yes, that makes one.

CYRANO [*drawing back to get him on the other side*].   And this too I could do:

Produce a whirlwind, and so take my flight,—

By rarefying air in a cedar chest

With burning mirrors in an icosahedron.

DE GUICHE [*taking another step*]. Two!

CYRANO [*still drawing back*].

Or, having skill of hand as well as brain,

On a grasshopper made with springs of steel,

Dart, with successive blasts of powder fired,

Through the blue pastures where the stars are grazing.

DE GUICHE [*following him without suspecting it, and counting on his fingers*].

Three!

CYRANO. And since all smoke must surely rise aloft,

Blow in a globe enough to bear me up.

DE GUICHE [*same action, more and more amazed*]. Four!

CYRANO. Since Diana, when her bow is smallest,

Loves, oh, ye oxen, to suck out your marrow!—

To anoint myself withal!

DE GUICHE [*in stupefaction*]. Five!

CYRANO [*who, while talking to him has led him to the other side of the street, near a bench*].   Finally,

Placing myself upon a plate of iron,

I take a magnet, and throw it in the air!

'Tis a good way—the iron rushes on

Fast as the magnet flies, and follows after.

Again I throw the magnet—there you are!

In this way I ascend without a limit.

DE GUICHE. Six! These be six good ways. What system, sir,

Of the six did you choose?

CYRANO.   I chose a seventh.

DE GUICHE. Really, what is it?

CYRANO.   You could never guess!

DE GUICHE. This rascal's growing interesting now.

CYRANO [*making the noise of the waves, with great, mysterious gestures*].

Hooüh! Hooüh!

DE GUICHE. Well?

CYRANO.   You guess?

DE GUICHE.   No.

CYRANO.   The tide!

At the hour when the moon doth draw the wave

I lay upon the sand,—after a bath,—

And the head led the way, my friend, because

The hair keeps so much water in its locks.

I rose in air, up, straight up, like an angel,

I ascended gently, softly, with no effort,

When suddenly I felt a shock,—then—

DE GUICHE [*carried away by curiosity, sitting down on the bench*].   Then?

CYRANO. Then—[*resuming his natural voice*]

The quarter hour has passed. I let you go.

The marriage is made.

DE GUICHE [*getting up with a bound*].

What! Come! Am I then drunk?

This voice?

[*The door of the house opens, and lackeys*

appear, carrying lighted candelabra. Light. CYRANO *takes off his hat with its lowered brim*]
This nose! Cyrano?
CYRANO [*bowing*]. Cyrano.
This very moment they've exchanged the rings.
DE GUICHE. Who are they?
[*He turns—Tableau. Behind the lackeys,* ROXANE *and* CHRISTIAN *hold hands. The* CAPUCHIN *follows them, smiling.* RAGUENEAU *also holds a torch.* THE DUENNA *closes the line, in great confusion, dressed in a wrapper*] Heavens! [*To* ROXANE]
You!
[*Recognizing* CHRISTIAN *with stupefaction*]
He?
[*Bowing to* ROXANE *with admiration*] A clever stroke!
[*To* CYRANO] My compliments, inventor of machines!
Your story would have made a saint stop short
At heaven's gate. Remember the details,
For it might well be turned into a book.
CYRANO [*bowing*].
Sir, that's advice that I engage to follow.
THE CAPUCHIN [*showing the lovers to* DE GUICHE, *and wagging his great white beard with satisfaction*].
A handsome pair, my son, joined there by you!
DE GUICHE [*giving him a frigid glance*]. Yes.
[*To* ROXANE] Be kind enough, Madame, to bid your husband
Farewell.
ROXANE. Why so?
DE GUICHE [*to* CHRISTIAN]. The troops are on the march.
Go join your regiment!
ROXANE. To go to war?
DE GUICHE. Of course.
ROXANE. But the Cadets, sir, do not go.
DE GUICHE. They'll go.
[*Drawing out the paper he had in his pocket*]
Here is the order.
[*To* CHRISTIAN] Take it, Baron!
ROXANE [*throwing herself into* CHRISTIAN'S *arms*].
Christian!
DE GUICHE [*sneeringly, to* CYRANO].
The wedding night is still far off!
CYRANO [*aside*]. To think that he believes that greatly pains me!
CHRISTIAN [*to* ROXANE]. Your lips again!
CYRANO. Come, come, that is enough!
CHRISTIAN [*continuing to embrace* ROXANE].
'Tis hard to leave her. You know not—
CYRANO [*trying to draw him away*]. Yes, I know.
[*Drums beating a march are heard in the distance*]
DE GUICHE [*who has retired to the background*].

The regiment is off!
ROXANE [*to* CYRANO, *holding back* CHRISTIAN *whom* CYRANO *still tries to draw away*]. I trust him to you!
O promise me that naught shall put his life
In danger.
CYRANO. I shall try—but cannot promise.
ROXANE [*same action*].
And promise that he shall be very careful!
CYRANO. Yes, I shall try, but—
ROXANE. In this fearful siege,
That he shall ne'er be cold.
CYRANO. I'll do my best
But—
ROXANE [*same action*]. That he shall be faithful—
CYRANO. Yes, of course,
But—
ROXANE [*same action*]. That he shall write often!
CYRANO [*stopping himself*]. That . . . I promise!

CURTAIN

FOURTH ACT

THE GASCON CADETS

The station occupied by CARBON DE CASTEL-JALOUX'S *company at the siege of Arras. In the background, a rampart crossing the entire stage. Beyond is seen a plain stretching away to the horizon; the country is covered with earth-works. The walls of Arras, and its roofs, silhouetted against the sky, in the far distance. Tents; arms scattered about, drums, etc. Day is about to dawn. The east is yellow. Sentinels stationed at intervals. Camp-fires. The* GASCON CADETS *are asleep, wrapped in their cloaks.* CARBON DE CASTEL-JALOUX *and* LE BRET *are on watch. They are pale and very thin.* CHRISTIAN *is asleep among the rest, wrapped in his cape in the foreground, his face lit by the firelight. Silence.*
LE BRET. 'T is frightful!
CARBON. Frightful!
LE BRET. Lord!
CARBON [*making a sign to him to speak lower*]. Swear in a whisper.
You'll waken them. [*To the* CADETS] Hush
Sleep. [*To* LE BRET] He who sleeps, dines
LE BRET. When one is sleepless, 't is lean far enough.
What famine!
[*Scattering shots heard in the distance*]
CARBON. Curses on these wretched shots!
They will awake my lads. [*To the* CADETS, *who raise their heads*] Sleep on!
[*They settle down again. More shots nearer*]

A CADET [moving]. The deuce! Again?

CARBON. 'T is nothing. Cyrano returns. [The heads which had been lifted fall again]

A SENTINEL [without]. Halt! Who goes there?

CYRANO'S VOICE. I! Bergerac!

THE SENTINEL ON THE RAMPART. The devil! Who's there?

CYRANO [appearing on top of the rampart]. Bergerac, fool!

LE BRET. Ah, thank the lord!

CYRANO [making a sign to him to awake no one]. Hush!

LE BRET. Wounded?

CYRANO. You know well they have a habit Of missing me each morning.

LE BRET. 'T is too much To risk your life to carry every day A letter—

CYRANO [stopping before CHRISTIAN]. But I gave my word he'd write. [Looks at him] He sleeps. He has grown pale. If the poor child Knew how he dies of hunger—but always fair!

LE BRET. Go straight to sleep.

CYRANO. Now do not scold, Le Bret— Know this: that where I pass the Spanish lines I've chosen a spot where they are always drunk.

LE BRET. Some day you should bring back some food for us.

CYRANO. I must go light to pass; and yet I know There'll be some news to-night. If I mistake not, The French will either eat or die.

LE BRET. Tell on!

CYRANO. No. I am not quite certain—you will see—

CARBON. To die of hunger while one lays a siege Is sorry warfare.

LE BRET. Ah! this siege of Arras Is a strange tangle, full of many knots: We besiege Arras;—caught in our own trap, The Cardinal-Prince of Spain besieges us.

CYRANO. Some one should come to besiege him in turn.

LE BRET. It is no laughing matter.

CYRANO. Oh!

LE BRET. To think That every day you risk a life like yours To carry— [Seeing him turn towards a tent] Whither now?

CYRANO. To write another! [Lifts the tent-flap and disappears. Day has just dawned. Rosy light. The town of Arras lies golden on the horizon. A cannon-shot is heard, followed immediately by a ruffle of drum, very distant, to the left. Other drums are heard near by.

The drum-beats answer each other, and coming together almost burst upon the scene; then withdraw towards the right, going through the camp. Noises of awakening. Distant voices of OFFICERS]

CARBON [with a sigh]. The reveille—alas! [The CADETS move in their cloaks and stretch themselves] Nourishing sleep! You cease; and what will be their cry I know Only too well!

A CADET [sitting up]. I'm hungry!

ANOTHER. I am dying!

ALL. Oh!

CARBON. Get up!

THIRD CADET. Not a movement!

FOURTH CADET. Not a step!

THE FIRST [looking at himself in a piece of his cuirass]. My tongue is yellow; this weather is unwholesome!

ANOTHER. My badge of barony for a bit of cheese!

ANOTHER. If no one will provide for my poor stomach Something on which the chyle may do its work, Achilles-like, I'll sulk within my tent.

ANOTHER. Bread!

CARBON [going into the tent into which CYRANO had entered: in a low voice]. Cyrano!

OTHERS. We're dying!

CARBON [still in a low voice, at the door of the tent]. To our aid! You who can always answer them so gaily, Come, cheer them up!

SECOND CADET [rushing at the first, who is chewing something]. What are you nibbling on?

THE FIRST. On cannon-wadding, fried with axle-grease, Cooked in a helmet. There is not much game Here around Arras.

ANOTHER [entering]. I'm just from the hunt.

ANOTHER [same action]. And in the river Scarpe I have been fishing.

ALL [standing and rushing upon the last comers]. What have you got—a pheasant, or a carp? Come, show them quickly!

THE FISHERMAN. A gudgeon.

THE HUNTER. And a sparrow.

ALL [exasperated]. Enough! Let's mutiny.

CARBON. Help, Cyrano! [It is now broad day]

CYRANO [coming out of his tent, placid, a pen over his ear, a book in his hand]. Well? [Silence. To the FIRST CADET] Why are you walking with this lagging step?

THE CADET. I've something in my heels which troubles me.

CYRANO. And what is that?

THE CADET.   My stomach.
CYRANO.   So have I.
THE CADET. Does it not trouble you?
CYRANO.   It makes me tall.
SECOND CADET. I have long teeth.
CYRANO.   You'll get the bigger bite.
A THIRD. My stomach's hollow.
CYRANO.   We'll use it for a drum.
ANOTHER. And as for me, I've buzzings in
    my ears.
CYRANO. No, no! A famished stomach, not
    your ears!
ANOTHER. Oh, to eat something—dressed
    with oil!
CYRANO [*taking off the* CADET's *helmet and
    putting it in his hand*].   Your sallet!
ANOTHER. Is there naught to devour?
CYRANO [*tossing him the book he holds in
    his hand*].   Try my Homer!
ANOTHER. The Minister at home has four
    good meals.
CYRANO. Should he send you a partridge?
THE SAME.   Well, why not?
And wine.
CYRANO. Some Burgundy, Richelieu, if you
    please!
THE SAME. By some good Capuchin.
CYRANO.   His highness gray?
ANOTHER. I'm hungry as a bear.
CYRANO.   Eat your own fat then!
FIRST CADET [*shrugging his shoulders*].
That is your way—to jest, to score your
    point.
CYRANO. Ah, yes, the jest, the point!—and
    well I hope
That I may die some night, 'neath rosy skies,
For a good cause, and making a good jest.
Oh, to fall by the only noble weapon,
Struck by a foeman worthy of one's self,—
Fall on the field of glory, not the sick-bed,
With point in heart, as well as on one's lips!
CRY OF ALL. I'm hungry!
CYRANO [*crossing his arms*]. Shame! you
    think of naught but food.
Come, Bertrandou, the fifer, once a shepherd,
Take from its leathern case one of your fifes.
Blow! and play for this pack of lazy gluttons
The old airs of our home, that hold us fast,—
In which each note is like a little sister;
In which are caught the tones of voices dear—
Airs sweet and slow, like to the curling smoke
That rises from the village of our birth,—
These melodies which speak our native tongue.
    [*The old man sits down and prepares his
    fife*]
And let the warlike fife, that grieves to-day,
Bethink itself a moment—while your fingers
Dance up and down its length like darting
    birds—
That ere 'twas wrought of ebony, 'twas a reed;
And let it marvel at its song, and find
Sweet memories of its peaceful, rustic youth.

    [*The old man begins to play airs of the
    South of France*]
List, Gascons,—'neath his fingers 'tis no longer
The camp's shrill fife, it is the forest's flute;
And from his lips no battle-blast is blown,
'T is the slow whistle of our humble goatherds.
List, Gascons,—'tis the vale, the plain, the
    forest;
The sunbrowned herdsman with his bonnet red;
The Dordogne, with its evenings green and
    sweet.
List, Gascons,—'tis the whole of Gascony!
    [*All heads are bowed; all eyes are dreamy.
    Tears are furtively wiped away on the
    backs of sleeves and corners of cloaks*]
    CARBON [*to* CYRANO, *aside*]. But you have
        made them weep.
    CYRANO.   Only homesickness.
A nobler ill than hunger: mind, not body.
'T is well their pains should strike another organ,
And that it is their hearts which now are wrung.
    CARBON. But when you touch their hearts
        you weaken them.
    CYRANO [*signalling to the drummer to ap-
        proach*].
Withhold your blame. The courage in their
    blood
Awakens quickly. 'T is enough—
    [*Makes a gesture. The drum is sounded*]
    ALL [*rising and rushing to arms*]. What!
        What!
    CYRANO [*smiling*].
One ruffle of the drum's enough, you see.
Farewell regrets, dreams, love, and province
    old!
The drum soon drives away what the fife
    brought!
    A CADET [*looking into the distance*].
Ah! There's Monsieur de Guiche.
    ALL THE CADETS [*murmuring*]. Hoo!
    CYRANO [*smiling*].   Flattering sound!
    A CADET. He wearies us!
    ANOTHER.   With his great ruff of lace
Over his armor—he comes to show it off.
    ANOTHER. It is like wearing cambric over
        steel.
    THE FIRST. It's good—if you have boils upon
        your neck.
    THE SECOND. A courtier still.
    ANOTHER.   The nephew of his uncle.
    CARBON. Yet he's a Gascon.
    THE FIRST.   Trust him not. He's false.
Because the Gascons—really—should be mad.
A Gascon with his wits is dangerous.
    LE BRET. He's pale.
    ANOTHER. He's hungry, like the rest of us
But since his armor's gay with silver-gilt
His belly-pangs but sparkle in the sun.
    CYRANO [*quickly*].
Let us no longer seem to be in pain.
Your cards, your pipes, your dice!—
    [*All quickly begin their games,—on the*

drums, on the benches, and on their cloaks spread on the ground; and they light long pipes of tobacco]
I read Descartes.
*[Walks up and down, and reads a little book which he has taken out of his pocket. Tableau—*DE GUICHE *enters; everyone seems absorbed and contented. He is very pale. He goes toward* CARBON]

DE GUICHE *[to* CARBON]. Good day! *[They both look at each other] [Aside, with satisfaction]* He's turning green.

CARBON *[same tone]*. He's naught but eyes.

DE GUICHE *[looking at the Cadets]*.
Are these the malcontents?—Yes, gentlemen,
I hear I am lampooned on every side:
And that, among your aristocracy
Bred on a mountain-side, in Périgord
Or Béarn, you cannot find hard words enough
For your commander,—calling me a trickster,
A shallow courtier; that it troubles you
To see a point-lace collar on my cuirass;
And that you never cease to take it ill
That every Gascon need not be a beggar.
[Silence. They play; they smoke]
Shall I then have you punished by your Captain?
No!

CARBON. I am free and give no punishments.

DE GUICHE. Ah!

CARBON. I've paid my company. It is my own:
And as a soldier only I obey.

DE GUICHE. Indeed! That is enough.
[Addressing the CADETS] I can despise
Your mockery. You know how I stand fire.
Yesterday, at Bapaume, you saw full well
How furiously I put to flight the Count
Of Bucquoi. Like an avalanche I hurled
My men on his: thrice and again I charged.

CYRANO *[without lifting his face from his book]*.
And your white scarf?

DE GUICHE *[surprised and satisfied]*. You know that detail too?
It came about, that as I wheeled my horse,
Rallying my soldiers for the final charge,
A pack of fugitives dragged me along
Close to the enemy's ranks. I was in danger
Of being taken prisoner and shot;
When I had wit enough to drop to earth
The scarf that showed my military rank,
And so was able to escape the Spaniards
Without their recognition,—then return,
Leading my rallied force, and win the fight!
—What say you of this feat?
[The CADETS *appear not to listen; but their cards and dice-boxes remain in the air, the smoke of their pipes in their cheeks. A pause]*

CYRANO. That Henry Fourth
Would never have agreed, 'gainst any odds,

To take one feather from his snow-white crest.
[Silent joy. The cards fall, the dice drop, the smoke escapes]

DE GUICHE. But still the ruse succeeded!
[Same wait; while games and smoke are suspended]

CYRANO. Like enough.
But it is not an honor lightly yielded,—
To be a target.
[Cards fall, dice drop, smoke rises, with growing satisfaction] Now, had I been there
When the abandoned scarf fell to the ground—
Our kinds of courage differ, sir, in this—
I should have picked it up and put it on.

DE GUICHE. Yes, Gascon boasting still!

CYRANO. You call it boasting?
Lend it to me,—and on this very night
I'll lead the assault, with the scarf draped about me.

DE GUICHE. Another Gascon offer! You know well
The scarf was lost within the foemen's lines,
By the River Scarpe, where, swept by leaden hail,
No one can go to seek it.

CYRANO *[taking the white scarf from his pocket, and handing it to him]*. Here it is!
[Silence. The CADETS *smother their laughter under their cards and dice-boxes. De* GUICHE *turns and looks at them; they immediately become serious again, and begin their games. One of them whistles the mountain melody played by the fife]*

DE GUICHE *[taking the scarf]*.
Thanks. With this piece of white I shall be able
To give a signal—I was loath to give.
[Goes to the rampart, climbs it, and waves the scarf several times in the air]

ALL. What?

THE SENTINEL *[on top of the rampart]*. See the man down there, who's running hither!

DE GUICHE *[coming down again]*.
He's a pretended spy. He renders us
Great service; for the tidings that he takes
To the enemy are those I give myself;
And so I have a chance to shape their plans.

CYRANO. A scurvy trick!

DE GUICHE *[carelessly tying on his scarf]*.
It works! As we were saying—
Ah, I was about to tell some news. To-night,
Making one effort more to get us food,
The Marshal goes to Dourlens, without drums.
The King's provision-trains are there. He'll join them
By going through the fields; but to get back
With ease, he's taken with him such a force
The foe will have a fair field for attack,
With half the army absent from the camp.

CARBON. Yes, if the Spaniards knew, it would go hard;
But do they know this sally?

DE GUICHE. Yes, they know.
They will attack us.

CARBON Ah!

DE GUICHE. My false spy came
To warn me of their near assault. He said:
"I can decide for them the very spot.—
At what point do you wish the battle fought?
I'll tell them that it is the least defended,—
And there they'll try their hand."

I answered him:
" 'T is well. Go from the camp. Watch the
whole line;—
'T will be the spot where I shall give the signal."

CARBON [to the CADETS].
Make ready, gentlemen.

[All rise. Noise of swords, and buckling of
belts]

DE GUICHE. 'T is in an hour.

FIRST CADET. Ah!

[All sit down again, and take up the
interrupted game]

DE GUICHE. You must gain time. The Marshal will return.

CARBON. And to gain time?

DE GUICHE. You will have the great kindness
To give your lives!

CYRANO. Ah,—is this vengeance, then?

DE GUICHE. I shall make no pretense that,
had I loved you,
I should have chosen you for this defense.
But since none vie with you in reckless daring,
I serve my King and satisfy my grudge.

CYRANO. Permit me, sir, to express my gratitude.

DE GUICHE. I know you like to fight—one
to a hundred!
You'll not complain that you lack such a task.

[Goes aside with CARBON]

CYRANO [to the CADETS].
'T is well! We shall add to the Gascon blazon,
Which bears six chevrons, sirs—azure and or,
One chevron more of gules—which still was
lacking.

[DE GUICHE talks aside with CARBON DE
CASTEL-JALOUX, in the background.
Orders are given. The defense is made
ready. CYRANO goes to CHRISTIAN, who
has remained motionless, his arms
crossed]

CYRANO [putting his hand on his shoulder].
Christian?

CHRISTIAN [shaking his head]. Roxane!

CYRANO. Alas!

CHRISTIAN. At least, I wish
That I might put my heart's farewell entire
Into one last sweet letter!

CYRANO. I had no doubt
The end would come to-day—
[Takes a letter from his doublet] And I have
made
Your farewells for you.

CHRISTIAN. Show it.

CYRANO. Do you wish?

CHRISTIAN [taking the letter].
Why, yes! [Opens it, reads and stops] Here?

CYRANO. What?

CHRISTIAN. This little spot?

CYRANO [taking the letter quickly and looking at it with an innocent air]. A spot?

CHRISTIAN. It is a tear.

CYRANO. Why, so it is! A poet
Is caught at his own game. That is the charm!
You understand—this note, 'tis very moving;
It made me weep, myself, while writing.

CHRISTIAN. Weep?

CYRANO. Why, yes; because—to die is noth-
ing much;
But—see her ne'er again! Aye, there's the rub!
For I shall never— [CHRISTIAN looks at him]
We shall ne'er— [Sharply] You will—

CHRISTIAN [snatching the letter from him]
Give me this letter.

[A noise in the distance in the camp]

VOICE OF A SENTINEL. Halt there! Who goes
there?

[Shots. Sounds of voices. Rattle of bells]

CARBON. What is 't?

THE SENTINEL [on the rampart]. A carriage.

CRIES. What, here—in the camp?
It enters! It seems from the enemy!
Fire— No! The driver shouts— Shouts what?
He shouts:
"On the King's service!"

[Everyone is on the ramparts looking out.
The bells approach]

DE GUICHE. What, the King?

[They come down and fall in line]

CARBON. Hats off!

DE GUICHE [from the wings].
From the King.—Take your places, wretched
rabble!
That he may enter in befitting state.

[The carriage enters at full speed,—
covered with mud and dust, curtains
drawn, two grooms behind,—and stops
short]

CARBON [shouting].
Beat the assembly! [Ruffle of drums. All the
CADETS uncover] Lower the step!

[Two men rush forward, the door opens]

ROXANE [jumping from the carriage]. Good
morning!

[The sound of a woman's voice raises the
whole line, which was bowing low. Blank
amazement]

DE GUICHE. On the King's service! You?

ROXANE. The sole King, Love!

CYRANO. Good God!

CHRISTIAN [rushing forward]. You! Why?

ROXANE. This siege was far too long.

CHRISTIAN. Why?

ROXANE. I'll tell you.

CYRANO [who at the sound of her voice has
remained motionless, rooted to the spot

without daring to turn his eyes toward her]. God! now dare I look at her!

DE GUICHE. You cannot stay here.

ROXANE [*gaily*].   Oh, yes—but I can!
Will you hand me a drum? [*Sits down on a drum which is handed to her. She laughs*]

There! Many thanks.
They fired on my carriage! [*Proudly*] A patrol!
It looks made of a pumpkin, does it not?
As in the fairy-tale; and the lackeys changed
From rats. [*Throwing a kiss to* CHRISTIAN]
Good morning! [*Looking at all of them*]
You do not look gay.
You know 'tis far to Arras? [*Seeing* CYRANO]
Cousin, I'm charmed!

CYRANO [*advancing*].
But how, Madame?—

ROXANE.   How did I find the army?
Heavens, my friend, 'twas simple: I but went
Where'er I saw the land laid waste. Such horrors!
I should not have believed, had I not seen.
If that, sirs, be the service of your King,
Mine is far better.

CYRANO.   Well, but this is mad.
Where did you pass, and how did you get through?

ROXANE. Where? Through the Spanish lines!

FIRST CADET.   An evil lot!

DE GUICHE. But how did you contrive to pass their lines?

LE BRET. It must have been no easy task.

ROXANE.   Why, yes!
I simply sent my carriage at full speed:
If a hidalgo showed his lofty air,
I merely beamed on him my sweetest smile.
And, as the Spaniards are the most gallant folk
In the world,—no offense to the French,—I passed.

CARBON. Yes, 'tis a passport sure, that smile of yours.
But still they often must have asked of you
Whither you went at such a pace, Madame?

ROXANE. They often did: and then I always answered:
"I go to see my lover!" Then the Spaniard,
E'en of the fiercest air, would gravely close
My carriage door,—and, with a courtly gesture
The King himself would envy, wave away
The guns already levelled at my breast;
And—gorgeous in his grace and in his pride,
While his spurs clanked beneath his mantle's train,
And his hat waved its sweeping plumes in air—
He would bow low, and say: "Pass, Señorita!"

CHRISTIAN. But—

ROXANE. I said, "My lover," yes; but, pardon me,—
You understand, if I had said, "My husband,"
None would have let me pass.

CHRISTIAN.   But—

ROXANE.   What's the matter?

DE GUICHE. You must depart.

ROXANE.   I?

CYRANO.   Quickly.

LE BRET.   Yes, at once!

CHRISTIAN. Yes!

ROXANE.   Why?

CHRISTIAN [*embarrassed*]. The fact is—

CYRANO [*same tone*]. In the next half-hour—

DE GUICHE [*same tone*]. About—

CARBON [*same tone*]. 'Tis better—

LE BRET [*same tone*].   You might—

ROXANE.   I shall stay.
A battle's near!

ALL.   Oh, no!

ROXANE.   This is my husband!
[*Throws herself in* CHRISTIAN'S *arms*]
Let me be slain with him.

CHRISTIAN.   What eyes you have!

ROXANE. I'll tell you why.

DE GUICHE [*in despair*]. This is a fearful post!

ROXANE [*turning*]. What! fearful?

CYRANO.   And in proof, he's given it
To us.

ROXANE [*to* DE GUICHE]. Ah! then you wish me widowed?

DE GUICHE. I swear!—

ROXANE. No, I am somewhat mad just now.
I shall not go away—and 'tis amusing.

CYRANO. What! Has Madame become a heroine?

ROXANE. Monsieur le Bergerac, I am your cousin.

A CADET. We will defend you.

ROXANE [*catching the fever more and more*].
Friends, that I believe!

ANOTHER [*in delight*].
The whole camp smells of iris.

ROXANE.   I have on
A hat which will look very well in battle.
[*Looking at* DE GUICHE]
Perchance 'tis time the Count should go away,—
They might begin!

DE GUICHE.   This is too much! I go
To inspect my cannon, and return at once.
You still have time; pray change your mind.

ROXANE.   No, never!
[*Exit* DE GUICHE]

CHRISTIAN [*pleading*]. Roxane!—

ROXANE.   No!

FIRST CADET [*to the others*]. She will stay.

ALL [*rushing about and jostling each other as they try to make themselves presentable*].   A comb— A brush—
Some soap— My clothes are torn; give me a needle—
A ribbon— Here, your mirror— Now, my gauntlets!—
Your curling-irons—and a razor,—quick!

ROXANE [*to* CYRANO, *who still pleads with her*].

No,—naught shall make me stir from out this
  place!
CARBON [*after having, like the rest, tightened
  his belt, dusted his clothes, brushed his hat,
  arranged his plume, and drawn on his
  gauntlets, advances towards* ROXANE *and
  with great ceremony*].
Perhaps it would be fitting to present,
Since the affair stands thus, these gentlemen,
Who'll have the honor to die before your eyes.
    [ROXANE *bows and waits, on* CHRISTIAN'S
      arm, standing. CARBON *introduces*]
Baron de Peyrescous de Colignac.
    THE CADET [*bowing*].   Madame!
    CARBON [*continuing*].
Baron de Casterac de Cahuzac;
The Vidame de Malgouyre Estressac Lésbas
  d'Escarabiot;
Chevalier d'Antignac-Juzet;
Baron Hillot de Blagnac-Saléchan de Castel-
  Crabioules.
    ROXANE. How many names has each of
      you?
    BARON HILLOT.   A string.
    CARBON. Open the hand that holds your
      kerchief.
    ROXANE [*opens her hand and the handker-
      chief falls*].   Why?
    [*The whole company rushes forward to
      pick it up*]
    CARBON [*picking it up quickly*].
My company had no standard. But, in faith,
The finest in the camp floats o'er it now!
    ROXANE [*smiling*]. 'T is rather small.
    CARBON [*tying the kerchief to the staff of his
      captain's lance*]. But it is all of lace.
    A CADET [*to the others*].
I should die gladly, having seen this vision,
If I had only one small bite to eat.
    CARBON [*who had heard him; indignantly*].
Shame,—speak of eating when a lady fair—
    ROXANE. But the camp's air is sharp,—I'm
      hungry too,—
Pasties, and game, and wines—that is my
  choice.
Will you be kind enough to bring them?
    [*Consternation*]
    A CADET.   All?
    ANOTHER. Good Lord! Where shall we get
      them?
    ROXANE [*tranquilly*].   In my carriage.
    ALL. What!
    ROXANE.   But they must be boned, and
      carved, and served.
Look at my coachman closer, gentlemen,
And you will recognize a very genius.
Each sauce shall be served hot, if you prefer.
    THE CADETS [*rushing towards the carriage*].
T' is Ragueneau. [*Acclamations*]
                  Oh, oh!
    ROXANE [*following them with her eyes*].
                  Poor boys!

CYRANO [*kissing her hand*]. Good fairy!
RAGUENEAU [*standing on the seat like a
  charlatan in a public square*].
Gentlemen—
    [*Enthusiasm*]
    THE CADETS. Bravo! Bravo!
    RAGUENEAU.   The Spaniards failed
To see the feast, when the feast of beauty
  passed.
    [*Applause.* CYRANO *talks aside to* CHRIS-
      TIAN]
    RAGUENEAU. So taken up with gallantry they
      were
They never saw [*takes from the seat a dish,
  which he lifts up*] the galantine!
    [*Applause. The galantine is passed from
      hand to hand*]
    CYRANO [*aside to* CHRISTIAN].   I beg you,
One word!
    RAGUENEAU. And Venus so filled every eye
That secretly Diana brought away [*Brandishes
  a leg of venison*]
The trophies of her hunt.
    [*Enthusiasm. The leg is seized by twenty
      outstretched hands*]
    CYRANO [*aside to* CHRISTIAN]. I must speak
      with you.
    ROXANE [*to the* CADETS, *who come down,
      their arms full of provisions*].
Spread this upon the ground. [*Lays a cloth
  on the grass, aided by the two footmen
  who were behind the carriage. To* CHRIS-
  TIAN]   Make yourself useful!
    [CHRISTIAN *goes to help her.* CYRANO
      makes a restless movement]
    RAGUENEAU. A truffled peacock!
    FIRST CADET [*radiantly, coming down while
      cutting a large slice of ham*]. Thunder!
      we shall have
One royal gorge at least, before we die—
    [*Quickly catching himself up as he sees* ROXANE]
—A royal feast, I mean,—I beg your pardon!
    RAGUENEAU [*tossing out the cushions of the
      carriage*].
The cushions are all stuffed with ortolans!
    [*Great tumult. The cushions are ripped up.
      Laughter and joy*]
    THIRD CADET. Ah!
    RAGUENEAU [*tossing out bottles of red wine*].
      Flasks of rubies!   [*Of white wine*]
                        Flasks of topaz, too!
    ROXANE [*throwing a folded tablecloth into
      CYRANO's face*].
Unfold this cloth—catch it—and look alive!
    RAGUENEAU [*waving one of the carriage-
      lamps, which he has wrenched off*].
And every lantern is a little cupboard.
    CYRANO [*aside to* CHRISTIAN, *while they to-
      gether arrange the cloth*].
I must speak with you, ere you speak to her.
    RAGUENEAU [*more and more rhapsodical*].
Even my whip-handle is a giant sausage!

ROXANE [*pouring wine and serving*].
Since they will kill us—heavens! let us laugh
At all the rest. Everything for the Gascons!
If De Guiche come, let no one bid him sit.
[*Going from one to another*]
There, you have time enough—don't eat so
fast—
But drink a little!—Why these tears?
FIRST CADET.   'T is too good!—
ROXANE. Tush!—red or white?—Bread for
Monsieur de Carbon.
A knife—your plate!—Some champagne? Or
a wing?
CYRANO [*who follows her, his arms full of
plates, helping her wait*]. I love her!
ROXANE [*going towards* CHRISTIAN]. You?
CHRISTIAN.   No, nothing.
ROXANE.   Yes, this biscuit,
Dipped in some muscatel,—two fingers only!
CHRISTIAN [*trying to detain her*].
Oh, tell me why you came!
ROXANE.   My duty now
Is to these luckless lads. Hush!—in a moment.
LE BRET [*who has gone to the background, to
hand up to the* SENTINEL *on the rampart a
loaf of bread on the end of a lance*].
De Guiche!
CYRANO. Quick, hide the bottles, plates, and
baskets!
Let us show nothing! [*To* RAGUENEAU]
Get back on your box!
Is all well hidden?
[*In a twinkling everything is pushed into
the tents, or hidden under their clothes,
their cloaks, or their hats.* DE GUICHE
*enters briskly—and stops suddenly, snif-
fing. Silence*]
DE GUICHE.   That smells good.
A CADET [*humming, with a preoccupied air*].
To-lo—
DE GUICHE [*stopping and looking at him*].
What is the matter with you? You're quite
red.
THE CADET. I? Nothing—'tis my blood.—
We'll fight—it starts—
ANOTHER. Poum, poum!
DE GUICHE [*turning*].   What's that?
THE CADET [*slightly intoxicated*]. Nothing
—a little song!
DE GUICHE. You're gay, my lad.
THE CADET. 'T is the approach of danger.
DE GUICHE [*calling* CARBON DE CASTEL-
JALOUX *to give an order*]. Here, Captain,
I—
[*Stops, looking at him*] The deuce! you're
cheerful too!
CARBON [*blushing scarlet, and hiding a bottle
behind his back with furtive movement*].
Oh!
DE GUICHE. There is left one cannon I've
had brought.
[*Points to a place in the wing*]

There, in the corner—use it, if you need.
A CADET [*strutting about*].
Charming attention!
ANOTHER [*smiling at him graciously*].
Kindly thoughtfulness!
DE GUICHE. Oh! they are mad! [*Drily*]
And being quite unused
To cannon, take good heed to the recoil.
FIRST CADET. Oh, pfft!
DE GUICHE [*going to him, furious*]. But!—
THE CADET.   Gascon guns never recoil.
DE GUICHE [*taking him by the arm and
shaking him*]. You're drunk!—on what?
THE CADET [*superbly*]. Upon the smell of
powder.
DE GUICHE [*shrugging his shoulders, push-
ing him away and going quickly to*
ROXANE]. Quick, Madame. What have you
resolved to do?
ROXANE. I stay.
DE GUICHE.   Flee!
ROXANE.   No!
DE GUICHE.   Well, since
the case stands thus,
Give me a musket!
CARBON.   What!
DE GUICHE.   I also stay.
CYRANO. But, sir, this savors somewhat of
bravado.
FIRST CADET. You are a Gascon, then, de-
spite your lace?
DE GUICHE. I do not leave a woman in
distress.
SECOND CADET [*to the* FIRST].
Really! I think we well might give him food.
[*All the provisions reappear as if by magic*]
DE GUICHE [*his eyes lighting up*].
Provisions!
THIRD CADET. Yes, they came from every
cloak.
DE GUICHE [*mastering himself, and with
dignity*].
Do you then think that I will eat your leavings?
CYRANO [*bowing*].
You're making progress now.
DE GUICHE [*proudly*]. I shall fight fasting.
FIRST CADET [*exulting with delight*].
There spoke a Gascon.
DE GUICHE [*smiling*]. I?
THE CADET.   He's one of us!
[*All begin to dance*]
CARBON DE CASTEL-JALOUX [*who has disap-
peared for a moment behind the rampart,
reappearing on top*].
I've placed my lancers there, in open order.
[*Points out a line of pikes over the top of
the rampart*]
DE GUICHE [*to* ROXANE, *bowing*].
Will you accept my hand for the review?
[*She takes it, and they go toward the ram-
part. Everyone uncovers, and follows
them*]

CHRISTIAN [*going to* CYRANO *quickly*].
Speak quick!

[*At the moment when* ROXANE *appears on
the top of the rampart, the lances disappear, lowered in the salute; a shout is
raised; she bows*]

THE LANCERS [*without*]. Hurrah! Hurrah!

CHRISTIAN. What was the secret?

CYRANO. If perchance Roxane—

CHRISTIAN. Well!

CYRANO. Should speak to you
Of letters—

CHRISTIAN. Oh, I know!—

CYRANO. Have not the folly
To show surprise.

CHRISTIAN. At what?

CYRANO. Well, I must tell you—
Oh, Lord! 'twas simple, as I see to-day,
When I see her. You have—

CHRISTIAN. Speak quick!

CYRANO. You have
Written her oftener than you think.

CHRISTIAN. How's that?

CYRANO. I took it on myself, and was your
spokesman!
I sometimes wrote, and never let you know.

CHRISTIAN. Ah?

CYRANO. It was simple.

CHRISTIAN. How did you contrive it?
Since the blockade—

CYRANO. Oh, I could pass ere daybreak.

CHRISTIAN [*folding his arms*].
And that was simple, too? How many times
A week have I then written—two? three?
four?

CYRANO. Oftener.

CHRISTIAN. Every day?

CYRANO. Yes—twice a day.

CHRISTIAN [*violently*].
And that made you so drunk with sheer delight
That you braved death—

CYRANO [*seeing* ROXANE *returning*]. Hush!
Hush! Not before her!

[*Quickly goes back into his tent*]

ROXANE [*running to* CHRISTIAN].
And now, Christian!—

CHRISTIAN [*taking her hands*]. And now;
now tell me why,
By frightful roads, through this rough soldiery,
You came to join me here?

ROXANE. It was your letters!

CHRISTIAN. What?

ROXANE. The worse for you, if I have
risked these dangers.
Your letters turned my head. Ah, think how
many
You've written me this month; and every
one
Was better than the last!

CHRISTIAN. What, for a few
Little love-letters—

ROXANE. Hush, you cannot know!

'T is true I've worshipped you since on that
evening,
Beneath my window—with a voice whose tones
I had not heard before—your soul began
To make itself known to me. Well, your letters,
You see, for this past month, have been the
same
As listening to your voice the livelong day,—
Your voice, as 'twas that evening, soft and
tender—
Like a caress. The worse for you, I came!
For had Ulysses written words like yours
Penelope would ne'er have stayed at home
And plied her spinning-wheel; but mad like
Helen
She would have sent her fleeces all a-packing,
And gone to seek her husband.

CHRISTIAN. But—

ROXANE. I read—
I read again. I felt myself grow faint.
I was your own; and every little page
Was like a petal flying from your soul.
I felt, in each word of your burning letters,
Your love—strong and sincere.

CHRISTIAN. Sincere and strong?
You felt it there, Roxane?

ROXANE. Indeed, I did!

CHRISTIAN. And you have come?

ROXANE. Oh, Christian!
Oh, my master!
(You'd raise me up if I should cast myself
Down at your knees! But 'tis my soul I cast;
And you will ne'er be able to raise that up.)
I come to crave your pardon. 'T is the hour
To pray for pardon—since death stands close
at hand—
For having lightly loved you at the first,
Moved only by your comeliness.

CHRISTIAN [*with alarm*]. Roxane!

ROXANE. Later, dear friend, growing less
frivolous,—
A bird that hops before he quite can fly,—
Your soul fast holding what your looks had
caught,
I loved you for them both at once!

CHRISTIAN. And now?

ROXANE. Now, 'tis yourself that doth out-
shine yourself;
And for your soul alone I love you now.

CHRISTIAN [*recoiling*]. Roxane!

ROXANE. Be happy, then; since to be loved
For what is but the fleeting moment's dress
Must wring with pain a noble, glowing heart.
But now your well-loved thought is what I see!
The comeliness with which you pleased me first
I see more clearly—yet I see it not.

CHRISTIAN. Oh!

ROXANE. You have doubts of such
a victory?

CHRISTIAN [*sadly*]. Roxane!

ROXANE. I know you cannot yet believe
This love of mine—

CHRISTIAN. I care not for this love!
I would be loved more simply, for—
ROXANE. For what
Women have loved in you until this hour?
Now let yourself be loved in nobler fashion!
CHRISTIAN. No. Better as it was!
ROXANE. You do not see!
'Tis now that I love more,—that I love most.
'Tis what makes you yourself that I adore;—
And even less fair—
CHRISTIAN. Hush!
ROXANE. I'd love you still,
If you should lose all comeliness at once—
CHRISTIAN. Oh, say not so!
ROXANE. 'T is what I mean!
CHRISTIAN. What! ugly?
ROXANE. Ugly. I swear it!
CHRISTIAN. God!
ROXANE. Your joy is deep?
CHRISTIAN [with smothered voice]. Yes.
ROXANE. What's the matter?
CHRISTIAN [pushing her away gently]. Nothing,—a word,—a moment.
ROXANE. But—
CHRISTIAN [pointing out a group of CADETS in the background].
From these poor lads my love takes you away!
Go,—smile on them a little, ere they die—
ROXANE [much moved]. Dear Christian!
[Goes toward the GASCONS, who crowd respectfully around her]
CHRISTIAN [calling toward CYRANO's tent]. Cyrano!
CYRANO [reappearing, armed for battle]. What? You are pale!
CHRISTIAN. No longer does she love me!
CYRANO. What?
CHRISTIAN. 'T is you.
CYRANO. No!
CHRISTIAN. 'T is my soul she loves.
CYRANO. No.
CHRISTIAN. Yes, 'tis so.
'T is really you she loves;—you love her, too!
CYRANO. I?
CHRISTIAN. I know it!
CYRANO It is true!
CHRISTIAN. Madly!
CYRANO. Yes, more!
CHRISTIAN. Tell her.
CYRANO. No!
CHRISTIAN. Why not?
CYRANO. Why look at my face!
CHRISTIAN. She'd love me—ugly.
CYRANO. Did she tell you so?
CHRISTIAN. She did.
CYRANO. Ah, I am glad she told you that!
But stop,—do not believe this foolish thing.
God! I am glad she even had the thought
To say so! Do not take her at her word.
Become not ugly;—she'd bear me a grudge!
CHRISTIAN. That's what I wish to see.

CYRANO. No!
CHRISTIAN. Let her choose!
For you shall tell her all.
CYRANO. No, not this torture!
CHRISTIAN. Shall I then kill your joy,—
since I am fair?
'T is too unjust!
CYRANO. And shall I bury yours?—
Because, thanks to the hazard of my birth,
I have the gift of putting into words
That which perchance you feel?
CHRISTIAN. Yes, tell her all.
CYRANO. He will insist on tempting me!
'T is sad.
CHRISTIAN. I'm weary of this rival in myself.
CYRANO. Christian!
CHRISTIAN. Our union—secret, all unknown—
May break, if we survive!
CYRANO. He still insists!—
CHRISTIAN. I must be loved myself, or not at all!
I go to see what is on foot—I go
To the end of our lines; then I return.
Speak! let her choose between us.
CYRANO. T' will be you.
CHRISTIAN. But—that I hope. [Calls] Roxane!
CYRANO. No! No!
ROXANE [running up]. What is it?
CHRISTIAN. Cyrano has important news to tell.
[She goes quickly to CYRANO. CHRISTIAN goes out]
ROXANE. Something important?—
CYRANO [in desperation]. He has gone—'Twas nothing.
He makes much out of little. You should know him
Better by this time.
ROXANE [quickly]. He did not believe
What I just said. I saw he had his doubts.
CYRANO [taking her hand].
But did you, then, tell him the very truth?
ROXANE. Yes, I should love him, e'en [hesitates a second]—
CYRANO [smiling sadly]. It troubles you
To say the word before me?
ROXANE. But—
CYRANO. 'Twill not
Hurt me.— E'en ugly?
ROXANE. Yes. [Musketry without] Ah, there's a shot!
CYRANO. Hideous?
ROXANE. Hideous!
CYRANO. Disfigured?
ROXANE. Yes.
CYRANO. Grotesque?
ROXANE. But naught could make him that to me!
CYRANO. You still would love him!

ROXANE. Yes, and even more!
CYRANO [*losing his head. Aside*].
My God,—perhaps 'tis true; and bliss at last!
[*To* ROXANE]
I—Roxane, listen—
LE BRET [*entering rapidly, calls in a low voice*]. Cyrano!
CYRANO [*turning*]. What?
LE BRET. Hush!
[*Speaks to him inaudibly*]
CYRANO [*dropping* ROXANE'S *hand with a cry*]. Ah!
ROXANE. What's the matter?
CYRANO [*to himself in stupefaction*]. It is done.
ROXANE. What now!
They fire?
[*Climbs up to look out*]
CYRANO. 'Tis done. I ne'er can tell you now.
ROXANE [*wishing to rush forward*].
What's going on?
CYRANO [*quickly stopping her*]. Nothing!
[*Some Cadets enter, concealing something which they are carrying; and forming a group, they prevent* ROXANE *from approaching*]
ROXANE. These men!
CYRANO [*drawing her away*]. Let be—
I was about to tell you? Nothing, nothing!
I swear it, Madame. [*Solemnly*] I swear that Christian's spirit
And Christian's soul were— [*stopping himself in alarm*] —are the greatest—
ROXANE. Were?
[*With a great cry*] Oh! [*Rushes forward and scatters every one*]
CYRANO. It is done!
ROXANE [*seeing* CHRISTIAN *wrapped in his cloak*] Christian!
LE BRET [*to* CYRANO]. The foe's first fire!
[ROXANE *throws herself on* CHRISTIAN's *body. More firing. Rattling of arms. Drums*]
CARBON [*sword in hand*].
'Tis the attack! To arms!
[*Followed by the Cadets, he goes to the other side of the rampart*]
ROXANE. Christian!
CARBON'S VOICE [*behind the rampart*].
Make haste.
ROXANE. Christian!
CARBON. Fall in!
ROXANE. Christian!
CARBON. Measure—fuses!
[RAGUENEAU *runs up, with water in a helmet*]
CHRISTIAN [*with dying voice*]. Roxane!
CYRANO [*quick and aside in* CHRISTIAN's *ear; while* ROXANE *distractedly dips into the water a piece of linen torn from her breast*

to bathe his wounds*]. I have told all. She loves thee still.
[CHRISTIAN *closes his eyes*]
ROXANE. What is't, my love?
CARBON. Draw ramrods!
ROXANE [*to* CYRANO]. Is he dead?
CARBON. Bite charges! Ready! Load!
ROXANE. I feel his cheek
Grow cold against my own.
CARBON. Take aim!
ROXANE. A letter
Upon him! [*Opens it*] 'Tis for me.
CYRANO [*aside*]. My letter!
CARBON. Fire!
[*Musketry, shouts, noise of battle*]
CYRANO [*trying to disengage his hand; which* ROXANE *holds, kneeling*]
Roxane, the fight is on!
ROXANE [*holding him back*]. Stay yet a while.
He's dead. You were the only one who knew him.
[*Weeps softly*]
—Was he not wonderful?—a chosen being?
CYRANO [*standing bareheaded*].
Yes, Roxane.
ROXANE. And a poet to adore?
CYRANO. Yes, Roxane.
ROXANE. And a lofty spirit?
CYRANO. Yes.
ROXANE. A mighty heart, undreamt of by the crowd,—
A glorious soul and charming?
CYRANO [*stoutly*]. Yes, Roxane!
ROXANE [*throwing herself on* CHRISTIAN's *body*]. He's dead!
CYRANO [*aside, drawing his sword*]. And only death is left for me—
Since she mourns me in him, and knows it not.
[*Trumpets in the distance*]
DE GUICHE [*reappearing on the rampart, helmet off, wounded in the forehead; with thundering voice*].
The promised signal! Hear the blaring brass!
The French will quickly reach the camp with food!
Hold hard a moment longer.
ROXANE. On his letter
Are blood and tears!
A VOICE WITHOUT [*shouting*]. Surrender!
CADETS' VOICES. No!
RAGUENEAU [*perched on his carriage, watching the battle over the rampart*]. The danger
Grows greater.
CYRANO [*to* DE GUICHE, *pointing out* ROXANE]. Take her hence. I'll join the charge.
ROXANE [*kissing the letter, with dying voice*]. His blood! His tears!
RAGUENEAU [*leaping from the carriage to run towards her*]. She's fainted!

DE GUICHE [*on the rampart, to the* CADETS, *in fury*].   Hold your ground!

A VOICE [*without*]. Lower your arms!

CADETS' VOICES.   No!

CYRANO [*to* DE GUICHE].   You have fairly proved.

Your courage, sir, already.   [*Pointing to* ROXANE] Flee, and save her!

DE GUICHE [*runs to* ROXANE, *and carries her away in his arms*].

So be it! But we still may win the day
If you gain time.

CYRANO.   'T is well! [*Calling to* ROX-ANE, *whom* DE GUICHE, *with* RAGUENEAU'S *help, carries off in a faint*]   Farewell, Roxane!

[*Confusion; shouts.* CADETS *reappear, wounded, and fall upon the stage.* CY-RANO, *rushing into the battle, is stopped on top of the rampart by* CARBON, *covered with blood*]

CARBON. Our line is broken! I have had two wounds!

CYRANO [*shouting to the* GASCONS].

Stand fast! Hold hard, my lads! [*To* CARBON, *whom he holds up*] Be not afraid.

Two deaths I must avenge: my friend,—my joy!

[*They descend.* CYRANO *brandishes the lance on which is fastened* ROXANE'S *kerchief*]

Float, little flag of lace that bears her name.

[*Plants it in the ground, and shouts to the* Cadets]

Fall on them! Crush them down! [*To the fifer*] And blow your fife.

[*The fifer plays. The wounded raise themselves.* CADETS, *climbing up the rampart, rally around* CYRANO *and the little flag. The carriage, transformed into a redoubt, is covered and filled with men, and bristles with arquebuses*]

A CADET [*appearing on top of the rampart, in retreat, but still fighting, shouts*].

They scale the rampart!

[*Falls dead*]

CYRANO.   Give them a salute!

[*The rampart is crowded in a moment with a terrible array of the enemy. The great Imperial standards appear*]

CYRANO. Fire!

[*General volley*]

A SHOUT IN THE ENEMY'S RANKS. Fire!

[*Murderous reply. The* CADETS *fall on every side*]

A SPANISH OFFICER [*uncovering*]. Who are these, who all court death!

CYRANO [*reciting, erect in the midst of the bullets*].

These be Cadets of Gascony,—
Carbon de Castel-Jaloux's men:
They fight, they lie full shamelessly,—

[*Darts forward, followed by a few survivors*]

—These be Cadets—

[*The rest is lost in the battle*]

CURTAIN

FIFTH ACT

CYRANO'S GAZETTE

Fifteen years after, in 1655. The park of the convent occupied by the Sisters of the Cross, at Paris. Superb foliage. To the left, the house; a great terrace upon which several doors open. An enormous tree in the centre of the stage, standing alone in the middle of a little oval opening. To the right, in the foreground, among boxwood bushes, a semi-circular stone bench. The rear of the stage is crossed by an avenue of chestnuts; which leads on the right (in the background) to the door of a chapel, half seen through the branches. Through the double curtain of trees formed by this avenue are seen stretches of lawn, other avenues, small groves; the perspective of the park; the sky. A little side door of the chapel opens on a colonnade, garlanded with reddened vines, the colonnade disappearing on the right in the foreground, behind the box. It is autumn. The foliage shows yellow above the green lawns. Dark spots of box and yew trees, still green. A circle of dead leaves under each tree. The leaves are scattered over the whole stage, crackle under foot in the avenues, and half cover the terrace and the benches. Between the bench on the right and the tree stands a large embroidery-table, in front of which a low chair has been placed. Baskets full of skeins and worsteds. A piece of embroidery already begun. When the curtain rises, SISTERS *are coming and going in the park; some are seated on the bench around an older nun. The leaves are falling.*

SISTER MARTHA [*to* MOTHER MARGARET].

Sister Claire glanced i' the mirror twice, to see
How sat her headdress.

MOTHER MARGARET [*to* SISTER CLAIRE]. It is very ugly.

SISTER CLAIRE. But I saw Sister Martha steal a plum,
This morning, from the tart.

MOTHER MARGARET [*to* SISTER MARTHA]. A naughty deed!

SISTER CLAIRE. But such a little look!

SISTER MARTHA.   So small a plum!

MOTHER MARGARET. I'll tell Monsieur Cyrano all, to-night.

SISTER CLAIRE [*alarmed*].

No, he will mock us.

SISTER MARTHA.   He will call the nuns
Very coquettish—

SISTER CLAIRE. Very fond of sweets—
MOTHER MARGARET [*smiling*].
And very good.
SISTER CLAIRE. But, mother, is't not so,—
He's come each Saturday these ten years past?
MOTHER MARGARET. Yes, longer! Ever since
    his cousin joined
Her worldly mourning to our linen robes,
And sought for peace with us,—fourteen years
    since;
Like some great black-plumed bird 'mid our
    white flock.
SISTER MARTHA. He only, since she first took
    refuge here,
Can charm away her never-lessening grief.
ALL THE SISTERS. He is so merry— 'T is
    cheerful when he comes—
He teases us— He's kind— We like him well—
We must prepare for him our choicest sweets—
SISTER MARTHA. But yet he is not a good
    Catholic!
SISTER CLAIRE. We shall convert him.
THE SISTERS.   Yes, yes!
MOTHER MARGARET.   I forbid!
That is a task you must not undertake.
Trouble him not. He might come less, per-
    chance.
SISTER MARTHA. But— God—
MOTHER MARGARET.   Be not dis-
    turbed! God knows him well!
SISTER MARTHA. Yet every Saturday he
    proudly tells me,
When he comes in, "I feasted yesterday!"
MOTHER MARGARET. He tells you that!—
    The last time that he came,
Food had not passed his lips for two whole
    days.
SISTER MARTHA. Mother!
MOTHER MARGARET.   He's poor.
SISTER MARTHA.   Who told you?
MOTHER MARGARET.   Monsieur le Bret.
SISTER MARTHA. He gets no help?
MOTHER MARGARET.   No, that
    would anger him.
    [*In an avenue in the background* ROXANE
    *appears, dressed in black, with a widow's
    cap and long veil;* DE GUICHE, *very ele-
    gant, but growing old, walks near her.
    They approach slowly.* MOTHER MAR-
    GARET *rises*]
We must retire—Madame Madeleine
Is walking with a stranger in the park.
SISTER MARTHA [*aside to* SISTER CLAIRE].
The Duc de Grammont?
SISTER CLAIRE [*looking*]. Yes, I think it is.
SISTER MARTHA. He has not come to see her
    for these months.
THE SISTERS. He's busy—with the Court—
    the Field—
SISTER CLAIRE.   The World!
    [*They go out.* DE GUICHE *and* ROXANE
    come down in silence, and stop near

the embroidery-table. An interval. DE
    GUICHE *is now the* DUC DE GRAMMONT]
THE DUKE. And you will stay here ever—
    vainly fair,
And always mourning?
ROXANE.   Always!
THE DUKE.   Faithful still?
ROXANE. Still faithful.
THE DUKE [*after an interval*]. And you
    have forgiven me?
ROXANE. Since I am here.
THE DUKE.   He was a noble soul.
ROXANE. You should have known him.
THE DUKE.   Ah?   Perhaps I should.
Perhaps I never knew him well enough.
Do you still wear his letter next your heart?
ROXANE. Like some dear relic, on this velvet
    band.
THE DUKE. You love him, e'en in death?
ROXANE.   Sometimes it seems
He is not wholly dead,—our hearts still meet,
His living love hovers about me still.
THE DUKE [*after another silence*].
Cyrano comes to see you?
ROXANE.   Often, yes.
He is for me a journal—this old friend,—
He comes at such a time. His chair is placed
Under this tree, whene'er the weather's fine.
I ply my needle, and I wait for him.
The clock strikes: and at the last stroke I
    hear—
For I no longer even turn my head—
His stick upon the steps. He seats himself;
He jests at my eternal needlework;
He tells me the week's doings. [LE BRET *ap-
    pears on the steps*]   Oh, Le Bret!
    [LE BRET *descends*]
How is our friend?
LE BRET.   Ill!
THE DUKE.   Oh!
ROXANE [*to* THE DUKE].   He tells it large.
LE BRET. 'T is all as I foretold. Alone and
    wretched—
His letters ever winning him new foes—
He levels his attacks at every sham:
Sham   nobles,—hypocrites,—sham   heroes,—
    wit
Stolen from others;—in short, at all the
    world.
ROXANE. But his sword still inspires a mighty
    dread;
No one will get the best of him.
THE DUKE [*shaking his head*]. Who knows?
LE BRET. But what I fear is not fair, open
    fight.
'T is solitude and hunger—winter cold,
Ent'ring his humble room with wolf-like
    tread,—
Such are the murderers who'll be his death.
—For every day he tighter draws his belt;
His nose is like some piece of antique ivory;
He has one single coat, of wretched black.

THE DUKE. Oh, he's no upstart rich! It is as well!
Waste not your pity on him!

LE BRET [*with a bitter smile*]. But, my Lord!

THE DUKE. Waste not your pity on him; he has lived
Without concessions, free in thought and deed.

LE BRET [*as before*]. Your Grace—

THE DUKE [*haughtily*].   I know
I've all things; he has naught,—
But I would gladly grasp him by the hand.
[*Bowing to* ROXANE]. Adieu!

ROXANE.   I will attend you.
[THE DUKE *bows to* LE BRET, *and turns toward the steps with* ROXANE]

THE DUKE [*stopping while she ascends*].
                             Yes, sometimes
I envy him. You see, when all one's life
Has brought too much success, too lightly won,
He feels—though he has done no downright wrong—
A thousand petty quarrels with himself,
Which all combined together only make
A dull disgust with life—yet not remorse;
And while one mounts the steps of worldly state,
Even the ermined mantle of a duke
Drags after it a host of vain regrets
And dead illusions; even as your gown—
While you mount slowly upward to these doors—
Drags after it the rustling fallen leaves.

ROXANE [*ironically*]. Are you a dreamer?

THE DUKE. Yes! [*Just as he is going out, quickly*] Monsieur Le Bret!
[*To* ROXANE]
By your leave? A word.
[*Approaches* LE BRET, *and in an undertone*]
                    'T is true, no one would dare
Attack your friend,—but many hate him well:
And yesterday they told me, at the Queen's,
"This Cyrano might die by some mishap!"

LE BRET. Ah?

THE DUKE.   Let him go out seldom, and be cautious.

LE BRET [*lifting his arms toward heaven*].
Cautious! He's coming. I shall warn him—
But!—

ROXANE [*who has remained on the steps, to a* SISTER *who advances towards her*]. What?

THE SISTER. Ragueneau would see you, Madame.

ROXANE. Bid him enter.
[*To* THE DUKE *and* LE BRET]
He comes to tell his woes. Having set out
To be an author, he has been in turn
Singer—

LE BRET. Bath-keeper—

ROXANE.   Actor—

LE BRET.   Beadle—

ROXANE.   Barber—

LE BRET. Lute-player—

ROXANE.   And what will he be to-day?

RAGUENEAU [*entering hurriedly*].
Ah, Madame! [*Sees* LE BRET] Sir!

ROXANE [*smiling*].   Now
you can tell your troubles
To Le Bret; I'll return.

RAGUENEAU.   But, Madame—
[ROXANE *goes out, without hearing him, with* THE DUKE. *He turns towards* LE BRET]
                             Well,
Since you are here, 'tis best she should not know—
As I was on my way to see your friend,
And still some twenty paces from his door,
I saw him coming out. I went to meet him,
And as he turned the corner of the street,
From out a window, under which he passed,
A lackey dropped a stave— By chance?
Perhaps!

LE BRET. The cowards—Cyrano!

RAGUENEAU.   I came and saw—

LE BRET. Frightful!

RAGUENEAU.   Our friend, Monsieur,
—our noble poet,
There on the ground, a great wound in his head.

LE BRET. He's dead?

RAGUENEAU.   No, but— Good
God!—I bore him
Up to his room. His room! Oh, you should see
His wretched pallet!

LE BRET.   He is suffering?

RAGUENEAU. No, sir, he is unconscious.

LE BRET.   A physician?

RAGUENEAU. One came by courtesy.

LE BRET.   Poor Cyrano!
We must not tell this all at once to Roxane.
What did the doctor say?

RAGUENEAU.   I hardly know.
He talked of fever; he spoke of the brain—
Oh, you should see him—his poor bandaged head!
Come quickly, there is no one at his side;
And if he rises, sir, he's like to die.

LE BRET [*drawing him toward the right*].
This way, 'tis shorter—through the chapel—come!

ROXANE [*appearing on the steps, and seeing* LE BRET *departing by the colonnade leading to the little door of the chapel*].
Monsieur Le Bret! [LE BRET *and* RAGUENEAU *escape without answering*] He goes when he is called!
'T is some new history of poor Ragueneau's.
[*Descends the steps*]
This last September day is very fair.
My sadness smiles,—in April wrapt in gloom,
But of a brighter hue when autumn comes.
[*Seats herself at her work.* TWO SISTERS

come out of the house, and carry a large arm-chair under the tree]
Here's the historic chair where my old friend
Will take his seat.

SISTER MARTHA. It is the best we have.

ROXANE. I thank you, Sister. [*The* SISTERS *withdraw*] He will come. [*Takes her seat. The clock strikes*] The clock
Is striking—my embroid'ry— It has struck.
I am amazed. Will he for once be late?
The Sister at the gate— Where is my thimble?
—Must be exhorting him to penitence.
I've found it now— [*An interval*] She is exhorting him.
He cannot tarry long— A fallen leaf!

[*With her finger she brushes away a leaf that has fallen on her work*]
Besides, nothing could keep him— Now, my scissors?
Here in my bag.

A SISTER [*appearing on the steps*]. Monsieur de Bergerac.

ROXANE [*without turning*].
What was I saying?

[*She sews.* CYRANO *appears, very pale, with his hat pulled down over his eyes. A* SISTER *ushers him in and retires. He starts to walk slowly down the steps, making a visible effort to hold himself erect, and leaning on his stick.* ROXANE *works at her embroidery*]
Ah, these faded shades!
Into what pattern shall I fashion them?

[*To* CYRANO, *in tones of friendly scolding*]
Late—for the first time in full fourteen years!

CYRANO [*reaching the arm-chair, and sitting down; speaking with a cheerful voice, in contrast to his expression*]
Yes, 'tis absurd, I am beside myself.
I was detained.

ROXANE. By what?

CYRANO. Oh, by a most
Untimely visitation!

ROXANE. By some churl
Troubling you with importunate demands?

CYRANO. Yes, cousin, and I soon must do
his bidding.

ROXANE. You bade him go?

CYRANO. Yes. "This is Saturday,"
I said: "a day when surely, rain or shine,
I must betake me to a certain house
And pay a visit there. So come again
Within an hour."

ROXANE [*lightly*]. Well, this friend of yours
Will have to wait for you a longer time—
I shall not let you go till evening falls.

CYRANO. But I may be constrained to go away
A little sooner.

[*He closes his eyes, and is silent for a moment.* SISTER MARTHA *crosses the park, from the chapel to the steps.* ROXANE *sees her, and signals to her with a little nod of her head*]

ROXANE [*to* CYRANO]. Oh! You will not tease
Poor Sister Martha?

CYRANO [*smartly, opening his eyes*]. Yes, I think I shall.

[*With a big, comical voice*] Sister, come here!
[*The* SISTER *glides towards him*] Ha, ha!
You carry still
Your bright eyes always lowered!

SISTER MARTHA [*lifting her eyes with a smile*] But— [*Sees his appearance, and makes a movement of surprise*] Oh!

CYRANO [*aside, indicating* ROXANE]. Hush!
'T is nothing. [*In a voice of burlesque boasting*] Yesterday I made a feast!

SISTER MARTHA. I understand. [*Aside*]
That's why he is so pale.
[*In a quick aside to* CYRANO]
Come to the dining-hall, and you shall take
A fine great bowl of broth. You will come, now?

CYRANO. Yes, yes; of course.

SISTER MARTHA. Now, I am glad to see
That for this once you can be reasonable.

ROXANE [*hearing them whispering*].
She's trying to convert you?

SISTER MARTHA. No, not I!

CYRANO. Yes, that is true! And yet the pious words
Fall from your lips in such a plenteous flow
I am amazed you do not preach to me.
[*With mock anger*]
Thunder and Mars! I shall amaze you, too,
For I shall suffer you this very night—
[*Pretends to be looking for a subject of raillery and to find it*]
—To pray for me at chapel!

ROXANE. Oh, oh, oh!

CYRANO [*laughing*]. The Sister's stricken dumb.

SISTER MARTHA [*gently*]. I waited not
For your permission.
[*Retires*]

CYRANO [*turning to* ROXANE, *who bends over her work*]. When shall I see the end
Of this interminable needlework?

ROXANE. I waited for that jest.
[*At this moment, a puff of wind starts the leaves falling*]

CYRANO. Look at the leaves.

ROXANE [*raising her head, and looking far off through the vista*].
They are Venetian yellow. Watch them fall.

CYRANO. Yes, watch them well—how gracefully they fall!
And in their journey short, from branch to earth,
How they put on a final fleeting charm!
And, although loath to molder on the ground,

They strive to give their fall the grace of flight!

ROXANE. What, are you sad?

CYRANO [*remembering himself*]. No, not at all, Roxane.

ROXANE. Let the leaves fall, and tell me all the news,—
My journal!

CYRANO. Here it is.

ROXANE. Ah!

CYRANO [*growing paler and paler, and struggling against his pain*]. Saturday,
The nineteenth of the month, His Majesty,
Having partaken of too many sweets,
Suffered a touch of fever, and was bled.
His illness was found guilty of high treason;
And now his august pulse is calm again!
At the Queen's ball, on Sunday, there were burned
Wax candles seven hundred sixty-three!
They say our troops beat John of Austria!
Four witches have been hanged! The little dog
Of Madame Athis needed medicine—

ROXANE. Monsieur de Bergerac, will you be still!

CYRANO. Nothing on Monday, but Lygdamire's new lover;—

ROXANE. Oh!

CYRANO. Tuesday the whole Court went to Fontainebleau;—
Wednesday De Fiesque had "No" from La Montglat;—
Thursday Mancini is Queen of France—almost!—
Friday La Montglat to De Fiesque said "Yes";
And on the twenty-sixth, on Saturday—
[*Closes his eyes; his head drops. Silence*]

ROXANE [*surprised at hearing nothing more, turns, looks at him; and getting up in fright*].
He's fainted? [*Rushes towards him, exclaiming*] Cyrano!

CYRANO [*opening his eyes; with muffled voice*]. What is it? What?
[*Sees ROXANE leaning over him; quickly settles his hat on his head, and draws back in alarm in his chair*]
No, no! 'T is nothing, nothing! Let me be!

ROXANE. Yet—

CYRANO. 'T is my wound—from Arras—which at times—
You know—

ROXANE. Poor friend—

CYRANO. 'T is naught. 'T will pass. [*Smiles, with an effort*] It has passed!

ROXANE. Each of us has his wound; and I have mine,—
An ancient wound that never heals,—just here.
[*Lays her hand on her breast*]

Here!—'neath this letter, with its yellowing folds!
Where still you see commingled blood and tears.
[*Twilight begins to fall*]

CYRANO. His letter! Once I think you promised me
That I might some day read it—

ROXANE. Do you wish?—

CYRANO. Yes, 'tis my wish, to-day—

ROXANE [*giving him the little bag which hangs about her neck*]. Here—

CYRANO [*taking it*]. I may open?

ROXANE. Open and read.
[*She returns to her work, folds it, and arranges her worsteds*]

CYRANO [*reading*]:
"Farewell, Roxane, my death is very near!"

ROXANE [*stopping in astonishment*]. Aloud?

CYRANO.
"This very night, my best-beloved,
My soul is heavy with unuttered love;
And now I die; and never, nevermore,
Shall my eyes feast on you their yearning gaze!"

ROXANE. But how you read his letter—with what voice!

CYRANO.
"Drunk with your beauty; kissing as they flit
Each little graceful movement that you make;
And one familiar gesture still I see—
The way you touched your forehead!"

ROXANE. How you read
This letter!
[*Night falls imperceptibly*]

CYRANO.
"And I fain would cry aloud
'Farewell!' "

ROXANE. You read—

CYRANO.
"My dearest! Oh, my love!
My treasure"—

ROXANE. With a voice—

CYRANO.
"My best-beloved"—

ROXANE. A voice that I have somewhere heard before.
[*Approaches softly, without his noticing it; goes behind his chair, leans over quietly, and looks at the letter. The darkness deepens*]

CYRANO.
"My heart has never left you for a breath;
And here, and in the world beyond the grave,
I am he whose love for you passed every bound."

ROXANE [*laying her hand on his shoulder*].
But how can you read now? The night has come.
[*He starts, turns; sees her close to him;*]

*makes a startled gesture, lowers his
his head. A long silence. Then, after it
has become quite dark, she says
slowly, clasping her hands*]
And for these fourteen years he's played this
part
Of the old friend who comes to cheer me up.

CYRANO. Roxane!

ROXANE. 'T was you!—

CYRANO. Ah, no, Roxane; not I!

ROXANE. I should have guessed it, when he
spoke my name.

CYRANO. Ah, no! It was not I.

ROXANE. 'T was you.

CYRANO. I swear—

ROXANE. At last I see it all—the generous
cheat!
You wrote the letters—

CYRANO. No!

ROXANE. The dear mad words
Were yours—

CYRANO. No!

ROXANE. The voice that night was yours.

CYRANO. I swear it was not!

ROXANE. And the soul was yours.

CYRANO. I loved you not!

ROXANE. You loved me—

CYRANO. It was he—

ROXANE. You loved me!

CYRANO. No.

ROXANE. But now you speak more soft.

CYRANO. No, no; my best-beloved, I loved
you not.

ROXANE. How many things since then have
come and gone!
Why have you held your peace for fourteen
years?
Since on this letter, which was naught to him,
These tears were yours?

CYRANO. But the blood was his!

ROXANE. Then why to-day should you decide to break
This noble silence?

CYRANO. Why?

[*Enter* LE BRET *and* RAGUENEAU, *running*]

LE BRET. What madness! I was sure—
There he is!

CYRANO [*smiling and straightening up*].
Why, yes; of course!

LE BRET. Madame, he's killed himself
By rising.

ROXANE. But just now, this weakness—

CYRANO. True,
My news was not yet finished: Saturday,
The twenty-sixth, an hour before he dined,
Monsieur de Bergerac was foully murdered.

[*Uncovers. His head is seen to be bandaged*]

ROXANE. What says he? Cyrano! Look at
his head,
Wrapped in a bandage! Oh! what have they
done
To you! Why?

CYRANO. *"By the good sword's thrust,
Struck by a hero, fall with point in heart!"*—
Yes, I said that. But Destiny's a mocker.
And here I am, caught by a coward's trick;
Struck from behind; felled by a faggot's blow
Wielded by hireling hands,—indeed 'tis well:
I shall have failed in all things,—e'en in
death.

RAGUENEAU. Oh, sir!

CYRANO. What are you
doing now, my colleague?

RAGUENEAU. I now am candle-snuffer—
for Molière.

CYRANO. Molière?

RAUGENEAU. But I shall surely leave
to-morrow!
Yes, I am angry with him. Yesterday
"Scapin" was acted; and I plainly saw
He'd stolen a scene from you—

LE BRET. A scene entire!

RAGUENEAU. The famous — "What the devil
did he there?"

LE BRET. Molière stole it from you!

CYRANO. Tush! He's done well!
The scene went off, I trust, with good effect?

RAGUENEAU [*sobbing*].
Oh, sir, they laughed, they laughed!

CYRANO. Yes, all my life
My part has been to prompt—and be forgot.
[*To* ROXANE]
Rememberest thou the night when Christian
wooed,
Under the balcony?— All my life is there!
While I remained below, hid in the dark,
Others have climbed to kisses and to fame!
'T is just; and on the threshold of my tomb,
I own Molière a genius—Christian fair.

[*At this moment the chapel-bell rings,
and the nuns are seen passing through
the avenue in the background, going to
mass*]
Their bell has sounded; let them go to prayers.

ROXANE [*rising to call for help*].
Come! Sister, Sister!

CYRANO. No, no! Go for no one!
When you return, I shall have gone away.

[*The nuns have entered the chapel. The
organ plays*]
Music was all I needed—there it is!

ROXANE. I love you! Live!

CYRANO. No, in the fairy-tale
'T is plainly written that when the humbled
Prince
Had heard the words—"I love you," his dis-
guise
Of horror fled like snow before the sun:
But you will see that I remain the same.

ROXANE. And I have wrought your sorrow
—even I!

CYRANO. You? No, not you! 'T is quite the opposite.
I ne'er knew woman's kindness. E'en my mother
Thought me not fair. I never had a sister.
Then I feared sweethearts with their mocking eyes!
But, thanks to you, I've had at least a friend;
And through my life a woman's robe has passed.
LE BRET [pointing out the moonbeams falling through the branches].
There comes your other friend to see you.
CYRANO [smiling at the moon]. Yes!
ROXANE. I loved but one—and now I lose him twice.
CYRANO. Le Bret, I'm going,—up to the shining moon,
And need devise no engine for this flight!
ROXANE. What did you say?
CYRANO. Yes, it is there, on high,
There am I sent to make my paradise.
More than one soul I love is exiled there:
Socrates—Galileo. I'll find them all.
LE BRET [rebelliously].
No, no! 'T is too absurd! 'T is too unjust!
So great a poet! Such a noble heart!
To die this way! To die—
CYRANO. Hear Le Bret scold!
LE BRET [bursting into tears]. Dear friend!
CYRANO [rising, his eyes wandering].
"These be Cadets of Gascony"—
The elemental substance— Yes—the "hic."
LE BRET. List to his science, even in his ravings.
CYRANO. Copernicus said—
ROXANE. Oh!
CYRANO. "What did he there?
And what the devil did he in the galley?"
Philosopher, physician,
Poet, swordsman, and musician,
And a traveller through the heavens to the moon!
His sword-point always ready,
His sword-arm always steady,
And a lover to whom love was not a boon!

Here lies Hercule-Savinien de Cyrano de Bergerac;
All things in turn he tried; and all things did he lack!

But pardon—I must go, I may not wait:
You see the moonbeams come to take me hence!
[Falls back into his seat. ROXANE's tears bring him back to realities. He looks at her, and caresses her veil]

I would not have you shed one tear the less
For Christian—fair and noble. All I ask
Is, when my body shall lie cold in death,
You give a double meaning to these weeds—
And let his mourning be my mourning too!
ROXANE. I swear it!
CYRANO [shaken with a great tremor, rises quickly] No, not there! Not in a chair!
[They rush towards him]
Let no one hold me up. [Leans against the tree] Only the tree— [Silence]
He comes! I feel already shod with stone,
And gloved with lead. [Stiffens himself] But since he's on the way,
I'll meet him standing upright— [Draws his sword]—sword in hand—
LE BRET. Cyrano!
ROXANE [fainting]. Cyrano!
[All draw back in terror]
CYRANO. He sees my nose!
Well! Let the flat-nose look me in the face!
[Raises his sword]
You say 'tis useless? That I know full well!
But I have never fought with hope to win.
No,—it is finer when 'tis all in vain.
Now, who are these—a thousand thronged about me?
I know you well— You are all ancient foes:
Falsehood! [Strikes with his sword in the air]
There, there! Ha, ha! And Compromise!
Bigotry! Cowardice! [Strikes] Shall I make terms?
No, never! never! There is Folly, too!
I knew that in the end you'd lay me low.
No matter. Let me fight! and fight! and fight!
[Swings his sword in circles, and stops, panting]
You snatch them all away—laurel and rose!
Snatch on! One thing is left in spite of you,
Which I take with me: and this very night,
When I shall cross the threshold of God's house,
And enter, bowing low, this I shall take
Despite you, without wrinkle, without spot—
[Rushes forward with brandished sword]
And that is—
[The sword falls from his hands. He staggers, and falls into the arms of LE BRET and RAGUENEAU]
ROXANE [leaning over him, and kissing his forehead]. What?
CYRANO [opens his eyes, recognizes her, and says with a smile]. My stainless soldier's crest!

CURTAIN

THE GREEN COCKATOO

A Grotesque in One Act

By ARTHUR SCHNITZLER

TRANSLATED FROM THE GERMAN BY ETHEL VAN DER VEER

CHARACTERS

EMILE, *Duc de Cadignan*
FRANCOIS, *Vicomte de Nogeant*
ALBIN, *Chevalier de la Tremouille*
MARQUIS DE LANSAC
SÉVERINE, *his wife*
ROLLIN, *a poet*
PROSPÈRE, *host of "The Green Cockatoo," formerly manager of a theatre*
HENRI
BALTHASAR
GUILLAUME
SCAEVOLA
JULES
ÉTIENNE   } *Prospère's troupe*
MAURICE
GEORGETTE
MICHETTE
FLIPOTTE
LÉOCADIE, *an actress, Henri's wife*
GRASSET, *a philosopher*
LEBRÊT, *a tailor*
GRAIN, *a tramp*
A SERGENT DE VILLE
ARISTOCRATS, ACTORS *and* ACTRESSES, *and* CITIZENS

The action occurs in Paris on the 14th of July, 1789, in the tap-room of "The Green Cockatoo."

THE GREEN COCKATOO

SCENE: *The tap-room of The Green Cockatoo. A not large cellar-room. Up right, a flight of seven steps, closed off at the top by a door, leads to the street. There is a second door up left, which is hardly visible. Almost the entire floor space is occupied by plain wooden tables surrounded by chairs. Left, is a kind of service bar, behind which are a number of casks, with spigots for drawing off wine. The room is lighted by oil lamps which hang from the ceiling. The proprietor,* PROSPÈRE, *is on the scene.*

[*Enter* GRASSET]

GRASSET [*on the steps*]. In here, Lebrêt. I know this place. My old friend the proprietor will have a barrel of wine hidden somewhere, even though the whole of Paris is dry.

[LEBRÊT *comes in*]

PROSPÈRE. Good evening, Grasset. I'm glad you've shown up at last. Gone sour on Philosophy? Looking for another engagement with me?

GRASSET. To be sure. But for the moment I am the guest and you are the host. So bring us some wine.

PROSPÈRE. Wine? Now where should I get wine, Grasset? Last night they emptied all the wineshops in Paris. And I'll wager you were mixed up in it, too.

GRASSET. Bring on the wine. Because the mob will follow us in an hour. [*Listening*] Do you hear anything, Lebrêt?

LEBRÊT. A rumble—like soft thunder.

GRASSET. Good—citizens of Paris. . . . [*To* PROSPÈRE] You have plenty for the mob. Bring some for us. My friend and admirer the Citizen Lebrêt, tailor of the Rue St. Honoré, will pay for everything.

LEBRÊT. Yes, certainly I'll pay.

[PROSPÈRE *hesitates*]

GRASSET. Show him you have some money, Lebrêt.

[LEBRÊT *displays his purse*]

PROSPÈRE. Well, I'll see if I— [*He fills two glasses from a spigot*] Where do you come from, Grasset? From the Palais Royal?

GRASSET. But yes, I just made a speech there. My friend, I'm in the running now. Can you imagine after whom I spoke?

PROSPÈRE. Well?

GRASSET. After Camille Desmoulins! Yes, I actually took the risk. And tell me, Lebrêt, who received the greater applause, Desmoulins or I?

LEBRÊT. You did—undoubtedly.

GRASSET. And how did I do?

LEBRÊT. Splendidly.

GRASSET. You hear that, Prospère? I climbed on the table . . . I looked as impressive as a monument . . . and thousands—five thousand, ten thousand, surrounded me—just as they did Camille Desmoulins . . . and how they applauded me!

LEBRÊT. It was a big demonstration.

GRASSET. And a very loud one. But they have heeded my words and have gone to the Bastile. And I promise you that before the night is over it will fall.

PROSPÈRE. If your speech could crumble the walls—

GRASSET. My speech indeed! Are you deaf? They are making an end of it. Our brave soldiers are with us. They will use their God-given courage on that damn prison. You know that behind those walls their fathers and brothers are confined. But they wouldn't have shot— if we hadn't talked. My dear Prospère, the power of the spirit is invincible. [*To* LEBRÊT] Where are the papers?

LEBRÊT [*producing them*]. Here.

GRASSET. Here are the latest pamphlets, which are now being distributed in the Palais Royal. Here is one from my friend Cerutti: RECORDS FOR THE PEOPLE OF PARIS. Here is one from Desmoulins, without doubt a better orator than a writer: FRANCE FREED.

PROSPÈRE. When is your own pamphlet going to appear, the one you are always talking about?

GRASSET. We don't need any more. The time has come for deeds. The man who sits at home these days is a coward. The real men are on the streets.

PROSPÈRE. Bravo! Bravo!

GRASSET. In Toulon they killed the Mayor. In Brignolles they have plundered a hundred houses. Only the Parisians have been sluggards and allowed themselves to remain passive.

PROSPÈRE. That can no longer be said.

LEBRÊT [*who has been drinking steadily*]. Rise, comrades! On to freedom!

GRASSET. Right! . . . Close up your shop, Prospère, and come along with us.

PROSPÈRE. I'll come freely, when the time is ripe.

GRASSET. Of course—when the danger is over.

PROSPÈRE. My dear friend, I love freedom as much as you do. But first I have my business to think about.

GRASSET. From now on there is only one

business for the citizens of Paris; to set your brothers free.

PROSPÈRE. That's all very well for those who have nothing else to do.

LEBRÊT. What does he say? . . . He is making fun of us!

PROSPÈRE. That never would occur to me. But get along now. My performance is about to begin. And I can't use you in that.

LEBRÊT. What kind of a performance? Is this a theatre?

PROSPÈRE. Certainly it's a theatre. Your friend here played with us for a fortnight.

LEBRÊT. You played here, Grasset? And do you let this fellow poke fun at you without punishing him for it?

GRASSET. Keep quiet . . . it's true. I have played here. But this is not a wineshop . . . it's a criminal's rendezvous. Come along.

PROSPÈRE. But first you'll have to pay.

LEBRÊT. If it's true that this is a criminal's hang-out, I'll not pay you a sou.

PROSPÈRE [to GRASSET]. Explain to your friend the kind of place he is in.

GRASSET. It's a remarkable place. People come here who play at being criminals, and also others who really are criminals and don't know it.

LEBRÊT. So—?

GRASSET. I should like to call your attention to the fact that what I just said was exceedingly witty. It could have been made the hit of an entire speech.

LEBRÊT. I fail to understand you.

GRASSET. I have told you that Prospère was once my manager. He now directs his comedies in a quite original manner. My old colleagues sit around here and act as if they were criminals. Do you understand? They tell hair-raising tales of lives they never lived, of crimes they never committed. . . . And the public that haunts this place feels the agreeable thrill of contact with the most dangerous characters of Paris—with thieves and crooks and murderers —and—

LEBRÊT. What kind of a public?

PROSPÈRE. The aristocrats of Paris.

GRASSET. Nobility . . .

PROSPÈRE. The Gentlemen of the Court—

LEBRÊT. Down with them!

GRASSET. This is the very thing for them. A sauce for their sated palates, a thrill for their blasé nerves. It was here my own aims began, Lebrêt. Here I made my first speech—in the manner of a jest. . . . And here is where I first began to hate the aristos, with their beautiful clothes, their perfumes and full stomachs. . . . And I am very glad, my good Lebrêt, to have you see the place where the greatness of your friend first began to take shape. . . . [In another tone] Say, Prospère, suppose this whole affair were to go up in smoke.

PROSPÈRE. Which affair?

GRASSET. My great political career. . . . Would you reengage me?

PROSPÈRE. Not for the world.

GRASSET [lightly]. Why not? Isn't there possibly a chance for any one besides your Henri?

PROSPÈRE. Perhaps, but in your case—I have always feared you would some day forget yourself and do an injury to one of my paying guests. You might sometime, under the excitement of the moment, let yourself go.

GRASSET [flattered]. Well, that would be possible.

PROSPÈRE. Yes. I have to use great restraint, myself. . . .

GRASSET. Truly, Prospère, I could admire your self-control—if I didn't know that you were a coward.

PROSPÈRE. Ah my friend, I am satisfied with the opportunities afforded by my profession. It gives me much gratification to tell those people exactly what I think of them, straight to their faces. I bawl them out to my heart's content while they regard it as a joke. It is an art to find an outlet for one's rancor. [He draws a dagger and allows the lights to play upon it]

LEBRÊT. Citizen Prospère, what does that mean?

GRASSET. Have no fear. I bet you that dagger isn't even sharpened.

PROSPÈRE. You might lose, my friend. Some day it may be that a joke will turn out to be deadly serious. And for that time I am prepared.

GRASSET. That day is near. We are living in great times. Come, Citizen Lebrêt, we must join our comrades. [To PROSPÈRE] Good-bye. You'll see me come back as a great man—or —never.

LEBRÊT [at the steps]. As a great man . . or . . . never.

[They go out. PROSPÈRE sits on a table opens a pamphlet and begins to read aloud]

PROSPÈRE. "Now the beast is in the noose —strangle it!" Hmm—he doesn't write badly this little Desmoulins. "Never has richer booty been offered for the taking. Forty thousand palaces and castles, two fifths of all the wealth of France, will be the reward of valor. The ones who believe themselves in power will be overthrown. The nation will be born anew."

[A SERGENT DE VILLE enters]

PROSPÈRE [looking him over]. Hmm—the rabble appears early to-night.

SERGENT. Spare me your wit, my dear Prospère. I am now the officer of your district.

PROSPÈRE. And what can I do for you?

SERGENT. I am ordered to attend your performance this evening.

PROSPÈRE. I am much honored.

SERGENT. That is not the intention. The authorities wish to know exactly what occurs here. During the last few weeks—

PROSPÈRE. This is a place of amusement, Mr. Sergent, nothing more.

SERGENT. Let me continue. For some weeks this place has been the scene of vile orgies.

PROSPÈRE. You've been misinformed, Mr. Officer. We just have a little fun, and that's all there is to it.

SERGENT. It may begin so, but my information goes further. You were once an actor?

PROSPÈRE. Director. Manager of an admirable company which last played in St. Denis.

SERGENT. That's immaterial. You came into a small inheritance?

PROSPÈRE. But not worth mentioning.

SERGENT. Your troupe was dispersed?

PROSPÈRE. Also the inheritance.

SERGENT. Good. So you opened this wine-room.

PROSPÈRE. It paid very little.

SERGENT. And then you got hold of an idea—which I must say was rather original.

PROSPÈRE. You make me very proud, Mr. Sergent.

SERGENT. No matter. You collected your troupe of actors and let them give a performance which I'm told is peculiar—and even questionable.

PROSPÈRE. Questionable? If it were, I could not hold my audiences—the finest audiences in Paris. The Vicomte de Nogeant is my daily guest. The Marquis de Lansac comes frequently, and the Duc de Cadignan, Mr. Sergent, is a warm admirer of my leading actor, the celebrated Henri Baston.

SERGENT. And he also admires the art—or the arts—of your actresses?

PROSPÈRE. Were you to see my little actresses, you couldn't blame any one for admiring them.

SERGENT. Enough. It is reported that the amusement offered by your—what shall I say—?

PROSPÈRE. The word "artists" would do.

SERGENT. I shall use the word "hirelings." The amusement offered by your hirelings goes far beyond what is permissible. We are told that your people make speeches here that are—what does my report say? [He reads from a notebook:] "that are not only immoral"—which would bother us very little—"but also seditious and inciting"—and in times like these—the State cannot wink at them.

PROSPÈRE. Mr. Officer, I answer these accusations only by a most polite invitation to attend the performance. You will then see for yourself that nothing seditious goes on here. Also that my audience is not one which would be susceptible to sedition. We give a theatrical performance, and that is all.

SERGENT. Naturally I cannot accept your invitation, as I must remain here in my official capacity.

PROSPÈRE. I believe I can give you excellent entertainment, Mr. Sergent. But you'll permit the advice that you remove your insignia and appear in civilian clothes? The presence of a police-officer, were it known to them, would make my actors self-conscious, and the mood of my audience would also suffer.

SERGENT. You are quite right. I will disappear for a while and return as a young man of fashion.

PROSPÈRE. Which should be easy for you, Mr. Officer. But even as a vagabond you would not attract attention. Only as an officer of the law.

SERGENT. Good-bye—for the moment.

PROSPÈRE [bows ironically after him]. When the blessed day arrives, when I see you and your like—

[GRAIN comes in. He is a tramp, ragged and dirty, and looks alarmed at seeing a policeman. The SERGENT DE VILLE looks him over, then smiles]

SERGENT [to PROSPÈRE]. One of your artists arriving? [Goes out]

GRAIN [whiningly, pathetically]. Good evening.

PROSPÈRE [after a long scrutiny]. If you are one of my players, then I certainly must compliment you, for I don't recognize you.

GRAIN. What do you mean?

PROSPÈRE. Stop your fooling and take off your wig. I want to know who you are. [He tugs at GRAIN's hair]

GRAIN. Ouch!

PROSPÈRE. By thunder . . . it's real hair . . . who the devil are you? You seem to be a genuine tramp.

GRAIN. But yes.

PROSPÈRE. What do you want, then?

GRAIN. I have the honor of speaking to the landlord of The Green Cockatoo?

PROSPÈRE. I am he.

GRAIN. My name is Grain . . . sometimes Carniche . . . some call me Whining Brimstone. But I was in prison under the name of Grain, so that's the most real to me.

PROSPÈRE. Ah—I understand. You wish me to engage you, so you at once begin to enact your part. Very good. Continue.

GRAIN. Citizen Prospère, please don't take me for a swindler. I am a man of honor. When I tell you that I have been in prison, that's the plain truth.

[PROSPÈRE regards him sceptically]

GRAIN [taking a paper from his pocket]. Look at this, Citizen Prospère. It will show you that I was released yesterday afternoon at four o'clock.

PROSPÈRE [looking at the paper]. After two

years of imprisonment. . . . By thunder, this is genuine.

GRAIN. Were you still in doubt?

PROSPÈRE. What did you do, that they locked you up for two years?

GRAIN. They would have hanged me, but happily I was still half a child when I murdered my poor aunt.

PROSPÈRE. Man alive! How could any one murder his aunt?

GRAIN. Citizen Prospère, I wouldn't have done it if my aunt had not been false to me, and with my best friend.

PROSPÈRE. Your aunt?

GRAIN. Yes. We were more to each other than is usual between aunts and nephews. Our family relationships were peculiar. . . . I was embittered, highly embittered. Shall I tell you about it?

PROSPÈRE. Go right ahead. Tell me the rest, and perhaps we can come to an agreement.

GRAIN. My sister was no more than half a child when she ran away from home. Could you guess with whom?

PROSPÈRE. I've no idea.

GRAIN. With her uncle. Then he left her in the lurch—with a child.

PROSPÈRE. With a whole child—I hope?

GRAIN. It is indelicate of you, Citizen Prospère, to make light of such matters.

PROSPÈRE. Let me tell you something, you Whining Brimstone. Your family affairs bore me. Do you think I'm here to listen to every chance ragamuffin's story of his murders? What is it to me? I take it you want something—

GRAIN. Yes indeed, Citizen Prospère. I've come to ask you for work.

PROSPÈRE [loftily]. Let me call your attention to the fact that this is a pleasure resort. There are no aunts to be murdered here.

GRAIN. Oh, one was enough for me. I wish to become an upright man. I was sent to you.

PROSPÈRE. By whom?

GRAIN. A most kindly young man who shared my cell with me for the last three days. Now he is there alone. His name is Gaston, and you know him.

PROSPÈRE. Gaston! Now I know why he hasn't shown up for three nights. He is one of my best men for the pickpocket act. Such stories as he can tell—they bring down the house.

GRAIN. Yes, yes. But now they have caught him.

PROSPÈRE. How could they catch him, when he has never really stolen?

GRAIN. But he has. Though it must have been for the first time, for he was incredibly clumsy. Imagine—[Lamentingly] on the Boulevard des Capucines—he simply ripped open a lady's pocket and pulled out her purse. A rank amateur. You've inspired me with confidence, so I'll confess to you that there was a time

when I also was up to little tricks like that. But never without my dear father. It was in my childhood days, and we all lived together, and my poor aunt was still alive—

PROSPÈRE. What are you lamenting? I think it very poor taste. Didn't you kill her yourself?

GRAIN. Too late. But the reason I came to ask you to take me on— I'll be just the opposite to Gaston. He first played the thief and then became one. While I—

PROSPÈRE. You look the part. I'll try you out. Then, at a given moment, you simply tell the whole story about your aunt. Just as it was. Some one will lead the way with a question.

GRAIN. I thank you, Citizen Prospère. And about my salary—

PROPÈRE. To-night you'll be playing on trial. For that I cannot pay. But you'll get plenty to eat and plenty to drink, and I'll hand you a couple of francs for your night's lodging.

GRAIN. I thank you. And you'll introduce me to your company as a visitor from the provinces?

PROSPÈRE. Oh no. I shall tell them at once that you are a real murderer. They will be delighted.

GRAIN. Excuse me—of course I want to put my best foot forward—but I don't exactly understand—

PROSPÈRE. You'll understand better after you've worked with them a little while.

[SCAEVOLA and JULES enter]

SCAEVOLA. Good evening, director!

PROSPÈRE. Host, if you please. How often must I tell you that if you address me as director, the whole show will be ruined.

SCAEVOLA. Whatever you say. But I don't believe we will play to-night.

PROSPÈRE. Why not?

SCAEVOLA. The people won't be in the mood. There is a terrific racket going on in the streets, and the mob in front of the Bastile is screaming with frenzy.

PROSPÈRE. What is that to us? For two months the noise has been going on, and our audience has never failed us. They enjoy themselves as always.

SCAEVOLA. Yes. Like the gaiety of people who are about to be hanged.

PROSPÈRE. Oh, that I may live to see it!

SCAEVOLA. Meanwhile, give us something to drink, to put us in the right mood. I haven't been in the right mood all day.

PROSPÈRE. That is frequently the case, my friend. I want to tell you that you were not very satisfactory last evening.

SCAEVOLA. In what way, may I ask?

PROSPÈRE. Your story of the burglary was utter piffle.

SCAEVOLA. Piffle?

PROSPÈRE. Precisely. It was absolutely unconvincing. Ranting alone is insufficient.

SCAEVOLA. I never rant!

PROSPÈRE. You always do. I'll have to re-hearse these things with you. I can't depend on your inspiration, as I do with Henri—

SCAEVOLA. Henri! Always Henri! Henri is nothing but a stage-hand compared with me. My burglary was a masterpiece. Henri couldn't equal it in a lifetime. If I am not satisfactory to you, my friend, I'll go to a regular theatre. This place is only a blot, a smear. [*He sees* GRAIN] Ah! Who is this? Not one of us. Have you already engaged a new performer, Pros-père? What sort of a make-up does he think that is?

PROSPÈRE. Don't get uneasy, he's not a pro-fessional actor, but a real murderer.

SCAEVOLA. Indeed! [*Goes to* GRAIN] De-lighted to make your acquaintance. My name is Scaevola.

GRAIN. I am called Grain.

[JULES *has all the while been walking back and forth in the tap-room, occasionally halting, like a man greatly disturbed in mind*]

PROSPÈRE. What's the matter with you, Jules?

JULES. I am rehearsing.

PROSPÈRE. As what?

JULES. A conscience-stricken soul. To-night you will see me as a man writhing under the pangs of conscience. Look at me—look at my furrowed brow. Isn't it effective? Don't I look as if the furies of hell were after me? . . . [*He paces back and forth*]

SCAEVOLA [*yells*]. Wine! Wine here!

PROSPÈRE. Keep quiet! The audience is not yet here.

[HENRI *and* LÉOCADIE *enter*]

HENRI. Good evening! [*With a light gesture of greeting*] Good evening, gentlemen.

PROSPÈRE. Good evening, Henri! What's this I see? You have Léocadie with you?

GRAIN [*who has been looking at* LÉOCADIE; *to* SCAEVOLA]. I know her . . . [*He goes on talking with* SCAEVOLA]

LÉOCADIE. Yes, my dear Prospère, it is I.

PROSPÈRE. Why, I haven't seen you for a year. Let me greet you. [*Makes to kiss her*]

HENRI. Here! Cut that out! [*His eyes rest on* LÉOCADIE *with pride, wistfulness, and a cer-tain anxiety*]

PROSPÈRE. But Henri . . . when we're such old friends . . . and your former manager, Léocadie!

LÉOCADIE. Ah, those were the days, Pros-père! . . .

PROSPÈRE. Why sigh about it—when you've made your way so well since? To be sure, a beautiful young woman always has it easier than—

HENRI [*sharply*]. Cut that out!

PROSPÈRE. Why do you flare up like that—when she's come here with you?

HENRI. Be still! . . . Since yesterday she has been my wife.

PROSPÈRE. Your wife! . . . [*To* LÉOCADIE] Is this a joke?

LÉOCADIE. No, he has really married me.

PROSPÈRE. Congratulations! . . . Here, Scae-vola, Jules . . . Henri is married.

SCAEVOLA [*going to them*]. My best wishes.

[JULES *shakes hands with her*]

GRAIN [*to* PROSPÈRE]. How strange! I saw this woman . . . just a few minutes after I was set free.

PROSPÈRE. How was that?

GRAIN. She was the first beautiful woman I had seen in two years. I was greatly thrilled. But there was another gentleman with her—[*He goes on conversing with* PROSPÈRE]

HENRI [*in an ecstatic, high-pitched tone, which must not be declamatory*]. Léocadie, my beloved, my wife! . . . All that has been is now forgotten. In a moment like this, the past exists no more.

[SCAEVOLA *and* JULES *have dropped back.* PROSPÈRE *comes forward*]

PROSPÈRE. What moment?

HENRI. We have been united by the Holy Sacrament. That is stronger than human vows. Now God is watching over us, we have for-gotten all that went before. A new day has dawned. Léocadie, everything between us is holy. Our kisses—once so passionate—from this day are sanctified. Léocadie, my beloved wife. [*He regards her glowingly*] Does she not look different, Prospère? Unlike when you knew her? Is her brow not purer, more serene? All that was is now no more. Is that not so, Léo-cadie?

LÉOCADIE. Of course, Henri.

HENRI. And all is well. To-morrow we leave Paris. Léocadie is playing to-night for the last time at the Porte St. Martin. And for the last time, also, I play here with you.

PROSPÈRE. Have you gone crazy, Henri? You can't think of leaving me. And surely the manager of the Porte St. Martin won't let Léocadie go. She is his greatest attraction. The young men, they say, go in streams to see her.

HENRI. Be still! Léocadie is going with me, and will never leave me. [*Brutally*] Tell them that you'll never leave me, Léocadie.

LÉOCADIE. I will never leave you.

HENRI. If you did, I should— [*Pause*] I'm weary of this life. I want rest—and rest I will have.

PROSPÈRE. But what will you do with your-self, Henri? It's ridiculous. I'll make you a proposition. Withdraw Léocadie from the Porte St. Martin—but let her come here with me. I can use an actress of talent.

HENRI. My mind is made up, Prospère. My decision is made. We leave the city. We go to the country.

PROSPÈRE. To the country? Where?

HENRI. To my old father, who lives alone in his poor village. I haven't seen him for seven years. He must have given up all hope of seeing his lost son. He'll receive us joyfully.

PROSPÈRE. And how are you going to support yourself and Léocadie? All over the land the people are dying of starvation. They are a thousand times worse off than we in the city. And don't think for a moment that you are the kind of man to labor in the fields.

HENRI. You'll find out that I am.

PROSPÈRE. There's hardly any wheat growing anywhere in France. You are going into certain misery.

HENRI. We are going into unimaginable happiness, Prospère. Isn't that so, Léocadie? Often we have dreamt about it. I look forward to the peace of the wide horizons. Yes, Prospère, in my dreams I see myself with her, walking over lush fields, in the stillness of eventide, the starry heavens above. We are escaping from this terrible and dangerous city, and great peace will enfold us. Isn't that so, Léocadie? Have we not often dreamt of it?

LÉOCADIE. Yes, we have often dreamt about it.

PROSPÈRE. Listen to me, Henri. You must think this over well. I will gladly increase your salary. And I will pay Léocadie the same as I pay you.

LÉOCADIE. Do you hear that, Henri?

PROSPÈRE. I really can't imagine who would take your place here. No one has such clever ideas as you. No one has ever been so loved by our audiences. . . . Don't go—

HENRI. I realize, of course, that no one could take my place.

PROSPÈRE. Stay with us, Henri. [A glance at LÉOCADIE informs him that she is in accord with him]

HENRI. The parting will be more painful for you than for me, I promise you. The regrets will all be yours. For to-night I have prepared the most dramatic of scenes, something that will cause everybody to shudder. There will be a presagement of the end of their world . . . for the end of their world is near at hand. We will hear of it from afar, Léocadie. They will tell us of it many days after it has occurred. But to-night you will all say only: Henri has never played so well before.

PROSPÈRE. What are you going to play? Do you know, Léocadie?

LÉOCADIE. Oh, I never know anything.

HENRI. Does any one realize the genius that is mine?

PROSPÈRE. We do, every one of us. That's why I insist it would be a sin to bury yourself in the country—with talents such as yours.

HENRI. I crave rest and serenity. You can-

not understand that, Prospère. You've never loved—

PROSPÈRE. Oh—?

HENRI. As I love! I feel that I must be alone with her. . . . Léocadie, only in that way can we forget, and thus find peace. . . . And never before will two people have been so happy. We shall have babies. You'll make a good mother, Léocadie, and a splendid wife. Everything unlovely will have vanished.

[A long pause]

LÉOCADIE. It's growing late. I'm due at the theatre. Good-bye, Prospère. I'm delighted to have seen your famous place, where Henri has achieved so many triumphs.

PROSPÈRE. And why have you never come before?

LÉOCADIE. Henri was not willing—on account of the young men with whom I should have to sit.

HENRI [who has drawn near to SCAEVOLA]. Give me a swallow of that, Scaevola.

PROSPÈRE [in a low tone, to LÉOCADIE]. A perfect fool, this Henri. If always you were only sitting with them—

LÉOCADIE. I won't let you speak to me so.

PROSPÈRE. Have a care, you little canaille— . . . Some day he'll kill you.

LÉOCADIE. What's the matter with you?

PROSPÈRE. Only yesterday you were seen with one of your fellows—

LÉOCADIE. That was no fellow, you dumbhead, that was—

HENRI [turning to them suddenly]. What's going on here? No monkey-business, please. And no more secrets. She's my wife.

PROSPÈRE. What did you give her as a wedding present?

LÉOCADIE. Oh, Henri doesn't think about things like that.

HENRI. Well, you'll have it this very evening.

LÉOCADIE. What will it be?

SCAEVOLA and JULES [simultaneously]. What are you going to give her?

HENRI [very seriously, to LÉOCADIE]. After you shall have finished your scene at the Porte St. Martin, I shall allow you to come here and see me act.

[The OTHERS laugh]

Never did a bride receive a more practical gift. Come, Léocadie. So long, Prospère, I will return shortly.

[HENRI and LÉOCADIE go out. FRANCOIS, the VICOMTE DE NOGEANT and ALBIN, CHEVALIER DE LA TREMOUILLE enter]

SCAEVOLA. What an insufferable braggart!

PROSPÈRE [as the guests appear]. Good evening, you swine.

[ALBIN draws back]

FRANCOIS [ignoring it]. Wasn't that the little Léocadie of the Porte St. Martin who just left with Henri?

PROSPÈRE. Surely it was. And I suppose that if she took the trouble, she could make you remember that you're something of a man?

FRANCOIS [laughing]. Possibly. It seems we have arrived rather early.

PROSPÈRE. Meantime you can amuse yourself with your country-bumpkin.

[ALBIN rises]

FRANCOIS. Let him alone. I've told you of the sort of thing that goes on here. [To PROSPÈRE] Good host, fetch us some wine.

PROSPÈRE. I will. But the time will come when you will be thankful to have water from the Seine.

FRANCOIS. Of course, of course. But to-day I want wine, and of the best.

[PROSPÈRE goes to the service-bar]

ALBIN. What a dreadful person!

FRANCOIS. You should bear in mind that it's all a joke. But there are other places where you might hear similar things spoken in earnest.

ALBIN. Is it not frowned upon?

FRANCOIS [laughs]. It's clear that you are fresh from the provinces.

ALBIN. Down our way things are almost as bad, nowadays. The peasants are becoming very insolent. But what is to be done about it?

FRANCOIS. What do you expect. The poor devils are hungry, and that's the whole trouble.

ALBIN. How can I help it? How can my great uncle help it?

FRANCOIS. Why do you mention your great uncle?

ALBIN. In our village they held a meeting— quite openly—where they actually called my great uncle, the Comte de la Tremouille, a grain-usurer.

FRANCOIS. Is that all!

ALBIN. Well, I should think—

FRANCOIS. To-morrow we will go to the Palais Royal. There you'll hear the monstrous speeches made by the mob. But we let them talk, it is better so. They are good fellows at heart, and that is the safest vent for their feelings.

ALBIN [indicating SCAEVOLA and JULES]. What suspicious characters! Look how they are staring at us. [He feels for his rapier]

FRANCOIS. Don't make yourself ridiculous. [To the OTHERS] You needn't begin yet. The performance may wait until more of an audience has arrived. [To ALBIN] They are the nicest people in the world, these actors. I warrant you have often sat at table with many worse knaves.

ALBIN. But they were better dressed.

[PROSPÈRE brings the wine. MICHETTE and FLIPOTTE enter]

FRANCOIS. Bless you, my little pigeons, come over here and sit down.

MICHETTE. Come along, Flipotte. She is still so shy.

FLIPOTTE. Good evening, young gentlemen.

ALBIN. Good evening, ladies.

MICHETTE. He's a nice little dear. [Sits on ALBIN's lap]

ALBIN. Please tell me, Francois, are these respectable women?

MICHETTE. What is he saying?

FRANCOIS. That is not quite the word. The ladies who come here . . . good heavens, Albin, but you are dense.

PROSPÈRE. What shall I bring for the duchesses?

MICHETTE. Sweet wine for me.

FRANCOIS [indicating FLIPOTTE] A friend of yours?

MICHETTE. We live together. We have only one bed between us.

FLIPOTTE [blushing]. Would you mind that, when you come to see her? [Sits on FRANCOIS's lap]

ALBIN. I wouldn't exactly call her shy—

SCAEVOLA [rises, comes threateningly to the table. To MICHETTE]. So I've found you at last! [To ALBIN] And you, you miserable seducer—she is mine.

[PROSPÈRE is looking on]

FRANCOIS [to ALBIN]. It's only a joke.

ALBIN. She isn't his—

MICHETTE. Go away. I shall sit where I like.

[SCAEVOLA stands with clenched fists]

PROSPÈRE [behind]. Easy there.

SCAEVOLA. Ha, ha!

PROSPÈRE. Ha, ha! [To SCAEVOLA, privately] You haven't a sou's worth of talent. Roaring —that's all you do.

MICHETTE [to FRANCOIS]. He used to do it much better.

SCAEVOLA [to PROSPÈRE]. I'm not in the right mood yet. I'll do better when there are more people present. You see, Prospère, I need an audience.

[The DUC DE CADIGNAN comes in]

DUC. Already in full swing?

[MICHETTE and FLIPOTTE go up to him]

MICHETTE. My sweet duke.

FRANCOIS. Good evening, Emile. [Introducing] My young friend Albin, Chevalier de la Tremouille—the Duc de Cadignan.

DUC. I am charmed to meet you. [To the girls, who are hanging on to him] Let go of me, children. [To ALBIN] You've come to have a look at this queer wine-room.

ALBIN. It quite bewilders me.

FRANCOIS [explaining]. The Chevalier has but recently come to Paris.

DUC [laughingly]. You've chosen a good time.

ALBIN. What do you mean?

MICHETTE. He still has that delicious perfume. No other man in Paris smells so sweet.

DUC. She's comparing me with the seven or

eight hundred other men she knows as well as she does me.

FLIPOTTE. May I play with your sword? [*She draws his sword from its sheath and holds it so that it reflects the light*]

GRAIN [*to* PROSPÈRE]. That's the man—the man I saw her with— [*He talks further to* PROSPÈRE, *who seems astonished*].

DUC. Henri not here yet? [*To* ALBIN] If you see Henri, you will not regret having come.

PROSPÈRE [*to the* DUC]. So you've turned up again, have you? I'm glad, because we won't have that pleasure much longer.

DUC. Why not? I find it very pleasant here.

PROSPÈRE. I believe that. But it's quite likely that you'll be one of the first to go. . . .

ALBIN. What does that mean?

PROSPÈRE. You understand me well enough. The most fortunate will become the most unfortunate. [*Returns to the service-bar*]

DUC. If I were the king I would make him my court jester.

ALBIN. What did he mean by saying you were too fortunate?

DUC. He means, Chevalier—

ALBIN. Oh please don't call me Chevalier. Everybody calls me Albin . . . simply Albin, because I look so young.

DUC [*smiling*]. Very good. But then you must call me Emile.

ALBIN. With your permission, Emile.

DUC. They have a sinister wit, these folk.

FRANCOIS. Why sinister? To me, it's very reassuring. So long as the populace remains in jesting mood, nothing serious can happen.

DUC. Their jests have a curious twist. Only to-day I learned of something that gives food for thought.

FRANCOIS. Tell us.

FLIPOTTE *and* MICHETTE. Yes, tell us, sweet Duke.

DUC. Do you know Lalange?

FRANCOIS. The village? Surely. The Marquis de Montferrat has one of his finest game preserves there.

DUC. Quite so. My brother is visiting him at his castle and has just written me of the affair. In Lalange they have a mayor who is very unpopular.

FRANCOIS. Can you name one that isn't?

DUC. Now listen. The women of the village paraded around the Mayor's house, carrying a coffin.

FLIPOTTE. Carrying a coffin! Oh, I wouldn't carry a coffin for anything.

FRANCOIS. Be still! Nobody wishes you to carry a coffin. [*To the* DUC] Well?

DUC. Some of the women entered the house and told the Mayor that it was necessary he should die, but that they would give him the honor of being buried.

FRANCOIS. And did they really kill him?

DUC. No, or at least my brother did not say so.

FRANCOIS. You see! . . . Blusterers, showoffs, clowns, nothing worse. To-day they are shrieking at the Bastile for a change—though they have done so half a dozen times before.

DUC. Well, if I were king I would have put a stop to it—long ago.

ALBIN. Is it true that the king is so kind and tolerant?

DUC. Have you not yet been presented to His Majesty?

FRANCOIS. The Chevalier is in Paris for the first time.

DUC. Yes, you are unbelievably young. May I ask your age?

ALBIN. It's only that I look young. I'm already seventeen.

DUC. Seventeen! How much is still before you. I have reached twenty-four and I begin already to regret how much of my youth I have squandered.

FRANCOIS. That is delicious, Duke—coming from you, who count that day as lost in which you have not won a woman or killed a man.

DUC. The pity is, one never wins the right woman, and always kills the wrong man. And so is youth wasted—just as Rollin says—

FRANCOIS. What does Rollin say?

DUC. I was thinking of his new piece they are giving at the Comédie—of that pretty simile —do you recall it?

FRANCOIS. I have no memory for verse.

DUC. Nor I, alas. I remember only the sense. He says that youth which is not enjoyed is like a feather ball left lying in the sand, instead of being tossed in the air.

ALBIN [*sagely*]. Quite true.

DUC. Is it not? The feathers gradually lose their color and fall out. Far better that it should drop into a bush, where it cannot be seen.

ALBIN. What should I understand by that, Emile?

DUC. It's more a matter of feeling. Could I only repeat the verse, you'd understand at once.

ALBIN. I believe you could write verse, Emile, if you tried.

DUC. What makes you think that?

ALBIN. Since you came in, all life has seemed to flame up.

DUC [*with a smile*]. Yes? Is life flaming up for you?

[*Meanwhile two more noblemen have entered and taken a distant table, where* PROSPÈRE *seems to be doing his best to insult them*]

FRANCOIS [*to the* DUC]. Won't you sit down with us?

DUC. I can't stop now. I will return later.

MICHETTE. Stay with us.

FLIPOTTE. Take me with you.

[*They try to hold him*]

PROSPÈRE [*joining them*]. Leave him alone. You are not nearly bad enough to suit him. He's going out now to meet some trollop of the streets.

DUC [*ignoring him*]. I can't stay now, but will surely be back in time to see Henri.

FRANCOIS. When we came in, Henri was just leaving with Léocadie.

DUC. He has married her. Did you know that?

FRANCOIS. Married, eh! What will the others say to that?

ALBIN. What others?

FRANCOIS. She is a general favorite, you know.

DUC. And he wants to take her away from Paris, or so I've been told.

PROSPÈRE [*meaningly*]. So you've been told?

DUC. It's very foolish. Léocadie was created to be a great courtezan. . . .

FRANCOIS. As every one knows.

DUC. And could anything be more unreasonable than to take people away from their true vocation?

[FRANCOIS *laughs*]

I'm not jesting. Like poets and conquerors, good courtezans are born, not made.

FRANCOIS. That is paradoxical.

DUC. I'm sorry for her—and for Henri. He should stay here—no, not here. I would put him in the Comédie—though there also, no one would appreciate him as I do. But then, I often have that feeling concerning artists. If I were not the Duc de Cadignan, I should love to be an actor, a conqueror—

FRANCOIS. Like Alexander the Great.

DUC [*smiling*]. Like Henri—or Alexander. [*To* FLIPOTTE] Give me my sword. [*He returns it to its scabbard. Slowly*] It is the choicest way to make sport of the world. He who can portray whatever he pleases is greater than the rest of us. [*As* ALBIN *regards him with astonishment*] Don't pay any attention to what I've said. It's true only at the moment. Goodbye.

MICHETTE. Give me a kiss before you go.

FLIPOTTE. Me, too.

[*They cling to him. The* DUC *kisses them both at once and takes his leave*]

ALBIN. A wonderful man.

FRANCOIS. Surely—in his way. But the fact that such men exist offers sufficient reason not to marry.

ALBIN. But who are these women?

FRANCOIS. Actresses—members of Prospère's troupe—

[GUILLAUME *rushes in breathlessly, goes to the table where the actors are sitting and theatrically puts his hand to his heart, apparently scarcely able to stand*]

GUILLAUME. Saved! I'm saved!

SCAEVOLA. What's happened? What ails you?

ALBIN. What's the matter with the man?

FRANCOIS. That's only play-acting. Now watch.

ALBIN. Ah—!

MICHETTE *and* FLIPOTTE [*running to* GUILLAUME]. What is it? What's the matter?

SCAEVOLA. Have a swallow—

GUILLAUME. More! More wine, Prospère! My tongue cleaves to my mouth. I've been running. They were at my heels!

JULES [*starts*]. Hush! They're ever at our heels!

PROSPÈRE. Come, tell us what happened. [*Coaching the actors*] More movement—livelier, there!

GUILLAUME. Women here—where are the women? Ah—! [*An arm about* FLIPOTTE] that gives me new life. [*To* ALBIN, *who is highly impressed*] The devil take me, my boy, if I thought I should ever see you again. [*Listening*] They are coming! They are coming! [*Runs to the steps*] No, it's nothing—they—

ALBIN. How strange! There really is a noise outside, as if throngs were hurrying past. Is that just part of the stage-effects?

SCAEVOLA [*to* JULES]. He does that trick every time. Silly realism.

PROSPÈRE. Now tell us why they are after you.

GUILLAUME. Nothing special—but if they get me—it will cost me my head. I set fire to a house—

[*During this scene, two more young noblemen drift in and sit at tables*]

PROSPÈRE [*coaching* GUILLAUME]. Go on—go on!

GUILLAUME. Go on? Isn't setting fire to a house sufficient?

FRANCOIS. You haven't told us why you set fire to the house.

GUILLAUME. Because the president of the Supreme Court lives in it. We chose him first—to show Parisian house-holders the danger of harboring tenants who have the power to send us poor devils to jail.

GRAIN. Good! That's very good.

GUILLAUME [*looks at* GRAIN *in surprise*]. All such houses must be burned. Three more men like me, and there won't be a judge left in Paris.

GRAIN. Death to the judges!

JULES. Yes . . . but there is perhaps one Judge whom we cannot do away with.

GUILLAUME. Who is that?

JULES. The Judge that dwells within us.

PROSPÈRE. That stuff is vapid. Come, Scaevola, roar! Now is the moment.

SCAEVOLA. Bring wine, Prospère, that we may drink to the death of all the judges of France.

[*During the last words, the* MARQUIS DE LANSAC, *with his wife,* SÉVERINE, *and* ROLLIN, *the poet, have come in*]

SCAEVOLA. Down with all those now in power! Down with them!

MARQUIS. You see, Séverine, this is the way they greet us.

ROLLIN. Marquise, I warn you.

SÉVERINE. But why?

FRANCOIS. Upon my word—the Marquise . . . allow me to kiss your hand. Good evening, Marquis. God bless you, Rollin. . . . Do you venture here, Marquise?

SÉVERINE. I've heard so much about this place. And besides, this is a day of adventure—isn't it, Rollin?

MARQUIS. Where do you suppose we've been? Yes, Vicomte, we've been to the Bastile.

FRANCOIS. Is the hullabaloo still going on there?

SÉVERINE. It looks as if they meant to storm the place.

ROLLIN [declaims].
It is like a river that washes away its own banks,
Like a flood that beats against the shore
In wrath that its own child, the earth,
Should dare resist its might.

SÉVERINE [to FRANCOIS]. We drove quite close and watched it from our carriage. It was very spectacular. Great crowds are so magnificent.

FRANCOIS. Yes, if only they didn't smell so vilely.

MARQUIS. And then my wife insisted that we bring her here.

SÉVERINE. What is there so remarkable about this place?

PROSPÈRE [to the MARQUIS]. So you're here, too, you dried-up old scoundrel! Did you bring your wife because you didn't think it safe to leave her alone at home?

MARQUISE [forcing a smile]. He is at least original.

PROSPÈRE. Be careful you don't lose her here. These fine ladies often get an urge to find out what a real rogue is like.

ROLLIN. I suffer unspeakably, Séverine.

MARQUIS. Dear child, I warned you—but there's still time to go.

SÉVERINE. What is troubling you? I think it quite charming. Let us sit down.

FRANCOIS. Permit me, Marquise, to present the Chevalier de la Tremouille, also here for the first time. Marquis de Lansac; Rollin, our distinguished poet.

[They exchange compliments and sit down]

ALBIN [in an undertone to FRANCOIS]. Is she one of the players? It's a little confusing.

FRANCOIS. Shake up your wits, Albin. That is the real wife of the Marquis—a lady of rank.

ROLLIN [to SÉVERINE]. Tell me that you love me.

SÉVERINE. Yes, yes, but don't ask me every few minutes.

MARQUIS. Have we missed anything?

FRANCOIS. Nothing much. That fellow over there is playing an incendiary.

SÉVERINE. Chevalier, are you not the cousin of the little Lydia de la Tremouille who was married to-day?

ALBIN. Yes, Marquise. That was one of my reasons for coming to Paris.

SÉVERINE. I recall now, having seen you at the church.

ALBIN [self-consciously]. I am flattered, Marquise.

SÉVERINE [to ROLLIN]. What a nice boy.

ROLLIN. Ah, Séverine, you never yet met a man you thought unpleasing.

SÉVERINE. Oh yes—but I married him at once.

ROLLIN. Yet I have a constant fear, Séverine, that there are moments when it is not safe for you to be with him.

PROSPÈRE [bringing wine]. Here's your wine. I wish it were poison, but at present I am not allowed to give you that.

FRANCOIS. That time will soon come, Prospère.

SÉVERINE [to ROLLIN]. What's the matter with those two pretty girls, that they haven't come to our table? Now that I'm here, I want to be in everything that's going on. Thus far it has been offensively dull.

MARQUIS. Just have a little patience, Séverine.

SÉVERINE. I think that nowadays the streets are more diverting. [To FRANCOIS] Did you hear what happened to us yesterday when we went for a drive down the Promenade de Longchamps?

MARQUIS. I beg of you, my dear Séverine. . . .

SÉVERINE. One fellow jumped on the step of our carriage and shouted in our faces: Next year you will walk behind your coach, while we shall be riding in it.

FRANCOIS. That's rather strong.

MARQUIS. I think it indiscreet to mention these things. Paris is a little feverish—but that will soon pass.

GUILLAUME [suddenly]. I see flames—everywhere flames—whichever way I look—red, leaping flames.

PROSPÈRE [in low-voiced protest]. You're playing a madman, not a criminal.

SÉVERINE. He sees flames?

PROSPÈRE. This is only a prelude, Madame la Marquise.

ALBIN. I can't tell you how bewildered I feel.

MICHETTE [goes to the MARQUIS]. I haven't greeted you yet, my sweet old pig.

MARQUIS [embarrassed]. She is just being playful, dear Séverine.

SÉVERINE. I doubt it. Tell me, little one, how many love affairs have you had so far?

MARQUIS [to FRANCOIS]. It's remarkable how my wife enters into the mood of this place.

ROLLIN. Quite.

MICHETTE [to the MARQUISE]. Could you count yours?

MARQUISE. When I was your age . . . but yes, certainly.

ALBIN [to ROLLIN]. Tell me, Monsieur Rollin, is the Marquise just acting—or is she really—? . . . I can't make it out.

ROLLIN. Reality . . . acting . . . can you always define the difference, Chevalier?

ALBIN. Why, I think so.

ROLLIN. I can't. And what I think so fascinating about this place, is that all apparent differences seem to be eliminated. Reality blends into illusion—illusion into actuality. Just look at the Marquise now, chatting with those creatures as if she were one of them. Yet she is—

ALBIN. Something entirely different.

ROLLIN. I thank you, Chevalier.

PROSPÈRE [to GRAIN]. How did it happen?

GRAIN. What?

PROSPÈRE. The story of your aunt, for whom you spent two years in the penitentiary.

GRAIN. I told you, I strangled her.

FRANCOIS. This fellow is weak. He must be an amateur. I've never seen him before.

[GEORGETTE comes in hastily, dressed as a prostitute of the lowest grade]

GEORGETTE. Good evening, friends! . . . Is my Balthasar here?

SCAEVOLA. Georgette, come and sit with me. Your Balthasar will show up soon. He will have settled his affair.

GEORGETTE. If he is not here within ten minutes, he won't come.

FRANCOIS. Watch her, Marquise. She is the real wife of this Balthasar who is about to come in. She represents a common street-walker, while Balthasar is her bully. But she's actually the most faithful wife in Paris.

[BALTHASAR arrives. GEORGETTE runs to him with an embrace]

GEORGETTE. My Balthasar! [Smiling, she puts her arms about him]

BALTHASAR. The matter is attended to. [The OTHERS listen] It was not worth the trouble— I felt almost sorry for him. You should size up your customers better, Georgette. I am sick of killing promising young men for the sake of a few francs.

FRANCOIS. Fine!

ALBIN. What—?

FRANCOIS. He gets his points over.

[The SERGENT DE VILLE returns in disguise; sits at a table]

PROSPÈRE [to the SERGENT]. You arrive at an excellent time, Monsieur le Sergent. This is one of my cleverest performers.

BALTHASAR. I'm going to look for another kind of a job. I'm not without courage, but on my soul, this is a hazardous way of earning a living.

SCAEVOLA. I believe you.

GEORGETTE [to BALTHASAR]. There's something else on your mind.

BALTHASAR. I'll tell you, Georgette. You are a little too nice to the young gentlemen.

GEORGETTE [to the OTHERS]. You see how childish he is? I have to be nice to them, to inspire confidence.

ROLLIN. Her words are profoundly true.

BALTHASAR [to GEORGETTE]. If I thought you had any feeling—

GEORGETTE. His silly jealousy will land him in his grave.

BALTHASAR. I heard a sigh, Georgette, at a moment when there already was plenty of confidence.

GEORGETTE. Of course, you can't stop pretending all of a sudden.

BALTHASAR. Beware, Georgette—the Seine is deep. [Wildly] You are deceiving me—

GEORGETTE. Never! I swear it!

ALBIN. I don't understand this at all.

SÉVERINE [to ROLLIN]. She has the right idea.

ROLLIN. You think so?

MARQUISE. We can still go, Séverine.

SÉVERINE. But why? I am beginning to enjoy it.

GEORGETTE [her arms about him]. My Balthasar, I adore you.

FRANCOIS. Bravo! Bravo!

BALTHASAR. What imbecile is that?

SERGENT. This is going too far . . . it is . . .

[MAURICE and ETIENNE appear, dressed as noblemen, but the shabbiness of their costumes is not observed]

THE PLAYERS. Who are they?

SCAEVOLA. Devil take me if it isn't Maurice and Etienne.

GEORGETTE. As I live, it is.

BALTHASAR. Georgette!

SÉVERINE. What handsome young men!

ROLLIN. It is painful, Séverine, that every handsome face excites you so.

SÉVERINE. What do you think I came here for?

ROLLIN. At least you might tell me that you love me.

SÉVERINE [with a look]. You have a short memory.

ETIENNE. Where do you suppose we've been to-day?

FRANCOIS. Pay attention, Marquis, these youths are very clever.

MAURICE. We've come from a wedding . . .

ETIENNE. You have to dress for that. Otherwise the confounded secret police are after you.

SCAEVOLA. Did you make a good haul?

PROSPÈRE. Let's see.

MAURICE [taking several watches from his pocket]. What am I offered for these?

PROSPÈRE. For that one, a gold louis.

MAURICE. You would.

SCAEVOLA. I'd pay more. It's worth more to me.

MICHETTE. That's a woman's watch. Give it to me, Maurice.

MAURICE. What do you offer me for it?

MICHETTE. You may look at me.

MAURICE. My dear child, that is not enough.

SÉVERINE [*in a low voice*]. I'll swear this is not just acting.

ROLLIN. There is an undercurrent—that's what makes it so fascinating—bits of the real flashing through.

SCAEVOLA. What wedding was it?

MAURICE. That of Mademoiselle de la Tremouille. She married the Comte de Bonville.

ALBIN. You hear that, Francois? I assure you they are real thieves.

FRANCOIS. Don't worry, Albin, I know this pair. I've seen them play a dozen times. They make a specialty of being pickpockets.

[MAURICE *extracts some purses from his coat*]

SCAEVOLA. You've done well by yourselves. Why not do well by us?

ETIENNE. It was a brilliant wedding. The entire nobility of France was there. Even the king was represented.

ALBIN [*excited*]. That is all true!

MAURICE [*throws gold pieces about upon the actor's table*]. That's for you, my friends, to show our loyalty.

FRANCOIS. Stage money, my dear Albin. [*He rises and picks up a few coins*] We can have some of it.

PROSPÈRE. Yes, take it—you never earned anything so honestly.

MAURICE [*holds aloft a garter set with diamonds*]. To whom shall I give this? [GEORGETTE, MICHETTE *and* FLIPOTTE *hasten to him and reach for it*] Patience, my sweet mice. We'll talk it over. . . . I'll give it to the one who invents a new caress.

SÉVERINE [*to* ROLLIN]. Would you allow me to compete with them?

ROLLIN. Séverine, you drive me mad.

MARQUIS. I think it is time for us to go.

SÉVERINE. By no means. I'm enjoying myself vastly. [*To* ROLLIN] I'm just getting into the spirit of it.

MICHETTE. How did you get that garter?

MAURICE. There was a great crowd in the church—and she thought I was making overtures . . .

[*All laugh. Meanwhile,* GRAIN *has "lifted"* FRANCOIS' *purse*]

FRANCOIS [*showing the money to* ALBIN]. All bogus—imitation money . . .

[GRAIN *is anxious to get out*]

PROSPÈRE [*follows him and says softly*]. Give me the purse you just took from that young man.

GRAIN. I?

PROSPÈRE. Be quick—or I'll have you set upon—

GRAIN. You needn't be rude about it. [*Gives him the purse*]

PROSPÈRE. I have no time to search you now, and dear knows what else you've pocketed. Go back to your place.

FLIPOTTE. I know I'll win that garter.

PROSPÈRE [*to* FRANCOIS, *throwing him the purse*]. There's your purse—you lost it out of your pocket.

FRANCOIS. Thanks, Prospère. [*To* ALBIN] You see how honest they are.

[HENRI, *who has come in and has been sitting in the rear unobserved for some time, now rises*]

ROLLIN. Henri! . . . Look, there's Henri!

SÉVERINE. The artist you told me about?

MARQUIS. He's the main attraction here—the reason for our coming.

[HENRI *strides forward in majestic silence*]

THE PLAYERS. What's wrong, Henri? What's the matter?

ROLLIN. Watch his expression . . . a world of suffering. He is playing the rôle of one who has committed a crime through soul-torment.

SÉVERINE. Splendid!

ALBIN. Why doesn't he commence?

ROLLIN. He's superb—watch him. . . . He's stunned by his own emotions.

FRANCOIS. But he overacts a little—seems to be preparing for a monologue.

PROSPÈRE. Henri, Henri, where have you been?

HENRI. I have just killed a man.

ROLLIN. What did I say!

PROSPÈRE. Who?

HENRI. My wife's lover.

[PROSPÈRE *looks at him and it dawns on him that it may be true*]

HENRI [*looks up*]. Yes, I've done it. Why do you stare at me so? It's the truth. It is so unexpected? You know what my wife is. It was bound to come.

PROSPÈRE. And she? Where is she?

FRANCOIS. You see, Prospère gives him his cue. How natural it all seems.

[*Noise outside, not too loud*]

JULES. What is that noise out there?

MARQUIS. You hear it, Séverine?

ROLLIN. It sounds like troops marching by.

FRANCOIS. Oh no, it's our beloved Parisian populace—growling.

[*Uneasiness in the cellar-room until the noise dies away*]

FRANCOIS. Go on, Henri, go on.

PROSPÈRE. Tell us, Henri, where is your wife? Where did you leave her?

HENRI. Oh, I'm not worried about her. She won't die of it. This one or that one—what do these women care? There are a thousand good-looking men in Paris. What matter whether this one or that one—

BALTHASAR. May the same fate take all men who take our women—

SCAEVOLA. All who take what belongs to us!

SERGENT [to PROSPÈRE]. These are inciting speeches.

ALBIN. It's frightful—these people are serious—mean every word they utter.

SCAEVOLA. Down with all the parasites of France. I'll wager that fellow he caught with his wife was one of the beasts who rob us of our bread.

ALBIN. I suggest that we go.

SÉVERINE. Henri! Henri!

MARQUIS. But Marquise, Séverine—!

SÉVERINE. Please, my dear Marquis, will you ask that man how he caught his wife? Or shall I ask him?

MARQUIS [unwillingly]. Will you tell us, Henri, how you succeeded in catching those two?

HENRI [who has been deep in thought]. Do you know my wife? She is the most beautiful and the most depraved being under the sun—and I love her. We have known each other for seven years . . . but only yesterday did she become my wife. In all those seven years, there was not one day that she did not lie to me. For everything about her lied—her eyes and her lips, her kisses and her smiles.

FRANCOIS. He overdoes it a trifle.

HENRI. Every young one and every old one—every one who attracted her, and every one who paid her—even every one who desired her—could have her . . . and I knew it.

SÉVERINE. Not every man could say as much.

HENRI. Yet nevertheless, my friends, she loved me. Can you understand that? From every one of those others, she came back to me. From the handsome ones and the ill-favored ones—from the clever ones and the stupid ones, from tramps, vagabonds, rapscallions and from cavaliers—always she came back to me.

SÉVERINE [to ROLLIN]. Now if you could only understand that this coming back is the only real love . . .

HENRI. What I suffered . . . tortures . . . tortures!

ROLLIN. It gives you the shivers.

HENRI. And yesterday I married her. We dreamed—I dreamed—of our going away together, to the solitude, the infinite peace of the open country. We dreamed too of having a child.

ROLLIN [tenderly]. Séverine! . . .

SÉVERINE. Yes, it's very good.

ALBIN. Francois, this man speaks the truth.

FRANCOIS. Of course, the love-story is true enough, but the murder—

HENRI. I had thought a new life had opened. But there was one man she had not yet forgotten. To-day, I returned unexpectedly and found them together. Now he is no more.

THE PLAYERS. Who? . . . Who? How did it happen? . . . Where is he? . . . Are they after you? . . . How did it happen? . . . Where is she?

HENRI [always erect; in crescendo]. I had left her at the theatre—it was to be her last appearance. She was on her way to her dressing room and I left her without a misgiving. But no more than a hundred steps away it began—a terrible unrest. It was as if something were compelling my return. And I did start back to the theatre, then I was ashamed and walked away again. But once more, after about a hundred steps, it pulled at me again—irresistibly. Her scene is soon over—she has only to stand for a moment on the stage, half-naked—then she is through. I waited before her dressing room . . . I held my ear to the door and heard whispers—I couldn't make out the words. The whispering ceased. I forced open the door . . . [With a cry like a wild animal] It was the Duc le Cadignan—and I killed him!

PROSPÈRE [fearing this is the truth]. Crazy fool!

[HENRI gazes fixedly at him]

SÉVERINE. Bravo! Bravo!

ROLLIN. What are you doing, Marquise? The moment you call Bravo! the illusion is lost and all the exquisite shivers are gone.

MARQUIS. I can't say I find the shivers so agreeable. Let us applaud, friends, so that we can shake off this unpleasant feeling.

[A murmur of Bravos! increasing in volume when all applaud]

PROSPÈRE [to HENRI]. Save yourself, Henri! Go!

HENRI. What . . . what?

PROSPÈRE. That will be enough—go, make haste!

FRANCOIS. Quiet! Let's hear what Prospère says.

PROSPÈRE [after a brief reflection]. I tell him he must flee, before the watch at the city gates are warned. [To HENRI] The handsome duke was a favorite of the king. He will break you on the wheel. Why didn't you put an end to that worthless wife of yours, instead?

FRANCOIS. What marvelous team-work . . . magnificent!

HENRI. Prospère, is it you that is crazy—or I? [He tries to read PROSPÈRE's eyes]

ROLLIN. It's extraordinary! We all know that he is acting. And yet, if at this moment the Duc de Cadignan should walk in, we would take him for a ghost.

[The tumult in the street has been growing in volume. Shouts and yells are heard, as the door bursts open and people press in, headed by GRASSET, with LEBRÊT following. Cries of "Vive la liberté!" outside]

GRASSET. Here we are, boys—in here.

ALBIN. What is this? Part of the programme?

FRANCOIS. No—I fear not.

MARQUIS. What is the meaning of this?

SÉVERINE. Who are the people?

GRASSET. Come in, children. My good friend Prospère always has a barrel of wine in reserve —and to-night we have earned it. [*Hullabaloo in the street*] Friends, brothers, we have taken it! We have taken it!

　　[*Shouts of "Vive la liberté!" outside*]

SÉVERINE. What is happening?

MARQUIS. Let us go! Let us go! The mob is pouring in.

ROLLIN. How do you think we can get out?

GRASSET. It has fallen—the Bastile has fallen!

PROSPÈRE. What's that you're saying? Is that true?

GRASSET. Don't you hear?

　　[ALBIN *would draw his sword*]

FRANCOIS. Leave it where it is—or we are all lost.

GRASSET [*reeling down the stairs*]. And if you hurry out, you'll see a merry sight. You'll see the head of our dear Delaunay stuck on the end of a pike.

MARQUIS. Is the fellow mad?

THE CROWD. Vive la liberté! Vive la liberté!

GRASSET. We lopped off the heads of a dozen of them. The Bastile is ours—the prisoners are free! Paris belongs to the people.

PROSPÈRE. Hear you—hear! Paris is ours!

GRASSET. Look how he gains courage! Yell if you like, Prospère, it can't harm you now.

PROSPÈRE [*to the* NOBLEMEN]. What do you say to that, you swine? The play is ended. The joke is over.

ALBIN. Didn't I tell you?

SERGENT. Silence! [*Laughter*] I prohibit the continuance of this performance.

PROSPÈRE. He has gone mad. What is that to you now? You killed him—there's nothing more you can do.

FRANCOIS. For God's sake—is this true or not?

PROSPÈRE. Yes, it is true.

GRASSET. Henri, from now on you'll be my friend. Vive la liberté! Vive la liberté!

FRANCOIS. Henri, do speak!

HENRI. She was his mistress—the Duke's mistress. And I never knew it. And he lives . . . he still lives.

　　[*There is a stir among the by-standers: intense interest*]

SÉVERINE [*to the Others*]. Well, what is the truth?

ALBIN. For heaven's sake—

　　[*The* DUC DE CADIGNAN *forces his way through the crowd on the stairs*]

SÉVERINE [*the first to observe him*]. The Duke!

THE OTHERS. The Duke! The Duke!

DUC. Why yes, but what of it?

PROSPÈRE. It's a ghost.

DUC. Not so far as I know. Let me get in there.

ROLLIN. I'm positive all this was prearranged. The mob out there belong to Prospère's troupe. Bravo! Prospère, you've done it well.

DUC. How is this? You don't mean you are still dawdling here, while outside . . . don't you know, then, what is going on? . . . I have seen the head of Delaunay go past me on the end of a pole. Why do you look at me that way? [*He steps down into the room*] Henri—

FRANCOIS. Watch out for Henri!

　　[HENRI *throws himself insanely upon the* DUC *and thrusts a dagger into his throat*]

SERGENT [*rises*]. That is going too far.

ALBIN. He is bleeding.

ROLLIN. A murder has been committed.

SÉVERINE. He is dying.

MARQUIS. I am distraught . . . dear Séverine, at having brought you to this place, and to-day of all days.

SÉVERINE [*a little unsteadily*]. Why? I think it's thrilling. It isn't every day that you can see a real duke really murdered.

ROLLIN. I don't understand it yet. It's bewildering.

SERGENT. Quiet! No one is to leave this room.

GRASSET. What does *he* want?

SERGENT [*going to* HENRI]. I arrest this man, in the name of the law.

GRASSET [*laughs*]. We make the laws now, simpleton. He who wipes out a duke is a friend of the people. Vive la liberté!

ALBIN [*with drawn sword*]. Out of the way, there! . . . Follow me, my friends.

　　[LÉOCADIE *elbows her way in and down the stairs*]

VOICES FROM THE CROWD. Léocadie!

OTHERS. His wife!

LÉOCADIE. Let me in! . . . I want to reach my husband. [*She runs forward, sees the* DUKE'S *body and screams*] Who did this? . . . Henri! [HENRI *looks at her*] Henri—why did you do this?

HENRI. Why? . . .

LÉOCADIE. But yes, I don't have to be told— it was for my sake—and I—I am not worth it.

GRASSET [*beginning a speech*]. Citizens of Paris! We wish to celebrate our victory. Chance has led us through the streets of Paris to this welcome resort. It couldn't have been a better one. Nowhere can the cry of Vive la liberté! sound more appropriate than over the dead body of a duke.

　　[VOICES FROM THE CROWD *call:* "Vive la liberté!"]

FRANCOIS. I think we had best go. The people are mad. Let's go at once.

ALBIN. Are we going to leave the duke's body—

SÉVERINE. Vive la liberté!

Marquis. Are you out of your head? Have you lost your wits?

[Citizens, *including* Players, *shout:* "Vive la liberté!"]

Séverine. Rollin, wait for me to-night in front of the house. I'll throw a key down as before. I feel greatly exhilarated.

Lebrêt. Stop these people—they are running away from us.

Grasset. Let them go . . . for to-day. Let them go . . . they will not escape us.

CURTAIN

THE MAN WHO MARRIED A DUMB WIFE

A Comedy in Two Acts

By ANATOLE FRANCE

TRANSLATED BY CURTIS HIDDEN PAGE

DRAMATIS PERSONÆ

MASTER LEONARD BOTAL, *judge*
MASTER ADAM FUMÉE, *lawyer*
MASTER SIMON COLLINE, *doctor*
MASTER JEAN MAUGIER, *surgeon*
MASTER SERAFIN DULAURIER, *apothecary*
GILES BOISCOURTIER, *secretary*
A BLIND FIDDLER
CATHERINE, *Botal's wife*
ALISON, *Botal's servant*
MADEMOISELLE DE LA GARANDIÈRE
MADAME DE LA BRUINE
THE CHICKWEED MAN
THE WATERCRESS MAN
THE CANDLE MAN
PAGE TO MADEMOISELLE DE LA GARANDIÈRE
FOOTMAN TO MADAME DE LA BRUINE
FIRST DOCTOR'S ATTENDANT
SECOND DOCTOR'S ATTENDANT
A CHIMNEY SWEEP
FIRST APOTHECARY'S BOY
SECOND APOTHECARY'S BOY

THE MAN WHO MARRIED A DUMB WIFE

ACT ONE

A large room in JUDGE LEONARD BOTAL'S *house at Paris.*

Left: Main entrance, from the rue Dauphine; when the door is open, vista to the Pont-Neuf.

Right: Door to the kitchen.

At the rear of the stage: A wooden stairway, leading to the upper rooms.

On the walls are portraits of magistrates, in gown and wig, and along the walls, great cabinets, or cupboards, full of books, papers, parchments, and bags of legal documents, with more piled on top of the cabinets. There is a double step-ladder on castors, with flat steps on each side, used to reach the top of the cabinets.

A writing-table, small chairs, upholstered arm-chairs, and a spinning-wheel.

(In Mr. Granville Barker's production the street is shown in front of the house, instead of being concealed behind it; so that the chimney-sweep, the chickweed-seller, the candle-man, etc., pass across the front of the stage.)

The street door of the house opens on a hallway, from which a door leads off to the kitchen, and a short stairway leads up, in a direction parallel with the front of the stage, past a double lattice window open to the street, to an upper room in which most of the action takes place.

This room has a large balcony and window-seat, and stands entirely open to the street. The writing-table, book-case (instead of cabinets), and step-ladder are seen within it. There is a bench or form, long enough to seat two or three people, in front of the table. A door at the right rear corner of the room is supposed to open on a stairway leading to the rooms above.)

*[*GILES *is discovered sitting on a small form in front of the table; on the rise of the curtain he turns to the audience, bows in flamboyant style, and then sits down again, with his back to the audience.*

The CHICKWEED MAN *goes by, calling:* "Chickweed! Chickweed! Good birdseed, good birdseed, good birdseed for saäle!"*

*[*Enter ALISON, *with a large basket under each arm. She curtsies to the audience.* GILES, *as soon as he spies her, runs to the street door and stands quiet beside*

it, so that she does not notice him. As she starts to enter the house, he jumps at her and snatches a bottle from one of the baskets]*

ALISON. Holy Mary, don't you know better than to jump at anybody like a bogie-man, right here in a public place?

GILES [*pulling a bottle of wine out of the other basket*]. Don't scream, you little goose. Nobody's going to pluck you. You're not worth it.

*[*Enter MASTER ADAM FUMÉE. *He bows to the audience*]

ALISON. Will you let the Judge's wine alone, you rascal!

*[*She sets down her baskets, snatches back one of the bottles, cuffs the secretary, picks up her baskets, and goes off to the kitchen. The kitchen fire-place is seen through the half-open door]*

MASTER ADAM [*slightly formal in manner and speech at first*]. Is this the dwelling of Mr. Leonard Botal, Judge in civil and criminal cases?

GILES [*with bottle behind his back, and bowing*]. Yes, sir; it's here, sir; and I'm his secretary, Giles Boiscourtier, at your service, sir.

MASTER ADAM. Then, boy, go tell him his old school-fellow, Master Adam Fumée, lawyer, wishes to see him on business.

GILES. Here he comes now, sir.

*[*LEONARD BOTAL *comes down the stairs.* GILES *goes off into the kitchen*]

MASTER ADAM. Good day, Master Leonard Botal, I am delighted to see you again.

LEONARD. Good morning, Master Adam Fumée, how have you been this long time that I haven't set eyes on you?

MASTER ADAM. Well, very well. And I hope I find you the same, your Honour.

LEONARD. Fairly so, fairly so. And what good wind wafts you hither, Master Adam Fumée?

*[*They come forward in the room]*

MASTER ADAM. I've come from Chartres on purpose to put in your own hands a statement on behalf of a young orphan girl . . .

LEONARD. Master Adam Fumée, do you remember the days when we were law students together at Orleans University?

MASTER ADAM. Yes, yes; we used to play the flute together, and take the ladies out to picnics, and dance from morning to night. . . . But I've come, your Honour, my dear old

school-fellow, to hand you a statement on behalf of a young orphan girl whose case is now
pending before you.

LEONARD. Will she give good fees?

MASTER ADAM. She is a young orphan
girl. . . .

LEONARD. Yes, yes, I know. But, will she give
good fees?

MASTER ADAM. She is a young orphan girl,
who's been robbed by her guardian, and he left
her nothing but her eyes to weep with. But
if she wins her suit, she will be rich again, and
will give plentiful proof of her gratitude.

LEONARD [taking the statement which MAS-
TER ADAM hands him]. We will look into the
matter.

MASTER ADAM. I thank you, your Honour,
my dear old school-fellow.

LEONARD. We will look into it, without fear
or favour.

MASTER ADAM. That goes without saying.
. . . But, tell me: Is everything going smoothly
with you? You seem worried. And yet, you are
well placed here . . . the judgeship's a good
one?

LEONARD. I paid enough for it to be a good
one—and I didn't get cheated.

MASTER ADAM. Perhaps you are lonely. Why
don't you get married?

LEONARD. What, what! Don't you know,
Master Adam, that I have just been married?
[They sit down on the form in front of the
table] Yes, only last month, to a girl from one
of our best country families, young and handsome, Catherine Momichel, the seventh daughter of the Criminal Court Judge at Salency. But
alas! she is dumb. Now you know my affliction.

MASTER ADAM. Your wife is dumb?

LEONARD. Alas, yes.

MASTER ADAM. Quite, quite dumb?

LEONARD. As a fish.

MASTER ADAM. And you didn't notice it till
after you'd married her?

LEONARD. Oh, I couldn't help noticing it, of
course, but it didn't seem to make so much
difference to me then as it does now. I considered her beauty, and her property, and
thought of nothing but the advantages of the
match and the happiness I should have with
her. But now these matters seem less important, and I do wish she could talk; that
would be a real intellectual pleasure for me,
and, what's more, a practical advantage for
the household. What does a Judge need most
in his house? Why, a good-looking wife, to
receive the suitors pleasantly, and, by subtle
suggestions, gently bring them to the point
of making proper presents, so that their cases
may receive—more careful attention. People
need to be encouraged to make proper presents.
A woman, by clever speech and prudent action,
can get a good ham from one, and a roll of cloth

from another; and make still another give
poultry or wine. But this poor dumb thing
Catherine gets nothing at all. While my fellow-
judges have their kitchens and cellars and
stables and store-rooms running over with good
things, all thanks to their wives, I hardly get
wherewithal to keep the pot boiling. You see,
Master Adam Fumée, what I lose by having a
dumb wife. I'm not worth half as much. . . .
And the worst of it is, I'm losing my spirits,
and almost my wits, with it all.

MASTER ADAM. There's no reason in that,
now, your Honour. Just consider the thing
closely, and you will find some advantages in
your case as it stands, and no mean ones
neither.

LEONARD. No, no, Master Adam; you don't
understand. Think!—When I hold my wife in
my arms—a woman as beautiful as the finest
carved statue, at least so I think—and quite as
silent, that I'm sure of—it makes me feel queer
and uncanny; I even ask myself if I'm holding
a graven image or a mechanical toy, or a magic
doll made by a sorcerer, not a real human child
of our Father in Heaven; sometimes, in the
morning, I am tempted to jump out of bed to
escape from bewitchment.

MASTER ADAM. What notions!

LEONARD. Worse yet! What with having a
dumb wife, I'm going dumb myself. Sometimes
I catch myself using signs, as she does. The
other day, on the Bench, I even pronounced
judgment in pantomime, and condemned a man
to the galleys, just by dumb show and gesticu-
lation.

MASTER ADAM. Enough! Say no more! I
can see that a dumb wife may be a pretty poor
conversationalist! There's not much fun in
talking yourself, when you get no response.

LEONARD. Now you know the reason why
I'm in low spirits.

MASTER ADAM. I won't contradict you; I
admit that your reason is full and sufficient.
But perhaps there's a remedy. Tell me: Is your
wife deaf as well as dumb?

LEONARD. Catherine is no more deaf than
you and I are; even less, I might say. She can
hear the very grass growing.

MASTER ADAM. Then the case is not hopeless. When the doctors and surgeons and apothe-
caries succeed in making the deaf-and-dumb
speak, their utterance is as poor as their ears;
for they can't hear what they say themselves,
any more than what's said to them. But it's
quite different with the dumb who can hear.
'Tis but child's play for a doctor to untie their
tongues. The operation is so simple that it's
done every day to puppies that can't learn to
bark. Must a countryman like me come to
town to tell you that there's a famous doctor
just around the corner from your own house
in Buci Square, at the Sign of the Dragon

Master Simon Colline, who has made a reputation for loosing the tongues of the ladies of Paris? In a turn of the hand, he'll draw from your wife's lips a full flood of mellifluous speech, just as you'd turn on a spigot and let the water run forth like a sweet-purling brook.

LEONARD. Is this true, Master Adam? Aren't you deceiving me? Aren't you speaking as a lawyer in court?

MASTER ADAM. I'm speaking as a friend, and telling you the plain truth.

LEONARD. Then I'll send for this famous doctor—and that right away.

MASTER ADAM. As you please. . . . But before you call him in, you must reflect soberly, and consider what it's really best to do. For, take it all in all, though there are some disadvantages in having a dumb wife, there are some advantages, too. . . . Well, good day, your Honour, my dear old school-fellow. [*They go together to the street door*] Remember, I'm truly your friend—and read over my statement, I beg you. If you give your just judgment in favour of the orphan girl robbed by her grasping guardian, you will have no cause to regret it.

LEONARD. Be back this afternoon, Master Adam Fumée; I will have my decision ready.

[*They bow low to each other. Exit* MASTER ADAM]

LEONARD [*at the door, calling*]. Giles! Giles! . . . The rogue never hears me; he is in the kitchen, as usual, upsetting the soup and the servant. He's a knave and a scoundrel. Giles! . . Giles! . . . Here, you rapscallion! You reprobate! . . .

GILES [*entering*]. Present, your Honour.

LEONARD [*taking him by the ear*]. Sirrah! Go straight to the famous doctor, Master Simon Colline, who lives in Buci Square, at the Sign of the Dragon, and tell him to come to my house at once, to treat a dumb woman. . . .

GILES. Yes, your Honour. [GILES *starts off, running, to the right*]

LEONARD. Go the nearest way, not round by the New Bridge, to watch the jugglers. I know you, you slow-poke; there's not such another cheat and loafer in ten counties.

[GILES *comes back, slowly, across stage, and stops*]

GILES. Sir, you wrong me. . . .

LEONARD. Be off! and bring the famous doctor back with you.

GILES [*bolting off to the left*]. Yes, your Honour.

LEONARD [*going up and sitting down at the table, which is loaded with brief-bags*]. I have fourteen verdicts to render to-day, besides the decree in the case of Master Adam Fumée's ward. And that is no small labour, because a decree, to do credit to the Judge, must be cleverly worded, subtle, elegant, and adorned with all the ornaments both of style and of thought. The ideas must be pleasingly conceived and playfully expressed. Where should one show one's wit, if not in a verdict?

[*The* WATERCRESS MAN *enters from the right and crosses to the left singing:* "Good watercress, fresh from the spring! Keeps you healthy and hearty! Six farthings a bunch. Six farthings a bunch." *When the* WATERCRESS MAN *is well on, enter the* CANDLE MAN *from left to right, singing:* "Candles! Cotton-wick candles! Burn bright as the stars!" *While he is passing,* CATHERINE *enters from the upper stairway door; she curtsies to the audience and then sits on the window-seat, embroidering. As the street-cries die away* LEONARD *looks up from his work at the table, and seeing* CATHERINE, *goes to her and kisses her as she rises to meet him. She makes a curtsy, kisses him in return, and listens with pleased attention*]

Good morning, my love. . . . I didn't even hear you come down. You are like the fairy forms in the stories, that seem to glide upon air; or like the dreams which the gods, as poets tell, send down to happy mortals. [CATHERINE *shows her pleasure in his compliments*] My love, you are a marvel of nature, and a triumph of art; you have all charms but speech. [CATHERINE *turns away sobbing slightly*] Shouldn't you be glad to have that, too? [*She turns back, intensely interested*] Shouldn't you be happy to let your lips utter all the pretty thoughts I can read in your eyes? Shouldn't you be pleased to show your wit? [*She waves her handkerchief in glee*] Shouldn't you like to tell your husband how you love him? Wouldn't it be delightful to call him your treasure and sweetheart? Yes, surely! . . . [*They rise.* CATHERINE *is full of pleased animation*]

Well, I've a piece of good news for you, my love. . . . A great doctor is coming here presently, who can make you talk. . . . [CATHERINE *shows her satisfaction, dancing gracefully up and down*] He will untie your tongue and never hurt you a bit.

[CATHERINE'S *movements express charming and joyous impatience. A* BLIND MAN *goes by in the street playing a lively old-fashioned country dance. He stops and calls out in a doleful voice:* "Charity, for the love of God, good gentlemen and ladies." LEONARD *motions him away, but* CATHERINE *pleads for him by her gestures, indicating that he is blind.* LEONARD *yields and goes back to his writing-table. She stands at the window listening while the* BLIND MAN *sings*]

THE BLIND MAN.

There's lots of good fish in the sea,
  La dee ra, la dee ra;
Now who will come and fish with me?
  La dee ra, la dee ra;
Now who'll with me a-fishing go?
My dainty, dainty damsel, O!
Come fish the livelong day with me,
  La dee ra, la dee ra,
And who will then be caught?—we'll see!
  La dee ra, dee ra, day.

[*Toward the end of the verse* CATHERINE
  glances at LEONARD *and sees that she is*
  unobserved; she steals to the street door
  as the BLIND MAN *begins the second*
  verse there; during this verse she dances
  to him and frolics around the stage as
  he sings]

THE BLIND MAN.

Along the rippling river's bank,
  La dee ra, la dee ra,
Along the wimpling water's bank,
  La dee ra, la dee ra,
Along the bank so shady O
I met the miller's lady, O
And danced with her the livelong day
  La dee ra, la dee ra,
And oh! I danced my heart away!
  La dee ra, dee ra, day.

[*The* BLIND MAN *stops playing and sing-*
  ing, and says, in a hollow and terrifying
  voice: "Charity, for the love of God,
  good gentlemen and ladies"]

LEONARD [*who has been buried in his docu-*
ments and noticed nothing, now drives the
BLIND MAN *off the stage with objurgations*].
Vagabond, robber, ruffian! [*And throws a lot*
of brief-bags and books at his head; then speaks
to CATHERINE, *who has gone back to her place*]
My love, since you came downstairs, I haven't
been wasting my time; I have sentenced fourteen men and six women to the pillory; and
distributed, among seventeen different people—
[*He counts up*]—six, twenty-four, thirty-two,
forty-four, forty-seven; and nine, fifty-six; and
eleven, sixty-seven; and ten, seventy-seven;
and eight, eighty-five; and twenty, a hundred
and five—a hundred and five years in the galleys. Doesn't that make you realise the great
power of a judge? How can I help feeling some
pride in it?

[CATHERINE, *who has stopped her work,*
  leans on the table, and smilingly watches
  her husband. Then she sits down on the
  table, which is covered with brief-bags]

LEONARD [*Making as if to pull the bags*
from under her]. My love, you are hiding great
criminals from my justice. Thieves and mur-

derers. But I will not pursue them, their place
of refuge is sacred.

[A CHIMNEY SWEEP *passes in the street,*
  calling: "Sweep your chimneys, my ladies; sweep them clear and clean"]

[LEONARD *and* CATHERINE *kiss across the*
  table. But, seeing the DOCTORS *arriving,*
  CATHERINE *runs off up the stairs. Enter,*
  in formal procession, GILES, *leading the*
  line and imitating a trumpeter, then the
  two DOCTORS' ATTENDANTS, *then* MAS-
  TER SIMON *and* MASTER JEAN. *The* AT-
  TENDANTS, *one carrying the case of*
  instruments, take their stand on either
  side of the door. The DOCTOR *and* SUR-
  GEON *bow formally to the audience*]

GILES. Your Honour, here's the great doctor
you sent for.

MASTER SIMON [*bowing*]. Yes, I am Master
Simon Colline himself. . . . And this is Master
Jean Maugier, surgeon. You called for our
services?

LEONARD. Yes, sir, to make a dumb woman
speak.

MASTER SIMON. Good! We must wait for
Master Serafin Dulaurier, apothecary. As soon
as he comes we will proceed to operate according to our knowledge and understanding.

LEONARD. Ah! You really need an apothecary
to make a dumb woman speak?

MASTER SIMON. Yes, sir; to doubt it is to
show total ignorance of the relations of the
organs to each other, and of their mutual interdependence. Master Serafin Dulaurier will
soon be here.

MASTER JEAN MAUGIER [*suddenly bellowing*
out in stentorian tones]. Oh! how grateful we
should be to learnèd doctors like Master Simon Colline, who labour to preserve us in health
and comfort us in sickness. Oh! how worthy of
praise and of blessings are these noble doctors
who follow in their profession the rules of
scientific theory and of long practice.

MASTER SIMON [*bowing slightly*]. You are
much too kind, Master Jean Maugier.

LEONARD. While we are waiting for the
apothecary, won't you take some light refreshment, gentlemen?

MASTER SIMON. Most happy.

MASTER JEAN. Delighted.

LEONARD. Alison! . . . So then, Master Simon Colline, you will perform a slight operation and make my wife speak?

MASTER SIMON. Say, rather, I shall order the
operation. I command, Master Jean Maugier
executes. . . . Have you your instruments with
you, Master Jean?

MASTER JEAN. Yes, Master.

[*He claps his hands; the* ATTENDANTS *run*
  forward into the room, and, each hold-
  ing one side, they unfold the large cloth
  case of instruments and hold it up, dis-

*closing a huge saw with two-inch teeth,
and knives, pincers, scissors, a skewer,
a bit-stock, an enormous bit, etc.*]

LEONARD. I hope, sirs, you don't intend to use all those?

MASTER SIMON. One must never be caught unarmed by a patient.

[*The* ATTENDANTS *fold up the case and give it to* MASTER JEAN; *then run back to their positions by the door, as* ALISON, *with a large tray, bottles, and glasses, enters from the kitchen*]

LEONARD. Will you drink, gentlemen?

[COLLINE *and* MAUGIER *take glasses from* ALISON *and drink, after* ALISON *has kissed* COLLINE'S *glass*]

MASTER SIMON. This light wine of yours is not half bad.

LEONARD. Very kind of you to say so. It's from my own vineyard.

MASTER SIMON. You shall send me a cask of it.

LEONARD [*to* GILES, *who has poured himself a glass full to the brim*] I didn't tell you to drink, you reprobate.

MASTER JEAN [*looking out of the window*] Here is Master Serafin Dulaurier, the apothecary.

[*Enter* MASTER SERAFIN. *He trots across the stage, stopping to bow to the audience*]

MASTER SIMON [*peering into the street*]. And here is his mule! . . . Or no—'tis Master Serafin himself. You never can tell them apart.

[MASTER SERAFIN *joins the group in the room*] Drink, Master Serafin. It is fresh from the cellar.

MASTER SERAFIN. Your good health, my Masters!

MASTER SIMON [*to* ALISON]. Pour freely, fair Hebe. Pour right, pour left, pour here, pour there. Whichever way she turns, she shows new charms. Are you not proud, my girl, of your trim figure?

ALISON. For all the good it does me, there is no reason to be proud of it. Charms are not worth much unless they are hidden in silk and brocade.

MASTER SERAFIN. Your good health, my Masters!

[*They* ALL *drink, and make* ALISON *drink with them*]

ALISON. You like to fool with us. But free gratis for nothing.

MASTER SIMON. Now we are all here, shall we go see the patient?

LEONARD. I will show you the way, gentlemen.

MASTER SIMON. After you, Master Maugier, you go first.

MASTER MAUGIER [*glass in one hand, case of instruments in the other*]. I'll go first, since the place of honour is the rear. [*He crosses to the left, and goes behind the table toward the door, following* BOTAL]

MASTER SIMON. After you, Master Serafin Dulaurier.

[MASTER SERAFIN *follows* MAUGIER, *bottle in hand.* MASTER SIMON, *after stuffing a bottle into each pocket of his gown, and kissing the servant,* ALISON, *goes up stage, singing*]

*Then drink! and drink! and drink again!
Drink shall drown our care and pain.
Good friends must drink before they part,
To warm the cockles of the heart!*

[ALISON, *after cuffing* GILES, *who was trying to kiss her, goes up last*]

[ALL *sing in chorus as they go out by the right upper door*]

Then drink! and drink! and drink again!

CURTAIN

ACT TWO

SCENE:—*the same. Four or five hours have elapsed.*

MASTER ADAM. Good afternoon, your Honour. How are you this afternoon?

LEONARD. Well, fairly well. And how are you?

MASTER ADAM. Well as can be. Excuse my besieging you, your Honour, my dear comrade. Have you looked into the case of my young ward who's been robbed by her guardian?

LEONARD. Not yet, Master Adam Fumée. . . . But what's that you say? You've been robbing your ward?

MASTER ADAM. No, no, never think it, your Honour. I said "my" out of pure interest in her. But I am not her guardian, thank God! I'm her lawyer. And, if she gets back her estate, which is no small estate neither, then I shall be her husband; yes, I've had the foresight to make her fall in love with me already. And so, I shall be greatly obliged to you if you'll examine her case at the earliest possible moment. All you have to do is to read the statement I gave you; that contains everything you need to know about the case.

LEONARD. Your statement is there, Master Adam, on my table. I should have looked through it already, if I hadn't been so besieged. But I've been entertaining the flower of the medical faculty here. [*Suddenly seizing him by the shoulders and shaking him*] 'Twas your advice brought this trouble upon me.

MASTER ADAM. Why, what do you mean?

LEONARD. I sent for the famous doctor you told me about, Master Simon Colline. He came, with a surgeon and an apothecary; he examined my wife, Catherine, from head to foot, to see if she was dumb. Then, the surgeon cut my dear Catherine's tongue-ligament, the apothecary gave her a pill—and she spoke.

MASTER ADAM. She spoke? Did she need a pill, to speak?

LEONARD. Yes, because of the interdependence of the organs.

MASTER ADAM. Oh! Ah! . . . Anyhow, the main point is, she spoke. And what did she say?

LEONARD. She said: "Bring me my looking-glass!" And, seeing me quite overcome by my feelings, she added, "You old goose, you shall give me a new satin gown and a velvet-trimmed cape for my birthday."

MASTER ADAM. And she kept on talking?

LEONARD. She hasn't stopped yet.

MASTER ADAM. And yet you don't thank me for my advice; you don't thank me for having sent you to that wonderful doctor? Aren't you overjoyed to hear your wife speak?

LEONARD [sourly]. Yes, certainly. I thank you with all my heart, Master Adam Fumée, and I am overjoyed to hear my wife speak.

MASTER ADAM. No! You do not show as much satisfaction as you ought to. There is something you are keeping back—something that's worrying you.

LEONARD. Where did you get such a notion?

MASTER ADAM. From your face. . . . What is bothering you? Isn't your wife's speech clear?

LEONARD. Yes, it's clear—and abundant. I must admit, its abundance would be a trial to me if it kept up at the rate which it started at.

MASTER ADAM. Ah! . . . I feared that beforehand, your Honour. But you mustn't be cast down too soon. Perhaps this flood of words will ebb. It is the first overflow of a spring too long bottled up. . . . My best congratulations, your Honour. My ward's name is Ermeline de la Garandière. Don't forget her name; show her favour, and you will find proper gratitude. I will be back later in the day.

LEONARD. Master Adam Fumée, I will look into your case at once.

[Exit MASTER ADAM FUMÉE. CATHERINE is heard off stage singing the BLIND MAN'S song; LEONARD starts, shakes his head, hurries to his writing-table, and sits down to work. CATHERINE, still singing, enters gaily, and goes to him at the table]

LEONARD [reading]. "Statement, on behalf of Ermeline-Jacinthe-Marthe de la Garandière, gentlewoman."

CATHERINE [standing behind his chair, and first finishing her song: "La dee ra, dee ra, day," then speaking with great volubility]. What are you doing, my dear? You seem busy. You work too much. [She goes to the window-seat and takes up her embroidery]

Aren't you afraid it will make you ill? You must rest once in a while. Why don't you tell me what you are doing, dear?

LEONARD. My love, I . . .

CATHERINE. Is it such a great secret? Can't I know about it?

LEONARD. My love, I . . .

CATHERINE. If it's a secret, don't tell me.

LEONARD. Won't you give me a chance to answer? I am examining a case and preparing to draw up a verdict on it.

CATHERINE. Is drawing up a verdict so very important?

LEONARD. Most certainly it is. [CATHERINE sits at the window singing and humming to herself, and looking out] In the first place, people's honour, their liberty, and sometimes even their life, may depend on it; and furthermore, the Judge must show therein both the depth of his thought and the finish of his style.

CATHERINE. Then examine your case and prepare your verdict, my dear. I'll be silent.

LEONARD. That's right. . . . "Ermeline-Jacinthe-Marthe de la Garandière, gentlewoman . . ."

CATHERINE. My dear, which do you think would be more becoming to me, a damask gown, or a velvet suit with a Turkish skirt?

LEONARD. I don't know, I . . .

CATHERINE. I think a flowered satin would suit my age best, especially a light-coloured one, with a small flower pattern.

LEONARD. Perhaps so. But . . .

CATHERINE. And don't you think, my dear, that it is quite improper to have a hoop-skirt very full? Of course, a skirt must have some fullness . . . or else you don't seem dressed at all; so, we mustn't let it be scanty. But, my dear, you wouldn't want me to have room enough to hide a pair of lovers under my hoops, now would you? That fashion won't last, I'm sure; some day the court ladies will give it up, and then every woman in town will make haste to follow their example. Don't you think so?

LEONARD. Yes! Yes! But . . .

CATHERINE. Now, about high heels. . . They must be made just right. A woman is judged by her foot-gear—you can always tell a real fine lady by her shoes. You agree with me, don't you, dear?

LEONARD. Yes, yes, yes, but . . .

CATHERINE. Then write out your verdict. shan't say another word.

LEONARD. That's right. [Reading, and making notes] "Now, the guardian of the said young lady, namely, Hugo Thomas of Piédeloup, gentleman, stole from the said young lady her—"

CATHERINE. My dear, if one were to believe the wife of the Chief Justice of Montbador the world has grown very corrupt; it is going to the bad; young men nowadays don't marry; they prefer to hang about rich old ladies; and meanwhile the poor girls are left to wither on their maiden stalks. Do you think it's as bad as all that? Do answer me, dear.

LEONARD. My darling, won't you please be silent one moment? Or go and talk somewhere else? I'm all at sea.

CATHERINE. There, there, dear; don't worry. I shan't say another word! Not a word!

LEONARD. Good! [Writing] "The said Piéde-loup, gentleman, counting both hay crops and apple crops . . ."

CATHERINE. My dear, we shall have for supper to-night some goose minced mutton and what's left of that goose one of your suitors gave us. Tell me, is that enough? Shall you be satisfied with it? I hate being mean, and like to set a good table, but what's the use of serving courses which will only be sent back to the pantry untouched? The cost of living is getting higher all the time. Chickens, and salads, and meats, and fruit have all gone up so, it will soon be cheaper to order dinner sent in by a caterer.

LEONARD. I beg you . . . [Writing] "An orphan by birth . . ."

CATHERINE. Yes, that's what we're coming to. No home life any more. You'll see. Why, a capon, or a partridge, or a hare, cost less all stuffed and roasted than if you buy them alive at the market. That is because the cook-shops buy in large quantities and get a big discount; so they can sell to us at a profit. I don't say we ought to get our regular meals from the cook-shop. We can do our everyday plain cooking at home, and it's better to; but when we invite people in, or give a formal dinner party, then it saves time and money to have the dinner sent in. Why, at less than an hour's notice, the cook-shops and cake-shops will get you up a dinner for a dozen, or twenty, or fifty people; the cook-shop will send in meat and poultry, the caterer will send galantines and sauces and relishes, the pastry-cook will send pies and tarts and sweets and desserts; and it's all so convenient. Now, don't you think so yourself, Leonard?

LEONARD. Please, please!

[LEONARD tries to write through the following speech, murmuring: "An orphan by birth, a capon by birth, an olla podrida," etc.]

CATHERINE. It's no wonder everything goes up. People are getting more extravagant every day. If they are entertaining a friend, or even a relative, they don't think they can do with only three courses, soup, meat, and dessert. No, they have to have meats in five or six different styles, with so many sauces, or dressings, or pasties, that it's a regular olla podrida. Now, don't you think that is going too far, my dear? For my part I just cannot under-

stand how people can take pleasure in stuffing themselves with so many kinds of food. Not that I despise a good table; why, I'm even a bit of an epicure myself. "Not too plenty, but dainty," suits my taste. Now, what I like best of all is capons' kidneys with artichoke hearts. But you, Leonard, I suspect you have a weakness for tripe and sausages. Oh, fie! Oh, fie! How can anyone enjoy sausages?

LEONARD [his head in his hands]. I shall go mad! I know I shall go mad.

CATHERINE [running to the table behind him]. My dear, I just shan't say another word —not a single word. For I can see that my chattering might possibly disturb your work.

LEONARD. If you would only do as you say!

CATHERINE [returning to her place]. I shan't even open my lips.

LEONARD. Splendid!

CATHERINE [busily embroidering]. You see, dear, I'm not saying another word.

LEONARD. Yes.

CATHERINE. I'm letting you work in perfect peace and quiet.

LEONARD. Yes.

CATHERINE. And write out your verdict quite undisturbed. Is it almost done?

LEONARD. It never will be—if you don't keep still. [Writing] "Item, One hundred twenty pounds a year, which the said unworthy guardian stole from the poor orphan girl . . ."

CATHERINE. Listen! Ssh-sh! Listen! Didn't you hear a cry of fire? [LEONARD runs to the window, looks out, and then shakes his head at CATHERINE] I thought I did. But perhaps I may have been mistaken. Is there anything so terrifying as a fire? Fire is even worse than water. Last year I saw the houses on Exchange Bridge burn up. What confusion! What havoc! The people threw their furniture into the river, and jumped out of the windows. They didn't know what they were about; you see, fear drove them out of their senses.

LEONARD. Lord, have mercy upon me!

CATHERINE. Oh! What makes you groan so, dear? Tell me, tell me what is the matter?

LEONARD. I can't endure it another minute.

CATHERINE. You must rest, Leonard. You mustn't work so hard. It isn't reasonable. You have no right to . . .

LEONARD. Will you never be still?

CATHERINE. Now, don't be cross, dear. I'm not saying a word.

LEONARD. Would to Heaven!

[MADAME DE LA BRUINE, followed by her FOOTMAN, crosses the stage during the following speech]

CATHERINE [looking out of the window]. Oh! Here comes Madame de la Bruine, the attorney's wife! She's got on a silk-lined hood and a heavy puce-coloured cape over her brocade gown. And she has a lackey with a face like a smoked herring. Leonard, she's looking this way; I believe she's coming to call. Hurry and arrange the chairs and bring up an arm-chair for her; we must show people proper respect according to their rank and station. She is stopping at our door. No, she's going on. She's gone on. Perhaps I was mistaken. Per-haps it was somebody else. You can't be sure about recognising people. But if it wasn't she, it was somebody like her, and even very much like her. Now I think of it, I'm sure it was she, there simply couldn't be another woman in Paris so like Madame de la Bruine. My dear. . . . My dear. . . . Would you have liked to have Madame de la Bruine call on us? [*She sits down on his table*] I know you don't like rattle-tongued women; it's lucky for you that you didn't marry *her;* she jabbers like a mag-pie; she does nothing but gabble from morn-ing to night. What a chatterbox! And some-times she tells stories which are not to her credit. [LEONARD, *driven beyond endurance, climbs up on his step-ladder and sits down on one of the middle steps, and tries to write there*] In the first place, she always gives you a list of all the presents her husband has received. It's a dreadful bore to hear her tell them over. [*She climbs up on the other side of the double step-ladder and sits down opposite* LEONARD] What is it to us, if the Attorney de la Bruine receives presents of game, or flour, or fresh fish, or even a sugar-loaf? But Madame de la Bruine takes good care *not* to tell you that one day her husband received a great Amiens pasty, and when he opened it he found noth-ing but an enormous pair of horns.

LEONARD. My head will burst! [*He takes refuge on top of one of the cabinets, with his writing-case and papers*]

CATHERINE [*at the top of the ladder*]. And did you see my fine lady, who's really no lady at all, wearing an embroidered cape, just like any princess? Don't you think it's ridiculous! But there! Nowadays everybody dresses above his station, men as well as women. Your court secretaries try to pass for gentlemen; they wear gold chains and jewelry, and feathers in their hats; all the same, anyone can tell what they are.

LEONARD [*on top of his cupboard*]. I've got to the point where I can't answer for the con-sequences; I feel capable of committing any crime. [*Calling*] Giles! Giles! Giles! The scoundrel! Giles! Alison! Giles! Giles! [*Enter* GILES] Go quick and find the famous Doctor in Buci Square, Master Simon Colline, and tell him to come back here at once for a matter far more needful and urgent than before.

GILES. Yes, your Honour. [*Exit*]

CATHERINE. What's the matter, my dear?

You seem excited. Perhaps the air is close. No? It's the east wind, then, don't you think?—or the fish you ate for dinner?

LEONARD [*frantically gesticulating on top of his cupboard*]. Non omnia possumus omnes. It is the office of servants to clean crockery, of mercers to measure ribbon, of monks to beg, of birds to drop dirt around everywhere, and of women to cackle and chatter like mad. Oh! How I regret, you saucy baggage, that I had your tongue loosed. Don't you worry, though —the famous doctor shall soon make you more dumb than ever you were.

[*He catches up armfuls of the brief-bags which are piled on his cupboard of ref-uge, and throws them at* CATHERINE'S *head; she jumps nimbly down from the ladder and runs off in terror, crying*]

CATHERINE. Help! Murder! My husband's gone mad! Help! help!

LEONARD. Alison! Alison!

[*Enter* ALISON]

ALISON. What a life! Sir, have you turned murderer?

LEONARD. Alison, follow her, stay by her, and don't let her come down. As you value your life, Alison, don't let her come down. For if I hear another word from her, I shall go raving mad,—and God knows what I might do to her—and to you. Go! Off with you!

[ALISON *goes upstairs. Enter* MASTER ADAM, MLLE. DE LA GARANDIÈRE, *and a* LACKEY *carrying a basket.* LEONARD *is still on top of the cabinet or book-case.* MASTER ADAM *and* MLLE. DE LA GARAN-DIÈRE *climb up on each side of the step-ladder. The* LACKEY, *with an enormous basket on his head, kneels in front, cen-tre*]

MASTER ADAM. Permit me, your Honour, with the object of softening your heart and arousing your pity, to present before you this young orphan girl, despoiled by a grasping guardian, who implores you for justice. Her eyes will speak to your heart more eloquently than my voice. Mlle. de la Garandière brings you her prayers and her tears; she adds there-unto one ham, two duck pies, a goose, and two goslings. She ventures to hope in exchange for a favouring verdict.

LEONARD. Mademoiselle, you arouse my in-terest. . . . Have you anything to add in de-fence of your case?

MLLE. DE LA GARANDIÈRE. You are only too kind, sir; I must rest my case on what my lawyer has just said.

LEONARD. That is all?

MLLE. DE LA GARANDIÈRE. Yes, sir.

LEONARD. She knows how to speak—and to stop. The poor orphan touches my heart. [*To the* LACKEY] Carry that package to the pantry.

[*Exit* LACKEY. *To* MASTER ADAM] Master Adam, when you came in, I was just drawing up the decree which I shall presently render in this young lady's case. [*He starts to come down from his cabinet*]

MASTER ADAM. What, up on that cupboard?

LEONARD. I don't know where I am; my head is going round and round. Do you want to hear the decree? I need to read it over myself. [*Reading*] "Whereas, Mlle. de la Garandière, spinster, and an orphan by birth, did fraudulently, deceitfully, and with injurious intent, steal, filch, and subtract from her lawful guardian, Squire Piédeloup, gentleman, ten loads of hay and eighty pounds of fresh-water fish, and whereas, there is nothing so terrifying as a fire, and whereas, the State's Attorney did receive an Amiens pasty in which were two great horns . . ."

MASTER ADAM. What in Heaven's name are you reading?

LEONARD. Don't ask me. I don't know myself. I think my brains have been brayed in a mortar, for two hours running, by the very devil himself for a pestle. [*He breaks down and weeps on their shoulders*] I'm a driveling idiot. . . . And all your fault, too, Master Adam Fumée. . . . If that fine doctor of yours hadn't restored my wife's speech . . .

MASTER ADAM. Don't blame me, Master Leonard. I forewarned you. I told you right enough, that you must think twice before untying a woman's tongue.

LEONARD. Ah, Master Adam Fumée, how I long for the time when my Catherine was dumb. No! Nature has no scourge more fearsome than a rattle-tongued female. . . . But I count on the doctors to recall their cruel gift. I have sent for them. Here's the surgeon now.

[*Enter* MASTER JEAN MAUGIER]

MASTER JEAN MAUGIER. Your Honour, I bid you good day. Here is Master Simon Colline coming forward upon his mule, followed by Master Serafin Dulaurier, apothecary. About him crowds the adoring populace: chambermaids, trussing up their petticoats, and scullions with hampers on their heads, form his escort of honour. [*Enter* MASTER SIMON COLLINE *and* MASTER SERAFIN DULAURIER *followed by the* TWO APOTHECARY'S BOYS] Oh! how justly does Master Simon Colline command the admiration of the people when he goes through the city clad in his doctor's robe, his square cap, his cassock and bands. Oh! how grateful we should be to those noble doctors who labour to preserve us in health and comfort us in sickness. Ohhhh! how . . .

MASTER SIMON [*to* MASTER JEAN MAUGIER]. Have done; 'tis enough.

LEONARD. Master Simon Colline, I was in haste to see you. I urgently beg for your services.

MASTER SIMON. For yourself? What is your disease? Where is the pain?

LEONARD. No! For my wife; the one who was dumb.

MASTER SIMON. Has she any trouble now?

LEONARD. None at all. I have all the trouble now.

MASTER SIMON. What? The trouble is with you, and it's your wife you want cured?

LEONARD. Master Simon Colline, she talks too much. You should have given her speech, but not so much speech. Since you've cured her of her dumbness, she drives me mad. I cannot bear another word from her. I've called you in to make her dumb again.

MASTER SIMON. 'Tis impossible!

LEONARD. What's that? You can't take away the power of speech which you gave her?

MASTER SIMON. No! That I cannot do. My skill is great, but it stops short of that.

[LEONARD *in despair turns to each of them in succession*]

MASTER JEAN MAUGIER. We cannot do it.

MASTER SERAFIN. Our greatest efforts would have not the slightest result.

MASTER SIMON. We have medicines to make women speak; we have none to make them keep silence.

LEONARD. You haven't? Is that your last word? You drive me to despair.

MASTER SIMON. Alas, your Honour! [*He advances to the centre, claps his hands for attention, and declaims*] There is no elixir, balm, magisterium, opiate, unguent, ointment, local application, electuary, nor panacea, that can cure the excess of glottal activity in woman. Treacle and orvietano would be without virtue, and all the herbs described by Dioscorides would have no effect.

LEONARD. Can this be true?

MASTER SIMON. Sir, you dare not so offend me as to doubt it.

LEONARD. Then I am a ruined man. There's nothing left for me to do but tie a stone around my neck and jump into the Seine. [*He rushes to the window and tries to jump out, but is held back by the* DOCTORS] I cannot live in this hubbub. [*The* DOCTORS *drag him back, set him down, and, with* MASTER ADAM, *stand in a circle in front of him*] If you don't want me to drown myself straightway, then you doctors must find me some cure.

MASTER SIMON. There is none, I tell you, for your wife. But there might be one for you, if you would consent to take it.

LEONARD. You give me a little hope. Explain it, for Heaven's sake.

MASTER SIMON. For the clack of a wife,

there's but one cure in life. Let her husband be deaf. 'Tis the only relief.

LEONARD. What do you mean?

MASTER SIMON. Just what I say.

MASTER ADAM. Don't you understand? That's the finest discovery yet. Since he can't make your wife dumb, this great doctor offers to make you deaf.

LEONARD. Make me really deaf? Oh! . . .

[*He starts to rise, but is pushed back by* MASTER SIMON, *who stands directly in front of him*]

MASTER SIMON. Certainly. I can cure you at once, and for all time, of your wife's verbal hypertrophy, by means of cophosis.

LEONARD. By cophosis? What is cophosis?

MASTER SIMON. 'Tis what is vulgarly called deafness. Do you see any disadvantages in becoming deaf?

LEONARD. Certainly I do!

MASTER JEAN MAUGIER. You think so?

MASTER SERAFIN. For instance?

MASTER SIMON. You are a Judge. What disadvantage is there in a Judge's being deaf?

MASTER ADAM. None at all. Believe me; I am a practicing lawyer. There is none at all.

MASTER SIMON. What harm could come to justice thereby?

MASTER ADAM. No harm at all. Quite the contrary. Master Leonard Botal could then hear neither lawyers nor prosecutors, and so would run no risk of being deceived by a lot of lies.

LEONARD. That's true.

MASTER ADAM. He will judge all the better.

LEONARD. May be so.

MASTER ADAM. Never doubt it.

LEONARD. But how do you perform this . . .

MASTER JEAN MAUGIER. This cure.

MASTER SIMON. Cophosis, vulgarly called deafness, may be brought about in several ways. It is produced either by otorrhœa, or by sclerosis of the ear, or by otitis, or else by anchylosis of the ossicles. But these various means are long and painful.

LEONARD. I reject them! . . . I reject them absolutely.

MASTER SIMON. You are right. It is far better to induce cophosis by means of a certain white powder which I have in my medicine-case; a pinch of it, placed in the ear, is enough to make you as deaf as Heaven when it's angry, or as deaf as a post.

LEONARD. Many thanks, Master Simon Colline; keep your powder. I will not be made deaf.

MASTER SIMON. What? You won't be made deaf? What? You refuse cophosis? You decline the cure which you begged for just now? Ah, 'tis a case but too common, and one calculated to make a judicious physician grieve,

to see a recalcitrant patient refuse the salutary medicament . . .

MASTER JEAN MAUGIER. And flee from the care, which would cure all his ailments . . .

MASTER SERAFIN. And decline to be healed. Oh!

MASTER ADAM. Do not decide too quickly, Master Leonard Botal; do not deliberately reject this slight affliction which will save you from far greater torment.

LEONARD. No! I will not be deaf; I'll have none of your powder.

ALISON [*rushes in from the stairs, stopping her ears*]. I can't stand it. My head will burst. No human creature can stay and listen to such a clatter. There's no stopping her. I feel as if I'd been caught in the mill-wheel for two mortal hours.

[CATHERINE *is heard off stage singing the* BLIND MAN'S *song*]

LEONARD. Wretch! Don't let her come down. Alison! Giles! Lock her in.

MASTER ADAM. Oh! Sir!

MLLE. DE LA GARANDIÈRE. Oh! Sir, can your heart be so cruel as to want to lock the poor lady up all alone?

[CATHERINE *is heard singing again.* LEONARD *starts for the ladder, and climbs it as she enters*]

CATHERINE. What a fine large assembly! I am your humble servant, gentlemen. [*She curtsies*]

MASTER SIMON COLLINE. Well, madam? Aren't you pleased with us? Didn't we do our work well in loosing your tongue?

CATHERINE. Fairly well, sirs; and I'm truly grateful to you. At first, to be sure, I could speak but haltingly, and bring out only a few words; now, however, I have some degree of facility; but I use it with great moderation, for a garrulous wife is a scourge in the house. Yes, gentlemen, I should be in despair if you could so much as suspect me of loquacity, or if you think for a moment that any undue desire to talk could get hold on me. [LEONARD, *on top of the cabinet, laughs wildly*] And so, I beg you to let me justify myself here and now in the eyes of my husband, who, for some inconceivable reason, has become prejudiced against me, and taken it into his head that my conversation bothered him while he was drawing up a decree. . . . Yes, a decree in favour of an orphan girl deprived of her father and mother in the flower of her youth. But no matter for that. [*She crosses to the ladder and starts to go up one side of it.* LEONARD *climbs down the other side, goes first to one doctor, then to another, and finally sits down on the bench in front of the table*] I was sitting beside him and hardly saying a single word to him. My only speech was my presence. Can a husband object to that? Can he take it ill when his wife stays with him and seeks to enjoy his company, as she ought? [*She goes to her husband and sits down beside him. During the rest of the speech all those present, one after another, sink down in exhaustion at listening to her*] The more I think of it, the less I can understand your impatience. What can have caused it? You must stop pretending it was my talkativeness. That idea won't hold water one moment. My dear, you must have some grievance against me which I know nothing about; I *beg* you to tell me what it is. You *owe* me an explanation, and as soon as I find out what displeased you I will see to it that you have no reason to complain of the same thing again—if only you'll tell me what it is. For I am eager to save you from the slightest reason for dissatisfaction. My mother used to say: "Between husband and wife, there should be no secrets." And she was quite right. Married people have only too often brought down terrible catastrophes on themselves or their households just because they didn't tell each other everything. That is what happened to the Chief Justice of Beaupréau's wife. To give her husband a pleasant surprise, she shut up a little sucking pig in a chest in her room. Her husband heard it squealing, and thought it was a lover, so he out with his sword and ran his wife through the heart, without even waiting to hear the poor lady's explanation. You can imagine his surprise and despair when he opened the chest. And that shows you must never have secrets, even for good reasons. My dear, you can speak freely before these gentlemen. I know I have done nothing wrong, so whatever you say can only prove the more clearly how innocent I am.

LEONARD [*who has for some time been trying in vain by gestures and exclamations to stop* CATHERINE's *flow of words, and has been showing signs of extreme impatience*]. The powder! Give me the powder! Master Simon Colline, your powder—your white powder, for God's sake!

MASTER SIMON. Never was a deafness-producing powder more needed, that's sure. Be so kind as to sit down, your Honour. Master Serafin Dulaurier will inject the cophosis powder in your ears.

[*The* DOCTORS *crowd about* LEONARD, *and inject the powder first in one ear and then in the other*]

MASTER SERAFIN. Gladly, sir, gladly.

MASTER SIMON. There! 'Tis done.

CATHERINE [*To* MASTER ADAM FUMÉE]. Master Adam, you are a lawyer. Make my husband hear reason. Tell him that he must listen to me, that it's unheard of to condemn a wife without letting her state her case; tell him it's not right to throw brief-bags at your wife's head—yes, he threw brief-bags at my head—unless you are forced to it by some very strong feeling or reason. . . . Or no!—no, I'll tell him myself. [*To* LEONARD] My dear, answer me, have I ever failed you in anything? Am I a naughty woman? Am I a bad wife? No, I have been faithful to my duty; I may even say I have loved my duty . . .

LEONARD [*his face expressing beatitude, as he calmly twirls his thumbs*]. 'Tis delicious. I can't hear a thing.

CATHERINE. Listen to me, Leonard, I love you tenderly. I will open my heart to you. I am not one of those light, frivolous women who are afflicted or consoled by airy nothings, and amused by trifles. [*She puts her arms about him and they rock back and forth,* LEONARD *grinning from ear to ear*] I need companionship. I need to be understood. That is my nature—I was born so. When I was only seven years old I had a little dog, a little yellow dog. . . . But you're not listening to me . . .

MASTER SIMON. Madam, he can't listen to you, or to anyone else. He can't hear.

CATHERINE. What do you mean he can't hear?

MASTER SIMON. I mean just that. He can't hear, as the result of a cure he has just taken.

[*The* BLIND MAN *is heard again, playing the same air*]

MASTER SERAFIN. A cure which has produced in him a sweet and pleasant cophosis.

CATHERINE. I'll make him hear, I tell you.

MASTER SIMON. No, you won't, madam; it can't be done.

CATHERINE. You shall see. [*To her husband, affectionately*] My dear, my beloved, my pretty one, my sweetheart, my better-half. . . . You don't hear me? [*She shakes him*] You monster, you Herod, you Bluebeard, you old cuckold.

LEONARD. I can't hear her with my ears, but I hear her only too well with my arms, and with my shoulders and back.

MASTER SIMON. She is going mad.

MASTER MAUGIER. She has gone mad! Stark staring mad!

LEONARD. Oh! How can I get away? [CATHERINE *bites his neck*] Oh! She has bitten me, I feel myself going mad, too.

[*The* BLIND MAN *has come forward, playing and singing the first verse of his song. Meanwhile* CATHERINE *and* LEONARD *go singing and dancing about, and bite the others, who likewise go mad and sing and dance wildly, all at the front of the stage. The other characters of the play come in—the* CANDLE MAN, CHIMNEY SWEEP, MADAME DE LA BRU-

INE, *etc.; all are caught and bitten, and join in the song and the dance, which resolves itself into the old-fashioned country "right and left," as they sing the second verse*]

ALL.
Along the rippling river's bank,
   La dee ra, la dee ra,
Along the wimpling water's bank,
   La dee ra, la dee ra,
Along the bank so shady O
I met the miller's lady O
And danced with her the livelong day,
   La dee ra, la dee ra,
And oh! I danced my heart away,
   La dee ra, dee ra, day.

[*As* LEONARD BOTAL *reaches the centre of the front stage, the dance stops a moment for him to say to the audience*]
LEONARD. Good gentlemen and ladies, we pray you to forgive the author all his faults.
[*The dance re-commences, and as the curtain falls all dance off left or right, singing the refrain*]

ALL [*diminuendo*].

I danced with her the livelong day,
   La dee ra, la dee ra,
And oh! I danced my heart away,
   La dee ra, dee ra, day.

CURTAIN

BLIND MAN'S SONG AND DANCE
(To the tune of "Dargason.")

There's lots of good fish in the sea, La dee - ra, la dee ra, Now who will come and fish with me? La dee - ra, la dee ra, Now who with me will fish - ing go, My dain - ty, dain - ty dam - sel, O, Come fish the live - long day with me, And who will then be caught, we'll see, La dee - ra, la dee - ra, La dee - ra, dee - ra - day.

DRINKING SONG
(To the tune of "The Beggar.")
See Folk Songs from Somerset, No. 82.

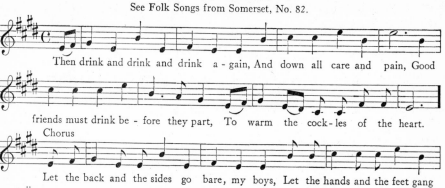

Then drink and drink and drink a-gain, And down all care and pain, Good

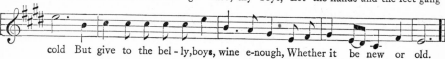

friends must drink be-fore they part, To warm the cock-les of the heart.

Chorus

Let the back and the sides go bare, my boys, Let the hands and the feet gang

cold But give to the bel-ly, boys, wine e-nough, Whether it be new or old.

STREET CRIES

Chickweed.

Chick-weed, Chick-weed, good bird-seed, good bird-seed, good bird-seed for sale.

Sweeps.

Sweep, Sweep, your chim-neys my la-dies, Sweep them clear and clean.

Water Cress.

Good wa-ter cress, fresh from the spring, keeps you health-y and

heart-y, Six farth-ings a bunch, Six farth-ings a bunch.

Candles.

Can-dles, Cot-ton-wick can-dles, burn bright as the stars.

SPRINGTIME FOR HENRY

A Farce in Three Acts

By BENN W. LEVY

CHARACTERS IN THE PLAY

MR. DEWLIP
MR. JELLIWELL
MRS. JELLIWELL
MISS SMITH

The action of the play takes place in the sitting-room of MR. DEWLIP'S *flat.*

SPRINGTIME FOR HENRY

ACT ONE

An extremely untidy room with two doors. It shows signs of a comfortable, wealthy owner but one not particularly house-proud. A very grand gramophone is noticeable, with a roulette wheel leaning haphazard against it. There are drinks available from a collapsible cabinet.

The central door [the one leading to the small front hall] is banged violently. Some one has left in a temper. Almost simultaneously from the door on the right leaps MR. DEWLIP. MR. DEWLIP *is also in a temper. He hurls after his late visitor a large handful of papers that he is carrying, but they flutter harmlessly against the banged door and fall to the ground like snow in a nightmare.* MR. DEWLIP, *a well-fed, well-groomed man a year or two under forty, grinds his teeth. He paces in rage. He picks up a tumbler and sends it hurtling into the fireplace. He kicks a chair off its balance. He is about to kick a heavy desk but recalls himself in time to drop a cushion as shock-absorber between desk and toe. On some of the papers scattered on the ground he deliberately wipes his feet. His eyes fall on a telephone directory and he searches for a number with a violence that leaves the book in tatters.* MR. DEWLIP, *in short, is in a rage.*

DEWLIP [*at the telephone*]. Regent 2403. . . . Yes. . . . [*While he waits, he seizes a cigarette, but, finding he has no matches within reach, chews it nervously. Soon his mouth is unpleasantly full of tobacco-ends, which he spits forth angrily*] What? . . . No, I didn't say anything. . . . Is that Regent 2403? This is Mr. Dewlip, Mr. Henry Dewlip. . . . I'm in a rage. . . . What? I say I'm in a rage. . . . Yes, my girl has just left me. The one you gave me. She bounced out of the place about two minutes ago. . . . No, bounced. . . . What? No, I was not rude to her. She called me names. . . . No, I didn't say a word about her. I said something about her mother but not a word about her. Then out she bounced. . . . No, bounced. . . . Yes, of course I want another girl and it *is* urgent. . . . No, I would not have the same one back. She was no good anyway. Besides she snored dreadfully and I never got a wink of sleep. . . . Well, let's come to the point. . . . Well, what have you got? . . . Yes? . . . Yes? . . . Efficient? . . . All

right, send her along as soon as you can. [*He replaces the receiver, lights a cigarette and, his temper improved, sets the gramophone playing. While he is sitting beside it, rather on the edge of his chair, the center door opens and* MR. JELLIWELL *comes in; a large, self-assured, humorless man of about the same age as* DEWLIP, *rather like the conventional idea of an Anglo-Indian, though he is not one*]

JELLIWELL. Morning, Henry.

DEWLIP. Hello, Johnny. Where did you spring from?

JELLIWELL. I was just passing; thought I'd look in. Rather wanted to have a word with you. What are you doing there?

DEWLIP. Playing the gramophone. I play it rather well.

JELLIWELL. But why are you sitting down to it?

DEWLIP. Is one supposed to stand up when playing the gramophone?

JELLIWELL. No; I just thought you looked rather peculiar sitting there alone with nothing in your hands. [*vaguely*] I don't know what it was. It was just your sitting there somehow. What are you playing?

DEWLIP [*getting up and stopping it*]. Be careful!

JELLIWELL [*starting*]. What of?

DEWLIP. Those papers. Don't stand on them, you fool. Those are all extremely important papers.

JELLIWELL. What a damn silly place to keep them.

DEWLIP. I don't keep them there. They're just there—temporarily.

JELLIWELL. Why?

DEWLIP. I have my own reasons.

JELLIWELL. Do you often put your papers—er—down there?

DEWLIP. I didn't put them there. I—I threw them at a lady.

JELLIWELL [*unsurprised*]. Did you hit her?

DEWLIP. No, I missed her.

JELLIWELL. How many shots were you allowed?

DEWLIP. One, and no prizes. You find me this morning in an extremely evil temper.

JELLIWELL. Pity. You're usually rather cocky.

DEWLIP [*severely*]. I have a sunny disposition but I am never cocky.

JELLIWELL. Sorry. What's gone wrong?

DEWLIP. My secretary's just thrown me over: without any warning.

JELLIWELL. Thrown you over? I'd no idea you were going to marry her.

DEWLIP. I had no intention of marrying her. I never marry my secretaries. I merely meant she'd thrown up her job: suddenly without notice. And here I am left helpless. Besides, I'd got used to her. She'd been with me longer than any of her predecessors: three weeks next Friday.

JELLIWELL. What was it all about? Did you—

DEWLIP. No, I never laid a finger on her.

JELLIWELL. So she left? Got anybody else?

DEWLIP. Got anybody else! After half-an-hour! You can't get a secretary as you'd get a rasher of bacon.

JELLIWELL. I don't see why not.

DEWLIP. As a matter of fact I'm expecting one to come and see me, at any time now: somebody who lives in this building. They're ringing her up. By the way, how did you get in? I didn't hear the bell.

JELLIWELL. I didn't ring it. I found the front door open so I walked in.

DEWLIP. Careless little slut!

JELLIWELL. Who the devil are you talking about?

DEWLIP. Not you: my secretary.

JELLIWELL. Oh, *she* left it open, did she! If you ask me I should say she's bust it. I couldn't shut it after me. Slammed it, eh? Temper, temper, temper.

DEWLIP. I suppose I'd better send for a locksmith. Whenever a secretary leaves me, I have to send for a locksmith. Anyhow what did you want to talk to me about?

JELLIWELL. Well, perhaps it will do some other time, as you're in such a foul temper to-day.

DEWLIP [*sourly*]. I am in a particularly good temper.

JELLIWELL. Well, you ought to know. But it *did* just seem to me you weren't quite as cocky as usual.

DEWLIP. Will you kindly stop calling me cocky! I tell you I am in a particularly good and cheerful humor to-day and at peace with all the world! Now! Try and get that into your thick head.

JELLIWELL. All right, old boy, all right. No need to be abusive even if you are at peace with all the world.

DEWLIP [*more quietly*]. It's merely that I happened to have a particularly late night last night and haven't had a bite of luncheon to-day.

JELLIWELL. Why haven't you had any luncheon?

DEWLIP. Because I didn't want any luncheon.

JELLIWELL. Have any breakfast?

DEWLIP. I had a strong breakfast and soda at eleven, but nothing since. [*Thoughtfully*] Perhaps that's what I need. [*He goes to the whisky*] Drink for you?

JELLIWELL. Thanks: I wouldn't mind one. [DEWLIP *hands one to* JELLIWELL *and retains one*] Your very good health, old boy. [*He drinks*]

DEWLIP [*complacently*]. My very good health. [*He drinks, settling himself comfortably*]

JELLIWELL. How did you come to be so late last night?

DEWLIP [*jerking his head toward the roulette wheel*]. Games of chance.

JELLIWELL. Oh, yes, I forgot. My wife was here.

DEWLIP. She was. Why don't you come next time?

JELLIWELL. Can't afford it, old boy. Nor could Julia for that matter, if she didn't always win.

DEWLIP [*a little uncomfortably*]. Julia's certainly very lucky. Anyway, that's not what you came to talk about. What was it?

JELLIWELL. Well, it's this. You've heard of Caribona Carburettors?

DEWLIP. I think so. Why?

JELLIWELL. Well, as a matter of fact, I *am* Caribona.

DEWLIP. The devil you are! Since when?

JELLIWELL. Since last Tuesday, to be exact. Me and one or two pals, we bought it up.

DEWLIP. My dear Johnny, you can't possibly say that.

JELLIWELL. Why not? It's true.

DEWLIP. It may be true, but it's not grammar. "Me and one or two pals bought it up!"

JELLIWELL. Well, what should it be?

DEWLIP. One or two pals and me bought it up.

JELLIWELL. Anyway, you knew what I meant.

DEWLIP. I did, but most people would not have known. Try and be a little more careful. Now go on.

JELLIWELL. Well, I *am* Caribona. That's the long and short of it. [*There is a silence*] Go on, old boy, say something.

DEWLIP. I'll say anything you like, but what does one say when a man bursts in and announces "I am Caribona"?

JELLIWELL. Oh, you say, "Well done, old boy" or "Congratulations, old boy" or something.

DEWLIP. Well done, old boy.

JELLIWELL. Thanks, old boy.

DEWLIP [*reflectively*]. Caribona Carburettors. They're no good, are they?

JELLIWELL. Oh, they're not too bad. They just want a bit of ginger put into them.

DEWLIP. Ginger?

JELLIWELL. You know what I mean. The

firm's been badly run; that's why we were able to get it comparatively cheap. The carburettors are all right: so we just said to ourselves, "All this show needs is a little ability and some ginger and guts and enterprise" and, if we've got any ginger and guts between us, we said, "by God we'll put them into it," we said.

DEWLIP. Well done, old boy.

JELLIWELL. And then I thought of you. "Here," I said to myself, "is a scheme by which we may both profit. What is the largest car-producing concern in Great Britain?" I said. "Dewlip Motors. Who is my oldest friend?" I said. "Henry Dewlip. What is the one complaint every one makes about Dewlip cars?" I then said. "Carburetion wonky."

DEWLIP. What's that?

JELLIWELL. Curburetion wonky, old boy.

DEWLIP. It's a lie; it's an ugly lie.

JELLIWELL. Oh no really; very wonky, I assure you. I've no reason to tell you wrong, have I?

DEWLIP. I don't believe you know a wonky carburettor when you see one.

JELLIWELL. Well, I ought to. After all I *am* Caribona.

DEWLIP. So I have gathered.

JELLIWELL. You see, wonkiness in a carburettor is a very tricky thing. Who makes your carburettors?

DEWLIP. I'm not sure. Draycott's, I think.

JELLIWELL [*snorting contempt*]. Draycott's!

DEWLIP. Well, what's the matter with Draycott's?

JELLIWELL. Oh nothing. Very good old-fashioned firm. You won't catch me running down a competitor. Ha! Draycott's! [*He affects a restrained laugh*] Anyway, why not let us have a shot? Of course one doesn't want to be sentimental, but after all, I *was* at school with you.

DEWLIP. So was Draycott.

JELLIWELL. I was in the eleven with you.

DEWLIP. You ran me out. Besides Draycott was in the Lower Third with me.

JELLIWELL. So was I.

DEWLIP. Yes, and you used to pinch my behind during Algebra.

JELLIWELL. Oh no, old boy be fair. I only used to pinch your behind during Divinity. And after all, every one else used to, also. It was, if you will forgive my saying so, that kind of behind.

DEWLIP. I will not forgive your saying so. I consider the conversation is on the verge of becoming personal. Besides it isn't true. I shall not give Caribona Carburettors a trial.

JELLIWELL. Oh well, of course, if I'd known that after twenty years you were going to throw your rotten old behind up at me, I shouldn't have wasted my time.

DEWLIP [*angrily*]. Will you kindly allude to my person with proper respect!

JELLIWELL. Oh come now, my dear chap; don't let's quarrel about a silly little thing like that.

DEWLIP [*still aggrieved*]. Silly little thing like what?

JELLIWELL. I didn't mean to slight it. Honestly I wouldn't say a word against it. I don't know how it ever pushed its way into the conversation. After all, it's not a very nice thing to talk about.

DEWLIP [*sulkily*]. I don't agree. I think it's a very nice think to talk about. Anyhow, now leave it alone.

JELLIWELL. Very well, I'd no idea you were sensitive about it. In any case I didn't come here to discuss—er . . . I came to discuss Caribona.

DEWLIP. And you have. I am very sorry not to be more helpful.

JELLIWELL. Is that your absolutely final decision? Won't you even let us send in a quotation?

DEWLIP. My dear Johnny, what's the use? You know I never interfere with the business.

JELLIWELL. You're chairman.

DEWLIP. That's only nominal. When my father died last year, he left me the business just as he left me his watch and chain. And I never tinker with either.

JELLIWELL. But you could, if you wanted to.

DEWLIP. Of course I could.

JELLIWELL. Very well then?

DEWLIP. My father built up the best motoring business in England and was satisfied with Draycott's carburettors. Am I to change a thing like that with my father not yet cold in his grave? God knows I'm not a good man, but at least I wouldn't touch his carburettors till my father's at least cold in his grave.

JELLIWELL. I don't want to be indelicate, old boy, but don't you think, after nearly twelve months, he—er—*might* be cold now?

DEWLIP. You never knew my father.

JELLIWELL. No, I'm afraid not.

DEWLIP. Mind you, Johnny, I don't want you to think I wouldn't do anything I could to help you, but that is just the kind of thing in which I never interfere. By Jove, is that the right time? My dear fellow, you must go. What a nuisance! I'm expecting some one.

JELLIWELL. That's all right. Don't make any compliments with me.

DEWLIP. Right. I won't. Ring me up sometime and we'll have lunch. Good-by.

JELLIWELL. Good-by, old boy.

[*He goes.* DEWLIP, *who has rather anxiously sped the parting guest, makes an erratic and ineffectual attempt to tidy his room. He moves many things but achieves only a different untidiness.*

Eventually satisfied, however, he sets the gramophone a-playing and sits by it again on the edge of his chair. Presently a lady opens the door; MRS. JELLIWELL. She is five or six and twenty; dark, self-assured, elegant, extremely handsome, exquisitely gowned and groomed. He does not at first notice her; so she watches him for a moment, then, moving behind him, clasps her hands before his eyes]

JULIA. Who is it?

DEWLIP [*ecstatically*]. Beatrice!

JULIA. Pig! [*She moves from him*]

DEWLIP [*a little discomforted*]. Julia! My mistake. That is an extremely silly trick of yours; a very silly trick. Numbers of happy lives have been wrecked by it.

JULIA. Rubbish. You were expecting me to tea. You knew perfectly well who it was. Didn't you?

DEWLIP [*sulkily*]. Yes.

JULIA. And you only said "Beatrice" in order to annoy me, didn't you?

DEWLIP. Yes.

JULIA. And there isn't a Beatrice, is there?

DEWLIP. I don't remember.

JULIA. And I want some tea.

DEWLIP. What kind?

JULIA. Martini. What exactly were you doing there?

DEWLIP. Playing the gramophone.

JULIA. But why were you sitting down to it?

DEWLIP. Is this a game?

JULIA. Can't you answer a civil question? I merely said, why were you sitting down?

DEWLIP. Because I am in love.

JULIA. Do you always sit down when you're in love?

DEWLIP. No, I adopt a variety of positions but that is the one I favor most.

JULIA. Why?

DEWLIP. Oh, stop asking me questions!

JULIA. Then stop the gramophone. It has that effect on me. [*He does so*] What about my drink? [*He goes to the cocktail cabinet, opens it, and proceeds to mix the drink. She lights a cigarette*] You're very silent?

DEWLIP. I was thinking.

JULIA. What about?

DEWLIP. About last night. You said you wanted to see me on a private matter and I said that was strange as I also wanted to see you on a private matter. I was wondering if it could be the same private matter.

JULIA. I hardly think so.

DEWLIP. Then let's hear yours first.

JULIA. Have you ever heard of Caribona Carburettors? [*He pauses in his shaking*]

DEWLIP. I think so.

JULIA. Well, it's about Johnny.

DEWLIP. Johnny *is* Caribona.

JULIA. Exactly. How did you know?

DEWLIP. Johnny left here about ten minutes ago.

JULIA. He never told me he was coming.

DEWLIP. The call was not premeditated. It was an inspiration. With a little bad luck you might have met him on the stairs.

JULIA. I came up by the lift. What a narrow escape. Johnny's so absurdly suspicious. [*He hands her a cocktail*] Thanks. Anyway, what did you decide?

DEWLIP. Decide?

JULIA. About Caribona. Did you give him the contract?

DEWLIP. No.

JULIA. Aren't you going to?

DEWLIP. No.

JULIA. But, Henry darling, you must! Why ever not?

DEWLIP. For a number of reasons. I explained them to Johnny.

JULIA. What were they?

DEWLIP. To begin with, my father's not quite cold in his grave.

JULIA. Rubbish. He's quite cold.

DEWLIP. Allow me to know best about my own father's—er—temperature.

JULIA. But I don't see what that's got to do with it.

DEWLIP. Naturally! You're a woman and aren't expected to understand business.

JULIA. But don't you realize that this contract is extremely important to Johnny—and to me? He had to borrow money to buy the business. We were counting on you.

DEWLIP. Confounded impertinence!

JULIA. I don't see why. I thought you liked me.

DEWLIP. I do like you. In fact I asked you here to-day with the express intention of making love to you.

JULIA. So I imagined. [*Impudently*] It seemed to me the two things might possibly be connected.

DEWLIP. You were wrong. I dislike men who do business for love or women who make love for business. It generally means that they do both badly.

JULIA. Then why are you so punctilious in paying my losses at roulette?

DEWLIP. Purely a question of ingratiation. Women should be stolen and not bought.

JULIA. But I am not conscious that you have even stolen me.

DEWLIP. I was about to do so this afternoon.

JULIA. I wonder.

DEWLIP. You don't believe me?

JULIA. Your welcome was scarcely ardent.

DEWLIP. I have my own methods. As a matter of fact only this morning I wrote you a letter so willfully, so blazingly indiscreet that no woman could fail to be touched by it.

JULIA. I shall receive it to-night. How lovely!

DEWLIP. Er—well, perhaps not to-night. More probably in the morning.

JULIA. To sweeten my morning coffee!

DEWLIP. However, now that the Caribona question is disposed of, perhaps you would prefer to go.

JULIA. But I couldn't dream of going. You haven't even attempted to make love to me yet. *My* mission has failed; aren't you going to see if yours does?

DEWLIP. Very well. Have another cocktail first.

JULIA. Thank you. In case I need it. [*He refills their glasses and sits beside her*]

DEWLIP. Will you drink to my mission?

JULIA. Yes, I think so. To your mission. [*They drink*] Come along; begin.

DEWLIP. Right. Do you mind holding that in your other hand? [*She moves the glass into her right hand*] Thanks. [*He takes her left in his and says a little prosaically*] I want you.

JULIA. Thrilling!

DEWLIP. I want you—er—very much indeed.

JULIA. Exhilarating!

DEWLIP. What are we going to do about it?

JULIA. Oh, the poetry of those words!

DEWLIP. Don't be frivolous, Julia.

JULIA. Frivolous in the face of such a passion?

DEWLIP. My dear, we're not schoolchildren. I pay you the compliment of omitting the frills.

JULIA. Still I rather like the frills.

DEWLIP [*with just a touch of impatience*]. I've put them in my letter. For the moment let's keep to the point.

JULIA. I've rather forgotten what the point is.

DEWLIP. Then suppose you pay a little attention. I repeat: I want you.

JULIA. Yes, I distinctly recall your saying that.

DEWLIP. Now the next question is, do *you* want *me?*

JULIA. I'm glad that's to be considered too.

DEWLIP. Well, do you?

JULIA. I suppose you remember that Johnny is your best friend?

DEWLIP. I do, and I also remember that when we were in the Lower Third together, he used constantly—but supposing you answer my question.

JULIA. Won't you repeat it?

DEWLIP. Do *you* want *me?* [*She regards him for a second, her head tilted to one side*]

JULIA. Yes. [*He beams at her, delighted. Then he finishes his cocktail*]

DEWLIP. Now I'm going to kiss you.

JULIA. It's taken you long enough. [*He takes her in his arms and kisses her at great length*]

DEWLIP [*at last*]. That was marvelous. Wasn't it?

JULIA. Yes.

DEWLIP. Happy?

JULIA. Yes; though it worries me when I think of Johnny.

DEWLIP. Johnny's a dear good fellow. Poor Johnny! [*He kisses her again*]

JULIA. Wouldn't it be dreadful if he walked in and found me here!

DEWLIP. I don't see why. It's the middle of the afternoon.

JULIA. You don't know Johnny as I do. He's got a strong Puritan strain in him. Besides he adores me.

DEWLIP. I suppose we ought to tell Johnny. I couldn't stand a hole-in-the-corner intrigue: it needs too much energy.

JULIA. Do you want to marry me?

DEWLIP [*clearing his throat*]. Well—that raises rather an interesting point.

JULIA. Not uninteresting.

DEWLIP. I'll have to tell you something that scarcely anybody knows; not even Johnny. To put it bluntly, I *am* married.

JULIA. No!

DEWLIP. I was two and twenty. It was in America. She used to live by Niagara Falls. I often think it was that that got on her nerves. I brought her over here and we were married quietly in Cumberland. For a year we were very happy; and then—and then—[*He taps his forehead significantly*] All to pieces. [*To conceal his emotion he blows his nose*] She became convinced that I was Durham Cathedral. You can't imagine how inconvenient that was.

JULIA. Poor Henry!

DEWLIP. Ever since of course she's had to remain in a—in a—[*But he can't go on*]

JULIA. Don't you say it, darling! Just forget it.

DEWLIP. In a home. They're very kind to her. It's in Glamorganshire. I try not to talk about it or think about it. But I wanted you to understand why I couldn't marry you.

JULIA. I understand. I shan't breathe it to a soul.

DEWLIP. Does it make any difference?

JULIA. Darling: of course not.

DEWLIP. Now what about telling Johnny?

JULIA. I don't quite see why we should.

DEWLIP. Well I think he'd like to know.

JULIA. What do you mean?

DEWLIP. I mean it seems only friendly.

JULIA. Supposing he shoots you?

DEWLIP. If he did, I should never forgive him. Do you think he would?

JULIA. I think at the worst he may shoot you, at the best he may pull your nose.

DEWLIP. Is that the best?

JULIA. What would you do?

DEWLIP. I don't know. I should probably pinch his— Have another cocktail?

JULIA. No, thank you.

DEWLIP. Well, I will.

[*As he goes to serve himself,* JELLIWELL *bubbling over with joyous excitement bursts into the room.* JULIA *gasps*]

JELLIWELL [*seeing* DEWLIP *only at first*]. I say, Henry! The most marvelous adventure. Happened almost as soon as I left the building. [*Suddenly seeing* JULIA, *he greets her amiably*] Hallo, Julia darling: fancy seeing you here. [*That is all: then he continues exuberantly, while the others remain speechless*] Damn nearly run over, she was. Had to leap ten feet into the air to save her skin. Wasn't touched, as it happened, but it gave her the shock of her life. Here; where's the whisky?

DEWLIP [*weakly*]. Here's the whisky.

JELLIWELL. Thanks. Do you mind if I take it down to her?

DEWLIP [*uncomprehending*]. She's downstairs, is she?

JELLIWELL. Of course, old boy. She lives downstairs: two small rooms in the basement.

JULIA. Do you mind, Johnny, trying to explain what has happened?

JELLIWELL. I've told you, darling. She was very nearly run over. I was passing and of course asked if I could do anything. At first, to my surprise, she said no.

DEWLIP. Did you explain that you *were* Caribona?

JELLIWELL. Don't be damn stupid, old boy. She said she was quite all right, thank you: but she looked a bit green, so I walked alongside of her to the door. On the way she did just stagger a little once—

JULIA. She was probably intoxicated.

JELLIWELL [*ignoring her*]. A kind of delicious, graceful stumble. You know what I mean, like this. [*He demonstrates*]

DEWLIP. Irresistible!

JELLIWELL. So I took her arm and brought her back to her room and laid her on her bed and opened her—er—opened her windows. And then I began hitting her in the face with a wet towel.

DEWLIP. Knotted?

JELLIWELL. Of course not, old boy. And then I just sat down and talked to her till the color came back to her cheeks.

JULIA. Which must surely have been instantaneous.

JELLIWELL. Anyway I must be getting back to her with the whisky.

JULIA [*a little severely*]. Just a moment, Johnny. Henry, I think you were right. We had better tell Johnny the news.

JELLIWELL. What news, darling?

JULIA. Henry will tell you.

DEWLIP. Perhaps really I should tell him alone.

JELLIWELL. What is it, old boy?

JULIA. It's about me, Johnny. I think I'll stay.

DEWLIP. Very well. Johnny, I have been seeing a great deal too much of your wife lately.

JELLIWELL. Well, it's no good blaming me. You didn't have to.

JULIA. Henry is not complaining that he's bored with me, darling.

JELLIWELL. I should think not. I happened to marry a damned amusing little woman, didn't I, old girl? A regular little comic in fact, eh? [*He pinches her cheek*]

JULIA. Don't do that!

DEWLIP. Listen to me, Johnny. I like your wife. Do you understand that? I like her very much.

JELLIWELL. Of course you do, my dear chap. I like her myself. And *we've* been married the best part of ten years.

JULIA. Six.

JELLIWELL. Six, is it? Thought it was more. I say I really must get along with the whisky. That poor girl's waiting.

DEWLIP. Johnny, I intend to deceive you.

JELLIWELL. You intend to what?

DEWLIP. I intend to wreck your married life.

JELLIWELL [*goodnaturedly*]. You know, I don't know *what* you're driveling about, old boy.

DEWLIP. I intend to steal your wife.

JELLIWELL. Who steals my wife steals trash. Who said that?

JULIA. Nobody said that. And one day you may be sorry that *you* did.

JELLIWELL. Oh, don't take offense, darling. No harm meant. The fact is you both seem to be talking such nonsense, I don't know where I am. Anyhow I mustn't wait any longer: really, Henry. [*He makes to go*]

DEWLIP. I will make one more effort. Johnny, I want your wife to come to me.

JELLIWELL. Well, I may be a fool, but I've not the least idea what you're talking about.

DEWLIP. It's perfectly simple. I want your wife.

JELLIWELL. But whatever for?

JULIA [*with indignation*]. Henry: kindly drive me home.

DEWLIP. Very well. [*He takes up his hat from a chair*] Johnny, my friend; you may be Caribona but you're a damn fool.

[*They go.* JOHNNY *looks after them in goodhumored perplexity for a moment, then goes to the whisky. He fills a glass but on his way to the door changes his mind and drinks it. While he is filling a second glass,* MISS SMITH *appears at the door. She is simply dressed, young, fair and with a certain ingenuous beauty that discords prettily with her rather independent manner*]

JELLIWELL. Hallo. I'm afraid I've been rather a long time.

MISS SMITH. It doesn't matter. I came up to find you: to tell you not to bother. I'm feeling quite all right now. Thank you for being so kind to me.

JELLIWELL [*a little distracted by the beauty of her*]. Oh not a bit. When a man sees a lady in the street suddenly leap ten feet into the air as though she'd been punctured, what else could he do? There's a certain code about these things, you know. Won't you sit down?

MISS SMITH. I ought really to be getting back. [*But she sits*] Is your friend out?

JELLIWELL. He went out about two minutes ago. What about your drink?

MISS SMITH. Oh no, thank you. I don't drink.

JELLIWELL. But you said downstairs you'd like something.

MISS SMITH. That was when I was feeling unwell. I only take it as medicine.

JELLIWELL. Do you? [*He looks longingly at the glass in his hand, then sets it down resolutely*] I don't care for it either. [*He sits beside her*] I say, I hope we meet again sometime. My—er—my first impressions of people never mislead me.

MISS SMITH. Your first impressions of me were of a young woman leaping ten feet into the air as though she'd been punctured. I don't always do that, you know.

JELLIWELL. Ah, I didn't quite mean that. As soon as I saw you, the thought flashed across my mind—if that woman's run over, it would definitely be—in my opinion at least—a pity.

MISS SMITH. No man could say more: especially as I went green with terror.

JELLIWELL. Did you?

MISS SMITH. Didn't I?

JELLIWELL. If you did, then I only wish all women were green.

MISS SMITH [*coolly*]. Is that a rather lame joke or an elephantine compliment?

JELLIWELL. I say, what do you take me for? I never make jokes.

MISS SMITH. It must therefore have been an elephantine compliment.

JELLIWELL [*rather on his dignity*]. It was a compliment certainly.

MISS SMITH [*softening*]. I didn't really mean to snub you but I hate compliments—at least after so short an acquaintance.

JELLIWELL [*responding eagerly*]. Of course you do. [*then rather overdoing the part*] I was a cad.

MISS SMITH. No, it's forgotten.

JELLIWELL. I say, do you realize, I don't even know your name?

MISS SMITH. Miss Smith.

[*He bursts out laughing*]

JELLIWELL. Oh, that's good! Miss Smith indeed!

MISS SMITH. What are you laughing at?

JELLIWELL. Oh I say! Miss Smith! Now you ask me what *my* name is.

MISS SMITH. Well, what *is* your name?

JELLIWELL. Mr. Brown! [*another paroxysm*]

MISS SMITH [*smiling a little*]. Oh *now* I see! What a strange coincidence! But honestly I don't think it's as funny as all that.

JELLIWELL. Perhaps it's not really. You see, I happen to have a particularly keen sense of humor. I always think a sense of humor is so important, don't you?

MISS SMITH [*skeptically*]. I do indeed.

JELLIWELL. I say, we *are* going to see some more of each other, aren't we?

MISS SMITH. That rather depends.

JELLIWELL. On what?

MISS SMITH. On you. You see, if we *are* to meet again, I shall have to take you in hand.

JELLIWELL. Will you? I don't quite know what you mean but I'm sure I shall love it.

MISS SMITH. How can I explain? Perhaps I'm not quite like most of the girls you meet. I like the Decent Thing.

JELLIWELL [*a little out of his depth*]. What's that?

MISS SMITH. I like men to be decent.

JELLIWELL. Well, what is there particularly indecent about me?

MISS SMITH. Why did you tell me you didn't care for drink?

JELLIWELL. But I don't.

MISS SMITH. Yet when I came into this room, I watched you gobble up the whisky you had prepared for me.

JELLIWELL. Oh not "gobble" really, Miss Smith.

MISS SMITH. I withdraw the "gobble" but you lied to me all the same. Why?

JELLIWELL. I don't know. I just had the idea that you might prefer me—er—not to care for drink.

MISS SMITH. You were right. I abominate men who reek of whisky. But I don't like liars either.

JELLIWELL. Oh I say, Miss Smith!

MISS SMITH. Then there's your attitude towards women.

JELLIWELL. What's wrong with that?

MISS SMITH. Shall we say a little—over-eager?

JELLIWELL [*indignantly*]. No, we shall not!

MISS SMITH. Of course I'm only judging by your attitude towards me.

JELLIWELL. Is it my fault that you happened to strike me as an extremely attractive young woman—when I saw you first?

MISS SMITH. Exactly. That was all that mattered to you. You never stopped to consider my soul.

JELLIWELL. Your what?

MISS SMITH [*quite firmly*]. My soul.

JELLIWELL. If I *had* stopped to consider it, you'd probably be run over by now. So possibly should I.

MISS SMITH. Instead you proceeded to deluge me with a bucketful of stale, gross, conventional, unconvincing, secondhand compliments to my body.

JELLIWELL. I may be gross but I prefer not to discuss your body till our acquaintance is a little older. Besides they weren't stale and secondhand: every nice thing I said (which by the way I now regret) rose to my lips as spontaneously as—as a dewdrop opens to the—er—the morning dew.

MISS SMITH [*more kindly*]. Perhaps then all I resented was your apparent facility.

JELLIWELL. Well, up to date you've managed to accuse me in the course of three minutes of being a liar, a drunkard, and a libertine. Are there any other complaints?

MISS SMITH. Yes; just one.

JELLIWELL. Oh. What's that?

MISS SMITH. I think every one ought to do a job of work. I don't like men who have nothing to do but kick their heels at half-past four in the afternoon.

JELLIWELL. Well, there you happen to be wrong, Miss Clever.

MISS SMITH. I beg your pardon?

JELLIWELL. I said, "There you happen to be wrong, Miss—Smith!"

MISS SMITH. I'm glad.

JELLIWELL. I have a very important job of work. As a matter of fact, I *am*—never mind. I only came here this afternoon for business reasons.

MISS SMITH. I'm afraid you'll think I've been very outspoken. It's only because if I like any one, I want them so terribly to be—you know —decent.

JELLIWELL [*softened at once*]. Then you do like me?

MISS SMITH. I hardly know you but I think I may.

JELLIWELL. In spite of all my—failings?

MISS SMITH. Perhaps I was wrong: perhaps after all you haven't so many.

JELLIWELL. Oh you weren't: I've led a worthless life. [*Piling it up*] I see it all now. I've been a bad man.

MISS SMITH [*ever so winningly*]. Don't you think that, if I helped you, you might start afresh, turn over a new leaf?

JELLIWELL. *Would* you help me? [*She nods*] I think I might. By God, I'll try.

MISS SMITH. Then for a start, try to stop swearing.

JELLIWELL. Miss Smith, you're wonderful. Already I begin to feel a better man. I say, I can't go on calling you Miss Smith.

MISS SMITH. What would you like to call me?

JELLIWELL. I think I should like to call you Andromache.

MISS SMITH. Why?

JELLIWELL. Don't you know the story of Andromache?

MISS SMITH. No.

JELLIWELL. Are you quite *sure* you don't?

MISS SMITH. Quite sure.

JELLIWELL. Well, the story of—er—Perseus and Andromache was a little like *our* story. Andromache was about the fastest girl they—er —ever had in Greece: a runner, you understand. She used to run after golden apples. So one day—er—Euripides offered a prize of half a pound of golden apples for the girl who—er— got there first. Well off they all went, hammer and tongs, tooth and nail,—er—Hades for leather, with Andromache leading of course by a good four lengths, when she suddenly caught her toe in something and tripped—just as you did just now in the street. Now it happened that Perseus was flying by at that moment with his Golden Fleece—just as I was just now, so to speak—and said to himself "By Jove, that's a —er—a maiden and a half! Poor little devil, she's crashed!" And down he swoops and picks her up. But no sooner had he set her down, topside up, than I'm blowed if Juno, who was always a bit of a cat, doesn't turn her into an oak-tree! And an extremely elderly oak-tree too. So of course they've called the place—er—Clytemnestra ever since.

MISS SMITH. What a divine story! I adore mythology.

JELLIWELL. Oh, wonderful people the Greeks

MISS SMITH. Are you a keen classical scholar?

JELLIWELL. Oh not really, you know. Not now. Haven't had time since I left school. But things come back to one. One doesn't really forget. [*He becomes the suitor again*] Anyway that's why I feel I must call you Andromache May I—Andromache?

MISS SMITH. Yes—Perseus [*Their eyes meet and remain held a moment. She speaks a little abruptly*] Honestly I must be getting back I'm expecting a telephone call. Besides it' dreadful settling in a strange man's flat like this.

JELLIWELL. Oh he wouldn't mind.

MISS SMITH [*looking about her*]. He's very untidy, your friend. What kind of a person is he?

JELLIWELL. Awful. You wouldn't like him. don't care much for my friend myself. He ha all the qualities that you dislike. He's disgustingly rich—

MISS SMITH. I don't dislike that. It's not hi fault.

JELLIWELL. He never does a stroke o work.

MISS SMITH. What about Dewlip Motors?

JELLIWELL. Inherited. He never goes near it. Then he drinks, swears, makes dreadfully long speeches and—and is very untruthful.

MISS SMITH. Oh dear, what a pity!

JELLIWELL. Gambling is about the only thing he devotes any time and attention to. He has giant roulette or "chemmy" parties here two or three times a week. [He nods towards the roulette wheel] And always loses. And as for women, no woman is really safe in the same county with him. Finally he has a vile temper and he—er—will answer back.

MISS SMITH. Perseus.

JELLIWELL. Yes?

MISS SMITH. I want to ask you something.

JELLIWELL. What's that?

MISS SMITH. Are you married? [He looks at her gravely for a moment; then rises, crosses to the window and stands staring through it]

JELLIWELL. You've raised a subject that I think I'd rather not talk about.

MISS SMITH. Oh, I'm so sorry.

JELLIWELL. No, it was not your fault. You couldn't know that it's a little painful to me. [proudly, bravely] I am married.

MISS SMITH. I see.

JELLIWELL. My marriage has not been a very happy one. My wife [speaking with some difficulty] is a mental invalid.

MISS SMITH. Oh, how dreadful!

JELLIWELL. Of course I don't mean she's dangerous—at least, I'm quite capable of looking after myself. But you can perhaps imagine that my married life has not been all roses.

MISS SMITH. Poor Perseus!

JELLIWELL. Oh no: don't think I'm asking for pity. I expect every one has his little cross to bear. All the same the divorce laws of this country are devilish unfair.

MISS SMITH [going to him and taking his hand]. I think there's something rather fine about you. I'm sorry I brought the subject up. Good-by, Perseus.

JELLIWELL. Good-by, Andromache. Can I see you down?

MISS SMITH. No, thank you. I'll go alone.

JELLIWELL. And we'll meet again? You know, you promised to help me. When?

MISS SMITH. You may ring me up. I'm in the book. Till then, don't forget: the Decent Thing. [Their hands grip tighter]

JELLIWELL [earnestly]. The Decent Thing.

[And she is gone. For a moment he stares, beaming, after her before wandering idly about the room in bland preoccupation. He halts instinctively by the whisky, flicks the decanter with his finger-nail, turns resolutely away. The telephone bell rings. He takes off the receiver and says without listening]

JELLIWELL. Number engaged. [He replaces it and saunters to the gramophone. As he winds it up, DEWLIP comes in]

DEWLIP [sourly]. Hallo. You still here?

JELLIWELL. Just off as a matter of fact. You mustn't think I've got nothing to do but kick my heels at half-past four in the afternoon.

DEWLIP. Who said anything about kicking your heels or kicking your anything else?

JELLIWELL [a little superior]. I must be getting along. They'll be waiting for me down at the office.

DEWLIP [still with a bad grace]. Just a minute. Do you still want that contract?

JELLIWELL [suddenly eager again]. Of course, old boy. Why?

DEWLIP. Then you'd better send in an estimate. Write to Davidson. I'll tell him to give you the details.

JELLIWELL [overjoyed]. But, my dear old boy! Why have you changed your mind? Why didn't you say that an hour ago?

DEWLIP. If I told you, you wouldn't understand.

JELLIWELL. I might. You never know. Try me.

DEWLIP. Because I happen to believe that women shouldn't be bought.

JELLIWELL. Why not, old boy? [an impatient movement from DEWLIP] Besides I don't see what that's got to do with it?

DEWLIP. I didn't suppose you would. [The telephone bell rings. DEWLIP answers it] Hallo. . . . Yes. . . . Yes, it is. Wait a moment, will you? [to JELLIWELL] If you're in a hurry, I may be some time.

JELLIWELL. All right. I'll get along. Jove, what a wonderful afternoon! I say, Henry, I'm most frightfully obliged to you.

DEWLIP. Not at all. Good-by.

JELLIWELL. Good-by.

DEWLIP [on the telephone]. What? . . . No, the line hasn't been engaged for nearly an hour. . . . Well they shouldn't have said so.

JELLIWELL. Tch, tch! The telephone service is a public scandal. [He goes]

DEWLIP. Yes. . . . Yes. . . . Efficient? . . . Won't come? . . . What do you mean "refuses point-blank"? Why? . . . Well I'd rather you did say. Kindly tell me what she said. . . . Yes, I do insist. . . . Yes. . . . Yes. . . . [ominously] Go on. . . . Go on. . . .

[MISS SMITH comes in, unnoticed, and stands quietly waiting]

DEWLIP. Go on. . . . [uttering with difficulty] What damned impertinence! What—damned impertinence! I'd teach her to "object to me on personal grounds"! I'd give her personal grounds! If she dared to show her nose in here now, I'd damn well tweak it. . . . No, you certainly will not try some one else. Did you think it necessary to telephone expressly to tell me that a common, little, knock-kneed, pigeon-chested, ugly, simpering chit of a girl [*She draws herself up*] had the impudence to comment upon my morals and habits? Good-by. [*He slams down the receiver, he hurls a cushion across the room, he searches on the desk for papers but, finding none, takes some from a drawer and deliberately sends them hurtling after the cushion. Then his eye lights on* MISS SMITH. *He addresses her aggressively*] Who the devil are you?

MISS SMITH [*coolly*]. Miss Smith.

DEWLIP. Who's Miss Smith?

MISS SMITH. Perhaps I'm interrupting.

DEWLIP. Get off those papers: they're important.

MISS SMITH [*moving aside*]. Really. Why are they there?

DEWLIP. They fell there.

MISS SMITH. I see.

DEWLIP. Who are *you?*

MISS SMITH [*still detached and self-possessed*]. I understand you are wanting a secretary?

DEWLIP. I am.

MISS SMITH. I am a secretary.

[*He has been watching her with growing admiration*]

DEWLIP [*quietly; pleased and surprised*]. The devil you are!

MISS SMITH. The Burlington Secretarial Bureau sent me.

DEWLIP. The devil they did! [*He just stares at her, fascinated, silent*]

MISS SMITH. What are you staring at?

DEWLIP [*absently*]. Staring at. What am I staring at? Let me see now: what am I staring at? Nothing: nothing at all.

MISS SMITH. Is that all you have to say?

DEWLIP. Yes, that's all.

MISS SMITH. Don't you want to know any particulars about me?

DEWLIP [*with a feeble effort at concentration*]. Oh yes, I want to know that. Let me see: how old are you?

MISS SMITH [*a little surprised*]. Twenty-four.

DEWLIP [*with a touch of ecstasy*]. Twenty-four! Wonderful! What do you weigh?

MISS SMITH. I don't think I heard you correctly.

DEWLIP. I mean what are your speeds?

MISS SMITH. Fifty and a hundred and thirty.

DEWLIP. A hundred and thirty! Delicious! Turn around.

MISS SMITH. Why?

DEWLIP [*his eyes beaming and never leaving her face*]. I don't know.

MISS SMITH. Do you want references?

DEWLIP. No. You're engaged.

MISS SMITH. When shall I begin work?

DEWLIP. Now.

MISS SMITH. Very well. [*She takes off her hat, adding casually:*] By the way, I'm not pigeon-chested. [*The fatuous complacency is suddenly washed from his face*]

DEWLIP [*slowly*]. What's that?

MISS SMITH. Nor knock-kneed.

DEWLIP. Are you . . . [*But he can get no further*]

MISS SMITH. I am. I'm the ugly little chit of a girl who had the impudence to comment unfavorably on your morals.

DEWLIP. Well, I'll be damned.

MISS SMITH. That was precisely my point.

DEWLIP. You're sacked.

MISS SMITH [*putting on her hat again*]. Very good. You owe me a week's wages.

DEWLIP. Do I indeed!

MISS SMITH. Have you forgotten already that you engaged me? Four pounds, I think it is. That's what the Bureau told me.

DEWLIP. You whistle for it!

MISS SMITH. I don't whistle.

DEWLIP. And I don't pay a week's wages for nothing.

MISS SMITH. Very well. Then I'll work for a week. [*She takes her hat off again.*]

DEWLIP. For heaven's sake stop taking that damned thing off and on. It's making me giddy.

MISS SMITH [*seating herself calmly at the desk and reaching for a pencil*]. Do you wish to dictate?

DEWLIP. So it was you who had the cheek to criticize my habits. Who the devil do you think you are, I'd like to know?

MISS SMITH. Miss Smith.

DEWLIP. And how, may I ask, do you come to know anything about me?

MISS SMITH. How? Mr. Henry Dewlip of Dewlip Motors is so well known.

DEWLIP. And may I also ask what exactly my conduct has to do with you?

MISS SMITH. Nothing except on general principles. I happen to be what you would probably call rather strait-laced.

DEWLIP. Oh do you! Well, you'll very soon come unlaced if you stay here a week. If one of us has to change, it won't be me.

MISS SMITH. And it certainly won't be I.

DEWLIP [*ignoring the correction*]. In that case I don't think you'll enjoy yourself here.

MISS SMITH. I don't expect to but I have my living to earn.

DEWLIP. Perhaps it may interest you to learn that my last five secretaries left me in tears.

MISS SMITH. Really? Do you cry a lot?

DEWLIP. It was them who cried.

MISS SMITH. Your grammar isn't very good, is it? Do you wish to dictate?

DEWLIP. My grammar is excellent and I do wish to dictate.

MISS SMITH. Have you a writing pad?

DEWLIP. You can take it down straight on to the machine. I shall not go fast.

MISS SMITH. Where is the machine?

DEWLIP. On the floor beside the desk.

MISS SMITH. It looks rather heavy. Will you kindly lift it for me? [*He is about to refuse but, reluctantly changing his mind, does what she asks*] Thank you.

DEWLIP. Kindly take two carbons.

MISS SMITH. Very good. [*She sets her machine in readiness*] I'm ready. [*He clears his throat, glances at her resentfully, takes a turn up the room; then, still scowling, proceeds in a crisp businesslike style.*]

DEWLIP. "May 23rd, 1932. Darling." [*He looks surreptitiously to see if she flinches but she doesn't*]

MISS SMITH [*prosaically*]. "Darling." Yes?

DEWLIP. "Darling, I have so much . . . to say to you . . . but somehow when I am with you"— Is that too fast?

MISS SMITH. Not in the least, thank you. "When I am with you"?

DEWLIP. "I can't say it. That is why . . . I am writing, although I shall be seeing you so soon."

MISS SMITH. "You so soon."

DEWLIP [*still very businesslike*]. "When I am with you, the scent of you—no, the luscious scent of you . . ."

MISS SMITH. "Luscious scent of you"? [*Her placidity enrages him*]

DEWLIP. "Seems to make me drunk."

MISS SMITH. "Drunk."

DEWLIP. Drunk. [*He ponders*] Drunk. "How I long to feel . . . your dear body shivering in my arms" . . . [*He looks to see if he has shocked her yet but alas, he has not.*]

MISS SMITH. "Body shivering in my arms."

DEWLIP. No, "quivering."

MISS SMITH. "Pulsing" is more usual.

DEWLIP. Very well: "pulsing." "Pulsing in my arms. When shall that be? Till then, all my love to you, Henry" . . . I want you to make—

MISS SMITH. Just a minute, please. I haven't quite finished. [*He waits impatiently while the machine clicks on*] Yes?

DEWLIP. I want you to make three copies of that. Send one to Mrs. J. Jelliwell, one to Lady Crighton and one to Miss Janet Harlowe. You'll find their addresses in the telephone book.

MISS SMITH [*quite unperturbed, noting down the names*]. Very good. Will you sign them yourself or shall I sign them per pro?

DEWLIP. I shall sign them myself of course. They naturally imagine I do my own typing.

MISS SMITH. I see. And shall I mark the envelopes "Private" or "Confidential"?

DEWLIP. Certainly. What do you expect to

mark them? O. H. M. S.? I want the one to Mrs. Jelliwell to catch the next post.

MISS SMITH. Very good.

[*He takes a turn or two*]

DEWLIP [*aggressively*]. I suppose I've shocked you?

MISS SMITH. Not in the least. I'm not a baby.

DEWLIP. I didn't suppose you were.

MISS SMITH. By the way, you haven't tweaked my nose yet. [*She begins to type the envelopes*]

DEWLIP. There's plenty of time.

MISS SMITH. You're annoyed not to have shocked me, aren't you? I'm sorry I couldn't oblige. You see, I knew what to expect.

DEWLIP. In that case why did you so suddenly change your mind and apply for the job?

MISS SMITH. If a traveler in a beautiful country comes across a slum, an eyesore, a plague-spot, he may either pass it by and put it out of mind or stop and try to do something about it. The second course has always seemed to me the more admirable.

DEWLIP. Meaning that I—correspond to the plague-spot?

MISS SMITH. Which I'm afraid it was my first impulse to pass by.

DEWLIP. God, if you were a man, if you were a man!

MISS SMITH. I very much doubt if I should have got this job. You asked me a question, and I answered you. Will you answer a question of mine?

DEWLIP. What is it?

MISS SMITH. Why did you engage me without references, tests or anything?

DEWLIP. Why? Because—er—because I was in urgent need of a secretary.

[*She smiles and shakes her head*]

DEWLIP. Why precisely should that make you grin like—like a cat on hot bricks?

MISS SMITH. Because I don't think that was a very truthful answer.

DEWLIP. Why do *you* think I engaged you?

[*She faces him boldly*]

MISS SMITH. Because you thought I was pretty.

DEWLIP. On the contrary I thought you quite revoltingly plain.

MISS SMITH. Then I was misled. As a rule when men think me plain, they don't beam fatuously and become incoherent in their speech.

DEWLIP. I am an exception. Ugly women make me extremely incoherent.

MISS SMITH [*still smiling*]. I see. Have you any other letters?

DEWLIP. Yes, I have. To L. P. Davidson, Dewlip Motors, Clerkenwell. [*a little absent-minded*] "May 28th, 1932. Dear—dear Davidson." [*He picks up the three letters she has typed*.] I'll post these myself. . . . "Dear Davidson" . . . What exactly was it that the traveler thought he ought to do about the plague-spot?

[*She turns from her machine and looks at him*]

MISS SMITH [*for the first time almost friendly*]. Let's drop that metaphor. It was rude of me.

DEWLIP. It was very rude of you.

MISS SMITH. You see I get a little carried away. Perhaps I'm rather different from most girls. I'm so tremendously keen on the Decent Thing.

DEWLIP. Go on.

MISS SMITH. Well, you rather put my back up; at least what I'd heard of you. You know what I mean: your idleness and cynicism and —and the drink and gambling and bad temper and the silly lies and—and the women. You know what I mean?

DEWLIP. You are lucidity itself.

MISS SMITH. So I thought perhaps, if only some one helped you all that might be changed. You might manage to make a fresh start.

DEWLIP. To turn over a new leaf, in fact?

MISS SMITH. Exactly. Won't you try? Do you think I could help you? What do you say?

DEWLIP. This is what I say. I say you are an impertinent, meddlesome, interfering little hussy with a vile complexion and I pray heaven that never again will a vindictive Providence visit me with such another. There!

MISS SMITH [*gazing back at him, smiling, unflinching*]. You know, you don't believe the bit about my complexion.

DEWLIP. I do.

MISS SMITH. Oh no, you don't. That was just bad temper. Still you believe the rest. I'm not discouraged. Much can happen in a week. I shall make my effort.

DEWLIP. If I catch you doing anything of the kind, I shall carry out my promise and pull your nose.

MISS SMITH. Then why not pull it now? [*She pushes it up at him impudently*]

DEWLIP. Is that a challenge?

MISS SMITH. It is. [*Slowly, deliberately he grasps her nose between his forefinger and thumb. She does not budge*]

DEWLIP. Let me ask you finally, once and for all, do you intend to reform me or not? [*Nasally she answers something inaudible*] What's that? [*She repeats it*] I can't hear a word you say.

MISS SMITH [*bellowing*]. How do you expect be to bake byself heard with fourteed-stode straphanging od by dose?

DEWLIP. Fourteen stone indeed! Under twelve stone.

MISS SMITH. That's quite edough.

DEWLIP. Do you intend to reform me or not?

MISS SMITH. I bost certaidly do.

DEWLIP. Very well. [*Very gently he tweaks her nose. For a moment or two they face each other, he in the acutest discomfort, she on the verge of tears.*]

MISS SMITH. You're a beast.

DEWLIP. I'm not. You insisted.

MISS SMITH [*trying not to cry*]. Will you kindly apologize?

DEWLIP [*trying to maintain his bold front*]. No: I will not. Do you expect me to say I did it by mistake?

MISS SMITH. You're not a gentleman.

DEWLIP. Isn't it lucky? If I were, you'd have nothing to reform.

MISS SMITH. I think we'll go on with the letters. [*There is a catch in her voice and, as she sits in front of the machine, the tears begin to flow. The fact distresses* DEWLIP *beyond measure but he manages not to surrender*]

DEWLIP [*unhappily*]. "May 28th, 1932. Dear Davidson." [*A long pause while he eyes her shaking shoulders wretchedly. Soon his glance lights on the letters in his hand*]—"Dear Davidson." [*Surreptitiously with his back turned to her, he tears the letters across, hiding the fragments in his pocket*] "Dear Davidson."

CURTAIN

ACT TWO

Nearly three months later. The room now presents one conspicuous contrast: it is tidy It is about half-past six, and MISS SMITH *is busy clearing up her chattels, when* MR. DEWLIP *comes in. His face is a little grave, but then immediately clears and assumes the benign expression of an amiable curate.*

DEWLIP. Well, well, Miss Smith! Half-past six and you still here? You ought to be resting I mustn't overwork you, you know. Let me help you tidy up.

MISS SMITH [*no less amiable*]. No, it's quite all right, thank you. I've practically finished I delayed on purpose really. I did so want to know what's happened about your carburet tors.

DEWLIP. How sweet of you to want to know

MISS SMITH. I expect you've had a terribly tiring day at the office?

DEWLIP. Well, I *was* pretty busy. But there I always say work does a man good. Kicking one's heels about idly is extremely damaging to the soul. Don't you agree?

MISS SMITH. Oh, I do.

DEWLIP. What I always say is, Satan find

work for idle hands. That's what I always say.

MISS SMITH. Do tell me about the carburettor. I'm so excited. Have you got all the details yet?

DEWLIP. We had them all before us this morning: estimates for installing our own plant, and everything. It really looks even rosier than I expected. According to conservative calculations we reckon that, by manufacturing ourselves carburettors of my design, we shall make an annual saving of over £9,000, and pay for the cost of installation inside five months.

MISS SMITH. Oh, how marvelous! Mr. Dewlip, you must be proud.

DEWLIP. Proud? Ah, pride is rather a dangerous thing, you know.

MISS SMITH. I think you're wonderfully modest. And your own invention, too!

DEWLIP. Hardly an invention: only a new design. Besides, I've always been fascinated by motors and mechanical things ever since I was a little tot. By George, I'm thirsty. [*He pours himself out and drinks a glass of iced water*] Has Mr. Jelliwell rung up here by any chance? Not a word from him at the office.

MISS SMITH. He hasn't rung up here. Were you expecting a message?

DEWLIP. I can't understand it. It's nearly a week since I wrote canceling his contract, and I haven't had a line in acknowledgment.

MISS SMITH. Perhaps he's sulking.

DEWLIP. Perhaps I ought not to have canceled it. After all, he *was* in the Lower Third with me.

MISS SMITH. I don't see that at all. Dewlip Motors is not a philanthropic institution. If your own carburettors are better and cheaper, you certainly ought to use them.

DEWLIP. Well, that was how I argued.

MISS SMITH. Have you come straight from the office?

DEWLIP [*with a forced lightness*]. Straight from the office? No, as a matter of fact I called on Dr. Bannerman: nice chap, old Bannerman.

MISS SMITH [*concerned*]. Weren't you well?

DEWLIP. Oh, not really bad, you know. It just happens that I haven't been feeling too fit sometimes lately. Periodical giddiness, and so on.

MISS SMITH. What did he say was the matter?

DEWLIP. He didn't know. He asked me to tell him. He's a doctor, you know.

MISS SMITH. And did you tell him?

DEWLIP. I told him it seemed to date from the moment I cut myself off from all alcohol.

MISS SMITH. What did he say?

DEWLIP. He said my heart might be a little affected as a result. He had known such cases. I should have dropped it gradually.

MISS SMITH. Disgusting man! He probably owns shares in a brewery. Why, every child knows that teetotalers have the strongest hearts. They learn that before they learn to run.

DEWLIP. Doctors certainly seem very unfamiliar with even the simplest scientific facts. Anyhow, I shall have to go steady: no strain, no excitement, no shocks.

MISS SMITH. It's a shame! I don't think doctors should be allowed. Poor Mr. Dewlip!

DEWLIP. No, you mustn't encourage self-pity! What is it the poet says? "If you can keep your head when all about you Are losing theirs and blaming it on you." Ponder a moment on those very remarkable words, Miss Smith. It is a pity they are not better known. But wait: I have another surprise for you. [*He takes a magazine from his pocket and hands it to her*]

MISS SMITH. What's this?

DEWLIP. That, Miss Smith, is the house-organ of Dewlip Motors Limited, a monthly journal compiled for and by the firm's employees. On page five you will see my first essay in journalism: an editorial contributed by the Chairman himself.

MISS SMITH. Oh, how lovely!

DEWLIP. I have called it: "That little sunny smile that helps." Do you think that's a good title?

MISS SMITH [*twinkling with pleasure as she scans the article*]. Are you sure it's not a little long?

DEWLIP. I didn't think so. It looks well in print, don't you think?

MISS SMITH. Indeed I do. No wonder you were late.

DEWLIP. Fancy being late, too, tonight of all nights!

MISS SMITH. Any one would think you'd never been to a theater before.

DEWLIP. Nor have I—with you.

MISS SMITH. But even I can't make a good play out of a bad one.

DEWLIP. Can't you? I wonder.

MISS SMITH [*amiably*]. Be careful. No compliments.

DEWLIP. Why would you never come out with me before?

MISS SMITH. I don't think it's right for a young woman to accept hospitality from her employer.

DEWLIP. Yet I am still your employer.

MISS SMITH. You were so persistent. Besides, you had done so many things to please me, it seemed only fair that I should do something to please you.

DEWLIP [*as who should say "Oh, my dearest!"*]. Oh, Miss Smith!

MISS SMITH. It's true.

DEWLIP. Have I really done so much to please you?

MISS SMITH. You have indeed. [*Earnestly*] And I'm so terribly, terribly grateful.

DEWLIP [*fondly again*]. Oh, Miss Smith!

MISS SMITH. But listen: there's just one other thing. [*She takes his lapel winningly in her fingers*]

DEWLIP [*enchanted*]. What is it, Miss Smith?

MISS SMITH. The thing I asked you about this morning: the roulette parties. I know you don't play yourself anymore, but I hate them turning your nice flat into a shambles two or three times a week. I suppose they're coming again tonight? It's Wednesday.

DEWLIP. Would it please you very much if I told you they weren't?

MISS SMITH. *Very* much.

DEWLIP. Well, they aren't. I let them know this morning, after you spoke to me, that there was to be no more gambling here and they must find somewhere else. Just for tonight I asked my mother to let them have a room. She's taken a house off Lowndes Square for the season. There! Are you pleased?

MISS SMITH [*genuinely delighted*]. Oh, Mr. Dewlip!

DEWLIP. Miss Smith!

MISS SMITH [*breaking at last from their held gaze*]. I must go down and change. I shall be late. I'll come up here as soon as I'm ready.

[*At the door she waves gaily. Rapt, he waves back. For a moment he contemplates the door through which she has passed; then goes into his bedroom himself to change. After a short silence a bell is heard: then another short silence; then the sound of the flat door being opened, and of voices speaking in the little hall.* JULIA *is at last audible*]

JULIA [*before she appears*]. You needn't announce us. We'll go in and wait.

[*She comes in, followed by her husband. A little grimly she seats herself by the table. Her fingers drum.* JELLIWELL, *clearly in a state of considerable perturbation, paces nervily. The house-organ, lying on the table, catches his eye. He picks it up*]

JELLIWELL. Listen to this. [*Reading*] "That little sunny smile that helps," by Henry Dewlip. [*With disgust*] That little sunny smile that helps! Good God!

JULIA. Of course, he's mad! I don't know what's happened to him, but there's no other way of explaining his conduct these last weeks. He's stark, staring mad.

JELLIWELL. It's so difficult to know how to deal with a man in his condition. I simply haven't an idea in my head.

JULIA. You never have.

JELLIWELL. Now don't be offensive, old girl. That won't get us anywhere.

JULIA. I can't help it. I'm sick to death of your dreary helplessness.

JELLIWELL. Well, I don't know that *you're* particularly helpful.

JULIA. Are you supposed to support me, or I you?

JELLIWELL. Well, aren't I supporting you?

JULIA. You are: but being supported on credit doesn't give one a very agreeable sense of security.

JELLIWELL. Now, for pity's sake don't start bullying me about my debts again. I don't know what's happened to us lately: nothing but scrapping. And we used to be such damn good friends.

JULIA. Perhaps we've been seeing too much of each other.

[DEWLIP *comes in. Disturbed in the process of changing, he is coatless, waistcoatless, collarless, and in his stockinged feet*]

DEWLIP. Hallo, Johnny. I thought I heard your voice.

JELLIWELL. Hallo, old boy

DEWLIP. And Julia! How nice to see you, Julia.

JULIA [*rather unfriendly*]. I should like a cocktail.

DEWLIP. There now: what a shame! I haven't a drop of anything in the place.

JULIA. Where's your cocktail cabinet gone?

DEWLIP. Well, the fact is, I sold it. It seemed such a useless kind of thing to lumber up the place with. One can somehow manage to keep the room much tidier without it. As a matter of fact, it was raffled at a bazaar for the Temperance Society.

JULIA [*indicating the article on the table*]. Did *you* write that?

DEWLIP [*proudly*]. I did.

JULIA. Why?

DEWLIP. Why? What a strange question, Julia dear. Have you read it? What do you think of it?

JULIA. I think your mind's affected. Johnny wants to speak to you.

DEWLIP. Of course, Johnny. What is it?

JELLIWELL. Well, old boy, it's about your letter.

DEWLIP. Yes, I've been expecting to hear from you.

[JULIA *lights a cigarette*]

JELLIWELL. Well, frankly, I didn't know what to say. It kind of bowled me over. So I thought it was best to come and have a chat about it.

DEWLIP. Very wise, dear friend. There's nothing like a good heart-to-heart talk between man and man.

JULIA. What did you call him?

DEWLIP. Dear friend. Johnny and I, you know, were in the Lower Third together.

JULIA. You must have been very bright boys.

JELLIWELL. Anyhow, to put the thing shortly, you can't do it, old boy, you just can't do it. It's like giving a chap a leg up for the sole purpose of giving him a good kick in the pants and letting him down again. Isn't that so, Julia?

JULIA. I couldn't have put it more elegantly myself.

DEWLIP. My dear Johnny, I am truly grieved that you should look at it like that. But after all, Dewlip Motors is not a philanthropic institution. If my own carburettors are better and cheaper, surely I ought to use them. The fact is, since I've taken a direct hand in the business, I have been lucky enough to introduce a number of small improvements, and this is one of them. The firm, if I may say so without vainglory—

JULIA. Without what?

DEWLIP. Without vainglory, Julia dear. The firm is already beginning to show signs of a general efficiency hitherto unsurpassed in its history. I do not boast. It is just that Providence has seen fit to bless me with a business flair of which, until a few months past, I was completely ignorant.

JELLIWELL. That's all very well, my dear fellow, but what about me? Do you realize it means red ruin for me?

DEWLIP [still beaming blandly]. That's a shame, my friend: it really is. But there! What does the poet say?

JELLIWELL [impatiently]. I don't know, old boy. What does he say?

DEWLIP. He says: "If you can make a heap of all your winnings And risk them on one turn of pitch and toss, And lose, and start again at your beginnings, And never breathe a word about your loss." [Dressed as he is, there is a touch of incongruity about this declamation]

JULIA [practically]. Johnny owes just on £4,000. With the Dewlip contract he would have been square inside a year. As it is, the creditors will be down on him as soon as they hear he's lost it. Also, having failed to secure any other contracts, he will have to sell the business. Also, being a congenital greenhorn, he paid too much for it, and he'll have to sell it at a loss.

[DEWLIP looks from one to the other; then goes to his desk, sits, and writes on a check-form]

DEWLIP. I am sorry. I cannot possibly give you back the contract. I am committed too far. But—well—what was the figure you mentioned, Julia?

JULIA. Four thousand pounds.

JELLIWELL. I say, old boy, it's frightfully good of you, but I really didn't mean that.

DEWLIP. Say no more about it, dear friend. We pass through this world but once; therefore, if there is any little good deed or kind action we can do, let us do it now. [The check is signed and blotted. He hands it to JELLIWELL] There.

JELLIWELL. No, really, old boy. I couldn't dream of accepting it.

JULIA [grimly]. Johnny, do you want me to leave you?

JELLIWELL. No, of course, darling, but—

DEWLIP. Julia is right. Accept it for the sake of old times.

JELLIWELL. Very well. But mind, I only accept it in memory of old times.

[The check changes hands]

DEWLIP. That's it. In memory of Stinker, eh?

JELLIWELL [with suppressed emotion as he grips DEWLIP's outstretched hand]. In memory of Stinker!

JULIA. Who was she?

DEWLIP [with hauteur]. Stinker was Divinity Master of the Lower Third.

JELLIWELL. Good-by, old boy. [At the door] Coming, darling?

JULIA. No, I want to speak to Henry. If you go home, I'll join you.

JELLIWELL. Very well, old boy—I mean, darling! [He goes]

DEWLIP. I hate to be inhospitable, my dear Julia, but you've got me at rather an inconvenient moment. I'm a little late already.

JULIA. I won't keep you long. But now that we're alone, please do me the favor of behaving like a human being.

DEWLIP. My dear Julia—

JULIA. Don't make speeches. Just answer my questions. [Crisply] Number one: do you want to kiss me?

DEWLIP. My dear Julia—

JULIA. The answer is Yes or No.

DEWLIP. No.

JULIA. Good. Number two: why not?

DEWLIP. My dear Julia—

JULIA. Number two: why not?

DEWLIP. I made a mistake in answering number one. To be perfectly truthful, I do want to kiss you. But I'm not going to.

JULIA. Why not?

DEWLIP. I don't think it would be right.

JULIA. Why not?

DEWLIP. Why not! Have you no moral sense at all? Do you think I'm the kind of man to go about the world kissing the wives of my best friend?

JULIA. Yes, I do.

DEWLIP. Well, I'm not.

JULIA. But you were.

DEWLIP. Very likely. I am, however, not the man I was. I have been fortunate enough to see the error of my ways.

JULIA. You'll get such a clout on the ear in a minute.

DEWLIP. I must finish dressing. Is there anything else?

JULIA [*still very businesslike*]. This is the first time for weeks I have been able to see you alone. You have been avoiding me. Question number three: why?

DEWLIP. Because I was not in the least anxious to receive a clout on the ear.

JULIA. You foresaw that that was likely?

DEWLIP. I foresaw that the interview might be delicate.

JULIA. Delicate?

DEWLIP. Disagreeable.

JULIA. Am I to understand, then, that this elaborate buffoonery of yours is no more than the outward manifestations of a reformed rake?

DEWLIP. If you choose to put it like that, yes.

JULIA. Number four: what precisely has reformed you?

DEWLIP. That is a point which at present I have neither the time nor the inclination to discuss. Suffice it that I have my own good reasons.

JULIA. Are you dining with them tonight?

DEWLIP. Since you ask me, I am: tonight.

JULIA. The reformed rake, accompanied by the source of his inspiration, takes to the tiles again: for one night only.

DEWLIP. As a matter of fact, I anticipate an extremely interesting evening. We are going to the Everyman Theater, where they are presenting for the first time in English, a play from the Jugo-Slav: "Three Sisters in search of a Character."

JULIA. Who is the woman?

DEWLIP [*loftily*]. Woman?

JULIA. Don't be affected. Who is she?

DEWLIP. My secretary: Miss Smith.

JULIA. How perfectly disgusting! You're a danger to the country. A poor little girl who is forced to endure you by the need of money!

DEWLIP. Julia! How dare you!

JULIA. Who probably has an old mother dependent on her, and as like as not a little crippled sister as well! What a subject for your middle-aged persecutions! Lend me your handkerchief. I feel a little sick.

DEWLIP. I shall not lend you a handkerchief. You have insulted me. I overlook it only because you have lost your temper.

JULIA. On the contrary I was never cooler. I shall ask you one more question, then you may go and dress. Number five, I think it is. Am I to understand that you have definitely and finally thrown me over? Answer very carefully, won't you, Henry?

DEWLIP. My dear Julia—

JULIA [*menacing*]. Yes or no, Henry. Am I to understand that that is the case?

DEWLIP [*defiantly*]. Yes. [*Hands behind his back, he strikes an attitude.* JULIA *grits her teeth with rage. She rises*]

JULIA [*as soon as she is able to articulate*]. Reptile!

[DEWLIP *does not budge. At length infuriated by his superb attitude, she goes to him and stamps her heel vigorously on his stockinged foot; then flounces, chin in air, out of the flat*]

DEWLIP [*in agony*]. God, you little swine!

[*But there is no sound in response, other than that of a slammed front door. Nursing his foot, he limps back to his bedroom. Presently there is the sound of voices in the hall again, and* JULIA *returns. She looks a little furtively to see that the bedroom door is closed; then takes her handbag from the table where she had left it. For a moment or two she moves about thoughtfully, and is arrested by the sound of an opening door.* MISS SMITH *comes in, just as* JULIA *is making as if to go. They stare at each other for a moment with mutual distrust*]

MISS SMITH [*at length*]. How do you do?

JULIA [*sullenly*]. How do you do?

MISS SMITH. Are you waiting for Mr. Dewlip? [*A little proprietarily*] I'll call him for you.

JULIA. Please don't trouble. He's changing, and is probably without a shirt. I never think Henry looks his best without a shirt, do you?

MISS SMITH. I haven't had the opportunity of judging.

JULIA. I see: you can't have known him long.

MISS SMITH. I think he won't keep you many minutes now.

JULIA. I'm not waiting for him.

MISS SMITH. Not?

JULIA. No. As a matter of fact, he's just left me.

MISS SMITH [*smiling with pleasure*]. Oh, how rude of him.

JULIA. Not at all. I trod on his toe.

MISS SMITH. That's no excuse for discourtesy. If a man doesn't want a woman's company at any time, he has no right to show it.

JULIA. Oh, Henry and I are such old friends. We don't make compliments. Did I leave the door open? I didn't hear you ring.

MISS SMITH [*enjoying herself*]. No: you see, I have my own latch-key. I'm in and out so much.

JULIA. You're Mr. Dewlip's typist, are you not?

MISS SMITH [*sweetly*]. His secretary, yes.

JULIA. My husband always gets his girls

from Baker's. He says they're so hardworking, and *quite* cheap. Were you trained at Baker's?

MISS SMITH. No. But then I probably wouldn't suit your husband. I'm not at all cheap.

JULIA. I understand Mr. Dewlip is taking you to the pictures or something tonight?

MISS SMITH. Yes; to the theater.

JULIA. Dear Henry! He's so good-natured. If he's late, you mustn't be cross with him. It's entirely my fault. Poor fellow, he hadn't seen me for so long. You may tell him you know whose fault it is.

MISS SMITH. But I don't.

JULIA. I am Mrs. Jelliwell. You may have heard Mr. Dewlip speak of me.

MISS SMITH. Oh, of course I have. He and I have discussed you often. [JULIA *stirs uneasily*] As a matter of fact, the very first letter I ever took from his dictation was to you: a kind of love-letter. I remember being surprised that he should have dictated a letter of that sort. Of course that was before I learnt how lightly Mr. Dewlip took such things. I don't think I ever saw your reply: or indeed, any of the replies. If so, I've forgotten them.

JULIA [*her foot tapping ominously*]. What exactly do you mean by "any of the replies"?

MISS SMITH. Oh, I had to send carbon copies of the letter to two or three other women.

JULIA [*in a fury*]. How dare you speak to me like that!

MISS SMITH. Oh, dear, have I said something indiscreet?

JULIA. I shall report you to Mr. Dewlip for impertinence.

MISS SMITH. I'm sorry, but it never occurred to me that you could have taken Mr. Dewlip seriously. Of course, if I'd guessed for a moment that you were in love with him—

JULIA. I am not in the least in love with him!

MISS SMITH. That's what I thought. After all, you have a husband, haven't you? And I expect he's really very fond of you, even if he does get his girls from Baker's.

JULIA. I have no intention of discussing my affairs with you.

MISS SMITH. Quite right. I think that's very proper and dignified. Still you've no cause really to resent my influence with him. I assure you it's in the right direction.

JULIA. Your influence? I was not aware that you had any.

MISS SMITH. A little, I think. You see, I happen to be rather a believer in the Decent Thing.

JULIA. In what?

MISS SMITH. In decency. [*Instinctively* JULIA, *who is seated, pulls down her skirt an inch or two*] Mr. Dewlip has come round to my point of view. [*A skeptical snort from* JULIA] For example, it was at my suggestion that he has given up gambling.

JULIA. What!

MISS SMITH. Yes, really. Then I don't think that is the kind of article he would have written three months ago.

JULIA. Well, I'm damned!

MISS SMITH. Again, I believe I'm responsible for his going to work in his own business, and therefore indirectly for his new carburettor designs. But for me the Caribona contract would still hold good.

JULIA [*rising, appalled*]. Do you dare to tell me that you were at the bottom of the Caribona affair?

MISS SMITH. Oh yes!

[JULIA *turns away, exsufflicate with rage*]

MISS SMITH. And finally, it's really thanks to me that he's given up the company of the many rather worthless women with whom he used to associate.

JULIA. I'll give you worthless women, my girl!

DEWLIP [*entering*]. Ah, Julia: I thought you had gone. [*He appears, dressed in immaculate tails, a white silk scarf wound about his neck, a silk hat in his hand*]

JULIA [*sullenly*]. I left my bag here and came back for it.

DEWLIP [*who is all benevolence*]. Ah, I hope you and Miss Smith have managed to entertain each other.

MISS SMITH. Oh, we have. Mrs. Jelliwell I think is really interested in your spiritual welfare.

DEWLIP. Dear Julia.

JULIA. On the contrary: I don't mind if he rots!

DEWLIP. Dear Julia: always such a tease.

JULIA. Henry, I warn you not to annoy me. How's your foot?

DEWLIP [*limping a few steps towards her*]. Oh, not very bad. It should be quite well in a week or two. I'm afraid I acted on a wicked impulse, Julia: I was wrong to reprove you. I am sorry. After all, you didn't do it on purpose.

JULIA. Rubbish. I did. What's more, if you come within range, I'll do it again.

DEWLIP. I think, my dear Julia, you are perhaps not quite yourself to-night. Furthermore I believe I can guess why.

JULIA [*rounding on him*]. I have no doubt you believe so! [*She launches upon a magnificent, a positively classical crescendo of fury*] And your girl here believes so! What else should one expect from a pair of minds so concentrated on vulgar, petty intrigue and scullery romanticism? What else should one expect from a complacent buffoon, a dreary, worn-out, used-up, sanctimonious, prematurely aged roué, so consumed with a pitiable, senile vanity as to imagine himself an object of adoration for any woman who allows a charitable impulse to disguise her natural instinct of contempt? In love with you, Henry Dewlip? In love with you, you poor, dim boob? When I fall in love, it's with a man: not with—with "a sunny smile that helps"! [*And with a magnificent sweep, she is gone. But* DEWLIP, *impervious, is still beaming*]

DEWLIP. How rude!

MISS SMITH. Poor Mr. Dewlip.

DEWLIP. I'm afraid I've kept you waiting. Mrs. Jelliwell delayed me.

MISS SMITH. Never mind. I'm not hungry.

DEWLIP. Aren't you? Nor am I. In any case it's almost too late for dinner now. Shall we cut it, and have supper after the show instead?

MISS SMITH. All right: that is, if we're hungry.

DEWLIP [*gravely*]. Miss Smith, people can have supper for other reasons than because they're hungry.

MISS SMITH. Can they? Tell me some.

DEWLIP. For example, because they wish to talk. There were certain things I had intended to say to you at dinner tonight.

MISS SMITH. Say them now. We've plenty of time.

[*He considers for a moment: then, his mind made up, sets down his hat on top of the gramophone next to the bowler which he has already left there on his first entrance. In silence, very deliberately, he seats himself, but changing his plans, he moves across and takes post standing with his back to the fire-place*]

DEWLIP. Miss Smith, a few moments ago we were not alone.

MISS SMITH. That was my impression.

DEWLIP. You will not easily believe me, but the lady who has just left us was until quite recently the object of my very warm regard.

MISS SMITH. Indeed, I can believe you very easily. Personally, I would have put it rather more strongly than that. Have you forgotten the very first letter you ever dictated to me?

DEWLIP. I never sent it.

MISS SMITH. I know, but it represented your feelings at the time. Besides, Mrs. Jelliwell is extremely beautiful. I'm not sure that she's quite the type that I personally admire, but she *is* beautiful.

DEWLIP. She is. But after all, what is beauty? Something quite unimportant. You have taught me that.

MISS SMITH [*smiling*]. That's a little clumsy, isn't it?

DEWLIP. Ah, don't make fun of me. You know what I mean. I merely mean that beauty was the only quality in a woman that used to interest me. She could be dishonest, unintelligent, unchaste, deceitful and quarrelsome. Those were faults for her husband to worry about, not me. I sought from women love always, companionship never. In my blindness, in my grossness, I used to say: among men one should look for friends, among women one should look for lovers. And so I had many friends, but not a woman among them; many lovers, but not a friend among them. Superficially it seemed to work well. At my club I was popular to a degree. The bachelors enviously regarded me as their ideal: the married men enviously regarded me as a cad. I was convinced that both were right: and I gloried in it. [*He drops his voice*] That is to say, until you came along.

MISS SMITH [*happily*]. And then?

DEWLIP. And then; and then for the first time in all these years I learnt what true love was: love of the spirit, pure love. That was it. Pure love for a pure woman. Gosh, it was great! My popularity at the club waned and perished. I became a bore; armchairs emptied magically when I entered. And I was proud of it. Which of those horrid men, I thought, had known a pure love for a pure woman? Not one. Several of them I asked that very question. Good afternoon, So-and-so, I would say, have you ever known a pure love for a pure woman? And So-and-so would look uncomfortable and walk away, so that I could draw but one conclusion: poor So-and-so had not. Probably he had not even known a pure woman. I do not want to make a speech, but in short that, my dear, my very dear Miss Smith, is what you have done for me.

MISS SMITH [*fondly*]. Are you happy; happier for the change?

DEWLIP. Do you doubt it? And you? Are you happy that you have caused the change? [*She nods gently, her eyes tender*] Miss Smith, I want to ask you something.

MISS SMITH. What is it?

DEWLIP. It's just this. Miss Smith—I say, I can't go through life calling you Miss Smith. What is your Christian name?

MISS SMITH. Why?

DEWLIP. Because I want to use it. May I use it?

MISS SMITH. Perhaps: at least outside office hours. It's Angela.

DEWLIP [*ecstatically*]. Angela!

MISS SMITH. What were you going to ask me?

DEWLIP. What I want to ask you is important. I don't expect an answer immediately, but I can't beat about the bush. It's just this.

[*The telephone bell rings*]

MISS SMITH. The telephone.

DEWLIP [*miles away*]. The telephone!

MISS SMITH. The telephone.

DEWLIP. Oh! The telephone! [*He goes to it*] Hullo. Yes, speaking. . . . Who? . . . Yes, she is. Hold on. [*To* MISS SMITH] It's the Hall-porter's wife. She wants to speak to you.

MISS SMITH [*taking the receiver from him*]. Thank you. Hallo? . . . Yes. . . . Yes. Asking for me? Is he? . . . Yes, I *know* he's in bed. I only left him ten minutes ago. . . . Oh, I *did* kiss him: it's not true. I kissed him again and again. . . . What? . . . Yes. . . . The darling! . . . All right. Tell him I'll come in again, but only for a minute. . . . Yes. Thank you so much. [*She replaces the receiver*] Darling Pierre! He's played this game before. Why, what's the matter? [*For just then she catches sight of* MR. DEWLIP'S *face. It is discolored with suppressed emotion*]

DEWLIP [*grimly*]. Who is Pierre?

MISS SMITH. Pierre? Why he's just— You're not ill, are you?

DEWLIP [*his voice rising*]. Who is Pierre?

MISS SMITH. Pierre is my son.

DEWLIP. Your what?

MISS SMITH. My little boy. The Hall-porter's wife looks after him for me. He says I didn't kiss him goodnight.

DEWLIP. Your son? And how in Heaven's name may I ask did *you* come by a son?

MISS SMITH [*beginning to take umbrage: a little haughtily*]. By the usual procedure, Mr. Dewlip.

DEWLIP. Are you completely shameless? You stand there brazenly and—and— Am I to understand—are you going to imply that you— you are married?

MISS SMITH [*proudly*]. Certainly we were married! I think you are a little forgetting yourself.

DEWLIP [*swallowing his feelings*]. Miss Smith, will you kindly hand me my hat. No, I need not trouble you. [*He crosses to the gramophone himself. On his way he stops and lays the theater-tickets on a table in front of her*] There are the theater-tickets. I shall not require my seat. Do me the favor of asking your husband to make use of it. [*Hat in hand he pauses at the door*] And if during the intervals you should have an opportunity for meditation, ponder on this thought, Miss Smith: there are more kinds of cheats than one. I wish you good evening.

[*He claps his hat on his head with a dignified gesture that is injured only by the fact that inadvertently he has picked up, not his silk hat, but his bowler. The front door is heard to bang, and* MISS SMITH *is alone*]

CURTAIN

ACT THREE

Eleven o'clock next morning. MISS SMITH *is alone, working at her machine. From time to time she halts to listen for somebody's arrival. At length the sound of the front-door bell is followed by the sound of* MR. JELLIWELL'S *voice in the hall.*

JELLIWELL [*bursting in*]. Where's Dewlip? [*He is in a fury*]

MISS SMITH. Perseus!

JELLIWELL. I'm sorry, my dear. But this is important. Where's your swine of an employer?

MISS SMITH. What do you want him for?

JELLIWELL. I want to wring his neck.

MISS SMITH. Why?

JELLIWELL. Don't ask me now, Andromache. I'm too angry to explain. It's just an impulse. Where is he?

MISS SMITH. Of course I don't want to interfere, but are you quite sure it would be right to wring his neck—you know what I mean—decent?

JELLIWELL. Quite sure. It would be the first decent thing I've done in my life.

MISS SMITH. Not the first, Perseus.

JELLIWELL. Dear child! You have such a soothing effect on a chap. All the same—where is he?

MISS SMITH. I don't know.

JELLIWELL. Oh come, old girl. You're his confidential secretary.

MISS SMITH. Very likely, but he's left me out of his confidence this time.

JELLIWELL. You know he's not at his office, don't you?

MISS SMITH. I do. But how did *you* know?

JELLIWELL. I telephoned. Is he in this flat?

MISS SMITH. No. [*She is standing in front of the bedroom door*]

JELLIWELL. Andromache, I believe you're shielding him.

MISS SMITH. Nonsense. Why should I?

JELLIWELL. Out of your sweet, generous nature.

MISS SMITH [*softened*]. I assure you I'm not.

JELLIWELL. Then why are you standing slap in front of his bedroom door?

MISS SMITH. Do you think it would be in better taste if I were standing behind it?

JELLIWELL. Andromache, I'm going into that bedroom.

MISS SMITH [*after contemplating him for a moment*]. As you please. [*She moves aside*]

[JELLIWELL *hesitates, then goes into the bedroom. Soon he comes out again*]

JELLIWELL. He's not there.

MISS SMITH. Oh, please don't apologize.

JELLIWELL. I'm sorry, old girl: but I had to make sure. I say, do you know, his bed's not been slept in!

MISS SMITH. I know.

JELLIWELL [*pulled up*]. Oh? And *how* do you know?

MISS SMITH [*sharply*]. Perseus! What's the matter with you this morning? How do *you* know it's not been slept in? Did you expect to find it still not made at eleven o'clock in the morning?

JELLIWELL. But it's all turned down; with his pajamas laid out and a black cat fast asleep on the trousers.

MISS SMITH. A black cat?

JELLIWELL. Yes, and, if I'm any judge, liable to have kittens at any moment.

MISS SMITH. Oh, how lucky!

JELLIWELL. It won't be lucky for him if I find him.

MISS SMITH. And where now do you propose to look?

JELLIWELL. I don't know. I've tried his club, and I've tried Vine Street. Can't you help me?

MISS SMITH. All I can tell you is that he left here about half-past seven last night, and hasn't been seen since.

JELLIWELL. Where was he going?

MISS SMITH. He *was* going to the theater, but he changed his mind. I want to find him just as much as you do.

JELLIWELL. *You* want him? Why?

MISS SMITH. They telephoned here for him from his mother's.

JELLIWELL. In the country?

MISS SMITH. No, she's taken a house in town for the season. Poor old lady!

JELLIWELL. Why, what's happened to her?

MISS SMITH. What's happened to her! She's only spent the night in jail.

JELLIWELL. No! What's she done?

MISS SMITH. She's done nothing. It was just bad luck. It appears that the tenant, who had the house just before Mrs. Dewlip, used to use it as a gambling-den, and the police had been watching it. Then as luck would have it, they needs must choose last night to raid it.

JELLIWELL. But suppose they did? Why arrest Mrs. Dewlip?

MISS SMITH. Because she's the present tenant. All Mr. Dewlip's regular roulette gang were playing there.

JELLIWELL. Why there?

MISS SMITH. Mr. Dewlip didn't want them here any more. He'd had enough; so he sent them to his mother's just for that one night.

JELLIWELL. I don't understand. You mean the police had been watching the place because the previous tenant had used it as a gambling house?

MISS SMITH. Exactly; and when they raided it last night, Mrs. Dewlip was arrested because her son's friends happened to be there playing roulette. Her solicitors are in the country, and she knew nobody here to get her out except Mr. Dewlip. They telephoned for him all over London, but he was nowhere to be found. I think it's a disgrace. If a man can't be at hand when his own mother's arrested, he ought to be ashamed of himself.

JELLIWELL. Dirty dog!

MISS SMITH. Anyway, it's not much use your searching any longer.

JELLIWELL [*stubbornly*]. Isn't it! I don't give up so easily. What's his mother's address?

MISS SMITH. Thirteen Horseshoe Gardens, Lowndes Square.

JELLIWELL. I shall go there and find out if they've heard anything of him.

MISS SMITH. But why do you want him?

JELLIWELL [*spluttering with indignation*]. Why do I want him? Can you ask why I want him? He—I—my wife—my own wife!!

MISS SMITH. No!

JELLIWELL. I tell you yes! My own wife! His best friend!

MISS SMITH. And I thought he had changed. Just think of it. That poor creature! Even her! Oh! [*She shudders*]

JELLIWELL. I tell you nothing is sacred to him.

MISS SMITH. Not even lunacy!

JELLIWELL. What? Oh. No. Quite.

MISS SMITH. Poor, poor Mrs. Brown!

JELLIWELL. Eh?

MISS SMITH. And poor, poor Perseus!

[*She takes his hand and grips it silently in both her own, considerately avoiding his eyes. He returns the pressure; then without another word, his head bowed, his lips manfully compressed, he leaves her. Alone, she ponders a moment, indignantly stamps her foot and returns to her work. Very soon* MR. DEWLIP *returns. He is unshaved: his evening clothes, white silk scarf and bowler hat —which he does not remove—are all soaking wet. She starts and rises quickly at his entrance. He ignores her*]

MISS SMITH. So you're back!

[*Without even looking at her, he walks to her desk, picks up his letters and begins to read them. Involuntarily he interrupts the perusal of them from time to time by some violent sneezing*]

MISS SMITH. You've caught a cold.

[*He glances toward her with an expression too negative to be called contemptuous*]

MISS SMITH. It's been raining.

[*Patiently he opens another letter*]

MISS SMITH. So you've made up your mind not to speak to me?

DEWLIP. On the contrary, I shall speak to you as soon as I have anything to say.

MISS SMITH. Then why don't you answer me?

DEWLIP. I am not conscious that you have asked me anything. During the last three minutes you have made three very striking observations. First you declared that I was back:

then that I had caught a cold: and finally, summoning all your resources for a dramatic climax, you announced defiantly that it has been raining. I agree with you in each respect. I *am* back. [*He sneezes*] I *have* caught a cold. It *has* been raining. Don't be stupid.

MISS SMITH. You hadn't got a cold last night.

[*He is ostentatiously patient—and silent*]

MISS SMITH. How did you catch a cold?

DEWLIP. By walking about the Park all night when it was raining.

MISS SMITH. Why did you do that?

DEWLIP. I like the Park. [*She is at a loss for a moment: he reads on. Then, still reading, he adds*] You have forgotten to ask me why it was raining.

MISS SMITH. How could you expect any one to find you when you were tucked away in the Park?

DEWLIP. I don't know what you mean by by "tucked away," but people *have* been found in the Park. Anyway, I didn't expect to be found.

MISS SMITH. Well, all London's been looking for you. Now you *are* here, you'd better hear the news. Your mother's been arrested.

[*He has just begun another letter and answers absently*]

DEWLIP. Eh?

MISS SMITH. I said your mother's been arrested.

DEWLIP [*miles away*]. Arrested.

MISS SMITH. Don't you understand me? Arrested. She's spent the night in jail.

[*He finishes the letter and walks across the room taking off his wet coat*]

DEWLIP [*almost to himself*]. Spent the night in jail. Yes, I know.

MISS SMITH. You know? How do you know?

DEWLIP [*a touch of anger in his voice*]. I called at Horseshoe Gardens this morning, and found out what happened—thanks to you!

MISS SMITH. Thanks to me? What had I to do with it?

DEWLIP. Oh, don't be so damned innocent! [*He strides up and down, his temper rising*] Wasn't it thanks to you that they played at my mother's house last night instead of here? Wasn't it thanks to you that I wasn't about when she needed me to bail her out? [*He takes off his hat and throws it viciously into a chair*] Oh!!

MISS SMITH [*herself coldly angry by now, her foot tapping*]. I'm glad you've at last had the courtesy to remove your hat.

[*For answer he retrieves it and jams it on again, well down to his ears*]

DEWLIP [*violently*]. There!

MISS SMITH. If you find it a comfort to be

childishly rude to me, I'm sure you're very welcome. Perhaps you would like to pull my nose again?

DEWLIP. I would: very much.

MISS SMITH. Isn't it lucky I'm here? A defenseless young woman must be a godsend in such moods as these.

DEWLIP. Defenseless! Why don't you run and tell your—your grotesque husband?

MISS SMITH. Only because I don't happen to have a husband.

DEWLIP. Oho. Now we're coming to the truth. Last night you said you had.

MISS SMITH. That also was the truth. I had.

DEWLIP. But you ceased to have one overnight?

MISS SMITH. On the contrary I ceased to have one over a year ago.

DEWLIP. What happened?

MISS SMITH. I shot him.

DEWLIP. You what?

MISS SMITH. I shot him in the Touraine. [*A long silence*]

DEWLIP. Rubbish!

MISS SMITH. You don't believe me?

DEWLIP. No.

MISS SMITH. Very well.

DEWLIP. What do you mean by that?

MISS SMITH. I mean it's no good my telling you any more.

DEWLIP. Go on: let's have it all. Suppose I did believe you. You shot him in the Touraine. Why?

MISS SMITH. He was a Frenchman.

DEWLIP. Any other reason?

MISS SMITH. Don't interrupt. He was a Frenchman, and we used to live in the Touraine. I was really very fond of Aristide—

DEWLIP. So you shot him in the Touraine.

MISS SMITH. Do you wish me to tell you or not?

DEWLIP. I'm sorry. Why did you shoot him?

MISS SMITH. I found out after a year that he had a mistress. That I could have put up with, for after all you must expect Frenchmen to be a little bit French. But he began bringing her home to tea. I used to say, "Please, Aristide, dear, don't bring that woman home to tea. Send her some tea, if you like, but it's not right to bring her here for it." He was very sweet to me in his own way and promised he would try not to. But he was rather weak, poor darling, and this was one of the temptations he really couldn't resist. It seemed to him innocent enough. A few months later I found out he had another mistress also; and the climax came when, after fighting against it for some time, he surrendered to an impulse, and invited them *both* to tea. I argued with him very nicely, and pointed out that it would be so bad for little Pierre to grow up thinking that mistresses for tea was in the natural course of things. So I bought a second-hand revolver and said that I was most terribly sorry but, if he did it again, I really would have to take the law into my own hands. Well, poor darling, he did it again. That's all.

Dewlip. Why weren't you hanged?

Miss Smith. Hanged? Why should I be hanged?

Dewlip. It's usual: at least in England.

Miss Smith. Well, it's not usual in France. The judge was most charming, and the jury were perfectly sweet. They said they wouldn't dream of convicting me. Everybody was extremely sorry for me. The judge declared that in a way I had performed a public service. If husbands began thinking they might bring their mistresses home to tea, he didn't know *what* would happen.

Dewlip. No doubt the demand for tea would very soon exceed the supply.

Miss Smith [*firmly*]. I assure you, to us it was not a laughing matter.

Dewlip. How long ago was this?

Miss Smith. About eighteen months. I was twenty-two.

Dewlip. Wasn't there something in the papers about it?

Miss Smith. Of course. The papers were full of it.

Dewlip. What was your husband's full name?

Miss Smith. Aristide Tantpis.

Dewlip. So you are Madame Tantpis?

Miss Smith. I am.

Dewlip [*almost to himself*]. I remember. So you're the notorious Madame Tantpis! Why do you call yourself Miss Smith?

Miss Smith. Madame Tantpis is too well-known. Smith is my maiden name. I preferred to work obscurely for my living as plain Miss Smith than to trade on my misfortune as Madame Tantpis. If I had wished, I assure you I could be earning a great deal more than four pounds a week. All the film companies, music-halls and newspapers in the world competed for my services.

Dewlip [*reflectively*]. Which you offered to me. [*He pauses*] Miss Smith, I owe you an apology. Last night I was over-hasty. I jumped to conclusions. I should have heard you out. [*He is beaming with pleasure now that she has cleared herself of the charge of matrimony*] I ask you only to make allowances for me, to consider my state of mind. For weeks you had been the center of all my hopes and plans. I had striven to please you and to please you only. I had trained myself to be what I hoped was a worthy companion for you. And then just as I was on the point of disclosing to you the tenderness that was in

my heart, I—[*He sneezes*]—I discover, as I think, that the prize is unattainable, that your affections are not only engaged elsewhere but engaged legally and irrevocably; and that the contract, moreover, is ratified by no less concrete and palpable a seal than little Pierre. Is it surprising that my equanimity temporarily deserted me? Miss Smith—Angela, was I really so very much to blame?

Miss Smith. Of course, I understand what you felt, but after all—

Dewlip. If you understand, that is enough. The old relationship is restored. We can begin from where we left off last night. We can turn over a new leaf. We can—

Miss Smith. Just one minute.

Dewlip. What is it, Angela?

Miss Smith. There's just one further point we may as well clear up.

Dewlip. What's that?

Miss Smith. How about Mrs. Brown?

Dewlip. Mrs. Brown?

Miss Smith. It will save trouble if you are frank.

Dewlip. Mrs. Brown?

Miss Smith. Exactly. Mr. Brown's wife.

Dewlip. Mrs. Brown?

Miss Smith. Do you consider the wife of your best friend fair game?

Dewlip. What are you talking about?

Miss Smith. Mrs. Brown.

Dewlip. Who's Mrs. Brown?

Miss Smith. Please don't pretend. Isn't it rather childish? Isn't it sufficient to have pretended all these weeks that you were a decent-living man with eyes for nobody but me, when all the time you were carrying on a squalid intrigue with Mr. Brown's poor mad wife?

Dewlip. Angela, my dear, I have had a very strenuous night and a most disagreeable morning: I implore you not to complicate my troubles by talking gibberish.

Miss Smith. The only complication is your lack of frankness.

Dewlip. Frank! Mrs. Brown! I tell you I don't know any Browns and never have. I know some people called Green and a number of other colors, but Browns, no.

Miss Smith. Let's drop the subject then, shall we? I see you've determined to be stubborn.

Dewlip. Perhaps at least you'll have the kindness to tell me where you got hold of this Brown story?

Miss Smith. Certainly. Mr. Brown called here this morning.

Dewlip. Oh, did he! Pity I was out. Did he borrow any money?

Miss Smith. I don't see why you should be spiteful.

Dewlip. I see. He's not that kind of Brown. Did he leave you in a rage?

MISS SMITH. He arrived in anger, he left more in sorrow. Why do you ask?

DEWLIP. Only because I see some fool's slammed the front door and burst the lock again.

MISS SMITH. You did that when you left last night.

DEWLIP [*he glances at her resentfully, then deliberately replaces his hat on his head*]. It is being gradually borne in upon me that the chances of our resuming pleasant relations are remote.

[*A short silence falls upon them*]

MISS SMITH. I'm afraid I haven't been very nice to you since you've come back.

DEWLIP. Not very.

MISS SMITH. I'm sorry. My nerves are upset. There was your dashing off and leaving me last night without a word; then this Brown business; then not knowing where to find you all the morning. Besides, you must admit you weren't very polite yourself to begin with.

DEWLIP. I wasn't; but I apologized.

MISS SMITH [*with a very friendly smile*]. So do I.

[*She offers her hand. Mollified, he takes it. The door opens suddenly. It is* MRS. JELLIWELL]

DEWLIP. Hallo, Julia!

JULIA. What are *you* doing?

DEWLIP. Well, as a matter of fact, we were shaking hands.

JULIA. A most original exercise! And that, I presume, is the regulation costume for it.

DEWLIP [*sneezes*]. Julia, please don't quarrel with me; I've got a cold.

JULIA. Has Johnny been here?

DEWLIP. No. Are you expecting him?

JULIA. He'll be here soon. I'll wait. [*She sits*]

DEWLIP. And in the meantime, what can I do for you?

JULIA. Anything you please except talk to me. Go on shaking hands if you like.

[MISS SMITH, *who has been busying herself with some filing, tosses her head*]

MISS SMITH. I've finished all the filing. I think I'll go down to my room till you want me. Perhaps you will ring through when you're ready.

[DEWLIP *nods gloomily. She goes. Alone with* JULIA, MR. DEWLIP *looks about him hopelessly for a moment, then seats himself, facing the same direction as she, staring glumly into space. Interminably they sit thus in unbroken silence. Presently he begins to shiver. He gets up, slopes off into the bedroom and returns with an eiderdown under one arm and the black cat under the other. The cat he deposits in the hall. Settling the eider-*

down about his shoulders but without removing his hat, he starts the gramophone again and sits miserably beside it. The record that happens already to be in position is "The Death of Asë." His expression unaltered, he resumes his seat. After a long while, MR. JELLIWELL *comes in*]

JELLIWELL [*aggressively*]. Oh: so you're back, are you!

DEWLIP [*gloomily*]. Hallo, Johnny.

JELLIWELL. Don't you talk to me!

DEWLIP [*after blinking a moment with mild incomprehension*]. So you're mad too this morning?

JELLIWELL. You'll soon find out whether I'm mad or not.

DEWLIP [*his gloom unrelieved*]. It's very strange: I go away for one night, and the consequence is that, by the time I return, the entire world has lost its balance.

JELLIWELL [*striding fiercely up and down*]. I'll give you balance if you talk to me!

DEWLIP. Therefore I will not talk to you. Julia and I were having a party on the same lines. Sit down and join us. We'll all be mad together.

JELLIWELL [*stopping the gramophone violently*]. I'll tell you what you are: you're vermin, old boy, vermin!

[DEWLIP *doesn't reply, so* JELLIWELL, *a little put out, continues to pace*]

JULIA [*to* JOHNNY]. Is that all you have to say?

JELLIWELL. Of course not: give us a chance, old girl. I've got this to say: there are some things no decent man will stand for. Heaven knows I'm not narrow-minded. I've knocked up with this one in my time and with—er—that one. I'm a bit of a Bohemian myself. Paris, Vienna, Budapest—I know 'em all. Why, before the War I was three weeks in Port Saïd all alone when—

JULIA. Suppose we skip Port Saïd.

JELLIWELL. Very well, darling. Anyway, Julia will bear me out; no one likes a joke or a bit of wholesome fun more than I do. I don't really even mind—

JULIA. Johnny, it would be so nice if you could come to the point.

JELLIWELL. All right, darling. The point is, for months and months you've been making love to my wife. Now: do you deny it?

DEWLIP [*without animation*]. *Deny it?* Three months ago I attempted to the best of my ability to inform you of it.

JELLIWELL. Three months ago. Exactly. Then Miss Smith came.

DEWLIP. What exactly has she got to do with it?

JELLIWELL [*turning on him warmly*]. Don't you cross-examine me, old boy. Perhaps it may interest you to know that you have wrecked my life—our lives.

DEWLIP [*not very interested*]. Have I, old boy? I hope Julia has been quite truthful with you.

JULIA. Oh, I have been perfectly truthful.

JELLIWELL. Three months ago Julia and I were extremely happy together. She used to see a lot of you, I know, and not very much of me. But when we *were* together, we were damn good pals: weren't we, Julia?

JULIA. We were, Johnny.

JELLIWELL. Then Miss Smith comes. And lo! Julia isn't good enough for my lord. Cools off, he does! Tells her she can go and—and boil herself! He's had enough of her: very sorry, but he doesn't love her any longer. Had enough of her indeed! Had enough of my wife!! Who the Hell do you think you are? After this morning you'll have learnt to treat my wife with some respect. If you think you can throw her away like an old glove or an old sock, you're mistaken! [*He pauses for want of breath*]

DEWLIP. I see.

JELLIWELL. Oh, you see, do you!

DEWLIP [*whose despondency throughout has been modified only by the mildest interest*]. I take it that you have come here this morning to put a formal end, in your own way, to our friendship?

JELLIWELL. Yes, old boy, I have.

DEWLIP. I see. [*He looks from one to the other; then goes to the telephone and removes the receiver*] Hallo, Mr. Dewlip here. Will you kindly ask Miss Smith to come up.

[*He replaces the receiver. JULIA turns quickly*]

JELLIWELL. What the devil are you going to do?

DEWLIP [*resuming his seat*]. While you have been speaking, I have been thinking. Sit down.

[*Wondering what is coming JELLIWELL sits*]

DEWLIP. So I have wrecked your lives, have I?

JELLIWELL. Yes, you have.

DEWLIP. The happiness you both enjoyed once has left you?

JELLIWELL. It has.

DEWLIP. Moreover, it has left you since I ceased to make love to your wife?

JELLIWELL. Precisely.

DEWLIP. How do you account for that?

JELLIWELL. Why, simply because now we see too much of each other. We get on each other's nerves. That never *used* to happen. It couldn't, when most of the week you used to take her off my hands.

JULIA. Johnny always puts things so gracefully.

JELLIWELL. No offense, old girl: but after all, that is the point, isn't it?

[MISS SMITH *comes in*]

MISS SMITH [*hesitating*]. Oh, I thought you'd be alone. [*Then she notices* JELLIWELL] Perseus!

JELLIWELL [*a little discomforted*]. Good morning. Er—hallo.

JULIA [*surprised*]. Do you *know* this woman?

JELLIWELL. Er—yes, as a matter of fact, I—er—do. Miss Smith is the lady I—er—met under the omnibus. I think I told you about it. We've—we've run across each other now and again since.

JULIA [*to* DEWLIP]. Did you know anything of this?

DEWLIP. Nothing.

MISS SMITH. Mr. Brown has been extremely kind to me.

JULIA. Mr. Who?

MISS SMITH. Mr. Brown.

DEWLIP. So *that's* Mr. Brown, is it?

MISS SMITH [*a little taken aback*]. Aren't you Mr. Brown?

JELLIWELL. Well, not—not altogether.

MISS SMITH. What do you mean by "not altogether"?

DEWLIP. He means he *is* Mr. Brown in places.

JULIA. And when not in those places, he is my husband, John Jelliwell.

MISS SMITH [*involuntarily*]. What? So that is your poor wife. [JULIA *bridles*] Oh, Perseus, why did you deceive me?

JELLIWELL. My dear, I didn't mean to deceive you. You said you were Miss Smith, and of course I didn't believe you; so I said I was Mr. Brown and never dreamed you believed *me!*

MISS SMITH [*smiling with relief at so credible an explanation*]. How absurd! You silly, my name really is Smith.

JELLIWELL. I'm most frightfully sorry, Andromache. After all, I'd nothing to conceal. You do believe me, don't you? [*She nods*] Am I forgiven?

MISS SMITH. Of course you are.

JULIA. Touching little scene!

DEWLIP. The scene being concluded, I propose to take the stage. Miss Smith, perhaps you will sit down. [*She does so*] Johnny, kindly be seated. [*With an inquiring eye on* DEWLIP, *he sits*] Julia?

JULIA. I prefer to stand.

DEWLIP. That would be a serious mistake.

JULIA. And why?

DEWLIP. Because I am about to make an exceedingly long speech. [*And so she consents. Very deliberately he takes up postiion in front of them, seated as they are in a row, and, in his own time, begins*] Ladies and gentleman, what I have to say is, I am afraid, largely autobiographical. I want you to call to mind for a moment the person who was Henry Dewlip three short months ago. I idled away my day and rioted away my night. My temper was short, I gambled and drank to excess, and the truth was not in me. I made love so promiscuously, so ubiquitously and, I may say, so successfully that I was a danger to the community. And no one did I pursue more strenuously than the wife of my best friend, Julia Jelliwell. I was, in short, an unconscionable blackguard. But what happened? Miss Smith happened. I will not conceal it from you: with Miss Smith I fell in love.

MISS SMITH. Oh, please.

DEWLIP. Allow me. In a sense it was for the first time. I had never loved quite in that fashion before. I realize now that all I had felt previously was a simple, unhallowed animal desire. [*He raises his hat politely in the direction of* JULIA] This was the first time that I had experienced what is known as a pure love: a pure love for a pure woman. What was the result? I gave up drink, I gambled no more, my temper improved, I worked like a slave, I acquired some ideals, I banished every ignoble thought of women from my mind. Julia adored me—

JULIA. Liar! Liar!

DEWLIP. But I was firm. She had to go. But were these the only results? Oh, no, there were others. I developed a weak heart; I became an outcast at my own club; the excellent business prospects of the man who was with me through the War and the Lower Third were destroyed at a blow; it cost me no less than four thousand golden sovereigns merely to postpone his bankruptcy; my mother spent a night in jail; Julia called me a reptile and trod on my toes; I lost all my friends; I ruined my evening clothes and caught a cold; I wrecked the hitherto happy lives of Johnny Jelliwell, who was my best friend, and of Julia Jelliwell, who has the best figure in London. But was it not worth it? It was all for love. Was it not a hundred times worth it? No, by Heavens, it was not! [MISS SMITH *rises, as if she had been pricked.* JULIA'S *eyes open wide with pleased surprise*] The world well lost for love! What craven, abject, pettifogging cur invented that most disgusting phrase? Some men are wolves and some are sheep, but nothing is more deplorable than the one masquerading as the other. Julia: will you kindly come here.

[*Very amiably,* JULIA *comes*]

JULIA. What is it, Henry?

DEWLIP [*setting his arm defiantly about her shoulders*]. Yesterday, I told you, Julia, that in my opinion it would be wrong to kiss you.

JULIA. You did, Henry.

DEWLIP. To-day, I have changed that opinion. It would be wrong not to. I am told on good authority that Ibsen said, "Be yourself." I have decided to do what Ibsen said. [*He kisses her.* MISS SMITH *turns her back and, betrayed only by a tapping foot, stares ostentatiously through the window*]

JELLIWELL [*only just able to express his delight*]. I say, old boy, this is splendid. Am I to understand that you're in love with Julia again?

DEWLIP. Love? I would not sully our relations with that tawdry word! I *want* her; simply and honestly, as primitive man wanted his mate, as any decent, self-respecting animal to-day wants his fellow-animal, as the eagle wants his fellow eagle, as the cow wants his fellow cow. Do I want her because I love her? Is this a pure love for a pure woman? Not it: not she. I want her because she has the best figure in London. Divorce her, if you like. Indeed, I wish it. You may even cite me as your co-respondent. It would do me good. I am so revolted with my last three months that nothing, I believe, will take away the unclean taste from my mouth until I have been through the relatively wholesome mud of the divorce courts.

JELLIWELL [*enthusiastically wringing the hand that is not engaged on* JULIA'S *shoulder*] My dear Henry, I withdraw all I said.

DEWLIP. My dear Johnny, it is already forgotten. As for you, Miss Smith, I can only regret the pain all this must be causing you. You had, I know, expected to marry me. [MISS SMITH *turns with an indignant protest on her lips: but he cuts in at once*] No, you need not say anything. Please do not blame yourself. I accept full responsibility. But we may as well be frank. During these last weeks you had learnt to reciprocate the affection I honestly imagined I felt for you. It is a pity, but that, my dear Miss Smith, is Life.

MISS SMITH [*icily*]. Will you kindly allow me to speak for a moment now? It is true I have been forced to be present at several rather odious and embarrassing "love-scenes," but in your self-preoccupation you no doubt omitted to observe that in each of them *I* played the rôle of resigned and slightly disgusted spectator. I was brought up to listen politely. It seems I was brought up just a little too well. As to marrying you, I assure you my mind has never even been crossed by that extremely obscene idea. Indeed, it was agreed very many weeks ago that, if ever he should be free again, I would marry Mr. Jelliwell.

JULIA. What!

DEWLIP. The devil it was!

JULIA. Johnny, is that true?

JELLIWELL. Well, old girl, it is more or less true.

DEWLIP. Well, I'm damned! And Johnny a married man! What became of your principles all of a sudden?

MISS SMITH. If it weren't for our unjust divorce laws, Johnny wouldn't *be* a married man.

DEWLIP. Unjust?

MISS SMITH. Do you consider it just that a man should be tied up all his life to a woman who's out of her mind?

JULIA. God, let me get at her!

[*But* DEWLIP *holds her back*]

DEWLIP. Julia, I entreat you, keep calm. Johnny, the lady appears to know a great deal about your private life: are you sure you know as much about hers? Did you know, for example, that she had a husband already?

JELLIWELL. A what?

DEWLIP. Husband, husband, husband.

JELLIWELL. Andromache!

DEWLIP. Oh, she hasn't got him any more. She shot him in the Touraine.

JELLIWELL. Don't be absurd, old boy. If she shot him, how could she be here now?

DEWLIP. You're allowed to in France. They have different rules.

JELLIWELL [*dazed*]. But why? Why should she?

DEWLIP. When they were married, they had mistresses for tea. There was therefore no alternative. It was the Decent Thing.

JELLIWELL. Andromache, darling, you hear what he's saying! He says you're a murderess, old girl! Is it true?

MISS SMITH. Quite true.

JELLIWELL. But, darling, why didn't you tell me?

MISS SMITH. I would have told you but you never asked me. After all, it's hardly the kind of thing one chatters about socially. [*Winningly*] Does it make any difference? Do you mind?

JELLIWELL. Of course I don't mind, old girl. You shoot what you like. But I would like to have been told.

DEWLIP. Perhaps she'll promise to tell you next time. [*But* JELLIWELL *and* MISS SMITH *are already gone. He looks at* JULIA *for a second and she at him. His toe taps complacently. And then he starts the gramophone. He is still absorbed in this favorite diversion when* JULIA, *lightly whistling the tune of the record, gets up and strolls aimlessly about the room. At first he doesn't notice that she has left his side but, when he does, he looks up and finds her hovering near the bedroom door—hovering and finally passing through it. For a second or two he is alone and then, girding his eiderdown about him, he proceeds to follow her. En route, however, he notices the battered hat still in his hand*] Oh, I don't need that. [*He puts it down carefully and continues on his way, closing the door behind him*]

CURTAIN

A KISS IN XANADU

A Pantomime in Three Scenes

By WINTHROP AMES

CHARACTERS

H. R. H. THE CROWN PRINCE OF XANADU
H. R. H. THE CROWN PRINCESS, *his wife*
FIRST LADY-IN-WAITING
FIRST GENTLEMAN-IN-ATTENDANCE
CAESAR, *the Prince's Page*
POMPEY, *the Princess's Page*
A POLICEMAN
A LAMPLIGHTER
FIRST WATCHMAN
SECOND WATCHMAN

SCENES

I. *The Royal Bedchamber.*
II. *A Public Park.*
III. *The Bedchamber Again.*

The numbers in parentheses in the text are music cues. Corresponding numbers will be found throughout the musical score which was especially composed for this pantomime by Deems Taylor. Although the text—without the music—can be used for the study of Pantomime, the musical setting will be necessary to an effective public presentation. The complete musical score can be had on application to Samuel French, 25 West 45th Street, New York City.

"A KISS IN XANADU"

SCENE ONE

THE ROYAL BEDCHAMBER

[1] The Curtain rises revealing an empty stage. The "Working Curtains" at the back are closed, hiding the window etc.

[2] The "working curtains" at the back part slowly, revealing the window with its steps and balustrade.

[3] From off-stage right, the canopied and curtained Bed of the Princess comes into view, apparently moving of its own accord, but really pushed from behind by a man concealed by the back curtains of the bed itself. It comes to right center stage. The front curtains of the bed are closed when it appears.

[4] From off-stage left, the Prince's Bed appears in the same manner and moves into its position on the opposite side of the stage.

The Scene now represents the Royal Bedchamber, except that the front curtains of both beds are closed, and that the bed-tables are not yet in place.

[5] Enter from left (above the bed) the Lady in Waiting, and from right the Gentleman in Attendance. They step stiffly and pompously like marionettes. They meet up center.

[6] They bow to each other. (Note: Whenever this "shake" occurs in the music, the Lady and Gentleman "shimmy"—the Lady agitating her fan, the Gentleman shaking his shoulders.) They then cross each other, the Lady going to the Princess's bed (right), the Gentleman to the Prince's bed (left).

[7] Again they "shake."

[8] At this point both the Lady and Gentleman take hold of the closed bed-curtains of their respective beds.

[9] They simultaneously slide open the bed-curtains, in five jerky movements, timed to the music. They then fold back and arrange the bed-covers.

At this same cue [9] while the Lady and Gentleman are engaged in the above business, enter simultaneously from right (above bed) the Prince's Page, and from left the Princess's Page. Each carries a small bed-table, with a lighted candle on it. They march stiffly, with high knee movements. Crossing each other up center, each puts down his bed-table at the upper end of his master's or mistress's bed. Then they march off, (again crossing each other), and go out at the entrances from which they came. They instantly reappear, the Princess's Page bearing a foot-pillow, which he lays on the floor in front of the Princess's bed; the Prince's Page carrying a "costumer" (or standard clothes-hanger), which he sets at the foot of the Prince's bed.

Each Page then stands at the foot of his respective bed. (This business of the Pages begins at [9] and ends at [11]. They must move briskly in order to be in position for cue [11].)

[10] The Lady and Lord each pick up from the bed a pillow and beat it, tapping it simultaneously in time to the five accents of the music. They then replace the pillows.

[11] All four—Lord, Lady, and the two Pages—kneel on the floor, the Lord and Lady at the head of their beds, the Pages at the foot. The Lord and Lady move rheumatically.

[12] With swinging movements, up and down along the floor, they all peer underneath the beds.

[13] Finding nobody, all rise to their knees and look at each other, spreading their arms with a triumphant gesture to signify "No Burglars!"

[14] All four rise. The Lord and Lady approach each other at up center, shake hands and, crossing each other, go out above the beds, the Lord going off right, the Lady off left.

[15] The Pages march to up center.

[16] They bow low to each other.

[17] They march out, the Prince's Page going off right, the Princess's Page off left.

[18] The stage is empty. The Palace clock strikes nine.

[19] The Princess of Xanadu enters slowly, from left, above the bed. (She is wearing the royal nightdress under her robe.) The Lady in Waiting follows the Princess, bearing her train. The Princess's Page follows the Lady in Waiting.

The Princess comes to down center, the Lady follows to up center. The Page stops by the Prince's bed-table.

[20] The Princess feels the lure of the night, and turns up toward right (but still standing center) to look out of the window. This forces the Lady, who is still holding the train, to skip rapidly around to the foot of the Princess's bed, where she drops the train, and stands panting from the exertion.

[21] The Princess goes slowly up toward the window, mounts the steps and stands on the platform, bathed in moonlight. She gazes out

309

into the alluring night, stretching her arms out yearningly. She longs to leave the tiresome Palace and steal away incognito.

[22] But she shakes her head sadly. She must not think of such temptation. She turns from the window, and coming down into the room again goes to beside her bed.

[23] She beckons the Lady to approach and undress her. Getting no response, she stamps her foot angrily. Still no response. Glancing across the room, she is amazed to spy the Lady nodding drowsily.

[24] Imperiously the Princess claps her hands.

[25] The Lady recovers with a start, hastens across to the Princess and removes her crown, which she lays on the bed-table. Then she starts to untie the cord of the Princess's robe.

[26] The Princess indicates that her Page (*who is still standing beside the Prince's bed-table*) may be watching.

[27] The Lady nods in understanding, marches up to the Page, moves him to up center, faces him away from the Princess; and, whipping from her pocket a large silk handkerchief, spreads it over his head—thus blindfolding him.

[28] Triumphantly she returns to the Princess (*who has watched the episode with amusement*) and standing just above her removes her robe (*throwing it over her—the Lady's—left arm*). This leaves the Princess clad only in her nightgown. The Princess sits on her bed, and the Lady, kneeling before her, takes off the Princess's slippers, (*which she leaves by the bed*) and strips off her garters and stockings.

[29] The Lady rises (*still carrying the robe, stockings and garters*), nods to her mistress, goes up to the left of the blindfolded Page, who has meantime been standing motionless up center.

[30] She turns the Page, still blindfolded, to face left, and, her hands on his shoulders, shakes him in time to the music.

[31] Raising her skirt, and with a well-directed foot, she kicks the Page. He stumbles off, out right, (*going above the bed*).

[32] Proudly the Lady follows him and marches out of sight.

The Princess, who has meantime got into bed, and slipped under the covers now—

[33–34] Closes her bed-curtains in two movements, timed to the music.

[35] But as soon as she thinks the Lady is out of hearing, she cautiously peeps out from between the bed-curtains.

[36] Seeing no one, she stealthily slides the curtains open again.

[37] From beneath her pillow she slyly draws a yellow-covered French novel.

[38] She reads it with varying emotions. The story is romantic. It is exciting. And, oh, it is a bit shocking.

[39] She hears someone coming. Hastily she hides the novel, puts out the light on her bed-table, and closes the bed-curtains.

[40] Now from the right, above the bed enters His Royal Highness the Prince of Xanadu, followed by his Gentleman in Attendance, who is in turn followed by the Prince's Page.

The Prince is crowned, and wears a gorgeous dressing-gown over his royal pajamas and slippers. He has a very slight, blond moustache, and carries a small box containing curl-papers for this moustache.

The three march on proudly, the Prince coming to down center, the Gentleman stopping on the left of the Prince, and the Page on the left of the Gentleman.

The Gentleman removes the Prince's crown, sash, and dressing-gown, passing them to the Page, who hangs them up on the "costumer" which stands at the foot of the Prince's bed.

[41] Ruefully the Prince opens the box of curl-papers and holds it out to the Gentleman. The Gentleman screws one curl-paper onto the left side of the Prince's budding moustache, twisting it tight to the evident discomfort of his Sovereign; then, passing behind the Prince, repeats the operation on the Prince's right.

(*The moustache curlers are affixed to the Prince's lip by a pellet of soft wax on the end of each paper. The Gentleman presses the wax into place as he pretends to twist the curlers.*)

[42] Returning the box to the Gentleman, the Prince dimisses his attendants with a wave of the hand, and goes to beside his bed-table. The Gentleman and Page retire, stepping backwards and bowing as they go. The Prince returns their bows. They disappear at right, going above the bed, the Gentleman going out first.

[43] From the shelf under his bed-table the Prince produces a small Phonograph and sets it on top of the table.

[44] He winds up the phonograph, giving the handle nine turns in time to the music—fast at first and then slower as the spring tightens.

[45] He practices his bed-time exercises—his "daily dozen"—in attitudes burlesquing the ordinary physical setting-up exercises.

[46] But the lure of Spring and the romantic night is upon him too. His motions become less vigorous.

[47] He goes up to the open window and stands on the balcony. He, too, yearns to steal away in quest of adventure.

[48] But conscience (*temporarily*) forbids half-heartedly he returns to the phonograph and resumes his exercising.

[49] Irresolute he stops, and glances toward the closed curtains of the Princess's bed. She must be asleep.

[50] He resolves to venture forth!

[51] Manfully he pulls off one moustache curler—

[52] And then the other.

[53] With a gesture he waves "I will go" toward the open window.

[54] But he glances down at his pajamas. "How shall he disguise himself?" Hastening to the costumer, he takes down and examines his dressing-gown. The lining is different from the rich outside. If the garment is turned inside-out it will serve to disguise him. Quickly he turns it inside-out, puts it on, and ties the sash (*also wrong side out*) round his waist. The result is a success. He smiles triumphant.

(*Repeat the music between* [54] *and* [55] *to give time for what follows.*)

What shall he wear on his head? The velvet lining of his crown answers that question. He rips it out, turns it inside-out, puts it on for a cap, and hangs the crown itself on the phonograph crank.

[55] Another good idea! The two small, black ostrich-feather plumes that ornament his crown will serve as a luxuriant moustache to hide his own. He plucks them from the crown and affixes them to his face. The Prince congratulates himself—his disguise is complete and satisfactory.

(*These small plumes are already shaped like a moustache when they ornament the crown, and like the moustache curlers, they are affixed to the face by a bit of wax.*)

[56] He tiptoes across and listens at the closed curtains of the Princess's bed. All is quiet. He is safe. He returns to his own bed, still on tiptoe.

[57–58] He closes the curtains of his bed in two stealthy movements.

[59] Turns out the light on his bed-table.

[60] Waves a mocking farewell toward the sleeping Princess.

[61] Runs up to the window, and stealthily climbing over the balcony rail, drops out of sight and disappears.

[62] For a moment there is no action on the half darkened stage.

[63] A beam of moonlight gradually shines out, brighter and brighter, illuminating the bed of the Princess.

[64] Awakened by it, the Princess slowly opens the curtains of her bed and, as if drawn by the beam, gets out of bed, bare-footed, and comes to the center of the stage, gazing up at the Moon. Then she turns toward the alluring night and, with outstretched arms, goes slowly up onto the balcony. Again she yearns to go. But no, (*she shakes her head sadly*) she must not. And yet why not? She glances at the

Prince's bed. He must be asleep—why not risk it?

[65] A smile lights her face. She decides to steal away. Clapping her hands in glee she quickly returns to the room, lights her bed-table light, and sitting on her bed, hastily puts on her slippers.

[66] Rising, she wonders how to dress herself. Why won't the fringed coverlet which lies folded over the foot of her bed serve as a shawl? The very thing! She pins it (*with a safety pin*) over her shoulder, shawl-wise, and admires the effect.

[67] But her head? For a moment she stands perplexed, her hands raised to her head. The music is silent for a second while she considers.

[68] An idea! She takes the beribboned lampshade from her bed-lamp. It makes a most becoming bonnet. She ties it under her chin by the ribbons that ornament it.

[69] But she should have something to hide her face. She has another inspiration! She runs to the Prince's bed-table, takes the candle-shade from his lamp, and makes a mask out of it by punching two holes through it with her forefinger. (*Timed to the music.*)

[70] The first punch.

[71] The second punch.

[72] Her disguise is now complete. She admires herself.

[73] In glee at the prospect of her coming adventure, she dances, whirling gaily about the room.

[74] Suddenly the Palace clock begins to chime midnight and warns her that time is precious. Quickly she closes the curtains of her bed, extinguishes her bed-lamp, runs up onto the balcony and, waving a little mocking adieu toward the Prince's bed, disappears, running off right.

[75] The lights on the stage fade to complete darkness.

INTERMEZZO

During this Intermezzo the Scene is changed in the dark.

The working curtains at the back are drawn shut, hiding the steps and window.

The Prince's and Princess's beds, and the bed-tables are carried off.

A Park Bench, with a flowering bush attached to the back of it, is set, up center.

On the right side of the stage is set another flowering bush.

On the left is set a third bush, from which rises a lamp-post.

(*With practice this change can be made during the music from* [75] *to* [76]; *but if more time is necessary, a short repeat can be arranged.*)

[76] Gradually the stage lights brighten, revealing:

SCENE TWO

A Public Park in Xanadu

[77] The Street lamp lights by itself, and by its light we discover the Prince, in his disguise, sitting disconsolate on the bench. No adventure has yet befallen him. He is disappointed and bored. He yawns. He hears in the distance the march-tune of the Park Watchmen, and turns up the collar of his dressing-gown to better hide his face.

[78] Enter from right, above the right bush, the Park Watchmen. First comes the Policeman, strutting pompously like a rooster, operaglass in hand to spy for malefactors.

He is followed by the Lamplighter with his lighted torch. He has a hopping gait that makes his long red beard and wired cap toss with each step.

He is followed by two diminutive Watchmen, each holding a long pistol stiffly before him.

They enter left above bush in procession and cross the stage toward right, following this path:—come down left, march around the left bush, then up and cross behind the bench, then down and around the lamp-post, then up and exit off right.

[79] As the Policeman passes the Prince he peers at him suspiciously through his operaglasses. The Prince turns away guiltily.

[80] The Watchmen are still marching.

[81] The Watchmen disappear, leaving the Prince alone. He is sunk in dejection at the failure of his escapade.

[82] And now, with a gay tripping step, the Princess appears. She enters from right, above the bush.

[83] She starts to come down center, when she sees a young man sitting alone on the bench, though he does not see her. She runs behind the right bush and, on tiptoe, peeps over it, and is rather attracted by his aspect.

[84] Pretending not to have noticed him, she circles the right bush, crosses up behind the bench, then down left, and circles the lamp-post.

[85] She trips off, up left, and disappears.

Meantime—during [84] and [85]—the Prince has observed her with growing admiration. Rising he takes a step or two as if to follow her; but his courage fails, and, as she disappears, he sinks back onto the bench again.

[86] Now the Princess reappears (*from up left*). Pretending that she has lost her way, she pauses for a moment by the lamp-post to read the street sign on it. Then she crosses, going in front of the bench, toward the right, as if to depart.

(*Whenever the Princess confronts the Prince she takes pains to keep her mask between them.*)

[87] As she passes in front of the Prince she drops her handkerchief (*by accident, of course!*) and as she reaches the right of the stage, pauses, pretending to discover her loss.

The Prince sees the handkerchief fall, and rising, picks it up.

[88] The Princess manufactures a sneeze. She hunts vainly for her lost handkerchief, and, seeing it in the Prince's hand, begs him to restore it. He does so with a timid bow.

[89] Feeling another sneeze coming on, the Princess has to sink down on the right end of the bench. At the same time the Prince also sits, shyly, at the opposite end. She sneezes.

[90] Somewhat emboldened, the Prince shyly tries to touch her left hand, which lies on the bench between them. But she draws it coyly away.

[91] Plucking a flower from the blossoming bush behind him the Prince lays it gently on her knee.

[92] She flicks it to the ground, at center, and with a roguish smile points up at the lighted street lamp. The Prince follows her gaze. At last he realizes what the trouble is.

[93] Rising, he strides over to the lamp and attempts to blow it out.

[94] He blows—(*the lamp flickers, but does not go out.*)

[95] And blows—(*again it flickers.*)

[96] And blows! On the third attempt he succeeds. The lamp goes out, and semi-darkness settles over the scene. We dimly see the Prince emboldened, attempt to steal a kiss, but he is interrupted, for now—

[97] A glimmer of light shows that the Watchmen, with their torch, are returning. The light increases as they draw near. The Prince and the Princess spring to opposite ends of the bench, as the Watchmen approach.

[98] From left, above the lamp-post, the Watchmen in procession reappear, in the same order as before. They start to march straight across the stage, toward right, but suddenly the Policeman perceives that the lamp is out! He points this out, and, with excited gestures, they all gather about the lamp-post.

[99] The Lamplighter relights the lamp and again the stage grows bright.

[100] The Watchmen reform in marching order, and start toward the right.

[101] Suddenly the Policeman, spying through his opera-glasses, sees a distant malefactor, off right, and rushes after him, followed by the other Watchmen who gallop after him with increasing speed.

[102] They disappear off up right, above the right bush.

[103] The Prince springs up, with a threatening gesture, toward the lamp. He resolves that it shall never shine again.

[104] He feels his biceps. Repeated "daily dozens" have made him strong.

[105] Striding toward the lamp-post he breaks it in two.

[106] And blows out the light for the last time.

[107] Again darkness hides the scene.

[108] But now the moon (which has apparently been hunting for the Princess) throws from the left a gradually increasing beam of moonlight down on the bench. Its occupants are discovered sitting very close together indeed.

[109] The startled Princess points out the intruding moon to her companion.

[110] The Prince rises, and with a royal gesture, bids the moon withdraw.

[111] He waves it away imperiously.

[112] Still more commandingly he waves.

[113] He waves again—with anger now. And, as in Xanadu, even the elements apparently obey their sovereign, the moon fades a little on each successive gesture, and at the last rapidly withdraws. For a moment the stage is again dark.

[114] Now from the opposite side of the stage (the right) the first faint rays of the morning sun throw a faint gleam upon the bench, and throughout what follows the light increases rapidly.

[115] In the distance the Palace Clock chimes four.

[116] Pointing at the rising sun the Princess springs up in alarm. She must go home at once. The Prince, too, rises, holding her hand and trying to detain her.

[117] She breaks from him, and runs in and out among the bushes, dodging behind them, trying to elude him. But he follows fast.

[118] At last, in a moment when he happens to be behind the center bush, she hides, kneeling before the bush on the right. Confused and dizzy, the Prince, thinking she has run away, follows in the direction he thinks she has gone, and

[119] Runs off right, above the bush.

[120] Sadly the Princess watches him out of sight. Then, she kisses her handkerchief, and lays it on the seat where he perhaps may find it.

[121] She spies on the ground the flower he laid on her knee. She picks it up and hides it in her breast as a tender souvenir.

[122] Hearing the Prince returning (right) the Princess runs off left, and

[123] Disappears, going above the left bush.

[124] Slowly, and with dragging feet, the Prince returns (from left). He has lost her!

[125] Disconsolate, he sinks mournfully down on the bench.

[126] Beside him he discovers the handkerchief she has left. He picks it up, gazes at it tenderly, and presses it to his lips. As he does so the scene gradually darkens.

[127] Musical Intermezzo in darkness while the scene is changed.

During this Intermezzo, the bench, bushes and lamp-post are removed, and the beds, bed-tables, costumer are set in their former positions, exactly as at the close of Scene I, except that the "working curtains" over the window at the back remain closed.

[128] Gradually the stage lights come up.

[129] The "working curtain" at the back slowly parts, showing the terrace, sky and trees now flooded with morning light.

SCENE THREE

The Royal Bedchamber Again

[130] The Princess comes running into sight, from the left, along the terrace.

[131] She blows a last kiss toward the unknown lover of last night, then comes down and listens at the closed curtains of the Prince's bed. He is quiet; he must be asleep. She is safe.

[132] She tiptoes hastily to her own bed.

[133] Pops quickly into it through the closed curtains.

[134] Steals a hand out between the curtains and drops one slipper on the floor.

[135] Drops the second slipper.

[136] The Prince appears, climbing stealthily over the balcony rail at the back. (He has removed his disguising moustache.)

[137] He sits on the steps, and, gazing with some apprehension toward the Princess's bed, furtively removes his slippers.

[138] Hastily he tiptoes to the Princess's bed and listens.

[139] Crosses, still on tiptoe, to his own bed.

[140] He tosses his slippers into his bed, strips off his robe and throws that, too, into the bed, and jumps in himself, making sure the curtains are tightly closed.

[141] The Palace Clock strikes eight, and it is breakfast time. While the clock strikes, both Prince and Princess stretch out a furtive hand through the bed-curtains, recover their crowns (his from the phonograph, hers from her bed-table), and draw them stealthily into bed.

[142] Enter simultaneously the Gentleman in Attendance and the Lady in Waiting. He comes from left above the Prince's bed. She from right above the Princess's bed. The Lady carries the Princess's morning dressing-gown, and a hand mirror and powder puff. The Gentle-

man brings a hand mirror and a small gold moustache comb. Bowing as they meet, they cross each other diagonally, she going to the head of the Princess's bed, he to the head of the Prince's bed.

[143] They knock (*in time to the music*) on the bed-tables to arouse the royal sleepers. The Prince and Princess pretend to wake, and emerge, with manufactured yawns from their respective couches.

The Lord and Lady robe them in their dressing-gowns. The Princess fluffs her hair and powders her cheeks, and the Prince combs his moustache while the Lady and Gentleman hold the hand mirrors for them.

Meantime, from [143] to [144] the two royal Pages enter together, from up right above the bed. They carry between them a small round table set for breakfast, with coffee pot, sugar bowl, plates, napkins and fruit. They place this table down center between the beds. Then they quickly march off, up right and up left, and immediately re-enter, each carrying a stool or small seat. These they set right and left of the breakfast table. They then march off, up right and up left, bowing as they disappear.

(*During this action by the Pages, the Gentleman and Lady are robing the Prince and Princess as above described.*)

[144] Now dressed, the Prince and Princess go to the breakfast table, she on the right, he on the left. The Lady and Gentleman stand together above the table.

[145] The Prince and Princess sit.

[146] The Lady and Gentleman withdraw backwards, up stage.

[147] They go off, up right and up left respectively, bowing as they disappear.

Meanwhile, beginning at [146], the Prince and Princess unfold their napkins. She pours a cup of coffee and passes it to the Prince who holds it in his outstretched hand. She takes from the sugar bowl a lump of sugar, and—

[148] Drops it into the cup.

[149] She drops in a second lump.

[150] A sudden silence. The Princess recollects a neglected rite. They have not exchanged the usual morning kiss. In the silence she rises and, standing in front of the table, presents an apathetic cheek. He recollects his duty, sets down the coffee cup, rises, and brushes her averted cheek with his lips. All this in silence. At the kiss, begin music [151].

[151] They both remember another—and, oh! what a different kiss last night.

[152] Slowly, and simultaneously, they turn away from each other to look back at the window through which they went adventuring.

[153] Still facing away from each other, they stealthily (*and simultaneously*) produce from the breasts of their gowns the flower and handkerchief exchanged last night, and gaze at them tenderly.

[154] Unseen by each other, they hide the souvenirs away again.

[155] Slowly they reseat themselves at the table.

[156] They spread their napkins over their knees.

[157] And, facing the audience, sit motionless and dreaming till

[158] The curtain falls.

LIMA BEANS

A Scherzo-Play in One Act

By ALFRED KREYMBORG

CHARACTERS

THE HUSBAND
THE WIFE
THE HUCKSTER

LIMA BEANS

The characters are four: HUSBAND, WIFE, *the voice of a* HUCKSTER *and—the* CURTAIN! HUSBAND *and* WIFE *might be two marionettes. The scene is a miniature dining-room large enough to contain a small table, two chairs, a tiny sideboard, an open window, a closed door leading to the other rooms, and additional elbow space. Pantomime is modestly indulged by* HUSBAND *and* WIFE, *suggesting an inoffensive parody, unless the author errs, of the contours of certain ancient Burmese dances. The impedimenta of occasional rhymes are unpremeditated. If there must be a prelude of music, let it be nothing more consequential than one of the innocuous parlor rondos of Carl Maria Von Weber. As a background color scheme, black and white might not prove amiss.*

As the curtain, which is painted in festoons of vegetables, rises gravely, THE WIFE *is disclosed setting the table for dinner. Aided by the sideboard, she has attended to her place, as witness the neat arrangement of plate, cup and saucer, and knife, fork and spoons at one side. Now, more consciously, she begins the performance of the important duty opposite. This question of concrete paraphernalia, and the action consequent thereupon, might of course be left entirely to the imagination of the beholder.*

THE WIFE [*wistfully whimsical*].
Put a knife here,
place a fork there—
marriage is greater than love.
Give him a large spoon,
give him a small—
you're sure of your man when you dine him.
A cup for his coffee,
a saucer for spillings,
a plate rimmed with roses
to hold his night's fillings—
roses for hearts, ah,
but food for the appetite!
Mammals are happiest home after dark!
[*The rite over, she stands off in critical admiration, her arms akimbo, her head bobbing from side to side. Then, seriously, as she eyes* THE HUSBAND'S *dinner plate*]
But what shall I give him to eat to-night?
It mustn't be limas,
we've always had limas—
one more lima would shatter his love!
[*An answer comes through the open win-*

dow from the dulcet insinuatingly persuasive horn of THE HUCKSTER]
THE WIFE. Oh, ah, ooh!
THE HUCKSTER [*singing mysteriously*].
I got toma*toes*,
I got pota*toes*,
I got new cabba*ges*,
I got *cauli*flower,
I got *red* beets,
I got *on*ions,
I got *lima* beans—
THE WIFE [*who has stolen to the window fascinated*]. Any fruit?
THE HUCKSTER. I got oran*ges*,
I got pineap*ples*,
black*ber*ries,
*cur*rants,
*blue*berries,
I got bana*nas*,
I got—
THE WIFE. Bring me some string beans!
THE HUCKSTER. Yes, mam! [*His head bobs in at the window*]
[THE WIFE *takes some coins from the sideboard. A paper bag is flung into the room.* THE WIFE *catches it and airily tosses the coins into the street. Presently, she takes a bowl from the sideboard, sits down, peeps into the bag, dramatically tears it open, and relapses into a gentle rocking as she strings the beans to this invocation*]
String the crooked ones,
string the straight—
love needs a change every meal.
To-morrow, come kidney beans,
Wednesday, come white or black—
limas, return not too soon!
The string bean rules in the vegetable kingdom,
gives far more calories, sooner digests—
love through with dinner is quicker to play!
Straight ones, crooked ones,
string beans are blessed!
[*Enter* THE HUSBAND *briskly. In consternation,* THE WIFE *tries to hide the bowl, but sets it on the table and hurries to greet him. He spreads his hands and bows*]
SHE. Good evening, sweet husband!
HE. Good evening, sweet wife!
SHE. You're back, I'm so happy—
HE. So am I—'twas a day—
SHE. 'Twas a day?

He. For a hot sweating donkey—
She. A donkey?
He. A mule!
She. My poor, dear, poor spouse—
He. No, no, my good mouse—
She. Rest your tired, weary arms—
He. They're not tired, I'm not weary—
I'd perspire tears and blood drops
just to keep my mouse in cheese.
In a town or in the fields,
on the sea or in a balloon,
with a pickaxe or a fiddle,
with one's back a crooked wish-bone,
occupation, labor, work—
work's a man's best contribution.
She. Contribution?
He. Yes, to Hymen!
She. Ah yes—
He. But you haven't—
She. I haven't?
He. You haven't—
She. I haven't?
He. You have *not*—
She. Ah yes, yes indeed!
[The Wife *embraces* The Husband *and
kisses him daintily six times*]
He. Stop, queer little dear!
Why is a kiss?
She. I don't know.
He. You don't?
She. No!
He. Then why do you do it?
She. Love!
He. Love?
She. Yes!
He. And why is love?
She. I don't know.
He. You don't?
She. No!
He. And why don't you know?
She. Because!
He. Because?
She. Yes!
He. Come, queer little dear!
[The Husband *embraces* The Wife *and
kisses her daintily six times*]
He [*solemnly*]. And now!
She [*nervously*]. And now?
He. And now!
She. And now?
He. And now I am hungry.
She. And now you are hungry?
He. Of course I am hungry.
She. To be sure you are hungry, but—
He. But?
She. But!
He. But?
[The Wife *tries to edge between* The
Husband *and the table. He gently elbows
her aside. She comes back; he elbows
her less gently. This pantomime is re-
peated several times; his elbowing is al-*

most rough at the last. The Husband
*reaches the table and ogles the bowl. His
head twists from the bowl to* The Wife,
back and forth. An ominous silence]
He. String beans?
She. String beans!
He. String beans?
She. String beans!
[*A still more ominous silence.* The Hus-
band's *head begins fairly to bob, only to
stop abruptly as he breaks forth:*]
He. I perspire tears and blood drops
in a town or in the fields,
on the sea or in a balloon,
with my pickaxe or my fiddle,
just to come home
footsore, starving, doubled with appetite
to a meal of—string beans?
Where are my limas?
She. We had—
He. We had?
She. Lima beans yesterday—we had them—
He. We had them?
She. Day before yesterday—
He. What of it?
She. Last Friday, last Thursday—
He. I know it—
She. Last Wednesday, last Tuesday—
He. What then, mam?
She. We had them
all the way since we were married—
He. Two weeks ago this very day—
She. I thought you'd have to have a change—
He. A change?
She. I thought you'd like to have a change—
He. A change?
You thought?
I'd like?
A change?
What!
From the godliest of vegetables,
my kingly bean,
that soft, soothing,
succulent, caressing,
creamy, persuasively serene,
my buttery entity?
You would dethrone it?
You would play renegade?
You'd raise a usurper
in the person of this
elongated, cadaverous,
throat-scratching, greenish
caterpillar—
you'd honor a parochial,
menial pleb,
an accursed legume,
sans even the petty grandeur
of cauliflower,
radish, pea,
onion, asparagus,
potato, tomato—
to the rank of household god?

Is this your marriage?
Is this your creed of love?
Is this your contribution?
Dear, dear,
was there some witch at the altar
who linked your hand with mine in troth
only to have it broken in a bowl?
Ah, dear, dear—
SHE. Dear, dear!
HE. You have listened to a temptress—
SHE. I have listened to my love of you—
HE. You, the pure, the angelic—
SHE. Husband, dear—
HE. Silence!
SHE. Husband!
HE. Silence!

[THE WIFE *collapses into her chair.* THE
  HUSBAND *seizes the bowl to this male-
  diction*]

Worms,
snakes,
reptiles,
caterpillars,
I do not know from whence ye came,
but I know whither ye shall go.
My love,
my troth,
my faith
shall deal with ye.
Avaunt,
vanish,
begone
from this domicile,
dedicated,
consecrated,
immortalized
in the name of Hymen!
Begone!

[THE HUSBAND *throws the bowl and beans
  out of the window. The customary crash
  of broken glass, off-stage, is heard. A
  smothered sob escapes* THE WIFE. THE
  HUSBAND *strides towards the door.* THE
  WIFE *raises her head*]

SHE. Husband!
HE. Traitress!
SHE. Love, sweet husband!
HE. Traitress, traitress!

[THE HUSBAND *glares at* THE WIFE, *and
  slams the door behind him.* THE WIFE
  *collapses again. Her body rocks to and
  fro. Silence. Then, still more mysteriously
  than the first time, the horn and the
  voice of* THE HUCKSTER. THE WIFE
  *stops rocking, raises her head and gets
  up. A woebegone expression vanishes before one of eagerness, of housewifely
  shrewdness, of joy. She steals to the
  window*]

THE HUCKSTER. I got oran*ges*,
I got pineap*ples*,
I got blackber*ries*,

I got c*u*rrants,
I got *blue*berries,
I got bana*nas,*
I got—
THE WIFE. Any vegetables?
THE HUCKSTER. I got toma*toes,*
I got pota*toes,*
new cabba*ges,*
*cauli*flower,
red beets,
I got *string* beans,
I got—
THE WIFE. Bring me some lima beans!
THE HUCKSTER. I got onions,
I got—
THE WIFE. Bring me some lima beans!
THE HUCKSTER. Yes, mam! [*His head ap-
pears again*]

[*The performance of paper bag and coins
  is repeated. Excitedly,* THE WIFE *takes
  another bowl from the sideboard. She
  sits down, tears open the bag, clicks her
  heels, and hastily, recklessly, begins splitting the limas. One or two pop out and
  bound along the floor.* THE WIFE *stops.
  Pensively*]

There you go,
hopping away,
just like bad sparrows—
no, no, more like him.
[*She smiles a little*]
Hopping away,
no, he's not a sparrow,
he's more like a
poor angry boy—and so soon!
[*She lets the beans slip through her fingers*]
Lima beans, string beans,
kidney beans, white or black—
you're all alike—
though not all alike to him.
[*She perks her head*]
It's alike to me
what's alike to him—
[*She looks out of the window*]
though I'm sorry for you,
crooked strings, straight strings,
and so glad for you,
creamy ones, succulent—
what did he say of you?
[*She returns to splitting the limas; with
  crescendo animation*]
Heighho, it's all one to me,
so he loves what I do,
I'll do what he loves.
Angry boy? No, a man
quite young in the practice
of wedlock—and love!
Come, limas, to work now—
we'll serve him, heart, appetite,
whims, crosspatches and all—
though we boil for it later!
The dinner bell calls us,

ding, dong, ding, dell!

[THE HUSBAND *opens the door and pokes in his head.* THE WIFE *hears him and is silent. He edges into the room and then stops, humble, contrite, abject. Almost in a whisper*]

Wife!

[*She does not heed him. He, louder*]

Sweet wife!

[*She does not answer. He, still louder*]

Beloved,
dear, dearest wife!

[*She does not answer. He approaches carefully, almost with reverence, watches her, takes the other chair and cautiously sets it down next to hers*]

HE. Wife!
SHE. Yes?
HE. Will you—
I want to—
won't you—
may I sit next to you?
SHE. Yes.
HE. I want to—
will you—
won't you
forgive me—I'll
eat all the beans in the world!

[THE WIFE *looks up at* THE HUSBAND *roguishly. He drops down beside her with the evident intention of putting his arm about her, only to jump up as, inadvertently, he has looked into the bowl. He rubs his eyes, sits down slowly, looks again, only to jump up again. The third time he sits down with extreme caution, like a zoölogist, who has come upon a new specimen of insect.* THE WIFE *seems oblivious of his emotion. He rises, looks from one side of her, then the other, warily. At last, rapturously*]

HE. Lima beans?

[*She looks up tenderly and invitingly, indicating his chair*]

SHE. Lima beans

[*He sits down beside her. With greater awe and emphasis*]

HE. Lima beans?
SHE. Lima beans!

[*A moment of elfin silence*]

HE. Sweet wife!
SHE. Sweet husband!
HE. Where—
whence—
how did it—
how did it happen?
SHE. I don't know.
HE. You do—
you do know—
SHE. I don't!
HE. Tiny miracle,
you do—

you're a woman,
you're a wife,
you're an imp—
you do know!
SHE. Well—
HE. Well?
SHE. Er—
HE. Eh?
SHE. Somebody—
HE. Yes, yes?
SHE. Somebody—
sent them—
HE. Sent them?
SHE Brought them!
HE. Brought them?
SHE. Yes!
HE. Who?
SHE. Somebody!
HE. Somebody who?
SHE. I can't tell—
HE. You can.
SHE. I—won't tell—
HE. You will—
SHE. I won't—
HE. You will—
SHE. Well!
HE. Well?
SHE. You ought to know!
HE. I ought to?
SHE. You ought to—
HE. But I don't—
SHE. Yes, you do!
HE. I do not—
SHE. You do!

[THE HUSBAND *eyes* THE WIFE *thoughtfully. She aids him with a gently mischievous smile. He smiles back in understanding*]

HE. I know!
SHE. You do not—
HE. Yes, I do!
SHE. Are you sure?
HE. Sure enough—
SHE. Who was it?
HE. I won't tell—
SHE. You will!

[*He points at the audience with warning, goes to the keyhole and listens, draws the window-shade and returns. She nods quickly and puts her head closer to his, her wide-open eyes on the audience. He puts his head to hers, his wide-open eyes on the audience, then turns quickly and whispers something in her ear. She nods with secret, uproarious delight*]

SHE. Yes!
HE. Yes?
SHE. Yes!

[*They embrace and click their heels with unrestrained enthusiasm.* THE WIFE *holds out the bowl to* THE HUSBAND *with mock solemnity. He grasps it and*] *together they raise it above their heads, lower it to their knees, and then shell the beans with one accord. They kiss each other daintily six times.* THE CURTAIN *begins to quiver. As before, but accelerando*]

HE. Stop, queer little dear! Why is a kiss?

SHE. I don't know.

HE. You don't?

SHE. No!

HE. Then why do you do it?

SHE. Love!

HE. Love?

SHE. Yes!

HE. And why is—

[*They are interrupted.* THE CURTAIN *comes capering down! The last we behold of the happy pair is their frantic signalling for* THE CURTAIN *to wait till they have finished. But curtains cannot see—or understand*]

A Dramatization of Charles Dickens's

A CHRISTMAS CAROL

By FRANK SHAY

CHARACTERS

SPEAKER OF THE PROLOGUE
EBENEZER SCROOGE
BOB CRATCHIT, *his clerk*
FRED, *his nephew*
FIRST GENTLEMAN
BOY IN THE STREET
THE GHOST OF JACOB MARLEY
THE GHOST OF CHRISTMAS PAST
SCROOGE, *as a schoolboy*
LITTLE FAN, *Scrooge's sister*
SCHOOLMASTER
FEZZIWIG, *Scrooge's master*
SCROOGE, *as an apprentice*
DICK WILKINS, *Scrooge's fellow-'prentice*
SCROOGE, *as a young man*
HIS FIANCÉE
A HUSBAND
THE GHOST OF CHRISTMAS PRESENT
MRS. CRATCHIT
BELINDA CRATCHIT
PETER CRATCHIT
MARTHA CRATCHIT
TINY TIM
MRS. FRED, *Scrooge's niece*
THE GHOST OF CHRISTMAS TO COME
FIRST MAN
SECOND MAN
THIRD MAN
FOURTH MAN
FIFTH MAN
JOE, *a fence*
MRS. DILBER, *a charwoman*
LAUNDRESS
UNDERTAKER'S MAN
FARMERS, TOWNSPEOPLE, GUESTS, PEDESTRIANS, ETC.

SCENE: *Scrooge's chambers.*
TIME: *Christmas Eve, 1842.*

A CHRISTMAS CAROL

PROLOGUE

The curtain rises on a completely darkened forestage. On the backstage, behind a gauze curtain, is the dimly lighted interior of the counting-room of Scrooge *and* Marley. *The action, during the reading of the Prologue, is entirely pantomimic. The* Clerk *is industriously adding columns of figures and trying to keep warm.* Scrooge *is doing similar work and, from time to time, looks sharply at the* Clerk.

The Speaker of the Prologue *takes his place to the right of the stage and reads or recites:*

Speaker.

Marley was dead, to begin with. There is no doubt whatever about that. The register of his burial was signed by the clergyman, the clerk, the undertaker and the chief mourner. Scrooge signed it. And Scrooge's name was good upon 'Change for anything he chose to put his hand to.

Old Marley was as dead as a door-nail.

Mind! I don't mean to say that I know, of my own knowledge, what there is particularly dead about a door-nail. I might have been inclined, myself, to regard a coffin-nail as the deadest piece of ironmongery in the trade. But the wisdom of our ancestors is in the simile; and my unhallowed hands shall not disturb it, or the Country's done for. You will therefore permit me to repeat, emphatically, that Marley was as dead as a door-nail.

Scrooge knew he was dead? Of course he did. How could it be otherwise? Scrooge and he were partners for I don't know how many years. Scrooge was his sole executor, his sole administrator, his sole assign, his sole residuary legatee, his sole friend, and sole mourner. And even Scrooge was not so dreadfully cut up by the sad event, but that he was an excellent man of business on the very day of the funeral, and solemnized it with an undoubted bargain.

The mention of Marley's funeral brings me back to the point I started from. There is no doubt that Marley was dead. This must be distinctly understood, or nothing wonderful can come of the story I am going to relate. If we were not perfectly convinced that Hamlet's Father died before the play began, there would be nothing more remarkable in his taking a stroll at night, in an easterly wind, upon his own ramparts, than there would be in any other middle-aged gentleman rashly turning out after dark in a breezy spot—say Saint Paul's Churchyard, for instance—literally to astonish his son's weak mind.

Scrooge never painted out Old Marley's name. There it stood, years afterwards, above the warehouse door: Scrooge and Marley. The firm was known as Scrooge and Marley. Sometimes people new to the business called Scrooge Scrooge, and sometimes Marley, but he answered to both names. It was all the same to him.

Oh! but he was a tight-fisted hand at the grindstone, Scrooge! a squeezing, wrenching, grasping, scraping, clutching, covetous old sinner! Hard and sharp as flint, from which no steel had ever struck out generous fire; secret, and self-contained, and solitary as an oyster. The cold within him froze his old features, nipped his pointed nose, shriveled his cheek, stiffened his gait; made his eyes red, his thin lips blue; and spoke out shrewdly in his grating voice. A frosty rime was on his head, and on his eyebrows, and his wiry chin. He carried his own low temperature always about with him; he iced his office in the dog-days; and didn't thaw it one degree at Christmas. External heat and cold had little influence on Scrooge. No warmth could warm, no wintry weather chill him. No wind that blew was bitterer than he, no falling snow was more intent upon its purpose, no pelting rain less open to entreaty. Foul weather didn't know where to have him. The heaviest rain, and snow and hail and sleet could boast of the advantage over him in only one respect. They often "came down" handsomely, and Scrooge never did.

Nobody ever stopped him in the street to say, with gladsome looks, "My dear Scrooge, how are you? When will you come to see me?" No beggars implored him to bestow a trifle, no children asked him what it was o'clock, no man or woman ever once in all his life inquired the way to such and such a place, of Scrooge. Even the blind men's dogs appeared to know him; and when they saw him coming on would tug their owners into doorways and up courts; and then would wag their tails as though they said, "No eye at all is better than an evil eye, dark master!"

But what did Scrooge care? It was the very thing he liked. To edge his way along the crowded paths of life, warning all human sympathy to keep its distance, was what the knowing ones call "nuts" to Scrooge.

Once upon a time—of all the good days in the year, on Christmas Eve—old Scrooge sat busy in his counting-house. It was cold, bleak, biting weather, foggy withal, and he could hear the people in the court outside go wheezing up and down, beating their hands upon their breasts and stamping their feet upon the pavement stones to warm them. The city clocks had only just gone three, but it was quite dark already—it had not been light all day—and candles were flaring in the windows of the neighboring offices, like ruddy smears upon the palpable brown air. The fog came pouring in at every chink and keyhole, and was so dense without, that, although the court was of the narrowest, the houses opposite were mere phantoms. To see the dingy cloud come drooping down, obscuring everything, one might have thought Nature lived hard by, and was brewing on a large scale. The door of Scrooge's counting-house was open, that he might keep his eye upon his clerk, who, in a dismal little cell beyond, a sort of tank, was copying letters. Scrooge had a very small fire, but the clerk's fire was so very much smaller that it looked like one coal. But he couldn't replenish it, for Scrooge kept the coal-box in his own room; and so surely as the clerk came in with the shovel, the master predicted that it would be necessary for them to part. Wherefore the clerk put on his white comforter, and tried to warm himself at the candle; in which effort, not being a man of strong imagination, he failed.

SCENE ONE

As the Speaker of the Prologue *finishes, the gauze curtain rises, clearly revealing* Ebenezer Scrooge *and his* Clerk. *For a moment or two the action is pantomime. A young man bursts into the room so quickly that this is the first intimation* Scrooge *has of his approach.*

Fred. A merry Christmas, Uncle! God save you!

Scrooge. Bah! Humbug!

Fred. Christmas a humbug, Uncle? You don't mean that, I am sure!

Scrooge. I do. Merry Christmas! What right have you to be merry? What reason have you to be merry? You're poor enough.

Fred [*gayly*]. Come, then. What right have you to be dismal? What reason have you to be morose? You're rich enough.

Scrooge. Bah! Humbug!

Fred. Don't be cross, Uncle.

Scrooge. What else can I be when I live in such a world of fools as this? Merry Christmas! Out upon merry Christmas! What's Christmas time to you but a time for paying bills without money; a time for finding yourself a year older

and not an hour richer; a time for balancing your books and having every item in 'em through a round dozen of months presented dead against you? If I could work my will, every idiot who goes about with "Merry Christmas" on his lips should be boiled with his own pudding and buried with a stake of holly through his heart. He should!

Fred [*pleadingly*]. Uncle!

Scrooge. Nephew, keep Christmas in your own way, and let me keep it in mine.

Fred. Keep it! But you don't keep it.

Scrooge. Let me leave it alone, then. Much good may it do you! Much good it has ever done you!

Fred. There are many things from which I might have derived good by which I have not profited, I dare say; Chrismas among the rest. But I am sure I have always thought of Christmas time, when it has come round—apart from the veneration due to its sacred name and origin, if anything belonging to it can be apart from that—as a good time; a kind, forgiving, charitable, pleasant time; the only time I know of, in the long calendar of the year, when men and women seem by one consent to open their shut-up hearts freely and to think of people below them as if they really were fellow passengers to the grave, and not another race of creatures bound on other journeys. And therefore, uncle, though it has never put a scrap of gold or silver in my pocket, I believe it *has* done me good and *will* do me good; and I say God bless it!

[*The* Clerk *in the tank involuntarily applauds, only to become immediately sensible of the impropriety, pokes the fire, and extinguishes the last frail spark*]

Scrooge. [*to* Clerk]. Let me hear another sound from *you*, and you'll keep your Christmas by losing your situation! [*Turning to his nephew*] You're quite a powerful speaker, sir. I wonder you don't go into Parliament.

Fred. Don't be angry, Uncle. Come! Dine with us to-morrow.

[*Under his breath* Scrooge *mutters he would see him in some dire extremity first*]

Fred. But why? Why?

Scrooge. Why did you get married?

Fred. Because I fell in love.

Scrooge. Because you fell in love. Good afternoon!

Fred. Nay, Uncle, but you never came to see me before that happened. Why give it as a reason for not coming now?

Scrooge. Good afternoon!

Fred. I want nothing from you; I ask nothing of you; why cannot we be friends?

Scrooge. Good afternoon!

Fred. I am sorry, with all my heart, to find you so resolute. We have never had any quarrel to which I have been a party. But I have made the trial in homage to Christmas, and I'll keep my Christmas humor to the last. So a merry Christmas, Uncle!

SCROOGE. Good afternoon!

FRED. And a happy New Year!

SCROOGE. Good afternoon! [*The* NEPHEW *leaves the room without an angry word. He stops at the outer door to bestow the greetings of the season on the* CLERK. SCROOGE *mutters*] There's another fellow, my clerk, with fifteen shillings a week, and a wife and family, talking about a merry Christmas. I'll retire to Bedlam.

[*The* CLERK *in letting out* SCROOGE'S *nephew lets two other people in. They are portly gentlemen, pleasant to behold*]

FIRST GENTLEMAN. Scrooge and Marley's, I believe. Have I the pleasure of addressing Mr. Scrooge or Mr. Marley?

SCROOGE. Mr. Marley has been dead these seven years. He died seven years ago this very night.

FIRST GENTLEMAN. We have no doubt his liberality is well represented by his surviving partner. [SCROOGE *frowns at the ominous word "liberality."*] At this festive season of the year, Mr. Scrooge, it is more than usually desirable that we should make some slight provision for the poor and destitute, who suffer greatly at the present time. Many thousands are in want of common necessaries; hundreds of thousands are in want of common comforts, sir.

SCROOGE. Are there no prisons?

GENTLEMAN. Plenty of prisons.

SCROOGE. And the Union workhouses? Are they still in operation?

GENTLEMAN. They are. Still I wish I could say they were not.

SCROOGE. The treadmill and the Poor Law are in full vigor, then?

GENTLEMAN. Both very busy, sir.

SCROOGE. Oh! I was afraid from what you said at first that something had occurred to stop them in their useful course. I'm very glad to hear it.

GENTLEMAN. Under the impression that they scarcely furnish Christian cheer of mind or body to the multitude, a few of us are endeavoring to raise a fund to buy the poor some meat and drink and means of warmth. We choose this time, because it is the time, of all others, when Want is keenly felt and Abundance rejoices. What shall I put you down for?

SCROOGE. Nothing!

GENTLEMAN. You wish to remain anonymous?

SCROOGE. I wish to be left alone. Since you ask me what I wish, gentlemen, that is my answer. I don't make merry myself at Christmas, and I can't afford to make idle people

merry. I help to support the establishments I have mentioned; they cost enough. Those who are badly off must go there.

GENTLEMAN. Many can't go there; and many would rather die.

SCROOGE. If they would rather die, they had better do it and decrease the surplus population. Besides, excuse me, I don't know that.

GENTLEMAN. But you might know it.

SCROOGE. It's not my business. It's enough for a man to understand his own business and not to interfere with other people's. Mine occupies me constantly. Good afternoon, gentlemen.

[*The* GENTLEMEN *withdraw and* SCROOGE *resumes his labors with an improved opinion of himself. Darkness has descended and outside the windows may be seen people running about with flaming lamps to light their way. The owner of one scant young nose, gnawed and mumbled by the hungry cold as bones are gnawed by dogs, stoops down at* SCROOGE'S *keyhole to regale him with a Christmas carol, but at the first sound of*

God bless you merry gentlemen,
May nothing you dismay

SCROOGE *seizes the ruler with such energy of action that the singer flees in terror. At length the hour of shutting up the countinghouse arrives. With ill-will,* SCROOGE *dismounts from his stool and signs to the* CLERK *in the tank, who instantly snuffs his candle out and puts on his hat*]

SCROOGE. You'll want all day to-morrow, I suppose.

CLERK. If quite convenient, sir.

SCROOGE. It's not convenient, and it's not fair. If I was to stop half-a-crown for it, you'd think yourself ill used, I'll be bound? [*The* CLERK *smiles faintly*] And yet, you don't think *me* ill used when I pay a day's wages for no work.

CLERK. Christmas comes but once a year, sir.

SCROOGE. A poor excuse for picking a man's pocket every twenty-fifth of December. But I suppose you must have the whole day. Be here all the earlier next morning.

[SCROOGE *walks out with a low growl. The office is closed in a twinkling, and the* CLERK, *with the long ends of his white comforter dangling below his waist, for he boasts no greatcoat, goes down a slide on Cornhill, at the end of a lane of boys, twenty times, in honor of its being Christmas Eve, and then runs home to Camden Town, as hard as he can pelt, to play at blindman's buff*]

CURTAIN

SCENE TWO

SCROOGE'S *chambers on the forestage.*
The door silently opens and SCROOGE *enters.*
He pauses for a moment, startled, staring at the
outer panel of the door. He is heard to mutter
"Pooh, pooh!" and closes the door with a bang.
Then he reopens it cautiously and peers out.
Before he recloses the door, he walks through
his rooms to see that all is right.

Sitting-room, bedroom, lumber-room. All as
they should be. Nobody under the table, nobody
under the sofa; a small fire in the grate; spoon
and basin ready; and the little saucepan of
*gruel (*SCROOGE *has a cold in his head) upon*
the hob. Nobody under the bed; nobody in the
closet; nobody in his dressing-gown, which is
hanging up in a suspicious attitude against the
wall. Lumber-room as usual. Old fireguard, old
shoes, two fish baskets, washing-stand on three
legs, and a poker.

Quite satisfied, he closes his door, and locks
himself in; double-locks himself in, which was
not his custom. Thus secured against surprise,
he takes off his cravat; puts on his dressing-
gown and slippers, and his night cap; and sits
before the fire to take his gruel.

It is a very low fire, indeed, nothing for such
a bitter night. He is obliged to sit close to it,
and brood over it, before he can extract the
least sensation of warmth from such a hand-
ful of fuel.

SCROOGE [*walking away*]. Humbug! [*After*
several turns, he sits down again. He glances at
an unused bell that hangs in the room and com-
municates, for some purpose now forgotten,
with a chamber in the highest story of the
building. As he looks, he sees the bell begin to
swing. It swings so softly that it scarcely makes
a sound; but soon it rings loudly, and so does
every bell in the house. The bells cease and are
followed by a clanking noise deep down below
as if some person were dragging a heavy chain
over the casks in the wine merchant's cellar.
Then the cellar door flies open with a boom-
ing sound, and the noise, much louder, is heard
coming up the stairs, then coming straight
toward the door] It's humbug still! I won't
believe it! [*Then as he sees who it is*] I know
him! Marley's ghost! [*For* MARLEY *it is.* MAR-
LEY *in his pigtail, usual waistcoat, tights and*
boots. The chain he draws is clasped about his
middle. It is long and wound about him like a
tail, and it is made of cash boxes, keys, padlocks,
ledges, deeds, and heavy purses wrought in
steel] How now! What do you want with
me?

GHOST. Much!
SCROOGE. Who are you?
GHOST. Ask me who I *was.*
SCROOGE. Who *were* you then? [*Then raising*
his voice] You're particular, for a shade.

GHOST. In life I was your partner, Jacob
Marley.
SCROOGE [*looking at him, doubtfully*]. Can
you—can you sit down?
GHOST. I can.
SCROOGE. Do it then.
[*The* GHOST *sits down on the opposite side*
of the fireplace as if he were quite used
to it]
GHOST. You don't believe in me.
SCROOGE. I don't.
GHOST. What evidence would you have of
my reality beyond that of your own senses?
SCROOGE. I don't know.
GHOST. Why do you doubt your own senses?
SCROOGE. Because a little thing affects them.
A slight disorder of the stomach makes them
cheats. You may be an undigested bit of beef,
a blot of mustard, a crumb of cheese, a frag-
ment of an underdone potato. There's more of
gravy than of grave about you, whatever you
are. [*The* GHOST *sits motionless while* SCROOGE
is talking] You see this toothpick?
GHOST. I do.
SCROOGE. You are not looking at it.
GHOST. But I see it nevertheless.
SCROOGE. Well, I have but to swallow this
and be persecuted for the rest of my days by
a legion of goblins, all of my own creation.
Humbug, I tell you, humbug! [*At this the*
GHOST *raises a frightful cry and shakes his*
chain with a dismal and appalling noise. SCROOGE
holds on to his chair to save himself from faint-
ing. But how much greater is his horror when
the GHOST *takes off the bandages from his*
head as if they are too warm to wear indoors
and his lower jaw drops down upon his breast.
SCROOGE *falls upon his knees*] Mercy! Dreadful
apparition, why do you trouble me?
GHOST. Man of the worldly mind, do you
believe in me or not?
SCROOGE. I do. I must. But why do spirits
walk the earth, and why do they come to me?
GHOST. It is required of every man that the
spirit within him should walk abroad among his
fellow men and travel far and wide; and if that
spirit goes not forth in life, it is condemned to
do so after death. It is doomed to wander
through the world, oh, woe is me! and witness
what it cannot share, but might have shared
on earth and turned to happiness. [*Again the*
GHOST *raises a cry and shakes his chains and*
wrings his shadowy hands]
SCROOGE. You are fettered. Tell me why.
GHOST. I wear the chain I forged in life. I
made it link by link and yard by yard. I girded
it on of my own free will and of my own free
will I wore it. Is its pattern strange to you?
[SCROOGE *trembles more and more*] Or would
you know the weight and length of the strong
coil you bear yourself? It was full as heavy
and as long as this seven Christmas Eves ago.

You have labored on it since them. It is a ponderous chain.

[Scrooge *glances at the floor as if he expects to find himself surrounded by some fifty or sixty fathoms of iron cable*]

Scrooge [*imploringly*]. Jacob! Old Jacob Marley, tell me more! Speak comfort to me, Jacob.

Ghost. I have none to give. It comes from other regions, Ebenezer Scrooge, and it is conveyed by other ministers to other kinds of men. Nor can I tell you what I would. A very little more is all permitted to me. I cannot rest; I cannot stay; I cannot linger anywhere. My spirit never walked beyond our countinghouse, mark me; in life my spirit never roved beyond the narrow limits of our money-changing hole; and weary journeys lie before me.

[*It is a habit with* Scrooge, *whenever he becomes thoughtful, to put his hands in his breeches pockets. Pondering on what the* Ghost *has said, he does so now, but without lifting up his eyes or getting off his knees*]

Scrooge. You must have been very slow about it, Jacob.

Ghost. Slow?

Scrooge. Seven years dead and traveling all the time?

Ghost. The whole time. No rest, no peace. Incessant torture of remorse.

Scrooge. You travel fast?

Ghost. On the wings of the wind.

Scrooge. You must have got over a great quantity of ground in seven years.

[*The* Ghost *sets up another wailing and clanking of his chains*]

Ghost. Oh! captive, bound and doubleoned, not to know that ages of incessant labor, by immortal creatures, for this earth, must pass into eternity before the good of which it susceptible is all developed. Not to know that any Christian spirit working kindly in its little sphere, whatever it may be, will find its mortal life too short for its vast means of usefulness. Not to know that no space of regret can make amends for one life's opportunities misused. Yet such was I! Oh! such was I!

Scrooge [*falteringly*]. But you were always good man of business, Jacob.

Ghost. Business! Mankind was my business. The common welfare was my business; charity, mercy, forbearance, and benevolence were all my business. The dealings of my trade were but a drop of water in the comprehensive ocean of my business. [*The* Ghost *lifts his chain aloft as if it were the cause of all his grief and then drops it heavily to the floor*] At this time of the rolling year, I suffer most. Why did I walk through crowds of fellow beings with my eyes turned down and never raise them to that blessed Star which led the Wise Men to a poor

abode? Were there no poor homes to which its light would have conducted *me?* [Scrooge *is so dismayed that he begins to quake*] Hear me. My time is nearly gone.

Scrooge. I will. But don't be hard upon me! Don't be flowery, Jacob. Pray!

Ghost. How it is that I appear before you in a shape that you can see, I may not tell. I have sat invisible beside you many and many a day. [Scrooge *shivers and wipes the perspiration from his brow*] That is no light part of my penance. I am here to-night to warn you that you have yet a chance and hope of escaping my fate. A chance and hope of my procuring, Ebenezer.

Scrooge. You were always a good friend to me. Thankee!

Ghost [*resuming*]. You will be haunted by Three Spirits.

Scrooge. Is that the chance and hope you mentioned, Jacob?

Ghost. It is.

Scrooge. I—I think I'd rather not.

Ghost. Without their visits you cannot hope to shun the path I tread. Expect the first tomorrow when the bell tolls one.

Scrooge. Couldn't I take 'em all at once and have it over, Jacob?

Ghost. Expect the second on the next night at the same hour. The third, upon the next night when the last stroke of twelve has ceased to vibrate. Look to see me no more; and look that for your own sake, you remember what has passed between us.

[*The* Ghost *takes his wrapper from the table and binds it about his head. Then he rises with his chain bound over his arm. As the* Ghost *walks backward, the window raises itself a little with each step. He beckons to* Scrooge *to approach. When they are within two paces of each other,* Marley's Ghost *holds up his hand, warning* Scrooge *to come no nearer. Incoherent sounds of lamentation and regret come through the open window. The* Ghost, *after listening for a moment, joins the mournful dirge and floats out upon the bleak, dark night. For a moment* Scrooge *stands staring out of the window. The noises cease, and he closes the window and examines the door by which the* Ghost *has entered. It is double-locked as he had locked it with his own hands, and the bolts are undisturbed. He tries to say "Humbug" but stops at the first syllable. Being in much need of repose, he goes straight to bed without undressing and falls asleep in an instant*]

CURTAIN

SCENE THREE

SCROOGE's *chambers.*

When SCROOGE *awakens it is so dark that looking out of bed he can hardly distinguish the transparent window from the opaque walls of his chamber. He is endeavoring to pierce the darkness with his ferret eyes when the chimes of a neighboring church strike the four quarters. So he listens for the hour. To his great astonishment the heavy bell goes from six to seven, and from seven to eight and regularly up to twelve; then stops. Twelve! It was past two when he went to bed. The clock is wrong. He looks at his watch. The church clock is right!*

SCROOGE. Why, it isn't possible that I can have slept through a whole day and far into another night! It isn't possible that anything has happened to the sun and this is twelve at noon! [*He scrambles out of bed and gropes his way to the window. He tries to rub the frost from the pane with the sleeve of his dressing-gown, and then he can see but little. He returns to bed again, carefully drawing his curtains. Almost immediately the chimes on the distant church begin ringing: Ding, dong!*] A quarter past. [*Ding, dong!*] Half past. [*Ding, dong!*] A quarter to it. [*Ding, dong!*] The hour itself and nothing else. [*As he finishes speaking, the hour bell sounds a deep, dull, hollow, melancholy one. The curtains of his bed are drawn aside by a hand, and* SCROOGE, *starting up to a half-recumbent attitude, finds himself face to face with an unearthly visitor. It is a strange figure, like a child; yet not so like a child as an old man. Its hair, which hangs about its neck and down its back, is white, as if with age; and yet the face has not a wrinkle in it. Its legs and arms are most delicately formed. It wears a tunic of the purest white, and round its waist is bound a lustrous belt. It holds a branch of fresh, green holly in its hand, and in singular contradiction to that wintry emblem, has its dress trimmed with summer flowers. Its cap is held under its arm*] Are you the Spirit, sir, whose coming was foretold to me?

GHOST. I am! [*The voice is soft and gentle*]

SCROOGE. Who and what are you?

GHOST. I am the Ghost of Christmas Past.

SCROOGE. Long past?

GHOST. No. Your past.

SCROOGE. I like your cap. Please be covered.

GHOST. What, would you so soon put out with worldly hands the light I give? Is it not enough that you are one of those whose passions made this cap and force me through whole trains of years to wear it low upon my brow?

SCROOGE. No offense, sir. May I inquire what business brings you here?

GHOST. Your welfare!

SCROOGE. I am much obliged, but I cannot help feeling that a night of unbroken rest would be more conducive to that end.

GHOST. Your reclamation, then. Take heed! [*It puts out its strong hand as it speaks and clasps him gently by the arms*] Rise and walk with me.

[SCROOGE *rises but finding that the* GHOST *is leading him toward the window through which* MARLEY'S GHOST *had gone, he clasps the* GHOST's *robe in supplication*]

SCROOGE. I am a mortal and liable to fall.

GHOST. Bear but a touch of my hand *there*, and you shall be upheld in more than this.

[*As* SCROOGE *and the* GHOST *disappear through the window, the stage darkens and the backdrop is lifted, revealing a country crossroads. There is a little schoolhouse at the left, a boy seated on the steps, disconsolate and alone. There are green fields to the right, and in the distance may be seen the little market town.* SCROOGE *and the* GHOST *carry on their conversation in the dark while travelers, farmers, townspeople, and children pass up and down the road*]

SCROOGE. Good Heaven! I was bred in this place. I was a boy here.

[*The* GHOST *gazes at him kindly*]

GHOST. Your lip is trembling. And what is that upon your cheek?

SCROOGE [*mumbling*]. A pimple, nothing else.

GHOST. You recollect the road?

SCROOGE. Remember it! I could walk it blindfold.

GHOST. Strange to have forgotten it for so many years.

[*Passers-by continue to move in both directions along the road*]

GHOST. They are but shadows of things that have been. They have no consciousness of us.

SCROOGE. I can name them, every one.

GHOST. See, the school is quite deserted. Only a solitary child, neglected by his friends, is left

SCROOGE [*in a whisper*]. My poor self, it is as I used to be. [*He sobs. The* GHOST *touches* SCROOGE's *arm and points to a strange man in foreign garments, wonderfully real and distinct to look at, with an ax stuck in his belt* Excitedly] Why, it's Ali Baba! It's dear, old honest Ali Baba! Yes, yes, I know! One Christmas time, when yonder solitary child was left here all alone, he *did* come, for the first time just like that. Poor boy! [*Other pedestrians appear on the highroad*] And there's Valentine and his wild brother, Orson; there they go. And what's his name, who was put down in his drawers, asleep, at the Gate of Damascus! Don't you see him? And the Sultan's Groom turned upside down by the Genii; there he is upon his head! Serve him right! I'm glad of it

What business had *he* to be married to the Princess? [SCROOGE, *halfway between laughing and crying, would make a strange picture to his business friends*] There's the parrot! Green body and yellow tail, with a thing like lettuce growing out of the top of his head; there he is! Poor Robin Crusoe, he called him, when he came home again after sailing round the island. Poor Robin Crusoe, where have you been, Robin Crusoe? The man thought the boy was dreaming, but he wasn't. It was the parrot, you know! And, there goes Crusoe's Man Friday, running for his life to the little creek. Halloa! Hoop! Halloa! [*Then, his attention returning to the solitary boy on the schoolhouse steps, he cries in pity*] Poor boy! I wish—but it's too late now.

GHOST. What is the matter?

SCROOGE. Nothing, nothing. There was a boy singing a Christmas carol at my door last night. I should like to have given him something, that's all.

[*The roads have cleared, and only the boy on the schoolhouse steps remains. He is not reading now but looking up and down despairingly. At last his face lights up in a smile as he discovers a little girl peering round the corner at him. Discovered, she rushes toward him*]

LITTLE FAN [*kissing him*]. Dear, dear brother. I have come to bring you home, dear brother. [*Laughing*] To bring you home, home, home!

BOY. Home, little Fan?

LITTLE FAN. Home for good and all. Home forever and ever. Father is so much kinder than he used to be that home is like Heaven! He spoke so me so gently when he told me to go and bring you home. And you're to be a man and are never coming back here. But first, we're to be together all the Christmas long and have the merriest time in all the world.

BOY. You are quite a woman, little Fan.

[LITTLE FAN *claps her hands and drags him laughing to the schoolhouse door. The* SCHOOLMASTER *appears at the door*]

SCHOOLMASTER [*in a terrible voice*]. Bring down Master Scrooge's box, there!

[*A* PORTER *appears with* MASTER SCROOGE'S *box on his back, and the little party starts off for the market town. The back scene fades and the lighting of the forestage reveals* SCROOGE *and the* GHOST *seated at the right*]

GHOST. Always a delicate creature, whom a breath might have withered. But she had a large heart. She was your sister?

SCROOGE. She was. You're right, Spirit, I will not gainsay it. God forbid!

GHOST. She died a woman and had, I think, children.

SCROOGE. One child.

GHOST. True. Your nephew.

SCROOGE [*faintly*]. Yes!

[*The lights on the forestage are again dimmed and the backstage reveals the interior of* FEZZIWIG'S *warehouse. There are several persons present, including the proprietor*]

GHOST. Recognize the place?

SCROOGE. Know it! Wasn't I apprenticed here? Why, there's old Fezziwig. Bless his heart; it's Fezziwig alive again.

[*Old* FEZZIWIG *lays down his pen, and looks up at the clock, which points to the hour of seven. He laughs to himself*]

FEZZIWIG. Yo ho, there! Ebenezer! Dick!

[SCROOGE'S *former self, now a grown young man, comes in briskly, accompanied by his fellow-'prentice*]

REAL SCROOGE. Dick Wilkins, to be sure! Bless me, yes. There he is. He was very much attached to me, was Dick. Poor Dick! Dear, dear!

FEZZIWIG [*on backstage*]. Yo, ho, my boys! No more work to-night. Christmas Eve, Dick. Christmas, Ebenezer! Let's have the shutters up before a man can say Jack Robinson! [*The two young men rush to obey the master's orders*] Hilli-ho! Clear away, my lads, and let's have more room here! Hilli-ho, Dick! Chirrup, Ebenezer!

[*Again they leap to obey the order of their beloved master. There is nothing they would not do for him, and in a minute the place is cleared, the floor swept, lamps adjusted, fuel heaped upon the fire and when they have finished the little room is snug, dry and as brightly lighted as a ballroom.*

In comes a fiddler with a music-book, and goes up to the lofty desk, and makes an orchestra of it, and tunes like fifty stomachaches. In comes MRS. FEZZIWIG, *one vast, substantial smile. In come the three* MISS FEZZIWIGS, *beaming and lovable. In come the six young followers whose hearts they broke. In come all the young men and women employed in the business. In comes the housemaid, with her cousin, the baker. In comes the cook, with her brother's particular friend, the milkman. In comes the boy from over the way, who is suspected of not having board enough from his master; trying to hide himself behind the girl from next door but one, who was proved to have had her ears pulled by her mistress. In they all come, one after another; some shyly, some boldly, some gracefully, some awkwardly, some pushing, some pulling; in they all come, anyhow and everyhow. Away they all go, twenty couple at once; hands half round and* back again the other way; down the middle and up again; round and round in various stages of affectionate grouping; old top couple always turning up in the wrong place; new top couple starting off again, as soon as they get there, all top couples at last, and not a bottom one to help them! When this result is brought about, old FEZZIWIG, clapping his hands to stop the dance, cries out, "Well done!" and the fiddler plunges his hot face into a pot of porter, especially provided for that purpose. But, scorning rest, upon his re-appearance he instantly begins again, though there are no dancers yet, as if the other fiddler had been carried home, exhausted, on a shutter, and he were a brand-new man resolved to beat him out of sight or perish.

There are more dances, and there are forfeits, and more dances, and there is cake, and there is negus, and there is a great piece of cold roast, and there is a great piece of cold boiled, and there are mince-pies, and plenty of beer. But the great effect of the evening comes after the roast and boiled, when the fiddler (an artful dog, mind! the sort of man who knows his business better than you or I could have told it him!) struck up "Sir Roger de Coverley." Then old FEZZIWIG stands out to dance with MRS. FEZZIWIG. Top couple, too; with a good stiff piece of work cut out for them; three or four and twenty pair of partners; people who are not to be trifled with; people who will dance, and have no notion of walking.

But if they were twice as many—ah, four times—old FEZZIWIG would be a match for them, and so would MRS. FEZZIWIG. As to her, she is worthy to be his partner in every sense of the term. If that's not high praise, tell me higher, and I'll use it. A positive light appears to issue from FEZZIWIG'S calves. They shine in every part of the dance like moons. You can't predict, at any given time, what will become of them next. And when old FEZZIWIG and MRS. FEZZIWIG have gone all through the dance—advance and retire, both hands to your partner, bow and courtesy, corkscrew, thread-the-needle, and back again to your place—FEZZIWIG "cuts"—cuts so deftly, that he appears to wink with his legs, and comes upon his feet without a stagger.

When the clock is striking eleven, this domestic ball breaks up. MR. and MRS. FEZZIWIG take their stations, one on either side of the door, and shake hand with every person as he or she goes out wishing him or her a merry Christmas When all have retired but the tw 'prentices they do the same to them, an thus the cheerful voices die away. Th lights fade.

During the whole of this time SCROOG has acted like a man out of his wits Suddenly he becomes conscious that th eyes of the GHOST are looking full upo him]

GHOST. A small matter to make these silly folks so full of gratitude.

SCROOGE. Small!

GHOST. Why! Is it not? He spent but a few pounds of your mortal money, three or four perhaps. Is that so much that he deserves thi praise?

SCROOGE [heatedly]. It isn't that, Spirit. H has the power to render us happy or unhappy to make our service light or burdensome; pleasure or a toil. Say that his power lies i words and looks, in things so slight and in significant that it is impossible to add or coun 'em up; what then? The happiness he gives i quite as great as if it cost a fortune. [He stoj abruptly]

GHOST. What is the matter?

SCROOGE. Nothing particular.

GHOST. Something, I think?

SCROOGE. No, no. I should like to be able t say a word or two to my clerk just now. Tha is all.

GHOST. My time grows short. Quick!

[This remark is not made to SCROOGE, bu it produces an immediate effect. Th backstage is again lighted, and agai SCROOGE sees himself. He is an older ma in the prime of life. He is not alone, fc at his side is a fair young girl in mourn ing dress]

YOUNG GIRL. It matters little to you, ver little. Another idol has displaced me; and if can cheer and comfort you in time to com as I would have tried to do, I have no ju cause to grieve.

YOUNG MAN. What idol has displaced you?

YOUNG GIRL. A golden one.

YOUNG MAN. This is an even-handed dealir of the world! There is nothing on which it so hard as poverty; and there is nothing professes to condemn with such severity as th pursuit of wealth.

YOUNG GIRL. You fear the world too muc All your other hopes have merged into th hope of being beyond the chance of its sord reproach. I have seen your nobler aspiration fall off one by one, until the master passio Gain, engrosses you. Have I not?

YOUNG MAN. What then? Even if I ha grown so much wiser, what then? I am n

anged towards you. [*She shakes her head*]
n I?

YOUNG GIRL. Our contract is an old one. It
s made when we were both poor and content
be so until in good season we could improve
r worldly fortune by our patient industry.
u *are* changed. When it was made, you were
other man.

YOUNG MAN. I was a boy.

YOUNG GIRL. Your own feeling tells you
t you were not what you are. I am. That
ich promised happiness when we were one
heart is fraught with misery now that we
two. How often and how keenly I have
ught of this, I will not say. It is enough that
ave thought of it and can release you.

YOUNG MAN. Have I ever sought release?

YOUNG GIRL. In words? No. Never.

YOUNG MAN. In what, then?

YOUNG GIRL. In a changed nature; in an
ered spirit; in another atmosphere of life;
other Hope as its great end. In everything
t made my love of any value in your sight.
this had never been between us, tell me,
uld you seek me out and try to win me
w? Ah, no!

YOUNG MAN. You think not.

YOUNG GIRL. I would gladly think otherwise
could. Heaven knows! When *I* have learned
ruth like this, I know how strong and ir-
istible it must be. But if you were free to-day,
morrow, yesterday, can I believe you would
ose a dowerless girl—you who, in your very
fidence with her, weigh everything by gain;
choosing her, if for a moment you were
e enough to your one guiding principle to
so, do I not know that your repentance and
et would surely follow? I do, and I release
. With a full heart, for the love of him you
e were. [*He tries to speak, but she turns her
d away and continues*] You may—the
mory of what is past half makes me hope
will—have pain in this. A very, very brief
e, and you will dismiss the recollection of
ladly, as an unprofitable dream, from which
appened well that you awoke. May you be
py in the life you have chosen. [*She rises
leaves him. The lights on the backstage
in fade*]

CROOGE. Spirit, show me no more! Conduct
home. Why do you delight to torture me?

HOST. One shadow more!

CROOGE. No more, no more. I don't wish to
it. Show me no more!

[*The* GHOST *is relentless and pinions*
SCROOGE'S *arms to his sides and com-
pels him to observe what follows. The
lights on the forestage fade and backstage is revealed another scene in*
SCROOGE'S *early life. They are in another scene and place; a room, not very
large or handsome, but full of comfort.*

*Near to the winter fire sits a beautiful
young girl, so like that last that* SCROOGE
*believes it was the same, until he sees
her, now a comely matron, sitting opposite her daughter. The noise in this
room is perfectly tumultuous, for there
are more children there than* SCROOGE *in
his agitated state of mind can count;
and, unlike the celebrated herd in the
poem, they are not forty children conducting themselves like one, but every
child is conducting itself like forty. The
consequences are uproarious beyond belief; but no one seems to care; on the
contrary, the mother and daughter laugh
heartily and enjoy it very much; and
the latter, soon beginning to mingle in
the sports, gets pillaged by the young
brigands most ruthlessly.*

*But now a knocking at the door is heard,
and such a rush immediately ensues that
she, with laughing face and figured dress,
is borne towards it, in the center of a
flushed and boisterous group, just in
time to greet the father, who comes
home attended by a man laden with
Christmas toys and presents. Then the
shouting and the struggling and the on-
slaught that is made on the defenseless
porter! The scaling him, with chairs for
ladders, to dive into his pockets, despoil
him of brown paper parcels, hold on
tight by his cravat, hug him round the
neck, pommel his back, and kick his legs
in irrepressible affection! The shouts of
wonder and delight with which the
development of every package is received! The terrible announcement that
the baby had been taken in the act of
putting a doll's frying pan into his mouth
and is more than suspected of having
swallowed a fictitious turkey, glued on
a wooden platter! The immense relief
of finding this a false alarm! The joy,
and gratitude and ecstasy! They are all
indescribable alike. It is enough that,
by degrees, the children and their emotions get out of the parlor, and, by one
stair at a time, up to the top of the
house, where they go to bed and so
subside.*

And now SCROOGE *looks on more attentively than ever, when the master of
the house, having his daughter leaning
fondly on him, sits down with her and
her mother at his own fireside; and when
he thinks that such another creature,
quite as graceful and as full of promise,
might have called him father and been
a springtime in the haggard winter of
his life, his sight grows very dim indeed*]

HUSBAND. Belle, I saw an old friend of yours this afternoon.

WIFE. Who was it?

HUSBAND. Guess!

WIFE. How can I? Tut, don't I know? [*Laughing*] Mr. Scrooge.

HUSBAND. Mr. Scrooge it was. I passed his office window; and as it was not shut up and he had a candle inside, I could scarcely help seeing him. His partner lies upon the point of death, I hear, and there he sat alone. Quite alone in the world, I do believe.

[*The light again fades*]

SCROOGE. Spirit! Remove me from this place.

GHOST. I told you these were shadows of things that have been. That they are what they are, do not blame me. [*He turns upon the* GHOST *and wrestles with it. The* GHOST *is undisturbed, and* SCROOGE *can only shout*] Leave me! Take me back! Haunt me no longer.

[*After a terrific effort* SCROOGE *is triumphant and finds himself, exhausted, in his own chambers. He has barely time to reel to his bed before he sinks into a heavy sleep*]

CURTAIN

SCENE FOUR

SCROOGE'S *Chambers.*

After the house is darkened and before the curtain rises, the chimes of the distant church may be heard tolling the quarter, half and three-quarter hour. Then, after a short pause, the deep sonorous one is tolled, and the curtain rises to reveal SCROOGE *staring at a strange visitor. It is clothed in one simple, deep green robe, or mantle, bordered with white fur. The mantle hangs loosely upon his figure, the feet are bare and the head crowned with a holly wreath, set here and there with icicles.*

GHOST. Look upon me! I am the Ghost of Christmas Present. [SCROOGE *leaves his bed to better view his visitor*] You have never seen the like of me before!

SCROOGE. Never.

GHOST. You have never walked forth with the younger members of my family, meaning my elder brothers born in these later years?

SCROOGE. I don't think I have. I am afraid I have not. Have you had many brothers, Spirit?

GHOST. More than nineteen hundred.

SCROOGE. A tremendous family to provide for. [*The* GHOST *bows.* SCROOGE *impatiently*] Spirit, conduct me where you will. I went forth last night on compulsion, and I learned a lesson which is working now. To-night, if you have aught to teach me, let me profit by it.

GHOST. Touch my robe!

[SCROOGE *obeys the* GHOST, *and the light on the forestage are dimmed and the action backstage begins. The scene is the kitchen and dining room of* BOB CRATCHIT'S *four-roomed flat.* MRS. CRATCHIT *stands at the stove preparing the Cratchit Christmas dinner.* BELINDA *and* PETER *her children, are gleefully helping her*]

MRS. CRATCHIT. What has ever got you precious father, then? And your brother, Tiny Tim? And Martha warn't as late last Christmas Day by half an hour.

MARTHA [*entering*]. Here's Martha, mother.

BELINDA. Here's Martha, mother!

PETER. Hurrah! There's *such* a goose Martha!

MRS. CRATCHIT [*holding* MARTHA *in her arm and kissing her a dozen times*]. Why, bless you heart alive, my dear. How late you are!

MARTHA. We'd a deal of work to finish up last night, and we had to clear away this morning.

MRS. CRATCHIT. Well! Never mind so long as you are here. Sit ye down by the fire, my dear, and have a warm. Lord bless you!

PETER. No, no! There's father coming. Hide Martha, hide!

[MARTHA *goes behind kitchen door*]

BOB CRATCHIT [*entering with* TINY TIM *on his shoulder*]. Why, where's our Martha?

MRS. CRATCHIT. Not coming.

BOB. Not coming! Not coming on Christmas Day!

[*But* MARTHA *cannot see her father disappointed, and she leaves her hiding place and runs to his arms. The two young* CRATCHITS *rush* TINY TIM *to the wash room*]

MRS. CRATCHIT. And how did Tiny Tim behave?

BOB. As good as gold and better. Somehow he gets thoughtful, sitting by himself so much and thinks the strangest things you ever heard. He told me, coming home, that he hoped people saw him in the church, because he was a cripple, and it might be pleasant for them to remember, upon Christmas Day, who made lame beggars walk and blind men see.

[TINY TIM, *on his active little crutch, re-appears and is escorted to a high stool by the stove from which he can observe all that is going on. All the* CRATCHITS *become very busy preparing for dinner*, MRS. CRATCHIT *making gravy,* BELINDA *mashing potatoes;* MARTHA *dusting the plates, and* PETER *arranging the chairs,* TINY TIM, *excited by all the bustle, beats on the table with his knife*]

TINY TIM. Hurrah!

[*The dinner is placed upon the table, and all are seated.* BOB CRATCHIT *takes tumbler and fills it with hot stuff from a jug*]

BOB. A merry Christmas to us all, my dears. God bless us!

ALL. A merry Christmas.

TINY TIM. God bless us every one!

[*While they are busy eating,* SCROOGE *looks toward the* GHOST]

SCROOGE. Spirit, tell me if Tiny Tim will live.

GHOST. I see a vacant seat in the poor chimney-corner, and a crutch without an owner, carefully preserved. If these shadows remain unaltered by the Future, the child will die.

SCROOGE. No, no! Oh, no, kind Spirit. Say he will be spared.

GHOST. If these shadows remain unaltered by the Future, none other of my race will find him here. What then? If he be like to die, he had better do it and decrease the surplus population. [SCROOGE *hangs his head as he hears his own words quoted*] Man, if man you be in heart, not adamant, forbear that wicked cant until you have discovered what the surplus is and where it is. Will you decide what men shall live, what men shall die? It may be that in the sight of Heaven you are more worthless and less fit to live than millions like this poor man's child. O God, to hear the insect on the leaf pronouncing on the too much life among his hungry brothers in the dust!

[SCROOGE'S *head sinks lower upon his breast*]

BOB [*standing and holding aloft a glass*]. Mr. Scrooge! I'll give you Mr. Scrooge, the founder of this feast.

MRS. CRATCHIT. The founder of the feast, indeed! I wish I had him here. I'd give him a piece of my mind to feast upon, and I hope he'd have a good appetite for it.

BOB. My dear, the children. Christmas Day.

MRS. CRATCHIT. It should be Christmas Day, I'm sure, on which one drinks the health of such an odious, stingy, hard, unfeeling man as Mr. Scrooge. You know he is, Robert! Nobody knows it better than you do, poor fellow!

BOB [*mildly*]. My dear. Christmas Day.

MRS. CRATCHIT. I'll drink his health for your sake and the day's, not for his. Long life to him! A merry Christmas and a happy New Year! He'll be very merry and very happy, I have no doubt!

[*The backstage is darkened, and* SCROOGE *is seen with his head bowed almost between his knees*]

GHOST [*peering as if into space*]. I see a place where miners live, who labor in the bowels of the earth. A light shines from the window of a hut. Inside there is a cheerful company around a glowing fire. There is an old, old man, his wife, their children, and their children's children, all in gay holiday attire. The old man is singing a Christmas carol. How can they be happy in such a hovel? [SCROOGE *groans*] Now I am traveling across a dark moor toward the sea. There are frightful rocks, and my ears are deafened by the thundering of the sea as it rolls and rages and roars among the rocks. Afar out to sea, upon a dismal reef of sunken rocks, there stands a lonely lighthouse. Inside I see two men joining their horny hands across the table at which they sit, drinking their grog, wishing each other a merry Christmas. How can they be happy in such a lonely place? [SCROOGE *groans again*] Now I am above the dark and heaving sea, and I am aboard a sailing ship. The helmsman is at the wheel, the officers on watch, the lookout on the bow, dark ghostly figures in their several stations. Each is humming a Christmas carol, each recalling some remembered Christmas among the loved ones at home. How can they be happy in the face of such danger?

[*The forestage darkens and a hearty laugh is heard from the backstage. As the lights are raised, there is revealed the home of* SCROOGE'S *nephew. A small group of people are seated in a bright gleaming room*]

FRED. Ha, ha! Ha, ha, ha, ha! He said Christmas was a humbug, as I live. He believed it, too.

MRS. FRED. More shame for him, Fred!

FRED. He's a comical old fellow, that's the truth, and not so pleasant as he might be. However, his offenses carry their own punishment, and I have nothing to say against him.

MRS. FRED. I'm sure he is very rich, Fred. At least you always tell me so.

FRED. What of that, my dear? His wealth is of no use to him. He don't do any good with it. He don't make himself comfortable with it. He hasn't the satisfaction of thinking—ha, ha, ha!—that he is ever going to benefit us with it.

MRS. FRED. I have no patience with him.

[*The guests nod their heads to show they are of the same opinion*]

FRED. Oh, I have! I am sorry for him: I couldn't be angry with him if I tried. Who suffers by his ill whims? Himself, always. Here, he takes it into his head to dislike us, and he won't come and dine with us. What's the consequence? He doesn't lose much of a dinner.

MRS. FRED. Indeed, I think he loses a very good dinner.

[*The guests nod their heads to show they are of the same opinion*]

FRED. Well, I'm very glad to hear it, because I haven't much faith in these young housekeepers. [*He laughs again*] I was going to say that the consequence of his taking a dislike to us and not making merry with us is, as I think, that he loses some pleasant moments, which could do him no harm. I am sure he loses pleasanter companions than he can find in his own thoughts, either in his moldy old office or his dusty chambers. I mean to give him the same chance every year, whether he likes it or not, for I pity him. He may rail at Christmas till he dies, but he can't help thinking better of it— I defy him—if he finds me going there, in good temper year after year and saying, "Uncle Scrooge, how are you?" If it only puts him in the vein to leave his poor clerk fifty pounds, that's something; and I think I shook him, yesterday.

[*Tea is served, and one of the guests plays music. A country dance, a song, and a game of blindman's bluff follow each other quickly*]

FRED. A merry Christmas and a happy New Year to the old man, whatever he is. He wouldn't take it from me, but he may have it, nevertheless.

[*The party breaks up, and the lights fade*]

SCROOGE. Are spirits' lives short?

GHOST. My life on this globe is very brief. It ends to-night.

SCROOGE. To-night!

GHOST. To-night at midnight. Hark! The time is drawing near. When the bell strikes I shall be gone.

[*After a pause the distant chimes begin to strike, and on the last stroke the* GHOST OF CHRISTMAS PRESENT *fades away*]

CURTAIN

SCENE FIVE

SCROOGE'S *chambers.*

SCROOGE *is awake and awaiting the advent of the* THIRD GHOST. *The distant chimes have hardly died away before a tall and stately figure enters, garbed in a long gray robe, the hood of which nearly covers his face. The robe reaches to the floor, and the sleeves are full and longer than they need have been.*

SCROOGE. I am in the presence of the Ghost of Christmas Yet to Come? [*The* GHOST *does not answer but points a long, bony finger off toward the distance*] You are about to show me shadows of the things that have not happened, but will happen in the time before us. Is that so, Spirit? [*Again the* GHOST *faces* SCROOGE. *He folds his arms and looks intently at the poor mortal before him*] Ghost of the Future! I fear you more than any specter I have seen. But as I know your purpose is to do me good, and as I hope to live to be another man from what I was, I am prepared to bear you company and do it with a thankful heart. Will you not speak to me?

[*The hand of the* GHOST *now points directly towards the backstage. The forestage dims and the backdrop rises,*

revealing a street corner in the city. Th *setting sun shines on one street; t* *other is dark and gloomy. Some me* *with whom* SCROOGE *had done busine* *only the day before, pass. Two, comi* *from opposite directions, greet ea* *other*]

FIRST MAN. How are you?

SECOND MAN. How are you?

FIRST MAN. Well! Old Scratch has got h own at last, hey?

SECOND MAN. So I am told. Cold, isn't it?

FIRST MAN. Seasonable for Christmas tim You're not a skater, I suppose?

SECOND MAN. No. No. Something else to thi of. Good morning!

[*The* SECOND MAN *goes off. Other gentl* *men come up and speak to* FIRST MA*]

FIRST MAN. Well! Old Scratch is dead. Wh did he die of?

THIRD MAN. I don't know much about I only know he is dead.

FOURTH MAN When did he die?

THIRD MAN. Last night, I believe.

FIFTH MAN. Why, what was the matter wi him? I thought he'd never die.

FIRST MAN. God knows! [*He stifles a yaw*]

FOURTH MAN. What has he done with h money?

THIRD MAN. I haven't heard. Left it to h company, perhaps. He hasn't left it to m That's all I know.

[*There is general laughter*]

FIFTH MAN. It's likely to be a very che* funeral, for, upon my life, I don't know of an body to go to it. Suppose we make up a par and volunteer?

FIRST MAN. I don't mind going if lunch provided. But I must be fed if I volunteer.

FOURTH MAN. Well, I am the most disinte ested among you, after all, for I never we black gloves and I never eat lunch. But I offer to go if anybody else will. When I cor to think of it, I'm not at all sure that I was his most particular friend, for we used to spe* to each other when we passed.

[*The group breaks up, and the men go* *the various tasks. Their places are tak* *first, by a man of sinister face in fad* *black, and several others, men a* *women, who bear sacks upon th* *shoulders*]

JOE [*a fence*]. One at a time. Let the cha woman be first, let the laundress be the seco and let the undertaker's man be third. [*T* CHARWOMAN *throws her bundle at his feet a* *stands looking at him with bold defiance*] Wh odds, then? What odds, Mrs. Dilber? Eve person has a right to take care of themselv He always did.

CHARWOMAN. That's true, indeed. No m more so.

JOE. Why, then, don't stand there staring as you were afraid, woman! Who's the wiser? We're not going to pick holes in each other's coats, I suppose?

LAUNDRESS. No, indeed! We should hope not.

CHARWOMAN. Very well, then. That's enough. Who's the worse for the loss of a few things like these? Not a dead man, I suppose?

LAUNDRESS. If he wanted to keep 'em after he was dead, a wicked old screw, why wasn't he natural in his lifetime? If he had been, he'd have had somebody to look after him when he was struck with Death, instead of lying gasping out his last there, alone by himself.

CHARWOMAN. It's the truest word that ever was spoke. It's a judgment on him.

LAUNDRESS. I wish it were a little heavier judgment, and it should have been, you may depend upon it, if I could have laid my hands on anything else.

CHARWOMAN. Open that bundle, old Joe, and let me know the value of it. Speak out plain. I'm not afraid to be the first, not afraid for them to see it. We knew pretty well that we were helping ourselves before we met here, I believe. It's no sin. Open the bundle, Joe.

[*The gallantry of the* UNDERTAKER'S MAN *will not permit this and he places his plunder before the fence. He presents seals, pencil case, a pair of sleeve-buttons, and a brooch of no great value*]

JOE. Sixpence, and not another ha' penny if I was to be boiled in oil for not giving it. Who's next?

LAUNDRESS. Me, I'm next.

[*Sheets, towels, a little wearing apparel, two old-fashioned silver teaspoons, a pair of sugar tongs, and a few boots*]

JOE. I always give too much to the ladies. It's a weakness of mine, and that's the way I ruin myself. [*Handing her some coins*] That's your account. If you asked me for another penny and made it an open question, I'd repent of being so liberal and knock off half a crown.

CHARWOMAN. And now undo my bundle, Joe.

[JOE *goes down on his hands and knees for greater convenience in opening it. He brings forth a large, heavy roll of some dark stuff*]

JOE. What do you call this? Bed curtains?

CHARWOMAN [*laughing*]. Ah! Bed curtains they are!

JOE. You don't mean to say you took 'em down, rings and all, with him lying there?

CHARWOMAN. Yes. I do. Why not?

JOE. You were born to make your fortune, and you'll certainly do it.

CHARWOMAN. I certainly shan't hold my hand when I can get anything in it by reaching it, for the sake of such a man as he was, I promise you, Joe. Don't drop that oil upon the blankets, now.

JOE. His blankets?

CHARWOMAN. Whose else's do you think? He isn't likely to take cold without 'em, I dare say.

JOE [*stopping his work and looking up*]. I hope he didn't die of anything catching? Eh?

CHARWOMAN. Don't you be afraid of that. I ain't so fond of his company that I'd loiter about him for such things, if he did. Ah! You may look through that shirt till your eyes ache; but you won't find a hole in it, nor a threadbare place. It's the best he had, and a fine one too. They'd have wasted it if it hadn't been for me.

JOE. What do you call wasting of it?

CHARWOMAN. Putting it on him to be buried in, to be sure. Somebody was fool enough to do it, but I took it off again. If calico isn't good enough for such a purpose, it isn't good enough for anything. It's quite becoming to the body. He can't look uglier than he did in that one. [JOE *takes out his bag with money in it to pay the* CHARWOMAN] Ha, ha! This is the end of it, you see! He frightened every one away from him when he was alive, to profit us when he was dead. Ha, ha, ha!

[*The ghouls take their pay and go their several ways. The lights fade*]

SCROOGE. Specter, something informs me that our parting moment is at hand. Tell me, what man was that who had neither friends to care that he had gone nor loved ones to protect him from the ghouls?

GHOST. There is yet one more scene. [*The inexorable finger begins again to point, and the lights on the backstage reveal a graveyard. Walled in by houses; overrun by grass and weeds, the growth of vegetation's death, not life; choked up with too much burying, fat with repleted appetite. The* GHOST *continues to point, but he points to a separate headstone that stands apart from its fellows*] Read!

SCROOGE. Ebenezer Scrooge! Was I that man who none loved? [*The* GHOST *continues to point to the tombstone*] Oh, no, Spirit. Oh, no, no, no! [*More calmly*] Spirit, hear me! I am not the man I was. I will not be the man I must have been but for this intercourse. Why show me this if I am past all hope? [*The* GHOST'S *hand appears to shake*] Good Spirit, your nature intercedes for me, pities me. Assure me that I may yet change these shadows you have shown me, by an altered life. [SCROOGE *falls to his knees and bows his head*] I will honor Christmas in my heart and try to keep it all the year. I will live in the past, the present, and the future. The Spirits of all three shall strive within me. I will not shut out the lessons that they teach. Oh, tell me that I may sponge away the writing on this stone!

[*When he lifts his head, he finds the* GHOST *has gone*]

CURTAIN

SCENE SIX

SCROOGE'S *chambers again. The curtains about the bed are yanked aside, and a man who looks like a younger* SCROOGE *leaps out with a halloa on his lips. He smiles and opens doors, curtains, shades, everything. Sunshine streams through the room.*

SCROOGE. I will live in the past, the present, and the future. The spirits of all three shall strive within me. O, Jacob Marley! Heaven and Christmas be praised for this! I say it on my knees, old Jacob, on my knees. [*Going to the curtains about the bed*] They are not torn down, they are not torn down, rings and all. They are here; I am here; the shadows of the things that would have been may be dispelled. They will be. I know they will be. [*He begins to dress*] I don't know what to do! I am as light as a feather; I am as happy as an angel; I am as merry as a schoolboy. I am as giddy as a drunken man. A merry Christmas to everybody! A happy New Year to all the world! Hallo here! Whoop! Hallo! [*He finishes dressing and skips about the room*] There's the saucepan that the gruel was in. There's the door by which the Ghost of Jacob Marley entered! There's the corner where the Ghost of Christmas Present sat! There's the window where I saw the wandering Spirits. It's all right; it's all true; it all happened. Ha, ha, ha! [*He acts very unlike the man we met in the first act*] I don't know what day of the month it is. I don't know how long I have been among the Spirits. I don't know anything. I'm quite a baby. Never mind. I don't care. I'd rather be a baby. Hallo! Whoop! Hallo there! [*He is checked in his transports by the ringing of the church bells, the lustiest peals he has ever heard. Running to the window, he opens it and sticks his head out. Calling to some one down below*] What's to-day?

BOY'S VOICE FROM STREET. Eh!

SCROOGE. What's to-day, my fine fellow?

BOY'S VOICE. To-day! Why, Christmas Day!

SCROOGE. It's Christmas Day! I haven't missed it. The Spirits have done it all in one night. They can do anything they like. Of course they can. Of course they can. [*Lustily*] Hallo, my fine fellow!

BOY'S VOICE. Hallo!

SCROOGE. Do you know the poulterer's, in the next street but one, at the corner?

BOY'S VOICE. I should hope I did.

SCROOGE. An intelligent boy. A remarkable boy! Do you know whether they've sold the prize turkey that was hanging up there? Not the little prize turkey, the big one?

BOY'S VOICE. What, the one big as me?

SCROOGE. What a delightful boy! It's a pleasure to talk to him! Yes, my buck!

BOY'S VOICE. It's hanging there now.

SCROOGE. Is it? Go and buy it.

BOY'S VOICE. Walk-er! *

SCROOGE. No, no! I am in earnest. Go and buy it and tell them to bring it here. Come back with the man, and I'll give you a shilling. Come back with him in less than five minutes, and I'll give you half a crown. [*The sound of the boy's footsteps are heard racing off*] I'll send it to Bob Cratchit's. He shan't know who sends it. It's twice the size of Tiny Tim. No, I've a better idea! [*Looking at the knocker on the door*] I shall love it as long as I live. It's a wonderful knocker!—Hallo! Whoop! Here's the turkey. How are you? Merry Christmas. [*The* BOY *and the* POULTERER *enter with an immense turkey*] Why, it's impossible to carry that to Camden Town. My fine fellow, do you know where Bob Cratchit, Mr. Robert Cratchit, of Scrooge and Marley's, lives? It's in Camden Town.

BOY. Yes, sir.

SCROOGE. Go at once and tell him that I must see him at once. I must see him and all his family. Tell him I most particularly want to see Tiny Tim. Take a cab. Here's a sovereign. Hurry! [SCROOGE, *now thoroughly animated by the spirit of Christmas, bustles about arranging things neatly. He washes and dons his best clothes. He tries to dance and sing and work all at the same time. Calling down the stair well*] Mrs. Bilder, merry Christmas, Mrs Bilder. Hallo, Mrs. Bilder. Can you roast a turkey for me, Mrs. Bilder? Whoop! Hallo! Come up here at once. [MRS. BILDER *appears and notwithstanding her surprise, hustles off with the turkey.* SCROOGE *at window again*] Hallo here! Fred! Whoop! Hallo! Come over here!

VOICE FROM THE STREET. Who is it?

SCROOGE. It's I. Your Uncle Scrooge. Go at once and bring your wife, my dear niece; bring everybody. You are all to have dinner with me. Will you come?

VOICE. We will. Merry Christmas.

SCROOGE. Hurry, then. Merry Christmas. [*He stands for a moment looking out the window.*] A merry Christmas to you, sir. Come up and see me. I hope you succeeded yesterday. Come up at once, sir!

[*The* FIRST GENTLEMAN *who visited* SCROOGE *in his countinghouse the day before appears at the door*]

FIRST GENTLEMAN. Mr. Scrooge?

SCROOGE. Yes, that's my name, and I fear it may not be pleasant to you. Allow me to ask

* (A slang word denoting incredulity.)

your pardon. And will you have the goodness—
[SCROOGE *whispers in his ear*]

FIRST GENTLEMAN. Lord bless me! Are you serious, my dear Mr. Scrooge?

SCROOGE. If you please. Not a farthing less. A great many back payments are included in it, I assure you. Will you do me that favor?

FIRST GENTLEMAN. My dear sir, I don't know what to say to such munifi—

SCROOGE. Don't say anything, please. Come and see me. Will you come and see me?

FIRST GENTLEMAN [*as if he meant it*]. I will!

SCROOGE. Thankee. I am much obliged to you. I thank you fifty times. Bless you! Merry Christmas. [*He returns to his place at the window. He sees the little boy who wanted to sing him a carol*] Oh, my fine young waif. Do you like turkey? Do you want some? Go home and wash your face and get back as fast as your legs will carry you. Ah, here comes Bob Cratchit. [*He sits in a chair and assumes his former stern visage. BOB enters. SCROOGE growls*] Hallo! What do you mean by coming here at this time of day?

BOB. I am very sorry, sir. I *am* behind my time!

SCROOGE. You are? Yes, I think you are. Step this way, sir, if you please.

BOB. It's only once a year, sir. It shall not be repeated. I was making rather merry last evening, sir.

SCROOGE. Now, I'll tell you what, my friend. I am not going to stand for this sort of thing any longer. And therefore [*poking BOB in the ribs*] and therefore, I am about to raise your salary! [BOB *stares wide-eyed*] A merry Christmas, Bob. A merrier Christmas, Bob, my good fellow, than I have given you for many a year!

I'll raise your salary and endeavor to assist your struggling family, and we'll discuss your affairs this very day over a Christmas bowl of smoking bishop, Bob! Make up the fires. Have your missus and children in. Have Tiny Tim in at once, sir! [*The* CRATCHIT *family enters, followed by* TINY TIM] Merry Christmas, everybody! Make yourself comfortable. Ah, here is my nephew, Fred, and my dear niece. And Old Topper, or I'm blind. Merry Christmas all! Merry Christmas!

[*He bustles about, finding first a punch bowl, then glasses and bottles. He mixes hot water with various ingredients, fills the glasses, and passes them about*]

ALL [*glasses aloft*]. Merry Christmas, all, merry Christmas and a happy New Year.

[*They drink*]

TINY TIM. God bless us, every one!

CURTAIN

PRODUCTION NOTES

The action involving SCROOGE *and the various* GHOSTS *takes place on the forestage. The scene in the countinghouse and all scenes within dreams are enacted on the backstage.*

Costumes, where not described in the text, are those of the Early Victorian Period.

Parts may be doubled or cut out at the discretion of the Director.

All action on backstage may be played before simple backdrops.

Curtain of backstage should be painted to resemble walls of SCROOGE'S *chamber.*

THE TWO SHEPHERDS

A Comedy in Two Acts

By G. MARTINEZ-SIERRA

ENGLISH VERSION BY
HELEN AND HARLEY GRANVILLE-BARKER

CHARACTERS

Doña Paquita.
Lucia.
Doña Gertrudis.
The Schoolmistress.
The Mayoress.
Rosita.
Niña.
A Young Lady.
Another Young Lady.
Don Antonio.
Don Francisco.
Don José María.
Don Juan de Dios.
Juanillo.
Mateo.
Demetrio.
Niceto.
The Mayor.
The Colonel of the Civil Guard.

SCENES

Act One: *The garden of the priest's house.*
Act Two: *The same. Four months later.*
        The Play Takes Place in a Castilian Village of Today.

THE TWO SHEPHERDS

ACT ONE

*The Scene is the garden of the priest's house.
The house itself is simple, almost humble; and
the scene is dominated by the side wall of the
church in which there is a small door, used
by the priest himself for going to and from his
duties. In another wall which divides the garden from the street, there is a gate. There are
a few flowers and a fruit tree or two . . . but
all as simple as the house itself. At this moment too, the laundry, personal and ecclesiastic,
has been hung out to dry, some amices, an
alb, a surplice, besides table cloths, dinner napkins and things. And when the play begins,*
JUANILLO, *a young rapscallion of fifteen, is taking them down under the direction of* DOÑA
PAQUITA, *the priest's sister, a woman of sixty-
five, and helping her to put them into two open
baskets. His attention wanders and he dodges
the work.*

DOÑA PAQUITA. Juan, you little nuisance!
What are you up to? Come here at once!

JUANILLO. Coming, Señora! I say, aren't we
in a temper all of a sudden!

DOÑA PAQUITA. And aren't you a more impertinent little idler than ever? Take down that
rochet, it ought to be dry by this.

JUANILLO [*picking up the rochet throws it
above his head, singing a stave of an evidently
ribald song*].

DOÑA PAQUITA. Silence, you young heathen.
And put the rochet in the basket. Sacred things
are not for playing about with.

JUANILLO [*throwing the rochet into the dark
basket*]. There she goes!

DOÑA PAQUITA. Not in that one. That's for
the house linen, can't you see?

JUANILLO. Oh my gracious goodness me!
What would a rochet say if it found itself
alongside a table napkin.

DOÑA PAQUITA. Will you listen to what *I*
say, please? Everything in its place and reverence where reverence is due! But what does
that mean to you, young limb that you are.
If you feared either God or the Devil—God
keep us from him [*Crossing herself*] . . . !
Shoo off that sparrow now, or he'll dirty the
altar cloth. [JUANILLO *scampers round after
the sparrow with great gusto*] But don't run,
you little fiend. The linen will be a nice sight,
won't it? with all the dust that you're raising.
Take down the amice now.

JUANILLO. I'll get the chair. [*From the chair

he can see* LUCIA *who is going along the street*]
So long, Lucia!

[LUCIA, *a pretty, demure minx of eighteen,
pauses at the gate, and looks in. She is
carrying a laundress's basket*]

LUCIA. Good afternoon, Godmother. I'll be
with you in a minute. I'm going to the sacristy
to get the linen.

DOÑA PAQUITA. God go with you, my dear.
Don't be too long about it.

JUANILLO [*to* LUCIA]. Father Antonio's been
asking for you.

LUCIA [*with alarm*]. For me?

JUANILLO. Yes . . . and you're not to go
without seeing him. He wants to talk to you!

LUCIA. To me?

JUANILLO. Get along with you to the church
then. It's just where you ought to be, asking
God on your knees to forgive you for taking
those walks, as you do, all alone in the woods
with Mateo. [LUCIA, *without a word, disappears.* JUANILLO *goes on in great delight*]
Aha, look at her, look at her! Did you see how
she blushed? So it's true!

DOÑA PAQUITA. Will you be quiet?

JUANILLO. Oh yes, I'll be quiet. But it's true.
Besides . . . I've seen them.

DOÑA PAQUITA. All right then . . . all right!
Unfasten the altar cloth. Take care it doesn't
drag! [JUANILLO, *after unfastening the altar
cloth, jumps to the ground*] Help me stretch it.
Take hold of that end. Pull! Carefully!!

JUANILLO. And to look at her you'd say that
she didn't know a goose from a gander! But
that's women all over. Follow their fancies and
when things go wrong, then it's the Saints must
get them out of the mess. Not that I wouldn't
rather like to be a Saint and have the dear re-
pentant creatures come and tell me all about it.

DOÑA PAQUITA. You imp of Satan . . . can't
anything or anyone be free from that wicked
tongue of yours.

JUANILLO. Wicked tongue, indeed! I should
think it was wickeder to commit the sin than
to talk about it.

DOÑA PAQUITA. Should you! Well, the
Church tells us to keep silent about the faults
of our neighbours. How do we know that the
stories are true?

JUANILLO [*with a very wise and ancient air*].
Now, how have you managed to grow so old
and to remain so very stupid!

DOÑA PAQUITA. You are a very rude boy!

JUANILLO. Oh, please don't be angry. Not

343

stupid then . . . but so easily taken in. Why, of course all the stories you hear are true. So are a great many more that you don't!

DOÑA PAQUITA. Juanillo, you horrify me! I can't think how such a piece of wickedness as you got loose in the world.

JUANILLO. Well . . . father and mother managed it somehow.

[*A tumbling of bells is heard; the sound of people, presumably coming out of the church, and the voices of children who are crying: A baptism! A baptism!*]

JUANILLO [*throwing away an amice which he has in his hand*]. The christening's over. They're coming out of the church. They'll be throwing the pennies. [*He disappears into the street*]

DOÑA PAQUITA. Juanillo! Off like a grey-hound! My amice on the ground! [*Picks up the amice, and goes to look over the wall*] Oh, but the godmother's smart, I must say.

[*The noise outside increases. Copper coins are heard falling, footsteps, the shouts and disputes of a crowd of children*]

A VOICE. Long live the godfather!

VOICES. A christening! Show us the baby!

A VOICE. Throw us the pennies!!

VOICES. A christening . . . a christening!!

1ST VOICE. That's mine!

2ND VOICE. I saw it first!

1ST VOICE. I picked it up!

VOICES. A christening!

3RD VOICE. Chuck us another one!

VOICES [*singing*].

He'll never grow up a Christian boy,
This little baby won't,
Nor his father's pride, nor his mother's joy.
For why? For why?
They christened him *under* the font!

1ST VOICE. That's mine!

JUANILLO. Oh, you want them all, don't you?

1ST VOICE. It *is* mine!

JUANILLO. Not if I know it!

[*A noise of blows and boys' voices*]

3RD VOICE. Let him have it!

2ND VOICE. Coward!

4TH VOICE. One for his nob!

[*During all these happenings DOÑA PA-QUITA is looking over the wall, crossing herself and making at the right moment the following comments*]

DOÑA PAQUITA. Ay Jesus! Now somebody's going to get their head broken. I do wish people wouldn't throw them money. That always raises the devil. Juanillo, *will* you come here when you're told? Yes, when he wants to, he will . . . not before. . . . Holy Virgin! They'll kill each other! Let go, you murderous little ruffian!

3RD VOICE. Look out . . . here's the sexton!

DOÑA PAQUITA. Oh, Benito, do pull them apart!

VOICE OF THE SEXTON. Now then, you young scoundrels . . . off with you!

VOICES [*singing*].
Where does the sexton get the wax
For the tapers he sells in bundles?
When he has bolted the door you can see through the cracks.
What? What?
He's nicking it off the candles.

[*A sound of cries and of children scampering*]

DOÑA PAQUITA. Be off! Run away home all of you!

[*JUANILLO, much ruffled from his fight, comes back*]

DOÑA PAQUITA. Good God, he's bleeding!

JUANILLO [*cleaning himself off with his sleeve*]. Don't be frightened. It's nothing to hurt.

DOÑA PAQUITA. You'll have no face left soon . . . nothing but scratches and bruises. And a nice way to spend your time, isn't it? Fighting . . . in the street!

JUANILLO. Call this a bruise? If you want to see bruises go and look at him. And he won't forget the kick he got from me either. No, by . . . !

DOÑA PAQUITA. Don't swear! It's a mortal sin to swear.

JUANILLO. And all for a halfpenny! That's a nice sort of godfather for you. And Papa was just as stingy. A shillingsworth of coppers. It's worth more than that I should think to walk along with your nose in the air behind the baby . . . even if the brat *isn't* your own after all!

DOÑA PAQUITA. What's that you say?

JUANILLO. Take it from me.

DOÑA PAQUITA. If you don't shut your wicked mouth you'll be struck dead by lightning, so you will. And suppose anyone going by had heard you say that . . . in the priest's own house too?

[*DON ANTONIO, the priest, comes out from the church. He is sixty years old, and has a benevolent, but at the same time, energetic air. He has rough white hair. He wears a cassock and carlotte He is carrying a small, very ancient figure of the Virgin and Child*]

DON ANTONIO. Well, another little lamb in the fold. [*He says this quite simply as if it were a current phrase*] And what's the matter with you, Paquita? You look very upset!

DOÑA PAQUITA. What's usually the matter? This Judas Iscariot of a boy will be the death of me!

DON ANTONIO. God bless my soul! What has he done now?

DOÑA PAQUITA. Ask him!

JUANILLO [*humbly*]. Nothing . . . nothing at all, Father. I was only picking up one of the coins thrown for the christening . . . and some stone or other must have hit me. But women always exaggerate, don't they . . . especially old women!

DOÑA PAQUITA. Old women! Do you hear that?

DON ANTONIO [*smiling*]. Ladies . . . and, when absolutely necessary . . . elderly ladies . . . would sound better. And how many thousand times have I told you to speak of my sister respectfully?

DOÑA PAQUITA. Respectfully!

DON ANTONIO. Now go in and wash that place clean and put some court plaster on it.

JUANILLO. No need. It's too hard to crack. [*He hits his head to give evidence of this*]

DON ANTONIO. I know that. But do as you're told.

[JUANILLO *goes into the house*]

DOÑA PAQUITA. Delightful! Yet let him off without a word. Of course he's a little angel . . . still it might do him some good to have his wings clipped.

DON ANTONIO. But what's the use of punishing him because he has had his head broken?

DOÑA PAQUITA. Oh, it isn't his broken head. It's his viper's tongue. But you're used to that by now, I suppose.

DON ANTONIO. I've got used to hearing you say so . . . for these five years.

DOÑA PAQUITA. And I'm to keep on saying it for another five, am I?

DON ANTONIO. But what do you want done with the lad? He has neither father nor mother nor anyone else. Wasn't it our duty to take him in, and how could we turn him out now? He's a good boy at bottom.

DOÑA PAQUITA. He's a perfect little earthquake.

DON ANTONIO. Sister, sister, we must learn to be patient. Rome wasn't built in a day . . . and it's more than a mile to Heaven.

DOÑA PAQUITA. Well, well . . . I'm not a saint like you!

DON ANTONIO. Has Don Juan de Dios come yet?

DOÑA PAQUITA. No.

DON ANTONIO. That's very odd. His train must have been in this half hour.

DOÑA PAQUITA. He'll come by the last.

DON ANTONIO. I think not. When he started this morning he said he only meant just to call in at the Bishop's palace to find out what was going on, and then that he'd come straight back . . .

DOÑA PAQUITA. As if you didn't know what he is. He'll be stopping at every church he comes to to say the Stations of the Cross.

DON ANTONIO. I daresay he will. He gets to be more and more devout.

DOÑA PAQUITA. And whose was the christening? For the baker's baby? Well, they might at least have asked you to the Breakfast! After all, but for you. the father would be rotting in jail at this very moment.

DON ANTONIO. Woman, woman, they *did* ask me! They did all that they ought to do. But I didn't happen to want to go.

DOÑA PAQUITA. And quite right not to, considering the sort of orgy it's likely to be. I should doubt if even the baby will finish up sober!

DON ANTONIO. Charity, charity, Paquita!

DOÑA PAQUITA. Do you want your chocolate?

DON ANTONIO. Thank you, I don't think I feel like it.

DOÑA PAQUITA. Aren't you well? Have you got a pain?

DON ANTONIO. No.

DOÑA PAQUITA. Worried?

DON ANTONIO. Now, why should I be!

DOÑA PAQUITA. Shall I send to the Convent and ask if Don Juan de Dios has got back?

DON ANTONIO. No, we shall hear soon enough.

DOÑA PAQUITA. Well, I do think the Archbishop might find some other way of amusing himself and leave his parish priests in peace.

DON ANTONIO. And what do you know of such things, pray? Be quiet, Paquita.

DOÑA PAQUITA. One needn't know much to know that there's no sense in making men of your age pass examinations as if they were charity schoolboys.

DON ANTONIO. His Grace knows what he's about. He wants to take stock of his shepherds and find out in what sort of hands his flocks are.

DOÑA PAQUITA. Then let him come here and see for himself! Here, among the flock is where the worth of the shepherd is known. Examinations in Latin and Theology, indeed! Let him come here, I say, and hear what this village was thirty years ago . . . and then see what it is today. Thanks to you and your toil and the heart's blood you've poured out for the sake of these sticks and stones . . . may God forgive me! And what do you gain by it?

DON ANTONIO. Heaven. Is that so small a thing to gain?

DOÑA PAQUITA. Oh yes, it'll pay you hereafter, no doubt. But what about *now*? Till this very moment has it ever occurred to the Archbishop to give you a thought? And here you've been slaving for thirty years . . . as *locum tenens* too. A *locum tenens* for thirty years! So that they could keep you on half pay!

DON ANTONIO. Quite so! And His Grace

when he came to the diocese found so many of us in like case, men who passed years and years working as parish priests and never being regularly made so, and therefore, as you say, on half pay . . . and he wanted to put that all right. After we've been examined we shall all be regular priests : . . on full pay. So cheer up!

DOÑA PAQUITA. A lot it will matter to me! For however much money comes into this house. . . .

DON ANTONIO. I know . . . there's always somebody wanting it, isn't there? So in any case, it won't come amiss.

[DOÑA PAQUITA, *while they are talking, has finished picking up the linen and folding it*]

DOÑA PAQUITA. And you don't want your chocolate? Then I'll hurry up supper. Are you coming in?

DON ANTONIO. I think I'd sooner sit out in the air.

DOÑA PAQUITA. Shall I take away the Virgin?

DON ANTONIO. No. Tell Juanillo to get out the tool box. I want to repair her crown. There are a few stones out of it.

[DOÑA PAQUITA *goes into the house, carrying one of the two baskets.* DON ANTONIO *sits down by the table upon which he has placed the Virgin; takes off her crown, extracts from his pocket a paper in which, carefully wrapped up, there are two or three imitation stones, and spreads it open.* NICETO *and* DEMETRIO *appear at the gate.* NICETO *is plainly a very ignorant sort of fellow.* DEMETRIO *is smooth, more effeminate and he makes many gestures. Both are men of the people*]

DEMETRIO. Glory be to God!

DON ANTONIO. Amen!

NICETO. May we . . .?

DON ANTONIO. Yes; come in.

NICETO. Good afternoon.

DON ANTONIO. Good afternoon to you.

DEMETRIO. My respects to you, Father.

DON ANTONIO. Well, what's the news?

DEMETRIO. Precious little, Father.

NICETO. And that's bad.

DON ANTONIO. God's will be done, you know. Sit down.

DEMETRIO. Thank you kindly. [*He sits*]

NICETO. I'm well enough as I am.

DON ANTONIO. Just as you like, my son. Well now, what is it?

DEMETRIO. I suppose, Father, we'd better begin at the beginning . . . because, as the saying is, there must be a beginning to everything. Therefore . . .

NICETO. Don't waste your time listening to him, Father. When he has got all his fine words off his chest it'll only have to be told all over again.

DEMETRIO. Well, tell it your own way then.

NICETO. If I hadn't had patience enough not to use my fists on you, you wouldn't be here to tell it at all . . . and if you weren't such a lath and plaster image of a man that anyone breaking your head for you would only be called a coward . . .

DEMETRIO. Which means that you are too much of a coward to try. . . .

NICETO. Am I! [*Looking at the priest*] You think you're safe now behind *his* petticoats. . . .

DON ANTONIO. Yes, yes . . . but come to the point. Use fine words or any other sort you can find. [*To* DEMETRIO] You!

DEMETRIO. Well. it's like this. I was the proprietor . . . with all due respect to you, Father . . . of an ass.

NICETO. Well, I suppose we must call it one.

DEMETRIO. And what do you mean by *that*?

NICETO. You can judge what a precious jewel of a beast it was when he sold it to me for three dollars and a half.

DEMETRIO. If you bought it for three dollars and a half, it couldn't have been so bad.

NICETO. I wanted something to work the pump, and I wasn't going to buy a young racehorse, was I? And even at that the poor beast was dear.

DEMETRIO. Dear or not, you took him away. And not a penny of the money have I seen.

NICETO. But didn't we agree that the money shouldn't be paid till I'd sold my pigs?

DEMETRIO. I don't remember that.

NICETO. Well, I do. For if I'd paid you the money down there and then, the half dollar was to have come off . . . making it three dollars cash.

DEMETRIO. Then as you didn't pay, the ass remained mine.

NICETO. Mine . . . because I'd settled to pay you, and I'm ready to stand to my word.

DON ANTONIO. But what in the name of ten thousand devils does all this matter? You've got him . . . and you're to be paid for him.

NICETO. No . . . no one has got him now, Father.

DON ANTONIO. How's that?

NICETO. He's dead.

DEMETRIO. Since yesterday, six o'clock.

DON ANTONIO. Ah . . . and in your possession when he died?

NICETO. Yes, I'd had him three days, Father.

DON ANTONIO. Well . . . pay for him then. And get along with you.

NICETO. That's what I say. Ready money. Here they are. Three dollars and a half. [*He starts to pay it down on the table*]

DEMETRIO. Keep your money.

NICETO. You won't have the offer of it again.

DEMETRIO. Three dollars and a half! Yes, a nice little bargain for you, isn't it?

DON ANTONIO. But . . .

NICETO. And I wouldn't pay you that, if he hadn't died as he did.

DEMETRIO. There, that's the sort of man he is, Father!!

DON ANTONIO. Now, do let me understand. What did the ass die of . . . and what has that to do with it?

NICETO. Well, Father, here's just how it was. Yesterday afternoon Paca . . . my wife . . . was bringing him home from where he's been having a bit of a feed. And such a state he was in even then . . . even *then* . . . that he hardly could stagger along. Well, as luck would have it, along comes a motor and frightened the brute, and he got in its way. And it hit him just about here [*Indicating the priest's head*] saving your presence. And as he wasn't what you might call strong . . . well, he lay where he fell. Then Paca . . . *you* know what women are, Father . . . started to weep and to wail, calling out she was ruined and that the ass was all that she and the children had to live on . . . and "What about the police" and "What had the law to say to it" . . . so the people in the car . . . they must have been weak in the head . . . just to put a stop to her noise, gave her a twenty dollar note and made off as quick as they could.

DON ANTONIO. Well, what more?

NICETO. Nothing more! Only now this fellow says that the twenty dollars are his.

DEMETRIO. Weren't they paid for the ass? And wasn't the ass mine?

NICETO. But hadn't I bought him from you?

DEMETRIO. But you hadn't paid *me*.

NICETO. Haven't I been trying to pay you these last two hours?

DEMETRIO. Thank you, but I've changed my mind. I don't care about selling him now.

NICETO. No, a bargain's a bargain.

DEMETRIO. Have you got it in writing?

NICETO. Writing! I'll write it out on your skin with my stick and seal it on your skull with my fist, so I will!

[*And a fight begins*]

DON ANTONIO. Stop that now! Keep your hands off each other and be quiet.

[*They separate*]

DON ANTONIO. Now what did you both come to me for?

NICETO. Well, we always do come to you, don't we, Father . . . to have you say which is in the right? And that's me! For this fellow didn't want to come . . . and he can't deny that.

DEMETRIO. I didn't want to trouble his reverence about such a thing.

NICETO. And why on earth shouldn't he be troubled? What else did he learn to be a priest for!

DON ANTONIO. Very well then. The ass was yours by legal right.

DEMETRIO. But Father, Father, consider a moment . . .

DON ANTONIO. I am considering . . . so be silent. Therefore the twenty dollars . . . though they were fraudulently obtained . . . are yours too.

NICETO [*turning away*]. Thank you . . . good afternoon.

DON ANTONIO. Wait. There's no doubt they are yours. But we will consider also that this man who was your friend trusted to your honour and handed you over the ass without getting his money for it. And ran the risk . . . you've told us so yourself . . . of never getting it at all if the beast had died on your hands. Therefore as the twenty dollars fell to you by chance, and you did not a thing for them, share them with him. Instead of the three and a half you owe him, pay him seven dollars . . . and let me hear no more about it.

NICETO. Seven dollars indeed . . . as if I was made of them!

DEMETRIO. What . . . and he gets thirteen!

DON ANTONIO. Yes, and you're three and a half to the good. And if you don't like my decision, go to law about it.

NICETO. No doubt . . . and be done out of the whole twenty dollars for costs. You're law enough for this village, Father.

DON ANTONIO. Very well then . . . fork out.

NICETO. But . . .

DON ANTONIO. What *now*?

NICETO. What's my wife going to say when I tell her I've parted with seven dollars?

DON ANTONIO. A lot you care what she says!

NICETO. Oh Father, you don't know what women are. . . . How should you?

DON ANTONIO. Are you master in your house or is she?

NICETO. I am! But it takes a lot of argument to convince my wife.

DON ANTONIO. Yes . . . and I've noticed that the stick's what you like to argue with . . . if she so much as opens her mouth to you.

NICETO. Well, Father, it's odd . . . but the more you beat 'em the more they seem to get their own way.

[DON FRANCISCO, *the village doctor, a man about* DON ANTONIO's *age, is seen in the gateway*]

DON ANTONIO. Who goes there?

DON FRANCISCO. Friend!

DON ANTONIO. Ah, doctor . . . come in. How are you?

DON FRANCISCO. What are you up to?

DON ANTONIO. Settling a quarrel, as usual.

DON FRANCISCO. Gratis?

DON ANTONIO. Of course. That's their only reason for preferring my judgment to the magistrate's. [NICETO and DEMETRIO laugh] Isn't that so, you scoundrels?

NICETO. Yes, Father. . . .

DON ANTONIO. Then . . . be off with you!

DEMETRIO. Good afternoon.

NICETO. Afternoon!

DON ANTONIO. Can't you even take the trouble to say thank you?

DEMETRIO. Oh . . . beg pardon, Father, I'm sure.

NICETO. But you know that we mean it, don't you!

[DEMETRIO and NICETO go out. JUANILLO comes in and sets a box on the table in which various tools, a hammer, pliers, etc., are neatly set out]

JUANILLO. Here is the tool chest. Anything else you want?

DON ANTONIO. Show the doctor your hurt.

JUANILLO. But it's nothing . . . I've cured it.

DON FRANCISCO [going up to JUANILLO and taking off the handkerchief which he is wearing on his head like a turban]. Let's have a look. What did you put on it?

JUANILLO. A slice of onion, salt and vinegar. What else should I put on it?

DON FRANCISCO. Kill or cure!

JUANILLO. Was that wrong?

DON FRANCISCO. Put your head in that water-butt. Wash the place well. [JUANILLO obeys] Now come here. Dry yourself. [He puts on a piece of court-plaster] There . . . that'll last till your next fight. Weeds are mighty hard to kill.

DOÑA PAQUITA [in the house]. Juanillo, bring in the black basket.

JUANILLO. Coming, Señora.

[JUANILLO takes up the black basket, and goes into the house, taking his time]

DON FRANCISCO. Where's your water jar? [He goes to fetch the round earthen jar with its spout and handle, which is under one of the stone seats beneath the arbour, and takes a long drink]

DON ANTONIO. It's warm today, isn't it?

DON FRANCISCO. The country's so hot it might be on fire. And I've had to walk all the way from the Venta Vieja. [Again drinks copiously] Ah, nothing like a good drink of cold water when you're thirsty. [He puts the water jar on the stone seat and goes up to the table] Nature has been very wise in giving us the greatest pleasures in life for nothing. We poor people should give thanks for that.

DON ANTONIO [smiling]. To Nature . . . or to God, Señor don Francisco?

DON FRANCISCO. To whichever you please, Señor Don Antonio. You and I are not going to quarrel over a word. Any news yet about that affair of yours?

DON ANTONIO. Nothing more so far. But I'm expecting Don Juan de Dios any minute. He went off to the Archbishop's this morning to find out what he could. Who's ill at the Venta Vieja?

DON FRANCISCO. The old grandfather. You'd better look in.

DON ANTONIO. Is he very poorly?

DON FRANCISCO. Blood poisoning. Anyone else would die of it. But he mayn't.

DON ANTONIO. What have you given him?

DON FRANCISCO. Oh, the usual thing. A bath. And plenty of water to drink with lemon juice squeezed in it.

DON ANTONIO. Well, that won't do any harm.

DON FRANCISCO. Or any good either, d'you think? Don't be too sure. Water's not touched him inside or out since the day he was christened. He has worked in the fields all his life. He's burnt up with wine and sun. Water . . . just for a change . . . may work a miracle.

DON ANTONIO. Perhaps you're right.

DON FRANCISCO. I've seen it happen. People talk of these "cures" . . . Anything may be a cure . . . for something. Yesterday they installed a regular medicine man in the dispensary. He has just got through his examinations in Madrid with flying colours . . . and he seems a clever boy. A little pedantic . . . but that's only natural . . . for he knows such a lot . . . such a devil of a lot. To hear him talk about serums and injections and immunity and all the while giving me a look from the corner of his eye as much as to say, "Now's your chance to pick up a tip or two." And I sat and laughed to myself. "Talk away, my lad," I thought. "These clodhoppers here are made of another clay than the sort your Madrid professors like to meddle with. Once upon a time I had book learning at my fingers' ends too. Wait a little, and you'll be glad enough to put your faith in lemon juice and water." Why, you might as well ask them when they come to confession, whether they'd been committing the unforgivable sin against the Holy Ghost. No, no . . . What good would the silk purse be to the sow anyway . . . she's better off with her ear. Leave learning to the learned!

DON ANTONIO. And theology to the Bishops. To get these folk to heaven I've to drag them by the scruffs of their necks . . . I know that!

DON FRANCISCO. Well, I have to vaccinate 'em by main force to keep them on earth a little longer. I went into the school yesterday afternoon, shut the door, and left El Tuerto in front of it with a thick stick. "Now," I said, "not a child leaves this room till he's been vaccinated." Lord, you should have heard them yell. Well . . . I'd had three of them die on my hands in two days and there's no mortal way of knocking sense into their mothers. The savages! When they're ill they still think they're possessed by the devil. I am . . . when I have to write small-pox on a death certificate. And now if one of these children that I stick a little calf lymph into goes and dies after all, the village will want to lynch me. So I ask myself . . . and you . . . for we're both in the same boat . . . since we get neither pay nor thanks . . . why on earth do we make such fools of ourselves?

Don Antonio. For the love of God, my dear doctor.

Don Francisco. Or is it that we just can't leave ill alone?

Don Antonio. Well, do you wonder? When most human beings . . . God forgive me for saying so . . . are hardly better than brute beasts, what should we do, if by God's grace we're a little less so, but lend them our strength and our brains? For it's not their fault, poor things.

Don Francisco. Don Antonio, Don Antonio . . . be careful. That sounds very like an attack upon Providence.

Don Antonio. Not at all! God made us all, and as he made us it is good to be. He has his reasons for all that he does.

Don Francisco. He may have . . . but I wish he'd confide 'em to us sometimes.

[Lucia *comes in from the street, and crosses the garden rapidly, making signs to someone outside, who cannot be seen, to wait for her. She is carrying a flat wicker basket, covered with a white cloth*]

Don Francisco. Hullo, Lucia!

Lucia. Good afternoon, Don Antonio . . . good afternoon, Don Francisco. [*She wishes to go on her way without being stopped*] Is my godmother in?

Don Francisco. You're in a great hurry.

Lucia. I've brought the surplices.

Don Antonio. Come here . . . I want to talk to you.

Lucia [*nervously*]. Yes, Father.

Don Antonio. Put that down. [*The basket*] Who are you making signs to?

Lucia. No one . . . no, indeed, Father. [Don Antonio *looks fixedly at her*] . . . that's to say, only to Mateo, who's waiting outside for me. But don't think . . .

Don Francisco. Mateo? Oho . . . so you mean to be my lady Mayoress, do you?

Lucia. I?

Don Francisco. Well, he'll be Mayor, I daresay, when his father dies. . . . So . . . it stands to reason . . . sauce for the gander is sauce for the goose, isn't it?

Lucia. What an idea!

Don Francisco. Oh . . . then you don't mean to marry him. It's a pity in that case you take so many walks with him in the woods of an evening.

Lucia. I?

Don Francisco. Yes, Miss . . . you. And he! Now don't deny it, because you've been seen.

Lucia. Who by?

Don Francisco. By me. So now!

Don Antonio. Listen to me, Lucia. I have heard of these walks too.

Lucia. Oh yes . . . from that little telltale Juanillo.

Don Antonio. Never mind how . . . for sooner or later, one way or another, it was bound to be known.

Lucia. Yes, I suppose so . . .

Don Antonio. Even then it's not people knowing it that matters . . . but that there should be anything to know. Do you understand me?

Lucia. Yes, Father.

Don Francisco. Well, that's something.

Don Antonio. And what do you think will be the end of this love-making in secret . . . ?

Don Francisco. . . . More or less . . . rather less by this time.

Lucia. Well . . . you see . . .

Don Antonio. You are as poor as a church mouse. He is well off. You're an orphan. His father's the Mayor of the village. Is he going to marry you for the sake of your pretty face?

[Lucia *doesn't answer*]

Don Antonio. Well?

Lucia. I love him.

Don Antonio. And does he love you, pray?

Lucia. He says so . . .

Don Antonio. You don't seem very sure of it.

Lucia. Well, you know what men are, Father!

Don Antonio. I suppose what you mean is that you think you do. Then what on earth are you about, throwing your reputation away in this insane fashion?

Lucia. I suppose I've a right to live my own life in my own way, haven't I?

Don Antonio. And what in Heaven's name do you mean by *that*?

Lucia. Oh, of course I'm nobody. I'm a country girl. I'm poor and I haven't been educated. But he's no better born than I am, and it isn't much good that his going to school has done him. Of course he has got money, or rather his father has. But is that any reason his mother should treat me like the dirt under her feet?

Don Antonio. Now what has his mother to do with it?

Lucia. Didn't she come on the feast of the

Virgin a year ago last August when I was dancing with Mateo in the Square . . . and that was no crime, was it? . . . and say before everybody that her son was too good for me . . . too good to be dancing with me, if you please? Well, I know that I'm poor, but why should that stop me from doing what I want to do? So I swore that I'd get the better of her for that . . . and I have.

DON ANTONIO. Can't you see that it's you will get the worst of it all?

LUCIA. Yes, I suppose so. But I *have* made her angry.

DON FRANCISCO. Which is always a comfort.

DON ANTONIO. Come here, you poor little fool. Here's a good lady that has done you no harm, and just to annoy her you think it worth while to disgrace yourself. Don't you know that your only dowry is your virtue and your good name, the fact that no one can say a syllable against you? And can't you understand, you feather-brain, that if when you're a good girl the Mayoress doesn't think you good enough for her son, you'll be good enough for nobody if you're a bad one? Where will you be I should like to know when everybody refuses to have anything to do with you? And if you could keep your shame a secret from them, can you keep it secret from God? You are a Christian, you have been dedicated to the Virgin Mother. You are committing deadly sin. Our Lady is watching you from Heaven with very sorrowful eyes. [LUCIA *hangs her head*] Well, what is it now?

LUCIA. I did tell Mateo that you'd think it very wrong if you knew.

DON ANTONIO. And what did he say to that?

LUCIA [*with much candour*]. He said it was none of your business.

[*The* DOCTOR *laughs*]

DON ANTONIO [*with almost comical indignation*]. None of my business! Whose business is it then I should like to know? You've no father, your mother's a helpless cripple. You're my sister's godchild. And even though you were not, I have known you since you were born . . . I baptised you . . . I've taught you the little catechism you know . . . your silly head wouldn't hold more . . . I gave you your first absolution . . . ah, and that's true, since Easter . . . four months ago, you haven't been to confession.

LUCIA. No . . . Mateo says he doesn't like me to go to confession.

DON ANTONIO. And why not, pray?

LUCIA. Well, he says that, after all, priests are only men just like he is . . . and they might easily take advantage of an innocent girl like me.

DON ANTONIO. Wrath of God!

DON FRANCISCO. Ho . . . ho! . . . he pre-fers to confess you himself, does he, under the pine trees.

DON ANTONIO [*to the shabby old figure of the Virgin*]. Mother of God . . . do you hear this? Give me patience. Don't let me be driven to violence. [*To* LUCIA] Take yourself out of my sight! No, come here. Now understand me once and for all. This scandalous nonsense is over, over and done with. For the future . . . from tonight . . . you will live here with your godmother, and she will see that you are kept properly employed. Your mother will go to the Hospital, where the Sisters will look after her far better than ever her gadabout daughter has done. As for Mateo, he can amuse himself by taking care of the kitten, for not so much as the tip of your skirt shall he ever touch again, I'll see to that.

LUCIA [*almost crying*]. Oh no, Father . . .

DON ANTONIO. Now, what is it . . . what's the matter?

LUCIA. I can't.

DON ANTONIO. What do you mean?

LUCIA. I simply can't.

DON ANTONIO. Why can't you?

LUCIA [*sobbing*]. Because I don't want to . . . and because I simply can't . . . now that there . . . isn't any help for it.

DON ANTONIO. What?

DON FRANCISCO. What's that?

LUCIA [*without stopping her crying*]. Well, you see . . . now . . . now . . .

DON FRANCISCO. Young woman . . . look me straight in the face. [*Then he smiles*] Oh, so that's it, is it? We've been sitting down to dinner before the bell rang! [*She cries like a child without answering*]

DON ANTONIO. You? You! Answer me . . . is this true? You, Lucia?

LUCIA [*choking*]. Yes . . . yes, Father. But you see I . . . that is, he said . . .

DON ANTONIO. Child of sin. Oh, but you're all alike. And wanting to keep your good name into the bargain. He said . . . ! Wait and see what'll be said to you now! Lord God . . . what is to be done with this village full of swine!

LUCIA [*weeping, but rather for the sake of the conventions, because, at bottom, she is glad to have got out of her difficulty*] Ay . . . Ay . . . Ay!

DON ANTONIO. Don't cry! And with that angel face! Too innocent if you please, to come to confession . . . and now we hear this! Well, and what are you going to do? Aren't you overwhelmed with shame? Where are you going? Who's to take care of you now . . .?

LUCIA [*knowing that she is sure of being looked after, but believing it an obligation upon her to show intense distress*] Ay . . . Ay! Whatever will become of me!

Don Antonio. Until . . . until . . .

Lucia. Ay . . . ay . . . ay!

Don Francisco. Come now, come . . . you mustn't go on like this. I'll let you know when it's time to start crying.

Lucia. Yes, Señor!

Don Antonio [*gruffly*]. Go into the house . . . and stop making an exhibition of yourself . . . here in the street almost. Paquita!

Lucia. Ay . . . don't tell my godmother.

Don Antonio. She'll know soon enough, won't she, whether we tell her or not? Paquita!

Doña Paquita [*appearing*]. What is it?

Don Antonio. The Doctor has a case for you.

Don Francisco [*supporting* Lucia]. Come along now, child . . . come along.

Doña Paquita. What's the matter . . . what has happened?

Don Francisco. Nothing more than usual, Señora. The flesh is weak, you know.

[*The three go in*]

Don Antonio. Holy Mother . . . Holy Mother! [*He addresses the Virgin, then turns and calls*] Mateo! [*As there is no answer, he goes out into the street and calls again*] Mateo! Come in. I want to speak to you.

Mateo. After you, Father.

Don Antonio. Go in.

Mateo. If you say so. May I ask what it is you want?

Don Antonio. Yes. I want you to go to-morrow morning and take out a license and bring it to me, so that I may send it to the Vicar of the Province. Because on Sunday the first banns must be published. You will be dispensed from the rest . . . and the week after you will be married.

Mateo. I?

Don Antonio. Yes, you.

Mateo. Who to?

Don Antonio. Who to! God bless my soul . . . to the mother of your child.

Mateo. So that cat's out of the bag, is it? I might have expected it. I believe if Lucia held her tongue for ten minutes she'd burst.

Don Antonio. But as if it could be kept a secret . . .

Mateo. Well, that remained to be seen, didn't it?

Don Antonio [*indignantly*]. What's that you say?

Mateo [*shamefacedly*]. Nothing, Father.

Don Antonio. So much the better for you. But you know what you've to do now anyhow.

Mateo. Look here, Father. I quite hate to disappoint you . . . but I'm really afraid that I can't.

Don Antonio. Can't you indeed! And why 'can't" you, I should like to know?

Mateo. Well . . . a man can't . . . so to speak . . . go against his own nature, can he?

Don Antonio. I see. And it's yours to behave like a scoundrel, is it?

Mateo. You needn't insult me.

Don Antonio. Well, please tell me what *you'd* call a man who just seduces an innocent girl, and then refuses to do his plain duty by her?

Mateo. Oh . . . innocent, Father. Come now . . .

Don Antonio. Yes . . . innocent beside you . . . and all such young blackguards. Shame on you, and doubly shame to speak like that of a woman that you yourself have disgraced. Yes, innocent till you came along . . . and an honest girl, till you dishonoured her. And if this is what men are like, why ever do women drag their skirts in the mud for them? That's what I ask! Your mother must be proud of you . . . very proud of the gentleman she has for a son!

Mateo. Look here . . . you know you can tell me I'm not a gentleman, and I've got to put up with it, because you're . . . what you are. But I wouldn't from anyone else. I mayn't be anything very out of the way, but my honour's all right.

Don Antonio. Indeed! And will it be when your child has been born fatherless, and his mother is drudging to keep him, or begging bread for them both in the streets . . . or worse?

Mateo. She shan't. They shall both be looked after as long as I live.

Don Antonio. As long, I daresay, as you're your own master. But wait six months . . . wait till you marry some woman of your own class, who can bring you the one thing on earth that you want no more of . . . the one thing this other poor girl hasn't got . . . money . . . money! Then you'll have other children, and a very good father you'll be, I don't doubt. Nothing that you and their mother can think of will you deny them. But this one, your first and more yours than the others can ever be, for he is to be the child of your youth and your illusions, he will go barefoot and hungry, with a bricklayer's hod on his shoulder . . . he'll go to prison, maybe, someday, for stealing his bread from his brothers . . . his own brothers.

Mateo. Father . . .

Don Antonio. Oh . . . no doubt you can answer . . . It's none of my business . . . she should have thought of all this sooner . . . and how am I worse than other men? . . . can I go against my nature . . . ?

Mateo. Father, it's not fair, to speak of me as if I were a . . . as if I weren't a . . .

Don Antonio. As if you were a scoundrel?

You are! As if you weren't a gentleman? You are not!

MATEO. I am. . . . I tell you I am. And I love her. . . . I tell you I love her. I swear it before those two (*The Virgin and Child*). And I can never love any woman else . . . that's true too. And the day that she told me . . . you know . . . about the baby . . . before ever it struck me what a mess I was in . . . I felt pleased . . . I did indeed . . . and almost proud . . . as if till that moment I'd never really known what . . . well, how would you put it now . . . what life was.

DON ANTONIO [*gently*]. And after that you still mean to leave her to her fate?

MATEO. But I don't! It can all go on just as before. I love her . . . I've said so.

DON ANTONIO. Not a bit of it, my son. You'll do what's right by her now, or you won't set eyes on her again. She may have made one mistake, but she's not a bad woman, I know . . . and you shan't see her again.

MATEO. Of course I'd marry her like a shot . . . but my father . . .

DON ANTONIO. Well?

MATEO. He's dead against it. And as for Mother . . . she says if I marry Lucia she'll die of it. And it's just the sort of thing she would do.

DON ANTONIO. All right! If she does, I'll give her Christian burial. But there's not much fear of that.

MATEO. You don't know her!

DON ANTONIO. I think I know you all . . . to my sorrow . . . and an evil worthless lot you are. Now, no more shuffling, my lad. You're going to get married. That's your duty, and it'll be the best thing for you too. The mother of your child is your wife by rights . . . there's no getting away from that. As to your mother . . . you leave her to me. And you can tell your father this to go on with . . . tell him I told you to . . . I know all about that business of the municipal slaughter houses . . . and there's more than one road by which a man may find himself in prison. He'll understand. So be off and break it to your parents . . . and I'll be by presently and assure them the news is true. Tomorrow before noon remember, I shall expect the license.

MATEO. All right. [*He goes*]

DON ANTONIO [*to the* VIRGIN]. Holy Mother, that's what these people are like. But you know it, you know it well. Stupid, cunning, greedy of money, their hearts as hard as their heads are empty. What can we do to save them? Holy Mother, whatever can we do? But remember, won't you, that sometimes in the end they do the right thing . . . why, now and then, even, you might almost think that one of them was a man. It costs us sweat and blood, Mother, doesn't it, to lead them to

the right path? But we must just be patient and keep on. Can your blessed Son ask more of us? Ah no; He knows, none better, the sort of flock that He has given to our care.

[JUANILLO *has entered*]

JUANILLO. It always sounds as if you were singing little songs to the Virgin.

DON ANTONIO. Now what do *you* want?

JUANILLO. I was listening to you . . . [*Looking at the Virgin*] Do you like talking to her . . . when she never answers back?

DON ANTONIO. And how do you know she never answers back?

JUANILLO [*with terror*]. Does she?

DON ANTONIO. She'll answer you someday . . . somewhere. . . .

JUANILLO [*incredulously*]. How does she do it? Does she give you a sign?

DON ANTONIO. What should Our Lady want, my child, with signs or words? She speaks to the soul, and in our souls we hear her voice.

JUANILLO. The soul . . . ?

DON ANTONIO. You'll know what that means someday. There's nothing kept from her and nothing that she doesn't understand. She never listens to idle gossip, and she never judges by appearances, and so her judgment is always right. And there's always good counsel on her lips for him who asks it from his heart . . . and healing in her heart if we bring our troubles to her. . . . She gives us her hand and asks her Son to pity us . . . for we want so to serve Him and yet we stumble . . . then she prevents our fall. Our Lady is our queen, you see. Well, we all want to be worthy to work for her in her kingdom.

JUANILLO. But what a silly face the child has, hasn't he?

[DON JUAN DE DIOS *appears at the gate*]

DON JUAN. Ave Maria Purissima. . . .

JUANILLO. Oh . . . it's Don Juan de Dios

DON ANTONIO. . . . *Concepta sine*. Come in.

DON JUAN. May God make the rest of the day a blessing to us.

DON ANTONIO. What about your journey

[DON JUAN DE DIOS *has a very troubled air. He is very nervous and keeps on turning his hat in his hands while repeating almost all his words*]

DON JUAN. Good . . . oh good! That is the journey itself was good. A little warm . . . one can't deny that. But good . . oh good . . . thanks be to God . . . so to speak.

DON ANTONIO. And did you find out anything?

DON JUAN. Yes . . . oh yes, my friend. did. Well . . . God's will is . . . is not always, quite naturally . . . does not always accord with the expectations of men . . . desires which seem, so to speak, quite natural that is, and legitimate. So that . . . well now I'm afraid . . . so to speak . . . that there's nothing more to do . . . but to bow . . . bow, you know . . . to the decrees of Providence.

DON ANTONIO. You mean that . . .

DON JUAN. Frankly . . . yes . . . frankly I do. And of course . . . submission . . . that's what it must come to in the end, mustn't it . . . so what's the use now . . . of saying . . . so to speak . . . anything? And I myself . . . well, I too . . . naturally . . .

DON ANTONIO. But you . . .

DON JUAN. Oh yes . . . both of us, I assure you . . . that's some comfort, isn't it . . . both of us, dear friend . . . both of us are suspended from office.

DON ANTONIO. You say they have suspended me from office!

DON JUAN. And me . . . and me! Oh yes, both of us . . . that's the truth.

DON ANTONIO. Are you quite sure?

DON JUAN. Oh, the secretary himself so to speak . . . His Grace, the Archbishop's secretary told me . . . that is, naturally in confidence, of course . . . but he told me. And the official communication . . . so to speak . . . will be sent next week.

DON ANTONIO. But what *for?*

DON JUAN. In my case . . . Latin, I'm afraid. . . . Yes, it was, so to speak, Latin. My translation . . . of St. Augustine. You, I fear, failed . . . that is . . . well, yes . . . failed in Theology.

DON ANTONIO. In Theology!

DON JUAN. Dogmatic . . . yes, dogmatic Theology. The secretary . . . well the secretary said that your answer to the question, "De vitiis religionis appositus per defectum . . ." was really . . . yes, "per defectum," was really almost a heresy.

DON ANTONIO. A heresy!

DON JUAN. Well, frankly . . . yes . . . he said . . . that from lack of true doctrine . . . of true doctrine . . . these villages were forgetting . . . so he said . . . the very alphabet of religion. Yes, that's how he put it.

DON ANTONIO. The very alphabet . . .

DON JUAN. For myself . . . I don't resent it . . so to speak . . . no, I don't resent it. God's punishment on me, no doubt . . . for pride . . . yes, for pride. A mere humble chaplain such as I, who thought . . . yes . . . that he could save souls. *Peccavi . . . peccavi!* My nuns though, my nuns of St. Clara . . . they'll resent it. Because they thought that they had as their chaplain a Chrysostom . . . so to peak . . . oh yes indeed a perfect Chrysostom . . . as it were.

DON ANTONIO [*first rebellious, then depressed*]. Suspended! Suspended! [*Then with serene resignation*] God's will be done.

DON JUAN. Why, of course, yes . . . God's will be done.

[DON FRANCISCO *and* DOÑA PAQUITA *come out of the house*]

DON FRANCISCO. Mostly nerves now! In ten minutes give her another glass of linden-flower water, and let her go home.

DOÑA PAQUITA. Good heavens . . . what a nuisance these girls are!

[JUANILLO *has been in a corner listening to the conversation of the two priests, goes up to* DOÑA PAQUITA *before she has finished coming down the door steps, and, taking hold of her skirts, says in almost tragic affliction*]

JUANILLO. Doña Paquita . . . they've suspended him!

DOÑA PAQUITA. What! What's that you say?

JUANILLO. They have! They've suspended him from office for failing in the examination. Yes, Señora . . . Don Antonio . . . and Don Juan de Dios . . . they've suspended them both.

DOÑA PAQUITA. It's not true! Oh, don't talk such nonsense. [*To her brother*] It's not true, is it?

DON ANTONIO. Yes, it's true, Paquita. And there's nothing to be done. We must just be patient.

DOÑA PAQUITA. D'you mean to tell me that you're no longer priest of this village?

DON ANTONIO. No . . . I've no right here at all.

DOÑA PAQUITA. And who will have . . . may I ask?

DON ANTONIO. Probably some young priest will be sent . . . who can pass the examination.

DOÑA PAQUITA. And you'll be put out in the street?

DON JUAN. Oh no . . . no, indeed . . . I'm sure that the Archbishop . . . that His Grace, the Archbishop, must take into account the years . . . so to speak . . . years of service. And he'll give him a chaplaincy . . . in an asylum, no doubt . . . or to a Convent . . .

DOÑA PAQUITA. Chaplain to a lot of nuns!

DON JUAN. Well now, I assure you it's not so bad. I have always found my sisters . . . very good, oh yes, indeed. A little tedious at times, perhaps . . . well, yes, I must confess . . . tedious . . . but very good.

DOÑA PAQUITA. Oh, please be quiet.

DON FRANCISCO [*to* DON ANTONIO]. How has it happened?

DON ANTONIO. Well, I'm afraid there's no doubt, that when it comes to dogmatic Theology . . . one has dropped a little behind. As we were saying just now, you know . . . with one's struggle, year in and year out, with these savages for their salvation, one forgets all about the sort of things that they put in examinations . . .

JUANILLO [*with indignation*]. Well, of course you do. . . . And here's the Virgin that knows everything . . . why, they'd stump her with their damned questions . . .

CURTAIN

ACT TWO

The same scene as in the first act. DOÑA PAQUITA, *the* DOCTOR *and* JUANILLO *are in the garden.* DOÑA PAQUITA *is seated, with an air of profound sadness, on one of the stone seats by the door:* JUANILLO *is doubled up on the step of the little door leading into the church, which is half open. The* DOCTOR *is walking up and down the garden with his hands behind his back.*

A ringing of bells is heard as the curtain rises.

DON FRANCISCO [*looking into the air, as if he were speaking to the sound of the bells*]. This is a great day.

DOÑA PAQUITA [*almost in tears*]. Oh . . . a great day indeed!

[*There is a pause, the sound of an organ inside the church can be faintly heard*]
DOÑA PAQUITA [*sighing*]. There . . . they've reached the Te Deum now.

JUANILLO. Yes . . . and hark at the organist flourishing away! . . . just to show off before the new priest!

DON FRANCISCO. Here . . . why aren't you in your surplice?

JUANILLO. Why should I be?

DON FRANCISCO. Aren't you an acolyte?

JUANILLO. Are we any of us anything now?

DON FRANCISCO. No indeed . . . no indeed, we're not!

JUANILLO. They've turned you out too . . . haven't they?

DON FRANCISCO. Yes, my lad, yes . . . they've turned me out too.

DOÑA PAQUITA [*rebellious and bitter*]. God will judge them for it.

DON FRANCISCO. Well, he may! . . . but what can we all expect in this progressive world? Is this enlightened village of ours the only one to be left behind in the great race of the millennium? We must follow the fashions, we must be brought up to date whether we like it or not! And what are our Town Councillors for but to push us along the path? So when it came to those seven illustrious gentlemen who read the papers once a week and are deep in the secrets of the Government, having to choose between an old doctor who had brought most of them into the world, by the grace of God and the exercise of his common

sense, and a brand-new medical gentleman who was ready to help them die in the very latest and most scientific style, hall-marked by Paris and Berlin—well, once again, what could you expect? Señora Doña Paquita. . . . We must be cosmopolitan, up to date. Hurrah for Progress! And if you don't like it, get out of the way . . . or be run over, if you like that better!

DOÑA PAQUITA. Well, then . . . God's will be done.

DON FRANCISCO. And the vote was unanimous . . . why the question, so they tell me, wasn't even argued. As with one voice they called aloud for the very latest thing! The first time, I believe, that they have ever agreed upon anything. Blessed progress . . . all-conquering youth!

[*There is another pause*]
JUANILLO. Andreson's wife, at the inn . . .

DON FRANCISCO. Well?

JUANILLO. She's having her baby today.

DON FRANCISCO. How do you know, pray!

JUANILLO. I saw that new doctor go by. They've called him in because he's a specialist . . . that's what he is . . . an acc—acc—something or other. Anyhow he went by on his motor bicycle like greased lightning.

DON FRANCISCO. Yes, he'd better not waste time. She doesn't.

DOÑA PAQUITA. Well, she's used to it . . . it's her seventh.

DON FRANCISCO. Eighth . . . the fourth time it was twins. Think of it! That's the first baby for twenty-five years to come into this world and this village without asking my leave! [*He tries to speak jestingly, but doesn't make a success of it*]

JUANILLO. And they say that that boy of Juana la Fea's was just dying . . . but the new doctor put water into him with a syringe and he got well at once.

DOÑA PAQUITA [*thinking* DON FRANCISCO's *feelings will be hurt*]. Hold your tongue now!

DON FRANCISCO. Are you going away this very day?

DOÑA PAQUITA. This very evening . . . as soon as they've finished in there [*Indicating the church with a glance, but without moving*] The van with the furniture has gone on already.

DON FRANCISCO [*to* JUANILLO]. How much longer will they be?

JUANILLO. There's the sermon to come still . . . he's just going up for it now.

DOÑA PAQUITA. Aren't you going in to hear it?

DON FRANCISCO. No, thank you!

JUANILLO. They say he's no end of a preacher. Well, since he's preached himself in here and preached us all out into the street I suppose it's true. He gets ten dollars a sermon

And the other day in the Cathedral at the Novenary of Souls he preached and he preached until the Canons almost died of it. [*He is at the church door*] And what a voice he has! You can hear it through the door. [*Repeating with gestures of admiration what it may be supposed he hears said by the preacher*] "Honoured servants of the Sanctuary . . . worthy authorities of this godly village . . . best beloved brothers, all, of the Sacred Heart of Jesus and the Sweetness of Mary." What rot! [*He hides himself behind the door so that he can go on listening*]

DOÑA PAQUITA. Shut that door . . . they don't want to hear every noise from the street in there.

DON FRANCISCO. It's a large congregation.

DOÑA PAQUITA. Every soul in the village. That's what novelty will do. Some of those people haven't set foot in the church for a matter of fifty years or so. The Mayor's there and the Schoolmaster and the Colonel of the Militia . . . even the District Judge . . . though he stands, if you please, for Sunday work at the Universities. . . . [*Crossing herself*] God save us from that at least!

DON FRANCISCO. But it seems that he is a bit of a prodigy.

DOÑA PAQUITA. Who . . . the judge?

DON FRANCISCO. No . . . our new priest.

DOÑA PAQUITA. He certainly is. [*Disdainfully*] He arrived today in a motor car.

DON FRANCISCO. Yes, the place will smell strong of petrol now . . . that's one sure sign of progress.

JUANILLO [*popping round the door*]. He says that the village is going to be a garden planted with carnations and roses and [*Scratching his head and trying to remember*] . . . that he . . . he means to be the gardener . . . and he'll make a nosegay of the gently opening flowers and suck from it honey for the honey-comb . . . which is the Church. He's a one-er ain't he? [*He disappears again*]

DOÑA PAQUITA. A garden of roses! With a few thorns among them he'll soon find.

DON FRANCISCO. These ceremonies take a long time.

DOÑA PAQUITA. Don't talk about it. First the Installation . . . then the Supplicatory Procession. Then a Te Deum . . . a sermon . . . and Heaven knows what else! Still this is the finish of it all, thank God. I tell you, what with one thing and another, we've had a pleasant four months.

DON FRANCISCO. Yes . . . the powers that be at the Archbishop's were a long time making up their minds.

DOÑA PAQUITA. Yes . . . and nobody pleased at the end. For don't imagine the young man likes coming here any more than the old man likes leaving. Do you notice that he uses a cigarette holder, so as not to stain his fingers? He will like it, won't he, when all the dirty nosed little children come kissing his hand?

DON FRANCISCO. Not quite the village, is it, for fastidious fingers to meddle with?

DOÑA PAQUITA. No, nor for his shiny shoes with their silver buckles. He's here because he's been put here and he has to do as he's told. Why, he has buttonholed everyone from Rome to Santiago to get himself into some church in Madrid. Preaching's what he likes. Showing off, getting talked about . . . he thought he'd be made a Bishop in no time. That's where he was wrong. He tried to be too clever . . . put things in the offices, they say, which were more than even they could stand. So like this world, isn't it? They take the old man from the corner he belongs in because they say he knows too little, and they send the young one to eat his heart out in a far-off village because they think he knows too much.

DON FRANCISCO. What else does one expect!

DOÑA PAQUITA. Oh well, time will put things right for the young man . . . but only death can do that for the old one.

DON FRANCISCO. Nonsense . . . what are you talking of . . . I never heard such nonsense! What your brother needs at his age . . . is a little rest . . . and peace and quiet.

DOÑA PAQUITA. Rest! You know him. He'll rest in his grave . . . not before. What has his life been? From morning till night, never stopping . . . was ever a single thing done in the village if his hand wasn't in it? Well, can you see him as chaplain to an old woman's almshouse . . . saying mass for them . . . sitting by while they gabble their prayers . . . hearing their confessions; the dreadful things they said to the cat when it stole the milk? He'll fret himself to death. Why you've only to look at him . . . ever since he knew it was settled. He says nothing . . . but what he's thinking and feeling! I know him so well. But so do you, oh, so do you. But he's all I have in the world, you see . . . he's brother and father and son to me, all in one. And I can't sit by and watch him suffer like this. I can't . . . I can't. What's to become of us!

[JUANILLO *comes from behind the door and turns towards the gate*]

DOÑA PAQUITA. Where are you going? Is the sermon over?

JUANILLO. No, Señora . . . there's a woman been taken ill . . .

DON FRANCISCO [*instinctively standing up; business-like*]. Where?

DOÑA PAQUITA. Who?

JUANILLO. I don't know . . . just someone in there. She was kneeling . . . and then she fell right over on the floor.

DoÑa Paquita. Fainted . . . they'd better bring her here.

Don Francisco. Let me see . . . let me see.

[At this moment Lucia comes in supported by Mateo and the Mayor, and followed by the Lady Mayoress. She is half fainting, or, rather pretending to be. She wears a black brocade silk dress, her wedding dress, very elaborate, a lace mantilla, a filigree rosary, diamond earrings and brooch, a mother-of-pearl fan and a lace handkerchief. She has all through the scene the manner of a very affected fine lady]

Don Francisco. What's the matter?

DoÑa Paquita. What has happened?

Juanillo. Well . . . if it isn't Lucia!

Mateo [very worried]. Get a chair please, somebody!

The Mayor. Please get a glass of water!

[Juanillo goes to the back to fetch the water and DoÑa Paquita pulls out a chair]

DoÑa Paquita. Loosen her dress.

Mateo [who hasn't noticed Don Francisco]. Will somebody please go for a doctor . . . at once.

Don Francisco. Now don't be frightened. Let's see what's the matter. Give her a chance to breathe.

The Mayor [with a mixture of confusion and annoyance]. Oh . . . oh . . . it's you, is it? Still here!

Don Francisco. Yes, Señor Alcalde . . . though not officially.

Mateo [at Lucia's side and afraid that this is going to be the death of his wife]. Don Francisco . . . for God's sake . . .

Don Francisco. Don't worry . . . don't worry . . . I am here.

[He goes up to Lucia who continues her pretence of a fainting fit]

Mateo [anxiously]. What's the matter with her?

The Mayoress. Nothing whatever.

Don Francisco. She fainted with the heat. She's coming to. It's all right.

Mateo. I warned her . . . I did warn her that in her most delicate condition she must not go into that crowded church!

Lucia [coming to very prettily]. Where am I?

Mateo. Here . . . safe with your husband.

Lucia [affectedly]. Oh!

Juanillo. Here's the water.

Mateo. Try to drink some, my darling.

The Mayor. But slowly . . . slowly.

Lucia. Oh . . . my fan!

Mateo [rushing to pick it up]. Here it is.

The Mayor. Shall I fan you? [He takes his wife's fan for the purpose]

Lucia. No, please . . . I can't bear it. My handkerchief.

The Mayor. Here it is!

Mateo. Take mine.

Lucia. Oh! Wipe my forehead please! Oh!

Mateo. Are you in pain?

The Mayor. Aren't you better?

Mateo. Would you like to go home?

The Mayor. Shall we have the carriage brought round for you?

Lucia. No, no . . . I'm better now, thank you. [She gets up] Oh . . . how my head swims!

Mateo. Sit down . . . please.

The Mayor. Keep still, child . . . just a little longer.

The Mayoress. Oh . . . for all our sakes! Suppose anything should happen to our precious jewel!!

Lucia. Mateo . . . Mateo!

Mateo. What is it?

Lucia. Your mother . . . your mother is insulting me . . . again.

The Mayor. My dear . . . will you be quiet?

The Mayoress. Yes, I will be when I choose!

Mateo. A nice thing, isn't it, to upset her now! Suppose anything happens . . .

The Mayor. . . . in her delicate condition!

The Mayoress. Delicate fiddlesticks! I've brought seven children into the world and never fainted over one of them.

Lucia. No doubt, Señora . . . but some of us are more sensitive, I suppose.

The Mayoress. I didn't hear of your fainting three months ago—before you were married—when you were still washing clothes in the river. And I understand that you'd every right to feel just as delicate then.

Lucia [collapsing]. Oh, Mateo! Oh Father, dear Father! Oh!!! [She affects the classic attack of nerves]

Mateo [furious, while he supports her on one side]. If it weren't that you are my mother . . .

The Mayor [threatening, while he supports her on the other]. If it wasn't that we are . . . where we are . . .

The Mayoress. And if you men weren't so easily taken in . . .

DoÑa Paquita. Please . . . please don't make so much noise. Every word you say can be heard in the church.

The Mayoress. By a dolly draggle-tail who was scrubbing floors three months ago and now if you please she can't lift a feather duster!

Lucia. Oh—oh—oh! Mateo . . . my heart

Don Francisco [who is losing patience]. Look here—young lady—will you stop this nonsense or shall I throw a bucket of water over you?

Juanillo. Shall I go and fetch one?

LUCIA [*taking hold of the doctor's hand*]. Oh, dear, dear Don Francisco!

JUANILLO. Turned into a fine lady in double-quick time, haven't you . . . fainting fits and all! You're no fool . . . I'll say that for you.

LUCIA. Is that Juanillo?

JUANILLO. Oh yes . . . the same old Juanillo as ever . . . and will be for ever and ever, amen! We can't all get up in the world by coming a cropper like you.

LUCIA. You are an impertinent boy.

JUANILLO. That's right—keep it going!— You do it very well.

MATEO. Get out of here . . . or I'll kick you out.

JUANILLO. All right . . . consider me kicked!

DOÑA PAQUITA. Well, Lucia . . . so you're better?

LUCIA [*a little shamefaced*]. Yes, Señora.

DOÑA PAQUITA. Let's have no more of these scenes then . . . unless you want to send your mother-in-law into a fit.

LUCIA. Suppose you ask her to stop driving me mad!

JUANILLO [*who has returned to his post by the small door leading to the church*]. The service is over! They're coming out . . . they're all coming . . .

[*A movement of curiosity on the part of everyone. LUCIA entirely forgetting her faint, goes forward with the others toward the church door. At the same time there come in from the street with huzzas, DOÑA GERTRUDIS, a lady of fifty summers, pretentiously dressed in black silk, with a mantilla; THE SCHOOL MISTRESS, a blue-stocking of twenty-five or thirty; ROSITA, a young girl of the village, about eighteen; a little girl; the Colonel of the "Guardia Civil"; and various other ladies, married and unmarried. Also some men*]

JUANILLO [*as the ladies appear, in a stage whisper*]. Ha—hum . . . enter the wise Virgins!

DOÑA PAQUITA. Be quiet . . . you blasphemous boy!

DOÑA GERTRUDIS. May we . . . ?

THE SCHOOL MISTRESS. Will you allow us to . . . ?

DOÑA PAQUITA. Yes . . . come in, come in.

DOÑA GERTRUDIS. Forgive us, dear Doña Paquita, won't you, for bursting in on you like this. But these girls . . . they felt they just must kiss our new Priest's hand and . . .

THE COLONEL. Only the girls . . .

DOÑA GERTRUDIS. Now . . . don't be mischievous, Colonel.

ROSITA [*to DOÑA PAQUITA*]. And you weren't there for the sermon. Oh, I never heard one like it.

DOÑA GERTRUDIS. Such feeling!

THE SCHOOL MISTRESS. And such erudition. [*They all talk*]

ROSITA. But what happened to you, Lucia?

LUCIA. It was nothing, dear . . . I felt a little faint. The heat I daresay . . .

THE MAYOR. She's so very delicate.

THE MAYORESS. And of course we were frightened . . .

DOÑA GERTRUDIS. And I'm sure that the sermon stirred you very deeply. Such depths of wisdom. You lost all the best of it.

ROSITA. What I liked best was the part about "godly womanhood."

DOÑA GERTRUDIS. Ah no, no! Remember "the mellifluent sweetness of our Redeemer's heart . . ."

THE SCHOOL MISTRESS. The best of all though was that passage about the soul as a butterfly taking flight, drawn by its intense desire to be consumed in the flame of the Love Divine. [*She looks softly at THE COLONEL*]

A LADY. And his voice . . . !

A YOUNG LADY. Such gestures . . . !

DOÑA GERTRUDIS. And what a beautifully embroidered rochet!

ROSITA. Made . . . was it not . . . from the fabric of the nipa-palm?

A LADY. It had lace half a yard wide.

THE COLONEL. Well . . . and did our respected school mistress enjoy herself?

THE SCHOOL MISTRESS. We all did!

THE COLONEL. Ah, but you discriminate. A thing must be really good before it pleases you.

DOÑA GERTRUDIS. Well, he brought tears to my eyes more than once . . . more than once!

LUCIA. Oh . . . he's coming!

[*DON ANTONIO and DON JOSÉ MARÍA, the new priest, come out of the small church door. The latter is a young man of about twenty-eight, he wears his mantle beautifully, elegantly gathered up in one hand, and in the other he is carrying his plush hat, small and tasselled. His hands are very white and perfectly cared for. He wears patent leather shoes with silver buckles. He comes forward slowly and bows with suave inclinations of the head. His eyes are cast down and he is smiling with honeyed sweetness. The actor must be careful to have the necessary affectations, without the slightest approach to caricature. DON ANTONIO, as in the first act, is wearing a sotana and threadbare cassock, with elastic boots, and has a breviary in his hand and an ordinary tile hat*]

DOÑA GERTRUDIS. So modest too!

ROSITA. Oh . . . but doesn't he remind one of St. Luiz Gonzaga!

THE COLONEL. Say something, Señora Dominie.

THE SCHOOL MISTRESS [*coquettishly*]. Colonel, Colonel, you know my name, don't you?

DON ANTONIO. This is the garden, you see . . . and that is the house. Shall we go in?

DON JOSÉ MARÍA. No . . . no thanks. Time enough . . . time enough!

DON ANTONIO. It's very convenient . . . one can come this way . . . without having to go through the street.

DON JOSÉ MARÍA. What a pretty garden . . . and how well kept!

DON ANTONIO. It has amused my sister to grow a potful of vegetables . . . and a bunch of flowers: Paquita . . . Don José María . . . My sister. [*He introduces them*]

DON JOSÉ MARÍA. So pleased, Señora . . .

DOÑA PAQUITA. Señor . . .

DON JOSÉ MARÍA. You're a great gardener, I see.

DOÑA PAQUITA. Oh . . . I love flowers. And the earth will always give something in return for one's care of it, will it not? It is easier to strive with than the hearts of men. [*She moves away*]

DON JOSÉ MARÍA. And these ladies and gentlemen?

DON ANTONIO. They all want to pay their respects to you, I think . . . if you don't mind.

DON JOSÉ MARÍA. No, no, of course . . . on the contrary . . .

DON ANTONIO. Don Francisco . . . [DON FRANCISCO *has been alone at the back*]. I have the honour to present to you Doctor Don Francisco Lasada . . . my best friend . . . my most valued comrade.

DON FRANCISCO. Your servant.

DON JOSÉ MARÍA. So delighted to know you.

DON ANTONIO. And I have never met his equal.

DON FRANCISCO [*smiling*]. Well . . . one's as good as one knows how to be!

DON ANTONIO. You'll come to value him too.

DON JOSÉ MARÍA. You're the Officer of Health for the village, of course.

DON FRANCISCO. I was . . . till a short while ago.

THE MAYOR [*putting in his oar where it isn't needed*]. Yes, there's been a new appointment. A younger man . . . your own age . . . and very clever . . .

DON ANTONIO. Our Mayor.

[DON FRANCISCO *and* DOÑA PAQUITA *retire together to one side*]

DON JOSÉ MARÍA. And so to remain, I hope, for many years.

THE MAYOR. Ah well . . . I'm on the way down hill now, you see. But here's my son [*Indicating* MATEO, *who comes forward with* *a certain perturbation*] ready to seize the staff of office . . . when I let it go.

MATEO [*not knowing what to say*]. What nonsense, Father!

THE MAYOR. Why, of course, you are . . . ready and anxious too. Don't be ashamed of it. Ready to put the whole world to rights, these young folk, aren't they? And quite right too . . . quite right [*To his wife*] Come here, my dear. Oh come along, come along . . . nobody's going to eat you. My wife!

DON JOSÉ MARÍA. Delighted to meet you, Señora.

THE MAYORESS [*bashfully kissing his hand*]. Oh no . . . I mean yes . . . the pleasure is yours . . . I mean mine . . .

[*A little whispered laughter in the group of women*]

THE SCHOOL MISTRESS [*quietly to the others*]. Now the Lady Mayoress has made her customary happy remark!

THE MAYOR [*taking* LUCIA *by the hand*]. And this is our daughter-in-law. Now you can boast that you know all the family. Now make him a pretty speech since you've got yourself up for the occasion.

LUCIA. I . . . oh yes, of course . . . [*She kisses the priest's hand*]

THE MAYOR. And we shall want your services soon. There's a christening coming! Ha, ha!

THE MAYORESS [*furious*]. Oh, of course . . . we don't escape *that* remark!

THE MAYOR. And remember . . . my house is yours . . . and everything in it. No compliments . . . I mean it.

DON JOSÉ MARÍA [*wanting to make an end*]. You are most kind . . . I'm much obliged . . .

DON ANTONIO [*presenting* DOÑA GERTRUDIS]. And here is the President of the Sisterhood of Our Lady of Sorrows.

DON JOSÉ MARÍA. Señora . . .

DOÑA GERTRUDIS [*kissing his hand*]. Your very devoted servant, Father. And we have such a beautiful image . . . oh but you must have noticed it . . . in the church.

DON JOSÉ MARÍA. I have indeed.

DOÑA GERTRUDIS. Ah, but she's not at her best now . . . as dowdy, I'm afraid as . . . well, as I am. We fully meant her to have a new mantle for the Novena. But it couldn't be managed. No, as usual, these girls [*Indicating* ROSITA] got everything.

ROSITA [*offended*]. Oh, you shouldn't say that!

DON JOSÉ MARÍA. I beg your pardon . . .

DON ANTONIO. This young lady, you see, is President of the Association of the Daughters of Mary.

ROSITA. Your reverence . . . [*She too kisses his hand*]

DON JOSÉ MARÍA. God bless you.

DOÑA GERTRUDIS [*persisting*]. But it is so . . . the Daughters of Mary get everything that's going. And I suppose it's natural, because they're young, and when it comes to begging, of course, people give more readily to a young girl than to an old woman.

ROSITA. Oh, but don't you think it's a little because our Virgin is so much prettier?

DOÑA GERTRUDIS. Certainly not, child . . . our Virgin is far more distinguished . . . and far more appealing too . . . with those tears on her cheeks.

ROSITA [*to* DON JOSÉ MARÍA]. Well . . . you must be the judge, Father . . .

DON JOSÉ MARÍA [*smiling*]. Ladies, ladies, there is but one Holy Virgin and her joy is the same in the worship offered to her through every one of her images.

THE SCHOOL MISTRESS. Oh, it's no use, Father, you'll never get them to believe that. It's to these villages one must come, I'm afraid, to find true materialism.

[DON JOSÉ MARÍA *looks at her with some alarm*]

DON ANTONIO [*smiling at the poor girl's inoffensive pedantry*]. This lady is the head of our elementary school.

THE SCHOOL MISTRESS. Yes . . . only a school teacher, and your humble parishioner, Señor. [*She kisses his hand*]

THE MAYOR. But she knows Latin!

DON JOSÉ MARÍA [*without enthusiasm*]. Does she indeed!

THE SCHOOL MISTRESS. A few words, oh, hardly more. Just enough to let me read the works of the Fathers in my moments of leisure.

DON ANTONIO [*going on with the introduction*]. Our commandant here, Colonel Manuel Ramirez of the Civil Guard.

THE COLONEL. At your command!

DON JOSÉ MARÍA. Señor . . .

[*They all surround him now, while he bows and smiles and the women kiss his hand in fierce rivalry*]

A LADY. Welcome . . . welcome from us all, Señor Cura . . .

A YOUNG LADY. And we hope that you'll stay here many, many years . . .

ANOTHER. And that you'll be so happy among us . . .

DEMETRIO. And preach us lots more sermons like today's . . .

NICETO. May we all be spared to hear 'em!

THE MAYOR. Come, come now . . . we mustn't tire him out.

DON JOSÉ MARÍA. Oh indeed, you do nothing of the sort!

DOÑA PAQUITA [*a little bitterly to* DON FRANCISCO]. They'll come to blows over him in a minute.

DON FRANCISCO. Children with a new toy!

DON JOSÉ MARÍA. Dear ladies . . . gentlemen . . .

SEVERAL PEOPLE. He's going to speak . . . he's going to speak!

DOÑA GERTRUDIS. Sh! Sh!

THE MAYOR. Hear, hear! Hear, hear!

DON JOSÉ MARÍA. No, really . . . I had no intention . . .

THE SCHOOL MISTRESS. Oh yes, yes, Father . . . say a word to us.

DON JOSÉ MARÍA. Why, I have nothing to say . . . [*But already he has dropped into his honeyed rhetorical tone*] . . . except that I am deeply, deeply grateful for the kindness . . . so little merited by me . . . and the warmth of my welcome to this enlightened village and for the trust with which it so readily begins to honour me . . .

THE MAYOR. The honour is ours . . . the honour is ours!

THE MAYORESS [*pulling his cloak*]. Don't interrupt him!

THE MAYOR. Don't interrupt *me!*

DON JOSÉ MARÍA. Today . . . this past hour . . . and above all this passing moment stamp an ineffaceable memory in my heart. I bring to your service little power of mind, no store of knowledge, much unworthiness . . . but leaning, in my feebleness upon the strength of Him to whom all things are possible, I do believe that I shall not quite utterly betray the hopes on which you build, when, with a simple and a touching faith, springing from the pure depths of love and fellowship, you hold out such a welcome to this unworthy servant of the Most High.

JUANILLO [*admiringly*]. Good Lord . . . you'd think he must have learnt it all by heart before.

DON JOSÉ MARÍA. But I . . . I ask your aid. Together we must labour in the mystic garden of our souls' Beloved. Alone I can do little. It will be your task . . . as when of old Aaron and Caleb so stood by Moses on the mountain . . . to strengthen and sustain the drooping hands I lift to God!

SEVERAL LOW VOICES. Yes, yes, indeed.

NICETO. That's the sort of priest for me!

DEMETRIO. Look out . . . there's the old one's sister listening . . .

DON JOSÉ MARÍA. But let me . . . taking up the staff that makes me shepherd of your fold . . . add now a word, inadequate I know, of gratitude and praise to him whom I succeed. For many years he has watched over you with patience and with skill that has indeed not had to be its own reward. The Will that orders all things calls him to well-earned repose. From his hands I take my sacred charge. In your name and my own I ask him, in the peace of his retreat, the evening of his days not to forget to pray for his old flock and for their new shepherd. [*He gives his hand to* DON ANTONIO *with signs of great emotion*]

[*There are murmurs of admiration*]

DON ANTONIO. God help you through your task. You'll find other things than roses in the garden . . . sometimes.

THE MAYOR. Well, come now . . . what have you had to complain of?

DON ANTONIO [*serene and grave*]. God did not ask me for complaints. We have been together—I among you all—for thirty years. I came so young . . . now that I leave you I'm so old that somehow all my life is left behind . . . I wish I could have laid my body here as well. But God has willed that otherwise . . . blessed be His name. Forgive me for the things in which I have offended you. I always wished you well. We all make mistakes. And I forgive, with all my heart indeed, any unkindness that has been done to me. And I'll never forget you . . . any of you . . . nor the village . . . as long as I live . . . because . . . I can't go on . . . I . . . God keep and help us all.

JUANILLO [*to steel himself against tears*]. Damn . . . !

[*There is a deep silence; no one moves, nor gives the least sign of approbation. After the flowers of rhetoric of the new priest, the other's simple speech leaves the assemblage cold,* MATEO, *alone, after a moment, goes up to the old man and presses his hand*]

MATEO [*with a little embarrassment*]. You know just how we feel . . .

DON ANTONIO [*more touched than he wants to show*]. Thank you . . . thank you, my dear boy.

THE MAYOR [*after another brief moment of silence*]. Well, well . . . we mustn't waste time here. There's a small—ah—collation ready in the Town Hall. [*To* DON JOSÉ MARÍA] You must honour us by coming.

DON JOSÉ MARÍA. Oh . . . but to go to all that trouble! With pleasure . . . with the greatest pleasure.

THE MAYOR. Let's be off then . . . or the chocolate will be getting cold. Come along, come along, everyone's welcome . . . plenty there for us all.

DON JOSÉ MARÍA [*to* DON ANTONIO]. Señor . . .

DON ANTONIO. No . . . forgive me if I don't come. I've a few little things still to pack . . . and my train goes at six.

DON JOSÉ MARÍA. But . . . are you going today?

DON ANTONIO. Yes, indeed . . . my sister will give the house keys to the sacristan.

THE MAYOR [*wishing to appear polite*]. But there's no hurry, you know . . . at least as far as the house is concerned. Don José María

can consider himself my guest for as long as he pleases. [*As* DON JOSÉ MARÍA *bows deprecatingly*] No, I mean it, I mean it.

DON ANTONIO. No, I've finished everything now. Besides . . . [*With a little smile*] my old ladies will be expecting me. There's my installation to think of, you know.

THE MAYOR. That's right . . . each in his turn! Well . . . till we meet again.

DON JOSÉ MARÍA. Good-bye, good-bye. And remember . . . anything I can do for you . . . at any time . . .

DON ANTONIO. Yes, yes. Good luck to your work here.

DON JOSÉ MARÍA [*to* PAQUITA *who bows but does not speak*] Señora. . . . [*To* DON FRANCISCO] Good afternoon, doctor.

DON FRANCISCO. Good afternoon.

[*They are all going out,* LUCIA *with the others, without paying any more attention to those who are left behind.* MATEO *detains her*]

MATEO [*to* LUCIA, *with a little reproach in his tone*]. Say a word to your godmother.

LUCIA [*as a duty and wanting to get it over*]. Anything I could do for you . . . if I stayed . . . ?

DOÑA PAQUITA. No, child, thank you . . . everything's done.

THE MAYOR [*from the gate*]. Lucia . . . Mateo . . . come along.

LUCIA. I'm just coming.

DOÑA PAQUITA. Yes . . . off with you!

MATEO. I shan't say good-bye . . . we'll be down at the station.

DON ANTONIO. All right . . . run away . . . run away!

[*Everyone goes out, except* DON ANTONIO, DON FRANCISCO, DOÑA PAQUITA *and* JUANILLO. *They don't speak. A gay peal of bells is heard; they are setting off rockets in the street, and a band of music, supposed to be stationed there, begins to play a quick-step, in front of the church, awaiting the exit of the new priest*]

JUANILLO [*who, on hearing the music and the rockets, forgets everything else, and dashes toward the street*]. Rockets!

DOÑA PAQUITA [*with deep reproach*]. Juanillo!

DON ANTONIO. Why . . . let him go, Paquita.

JUANILLO [*very conscience-stricken*]. No, Father, I wasn't going . . . wasn't really.

DOÑA PAQUITA [*making an effort to appear calm*]. I'll make sure that nothing has been forgotten. [*To* JUANILLO] You come with me.

DON ANTONIO. Very well . . . fetch me when you're ready.

[DOÑA PAQUITA *and* JUANILLO *go out. The sound of music and bells goes on for an instant. The last rockets are fired off.* DON ANTONIO, *overcome by emotion, falls on a chair, and leaning his head on the stone table sheds a few tears; afterwards he makes a great effort to be calm, and succeeds*]

DON ANTONIO [*in a broken voice*]. God's will be done . . . His will be done. [*He dries his eyes with his bare hands*] Ay . . . ay! [*To* DON FRANCISCO *bitterly*] all that my courage really comes to, you see. Don't despise me.

DON FRANCISCO. Well—if you mean to begin trying to hide things from me at this time of day . . .

DON ANTONIO. Our work's done, my friend.

DON FRANCISCO. Yes, indeed . . . over and done with.

DON ANTONIO. Oh, this village . . . this village!

[*They both speak excitedly and with emotion, and at first, each one as if he were talking only to himself and with himself*]

DON FRANCISCO [*walking from one side to another*]. I remember the day I came. What a hideous and impossible place I thought it. I said to my wife—I won't stay here a week. Well . . . that's thirty years ago.

DON ANTONIO. More.

DON FRANCISCO [*a little grudgingly*]. And the odd thing is that one ends by having some sort of feeling . . . an affection . . . for all the savagery and indecency of it.

DON ANTONIO. And for this hard dry land beyond . . . and . . . oh the harder hearts of its people.

DON FRANCISCO. Yes . . . I suppose if we labour at the plough long enough the ass-thistles in the furrows get to look like roses . . . we see no others.

DON ANTONIO. Well . . . at least we *have* laboured!

DON FRANCISCO. We have! When I think how I've travelled these roads . . . in the glaring sun . . . not a tree on all the length of them . . . summer after summer . . .

DON ANTONIO. And these hearts of stone . . . knocking at them day by day. . . .

DON FRANCISCO. I sold my horse yesterday. Well, I've no use for him now. My wife cried when they took him away.

DON ANTONIO. And you're staying on, are you . . . to watch your successor? That takes some courage.

DON FRANCISCO. Does it! But where am I to go at my age? The boys will be breaking loose—they've their own way to make. I have a bit of land, you know. My wife and I can live very simply . . . and she thinks stopping on in the house where they were born . . . where they were children . . . will be almost like having

them with her still. Women will indulge themselves in these fancies. But there's nothing else left for me . . . except to be lazy while the other man does his work . . . my work . . . ! and to console myself by thinking—though it mayn't be at all true—that I should be doing it better. Time heals all wounds!

DON ANTONIO. God heals them, Señor Don Francisco.

DON FRANCISCO. The same thing!

DON ANTONIO [*passionately*]. It is not . . . it is not the same thing. Do you think if I didn't *know* it was the will of God that I could be patient while my life . . . my whole life . . . was torn up by its roots?

DON FRANCISCO. Well, you know . . . what can't be cured must be endured.

DON ANTONIO. Yes . . . if God gives us strength to endure. Beneath the wings of his pity we are still. His will be done, we say.

DON FRANCISCO. Oh yes, we keep still because a wise instinct teaches us that keeeping still is the proper prescription for dangerously wounded men.

DON ANTONIO. And you are content to believe, are you, . . . even in such an hour as this . . . that there's no God watching over you . . . that you must stand in this friendless world alone?

DON FRANCISCO. I'm not alone! What about my wife? We've been happy together these forty years. What about you? And if I lost everything else I'd have my conscience still.

DON ANTONIO. But doesn't that whisper to you . . . doesn't it? . . . of something beyond and above, something more enduring that can give us the answer to this desperate riddle of our life?

DON FRANCISCO. I shall be quite content to have lived it honourably.

DON ANTONIO. I don't understand . . . no, I do not understand how you can so have lost your faith.

DON FRANCISCO. Bless you, I haven't . . . I never had any . . . and never felt the need of it.

DON ANTONIO. You've never prayed . . . your heart has never turned to God . . . you mean to die and not to ask him to go with you upon that unknown journey?

DON FRANCISCO. When I was a child I used to pray with my mother . . . to please her. I still have the rosary that she said so many paternosters over . . . and that I fell asleep over so many times. When I was first married I went to Mass with my wife . . . to please *her*. If I die first, I'll have them call a priest . . . to set her mind at rest. If she has gone before me, I shall die quietly enough, without ceremony. What is there to fear? One will fall asleep like a child in his mother's arms.

DON ANTONIO. Oh, Señor Don Francisco.

Don Francisco. No, believe me, dear old friend . . . there's only one thing that matters . . . to be an honest man. And I'm sometimes afraid that is settled for each of us . . . whether or no . . . when we're born. And everything else is illusion . . . hysteria in some people . . . gross superstition in others. Your dreams are very beautiful, my friend, because . . . well, it is your own nature makes them so. You have faith in God, you hope for Heaven. But tell me now, truthfully . . . suppose you were to lose all faith, all hope, could you, for any price the world might offer . . . could you do a wicked thing?

Don Antonio [*humbly and sweetly*]. I don't know . . . really I don't know. We are all weak creatures.

Don Francisco. Weak . . . and brave!

[Doña Paquita *and* Juanillo *enter.* Doña Paquita *is carrying the image of the Virgin, a small bag and a case containing a chalice and paten.* Juanillo *has a basket with food for the journey and other packages.* Doña Paquita *shuts and locks the door of the house*]

Doña Paquita [*turning the key*]. There . . . that's done.

Don Antonio. Everything?

Doña Paquita. Every single thing. I'm going to hand over the keys. [*She calls into the church*]. Benito! Benito! [*There is no answer*] Juanillo, take them to the Sacristy.—Here.

Juanillo. He's off to the Town Hall . . . if there's chocolate going. [*He starts to go out with the keys and the basket*]

Doña Paquita. Leave that basket now. If you lose that we'll have no lunch. [Juanillo *goes off*] Have you anything to put in the bag?

Don Antonio. My breviary. [*He gives her the breviary which is bound in coarse black cloth and* Doña Paquita *packs it in the bag*]

Don Francisco [*taking up the case with the chalice in it*]. What's this?

Doña Paquita. His chalice. That's our only valuable.

Don Antonio. My godmother gave it me when I said my first Mass. Yes . . . it had better go in the bag.

[Doña Paquita *packs the case with the chalice in the bag*]

Doña Paquita. I'll wrap the Virgin in a handkerchief . . . then she can go in too.

Don Antonio. No, no . . . I'll carry her.

Doña Paquita. Here's the carriage already.

Don Antonio. Well now . . . you go on with Juanillo . . . and I'll walk. That won't be so conspicuous.

Doña Paquita. We shan't be noticed anyway if we take the short cut. [*To* Don Francisco] Are you coming?

Don Francisco. Yes, Señora.

[Juanillo *comes back*]

Juanillo [*licking his lips*]. Oh yes . . . he was there! And I tell you they're having no end of a time. They gave me a meringue through the window.

[Paquita *suddenly breaks down, and bursts into tears*]

Doña Paquita. Oh God . . . Oh God!

Don Antonio [*trying to quiet her*]. Come now, Paquita . . . Come . . .

Doña Paquita. We're so old . . . we're all so old . . . such a little time left us. Surely . . . surely . . . you'd think they could have waited . . . just for a little.

Don Francisco. Young people have no patience, Señora.

Doña Paquita [*with passionate grief*]. No, nor pity.

Don Antonio. Remember that God knows what is best for us, my dear. There now, go along . . . and don't let them see you crying.

Don Francisco. Yes . . . yes. Come . . . come.

[*He gives his arm to* Doña Paquita, *and picks up the bag—*Doña Paquita *takes some of the packages, and they go*]

Juanillo [*breaking out uncontrollably*]. I can't stand it . . . I won't stand it! And that brute in there stuffing himself with sweets and wine and everything! Shall I go wait at the Plaza and throw a stone at him when he comes out? Shall I? Shall I?

Don Antonio [*horrified*]. God preserve us . . . certainly not! Do you know what you are saying! [*He gently draws the lad to him*] Now listen, my child. This that has happened is God's will . . . and no one . . . do you understand? . . . no one is to blame. Never speak like that again. And never think of committing such a mortal sin.

Juanillo [*vaguely comprehending, from the priest's agitation, that he has said something atrocious*]. No, Father . . . I won't . . . If you say so . . . but I . . . [*He bursts into tears*]

Don Antonio. There then . . . run along . . . take the basket . . . we'll say no more about it.

[Juanillo *takes the basket and goes out.* Don Antonio *remains alone for a moment, takes a long look about the garden, as if to say good-bye to it, sighs, and going slowly to the table, takes the image of the Virgin in his arms, and says to it, with love and resignation, but simplicity*]

Don Antonio. And now . . . we must go too, Holy Mother. [*He lifts the little statue and goes*]

CURTAIN

THE BUTTER-AND-EGG MAN

By GEORGE S. KAUFMAN

CHARACTERS

PETER JONES
JANE WESTON
JOE LEHMAN
FANNY LEHMAN
JACK MCCLURE
MARY MARTIN
A WAITER
CECIL BENHAM
BERNIE SAMPSON
PEGGY MARLOWE
KITTY HUMPHREYS
OSCAR FRITCHIE
A. J. PATTERSON

SYNOPSIS OF SCENES

ACT I: *Office of Lehmac Productions, Inc., New York City.*

ACT II: *A Hotel Room in Syracuse.*
  SCENE I: *Just before the Opening.*
  SCENE II: *Just after the Opening.*

ACT III: *The Office. A few weeks later.*

THE BUTTER-AND-EGG MAN

ACT ONE

SCENE: *The office of Lehmac Productions, Inc. It is situated in any one of the buildings that sprinkle Broadway above Forty-second Street.*

The Lehmac office has been only lately taken possession of. A pile of miscellaneous junk from an old office occupies a large part of the rear wall. There are great bundles of newspapers, most of them copies of Christmas issues of "The Morning Telegraph," containing MR. LEHMAN'S *advertised seasonal greetings to all artists everywhere; there are a few mouldy box files, part of a stray, bespangled costume, and even a ballet dancer's slipper. Except for a huge and shining and obviously new desk, the pile is the most prominent object in the room.*

The other furniture is likewise new; a swivel chair at the desk left center, a visitors' chair in front of it, a smaller chair left. There is a filing cabinet right of center door, but from the outside it looks as if there were nothing in it. A water-cooler left of center door. Some sixty or seventy photographs of artists are on the walls in interesting disarray. They are all inscribed. "With love to Joe," "To Joe from La Belle Marguery," "To the Greatest Agent in the World"—inscriptions, plainly, that bespeak a business affiliation rather than a personal bond.

There are two doors; one to a small office at the Right, the other directly to the outer hallway. The door at the Right is unlettered; when it is opened one catches a glimpse of the reception room without. The other door is exactly center, and is lettered as follows on the reverse side of its frosted glass:

ROOM 806

LEHMAC PRODUCTIONS,

INC.

Entrance Room 805

Across the hall, when the center door is opened, is another office door; a door announcing that it is the office of "Stein, Birchfelder & Blaumann, Attorneys-at-Law," and setting forth, in a corner below, the additional names of "Leo Heymann" and "A. J. Carmody."

The rising curtain—reveals MR. LEHMAN *and his confrère,* JACK MCCLURE, *deeply and none too amiably in thought.* JOE LEHMAN *is about forty. Except for a colored shirt, his clothes are not of the kind known as loud, and yet he has the knack of making them seem a bit exaggerated. He bulks large and forceful as he sits in his desk chair—cigar in mouth, derby hat on head, one clenched fist thoughtfully pounding an open palm.* JOE LEHMAN *gets his effects by solid driving.* JACK MCCLURE *is a more ingratiating type.* MAC, *as a matter of fact, is even rather attractive. About thirty-five. His attire is up to the minute and a shade beyond it; he wears a fashionable gray soft hat. The hats of* LEHMAN *and* MCCLURE *remain on their heads throughout the three acts; they are a part of them, and you could hardly imagine them bareheaded.*

MAC *discovered in chair right of desk, lighting cigarette, straw hat on back of head.* LEH-MAN *discovered sitting left of desk, feet up, cigar in mouth, derby over eyes.*

LEHMAN [*pauses, rises, crosses up left; gets idea, snaps fingers, crosses to 'phone on upper end of desk, takes off receiver and jiggles receiver piece*]. Get me Sol David. [*Hangs up*] He come through for that Jenny show last year.

MAC. Never got a nickel back. [*Tosses burnt match to ashtray on desk*] I saw the statements.

LEHMAN [*crosses down left*]. Anybody comes in on this trick'll clean up. I can do it for fifteen thousand. I'd take twelve.

MAC. You'd take one.

LEHMAN [*crosses to left of desk*]. You don't say? Let me tell you this, Sweetheart—there ain't going to be no bargains, not if I have to throw—['*Phone rings*]—it in the ashcan. [*Picks up 'phone, takes off receiver and holds mouthpiece against chest as he still talks to* MAC] This show's a pipe, and any bird that comes in is going to make plenty. [*Speaks in 'phone*] Hello! Right! Is Sol David there?— This is Joe Lehman talking. Oh—no. [*Hangs up*] Bermuda. Beats hell how far away they can get when you're trying to raise coin. [*Crosses down left*]

MAC. Here's a slant! Remember them income lists the papers published—taxes?

LEHMAN. We ain't got no time to—[*Crosses up around desk to center*]—follow them up. I got to get a bankroll before morning or I can't rehearse no longer. [*Turns to* MAC *as he reaches center*] Huh! That's Equity for you!

MAC. Tough luck they had to grab Ackerman just when they did.

LEHMAN. I woulda had his check this morning. [*Starts up around desk again to left*] Then he has to go and get pinched with them four cases in the car— I don't link up with no more bootleggers. [*Crosses down left and hold*]

MAC [*thoughtfully*]. There's a fellow makes lithographs. He sunk some coin in a two-for-one last year—Everson.

LEHMAN. A bowl of cherries. When you going to meet this other bird?

MAC. Lots of time—it's right downstairs. Anyway, he wants a musical—you know— girl stuff.

LEHMAN. Ten thousand, I could do this trick of mine for. [*Looking front*]

MAC. Say—there was two fellows named Levi, in ladies' shirtwaists—

LEHMAN. They got bit. [*Crosses up to left end of desk*] When I think the way—[*Leans over upper end of desk*]—them ham managers can go out and get bank accounts for bum shows—and here I got the best proposition in twenty years.

MAC [*still seated*]. You know what that downtown bunch got set back for half of Sid Ehrman's show? I got the inside on it—ninety grand.

LEHMAN [*crosses away to left*]. You'd think they'd get wise after awhile, with them shows they put on. Ain't nothing but luck puts half of 'em over. That one of Ziegfeld's the other night. [*Crosses back to left of desk; leans over on center*] You seen it.

MAC. A turkey.

LEHMAN. Junk scenery— [*Crosses left*] Bunch of costumes I wouldn't send over the Pan time. But he gets away with it. Dumb luck! [*Cigar in mouth, looking front*]

MAC. The public'll get on to him some day.

LEHMAN. Comedy bits they kicked off the— [*Leaning over center of desk*]—Columbia Wheel ten years ago. And here I am with a compact little drama, up to the minute, and I can't grab even eight, ten thousand to get the curtain up. [*Sits left of desk*]

MAC [*leans over in chair*]. Listen, Joe—on the level, can't you get it out of Fanny? [*Turns to left on chair*]

LEHMAN. Do I look like a sap? Ain't I told you me and her was up to six o'clock this morning, jawing about it? There ought to be some law against a wife having a lot of property in her own name. [*Looks front left, elbow on arm of chair, cheek resting on palm of hand*]

MAC. But look what you done for her. You took her out of that five-a-day and put her on Broadway. Didn't you tell her that?

LEHMAN. I didn't tell her nothing else for four hours. And she ain't only got the shack in Freeport—she's got a hunk in the bank come due on a bond or something, and she's going to buy another slice of Long Island with it. Beats all how them vaudeville hams ain't happy unless they're buying up a bunch of bum lots. [*Feet on table*]

MAC [*rises; crosses up to door*]. Well—it's about time for me to slide down.

LEHMAN. Don't bring nobody up here without you ring me. [FANNY *knocks once off center*] Open up—it's Fanny.

[MAC *throws open the door.* FANNY LEHMAN *stands without—a woman in the late thirties, perhaps, with an enormous poise and an insolent assurance acquired in years of touring the South Bends and the Wichitas. She does not even give* MAC *a contemptuous glance. Instead, her eyes go to* LEHMAN, *who is leaning far back in his swivel chair, his feet on the desk.* FANNY *drifts down to the desk and plants herself squarely in* LEHMAN's *line of vision. She has fortified herself with evidence with which to continue the battle begun at home, and she feels pleasantly sure of herself. There is a world of insolence in her opening speech*]

LEHMAN. Well? [MAC *stays up center by filing cabinet*]

FANNY. I just been taking a peep at that trick troupe of yours.

LEHMAN. Yeh? Well, you keep out of them rehearsals, you hear me? [*Rises, crosses down left*]

FANNY. You got a show there that's going to make history, do you know it? They're going to date things from the time you—[*Leaning against lower right end of desk*]—open this one.

LEHMAN [*looking at her*]. I ain't asked you what you think about it.

FANNY [*still leaning on right end of desk*]. I caught that bit where the leading lady was supposed to be sixteen or something and climbing up apple trees. The thing to make them trees out of is reinforced concrete.

LEHMAN. All right. It ain't your money, is it?

FANNY. No. You bet it ain't, dearie. [*Puts purse on table; crosses in front below desk*] And I gather that so far it ain't nobody else's. [LEHMAN *crosses to water-bottle up left-center*]

MAC. Now, listen—[*Crosses down to her, below desk left-center*]—Fanny—Joe's in a hole.

FANNY. Well, if it ain't Close-mouth!

MAC [*to* FANNY *at left center*]. I only want to help you both. Now, Joe's got a nice little entertainment—that's all it is, a good entertainment— [JOE, *at water-bottle up left-center, fills glass*] Ain't it, Joe? And he can ring up on it for ten thousand. Now, you're his own wife and he's your husband, and you got all this property—

FANNY. Save your voice for the sucker. [MAC starts right]

LEHMAN [at water-bottle]. Let her alone. [Up left-center. Crosses to center] She don't care nothing about me. That's women. [MAC up right center] You wouldn't 'a' had a sou if I hadn't dug you out of that Texas honky-tonk and steered you onto Broadway. I put you in regular vaudeville, that's what I done for you.

FANNY [leaning on front of desk]. Well—you got yours, didn't you? All the acts is on to agents like you. Twenty-per-cent Joe.

LEHMAN. Fanita, the world's greatest juggler! Hah! If it wasn't for me you'd be keeping four clubs in the air right now for some Gus Sun that nobody ever heard of.

FANNY [crosses right to JOE]. Don't you four-club me! I done six clubs for the wow at the finish, and done it for years.

LEHMAN. Aaah! There ain't a stage between here and California ain't got dents in it from them clubs of yours. [FANNY crosses to lower end of desk. MAC gets up in front of filing cabinet] They wouldn't let nobody sit in the first five rows. [She gives LEHMAN a look. LEHMAN crosses up and back] Fanita!

FANNY. Yes, Fanita. And I'm as good today as I ever was.

LEHMAN. Just about. [Crosses right, hands behind back, cigar in mouth]

FANNY. All right, all right. I was a bum juggler and you were a great agent. But—I got the house and lot in Freeport and you're trying to get it. [She looks front. LEHMAN gives her a look and as MAC speaks turns his back to foots]

MAC [takes couple of steps down to her]. What are you going to do with your money, Fanny—leave it to a home for jugglers?

FANNY. Say, listen, don't you go worrying none about the jugglers. They can take care of themselves. [Hold at desk] They ain't none of—[Takes a couple of steps up, back to footlights]—them hanging on to the edge of show business, pretending to know all about it just because they bum a lunch at the Astor every day. [Angrily] And what are you doing in here, anyhow? Me and Joe can get along without you.

MAC [at door center]. I'll go down and meet that certain party. [Exits center]

LEHMAN [crosses up around desk. FANNY watches him. As she places hand on hip, he takes a startled step away, still crossing left] Why don't you go home if— [Sits] you're so crazy about it? [Cigar in mouth]

FANNY. Now, listen— [Crosses to right of desk] Joe—this ain't your game. Why don't

you go back to agenting, where you know the ropes?

LEHMAN. Because I don't want to,— [Slaps table] see? I'm in the legit from now on.

FANNY. All right. But you ain't going to get anyone to sink any money in that junk show— I seen a rehearsal. [Sits right of desk]

LEHMAN. I don't want no advice. [Rises] Go on home. [Crosses down left]

FANNY. All right, go on and produce it. Produce it with some butter-and-egg man's coin and that dame of the Colonial Revolution that you got in the leading role.

LEHMAN [crosses below desk to right]. Never you mind about Martin. She's going to make the hit of her life. [Looks front, cigar in mouth]

FANNY. I ain't got nothing against her. I suppose she either had to join up with your troupe or go back to her original role in "The Two Orphans." [LEHMAN gives her a look] Who tipped you off to her, the British Museum?

LEHMAN. Just because— [Crosses back of desk] you ain't never heard of her, don't say she ain't good. [Crosses to windows left, and looks out, smoking]

FANNY. Say—my not hearing of her don't prove nothing. They didn't have no rotogravure sections in them days. What's her name again?

LEHMAN. Her name is Mary Martin and it'll —[Sits, looks front, cigar in mouth] be up in lights.

FANNY. Mary Martin. And what a temper she's got! Why, I wasn't even talking to her.

LEHMAN [turns and looks at her, takes ashtray and carefully places it on left of desk] You mean you let fly one of them wisecracks at that rehearsal?

FANNY. I never opened my mouth.

LEHMAN. What did you say?

FANNY. I merely asked a question.

LEHMAN. What was it—when was she born?

FANNY. I told you I caught her in that scene where she's mama's little darling—playing around cherry trees.

LEHMAN. Well—and what was your question?

FANNY. I says to the Director—"What does she wear in that scene?"

LEHMAN. Go on.

FANNY. And he says—"Blue pants."

LEHMAN. Then comes the gag.

FANNY. I just says—"Drop your curtain on that laugh." [Rises, crosses up right center]

LEHMAN [crosses above desk to FANNY right center]. Oh, you did, did you? And if Martin goes and has hysterics on me, I suppose that don't mean nothing to you, does it?—But what about me? I suppose you're trying to see how much you can help, when here I am sweating blood trying to get this show on and worried all the time about— [*Cries and crosses away to left*]

> [JANE WESTON *enters somewhat uncertainly from the reception room. She is twenty or so, and, since she is the heroine of this fable, she is good-looking and neatly dressed. She is* LEHMAN's *stenographer and office girl. She closes the door and stands*]

LEHMAN. I'd think the least a— [*Crosses back to* FANNY] man's wife could do— What is it?

JANE [*at door*]. Miss Martin is outside.

FANNY. Wheel her in.

LEHMAN [*looks at* FANNY]. Take them small-time jokes and get out of here. [*Starts left; stops at center*] Is she behaving all right? [*Crosses left to desk at upper end*]

JANE. Why—yes, sir.

LEHMAN. Not crying or nothing?

JANE. No, sir.

FANNY. Has she got a knife?

LEHMAN [*above desk left center and hold*]. You get out! Bring her in! Go on, I don't want no scenes in here! [JANE *opens door right*]

FANNY [*indicating distance from door to desk*]. I want to see if she can make it to the desk.

JANE [*enters, holds door open for* MARTIN]. Miss Martin.

> [MARY MARTIN *enters right. She is the familiar type of slightly passée actress. She stops short as she sees* FANNY; *draws herself up*]

FANNY [*up to center door*]. Can you imagine? Blue pants. [*Exits up center.* JANE *exits right*]

[*READY 'Phone*]

MARTIN [*after* FANNY *and* JANE *exit*]. Well—

LEHMAN [*crosses to back desk*]. Don't pay no attention to her. [*Sits*] She's loco. What's on— [*Looks at papers*] your mind?

MARTIN [*crosses to desk*]. It's a check of yours, Mr. Lehman. It just came back to me for the third time. [LEHMAN *looks at check*] What does that entitle me to—permanent possession?

LEHMAN [*looking over check*] Wait a while and put it through again. [*Hands her back check*]

MARTIN. I want the money. I need it.

LEHMAN [*looking through papers*] All right —you're going to get it. You just got to wait. That's all.

MARTIN. Mr. Lehman, I think a shoestring would be big for what you're operating on. And unless I get fifty right now— [*Raps on desk with right hand*] I'm going straight to Equity and tell the whole story. They'll call out the company.

[*Turns back on* LEHMAN. JANE *starts typ-ing off right and keeps it up until* LEHMAN *opens door*]

LEHMAN [*rises and leans on desk*]. Now listen, Sweetheart. You got a great part in a great show and you're going to be great in it. [*Pats her on left shoulder*] We're all going to make a pile of coin, and if you just string along with us—

MARTIN [*angry*]. That's what you said the last time. This time I want the money.

LEHMAN. Well, you don't get it, see? Not till I'm good and ready. [*Sits*] A lot of real stars would give their eye teeth to play the part you got. [*'Phone rings*]

['PHONE]

MARTIN. Well, if that's the way you feel about it— [*Crosses right center*]

LEHMAN [*at 'phone impatiently*]. Yes? Mac? What is it? She's gone. What is it—a live one? Bring him up. Where are you, downstairs? Right! Hey, keep a hold of his arm. [*Hangs up*] Now clear out. [*Rises, crosses to* MARTIN] I got business.

MARTIN [*crosses to* LEHMAN]. And the money?

LEHMAN. Listen! You'll get your money. We're taking in a partner, a millionaire. See? [*Starts right*] Miss Weston—

MARTIN. When do I get it?

LEHMAN [*crosses down right to door*]. Come back in half an hour you can have all the money you want. I tell you he's a big millionaire. Miss Weston! [*Opens door right*]

JANE [*discovered typing, enters right*]. Yes, sir?

LEHMAN [*to* JANE]. Now, get this— [*Then to* MARTIN] Will you get the hell out of here?

MARTIN. I'll give you just half an hour. Then I'm coming back. [*Exits up center*]

LEHMAN [*crosses left to desk*]. Clean this place up. There's a big butter-and-egg man coming.

JANE. Yes, sir. [*Shuts door right and crosses to up right center*]

LEHMAN. And shake a leg. [*Clears desk, putting papers in drawers*]

JANE. Yes, sir. [*Crosses up center. Picks up papers from floor*] Who did you say was coming, Mr. Lehman?

LEHMAN [*busy at desk*]. A butter-and-egg man. Don't you know what a butter-and-egg man is? A millionaire! A millionaire! He's going to put money in the show.

JANE. Oh, I'm glad of that. [*Picking up papers and puts them in drawer of filing cabinet*]

LEHMAN. I thought you'd get it after a while [*Sits, looks in cigar box in drawer on upstage end, and shuts drawer*]

JANE [*crosses down to right of desk; she has three or four sheets of typed paper*]. Yes, sir [*Slight pause*] Does that mean you'll pay me my salary then?

LEHMAN [*stops, takes cigar out of mouth*]. You're going to begin, too, huh?

JANE. I've been here four weeks.

LEHMAN [*closes drawer, which he has left open on down stage end*]. All right. You'll get it.

JANE. Thanks. [*Crosses up to filing cabinet again*]

LEHMAN [*gets idea as he closes drawer, crosses to* JANE *at left of filing cabinet*]. And look here— when this guy's been in here a while, you make an entrance with a piece of paper, see? A letter, anything—make it busy. Put it on my desk.

JANE. Yes, sir. [*Holds position up right center*]

LEHMAN. Don't stop to take no bows—just exit. [*Starts back to desk*]

JANE. Yes, sir. [*Mac enters right, closes door and crosses to center*]

LEHMAN [*crosses to* MAC *center*] Is he there?

MAC. With his hat off.

LEHMAN. What's the low down?

MAC. Built to order. A big butter-and-egg man from the West.

LEHMAN. Where'd you get him?

MAC. I'm waiting for this other bird when up blows Sid Bloom with this kid in tow— He's just a kid. I seen in a minute he was our oyster, and a second later he tells me he's looking to get into show business— [*Pause. He extends his hands, as though indicating a platter*] With watercress.

LEHMAN. Shoot him in. [*Crosses around above desk; sits*] All right, you! [*Jane crosses to right door; holds it open*] And don't forget that letter stuff. [*Sits at desk, feet up*]

MAC. Come right in, Mr. Jones. [*Peter enters right, hat in hand, rather timidly. Peter is a boy of twenty-one or so, and it may be said without exaggeration that there are some things he does not know about the world. For the rest, he is simple, likable, and just about average. His gaze is on the room at large, and his eyes never go to* JANE WESTON. JANE, *however, notices him*] This is Mr. Peter Jones. JANE *exits right*] Mr. Lehman, Mr. Jones. *Right center*]

PETER. I'm very glad to met you, Mr. Lehman.

LEHMAN. How are you, Sweetheart? [*Peter looks behind him*] Sit down. [*Takes feet down. Mac places chair, Peter crosses to desk; sits right of desk*] Cigar?

PETER [*seated right of desk,* LEHMAN *left of desk,* MAC *right center*]. No, thanks.

LEHMAN. Where you from?

PETER. Chillicothe— [*Pause*] Ohio.

LEHMAN. Great place. I never played it myself, but they all tell me.

PETER. Mr.—er—this gentleman said you

were about to make a theatrical production. [*Looks at* MAC *at right center*]

LEHMAN. I'm doing a wow.

PETER. What?

LEHMAN. Listen, Sweetheart— [*Pulls chair closer*] I got a show that's the greatest dramatic novelty in twenty years. There ain't never been nothing like it, see?

MAC [*at right center*]. I was telling Mr. Jones that, providing he acts quick, maybe he could get in on it.

LEHMAN. Ever been in show business, Mr. Jones?

PETER. Oh, yes. We put on two shows last year in Chillicothe—during the hospital drive.

LEHMAN. I see.

PETER. During the second one I had charge of everything—told them what to do—the actors. Made over a hundred dollars.

LEHMAN. Well— [*Leans back and humors him*] Then you know how them things are.

PETER. Yes, sir.

LEHMAN. Of course, here in New York, it's just like Mr. McClure says—you got to make quick decisions—think on your feet.

PETER. Yes, sir.

MAC [*crosses to* PETER]. There was a friend of ours could have bought in on "Abie's Irish Rose" if he'd snapped it up. He waited 'til the next day and it was too late. [*Crosses away a little*]

LEHMAN [*snaps fingers*]. That's the show game.

PETER. Well, I'm a believer in quick decisions myself, if it's an A-Number-One proposition. Only, of course, I've got to be careful.

LEHMAN [*leans back*]. Just the kind of man I like, Sweetheart. What line you been in?

PETER. I was—in a hotel.

LEHMAN. Working there, you mean—had a job?

PETER. Yes, sir.

LEHMAN. Out in that town?

PETER. Um hm. Chillicothe. [*Mac looks at* PETER]

LEHMAN [*considers*]. This coin—you didn't make it yourself, then?

PETER. No, sir. It was—left me.

LEHMAN. How much do you want to put up?

PETER [*pauses*]. I'd want to know more about your proposition first. I've got to be careful.

LEHMAN. I ain't asking you to go in blindfold. [*Puts hat on back of head*] I got a great gag and I ain't afraid to show it. I got a show that's going to catch everybody, see? It ain't highbrow and yet it ain't lowbrow.

PETER. Sort of—medium brow?

LEHMAN [*humors him again*]. That's it. It's the first good medium-brow show they've had, and it's going to be a knockout.

PETER. How much money do you figure it's going to make?

LEHMAN. Say—ask Sam Harris what he's knocking down out of this "Rain" show. Ask that woman what she's making out of "Abie's Irish Rose." Ask Bill Brady what he cleaned up out of "The Man Who Come Back." [*Leans over desk to* PETER]

PETER. You want *me* to ask them?

LEHMAN. I'll tell you, Sweetheart! Millions!

PETER. That's what I'd like. Only I'd want it to be safe.

LEHMAN. I'll guarantee it personally. So will my friend here. Won't you, Mac?

MAC. Sure! [PETER *looks at* MAC]

LEHMAN. Now—what do you say?

PETER. Well—

MAC. Think on your feet—that's show business.

PETER. Oh, I couldn't possibly decide that quickly.

LEHMAN. You couldn't.

PETER. No, sir. I've got to be careful.

LEHMAN. Well, when do you think you could decide?

PETER. I'd want to investigate it first. Maybe I could read the play, huh?

LEHMAN. Oh! Well—think we could dig up a script for— [PETER *looks right at* MAC] Mr. Jones, Mac? [*He shakes his head for* MAC *to say "no"*]

MAC [*quickly*]. No, afraid not. You see, the troupe's in rehearsal, Mr. Jones, and they're using 'em all.

LEHMAN. I'll show you where it's sure-fire. [MAC *gets chair left. Brings it to lower end of desk; sits, back to audience*] Now, look! It's a play about a dame, see? Only it starts this way. There's a prologue—with a playwright in it, that's in love with this girl. So he asks a bunch of people to come around and hear him read his new play. Now— [*Rises*] he starts in to read, and he says, "The first scene is in an orchard"—and when he says "orchard," instead of his going on reading, we work that new trick everybody's talking about. [PETER *looks at* MAC]

MAC. We call it the "cut-back."

LEHMAN. Black out, quick change, lights up, and it's this orchard. Get it?

PETER. Um-hm. Just the way he said. [*Points to* MAC]

LEHMAN. You got it. Then all the rest of it is his play. First, here she is in the orchard— [*Indicates orchard*] only it's the same dame you seen in the prologue. Neat?

PETER. You bet.

LEHMAN. She's younger, see? About seventeen and playing around the trees. Then along comes this guy—

PETER. Who?

MAC. The same fellow that was the playwright.

LEHMAN. He makes love to her, only he's too nice about it. She wants some bozo that'll give her a lot of hot stuff. You know women. [*Leans over desk*]

PETER. Say— [*Business of hand as if he knew all about them*]

LEHMAN. So this fellow does a getaway and in blows this other baby. From New York, see, and dressed sorta loud. He gives her an earful about how beautiful she is, and anyhow, she falls for him.

MAC. Don't forget the priest.

LEHMAN [*over desk*]. Oh, yeh. There's a priest comes in and there's some gab with him. Now! The next scene the dame's hitched up to this baby, and having a swell time. It's a big cabaret in New York, music and dancing—

MAC. *You* know! [*Indicates short skirts*]

LEHMAN. One thing after another happens—anyhow—a guy comes along and insults her. And her husband he says, "What the hell!"— [LEHMAN *backs away*] and back and forth, and out with a gun, and— [*Snaps fingers, leans over desk*]

PETER. Who does?

MAC. The fellow she's married to croaks the guy that insulted her.

PETER. That's a good thing. I'm glad of that.

LEHMAN [*backs away*]. Music stops, police, —who done it? [*Bends over desk*] She says she done it.

PETER. But—weren't there a lot of people around at the time?

LEHMAN. Sure they was.

PETER. Then don't they see the husband shoot him?

LEHMAN. No. They're all looking the other way. [PETER *nods*] And now—comes the trial scene. She don't recognize this judge, see?

MAC. He has a beard on.

LEHMAN. Yeh—the judge has got a long beard on— [*Indicates beard*] and she don't— [*Snaps fingers*] I forgot to tell you this part. When she run off with this guy her father kicked her out,— [PETER *starts to talk*] see—didn't want no more to do with her, and she ain't seen him since. Got it?

PETER. Well, I'm not—

LEHMAN. *Wait* for the surprise! A lot of trial stuff, so-and-so and so-and-so and so-and-so—she keeps on saying she done it, and finally this judge he gives her *fifteen years* [*Reads the last part like giving a sentence to some one*]

PETER. Gee! [*Shakes head*]

LEHMAN. Then— [*Steps back*] everybody does an exit, she's just there with him, and who does the judge turn out to be but her *own father*. [*Leans over table*]

PETER. That's a great—coincidence.

MAC. The father used to be a lawyer.

LEHMAN. Yeh. Anyhow, it goes back and forth, and she gets crying, and more and more, and goes crazy sorta—and finally they drag her off, cursing like a trooper. That's your first act. [*Starts up center*]

PETER. It's a great start, all right. [*Puts hat on table*]

[LEHMAN *takes off coat and throws it up center*]

MAC. The name of it is "Her Lesson."

LEHMAN [*crosses down to center*]. Yeh— "Her Lesson." It's a big moral play, see—we get all the women.

PETER. Good.

LEHMAN. Second act. Ten years later, and she's just getting out of jail. And she's sore— she's out to get square, and she's doped out a way to skin rich men out of their coin, and still they can't do nothing to her.

MAC. She stays within the law.

PETER [*looks at* MAC]. Say, "Within the Law" would be a good name for a play, wouldn't it?

LEHMAN. Now! She's laying plans to fleece a guy that's coming to see her! She don't know his name, see? And *who* does it turn out to be but this other guy that wanted to marry her.

PETER. What's he say?

LEHMAN. He gives her a long spiel, and she makes up her mind to go straight. But she can't. She tries it on the next guy and he won't stand for it. So she says what the hell, and men is all alike, and me for the easiest way. [*Standing feet slightly apart, palms turned out, hands down*]

PETER. That was the name of a play.

MAC. Made half a million.

LEHMAN. Sure fire. And now comes the big punch. [*Crosses to* PETER *a little*] Next is the brothel scene. [PETER *pauses, looks at* MAC] The dame has been going down hill and there he is, see? Only—before anything terrible can happen, who comes along but this priest. Remember him?

PETER. He used to be in the orchard. [*Points left*]

LEHMAN. That's him.

MAC. He wants to close this place up.

LEHMAN. Of course there's a big scene when he finds the girl in there. Everybody's standing round, he opens up on her, then *zowie!*—she comes back at him.

PETER. That's fine. I thought she would. [*Starts to rise*]

LEHMAN. That's where we bring in the strong talk. She calls him all kinds of names—we go the limit. Then she says, "you priests and missionaries— [*Shakes finger in* PETER's *face*] is all alike. You don't give a girl no chance," and so— [*Backs away to right*] and-so and so-and-

so and so-and-so—she faints dead away and somebody says, "Everybody get out of here, she's sick." That's your second act.

MAC [*rises*]. Want me to tell the rest?

LEHMAN. No!—Act Three is her dream. She's delirious, see, and dreams she's dead and gone to Heaven. Here's where we got all these angels coming down the aisles— [*Indicates aisles*]

MAC. With long veils over them.

LEHMAN. There was a show done it last year and it was a wow. [*Points up with thumb*] Everything's all mixed up in this act. Her father's up there, the Judge, see—only he's supposed to be God.

PETER. Is that all right to do?

LEHMAN. There was a big *hit* done it. Anyhow, we don't really say it, see?

MAC. Don't forget the priest.

LEHMAN. Oh, yeh. This priest comes in and he's got a rabbi with him, see? And they talk about how everybody's the same underneath, and it doesn't matter none what religion they got. Anyhow, just as they're starting to execute her, she wakes up. And this fellow, the good one, has got her in his arms, and she says "the bluebird— [*Hands clasped*] of happiness was at home all the time," kiss, lights out, finishing reading the play, everybody says great, the fellow and the girl gets married, fade out, and curtain. [*Indicates these things*]

[LEHMAN *gets coat and takes it and crosses to left of desk*]

MAC [*Rises, puts chair back left and crosses center in front of desk*]. How do you like it?

[LEHMAN *crosses above desk, to left of it. Business with coat*]

PETER. My—my—my! I *tell* you. Who wrote it?

MAC [*crosses to center*]. It used to be a short story.

LEHMAN [*at left of desk*]. Yeh, it was a story, see? A story in a highbrow magazine. Then some fellow makes a play out of it, a long time ago. Only he died, so of course we don't have to pay no royalties. You can't lose with it, Sweetheart. Can you imagine what a picture it'll make for this Swanson baby? [*Leaning over desk to* PETER]

PETER. Would it take very much money to produce it?

LEHMAN [*sits quickly in chair.* MAC *crosses up to end of desk. Quickly*]. Here's the angle. We're willing to let you have half of it, see— forty-nine per cent.

PETER. Of course, I'd be a producer, too?

LEHMAN. Sure. Now—how much was you thinking of putting up?

PETER. I'd rather you'd tell me, first.

LEHMAN. I'll let you in on the ground floor. You can have forty-nine percent for—thirty— [*His head comes forward just a little*] thousand dollars.

PETER [*turns in his chair.* MAC *puts his hand on his shoulder*]. Oh, I couldn't think of paying that much.

MAC [*pleads*]. Can't you shave that a little, Joe, for Mr. Jones?

LEHMAN [*considers*]. I'll tell you what I'll do. Give me a quick Yes and I'll take twenty-five.

PETER. I guess we've got to let the whole matter drop. [*He starts to go*]

LEHMAN [*rises and both move as if to stop* PETER]. Hold on! This coin of yours—you ain't got it some place out West, have you?

PETER. Why?

LEHMAN. Because if it was where you could dig it up in a hurry, maybe we can do business.

PETER. It's right down the street—in a bank.

[LEHMAN *and* MAC *give a sigh of relief*]

LEHMAN. I wasn't going to let it go for this, —[*Sits*] but you give me your check for twenty thousand and forty-nine percent of the show is yours. And it's a bargain, ain't it, Mac?

MAC. He couldn't have bought in on "Sally" for that. [*Crosses down to center*]

LEHMAN. And *that* was a big hit, too. Now, what do you say?

PETER. Twenty thousand?

LEHMAN. That's the dope.

PETER. Twenty thousand?

LEHMAN. And it's a bargain.

PETER. Twenty thousand? [*Faces front, hat in lap*]

MAC. Think on your feet.

[LEHMAN *places hand on pen*]

PETER [*rises*]. Well—I might—

LEHMAN. Set!

[*Dips pen in ink,* MAC *crosses above table, takes* PETER'S *hat,* LEHMAN *offers pen quickly,* PETER *takes pen and sits, starts to write*]

PETER. It's check number one.

[LEHMAN *writes receipt*]

MAC [*looks over* PETER'S *shoulder*]. Chatham and Phoenix, eh?

PETER. Yes, sir.

MAC. Joe Lehman. L-e-h-m-a-n. [*Crosses center*]

LEHMAN [*making out receipt, tears it out of book and leaves it on blotter*]. You're a smart baby, Mr. Jones, and you're going to clean up.

[FANNY *starts in center on the last two words*]

MAC. Now, just *sign it*. [*Crosses down right*]

FANNY [*enters angrily up center, slams door and crosses down center a little*]. Well!

LEHMAN. Ain't you got no sense at all? Get out of here! Get out of here! [*Up to center*]

[PETER *partly rises,* MAC *reassures him,* PETER *sits*]

FANNY. Listen, you four-flushing bum!

LEHMAN. Now, Fanny— [*Tries to hush her*]

MAC. Fanny, for the love of— [*Indicates to* PETER *to sit down; that it is all right*]

FANNY. I just come from my bank. And the paying teller says there was a guy around there this morning with black hair and a checked suit and a trick tie trying to find out how big my balance was.

MAC. Fanny—

LEHMAN. Now, now, I don't know nothing about it. Come back after a while.

FANNY. If you show up around there again they got instructions to shoot on sight. That's all I come to tell you.

MAC. Don't—

LEHMAN. Then get out. [*Crosses left to upper left end of desk and hold*]

FANNY [*crosses to center door*]. I ain't staying! But don't you go snooping around my money, because you ain't going to get a nickel of it! Not for a rotten show like that. [*Exits up center; slams door*]

[LEHMAN, *cigar in mouth, turns head slowly front.* PETER *looks after her exit. He looks at* LEHMAN *and he gives a sickly smile. Starts to write, then looks around again.* MAC *and* LEHMAN *eye* PETER]

PETER [*starts to sign check*]. Did she say rotten?

LEHMAN. She wasn't talking about this show. [*Crosses to left of desk*]

MAC. It's another one we got. [*Crosses left to* PETER]

LEHMAN. She don't even know nothing about this one.

PETER. Who was it? A friend of yours?

LEHMAN. My old lady.

PETER. Oh, your mother, huh?

LEHMAN [*sits left of desk*]. Now, listen, you got judgment of your own, ain't you? A smart guy like you. I told you about the show. Don't it sound like a wow?

PETER. But you see—there are reasons why I don't want to lose this money.

LEHMAN. You ain't going to lose it. Did I tell you about the bookings? [*To* MAC] Did I tell him about the bookings?

MAC. Not yet. [*Crosses to back of upper end of desk*]

PETER. Bookings?

LEHMAN. The towns we play in—the theatres. [*Takes out route sheet of top drawer in the down end of desk*]

PETER. Oh!

LEHMAN. We got the cream. Look! We open in Syracuse. A great show town. And we play there a *full* week.

PETER. A week, eh?

MAC. Most shows only get three days.

LEHMAN. Then we go to Providence, Worcester, Albany—all them soft spots.

PETER. I guess they're nice towns, but—

LEHMAN. They're great.

PETER. But you see—it's just as I was telling you—I got a special reason why I wouldn't want to lose this money—

[JANE *enters right, slamming door, with typed paper; crosses above desk to* LEHMAN, *lays paper on desk, smiles at* PETER, *exits right.* MAC *takes look at paper over* LEHMAN'S *shoulder*]

PETER [*eyes* JANE; *hesitates. Looks right after her exit*]. Well—would I be working right in this office?

LEHMAN. Sure. Give you a desk right in here.

PETER [*looks at door right*]. Well—either here or—out there.

LEHMAN. Whatever you say.

[JANE *types outside of door right.* PETER *looks at door right.* MAC *and* LEHMAN *exchange looks*]

PETER [*signs check. As he tears it out of checkbook* LEHMAN *grabs it*] Look out! It's wet!

LEHMAN [*rises.* MAC *shakes* PETER'S *hand, both in hurry to get away*] I'll dry it. You're a partner now, Sweetheart. [*Hands* PETER *receipt*] There's your receipt and we'll draw up the papers later. [*Crosses up center*]

PETER [*rises*]. Wait a minute. I guess maybe I shouldn't have done it.

LEHMAN [*at right of center door*]. You ain't going to start worrying?

PETER. Shouldn't I?

LEHMAN. I should say not. Now, Mac and me'll be right back. You wait here, see? Right in this room. [*Crosses up a little*]

PETER. But shouldn't I go with you to the bank?

LEHMAN. You look after things here, see?

PETER. But you see, my check—

MAC [*is holding door open, hand on the outside knob. They start again*]. The bank knows us.

PETER. But that isn't what I meant. I—

LEHMAN. Now don't worry. Just stay right here, because we want to talk to you when we get back, see? I'll tell you what! [*Starts to door right*]

PETER. What?

LEHMAN [*calls*]. Miss Weston!

PETER. Is that the name of—?

LEHMAN. Miss Weston! [*Opens door right*] Mac. That's her. [JANE *enters right*]

LEHMAN [*at door right*]. Look out for Mr. Jones 'til we come back. He's a regular partner. [*Starts up center*] Come on, Mac. [*Exits up center*]

[MAC *looks at* JANE, *exits up center, closing door. A pause as* JANE *and* PETER *face each other*]

JANE [*smiles; is thoroughly at ease*]. It wasn't much of an introduction, was it?

PETER. I don't mind if you don't.

JANE [*at center*]. Mr. Lehman says you've invested money in the play.

PETER. Yes, I—did put some in—a little. [*Picks up checkbook from desk*]

JANE. I hope it'll be very successful.

PETER [*rather stiffly*]. Thank you. [*They come closer together center*]

JANE. I've often wondered how it would feel to be able to do that.

PETER. You mean to be a producer?

JANE. Anyhow, to have enough money to be one.

PETER [*is a bit at a loss as to how to proceed*]. It—doesn't feel any way in particular yet. [*Looking at checkbook*]

JANE [*at right*]. Then if I had a *great deal* of money—well, like you—I might go ahead and *be* one.

PETER [*not quite getting the full implication, but coming close enough to be disturbed*]. How's that?

JANE. I say, if I could afford to *risk* part of the money, I'd *be* a producer.

PETER. Risk it? [*Crosses to her a little*] Don't you think it's a good business, putting plays on?

JANE. Well, of course, it depends. You see—

PETER [*grows a little panicky*]. But this—this play of Mr. Lehman's—it's good, isn't it? You think it'll be a hit? Don't you?

JANE [*a new doubt has come to her; regards him*]. Tell me something.

PETER. Don't you really?

JANE [*now sparring for information*]. It—it will be a hit, of course. But—I'm sure you wouldn't care, would you? A millionaire like you?

PETER. Like me? I'm not anything like that. It was all I could do to— [*Crosses up around desk to left of desk*] Well, I hope it turns out all right.

JANE [*still sizing him up*]. You're not a New Yorker, are you, Mr. Jones?

PETER. No, I'm from Chillicothe.

JANE. Oh—you—you haven't been connected with the theatrical business before, then?

PETER. Oh, yes. In a way—we made several productions last year in Chillicothe, sort of.

JANE [*sits right of desk left center*]. I see.

PETER. It's all right, isn't it? Mr. Lehman's play, I mean? You don't think anything could happen to it?

JANE. No, it isn't that, but— [*Leans toward him*]

PETER. It sounded great, I thought. But it'd be terrible if it wasn't a go.

JANE. What I was going to ask you was—of course it isn't any of my business, but—I was wondering how you happened to be here. In this office, I mean. How you ever happened to pick the theatrical business to invest in.

PETER. Oh, it's always kind of appealed to me.

JANE [pauses]. Did you give Mr. Lehman—much money?

PETER. Why? There isn't anything the matter, is there? [Over desk]

JANE. No, no. The only reason I asked—

PETER. Oh, if there were— [Turns head away and back] Plays do make a lot of money, don't they?

JANE. I'm sure it'll be all right. You mustn't worry.

PETER. All right. If you feel that way about it, why—all right.

JANE. Well, I—I appreciate your trusting me, of course, but—

PETER. Why—you're being here is one of the reasons I went into it. Partly.

JANE. How's that?

PETER. I felt pretty sure it was all right or you wouldn't be connected with it at all.

JANE. I'm not sure that I understand.

PETER. Well, when you came in—while they were here, you—sort of smiled at me. [She looks away] Maybe you didn't. I thought you did.

JANE. You did it because I smiled?

PETER. I didn't mean—

JANE. Oh, it's all right, only—it just makes me feel a good deal of responsibility, that's all. Was it all your money that you invested?

PETER. Oh, no. I've got—some left. A little.

JANE. Money you'd saved?

PETER. No, we couldn't save much. I wasn't earning enough. Grandfather had this money he'd saved, and then last June he died. And he left the money to us—mother and me.

JANE. Was it much?

PETER. Um-huh. Twenty-two thousand four hundred dollars.

JANE. How much did you invest?

PETER. Well, first I want to tell you. You see, if you just take the interest on that, why, it isn't very much to get along on. Because, of course, I wasn't getting very much. Then Mr. Madden—that's the man who owns the hotel —he heard I was getting this money, only he thought it was more,—and he was sort of tired of running the hotel, anyhow—and he said if I could pay him fifty thousand dollars he'd let me have it. It makes a lot of money.

JANE. I see.

PETER. That's when I thought, if I could take this money we had—and make more out of it, quickly—everything would be fine. So, of course, I thought of the theatrical business, because I'd been connected with it, sort of. Mother thought too it would be a good thing, and so I left fourteen hundred dollars with her, and I came to New York to look around. That was last week.

JANE. You brought twenty-one thousand with you?

PETER. Well, the bank there put it in a bank here for me. So all I had to do was give Mr Lehman a check.

JANE. For—all of it?

PETER. Oh, no. Only twenty thousand.

JANE [rises angrily. Crosses center, looking at door where LEHMAN has just left]. Oh!

PETER. What's the matter?

JANE. Nothing. [Starts right]

PETER. You're not—going, are you?

JANE [still half afire with rage at LEHMAN] Yes, I—I think I must.

PETER. Thank you very much for coming in and talking to me.

JANE [turns to him, her mind still half on LEHMAN]. I hope again that it's a big success. The play.

PETER. Oh, I feel better about that now, since you talked to me. You see, it's the first time I've talked regularly with anyone since I left home. I mean, you're the first person that's—
   [MARY MARTIN enters at right]

MARTIN. Sorry. Mr. Lehman's not here, I see

JANE. He'll be back soon, Miss Martin.

MARTIN. I'm afraid I can't wait. It's important. I told him I was coming back. [Start to go; takes hold of doorknob]

PETER. Is it— [Crosses to right of desk]—something to do with the firm?

MARTIN. How's that? [Stops at door]

PETER. I say, if it's something to do with the firm, maybe I can do it for you.

MARTIN. Oh! [Crosses to PETER center] I wonder if this is the young man Mr. Lehman spoke about? That was—coming into the company?

PETER. Yes, ma'am.

MARTIN. Oh—then of course you can do it [Dismisses JANE with a look. JANE starts to go]

PETER. You needn't go, Miss Weston.

JANE [opens door]. I will, if you don't mind [Exits right]

MARTIN [crossing to PETER]. I don't believe Mr. Lehman mentioned your name.

PETER. Jones, Peter Jones.

MARTIN. I'm Mary Martin, Mr. Jones. [She puts her hand out and he takes it] I'm with the show.

PETER. Really? Our show?

MARTIN. Yes. So you and I will probably see a good deal of each other.

PETER. We will, huh?

MARTIN. Oh, indeed, yes.

PETER [pauses, embarrassed]. Which one are you? In the show— [Let go of hands] I mean

MARTIN. Oh, the lead.

PETER. The what?

MARTIN. The leading part.

PETER. Oh, yes, that's a great rôle. I mean she gets in a lot of trouble.

MARTIN. I hope you're coming to rehearsal

soon, Mr. Jones. I'm sure we will want to get your ideas.

PETER. My ideas?

MARTIN. Of course. I do particularly.

PETER. Oh, I don't know that I'd be much good at—

MARTIN. You'd be wonderful. [*Looks at him*] And I can tell.

PETER. Oh, I did make a few productions out in Chillicothe.

MARTIN [*flatters him*]. There, you see! I knew the minute I saw you. Now I want you to promise you'll come to rehearsals and that whenever you have any suggestions for me you'll tell me.

PETER. All right.

MARTIN [*crosses to center*]. I can't tell you how relieved I am that you've come in to take charge of things.

PETER. Oh, I'm not going to take charge.

MARTIN. Oh, yes, you will. [*Snaps fingers as if remembering something*] I knew there was something, Mr. Jones. [*Crosses to* PETER] I wonder if you'd do me a very great favor?

PETER. Yes, ma'am.

MARTIN. I don't like to trouble you, but I left my checkbook at home this morning. And just now I saw the darlingest frock and they won't *hold* it. [*Puts on air*]

PETER. Why—that's all right. [*Sits right of desk; starts to write check*]

MARTIN. That's lovely of you. I hate to *bother* you. It will be taken out of my salary. Just a hundred. [*Looking over his shoulder*]

PETER. Just a hundred. [*Starts to write a check*]

MARTIN. Just make it to cash. I think it's wonderful, your coming in with us, Mr. Jones. It makes everything seem so different. [*After he finishes and tears check out*] Oh, that's just fine. [*He rises and blots check on desk pad*] I'm ever so much obliged. [*Takes check*] Thank you.

PETER. You're welcome.

MARTIN. Now, don't forget. You're coming to rehearsals. And you're going to tell me just what you think.

PETER. There was something—when they were— Oh—I was thinking, a little while ago —that is, if you're sure you don't mind?

MARTIN. Mind? I'm crazy for suggestions. [*Backing away from him to right center*]

[*WARN Curtain*]

PETER. You know that part where you're in —that place?

MARTIN. Place? I'm not sure just which scene—

PETER. You know. The place—that you go to—?

MARTIN. You don't mean the Heaven scene?

PETER. No, ma'am. Just before the Heaven scene.

MARTIN. Oh, the brothel.

PETER. Yeh. [*Coming center*] That's the place. That's where, if I were you, I'd really do some of my best acting—where you bring in the strong talk— "You priests and missionaries are no better than a lot of rabbis—"

MARTIN. Oh, yes—indeed I will, Mr. Jones. [*Puts check in purse*] And thank you.

PETER. You're welcome. I'll come to rehearsals myself tomorrow.

MARTIN. I can go out this way, can't I? [*Starts up center*]

PETER. Yes, ma'am. [*Opens door center*]

MARTIN. It's been a great pleasure, Mr. Jones.

PETER. It has been for me, too.

MARTIN [*they shake hands*]. Something tells me we're going to be very good friends. Because I know you'll produce other plays, too, won't you?

PETER. I don't know.

MARTIN. Of course you will—a man like you.

PETER. Well, maybe a couple.

MARTIN. And now, good-bye until tomorrow. And I want to tell you what a pleasure it is to be under your management. Good-bye. [*Exits to right*]

PETER. Good-bye.

[*As he stands in door looking after her he puts left hand to head in a nervous manner, as if he had just passed through a great strain. He looks at name on the outside of the door, closes door, looks at name on door inside; satisfied, looks about room, feels desk, crosses down, looks at route sheet, sits in chair, tries it, then forgets and leans back and chair goes back with him, giving him a start; pulls chair closer, puts on hat, puts feet on desk, then tips hat forward over eyes*]

CURTAIN

ACT TWO

SCENE I

A hotel room in Syracuse, shortly before the curtain rings up on "Her Lesson." It is in all respects a typical hotel room, from the heavy maroon hangings on the windows to the picture of the signing of the Declaration of Independence on the wall. There is but a single door, set in an alcove up left, and when it swings wide enough you can read the room number, 726. Across the outside hall the edge of another door is barely visible.

The room is our hero's, of course. Being the gentleman who made the production possible, he has been favored with ample quarters. At the right are two windows, and between them a dresser. Set in the rear wall, toward the right, is a clothes closet; adjoining it on the left is a chiffonier, and then comes the inevitable bed, set at right angles to the footlights. There is a writing-table against the wall at left; there are two or three small chairs and one more comfortable.

It is evening—eight o'clock or thereabouts.

PETER *discovered in evening dress, tie around collar but not tied. Dress coat hanging on hall tree up right center. He has dress vest on. He is standing down right center, and as the curtain rises crosses hurriedly up stage to closet up right center and hangs up top coat which he has already on a hanger to save time. Comes out of closet and shuts door; starts for dresser right.*

LEHMAN *knocks off up left.*

PETER. Come in! [PETER *starts to tie tie at dresser*]

LEHMAN [*enters up left. Same clothes as Act I*]. How are you, Sweetheart? [*Crosses down left center*]

PETER. Oh, hello. [*Turns, then crosses to* LEHMAN] I was looking for you.

LEHMAN [*noticing dress clothes*]. Say!

PETER. Aren't the—rest of them doing it? [*Crosses right center*]

LEHMAN [*crosses to foot of bed*]. That don't make no difference. How's the kid? [*Sits at foot of bed*]

PETER. I thought—being an opening—

LEHMAN. Sure! And it's going to be some opening. The biggest Syracuse has ever seen.

PETER [*crosses to* LEHMAN *at foot of bed*]. Well, then look. What I wanted to say was—if a lot of people come to see it this week—and they will, won't they?

LEHMAN. We'll be turning 'em away.

PETER. Then would it be possible for you, before we leave here, to let me have a little money back? Just some of the profits?

LEHMAN [*rises from bed*]. I'll tell you, Sweetheart, this is sort of an expensive show, see? We might be out on the road a couple of weeks before we really start cleaning up. Big, I mean.

PETER. You won't—have any money here?

LEHMAN. Not to split up. But don't you worry none about your coin. If this show ain't a hit, I'll eat it.

PETER. Well, as long as I get some pretty soon— [*Starts right for dresser and has hold of tie as if to tie it*]

LEHMAN. Sure you will. [*Looks at watch*] Ready? Pretty near curtain— [*Crosses left*] time.

PETER. Why—just about. [*Crosses back to* LEHMAN] I don't suppose you could tie a bow tie, could you, Mr. Lehman?

LEHMAN [*comes back to center*]. Afraid not.

PETER. Well, I'll try it again. [*Crosses to dresser right and starts to tie tie again*]

MAC [*enters up left*]. Are you coming? How are you, Mr. Jones? [*Crosses to* LEHMAN *down center*]

PETER. Oh, hello. [*Looks around to* MAC]

LEHMAN. What room's Weston in?

MAC. Down the way. You want her?

LEHMAN. Yeh. And tell Fanny I'm here in twenty-six.

MAC. O.K. [*Exits up left to left hurriedly*]

LEHMAN [*looks around room*]. Oh—er—the reason I come in, Sweetheart—you got such a nice big room, I thought mayb: you wouldn't mind if we was to get together up here after the show.

PETER [*faces* LEHMAN *but stands at dresser, still holding ends of tie*]. Tonight?

LEHMAN. Sure.

PETER. You mean—to celebrate? [*Lets go of tie*]

LEHMAN. Well—sort of talk things over. There might be some changes or something.

PETER. Changes— [*Crosses right center toward* LEHMAN] in the play?

LEHMAN. In case there is any.

PETER. Isn't it all right?

LEHMAN. Great. But there might be something, see? Just a line.

PETER. Oh!

LEHMAN. I and the wife is cooped up in twenty-eight, next door—but this is good and big so we can all get in.

PETER. All who?

LEHMAN. Well—whoever comes. You see, after a show's opened you always have a sort of conference—talk it over.

PETER. You mean for me to be here too, don't you?

LEHMAN. Sure. We'll want to know what everybody *thinks*, see? [*A couple of steps to* PETER] I'll tell you—you take a wad of paper at the show tonight and put down anything you see that's wrong.

PETER. Anything about the play?

LEHMAN. Play, acting, scenery, anything. Make a note of it—then we'll talk it over.

PETER. What I thought you did after a play has opened is—sort of have a supper, and celebrate.

LEHMAN. We can do that, too. Great.

PETER. I'd like that. Miss Weston could come couldn't she?

LEHMAN. Sure. You invite her. [*Crosses to left center*]

PETER [*crosses to* LEHMAN]. And don't they usually— Do you think they'd let us have some champagne? If I asked them.

LEHMAN. I'll introduce you to the manager. Only look out for him—he's show-crazy.

PETER. He's what?

LEHMAN. Show-crazy. Off his nut about show business.

PETER. Why?

LEHMAN [*starts for door upper left*]. Are you coming?

JANE [*enters up left.* PETER *sees* JANE, *crosses up to hat tree quickly and puts on dress coat*]. Yes, Mr. Lehman? [*Down to* LEHMAN *left center*]

LEHMAN. Oh! I want you right beside me during the play, see? Take notes as I dictate 'em. We're going right over. [MAC *crosses past door, going from right to left in hall*] Mac— [*Exits up left*]

JANE [*at upper left*]. Very well. [*Turns to go*]

PETER. Oh, Miss Weston! [*At hat tree up right center*] Miss Weston.

JANE. Hello.

PETER [*crosses to right center*]. Would you come to a sort of party tonight, here in this room, to celebrate the success of the show? There'll be other people here.

JANE. Why—of course. I'd be delighted. [*Starts out*]

PETER. Please don't go yet. I haven't seen you for a long time, to talk to at all. I almost thought you—didn't want to talk to me.

JANE. Why shouldn't I want to talk to you? [*Hold up by door*]

PETER. Won't you, for a minute now, then? The—door's open—that makes it all right.

JANE [*looks toward door*]. I think Mr. Lehman wants me soon.

PETER. He'll call for you again— [JANE *comes down to foot of bed*] You haven't said anything to me about the play, and it's the opening night. I'm a producer. [*Crosses to foot of bed right*]

JANE. I wish you the best of luck.

PETER. Thanks.

JANE. I can't bear to think of its being anything but a—great success.

PETER. Neither can I. It's bound to be, don't you think?

JANE. Well—remember, if it isn't just perfect tonight, it can probably be fixed.

PETER. I'm going to take notes of whatever's wrong.

JANE. That's right.

PETER [*crosses up to her*]. Look—I didn't want to ask Mr. Lehman about this, but you don't think there's any chance of—my having to make a speech, do you—tonight?

JANE. I—don't—think so.

PETER. I didn't really think there was, but—just in case it should happen—that was the reason I wore this. One of the reasons. [*Indicates dress suit*]

JANE. I see.

PETER. Oh, look! [*Notices tie still undone*] Can you tie a bow tie?

JANE [*crosses to him at foot of bed*]. Why, yes— [*Does so*]

PETER. You see, at home my mother always did it for me when I wore it. I only wore it once. They gave a big dance at the hotel. We had it all fixed up— Oh, it was beautiful—

JANE. There! [*Finishes tie*]

PETER. Is it finished? Thanks. [*Looks at her*] Oh—wait a minute. [*Gets roses in box from closet upper right*] I got these for you for tonight on account of the opening.

JANE. Oh! Why—that was lovely of you. [*She takes box*]

PETER [*points to box as he steps back a few steps*]. They're flowers.

JANE [*puts box on bed; takes off cover*]. They're beautiful. [*She takes them in her arms and faces* PETER] You shouldn't have done that.

PETER. Well, on account of the opening, and besides—I wanted to. You know, you look awfully lovely with them—I mean—the way you're standing there—and the way— Gosh! [JANE *puts flowers in box on bed with a sudden gesture*] What's the matter?

JANE. I'm the last person—that you should give flowers to.

PETER. Last—why, you're the first. You're the only one I want to give any to—the only one I ever wanted to give any to. That's— the truth.

JANE. I can't let you say those things.

PETER [*a few steps to her*]. But I can't help it. And I've got to say something more. I— I've just got to. I want to know whether— some day—you think you could ever—marry a theatrical producer?

JANE. Please—

PETER. I don't mean just a producer with forty-nine percent of one show—but there'll come a time when I'll have my own theatre— and—

JANE. Peter, don't! You're going to hate me! Just—hate me!

[*WARN Curtain*]

PETER. Not much. I'm going—to love you. I do now, Jane. That's what I've been trying to get at—

JANE. Please—

PETER. Only I guess—I know it's kind of nervy of me, but—

LEHMAN [*enter up left from left*]. How about you in there? Ready? [MAC *enters up left after* LEHMAN *from left*]

PETER. I'll get my things. [*Starts for closet up right*]

JANE. I'll be at the theatre. [*Starts for door up left*]

PETER [*stops*]. Aren't you going with us?

JANE. I've some things—to attend to—if you don't mind. [*Exits up left*]

PETER. Well, I'll see you over there. [*En-*

ters closet for cane, silk hat and top coat]
LEHMAN. Ready?

PETER. Yes, sir. [*Comes out of closet with top coat over left arm, cane in left hand, silk hat in right hand*] Well, here we go.

LEHMAN. Right! And it's going to be a big night! Come along! [*Starts left*]

PETER. Shouldn't we wish each other—good luck, or something?

LEHMAM [*stops*]. Why, of course. [*Crosses to* PETER, *and shakes hands*] Good luck, Mr. Jones!

PETER. Good luck to you! [LEHMAN *crosses left*]

MAC [*at right center crosses to* PETER]. Good luck! [*Shakes hands with* PETER]

PETER. Good luck to you, Mr. McClure!

LEHMAN [*at left*]. A whale of a hit, Sweetheart! That's what we're going to have—a whale of a hit!

MAC. You bet we are! [*Slaps* PETER *on back*] Aren't we?

PETER. Yes, sir! A whale of a hit! [*Puts on silk hat*] Sweetheart. [*Swings cane and starts out*]

[*As he takes about two steps, ring Curtain.* LEHMAN *starts out first, followed by* MAC, *then* PETER]

CURTAIN

ACT TWO

Scene II

Curtain down only a few seconds, providing for the lapse of several hours. When it rises the room is in near darkness—only a small lamp on the bed table is lighted. Immediately the sound of a key is heard in the door. The door opens, and for a second the figure of PETER, *stick, high hat and all, is silhouetted against the brightly lighted hallway. He presses the lights on; leaves the door open behind him and comes into the room, whistling gaily. Still whistling, he hangs up his coat.* LEHMAN, *a disconsolate figure with hands in pockets and eyes on the floor, comes slowly into the room. He is followed, at a respectful distance, by* MAC—*a much repressed* MAC. LEHMAN *drops onto the bed, with a sigh, and* MAC *slumps into the chair at the writing table.* PETER *is vastly puzzled. He regards them for a second, then finally gets up courage to ask* LEHMAN *a question.*

PETER. Is something the matter? I thought it was all right. Except—here and there, maybe.

LEHMAN [*rises, crosses to chair right*]. Oh— [*Sits*]

PETER. Isn't it any good at all?

FANNY [*enters up left, clears throat, crosses to center and plants herself*]. First—

LEHMAN [*rises*]. Now, one thing we ain't going to have none of is wisecracks. They can't nobody tell me we ain't got a great show—when it's fixed. [WAITER *starts to enter off left in hall*] Just because this bunch tonight give us the raspberry don't prove nothing. Syracuse is the bummest show town in the world.

WAITER [*arrives down left center with tray on left shoulder, six wine glasses, three knives, three forks, three plates, service table in right hand*] Is this where the party's going to be? [*Looking at* FANNY]

FANNY [*crosses to foot of bed*]. Party is right.

PETER [*turns to* WAITER]. If you'll just bring the things—

WAITER. Yes, sir. [*Crosses up right center and puts tray on serving table*]

PETER [*turns back to* LEHMAN]. It's just a little thing, isn't it—the matter? I mean, the play's a success?

WAITER [*crosses down to* PETER *at his left*]. Mr. Fritchie says he'll be up later to see if everything is all right.

PETER. What?

WAITER. Mr. Fritchie, the assistant manager. He says—

LEHMAN. Never mind.

WAITER [*looks at* LEHMAN]. Yes, sir. [*Exits up left to left*]

LEHMAN. All I need is that nut.

FANNY [*sarcastic apology*]. May I ask a question? [*At center*]

LEHMAN. Go easy with me.

FANNY. Are you going to put anything in that five-minute spot where Martin couldn't think of the next line?

PETER [*at right*]. Oh, yes. I noticed that.

FANNY. Because if she's going to wait like that every night I figure it'd be a great place for a specialty. I could come on with the clubs— [*Crosses up center to chiffonier*]

LEHMAN. I know you don't like her. Now lay off! Did you tell that ham Director we was meeting here?

MAC. Be here any minute.

LEHMAN. How about Bernie—is he ever coming?

MAC. I give him the room.

LEHMAN. And where's Weston with them notes? I don't get no co-operation.

MAC. I'll get her. [*Crosses up left*]

PETER. Here are my notes, Mr. Lehman, if— [*At right*]

LEHMAN. Better give Bernie a ring—get him up here.

MAC. Right. [*Exits up left off to right*]

LEHMAN. Was he at the show? I didn't see him.

FANNY. I saw him. [*Up center*]

LEHMAN. What did he say? [*She starts to speak*] Don't tell me.

PETER. Mr. Lehman,— [*Crosses down to him at* LEHMAN's *left*] here are the notes that I put down, if—

LEHMAN. What?—Oh—

JANE [*enters up left from right with notes and Mss. and notebook, pencil*]. Did you want me, Mr. Lehman?

[MAC *re-enters up left from right to 'phone*]

LEHMAN [*takes off coat and throws it on foot of bed*]. Give me them notes. And bring that table over here to the light. [*Indicates writing-table against wall left*]

PETER. Wait a minute. I'll get it. [*Does so*]

MAC. Kitty, give me four thirteen. [*Short pause*] How'd you like the show? [*This to the 'phone operator*]

PETER [*to* JANE]. How'd you like it? [*As he carries table*]

[WAITER *enters up left with two bottles of wine in two coolers, places one on each side of serving-table*]

LEHMAN. Hey—hey—

[*Sets table right with enough room for a chair between the right of table and* FANNY's *chair, which is also right. As* PETER *gets table placed at right,* LEHMAN *puts chair he has just taken from right corner and puts it above table.* PETER *sees this chair and takes it and puts it right of table for* JANE *and she sits.* LEHMAN *gives* PETER *a look.* PETER *crosses to left again and gets the other chair for* LEHMAN; *he sits*]

MAC [*on the 'phone*]. Well, I wouldn't go as far as that. [*This speech is read through the above business*] Of course we've got a little work ahead. You got to make allowances for it being an opening. By the time it reaches the big burg we'll have it clicking all along the line.

LEHMAN [*to* JANE]. Now—you take down anything that—[PETER *comes down to* JANE] comes up, see? [*To* PETER] Let her alone.

[WAITER *has arranged glasses on tray*]

FANNY [*picks up wine bottle at left of serving-table*]. Well, now, who did all this?

PETER. Huh? [*Crosses up right center*] Oh, it's to celebrate the success of the show. It's champagne.

FANNY [*to* PETER]. Do they open?

PETER. Yes, ma'm.

FANNY. Soon?

PETER. Oh, excuse me. Ah—waiter—open some champagne.

WAITER [FANNY *hands* WAITER *bottle*]. Yes, sir. [*Opens bottle. Fills glass nearest* FANNY *first*]

MAC [*in 'phone*]. Bernie?—Mac—

LEHMAN. Tell him to hurry up.

MAC. We're getting together up here in seven twenty-six, whenever you're ready—O. K. [*Hangs up. Crosses down left*]

[WAITER *fills two other glasses with wine*]

FANNY. I don't like to seem in a hurry, but you see, I saw all three acts. [*Picks up glass of wine*]

[WAITER *gives her a look as he finishes pouring third glass*]

LEHMAN [*to* JANE]. Where's all them second-act notes? Lose 'em?

[WAITER *puts bottle under serving-table in cooler left, cork out*]

JANE. No, sir. They're right here.

LEHMAN. Oh!

PETER [*crosses down right to* JANE]. Will anyone else—have some champagne? Miss Weston?

[WAITER *takes cork out of second bottle, right of serving-table, but leaves it in cooler*]

JANE. No, thank you.

LEHMAN [*to* FANNY]. You're beginning that, huh? Is that— [WAITER *starts left*]—Director coming or ain't he? And where's Bernie?

MAC. They'll be along.

WAITER [*stops left center. To* PETER]. Mr. Fritchie says—how soon do you want the food served?

PETER [*crosses to* WAITER, *left center*]. Oh, yes. Do you want the food served right away? Chicken a la King.

LEHMAN. I don't care. Only keep that nut Fritchie away from here.

WAITER [PETER *starts to speak*]. Yes, sir. [*Exits up left off to left*]

FANNY [*toast*]. To Mary, Queen of Stage Waits. [*Takes wine bottle in left hand and glass of wine in right, crosses to big chair at right; chair has arms wide enough to put glasses of wine on*]

LEHMAN [*at center*]. Will you shut that door—? Now where is everybody? I don't get no co-operation, that's the trouble. I pay a director three hundred a week—where is he? I bring Bernie Sampson up from New York—where is he?

PETER [*down to* LEHMAN]. Three hundred dollars, did you give him?

[BENHAM *knocks door up left*]

LEHMAN [FANNY *pours drink, standing in front of chair*]. Answer that, will you?

PETER. Who—me? [*Starts up.* FANNY *sits down right in chair*]

LEHMAN [*at right center, crosses to table, bends over papers*]. If you don't mind. [PETER *opens the door.* CECIL BENHAM *enters*] Thank God! What the hell happened to that scenery?

BENHAM [*a calm, reserved and dignified Englishman, who is even able to wear a monocle without suggesting musical comedy. Coming down left center, hat in hand*] I beg your pardon?

LEHMAN. I said, what happened to the scenery? It was crooked—all through the show.

PETER [*at left center*]. I got a note of that.

BENHAM. My dear Mr. Lehman, I was hardly in position to prevent that.

LEHMAN. You're the director, ain't you?

BENHAM. Permit me to point out that not even a director can be everywhere. You may not realize it, but I was holding book all evening.

PETER [*to* MAC *at left*]. What was he holding?

[MAC *explains by pantomime*]

LEHMAN. Oh! Well, if you were holding book, where were you during that stage wait of Martin's in the second act? Couldn't you throw her the line?

BENHAM. I gave Miss Martin the line four times. She seemed to be nervous.

PETER [*crosses to center, between* BENHAM *and* LEHMAN]. She wasn't feeling well.

LEHMAN. What?

PETER. I say, she told me she wasn't feeling well.

LEHMAN. When did you see her?

PETER. In her dressing-room between the acts. I was giving her some notes.

LEHMAN. *You* were?

PETER. Yes, sir.

LEHMAN. Well, for the— [*A knock on the door upper left.* LEHMAN *controls himself*] Answer that, will you? [PETER *goes up.* BENHAM *crosses up and sits on left of bed*] If that's Bernie, we can get at this.

[PETER *opens door.* BERNIE *enters up left, straw hat on, street suit*]

MAC. It's Bernie.

[PEGGY *enters up left after* BERNIE *and at his left, cigarette in holder*]

BERNIE [BERNIE SAMPSON *is a slightly Semitic young man with that air of sophistication about him that can be acquired only through long service on Broadway.* PEGGY MARLOWE *is a smartly dressed and ever so good-looking chorus girl*] Hello, people. Hello, Joe.

LEHMAN. Hello!

BERNIE. How are you, Mackie?

MAC. Hello!

BERNIE. Come on, baby. I just happened to have a young lady with me.

[BENHAM *rises, leaves hat on bed, stands by bed*]

MAC. That's all right.

[LEHMAN *sits at table right center*]

BERNIE [*at foot of bed*]. This is Miss Marlowe, folks.

PEGGY [*right of* MAC, *down left*]. How are you? [*Nods, blowing out cloud of smoke*]

MAC [PETER *comes down left*]. Let's see. This is Mrs. Lehman—Mr. Lehman—Mr. Benham— [BENHAM *up left center*] and Mr. Jones.

[PETER *at left*]

FANNY [*on* "Mrs. Lehman"]. Hi—

PEGGY [*looks coldly about room*]. Aren't there any chairs in this dump? [*Starts to walk slowly to right of bed*]

BERNIE [BENHAM *crosses up by suitcase left*]. Sit on the bed. [*He tosses hat on bed*]

PEGGY. Sit on it yourself. [*Crosses to right of bed, takes off coat and tosses it on center of bed*]

PETER. I'm sorry—there don't seem to be any more chairs. Maybe—

MAC. Mr. Jones, will you run into my room and get some—twenty-two—the door's open.

[PEGGY *walks slowly to serving-table up right center*]

PETER. Well—don't decide anything 'til I come back. [*Exits up left off left*]

PEGGY. Well, if it isn't my old friend, liquor. [*Picks up glass of wine and drinks, and holds position*]

LEHMAN [BENHAM *crosses to left corner of bed*]. Now, Bernie, I want you to tell us just what you think of it. [PEGGY *takes off hat, looks in mirror right, but holds her position by tray.* LEHMAN *to* BENHAM, *who is at foot of bed*] Mr. Sampson here came up from New York to see the show, and maybe do some work if it needs it.

BENHAM. Is that so?

[PEGGY *picks up knife and fork from serving-table up right center*]

LEHMAN. Now, we're all going to give our frank opinions, see?

FANNY [*starts to rise*]. Well—

LEHMAN. That's enough! [*Puts hand up to* FANNY] Bernie, you're first. [BENHAM *crosses over left.* To JANE] Take this down.

[PEGGY *starts down to right of* BERNIE]

PEGGY [*holds up knife and fork*]. Does anything go with these? [*To* BERNIE]

LEHMAN. Shut up! Oh—I thought it was Fanny. [PEGGY *turns quickly to* LEHMAN, *then away to the tray, and then sits on bed*] All right, Bernie.

BERNIE [*at center foot of bed*]. Well, I'll tell you—

PETER [*enters up left with two chairs from left*]. Was anything decided?

LEHMAN. Will you shut that door, please? [PETER *puts chairs down left center, crosses up, shuts door up left.* MAC *takes chair, sits astride it at left.* BENHAM *takes the other, sits and smokes cigarette on* MAC's *right. Chairs close together*] Bernie! Go ahead!

BERNIE [*at center*]. Well, of course there

ain't no doubt but what it needs some work.
Now, when I catch a show I don't look at the
show so much. I look at the audience. They'll
tell you every time. Now, your prologue is
great. [MAC *and* PETER *pleased*] It's a great
idea—him reading the play. And it held 'em.
It's a novelty. But after that they begun to
slip away from you.
PETER [*to* BERNIE]. I'd like to talk to you
about that. [*Crosses to* BERNIE *at center*]
BERNIE. Who's the kid? [*Turns to* PETER]
LEHMAN. If you don't mind, Mr. Jones.
PETER. Well, I just wanted to talk to him—
LEHMAN. All right! Go on, Bernie!
[PETER *crosses back of* BERNIE *to right of*
BERNIE, *up right center*]
BERNIE. Well, I'll tell you. Some of them
scenes—they don't click. [*He snaps his fingers*]
Now I got a scene,— [PEGGY *crosses to left of*
PETER] that I done in a show called—ah—
PEGGY. Hello, Cutie— [*At* PETER's *left*]
PETER. Hello.
BERNIE [*to* PEGGY *and* PETER]. Say, what's
going on here?
PEGGY. Mind your business.
LEHMAN. Bernie, can't you get rid of her
somehow?
PEGGY. Let him try! What I got on him!
[BERNIE *nervous business.* PEGGY *turns and
looks at* PETER]
LEHMAN. Are we going to get anything done
here, or ain't we?
FANNY. I vote "no." [*Pours wine*]
LEHMAN. Go ahead, Bernie—you was say-
ing?
BERNIE. Well—if this kid's going to butt in.
[*Eyes* PETER]
PETER. I was just listening. [FANNY *drinks*]
LEHMAN. Oh—go on, Bernie.
[PEGGY *sits on right of bed*]
BERNIE. Where was I?
LEHMAN. You was saying you got a scene.
BERNIE. Oh, yah. You got to put something
in the place of that cabaret scene. Of course,
it may be the way it was put on. I don't know
who done it for you, but of all the lousy di-
recting—
BENHAM [*rises, crosses to* BERNIE]. I beg
your pardon, Mr. Jackson.
MAC [*to* BENHAM]. Now, that's all right.
BERNIE [MAC *stands between the two
center*]. Bernie Sampson is my name.
BENHAM. It's quite possible that you don't
know who I *am*.
BERNIE. That's only part of it.
BENHAM. I was associated for ten years
with Sir John Hare, and I've been with Sir
Charles Wyndham and Sir Beerbohm Tree.
FANNY [*looks at* BENHAM]. And where are
they now?
BENHAM. I am not accustomed to having

my direction described by that adjective.
[FANNY *drinks*]
BERNIE. Listen, I come up from New York
as a favor to Joe here—
BENHAM. Nevertheless, I must insist—
LEHMAN. Now don't let's get scrapping.
BENHAM. But if he's to be permitted—
MAC [*between* BERNIE *and* BENHAM]. Now,
there's no use flying off the handle— [*Holds*
BENHAM *back*]
BENHAM. Yes, but—but—
MAC. He didn't mean anything. [*Pushing*
BENHAM *in chair left*]
BENHAM. Well—I— [*Sits*]
MAC. That's the stuff.
PEGGY. Is that going to be all?
BERNIE. Now, baby—
PEGGY. Well—call me if it gets good. [*Lies
on bed*]
LEHMAN. Go on, Bernie.
BERNIE [*a nod of head toward* BENHAM].
What's this guy so touchy about?
BENHAM [*starts to rise.* MAC *lays a restrain-
ing hand on his shoulder*]. Well—
LEHMAN [*to* BERNIE]. Never mind, Bernie!
What's this scene you got?
BERNIE. Well, I'll tell you. It'll drop right in
where your cabaret is, see? It was a wow
scene, but the show never come to New York,
so it'll be new. There's never been anything
like it. It was a hop joint in Hongkong.
BENHAM [*with great dignity*]. It would not
possibly do.
LEHMAN. We got to stick to the story,
Bernie. We can't throw away the whole play.
FANNY. Why not? [*Drinks at end of laugh*]
[BERNIE *crosses up right center between
bed and serving-table*]
LEHMAN. Now, I'll tell you. Suppose we
start at the beginning—
[FANNY *puts glass on arm of chair.* MARTIN
knocks at door up left. PETER *crosses
left to door*]
LEHMAN. Who's this?
FANNY. Oh—you can't tell.
[PETER *opens door.* MARTIN *enters up left,
walks down left center as* FANNY *applauds. Stops and gives* FANNY *a dirty
look.* FANNY *applauds and rests head on
hand*]
MARTIN [*at center*]. Now, before anything
is said—that stage wait was not my fault.
LEHMAN. All right, all right. [PETER *crosses
to right of bed again*]
MARTIN. Maxwell gave me the wrong cue—
a cue out of the third act. So, of course, I had
to stop and think.
FANNY [*rises a little and leans on arm of
chair*]. Well, you certainly had a lovely evening for it.
MARTIN [*turns to* BENHAM *at left*]. And

then—you'd think there'd be someone in the wings to throw me a line. But no.

BENHAM. That's not true, [*Rises*] Miss Martin. I gave you the line distinctly.

MARTIN [*angry*]. Well, I certainly didn't hear it. [*Crosses to* BENHAM]

PEGGY [*sitting up*]. Oh, goody, a scrap— [*Then sits up on bed*]

LEHMAN. Now, stop—

MARTIN [PETER *gets up right center, above* LEHMAN, *right of* MARTIN]. Besides—I've had a raging headache all day. And if you think it's easy to give a performance of a *star* part, with people coming back into your dressing-room all the time—[*She eyes* PETER] trying to tell you what to do—

[ALL *eye* PETER *and he backs away a couple of steps*]

PETER. You said if I had any suggestions—

[FANNY *nearly finishes glass of wine*]

MARTIN. Well, really, Mr. Jones—I've been in the profession longer than you have.

FANNY [*drops arm and glass over right arm of chair, holds glass*]. And that's no fairy tale.

MARTIN [BERNIE *takes* PEGGY'S *cigarette and puts ashtray on chiffonier.* BENHAM *sits in same chair again.* MARTIN *is angry*]. I beg your pardon!

[MAC *crosses up and puts cigarette on 'phone table*]

LEHMAN [*rises*]. Oh, stop it—you two! Sit down, Mary. [MARTIN *takes chair left and turns back on* BENHAM *and* BENHAM *does the same*] Now— [*Looks at papers*] We're going to begin at the beginning and go right through the show.

MAC [*crosses down left center*]. Joe—do you want some good, straight dope? A fresh viewpoint?

LEHMAN. Who?

MAC. There's a little girl down on the switchboard, smart as a steel trap. She sees everything that comes here, and I slipped her a couple tonight. Now—

LEHMAN. Good idea. Get her up. Anybody but that nut Fritchie. [*Sits at table right center*]

MAC. Right!

PEGGY. Did he say on the switchboard? [*Crosses down right center of* LEHMAN]

[MAC *talks pantomime at 'phone*]

BERNIE. Now, baby—

PEGGY. Is there more than one operator in this hotel?

BERNIE. Never mind.

PEGGY. Because I just had a run-in with one of them and I'd like to know.

LEHMAN. Bernie—can't you get this dame to sit down or something?

BERNIE. Some other time, baby—

PEGGY. Well—just in case she *is* the one,

I'll take another drink. [PETER *hands her glass; she takes drink*]

MAC [*during last seven lines, above, but sotto voce*]. Kitty? This is Mr. McClure—Jack. Can you leave there for a minute and come to seven twenty-six? I'll tell you when you get here— That's right. Thanks. [*Hangs up on* PEGGY'S *word "drink."* BERNIE *gets* PEGGY *to sit on bed*]

LEHMAN. Now—please. We ain't going to have no more interruptions. [*Looks at* FANNY] We're going to take up the scenes as they come along. Now—we're set on the prologue.

BERNIE. Right. }
MAC. O. K.   } [*Together*]

LEHMAN. How about you, Benham—prologue O. K.?

BENHAM [*angry*]. Oh, I am quite satisfied. [*Turns chair left*]

LEHMAN. Well, don't get sore about it. Make a note—Prologue O. K.

PETER [*up right center*]. O. K. [ALL *look at him*]

MARTIN [*in chair left*]. May I say something?

LEHMAN [*to* MARTIN]. What is it?

MARTIN [*rises; crosses to center*]. The trouble with your play is that the leading character doesn't have sympathy. I'm fighting the audience all the time. I feel it. They don't like me.

FANNY [*rises slowly*]. Well, I think you were fine. I really do. [*Sits slowly*] That'll give you a rough idea of *my* condition. [*Settles self in chair*]

MARTIN [*furious tapping of toe, trying to control herself*]. Really, Mr. Lehman, if I'm to be required—

LEHMAN. Shut up, Fanny! [*To* MARTIN] What is it?

MARTIN [*a little left of bed*]. I'm *trying* to tell you that I'm not getting sympathy. Something ought to be put in to show that I'm really all right at heart.

PEGGY [*on lower end of bed*]. How about giving out pamphlets?

BERNIE. Hey! Baby!

MARTIN [*a glare at* PEGGY, *then turns to* LEHMAN *again*]. If I could have a scene early in the play that would show me in a more sympathetic light—say a scene with a baby.

LEHMAN. We'll come back to it. [*To* JANE] Make a note. Sympathy for Miss Martin.

PETER. If it's early in the play, Mr. Lehman, it can't be a baby, because she isn't married then.

LEHMAN. All right. [*Loud knock by* WAITER *off upper left*] All right. See who that is. [PETER *goes up*] Now we're going ahead from the prologue.

[PETER *opens the door. The* WAITER *enters*

with food, crossing around bed to up right center]

PEGGY [*as* WAITER *passes bed*]. Ah! The troops!

BERNIE [*WAITER puts container up right and passes sandwich to* PEGGY; *she is the only one he passes any to; puts tray on chiffonier*] Sssh!

LEHMAN [*with emphasis, rises*]. We are going ahead from the prologue. The next is the orchard scene.

PETER [*crossing to* LEHMAN]. I want to say something about that, Mr. Lehman.

LEHMAN [*at center*]. You don't tell me!

PETER. Yes, sir. I was just waiting till you reached it. You see—

LEHMAN. Would you mind letting *me* talk for a minute?

PETER. No, sir.

LEHMAN. Much obliged. [*To* JANE] Give me that stuff.

[PETER *gets over back of* LEHMAN. KITTY HUMPHREYS, *a pretty switchboard girl, enters up left from left*]

MAC [KITTY *crosses down to* MAC *on his right at left center*] Oh, here's Kitty, Joe!

LEHMAN, What? [*Sits back of table again*]

MAC. Here's Kitty from the switchboard.

LEHMAN. Oh!

MAC. Come on, Kitty.

FANNY. Now we're going to get the real lowdown. [WAITER *looks at* FANNY]

MAC. This is Miss Humphreys, everybody. Kitty, here's the angle. We want you to tell us just what you think of the show tonight, see? Straight from the shoulder. Now, you see all the shows that come here. We want to know your real opinion.

[PEGGY, *on bed, eyes* KITTY *angrily*]

KITTY. Well, I'll tell you, Jack—er—Mr. McClure. You see, Syracuse is a funny town.

FANNY. Oh, *that's* it?

KITTY [*to the people on her right*]. It's a hard town to please, sort of—because you see we get *all* the new shows. The managers all bring their shows here, because they know if it goes *here*, it'll go *any* place. You see, the people here are funny, sort of. If they *like* a show they'll *go* to it, but if they don't like it—they *won't*.

LEHMAN. Well, that's a hot lot of news.

WAITER [*crosses to left of* LEHMAN] Excuse me. I can tell you what's wrong with your show. I wasn't there, but the chambermaid on Number four—

LEHMAN [*rises and yells*]. Mac—Mac—

[PEGGY *rises and crosses to tray up right center*]

MAC. Just a minute. We want this young lady to—

(WAITER *looks at* MAC).

WAITER. Oh, I beg your pardon. [*Back up center a few steps.* PEGGY *crosses to center*]

KITTY. Well—

PEGGY [*crosses center to direct front of* KITTY]. Are you the operator that took— z

BERNIE [*gets off of bed, crosses to* PEGGY *at her right*]. Baby—

PEGGY. A New York call out of four thirteen this evening?

BERNIE. Now, baby—

PEGGY. Are you?

KITTY. I may have been.

BERNIE. Now don't—

MAC. Now— } [*In unison*]

LEHMAN. Say—

PEGGY. You were pretty fresh, weren't you?

KITTY. I don't think so.

MAC. Kitty—

PEGGY. Well, I do—

BERNIE. Now—now—

PEGGY. And if you ever try it on me again—

LEHMAN. Get them out of here, will you?

MAC. Now listen, girls— }

PEGGY. Are you or are you not } [*In unison*] supposed to be respectful? }

BERNIE. Now, baby—

KITTY. I'm always respectful, madam, when I'm speaking to a lady.

PEGGY [*very calmly*]. I'll push your goddamn face in!

BERNIE. Baby— [*Grabs* PEGGY]

[MAC *grabs* KITTY *and swings her upstage in front of him, holding her by the arm*]

LEHMAN. Get her out, Mac. }

FANNY. Hurrah—[MAC *takes* KITTY *up left*]

KITTY [MAC *and* KITTY *stop up left*]. You know where you can find me. } [*Together*]

PEGGY [*up at head of bed on right side*]. I can guess. [KITTY *exits up left.* PEGGY *sits on bed and fixes pillow behind her back; she eyes* LEHMAN]

BERNIE. Now stop it.

LEHMAN. Stop—everybody. [*Crosses to left and back to table*] How are we going to get anything decided with all this—a-a-ah! [*Sits back of table right center*]

FANNY. I vote we make this a permanent organization and meet once a week.

LEHMAN. We're here to decide about this show.

WAITER [*crosses down to* LEHMAN *on his left*]. I was going to tell you what this chambermaid said—

LEHMAN. I don't want to know! Get out!

WAITER. Yes, sir. [*Crosses to left of bed*] Here's the check. [*Looks at* PETER]

PETER [*down, takes it, pays it*]. Gosh!

LEHMAN. Where were we?

[BERNIE *sits on bed*]

MAC. You were up to the prologue.

PETER. All right. [*Pays* WAITER]

WAITER. Much obliged. [*Exits up left*]

LEHMAN. All right. Now—the orchard scene.

PETER. The trees aren't planted right.

MAC. Take it easy, Joe.

LEHMAN. Oh, they ain't, huh?

PETER. No, sir. In a real orchard—

LEHMAN [*rises*]. Now, listen. I'm pretty near fed up—get me? You been interrupting all night—one fool idea after another—and I had all I can stand.

PETER. But—but this isn't a—fool idea. I'm right about it.

LEHMAN. All right, and I tell you I don't want to hear about it. Who's producing this show, anyhow?

PETER. Well, I'm part producer of it, and—

LEHMAN [BERNIE *rises and watches scene*] Yah? Well, I'm the main producer. Get me? And I'm going to do the talking! Forty-nine per cent—that's what you got.

PETER. Well—I didn't mean to—do anything, but—you told me to take notes, and—

LEHMAN. You're going to keep on, are you?

PETER. No, sir, but if I see something I know is wrong. An orchard isn't planted that way. The trees—

LEHMAN [*exasperated beyond control*]. Good gawd! You half-wrecked the show, prowling around back stage, and then come here and— What in blazes do you know about show business? I been all my life in it and you come green out of the country trying to tell me— *I'm* running this show—you're nothing but a butter-and-egg man. Now, keep still! [*Crosses back to table; sits*]

MAC [*pacifying*]. Now, this ain't no way—

PETER [*turns to* MAC *at center*]. What—what did he say I was?

LEHMAN. Never mind! Only I want you to butt out of this show, see? I had all I can stand, and I want you to keep out!

JANE [*rises, stands at table*]. Mr. Lehman, that isn't fair. He hasn't done half as much as the others.

[PETER *back to audience*]

LEHMAN. Oh— [*Fast and mean*] Now it's your business, is it?

JANE. I simply say you're being unfair to him. I think—I think it's an outrageous way to treat him. You take his money—all you can get —for a play you must have known was worthless—

LEHMAN [*rises*]. Oh, I did, eh! And who asked you to say anything? Huh?

JANE. I've stayed silent as long as I can.

LEHMAN. Then suppose you get the hell out of here—and you needn't come back.

PETER. Hold on, there!

JANE. Peter! }

LEHMAN. What? } [*Together*]

PETER. This is *my* room. You can't order her out.

LEHMAN. I can't, eh? [*Crosses down one step*]

PETER. No, sir. I mean *no*.

LEHMAN. I warn you to lay off me.

PETER. Well—well, I won't. You—you can't talk to her like that here—or any other place.

LEHMAN. I'll talk to her anyway I want to —and you too.

PETER. Well, you won't. Because—I won't let you. [*Crosses up to bed and down center again*]

LEHMAN. Oh! Besides running the show you're going to run me? Go on back to your sap town, whatever it was. And you can take her with you, because she's fired.

PETER. She wouldn't work for you anyhow, any longer. Do you want to know why?

LEHMAN. I'd love to.

PETER [*at center*]. Because she's going to work for me. You think I don't know anything, huh? I'm just a bread-and-butter man? [*Looks left, then to* LEHMAN] And I don't know anything about shows, huh? [*Crosses up center a little*]

LEHMAN. How'd you guess it?

PETER [*crosses to* LEHMAN]. Well, I'll show you whether I know anything about them. And I'll show you whether you can talk to people like that. Do you want to sell the rest of it— to me—the show?

[MARTIN *rises*]

JANE. Peter, you can't.

PETER [*left of* MAC]. Do you?

LEHMAN [*pauses. Crosses around* PETER *to* MAC, *left center. Pauses. To* PETER, *who is left of table right center*] I might, for a price. It's a valuable property.

PETER. How much?

LEHMAN. What do you say, Mac?

MAC. Up to you, Joe.

LEHMAN. McClure and me is in together. Give us—ten thousand apiece and the show's yours. [JANE *touches* PETER's *arm not to do it*]

PETER. I'll give you five thousand apiece.

LEHMAN. Seventy-five hundred.

PETER. Five thousand.

LEHMAN. Cash?

PETER [*takes money from pants pocket, looks down at it, not at them*] You give me— an option—'til this time tomorrow—and I'll give you—five hundred dollars for it. It's about all I have—with me.

JANE. Peter, you can't.

PETER. You're all witnesses. [*Looks up*]

LEHMAN. Five thousand apiece for the rest of the show. Ten thousand altogether.

PETER. For Lehmac Productions—all of it.

LEHMAN. And a one-day option. That goes. [*Crosses to* PETER *for money*] Give me the five hundred.

PEGGY. Thank God! That's settled.

[PETER *gives money to* LEHMAN *and he puts it in pocket. Then* LEHMAN *and* MAC *shake hands*]

PETER. You all know the arrangement.

FANNY. I'm a witness. [*Gets up, takes glass, but leaves bottle*]

LEHMAN [*picks up coat off foot of bed*]. Well, I guess that's that. [*Puts on coat, takes out cigar*]

PEGGY. Can we go now? [*Rises, putting on hat, looking in mirror at right*]

MARTIN [*sweetly. At left*]. Well, Mr. Jones—

PETER. Now, if you all wouldn't mind leaving—

PEGGY [BERNIE *helps her put coat on*]. Mind —did he say?

LEHMAN. I wish you luck and I hope you take up the option. [*Starts out, cigar in mouth*]

PETER. I'll take it up.

LEHMAN. Coming, Fanny? [*As he crosses up left center*]

FANNY. Ya. [*Puts glass of wine on serving-tray up right center*]

MAC. Good night, Mr. Jones—you know me. [*Crossing out*]

PETER. Yah.

[LEHMAN *exits up left.* MAC *exits up left after* LEHMAN]

BENHAM [*at left center*]. Will you require my services, Mr. Jones?

[PEGGY *crosses in front of* BENHAM *to up left center*]

PETER. I'll let you know tomorrow.

BENHAM [*bows and turns up left; gets hat off bed*]. Thanks.

PEGGY [*stops*]. Well, it was a dandy trip. [*Exits up left*]

BENHAM [*turns to* PETER, *hat in hand*]. Good evening. [*Exits up left*]

PETER. Good evening.

BERNIE [*a wave of the hand, crosses up left center*] Good luck to the show. [*Stops up left*] All you need is to fix it. [*Puts hat on and exits left*]

MARTIN. Don't forget. Anything at all that you want to tell me [*Exits up left*]

[*As* MARTIN *goes,* FANNY *crosses from right of bed to left of bed*]

FANNY Something tells me you haven't got the money.

PETER. I'll get it—some place.

FANNY. Well—anyhow— [*Exits up left; shuts door*]

PETER. Well!

JANE. Why did you do it? Why?

PETER. He just got me mad, I guess. [*Crosses up left. Crosses back to* JANE] What was that he said I was—about butter?

JANE. Never mind.

PETER. Butter—a butter-and-egg man, that was it. What's that mean?

JANE. It isn't anything.

PETER. It must mean something.

JANE. It's—it's just a man that invests money, that's all. That puts money into something.

PETER. Oh!

JANE. Peter, you must think what you're going to do. You gave him all your money, didn't you—that five hundred? Oh, Peter, it was foolish.

PETER [*crosses away and back*]. I couldn't help it. I couldn't help it when he started talking to you like that.

JANE. I got you into it again.

[*READY 'Phone*]

PETER. Oh, no! You didn't. I mean, I'm glad you did. I mean I'm glad I feel that way about you. I know why you thought I was going to hate you. Because the play wasn't good. As if I could.

JANE. But, Peter, where are you going to get the money? Ten thousand dollars.

PETER. He—he got me so mad I thought sure I could get it some place. [*Turns and looks front*]

JANE. Do you know anyone here in Syracuse?

PETER [*shakes his head*]. I don't know anyone anywhere, with—ten thousand dollars.

JANE. Think hard! Peter—is there anyone in Chillicothe?

PETER [*pauses, as the mention of Chillicothe reminds him*]. I sent her a telegram just after the show, saying it was a big success. [*Looks at* JANE]. My mother, I mean.

JANE. Peter! Now, it's going to be one yet!

PETER [*shakes his head*]. I—I'm just beginning to realize what's happened. I gave him about everything I had left and—that's all there is to it. It's gone. I guess I'm done for. [*Crosses up right center and to chair at table*]

JANE. Peter, you're not.

PETER [*at table right center*]. No. It's gone, all right. And she expected me to do such big things— I'm not ever going home again.

JANE. Peter! Don't say that!

PETER. I was a fool— [*Looks through scripts and piles them on left side of table*] all right —thinking I knew anything about shows. She was depending on me, too—and now look what I've done to her—I'm going to kill— [*Sits*] myself.

JANE [*crosses to him quickly*]. Peter, don't talk like that! You're breaking my heart. I know things are going to be better. I just *feel* that something is going to *happen*. ['Phone *rings once*] That may be something now— ['Phone *rings again*]

PETER [*looks up at* Jane, *worried; rises; 'phone rings again; he starts for 'phone and it rings until he reaches it. At 'phone up left*]

Hello. Yah, this is Mr. Jones. Why, no—there isn't any— Oh, yes—there is. All right. Right away. [*Hangs up and places 'phone on table*]

JANE. Well?

PETER. You're not allowed to stay here any longer. It's against the rules.

JANE [*at right of bed*]. Oh, well—we'll meet first thing in the morning and plan something then. Won't we? And you're not going to be unhappy? [*Crosses down to foot of bed*]

PETER. No matter what happens, I met you.

JANE. If only you hadn't.

PETER [*crosses down to foot of bed*]. Oh, but I love you, Jane. I do, terribly. And if ever I get out of this trouble—don't you think—really—

JANE. Peter—I think you're just the finest person that ever lived. But I've got you into an awful mess. I didn't mean to, but I have. And that's why I can't—

PETER. Well— [*Crosses away to left*] I'll get out of it some way. You just see if I don't. I'll get the money some place and—the play— [*Crosses back to her in front of bed*] It might be a success in New York, don't you think?

JANE. It—might.

PETER. I mean—even if it isn't awfully good. That isn't supposed to matter so much in New York, is it?

JANE. Oh, Peter, I'm afraid—

PETER. It—it just *can't* be a failure, that's all. It just can't be. I bet if they'd just wait till we got a little money some place. [OSCAR *knocks at door up left.* PETER *looks at* JANE. OSCAR *counts seven; knocks again.* PETER *turns to door*] Who's there?

OSCAR [OSCAR FRITCHIE *is a sufficiently nice-looking young man, but just a little dumb*]. This is Mr. Fritchie.

PETER. Who?

OSCAR. Mr. Fritchie. The assistant manager.

PETER [*crosses to* JANE; JANE *crosses a couple of steps to* PETER]. He's the man that got us the champagne. [*A couple of steps to door*] What do you want?

OSCAR. Can I come in?

[PETER *looks at* JANE; *she nods "yes."* PETER *crosses up and opens door.* OSCAR *enters up left*]

PETER. The door wasn't locked.

JANE. I was just leaving.

OSCAR [*up left center*]. Huh? Oh, broke up early, eh?

PETER [*at door*]. This is—Mr. Fritchie, Miss Weston.

JANE. How are you?

OSCAR. Hello.

PETER. Miss Weston was just going out when you—she was just going out— [*Crosses down to* OSCAR *on his left*]

OSCAR. Oh. Well, don't let me disturb you. I just—

PETER. Isn't that what you came about?

OSCAR. Huh?

PETER. They just telephoned me from downstairs—on account of Miss Weston being here.

OSCAR. Oh, that's all right. They didn't know you were friends of mine. [*Crosses right center*]

PETER. Thank you very much, Mr. Fritchie. Is there something— [*Crosses to center after* OSCAR] we can do for you?

OSCAR [*at center*]. Oh, no, no—no. I just— [*Turns to* PETER] how was everything, all right—the supper?

PETER. Oh, yes. Fine, thanks.

OSCAR. And the champagne—did you get it all right?

PETER. Yes. Thanks.

OSCAR. You see, we get show troupes right along, up here, and—I know they got the habit of getting together, sort of—and—I like to—do whatever I can.

PETER. That's fine—thanks, Mr. Fritchie.

OSCAR [*crosses to table right center, the same table* LEHMAN *used*]. I—I'm kind of sorry your party's broken up.

JANE. Yes. We are, too.

OSCAR [*at right center*]. I've always a kind of a liking for theatrical people, and of course, they stop here at the hotel a lot—and some of them sort of let me come around. [*A couple of steps toward them*] Just talk.

PETER [*turns to* JANE]. Why, sure—we—huh?

JANE. Why—yes.

PETER. Yes.

OSCAR. Louis Mann was here last year. [*Hands in pockets*] We had quite a *long* talk.

PETER. Well, we don't mind talking at all—if— Is there something special you want to talk about?

OSCAR [*crosses back of table right center*]. Oh, no—no—nothing in particular. You know how it is— [*Turns to them*] You get a liking for something—the theatre— All my life I've —I've just kind of liked to talk about it, that's all. I guess maybe it's because I've always had a sort of feeling that some day I might get into it— [*Puts hands in pockets*] myself. [OSCAR *looks front.* PETER *has hand to head during this speech*]

PETER [*takes hand from head, crosses a little to center. Long pause*]. Would you mind saying that again?

OSCAR. The show business. I say—some day I'm going to get into it.

PETER [*a couple of steps to* OSCAR]. You don't mean—as a producer?

OSCAR [*pleased, looks front*]. That's what. [*Pause.* PETER *looks at* JANE, *looks at* OSCAR, *shakes his head, crosses up, crosses down, looks at* JANE]

PETER. Sit down, Sweetheart. [*Places chair back of* OSCAR, *then crosses up left*]

OSCAR. Who, me? [*Puzzled.* PETER *nods*] I don't mean to butt in. I just—

PETER [*crosses to back of table right center*]. That's all right.

OSCAR. Well—much obliged. [*Sits*]

JANE [*crosses to left of table*]. You—you said you were the assistant manager?

OSCAR. Yah. Mr. Hemingway is the manager.

PETER [*crosses to right of table*]. I used to work in a hotel, before I went into the theatre business.

OSCAR. That so?

PETER [*hand on back of chair right of table*]. That must be a fine job you have here. You must make a lot of money?

OSCAR. Oh, I don't suppose you folks would call it much.

JANE. Oh, yes, we would.

PETER. Look, Mr. Fritchie. Have you—that is, have you been able to—in all this—have you got any saved up—I mean money?

OSCAR. Huh?

JANE. Mr. Jones has known so many hotel men who didn't save. He just hopes you're different.

OSCAR. That's right. A lot of them don't.

PETER [*bending over* OSCAR]. I know. But you *do*, don't you? That's what we want to get down to.

OSCAR. You bet your life I do.

PETER. That's fine. [*Turns right*]

OSCAR. What's the matter?

JANE. Not a thing.

PETER. Nothing. [*Alone*] Would⎫ you like a glass of champagne? ⎬ [*Together*] [*Crosses up and gets it*] ⎭

OSCAR [*still in chair*]. Say—that's not a bad idea. [*Turns left to* JANE] You know, I like you folks. You make a fellow feel nice.

PETER [*at* OSCAR'S *right with glass of wine*]. Here, drink this first. [*Puts glass on table and stands by dresser*]

OSCAR. Well, here's to you. [*Drinks.* PETER *salutes toast*]

JANE [*as he finishes*]. Some more? [*Crosses up; gets champagne*]

OSCAR. I'm not robbing you?

PETER. No—no—it's all right.

[JANE *crosses to right of* OSCAR; *pours champagne in same glass*]

OSCAR. Yes, sir—I always say show folk are nice people. Not stuck-up, you know—make a fellow feel at home. [*Finish pouring*] Oh, thanks.

[PETER *puts bottle back up stage after* OSCAR *ends drink.* PETER *crosses around and to* OSCAR, *at his left*]

PETER [*puts hand on* OSCAR'S *shoulder*]. Er—

OSCAR. Huh?

PETER [*worried*]. Nothing—yet. [*Crosses to left of bed*]

OSCAR. Say—what's going on here?

JANE. Mr. Jones has a proposition to make to you. He's going to give you a chance to invest in this play that opened tonight. It's going to make an awful lot of money—

OSCAR. Well, I don't want to invest. [*Rises*]

PETER [*crosses to* OSCAR]. Now wait! You didn't see the play tonight, did you?

OSCAR. No.

PETER. That's fine. It's going to be much better. It's a big drama, see, with this girl in it and—and—do you know how much money a lot of shows have made?

OSCAR. You bet your life I do. "Madame Sherry" made seven hundred and fifty thousand dollars. "Potash and Perlmutter" made half a million. "Within the Law" made—

PETER. There you are! Isn't that wonderful?

JANE. Mr. Jones'll tell you what a wonderful play this is, Mr. Fritchie. And he has a chance to get hold of the whole thing—all of it. It's a real chance—the chance of a lifetime.

PETER. Do you know what a brothel is? Do you?

OSCAR [*looks at* JANE, *bashful*]. Huh? Why—yes, I guess I do. [*Sits*]

PETER. Well, we've got one in this play and it's great, see? A priest and a rabbi come into it—it's a great big scene. [OSCAR *looks at* PETER] It's going to be a knockout—everything happens to this girl—she marries a fellow and there's another fellow and she gets into a lot of trouble—only she's got to have more sympathy—so she's going to have a baby—it's going to make millions of dollars—thousands.

OSCAR [*rises*]. I don't think I want to—

PETER. Everything is changed around—it's going to have Hong Kong in it—in place of where the trial scene is now—it's going to be a hop joint in Hong Kong. It's a wow, and he turns out to be her father—with a long beard on—that's where we bring in the strong talk and so and so, and so and so, and so and so. That's your first act. [*Crosses over to foot of bed, taking off dress coat as he goes, throws coat on bed, crossing back to* OSCAR] Then we go on from there.

OSCAR. Now—now—you got to stop, if you want me to— [*Considers*] Go into the theatrical business, eh? It would be fun.

PETER. Oh, it's an awful lot of fun—you haven't any idea.

OSCAR. Would it cost much money?

PETER. No. You can have half of it—that is —forty-nine percent—for thirty thousand dollars. [*Crosses away toward center*]

OSCAR [*crosses to* PETER *and* PETER *back to left*]. Thirty thousand dollars!

PETER. Twenty-five thousand!

OSCAR. Twenty-five thousand?

PETER. Twenty! Fifteen!

JANE. And that's— [*Slaps table*] the very lowest, Mr. Fritchie!

OSCAR [crosses to table; sits]. It's a lot.

JANE. Oh, no, it's a bargain.

PETER [reads fast]. Yes. Only you have to decide quickly—because the man that decides right away—I mean standing up— [Motions up with hands. OSCAR rises slowly] You see, Mr. Fritchie, everything in the show business is done like that— [Makes a poor attempt at snapping fingers] We read about a fellow who could have bought some of the "Follies" once, only he didn't—and look, it's all gone now.

OSCAR. Now, wait. I—I don't know what to say. I know I'd like the theatrical business, and I been— [Looks front] getting kind of tired of the hotel lately—

PETER. Of course you would. You're not the kind of man to stay cooped up in a hotel all his life.

JANE. Mr. Jones got out, and look at him.

PETER [backs away toward center a couple of steps]. Yes. Look at me.

JANE. It's going to make an awful lot of money.

OSCAR [looks front]. I'd love to quit and tell Mr. Hemingway what I thought of him.

PETER [crosses to OSCAR]. That's the stuff!

JANE. Then why don't you?

OSCAR. I'm scared.

PETER. Well, this is your chance.

JANE. A chance to leave this old hotel behind you.

PETER. I guess— [Crosses away to left again] when he looks back at an opportunity he's missed, like this, it will make him feel pretty terrible. When it's a big success in New York—

OSCAR [crosses to PETER center]. Now—now wait. I haven't said I wouldn't, yet.

PETER. You've got to act quick with us, if you want it.

OSCAR. You say it's—a good play?

PETER [at left center]. Good! There's never been anything like it.

OSCAR [at center]. There are certainly some things I'd tell Mr. Hemingway, the big stiff.

PETER [crosses to JANE at right quickly]. Make out a receipt, Jane.

[JANE picks up pad and crosses to dresser right quickly. Starts writing receipt]

OSCAR [crosses back of table]. Now, wait.

PETER [at right of table]. No, unless you can give us your check right away, we can't do it at all. Can you?

OSCAR. I haven't said I was going to at all, yet.

JANE [play very fast. Turns to OSCAR from dresser]. But if you do it right away, you can go to Mr. Hemingway tonight and tell him all those things. Just think. [Continues writing receipt]

OSCAR [behind table right center]. He made me work twelve hours a day.

PETER. You don't have to work at all in the theatre.

OSCAR. He'd be sore, all right.

PETER. There's no reason why we have to produce just this one show. We could go ahead and do a lot more.

OSCAR [takes out checkbook from inside coat pocket and stands with it in his hands, undecided]. Could we?

PETER. Of course—couldn't we?

JANE. Of course.

PETER [at right of table]. Why, we can be the biggest producers there are. All kinds of shows— Can I open that for you? [Starts to open. OSCAR scans checkbook]

OSCAR [sits at table]. No. No.

PETER [at OSCAR's right]. Well, here is ink and pen and everything. You just make the check out to me—Peter Jones.

[WARN Curtain.]

JANE. What's your first name, Mr. Fritchie, and how do you spell this one?

OSCAR. Oscar Fritchie. F-r-i-t-c-h-i-e.

PETER [crosses to JANE]. F-r-i-t-c-h-i-e. Got it?

OSCAR [continues as PETER spells name]. But I haven't made up my mind yet.

PETER. How are you coming here? Have you started yet?

OSCAR. I don't know. You got me all excited —but—

JANE [reads fast]. Here's the receipt. [Crosses to right of table; puts the receipt on it] It just says you're giving us the money for forty-nine percent of. [Crosses to left of OSCAR] Is that all right?

PETER. That's fine. Here's the receipt. Now all you have to do is to sign the check, see? Here, I'll help you. Oscar, it should be—

OSCAR [as PETER starts to help him, OSCAR stops] Do you think I ought to?

PETER. Of course you ought to. It's a great big drama, and there's an orchard in it, and Mr. Hemingway comes in, and he's got a long beard on. Oh! Did I tell him about the bookings yet? Did I? We go from here to Providence, then Albany, and Seattle—

OSCAR. Look out— [Tears out check and PETER grabs it] It's wet.

PETER. I'll dry it. [Ring curtain] It's going to be a whale of a hit, Sweetheart, a whale of a hit.

[As curtain falls, OSCAR mops his head with handkerchief and JANE shakes his hand. PETER ad lib. as curtain falls]

CURTAIN

ACT THREE

SCENE: Same as Act I; a few weeks later. All that is missing is the overwhelming pile of papers that had stood against the rear wall.

JANE [*is seated at the desk at rise, looking over newspaper notices. 'Phone rings as curtain is up; it is out of her reach; she gets up to answer it*]. Hello— No, Mr. Jones hasn't come in yet— Well, if you try a little later— Yes, it looks like a very big hit. At least, they seem to think so at the theatre, but of course it's a little early to tell— Good-bye. [*There is a knock at right. She hangs up*] Come in!
[*Crosses center, but the door is opened before she reaches it. It is A. J.* PATTERSON *who enters, with brief case*]

PATTERSON [*is a middle-aged business man, rather formidable in manner. Crosses right center after a quick look around the office*]. Pardon me. [*Takes hat off*] Mr. Jones is not in?

JANE. No, sir—he isn't. Is there anything I can do for you?

PATTERSON. His partner is not here either?

JANE. Mr. Fritchie? No. I'm expecting them any minute.

PATTERSON [*considers; nods*]. I'll return.

JANE. Isn't there any message? Can't I give them your name?

PATTERSON [*turns as he is about to go out*]. Oh, this new play of theirs— I understand that it's successful. Is that right?

JANE. Yes, sir—I think so. But of course it only opened last night.

PATTERSON. I see. Thank you. [*Turns to go; puts hat on*]

JANE. You—you still won't tell me who it is?

PATTERSON [*left hand on doorknob, turns back*]. You needn't worry. I shall return. [*He goes out at right*]

[JANE, *impressed by his manner and a little worried, stands for a second looking at the closed door, then turns back to the desk. She has just taken up a newspaper again when* PETER *enters center, derby on, cigarette in holder-case, dark street suit*]

PETER [*enters snappily*]. Well! [*Crosses center, smiling, takes hat off*]

JANE [*crosses below desk to right of it*]. Peter!

PETER [*pleased*]. Well, I guess I was right, wasn't I?

JANE. What?

PETER. The play's a hit. Remember— [*Crosses to hat tree up right center, just puts cane on it*] I told you it would be, when it came to New York? [*Crosses back to her*]

JANE. Yes, Peter! I can hardly believe it. People are lined up over at the theatre, buying tickets. Isn't it wonderful?

PETER. Oh, I don't know. It wasn't any surprise to me. [*Crosses to left of desk*] Is there any mail? [*Puts hat on desk and starts piling up newspapers on center part of desk*]

JANE. Ah—why, no. Some people have been telephoning, and there was a gentleman here just now, but he wouldn't leave his name.

PETER [*business-like*]. Did he state his business?

JANE. No, he didn't.

PETER. Always ask them to state their business. And—ah—if anybody else comes, bring in their cards first, please, to see if I'll see them. [*At center of desk; looks at papers*]

JANE. All right.

PETER. You see, Jane, the reason you mustn't ever be surprised at a play like this being a hit is because it's so full of heart interest— *that's* what the public wants—*heart* interest— and *menace*. The moment I first heard of this play I knew it would be a success. [*Picks up newspapers again and holds them in his hands*]

JANE [*crosses to desk*]. I'm terribly happy, Peter, that you were right.

PETER. It doesn't amount to anything, once you learn how. Probably all of my productions will be successes now. [*He starts reading through two or three different papers*]

JANE. That would be nice.

PETER [*looks at* JANE]. Did you read these— the criticisms? [*Pointing to criticism in paper*]

JANE. Yes.

PETER. This fellow missed the whole idea of the play. [*Stands and puffs cigarette*] And he thought the performance was only adequate. A lot they know about it—the critics. I'm thinking of not letting them come at *all* the next time. [*'Phone rings. Picks it up* ['PHONE] *quickly*] Hello— Yes, this is Mr. Jones speaking— Thank you— Yeh, I guess it's about the biggest that's ever been produced— Huh? [*Sits on desk*] Oh, no— I'm going to produce it *myself* in London. Budapest, too— Yeh—a sort of international producing company.— Well, it wouldn't be any use of your coming over, because when I make up my mind I'm like that. Good-bye. [*Hangs up. Rises from desk*] I'm going to produce it all over the world.

JANE. Do you want anything more from me now? [*Starts right*]

PETER [*crosses front of desk to* JANE]. What's the matter, Jane?

JANE [*crossing to right*]. Nothing.

PETER. Aren't you glad the play's a success?

JANE. Of course. I'm very happy for you. I wish you just all the success in the world. [*Back turned to him*]

PETER [*crosses to her*]. It means an awful lot to us, Jane.

JANE [*turns to him. Eagerly*]. Does it, Peter?

PETER [*at center*]. Oh! I forgot to tell you about a man I met this morning. He wants to build a theatre for me—the Peter Jones Playhouse.

JANE. I'll hardly know you, will I?

PETER [*just right of center door at center*]. Jane, what would you say to changing the name of the firm, now that they're out of it? Don't you think it would be simpler to have it just Jones Productions, Inc.?

JANE. Yes, I suppose it would be simpler.

PETER. Do you think—do you think my picture would make a good trademark?

JANE. If you—want it.

PETER. And oh, Jane— [OSCAR *enters right. Pauses, hat in hand*] Well?

OSCAR. Good morning!

JANE. Good morning, Mr. Fritchie.

OSCAR. Good morning, Miss Weston!

PETER. How do you feel now?

OSCAR. What are all those people doing over at the theatre?

PETER. The play's a big success.

OSCAR. Who says so?

PETER. Everybody. We're nearly sold out for tonight.

OSCAR. Yes—who'll come tomorrow night?

PETER [*crosses up, then to left of desk*]. Wait till you hear all the plans I've got. Get Jane here to tell you about the Peter Jones Playhouse. [*Throws papers in waste-basket*]

JANE. I—I think there's someone in the outer office. [*Crosses to door right in front of* OSCAR]

PETER. Well, don't forget about bringing in their cards. [*Sits at desk*]

JANE [*in door*]. I won't. [*Exits right, closing door*]

OSCAR [*crosses to desk*]. Now on the level, how are things?

PETER [*smokes cigarette in holder*]. It's one of the biggest successes ever produced.

OSCAR [*leans over desk*]. She's gone—you can tell me.

PETER. People are calling up to buy it for London and every place.

OSCAR [*over desk, speaks quickly*]. How much did you get?

PETER. I wouldn't sell it.

OSCAR. Now look—I think if we can get *any* money we ought to, because—I don't feel just right yet, see? [*Turns away*]

PETER. When we go ahead and produce the Peter Jones "Follies" you'll feel right.

OSCAR [*turns back*]. Do you think we ought to do that?

PETER. And this afternoon I'm seeing a man about the Hippodrome. [*Smokes*]

OSCAR. I think— [*Crosses to center*] maybe I ought to get out. [*Picks up hat from table*]

PETER [*puts cigarette down, picks up pen and receipt book*]. All right. I can handle it myself.

OSCAR [*crosses back to desk quickly*]. Would you be willing to buy my share back?

PETER [*opens receipt book as if to write*]. You bet I would.

OSCAR. Well—then I don't know. [*Crosses away a couple of steps*]

PETER [*rises, crosses to* OSCAR *center*]. Do you know what I'm going to do if you stay with me? I'm going to get all the playwrights there are in this country, and put them under contract, and then we'll tie up all the foreign plays.

OSCAR. But suppose something happens?

PETER. What can happen in the theatrical business? [*Puts cigarette on tray on desk*] Now, look! When we've got all the plays tied up, then the thing to do is to get all the theatres.

OSCAR. You don't think it could go wrong some place?

PETER. No. You can't make a mistake—all you got to do is to give the public what they want.

OSCAR. Yah, but—but—but how do you know what they *want*?

PETER. It's easy. They always want the same thing.

OSCAR [*shakes his head*]. Sure as I went into it they'd change their minds.

PETER. We'll put another— [JANE *enters right with a card*]—company in Chicago— [*Sees* JANE; *crosses to her in front of* OSCAR] See? A card! People are starting to come in already.

JANE. It's the gentleman who was here before.

PETER. Yah? I've never heard of him. [*Crosses to* OSCAR] Did you?

OSCAR [*at right center, looking at card; shakes head*]. No. And I don't know *why*, but I've got a feeling it's *bad* news.

PETER [*reading card*]. A. J. Patterson.

OSCAR [*also reading*]. Attorney-at-law. [*Quickly*] That's the part I don't like. [*Takes step left*]

PETER. Did he say what he wanted?

JANE. No, he didn't.

PETER [*to* OSCAR]. Oh, well, he's probably just come to make an offer. Huh?

OSCAR. No—they don't make offers, attorneys-at-law.

PETER. You're getting me nervous now.

OSCAR. I bet we've got the show in the wrong theatre.

PETER [*to* JANE]. Will you tell him to come in?

JANE. Yes, sir. [*Crosses to door, opens and holds it open*] Will you please come in, Mr. Patterson?

[*He enters and she closes door and stands with back to same.* PATTERSON *enters right, comes in a few steps and holds*]

PETER. Did you want to see me?

PATTERSON [*looks at* OSCAR]. Which is Mr. Peter Jones?

OSCAR [*sidesteps a little to the left*]. He is.

PATTERSON. Is this Mr. Oscar Fritchie?

OSCAR. Yep.

PATTERSON. I called on you gentlemen earlier and left word that I would return.

OSCAR. Yah? I—wish I'd *known*. [*Another step left*]

PATTERSON. You have my card?

PETER. Yes.

PATTERSON. My name is Patterson.

PETER [*looks at card*]. That's right.

PATTERSON. I'm an attorney-at-law.

OSCAR. A lawyer, huh? [*Steps toward* PATTERSON]

PATTERSON [*sternly*]. An attorney-at-law.

OSCAR [*turns and steps away to left one or two steps*] Oh!

PETER. Is there something we can do for you, Mr. Patterson?

PATTERSON. There is. May I— [*Indicates desk left center*]

PETER [JANE *steps down below door right and holds*]. Yes. Surely.

[PATTERSON *crosses to upper end of desk, puts on glasses, takes documents from case, magazine, arranges them. Long pause.* PETER *and* OSCAR *look at* PATTERSON, *then each other, worried.* PATTERSON *clears throat, looks at legal paper*]

PATTERSON. You are the owners of Lehmac Productions, Incorporated, Fourteen Hundred and Sixty-eight Broadway, New York, New York. A New York corporation. [*Looks at* PETER]

PETER. We are. [*Raises right hand*]

OSCAR. He owns most of it. [*Indicates* PETER]

PATTERSON [*crossing left*]. Said corporation being the producers of a dramatic composition or play, entitled "Her Lesson."

PETER. Is it s-something about the play? [*Crosses to* PATTERSON *in front of* OSCAR]

PATTERSON [*back of desk*]. In November, Nineteen— [*Picks up magazine, reads year and date from magazine*] Hundred and Sixteen there appeared in this magazine, "Peppy Tales," published in New York City, an article of fiction, or short story, entitled "A Woman's Honor." Said story— [*Crosses to left*] having been written by my client, Mr. Rodney Rich, of Northampton, Massachusetts— [*Crosses back to desk*] and, as we shall duly prove in court—

OSCAR. In court?

PATTERSON [*puts magazine on desk and again picks up legal paper*]. In court.

OSCAR. I thought you said court.

PATTERSON. The said story was, on— [*Reads from legal paper*] January Eight, Nineteen

Hundred and Seventeen, accepted as the basis of a play by one Harley Thompson, since deceased.

PETER [OSCAR *looks to* PETER *to explain*]. Dead.

PATTERSON. Subsequently, as we shall prove, the said play was purchased, or acquired, by one Joseph Lehman— [PETER *looks at* OSCAR] and by him duly produced. It will be shown that the said dramatic composition, or play, is similar to the aforesaid short story at— [*Looks at legal paper again*] one hundred and forty-six points.

PETER. One hundred and forty-*six*? [*Turns to* PATTERSON *again*]

PATTERSON. And that no less than *six* characters in the aforesaid play bear the same names as those in the aforesaid short story. [*Looks at* PETER]

PETER [*a few steps to* PATTERSON]. Well, was the aforesaid—?

PATTERSON. One moment, please. [*Crosses down on right side of desk*] My client, Mr. Rodney Rich, has received no payment for this play, nor has his permission been sought in any way. [*Stops at lower end of desk*] It is, gentlemen, a clear case of plagiarism— [*Crossing up on left side of desk*] and one of the most flagrant that it has *ever* been my privilege to encounter. [*Arrives again at upper end of desk*]

OSCAR. But—but—but—look here—

PETER. We didn't know anything about it. I bought it from Mr. Lehman, and then Mr. Fritchie here—

PATTERSON. Unfortunately— [*Looks at legal papers again*]

OSCAR. That's a *bad* word.

PATTERSON [*at upper end of desk*]. My client cannot take that matter into account. His composition has been produced in dramatic form without his consent. Not unnaturally he seeks redress.

OSCAR. Seeks what?

PATTERSON [OSCAR *looks at* PETER *for him to explain*]. Redress.

PETER. Money.

PATTERSON. My purpose in placing these facts before you, prior to bringing suit—is to afford you the opportunity,—if you so desire, of adjusting the matter outside of court. [*Places legal paper on desk.* OSCAR *indicates* PETER *to do something*]

PETER. Well—well—what are we supposed to do? [*Crosses a couple of steps to* PATTERSON]

PATTERSON. My client will accept sixty-six and two-thirds per centum of all profits derived from said play, when, if and as produced, and in those circumstances will permit the play to continue. Failing to receive sixty-six and two-thirds per centum—

OSCAR [*nods head to* PETER]. That's money, too.

PATTERSON. He will apply for an injunction and cause the play to be closed at once.

PETER. He'll close it?

PATTERSON. He will close it.

OSCAR. Close it?

PATTERSON [*very firm and fierce*]. You understand me. [*Turns and puts magazine and papers in case and shuts it, puts glasses in pocket*]

OSCAR. Yah. Look. Most of it's yours, see? I don't know much about law, see? You—do something, and I'll go over and see if the theatre's burned down yet. [*Puts hat on, exits right, closing door*]

PETER [*crosses upper right after* OSCAR'S *exit*]. What are we going to do?

JANE [*crosses to center*]. Must Mr. Jones give an answer immediately?

PATTERSON. I regret that he must.

PETER [*crosses down right center on* JANE'S *right*]. But—I haven't had time—

JANE [*at center*]. Can't we—even talk it over? That is, Mr. Jones and I?

PATTERSON [*crosses down to them right center*]. This young lady is your adviser?

PETER. Yes, indeed.

PATTERSON [*crosses right to door*]. At best, I could allow but a brief time. [*Opens door*]

PETER. Well, that would be better than—

PATTERSON [*in door*]. Shall we say—fifteen minutes?

PETER. Shall we?

PATTERSON. Very well. [*Puts on hat*] I shall return for your decision in fifteen minutes. [*Exits right, closing door*]

PETER. Oh, Jane!

JANE. Oh, Peter, you mustn't worry.

PETER [*crosses left to right side of desk*]. Oh, Jane—just when everything was going along so fine, to have—

JANE [*at center*]. But you mustn't get discouraged. He—may not be right at all.

PETER [*at lower end of desk, his back to her*]. Oh, yes, he is. I remember Mr. Lehman said something about its being a story, that very first day.

JANE [*crosses to* PETER *at his right*]. But this may not be it. Now, when he comes back we'll make him show all his proofs—

PETER. It's no use, Jane— Sixty-six and two-thirds per centum— And I was going to do such big things. [*Sits right of desk*]

JANE. You will yet, Peter.

PETER. I guess I wasn't supposed to do them. Some people that sort of naturally do big things, and others that—like— I wouldn't care if it weren't— [*Puts elbows on table, rests chin in hands*] for—everything.

JANE [*pauses; backs away a step*]. Peter— may I tell you something? I love you.

PETER [*rises; crosses to her*]. Do you?

JANE [*at center*]. I wanted to tell it to you now, when things are—looking black. It—it may be wrong, but—I'm glad this has happened.

PETER [*takes her hands*]. Glad?

JANE. Of course—I'm sorry about the money, but I'm awfully glad for you.

PETER. How do you—mean, Jane?

JANE. I did want you to be successful, but somehow you lost something that was you. It's just as you said, Peter—you're not that kind of person—you never could be. You belong back in Chillicothe, in the hotel. You're sweet and—simple and—you don't really like all this, do you?

PETER. I don't know. I thought I did, but— I don't know. [*Turns away; she still holds his right hand*]

JANE. Don't you see—how little it amounts to, really? You're too fine for it, Peter.

PETER [*turns to her*]. Did you mean that, about—loving me? [*Hands on her arms*]

JANE. More than anything that ever was. [*Head on his shoulder; pause*] I thought— [*Raises head*] for a while you'd gone away from me, but now I know you never can. It made me so unhappy to think that—but now it's all over.

PETER [*crosses to lower end of desk*]. It's over, all right. Being a success is all over.

JANE. You mustn't mind.

PETER. I wanted it to go, on account of you, and now there isn't anything and that lawyer'll be coming back and—

JANE. But suppose you gave him what he wanted—what difference does it make?

PETER. I couldn't. I hardly have a thing left. Besides, I got Oscar to go into this and— [JANE *crosses to center. Knock on center door*] He wouldn't be here already, would he?

JANE [*crosses up; opens center door*]. Mrs. Lehman.

FANNY. Hello. [*Enters up center*]

PETER [*at lower end of desk*]. Oh—hello.

FANNY [*crosses to center*]. Hello! Well, you ought to be peppier than this. Do you know you've got a hit?

PETER [*at* FANNY'S *left*]. Yes, ma'am.

FANNY. Yes, sir—a hit. I don't know what that proves about the public, but it's certainly something.

JANE [*crosses down to* FANNY'S *right*]. You've come to tell us something.

FANNY. You're pretty cute.

JANE. Well?

FANNY. You've got company coming.

JANE. Mr. Lehman?

FANNY. Right.

JANE. Soon?

FANNY. On the fire.

PETER. What's he want?

FANNY. He's smoked out a bankroll and he wants to buy back the show.

PETER. No?—Oh— [*To* JANE] S-a-y— [*Then right and back down right center*] Look. You don't think he will get here pretty soon— [*Looking at watch*] in less than fifteen minutes, do you think?

FANNY. What's going on?

PETER. Do you?

FANNY [*nods*]. I just shot ahead of him to tell you that he's picked up a little tip.

PETER. Huh? ⎫
JANE. What is it? ⎭ [*Together*]

FANNY. You know I got a kind of a fool liking for you two. Somehow, suckers always did appeal to me.

PETER. You were going to tell us? He might get here, and—

FANNY. It's this. You've got about three times as big a hit as you think you have.

PETER. No!

FANNY. You know that brothel scene?

PETER. Yes, indeed.

FANNY. The police are going to try to close the show. That means you'll be hanging 'em up on the rafters.

PETER. Gosh! [LEHMAN *knocks up center door. Backs away*]

FANNY. Joe raised the money on that tip. He's got it on him in certified checks.

JANE. How much?

FANNY. I don't know. [LEHMAN *knocks again*]

PETER. A butter-and-egg man.

[*They hold till* PETER *sits at desk, and puts feet up.* FANNY *crosses to right.* JANE *crosses to up center door.* PETER, *hat on, feet upon desk a la* LEHMAN. JANE *opens center door.* LEHMAN *pauses, enters up center*]

JANE. Good morning, Mr. Lehman.

LEHMAN [*to* JANE]. Hi— [*Looks at* FANNY *and comes center*] Morning.

PETER [*pauses, as* LEHMAN *gets down center*]. How are you, Sweetheart?

LEHMAN [*to* FANNY]. What are you doing here?

FANNY. Just visiting.

LEHMAN [*at center*]. Get out!

JANE [*crosses down center on* LEHMAN'S *right*]. I—I think Mrs. Lehman ought to stay.

PETER. You're not going to start putting people out of places again, are you? Now, let's all sit down and—visit. Unless there's something particular you want to say.

LEHMAN. I don't know what she's been handing you, but don't start in believing it. [*Hands in vest pockets*]

PETER. About what?

LEHMAN. We can skip all that. I came

around to give you your coin back—and let you out clean.

PETER. Oh, you mean you want to buy the show?

LEHMAN [*at center*]. I'll give you what you paid for it—twenty and ten—thirty thousand. You won't lose a thing.

PETER [*laughs*]. You won't either, will you?

LEHMAN. What?

PETER. The point is, it's a valuable property, see? It starts with a prologue and it's—

LEHMAN [*crosses to upper end of desk*]. You're going to believe that stuff of hers, huh? Listen, Sweetheart, I'm an old hand at this game—I can make something out of this show, but you can't.

PETER. The judge has got a long beard on.

LEHMAN. I'll give you forty—and I've got the certified checks in my pocket. Set? [JANE, *at center, shakes her head.* PETER *shakes his head*] Forty-five, and that's all. That's netting you fifteen. [JANE *shakes her head.* PETER *shakes his head*] I only got fifty— Do you want it all?

MAC [*bursts in center door*]. So— [*To down center to right of* JOE *and holds*]

[LEHMAN *looks around*]

FANNY. The boy-friend. [*All look at* FANNY]

MAC [*swings door shut*]. I thought so.

LEHMAN. Thought what?

MAC. Trying to double-cross me? Eh? Have you sold it to him yet? [*Crosses down right of desk*]

[LEHMAN *crosses to center right of* MAC]

PETER. Why?

MAC [*at right of desk*]. If you haven't—don't—because he's going to skin you.

PETER. Mr. Lehman?

MAC. He didn't tell you about the police, did he?

FANNY. I did. [ALL *look at* FANNY *again*]

LEHMAN. Just a pal.

MAC. Now listen. I'll give you fifty thousand dollars. I've got it right here.

PETER [*rises, crosses to* LEHMAN]. Fifty thousand? That's ridiculous. Why, even Mr. Lehman offered that much.

MAC. He did?

PETER. Do you want to go any— [*Turns to* MAC] higher? It's a great play—there's a priest in it—

MAC [*turns to* LEHMAN]. How about you, Mr. Lehman?

LEHMAN [*steps up center a little. To* FANNY]. I'm going to brain you.

JANE. I know a way to fix things. Mr. Lehman has fifty thousand dollars and so has Mr. McClure.

LEHMAN [*steps down again*]. Well?

JANE. Why shouldn't they—buy it together?

PETER [*smiles*]. Yah! That's an idea. Very

good. [*Pats her on shoulder*] A hundred thousand dollars.

LEHMAN. What?

JANE. That's the price, Mr. Lehman.

LEHMAN. A hundred thousand?

PETER. Umhuh. [MAC *starts to sit*] And think on your feet.

[MAC *rises.* PETER *crosses to left of desk and sits, puts hat on desk*]

LEHMAN [*looking to* PETER *at desk*]. That's final?

PETER. Yep.

FANNY [*crosses to filing cabinet near door center*]. Five-Star.

PETER [*writing receipt*]. Only I got to know right away. [*Snaps fingers*] That's the show game.

LEHMAN. Come out here a minute, Mac.

MAC. O. K. [MAC *exits first, center*]

LEHMAN [*to* PETER]. We'll be right back. [*Gives* FANNY *a look as he goes out center*]

PETER. Do. [*Rises. Crosses center.* JANE *on his right.* FANNY *crosses to his left*] You think they'll do it?

JANE. I think so. Oh, I hope so.

PETER. But suppose that lawyer comes back before they—

FANNY. What lawyer?

PETER. Don't tell them, see—but there was a lawyer came in—

[OSCAR *knocks; enters.* FANNY *crosses up to center door*]

PETER. There he is! ⎱ [*Together*]
JANE. I'll keep him out here— ⎰

OSCAR [JANE *crosses up center to* FANNY]. Has he gone?

PETER [*crosses right to* OSCAR]. Listen. Everything has changed, see? I haven't got time to tell you, but don't be nervous, and—and don't ask any questions.

OSCAR. Huh?

JANE. Don't say anything. [*Crosses down to left desk; sits*]

OSCAR. What's going on? [LEHMAN *enters center door and crosses down center,* MAC *on his left*] Look, look— [*As they come down center*] Hello.

MAC. Hello, how are you?

OSCAR. Not bad. My throat's a little bit—

PETER [*to* LEHMAN]. Have you—decided?

LEHMAN. Now look here a minute—

[*KNOCK*]

[PATTERSON *knocks off right*]

OSCAR. I'll go.

PETER [*locks door and looks at watch*]. No, no! It's—it's— I know what it is, see? [*To* LEHMAN] You were going to say whether you'd decided.

OSCAR. But if there's somebody out there—

PETER. There isn't anybody out there. [*Long knock*] [*KNOCK*]

OSCAR. I'll take your word for it.

PETER. The point is—whether you've decided.

LEHMAN. Who's out there?

PETER. It's not anybody. Maybe a book agent. Do you want the show or don't you?

LEHMAN. Now look here, Sweetheart, that's a big bundle of coin. You can't expect us— [*A more insistent knock*] Oh, for Heaven's sake! Why don't you send him away?

[*KNOCK*]

PETER. Don't worry about him. [*Gets idea*] I can't send him away—anyway—I can't send him away—till you've decided.

LEHMAN. What?

PETER. Do you want to know who it is? I'll tell you—

LEHMAN. I don't care as long as he stops his racket.

PETER. All right. I'll tell you who it is—if you really want to know. That's a fellow who wants to take over most of the show—that's who that is.

[*Pause.* MAC *turns quickly to right and* LEHMAN *looks at him*]

OSCAR. Is it?

PETER. Yes, sirree. You'd be surprised if you knew who that was. [*KNOCK*]

LEHMAN [*knock*]. Who is it?

PETER. He's a man that does things just like that [*Snaps fingers*] and if you don't want it, all right. I'll open the door right up, and—

LEHMAN. Wait a minute. Mac! Hurry up.

PETER. If you want it you'd better give me your checks before he comes in, or—

LEHMAN. Hurry up, Mac! [*Hands* PETER *check*] Here! Now it's ours. [*Business with money and receipt*]

OSCAR. What's going on here?

PETER [*gets checks*]. That's all right. They've just bought the show back again.

OSCAR. I—I get my money back?

PETER. I should say you do. They've just paid a hundred thousand dollars for thirty three and a third per centum— [*Crosses to door on laugh*]

LEHMAN. For what?

PETER [*unlocks and opens door right*]. This gentleman will tell you all about it. Oh, Mr Patterson— [PATTERSON *enters right*] This gentleman is Mr. Patterson—Mr. A. J. Patterson—a lawyer at law, and he wants sixty six and two-thirds percent on account of that short story. Remember?

LEHMAN. Oh, he does, eh?

PETER. Mr. Lehman has just bought the show back again, Mr. Patterson. [*Crosses to* JANE *at desk; gives her checks, which she keeps*]

PATTERSON. Indeed?

OSCAR [*takes up center*]. Yes, indeed.

LEHMAN [*crosses to* PATTERSON]. Yah, an

I know all about that phoney case. You ain't got no more grounds than a rabbit.

PATTERSON. We have a perfect case.

LEHMAN. Yah? Well, there's one thing you don't know. [*Looks at others*] There ain't been a hit produced in twenty years that—[*Leads PATTERSON off right*] some guy ain't said it was swiped from him. [*Both exit right; shuts door*]

MAC [*crosses right*]. You certainly disappointed me. [*Exits right, closing door*]

LEHMAN [*voice off right*]. Last year in London—

OSCAR. Gee, this is great! You mean it—I get my money back?

PETER. You get forty-nine thousand dollars.

OSCAR. This is going to be an awful lesson to me.

LEHMAN [*voice off stage*]. And there's another thing you don't know—

OSCAR [*crosses to door right and opens*]. I want to hear what he's saying.

LEHMAN [*off right*]. Ten years ago from a guy named Sheridan—

[*OSCAR exits. Closes door right. PETER at door right, listens*]

FANNY. And I came here to look after you two. [*Crosses to down to center*]

JANE [*rises; crosses to FANNY's left*]. We couldn't have done it without you. And we do appreciate it—enormously.

PETER [*at FANNY's right*]. I should say we do. I'll never forget it. I'll never forget the whole thing. And if Mr. Lehman does anything to you, just you let me know.

FANNY [*nods head*]. I'll get along all right.

[*OSCAR enters right*]

LEHMAN [*off right*]. And you're getting a bargain, too.

OSCAR [*closes door right*]. I just came in to tell you the good news.

PETER. What?

OSCAR. Mr. Lehman is going to let me buy my share *back* again.

[*PETER crosses up and leans on file cabinet.*]

FANNY, center, looks at JANE, left center]

FANNY. Let me out first. [*Crosses right*] Oh, well—good-bye.

PETER [*crosses to center*]. Good-bye.

FANNY. At that maybe you're not such a sucker. You certainly put it over. But how that charade ever turned out to be a hit is a mystery to your Aunt Sadie. [*Opens door right and exits, closing door*]

OSCAR. Could you let me have my share of the money right away—to give Mr. Lehman?

PETER. Now—now look here, Oscar—

OSCAR. But I'm afraid Mr. Lehman won't wait.

PETER. He'll wait, but— Gosh! You don't want to go back into the theatrical business. [*To JANE*] Does he?

[*WARN Curtain*]

JANE. Of course not.

OSCAR. Don't I?

PETER. You know where you ought to be— a man like you? In the hotel business. Shouldn't he?

JANE. Of course.

OSCAR. But last time you said I ought to get out of it.

PETER. Oh, that was different. Listen, have you ever been in Chillicothe?

OSCAR. No.

PETER. Well, it's a wonderful place—there's a wonderful town, Oscar. Jane and I are going there. Aren't we, Jane? [*Crosses to JANE*]

JANE. I hope so.

PETER [*crosses back to OSCAR*]. You bet we are! We're going back to Chillicothe, and buy a hotel, see—for fifty thousand dollars—and with your money too it could be made one of the greatest hotels in the world—anywhere.

OSCAR. But now—now, wait—

JANE. It's a real chance, Mr. Fritchie. The chance of a lifetime.

PETER. It'll be wonderful, see? We'll build a great big addition— It'll be the greatest hotel that—I'll sell you forty-nine percent of it for—here—sit down, Sweetheart— [*As FRITCHIE sits in chair right of desk. Ring curtain*] Now, look. This is going to be one of the— [*Ad lib. as Curtain falls*]

CURTAIN

HOUSEPARTY

A Play in Three Acts

By KENNETH PHILLIPS BRITTON
and ROY HARGRAVE

CHARACTERS

ALAN BRADFORD
RONALD EVANS
SALLY ANDREWS
FLORENCE
HORTENSE PFEIFFER
MRS. MILLIGAN
MRS. WHITE
MRS. RUTHERFORD
EDWARD CANBY
DARROW JENCKES
DORIS CALLANDER
MALCOLM F. R. WHITE
BILL WARREN
CHICK SMYTH
MARRIANNE GUION
BOB DAVIS
BETTY CREELING
JAMES
STUDENTS AND HOUSEPARTY GUESTS

SCENES

The entire action of the play takes place in the Library of a fraternity house at Williams College, Williamstown, Massachusetts, during houseparties.

ACT I: *Autumn. The end of the afternoon tea-dance.*
ACT II: *Autumn. The dinner-dance, later that same evening.*
ACT III: *Spring. Six months later. The dinner-dance.*

HOUSEPARTY

The scene is the library of a fraternity house at Williams College.

The room is dominated by a wide panelled fireplace, on either side of which are French doors. Those on the right lead onto an open terrace, giving a view of autumn lawn and shrubbery and, beyond, the great elms that are typical of Williamstown. The doors to the left of the fireplace lead into the living room, one end of which, cleared for dancing, is visible. On the left, down-stage, is an ordinary door, opening onto the hall and leading thence to the bedrooms upstairs. Thus, the library is a backwater, quiet and not greatly frequented by the boys and their guests, although the life of the fraternity house flows around it on the terrace, in the living room, and in the hall.

Most of the wall space is covered from floor to ceiling with built-in bookshelves; the lower shelves have panelled doors (about three feet from the floor in height). The rest of the shelves are filled with books with the exception of the top shelves on which are arranged the class-cups, swimming trophies, prizes, etc., of the fraternity.

In front of the fireplace, facing into it, and hiding the hearth completely from the rest of the room, is a long deep davenport backed by a wide table. On the table are lamps, one or two books, a low bowl of flowers and a silver-mounted elephant's tusk on a standard. On the left wall hangs a large painting of the first president of the fraternity. Beneath it is another davenport. Large richly upholstered chairs, occasional tables, standard ashtrays, complete the furnishings of the room.

The rug, the hangings, the upholstery, as well as the bindings of the books and all the accessories of the room are very expensive and in the best taste. The entire atmosphere is one of well-bred luxury carefully maintained for the sons of wealth who are members of the club. There are no pennants, no stolen signs, no chorus girls' slippers, such as are usually supposed to decorate the living quarters of college undergraduates. The cups and trophies unostentatiously arrayed are the only collegiate tokens. Nor do the boys in the play wear over-baggy knickers, skullcaps or turtle-neck sweaters. The girls are attractive, well-groomed, vivacious students at Smith, Vassar, Dana Hall, Spence, and similar eastern schools; there are no Clara Bow jazz-flappers, and no feminine hip-flasks visible.

The entire action of the play takes place during houseparties, at which time the boys are dressed in their newest Rosie or Brooks clothes, well shaven, and on their best behavior.

ACT ONE

An orchestra is playing, and as the curtain rises, the tea dance of the first day of house-party is coming to a close.

The room is filled with autumn flowers, chrysanthemums, wild asters, colored leaves, and through the terrace windows floods the deep gold of late afternoon.

On the terrace and in the living-room dancing couples are seen weaving patterns in motion and color, while in the library MRS. RUTHERFORD, MRS. WHITE, PROFESSOR WHITE *and* EDDIE CANBY *are discovered playing bridge at a folding table left. The hand has just been dealt, but* MRS. RUTHERFORD *resolutely continues her inconsequential commentation.*

MRS. RUTHERFORD. Did you ever see such clothes as people wore to the President's reception? Now, that Mrs. Plendon, she was in fuchsia.

MRS. WHITE. One heart.

PROFESSOR WHITE. One spade.

[EDDIE *is paying no attention, having escaped momentarily into an imaginary world where duty and suffering are unknown and freshmen are never called upon to make a fourth for faculty bridge*]

MRS. WHITE. Spade bid, Edward.

EDDIE. Oh, yes. Uh—two hearts.

MRS. RUTHERFORD. Two spades.

MRS. WHITE. Three hearts.

PROFESSOR WHITE. Pass.

MRS. WHITE. Your turn, Edward.

EDDIE. Oh . . . uh . . . pass. [*He smiles warmly at* MRS. WHITE, *whom he considers to be beautiful, sympathetic, intelligent, and probably misunderstood by her husband*]

MRS. RUTHERFORD. Three . . . uh-h. No, I pass. Your play, partner. [PROFESSOR WHITE *leads.* EDDIE *gladly lays down his hand*] Very good support [MRS. WHITE *follows from dummy.* MRS. RUTHERFORD *plays after much hesitation.* MRS. WHITE *trumps the trick*] She hasn't any spades. We should have gone to three spades.

PROFESSOR WHITE [*seeing an honor in spades*

in EDDIE's *hand, points it out to* MRS. RUTHER-FORD]. Sh-h-h.

EDDIE [*would like to rush right over to the door and watch the dancing, but etiquette demands that he show the chaperons some attention first. Seeing a cigarette box on the table, he passes it gallantly to* MRS. RUTHERFORD]. Will you have a cigarette, Mrs. Rutherford?

MRS. RUTHERFORD [*with the frigidity of one whose virtue has been doubted—publicly*]. No, thank you.

EDDIE. Will you have one, Mrs. White?

MRS. WHITE. Yes, thanks.

MRS. RUTHERFORD [*torn between propriety and adventure, decides to emulate* MRS. WHITE]. Oh, Mr. Canby, I've changed my mind, I will have one.

[*While* MRS. RUTHERFORD *puffs valiantly at her cigarette, the game is delayed. Finally* PROFESSOR WHITE *calls her attention to the cards*]

PROFESSOR WHITE. You may play, whenever you are ready, Mrs. Rutherford.

MRS. RUTHERFORD. Oh, yes. I'm so sorry. [*She discards*]

PROFESSOR WHITE. Having no trumps, partner?

MRS. RUTHERFORD. Oh, I'm so sorry. [*She carefully selects another card*] Honestly, I don't see why she picked that fuchsia color. It isn't as though she were in the Romance Language Department. [MRS. WHITE *has led again and* MRS. RUTHERFORD *plays wrong card*]

PROFESSOR WHITE. Still having no trumps, partner?

MRS. RUTHERFORD [*taking back the card and substituting a trump*]. Oh, I'm so sorry. It was in there among my diamonds. Even in the English Department a dress like that would be a trifle ridiculous, but in the Political Sciences!

[*Several hands are played,* MRS. WHITE *leads hearts again.* MRS. RUTHERFORD, *this time triumphant, plays a higher heart, overtrumping* MRS. WHITE]

MRS. RUTHERFORD. There, I played right that time.

PROFESSOR WHITE [*sotto voce*]. Remarkable. [*On the next trick,* PROFESSOR WHITE *has to discard, having no trumps*]

MRS. RUTHERFORD. No trumps, partner?

PROFESSOR WHITE. No trumps.

[EDDIE, *temporarily released from bondage, has wandered over to the windows leading to the terrace.* BEATRICE *and* JACK, *who are dancing, stop and come into room*]

BEATRICE. Come on out, Eddie.

EDDIE [*pointing to the bridge game*]. I can't.

BEATRICE. Oh-h-h. [*She and* JACK *dance away*]

[*During this business another trick is played and* MRS. RUTHERFORD *discards*]

MRS. RUTHERFORD. Have you seen my cigarette, Mrs. White?

MRS. WHITE. No, I haven't.

MRS. RUTHERFORD. Have you seen my cigarette, Professor White?

PROFESSOR WHITE. You had it in your hand a moment ago.

[*The game stops while they search for the cigarette*]

MRS. RUTHERFORD. Whatever in the world could I have done with it? Oh well, never mind, it will turn up.

[*Play continues.* MRS. RUTHERFORD *plays a trump on* MRS. WHITE's *lead*]

MRS. RUTHERFORD. There. That's ours.

MRS. WHITE. You revoked.

MRS. RUTHERFORD. Why, no. I followed suit right along.

MRS. WHITE [*turning up the last trick played*]. Here is the last trick. I led hearts and you discarded.

MRS. RUTHERFORD. Why uh— [*She screams and rises*] Oh-oh—oh!

EDDIE [*rushing down from window*]. What's the matter? Can I help you?

MRS. RUTHERFORD [*clutching her bosom frantically*]. It's the cigarette. It's in there.

[EDDIE *slaps her on the stomach in a commendable effort to be of some use and attempts to recover the offending cigarette in a simple and straightforward manner.* MRS. RUTHERFORD *indignantly removes* EDDIE's *hand from her dress*]

MRS. RUTHERFORD. Mr. Canby! I can attend to it. [*She exits hurriedly through door left. The other three are in spasms of laughter*]

EDDIE [*with a wide mammiform gesture*]. I don't see how that could happen to Mrs. Rutherford.

PROFESSOR WHITE. Anything is liable to happen to Mrs. Rutherford.

EDDIE [*innocently trying to make a joke*]. I'll bet that is the hottest she's been in a long time.

MRS. WHITE [*reprovingly, but laughing all the time*]. Eddie! You shouldn't say such things.

[EDDIE *is embarrassed at the realization of what he has said, and* MRS. WHITE *and* THE PROFESSOR *again burst into uncontrollable laughter.* MRS. RUTHERFORD *re-enters*]

MRS. WHITE [*trying to conceal her laughter*]. Are you all right, Mrs. Rutherford?

MRS. RUTHERFORD [*resuming her place at bridge table*]. Quite all right, thank you. It's happened before. It's nothing but what can be replaced. Now let's see. Where was I?

MRS. WHITE. Well if you remember, you revoked.

MRS. RUTHERFORD. Oh, so I did. Didn't I? That comes from people talking to me, Professor White. Really, I never can play when people talk.

MRS. WHITE. That gives us game and rubber.

MRS. RUTHERFORD [*dismissing the game without another word*]. Now let me see. What was I saying? Oh yes, the Political Sciences. Blue or gray would have been much more sensible, don't you think so, Mr. Canby?

EDDIE [*who has been yearning slightly at* MRS. WHITE *beyond* PROFESSOR WHITE'S *range of vision*]. Huh—?

MRS. RUTHERFORD. Don't you think blue or gray would have been much more sensible?

EDDIE. Oh, sure.

MRS. WHITE. I don't believe that Mr. Canby is interested in these details of faculty wardrobe.

EDDIE. Oh, yes, I am.

MRS. WHITE. By the way, don't you dance, Edward?

EDDIE. Oh yes, Mrs. White, I dance.

MRS. RUTHERFORD. Perhaps you prefer bridge?

EDDIE. Oh yes, I'm very fond of bridge.

PROFESSOR WHITE. Besides, Edward's inamorata is not attending the festivities.

EDDIE. Beg Pardon?

PROFESSOR WHITE. You haven't got a girl up.

EDDIE. No, sir. They don't let freshmen have girls up for the Fall parties.

MRS. RUTHERFORD. Don't they let them dance either?

EDDIE. Yes, but . . .

MRS. WHITE [*with a knowing glance at* PROFESSOR WHITE]. But you really prefer playing bridge with the chaperons?

EDDIE. Yes'm. [*With great daring*] With you.

MRS. WHITE [*is pleasantly conscious of* EDDIE'S *infatuation, but prefers to ignore it until* PROFESSOR WHITE *goes down to that convention in New Haven*]. And this evening— what time does the dancing begin?

EDDIE. About ten.

MRS. WHITE. Well, the chaperons will be at the bridge table at nine forty-five, waiting for you.

EDDIE. I don't believe I can play tonight. I'm on the towels.

MRS. RUTHERFORD. On the towels?

EDDIE. Yes'm. That means I have to see that there are fresh towels in the periwinkle—I mean the lavatory—and watch the coats and tell people where to go and—

MRS. WHITE. Oh, you're vestiaire? That must be fun. And did you volunteer for that?

EDDIE. No. I drew it. That is—the freshmen have certain duties—I mean—

PROFESSOR WHITE. What you mean, Edward, is that the dirty work of supervising the lavatories and entertaining the chaperons is delegated to the newly initiated brothers.

EDDIE. Yes, sir.

MRS. WHITE. Did you draw first choice, Edward?

EDDIE [*complacently*]. Yes.

MRS. WHITE. Wasn't that nice? Then as a choice of two evils, you chose the towels.

EDDIE. Yes.—I mean, no—

PROFESSOR WHITE. Of course Edward didn't mean that. He'd much prefer to spend the evening playing bridge with us. Wouldn't you, Edward?

EDDIE. Yes, sir.

PROFESSOR WHITE. I'll speak to Dar Jenkes then and tell him that we like you so much as a bridge partner that we must have you again for tonight.

EDDIE. Yes, sir.

PROFESSOR WHITE. Then we'll count on you. But no doubt the ladies will become extremely bored with the cards after an hour and we'll excuse you—

EDDIE. Oh, you mean—

MRS. WHITE. That I often get dizzy spells after looking at the cards too long.

EDDIE. Thank you. Oh—I mean I'm sorry— for your dizzy spells.

PROFESSOR WHITE. Good-bye, Edward.

EDDIE. Good-bye, sir.

MRS. WHITE. We've enjoyed this afternoon so much.

MRS. RUTHERFORD. It's been delightful, Mr. Canby. [EDDIE *helps her with her wrap, trying manfully to keep a joyous nunc dimittis from his face and voice*] Thank you. Don't forget to put the table in the hall near the dancing. The nearer it is, the better it will be for all of us. Then perhaps after the bridge, we can have a little dance.

EDDIE. It's been a great pleasure, Mrs. Rutherford. I've certainly enjoyed this afternoon, a lot, Mrs. White. I shall look forward to the game this evening.

[*They exeunt.* MRS. WHITE *comes back immediately*]

MRS. WHITE [*with that faintest degree of the maternal which safeguards experienced faculty-wives*]. Edward, I'll see that Professor White cuts in on your dance with Mrs. Rutherford.

EDDIE. That will be fine. Then perhaps I can dance with you.

MRS. WHITE. I'll enjoy that. Good-bye, Edward.

EDDIE [*more convinced than ever that her husband cannot appreciate her pure and shining spirit*]. Good-bye.

[*He stands watching her for a moment as she leaves. Then closing the door softly, he leans against it in ecstatic revery; it is of short duration, however, for* RONNIE *and* SALLY *have entered from the living-room and are watching this exhibition with unconcealed interest*]

RONNIE. Well, what's the matter with you?

EDDIE [*with rapidly acquired dignity, draws himself to his full height*]. It's nothing. Nothing you would understand. [*He strides aloofly across the room, but dropping his elaborate condescension at the door, he rushes across the terrace, shouting*] Oh, Chick! Chick!

RONNIE. Mad! Quite mad!

SALLY. Wouldn't you be mad if you had to play bridge tonight with the chaperons?

RONNIE. I don't know. I might be able to get a word in edgewise with my partner at odd moments. That's more than I do dancing with you.

SALLY. But I've told you, Ronnie, that you mustn't talk to me when we're dancing. I get out of step when my heart flutters.

RONNIE [*who has said the same thing before*]. Heart! I don't believe you have one.

SALLY [*to whom the remark is far from novel*]. That's because it isn't exposed. You're used to the obvious. That's the only thing I hold against Mary Lou and Babbie and all those other girls. They've spoiled you for short sleeves. They made you lose your appreciation of the subtleties.

RONNIE. There's certainly nothing very subtle about your dirty digs.

SALLY. No?

RONNIE. No.

SALLY. I told you you were spoiled.

RONNIE. Sally, don't you suppose that maybe down underneath all your snootiness you really do like me the way I like you?

SALLY. Ronnie, my dear, I wouldn't be so unkind as to like you the way you like me. *You* wouldn't enjoy doing extra work in a mob scene.

RONNIE. Honestly, Sally, how many times do I have to tell you that you're really and truly the only girl I care a darn about. [*Intensely*] Sally, I . . .

SALLY. Stop it, Ronnie, and listen to me. I've roomed with two of the girls who used to be on your extensive—to say nothing of expensive—list. I've listened to them when they came back from proms with you. And I was present on that unfortunate evening when they compared notes on your letter writing and your technique. Now, really, Ronnie, do you expect me to believe that you love me, always have loved me, and always will?

RONNIE. Yes.

SALLY. The Lord giveth and the Lord taketh away.

RONNIE. What?

SALLY. The Lord gave you your slippery line and the Lord took away your sense of humor. [*Impatiently*] Come on, let's pretend it's funny. Let's both laugh.

RONNIE. Maybe I did lose my sense of humor, but that was because I met you.

SALLY [*with mock indignation*]. And now who's making the dirty digs? Nothing like telling a girl she's the only joke in life you can't see.

RONNIE [*smiling in spite of himself*]. I give you up. You're the only riddle in life I can't answer.

SALLY [*gaily*]. There! That's right to the point. I don't want to be answered. Least of all answered back. I want to be Sally the unsolved. The greatest mystery of the twentieth century! Step right up, ladies and gentlemen. But don't try to find out what makes her go.

RONNIE. At least it isn't a heart. Just some sort of clockwork that has no feelings.

SALLY [*thoughtfully*]. It seems to me I've heard that before.

RONNIE [*trying to put an arm around her*]. But seriously, Sally . . .

SALLY [*moving away—but not too far away*]. Duty or recreation, Ronnie?

RONNIE [*visibly embarrassed*]. Why . . . what do you mean?

SALLY [*who planned this speech, word for word, during a physiology lecture three weeks before* RONNIE *even decided to ask her to houseparty*]. As I remember, you once wrote to Babbie—or was it Jane Shaw? Jane, I guess; yes, that would be it; Jane came in about May of last year; say from the sixth to the twenty-first of May—anyway, *you* were the one who wrote: necking is either a duty or a recreation. If it's a duty, avoid it. If it's a recreation, pursue it until it becomes a duty.

RONNIE [*angrily*]. Don't you girls do anything except read each other's letters? It seems to me, if you had any decency . . .

SALLY [*helpfully*]. Yes?

RONNIE [*lamely*]. Well, you'd respect a fellow's feelings.

SALLY. Oh, but we do! You can't imagine how much we respect your feelings, Ronnie; why we sit around and watch and wait for a new manifestation of Ronnie Evans' feelings. It's ever so much more thrilling than going to the movies now that Valentino's dead.

RONNIE. If you wouldn't go flying off on these tangents of imagination, we might be able to talk sensibly. [*Moving towards her*] Sally, let's talk this thing out.

SALLY [*pushing him away lightly*]. Bring out your best arguments and I'll guarantee to laugh.

RONNIE [*earnestly*]. I don't see why you always have to be snooty to me.

SALLY [*calmly*]. Don't you? Well, I do. For exactly the same reason that you have such a smooth and slippery line that every time you whisper sweet nothings to a girl it re-echoes all over Smith, Vassar, and Wellesley. You can't help your actions any more than I can help my reactions. You're just made that way. No doub it's a gift. But I don't accept presents that have been used before.

[BILL *and* CHICK *enter, left*]

RONNIE [*forcefully*]. But damn it, Sally, I tell you that . . .

SALLY. Oh, Ronnie . . .

RONNIE [*seeing the boys*]. Oh, hello.

BILL [*laughing*]. I'm afraid we're interrupting one of the Sally-Ronnie Battles of the Century.

SALLY [*airily*]. Not at all. Not at all. Ronnie's idea of fighting is to be up in arms with a girl. So I called it off.

CHICK. Well, now it's my turn. How about giving me a chance. Let's wrestle.

RONNIE. Lay off, Chick. Any results from the football manager competition yet?

BILL. Haven't heard of any.

RONNIE. I'm afraid Alan is pretty worried waiting to find out about it. Have you seen him?

BILL. Yes, indeed! He's still trying to entertain that girl of Jerry's!

SALLY. Poor Alan. Someone ought to help him out. He's been stuck with her all afternoon.

RONNIE. I'd better go.

BILL. Oh, leave him alone. He's intelligent enough to take care of himself. [*Looking angrily at* RONNIE] Everybody's always treating Alan as though he were a baby.

RONNIE. Including our Bill.

BILL. Anyway, he's probably so bowed down with grief because his Patricia couldn't come to the party that he doesn't know whether he's dancing or not.

SALLY. Pat's a darling! I don't blame Alan for being crazy about her.

RONNIE. He'll get over it. That is, in a week or two. One does.

SALLY. How long did you say it takes, Ronnie?

RONNIE. I was talking about Alan, not myself.

SALLY. Oh!

CHICK. Say, why don't you two do a book on domestic harmony?

RONNIE. What I mean is, Alan is not really in love. If he didn't see Pat's beautiful face every day, he'd forget about her in a week. And you know what I mean.

SALLY. And who should know better!

BILL. Well, let him at least fall in and out of love for himself. He's capable.

SALLY. Alan's sweet.

BILL. I know, you feel as though you ought to see if he's washed behind the ears.

[*Enter* DARROW JENCKES *and* DORIS CALLANDER *from lower right*]

DARROW [*as usual taking his presidential duties most seriously*]. Who hasn't washed behind his ears?

RONNIE. Here comes Papa Darrow, our newly elected head of the house.

DORIS. And father of all the freshmen.

BILL. All except Eddie Canby. He's an example of mass production.

RONNIE. Dar is our supreme authority on everything.

DARROW. You can see all the authority I have. I told Eddie Canby to clean up after they were through. Where did he go?

RONNIE [*pointing to terrace*]. He went mad in that direction.

DARROW [*going to terrace door and calling*]. Canby. Eddie Canby.

EDDIE [*off right*]. Yes, Dar.

DARROW. Come here.

RONNIE. Don't let him bite you when he comes in.

EDDIE [*appearing disheveled in door*]. Yes, Dar?

DARROW. Come in here.

EDDIE. Come in?

DARROW. Yes, come in! Clean up those cards as I told you to do and put that table away.

[MARIAN *and* CHICK *follow* EDDIE *in, going through force of habit directly to a couch*]

EDDIE [*hastily and cheerfully*]. Oh, yes, I forgot. [*He gathers up the cards, tossing them hurriedly on top of the books in the case, and and folds up the table, whistling merrily*]

DARROW. The cards don't belong there.

EDDIE [*folding up bridge table*]. I know, but I'll be needing them again before long.

DORIS. Oh, Dar, you make him work so hard.

DARROW. Well, after all why not? He came to college for an education.

BILL. What are you so pleased about?

EDDIE [*bursting with enthusiasm*]. Professor White fixed things up with Dar so that I could play bridge with the chaperons. Isn't that swell?

BILL. Really, I don't believe he's well. Imagine all that enthusiasm over taking care of the chaperons. Are you in love with one of them?

EDDIE. Well, suppose I am?

DARROW. What?

EDDIE. Well, after all why not? I came to college for an education.

DARROW [*vehemently*]. Are you inviting chastisement?

[EDDIE *dashes out the door left with the card table*]

SALLY. I think this afternoon's game touched his brain. They do say that a mind will give way under great suffering.

DORIS. I didn't know freshmen were supposed to have brains.

SALLY. Come! Come! Be true to your alma mater, Doris. That's a Radcliffe line. You have to wear groundgrippers and horn spectacles in order to belittle the freshmen. At Smith we're capable of belittling seniors. And they do tell me that there is a girl at Vassar who once put a college president in his place.

DARROW. Say! This is sub-rosa; so don't say anything about it, but I just saw Herb Schnell; he's been counting votes all day for the Athletic Council and he says that Alan's got the managership hands down. Isn't that swell?

CHICK. No? Gee, that's great.

RONNIE [*with a sigh of relief*]. Well, I'm glad of that. Alan's been worried to death for the past week.

BILL. I hope it doesn't make him swell-headed.

DARROW. They haven't got the final count yet, but Herb said it looked certain. Bud Pendergrast is runner-up. [*Gloatingly*] Well, I guess that means a man tapped for Gargoyle in your delegation; I was beginning to give up hope.

RONNIE. Well, I don't give a darn about your Gargoyle, but I'm certainly glad the kid got it. He'd have felt pretty sick if he'd lost out.

MARIAN. Is the football managership so important?

CHICK. Football managership is one of the biggest jobs around college. [*He takes advantage of the others' interest to share a moderate kiss with* MARIAN, *whom he invited up for that purpose*]

DARROW [*complacently*]. Alan's a good worker; takes things seriously.

[BILL *turns away with disgust*]

SALLY [*looking archly at* RONNIE]. A trait I admire—taking things seriously.

RONNIE. One of the reasons why you're so fond of me, no doubt.

DORIS. Sally! Are you getting fond of Ronnie?

SALLY [*judiciously*]. Well, I shouldn't say that. He interests me. He's sort of a museum piece; I like to take him out occasionally and admire him; but I'd be scared to death to have him around the house.

DORIS. He has that priceless quality. I imagine he is the incarnation of Don Juan anyway.

SALLY. And maybe Apollo Belvedere and Lord Byron thrown in.

RONNIE. And you represent the fatal blending of Lilith and Helen of Troy.

SALLY. "Sweet Helen, make me immortal with a kiss!" I can see the quotation you're leading up to.

RONNIE. I was merely going to ask "Is *that* the mouth that staunched a thousand lips?"

BILL [*dragging up a chair*]. Get your ring-side seats! The battle is on!

RONNIE. No battle! Sally wins by default. I admit she's a knockout.

[ALAN *appears in door right*]

DORIS [*casually, seeing* ALAN]. Hello, Alan.

[ALAN *hesitates with a sensitive person's innate fear of intruding*]

SALLY [*looking around*]. Well, well, well. If it isn't our own little Alan. Come in.

ALAN [*still hesitant*]. What are you talking about?

SALLY [*gaily*]. Why, Alan, we've just been waiting for you; come in and say hello nicely to everybody.

[ALAN *enters*]

CHICK. Congratulations!

MARIAN. Sh-h!

ALAN [*starting up; his face bright with anticipation*]. What for?

[DARROW *frowns at* CHICK, *shaking his head to signify silence*]

CHICK. Oh—er—for picking such a marvelous partner to dance with all afternoon.

ALAN [*his anticipation fading visibly; embarrassed that he has given his anxiety away*]. Oh—yes.

[*Boys frown angrily at* CHICK]

BILL [*sarcastically*]. And what did you do with your beautiful and intellectual partner?

RONNIE. How did you get rid of Hortense?

ALAN. I didn't get rid of her. I just left her.

SALLY. But, Alan, you didn't just walk off and leave her?

ALAN. Why, no. Not exactly—Steven Rand-some was there talking to her. So I came in here. That was all right, wasn't it?

SALLY. Well, you might at least have said you wanted a glass of water.

ALAN. Well, I told her I was going up to look after my dogs and she said she believed me.

DORIS. Oh, how *is* Marie Antoinette, Alan?

ALAN. She didn't seem so well this afternoon, when I went up to see her. She's up at the vet's. You see, she just had some puppies, three of them. One of them died. [*Without any self-consciousness he draws some sketches from his pocket*] Here's a picture of the one that died.

SALLY. Oh, it's sweet.

DORIS. I've never seen any of your drawings, Alan; let me see it.

ALAN. I've got some others here.

RONNIE. They're awfully good.

CHICK. I like the face on this one. Sort of embarrassed as though he had done something he shouldn't.

SALLY. I can't bear to think of that little one being dead.

ALAN [*with the sincerity of an ardent theorist*]. You know, it seems to me that a dog probably feels just like a human being about its children. What I mean is, the littlest puppy died and she misses it and the more she thinks about it, the more perfect it seems to have been. Just the way people always think of all the good things about a relative after he's dead.

DORIS. Why, Alan, you have the style of Beardsley. [*Laughter from* ALAN] Well, it does look like Beardsley, doesn't it, Bill?

BILL. I think it looks more like Eddie Canby.

ALAN. So I go up there and play with the other puppies in front of her so that she will pay more attention to them. Then maybe she'll get better. Do you think that's silly, Doris?

DORIS. No, I think it's sweet.

BILL. Sounds like a two year old.

ALAN [*confused by* BILL'S *sharpness*]. Well, I didn't intend to talk so much about it, Bill. I'd better go out and see how Hortense is.

RONNIE. Never mind. She'll take care of herself.

DORIS. Where's the man Hortense came with?

CHICK. He's drinking.

BILL. I think he must have been drinking before he asked her.

RONNIE. Don't be vindictive. It's not Jerry's fault. She was a blind date—Marian Meggs' room-mate. Jerry never saw her before she arrived in town.

ALAN. He's certainly doing his best never to see her again. Gee, I had to dance with her all afternoon while Jerry's down in Fayerweather Hall drinking his head off.

DORIS. *Now* I know why they call it a *blind* date.

DARROW. Don't start that. You sound like Alan and Ronnie when they get under way.

RONNIE [*turns suddenly to* ALAN *with his best vaudeville manner*]. Hello, Charlie. I've got a new job.

BILL [*with deep disgust, turning his back on them and walking to the window*]. Oh, my God!

DARROW [*mournfully*]. I knew you'd get them started.

ALAN [*assuming a minstrel pose*]. You don't say, Charlie. And what is it?

RONNIE [*clowning a bit*]. I'm a furnace man.

ALAN. A furnace man? And how do you like it?

RONNIE. Great!

[DORIS *and* SALLY *laugh, but the boys all groan*]

ALAN [*with the glibness of long practice*]. Well, well, Charlie. I have a new job myself.

RONNIE Is that so, Charlie? And what is it?

ALAN. I'm a traveling salesman for a salt company.

RONNIE. Ah, a salt seller!

ALAN *and* RONNIE [*clasping hands dramatically*]. Shake!

DARROW. Enough! Enough!

ALAN [*to* RONNIE]. Shall we give them the one about being married?

BOYS. No!

RONNIE. Bum audience. [*He sits by* SALLY *on couch right*]

DORIS. Why, I think they're cute.

BILL [*suave, but really nettled*]. You wouldn't if you heard it all day long. It's a disease they picked up in a cheap vaudeville

theatre, and only Death the Great Healer can put an end to it.

DARROW. And Death the Great Healer will if I wake up again in the middle of the night to hear one hyena yelling down the hall to the other, "Hey, Charlie. I've got a new job."

BILL [*with disgust*]. They lie awake nights trying to think up new combinations.

RONNIE [*undaunted*]. Combinations . . . that gives me an idea for a new one! Hey, Charlie—

EDDIE [*entering breathlessly*]. Say, Dar! What do you know? The finals for the football manager are up and Alan didn't get it. [*Seeing* ALAN *for the first time*] Oh. . . .

DARROW. You're crazy. I just saw Herb Schnell . . . [*He looks earnestly at* EDDIE, *who merely shakes his head silently*]

[*They all stand awkwardly looking at* ALAN, *surprised, and silent*]

EDDIE. But I tell you I—

DARROW. Shut up.

ALAN [*grips the table in a terrific effort not to show his disappointment. At last he manages a half-smile*]. Don't look so surprised. I—I really didn't expect it.

DARROW [*patting his shoulder*]. Too bad, Alan. You worked hard for it.

CHICK. It's a dirty shame, feller; you certainly deserved it.

[RONNIE *goes to* ALAN, *laying his hand sympathetically on his shoulder, saying nothing*]

ALAN. Thanks! That's all right. It doesn't make any difference to me. [*He struggles to control his disappointment*] Bud Pendergrast got it?

DARROW. Yeah. The Dekes again.

BILL. Damn them!

ALAN. Anyway, I'm glad Bud got it. He's a swell boy. We worked together most of the time. I'll have to telephone him.

RONNIE. Don't bother. You can phone him later.

ALAN. Maybe that would be better. [*He draws himself up, resolutely cheerful*] Oh, well, the competition kept me busy this Fall anyway. I saved a lot of money by not having time to go to the movies. [*Laughing forcedly*] Gee, everybody conspires to save me money. Think how much I've saved because Pat flunked an exam and couldn't come up to houseparty. Well, I'll have to buy you and Doris some flowers tomorrow, Sally, with my hard-earned savings!

SALLY [*going directly to him*]. Alan, you're a sporting gentleman. [*She kisses him lightly*]

ALAN. Thank you, Sally. It didn't make any difference really. [*With a leer at* RONNIE] How do you like that, Ronnie?

RONNIE [*stepping right up for his*]. Hey! Hey! I'm going out for the golf team, Sally.

I'm sure not to make it, so you might pay me in advance.

SALLY. No, indeed, I know my banking. Pay you in advance and I'd lose interest.

BILL. I've got to go and meet the seven-thirty-four.

SALLY. That sounds suspiciously like our cue to go and change for dinner. [*To* ALAN] What time *is* dinner?

ALAN. Eight o'clock.

SALLY [*with an elder-sister air*]. Well, be sure your tie is straight, and don't forget to shave.

BILL [*disagreeably*]. And wash behind your ears, Alan.

DARROW. And you might even put on some of that highly scented powder Bill coats himself with.

DORIS. Oh, is that why Bill always looks so pale?

CHICK. That's the reason.

BILL [*furtively wiping his chin and trying to appear dignified*]. Don't you know that a man puts powder on his face for one of two reasons: either he *has* shaved or he *hasn't?*

RONNIE. Bill the epigrammatic!

HORTENSE [*calling from the next room*]. Alan, Alan—where are you?

ALAN. Oh, Hell!

[*Everyone jumps up to flee from* HORTENSE. *It is apparent immediately upon her entrance that their precipitance is justifiable*]

DARROW. My God! Hortense! Come on, Doris.

[*Exit down right.* CHICK *and* MARIAN *exeunt to terrace right*]

HORTENSE [*flying into the room*]. Oh, there you are. [*Going to* ALAN] Oh, you poor dear child. I've heard all about it. Isn't it terrible about your not making the football managership? I think it's the most awful thing I ever heard. I only hope—

SALLY [*taking* ALAN *away from* HORTENSE]. Come on, Alan, take me to the door.

ALAN. Excuse me.

HORTENSE. Oh, but Alan, aren't you going to take me over to Mrs. Mac's?

ALAN. Oh . . . Oh . . . Uh . . . Ronnie said *he* wanted to take you to Mrs. Mac's. I think he wants to talk to you.

[*They* ALL *go out laughing, leaving* RONNIE *at the mercy of* HORTENSE]

HORTENSE. Oh, did you, Ronnie? Did you really, Ronnie?

RONNIE [*trying politely to hide his chagrin*]. Hadn't we better be getting dressed? We'll be late.

HORTENSE [*settling down comfortably*]. Oh, I don't mind if we are. I'm having much more fun with you.

RONNIE [*helplessly*]. Still, it's not very long before dinner.

HORTENSE. Oh, there's nearly an hour and a half. And it doesn't take me long to dress. And I'm staying just across the street. Do the boys all live in the frat houses? [*Her mind works even more quickly than her tongue with the result that many of her remarks seem to be non sequiturs*]

RONNIE [*snootily*]. Fraternity houses. Only a few colleges have frat houses and we don't have chapters there.

HORTENSE [*unconscious that she has been corrected*]. But do the boys all *live* in the frat houses?

RONNIE. All except the freshmen.

HORTENSE [*asks questions mechanically, having read somewhere that the secret of success lies in making the man do the talking*]. Where do the freshmen live?

RONNIE [*wearily*]. In the dormitories. [*Brightening for a moment*] Wouldn't you like to see them? You can see them from the house where you're staying. If you go over there . . .

HORTENSE [*her eyes wandering around the room*]. Now that I'm here I think I'd better see a frat house first. Can I go upstairs? [*Points to portrait on wall*] Who is that funny man with the beard?

RONNIE [*patiently*]. That's the founder of this fraternity.

HORTENSE [*squealing*]. Oooo! Did I say something awful?

RONNIE. No! You said just what almost every girl says when she comes into this room.

HORTENSE. Did I? I'm glad of that. [*Confidentially*] You see, I've never been to a college houseparty before. You didn't know that, did you?

RONNIE. Well, I rather guessed as much.

HORTENSE. You must be awfully clever.

RONNIE. No.

HORTENSE. Oh, but you must be to have guessed that. [*Pointing suddenly to the elephant's tusk on the center table*] Oh-h-h. Is that a real elephant's tusk?

RONNIE. Yes, I think so. They don't imitate elephants very much any more.

HORTENSE. Isn't it cute? Do you like to go to circuses? [*Looking around*] I just adore circuses. What are those cupboards for? My don't they look mysterious? [*She goes over to the cupboards under the bookcase left of fireplace*] Are they locked? What do you keep in them?

RONNIE [*with overbearing patience*]. No they're not locked. No, they're not at all mysterious. We keep magazines and text books and exam papers there. And a few old shoes and hats and sweaters that the boys leave around [*With deep thought*]— And, oh yes, two bound volumes of St. Nicholas for 1904.

HORTENSE [*who hasn't been listening to any*

thing he said]. St. Nicholas? I love St. Nicholas.

RONNIE. We don't use them very much ourselves. We keep them there for some of the girls who occasionally come up to houseparties. Would you like to see one of them now?

HORTENSE. No. *You* entertain me.

RONNIE. What shall I do, recite?

HORTENSE. Can you recite "The Night before Christmas?"

RONNIE. Not as a rule. I'm usually too tight the night before Christmas.

HORTENSE [*whose sense of humor is too rudimentary for that one*]. And don't you just adore James James Morrison Morrison Weatherby George Dupree took very good care of his mother although he was only three?

RONNIE [*taking her firmly by the hand*]. Only three. Yes. And now, don't you think you had better go get dressed?

HORTENSE [*breaks away from him with what she fondly supposes is a flirtatious gesture*]. Oh, no. I want to look around some more. You know, I feel just as though I was at my grandmother's. What do you keep in those drawers? [*Going to drawer of the center table, she opens it*] Oh, look! It's a gun! [*Reaching in, she pulls out a revolver and holds it up*]

RONNIE [*jumping up and taking it from her*]. Now, Hortense, don't you think you've seen about enough? [*He replaces the revolver and closes the drawer*] I'll tell you what I'll do. I'll play games with you sometime this evening.

HORTENSE. When? During the dance?

RONNIE. Perhaps during supper.

HORTENSE. During supper? Oh, I just love games. Did you ever play "I packed my trunk"? That's a great game. I'm awfully good at that.

RONNIE. Yes, I'll bet you are.

HORTENSE. But why do you have a gun?

RONNIE [*taking her by the elbow and propelling her towards the door*]. I can think of one very good reason for it, but it really belongs to James, the steward. There were some burglaries in town last Fall and James fears for the family plate.

HORTENSE. You mean the silver? Can I see it?

RONNIE. When you come back to dinner it will be all spread out on the table for you.

[ALAN *enters down stage left in shirtsleeves, coat and tie in hand*]

HORTENSE. Hello, Alan, Ronnie's been showing me the library. We've had a time, haven't we, Ronnie?

RONNIE. I should say so! [*To* ALAN, *mock-threateningly*] Just wait here until I come back.

ALAN. Good-bye, Hortense.

HORTENSE. Oh, good-bye. I'll see you soon. We're all going to play games during supper. Ronnie said so.

[RONNIE *drags her off by main force,* HOR-

TENSE *squealing with delight, having read of the desirability of strong forceful men.* ALAN *throws down his coat and tie and flings himself despondently into a chair*]

RONNIE [*re-appears in the doorway, briskly cheerful, and hurls a pillow at* ALAN]. A great guy you turned out to be!

ALAN [*tossing the pillow aside disconsolately*]. I know. But don't rub it in.

RONNIE [*perplexed*]. Rub it in?

ALAN. I suppose all the fellows are sore because I failed.

RONNIE [*quickly sympathetic*]. Why, I didn't mean that, Alan. I was talking about your sicking Hortense on me.

ALAN. Oh, yes.

RONNIE [*going to him*]. It was tough about the managership, kid. But get this idea that the fellows are sore out of your head. Why, they don't feel that way at all. [*He tousles* ALAN *affectionately*] Now, come on, don't let it spoil your party.

ALAN [*tries to respond to* RONNIE's *mood*]. The dean at Smith did that when she wouldn't let Pat come up.

RONNIE. Deans don't seem to have any finer feelings.

ALAN. I know it. [*He returns to the subject uppermost in his mind*] I called up Bud; he was all excited. That guarantees him Gargoyle, practically. Any other senior honors he wants, too.

RONNIE. Hell! There's plenty of fun in college without having a string of charms hanging on your watch chain.

ALAN. Yes. I suppose so.

RONNIE [*emphatically*]. Now, listen here, kid. Don't go and get all down in the mouth simply because you didn't get elected. That doesn't make you a nigger. You were runner up. [ALAN *sits down, attentive, while* RONNIE *goes on argumentatively*] Lord! That virtually amounts to your being elected the second most popular man in the class. What more do you want? Anyway, the Dekes have a bigger delegation than we have or you might have been first.

ALAN [*slowly, smiling shamefacedly*]. I guess you're right. But that doesn't bother me any more.

RONNIE. Yeah? I saw the gloom come over your face when Eddie brought in the bad news.

ALAN. You see too damn much. I always do get in a stew over things. And most of the time they don't really count, do they, Ronnie?

RONNIE [*impatiently*]. But you shouldn't. Don't be so darn sensitive. [*He sits down beside* ALAN, *continuing more kindly*] If you'd only forget your imaginary injuries as easily as you do your eight o'clock classes, you'd enjoy life a lot more. Honestly, I'd hate to think what you'd do if anything real ever happened to you.

ALAN [*laughing ruefully*]. That sounds familiar. I listened to just those same words all last year when I was rooming with Bill. You two have the same technique in bawling me out.

RONNIE [*gruffly to hide his real feeling*]. Well, you need to be bawled out.

ALAN. I know it. I need it. I don't seem to be able to snap out of things by myself. I seem to need someone pulling at me and telling me what not to do and slapping me on the back all the time. Damn silly.

RONNIE. I'll say it's damn silly—

[BILL *enters from the door down right. He goes over to the center table and takes a cigarette and begins to light it*]

ALAN. Going to the train, Bill?

BILL [*brusquely*]. Yes!

ALAN. You're going to get Jack's girl, aren't you?

BILL. Yes!

ALAN. You'd better hurry. You know she hates to be kept waiting.

BILL [*going to the door down left. Impatiently*]. Yes, I know—I know— [*He goes out*]

ALAN [*sits for a second in deep thought and then seriously turns to* RONNIE *who is lying on the sofa, right, planning a speech for* SALLY] Say, Ronnie. What's the matter with Bill?

RONNIE. Matter? I haven't noticed anything different about him.

ALAN [*very seriously*]. I don't think he likes me.

RONNIE [*emphatically*]. Of course he likes you.

ALAN. No. He's always making dirty cracks in my direction.

RONNIE [*laughing assuringly*]. My good God! Bill's always making dirty cracks in everybody's direction. That's Bill's way of being pleasant.

ALAN [*only partly convinced*]. I suppose so, but . . .

RONNIE [*impatiently*]. There you are. Brooding over something that hasn't happened at all.

ALAN [*turning to argue*]. He always made cracks at me and I never used to mind, but now they seem to be more . . . more aggressive. As though he really meant them. Gee, I ought to understand Bill. He used to be my closest friend.

RONNIE [*looking away*]. That's just it. [*Turning suddenly to* ALAN, *flinging off his embarrassment*] Don't you see? He *used* to be your closest friend. You and he grew up together. And he bossed you around and bawled you out and spanked your bottom for you. . . . [*Laughing*] God knows you probably needed it! . . . and then you two came to college together and roomed together last year— and now you and *I* are sharing a study and *I* spent Christmas vacation at your home and

you make the night hideous with your wails when *I* paddle your tail and tell you what a damn fool you are. Naturally Bill is a trifle glum. So he makes sour cracks just to show that he doesn't care. [*Bitterly*] I know just how it is. I do the same thing sometimes when I'm with Sally. [*Intensely*] Gee, but I like her. [*Then furiously*] But, damn it, she gripes me! She laughs at everything I say to her. Thinks I'm always trying to be funny. [*He ponders that problem for a moment and then cheerfully dismisses it*] Oh, well. I'll snap out of that and convince her.

ALAN [*with slow admiration*]. I wish I were like that. I guess I haven't got enough guts.

RONNIE [*goes to him and lays his arm on* ALAN'S *shoulder*]. You know I'm all for you, kid.

[*They stand there a moment in silence. Suddenly they realize that they are perilously near expressing in words their real fondness for each other. They move quickly apart*]

ALAN [*vigorously*]. Let's get dressed. Oh, by the way! I have a new job, Charlie.

RONNIE. Oh, have you, Charlie? [*He flings himself on* ALAN; *the two scuffle boisterously*] Well, I have one myself—chastising you for leaving me with Hortense. Stand up while I sock you one! Of all the dirty tricks, deliberately saddling me with that woman. I'll get you a new job, Charlie, my boy. One that you will be just coffin over.

ALAN. Let go my shirt, will you. Ow!

RONNIE. Apologize.

ALAN. Like hell I will! [RONNIE *gets a painful grip on him*] Hey, you're killing me. Cut it out, will you?

RONNIE. Apologize.

ALAN. Ouch! I apologize.

RONNIE [*still holding him*]. And I'm a pretty good guy?

ALAN. Yes. You're a prince. [RONNIE *lets him up. His shirt is completely pulled out*] But you know how I spell prince!

[RONNIE *throws a pillow at him*]

JAMES [*entering left*]. Pardon me, Mr. Bradford, but there's someone to see you. [*He shows disapproval*] A lady, sir.

ALAN. For me?

JAMES. Yes, sir.

ALAN [*perplexedly*]. Who the devil . . . [*Reaching for his shirt*] I can't go and see anyone this way. Ronnie, you go out and see who it is.

RONNIE [*good naturedly*]. All right.

[*He goes out, followed by* JAMES. ALAN *hurriedly arranges his clothes. In a minute* RONNIE *returns, partly amused partly perplexed*]

ALAN. Who is it?

RONNIE. Of all people—Florence.

ALAN. Who?

RONNIE. Florence.

ALAN. What's she coming up here for? I don't want to see her.

RONNIE [cheerfully]. Don't ask me. You know her better than I do.

ALAN [peevishly]. I don't know her at all. I've only been out with her once. . . . [Aggrievedly] I don't want to see her. [Appealingly] You see her.

RONNIE [emphatically, laughing]. No, sir! She asked very especially for you. [Seriously] Find out what she wants and tell her you're in a hurry to dress. [He exits left, turning to laugh over his shoulder]

[ALAN walks nervously to the door, left, frowning with perplexity. FLORENCE enters from the living-room. She is a pretty, young woman of perhaps twenty-eight years, slightly common. She wears copies of the sport clothes of the house-party girls she has seen on the campus, clothes a trifle too bizarre in cut and too cheap in material. The same might be said of her manners. She enters the room with an assurance so pronounced as to suggest bravado and a slight tensity may be detected under her easy appraisal of the library. Obviously she has not been there before, may never be there again, but she is coolly at ease, conscious that whatever situation may evolve it will be entirely in her control]

FLORENCE [casually]. Hello, Alan!

ALAN [turning suddenly]. Hello, Florence.

FLORENCE [looking around the room]. Attractive room.

ALAN. Yes. It is, isn't it?

FLORENCE. I don't usually get any further than the back porches of fraternity houses. [Advancing calmly towards a comfortable chair] Well, aren't you going to ask me to sit down?

ALAN [confused by her nonchalance]. Oh, yes. Certainly! Won't you sit down, Florence?

FLORENCE [sitting]. Thank you. Nice of you to ask me.

ALAN. Is there anything I can do for you, Florence? [Apologetically] You see—we're having a houseparty.

FLORENCE [in mock surprise]. Oh, really! A houseparty. [Sitting back comfortably] Then I must be intruding.

ALAN. Well, not exactly—look, can't I see you some other time?

FLORENCE. I'm afraid not. Won't you sit down?

ALAN. Oh, thanks—but really I like standing up.

FLORENCE. It's all the same to me. We may have to talk for a while and I wanted you to feel at home. [ALAN sits facing her. She scru-

tinizes him carefully, to his discomfort] Yep. You're the one.

ALAN [uncomfortably]. The one?

FLORENCE [in a tone of idle curiosity]. The girls back yet from dressing?

ALAN. I think some of them are. They'll be here shortly; we're eating at the house tonight. I shall have to dress right away. Florence, I wish you'd tell me if there's something I can do.

FLORENCE [easily]. Yes, Alan, you can do something for me. There's something I want.

ALAN. Look—can't you tell me on Monday?

FLORENCE [sarcastically]. You boys certainly are in an awful hurry on your own grounds. It's different when you're walking home with a girl. . . .

ALAN. You mean that night after the movies? I'm sorry. I didn't realize how late it was. And it was such a swell night, too. Was your mother angry?

FLORENCE. I'll say! She wanted to know what I was doing out so late. I told her I was out with you. And then she wanted to know what I was doing with you. [She winks maliciously] I didn't tell her. Thought I'd just let her guess. [She laughs knowingly] She did!

ALAN [protests]. But Florence! Why didn't you explain to her that we were just walking. You shouldn't let her think . . . You mean, she does think . . . ?

FLORENCE. And how! She'll be out gunning for you, if she doesn't decide to see the Dean first. Ma can make an awful row when she gets started. Don't you think perhaps you ought to do right by your Florence?

ALAN [startled by the undercurrent of determination in her voice]. What do you mean? I don't understand, Florence. I'm sorry I got you home late. And I'm sorry your mother was worried. I'd be very glad to apologize.

FLORENCE [laughing boisterously]. Alan, you're a wow! Offering apologies. That's something no one ever offered me before. But it's not what I want.

ALAN [fidgeting uncomfortably]. But Florence, what is it you want? [The voices of a few boys and girls returning across the lawn remind them both of the approaching dinner. ALAN rises hastily] Or perhaps I could see you later. This is rather a bad time, you know.

FLORENCE. Oh, it's a bad time is it? Then I guess I'll tell you now. I do want something, but it isn't an apology.

ALAN. You mean, you want . . .

FLORENCE. Right! I want some money.

ALAN [bewildered]. Of course, Florence, if I can help you. . . . Only I haven't very much . . . [He reaches for his wallet]

FLORENCE. Put your wallet away. I don't believe you carry around the amount I want.

ALAN. How much do you need?

FLORENCE. Ten thousand!

ALAN [sits down again, stunned by the demand]. What!

FLORENCE. Ten thousand.

ALAN. But, Florence, I haven't got that much. I haven't got that much in the world.

FLORENCE. I know it. But your old man has.

ALAN [becoming disturbed at her casualness]. I can't go and ask my father for ten thousand dollars.

FLORENCE [almost wearily]. You won't have to. I'll tend to that.

ALAN [completely bewildered]. But you can't just go and ask Dad for money. What are you after, Florence? What do you want it for? You can't just step up and ask for ten thousand dollars without any reason. You're . . . why, you're crazy, Florence. . . . I don't . . .

FLORENCE [with threatening deliberation]. Suppose I said I was going to have a . . . baby?

ALAN. Florence! . . . [Completely at a loss] Are you going to have . . .

FLORENCE. No. But supposing I said so? [ALAN stares at her uncomprehending] Supposing I mentioned you?

ALAN. But you couldn't. It wouldn't be true. You and I . . . Why, they could prove it was a lie.

FLORENCE. Sure. After it was in all the papers. All the papers. Anything connected with your old man would be on the front page. But maybe it won't get in the papers. . . .

ALAN. Florence, I don't understand. I don't know what you're talking about.

FLORENCE. You'll understand in a minute. It's a great idea. A fellow I know in Pittsfield who has been a lawyer mapped it all out for me. I've been fooling around this town for ten years now, waiting to hang something on someone, and now it's all set. Florence is all fixed from now on. Good fellows, good dresses, New York if I want.

ALAN [recovering his poise]. I know just how you must feel, Florence, after ten years here. I don't blame you for wanting to get away. But of course, asking Dad for money is impossible. [With a burst of boyish sympathy] Gee, it must be tough to be tied down to a town where you don't really know anyone and don't like it. You know I haven't got much money except the allowance that Dad gives me, but I'd be glad enough to try to scrape up something, and perhaps you could get a job in New York. . . .

FLORENCE. Perhaps . . . [Irritated by ALAN's naive unselfishness] Say, listen! If you wouldn't talk so damned much, I'd be able to explain this thing so you could understand it. [Reaching in her bag, she draws out a paper] Here, baby! There it is all in black and white!

ALAN [switches on table lamp and reads the letter. FLORENCE takes advantage of his preoccupation to survey the living-room. As she returns, ALAN looks up]. Why, I never wrote this, Florence. I never said that I loved you, that I wanted to marry you. And I never even thought of calling you—of calling you—well of using such names. I don't express myself quite that way.

FLORENCE. Of course you didn't write it. I wrote it for you. All you have to do is copy it and sign it. You can leave out one or two of the pet names if you want; the marriage part is what's worth money to me. [She smiles complacently at her own cleverness] You see, it's the simplest thing in the world. A straight breach of promise suit settled out of court. Settled out of court for ten thousand dollars. I think it would be worth that to your old man to keep his name out of the paper.

ALAN. Why, I wouldn't think of doing that to Dad. You don't know Dad; he's a prince. I wouldn't play a dirty trick like that on him for anything.

FLORENCE [angry at his unexpected resistance]. It would be a dirtier trick to fill the papers with a lot of scandal, wouldn't it? And I can do it. All the papers. Say, anything connected with your old man would be on the front page. Now, I'm letting you off easy. I even brought you a piece of paper and a fountain pen. [FLORENCE takes out pen and paper from bag and then throws her bag on couch]

ALAN. You're crazy, Florence. I'm not going to sign that letter. Why, it's just blackmail.

FLORENCE. Oh, no. That's not blackmail. The blackmail part's coming. Now, I don't want to have to do this. I don't want to be any scrimier than I have to, but this little deal is going through, Alan, and here's what happens if you don't start copying that letter right away: now, get this: Florence screams—and I can scream the house down if necessary—and then falls in a faint on the sofa. That's why I picked this hour of the day to come calling. Everybody rushes in, the boys and girls, and maybe a couple of professors and their wives, and what do they find? You and Florence. And Florence in a faint. And when poor Florence comes to, she starts telling them all about how you've played her dirt. I don't think you will get very far trying to laugh that off.

ALAN [completely aghast at her callousness]. You mean . . . you mean you would actually make a scene like that? That you'd do that in order to . . . Why, you couldn't! And it would be a lie. I could prove it.

FLORENCE. Maybe you could prove it. But by the time you do, your name and your father's name will be damn well known around this country. I don't care about my name; I could probably get a good job on the strength of it, but I'm willing to be decent. I'm giving you a chance to keep this quiet. But that's what happens if you don't get down to business.

ALAN. You *can't* do that, Florence. You can do what you want to me, but you can't do that to my father and mother. It would kill them. Dad hates anything of that sort. I'm their only son. I can't help you to hurt them that way. It isn't the money; it's what they'd think. [*Imploringly*] Please go, Florence. I'll come and see you next week.

FLORENCE. No, Alan, we'll settle this now.

ALAN [*is becoming terrified at her cold insistence*]. Florence, you can't be so hard. Honestly, Florence, I can't do it. Please, Florence, won't you go home now? I'll promise to come and see you next week. I'll promise to do anything I can to help you. Only please go now.

FLORENCE [*calmly*]. No.

ALAN. Please, Florence. You must be decent. [*Weakly*] I don't know what to do. I'll have to ask Ronnie. [*With a visible effort he gets some control of himself*] Listen, Florence. I won't do anything about that letter until I've talked it over with someone. You can wait here, if you want— [*He starts towards the door*]

FLORENCE [*seeing her plan failing, loses all her artificial calm and springs up, her voice rising*]. No, you don't. You stay right here. And I'll give you about three to get to work on that letter or I'll scream.

ALAN [*frantically locking the door*]. Sh!! Florence! Please don't make so much noise! [*He crosses to the living-room doors and closes them*]

[FLORENCE *is now standing on the hearth of the fireplace, directly behind the davenport*]

FLORENCE [*suddenly striking her hands together and crying in a hard, loud voice*]. Well!!! [ALAN *stands stock still, paralyzed by her sudden savageness. She remains immovable, rigidly erect, dominant.* ALAN *falteringly moves toward the paper and pen lying conspicuously on the table. As he approaches it, he hesitates a moment*] Well! [*In an agony of uncertainty, he picks up the pen. After a moment he starts to write, and then, pausing, looks helplessly toward* FLORENCE. *For a moment there is silence; the boy mutely eloquent with appeal . . . the woman tense and determined, the epitome of menace, as she stands before the fireplace. Suddenly* ALAN *throws down the pen and steps back from the table.* FLORENCE *cries out sharply*] All right, then.

ALAN [*as she opens her mouth to scream, rushes toward her, galvanized into instinctive action by her voice*]. Florence! For God's sake! . . . [*He seizes her, clapping his hand desperately over her mouth. As she strikes out viciously at him, pushing him violently away from her, she loses her balance. Her head hits against the stone of the high mantelpiece and* she falls onto the hearth behind the davenport. One of the great metal andirons is overturned with a menacing thud and the fire-irons clatter on the stone hearth.* ALAN *bends down quickly over the girl, and with a terrific effort pulls the heavy andiron off her*] Oh, Florence, I'm sorry! I didn't mean— [*He disappears behind the davenport. His voice comes sharply*] Florence!! . . . Florence!! [*And then there is a complete, frightening silence. . . . Slowly from behind the couch,* ALAN *rises, staring downwards, . . . his face stiff with horror. There is blood on his hands and unconsciously he rubs them together*] Florence! Stop staring like that. Get up.

[*He tries to lift her, but her body falls heavily to the floor. As he stands by the fireplace, dazed by the suddenness of the catastrophe, he becomes aware of the blood on his hands and drawing out his handkerchief, he wipes them mechanically. With that act comes a realization of disaster and with realization, panic. In the midst of* ALAN's *frantic uncertainty,* JAMES *the steward, enters silently*]

JAMES. Can I do anything, sir? [ALAN, *with a start, swings around*] Is there anything wrong, sir? Is there anything I can do?

ALAN [*slips rapidly to the end of the couch, hiding the body from* JAMES. *After a brief moment he has recovered his breath and enough self-control to reply*]. No. It's all right, James. [*He makes a feeble gesture of dismissal.* JAMES *stares at him curiously, but turns to leave.* ALAN *stops him*] James. Wait a minute. Tell Mr. Evans I want him. Tell him to come down right away.

[JAMES *crosses the room, flashing an inquiring glance at* ALAN *when it becomes necessary to unlock the door, and leaves to call* RONNIE. ALAN *stands, silent and taut, trying to force some order into the bewildering chaos of his mind. At length he returns to the hearth, staring down at what lies there until horror and disgust force him to turn away. He trembles slightly as though about to collapse, and steadies himself against the table*]

RONNIE [*enters down stage left. He is immediately startled at* ALAN's *appearance*]. Alan!

ALAN [*almost hysterically*]. Look, Ronnie. Look! Look what happened. . . . [*He sways as though about to fall*]

RONNIE [*starting towards him*]. Steady, kid. What's the trouble?

ALAN [*suddenly terrified lest* RONNIE *see the body, throws himself at the other boy*]. No, Ronnie! No! No! Don't!

RONNIE [*taking him forcibly by the shoulders and trying to lead him to a chair*]. Alan! Stop that! Alan, what's the matter?

ALAN [*resisting him. He seeks feverishly for a reason to get* RONNIE *out of the room*]. No, Ronnie, no! Listen, Ronnie! Listen! Listen, Ronnie. You've got to go. You've got to. Florence was here. She's gone, Ronnie. She's gone down town. She's gone down to the Dean's office, Ronnie. She's going to make trouble. You've got to stop her. Hurry, Ronnie. You've got to stop her! [*He pushes him violently towards the door*]

RONNIE [*trying to calm him*]. Wait a minute, Alan! Wait a minute, kid! Sit down!

ALAN [*flings himself at him with all his force*]. No, Ronnie. No! I'm all right. But you've got to go. You've got to! [*Almost crying*] Ronnie, please . . . [*He forces him to the door*]

RONNIE [*lets go of* ALAN *in the hope of calming him by giving in*]. All right. I'll go. [*As he crosses the room he warns* ALAN] But you stay here. I'll be right back. [*He runs out of the room*]

[*As soon as he has gone,* ALAN *flings the doors shut, locking them. Then he turns, an instinctive hunted look beginning to show in his face as he looks rapidly around the room. Across the lawn beyond the terrace come the voices of boys approaching, laughing and talking, drawing nearer and nearer every second. Feverishly* ALAN *searches the room in which he may be trapped with* FLORENCE'S *body. Then he rushes to the cupboard below the bookcase, throwing it open, and as the boys pass beyond the closed and curtained window, he commences to drag the mangled corpse toward the cupboard, murmuring in distracted terror*]

ALAN. Oh, my God.

THE CURTAIN FALLS

ACT TWO

It is about ten o'clock. The stage is not lighted, but the festively brilliant living-room and the gay lanterns of the terrace throw conflicting shadows across the deserted library. Through the doors can be seen the dancers, noisy and colorful, while on the stage ALAN *keeps a secret vigil in the dark. As one of the orchestra sings the refrain of a popular ballad,* ALAN *crosses slowly, almost stealthily, to the cupboard to the left of the fireplace. He does no more than stand in front of it, however, for at that moment the door left opens and* JAMES *appears carrying a bowl of punch.* ALAN *retreats silently through the door down right as* JAMES *places the punch bowl on the center table.*

JAMES *switches on the lights in the library, attracting the attention of the boys and girls, many of whom enter at once in a search of refreshment.* DARROW, DORIS *and* BILL *are among the first;* CHICK *and* MARIAN *are among the most loudly enthusiastic; others come and go gaily. One of the girls,* BEATRICE, *has just settled into a chair for a comfortable smoke with her escort, when* HELEN *enters and rushes over to them.*

HELEN [*is just the type of girl one would expect to be the fiancée of a boy known to all his fraternity brothers as Peter the Prim*]. Darling give me a drag of your cigarette before Pete catches me.

[*She snatches* BEATRICE'S *cigarette and has just taken a puff as* PETE *enters*]

PETE [*conversely, is just the type who would get engaged to a girl like* HELEN *and be called Peter the Prim by all his fraternity brothers. He goes quickly to* HELEN, *slapping the cigarette out of her hand*]. Helen, you know I don't like your doing that!

HELEN. Why can't *I* smoke if Beatrice does? . . .

PETE [*primly*]. Don't forget she comes from Smith, and after all, you're from Bordentown. . . .

HELEN. Hush! . . . I'm trying to forget the beloved seminary! . . . Pick up that cigarette, Peter the Prim!

PETE. I don't like that either! [*He picks up the cigarette and throws it into the fireplace*]

HELEN. I suppose he'd rather be called "Peter the Great." [*Having made what she considers to be an unanswerably clever remark, she goes over to inspect the punch bowl*] What kind of punch is this, Bill? Grape juice?

DORIS. You didn't expect champagne, did you?

BEATRICE. At Princeton they once popped paper bags in the pantry and four girls got the vapors, thinking they were drinking champagne.

PETE [*vaguely*]. The vapors . . . ?

CHICK. It's a polite form of intoxication, Peter. . . .

BEATRICE. And, believe me or not, they actually served lobster patties and *not* chicken à la king!

CHICK. Don't you believe it!

DORIS. *I* have it on Dar's good authority it *will* be lobster patties tonight!

CHICK. Who ever heard of such a thing! It's bound to be chicken à la king. This evening, promptly at eleven, in fifteen fraternity houses in Williamstown, hundreds of happy unsuspecting guests will be handed plates of chicken à la king.

RONNIE [*entering from the terrace and crossing to the back hall door*]. Hello, people. Where is Alan, do you know, Bill?

BILL. How should I know? *I'm* not his guardian. . . .

MARIAN. Where's Sally, Ronnie?

RONNIE. She's over at the Beta house. I just ran back for her shawl. [*He goes out through the hall door*]

[PETER *and* HELEN, *who have been quarrelling over the amount of punch* HELEN *has been drinking, pass belligerently onto the terrace as* DARROW *enters from living-room in search of his partner*]

DARROW. Come on, Doris. We'll have one dance at least.

[DARROW *and* DORIS *lead the way, followed by all the boys and girls except* BILL, *who stands in the door listening to the music, and* CHICK *and* MARIAN, *who have been waiting for this moment. They lose no time in taking advantage of the comparative privacy, with the result that their eyes are closed when* EDDIE *enters, down-stage left.* MRS. WHITE *has just had her dizzy spell, and* EDDIE *is happily engaged in putting the cards away. He goes to the cupboard to the left of the fireplace, but finding it locked, tosses the cards into another cabinet. Attracted by a faint sound from the occupants of the sofa, whose eyes are still closed, he approaches them and stands watching with that eager thirst for knowledge that marks a freshman who will go a long way. Unfortunately,* MARIAN *and* CHICK *suddenly see him and, springing up, put an end to what might have been a valuable lesson*]

CHICK [*angrily*]. Haven't you got any respect for love? [*He and* MARIAN *retire to the safer shadows beyond the terrace*]

EDDIE [*undismayed, takes his ingenuous enthusiasm to* BILL *and stands beside him, listening to the music*]. They're good. That's the sort of music I like.

BILL. You don't know anything about decent music.

EDDIE. Well, I met George Gershwin once in New York.

[HORTENSE, BOB *and* BETTY *enter from living-room*]

HORTENSE. Oh, did you? Did you, Eddie? I met Rin-tin-tin once. I patted his head. [*A shocked glance from* EDDIE *leads her to the discovery that her dress is very much undone. She giggles tranquilly*] Oh, I'm all broken out. Will you hook this, Eddie?

[EDDIE *hooks* HORTENSE *up, a painfully embarrassing process, but man is often ennobled by suffering*]

HORTENSE. Oh, don't! You tickle.

EDDIE [*petulantly*]. Stand still, will you?

BOB. This is Hortense's coming-out party.

BETTY. How embarrassing for you, Hortense.

HORTENSE. I am not embarrassed at all. [*She turns to address them while* EDDIE *struggles to find the hooks and eyes.*] My Sociology professor says that one of the finest points of the modern generation is the calm efficiency with which young womanhood has learned to meet the calamities of everyday, workaday existence. Hurry up, Eddie.

EDDIE. Stand still a minute. I can't see anything.

BETTY. You shouldn't try to see. This is a calamity, not an excursion.

DARROW [*entering from the living-room with* DORIS, *comes upon a giggling* HORTENSE *attended by an ostrich-like* EDDIE]. Why aren't you out playing bridge with the chaperons?

HORTENSE. Gracious! You scared me!

EDDIE. They don't want to play any more. They said I could do what I wanted.

DORIS. Well, just what is it you're doing?

BOB. "And he learned about women from her!"

[EDDIE, *mortified, tries to escape through the living-room, but* DAR *stops him*]

BILL. He certainly has got a drag with the chaperons.

DARROW. I think he ought to be made to work next June to make up for all the freedom he's had at this party.

EDDIE. Oh, I wouldn't have to do that, would I, Dar? I thought freshmen could have girls up next party. I was planning to ask my girl.

DORIS [*with deliberate malice*]. Isn't that nice, Hortense? Have you accepted?

[EDDIE *protests silently, but* DORIS *refuses to see him*]

HORTENSE. Oh, he hasn't asked me yet.

DORIS. I see. That's why he was looking you over. He wanted to be sure about you first.

EDDIE. I think perhaps I had better go and see— [*He makes a dash to the door left, but* BILL, *who is standing near it, blocks him*]

BILL. You're pretty much a man of the world, Eddie. Are there certain requirements a girl has to fulfill before you ask her up?

HORTENSE [*pleased at being the center of so much attention, but not knowing what it is all about*]. You must be awfully particular.

DARROW [*interrupts the baiting for a moment*]. Take care of Doris, will you, Bill? I ought to see if the cook's planned on supper for the orchestra. Don't let Eddie trifle with your girlish affections, Hortense. He's a terrific philanderer. [*Exit* DARROW *through living-room*]

HORTENSE [*turning to* EDDIE *in awe*]. Oh-h-h . . . what do I have to do now?

BILL. It seems to me that the next move should be Eddie's. . . .

EDDIE. Perhaps I ought to go and see . . .

BOB [*standing between* EDDIE *and the door*]. He's shy.

HORTENSE. Beatrice Fairfax says that shyness is a good sign in a man. It shows sincerity.

DORIS. Oh, Eddie's terribly, terribly shy.

EDDIE [*backs away from* HORTENSE, *having made up his mind that his only safety lies in retreat*]. Hortense, I simply have to ask you . . . [*Unfortunately* BOB *gives him a terrific shove just at this moment, and before he can regain his breath, all is lost*]

HORTENSE. Oh, thank you, Eddie. I'd love to.

EDDIE. What?

HORTENSE. Come up to June houseparty. Isn't that what you wanted to ask?

EDDIE. Why, I . . . really, Hortense . . . you see . . .

BILL. Yes, that is what he wants, Hortense.

DORIS. Well, now that we have Eddie's budding romance all propped up, let's dance.

EDDIE [*rushes imploringly to* DORIS]. Can I have this dance, Doris?

BILL. Sorry, Doris has this dance with me. [*He and* DORIS *join the dancers, leaving* EDDIE *to* HORTENSE]

[ALAN *enters from terrace through door right, tired and dazed with anxiety. He flashes a rapid glance at the bookcase before he succeeds in summoning a painful attitude of nonchalance; when he speaks, his voice strains itself to sound casual*]

EDDIE [*brazenly indicating* HORTENSE]. Aren't you . . . aren't you dancing, Alan?

ALAN. What? Oh, no. No, I'm not dancing. I've got a headache.

HORTENSE. Don't you want to dance with me, Eddie?

EDDIE. You don't want us to leave you, Alan?

ALAN. Go right ahead. I don't mind at all.

EDDIE. Oh, all right. Only, if you have a headache . . .

ALAN [*impatiently*]. I'm all right. Don't worry about me. Run along and dance.

EDDIE. But . . .

HORTENSE. Come on, Eddie. [*She takes him firmly by the hand and leads him towards the living-room*] You mustn't mind Eddie, Alan. It is a form of shyness. [*Exeunt*]

[ALAN *relaxes with relief now that he is alone at last. He walks uncertainly across the room and then turns as though to go to the bookcase*]

RONNIE [*enters from the hall, right*]. There you are. I want to see you.

ALAN [*attempts to brush past him*]. Where's Sally? I want to dance with her.

RONNIE [*blocking his way*]. Sally's over to the Beta house for a couple of dances. I just came over to get her scarf. [ALAN *tries to leave*] Now, listen! Quit trying to avoid me. I want to talk to you.

ALAN. But I ought to dance. Dar said everybody ought to dance.

RONNIE. You can dance in a minute. I want to find out what this is all about.

ALAN. What?

RONNIE. You know well enough what. What's the idea of trying to avoid me in the first place? And what was the idea of telling me Florence had gone down to the Dean's office when you knew darn well she hadn't?

ALAN. But . . . But . . . I didn't know. I didn't know she hadn't.

RONNIE. Anyway, I'm not much interested in Florence Milligan. What's more important is why are you trying to avoid me?

ALAN. Well, I—

RONNIE. Now, look here—you send me off on a wild goose chase and when I come back you're in your room with the door locked and I nearly have to batter it down before you let me in. And then you refuse to talk to me.

ALAN. Well, I had nothing to say.

RONNIE. Now, listen, Alan, I'm not asking you to tell me anything you don't want to. But this is the first time you ever held anything out on me. There is no use insisting there is nothing wrong, because I know damn well there is.

ALAN. You're right, Ronnie, something is wrong. It's about Florence. But it's my affair and I'm not going to let you get mixed up in it. But I know I shouldn't have tried to avoid you just because of that. I'm sorry.

RONNIE. All right, Charlie. We'll let the matter drop. I just didn't want any pretense between us. I won't pester you any more. [*He assumes their customary mood of friendly banter*] But look here, if you ever start acting like this around me any more, you're not going to be my best man.

ALAN. You mean, you and Sally—

RONNIE. Well, not yet. But I'll fix that before long.

ALAN [*trying to be gay*]. I'll just take one look at that face of yours and I'll know when.

RONNIE. I should say you will. Well, I've got to barge along and get Sally. So long, kid. [*As he opens door into living-room, he thinks of a new gag*] I've got a new job, Charlie.

ALAN [*forces himself to ask*]. What is it, Ronnie?

RONNIE. I'm working for the the telephone company, trying to give Sally a ring. [*He runs off, leaving* ALAN *to sink wearily into a chair*]

[DARROW *enters*]

DARROW. You're a great help to the party.

ALAN. Who? Me?

DARROW. Yes, you. You're doing a lot to enliven the evening. Just because your girl couldn't come is no reason for taking the veil. I wish you'd snap out of it.

ALAN. But I have a headache, Dar.

DARROW. Horses! You're just stubborn! [*With ill-natured resignation*] All right. I don't care. Let the party fall flat. I'll never take charge of a houseparty again; you can be darn sure of that.

ALAN. I'm sorry, Dar.

[DARROW *shrugs impatiently and starts to leave*]

EDDIE [*enters breathlessly*]. Oh, Dar, I've been looking for you.

DARROW [*groaning*]. Oh, God, what's wrong now?

EDDIE. Has anybody got a girl here named Milligan?

DARROW. Not that I know of.

EDDIE. Well, I looked through the list and I couldn't find anybody by that name, but she insists she's here.

DARROW. Talk sense. Who insists she's here?

EDDIE. She says she's her mother and she's called twice now and she won't hang up until I find her. She says that her daughter said this afternoon that she was coming up this afternoon and she hasn't come back yet and there's an important telephone call for her at her home and she's to come back at once.

DARROW. Milligan? . . . Where is she telephoning from? Here in town?

EDDIE. Yes.

DARROW. Well, it's a joke. The only Milligan around here is that Florence woman. And it stands to reason that she's not up here. Isn't that so, Alan?

ALAN [*hastily*]. No. No. She wouldn't be up here. It's a joke. That's what it is, a joke.

EDDIE. I don't think it's a joke. At least, her mother seems terribly insistent and serious. She's called twice.

DARROW [*impatiently*]. But Florence is the —she wouldn't be up here.

EDDIE. No?

ALAN. No. Of course not. Florence wouldn't be up here.

EDDIE. But what shall I do?

DARROW. Tell her mother you're looking for her and you'll call her back when you find her.

EDDIE. All right, but where shall I look?

DARROW. Look?

EDDIE. Didn't you say to look for her?

DARROW. Gee, you're dumb! Sure, go ahead and look for her. Ask all the boys if they brought Florence up to the party. [*Laughing*] That ought to liven things up a bit. [EDDIE *looks at him doubtfully, but* DARROW *dismisses him unsmilingly*] Go on. Ask everyone if they've seen Florence. [*He winks knowingly to* ALAN]

ALAN. No! No! [*Attempting to sound casual*] I wouldn't do that, Dar. I don't think that's right.

[EDDIE *starts out on his errand without hearing him*]

DARROW. I just want to see the expression on Pete the Prim's face when Canby asks him if he brought Florence to the houseparty.

[*He chuckles, stumping out his cigarette, but becomes grouchy again at once*] Well, I suppose I've got to go out and comfort the cook. I don't even have a chance to smoke a cigarette. [*He leaves, grumbling*]

[ALAN, *able to relax for a moment, stumbles wearily to a chair, but a moment later he rises, frightened, and searches the room with his eyes as though to find a new place to hide the body. At length he goes uncertainly to the cupboard and taking the key from his pocket, inserts it in the door*]

PROFESSOR WHITE [*sauntering in from terrace to punch bowl, views* ALAN *with the complacent good nature of the professor who knows he is popular with the boys*]. Tidying up, Alan? You boys are a lot neater than we were when I was in college. [ALAN, *startled and guilty, hastily puts the key in his pocket.* PROFESSOR WHITE *laughs knowingly*] Or do some of you boys keep a little contraband in a handy place?

ALAN. No, no, sir. . . .

PROFESSOR WHITE [*with self-conscious tolerance*]. Well, Alan, as long as I don't see it —or its too flagrant results—I shall have nothing to report to the Dean. [*He crosses the stage casually*]

ALAN. Yes, sir . . . thank you, only . . . [*Breathlessly*] Sir, I wanted to ask you sometime about my marks in the course. I thought perhaps I might have . . . [BILL *enters, returning a couple of empty punch glasses*] Oh, hello, Bill.

BILL. Seen Doris? Oh, excuse me, Professor White.

PROFESSOR WHITE [*knowingly*]. Another one of the conspirators, Bill?

BILL. Conspirators, sir?

PROFESSOR WHITE. I've frightened poor Alan so he's taken to discussing his marks. I'll leave you—but remember, just don't let me know anything about it. [*He strolls off, chuckling*]

BILL. What's he talking about?

ALAN. I don't know, Bill. That is, I guess he thought I had some liquor on me.

BILL [*angrily*]. Say, Alan, who told Eddie Canby to go around asking everyone if his girl was Florence Milligan? Why, Pete Slosser will kill him. Pete's got his fiancée up from the seminary.

ALAN. Do you mean to say he's asking everybody?

BILL. Eddie's out there organizing a search party for Florence. And then Chick and Bob and that crazy gang are getting ready to tear the house down pretending that she's hiding somewhere.

ALAN [*for a second is panic-stricken*]. You mean, they're looking . . . [*But he manages to control himself*] They shouldn't do that. Damn fool idea of fun. Canby ought to know better even if he is a freshman.

[*With a great deal of laughter and noise,* CHICK *leads the boys and girls in from the terrace in a hilarious burlesque search.* EDDIE, *protesting, is pushed from side to side, while the boys call "Here, Florence. Here, Florence," and the girls peer under the chairs and in the corners.* HORTENSE *alone is conducting a serious search and she stays only long enough to assure herself that* FLORENCE *isn't up the chimney before wandering into the living-room, followed by* EDDIE *and one or two of the boys*]

[ALAN *by this time is in a state of panic, and as* MARIAN *goes toward the bookcase to the left of the fireplace, he rushes to her and hurls her back so violently that she almost falls. Astonished at his inexplicable display of anger, the boys stop their mock search, listening to* ALAN *as he turns on them furiously*]

ALAN. Say, what's the idea of stirring up that kid, Canby? He'll believe anything you tell him. If you kid him like this about Florence, he'll think she's actually here.

CHICK. Sure he will. What difference does it make?

ALAN [*unable to answer, falters*]. Well, a lot. The first thing you know it's going to be all over the campus that somebody invited Florence to the houseparty. You ought to have sense enough, Chick.

CHICK. Oh, you're crazy.

BOB. No one takes it seriously except Eddie . . . and *you.*

BETTY. What harm does it do?

BILL. Alan's right. You ought to know better.

MARIAN. What's the harm?

ALAN. You oughtn't to do it. You oughtn't to egg him on.

CHICK. Why?

ALAN. Because . . . because . . . because rumors get around.

CHICK. Rumors?

MARIAN AND BETTY. Rumors?

BOB. Anyone would think you were afraid we were going to find Florence up in your room.

[ALAN *turns suddenly from them*]

CHICK [*teasingly*]. Oh, Alan, shame. . . .

BILL. Leave him alone. He isn't feeling well.

CHICK. Sorry.

BETTY. We didn't mean any harm, Bill.

JACK. There isn't any harm in it.

BILL. I know, I know.

DARROW [*entering down left*]. What's all the racket? [*Everybody laughs*]

ALAN [*turns angrily to him*]. It's all your fault. You started this damned hunt.

DARROW. Hunt! Hunt? What hunt?

ALL. For Florence.

DARROW. My God! Did Eddie really start that? Jack, go and tell him to stop it right away.

BEATRICE [*in mock disappointment*]. I thought we were going to look at the rooms upstairs.

MARIAN. I wanted to see how many girls' pictures Chick had on his bureau.

BETTY. And Hortense wanted to see the cellar.

[EDDIE *and* HORTENSE *enter excitedly from the terrace,* EDDIE *holding* ALAN's *bloodstained handkerchief conspicuously before him*]

HORTENSE. Look, Dar. Look at what we found. Show them, Eddie.

[EDDIE *gingerly exhibits the handkerchief to the amusement of all the boys and girls*]

DARROW. Put that thing away.

EDDIE. She found it on the terrace behind one of the bushes.

DARROW [*impatiently*]. Well, you don't have to drag it out in front of everybody.

[ALAN *stares fixedly at the handkerchief*]

HORTENSE. But it looks like blood and we thought it might be a clue or something.

[*The* BOYS *and* GIRLS *burst out laughing* DARROW *tries politely not to smile*]

DARROW. Clue to what?

HORTENSE. I don't know. Just a clue. I love search parties, don't you, Betty?

BETTY. I adore them.

DARROW. Didn't it occur to you that someone might have cut himself?

HORTENSE. Oh . . . I thought it might be a murder or something.

[EDDIE *looks so crestfallen that the* BOYS *and* GIRLS *try to control their mirth. A second later their attention is focused on* ALAN, *who without warning suddenly faints*]

DARROW. Steady!

BILL. Hold it, kid! [*Everybody rushes to* ALAN *exclaiming*] My God! He's fainted.

BETTY. Eddie, get some water. Quick.

[RONNIE *and* SALLY *enter from down left talking casually*]

RONNIE. What's the matter?

MARIAN. Alan's fainted.

RONNIE [*rushing over to the group*]. Here, let me take him.

[RONNIE *carries* ALAN *across the room and lays him gently on the couch. The others, of course, crowd around*]

SALLY. Here, don't crowd around him so.

RONNIE. Give him air.

HORTENSE. My, isn't he white? Do you think he's dead?

SALLY. Hortense, leave him alone.

RONNIE. How did it happen?

BILL. He just fainted, that's all.

BETTY. He hasn't been feeling well all evening.

BOB. No, he said he didn't feel very well this afternoon.

HORTENSE. Do you suppose it could have been the bloody handkerchief?

[*Everyone laughs, not at the idea, but simply because it came from* HORTENSE]

DARROW. I don't see why he should faint just at the sight of blood.

BETTY. Some people can't stand seeing blood.

BEATRICE. That's right. It does affect some people that way.

HORTENSE. Oh, I always faint at the sight of blood. Only this time I was too excited.

RONNIE. What blood?

DARROW. Nothing. Just this handkerchief. [*He puts it away and addresses the* BOYS *authoritatively*] You all might as well dance. There is nothing you can do.

[EDDIE *returns with a glass of water which he hands to* SALLY]

BETTY. Perhaps we'd better go, unless we can be of some help.

SALLY. No, I don't believe so, thanks. He's all right now. [*The* BOYS *and* GIRLS *exeunt, chattering excitedly*] Aren't you? Drink this. Come on, honey— That's a good boy. Don't try to sit up.

HORTENSE [*who never leaves voluntarily*]. Oh! His pupils are all rolled up.

DARROW. Hortense, will you—Eddie, will you take Hortense out on the terrace?

HORTENSE. But I want to see him when he comes to. He might throw a fit or something—

DARROW. Yes—yes—yes— [*He escorts her onto the terrace with* EDDIE *in tow*]

BILL. Don't suppose I can do anything either.

SALLY. Stay if you want to, Bill. [*To* DARROW *who has gone to close the terrace doors*] Leave them open, Dar. Fresh air is good for him.

DARROW. He's all right now, isn't he? [*Going to sofa*] Feeling better?

ALAN. I'm all right, thanks.

RONNIE. You run along, Dar. Sally and I will take care of him.

DARROW [*hesitatingly*]. Well, I *have* got a lot to do, but it seems too bad for you and Sally—

RONNIE. That's all right. We weren't going to dance, anyway.

SALLY. We were just looking for a battlefield as usual.

DARROW. Then I'd better run before I get picked off by stray shot. So long, Alan. Don't pull any more of these tricks.

ALAN. I'm sorry, Dar.

[*Exit* DARROW]

SALLY [*lightly*]. I should think you would be. I'm ashamed of you! Why didn't you tell Sally you were bilious? I should have given you some castor oil.

ALAN [*sitting up*]. I feel better now.

RONNIE. Just mention castor oil and he's cured. [*Solicitously*] Say, what is this all about, Charlie?

ALAN. I . . . I . . . don't know. I just felt dizzy, I guess. I'm awfully sorry.

SALLY. I think some bi-carb would fix you up. Does your stomach feel all right?

RONNIE. I'll find some.

BILL. What you need is a little fresh air. You come on out on the terrace with me.

ALAN. But I don't want to go out on the terrace.

BILL. Come on.

SALLY. Alan, fresh air will do you good.

BILL. Come on.

ALAN [*would like to go outdoors, but is afraid to leave the room*]. But I don't want to, Bill.

BILL [*taking him firmly by the shoulder and leading him to the terrace*]. Come on; don't be like that.

RONNIE. Don't let him walk around too much Bill.

BILL. You leave him to me.

ALAN. No, I don't want to.

BILL. Come on, will you!

[ALAN *hesitates at the door, but accompanies* BILL *onto terrace*]

SALLY. Now, what do you make of that? Something bothering him?

RONNIE. Yes.

SALLY. What?

RONNIE. I don't know. He wouldn't tell me. Nothing much, I suppose. Alan can get more in a stew over a lost collar button than most fellows would in flunking out. Only I wish he wouldn't spoil his own fun.

SALLY. I suppose it all started when he found that Patsie couldn't come up to houseparty.

RONNIE. I suppose it probably did. [*Which gives him the sentimental opportunity he has been waiting for; he comes very close to* SALLY] Don't you feel awfully, awfully sorry for poor devils that fall in love?

SALLY [*who knew it was bound to come, sighs exaggeratedly*]. Now it's coming. The same old story.

RONNIE. The same old story. I love you, Sally!

[*He kisses her and she offers no resistance for a moment. Then she pushes him away and sits down in a chair by herself, pensive*]

SALLY. Perhaps you do, Ronnie. But how long is it going to last?

RONNIE. Always.

SALLY. I wonder . . . [*She becomes suddenly brisk, almost flippant, in an attempt to explain what is in her mind without revealing what is in her heart*] No, Ronnie. Sally is the original burnt child. I fell in love badly once with a gay young blade like you and lo! he rode away into the West and this lily maid almost went out and built a raft for herself. Wouldn't I have looked swell floating down the Connecticut river on a raft, all dressed up in my new white tulle evening gown and a big smack of daisies on my chest! I'll bet that would have brought the simple burghers of Holyoke, Springfield, and Warehouse Point to the brink of tears. Can't you just see the weeping throngs lining the river banks? Though probably all the grubby little boys would have thrown stones at me and the local yokels would have made books on which one would sink me first. On after thought, perhaps it was just as well I decided to stay in college and major in anthropology. [RONNIE *sits perfectly still, looking at her and she realizes that she is talking against time*] No, Ronnie. I'm not going to let that happen again.

RONNIE. But it won't, Sally.

SALLY [*laughing whimsically*]. Don't make me flatter you all the time, Ronnie, by reminding you of your infinite capacity for falling in love with different girls. With reciprocation! [*She decides to try a new argument*] Besides, it would spoil your fun, you know, to be tied down to one girl. And I should insist upon that.

RONNIE. I wouldn't mind.

SALLY. Perhaps not for the first month.

RONNIE. You're wrong, Sally.

SALLY [*wistfully*]. I wish I thought so.

RONNIE. You wait and see.

SALLY [*softly*]. Yes, I'll wait and see.

RONNIE [*tremendously excited*]. Is that a sort of a promise, Sally? Do you mean you'll try me out and we can be . . .

SALLY. Not so fast, Ronnie. I merely said I'd wait and see. [*As his enthusiasm fades*] Oh don't you see, Ronnie? I'm not made for this fly-by-night, let's-be-engaged-for-a-week sort of love. When it comes I'll take it seriously, and I want the man to take it seriously, too. I like you enormously, Ronnie, but you're a bad risk. You've never taken anything seriously except yourself. And I refuse to toss my heart out for you to play ball with. There. Now you see how I stand? [*She goes quickly from him, studying the titles of the books in the case abstractedly*]

RONNIE [*thoughtfully*]. I suppose you're right. But give me a little time, Sally, I'll show you I can be serious.

SALLY [*goes to fireplace*]. You can have all the time you want, Ronnie.

RONNIE [*goes enthusiastically to her*]. Think what we're missing, Sally.

SALLY [*evades him, laughing*]. That sounds to me like a prelude to petting. [*She discovers something on the sofa*] Look! Someone else has been getting engaged here. These sofas are a most incriminating form of furniture. [*She draws* FLORENCE'S *handbag from the sofa and rising, she starts to open it*] Some poor girl is probably wild at having lost it.

ALAN [*looking into the room, sees* SALLY *and rushes in*]. Sally! That's mine. That is, I know who it belongs to. [*He seizes the bag, and stands looking bewildered at them*]

RONNIE [*taking* ALAN *by the arm, addresses him seriously*]. Listen, kid, you've got to stop acting like this. It's getting beyond a joke. Sally and I have been noticing it all evening.

SALLY. It's not only that, Alan. It doesn't make any difference about us. We understand you, but other people are beginning to notice it, too.

RONNIE. People are beginning to whisper about it. You've got to snap out of it, Charlie. You don't want the chaperons to start talking too. [*He waits for an explanation, but* ALAN *does not answer*] I don't want to butt in. But I think I can tell you something that will clear this up. Sally, do you mind waiting outside a moment?

ALAN [*hastily intervenes*]. No, I would rather Sally stayed here. I answer too many questions when I'm alone with you. And, Ronnie, I told you I'm not going to let you get mixed up in this affair.

SALLY. Come on, Alan, tell me about it. This is really not fair to Ronnie. He has been worried to death about you all evening. Go ahead. You can say anything you want in front of me.

ALAN [*decides to tell at least part of the truth*]. All right, I'll tell you. There's no sense in bluffing any more. Well, as I told you, Florence said she was going down to the Dean's office. . . . She threatened to . . . [*He loses control of himself for a moment as he realizes how impossible it is for him to tell them. He throws himself on the sofa, covering his face with his hands*] Oh, I can't face this thing any more. I've got to get away.

SALLY. Run away!

ALAN. Yes, run away.

RONNIE. Alan, this isn't as serious as you think. I don't know what Florence has threatened to do, but, honestly, kid, she can't get away with it. She can't do a thing to you. Now I'll promise you that Sally and I will get you out of this. But we can't do anything now. Keep calm until the parties are over and we'll fix everything.

EDDIE [*enters from living-room and proceeds to terrace shouting*]. Supper is served in the dining-room.

RONNIE. Now listen, Alan. We'll go in and get some food and we'll forget about this for now

[ALAN *recovers his poise as a new plan begins to form in his mind*]

SALLY. That's the idea. It will do you good, Alan.

ALAN. Yes, sure, that's fine. [*He smiles at them as though he had dismissed all his troubles*] I want to fetch something up stairs. You and Sally go on in and I'll join you in a minute.

RONNIE. O. K. We'll be waiting for you.

SALLY. And no more talk of running away.

DORIS [*entering from terrace, joins* SALLY *and* RONNIE]. Supper, Sally. I'm going to win my bet.

SALLY. You are like fun.

[*Crowds of* BOYS *and* GIRLS *can be seen going from the terrace through the living-room off left to the dining-room.* SALLY, DORIS, *and* RONNIE *join the gay procession.* ALAN *remains watching them. Then when the last couple has disappeared into the other part of the house and the rooms are all deserted, he dashes through the door down right and can be heard running up the stairs*]

[CHICK *and* MARIAN *enter from living-room*]

CHICK. Thank God, there's no one here. I hate crowds!

MARIAN. So do I.

CHICK. I like to eat and love in private.

MARIAN [*wearily fending him off*]. Can't you concentrate on eating for a while?

[RONNIE *and* SALLY *enter from the living-room with food*]

RONNIE. Swell idea of yours, Sally. We can be alone in here with Alan.

SALLY [*seeing* CHICK *and* MARIAN]. Oh— Oh—

RONNIE. Wouldn't you know it!

SALLY. I thought we would be the only ones who would think of avoiding the subway rush.

CHICK. We have our instincts, too.

RONNIE. Well, there's still the terrace. Alan can find us out there. Come on, Sally.

SALLY. I like the terrace anyway.

[RONNIE *and* SALLY *start toward the terrace, but* HORTENSE *rushes madly in, catching* RONNIE *by the arm*]

HORTENSE. I found you. I found you. I thought I saw you going out of the dining-room. You said you were going to play games with me.

RONNIE. Excuse me, Hortense, but I can't. Come on, Sally.

[*He tries to escape, but the door is blocked by two of the boys who have followed* HORTENSE, *knowing that where she is, there excitement of some sort will be*]

FIRST BOY. Oh, no, you don't.

SECOND BOY. I guess you're in a jam.

RONNIE. What are you talking about?

FIRST BOY. You're going to play games with her.

SECOND BOY. And we're going to watch you.

RONNIE. I'm afraid I can't, Hortense. Sally and I have an engagement.

HORTENSE. Oh, spooning!

RONNIE. Couldn't you play solitaire?

HORTENSE. That's no fun. It must be something we all can play.

RONNIE. Let's all juggle our food. Sorry, Hortense, but we have an engagement with Alan.

HORTENSE. But you promised.

SALLY. If you make promises, Ronnie, you've got to keep them.

SECOND BOY. Don't be a welcher.

SALLY. Come on, Ronnie, let's stay.

RONNIE. It's all right by me. Let's eat.

CHICK [*rises from his comfortable seat, thoroughly disgruntled*]. This place has all the privacy of the Grand Central Terminal. Come on, woman.

[CHICK *and* MARIAN *exeunt. As the others sit down,* DARROW *and* DORIS *enter*]

DORIS [*to* SALLY]. I hope you choke!

SALLY. Oh, hello! I won.

DORIS. You probably cheated.

SALLY [*turns to* RONNIE]. I bet we would have chicken à la king and salad rolls. Did you ever know a fraternity dance to serve anything else? But Doris was greedy enough to bet on lobster patties. You might think she had never been to a houseparty.

DORIS. Well Dar told me . . . Dar, you told me and now you'll have to pay. Give Sally a quarter.

[DARROW *hands over the coin*]

HORTENSE. I like chicken à la king. But aren't we going to play something?

RONNIE. Pete's playing the piano.

DORIS [*sees someone on the terrace and calls out*]. What is Alan doing with his valise. Alan! Alan! [*She runs off and returns with* ALAN, *who has on a top coat and is carrying a suitcase*]

RONNIE. Where are you going?

DARROW. What's the idea of the baggage?

[BETTY *and* BOB *enter and stand watching with amused curiosity*]

ALAN [*confused*]. I? I'm . . . why, no-where. . . . [*He stands irresolutely in the door*]

SALLY [*sharply*]. Alan, you said . . .

ALAN [*quickly*]. You see, that's just laundry, Sally—just laundry. I've been meaning to take it down to the chink's for weeks and I suddenly thought of it and I thought that perhaps if I brought it downstairs and left it where I could see it, perhaps—perhaps I might remember it tomorrow. [*He stands frightened in the doorway. There follows a long tense silence*]

BOB. Laundry! He only owns one shirt.

[BILL *and* RONNIE *are looking steadily at* ALAN, *who concludes lamely*]

ALAN. That's all it is, really. [*He puts the suitcase down*]

SALLY [*laughing forcedly and crossing to* ALAN]. I'll have to explain. You see, I asked Alan to show me some of his paintings. I really didn't expect a whole crate of them, Alan. And then when he comes in he finds a whole audience waiting for them.

HORTENSE [*by this time has reached over from couch right and has gotten hold of the bag which she places on the couch*]. Pictures! I just love pictures! Have you any animal pictures! [*She attempts to undo the straps*]

SALLY [*sharply*]. Hortense! Leave that alone! Alan was going to show those pictures to me. [*She takes the suitcase away from her*]

HORTENSE. Oh, I want to see the pictures.

SALLY [*impatiently*]. Oh, Hortense! [*To RONNIE, with hidden meaning*] Ronnie, take the suitcase upstairs.

[RONNIE *takes the suitcase, at the same time helping* ALAN *off with his coat*]

ALAN. I-I'll take it up!

SALLY. No, Ronnie will do it. [RONNIE *goes upstairs with the coat and suitcase. The others resume their eating and chatting as* SALLY *leads* ALAN *to a chair beside her*] You come over here and entertain me. Sit here. You see, what I really want is to get rid of Ronnie. He's been hanging around all day and it spoils my chances of seeing anyone else. He'll be frightfully jealous.

HORTENSE. Oh, I didn't get a pickle. I just love pickles.

[*She spears a pickle from* CHICK'S *plate.* CHICK, *who is sitting next to her on the couch changes places with* MARIAN; *neither* MARIAN *nor* HORTENSE *are particularly pleased*]

BILL [*enters from living-room*]. Everybody got food? You haven't, Alan. Here, take this.

ALAN. I'm not hungry. I don't feel like eating.

SALLY. Oh, yes, you do. Have some of mine. [*She insists on feeding him*]

HORTENSE. Ooh! aren't they intimate.

[RONNIE *enters from door right*]

DORIS. Ronnie, you ought to be frightfully jealous.

RONNIE. Should I? I'll give you a dollar for the low down. [DORIS *refuses and* RONNIE *goes over to where* SALLY *and* ALAN *are sitting.* ALAN *rises at once and crosses to another part of the room*] That's all right, Alan; stay where you are.

ALAN. I'm all right here.

DARROW. Don't be so exclusive.

[*While the boys and girls chatter gaily in the brightly lighted library, the tall gaunt figure of an elderly woman moves silently through the blue shadows of the lantern-hung terrace. She stands by the door, meanly dressed in black, but sinisterly impressive, unseen by the young people whom she watches so intently*]

DORIS. Come on over here, Alan.

ALAN. I'm all right, thanks. I'm all right here. I don't feel very much like talking.

RONNIE. With these girls you wouldn't get a chance to do much talking. Give us the dirt on Smith, Doris.

DORIS. Do I look like a girl who knows all the dirt?

RONNIE. Well, I wouldn't say that. But muddy water runs deep.

DORIS. Oh, someone be gallant and stand up for me.

BETTY [*turning to toss a bantering remark to* DORIS, *notices the figure on the terrace and stops, startled*]. Look, Dar, there's someone out there on the terrace.

DARROW [*goes inquiringly to the terrace door*]. Are you . . . Can I help you? .

THE WOMAN IN BLACK [*does not answer for a moment. Then coldly, stolidly, she walks through the doors into the room and stares straight at* DARROW]. I'm Mrs. Milligan. . . .

[*There is a quick pause. One or two of the boys rapidly exchange glances. The rest keep their eyes rivetted on the woman*]

DARROW [*awkwardly, as the woman suddenly sweeps the room with a swift movement of her eyes*]. Well . . . Is there anything I can do for you?

MRS. MILLIGAN. I'm looking for Florence. She's my daughter. . . .

[ALAN *fumbles in his pocket and draws out a package of cigarettes. His hand trembles violently as he lights one, but the attention of everyone is focused on the woman*]

DARROW [*replying courteously, but with an undercurrent of exasperation in his voice*]. Florence? Florence? . . . But, my dear lady, she isn't here. We've already told you over the telephone.

MRS. MILLIGAN [*impatiently*]. I know—but the point is— [*She is embarrassed by too great a knowledge of her daughter's plans*] You see, I happen to know that Florence came up here this afternoon . . . and she hasn't been home since.

[ALAN *sits down suddenly, his back half turned, and concentrates upon his cigarette*]

DARROW [*less effectively concealing his irritation*]. Well, we're sorry, but after all that's hardly our fault, is it? Really, I'm sorry, but you must be mistaken. You see, I'm quite sure that Florence hasn't been here. We're having a houseparty—

MRS. MILLIGAN. Yes, I know. . . .

DARROW. Well then, of course, if Florence *had* been here, surely someone would have noticed her. And as far as I know, no one has seen her. I assure you I've already made inquiries. [MRS. MILLIGAN *makes no sign of leaving*] After all, couldn't *you* be mistaken—couldn't Florence have gone some other place?

MRS. MILLIGAN. No! No! I happen to know what she came here for. [*She scrutinizes the faces of the boys in the room*] It was kind of important. And she would have come back home.

HORTENSE. Oh, Mrs. Milligan, do you suppose she could have lost herself?

SALLY [*angrily*]. Hortense! For heaven's sake!

[*The entire room glowers at* HORTENSE, *who for once is squelched*]

DARROW. Please excuse it, Mrs. Milligan.

MRS. MILLIGAN. This ain't any more pleasant for you than it is for me. Now I want to know what happened to Florence and I'm gonna find out. She came up here this afternoon and— [ALAN *barely covers a gasp of dismay by smoking rapidly.* MRS. MILLIGAN, *who has been watching him carefully crosses over to him*] Excuse me, are *you* Mr. Bradford?

ALAN. Why, yes. . . .

MRS. MILLIGAN. *You* didn't happen to see Florence, did you?

ALAN. Why . . . Why, no. . . . What makes you think that?

MRS. MILLIGAN. I don't know, I just thought you acted as though you might have known something about her—that's all. . . .

RONNIE [*interrupts hastily*]. Pardon me, Mrs. Milligan, but I've been with Mr. Bradford all evening. As a matter of fact, I heard one of the boys say he had seen Florence near the North Adams trolley station late this afternoon. Perhaps she decided to go over there.

DARROW. There, you see— [*With a faint touch of sarcasm*] You know how it is with *these girls*, Mrs. Milligan. . . . They sometimes *will* stay out later than they should!

[*This wins a slight laugh from* HORTENSE]

MRS. MILLIGAN [*sharply*]. That remark ain't necessary! I know what you think of us, and how we ain't welcome here. [*Bitterly*] Because we don't have no money. But I got a right to know where Florence is and I'm going to find out. Now, she came up here this afternoon and she— [*She realizes that she cannot make any accusations without disclosing* FLORENCE's *shady plans*] Oh, I know I can't prove anything. I guess I can't do anything more now, but just you remember: other people's got their rights just the same as you. And you remember that, too, Mr. Bradford! [*She turns toward the terrace doors again*] Well . . . I'll be goin' now. . . .

DARROW. Won't you go out the front door; it's nearer the street.

MRS. MILLIGAN [*with the bitter resignation of one who "knows her place"*]. No. No, I'll go the way I come. [*She walks heavily out of the room onto the terrace and disappears from sight*]

[*For a minute there is silence*]

ALAN [*stumps out his cigarette with an awkward laugh*]. I wonder why she picked on me?

RONNIE [*goes quickly over to him taking hold of his arm*]. Don't pay any attention to her, kid. She's probably tight. Come on, we were going to play games with Hortense, weren't we?

HORTENSE [*hoping to be funny*]. No. I want to know what became of . . .

RONNIE [*interrupts her sharply*]. Hortense, don't you ever know your own mind?

DARROW. Of all the fool women, that Mrs. Milligan! I hated to suggest that that daughter of hers had probably stayed out later than this before.

HORTENSE. Maybe she had something for supper that wouldn't keep. It always makes my mother furious if she has a soufflé and I'm late.

DARROW. Don't worry. The local police aren't going to investigate very far just because Florence didn't come home for supper.

ALAN [*straining to sound casual*]. I wouldn't let her do that, if I were you, Dar. The authorities . . . you wouldn't want the police coming around on some wild goose chase.

[ALAN's *misunderstanding draws forth hearty laughter from most of the boys and girls, who think the entire situation most amusing*]

DARROW. Who said anything about getting the police?

RONNIE [*irritably*]. Oh, for God's sake, let's forget about Florence and her mother! Come on, Hortense, let's get started with your game.

HORTENSE [*gaily*]. Yes! We're going to play "I packed my trunk." [*To* DARROW] Do you know how?

DARROW. Is that the game where you eat a cracker and whistle the national anthem?

SALLY. Oh, I hope not!

BILL. No, that's the one where you keep adding names of things all through the alphabet.

HORTENSE. That's the one! That's the one! Oh, isn't it nice that everyone knows how to play it. Let's start!

DORIS [*who has tried refusing* HORTENSE *before*]. I suppose we might as well play, too, Sally. It's the easiest way out.

[*They have all just settled themselves as* EDDIE *enters with the chaperons and* PROFESSOR WHITE]

MRS. RUTHERFORD [*is still talking*]. . . . Really Mr. Canby, I don't know when I've had so much fun at a party. [*To boys and girls*] Oh, don't get up. You look so comfortable.

MRS. WHITE. Oh, do please sit down. I'm afraid we're interrupting you.

PROFESSOR WHITE. As long as there are so many of them I don't believe the interruption will be seriously offensive.

[*With a great deal of gallantry on the part of the boys and polite insincere smiles on the part of the girls, the chaperons are seated*]

MRS. RUTHERFORD [*continues effusively*]. Mr. Canby has been so faithful all evening. I can't understand it. Why, Mr. Jenckes, he even asked me to dance as though he really wanted to. I think it's marvelous the way you train the freshmen.

[*Under cover of her heavy sprightliness* EDDIE *escapes—to* MRS. WHITE]

HORTENSE. We're going to play "I packed my trunk." Don't you want to play, too?"

MRS. WHITE. Oh, I think not. We'll watch you.

MRS. RUTHERFORD. Oh, we played that one night at the Griscoms. We had a baby party. *Don't* ask Professor White. He thinks up the most dreadful words.

PROFESSOR WHITE. Mrs. Rutherford has never forgiven me for "eleemosynary elements."

MRS. RUTHERFORD. Isn't that a dreadful word? That's where I dropped out.

PROFESSOR WHITE. Don't let us keep you from playing.

HORTENSE. Shall I start?

DARROW. Sure. Go ahead.

HORTENSE. All right. Let me see. [*To* PROFESSOR WHITE] My, I wish I had your vocabulary. I never can think of hard ones. Well, let me see . . . I packed my trunk and in it I put . . . in it I put . . . an . . . an . . . wait a minute . . . in it I put an . . . an . . . [*Triumphantly*] An apple.

CHICK. Hurrah!

HORTENSE. You go next, Alan.

ALAN [*rising, looks helplessly around him, but he cannot escape; he is trapped in a group of smiling, unsuspecting people*]. I don't really feel like playing. I don't know how.

HORTENSE. Of course you do. You just repeat that and add another word beginning with A.

SALLY [*who partially understands his bewilderment and wants to help him*]. It's easy. Just say: "I packed my trunk and in it I put an apple and . . ."

ALAN. An automobile.

SALLY. I packed my trunk and in it I put an apple, an automobile and an armadillo.

PROFESSOR WHITE. "Dillowing in his armor."

[*Laughter from all the boys, none of whom think it is funny, nor recognize it as a quotation*]

HORTENSE. That's great. Don't you get left out, Ronnie.

RONNIE. I packed my trunk and in it I put an apple, an automobile, an armadillo, and an agate.

DARROW. I packed my trunk and in it I put an apple, an automobile, an armadillo, an agate and an antler.

DORIS. A what?

DARROW. An antler. [*He wiggles his fingers at the side of his head in order to make his selection clear*]

BILL. I packed my trunk . . .

DORIS [*who is a little schemer*]. Don't leave me out. I packed my trunk, and in it I put an apple, an automobile, an armadillo, an antler and . . .

HORTENSE. No. No. You're out. You forgot the agate.

DORIS [*in mock dismay*]. Oh, shucks. Isn't that a shame! Now I can't play any more. [*She leaves the circle of players*]

DARROW. I'll be with you in a minute.

BILL [*irritatingly slow, continues with many sarcastic glances at poor* HORTENSE]. I packed my trunk and in it I put an apple, think of that, an apple, an automobile, an armadillo, an agate, an antler and an antimacassar.

HORTENSE. That's just the word I was thinking of. You must have read my mind. Don't you think he reads my mind, Professor White?

PROFESSOR WHITE. I shouldn't be at all surprised.

HORTENSE. Do you read minds, Bill?

BILL. No, and I don't stuff birds either.

MRS. RUTHERFORD [*who has no idea what* BILL *means, is convulsed with laughter*]. Stuffed birds—

[*All the boys, and one or two more sophisticated girls laugh uproariously*]

DARROW. Order. Order.

HORTENSE. Well, I never said you did. Go on, Eddie.

EDDIE. No, I can't play. I may have to answer the telephone or something.

HORTENSE. Oh, all right. Only let's hurry. It's much more fun if you hurry. It's your turn, Chick, and then Marian, and then—

CHICK. No—we're none of us playing. We'll just watch you. It's more fun!

HORTENSE. All right. Let me see, it's B now, isn't it? B. I packed my trunk and in it I put an apple, an automobile, an armadillo, an agate, an antler, an antimacassar, and . . . and . . . a bug. [*Everybody cheers*] Come on, Alan. It's your turn.

ALAN [*begins with an effort.* SALLY *and* RONNIE *knowing his mental disturbance and hoping to hide it, keep him in the game with whispered instructions*]. I packed my trunk and in it I put an apple, an automobile, an armadillo, an agate, an antler, an antimacassar, a bug. . . .

SALLY. B is easy, Alan. Just look around you.

ALAN. Look around? . . .

[RONNIE *points to the books*]

ALAN. Books.

[*He cannot control a shudder at the thought.* SALLY *shows some alarm at his condition and glances to* RONNIE *who reassures her with a look*]

SALLY. I packed my trunk and in it I put an apple, an automobile, an armadillo, an agate . . . [RONNIE *borrows* DARROW'S *gesture, wig-*

gling his hands wildly] Don't do that to me . . . an antimacassar. . . .

BILL. Wrong. You're out. You forgot the antler.

SALLY. There I told you not to do that to me, Ronnie. Oh, well, now I'll have a chance to go and talk to Doris. [*She leaves her chair and goes over to* DORIS]

DARROW. It's a plot! It's a plot! I packed my trunk . . .

JAMES [*entering from living-room*]. Pardon me, Mr. Jenckes. The orchestra leader would like to see you a moment.

DARROW. Hah, that lets me out nicely.

[*He leaves with great willingness and the boys and girls seize his interruption as an opportunity to forget the game. In the attendant resetting,* MRS. RUTHERFORD *recaptures* EDDIE]

HORTENSE. Come on! Come on! We haven't stopped playing. [*Looking over at* MRS. RUTHERFORD *and* EDDIE] Stop flirting you two. Come on, Bill, you're next.

BILL [*resignedly*]. I packed my trunk and in it I put an apple, an automobile, an armadillo, an agate, an antler, an antimacassar, a bug, books and beer.

HORTENSE. Oh, I can think of two good ones beginning with C. I don't know which one . . .

RONNIE. Use them both.

HORTENSE. Oh, I couldn't. I packed my trunk and in it I put an apple, an automobile, an armadillo, an agate, an antler, an antimacassar, a bug, books, beer and a cannibal! Go on, Alan.

ALAN. I don't know if I can. I packed my trunk and in it I put an apple, an automobile . . . an armadillo . . . an agate . . . an antler . . . [*He slumps weakly under the effort*] I . . . I . . . I . . . can't think of anything.

HORTENSE. Go on, Alan. Go on.

SALLY. No, I'll take his place; he isn't feeling well. I packed my trunk and in it I put an apple, an automobile, an armadillo, an agate, an antler, an antimacassar, a bug, books, beer, a cannibal, and a . . .

HORTENSE. Oh, I know a beauty. It's my other one—I'll give it to you. . . . Look, Sally. Look. [*She leans over and whispers with hoarse enthusiasm*] Corpse. Corpse, Sally. Corpse.

ALAN [*springs up so suddenly he knocks over a chair with a crash*]. I told you I didn't want to play this game. I won't. Do you hear? I won't play this God damned game!

RONNIE [*catching hold of him*]. Steady, Charlie. Steady. Now what is it?

ALAN. No, leave me alone. [*During the shocked silence that follows he recovers himself enough to apologize*] I'm sorry. I'm sorry, Mrs. Rutherford. I beg your pardon Mrs. White. I guess I don't feel very well. I don't believe I'll play any more.

MRS. WHITE. Of course, Alan.

SALLY [*explains to the chaperons*]. After all, the boy is sick. You know he fainted a little while ago.

ALAN. I don't believe I'll play any more.

[*He goes slowly to the terrace door, inhaling deeply, trying to steady himself. Everyone looks perplexedly at one another, saying nothing.* RONNIE *moves as though to go to* ALAN, *but* BILL *shakes his head. By tacit consent they try to act as though nothing has happened*]

DARROW [*entering*]. What's up? A silent game?

HORTENSE. I think we ought to play Ghosts. [*The suggestion is not greeted enthusiastically*] Shall I start?

BILL. Where to?

HORTENSE. Playing Ghosts, silly. We're going to play, aren't we?

DARROW. Well, since the orchestra's still eating, we might as well.

HORTENSE. I love Ghosts. Sally, don't you adore it?

SALLY. I can't say I ever considered spelling words around in a circle very exciting.

HORTENSE. Oh, if you allow proper names, and apostrophes, and hyphens, it's terribly exciting. Shall I start?

DARROW. Yes, I guess so. Go ahead. [*There is a long pause*] Well?

HORTENSE. I'm trying to think of a letter.

BOB. Don't write. Telegraph.

HORTENSE. B.

RONNIE. B? All right. U.

SALLY. D.

DORIS. That's a word.

HORTENSE. Three-letter words don't count.

DORIS. All right. Names of places allowed?

DARROW. Anything's allowed.

BILL. Go the limit.

DORIS. A.

DARROW. B . . . U . . . D . . . A . . . ? B . . . U . . . D . . . A . . . ? Let me think. Oh, sure. That's easy. I shall add a hyphen.

BILL. What?

DARROW [*complacently*]. A hyphen.

RONNIE. B . . . U . . . D . . . A . . . Hyphen?

DARROW. Yep.

BILL. I think you're wrong.

DARROW. Do you challenge me?

BILL. If it's the word I'm thinking of, you're wrong.

DARROW. Challenge me.

DORIS. Challenge him, Bill. He never could spell.

BILL. B . . . U . . . D . . . A . . . hyphen? All right. I'll challenge you.

DARROW. Budapesth.

MRS. RUTHERFORD. Budapesth. Of course.

BILL. No hyphen. How about it, Professor White?

SALLY. Bill's right.

PROFESSOR WHITE. I shouldn't like to set myself up as an authority on the spelling of foreign capitals, but I don't believe I've ever seen it spelled quite like that.

DARROW. I'm sure of it.

RONNIE. I think you're wrong. But look it up.

DARROW. It's spelled both with and without a hyphen. There used to be two cities, Buda and Pesth. One on each side of the river.

SALLY. That sounds good, but I don't think you're going to get away with it.

DARROW [going to bookcase]. I'll prove it to you.

[BILL follows]

ALAN [turning suddenly and getting in front of DARROW]. What do you want?

DARROW. I want to look up a word in the encyclopaedia.

ALAN. Oh. . . . [He crosses stage and stands watching DARROW and BILL nervously]

DARROW [searching for dictionary]. B . . . B . . . U . . . B . . . U . . . D . . .

BILL. No! You're wrong. There's no hyphen.

DARROW [replacing volume]. That's funny. I swear I've seen it spelled that way.

[They return to their seats]

HORTENSE. You're a third of a ghost.

BILL. It won't be long now. Do I start?

DARROW. I have it. I know where I saw it. In that London Illustrated News that Pete had. There's an article there about the Boundaries of Central Europe before and after the War. [Rising] It's up in his room. It must be the English spelling.

RONNIE. I brought it downstairs yesterday. It's around here somewhere.

EDDIE. All the magazines are in the cupboard under the bookcase.

ALAN [aghast]. No. No. [Trying to laugh] Dar's a ghost. Dar's a ghost.

DARROW. Not if I can prove my point. [He takes a step towards the bookcase]

ALAN [clapping his hands]. Listen, everybody. Listen. I tell you what let's do. Let's dance. Let's dance, Ronnie. Tell them to play. [To the orchestra which has assembled informally] Play! Go on, play! Will you?

[The orchestra starts, and a few boys and girls, hearing ALAN, enter from the terrace]

RONNIE [with an understanding nod at BILL]. Come on, Sally. Come on, Bill. We might as well dance. Come on, Charlie.

[ALAN holds back]

DARROW. All right, if you want to. I'll be with you in a minute. But I'm going to look this up for my own satisfaction. [He goes to the cupboard, pulling it] Why, it's locked.

ALAN [in his furious attempt to divert him grabs EDDIE, and turns to the chaperons who have risen to leave]. Did you ever see Eddie dance, Mrs. Rutherford? Did you ever see Eddie dance, Dar? He's a great dancer. [Shaking EDDIE hysterically] Dance, Eddie, dance!

[More couples enter, attracted by the noise]

EDDIE [frightened by ALAN's violence]. I . . . I don't dance. At least, not that way. Please, Alan. [He tears himself away]

DARROW. Quit trying to be funny, Alan. Let Eddie alone. Who has the key to the cupboard and what's the idea of locking it?

[As a last desperate, hysterical attempt to keep DARROW from the cupboard, ALAN sweeps a tray of punch glasses from the table. Everyone leaps to his feet with surprise and couples look in curiously from the terrace and the living-room. The orchestra begins to waver, stopping piece by piece]

MRS. RUTHERFORD. Mr. Bradford! Really I think he's been drinking.

PROFESSOR WHITE [sternly]. Alan, you know what I told you.

DARROW [striding over towards him]. Now, listen. Just what's the big idea?

ALAN [weakly, futilely]. I . . . I . . . guess I knocked over the punch glasses. Look Ronnie, look. Look what happened, Ronnie. . . . [He laughs hysterically]

RONNIE [taking him by the arm]. Come on, kid. We'll take a little walk.

DARROW. There's something funny here. I've felt it all evening. [To RONNIE] What's it all about?

RONNIE. I don't know, Dar. But it's all right. Leave the kid alone.

BILL [taking ALAN's other arm as he starts to collapse]. Can't you see he isn't feeling well? Leave him alone.

DARROW. Leave him alone when he's going crazy and smashing things up?

ALAN. I'm all right! I'm all right!

DARROW. No, you're not. There's something wrong with you and it's not just a headache either. I want to know what there is about that cupboard that's got your nerve so. [He goes rapidly towards the bookcase] There's something darn funny here, and I'm going to know what it is.

ALAN [wrenches himself away from RONNIE and BILL and dives ahead of DARROW, throwing himself with all his force against the cupboard]. Don't, Dar! Don't! Don't come near here! Don't come near here! . . . I'll tell you what it is. I'll tell you what's in the cupboard. It's Florence! Florence! and she's dead! Do you hear me, everybody? Horribly, terribly dead! [A mad, terror-stricken confusion gathers force among the people in the room] But it wasn't my fault! It wasn't my fault! [In the ensuing confusion, RONNIE and BILL try to drag ALAN away from before the cupboard, but he

clings madly to it, screaming] No, don't!
Don't! . . . For God's sake, don't look!!

THE CURTAIN FALLS SWIFTLY

ACT THREE

*It is a spring night, six months later. The
tree on the terrace is a mass of white blossoms,
under the moonlight, and within the room, in
place of the autumn leaves, is a profusion of
spring flowers. A few pieces of furniture have
been rearranged, but otherwise the room is
very much the same as in Acts One and Two.
And once again it is houseparty time, with its
music, its laughter, its soft flow of color.*

*The library is dimly lighted by one or two
lamps and at first sight seems to be deserted.
In the living-room and on the terrace the same
boys and many of the same girls can be seen
dancing.*

As the dancing stops for a moment, CHICK
and BEATRICE *disengage themselves from the
crowd and stroll into the library.*

CHICK. Can I have the next dance, Beatrice?

BEATRICE. No, it's too hot. Let's sit down for
a while. Have you got a cigarette?

CHICK [*feeling his pockets*]. I haven't. Wait
till I light the lights. There may be some in the
cigarette box.

[*He turns on the lights and* EDDIE *is discovered curled up into a ball on one of
the couches*]

BEATRICE. What are you doing here?

EDDIE [*shrinks into a corner, pleading in a
hoarse whisper*]. Turn out the lights; I'm hiding from Hortense.

BEATRICE. Aren't you ashamed of yourself
for neglecting that poor unfortunate woman
that way?

CHICK. Yes, you ought to dance with her,
Eddie. [*He prods him out of his hiding place*]

EDDIE. Oh, I'm exhausted.

CHICK. This cigarette box is empty.

EDDIE [*tossing him his case*]. Here. But give
them back this time.

CHICK. You see Eddie has taken to smoking.
He'll soon be a man at this rate.

EDDIE [*with a loftiness unbecoming a freshman*]. Oh, you'd be surprised. [*He ignores
them, lying down out of sight on the center
davenport*]

BILL [*and* DORIS *enter from the terrace, followed by* BOB. BILL *is in a bad humor*]. I tell
you, Doris, I don't know! You're getting worse
than Hortense at asking questions. Where's
Dar? He can tell you as much as I can.

DORIS [*petulantly*]. How should I know
where Dar is? You know him at a houseparty.
Running around and managing things. He left
me to go to the telephone and that's the last

I've seen of him for half an hour. I hate to
think of you boys keeping things from me.

BOB. We don't know any more than you,
Doris.

BEATRICE. What are you talking about?

DORIS. Alan.

EDDIE [*without moving from his hiding
place*]. I wish we did. We'd tell you if we did.

DORIS [*starts with fright at* EDDIE'S *voice*].
Oh, what's that!

BOB. Little Eddie Canby. [*He tosses a pillow
at him*]

EDDIE [*dodging the pillow without loss of
dignity*]. Nobody knows where Alan is.

DORIS [*shuddering*]. It gives me a funny
feeling to think of him around somewhere all
alone tonight and none of his friends knowing
where. He must be frightfully lonely. . . .

BILL. His father's with him.

BOB. I imagine they're in New York.

BILL. He might be down at the Fordyce's.
Mr. Fordyce is an old friend of his father's.

CHICK. Where's that?

BOB. You know that big place down on the
South Williamstown road.

CHICK. I don't see why he'd go there.

BILL. You didn't expect him to stay in Pittsfield, did you? With that mob of reporters and
sob sisters and curiosity hounds?

BOB. Dar said that three minutes after Alan
had been acquitted the street in front of the
court house was packed solid with people.

CHICK. Women mostly.

EDDIE. Gee, but I was excited when the news
came in this afternoon that he had been acquitted.

BILL. Quit being ingenue! If you had any
sense you'd have known he'd be acquitted.

BOB. Yeah? I noticed you gnawing your
fingernails pretty thoroughly all last week.

BILL. Well, it wasn't an acquittal I was
worrying about.

EDDIE. What were you worrying about?

BILL. Nothing you'd understand.

DORIS. You mean—how Alan would take it?

BILL. Yes.

DORIS. How has he taken it?

BILL. Well. You know Alan.

CHICK [*defensively*]. He didn't look so badly
when I saw him.

BOB. Oh, I don't know. There's a funny look
in his eyes that doesn't seem to go away—as
though he were straining for something . . .
as though he were sort of fighting things out
all the time inside himself.

DORIS. Alan would do that.

EDDIE [*sitting bolt upright*]. Introspective!

BEATRICE. Why, Eddie, wherever did you
find a word like that?

CHICK. From Mrs. White.

[EDDIE *is injured and lies down again*]

DORIS. Alan will get over it.

BOB. Oh, sure. He'll get over that. When he gets to Paris and gets started studying art, he'll forget all about what's happened.

BILL. Maybe.

EDDIE. I wish he'd come back to college.

DORIS. He couldn't do that.

BILL. No.

BEATRICE. Why not? The college will let him, won't it?

CHICK. Of course.

DORIS. I didn't mean that. I was thinking of Alan.

BILL. You know how upset he used to get over little things. How do you think he'd be now?

EDDIE. Well, he always liked the fellows so much, and he and Ronnie always played around together all the time, I should think he'd hate to go off to some other country.

DORIS [to BILL]. Alan always sort of relied on you and Ronnie, didn't he?

BILL. I guess he put a lot of stock in Ronnie's advice.

BOB. I'd hate to come back, if I were Alan. I'd be sort of embarrassed to see everybody.

CHICK. Embarrassed?

EDDIE. I know what Bob means.

BILL. That's exactly what I'm afraid of now. He's too darned sensitive.

DORIS. This room gives me an unpleasant shiver every time I come into it. It wouldn't be possible to come back, if . . . Oh, hello, Dar.

[She breaks off as DARROW enters, excitedly, down-stage, left]

DARROW. Hello, listen everybody. [Closes the door silently behind him, excited, but conscious that his news is dramatic] Alan is going to spend the night here.

BILL. What!

DARROW. Yes. His father just telephoned me.

BILL. Where is he?

DARROW. At the Fordyces.

BILL. I thought so.

CHICK. What's he coming here for?

DARROW. He wants to see the fellows before he goes. And then, of course, he's got a lot of stuff in his room.

BILL. That could be packed up and sent to him.

DARROW. Yes, I suppose so.

CHICK. That's a funny one.

DARROW [angrily]. I should think you fellows would be glad to have him come back.

CHICK. Lord, yes. I'm glad. I was just surprised.

EDDIE. I am.

BOB. I'd like to see Alan again.

DARROW. His father seemed to think it would be a good idea if he saw that all the fellows felt just the same towards him as before.

BOB. There's something in that.

CHICK. Sort of cheer him up.

BILL. Was it his father's idea?

DARROW. No, Alan suggested it himself.

BILL. That's funny.

DORIS. I think that's awfully nice.

[BILL lapses into a puzzled silence]

DARROW. Now let me see. We've got a lot to do. We can't have a dance going on when he arrives. I spoke to Pete Chapman and he's invited the whole party over to the Deke house.

EDDIE. The whole party?

DARROW. Yes, the whole party. Even Hortense.

BOB. That's a great idea. We can't have a dance going on if Alan's coming back.

CHICK. That would be a bit thick.

DARROW. I guess I'd better let everyone know right away and get them to clear out. And then we can get the house straightened out so it won't look like a party. [CHICK starts to push the chairs into place] I'll give them one more dance. A short one. [To CHICK] Of course we'll have to pay for the orchestra anyway. [He starts towards the living-room]

BILL. Dar.

DARROW. Yes?

BILL. You were in Pittsfield this morning. How did Alan seem?

DARROW. Awfully nervous, but making a splendid effort to be cheerful.

BILL. Did he say anything about wanting to see the fellows?

DARROW. I don't think so. Why?

BILL. I just wondered. [He sits puzzled and silent]

DARROW. Come on, Doris. We'll have the last dance after I make the announcement. [He goes to the orchestra, speaking to the leader.]

[DORIS follows him]

JACK [entering from terrace]. Come on, Bea. This is the last dance.

[JACK and BEATRICE exeunt to terrace]

BOB. Gee, can you beat that!

CHICK [rising]. Say, that's guts for you. To come back here just to say good-bye to the fellows.

EDDIE. I don't think I'd do it.

BOB. I'm darn sure I shouldn't.

BILL. I'm not sure Alan would.

[The drums roll and the dancers stop. DARROW can be seen in the living-room, addressing the boys and girls]

CHICK. Say, there's one thing I certainly do not understand.

EDDIE. What's that?

CHICK. Ronnie.

BILL. What do you mean?

CHICK. Why, the way he's acted. It seems to me darn funny that a fellow who was such a close friend of Alan's as Ronnie was shouldn't go down to the trial even once. Why, he never even went down to Pittsfield, he made no attempt to see Alan.

BOB. Yes, that's right. He was the only fellow in the house who didn't go down.

EDDIE. I guess he was the only fellow in college who didn't.

BILL [*rising*]. You'd think it was a three ring circus, the way the college raced down there. [*He goes out, slamming the door*]

CHICK. He's become the most persistent grouch I ever saw.

DARROW [*re-entering*]. Keep Alan's visit under your hat will you! We don't want a flock of reporters busting in.

EDDIE [*nervously*]. Maybe I'd better speak to Hortense.

CHICK. Maybe you had.

BOB. Maybe you'd better gag her. [EDDIE *hastens off to do what he can*] Poor Eddie. [RONNIE *appears in the doorway, watching the dancers*] Guess I'll dance before it's all over.

CHICK [*getting up*]. So'll I. I want to dance with Marian. [RONNIE *enters*] My woman out there?

RONNIE. I think so. I saw her just a minute ago.

[*The* TWO BOYS *exit.* RONNIE *sits down, busy with his thoughts*]

DARROW. Hello, Ronnie.

RONNIE. Oh, hello, Dar.

DARROW. Going over to the Deke House to dance?

RONNIE. No. Win's going to take care of Sally. They're just leaving.

DARROW. Oh . . . [*Casually*] Going to stay around here?

RONNIE. Sure.

DARROW. Going to be here when Alan arrives?

RONNIE. Naturally. Why?

DARROW. I don't know. I just wondered. [*He looks at* RONNIE *questioningly*] You're not . . . you don't hold anything against Alan, do you?

RONNIE. I? Why, no. What made you think that?

DARROW. Oh, I don't know. I thought perhaps you might be sore at him.

RONNIE. Don't be foolish.

DARROW. Well, you didn't go down to Pittsfield to see him at all during the trial.

RONNIE. Oh . . . I see . . . No, I didn't go down to Pittsfield.

DARROW. It looked darn funny, you being his best friend. Everybody in the house thought it was funny.

RONNIE. Yes?

DARROW. Yes. It didn't look very well for the house. People talked about it on campus.

RONNIE [*angrily*]. People talked about it. You and your damn worries about the house reputation make me sick.

DARROW [*persistently*]. I certainly can't understand why you never went down.

RONNIE. There are lots of things you don't understand.

DARROW. Well, you don't have to get sore.

RONNIE. I'm not sore.

CHICK [*entering with* MRS. WHITE, *who is looking particularly well,* PROFESSOR WHITE *being confined to his house with a cold. Behind her follow* BOB *and two other anxious swains*] Oh, Dar, Mrs. White's looking for you.

MRS. WHITE. I hope I'm not intruding.

RONNIE. No, I was just leaving. Will you excuse me, Mrs. White? [*He leaves through the door down right*]

MRS. WHITE. It's so splendid about Alan's coming back, Darrow. I know how excited you must be. You realize, of course, how much he must have wanted to see you all; it takes a lot of courage to come back and face all his friends in the same place.

DARROW. Yes, it certainly does.

MRS. WHITE. And I think that's a fine idea of yours to send all the boys and girls somewhere else to dance.

DARROW. It wasn't really all my idea. But I think everyone will have just as good a time.

MRS. WHITE. I'm sure of it. I'll run along now, Darrow. The girls will be going on to the other house now, and I can get in a game of cribbage with Professor White before going to bed. He won all the kitchen money last night, and I've got to get it back in order to feed him.

FIRST BOY. Can I take you home, Mrs. White?

BOB. Can I take you home?

SECOND BOY. No, I'll do it.

MRS. WHITE. Well—I—

BEATRICE [*entering from living-room with one of the other girls*]. Say Chick, where's Tommy? I can't find my coat.

CHICK. I haven't seen him.

BEATRICE [*totally uninterested*]. Going over to the Deke House, Mrs. White?

MRS. WHITE. No, I think not.

BEATRICE [*as one woman to another*]. Oh, I'm sorry. Good-night. We'll miss you.

[*The two girls hasten off to express their opinions of giddy chaperons*]

MRS. WHITE. Do give Alan our very best, and tell him that Professor White and I will always be delighted to see him any time he is in town. Any time.

[EDDIE *enters from living-room searching vigorously for something*]

DARROW. Thank you, Mrs. White, I'll do that. [*Bidding her good-night, he leaves her to her escorts*]

MRS. WHITE. You boys are coming over to tea Sunday?

BOYS. Oh, yes, Mrs. White.

MRS. WHITE. You're coming too, Edward?

EDDIE. Oh, of course, Mrs. White. I'm sorry I

couldn't dance with you tonight, but I had Hortense on my hands.

MRS. WHITE. Well, I'll forgive you this time. Good-night.

[*She leaves with a boy on each side, one of whom slams the door triumphantly in the faces of* BOB *and* CHICK. EDDIE *disconsolately continues his search*]

BOB. Well, I see you're getting along famously with your education, Eddie.

EDDIE. I don't need any tutoring from you.

BOB. Lost something, Eddie?

EDDIE. No. But Hortense has. She can't find her powder. I'd give about ten dollars not to have to take her to that dance tonight.

CHICK. Did you say ten dollars?

BOB. Ten dollars is a lot of money.

EDDIE. I know, but it would be worth it. She doesn't know a soul over there and I'll have to dance with her all evening.

BOB. There's a box over there on the table, Eddie.

HORTENSE [*enters vaguely from the living-room*]. There you are. My! I seem to spend more time looking for people. Did you find my powder?

EDDIE. Is that it?

HORTENSE. Oh, aren't you clever! I never could have found it. Come on, let's go over to the Deke House.

CHICK. Oh, Hortense. [*With a conspirator's wink at* BOB] You look pretty tired to me, Hortense. Doesn't she look tired to you, Bob?

BOB. Oh, awfully tired. [*He yawns*]

CHICK. Awfully tired. [*He gets* EDDIE's *attention, raising ten fingers inquiringly with a nod at* HORTENSE. EDDIE *agrees*]

HORTENSE. Do I? Do I, really? Do I need some lipstick? [*She applies the lipstick*] There, do I look rested?

BOB. A little bit. But it shows in your eyes.

HORTENSE [*dabbing at her eyes*]. The lipstick? My, but I'm messy!

CHICK. It's a hard trip up from Northampton, isn't it? [*He yawns*]

HORTENSE. Yes it is. [*Yawning with him*] I had to wait two hours in the Greenfield station. Do you know, they haven't a single weighing machine that works in that station. And I do so love to get weighed.

BOB. There's nothing more wearying than waiting around a station. [*He and* HORTENSE *yawn together*]

HORTENSE. There isn't, is there?

CHICK. And no one wants to look weary, do they, Hortense?

BOB. What a fellow really wants is a girl who looks all fresh and rosy in the early morning. [*He yawns*]

CHICK. Madame Rubenstein says that little rest periods are what keep a woman young and radiant.

BOB. That's the right idea. Rest and a good mattress. You've got to be careful about your mattress.

HORTENSE. Oh, I am careful about my mattress!

RONNIE [*entering from right*]. Aren't you going over to the dance, Hortense?

CHICK [*waving frantically*]. No, Hortense is going to bed.

RONNIE. So early?

EDDIE. Hortense is awfully tired.

HORTENSE [*who has learned a great deal in six months*]. Yes I'm awfully tired. Good-night everybody. [*She goes to door left as though leaving, but instead stands there watching the boys who are dividing up the ten dollars with glee*]

CHICK. You should major in psychology, Eddie.

HORTENSE [*strolls over to them and takes* EDDIE *by the hand*]. Yes, you should major in psychology, Eddie. That's what I've been doing. My professor says that even so immature a human mind as you boys apparently possess should develop the faculty of ratiocination a short period after puberty. Come on, Eddie, we're going to that dance. [*She leads him to door left, taking the two five dollar bills out of his hands*] And thanks for the money. I'll use it for the upkeep of my mattress. Come on, Eddie. [*She drags the bewildered* EDDIE *out the door left, leaving two thoroughly wilted sophomores behind*]

RONNIE. What in the world has happened to Hortense?

[BOB *and* CHICK *can only stand and gape*]

DARROW [*entering from the living-room*]. Say, will you help me put down the hall rug?

BOB. Sure.

CHICK. You wouldn't like to pay us ten dollars to do it, would you?

DARROW. I would not.

CHICK. All right, only we just lost ten dollars. Come on, Bob, snap out of that trance.

BOB. Right you are.

[*They all go together into the living-room. As* RONNIE *stands for a moment thinking,* SALLY *enters from terrace*]

SALLY. Hello, Ronnie. Has Alan come yet?

RONNIE. Hello, Sally. No, not yet. He ought to be along any minute now. I am afraid you aren't having a good time at the party.

SALLY. Oh, I'm having a great time. It's a marvelous party. Only I wanted to speak to you for a second. I haven't had a moment with you all day.

RONNIE. I am awfully sorry, Sally. I haven't been very entertaining, I know. Thinking of other things I guess. [*He sits down beside her*]

SALLY. Ronnie, are you worried about meeting Alan?

RONNIE. Gee, yes, Sally. I won't know how to begin.

SALLY. Of course you will. You've been such a bisected Siamese twin these last six months, that you'll probably be yourself again when you see him.

RONNIE. Yes, but I won't know what to say.

SALLY. Of course you will. [*She moves over close to him invitingly*] You always know what to say, Ronnie.

RONNIE [*however, is too busy planning his reunion with* ALAN *to notice* SALLY'S *changed attitude*] It would be easier, of course, if the others saw him first. I'll wait until he gets upstairs. . . . Don't you think I'm right?

SALLY [*leaning towards him*]. Yes, Ronnie, I think you're always right.

RONNIE. I'd hate to see him in front of everybody. Oh, Sally, I know I've been an awful bore tonight. I am ashamed of myself for not giving you a better time.

SALLY. I'm having a wonderful time now. As a matter of fact, Ronnie, I've never been happier.

RONNIE. I'm glad of that. But I wish I had done more to make you feel that way.

SALLY. You've done everything, Ronnie. You're the reason why I'm so happy.

RONNIE. I?

SALLY. You, goose.

RONNIE. I haven't done much except mope around, I'm afraid.

SALLY. Ronnie, my dear, I wanted you to show signs of seriousness, but I didn't want you to become thickwitted.

[*Boys' voices are heard off left, greeting* ALAN. *A few seconds later they pass through the living-room and across the terrace with* ALAN. RONNIE *and* SALLY *go to terrace door and watch them. Their voices die away as they go upstairs*]

SALLY. You remember Ronnie, I told you I might believe in you if you ever took anything or anybody seriously except yourself?

RONNIE. Yes?

SALLY. Well, now, don't you see? I can believe in you now.

RONNIE [*going toward her*]. Sally, you mean—

SALLY. Oh Ronnie, I love you. I love you.

[*She runs to him, throwing her arms around him and kissing him passionately. Then she slides gently out of his arms and glides through the terrace door.* RONNIE *stands watching her until she is out of sight. Then he pulls the curtains over the terrace doors and goes slowly around the room turning off the lamps until only one or two are left.*

[*The door opens and* ALAN *appears. He shows all the signs of his six months'*

imprisonment. *The two boys stand in silence looking at each other, too embarrassed by their deep feeling to speak. Then* ALAN *closes the door behind him and enters the room*]

ALAN [*simply*]. Hello, Ronnie.

RONNIE. Hello, Alan. [*They shake hands awkwardly, looking silently at each other*] How did you know I was here?

ALAN. Oh, I don't know. I just thought so.

RONNIE. Well . . . you look great, kid.

ALAN [*straining to be cheerful*]. Oh, I feel great. You look well.

RONNIE. Yes, I'm well. How's your father?

ALAN. He's fine.

RONNIE. I'm glad of that. Pretty hot for— come on and sit down, kid.

ALAN. Thanks. [*They sit down uncomfortably on the edge of their chairs, facing each other*]. . . . It was sort of cool coming up—I mean, for this time of the year . . . [*He stops awkwardly*] . . . I . . . [*Then suddenly softly*] Ronnie, it's good to see you again.

RONNIE. It's good to see you, kid.

ALAN. And Ronnie, thanks for not coming down to Pittsfield.

RONNIE. That's all right, Alan.

ALAN. And thanks for your letters. They were great. I don't know if you can understand why I didn't want you to come down, Ronnie. You see . . . well . . . Mother wanted to come down too, but I asked her not to. I couldn't help about Dad. He had to be there, you know, but I hated it. I just wanted Mother to pretend I wasn't there, but, you know, some other place. Mother wrote me almost every day. That helped a lot. But somehow, I couldn't have stood her seeing me up there like that. It would have hurt her so. And . . . and I didn't want you, either, to . . . Well do you see what I mean, Ronnie . . . ?

RONNIE. Yes, I see. [*He goes to the window so that* ALAN *won't see his face. When he turns, he is determinedly cheerful*] Well, everything's all right, now, Alan. It's all over isn't it, kid?

ALAN [*trying to be cheerful, too*]. Yes. That's right. Everything's all right now.

RONNIE. It's certainly great to see you. I didn't think you would be coming back here again.

ALAN. Well, I . . . I wanted to see the fellows again before I went.

RONNIE. Of course. When do you sail, Wednesday?

ALAN. Yes, Wednesday.

RONNIE. Paris will be great at this time of the year.

ALAN. Yes, it ought to be great at this time of the year.

RONNIE. And in the Fall it will be great, too. You're going to start studying in the Fall?

ALAN. Yes, I'm going to start studying in the

Fall. I think it ought to be awfully interesting.

RONNIE. At Juliens?

ALAN. Yes. I think so. Or maybe the Grand Chaumière.

RONNIE. If you're at the Grand Chaumière, you ought to take a course in sculpture. Bourdelle's there. They say he's a wonderful teacher.

ALAN. Yes.

RONNIE. All the boys will want to hear from you.

ALAN. Oh, yes. Yes, I'll write.

RONNIE. They're awfully glad you're back. You feel that, don't you. Why, even all the faculty would like to have you for tea. [ALAN *nods in acquiescence. After a minute* RONNIE *says softly*] Of course you're going away and we won't see much of each other . . . again, I guess. But . . . but we'll be the same, Alan.

ALAN [*not able to look up—scarcely trusting his voice*]. Sure. Sure. We'll be the same.

RONNIE. That's the way for you to feel Alan. You've got to feel that nothing's happened. Remember the way we used to fool around here and go to Hamp on parties and get Bill's goat and kid Eddie Canby?

ALAN. Of course I remember.

RONNIE. Hey, Charlie, I've got a new job—

[ALAN *looks up and smiles; then he turns his head away and covers his face with his hands quickly, muffling his sobs*]

RONNIE. Aw, now, Alan, please! Please don't do that, kid. Please!

ALAN. Oh, I'm tired of pretending any more, Ronnie. What's the use? Things aren't the same and they never will be. [*He raises his head and looks* RONNIE *squarely in the eye; his voice is unexpectedly strained and hard*] Do you want to know why I came back here tonight? Do you want to know why I came down here? I didn't come back to see you. I didn't know you were here. I didn't come back to see the fellows. I'll tell you why I came back. [*Hoarsely*] I came back because I wanted to see this room!

RONNIE. Alan!

ALAN [*fiercely*]. That's the reason why I came back. Now do you think everything's O. K.?

RONNIE [*frightened*]. Cut that out, Alan.

ALAN [*roughly*]. You think I've been down in Pittsfield all the time, don't you? Don't you? Well, do you know where I have been? [RONNIE *stares at him fearfully as* ALAN *leans suddenly towards him*] Do you know where I've been?

RONNIE [*grasping* ALAN *sternly*]. Shut up, Alan. Shut up. Do you hear!

ALAN. Right here in this room! [*He winces and pulls away from* RONNIE, *rising and walking up and down the room*] All day long in that cell, I've been up here. Right here. Looking at the cupboard. Looking at it. Waiting for someone to open it. Waiting. And looking all day long. And all night long. All night, every night, I've dreamed I was here.

RONNIE [*terrified, but trying to control himself*]. But Alan! Alan, listen to me. That's all over. Everything is different now, you're acquitted.

ALAN. Acquitted? Yes, I'm acquitted. But it happened. I can't forget that. A jury can't wipe that out. It's there. Inside me. And it's going to keep on that way. On and on and on. It won't be any better in Paris. Only worse, because I'll be so far away from it. I know I'm going to be right here all the time. Looking at the cupboard. Waiting for someone to open it. You can say what you want. You can be as Pollyanna as you like, but I know it. I've been wanting to be here. And now I am. Right where I've been for the last six months. Right here in this room. Where I can see everything again. Clearly. [RONNIE *tries to restrain him as he points fiercely to the hearth and cupboard*] That's where it happened. You see? [*Boys are heard entering the house*] And that's the cupboard where I put . . .

RONNIE [*shaking him violently*]. Alan. Listen to me, Alan. You've got to stop that. You've got to! You've got ·to quit thinking about it.

ALAN [*dazedly*]. But that's the cupboard.

RONNIE [*shaking him*]. The fellows are coming in! Stop it, Alan!

[BILL *enters followed by four other boys*]

JACK. Hello, Alan.

ALAN [*trying to recapture his synthetic gaiety*]. Hello, Jack.

JACK [*casually*]. You look fine, Alan.

ALAN. Yes, I'm feeling fine. Hello, Pete.

[BILL *drops back and watches* ALAN *silently*]

PETE. Hello, Alan. It's great to see you back again.

ALAN. Yes. It's fine to be here again. Well, Chick.

CHICK. Hello, Alan.

ALAN. And Bob.

BOB. Hello, Alan.

JACK. When did you get in?

ALAN. Just a little while ago.

PETE. Going to stay with us long?

ALAN. No. Just over night.

JACK. Wish I were going to Paris.

PETE. So do I. How long will you be gone?

ALAN. I don't know exactly.

PETE [*starts with the others towards the door*]. Well, you'll be coming back from time to time, I suppose.

ALAN. Oh, yes. [*Avoiding* RONNIE's *eye*] Yes . . . I'll be coming back here . . . often.

PETE. Good-night, Alan.

JACK. Good-night, Alan.

ALAN. Good-night.

CHICK. Coming over to the Deke House, Bill?

BILL. No, Dar has wished me the pleasant job of seeing that our athletes get the bed. That means you, Jack.

[*Exeunt all but* BILL, *who stands by the door, hesitant, looking at* ALAN *and* RONNIE. *Then he comes back, hand outstretched*]

BILL [*with deep feeling*]. Alan—I . . .

ALAN [*taking his hand*]. Thank you, Bill.

BILL. I . . . I . . . [*He turns sharply*] Good-night, kid.

ALAN. So long, Bill.

[BILL *leaves. Now the two boys are alone again.* ALAN *seats himself wearily.* RONNIE *paces up and down the room behind him, at a loss as to where to begin*]

RONNIE. Now listen here, kid . . .

ALAN. I know—I know—don't lecture me. . . .

[*Again there is silence*]

RONNIE. But Alan, this is horrible.

ALAN. I know it. You don't have to tell me that. I know it just as well as you do.

RONNIE. Well, then, why don't you—

ALAN. There's no use in talking, Ronnie. I know everything you can say! . . . It disgusts me just as much as it does you! . . . How do you think *I* feel to have thoughts like this? My God, I wouldn't even dare tell you about some of them! [*Pause*] You know, Ronnie, sometimes it seems as though this thing couldn't really have happened . . . as though it were just a rotten dream. . . . How is it? Why is it, Ronnie? Do you understand?

RONNIE. Things just happen, I guess.

ALAN [*with a weariness that seems almost like physical pain*]. Sometimes I wish that I could rub it all clean up here, so that there was no more memory of things—like wiping a slate clean with a sponge. . . . [*His voice takes on a strange, soft quality that is in some vague fashion morbidly fascinating.* RONNIE *watches him closely*] At night, I often try to think of a whiteness . . . a negativeness . . . but it doesn't last long . . . soon spots appear and then . . . [*His voice trails off into nothingness.* RONNIE, *half frightened, lays his hand on* ALAN's *shoulder. There is a pause. Then* ALAN *shakes his head slowly*] No, Ronnie . . . no. . . Acquitting a person doesn't wipe away memory. . . . [*Suddenly swinging around*] Don't you suppose if I could get over this thing, I would? Do you think I like being this way? I want to be like . . . like you . . . like other boys. . . . But what am I going to do? I just can't help it. . . .

[*There is silence*]

RONNIE [*turning suddenly on* ALAN, *determined, as a last resource, to let him have it straight from the shoulder*]. Then I guess you're right. I just guess you haven't any guts. If you feel that way, if you haven't got enough strength within yourself, I suppose it will be just as bad in Paris, or wherever you are. It's entirely up to you, Alan. We can't do anything now. Oh, we can open your windows for you and give you advice and spank your tail, but we can't clear this thing upon your mind for you. You've got to do that yourself. You've got to want to. I can't help you. But here's what I can do. Here's what I will do. If you can't pull yourself out of this by yourself—over in Europe—then I'm going to Europe with you! Perhaps I can't help much, but I can try.

ALAN [*startled*]. But you can't do that.

RONNIE. Yes, I can. I've no ties.

ALAN. But you'd hate to leave college. You love it here.

RONNIE. Yes, I do. But I'd leave. Willingly.

ALAN. And Sally. You couldn't leave Sally.

RONNIE. Sally will have to wait, because that's just what I'm going to do if you can't pull yourself out of this.

ALAN. Yes; but, Ronnie, I—

RONNIE. Nothing you can say will prevent me from doing it. [ALAN *sits in complete silence, not moving.* RONNIE *stands looking at him for a moment. At last he goes to* ALAN, *laying a hand on his shoulder gently*] And now you'd better go to bed, kid.

[ALAN *and* RONNIE *start toward door right. When they get to couch* RONNIE *leans over to turn off the lamp*]

ALAN [*grasps his arm*]. Ronnie, I'm not going to let you do it. Why should you throw away all your chances of success just for me?

RONNIE. There's no use arguing, kid.

ALAN. But Ronnie, you don't understand what it means. It would mean the end of school for you. It would probably mean a separation between you and Sally. I've done enough already. I've made enough of a mess of my own life without making a mess of yours also. I'm not going to let you do it, Ronnie.

RONNIE. There's no use arguing.

ALAN [*desperately*]. But, Ronnie, you're putting so much responsibility on my shoulders.

RONNIE [*slowly as he looks* ALAN *full in the eye*]. Yes, I am.

[RONNIE *turns off the lamp and the two of them go out of the door right still talking. There is silence for a moment as they climb the stairs. Then voices can be heard from the upper rooms*]

1ST VOICE. Hello, Alan.

[*Silence for a moment*]

2ND VOICE. Hey, Willie, Willie. For Pete's sake will you turn off that shower. How do you expect anyone to sleep with that thing going!

3RD VOICE. At least I don't snore.

1ST and 2ND VOICE. The hell you don't.

3RD VOICE. Aw, nuts.

4TH VOICE. Shut up, all of you.

1ST VOICE. Hey, what's the big idea! Who took my pajamas? Hey, who took my pajamas?

3RD VOICE. It's warm tonight. Why worry?

1ST VOICE. That's a dirty trick.

4TH VOICE. For Pete's sake, will you shut up!

[*The voices cease abruptly and there is silence throughout the house. Moonlight fills the deserted library. The strains of an orchestra can be heard from far across the campus. There is a distant murmur of voices; of laughter; of boys' voices singing fragments of "The Mountains"*

[*Suddenly the door down right opens and* ALAN *enters, closing the door behind him. He leans heavily against it as he turns the key in the lock. He looks around the room, then suddenly runs to the cupboard. As soon as he touches it, he draws back and his body stiffens. He sinks to the floor, covering his face with his hands. The chimes in the chapel tower begin to strike the hour. After a moment he wearily lifts his head. The center table looms up in the moonlight and* ALAN *stares at it. He crosses to it, pulling open the drawer, and takes out a*

gun. *He runs quickly in back of the couch and stops before the cupboard. Swaying there, he raises the gun slowly to his head*]

[*At this moment* RONNIE's *voice is heard from upstairs. It is urgent, startled*]

RONNIE [*sharply*]. Alan! Alan!

[RONNIE *is heard running down the stairs and there is a furious and imperative pounding on the locked door.* ALAN *raises the gun again.* RONNIE's *voice rings out fiercely, but firmly, with a tense undercurrent of challenge*]

RONNIE. Hey, Charlie, I've got a new job!

[ALAN *stares toward the door. There is a long silence*]

RONNIE [*shouting, pleading*]. Hey, Charlie, I've got a new job!

ALAN [*half whispering, in spite of himself*]. Is—is that so Charlie? [*Louder, his voice breaking*] And what is it? [*Rushing to door right and flinging the gun aside. Hysterically, joyfully*] What is it, Charlie? [*He flings open the doors wildly and rushes out*] . . . Charlie! . . . Ronnie!

[*The light from the hall falls across the stage upon the revolver on the floor as*

THE CURTAIN FALLS

THE MOON OF THE CARIBBEES

A Play In One Act

By EUGENE O'NEILL

·

CHARACTERS

YANK
DRISCOLL
OLSON
DAVIS } *Seamen of the British tramp steamer, Glencairn*
COCKY
SMITTY
PAUL
LAMPS, *the lamptrimmer*
CHIPS, *the carpenter*
OLD TOM, *the donkeyman*
BIG FRANK,
DICK
MAX } *Firemen on the Glencairn*
PADDY
BELLA
VIOLET
SUSIE } *West Indian Negresses*
PEARL
THE FIRST MATE
Two other seamen—SCOTTY AND IVAN—and several other members of the stokehole-engine-room crew.

THE MOON OF THE CARIBBEES

SCENE—*A forward section of the main deck of the British tramp Steamer* Glencairn, *at anchor off an island in the West Indies. The full moon, half-way up the sky, throws a clear light on the deck. The sea is calm and the ship motionless.*

On the left, two of the derrick booms of the foremast jut out at an angle of forty-five degrees, black against the sky. In the rear the dark outline of the port bulwark is sharply defined against a distant strip of coral beach, white in the moonlight, fringed with coco palms whose tops rise clear of the horizon. On the right is the forecastle with an open doorway in the center leading to the seamen's and firemen's compartments. On either side of the doorway are two closed doors opening on the quarters of the Bo'sun, the ship's carpenter, the messroom steward, and the donkeyman—what might be called the petty officers of the ship. Near each bulwark there is also a short stairway, like a section of fire escape, leading up to the forecastle head (the top of the forecastle)—the edge of which can be seen on the right.

In the center of the deck, and occupying most of the space, is the large, raised square of the number one hatch, covered with canvas, battened down for the night.

A melancholy negro chant, faint and far-off, drifts, crooning, over the water.

Most of the seamen and firemen are reclining or sitting on the hatch. PAUL is leaning against the port bulwark, the upper part of his stocky figure outlined against the sky. SMITTY and COCKY are sitting on the edge of the forecastle head with their legs dangling over. Nearly all are smoking pipes or cigarettes. The majority are dressed in patched suits of dungaree. Quite a few are in their bare feet and some of them, specially the firemen, have nothing on but a pair of pants and an undershirt. A good many wear caps.

There is the low murmur of different conversations going on in the separate groups as the CURTAIN *rises. This is followed by a sudden silence in which the singing from the land can be plainly heard.*

DRISCOLL [*a powerfully built Irishman who is sitting on the edge of the hatch, front—irritably*]. Will ye listen to them naygurs? I wonder now, do they call that keenin' a song?

SMITTY [*a young Englishman with a blond mustache. He is sitting on the forecastle head looking out over the water with his chin supported on his hands*]. It doesn't make a chap feel very cheerful, does it? [*He sighs*]

COCKY [*a wizened runt of a man with a straggling gray mustache—slapping SMITTY on the back*]. Cheero, ole dear! Down't be ser dawhn in the marf, Duke. She loves yer.

SMITTY [*gloomily*]. Shut up, Cocky! [*He turns away from COCKY and falls to dreaming again, staring toward the spot on shore where the singing seems to come from*]

BIG FRANK [*a huge fireman sprawled out on the right of the hatch—waving a hand toward the land*]. They bury somebody—py chiminy Christmas, I tink so from way it sound.

YANK [*a rather good-looking rough who is sitting beside DRISCOLL*]. What d'yuh mean, bury? They don't plant 'em down here, Dutchy. They eat 'em to save fun'ral expenses. I guess this guy went down the wrong way an' they got indigestion.

COCKY. Indigestion! Ho yus, not 'arf! Down't yer know as them blokes 'as two stomacks like a bleedin' camel?

DAVIS [*a short, dark man seated on the right of hatch*]. An' you seen the two, I s'pect, ain't you?

COCKY [*scornfully*]. Down't be showin' yer igerance be tryin' to make a mock o' me what has seen more o' the world than yeself ever will.

MAX [*a Swedish fireman—from the rear of hatch*]. Spin dat yarn, Cocky.

COCKY. It's Gawd's troof, what I tole yer. I 'eard it from a bloke what was captured pris'ner by 'em in the Solomon Islands. Shipped wiv 'im one voyage. 'Twas a rare treat to 'ear 'im tell what 'appened to 'im among 'em. [*Musingly*] 'E was a funny bird, 'e was—'ailed from Mile End, 'e did.

DRISCOLL [*with a snort*]. Another lyin' Cockney, the loike av yourself!

LAMPS [*a fat Swede who is sitting on a camp stool in front of his door talking with CHIPS*]. Where you meet up with him, Cocky?

CHIPS [*a lanky Scotchman—derisively*]. In New Guinea, I'll lay my oath!

COCKY [*defiantly*]. Yus! It *was* in New Guinea, time I was shipwrecked there.

[*There is a perfect storm of groans and laughter at this speech*]

YANK [*getting up*]. Yuh know what we said yuh'd get if yuh sprung any of that lyin' New Guinea dope on us again, don't yuh? Close that trap if yuh don't want a duckin' over the side.

COCKY. Ow, I was on'y tryin' to edicate yer a bit. [*He sinks into dignified silence*]

YANK [*nodding toward the shore*]. Don't yuh know this is the West Indies, yuh crazy mut? There ain't no cannibals here. They're only common niggers.

DRISCOLL [*irritably*]. Whativir they are, the divil take their cryin'. It's enough to give a man the jigs listenin' to 'em.

YANK [*with a grin*]. What's the matter, Drisc? Yuh're as sore as a boil about somethin'.

DRISCOLL. I'm dyin' wid impatience to have a dhrink; an' that blarsted bumboat naygur woman took her oath she'd bring back rum enough for the lot av us whin she came back on board to-night.

BIG FRANK [*overhearing this—in a loud eager voice*]. You say the bumboat voman vill bring booze?

DRISCOLL [*sarcastically*]. That's right—tell the Old Man about ut, an' the Mate, too. [*All of the crew have edged nearer to DRISCOLL and are listening to the conversation with an air of suppressed excitement. DRISCOLL lowers his voice impressively and addresses them all*] She said she cud snake ut on board in the bottoms av thim baskets av fruit they're goin' to bring wid 'em to sell to us for'ard.

THE DONKEYMAN [*an old gray-headed man with a kindly, wrinkled face. He is sitting on a camp stool in front of his door, right front*]. She'll be bringin' some black women with her this time—or times has changed since I put in here last.

DRISCOLL. She said she wud—two or three—more, maybe, I dunno.

[*This announcement is received with great enthusiasm by all hands*]

COCKY. Wot a bloody lark!

OLSON. Py yingo, we have one hell of a time!

DRISCOLL [*warningly*]. Remimber ye must be quiet about ut, ye scuts—wid the dhrink, I mane—ivin if the bo'sun is ashore. The Old Man ordered her to bring no booze on board or he wudn't buy a thing off av her for the ship.

PADDY [*a squat, ugly Liverpool Irishman*]. To the divil wid him!

BIG FRANK [*turning on him*]. Shud up, you tamn fool, Paddy! You vant make trouble? [*To DRISCOLL*] You und me, ve keep dem quiet, Drisc.

DRISCOLL. Right ye are, Dutchy. I'll split the skull av the first wan av ye starts to foight.

[*Three bells are heard striking*]

DAVIS. Three bells. When's she comin', Drisc?

DRISCOLL. She'll be here any minute now, surely. [*To PAUL, who has returned to his position by the bulwark after hearing DRISCOLL's news*] D'you see 'em comin', Paul?

PAUL. I don't see anyting like bumboat.

[*They all set themselves to wait, lighting pipes, cigarettes, and making themselves comfortable. There is a silence broken only by the mournful singing of the negroes on shore*]

SMITTY [*slowly—with a trace of melancholy*]. I wish they'd stop that song. It makes you think of—well—things you ought to forget. Rummy go, what?

COCKY [*slapping him on the back*]. Cheero, ole love! We'll be 'avin our rum in arf a mo', Duke. [*He comes down to the deck, leaving SMITTY alone on the forecastle head*]

BIG FRANK. Sing someting, Drisc. Den ve don't hear dot yelling.

DAVIS. Give us a chanty, Drisc.

PADDY. Wan all av us knows.

MAX. We all sing in on chorus.

OLSON. "Rio Grande," Drisc.

BIG FRANK. No, ve don't know dot. Sing "Viskey Johnny."

CHIPS. "Flyin' Cloud."

COCKY. Now! Guv us "Maïd o' Amsterdam."

LAMPS. "Santa Anna" iss good one.

DRISCOLL. Shut your mouths, all av you. [*Scornfully*] A chanty is ut ye want? I'll bet me whole pay day there's not wan in the crowd 'ceptin' Yank here, an' Ollie, an' meself, an' Lamps an' Cocky, maybe, wud be sailors enough to know the main from the mizzen on a windjammer. Ye've heard the names av chanties but divil a note av the tune or a loine av the words do ye know. There's hardly a rale deep-water sailor lift on the seas, more's the pity.

YANK. Give us "Blow The Man Down." We all know some of that. [*A chorus of assenting voices:* Yes!—Righto!—Let 'er drive! Start 'er, Drisc! *etc.*]

DRISCOLL. Come in then, all av ye. [*He sings:*] As I was a-roamin' down Paradise Street—

ALL. Wa-a-ay, blow the man down!

DRISCOLL. As I was a-roamin' down Paradise Street—

ALL. Give us some time to blow the man down!

CHORUS

Blow the man down, boys, oh, blow
    the man down!
Wa-a-ay, blow the man down!
As I was a-roamin' down Paradise
    Street—
Give us some time to blow the
    man down!

DRISCOLL. A pretty young maiden I chance for to meet.

ALL. Wa-a-ay, blow the man down!

DRISCOLL. A pretty young maiden I chance for to meet.

ALL. Give us some time to blow the man down!

CHORUS
Blow the man down, boys, oh, blow
the man down!
Wa-a-ay, blow the man down!
A pretty young maiden I chanced
for to meet.
Give us some time to blow the
man down!

PAUL [*just as* DRISCOLL *is clearing his throat preparatory to starting the next verse*]. Hay, Drisc! Here she come, I tink. Some bumboat comin' dis way.

[*They all rush to the side and look toward the land*]

YANK. There's five or six of them in it—and they paddle like skirts.

DRISCOLL [*wildly elated*]. "Hurroo, ye scuts! 'Tis thim right enough. [*He does a few jig steps on the deck*]

OLSON [*after a pause during which all are watching the approaching boat*]. Py yingo, I see six in boat, yes, sir.

DAVIS. I kin make out the baskets. See 'em there amidships?

BIG FRANK. Vot kind booze dey bring—viskey?

DRISCOLL. Rum, foine West Indy rum wid a kick in ut loike a mule's hoind leg.

LAMPS. Maybe she don't bring any; maybe skipper scare her.

DRISCOLL. Don't be throwin' cold water, Lamps. I'll skin her black hoide off av her if she goes back on her worrd.

YANK. Here they come. Listen to 'em gigglin'. [*Calling*] Oh, you kiddo!

[*The sound of women's voices can be heard talking and laughing*]

DRISCOLL [*calling*]. Is ut you, Mrs. Old Black Joe?

A WOMAN'S VOICE. Ullo, Mike!

[*There is loud feminine laughter at this retort*]

DRISCOLL. Shake a leg an' come abord thin.

THE WOMAN'S VOICE. We're a-comin'.

DRISCOLL. Come on, Yank. You an' me'd best be goin' to give 'em a hand wid their truck. 'Twill put 'em in good spirits.

COCKY [*as they start off left*]. Ho, you ain't arf a fox, Drisc. Down't drink it all afore we sees it.

DRISCOLL [*over his shoulder*]. You'll be avin' yours, me sonny bye, don't fret. [*He and YANK go off left*]

COCKY [*licking his lips*]. Gawd blimey, I can do wiv a wet.

DAVIS. Me, too!

CHIPS. I'll bet there ain't none of us'll let any go to waste.

BIG FRANK. I could trink a whole barrel mineself, py chimminy Christmas!

COCKY. I 'opes all the gels ain't as bloomin'

ugly as 'er. Looked like a bloody organ-grinder's monkey, she did. Gawd, I couldn't put up wiv the likes of 'er!

PADDY. Ye'll be lucky if any of thim looks at ye, ye squint-eyed runt.

COCKY [*angrily*]. Ho, yus? You ain't no bleedin' beauty prize yeself, me man. A 'airy ape, I calls yer.

PADDY [*walking toward him—truculently*]. Whot's thot? Say ut again if ye dare.

COCKY [*his hand on his sheath knife—snarling*]. 'Airy ape! That's wot I says!

[PADDY *tries to reach him but the others keep them apart*]

BIG FRANK [*pushing PADDY back*]. Vot's the matter mit you, Paddy. Don't you hear vat Driscoll say—no fighting?

PADDY [*grumblingly*]. I don't take no back talk from that deck-scrubbin' shrimp.

COCKY. Blarsted coal-puncher!

[DRISCOLL *appears wearing a broad grin of satisfaction. The fight is immediately forgotten by the crowd who gather around him with exclamations of eager curiosity. How is it, Drisc? Any luck? Vot she bring, Drisc? Where's the gels? etc.*]

DRISCOLL [*with an apprehensive glance back at the bridge*]. Not so loud, for the love av hivin! [*The clamor dies down*] Yis, she has ut wid her. She'll be here in a minute wid a pint bottle or two for each wan av ye—three shillin's a bottle. So don't be impashunt.

COCKY [*indignantly*]. Three bob! The bloody cow!

SMITTY [*with an ironic smile*]. Grand larceny, by God.

[*They all turn and look up at him, surprised to hear him speak*]

OLSON. Py yingo, we don't pay so much.

BIG FRANK. Tamn black tief!

PADDY. We'll take ut away from her and give her nothin'.

THE CROWD [*growling*]. Dirty thief! Dot's right! Give her nothin'! Not a bloomin' 'apenny! etc.

DRISCOLL [*grinning*]. Ye can take ut or lave ut, me sonny byes. [*He casts a glance in the direction of the bridge and then reaches inside his shirt and pulls out a pint bottle*] 'Tis foine rum, the rale stuff. [*He drinks*] I slipped this wan out av wan av the baskets whin they wasn't lookin'. [*He hands the bottle to* OLSON *who is nearest him*] Here ye are, Ollie. Take a small sup an' pass ut to the nixt. 'Tisn't much but 'twill serve to take the black taste out av your mouths if ye go aisy wid ut. An' there's buckets more av ut comin'.

[*The bottle passes from hand to hand, each man taking a sip and smacking his lips with a deep "Aa-ah" of satisfaction*]

DAVIS. Where's she now, Drisc?

DRISCOLL. Up havin' a worrd wid the skipper, makin' arrangements about the money, I s'pose.

DAVIS. An' where's the other gels?

DRISCOLL. Wid her. There's foive av thim she took aboard—two swate little slips av things, near as white as you an' me are, for that gray-whiskered auld fool, an' the mates—an' the engineers too, maybe. The rist av thim'll be comin' for'ard whin she comes.

COCKY. 'E ain't 'arf a funny ole bird, the skipper. Gawd blimey! 'Member when we sailed from 'ome 'ow 'e stands on the bridge lookin' like a bloody ole sky pilot? An' 'is missus dawn on the bloomin' dock 'owlin fit to kill 'erself? An' 'is kids 'owlin' an' wavin' their 'andkerchiefs? [*With great moral indignation*] An' 'ere 'e is makin' up to a bleedin' nigger! There's a captain for yer! Gawd blimey! Bloody crab, I calls 'im!

DRISCOLL. Shut up, ye insect! Sure, it's not you should be talkin', an' you wid a woman an' childer weepin' for ye in iviry divil's port in the wide worrld, if we can believe your own tale av ut.

COCKY [*still indignant*]. I ain't no bloomin' captain, I ain't. I ain't got no missus—reg'lar married, I means. I ain't—

BIG FRANK [*putting a huge paw over Cocky's mouth*]. You ain't going talk so much, you hear? [COCKY *wriggles away from him*] Say, Drisc, how ve pay dis voman for booze? Ve ain't got no cash?

DRISCOLL. It's aisy enough. Each girl'll have a slip av paper wid her an' whin you buy anythin' you write ut down and the price beside ut and sign your name. If ye can't write have some one who can do ut for ye. An' rimimber this: Whin ye buy a bottle av dhrink or [*With a wink*] somethin' else forbid, ye must write down tobacco or fruit or somethin' the loike av that. Whin she laves the skipper'll pay what's owin' on the paper an' take ut out av your pay. Is ut clear to ye now?

ALL. Yes—Clear as day—Aw right, Drisc—Righto—Sure, etc.

DRISCOLL. An' don't forgit what I said about bein' quiet wid the dhrink, or the Mate'll be down on our necks an' spile the fun.

[*A chorus of assent*]

DAVIS [*looking aft*]. Ain't this them comin'? [*They all look in that direction. The silly laughter of a woman is heard*]

DRISCOLL. Look at Yank, wud ye, wid his arrm around the middle av wan av thim. That lad's not wastin' any toime.

[*The four women enter from the left, giggling and whispering to each other. The first three carry baskets on their heads. The youngest and best-looking comes last. YANK has his arm about her waist and is carrying her basket in his other hand. All four are distinct negro types.*

They wear light-colored, loose-fitting clothes and have bright bandana handkerchiefs on their heads. They put down their baskets on the hatch and sit down beside them. The men crowd around, grinning]

BELLA [*she is the oldest, stoutest, and homeliest of the four—grinning back at them*]. Ullo, boys.

THE OTHER GIRLS. 'Ullo, boys.

THE MEN. Hello, yourself—Evenin'—Hello —How are you? etc.

BELLA [*genially*]. Hope you had a nice voyage. My name's Bella, this here's Susie, yander's Violet, and her there [*Pointing to the girl with Yank*] is Pearl. Now we all knows each other.

PADDY [*roughly*]. Never mind the girls. Where's the dhrink?

BELLA [*tartly*]. You're a hawg, ain't you? Don't talk so loud or you don't git any—you nor no man. Think I wants the ole captain to put me off the ship, do you?"

YANK. Yes, nix on hollerin', you! D'you wanta queer all of us?

BELLA [*casting a quick glance over her shoulder*]. Here! Some of you big strapping boys sit back of us on the hatch there so's them officers can't see what we're doin'. [DRISCOLL *and several of the others sit and stand in back of the girls on the hatch.* BELLA *turns to* DRISCOLL] Did you tell 'em they gotter sign for what they gits—and *how* to sign?

DRISCOLL. I did—what's your name again— oh, yis—Bella, darlin'.

BELLA. Then it's all right; but you boys has gotter go inside the fo'castle when you gits your bottle. No drinkin' out here on deck. I ain't takin' no chances. [*An impatient murmur of assent goes up from the crowd*] Ain't that right, Mike?

DRISCOLL. Right as rain, darlin'. [BIG FRANK *leans over and says something to him in a low voice.* DRISCOLL *laughs and slaps his thigh*] Listen, Bella, I've somethin' to ask ye for my little friend here who's bashful. Ut has to do wid the ladies so I'd best be whisperin' ut to ye meself to kape them from blushin'. [*He leans over and asks her a question*]

BELLA [*firmly*]. Four shillin's.

DRISCOLL [*laughing*]. D'you hear that, all av ye? Four shillin's ut is.

PADDY [*angrily*]. To hell wid this talkin'. I want a dhrink.

BELLA. Is everything all right, Mike?

DRISCOLL [*after a look back at the bridge*]. Sure. Let her droive!

BELLA. All right, girls. [*The girls reach down in their baskets in under the fruit which is on top and each pulls out a pint bottle. Four of the men crowd up and take the bottles*] Fetch a light, Lamps, that's a good boy. [LAMPS *goes to his room and returns with a candle. This i passed from one girl to another as the men sign the sheets of paper for their bottles*] Don't you boys forget to mark down cigarettes or tobacco or fruit, remember! Three shillin's is the price. Take it into the fo'castle. For Gawd's sake, don't stand out here drinkin' in the moon-light.

[*The four go into the forecastle. Four more take their places.* PADDY *plants himself in front of* PEARL *who is sitting by* YANK *with his arm still around her*]

PADDY [*gruffly*]. Gimme thot!

[*She holds out a bottle which he snatches from her hand. He turns to go away*]

YANK [*sharply*]. Here, you! Where d'yuh get that stuff? You ain't signed for that yet.

PADDY [*sullenly*]. I can't write me name.

YANK. Then I'll write it for yuh. [*He takes the paper from* PEARL *and writes*] There ain't goin' to be no welchin' on little Bright Eyes here—not when I'm around, see? Ain't I right, kiddo?

PEARL [*with a grin*]. Yes, suh.

BELLA [*seeing all four are served*]. Take it into the fo'castle, boys. [PADDY *defiantly raises his bottle and gulps down a drink in the full moonlight.* BELLA *sees him*] Look at 'im! Look at the dirty swine! [PADDY *slouches into the forecastle*] Wants to git me in trouble. That settles it! We all got to git inside, boys, where we won't git caught. Come on, girls.

[*The girls pick up their baskets and follow* BELLA. YANK *and* PEARL *are the last to reach the doorway. She lingers behind him, her eyes fixed on* SMITTY, *who is still sitting on the forecastle head, his chin on his hands, staring off into va-cancy*]

PEARL [*waving a hand to attract his atten-tion*]. Come ahn in, pretty boy. Ah likes you.

SMITTY [*coldly*]. Yes; I want to buy a bot-tle, please.

[*He goes down the steps and follows her into the forecastle. No one remains on deck but the* DONKEYMAN, *who sits smoking his pipe in front of his door. There is the subdued babble of voices from the crowd inside but the mournful cadence of the song from the shore can again be faintly heard.* SMITTY *reappears and closes the door to the forecastle after him. He shudders and shakes his shoul-ders as if flinging off something which disgusted him. Then he lifts the bottle which is in his hand to his lips and gulps down a long drink.* THE DONKEYMAN *watches him impassively.* SMITTY *sits down on the hatch facing him. Now that the closed door has shut off nearly all the noise, the singing from shore comes clearly over the moonlit water*]

SMITTY [*listening to it for a moment*]. Damn that song of theirs. [*He takes another big drink*] What do you say, Donk?

THE DONKEYMAN [*quietly*]. Seems nice an' sleepy-like.

SMITTY [*with a hard laugh*]. Sleepy! If I listened to it long—sober—I'd never go to sleep.

THE DONKEYMAN. 'Tain't sich bad music, is it? Sounds kinder pretty to me—low an' mournful—same as listenin' to the organ out-side o' church of a Sunday.

SMITTY [*with a touch of impatience*]. I didn't mean it was bad music. It isn't. It's the beastly memories the damn thing brings up—for some reason. [*He takes another pull at the bottle*]

THE DONKEYMAN. Ever hear it before?

SMITTY. No; never in my life. It's just a something about the rotten thing which makes me think of—well—oh, the devil! [*He forces a laugh*]

THE DONKEYMAN [*spitting placidly*]. Queer things, mem'ries. I ain't ever been bothered much by 'em.

SMITTY [*looking at him fixedly for a mo-ment—with quiet scorn*]. No, you wouldn't be.

THE DONKEYMAN. Not that I ain't had my share o' things goin' wrong; but I puts 'em out o' me mind, an' fergets 'em.

SMITTY. But suppose you couldn't put them out of your mind? Suppose they haunted you when you were awake and when you were asleep—what then?

THE DONKEYMAN [*quietly*]. I'd git drunk, same's you're doin'.

SMITTY [*with a harsh laugh*]. Good advice. [*He takes another drink. He is beginning to show the effects of the liquor. His face is flushed and he talks rather wildly*] We're poor little lambs who have lost our way, eh, Donk? Damned from here to eternity, what? God have mercy on such as we! True, isn't it, Donk?

THE DONKEYMAN. Maybe; I dunno. [*After a slight pause*] Whatever set you goin' to sea? You ain't made for it.

SMITTY [*laughing wildly*]. My old friend in the bottle here, Donk.

THE DONKEYMAN. I done my share o' drinkin' in my time. [*Regretfully*] Them was good times, those days. Can't hold up under drink no more. Doctor told me I'd got to stop or die. [*He spits contentedly*] So I stops.

SMITTY [*with a foolish smile*]. Then I'll drink one for you. Here's your health, old top! [*He drinks*]

THE DONKEYMAN [*after a pause*]. S'pose there's a gel mixed up in it someplace, ain't there?

SMITTY [*stiffly*]. What makes you think so?

THE DONKEYMAN. Always is when a man lets music bother 'im. [*After a few puffs at his pipe*] An' she said she threw you over 'cause you was drunk; an' you said you was drunk 'cause she threw you over. [*He spits leisurely*] Queer thing, love, ain't it?

SMITTY [*rising to his feet with drunken dignity*]. I'll trouble you not to pry into my affairs, Donkeyman.

THE DONKEYMAN [*unmoved*]. That's everybody's affair, what I said. I been through it many's the time. [*Genially*] I always hit 'em a whack on the ear an' went out and got drunker'n ever. When I come home again they always had somethin' special nice cooked fur me to eat. [*Puffing at his pipe*] That's the on'y way to fix 'em when they gits on their high horse. I don't s'pose you ever tried that?

SMITTY [*pompously*]. Gentlemen don't hit women.

THE DONKEYMAN [*placidly*]. No; that's why they has mem'ries when they hears music.

[SMITTY *does not deign to reply to this but sinks into a scornful silence.* DAVIS *and the girl* VIOLET *come out of the forecastle and close the door behind them. He is staggering a bit and she is laughing shrilly*]

DAVIS [*turning to the left*]. This way, Rose, or Pansy, or Jessamine, or black Tulip, or Violet, or whatever the hell flower your name is. No one'll see us back here.

[*They go off left*]

THE DONKEYMAN. There's love at first sight for you—an' plenty more o' the same in the fo'c's'tle. No mem'ries jined with that.

SMITTY [*really repelled*]. Shut up, Donk. You're disgusting. [*He takes a long drink*]

THE DONKEYMAN [*philosophically*]. All depends on how you was brung up, I s'pose.

[PEARL *comes out of the forecastle. There is a roar of voices from inside. She shuts the door behind her, sees* SMITTY *on the hatch, and comes over and sits beside him and puts her arm over his shoulder*]

THE DONKEYMAN [*chuckling*]. There's love for you, Duke.

PEARL [*patting* SMITTY'S *face with her hand*]. 'Ullo, pretty boy. [SMITTY *pushes her hand away coldly*] What you doin' out here all alone by yourself?

SMITTY [*with a twisted grin*]. Thinking and, —[*He indicates the bottle in his hand*]—drinking to stop thinking. [*He drinks and laughs maudlinly. The bottle is three-quarters empty*]

PEARL. You oughtn't drink so much, pretty boy. Don' you know dat? You have big, big headache come mawnin'.

SMITTY [*dryly*]. Indeed?

PEARL. Tha's true. Ah knows what Ah say. [*Cooingly*] Why you run 'way from me, pretty boy? Ah likes you. Ah don' like them other fellahs. They act too rough. You ain't rough. You're a genelman. Ah knows. Ah can tell a genelman fahs Ah can see 'im.

SMITTY. Thank you for the compliment; but you're wrong, you see. I'm merely—a ranker. [*He adds bitterly*] And a rotter.

PEARL [*patting his arm*]. No, you ain't. Ah knows better. You're a genelman. [*Insinuatingly*] Ah wouldn't have nothin' to do with them other men, but [*She smiles at him enticingly*] you is diff'rent. [*He pushes her away from him disgustedly. She pouts*] Don' you like me, pretty boy?

SMITTY [*a bit ashamed*]. I beg your pardon. I didn't mean to be rude, you know, really. [*His politeness is drunkenly exaggerated*] I'm a bit off color.

PEARL [*brightening up*]. Den you do like me —little ways?

SMITTY [*carelessly*]. Yes, yes, why shouldn't I? [*He suddenly laughs wildly and puts his arm around her waist and presses her to him*] Why not?

[*He pulls his arm back quickly with a shudder of disgust, and takes a drink.* PEARL *looks at him curiously, puzzled by his strange actions. The door from the forecastle is kicked open and* YANK *comes out. The uproar of shouting, laughing and singing voices has increased in violence.* YANK *staggers over toward* SMITTY *and* PEARL]

YANK [*blinking at them*]. What the hell— oh, it's you, Smitty the Duke. I was goin' to turn one loose on the jaw of any guy'd cop my dame, but seein' it's you— [*Sentimentally*] Pals is pals and any pal of mine c'n have anythin' I got, see? [*Holding out his hand*] Shake, Duke. [SMITTY *takes his hand and he pumps it up and down*] You'n me's frens. Ain't I right?

SMITTY. Right it is, Yank. But you're wrong about this girl. She isn't with me. She was just going back to the fo'c's'tle to you.

[PEARL *looks at him with hatred gathering in her eyes*]

YANK. Tha' right?

SMITTY. On my word!

YANK [*grabbing her arm*]. Come on then you, Pearl! Le's have a drink with the bunch.

[*He pulls her to the entrance where she shakes off his hand long enough to turn on* SMITTY *furiously*]

PEARL. You swine! You can go to hell! [*She goes in the forecastle, slamming the door*]

THE DONKEYMAN [*spitting calmly*]. There's love for you. They're all the same—white, brown, yeller 'n' black. A whack on the ear's the only thing'll learn 'em.

[SMITTY *makes no reply but laughs harshly and takes another drink; then sits staring before him, the almost empty bottle tightly clutched in one hand. There is an increase in volume of the muffled clamor from the forecastle and a moment later the door is thrown open and the whole mob, led by* DRISCOLL, *pours*] out on deck. *All of them are very drunk and several of them carry bottles in their hands.* BELLA *is the only one of the women who is absolutely sober. She tries in vain to keep the men quiet.* PEARL *drinks from* YANK'S *bottle every moment or so, laughing shrilly, and leaning against* YANK, *whose arm is about her waist.* PAUL *comes out last carrying an accordion. He staggers over and stands on top of the hatch, his instrument under his arm*]

DRISCOLL. Play us a dance, ye square-head swab!—a rale, Godforsaken son av a turkey trot wid guts to ut.

YANK. Straight from the old Barbary Coast in Frisco!

PAUL. I don' know. I try. [*He commences tuning up*]

YANK. Ataboy! Let 'er rip!

[DAVIS *and* VIOLET *come back and join the crowd.* THE DONKEYMAN *looks on them all with a detached, indulgent air.* SMITTY *stares before him and does not seem to know there is any one on deck but himself*]

BIG FRANK. Dance? I don't dance. I trink! [*He suits the action to the word and roars with meaningless laughter*]

DRISCOLL. Git out av the way thin, ye big hulk, an' give us some room.

[BIG FRANK *sits down on the hatch, right. All of the others who are not going to dance either follow his example or lean against the port bulwark*]

BELLA [*on the verge of tears at her inability to keep them in the forecastle or make them be quiet now they are out*]. For Gawd's sake, boys, don't shout so loud! Want to git me in trouble?

DRISCOLL [*grabbing her*]. Dance wid me, me cannibal quane.

[*Some one drops a bottle on deck and it smashes*]

BELLA [*hysterically*]. There they goes! There they goes! Captain'll hear that! Oh, my Lawd!

DRISCOLL. Be damned to him! Here's the music. Off ye go!

[PAUL *starts playing* "You Great Big Beautiful Doll" *with a note left out every now and then. The four couples commence dancing—a jerk-shouldered version of the old Turkey Trot as it was done in the sailor-town dives, made more grotesque by the fact that all the couples are drunk and keep lurching into each other every moment. Two of the men start dancing together, intentionally bumping into the others.* YANK *and* PEARL *come around in front of* SMITTY *and, as they pass him,* PEARL *slaps him across the side of the face with all her might, and laughs viciously. He jumps to*

his feet with his fists clenched but sees who hit him and sits down again smiling bitterly. YANK *laughs boisterously*]

YANK. Wow! Some wallop! One on you, Duke.

DRISCOLL [*hurling his cap at* PAUL]. Faster, ye toad! [PAUL *makes frantic efforts to speed up and the music suffers in the process*]

BELLA [*puffing*]. Let me go. I'm wore out with you steppin' on my toes, you clumsy Mick. [*She struggles but* DRISCOLL *holds her tight*]

DRISCOLL. God blarst you for havin' such big feet, thin. Aisy, aisy, Mrs. Old Black Joe! 'Tis dancin'll take the blubber off ye.

[*He whirls her around the deck by main force.* COCKY, *with* SUSIE, *is dancing near the hatch, right, when* PADDY, *who is sitting on the edge with* BIG FRANK, *sticks his foot out and the wavering couple stumble over it and fall flat on the deck. A roar of laughter goes up.* COCKY *rises to his feet, his face livid with rage, and springs at* PADDY, *who promptly knocks him down.* DRISCOLL *hits* PADDY *and* BIG FRANK *hits* DRISCOLL. *In a flash a wholesale fight has broken out and the deck is a surging crowd of drink-maddened men hitting out at each other indiscriminately, although the general idea seems to be a battle between seamen and firemen. The women shriek and take refuge on top of the hatch, where they huddle in a frightened group. Finally there is the flash of a knife held high in the moonlight and a loud yell of pain*]

DAVIS [*somewhere in the crowd*]. Here's the Mate comin'! Let's git out o' this!

[*There is a general rush for the forecastle. In a moment there is no one left on deck but the little group of women on the hatch;* SMITTY, *still dazedly rubbing his cheek;* THE DONKEYMAN *quietly smoking on his stool; and* YANK *and* DRISCOLL, *their faces battered up considerably, their undershirts in shreds, bending over the still form of* PADDY, *which lies stretched out on the deck between them. In the silence the mournful chant from the shore creeps slowly out to the ship*]

DRISCOLL [*quickly—in a low voice*]. Who knoifed him?

YANK [*stupidly*]. I didn't see it. How do I know? Cocky, I'll bet.

[*The* FIRST MATE *enters from the left. He is a tall, strongly-built man dressed in a plain blue uniform*]

THE MATE [*angrily*]. What's all this noise about? [*He sees the man lying on the deck*] Hello! What's this? [*He bends down on one knee beside* PADDY]

DRISCOLL [*stammering*]. All av us—was in a bit av a harmless foight, sir,—an'—I dunno—

[*THE MATE rolls PADDY over and sees a knife wound on his shoulder*]

THE MATE. Knifed, by God. [*He takes an electric flash from his pocket and examines the cut*] Lucky it's only a flesh wound. He must have hit his head on deck when he fell. That's what knocked him out. This is only a scratch. Take him aft and I'll bandage him up.

DRISCOLL. Yis, sor.

[*They take PADDY by the shoulders and feet and carry him off left. THE MATE looks up and sees the women on the hatch for the first time*]

THE MATE [*surprised*], Hello! [*He walks over to them*] Go to the cabin and get your money and clear off. If I had my way, you'd never— [*His foot hits a bottle. He stoops down and picks it up and smells of it*] Rum, by God! So that's the trouble! I thought their breaths smelled damn queer. [*To the women, harshly*] You needn't go to the skipper for any money. You won't get any. That'll teach you to smuggle rum on a ship and start a riot.

BELLA. But, Mister—

THE MATE [*sternly*]. You know the agreement—rum—no money.

BELLA [*indignantly*]. Honest to Gawd, Mister, I never brung no—

THE MATE [*fiercely*]. You're a liar! And none of your lip or I'll make a complaint ashore tomorrow and have you locked up.

BELLA [*subdued*]. Please, Mister—

THE MATE. Clear out of this, now! Not another word out of you! Tumble over the side damn quick! The two others are waiting for you. Hop, now!

[*They walk quickly—almost run—off to the left. THE MATE follows them, nodding to THE DONKEYMAN, and ignoring the oblivious SMITTY*]

[*There is absolute silence on the ship for a few moments. The melancholy song of the negroes drifts crooning over the water. SMITTY listens to it intently for a time; then sighs heavily, a sigh that is half a sob*]

SMITTY. God! [*He drinks the last drop in the bottle and throws it behind him on the hatch*]

THE DONKEYMAN [*spitting tranquilly*]. More mem'ries? [*SMITTY does not answer him. The ship's bell tolls four bells. THE DONKEYMAN knocks out his pipe*] I think I'll turn in. [*He opens the door to his cabin, but turns to look at SMITTY—kindly*] You can't hear it in the fo'c's'tle—the music, I mean—an' there'll likely be more drink in there, too. Good night. [*He goes in and shuts the door*]

SMITTY. Good night, Donk. [*He gets wearily to his feet and walks with bowed shoulders, staggering a bit, to the forecastle entrance and goes in. There is silence for a second or so, broken only by the haunted, saddened voice of that brooding music, faint and far-off, like the mood of the moonlight made audible*]

THE CURTAIN FALLS

THE DRUMS OF OUDE

A Drama in One Act

By AUSTIN STRONG

CHARACTERS

CAPTAIN HECTOR MCGREGOR
LIEUTENANT ALAN HARTLEY
SERGEANT MCDOUGAL
STEWART, *the sentry*
TWO HINDUSTANI SERVANTS
MRS. JACK CLAYTON, *Hartley's sister*
A PRIVATE
SCENE: *An interior of a palace in Northern India, occupied by British troops.*
TIME: *Spring of 1857.*

The acting rights of this play are fully protected by law. For permission to perform, either by professionals or amateurs (whether to read in public, or in private), to cause to be performed or represented, read in public, produce or to in any way utilize this play, application should be made to Samuel French, at 25 West 45th St., New York N. Y., or at 811 W. 7th St., Los Angeles, Calif.

As Reading by performance of the Author and Samuel French.

THE DRUMS OF OUDE

Music before curtain rises to be of that mysterious, nervous Indian quality, in a minor key, with the barbaric drum-beat measure throughout.

All lights out. Theater in total darkness. Drumming is heard from beyond the stage, mingled with faint cries. This drumming must be great in volume, yet low in key. It stops short.

Repeats itself and again stops short. The curtain has gone up in the darkness. The audience first becomes aware of the moonlit Indian City, in the distance, over the top of an intervening forest.

Then they see the outline of the archway and the stage itself, which is a store-room in an old Indian Palace, now occupied by the British. There is no furniture in the room except a piano, right, and a business desk, right, rear. A large Indian carpet is upon the floor. The only decorations are two crossed swords on either side of the arch.

Sentry STEWART, *in Highland uniform, passes beyond the arch, in the moonlight, from right to left. Pause. He returns. Pause. Then again from right to left. The drumming swells in the distance and seems to come from the Indian City. As the* SENTRY *appears on his return beat, the drumming ceases. He halts center of archway and turns a puzzled face towards the audience and listens intently. Dead silence.*

He is seen to breathe a sigh of relief, straighten himself and continue his stolid march. Silence.

Then with a crash, door left bursts open and MCGREGOR *slides in. He shuts the door softly and swiftly and listens intently with his ear to the panels. He gives a glance at the open arch, then takes three steps center, stoops, takes hold of the corner of carpet and flings it back. Rises, goes back to door left, and listens at panels again. Then returns center and opens a trap-door which was beneath the carpet. The trap-door is three feet square and eight inches thick.*

He looks carefully in and then closing it returns the carpet to its place, stands on it, and listens intently, his eyes to the audience. He then draws from his left-hand coat pocket a large leather cigar case. Chooses a cigar and returns case. He then slowly backs to wall right. When he reaches it he strikes a match upon it with a downward sweep of his hand. He lights cigar and carefully putting out the match, he assumes a graceful, easy position, his

back against the wall, his hands rammed deep in his coat pockets and his right foot crossed over his left, his eyes always on the corner of the carpet.

STEWART, *the sentry, is seen to pass at rear. He halts again and listens as if he heard something. He turns his face towards the audience to listen better, and with a start becomes aware of* MCGREGOR's *presence. He brings his musket sharply to the shoulder, comes down the stage and halts three paces from* MCGREGOR, *his face towards the audience. He makes the stiff soldier's salute, right hand across the body.*

[MCGREGOR *continues smoking and regarding the carpet. Pause*]

MCGREGOR [*cigar between his teeth*]. Well, Stewart?

STEWART. Please, sir! Beg pardon, sir, but did you 'ear anything, sir?

MCGREGOR. Eh?

STEWART. Listen, sir!

[MCGREGOR *removes the cigar from his mouth and listens. Dead silence*]

MCGREGOR. What do you mean?

STEWART [*intensely*]. Listen, sir! [*The drumming heard. It stops abruptly*] There, sir!

MCGREGOR. Well?

STEWART. Beg pardon, sir—but me and the men don't fancy it, sir.

MCGREGOR. That will do, Stewart.

STEWART. Yes, sir! [*Salutes stiffly—faces about—marches out and resumes sentry duty, and is seen at stated intervals passing and repassing beyond the arch*]

[*Door left softly opens and two* HINDUSTANI SERVANTS *enter, one bearing a standard lamp with a red shade. The lamp is lighted. The other bears a small table which he places at left center. The standard lamp is placed near the business desk.* SERGEANT MCDOUGAL *enters left with* PRIVATE, *both in Highland uniform and carrying telegraphic apparatus. They cross the stage and exeunt door right. After a moment ticking is heard from that room. The two* SERVANTS *have by this time returned with the two wicker chairs, which they place right and left and then exeunt.* SERGEANT MCDOUGAL *and* PRIVATE *return through door right. The* PRIVATE *crosses stage and exits door left.* SERGEANT MCDOUGAL *comes down center. Enter* FIRST *and* SECOND HINDUSTANI SERVANTS *through door left.*

They go over to McGregor *and salaam deeply before him*]

McGregor. I want you to serve supper up here for two. [*They do not move. A pause*] Did you hear what I said? I said—serve supper —supper—up here for two.

[*They salaam and exeunt softly*]

McDougal. The telegraph is in working order, sir! [*He faces about and goes towards door left. Just as he is about to exit—*]

McGregor. Sergeant!

McDougal [*stopping abruptly*]. Y-y-yes, sir!

McGregor. How many men on guard duty?

McDougal [*in a surprised tone*]. Seven, sir! [*Pause*]

McGregor. Wake the others up!

McDougal [*his tone more surprised*]. B-b-beg p-pardon, sir!

McGregor. Double the sentries. Put Neill and ten men on the ground floor with orders to let no one enter except women and civilians. Take the rest yourself and string them along the walls. North and West sides as much as possible, towards the dome.

McDougal. Yes, sir! [*Is about to exit*]. Pardon, sir—but—but do you know when the regiment will be back?

McGregor. Can't say, McDougal.

McDougal. Thank you, sir. [*Is about to exit*]

McGregor. Sergeant!

McDougal. Yes, sir!

McGregor. Lieutenant Hartley will take command. Kindly wake him up with my compliments and ask him up here.

McDougal. Yes, sir. [*Exits*]

[*Drumming is heard again.* Sentry *is seen to pass from right to left, then left to right.* McGregor *still regards the corner of the carpet, the cigar between his teeth. Door left opens and* Lieutenant Hartley *enters; a tall fair-haired English lad, garrulous and pink-cheeked. He is buttoning his tunic and wears the expression of one who has been aroused from a deep sleep. He looks vaguely about for* McGregor, *but does not see him*]

McGregor. Ah, Hartley.

Hartley [*in a thick, sleepy voice*]. Oh, there you are—didn't see where you were at first. Why in thunder— [*Yawns*]—d-d-did y-y-you w-wake me u-up at this hour? Must be near one or two or something—your man bounced me out of bed as if the house was afire. [*Goes over to table and mixes brandy and soda*] And why have you moved up to this outlandish store-room? [*Drinks glass, his voice becoming more awake*] Shifted all your things, too! [*He pauses, and then becoming wide awake he suddenly asks*] I say, McGregor, what's up?

McGregor. Listen!

[*The drumming a shade louder*]

Hartley. Oh, that's the Mohurrum business they're having. Guess the beggars will keep it up all night. They tell me it is a religious festival they hold here once a year. [Hartley *takes a few strides nearer* McGregor] I say, you don't think there is anything nasty about it, do you?

McGregor. India is a queer place, Hartley.

Hartley. By Jove—come to think of it—I— did you hear that queer rumor this morning?

McGregor. Rumors. You're all alike, you youngsters. I was the same myself once—well, out with it!

Hartley. Something about a small cake—!

McGregor [*sharply*]. What?—Quick—where was it seen?

Hartley [*blithely*]. The chaps I was talking to said that it was a sure sign that these devils meant mischief. They called it the fiery cross of India and they said that this little cake passes from hand to hand—from village to village—and the message which means mutiny and disaster flies faster than our telegraph!

McGregor. Oh, yes—I know all that— But where was it seen?

Hartley. This morning on the steps of the Mission! [*A pause while* Hartley *watches face of* McGregor *who goes on smoking.* Hartley, *in an eager voice*] I say—by Jove— you don't think there's a chance for a row, do you?

McGregor. Hartley.

Hartley. Yes, old chap?

McGregor. You are standing over forty tons of gunpowder!

Hartley [*standing back and looking down at the carpet*]. What!

McGregor. Beneath you is the magazine!

Hartley. The magazine! [*Stooping and lifting edge of carpet*] I didn't know it was here! Thought it was by the Colonel's quarters.

McGregor. Hartley, these Sepoys want that powder.

Hartley. Eh?

McGregor. I'm afraid they will be disappointed.

Hartley. I say, McGregor—do you really think—

McGregor. The regiment is away—we don't know when it will be back. The town is full of strangers. . . . [*Pause*] Hartley, there are women in this town—white women—English women.

Hartley. Rather. And, by Jove, there's my sister, Mrs. Clayton, the widow—I hadn't thought of her!

McGregor. Well, you see—I had, Hartley!

Hartley [*surprised*]. Why, what do you mean . . . ?

McGregor. Only that I bribed her woman— her faithful ayah—to bring her here tonight under some pretext or other. I expect her any minute now.

HARTLEY. I say, that was clever of you! [*Pause.* MCGREGOR *goes over center for the first time and looks through archway.* HARTLEY, *in a queer voice*] You have known my sister, Mrs. Clayton, a long time out here, haven't you?

MCGREGOR. I remember her before she left England—when you were still at Sandhurst.

HARTLEY. She used often to write me of you.

MCGREGOR [*turning*]. She did?

HARTLEY. You have been a better friend to her than ever Clayton, her husband, was.

MCGREGOR. The man's dead, Hartley.

HARTLEY. Oh yes, I know—but it was all the mater's fault she ever married him. [*Pause.* HARTLEY *goes over to* MCGREGOR *in a shy, boyish manner*] I say, McGregor— give us a chance if there's a row?

MCGREGOR [*smiling*]. I woke you up for that purpose. You'll take command of the walls in a few minutes. I don't trust anyone here except myself. That is why I had my things shifted. [*Takes out watch*] The Colonel ought to be near Bandagaar by this time. You stay here a moment—I'll telegraph along the line. [*Goes toward the door at right*]

HARTLEY. McGregor!

MCGREGOR. Eh?

HARTLEY. You're a brick to give a fellow such a chance—thanks!

MCGREGOR [*laughing*]. Don't be too sanguine, Hartley—it's a bad habit. Perhaps, after all, this is nothing. [*Exits into next room, at right, and after a moment is heard telegraphing*]

[HARTLEY *takes another look at the magazine, then goes to the center of the archway and listens a moment to the drumming, which, by fine degrees has grown louder. The* SENTRY *passes at rear, but doesn't see* HARTLEY. HARTLEY *goes over right to business desk and idly looks over it. Picks up a newspaper, looks at it a moment, and then drops it. He sees writing materials upon the desk. He seats himself, spreads paper, leans forward and dips pen in ink*]

HARTLEY [*as he writes*]. "Dear mater . . . This is the slowest station in Northern India . . . there is nothing to do . . . no society . . . nothing! Sis is practically the only English-woman of any account, except the Major's wife and Mrs. Indermaur. By the way, Captain McGregor, my senior, you remember him . . . the chap Sis used to write us about. . . . Well, he's a thoroughbred and dead nuts on Sis . . . has been all his life, it seems. I think McGregor is the only man Sis ever cared a straw about, but she won't have a word said against Clayton's memory.". . . [HARTLEY *leans back in his chair,*

lifting his pen and searching the ceiling for ideas. Then leans forward and continues writing in silence]

[*Door left softly opens and* FIRST *and* SECOND SERVANTS *glide noiselessly in, walking as Orientals do, straight from the hips. They move about quietly setting the table. The drumming ceases suddenly. The* SERVANTS *raise their heads slowly and look deep into each other's eyes, across the table. They both come forward center without changing their relative positions or shifting their gaze from each other's eyes. They stand center a moment listening. Then a small white cake, the size of a griddle cake, flies through the archway and falls between the* SERVANTS. *The* FIRST SERVANT *drops on one knee and covers the cake with his right hand, and watches his companion.* SECOND SERVANT *takes four deliberate steps backwards, which brings him immediately behind* HARTLEY, *who is deep in his letter.* SECOND SERVANT *slowly draws from his bosom a pistol which he levels at* HARTLEY'S *neck, about two feet distant.* HARTLEY *blots letter with a satisfied air, throws down pen, leans far back in his chair, which brings the muzzle of the pistol within two inches of his neck. He passes his hand through his hair and reads. Reading in a satisfied air*]

. . ."and I always wear my flannels as you asked me to, and take my two grains of quinine regularly. I forgot to say in my last letter that Spiffy Watkins may have my cricket bat. I shan't need it again, but don't let anyone touch my fishing rod on any account! [*Leans forward to underline—"any"*] You needn't be anxious about me, mother dear—there is no danger in India. It's positively dull, it's so safe. Love to everybody—shall write the girls next mail. Your affectionate son, Alan Hartley. P.S. —I repeat—don't let anyone touch my fishing rod."

[*The ticking of the telegraph is heard to stop suddenly.* SECOND SERVANT *hides pistol in his bosom.* FIRST SERVANT *rises and hides cake in his sash. Both assume position at door left, one immediately behind the other—watching* HARTLEY *intently.* HARTLEY *rises, folds letter, slips it into envelope, and is about to lick it when he becomes aware of the two Indians staring at him. He is taken aback. They drop their eyes—salaam, and exeunt together*]

HARTLEY [*taking five paces after them and stopping with a startled expression*]. By Gad, I didn't know those men were in the room. I wish these servant fellows would laugh or make a noise, or anything—instead of bowing and gliding about. [*With a slight shudder*] Makes a fellow feel deuced uncanny!

McGREGOR [*entering with papers which he throws on business desk, then comes center, sits*]. Can't get the Colonel yet. They haven't reached the station—or they have passed it.

HARTLEY [*still looking after the servants*]. I say, McGregor, do you trust those two servants of yours?

McGREGOR [*laughing and coming forward*]. Implicitly. . . . Come, my dear boy, take a seat and have some supper. [*Motions* HARTLEY *to a seat opposite to him at the table*] I would trust those two men with my life.

HARTLEY. Well, I suppose you know. For myself, I don't like them. Fact is, I never liked the looks of any of these vermin—they're so damned slippery.

McGREGOR. Hartley, may I give you a piece of advice?

HARTLEY [*taking a large piece of toast. His mouth full*]. Go ahead.

McGREGOR. You are new to India—you have only joined the regiment three weeks, and you have an imagination. . . . My boy, quell it—stifle it—for if you let it grow in this hotbed of rumors and strange noises, it will devour you! I have seen brave men made cowards by it. . . . Sherry?

HARTLEY. Thanks. [McGREGOR *pours it out*] Perhaps you're right, but talking of rumors—do tell me more about this chuppattie cake!

McGREGOR. Fact is, no one knows much about them. A chuppattie cake is the commonest thing in India. Why, it's the food of the people—it's their bread.

HARTLEY. These chaps told me it was a signal of mutiny—they told me of a sentence that went with it—do you know it?

McGREGOR. "Sub lal hogga hi." (*Pronounced* "Sub lal hoyarggi.*")

HARTLEY. And what does that mean, pray?

McGREGOR [*slowly*]. Everything is to become red!

HARTLEY [*watching* McGREGOR, *who goes on calmly eating*]. Do—do you believe in it?

McGREGOR. Depends, Hartley, where I saw one.

HARTLEY. What do you mean?

McGREGOR. If I saw a chuppattie in an out-of-the-way place—

HARTLEY [*eagerly*]. Yes?

McGREGOR [*smiling*]. India's a queer place, Hartley. [*Pause*] I remember when I was with a Sepoy regiment once, the Colonel had us out on a surprise inspection one night, and we found that a corporal had two chuppatties under his pillow. . . . [*Pause*] We had a narrow escape that night. [*They both rise suddenly to their feet*]

HARTLEY. Did you hear that?

McGREGOR [*listening*]. Yes.

HARTLEY. Sounded like . . . sounded like a whistle!

McGREGOR. Sit down! [*They both sit down*] [*Enter the* TWO HINDUSTANI SERVANTS *with more dishes for dinner*]

McGREGOR [*to* FIRST SERVANT]. Abdul, that lamp is smoking—turn it down.

[FIRST SERVANT *crosses the stage to right to standing lamp, which he lowers. He listens all the while intently, with his eyes fixed upon his companion, who is immediately behind* HARTLEY. *As he reaches center of stage on his return, unnoticed by himself or any of the others, the chuppattie falls from his sash to the floor near* McGREGOR. *Exeunt* SERVANTS *softly*]

HARTLEY [*using a siphon*]. I don't like those two men!

McGREGOR. Oh, you will get over that, Hartley.

[*Door left bursts open and* SERGEANT Mc-DOUGAL *enters, breathless—he salutes and stands*]

McGREGOR [*going on eating*]. Well, McDougal?

McDOUGAL [*breathlessly*]. Please, sir—Mrs. Cameron, Miss Williams and five other ladies, Mr. Palmer and Judge Lawson with some civilian gentlemen, have come into the walls, sir! They seek protection, sir! They're afraid of a rising, sir!

McGREGOR. Ah! Is—is Mrs. Clayton with them?

McDOUGAL. N-n-no, Sir! P-p-please, s-sir —what'll I do with them, sir?

McGREGOR [*thoughtfully*]. Well, I can't very well leave this room. . . .

HARTLEY [*rising abruptly*]. I'll go!

McGREGOR. Sit down— I want you here, Hartley! McDougal, put the ladies in the Mess Room and see that they are properly cared for. Give the gentlemen muskets and put them on the North Side as much as possible. Lieut. Hartley will take command in a few minutes. McDougal!

McDOUGAL. Yes, sir! [*About to exit*]

McGREGOR. And McDougal—

McDOUGAL. Yes, sir!

McGREGOR. If Mrs. Clayton comes, show her up here.

McDOUGAL. Yes, sir. [*Salutes and exits*]

[*They go on eating in silence,* HARTLEY *tries to hide his excitement and watches* McGREGOR *excitedly. At last, with a great show of unconcern he drains his cup of coffee, uses a napkin, throws it down, and speaks in an obviously careless manner*]

HARTLEY. My sister. . . . You think she will get here safely?

McGREGOR. I have known this servant of hers for years. Your sister will be here—don't you worry. [*Rises—another pause.* HARTLEY *tries again to hide his excitement*]

HARTLEY [*obviously making conversation*]. I say, McGregor— I am interested about these chuppattie cakes—tell me what does one look like?

McGREGOR [*going over to business desk. He gets cigar box from a drawer and returns across stage. He pauses in the center and looks out into the moonlight*]. Hartley, I don't see that sentry! [*He remains silent a moment, looking out, then comes over to the table and throws the cigar box among the dishes*] Have a cheroot? [*Business of* HARTLEY *choosing one.* McGREGOR *put a match into the candle and facing audience holds it in the air, his eyes to the ceiling*] What's a chuppattie look like? Why, let me see if I can describe it to you. [*Lights cigar thoughtfully—then looks upon the floor, match still burning in his right hand. Sees cake at his feet. Shakes out the lighted match slowly. Puts it carefully in the saucer. Takes a draw at his cigar, all the while examining the cake intently*] Well, it looks like a griddle cake . . . it's thick—and—er—white. [*Leans down and picks up with his right hand and weighs it*] Weighs about an ounce—looks deuced indigestible! [HARTLEY *at this word is in the act of lighing his cigar under the candle shade.* McGREGOR *carelessly throws cake on table and it falls with a clatter among the dishes*] Something like that, Hartley.

HARTLEY [*sternly, back*]. My God—how did that get here?

McGREGOR [*looking over the heads of the audience*]. I told you India was a queer place, Hartley.

[HARTLEY *puts his cigar on his plate and watches* McGREGOR'S *face excitedly*]

McGREGOR [*slowly*]. The first thing to be done, Hartley, is to see if that sentry is there.

HARTLEY [*quickly*]. I'll go and see! [*Turns and runs towards arch*]

McGREGOR. Stop! [HARTLEY *stops abruptly*] Are you armed?

HARTLEY [*with a rising inflection*]. No! [*Looks about*]

McGREGOR. You will find one in the left-hand drawer of my desk. [HARTLEY *goes to desk, opens drawer, takes out pistol, comes back center holding the pistol in front of him. Is seen to collect himself, square his shoulders and march out into the moonlight with military step. Halts without, his back to the audience*] What do you see?

HARTLEY. All the men seem to be at their posts. I see Mr. Palmer and Judge Lawson— they have given them muskets.

McGREGOR. And Stewart—the sentry?

[HARTLEY *disappears right of archway,* then returns at a run. He arrives breathless at* McGREGOR'S *side*]

HARTLEY [*in a whisper*]. They've cut his throat!

McGREGOR. Hartley! Hartley! [*Draws his cigar sharply from his mouth. Pause*] Hartley, would you mind going into that room and telegraphing?

HARTLEY [*flying to the door right, breathless with excitement*]. What will I say?

McGREGOR. Get Bandaggaar. . . . If they don't answer get Sir John at Hadraa . . . then the Bulbud Residency. . . . Repeat the one word "massacre" till someone answers you!

[*Exit* HARTLEY, *banging the door. Then the sound of the machine repeating the same message over and over again. Drumming begins again.* McGREGOR *stands a moment longer looking over the heads of the audience, then goes quickly to the business desk and begins pulling out with feverish hurry papers and documents which he tears to pieces. His cigar between his teeth. Door left opens with a bang and the* Two HINDUSTANI SERVANTS *burst into the room, wildly searching for the lost chuppattie cake.* FIRST SERVANT *is seen feeling in his sash.* McGREGOR *turns sharply around*]

What the devil— [SERVANTS *immediately salaam and make a pretense of going towards the table*] Oh yes, we have finished—you may clear away the things.

[*He turns his back to them and goes on tearing up the papers. As soon as his back is turned,* FIRST SERVANT *signals through door at left and out troop all the other* SERVANTS. *They tiptoe down stage, all with their eyes on* McGREGOR'S *back. They pass through arch and one by one leap lightly over the parapet and out of sight. When all have gone—* McGREGOR *speaks through his teeth. still tearing up his papers, his back to the empty stage*]

Look here, you men— I didn't like the way you burst into the room just now! [*Pause, he goes on tearing up papers*] What did you mean by it? [*Pause*] I said, what did you mean by it? [*He turns sharply*] Look here, when I ask a question I expect an answer. . . . [*The words die on his lips as he sees the empty stage*]

[*Stands silent a moment, looking at the untouched supper table. Then takes three deliberate steps backwards, which brings him to right of arch. He raises his hand and unhooks one of the Indian swords that decorates the wall, and throws it lightly on the desk within easy reach. He then leans comfortably on the side of the archway, looking out into the moonlight, smoking his cigar. A sound of running feet approaching.* McGregor's *hand is seen to move towards the sword on the desk. He continues smoking and looking out*]

A Woman's Voice. Captain McGregor! Captain McGregor!

[McGregor *removes the cigar from his mouth and gives a quick look at the magazine door. Then, breathless and half crying with excitement,* Mrs. Clayton *enters wildly and leans fainting against wall left of archway. She covers her eyes with her arm*]

Mrs. Clayton [*wildly*]. Captain McGregor . . . your men . . . your men showed me up here . . . the town is rising! Save me! Save me!

McGregor [*in a polite voice, carefully putting cigar out in a small ash-tray beside him on the desk*]. Why, how do you do, Mrs. Clayton?

Mrs. Clayton. No—no—no—the Sepoys—they're rising—where is my brother?—I escaped just in time! . . .

McGregor [*wheeling on an easy chair towards her*]. I know, but won't you sit down? . . . Your brother is here . . . in the next room.

Mrs. Clayton. Can't you hear them? . . . they're coming . . . we'll all be massacred!

McGregor. Come, Mrs. Clayton. . . . [*Forces her gently into a chair*] Sit down. Your nerves are all awry. Calm yourself!

Mrs. Clayton. Calm myself! . . . Listen! [*They listen a moment to the drumming*]

McGregor [*going over to the table, taking a decanter with which he fills a small glass*]. Why, you know what that is, Mrs. Clayton; it's the Mohurrum business—religious affair—pious riot—quite harmless. Won't you try some of my sherry? [*Offers glass*]

Mrs. Clayton [*waving glass aside*]. Captain McGregor, the natives are pouring into the town by thousands! They are collecting at the bazaar! There is danger! I feel it here! [*Puts hand on heart*]

McGregor. Do you think, Mrs. Clayton, that if there was much danger I would be here enjoying a cigar alone?

Mrs. Clayton. I—I—I—suppose—after all —I—I—I—I have let my nerves get the better of me . . . but, oh, Captain McGregor—just as I was going to bed I began to hear that horrid, queer noise they are making! [*Listens a moment*] I called Rebottie—you know her—my faithful ayah. Well, she told me that all the servants had fled!

McGregor [*laughing*]. You can no more keep a native from a Mohurrum than a small boy from a circus. My servants have left me, too!

Mrs. Clayton. But this kind of thing never

happened to me before! We flew to the stables to saddle our own horses, but they were all gone—they had taken them too. . . . So we ran here on foot—choosing the back street. I could see the town was full of strangers—they are pouring from all quarters! When we came to your gates they sent me up here!

McGregor. They did right—but after all this, you must calm yourself. [*Gives her the glass again, which she reluctantly drinks. While she is in the act, he turns his head slowly and looks through the archway*]

Mrs. Clayton [*weakly*]. I'm afraid I've made an awful fool of myself. You'll have to forgive me, Captain McGregor. You know, really, I am not often frightened, but India has always been a land of horror to me. Full of sounds and strange noises—terrible—terrible silences . . . and always those eyes looking at you! One can't help thinking of what these Sepoys will do when they are once let loose! Remember that Oude massacre. . . . Massacre! Massacre! . . . I can't get that word out of my brain.

McGregor [*still listening and not looking up*]. Come—rest a bit. You're worn out!

Mrs. Clayton [*suddenly, after a pause*]. But I can't stay here—it's late! If you really think, Captain McGregor, that there is no cause for alarm, will you forgive a silly woman and let her return home?

McGregor [*slowly*]. Won't you stay a bit? . . . Your brother is here.

Mrs. Clayton. I'd like to . . . [*Laughing*] —but it's growing very late!

McGregor. Then I'll call Stewart and have him take you home. [*Goes toward arch, thinking deeply. Then stopping*] By the way, won't you in the meantime play me something on my new piano? I had it shifted up here with my other things— I want you to try it for me.

[*Reluctant, yet to humor him, she pulls off her gloves and goes towards the piano. She pauses to put her gloves upon the table, and sees the chuppattie cake lying among the dishes. She turns quickly with a face full of horror to* McGregor, *who is leaning against the archway and looking out*]

Mrs. Clayton [*in an awed and intense voice*]. How did this get here?

McGregor. Eh? . . . Oh . . . the chuppattie. . . . Why, you know, I rather like them. Always have them for supper. . . . I'm quite an Indian in my tastes.

Mrs. Clayton [*with a short laugh of relief*]. You must think I'm an awful coward—but you know the rumor of these cakes, and that awful sentence, "All is to become red!" [*Stands still, looking down at it with a frightened face*]

McGregor. Come—you have been badly frightened, and I don't blame you. Do try my piano and forget for a moment this country which you detest so heartily!

[MRS. CLAYTON *goes over to the piano, seats herself and commences playing* "THE WATER LILY" *softly and with deep feeling. The drumming goes on.* HARTLEY *is heard repeating the one word incessantly on the telegraph,* MCGREGOR *keeps his position at the side of the archway, looking out.* MRS. CLAYTON *plays for some time in silence*]

MRS. CLAYTON [*stopping abruptly, and in a queer voice*]. Did you call that man to take me home, Captain McGregor?

MCGREGOR. Yes.

MRS. CLAYTON. I didn't hear you.

MCGREGOR [*coming down stage and leaning over the edge of the piano*]. He will be here in a moment. [*She goes on playing again, looking up at him. His voice changes to one of emotion*] That was the melody you played at the Maharajah's ball.

MRS. CLAYTON. You remember that?

MCGREGOR. Remember! . . . My life is made up of memories. [*Pause*] I remember the day when a fresh, young English girl arrived on the decks of a great East Indiaman—and how we cheered her pretty face! I remember a military wedding at Calcutta and Mrs. Jack Clayton, the toast of the regiment. And then I remember when I first saw you in mourning. . . . I remember many things! [*Sighs*]

[*Here a long pause.* MCGREGOR *turns his face slowly and looks through archway*]

MRS. CLAYTON [*her voice low and full*]. You have been a loyal friend! [*She plays*]

MCGREGOR [*turning to her with a smile*]. How wonderfully you play! [*A pause*] What a strange and beautiful thing awakened memory is! One can live again those hours one has thought forever lost. Do you—can you—remember and live over those wonderful days—in the old bungalow by the river—the queer lights and tall shadows—when in the gaiety of your heart you called me Major Dobbin?

MRS. CLAYTON. Because you were so awkward and were always upsetting my tea cups and things—oh, yes—I remember.

MCGREGOR. I thought you called me Major Dobbin because I was so faithful.

MRS. CLAYTON. Perhaps I did. [*She plays on a moment, and then stops and sits looking out into the moonlight in silence,* MCGREGOR *watching her intently the while*] What a dear fellow you were, Major Dobbin! Ah, a woman never forgets a man's friendship in a time like that—and it seems I can never get the chance—[*turning to him*] to thank you enough!

MCGREGOR. Thank me! . . . Why, I stood by you, as you call it, because I couldn't help myself—because you're the only woman worthy

of the name . . . because you took your trouble like a thoroughbred . . . because . . . because you are beautiful . . . because you're straight and tall and your hair is brown . . . because you're true, and clean-hearted . . . because, old friend, I have loved you all my life!

MRS. CLAYTON [*her voice broken*]. Major Dobbin!

MCGREGOR [*coming to her side and kneeling on one knee*]. Aye—Major Dobbin—as ever was!

MRS. CLAYTON [*putting her hand on his shoulder and looking down into his eyes*]. You know 'way down deep in your heart that you were the first and only one—and now, old friend, tried and trusted—after all these years of silence and pain—here is your reward. [*With a low laugh*] A poor thing, Major, but myself —my honor—my life—my—my— [*tenderly drawing his head with both hands to her bosom and putting her lips to his hair*] . . . my Major Dobbin!

[MCGREGOR *raises his head and their lips meet.* MCGREGOR *then stands straight and breathes deep*]

MCGREGOR. It was worth it—it was worth the waiting for!

[*The sound of a chair being violently overturned in room at right*]

MRS. CLAYTON. What is that?

[*Door bursts open and* HARTLEY *bursts in*]

HARTLEY [*shouting*] McGregor! McGregor!

MCGREGOR [*going quickly up to him and speaking in a calm, rapid voice*]. Ah, Hartley . . . [*turning*] here is Mrs. Clayton, your sister . . . she sought our protection, thinking that perhaps this Mohurrum was a Sepoy rising, but I have assured her that there is no cause for alarm.

HARTLEY [*breathlessly*]. It's all right, Sis . . . you needn't be alarmed . . . —I—I—I— if there had been any danger we would have heard of it.

MRS. CLAYTON. You must forgive us poor women our cowardice, Alan—it is only when we realize our helplessness that we are frightened. Sometimes I wish that I were a man—a soldier—a Highlander like yourselves—instead of a woman who has to wait and listen . . . and listen . . . and listen!

HARTLEY [*blatantly*]. It is not all beer and skittles being a man, I can assure you, Sis . . . Why, do you know—just now . . . !

MCGREGOR [*sharply*]. Hartley!

HARTLEY. Eh?

MCGREGOR. Would you kindly take a message for me?

HARTLEY. Pardon me, Sis. [*She inclines her head and goes on playing, her eyes to the keys*]

[HARTLEY *goes over to* MCGREGOR *and both watch her as they speak*]

McGregor [*in an undertone*]. Well, what is it?

Hartley [*in an excited whisper*]. They have cut the wires!

McGregor. Ah—I thought as much!

Hartley. Sir John says, don't let them get the powder!

McGregor. He needn't worry.

Mrs. Clayton [*stopping her playing and looking up*]. Is your man ready, Captain McGregor? [*Politely*] It is growing very late!

McGregor. I am sending your brother to hurry him up.

[Mrs. Clayton *goes on playing*]

Hartley [*to McGregor*]. Well?

McGregor. You'll take command now at once, as they will be on us in a moment. Hold them off as long as possible. I'll stay here and watch that powder [*Points to the corner of the carpet*] I daren't trust anyone in this room except myself. If they once get over the walls. . . .

Hartley. We're lost!

McGregor. If they once do, Hartley. . . .

Hartley. Yes?

McGregor. Have the bugler sound the charge so that I can hear it. Make him play it loudly, mind you!

Hartley. And then—?

McGregor. I shall blow up the magazine!

Hartley. By Jove—

McGregor. Quick—say a word to your sister, and go!

[Hartley *backs down stage, watching McGregor, who is looking out into the moonlight—he feels the air behind him for his sister*]

Hartley [*as he reaches her. She continues to play*]. I say, Sis, I'm going for the man. I won't be back myself—he'll see you safe home. I want to say good—good-night!

Mrs. Clayton [*continuing her music*]. Good-night, old fellow!

Hartley. Sis?

Mrs. Clayton [*stopping and looking around*]. Yes, Alan?

Hartley. Pardon my asking, but—has McGregor said anything to you?

Mrs. Clayton [*looking up and smiling*]. Yes.

Hartley [*with enthusiasm*]. I'm glad! [*Bending and kissing her tenderly*] Good-night, old girl!

Mrs. Clayton. Good-night, my brother!

Hartley [*goes up to McGregor and gives him his hand in silence*]. I congratulate you. . . . By Jove, you are a brick. . . . [*Lower*] Good-bye!

[McGregor *gives him his hand in silence and Hartley exits, drawing his pistol. McGregor remains a moment looking after him, and then comes down stage and leans on the piano and watches Mrs. Clayton as she continues to play softly.*]

A Sepoy's head and shoulders rise up stealthily from behind the balustrade—beyond the arch. First an arm appearing, then a turban, and then a white-trousered leg is thrown over the balustrade. McGregor turns quickly and sees the Sepoy who instantly drops out of sight. Mrs. Clayton has seen nothing and continues playing dreamily. McGregor goes at once to the desk and quickly opens a drawer and takes out a black coil of fuse. He comes down center. He throws back the corner of the carpet, opens the magazine door, gives a quick look through the archway, and lowers one end of the fuse deep into the magazine]

Mrs. Clayton [*not looking up*]. Ah! I'm so happy. . . . Tell me, dear, you like my brother?

McGregor [*backing and uncoiling fuse*]. Rather! [McGregor *leaves end of fuse near center*]

Mrs. Clayton. I suppose India will spoil him like all the rest—but it's like a breath of old England to see his boyish honest face!

McGregor. Rather. . . . [*He says this as he is in the act of taking one of the silver candlesticks, removes the shade, and places it with the lighted candle near the end of the fuse*]

Mrs. Clayton. I remember when I first saw India—how terrified I was—the bronze and blackened faces. . . . [*She happens to look around*]

[*She stops playing and rises slowly. McGregor is standing over the lighted candle with his hands rammed in his coat pockets. He is looking out into the moonlight. She looks from him to the open magazine, and back to him again*]

Mrs. Clayton. What are you doing?

McGregor [*turning his face towards the audience*]. You will pardon me—I have lied to you. I am afraid, after all, there is danger. [*A pause—*Mrs. Clayton *remains perfectly still*] I thought perhaps I'd spare you unnecessary alarm, but I'm afraid I can't—you see, the regiment is not on time. I know you for a thoroughbred—you've the blood of soldiers in your veins. So I can tell you plainly how we stand.

Mrs. Clayton [*after drawing a quick breath*]. Tell me!

McGregor. That door you see open is the powder magazine. . . . *You* know what it means if these Sepoys capture it—*You* know what it means if I let them capture you. *You* know what it means when they get an Englishwoman in their power! My Highlanders will hold them off as long as possible, and if they fail . . . you see my duty?

Mrs. Clayton [*after a pause, while she struggles with herself*]. Yes!

McGREGOR. I thought it would seem a hard thing to do, but with you beside me—why, girl, I am going to blow up that magazine. . . . Will you stand by me?

MRS. CLAYTON. With my last breath!

[*The sound of musket shooting without, rapid and terrifying*]

McGREGOR. Ah, they've begun already! [They *stand listening*] Tell me if you hear the bugle call! [*The noise without becomes deafening. Savage yells, hoots, and firing. The sky through the archway turns scarlet as if the city were afire. Suddenly the standing lamp at right is shot to pieces by a stray bullet.* MRS. CLAYTON *screams, but still stands beside piano*] What's that?

[*They listen. A sudden lull in the battle and a tiny call is heard gallantly playing in the distance.* McGREGOR *slowly leans down and takes the lighted candlestick in his hand and looks up at* MRS. CLAYTON. *She goes to him. He then slowly and carefully touches the fuse with the lighted candle. It burns with great display towards the magazine. Together they watch the fuse as it hisses and splutters towards the yawning pit. The*

noise without becomes deafening. The red light flares more brilliantly—when suddenly the noise stops. Dead silence]

MRS. CLAYTON [*dashes for* McGREGOR's *side*]. Stop it! Stop it! [*She flies to the fuse and stamps it out*] Can't you hear it? . . . Listen!

[*Pause. They both listen. Then far away in the distance is heard fife, drum and bagpipes playing, "The Campbells Are Coming, Ye Ho, Ye Ho." It swells louder at each approaching step.* HARTLEY *enters wildly, his coat torn off his back; he carries his smoking revolver, which he waves madly*]

HARTLEY [*hoarsely, and with excitement*]. McGregor—McGregor—it's all right! The Highlanders are here! We're saved—saved!

[*Exits reeling and shouting.* McGREGOR *puts the candle out by striking the flame with his open palm and catches* MRS. CLAYTON *just as she faints, falling backwards into his arms. Curtain falls on this tableau now lit with red fire smoke and resounding with rousing British cheers, drums and bagpipes*]

CURTAIN

THE LORD'S WILL

A Tragedy in One Act

By PAUL GREEN

CAST OF CHARACTERS

LEM ADAMS, *a country preacher and tenant farmer*
MARY, *his wife*
MRS. JONES, *wife of the farm owner*
SCENE: *A North Carolina tenant farm home.*
TIME: *The present, the late afternoon and evening of an autumn day.*

THE LORD'S WILL

The scene is laid in the kitchen-dining room of the Adams home, a home typical of the tenant farmer class. It is weather-boarded on the outside, with rough joists and rafters showing inside. In the center is a table covered with striped oil-cloth. Two or three splint-bottomed chairs are set around it. Directly behind the table is a child's high chair. At the right front is a stove with a fire going, and beside it a wood-box. Through the rear center wall a door leads into a shed room, to the right of which is a window. To the left rear are a cupboard and a flour barrel. Near the center of the left wall a door opens to the outside. On a string behind the stove dishcloths hang drying. At the right a door leads into a bedroom. Between this door and the window at the rear hang several old coats, a shawl and two or three ragged hats. An old organ is beside the door. Near the right front is a large homemade chest.

When the curtain rises, MARY ADAMS *is at the table ironing on a spread-out quilt. Through the window at the rear the sun can be seen setting behind a wide cotton field fringed in by trees glowing with autumn color. Beyond the rim of the woods a country church with its surrounding tombstones stands white on the hill. Somewhere far off a dog barks. Then there is the rattle of a wagon and the sound of the driver hurrying on his team. A great gap of silence hushes these sounds, and nothing is heard except the slipping of the iron on the clothes and the sudden "blump" as* MARY *sets it on the holder to turn the garment.*

MARY *is a thin-chested woman about twenty-five years old, tall and pale of face, yet retaining a sort of wistful beauty. Her dress is poor but clean. Her eyes are red and dark-circled with weeping and sleeplessness.*

Lazily and clear from the cotton fields on the creek rises a song:

"They'll be no stranger there,
They'll be no stranger there,
I'll take my golden rocking-chair
To the River and set down.

"Look up, look up that lonesome road,
Where me and my pardner's got to go—"

The day's work is done, and the negroes, with their cotton weighed up, are going home. MARY *stops ironing and, holding the iron in her hand, listens with something of a rapt expression on her face. She goes to the window and stands looking out at the cold streaks of the sunset. Fainter and farther away comes a single negro's voice yodeling high in the gathering dusk. "O——ee! O——ee! Hi—yo—o-o-o—ee!" It too passes out of hearing. She turns from the window with a sigh. In a childish sort of helplessness she brushes her hand across her forehead and into the hair loosely done up at the back of her head. She returns to the table, sets the iron down, and takes up the garment which she has been ironing. It is a child's dress, suitable for a girl of four or five. Placing a chair near the stove, she hangs the dress on it and begins ironing another.*

The sound of a childish rattling cough comes from the room at the rear. MARY *drops her iron and hurries quietly through the door, leaving it ajar. The indistinct outlines of a low wooden bed are seen. The spell of coughing passes, the words "My precious!" are heard, and* MARY *comes back into the room. Closing the door softly behind her, she stands wiping the tears from her eyes. Then she clasps her hands and lifts her head as if to pray. But a look of rebellion comes over her face. Vehemently she throws her hands apart.*

Footsteps are heard coming up the porch. She starts impetuously toward the door, but stops and goes slowly back to her work.

MRS. JONES *comes in at the left. She is a stout woman about forty, dressed in a cheap dark dress, bareheaded, and puffing with the exertion of walking. She is carrying food on a tray with a napkin spread over it. For a moment she stands just inside the door as if undecided as to what to do.*

MARY [*in surprise*]. Why, Mis' Jones, I thought it was—

MRS. JONES. Never mind, Mary, I just stepped over for a minute. [*She comes toward the table*] Was you expecting somebody else?

MARY. It's about time for Lem to be coming. I thought it was him.

MRS. JONES [*somewhat laconically*]. Yes, Lem!

MARY. But come in and take a seat. [*She places a chair for her.* MRS. JONES *puts the tray on the table*] I shore am surprised to see you.

MRS. JONES. Well, it's a sort of surprise to me. But I'd cooked up some different things for supper; and a-setting there waiting for

457

John to come from the gin, I thought I'd run down here and bring something. Perhaps Ruth could drink a little of the chicken soup, and maybe you'd like a piece of fruit cake yourself. [*She turns towards* MARY *and looks around the room*] Where is she? She ain't bad off enough to be in bed, is she?

MARY. I don't know—she's in there asleep. [*With a motion of her head towards the room at the rear*] Yistiddy she said she wanted to lay down. [*After a moment*] Maybe she's better there in bed.

MRS. JONES [*looking rather directly at* MARY *and then away*]. I reckon so. Guess you know best. [*She uncovers the food*] This is shore-'nough cake, Mary, if I did make it myself. It's got some of John's scuppernong wine in it I snitched from the bottom of his trunk.

MARY [*gazing hungrily at the food and then turning off*]. You're mighty good, Mis' Jones. Set down and rest.

MRS. JONES [*blowing her nose in her apron*]. No, no. Lord help my life. I got to be hitting the grit in a minute. John'll be home after while and want his supper. And Dick's there waiting for hisn. You know how men folks is. And John's on the puny list too.

[MARY *replenishes the fire from the wood-box*]

MARY. Oh, set down, Mis' Jones—if you can spare the time.

MRS. JONES. Wisht I could, but there's my greens I left a-cooking. The thrasher's coming tomorrow and they'll be a passel of hands to feed. But—there I go about my fixings. How's the child tonight?

MARY [*with a troubled look*]. I don't know. This morning she seemed to be better, but about five o'clock she tuck to coughing worse'n usual. Onct or twice she had a spell of choking with the phlegm. I—I—oh, I don't know how she is. [*She goes to the window*] Take a seat.

[MRS JONES *stands watching her.* MARY *turns from the window, puts the iron back on the stove, folds the quilt up and places it in the chest along with the dress. Then she lights the lamp and sets it on the table*]

MRS. JONES. The soup'll soon be cold. You reckon you'd better see if she'll drink some now? [*Accusingly*] Is that her coughing so? [*As the child coughs*]

MARY [*in alarm*]. Yes, but I—I think she'll be all right soon. Shore 'nough she ain't bad off. [MRS. JONES *starts toward the door*] Better not go in. She's sleeping now. And the soup can warm on the stove. We sure appreciate it. If you hadn't brought the soup and cake I hardly know what we'd 'a' done—for supper. [*She sighs*]

MRS. JONES. There, there. Don't go taking on so. I ain't done nothing for you but what I

ought. It ain't more'n human for folks to help each other out in spells of trouble.

MARY. Yes, but—I didn't think—and the way things has turned out!

MRS. JONES. Now, now, that's all right. I have been hopping mad about the way Lem's done, but—well, just because you live on our land ain't no reason we can't be neighbors. You know, Mary, we'd ought to sorter pull together.

MARY. Yes, oh, yes, we had ought.

MRS. JONES. And if John does stay mad about the way Lem's done him, it don't mean that I can't be kind to his wife and baby, does it?

MARY. But Mr. Jones, he don't feel for—oh, I reckon women folks hadn't ought to fall out when they men can't gee horses—and I'm thankful for—

MRS. JONES. Yes, yes, and soon as Sue told me this evening about Ruth being sick, I thought I'd better fix some soup and bring her. [*Impulsively*] 'Tain't as if I had a houseful of little uns of my own, Mary. And you know Ruth sorter tuck to me the time you was at your daddy's nussing the fever.

MARY. That's so. She loves you about as much as she does me. She takes natural to most everybody.

MRS. JONES. Now you see, I wanted to. And besides it's my duty.

MARY. Yes, but they's plenty of folks in this world don't do they duty.

MRS. JONES. That they is. And one of 'em don't live far from here neither.

MARY [*turning quickly toward her*]. Don't, Mis' Jones. Don't start on that. He ain't never said a harm word ag'in' Mr. Jones.

MRS. JONES. I reckon not. [*She shivers*] Well—I feel a draught from som'ers. I got hot digging across the plowed ground, and now I'm about to have the shivers. [*She looks around at the unceiled room*] Mary, tell me, you reckon she caught that cold on account of this house being so airish?

MARY. I think not. 'Tis terribly cold, but she got the starting of it last week. That cold day, the Saturday Mr. Matthews killed hogs, I washed up Lem's clothes for the meeting at Prospect Church; and she kept playing around the pot in the cold. I tried to git Lem to keep her in the house with him, but he was reading the Bible and working at his sermons. He didn't have no time to fool with her he said. That night she was all stopped up. And she's been gitting worse ever since.

MRS. JONES [*explosively*]. Well, I never in all my born days! There—again, always—but —[*Seeing* MARY's *accusing face*]—I was sorter afraid she'd caught it all from the openness here. I been after John to ceil the house before the roaring gusts sets in, but [*stopping*] somehow he won't take much stock in doing it.

[MARY *sits down at the table resting her chin in her hand*]

MARY. I know, I know. Set down.

MRS. JONES. Well, I will a minute. [*She sits*] Don't notice what I said. They's more ways than one to git a house ceiled, and I reckon I'll see to it or break a trace. [*Sympathetically*] Must be powerful lonesome here at times, ain't it?

MARY [*persistently*]. I know the reason he won't ceil the house. It's account of Lem, ain't it?

MRS. JONES. Well, I do say! How come you to think of such a thing? I never said a word about it.

MARY. But that's just the reason, ain't it? He don't want us another year.

MRS. JONES. Aw, Mary, don't go digging up trouble before your joy's spread.

MARY [*bitterly*]. I know, though. He's goin' to git niggers to move in next year and plant a lot of cotton. Sue come from the cotton patch this evening to git a drink of water, she said, but it was just to tell me that Mr. Jones had rented to them another year.

MRS. JONES [*wrathfully*]. The black hussy! What's she talking to you like that for! You just let her come back to pick cotton a-Monday and I'll make her cut a dido for that very thing.

MARY. Oh, I don't blame him for wanting to git rid of us, with nobody to work. There's our cotton standing in our field not touched expect for the little dab I picked. And I ain't picked none since Ruth was tuck.

MRS. JONES [*taking out her snuff-box*]. Mary, it ain't that I blame you. You've done your level best. But— [*Blurting out*]—Lem's jest no 'count for farm work.

MARY [*wearily, without seeming surprised*]. Maybe not. He's plumb carried away with his preaching. Says that's what he's made for. And—you know the way he feels about it.

MRS. JONES. It may be what he's made for. But he told John, when he come to rent from him, that he'd let preaching go and count his crop first. And look what he's done. A quair thing when preachers can't tell the truth. [*Scornfully*] Been off to tent meetings, and holding revivals and brush meetings ever since last July. And here it is the first of November with just a day now and then at home. Never got all his fodder pulled even. Left it all for you to do.

MARY. Don't blame him, Mis' Jones. You can't understand how much his preaching means to him. He's just filled up with it. You know he's good to me in his way. I understand him. But his religion's everything to him, it is that.

MRS. JONES [*resolutely calming down and taking snuff*]. Well—but anyhow people has different ideas on that. Have some snuff?

MARY [*looking at her hungrily as she lifts*

a huge brushful to her mouth*]. I'd be plumb glad to, but I quit it long ago. Lem said 'twon't right to dip, and so I ain't teched it since we was married. [*Leaning forward*] That smells like Sweet Scotch, is it?

MRS. JONES [*holding the box toward her*]. Yes, that's the kind 'tis—good too.

MARY. It's what I used to dip.

MRS. JONES. Then try a dust of it. Lem won't know. [*With a sudden thought*] Now if John Jones'd try to stop me from my snuff I'd—

MARY [*pushing the box from her*]. But he ain't like Lem. You can reason with Mr. Jones. And he kinder lets you have your way at times. But they's something slow and awful in the way Lem does things. You couldn't go ag'in him. He used to chew tobacco, but on the road one day God told him to quit it. And he ain't never had none in his mouth since.

MRS. JONES [*bursting out*]. There you go, Mary Adams! You're a plumb fool to be belly-banged around the way Lem Adams does you. Set here and eat your heart out from pure lonesomeness, not a ray of pleasure in the world. And he off preaching trying to save souls. He'd better sight be here saving his crop. [*With gathering wrath*] He ain't even been here since Ruth got sick, I bet you on it.

MARY. She ain't been sick long. I sent word to Mr. Matthews this morning that she had a cold. The meeting breaks today and he'll be shore to come home tonight. I been expecting him all the evening. I thought at first that you was him.

MRS. JONES. It's his own good time he'll take leaving that meeting. Oh Lord, child, I'm sorry for you. My man's hard enough to endure, but if I was tied—don't look at me that way, for I'm going to say it— Yes sirree, if I'd married a spindle-shanked fool like that, always dribbling gospel from his jaws—oh, I'd been in the asylum long ago. Cussing and fighting is better'n too much praying for me. [*Her snuff-brush works up and down with excitement.* MARY *rises from her seat*] And what's any of it worth? Far as I can see—and God'll forgive me for saying it—far as I can see, his preaching ain't worth a cent. He might as well spend his time catching doodles. Yes, I do mean it! [*She also rises from her seat.* MARY *turns from her in pain*] He ain't fit for nothing but to stake out cows. Here he goes up and down the country roaring out the word of God, and he might as well be on a hill in a dark night calling *cooshy, cooshy* to a dead sheep. Suit him better —and he a treating you like pizen.

MARY [*half in tears*]. You hadn't ought to—

MRS. JONES [*continuing*]. I ain't never heard him preach but once, thank God! And I didn't understand a word he said, and I don't believe he did. The way he throwed his hands around in the air made me think of my old cat the day he got caught in a whirlwind of sand. [*She stops for lack of breath*] But, oh, Lord, what's the use of my preaching too. And you, a-standing there, pale and plumb wore out.

MARY [*turning on her in sudden rage*]. Stop that! You ain't got no right to run him down behind his back. [*Half sobbing*] You're trying to tear up my belief in him. But he'll show you all some day what a man he is. He's got a great work to do. I married him believing in him, and I'll keep on till everybody puts confidence in what he's trying to do.

MRS. JONES [*sadly, sympathetic, but firm*]. What he's trying to do! He ought to be here trying to take care of his family.

MARY. Oh, it's been hard, lonesome—doing without enough to eat even, working my fingers to the bone, believing in him, trusting in him, knowing that some these days it'd come all right and folks'd see in Lem what I see in him. But—now— [*She looks at the floor to hide her tears*]

MRS. JONES. There, there, Mary. Don't. [*Blowing her nose*] I—I shore sympathize with you.

MARY [*wildly*]. Don't keep on telling me how sorry you are for me and what a hard time I have in this world. Don't I git to the place sometimes I can't hardly stand it? If I hadn't had Ruth I'd done been raving distracted. [*She goes to the window and looks out*]

[*Several negroes are passing the road singing . . . a medley of high-keyed women's and low husky men's voices— mingled into a far-away harmony—*]

"We are climbing Jacob's Ladder,
We are climbing Jacob's Ladder,
We are climbing Jacob's Ladder,
Soldiers of the Cross.

"We will wear them golden sandals,
We will wear them golden sandals,
We will wear them golden sandals,
Soldiers of the Cross."

[*An expression of almost delight comes over her eager face. The singing passes down the road dying into a faint wisp of song. . . .*]
"Soldiers of the Cross."

MRS. JONES [*casually*]. That's purty, ain't it?
MARY [*almost in awe and forgetful for a moment*]. Ain't it! And don't it make you think of sorter way-off things—with the sky so glowsy and cold and everything so still-like. [*She glances shyly at* MRS. JONES]
MRS. JONES [*a little gruffly*]. Them lazy niggers! They'll chouce you out'n a piece of meat and a peck of meal slicker'n nothing, talking of how po'ly they's getting along, and go home at night singing all the way like you hear 'em there. They don't feel trouble no more'n goats.

MARY. Yes, but they ain't no telling what they's remembering back of all they's singing. [*A tear slides down her cheek*]

MRS. JONES [*embarrassed*]. Don't—don't let a little music make you babyish.

MARY. That there music sorter makes me think of all I've wanted and ain't never had— and—

MRS. JONES. Oh, Mary, don't carry on so— and be foolish now. [*She stops, at a loss as to what to do*]

MARY [*growing calm again and speaking dully*]. Oh, well, they ain't a bit of use of complaining. [*In a queer abstracted fashion she begins picking at her finger nails, now and then wringing her hands together*] But Lem keeps saying put all your troubles on the Lord and if you want anything to ask for it. He seems to understand it all. But everything is numb and cold when I pray. I ain't never had no prayer answered. Lem says I ain't never been changed from nature to grace.

MRS. JONES. Changed! The idea!

MARY. It's all a mystery to me. I can't understand it. [*Helplessly*] But he seems so certain about it all. He don't even git worried no more—says the Lord's tuck away his troubles.

[*The child has another coughing spell*]

MRS. JONES. Let me go to her. She's coughing

MARY [*with her hand on the door latch*] I'll 'tend to her. She may just be restless in her sleep. And one she ain't used to might wake her. [*She passes through the door*]

[*The rattling breathing of the child is heard more distinctly.* MRS. JONES *raises her head quickly with a sharp movement of uneasiness.* MARY *comes back into the room, her face even more haggard than before. She closes the door softly*]

MRS. JONES [*catching* MARY *by the shoulders*]. Look here. Why didn't you let me know how sick that child was? From the way she's breathing she's—

MARY [*frantically catching her hands*]. Tell me, tell me! She ain't real sick, is she? No, no! What you mean! They can't be no danger can they!

MRS. JONES [*pushing her firmly down in chair*]. Set still, Mary, and I'll go in and see her. No, I won't wake her. [*As* MARY *starts to interpose*] They mayn't be nothing much the matter. [*Her face belies her words. She goes into the room*]

[MARY *rises and follows her with her eyes, clasping and unclasping her hands and looking around the room as if pursued by a nameless fear.* MRS. JONES *reappears in the door.* MARY *runs to her frightened by what she sees in her face]*

MARY. Oh, Mis' Jones!

MRS. JONES. Child, child, why didn't you let me know? She's burning up with a fever.

MARY. I knowed she's awful warm, but I didn't think it was wors'n croup.

MRS. JONES. Croup! She's got pneumony in both sides, bless God, if I'm any judge.

MARY [*fear blanching her face*]. Pneumony! But they ain't no danger, is they? Oh, they ain't! [*Looking at her beseechingly*]

MRS. JONES. They may be. We got to git a doctor quicker'n that. I'll run home and hurry Dick to Dr. McKay's. And he'll be here in no time. Oh, why didn't you let me know? [MARY *stands at the stove with a lost look on her face*] What sort of medicine you been giving her?

MARY [*coming to with a start*]. You, you know Lem don't believe in medicine. [*Wildly*] I prayed and prayed for her all last night and all day yistiddy. But it don't do no good. Lem says you must have faith.

MRS. JONES [*exasperated to the limit*]. Faith! Lord 'a' mercy! Here, I'll kite across the fields and send for the doctor. Then I'll come right back. Don't be uneasy now.

MARY. No, no. Lem won't have no doctor. It's ag'in' his religion. You know that.

MRS. JONES. It may be ag'in' his religion, but it ain't ag'in' common sense. [*Taking a salve box out of her pocket*] I brought some pneumony cure with me. Git a piece of flannel and we'll fix a poultice quick.

[MARY *goes hesitatingly towards the chest. The sound of a buggy is heard outside*]

MARY. I can't do it. There's Lem now, I believe. Somebody must 'a' brought him from the meeting.

MRS. JONES. Go at the door and see if it is. [*She rummages around in the chest*]

MARY [*at the door*]. Lem!

A VOICE [*replying from the outside*]. All right, Mary. I'll be there in a minute.

MRS. JONES. It's him, ain't it? [*She lets the lid fall with a bang.* MARY *closes the door*] Well, it won't do to have no trouble with him now, Mary.

MARY [*somewhat hopefully*]. Maybe Lem can—oh, maybe he can—

MRS. JONES. Maybe nothing. You can believe in prayer if you want to. But you just do what I tell you. Don't say nothing to Lem about how sick Ruth is till I git back. We'll have the doctor then and let him do his do when he comes. If you'd let him git in there to her now, he'll like as not pray over her so loud he'd bring the death sweat on her from pure fear. Now keep him from her if you have to scratch his eyes out.

[*She hurries out through the door at the left and is heard greeting* LEM *as he comes up the walk.* MARY *straightens*

up, wipes her eyes, hurriedly tidies the room, goes to the stove and replenishes the fire, through every motion acting like one numbed with the horror of the news she has just heard.*

The last faint streak of day has died out. Now and then a stray negro going home from the cotton fields can be heard far away giving his holler. MARY *goes to the cupboard and brings out some cold food. She breaks off a piece of cake and nibbles at it hungrily. The remainder she puts back in the cupboard.*

LEM ADAMS, *about forty years old, tall and stoop-shouldered, enters carrying a small ill-looking handbag made of imitation leather and split at the sides. He wears cheap clothes, rough shoes, a derby hat, home-laundered collar without a tie*]

LEM [*in a voice hoarse from the week's preaching*]. Well, how you been, Mary? [*He looks at her kindly*]

MARY. All right, I reckon. Supper's about ready. [*He hangs his hat up and starts through the door at the rear.* MARY *calls out sharply, but half-afraid*] Don't go in there. Ruth's asleep. You mustn't wake her. Please don't.

[LEM *slowly sets his bag down and turns towards* MARY. *His face is ignorant and kind. There is a deadly sort of seriousness, a powerful will shown in his every action and word. He has the way of a man absorbed in the power of a belief or idea*]

LEM. Yes, I'd forgot about Ruth. Brother Matthews told me she had a bad cold. How's she tonight? [*Without waiting for her reply, he opens his satchel and takes out a well-worn Bible*]

MARY [*bringing out knives and forks*]. She's better now, I think. Anyhow she's asleep.

[*He lays the Bible on the table, buttons up his coat, the sleeves of which are far too short for his arms, and goes over to the stove*]

LEM [*rubbing his hands together*]. It's going to be cold tonight, and think of the poor suffering homeless ones with no place to lay their head. We sure ought to be thankful that we're living in peace here, keeping our health and strength. [*Stands musing*] I'as sorter surprised to see Mis' Jones. What'd she want?

MARY [*wiping a plate with a dishcloth*]. Nothing, she just come down to see how we're making out.

LEM. I thought she'd been a-giving you a piece of her mind about me. She's a right good woman if she won't so wild in her talk. But, Mary, it's set forth plain as light concerning them as talks about they neighbors the way she does. Sometimes— [*Hurriedly*] I don't mean no harm by saying that either. [MARY *stands near the door to the sick-room, as if listening for the child's breathing*] You say the baby's gittin' 'long better?

MARY [*coming towards the stove*]. I think she's better.

LEM. When'd she begin to mend?

MARY [*calculating*]. She must have had a change this evening about five o'clock.

LEM [*his voice thrilling*]. It was just about that time, Mary, as I was coming along the road I felt a strong desire to pray for her. And right there on my knees I asked the Lord to do as He saw best. And He's seeing fit to restore her to health. Few knows the power of prayer.

    [MARY *impulsively starts to reply, but controls herself*]

MARY. Yes. Oh, yes, I hope so.

LEM [*earnestly, with a worried note in his voice*]. Hope? It ain't hope that saves, Mary, it's faith—faith in the Lord Jesus Christ. If you could have seen what faith did in our meeting! Old Miss Campbell, who's been crippled for five long years, is walking about tonight because she had faith—faith in our prayers for her. Walking, Mary, walking! Praise His name!

MARY. Yes,—faith. [*Bursting forth*] But I ain't got no faith.

LEM. What?

MARY [*frightened*]. No, no. I mean it's so awful hard to—to have faith.

LEM. Yes, that's so. You sorter scared me at first with that wild talk. It made me think of your pa, and he such a cussing man, and how you's raised in the times back there before I married you. [*More kindly*] But you know what it says about it. [*He throws his long right arm out in a gesture*] Repentance, saith the Lord.

MARY. Better eat your supper, Lem.

LEM [*quieting down*]. Mary, you're a good woman, but you ain't reached to the state of the holy life. When you do and are redeemed, you won't have no doubts. It'll be like a stone rolled from your heart. Oh, Blessed Jesus!

MARY [*glancing at the door*]. Le's eat. The towel's by the stove.

    [LEM *runs his fingers through his thin hair. He goes to a towel hanging behind the stove and gives his hands a dry wash. Then they sit down at the table*]

LEM [*hesitatingly*]. Ain't you going to put Ruth in her high chair?

MARY. Let her sleep. It's better.

LEM. I'd sorter like—never mind. Le's give thanks.

We thank thee, our Father, for what we receive. Make us truly thankful for all blessings, all things that come from thee. Do with us as thou seest fit. We ask thy kind mercy on the deeds done in the body. All is in thy hands. Thou givest and thou takest away. Save us— [*Here the child begins coughing and* MARY *in her nervousness knocks over a cup*] For Jesus' sake, Amen!

MARY [*breaking out*]. I just can't stand to hear her cough so much.

LEM [*speaking kindly, but rebukingly*]. You hadn't ought to break right in on the blessing like that. [*He looks at her and then at the meal before him*] Why, where is all your supper, Mary?

MARY. I ain't got nothing but this. The flour give out two or three days ago. And—and— yes, I was about to forget a special I had for you. [*She rises and goes to the cupboard and gets the cake*] Here's some fruitcake. It's a sort of surprise.

LEM [*looking at her with a manner of affection and smiling somewhat boyishly*]. It shore was good of you to save it for me. [*He buries his teeth in it*] It's fine, all right. Ain't you going to eat?

MARY. No, I don't want nothing. I et just before you come in. [*She goes to the stove and replenishes the fire*]

LEM [*roused by the noise of the stove door and the crackle of the flames*]. Ironing ag'in, air you?

MARY. I'm trying to. They ain't been a thing ironed since you left. But the irons won't heat with nothing to burn but chips and pine bark

LEM [*rising from the table*]. I'll cut you some wood a-Monday. You ironed that streaked shirt and low collar yet?

MARY. I was just fixing to. They're out on the line now. I better git 'em. [*She goes through the door at the right*]

    [LEM *finishes eating, crosses the room to the organ and sits down. Pedaling with one foot, he begins to play chords to "The Ninety and Nine." He sings:*]

"There were ninety and nine that safely lay
In the shelter of the fold.
But one was out on the hills away
Far off from the gates of gold.
Away on the mountains, wild and bare,
Away from the tender Shepherd's care.

"Lord, whence are those blood drops all the way
That mark out the mountain track?
They were shed for one that had gone astray
Ere the Shepherd could—"

With a rush MARY *comes back into the room carrying the shirt and collar. She runs to* LEM *and pulls at his arm*]

MARY. Lem, Lem, don't do that. Ruth can' sleep. Please quit.

    [*After a minute he stops playing*]

LEM [*turning around slowly as he closes the organ*]. Oh, I forgot, Mary. But that won't wake her, will it? And what you want her to go to sleep for right here at dark?

MARY. It might wake her. And I just got her to sleep a while ago.

LEM [*coming towards the table*]. It seems so natural to play a piece after supper that I —well, go ahead and iron them things. I'll need 'em tomorrow, if the Lord's willing.

MARY. You ain't going off to preach ag'in, are you, Lem?

LEM. Don't ask me not to, Mary.

MARY. I—I—kinder thought you'd—

LEM [*turning away his face*]. Don't start that old tale ag'in. [*He stands in silence a moment and then flames out*] Can't you see? It's my work. [*Fiercely*] I got to. I ain't one of them highfaluting preachers serving God for the money. I'm called to do it. They ain't no rest for me 'less I'm preaching. [*His eyes flash and he nervously clutches the Bible as it lies on the table*]

MARY. I know. [*Somewhat timidly*] But you—

LEM [*hurrying on*]. People don't understand me. They abuse me, talk about me, and accuse me. But let 'em talk. Didn't they persecute the Master? And He said in His Holy Writ: Blessed are ye, when men shall revile you, and persecute you, and shall say all manner of evil against you falsely for my sake. Didn't He say for us to be glad of it? For so they persecuted the prophets. And great shall be my reward in Heaven. Praise His name! [*His voice is earnest, glowing with the power of his feeling*]

[MARY, *no longer able to contend against him, sits down, holding the ironing cloth idly in her hand. The strained and hunted look in her face grows more accentuated.*

For a moment LEM *stands silently looking at the Bible.* RUTH *coughs and struggles for breath.* MARY *springs to her feet and runs to the door.* LEM, *on whose face has come a look of pain at hearing the child cough, also starts towards the rear room.*

MARY. Don't bother to come in, Lem. I'll just smooth out her pillow so she can sleep better. 'Tain't nothing much. [LEM *seems to mistrust her and makes a move as if to go into the room. In fright* MARY *clutches his arm*] Let me 'tend to her. A touch of croup ain't nothing. [*She pushes him from the door, and closes it behind her*]

[LEM *clearly shows that he realizes something is wrong. He falls on his knees and prays in a barely audible voice, clasping and unclasping his hands. Now and then the words,* "Heal her, Lord! Heal

her, Lord! if it is Thy will," *are heard. As* MARY *comes back into the room, he rises and taking a dirty blue and white-striped handkerchief from his pocket, wipes his moist face with trembling hands*]

MARY [*feelingly*]. She's resting all right. [*Loudly, as if trying to calm herself as well as* LEM] 'Tain't nothing but a bad cold. She'll be plumb well in the morning and wanting to set in her chair.

LEM [*visibly relieved*]. I'm shore glad tain't nothing worser'n that. I wanted to come home soon's I heard about it this morning, but I couldn't leave the meeting. [*Piously*] What a privilege it is to have a Friend who will take all our sorrows upon Him—and we can know that all things work for the good of those that love the Lord—and He alone knows how I love Him.

MARY [*briskly*]. It's all right. I been ironing a dress so me and her could go down to pa's tomorrow. Anyhow I was ironing it—an— [*She suddenly sobs*]

LEM [*half amazed*]. Why, what's there to be crying about? [*With a sudden light dawning on him*] Now, if it's Ruth you're worrying about, don't you know you needn't do it? The Lord'll take care of her. He knows what is best. Put your trust in Him. [*He speaks kindly but firmly, like one reasoning with a child*]

[*With an effort* MARY *holds back her tears and begins clearing away the dishes.* LEM *picks up his Bible and sits down near the lamp. From his jacket pocket he pulls out a pair of steel-rimmed spectacles and puts them on. He begins thumbing the leaves of the book.* MARY *sits a moment as if lost in thought and then springs up suddenly, spreads the quilt back on the table, goes to the stove for the iron and begins ironing*]

LEM. We hadn't ought to worry about what we ain't got no control over. The Lord of Hosts has got this world in His keeping. Listen here. [*Reading*]

See now that I, I am He, and there is none good besides Me. I kill and I make alive. I wound and I heal. Ain't that plain? [*He turns the leaves*] Listen. [*Reading*] Come and let us return unto the Lord, for He hath torn and He will heal us. He hath smitten and He will bind us up.

MARY. It might be so, yet I can't, I can't understand it. But Lem, if Ruth—if Ruth's sick tomorrow, you won't go off, will you?

LEM. I'd love to stay with her, but— [*Closing the Bible firmly*] You know I ain't going to let nothing stand in the way of service, Mary. I can't neglect my duty. I'll leave her in the hands of God.

MARY [*coming around the table towards*

him]. Lem, I—I—wish you wouldn't go. It's so lonesome here. Why can't you stay at home and let the preaching be for *one* time? [*Somewhat defiantly*] What's it all for anyhow?

LEM [*more amazed*]. What you mean by saying that? Can't you understand? Mary, it's writ out as plain as it can be, and a fool, though a wayfaring man, can understand. Why, why do you act like you do? Here's the Book sent as a lamp to your feet and you won't heed it. Don't you remember He said, Go ye into all the world and preach the Gospel—and whosoever he be of you that forsaketh not all that he hath, he cannot be my disciple? [*He stands up and speaks humbly*] I felt His power this morning in the meeting. I know He speaks through me—to help save this poor sinful world. Oh, don't tempt me from my duty!

MARY [*with a sob in her voice*]. And what sort of people is it you preach to? All the common trash in the neighborhood. The best folks, them that has work to do, don't waste their time at meetin's when they're housing their crops.

LEM. Mary, you ought to be thankful that people is people in His sight.

MARY [*doggedly*]. Lem, I always let you convince me because I wanted to believe in you. But somehow, it's changed now, and something's got to be done. For one thing, we can't live on your preaching. It takes money.

LEM. Money don't count, Mary. Wasn't He a poor man? [*Sympathetically*] I know we have got to have some money. I'll try to fix it somehow. They took up a collection for me down at the meeting. But Brother Jenkin's family is all down with the flus, and I turned it over to them, remembering it is more blessed to give—

MARY [*now angry*]. And here your own child sick and we with hardly a bite.

LEM [*trying to be patient*]. But, Mary, can't I convince you? Listen here— [*Turning through the Bible*]

MARY [*half turning upon him*]. Ain't— Oh, who could answer your scriptures!

LEM. It ain't never seemed right to think of money when serving God. Didn't He tell His disciples to take no thought of money or clothes? [*Firmly*] Now let's have no more words about it.

MARY [*her voice rising high and nervous*]. I'm going to have it out about this preaching. [*Half sneering*] Preaching! I heard them niggers yistiddy laughing about you being off preaching. [*Vehemently*] They even make fun of you and your education.

LEM [*hurt and angered, looking at her*]. What ails you tonight? You ain't never talked to me this way. [*Letting his arms fall in a despairing gesture. In a hurt, proud voice*] Them niggers laughed at me! Well it's not them

I heed. And what's education got to do with it! If God wants you to preach, He'll put words in your mouth. I ain't never lacked for nothing to say.

MARY [*hysterically*]. Why? Why? But, Lem, look what you promised Mr. Jones about the crop—and—

LEM. Hush, Mary. I told you it was wrong in me to promise when I didn't know what work the Lord would call on me to do. I got forgiveness for that promise— [*Raising his hand*]—and I'll never make another'n like it ag'in. [*Forgetting himself*] It was all on account of you that I promised. No—no—I didn't mean that, Mary.

MARY [*with growing wrath*]. Yes, account of me!

LEM. After tomorrow I am going to work on the crop, shore 'nough I will and that's a fact. They won't be much more preaching until next summer. But you ought to help me, Mary, encourage me and not do all you can to pull me down. They ain't nothing bigger than the Lord's work. Why can't it be like it was when we started out together? It's hard, I know. But I will get beyond this—and bring the people to the fold—and you shan't want, and then on to bigger things for His name's honor and glory. But I need your help, Mary, you must help me.

MARY [*fighting to understand, and yet helplessly angry at him*]. I've helped you all I can and nothing don't come of it. I reckon you wisht I was out of the way. I've always been a drawback to you.

LEM [*contritely*]. Don't say that, Mary. Let's not quarrel. We must help each other. You know we'd ought to sorter pull together.

MARY. Yes, I have been a hindrance to you and you know it. We wa'n't made for each other. We wa'n't. I love to work on the farm and live respectable and have things a woman likes. [*Recklessly*] And you're fit for nothing but preaching and praying and reading that old Bible.

LEM [*horrified*]. Mary, what you saying!

MARY [*her face twitching*]. I mean it! I—I hate it. Why don't you leave me, you and your scripture! I don't understand it, I— [*Helplessly*] Oh, everything is—in a mess! You, you, ain't got no feelings for nothing but your Jesus and God and—

LEM [*sternly*]. Stop that talk!

MARY [*crying out*]. I won't, I won't! What's He ever done for me but hurt me!

LEM [*thundering*]. Stop saying that!

MARY [*sobbing*]. I hate it, I hate God—all of it! [*Wildly*] Oh, I ain't afraid of your hell fire—and brimstone and burning pit—

LEM [*in awe*]. That's blasphemy. It's a wonder He don't strike you dead.

MARY [*coming towards* LEM]. I tell you

they ain't no God. It's all lies and talk. He wouldn't allow things to be like this if—if— [*Her voice is lost in a senseless stammer*]

[*The terrified expression deepens on* LEM'S *face. He moves away from her.* MRS. JONES *is heard coming up the steps. She hurries in out of breath. Her eyes show that she has been weeping*]

MRS. JONES. Mary, I sent for him, and he'll be right along. [*With a defiant look at* LEM] And I brought some medicine back, too.

LEM [*staring around him as in a dream*]. What's all this mean? Is there— [*Turning quickly towards* MARY] Mary—Oh, Mary!—

[*Suddenly from the sick-room comes a scream and the sound of the child struggling for breath, then a cry:* "Mamma! Mamma!" *With a bound* MARY *is in the room and at the bed.* MRS. JONES *hurries after her.* LEM, *left alone, stands a moment as if dumbfounded, and then runs to the bedside of the child. After a moment* MRS. JONES *kindly leads* LEM *back into the kitchen. She wipes the tears from her eyes and goes back into the room.* LEM *mechanically twists his hands together, crying out*]

LEM. Oh, Lord, it can't be so! It can't be so! Spare me! Spare me!

[*With a hysterical cry* MARY *comes through the door. Her eyes are almost wild now. As she sees* LEM, *a look of hatred comes over her face. With a scream she throws herself at him, clutching wildly at his throat. Dazed and uncomprehending, he holds her from him*]

MARY. It is so! It is so! She's gone—gone!

[LEM *catches sight of the Bible. Eagerly he picks it up. Outside the singing of the home-going negroes can be heard*]

"See them children come dressed in red,
  Don't you see?
See them children come dressed in red—
Must be the children what Pharyoh led.
  I got a home in the rock,
  Don't you see?"

LEM [*half sobbing*]. Mary, we still got His blessed Word with its promise. [*He looks indefinitely around the room as if seeking aid from the bare walls. Dropping the Bible, he starts toward* MARY, *a sob in his throat*] We've got each other, Mary, and—

MARY [*with a great cry, her voice rising high in a crescendo of final hopeless yielding*]. She's dead—dead! You hear! Ruth's dead—dead! and, oh— [*Her voice goes out of her with a gasp. Sinking into a chair, she bursts into a wild scornful laugh.* LEM, *as if in a maze, brushes his hand across his forehead again and again. The singing of the negroes passes out of hearing. Suddenly she springs up and throwing back her head, cries out to the empty air*] It's You! You! Setting up there on your golden throne! [*She begins laughing and moaning again*]

[LEM *covers his face with his arm to escape from her wrath and goes into the room at the rear and falls upon his knees by the bed. Far away a single negro's voice comes back cold and high:*]

O—ee—O—ee—O—ee!—O!

CURTAIN

"L"

By LEOPOLD L. ATLAS

.

CHARACTERS

Milkman
Cop
Beggars
Tradesmen
The Morning Crowd
Director
Newsboys
Speechmonger
Madonna
Daughter
Girl
Boy

"L"

SCENE: *The curtain rises on a street over which an elevated line runs. The L posts stand close to the curb—heavy massive pillars zigzagging upwards, or perhaps crawling downwards, a matter of how you look at it. At the left corner of the stage is a stairway leading up to the L station. In the rear is a solid wall of business shops, looking like a painted backdrop. The sidewalk is between this wall and the L pillars. The corner building on the extreme right of the stage or even in the auditorium, near stage, is a movie palace over which an electric sign flamboyantly announces Antonio Rudolpho in "Passionate Nights." Next to this, but on stage surely, is a pawnshop with its emblem of three golden balls, and then a butcher's shop, and a music store (about the center of the street) with a large exaggerated radio horn over it, and a bakery, and a barber shop with its red and white pole, a drugstore and a grocery.*

All through the play the lighting of the scene progresses as that of a twenty-four hour day.

At present it is just before dawn. The street is a mass of shadows, moonlit and still.

The hollow resounding clack-clack of heels striking the pavement breaks through the intense blue silence of the night. A COP walks down the street, yawning and swaying to and fro as he looks vacantly at the blank-eyed buildings. His club wags behind him.

There is the rattle of a milk wagon over cobblestoned streets and a long drawn "Whoa."

A MILKMAN enters, white-jacketed, carrying a lantern and basket.

MILKMAN [*wearing big rubbers that clump, clump*]. 'Lo Mike.

COP [*warming himself by his swinging arms*]. 'Lo Pete.

MILKMAN. Well, another day—

COP. Yep, another day—

MILKMAN [*joshingly*]. Still watching the world?

COP [*same*]. Yep—still feeding the world?

MILKMAN. Well, 'at's the way it goes.

COP. Yep—

MILKMAN. Well, so long Mike.

COP. Yep, so long Pete, see yuh t'morrer.

[*The* MILKMAN *goes out,* COP *yawns again, and slowly walks down the street whistling to himself. The street is deserted for a moment and then several shadowy figures, as if waiting for the* COP *to leave, sneak their way one by one,* oblivious each of the other, to the L station. As they meet and become aware of one another, in husky surprised whispers:*]

ONE. You here—

THREE. What are you doing here—

FIVE [*sliding around corner of steps*]. This is my place—

TWO. Where'd ya learn that, first come first served, it's mine—

FOUR. No, it's mine—

ALL [*in unison*]. It's mine, I came first— Like hell you came first—

THREE. Listen to them, will yuh; it's my place—

FIVE. Where d'ya get off with that stuff—

TWO. I'm telling you this is my place. I've begged here nearly two years and I'm gonna beg here to the end of my life—now beat it—

FOUR. Who're ya pushin'—

ONE. Easy with the hands there—

TWO. Who's asking you—

THREE. Mind your own business—

FOUR. This is my business and my place—

FIVE. Take your hands off me—

ONE. Watch your mitts there— ⎫
THREE. Who's gonna make me— ⎪
FIVE. Leggo. It's my place and— ⎬ [*together*]
TWO. Ouch. You damn lousey— ⎪
FOUR. It's my place— ⎭
ALL. Mine— Mine— Mine—

ONE. Leggo—

TWO. Oh you—

THREE. Leggo—

FOUR. Ouch—

FIVE. I tell you—

ONE. Shut up, will yuhze, yu'll have the cops on yuhze—

[*Pause*]

THREE. Quit yer fightin'—

FIVE. Shut yuh trap—

TWO. It's my place, good people, fellow beggars—

FOUR. Like hell it is—

ONE. Quiet, wanna get pinched—

TWO. Good people, I'm an old man—

THREE. We'll bury yuh—

FIVE. 'Bout time y' kicked off.

TWO. But, good people, I'm old and a cripple. I've got six children, they're starving—

ONE. Aw, become a beggar—

THREE. Go to the charity sassieties if you're that bad off—

TWO. Friends—

469

FOUR. Oh listen to this guy—
FIVE. First he hits and then he yells friends—
TWO. Friends, listen to me—please—I haven't got a nickel to my name—this is the best place in town for begging— I used to be well-to-do but I've spent all my money sending a son to law school and a daughter to medical school—help me, friends, help me—
ALL [*in unison*]. Haw—haw—haw—haw—
FOUR. What do you want help for—
ONE. You've raised a true beggar's family—ha-ha—
THREE. A lawyer and a doctor—hee-hee—
FOUR. The bourgeois cultured-beggars—
ALL [*in unison*]. Begging for justice—
For diseases—
For clients—
ONE. Hoodwinking the wide-awake American public—ha-ha—
THREE. Ha-ha—a beggar's family—
TWO. Friends, please give me the place—
ONE. No—no—
TWO. Give it to me—
THREE. To me—
FIVE. To me—
} [*together*]
FOUR. Silence!
[*A figure leaps out of their midst*]
ONE. Who for—
THREE. We're free American citizens—
FOUR. Silence! Gentlemen, this is the best begging spot in the city, isn't it—
TWO. You bet—
FIVE. It's mine—
ONE. Mine—
TWO. Mine—
THREE. Mine—
FOUR. Mine—
FIVE. Mine—
} [*together*]
FOUR. Silence! I'm not asking you whose place it is, I'm telling you. To the best goes the best. I'm the greatest beggar of you all—
ONE. Dirty liar—
TWO. Braggart—
THREE. What are you—
ONE. Hypocrite—
TWO. You lie—
THREE. Faker—
FIVE. Who are you—
} [*together*]
FOUR. I am a poet—
ONE. What about it—
TWO. What the hell difference does that make—
THREE. Who wants to know—
} [*together*]
FOUR. I'm the greatest beggar of you all—
ALL [*whine*]. Yeah!
FOUR. I wear my heart on my sleeve— I broadcast my perversities— I parade my nervous ills—my deformities—my agonies— I beg wholesale—buy books, pamphlets, magazines, papers. I flaunt my ills. I beg for their ears, their eyes, their time, their money, their praise,

and everybody sympathizes and pities and pays me. That's the trick a beggar must learn—make them believe in you. That's me. I vivisect and put myself in a paper cage and people like it. I tell them my hard-luck stories in a way that hits them. Women kiss my feet for it. I tell them how great I am and that nobody is greater than the poet; and I don't tell this to just one or two like you do—I tell the whole wide world—
ONE. Can the sales talk—
THREE. If you're so damn successful, then what do you want this place for?
FOUR. Well, you see I'm just a beginner—[*Another jeering general whine— "Yeah"*] and I was telling you how the big men in my line got started.
ONE. Get down, you humbug.
TWO. Mob him—
THREE. Chase him—
FIVE. Shyster—
} [*together*]
ONE. Tryin' t' steal my place—
TWO. Your place—it's mine—
ONE. Liar—
TWO. I came first—
THREE. I did—
FOUR. I did—
FIVE. How d'ya like this—
ONE. Yuh will, will yuh—
TWO. Leggo—
THREE. Stop—
FOUR. Mine—
FIVE. Like hell—
} [*together*]
[*They are fighting again and raising a subdued hubbub. The light has gradually become that of dawn. Three shop doors open simultaneously and out walk the Butcher, the Baker and the Candlestickmaker at the same moment with military precision. They are dressed in their white-aproned trade regalia and armed with broomsticks. The Butcher is hale, hearty, rosy-cheeked, bloodstained, and coarse; the Baker, short, dumpy, dough-faced and rolling-bodied; the Candlestickmaker, tall, thin, stringy-haired, wax-faced, and sharp-eyed. They march on the BEGGARS who cringe before them*]
TRADESMEN [*all together*]. Onward.
[*One step forward*]
ONE. For Law.
TWO. And Order.
THREE. And Peace.
ALL. Onward. [*Another step forward*]
BEGGARS
[*Whispering as they go three steps backward*]
ONE. Cheese it—
TWO. Help—
THREE. They'll beat us—
FOUR. The Forces—

FIVE. Help—
                    TRADESMEN
ONE. Scat—
TWO. Beat it—
THREE. Don't disturb honest people in their sleep.
                    BEGGARS
[Edging forward]
ONE. We're just as honest as you are.
FOUR. We're professional men.
THREE. The oldest in the world.
FIVE. Beggars—
                    TRADESMEN
ONE. Shut up.
TWO. Clear the streets.
THREE. They're ours.
ONE. We paid for them.
                  ALL TRADESMEN
Beat it!
    [They flourish their brooms menacingly.
    The BEGGARS scamper away for safety,
    whining. With a haughty "haw" the
    TRADESMEN wheel about and tramp
    heavy-footed to their individual shops
    and immediately with the same stroke
    begin sweeping the walks in front of
    them]
                   TRADESMEN
    [With each stroke of the broom]
THREE. Law.
TWO. And Order.
ONE. For Business.
TWO. Business is good.
ONE. Business is bad.
ALL. Business is business.
ONE. Sweep the streets for business.
TWO. Keep them clean.
THREE. Keep them in order.
ONE. Order in the temple of business.
TWO. And Reverence.
THREE. And awe. [They have reached the curb]
ONE [in alarm]. We're sweeping the dirt on our patrons.
TWO. Oh, that's all right.
THREE. They'll get plenty of dirt before the day is done.
ONE. It's bad business.
TWO. It's good business.
THREE. Give them the dirt.
ALL [in unison]. They like it— They live it— They eat it
    [A loud irritating ringing of many small
    alarm clock bells all over the street.
    Day has begun. The three TRADESPEOPLE
    return with hurrying steps to their posts
    in front of their stores and stand erectly
    waiting. A moment and the crowd
    streams * in, yawning, chattering, stretch-

* 1. EARLY RISERS.
    (Very slow—dragging feet—head down—
    clump, clump—round shoulders—arms
    hanging down limp.)

ing, mumbling, all hurrying to the L
station—a continuous unending flow.
They stamp up the steps with the
rhythmic thump of heels on stairs, up,
and across, and around, and still up.
Turnstile sets rhythm]
[As they pass, the Shopkeepers nod regularly "Good-morning, good-morning" to
no one in particular and to the great
mass in general. The hurrying and scurry-
ing of feet; the movement of heads, arms,
faces, sounds, bodies; the shambling, the
thumping, the clacking,—all make a continuous motion. The crowd is the same
all the time—they talk as the Shopkeepers
do to no one in particular. The COP
comes down the street and leaning
against an L post watches the crowd
weariedly]
MORNING CROWD.* Oh hell—can't get a wink
of sleep—sleep—sleep—what do you think I
was dreaming about last night—work—to hell
with work—lousy work—always go to work—
day in day out—work—work—work—so I says
to her— Gee, I couldn't pull myself outa bed—
nice morning—great morning—beautiful morning—but it's better to lie in bed—bed—oh sweet
bed—
    [First crescendo]
Hurry we'll be late—can't finish breakfast anymore—just a cup of coffee—anahunkabread—
and some eggs—scrambled—soft-boiled—
poached—just a cup of coffee and some bread—
There goes our train—they come every three
minutes—every two minutes—every minute—
every second—oh boy, I could sleep for two
years straight and never catch up—what a
dance last night, God!—what's your hurry—
    [Second crescendo]
    2. YAWNERS AND STRETCHERS.
        (Same rhythm—slow exaggerated arm and
        head movements.)
    3. SLOW DRESSERS.
        (Same rhythm—buttoning collars—coats.
        Adjusting ties—smoothing hair—putting
        on overcoats.)
    4. EATERS.
        (Same rhythm—coffee—bread—knife and
        fork.)
    5. NEWSPAPER READERS AND MONEY-
        COUNTERS.
        (Goose step—reading down column in four
        head jerks—turning page every sixteen
        beats. Money-counters reaching into pock-
        ets and counting coins.)
    6. BRISK WALKERS.
        (Four-four time—low goose-step and
        swinging arms—heads up.)
    7. PUSHERS.
        (Bending forward—1—2—3—4—5—6—
        three steps forward and three back. Arms
        out—palms up for first three steps for-
        ward.)
    8. RUNNERS.
        (Arms alternating back and forward—
        sliding run—not much knee action.)
* What follows is Business. The scene may be
divided as Producer thinks best among the eight
groups mentioned in the just preceding footnote.

Hurry—hurry—hurry!—I read in the papers last night—is that so, now would you believe it—it's all in the game you know—if I can't make more money—money—money— Great Scott and Little Wales— Charity begins at home — Law is the game you want to get into— I'm so tired I could drop from sleep—sleep—sleep —what a dame—what a dame—couldn't teach her nuthin'—

[*Third crescendo*]

Come on let's hurry—hurry—hurry!—there goes a train—

[*From above*]

Washastep—washastep— Ohriodonavanoo-nesstop—washadoors—washadoors—hurry — run—we'll miss it—on the go—run run run— it's late—late—late—run—push—rush—crush— dash — smash — crash — run — late — hurry— hurry—run run run—

[*The movement has become more electric now. People rush through the street in a maddening zig-zag weaving—coming from no place—going no place—coming from everywhere—going everywhere— shouting—gesticulating—pushing— here, there, everywhere.*

Ten of the crowd who are to play the Business scene are left at center * as the rest group at back as if in offices. Business is in full swing—typewriters clicking, telephones ringing, and tickers rattling.]

ONE. Dictation—

SIX. Dictation—

TWO. Dictation, miss—

FOUR. Dear sir, Gentlemen, Madam,—

THREE. Yours very truly—

* BUSINESS SCENE.
(Typewriters give the rhythm)
Four men, and two girls, on high stools set thus:

XXXX
X   X

Girl walking up and down on each side, one stage right—one stage left—big cuffs.
Man walking from left to right at back— eye shade.
Man walking from right to left at front— eye shade.
When A and B and C and D meet they say "O. K.!"
When A and D and B and C meet they say "Cheque!"

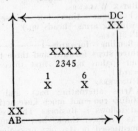

FIVE. 84—92—16—471 dollars—dollars—cents—

TWO. 58—49—39 debit—

THREE. Credit—

FOUR. Profit—

FIVE. Loss—

ONE. Sorry, sir—

SIX. Sorry, sir—

FIVE. Got no time—

FOUR. Busy—

THREE. Busy—

TWO. Busy—

ONE. Your letter of the twelfth inst. on hand and beg to note—

TWO. Report of inventory for the year 1927 —in stock 4793—sold 3421 on hand 1372 corkscrews—

THREE. Corkscrews—

FOUR. Corkscrews—

TWO. Business—

THREE. Business—

FOUR. Business—

FIVE. Business— Hello, operator—operator please, gimme Bryant 4265. Thank you—

SIX. You're welcome, excusit please—

THREE. Operator, operator, a little service please—

TWO. Get in on this deal; it's the best thing you ever saw, small investment big returns—

THREE. Money—

FOUR. Money—

FIVE. Money—

ONE. Opening report stock market—

TWO. International Nickel 82—$\frac{1}{8}$—

THREE. Omnibus 12—$\frac{1}{4}$—

FOUR. Pan Pete B 41$\frac{1}{2}$—

FIVE. US Rubber 55—

ONE. Whom do you wish to see—name sir— sorry sir—in conference—

SIX. Sorry sir—sorry—

FIVE. Miss Remington—

FOUR. Dictation—

THREE. Dictation—

TWO. Dear sir— Beg to note—yours very truly— Got it?

ONE. Yes sir— Dear sir— Hope Joe takes me for lunch to-day—yours forever—

TWO. Right—

THREE. Right—

FOUR. Right—

THREE. Speed—

TWO. Speed—

FIVE. Speed—

FOUR. Time is money—

ONE. Almost time for lunch—

SIX. Can't come too soon—

FIVE. 236—943—158 net assets 2487—

FOUR. Yes sir—thank you sir—

TWO. See you for lunch sir—

THREE. Yes sir—

FOUR. Hello—hello, operator, meet me fo lunch at one—

Six. Whom do you wish to see—sorry sir—out for lunch—

One. Oh God when does that lunch hour begin—

[*Noon whistle. Everything stops, transfixed*]

All. Anybody calls tell them I'll be back in an hour—

Woman. D'ja see that dress, knock your eye out.

Man. I always like to walk around during lunch-hour—

Second Man. Hello, Charlie, how're you—

Third Man. My old man's all right, he knows a thing or two—

Fourth Man. Cross my heart I took her out and it cost me twelve smacks cash—

Fifth Man. Where do you eat—

Sixth Man. If you've got the dough you're all right—

Seventh Man. God almighty, I wouldn't wanna be in his boots—

Second Woman. I like Child's better than the tea rooms—

Eighth Man. Yes the wife and I are goin' to build a beautiful bungalow in Brooklyn—

Ninth Man. Aw you give me a swift pain in the neck—

Third Woman. Gee I'm almost starved—starved—starved—

Tenth Man. Starved—

Third Woman. Starved—

First Woman. They've got a sale over at Feltman's—

Fourth Woman. Look at that hat she's wearing—

Eleventh Man. Can't get a look in on those things, politics, 'atsall politics—

Third Man. Those ain't legs those are piano stools—

Twelfth Man. No listen, Mary, don't start up with me—

Thirteenth Man. Boy did I pack in a meal—

First Man. I'll walk it off—

Fourteenth Man. Walk around—walk around—

Fifth Woman. Look there's Sadie—

Sixth Woman. Do you like my gloves—

[*They are now walking around in a leisurely way but with an inherent briskness, looking in shop windows, chatting, greeting each other, Men eyeing the Women and the Women returning their stares with feigned aloofness. In general, strolling about during the lunch-hour and having a good time of it. The stream is continuous, the same people coming and going. Then suddenly a Woman's scream from the L Station. For a second the Crowd stops dead in its tracks and runs wildly hither and thither like so many ants. The Tradesmen seek safety in their stores. A second scream and the Crowd stops as though suddenly petrified. A Camera Man and Movie Director run down the street (a theatre aisle) focusing on the scene. The action starts flickering like a motion picture. A Reporter carrying a large typewriter runs on the street ready for work. Newsboys mass at a corner, laden with "extras," waiting to rush on the street as soon as the crime is committed*]

Director. Everybody hold it—look alive—get some action in this—Ready—Shoot—

[*The action begins—a Woman screams—the camera grinds—typewriters click away—the tempo is one and a half times the speed of a movie—jerky—electric. Simultaneously with the scream, the Cop comes from behind an L post—a Masked Man gun in hand runs wildly down the station steps—Cop spying him makes a grab for his gun— A shot! Cop drops—another scream—Thief runs around the corner—the whir of an automobile motor*]

Director [*ordering the action just before it occurs*]. Come on, scream—cop—crook—run—shoot—fall—crowd scream—and away—[*Temperamentally*] Great—stupendous—lavish epic—Realism in Art!—Cut!

[*At the word "cut" silverscreen flicker stops. Director, Camera Man, Reporter leave on the run; the Crowd makes a mad rush and forms a circle around the body of the Policeman; Newsboys run in shouting and selling their newspapers to the Crowd on the street and in the audience*]

Newsboys

[Newsboy One *starts with Section 1 of what follows, running down right aisle.* Newsboy Two *starts with Section 2, then 3, then 1, running down center aisle.* Newsboy Three *starts with Section 3, following it with Section 1, then Section 2, running down left aisle*]

One. Wudextra—wudextra—big murder just committed on Wall Street—Read all about it—Babe Ruth walked three times—Wudextra—Read about it—read about it—read about it—Worldtimesnews mirror—Wha pape ya read—Mrs. Killman acquitted—Cop shot defending wife and children—

Two. Paper — paper — paper — paper — All about big scandal not yet committed—Pictures of girl in strip poker game on front page—Five different views all for three cents—Fire—Fire—Murder—Wudextra—terrible news abroad, Giants lose double header to Cincinnati—Paper you read—

Three. Paper you read—paper you read—High school student shoots self—Love affair with pretty bobbed-hair teacher—Man killed defending humanity—Private life and diary of Marie of Romania—O de O de O de O de Extra —Scandal—scandal—murder—fire—big divorce case—now going on—wha pape yuh read— Wudextra—Wudextra—Goin' like hot cakes—

[*They sell their papers to the audience. Suggestion: the papers are of the following type. A large sheet of blank paper folded over tabloid size—Name "Daily Blank"—Motto—"All news fit for Americans to read"—The paper is entirely blank except for the headline. It is now late afternoon and getting darker. A great moan rises from the* CROWD *circled around the body of the* POLICE-MAN]

ONE. Oh God, my fish is burning—

TWO. Frances loves John but I don't care—

THREE. Business is lousey—burn it—burn it —burn it—collect insurance—

FOUR. He says "Mother is the necessity of invention" but he's all wrong—

FIVE. Boy, she's hot, look at those legs, ain't they terrible—

ALL [*in a deep rising groan*]. Oh terrible— terrible—terrible—

ONE. All I've got to do is buy phosphorus and insurance—

TWO. My old man said to get the hell outa the house—

THREE. Exteriority complex, moriarity complex, interiority complex—

FOUR. Oh my God I left my baby all alone—

FIVE. So I went and saw that movie and was it terrible—

ALL [*again in a deep rising groan*]. Oh terrible —terrible—terrible—

ONE. There's nothing like a good homemade meal—

TWO. Oh girl what a sheik, look at him—

THREE. If I don't get a raise I'll tell the boss where he gets off—

FOUR. Doing anything to-night kid—atsa stuff, get hot—

FIVE. We've got to get back to wirk—ain't that terrible!

ALL [*beginning to spread apart and go their different ways, moaning all the time*]. Oh terrible—terrible—terrible—

[*The breaking up of the circle around the* COP *discloses a ragged bony* WOMAN, BABE *in arms and a little ragged* GIRL *at her skirts. The* WOMAN *is a living model of the "Give until it hurts" poster,— hollow-cheeked, glaze-eyed, grim, toothless, bony arm outstretched. It has become dark now. The store and house lights spring into being one by one every now and then. The* CROWD *goes off. A spotlight plays a halo around the head of the* WOMAN *giving her an almost ma-donna-like effect. As the* CROWD *continues moving and moaning a* MAN *and four* WOMEN *rush into the street and begin haranguing the* CROWD. *The* MAN *in dress and speech is a composite picture of the three great speechmonging types of America—the radio minister, the frockcoated senator, and the sideshow barker. His speech rolls from the solemn, ominous, moral-giving intonations of the minister, to the stentorian, pompous, weighty-worded tones of the senator, to the short, snappy bark of the sideshow man. The* WOMEN *are composites of the Salvation Army lassie, cigarette girl, and Red Cross nurse. While the* SPEECH-MONGER *stands on the platform belaboring the* CROWD, *the* GIRLS *run into the midst of them, raising collections and chiming into the different moods of the* SPEECHMONGER. *The radio screams hoarsely*]

Station LMNOPQ—United Press—press—press Association announcing—Give until it hurts— hurts—hurts—hurts—Bla - a - a - a—Give— Press—Station—Hu - u - rts—hurts—hurts— hurts—Bla - a - a - a—

SPEECHMONGER [*haranguing the* AUDIENCE *fierily, up and down the platform*]. Listen to the voice of God Almighty, oh brethren—Give— give—Give until it hurts—dig down—learn the true blessing of religion—God so loved the world —Give—give—give—to this poor christian holy mother of children—look at her as she stands there forlorn, forsaken, uncared for—look at her—look at her—look at her—

SPEECHMONGER. The only one in captivity ladies and gents—captured in the wilds of Kalamazoo—at the expense of the lives of two men and four horses—captured only after the fiercest battle ever waged in any primeval forest in the wide world—she jigs in the cold—cringes with hunger—cries with pain—

ONE. Hey, Professor, can she do the hootchy-cootchy?

SPEECHMONGER. Knows all the primitive agonies of famine, thirst, bloodshed, work—

TWO. Now give us a hot number!

SPEECHMONGER. And misery—gives an exhibition dance of each inside folks—all going on—

FOUR. Show now going on—get your tickets —only one quarter—

SPEECHMONGER. Fifty other attractions—only two bits—five nickels—two and a half dimes— twenty-five pennies—one quarter—

THREE. Some dame—whatta shape— Oh Boy!

SPEECHMONGER. Imagine only that little part and you make the world safe for democracy— [*Applause*] Don't be a yellow slacker—your country needs our money—we are engaged in a great world war—

WOMEN [*breaking out*]. Buy Liberty Bonds—

liberty—liberty—liberty—save the world with war—war—War Saving stamps—Help your country in its time of need—Do your bit—Come across or go across—Help—Liberty—War—war—saving stamps—Four and a quarter percent interest—

ONE. Put me down for $200—

WOMEN. Buy—buy—buy—

SPEECHMONGER. Democracy over all—buy the bonds of liberty—

THREE. It's a fake—

SPEECHMONGER. The stamps of war—There's fire and flood and famine—I swear to do away with all this when I'm in Congress—congress—congress—people, the Almighteh Church of our Grand and Glorious Countreh—the Sanctimonious Cathedral of American Inspiration and Justice—may this flag wave eternally over the broad expanses of our mighty nation—this beautiful symbol of the American people—

THREE. Hurray for the American flag!

SPEECHMONGER. Red for the blood spilled on our soul—white for the purity of our people—

THREE. Three cheers for our side—yah!

SPEECHMONGER. And blue for the heavens that shall never cease casting their light over us—and stars like that which hung over Bethlehem shall lead us into a truer life—

ONE. How 'bout Prohibition?

SPEECHMONGER. In this land of Justice—Free Speech and Golden Opportunity—

TWO. Why don't you get yourself a job?

SPEECHMONGER. If you vote for me I shall keep this going—going—going once—do I hear a bid—going—going twice do I hear a bid—whatsamatter with you folks—will you let a valuable pure old genuine guaranteed—

THREE. It's a fake!

SPEECHMONGER. Article like this be given away for nothing—it's a crime—

FOUR. That looks pretty good—I think I'll put in a bid.

SPEECHMONGER. I've been in the business for fifteen years and never has an article like this been given away so cheaply—It's a shame—an atrocity—a sin—an unpardonable sin against God and Church—Oh Lord, here's this poor forsaken woman whose husband has sacrificed his life for you and you and you, and you sit there heartlessly, coldbloodedly looking on while the greatest show in Coney Island—the greatest show in the United States—the greatest show in the whole wide world is going on—

ONE. Get your ice cold soda—

TWO. Popcorn—chewing gum—ice cream—

THREE. It's a fake!

FOUR. Peanuts—frankfurters—all hot!

SPEECHMONGER. Fifty different marvelous and astounding attractions now being shown inside—this woman is only one of the many we have to offer—see the limbless father of ten children—the headless poet—see—see—see—

the glorious golden banners of God and Country and American Womanhood flourished aloft again—into the topless towers of the sky—into the peace and good-will of our Glorious Country— [Applause] Dig into your pockets and give until it hurts—give—give—this woman's husband died in the trenches fighting for womanhood—give—give—give me your votes until it hurts—turn your purses inside out and give these women—these girls who Glorify American Womanhood—Oh in this great and prosperous nation of ours let there be no strife —no bloodshed—no turmoil—only peace and brotherly love and unity and to those who dare to desecrate and profane American Ideals show no mercy—kill the radicals—reds—the agitators—the unions—lynch them—murder them—deport them—beat them—exclude them—

ONE. Kill 'em—

SPEECHMONGER. Hang them—

THREE. That's right—

SPEECHMONGER. Jail them—

FOUR. Dam foreigners—

SPEECHMONGER. And make the world safe for Democracy— [Applause] See America First —Vote the Straight Ticket—Glorify the American Girl—Fight for God and Country—

THREE. Three cheers for the American flag!

SPEECHMONGER. Uphold American Justice—Sin no more—and folks, the biggest show in the world is now going on—only a quarter—twenty-five pennies—every little bit helps—step right up—come on don't be afraid—come up closer and give—give—give—

[He finishes his speech with a magnificent toss of his leonine head. His accompanying women, now in the CROWD, start shouting loudly]

ONE. The Salvation Army—your country needs you—

TWO. Save your souls with a few pennies—

THREE. Dig into your pockets—who's next? —get 'em right over here.

ONE. Liberty Bonds—War Saving Stamps—Do your bit—

TWO. Save your souls, sinners, with purity, faith, money—

THREE. Cigars—cigarettes—candies—refreshments—

ONE. Give for the uplifting of American Ideals—

TWO. Come on folks—Come on and help—

ALL [together].

Help—help—help—help—

Give—give—give—give—

[A whistle sharply blown by the SPEECHMONGER]

SPEECHMONGER [lifting his arm as though halting traffic]. All right, folks—give these little girls a big hand— [Starts applause] All right, Glorious Glories, step right up and let's see how much our generous public has contributed!

[*The girls mount the platform*]

SPEECHMONGER [*holding out a bag*]. Pour all the money in here, girls, into the Central Bureau of All Charitable, Patriotic and Fraternal Orders— [*As each one passes and pours the money into the bag*] God will do right by you sweet child—Dear Madam: I take this appropriate moment to thank you for your untiring efforts in making our campaign a success, Yours very truly—Great show you put on, kid— [*They have all emptied their contribution boxes into the bag*] All right—Come on, girls, let's go—

[*They start to go off*]

MADONNA [*in a loud coarse voice*]. Hey you, where the hell d'yuh think you're going—Come across with my share—

SPEECHMONGER [*turning*]. Now my dear young lady—

MADONNA. Can 'at stuff—Who d'yuh think I am, the audience? What d'yuh think I was doin' there—posin' for animal crackers?—Come across—

SPEECHMONGER. My dear lady—I believe you're laboring under some misunderstanding. Exactly what is it you desire?

MADONNA. Dough—

SPEECHMONGER. Oh, I see—why of course—

MADONNA. Well then, come across—

SPEECHMONGER. Yes, certainly, madam; that is, after we have made our distributions. You see we have solicitors, campaigners, office workers, advertisers, executive staffs, investigators—

MADONNA. Hey, where do I come off—

SPEECHMONGER. Exactly— [*Turns into exit position*] Ta—ta—come on, girls!

[*He and the girls trip away gaily*]

MADONNA. Come back here—I'll have the law on you—Where do you get off with that stuff—Don't I ever get a break in this mess—Come on back you—you—Oh—hell—

[*The* CROWD *has become discernible again. They are coming home from work*]

DAUGHTER [*starting to cry*]. Hey—mom—mom—gimme back my dolly—mam-ma—

MADONNA. Oh shut up for a minute. I've got enough troubles without you—

DAUGHTER. I don't care, I want my doll—it's mine—gimme it—

[*Enter* CROWD]

MADONNA. Here— [*She flings the babe in arms to her daughter*] And shut up—I wanna think—

[*The* CROWD *with tired voices flows past them*]

Going home from work—Tired—Home—Eat—Eat — Eat — Warm — Nice — Tired — Wife — Kids — Eat — Eat — Paper — News — Jokes — Sit — Sports — Sit — Sit — Radio — Jazz — Tired — Home — Home — [*As the*

movie entrance lights up, with a sudden outburst*] Movies —

[*The movie sucks them in, leaving the* MADONNA *and the* GIRL *alone on the street. After a moment a* MAN *enters. It is the* SPEECHMONGER *now wearing a top-hat, cane, and spats. The* MADONNA *spies him and as he comes down the street she walks across his path, making up to him. He stops and looks at her appraisingly*]

HE. Your name please!

MADONNA. Mazie M'Gurk—

HE. Ah, working girl! We ought to get along well together—

MADONNA. Yeh, Labor an' Capital—

HE. Are you a union girl?

MADONNA. No, mister, I'm just a poor working girl—

HE. Why don't you join a union? Don't you realize the benefits to be derived from such an affiliation? By staying out of their organization you frustrate the unions in organizing a universal war for more pay and less work—

MADONNA. But mister, I only want enough work and enough pay to live on—

HE. Can't you understand that the labors of mankind are founded on the principle of doing as little work as possible for the greatest monetary return? Now, don't tell me you still believe in the fairy tale that people work for the love of the job. Rats, we're not living in the dark ages—we're modern people in a modern age— If you ignorant working people would only learn—

MADONNA. I'm sorry—I'll learn—

HE. I don't want you to learn—I want you to know!

MADONNA. Well, what do you want me to do?

HE. My God, I've been standing here for ten minutes telling you to join the union!

MADONNA. All right!—I—I'll join the union—

HE. Now that's talking the way I like to hear talk— [*He takes out a large book*] Here's an application blank. All you have to do is sign here and pay me the initiation fee of—oh, by the way, have you any money?

MADONNA [*hunting through her pockets*]. Only—only a quarter—

HE. Oh ye Gods—

MADONNA. How much do you need to join a union—

HE. Only a couple of hundred dollars— [*Going*] Well, I'm sorry I can't waste any more time here. I can only do business with union women—

MADONNA [*running after him*]. Wait a minute —mister—wait a minute—

HE [*turning*]. Well—

MADONNA What—what if I work out my initiation fee?

HE [*musing*]. Well— [*Then*] Well, that doesn't sound so bad—all right, three years' apprenticeship—and remember I'm doing this only because there is still something of the age of Chivalry in me. Come—

[*They start*]

DAUGHTER [*crying out*]. Mama—mama—I wanna go too—

HE. What's that?

MADONNA. That's my little girl—she wants to go with us—

HE [*looking the little girl over*]. No—she's too young yet—too frail—Child Labor Laws— got to give her a proper education first— [*To the mother*] Give me your quarter— [*She gives it to him, and he in turn hands it to the girl*] Here's a quarter, and go to the movies. And remember—the movies are the greatest institution for learning in the world. Go on—

DAUGHTER [*running joyfully to the movies*]. Hurray—"Nights of Passion" with Antonio Rudolpho— [*She goes in*]

HE. Let's go—

MADONNA. Say, who are you?

HE. Cornelius Algernon D'Arcy Rockeford, the 2nd—

MADONNA. Ah, money!

HE. Come now— Let's hurry! We'll go to my luxurious ancestral mansion on Fifth Avenue—let's go!

[*They leave. The electric lights have been going out one by one—the street is empty. Then the movie palace lights go out and the doors open wide. The people stream forth. They walk in all directions toward their homes. This, spoken in flowing rhythm, by a group of (1) yawning people; (2) a group of boys and girls, their arms around each other; and (3) a group spellbound by the performance*]

THREE. What a picture—

TWO. Red—red—hot—soul kisses—red hot mamma—

ONE. Tired—tired—

TWO. Oh boy one night with Antonio and I'd die glad—

THREE. Hot—hot—red hot—

TWO. That's what happens to a wife—to a boy—to a father—to a bachelor—to a girl— to a mother—to a husband—

ONE. Oh boy tired.

TWO. Antonio—Antonio—Antonio—

ONE. Goin' to bed—

THREE. Some picture—sleep—sleep—some show—

ONE. Sleep—sleep—sleep—

[*The street is empty again. A violin or piano plays softly on the Radio. A GIRL runs in shyly, love enraptured, followed by a love-stricken YOUTH*]

GIRL [*looking up happily at the moon, and singing in time to music*].

Blue skies smiling at me
Nothing but blue skies do I see—

BOY [*in time to music*].

Never saw the moon shining so bright
Never saw things going so right

GIRL [*saying lines in time to music*].

Dawn of to-morrow
Take every sorrow
Bring back the sunshine
I long to see—

BOY [*in same way*].

So tired of waiting, lonely without you
Dawn of to-morrow, bring you back to me—

[*As BOY finishes the saying of the lines to music, he and the GIRL embrace. The GIRL is facing stage left and sees the COP who has started to stroll on stage in their direction. She drops the embrace and goes, right. The BOY turns to go, left, almost collides with COP, proceeds off stage, left, as COP leans against lamp post and yawns as in first scene. There is the sound of an elevated train whizzing by. The COP sways to and fro as he looks vacantly at the blank-eyed buildings. The rattle of a milkwagon over a cobble-stone street is heard, with a long drawn-out "Whoa." A MILKMAN enters as in the first scene.*]

MILKMAN. 'Lo, Mike.

COP. 'Lo, Pete.

MILKMAN. Well, another day—

COP. Yep, another day—

MILKMAN. Still watching the world?

COP. Yep—still feedin' the world?

MILKMAN. Yep—'at's the way it goes.

COP. Yep—

MILKMAN. Well so long Mike.

COP. So long Pete, see yuh t'morrer.

[*MILKMAN goes. COP yawns again, beginning to stroll down the street again as*]

THE CURTAIN FALLS

OFF-STAGE NOISES AND MUSIC CUES

Milkman and Cop

Count 10 from rise of curtain, then follow with

1. APPROACH OF HORSE AND WAGON

Slow at Milkman's "Whoa!" to gradual stop; begin

2. CLINK OF MILK BOTTLES
Continue same until exit of Milkman. Then

3. DEPARTURE OF HORSE AND WAGON
Which dies away in distance. Then start

4. ELEVATED TRAIN
Approach and die away in distance.
Beggar Scene
Nothing.
Tradesmen Scene
At word "Law" commence

5. SWEEPING
Synchronizing with rhythm of lines. Stop
at "and awe."
At cue "They eat it!" Commence

6. ALARM CLOCKS
Begin with one, add in 2, 3, 4, 5, 6, 7, 8
until all are ringing, then

7. ELEVATED TRAIN
Approaches as

8. ALARM CLOCKS
Are shut off, one by one, as

9. ELEVATED TRAIN
Dies in distance
Morning Crowd Scene
At cue "Oh Hell" start

10. TURNSTILES
Slow at first, in rhythm of crowd. At cue
"Oh sweet bed" accelerate tempo as per
direction. At cue "What's your hurry?"
accelerate tempo. At cue "Come on, let's
hurry!" accelerate tempo, and start

11. ELEVATED TRAIN
Approach and stop. At cue "Run, run,
run!" start train and stop

12. TURNSTILES AND START RIVETTER, AND START
BUSINESS NOISES
Business Scene
After Elevated Train has died in distance
start

13. TYPEWRITERS

14. TELEPHONE BELL.
Spasmodic ringing every 10 seconds.

15. TICKER
At cue "Oh God, when does that Lunch-
hour begin?" Blow

16. NOON WHISTLE
Stop all other noises; start

17. DISHES AND SILVER
Elevated train (approach and die away)
Lunch-hour Scene
At Scream stop

18. DISHES AND SILVER
Movie Scene
At cue "Shoot!" start

19. MOVIE CAMERA CLICK

20. GUN SHOT
At cue, "Cut!" stop

21. MOVIE CAMERA CLICK
Crowd "Terrible" Scene
Nothing. We have to get back to work.
Terrible, Terrible. Start Radio and Organ.
Speechmonger Scene

At cue, "Your logic's terrible!" start

22. RADIO
Repeat announcement as per direction. As
Spotlight comes on Madonna, start

23. ORGAN
Play eight bars of Doxology and stop. Continue with very soft

24. RADIO
during Organ; at end of Organ, come up
forte, finish announcement.
At start of Speechmonger's Spiel, start

25. ORGAN
At first "Look at her!" die out on Organ
and start

26. TOM-TOM
At cue "only two bits" start

27. DRUMS [Snare and Base]
Military March Time—very softly at first,
gradual increase. At same time start dying
out with

28. TOM-TOM
And stop. At cue, "We are engaged in a
great world war" play

29. BUGLE [*or trumpet*]
Reveille, loud at first gradually dying out.
However, keep

30. DRUMS
At march time until cue "American Inspiration and Justice" when drums come
up forte and

31. BUGLE
Play "Semper Fidelis" once through.
Soften.

32. DRUMS
At cue "I shall keep this going." Drums die
away and start

33. AUCTIONEER'S HAMMER
Synchronizing with Speechmonger until
cue "A sin!" stop Hammer and start

34. ORGAN
It's a Shame
"Nearer My God To Thee" until cue "You
and you and you!" At same cue start

35. TOM-TOM
At cue, "The headless poet" start

36. DRUMS
Military march time. Bring up gradually.
At cue "See, see, see!"
Die out

37. TOM-TOM
After cue "Kill the radicals!"

38. GUN SHOT
Follow quickly with one shot after each
word as follows:
"The Reds!" [SHOT]
"The Agitators!" [SHOT]
"The Unions!" [SHOT]
"Lynch them!" [SHOT]
"Murder them!" [SHOT]
"Deport them!" [SHOT]
"Beat them!" [SHOT]
"Exclude them!" [SHOT]

"Hang them!" [SHOT]
"Jail them!" [SHOT]
At cue, "Show is going on" come up forte on

39. DRUMS
When Speechmonger puts finger to mouth, blow

40. TRAFFIC COP'S WHISTLE
And stop

41. DRUMS.
As girls dump money into bag, synchronize with

42. CLINK OF COINS
On exact cue "Ta, ta—come on, girls"

43. LONG CHORD IN G ON PIANO

44. LONG ROLL OF DRUMS
Until Speechmonger and Girls exit, then follow with quick

45. CYMBAL CRASH

Crowd Coming Home Scene
At cue "I wanna think!" Start slow

46. TURNSTILES AND ELEVATED TRAIN
At cue "Movies!" stop. Then start

47. PIANO
Play until exit of crowd.—Sequi into "Villain entrance" and stop.

Capitalist Scene
At cue "Passionate Nights With John Gilbert" play

48. PIANO
Four bars, and stop.

Crowd Leaving Movies Scene
Organ. Exit march
Nothing as yet.

Boy and Girl Scene
At exit of crowd start

49. VIOLIN

Milkman and Cop Scene
Count 10 after Cop enters then follow with

50. APPROACHING OF HORSE AND WAGON
Slow at Milkman's "Whoa" to gradual stop; begin

51. CLINK OF MILK BOTTLES
Continue same until exit of Milkman. Then

52. DEPARTURE OF HORSE AND WAGON

LILIOM

A Play in Seven Scenes

By FERENC MOLNAR

TRANSLATED FROM THE HUNGARIAN BY
BENJAMIN F. GLAZER

CHARACTERS

LILIOM
JULIE
MARIE
MRS. MUSKAT
LOUISE
MRS. HOLLUNDER
FICSUR
YOUNG HOLLUNDER
WOLF BEIFELD
THE CARPENTER
LINZMAN
THE DOCTOR
THE MAGISTRATE
TWO MOUNTED POLICEMEN
TWO PLAINCLOTHES POLICEMEN
TWO HEAVENLY POLICEMEN
THE RICHLY DRESSED MAN
THE POORLY DRESSED MAN
THE GUARD
A SUBURBAN POLICEMAN

SYNOPSIS OF SCENES

PROLOGUE—*An amusement park on the outskirts of Budapest.*
FIRST SCENE—*A lonely place in the park.*
SECOND SCENE—*The photographic studio of the* HOLLUNDERS.
THIRD SCENE—*Same as scene two.*
FOURTH SCENE—*A railroad embankment outside the city.*
FIFTH SCENE—*Same as scene two.*
SIXTH SCENE—*A courtroom in the beyond.*
SEVENTH SCENE—JULIE'S *garden.*

LILIOM

THE PROLOGUE

An amusement park on the outskirts of Budapest on a late afternoon in Spring. Barkers stand before the booths of the sideshows haranguing the passing crowd. The strident music of a calliope is heard; laughter, shouts, the scuffle of feet, the signal bells of merry-go-round.

The merry-go-round is at center. LILIOM stands at the entrance, a cigarette in his mouth, coaxing the people in. The girls regard him with idolizing glances and screech with pleasure as he playfully pushes them through entrance. Now and then some girl's escort resents the familiarity, whereupon LILIOM's demeanor becomes ugly and menacing, and the cowed escort slinks through the entrance behind his girl or contents himself with a muttered resentful comment.

One girl hands LILIOM a red carnation; he rewards her with a bow and a smile. When the soldier who accompanies her protests, LILIOM cows him with a fierce glance and a threatening gesture. MARIE and JULIE come out of the crowd and LILIOM favors them with particular notice as they pass into the merry-go-round.

MRS. MUSKAT comes out of the merry-go-round, bringing LILIOM coffee and rolls. LILIOM mounts the barker's stand at the entrance, where he is elevated over everyone on the stage. Here he begins his harangue. Everybody turns toward him. The other booths are gradually deserted. The tumult makes it impossible for the audience to hear what he is saying, but every now and then some witticism of his provokes a storm of laughter which is audible above the din. Many people enter the merry-go-round. Here and there one catches a phrase "Room for one more on the zebra's back," "Which of you ladies?" "Ten heller for adults, five for children," "Step right up"—

It is growing darker. A lamplighter crosses the stage, and begins unperturbedly lighting the colored gas-lamps. The whistle of a distant locomotive is heard. Suddenly the tumult ceases, the lights go out, and the curtain falls in darkness.

END OF PROLOGUE

SCENE ONE

SCENE: *A lonely place in the park, half hidden by trees and shrubbery. Under a flowering acacia tree stands a painted wooden bench. From the distance, faintly, comes the tumult of the amusement park. It is the sunset of the same day.*

When the curtain rises the stage is empty.

MARIE *enters quickly, pauses at center, and looks back.*

MARIE. Julie, Julie! [*There is no answer*] Do you hear me, Julie? Let her be! Come on. Let her be. [*Starts to go back*]

[JULIE *enters, looks back angrily*]

JULIE. Did you ever hear of such a thing? What's the matter with the woman anyway?

MARIE [*looking back again*]. Here she comes again.

JULIE. Let her come. I didn't do anything to her. All of a sudden she comes up to me and begins to raise a row.

MARIE. Here she is. Come on, let's run. [*Tries to urge her off*]

JULIE. Run? I should say not. What would I want to run for? I'm not afraid of her.

MARIE. Oh, come on. She'll only start a fight.

JULIE. I'm going to stay right here. Let her *start* a fight.

MRS. MUSKAT [*entering*]. What do you want to run away for? [*To* JULIE] Don't worry. I won't eat you. But there's one thing I want to tell you, my dear. Don't let me catch you in my carousel again. I stand for a whole lot, I have to in my business. It makes no difference to me whether my customers are ladies or the likes of you—as long as they pay their money. But when a girl misbehaves herself on my carousel—out she goes. Do you understand?

JULIE. Are you talking to me?

MRS. MUSKAT. Yes, you! You—chambermaid, you! In my carousel—

JULIE. Who did anything in your old carousel? I paid my fare and took my seat and never said a word, except to my friend here.

MARIE. No, she never opened her mouth. Liliom came over to her on his own accord.

MRS. MUSKAT. It's all the same. I'm not going to get in trouble with the police, and lose my license on account of you—you shabby kitchen maid!

JULIE. Shabby yourself.

MRS. MUSKAT. You stay out of my carousel! Letting my barker fool with you! Aren't you ashamed of yourself?

JULIE. What? What did you say?

MRS. MUSKAT. I suppose you think I have no eyes in my head. I see everything that goes on in my carousel. During the whole ride she let Liliom fool with her—the shameless hussy!

JULIE. He did not fool with me! I don't let any man fool with me!

MRS. MUSKAT. He leaned against you all through the ride!

JULIE. He leaned against the panther. He always leans against something, doesn't he? Everybody leans where he wants. I couldn't tell him not to lean, if he always leans, could I? But he didn't lay a hand on me.

MRS. MUSKAT. Oh, didn't he? And I suppose he didn't put his hand around your waist, either?

MARIE. And if he did? What of it?

MRS. MUSKAT. You hold your tongue! No one's asking you—just you keep out of it.

JULIE. He put his arm around my waist—just the same as he does to all the girls. He always does that.

MRS. MUSKAT. I'll teach him not to do it any more, my dear. No carryings on in my carousel! If you are looking for that sort of thing, you'd better go to the circus! You'll find lots of soldiers there to carry on with!

JULIE. You keep your soldiers for yourself!

MARIE. Soldiers! As if we wanted soldiers!

MRS. MUSKAT. Well, I only want to tell you this, my dear, so that we understand each other perfectly. If you ever stick your nose in my carousel again, you'll wish you hadn't! I'm not going to lose my license on account of the likes of you! People who don't know how to behave, have got to stay out!

JULIE. You're wasting your breath. If I feel like riding on your carousel I'll pay my ten heller and I'll ride. I'd like to see anyone try to stop me!

MRS. MUSKAT. Just come and try it, my dear—just come and try it.

MARIE. We'll see what'll happen.

MRS. MUSKAT. Yes, you will see something happen that never happened before in this park.

JULIE. Perhaps you think you could throw me out!

MRS. MUSKAT. I'm sure of it, my dear.

JULIE. And suppose I'm stronger than you?

MRS. MUSKAT. I'd think twice before I'd dirty my hands on a common servant girl. I'll have Liliom throw you out. He knows how to handle your kind.

JULIE. You think Liliom would throw me out.

MRS. MUSKAT. Yes, my dear, so fast that you won't know what happened to you!

JULIE. He'd throw me— [Stops suddenly, for MRS. MUSKAT has turned away]

[Both look off stage until LILIOM enters, surrounded by four giggling servant girls]

LILIOM. Go away! Stop following me, or I'll smack your face!

A LITTLE SERVANT GIRL. Well, give me back my handkerchief.

LILIOM. Go on now—

THE FOUR SERVANT GIRLS [simultaneously]. What do you think of him?—My handkerchief! —Give it back to her!—That's a nice thing to do!

THE LITTLE SERVANT GIRL [to MRS. MUSKAT]. Please, lady, make him—

MRS. MUSKAT. Oh, shut up!

LILIOM. Will you get out of here? [Makes a threatening gesture]

[The four servant girls exit in voluble but fearful haste]

MRS. MUSKAT. What have you been doing now?

LILIOM. None of your business. [Glances at JULIE] Have you been starting with her again?

JULIE. Mister Liliom, please—

LILIOM [steps threateningly toward her]. Don't yell!

JULIE [timidly]. I didn't yell.

LILIOM. Well, don't. [To MRS. MUSKAT] What's the matter? What has she done to you?

MRS. MUSKAT. What has she done? She's been impudent to me. Just as impudent as she could be! I put her out of the carousel. Take a good look at this innocent thing, Liliom. She's never to be allowed in my carousel again!

LILIOM [to JULIE]. You heard that. Run home, now.

MARIE. Come on. Don't waste your time with such people. [Tries to lead JULIE away]

JULIE. No, I won't—

MRS. MUSKAT. If she ever comes again, you're not to let her in. And if she gets in before you see her, throw her out. Understand?

LILIOM. What has she done, anyhow?

JULIE [agitated and very earnest]. Mister Liliom—tell me please—honest and truly—if I come into the carousel, will you throw me out?

MRS. MUSKAT. Of course he'll throw you out.

MARIE. She wasn't talking to you.

JULIE. Tell me straight to my face, Mister Liliom, would you throw me out?

[They face each other. There is a brief pause]

LILIOM. Yes, little girl, if there was a reason —but if there was no reason, why should I throw you out?

MARIE [to MRS. MUSKAT]. There, you see!

JULIE. Thank you, Mister Liliom.

MRS. MUSKAT. And I tell you again, if this little slut dares to set her foot in my carousel, she's to be thrown out! I'll stand for no indecency in my establishment.

LILIOM. What do you mean—indecency?

MRS. MUSKAT. I saw it all. There's no use denying it.

JULIE. She says you put your arm around my waist.

LILIOM. Me?

MRS. MUSKAT. Yes, you! I saw you. Don't play the innocent.

LILIOM. Here's something new! I'm not to put my arm around a girl's waist any more! I suppose I'm to ask your permission before I touch another girl!

MRS. MUSKAT. You can touch as many girls as you want and as often as you want—for my part you can go as far as you like with any of them—but not this one— I permit no indecency in my carousel.

[*There is a long pause*]

LILIOM [*to* MRS. MUSKAT]. And now I'll ask you please to shut your mouth.

MRS. MUSKAT. What?

LILIOM. Shut your mouth quick, and go back to your carousel.

MRS. MUSKAT. What?

LILIOM. What did she do to you, anyhow? Tryin' to start a fight with a little pigeon like that . . . just because I touched her?—You come to the carousel as often as you want to, little girl. Come every afternoon, and sit on the panther's back, and if you haven't got the price, Liliom will pay for you. And if anyone dares to bother you, you come and tell *me*.

MRS. MUSKAT. You reprobate!

LILIOM. Old witch!

JULIE. Thank you, Mister Liliom.

MRS. MUSKAT. You seem to think that I can't throw you out, too. What's the reason I can't? Because you are the best barker in the park? Well, you are very much mistaken. In fact, you can consider yourself thrown out already. You're discharged!

LILIOM. Very good.

MRS. MUSKAT [*weakening a little*]. I can discharge you any time I feel like it.

LILIOM. Very good, you feel like discharging me. I'm discharged. That settles it.

MRS. MUSKAT. Playing the high and mighty, are you? Conceited pig! Good-for-nothing!

LILIOM. You said you'd throw me out, didn't you? Well, that suits me; I'm thrown out.

MRS. MUSKAT [*softening*]. Do you have to take up every word I say?

LILIOM. It's all right; it's all settled. I'm a good-for-nothing. And a conceited pig. And I'm discharged.

MRS. MUSKAT. Do you want to ruin my business?

LILIOM. A good-for-nothing? Now I know! And I'm discharged! Very good.

MRS. MUSKAT. You're a devil, you are . . . and that woman—

LILIOM. Keep away from her!

MRS. MUSKAT. I'll get Hollinger to give you such a beating that you'll hear all the angels sing . . . and it won't be the first time, either.

LILIOM. Get out of here. I'm discharged. And you get out of here.

JULIE [*timidly*]. Mister Liliom, if she's willing to say that she hasn't discharged you—

LILIOM. You keep out of this.

JULIE [*timidly*]. I don't want this to happen on account of me.

LILIOM [*to* MRS. MUSKAT, *pointing to* JULIE]. Apologize to her!

MARIE. A-ah!

MRS. MUSKAT. Apologize? To who?

LILIOM. To this little pigeon. Well—are you going to do it?

MRS. MUSKAT. If you give me this whole park on a silver plate, and all the gold of the Rothschilds on top of it—I'd—I'd— Let her dare to come into my carousel again and she'll get thrown out so hard that she'll see stars in daylight!

LILIOM. In that case, dear lady [*takes off his cap with a flourish*], you are respectfully requested to get out o' here as fast as your legs will carry you— I never beat up a woman yet—except that Holzer woman who I sent to the hospital for three weeks—but—if you don't get out o' here this minute, and let this little squab be, I'll give you the prettiest slap in the jaw you ever had in your life.

MRS. MUSKAT. Very good, my son. Now you *can* go to the devil. Good-bye. You're discharged, and you needn't try to come back, either. [*She exits*]

[*It is beginning to grow dark*]

MARIE [*with grave concern*]. Mister Liliom—

LILIOM. Don't you pity me or I'll give *you* a slap in the jaw. [*To* JULIE] And don't you pity me, either.

JULIE [*in alarm*]. I don't pity you, Mister Liliom.

LILIOM. You're a liar, you *are* pitying me. I can see it in your face. You're thinking, now that Madame Muskat has thrown him out, Liliom will have to go begging. Huh! Look at me. I'm big enough to get along without a Madame Muskat. I have been thrown out of better jobs than hers.

JULIE. What will you do now, Mister Liliom?

LILIOM. Now? First of all, I'll go and get myself—a glass of beer. You see, when something happens to annoy me, I always drink a glass of beer.

JULIE. Then you *are* annoyed about losing your job.

LILIOM. No, only about where I'm going to get the beer.

MARIE. Well—eh—

LILIOM. Well—eh—what?

MARIE. Well—eh—are you going to stay with us, Mister Liliom?

LILIOM. Will you pay for the beer? [MARIE *looks doubtful; he turns to* JULIE] Will you? [*She does not answer*] How much money have you got?

JULIE [*bashfully*]. Eight heller.

LILIOM. And you? [MARIE *casts down her eyes and does not reply*. LILIOM *continues sternly*] I asked you how much you've got?

[MARIE *begins to weep softly*] I understand. Well, you needn't cry about it. You girls stay here, while I go back to the carousel and get my clothes and things. And when I come back, we'll go to the Hungarian beer-garden. It's all right, I'll pay. Keep your money. [*He exits*]

[MARIE *and* JULIE *stand silent, watching him until he has gone*]

MARIE. Are you sorry for him?

JULIE. Are you?

MARIE. Yes, a little. Why are you looking after him that funny way?

JULIE [*sits down*]. Nothing—except I'm sorry he lost his job.

MARIE [*with a touch of pride*]. It was on our account he lost his job. Because he's fallen in love with you.

JULIE. He hasn't at all.

MARIE [*confidently*]. Oh, yes! he is in love with you. [*Hesitantly, romantically*] There is someone in love with me, too.

JULIE. There is? Who?

MARIE. I—I never mentioned it before, because you hadn't a lover of your own—but now you have—and I'm free to speak. [*Very grandiloquently*] My heart has found its mate.

JULIE. You're only making it up.

MARIE. No, it's true—my heart's true love—

JULIE. Who? Who is he?

MARIE. A soldier.

JULIE. What kind of a soldier?

MARIE. I don't know. Just a soldier. Are there different kinds?

JULIE. Many different kinds. There are hussars, artillerymen, engineers, infantry—that's the kind that walks—and—

MARIE. How can you tell which is which?

JULIE. By their uniforms.

MARIE [*after trying to puzzle it out*]. The conductors on the street cars—are they soldiers?

JULIE. Certainly not. They're conductors.

MARIE. Well, they have uniforms.

JULIE. But they don't carry swords or guns.

MARIE. Oh! [*Thinks it over again; then*] Well, policemen—are they?

JULIE [*with a touch of exasperation*]. Are they what?

MARIE. Soldiers.

JULIE. Certainly not. They're just policemen.

MARIE [*triumphantly*]. But they have uniforms—and they carry weapons, too.

JULIE. You're just as dumb as you can be. You don't go by their uniforms.

MARIE. But you said—

JULIE. No, I didn't. A letter-carrier wears a uniform, too, but that doesn't make him a soldier.

MARIE. But if he carried a gun or a sword, would he be—

JULIE. No, he'd still be a letter-carrier. You can't go by guns or swords, either.

MARIE. Well, if you don't go by the uniforms or the weapons, what *do* you go by?

JULIE. By— [*Tries to put it into words; fails; then breaks off suddenly*] Oh, you'll get to know when you've lived in the city long enough. You're nothing but a country girl. When you've lived in the city a year, like I have, you'll know all about it.

MARIE [*half angrily*]. Well, how *do* you know when *you* see a real soldier?

JULIE. By one thing.

MARIE. What?

JULIE. One thing— [*She pauses.* MARIE *starts to cry*] Oh, what are you crying about?

MARIE. Because you're making fun of me. . . . You're a city girl, and I'm just fresh from the country . . . and how am I expected to know a soldier when I see one? . . . You, you ought to tell me, instead of making fun of me—

JULIE. All right. Listen then cry-baby. There's only one way to tell a soldier: by his salute! That's the only way.

MARIE [*joyfully; with a sigh of relief*]. Ah —that's good.

JULIE. What?

MARIE. I say—it's all right then—because Wolf—Wolf— [JULIE *laughs derisively*] Wolf— that's his name. [*She weeps again*]

JULIE. Crying again? What now?

MARIE. You're making fun of me again.

JULIE. I'm not. But when you say, "Wolf—Wolf—" like that, I have to laugh, don't I? [*Archly*] What's his name again?

MARIE. I won't tell you.

JULIE. All right. If you won't say it, then he's no soldier.

MARIE. I'll say it.

JULIE. Go on.

MARIE. No, I won't. [*She weeps again*]

JULIE. Then he's not a soldier. I guess he's a letter-carrier—

MARIE. No—no—I'd rather say it.

JULIE. Well, then.

MARIE [*giggling*]. But you mustn't look at me. You look the other way, and I'll say it. [JULIE *looks away.* MARIE *can hardly restrain her own laughter*] Wolf! [*She laughs*] his real name. Wolf, Wolf, Soldier—Wolf!

JULIE. What kind of a uniform does he wear?

MARIE. Red.

JULIE. Red trousers?

MARIE. No.

JULIE. Red coat?

MARIE. No.

JULIE. What then?

MARIE [*triumphantly*]. His cap!

JULIE [*after a long pause*]. He's just a porter, you dunce. Red cap . . . that's a porter—and he doesn't carry a gun or a sword, either.

MARIE [*triumphantly*]. But he salutes. You said yourself that was the only way to tell a soldier—

JULIE. He doesn't salute at all. He only greets people—

MARIE. He salutes me. . . . And if his name *is* Wolf, that doesn't prove he ain't a soldier—he salutes, and he wears a red cap and he stands on guard all day long outside a big building—

JULIE. What does he do there?

MARIE [*seriously*]. He spits.

JULIE [*with contempt*]. He's nothing—nothing but a common porter.

MARIE. What's Liliom?

JULIE [*indignantly*]. Why speak of him? What has he to do with me?

MARIE. The same as Wolf has to do with me. If you can talk to me like that about Wolf, I can talk to you about Liliom.

JULIE. He's nothing to me. He put his arm around me in the carousel. I couldn't tell him not to put his arm around me after he had done it, could I?

MARIE. I suppose you didn't like him to do it?

JULIE. No.

MARIE. Then why are you waiting for him. Why don't you go home?

JULIE. Why—eh—he *said* we were to wait for him.

[*Liliom enters. There is a long silence*]

LILIOM. Are you still here? What are you waiting for?

MARIE. You told us to wait.

LILIOM. Must you always interfere? No one is talking to you.

MARIE. You asked us—why we—

LILIOM. Will you keep your mouth shut? What do you suppose I want with two of you? I meant that one of you was to wait. The other can go home.

MARIE. All right.

JULIE. All right. [*Neither starts to go*]

LILIOM. One of you goes home. [*To* MARIE] Where do you work?

MARIE. At the Breier's, Damjanovitsch Street, Number 20.

LILIOM. And you?

JULIE. I work there, too.

LILIOM. Well, one of you goes home. Which of you wants to stay? [*There is no answer*] Come on, speak up, which of you stays?

MARIE [*officiously*]. She'll lose her job if she stays.

LILIOM. Who will?

MARIE. Julie. She has to be back by seven o'clock.

LILIOM. Is that true? Will they discharge you if you're not back on time?

JULIE. Yes.

LILIOM. Well, wasn't I discharged?

JULIE. Yes—you were discharged, too.

MARIE. Julie, shall I go?

JULIE. I—can't tell you what to do.

MARIE. All right—stay if you like.

LILIOM. You'll be discharged if you do?

MARIE. Shall I go, Julie?

JULIE [*embarrassed*]. Why do you keep asking me that?

MARIE. You know best what to do.

JULIE [*profoundly moved; slowly*]. It's all right, Marie, you can go home.

MARIE [*exits reluctantly, but comes back, and says uncertainly*]. Good-night.

[*She waits a moment to see if* JULIE *will follow her.* JULIE *does not move.* MARIE *exits. Meantime it has grown quite dark. During the following scene the gaslamps far in the distance are lighted one by one.* LILIOM *and* JULIE *sit on the bench. From afar, very faintly, comes the music of a calliope. But the music is intermittently heard; now it breaks off, now it resumes again, as if it came down on a fitful wind. Blending with it are the sounds of human voices, now loud, now soft; the blare of a toy trumpet; the confused noises of the show-booths. It grows progressively darker until the end of the scene. There is no moonlight. The spring irridescence glows in the deep blue sky*]

LILIOM. Now we're both discharged. [*She does not answer. From now on they speak gradually lower and lower until the end of the scene, which is played almost in whispers. Whistles softly, then*] Have you had your supper?

JULIE. No.

LILIOM. Want to go eat something at the Garden?

JULIE. No.

LILIOM. Anywhere else?

JULIE. No.

LILIOM [*whistles softly, then*]. You don't come to this park very often, do you? I've only seen you three times. Been here oftener than that?

JULIE. Oh, yes.

LILIOM. Did you see me?

JULIE. Yes.

LILIOM. And did you know I was Liliom?

JULIE. They told me.

LILIOM [*whistles softly, then*]. Have you got a sweetheart?

JULIE. No.

LILIOM. Don't lie to me.

JULIE. I haven't. If I had, I'd tell you. I've never had one.

LILIOM. What an awful liar you are. I've got a good mind to go away and leave you here.

JULIE. I've never had one.

LILIOM. Tell that to someone else.

JULIE [*reproachfully*]. Why do you insist I have?

LILIOM. Because you stayed here with me the first time I asked you to. You know your way around, you do.

JULIE. No, I don't, Mister Liliom.

LILIOM. I suppose you'll tell me you don't know why you're sitting here—like this, in the dark, alone with me— You wouldn't 'a' stayed so quick, if you hadn't done it before—with some soldier, maybe. This isn't the first time. You wouldn't have been so ready to stay if it was—what *did* you stay for, anyhow?

JULIE. So you wouldn't be left alone.

LILIOM. Alone! God, you're dumb! I don't need to be alone. I can have all the girls I want. Not only servant girls like you, but cooks and governesses, even French girls. I could have twenty of them if I wanted to.

JULIE. I know, Mister Liliom.

LILIOM. What do you know?

JULIE. That all the girls are in love with you. But that's not why *I* stayed. I stayed because you've been so good to me.

LILIOM. Well, then you can go home.

JULIE. I don't want to go home now.

LILIOM. And what if I go away and leave you sitting here?

JULIE. If you did, I wouldn't go home.

LILIOM. Do you know what you remind me of? A sweetheart I had once—I'll tell you how I met her— One night, at closing time, we had put out the lights in the carousel, and just as I was—

[*He is interrupted by the entrance of two plainclothes policemen. They take their stations on either side of the bench. They are police, searching the park for vagabonds*]

FIRST POLICEMAN. What are you doing there?

LILIOM. Me?

SECOND POLICEMAN. Stand up when you're spoken to! [*He taps* LILIOM *imperatively on the shoulder*]

FIRST POLICEMAN. What's your name?

LILIOM. Andreas Zavoczki. [JULIE *begins to weep softly*]

SECOND POLICEMAN. Stop your bawling. We're not goin' to eat you. We are only making our rounds.

FIRST POLICEMAN. See that he doesn't get away. [THE SECOND POLICEMAN *steps closer to* LILIOM] What's your business?

LILIOM. Barker and bouncer.

SECOND POLICEMAN. They call him Liliom, Chief. We've had him up a couple of times.

FIRST POLICEMAN. So that's who you are! Who do you work for now?

LILIOM. I work for the widow Muskat.

FIRST POLICEMAN. What are you hanging around here for?

LILIOM. We're just sitting here—me and this girl.

FIRST POLICEMAN. Your sweetheart?

LILIOM. No.

FIRST POLICEMAN [*to* JULIE]. And who are you?

JULIE. Julie Zeller.

FIRST POLICEMAN. Servant girl?

JULIE. Maid of All Work for Mister Georg Breier, Number Twenty Damjanovitsch Street.

FIRST POLICEMAN. Show your hands.

SECOND POLICEMAN [*after examining* JULIE's *hands*]. Servant girl.

FIRST POLICEMAN. Why aren't you at home? What are you doing out here with him?

JULIE. This is my day out, sir.

FIRST POLICEMAN. It would be better for you if you didn't spend it sitting around with a fellow like this.

SECOND POLICEMAN. They'll be disappearing in the bushes as soon as we turn our backs.

FIRST POLICEMAN. He's only after your money. We know this fine fellow. He picks up you silly servant girls and takes what money you have. Tomorrow you'll probably be coming around to report him. If you do, I'll throw you out.

JULIE. I haven't any money, sir.

FIRST POLICEMAN. Do you hear that, Liliom?

LILIOM. I'm not looking for her money.

SECOND POLICEMAN [*nudging him warningly*]. Keep your mouth shut.

FIRST POLICEMAN. It is my duty to warn you, my child, what kind of company you're in. He makes a specialty of servant girls. That's why he works in a carousel. He gets hold of a girl, promises to marry her, then he takes her money and her ring.

JULIE. But I haven't got a ring.

SECOND POLICEMAN. You're not to talk unless you're asked a question.

FIRST POLICEMAN. You be thankful that I'm warning you. It's nothing to me what you do. I'm not your father, thank God. But I'm telling you what kind of a fellow he is. By tomorrow morning you'll be coming around to us to report him. Now you be sensible and go home. You needn't be afraid of him. This officer will take you home if you're afraid.

JULIE. Do I *have* to go?

FIRST POLICEMAN. No, you don't *have* to go.

JULIE. Then I'll stay, sir.

FIRST POLICEMAN. Well, you've been warned.

JULIE. Yes, sir. Thank you, sir.

FIRST POLICEMAN. Come on, Berkovics.

[*The* POLICEMEN *exit.* JULIE *and* LILIOM *sit on the bench again. There is a brief pause*]

JULIE. Well, and what then?

LILIOM [*fails to understand*]. Huh?

JULIE. You were beginning to tell me a story.

LILIOM. Me?

JULIE. Yes, about a sweetheart. You said, one night, just as they were putting out the lights of the carousel— That's as far as you got.

LILIOM. Oh, yes, yes, just as the lights were going out, someone came along—a little girl

with a big shawl—you know— She came—eh
—from— Say—tell me—ain't you—that is, ain't
you at all—afraid of me? The officer told you
what kind of a fellow I am—and that I'd take
your money away from you—

JULIE. You couldn't take it away—I haven't
got any. But if I had—I'd—I'd give it to you—
I'd give it all to you.

LILIOM. You would?

JULIE. If you asked me for it.

LILIOM. Have you ever had a fellow you gave
money to?

JULIE. No.

LILIOM. Haven't you ever had a sweetheart?

JULIE. No.

LILIOM. Someone you used to go walking
with. You've had one like that?

JULIE. Yes.

LILIOM. A soldier?

JULIE. He came from the same village I did.

LILIOM. That's what all the soldiers say.
Where *do* you come from, anyway?

JULIE. Not far from here.

[*There is a pause*]

LILIOM. Were you in love with him?

JULIE. Why do you keep asking me that all
the time, Mister Liliom? I wasn't in love with
him. We only went walking together.

LILIOM. Where did you walk?

JULIE. In the park.

LILIOM. And your virtue? Where did you
lose that?

JULIE. I haven't got any virtue.

LILIOM. Well, you had once.

JULIE. No, I never had. I'm a respectable girl.

LILIOM. Yes, but you gave the soldier something.

JULIE. Why do you question me like that,
Mister Liliom?

LILIOM. Did you give him something?

JULIE. You have to. But I didn't love him.

LILIOM. Do you love me?

JULIE. No, Mister Liliom.

LILIOM. Then why do you stay here with
me?

JULIE. Um—nothing.

[*There is a pause. The music from afar is
plainly heard*]

LILIOM. Want to dance?

JULIE. No. I have to be very careful.

LILIOM. Of what?

JULIE. My—character.

LILIOM. Why?

JULIE. Because I'm never going to marry.
If I was going to marry, it would be different.
Then I wouldn't need to worry so much about
my character. It doesn't make any difference
if you're married. But I shan't marry—and
that's why I've got to take care to be a respectable girl.

LILIOM. Suppose I were to say to you—I'll
marry you.

JULIE. You?

LILIOM. That frightens you, doesn't it?
You're thinking of what the officer said and
you're afraid.

JULIE. No, I'm not, Mister Liliom. I don't
pay any attention to what he said.

LILIOM. But you wouldn't dare to marry
anyone like me, would you?

JULIE. I know that—that—if I loved anyone
—it wouldn't make any difference to me what
he—even if I died for it.

LILIOM. But you wouldn't marry a rough
guy like me—that is,—eh—if you loved me—

JULIE. Yes, I would—if I loved you, Mister
Liliom.

[*There is a pause*]

LILIOM [*whispers*]. Well,—you just said—
didn't you?—that you don't love me. Well,
why don't you go home then?

JULIE. It's too late now, they'd all be asleep.

LILIOM. Locked out?

JULIE. Certainly.

[*They are silent a while*]

LILIOM. I think—that even a low-down
good-for-nothing—can make a man of himself.

JULIE. Certainly.

[*They are silent again. A lamp-lighter
crosses the stage, lights the lamp over
the bench, and exits*]

LILIOM. Are you hungry?

JULIE. No.

[*Another pause*]

LILIOM. Suppose—you had some money—
and I took it from you?

JULIE. Then you could take it, that's all.

LILIOM [*after another brief silence*]. All I
have to do—is go back to her—that Muskat
woman—she'll be glad to get me back—then
I'd be earning my wages again.

[*She is silent. The twilight folds darker
about them*]

JULIE [*very softly*]. Don't go back—to
her— [*Pause*]

LILIOM. There are a lot of acacia trees around
here. [*Pause*]

JULIE. Don't go back to her— [*Pause*]

LILIOM. She'd take me back the minute I
asked her. I know why—she knows, too—
[*Pause*]

JULIE. I can smell them, too—acacia blossoms—

[*There is a pause. Some blossoms drift
down from the tree-top to the bench.
LILIOM picks one up and smells it*]

LILIOM. White acacias!

JULIE [*after a brief pause*]. The wind brings
them down.

[*They are silent. There is a long pause
before*]

THE CURTAIN FALLS

SCENE TWO

SCENE: *A photographer's "studio," operated by the* HOLLUNDERS, *on the fringe of the park. It is a dilapidated hovel. The general entrance is back left. Back right there is a window with a sofa before it. The outlook is on the amusement park with perhaps a small Ferris-wheel or the scaffolding of a "scenic-railway" in the background.*

The door to the kitchen is up left and a black-curtained entrance to the dark-room is down left. Just in front of the dark-room stands the camera on its tripod. Against the back wall, between the door and window, stands the inevitable photographer's back-ground-screen, ready to be wheeled into place.

It is forenoon. When the curtain rises, MARIE *and* JULIE *are discovered.*

MARIE. And *he* beat up Hollinger?

JULIE. Yes, he gave him an awful licking.

MARIE. But Hollinger is bigger than he is.

JULIE. He licked him just the same. It isn't size that counts, you know, it's cleverness. And Liliom's awful quick.

MARIE. And then he was arrested?

JULIE. Yes, they arrested him, but they let him go the next day. That makes twice in the two months we've been living here that Liliom's been arrested and let go again.

MARIE. Why do they let him go?

JULIE. Because he is innocent.

[MOTHER HOLLUNDER, *a very old woman, sharp-tongued, but in reality quite warm-hearted beneath her formidable exterior, enters at back carrying a few sticks of firewood, and scolding, half to herself*]

MOTHER HOLLUNDER. Always wanting something, but never willing to work for it. He won't work, and he won't steal, but he'll use up a poor old widow's last bit of firewood. He'll do that cheerfully enough! A big, strong lout like that lying around all day resting his lazy bones! He ought to be ashamed to look decent people in the face.

JULIE. I'm sorry, Mother Hollunder. . . .

MOTHER HOLLUNDER. Sorry! Better be sorry the lazy good-for-nothing ain't in jail where he belongs instead of in the way of honest, hard-working people. [*She exits into the kitchen*]

MARIE. Who's that?

JULIE. Mrs. Hollunder—my aunt. This is her [*with a sweeping gesture that takes in the camera, dark-room and screen*] studio. She lets us live here for nothing.

MARIE. What's she fetching the wood for?

JULIE. She brings us everything we need. If it weren't for her I don't know what would become of us. She's a good-hearted soul even if her tongue is sharp.

[*There is a pause*]

MARIE [*shyly*]. Do you know—I've found out. He's not a soldier.

JULIE. Do you still see him?

MARIE. Oh, yes.

JULIE. Often?

MARIE. Very often. He's asked me—

JULIE. To marry you?

MARIE. To marry me.

JULIE. You see—that proves he isn't a soldier. [*There is another pause*]

MARIE [*abashed, yet a bit boastfully*]. Do you know what I'm doing—I'm flirting with him.

JULIE. Flirting?

MARIE. Yes. He asks me to go to the park—and I say I can't go. Then he coaxes me, and promises me a new scarf for my head if I go. But I don't go—even then. . . . So then he walks all the way home with me—and I bid him good-night at the door.

JULIE. Is that what you call flirting?

MARIE. Um-hm! It's sinful, but it's so *thrilling*.

JULIE. Do you ever quarrel?

MARIE [*grandly*]. Only when our Passionate Love surges up.

JULIE. Your passionate love?

MARIE. Yes. . . . He takes my hand and we walk along together. Then he wants to swing hands, but I won't let him. I say: "Don't swing my hand"; and he says, "Don't be so stubborn." And then he tries to swing my hand again, but still I don't let him. And for a long time I don't let him—until in the end I let him. Then we walk along swinging hands—up and down, up and down—just like this. *That* is Passionate Love. It's sinful, but it's awfully *thrilling*.

JULIE. You're happy, aren't you?

MARIE. Happier than—anything— But the most beautiful thing on earth is Ideal Love.

JULIE. What kind is that?

MARIE. Daylight comes about three in the morning this time of the year. When we've been up that long we're all through with flirting and Passionate Love—and then our Ideal Love comes to the surface. It comes like this: I'll be sitting on the bench and Wolf, he holds my hand tight—and he puts his cheek against my cheek and we don't talk . . . we just sit there very quiet. . . . And after a while he gets sleepy, and his head sinks down, and he falls asleep . . . but even in his sleep he holds tight to my hand. And I—I sit perfectly still just looking around me and taking long, deep breaths—for by that time it's morning and the trees and flowers are fresh with dew. But Wolf doesn't smell anything because he's so fast asleep. And I get awfully sleepy myself, but I don't sleep. And we sit like that for a long time. That is Ideal Love—

[*There is a long pause*]

JULIE [*regretfully; uneasily*]. He went out last night and he hasn't come home yet.

MARIE. Here are sixteen Kreuzer. It was supposed to be carfare to take my young lady to the conservatory—eight there and eight back —but I made her walk. Here—save it with the rest.

JULIE. This makes three gulden, forty-six.

MARIE. Three gulden, forty-six.

JULIE. He won't work at all.

MARIE. Too lazy?

JULIE. No. He never learned a trade, you see, and he can't just go and be a day-laborer—so he just does nothing.

MARIE. That ain't right.

JULIE. No. Have the Breiers got a new maid yet?

MARIE. They've had three since you left. You know, Wolf's going to take a new job. He's going to work for the city. He'll get rent free, too.

JULIE. He won't go back to work at the carousel either. I ask him why, but he won't tell me— Last Monday he hit me.

MARIE. Did you hit him back?

JULIE. No.

MARIE. Why don't you leave him?

JULIE. I don't want to.

MARIE. I would. I'd leave him.

[*There is a strained silence*]

MOTHER HOLLUNDER [*enters, carrying a pot of water; muttering aloud*]. He can play cards, all right. He can fight, too; and take money from poor servant girls. And the police turn their heads the other way— The carpenter was here.

JULIE. Is that water for the soup?

MOTHER HOLLUNDER. The carpenter was here. There's a *man* for you! Dark, handsome, lots of hair, a respectable widower with two children—and money, and a good paying business.

JULIE [*to* MARIE]. It's three gulden sixty-six, not forty-six.

MARIE. Yes, that's what I make it—sixty-six.

MOTHER HOLLUNDER. He wants to take her out of this and marry her. This is the fifth time he's been here. He has two children, but—

JULIE. Please don't bother, Aunt Hollunder, I'll get the water myself.

MOTHER HOLLUNDER. He's waiting outside now.

JULIE. Send him away.

MOTHER HOLLUNDER. He'll only come back again—and first thing you know that vagabond will get jealous and there'll be a fight. [*Goes out, muttering*] Oh, he's ready enough to fight, he is. Strike a poor little girl like that! Ought to be ashamed of himself! And the police just let him go on doing as he pleases. [*Still scolding, she exits at back*]

MARIE. A carpenter wants to marry you?

JULIE. Yes.

MARIE. Why don't you?

JULIE. Because—

MARIE. Liliom doesn't support you, and he beats you—he thinks he can do whatever he likes just because he's Liliom. He's a bad one.

JULIE. He's not really bad.

MARIE. That night you sat on the bench together—he was gentle then.

JULIE. Yes, he was gentle.

MARIE. And afterwards he got wild again.

JULIE. Afterwards he got wild—sometimes. But that night on the bench . . . he was gentle. He's gentle now, sometimes, very gentle. After supper, when he stands there and listens to the music of the carousel, something comes over him—and he is gentle.

MARIE. Does he say anything?

JULIE. He doesn't say anything. He gets thoughtful and very quiet, and his big eyes stare straight ahead of him.

MARIE. Into your eyes?

JULIE. Not exactly. He's unhappy because he isn't working. That's really why he hit me on Monday.

MARIE. That's a fine reason for hitting you! Beats his wife because he isn't working, the ruffian!

JULIE. It preys on his mind—

MARIE. Did he hurt you?

JULIE [*very eagerly*]. Oh, no.

MRS. MUSKAT [*enters haughtily*]. Good morning. Is Liliom home?

JULIE. No.

MRS. MUSKAT. Gone out?

JULIE. He hasn't come home yet.

MRS. MUSKAT. I'll wait for him. [*She sits down*]

MARIE. You've got a lot of gall—to come here.

MRS. MUSKAT. Are you the lady of the house, my dear? Better look out or you'll get a slap in the mouth.

MARIE. How dare you set foot in Julie's house?

MRS. MUSKAT [*to* JULIE]. Pay no attention to her, my child. You know what brings me here. That vagabond, that good-for-nothing, I've come to give him his bread and butter back.

MARIE. He's not dependent on you for his bread.

MRS. MUSKAT [*to* JULIE]. Just ignore her, my child. She's just ignorant.

MARIE [*going*]. Good-bye.

JULIE. Good-bye.

MARIE [*in the doorway, calling back*]. Sixty-six.

JULIE. Yes, sixty-six.

MARIE. Good-bye. [*She exits*]

[JULIE *starts to go toward the kitchen*]

MRS. MUSKAT. I paid him a krone a day, and on Sunday a gulden. And he got all the beer and cigars he wanted from the customers. [JULIE *pauses on the threshold, but does not answer*] And he'd rather starve than beg my pardon. Well, I don't insist on that. I'll take him back without it. [JULIE *does not answer*] The fact is the people ask for him—and, you see, I've got to consider business first. It's nothing to me if he starves. I wouldn't be here at all, if it wasn't for business—

[*She pauses, for* LILIOM *and* FICSUR *have entered*]

JULIE. Mrs. Muskat is here.

LILIOM. I see she is.

JULIE. You might say good-morning.

LILIOM. What for? And what do *you* want, anyhow?

JULIE. I don't want anything.

LILIOM. Then keep your mouth shut. Next thing you'll be starting to nag again about my being out all night and out of work and living on your relations—

JULIE. I'm not saying anything.

LILIOM. But it's all on the tip of your tongue —I know you—now don't start or you'll get another. [*He paces angrily up and down*]

[*They are all a bit afraid of him, and shrink and look away as he passes them.* FICSUR *shambles from place to place, his eyes cast down as if he were searching for something on the floor*]

MRS. MUSKAT [*suddenly, to* FICSUR]. You're always dragging him out to play cards and drink with you. I'll have you locked up, I will.

FICSUR. I don't want to talk to you. You're too common. [*He goes out by the door at back and lingers there in plain view*]

[*There is a pause*]

JULIE. Mrs. Muskat is here.

LILIOM. Well, why doesn't she open her mouth, if she has anything to say?

MRS. MUSKAT. Why do you go around with this man Ficsur? He'll get you mixed up in one of his robberies first thing you know.

LILIOM. What's it to you who I go with? I do what I please. What do you want?

MRS. MUSKAT. You know what I want.

LILIOM. No, I don't.

MRS. MUSKAT. What do you suppose I want? Think I've come just to pay a social call?

LILIOM. Do I owe you anything?

MRS. MUSKAT. Yes, you do—but that's not what I came for. You're a fine one to come to for money! You earn so much these days! You know very well what I'm here for.

LILIOM. You've got Hollinger at the carousel, haven't you?

MRS. MUSKAT. Sure I have.

LILIOM. Well, what else do you want? He's as good as I am,

MRS. MUSKAT. You're quite right, my boy. He's every bit as good as you are. I'd not dream of letting him go. But one isn't enough any more. There's work enough for two—

LILIOM. One was enough when *I* was there.

MRS. MUSKAT. Well, I might let Hollinger go—

LILIOM. Why let him go, if he's so good?

MRS. MUSKAT [*shrugs her shoulders*]. Yes, he's good. [*Not once until now has she looked at* LILIOM]

LILIOM [*to* JULIE]. Ask your aunt if I can have a cup of coffee. [JULIE *exits into the kitchen*] So Hollinger is good, is he?

MRS. MUSKAT [*crosses to him and looks him in the face*]. Why don't you stay home and sleep at night? You're a sight to look at.

LILIOM. He's good, is he?

MRS. MUSKAT. Push your hair back from your forehead.

LILIOM. Let my hair be. It's nothing to you.

MRS. MUSKAT. All right. But if I'd told you to let it hang down over your eyes you'd have pushed it back—I hear you've been beating her, this—this—

LILIOM. None of your business.

MRS. MUSKAT. You're a fine fellow! Beating a skinny little thing like that! If you're tired of her, leave her, but there's no use beating the poor—

LILIOM. Leave her, eh? You'd like that, wouldn't you?

MRS. MUSKAT. Don't flatter yourself. [*Quite embarrassed*] Serves me right, too. If I had any sense I wouldn't have run after you— My God, the things one must do for the sake of business! If I could only sell the carousel I wouldn't be sitting here. . . . Come, Liliom, if you have any sense, you'll come back. I'll pay you well.

LILIOM. The carousel is crowded just the same . . . *without me?*

MRS. MUSKAT. Crowded, yes—but it's not the same.

LILIOM. Then you admit that you *do* miss me.

MRS. MUSKAT. Miss you? Not I. But the silly girls miss you. They're always asking for you. Well, are you going to be sensible and come back?

LILIOM. And leave—her?

MRS. MUSKAT. You beat her, don't you?

LILIOM. No, I don't beat her. What's all this damn fool talk about beating her? I hit her once —that was all—and now the whole city seems to be talking about it. You don't call that beating her, do you?

MRS. MUSKAT. All right, all right. I take it back. I don't want to get mixed up in it.

LILIOM. Beating her! As if I'd beat her—

MRS. MUSKAT. I can't make out why you're so concerned about her. You've been married to her two months—it's plain to see that you're sick of it—and out there is the carousel—and the show booths—and money—and you'd throw it all away. For what? Heavens, how can anyone be such a fool? [*Looks at him appraisingly*] Where have you been all night? You look awful.

LILIOM. It's no business of yours.

MRS. MUSKAT. You never used to look like that. This life is telling on you. [*Pauses*] Do you know—I've got a new organ.

LILIOM [*softly*]. I know.

MRS. MUSKAT. How did you know?

LILIOM. You can hear it—from here.

MRS. MUSKAT. It's a good one, eh?

LILIOM [*wistfully*]. Very good. Fine. It roars and snorts—so fine.

MRS. MUSKAT. You should hear it close by —it's heavenly. Even the carousel seems to know . . . it goes quicker. I got rid of those two horses—you know, the ones with the broken ears?

LILIOM. What have you put in their place?

MRS. MUSKAT. Guess.

LILIOM. Zebras?

MRS. MUSKAT. No—an automobile.

LILIOM [*transported*]. An automobile—

MRS. MUSKAT. Yes. If you've got any sense you'll come back. What good are you doing here? Out there is your *art,* the only thing you're fit for. You are an artist, not a respectable married man.

LILIOM. *Leave her—this little—*

MRS. MUSKAT. She'll be better off. She'll go back and be a servant girl again. As for you —you're an artist and you belong among artists. All the beer you want, cigars, a krone a day and a gulden on Sunday, and the girls, Liliom, the girls—I've always treated you right, haven't I? I bought you a watch, and—

LILIOM. She's not that kind. She'd never be a servant girl again.

MRS. MUSKAT. I suppose you think she'd kill herself. Don't worry. Heavens, if every girl was to commit suicide just because her— [*Finishes with a gesture*]

LILIOM [*stares at her a moment, considering, then with sudden, smiling animation*]. So the people don't like Hollinger?

MRS. MUSKAT. You know very well they don't, you rascal.

LILIOM. Well—

MRS. MUSKAT. You've always been happy at the carousel. It's a great life—pretty girls and beer and cigars and music—a great life and an easy one. I'll tell you what—come back and I'll give you a ring that used to belong to my dear departed husband. Well, will you come?

LILIOM. She's not that kind. She'd never be a servant girl again. But—but—for my part—if I decide—that needn't make any difference. I can go on living with her even if I do go back to my art—

MRS. MUSKAT. My God!

LILIOM. What's the matter?

MRS. MUSKAT. Who ever heard of a married man—I suppose you think all the girls would be pleased to know that you were running home to your wife every night. It's ridiculous! When the people found out they'd laugh themselves sick—

LILIOM. I know what you want.

MRS. MUSKAT [*refuses to meet his gaze*]. You flatter yourself.

LILIOM. You'll give me that ring, too?

MRS. MUSKAT [*pushes the hair back from his forehead*]. Yes.

LILIOM. I'm not happy in this house.

MRS. MUSKAT [*still stroking his hair*]. Nobody takes care of you.

[*They are silent. JULIE enters, carrying a cup of coffee. MRS. MUSKAT removes her hand from LILIOM's head. There is a pause*]

LILIOM. Do you want anything?

JULIE. No. [*There is a pause. She exits slowly into the kitchen*]

MRS. MUSKAT. The old woman says there is a carpenter, a widower, who—

LILIOM. I know—I know—

JULIE [*reëntering*]. Liliom, before I forget, I have something to tell you.

LILIOM. All right.

JULIE. I've been wanting to tell you—in fact, I was going to tell you yesterday—

LILIOM. Go ahead.

JULIE. But I must tell you alone—if you'll come in—it will only take a minute.

LILIOM. Don't you see I'm busy now? Here I am talking business and you interrupt with—

JULIE. It'll only take a minute.

LILIOM. Get out of here, or—

JULIE. But I tell you it will only take a minute—

LILIOM. Will you get out of here?

JULIE [*courageously*]. No.

LILIOM [*rising*]. What's that!

JULIE. No.

MRS. MUSKAT [*rises, too*]. Now don't start fighting. I'll go out and look at the photographs in the show-case a while and come back later for your answer. [*She exits at back*]

JULIE. You can hit me again if you like—don't look at me like that. I'm not afraid of you. . . . I'm not afraid of anyone. I told you I had something to tell you.

LILIOM. Well, out with it—quick.

JULIE. I can't tell you so quick. Why don't you drink your coffee?

LILIOM. Is that what you wanted to tell me?

JULIE. No. By the time you've drunk your coffee I'll have told you.

LILIOM [*gets the coffee and sips it*]. Well?

JULIE. Yesterday my head ached—and you asked me—

LILIOM. Yes—

JULIE. Well—you see—that's what it is—

LILIOM. Are you sick?

JULIE. No. . . . But you wanted to know what my headaches came from—and you said I seemed—changed.

LILIOM. Did I? I guess I meant the carpenter.

JULIE. I've been—what? The carpenter? No. It's something entirely different—it's awful hard to tell—but you'll have to know sooner or later—I'm not a bit—scared—because it's a perfectly natural thing—

LILIOM [*puts the coffee cup on the table*]. What?

JULIE. When—when a man and woman— live together—

LILIOM. Yes.

JULIE. I'm going to have a baby. [*She exits swiftly at back*]

[*There is a pause.* FICSUR *appears at the open window and looks in*]

LILIOM. Ficsur! [FICSUR *sticks his head in*] Say, Ficsur,—Julie is going to have a baby.

FICSUR. Yes? What of it?

LILIOM. Nothing. [*Suddenly*] Get out of here. [FICSUR'S *head is quickly withdrawn.* MRS. MUSKAT *reënters*]

MRS. MUSKAT. Has she gone?

LILIOM. Yes.

MRS. MUSKAT. I might as well give you ten kronen in advance. [*Opens her purse.* LILIOM *takes up his coffee cup*] Here you are. [*She proffers some coins.* LILIOM *ignores her*] Why don't you take it?

LILIOM [*Very nonchalantly, his cup poised ready to drink*]. Go home, Mrs. Muskat.

MRS. MUSKAT. What's the matter with you?

LILIOM. Go home [*sips his coffee*] and let me finish my coffee in peace. Don't you see I'm at breakfast?

MRS. MUSKAT. Have you gone crazy?

LILIOM. Will you get out of here? [*Turns to her threateningly*]

MRS. MUSKAT [*restoring the coins to her purse*]. I'll never speak to you again as long as you live.

LILIOM. That worries me a lot.

MRS. MUSKAT. Good-bye!

LILIOM. Good-bye. [*As she exits, he calls*] Ficsur! [FICSUR *enters*] Tell me, Ficsur. You said you knew a way to get a whole lot of money—

FICSUR. Sure I do.

LILIOM. How much?

FICSUR. More than you ever had in your life before. You leave it to an old hand like me.

MOTHER HOLLUNDER [*enters from the kitchen*]. In the morning he must have his coffee, and at noon his soup, and in the eve-

ning coffee again—and plenty of firewood— and I'm expected to furnish it all. Give me back my cup and saucer.

[*The show booths of the amusement-park have opened for business. The familiar noises begin to sound; clear above them all, but far in the distance, sounds the organ of the carousel*]

LILIOM. Now, Aunt Hollunder.

[*From now until the fall of the curtain it is apparent that the sound of the organ makes him more and more uneasy*]

MOTHER HOLLUNDER. And you, you vagabond, get out of here this minute or I'll call my son—

FICSUR. I have nothing to do with the likes of him. He's too common. [*But he slinks out at back*]

LILIOM. Aunt Hollunder!

MOTHER HOLLUNDER. What now?

LILIOM. When your son was born—when you brought him into the world—

MOTHER HOLLUNDER. Well?

LILIOM. Nothing.

MOTHER HOLLUNDER [*muttering as she exits*]. Sleep it off, you good-for-nothing lout. Drink and play cards all night long—that's all you know how to do—and take the bread out of poor people's mouths—you can do that, too. [*She exits*]

LILIOM. Ficsur!

FICSUR [*at the window*]. Julie's going to have a baby. You told me before.

LILIOM. This scheme—about the cashier of the leather factory—there's money in it—

FICSUR. Lots of money—but—it takes two to pull it off.

LILIOM [*meditatively*]. Yes. [*Uneasily*] All right, Ficsur. Go away—and come back later.

[FICSUR *vanishes. The organ in the distant carousel drones incessantly.* LILIOM *listens a while, then goes to the door and calls*]

LILIOM. Aunt Hollunder! [*With naïve joy*] Julie's going to have a baby. [*Then he goes to the window, jumps on the sofa, looks out. Suddenly, in a voice that overtops the droning of the organ, he shouts as if addressing the far-off carousel*] I'm going to be a father.

JULIE [*enters from the kitchen*]. Liliom! What's the matter? What's happened?

LILIOM [*coming down from the sofa*]. Nothing. [*Throws himself on the sofa, buries his face in the cushion*]

[JULIE *watches him a moment, comes over to him and covers him with a shawl. Then she goes on tip-toe to the door at back and remains standing in the doorway, looking out and listening to the droning of the organ*]

THE CURTAIN FALLS

SCENE THREE

SCENE: *The setting is the same, later that afternoon.* LILIOM *is sitting opposite* FICSUR, *who is teaching him a song.* JULIE *hovers in the background, engaged in some household task.*

FICSUR. Listen now. Here's the third verse. [*Sings hoarsely*]

"Look out, look out, my pretty lad,
The damn police are on your trail;
The nicest girl you ever had
Has now commenced to weep and wail:
Look out here comes the damn police,
The damn police,
The damn police,
Look out here comes the damn police,
They'll get you every time."

LILIOM [*sings*].

"Look out, look out, my pretty lad,
The damn police—"

FICSUR, LILIOM [*sing together*].

"Are on your trail
The nicest girl you ever had
Has now commenced to weep and wail."

LILIOM [*alone*].

"Look out here comes the damn police,
The damn police,
The damn police—"

[JULIE, *troubled and uneasy, looks from one to the other, then exits into the kitchen*]

FICSUR [*when she has gone, comes quickly over to* LILIOM *and speaks furtively*]. As you go down Franzen Street you come to the railroad embankment. Beyond that—all the way to the leather factory—there's not a thing in sight, not even a watchman's hut.

LILIOM. And does he always come that way?

FICSUR. Yes. Not along the embankment, but down below along the path across the fields. Since last year he's been going alone. Before that he always used to have someone with him.

LILIOM. Every Saturday?

FICSUR. Every Saturday.

LILIOM. And the money? Where does he keep it?

FICSUR. In a leather bag. The whole week's pay for the workmen at the factory.

LILIOM. Much?

FICSUR. Sixteen thousand kronen. Quite a haul, what?

LILIOM. What's his name?

FICSUR. Linzman. He's a Jew.

LILIOM. The cashier?

FICSUR. Yes—but when he gets a knife between his ribs—or if I smash his skull for him—he won't be a cashier any more.

LILIOM. Does he have to be killed?

FICSUR. No, he doesn't *have* to be. He can give up the money *without* being killed—but most of these cashiers are peculiar—they'd rather be killed.

[JULIE *reënters, pretends to get something on the other side of the room, then exits at back. During the ensuing dialogue she keeps coming in and out in the same way, showing plainly that she is suspicious and anxious. She attempts to overhear what they are saying and, in spite of their caution, does catch a word here and there, which adds to her disquiet.* FICSUR, *catching sight of her, abruptly changes the conversation*]

FICSUR. And the next verse is:

"And when you're in the prison cell
They'll feed you bread and water."

FICSUR AND LILIOM [*sing together*].

"They'll make your little sweetheart tell
Them all the things you brought her.
Look out here comes the damn police,
The damn police,
The damn police.
Look out here comes the damn police
They'll get you every time."

LILIOM [*sings alone*].

"And when you're in the prison cell
They'll feed you bread and water—"

[*Breaks off as* JULIE *exits*]

And when it's done, do we start right off for America?

FICSUR. No.

LILIOM. What then?

FICSUR. We bury the money for six months. That's the usual time. And after the sixth month we dig it up again.

LILIOM. And then?

FICSUR. Then you go on living just as usual for six months more—you don't touch a heller of the money.

LILIOM. In six months the baby will be born.

FICSUR. Then we'll take the baby with us, too. Three months before the time you'll go to work so as to be able to say you saved up your wages to get to America.

LILIOM. Which of us goes up and talks to him?

FICSUR. One of us talks to him with his mouth and the other talks with his knife. Depends on which you'd rather do. I'll tell you what—you talk to him with your mouth.

LILIOM. Do you hear that?

FICSUR. What?

LILIOM. Outside . . . like the rattle of

swords. [FICSUR *listens. After a pause*, LILIOM *continues*] What do I say to him?

FICSUR. You say good evening to him and: "Excuse me, sir; can you tell me the time?"

LILIOM. And then what?

FICSUR. By that time I'll have stuck him— and then you take *your* knife— [*He stops as a* POLICEMAN *enters at back*]

POLICEMAN. Good-day!

FICSUR, LILIOM [*in unison*]. Good-day!

FICSUR [*calling toward the kitchen*]. Hey, photographer, come out. . . . Here's a customer. [*There is a pause. The* POLICEMAN *waits.* FICSUR *sings softly*]

"And when you're in the prison cell
They'll feed you bread and water
They'll make your little sweetheart tell."

LILIOM, FICSUR [*sings together, low*].

"Them all the things you brought her.
Look out here comes the—"

[*They hum the rest so as not to let the* POLICEMAN *hear the words "the damn police." As they sing,* MRS. HOLLUNDER *and her son enter*]

POLICEMAN. Do you make cabinet photographs?

YOUNG HOLLUNDER. Certainly, sir. [*Points to a rack of photographs on the wall*] Take your choice, sir. Would you like one full length?

POLICEMAN. Yes, full length.

[MOTHER HOLLUNDER *pushes out the camera while her son poses the* POLICEMAN, *runs from him to the camera and back again, now altering the pose, now ducking under the black cloth and pushing the camera nearer. Meanwhile* MOTHER HOLLUNDER *has fetched a plate from the dark-room and thrust it in the camera. While this is going on,* LILIOM *and* FICSUR, *their heads together, speak in very low tones*]

LILIOM. Belong around here?

FICSUR. Not around here.

LILIOM. Where, then?

FICSUR. Suburban. [*There is a pause*]

LILIOM [*bursts out suddenly in a rather grotesquely childish and overstrained lament*]. O Gőd, what a dirty life I'm leading—God, God!

FICSUR [*reassuring him benevolently*]. Over in America it will be better, all right.

LILIOM. What's over there?

FICSUR [*virtuously*]. Factories . . . industries—

YOUNG HOLLUNDER [*to the* POLICEMAN]. Now, quite still, please. One, two, three. [*Deftly removes the cover of the lens and in a few seconds restores it*] Thank you.

MOTHER HOLLUNDER. The picture will be ready in five minutes.

POLICEMAN. Good. I'll come back in five minutes. How much do I owe you?

YOUNG HOLLUNDER [*with exaggerated deference*]. You don't need to pay in advance, Mr. Commissioner.

[*The* POLICEMAN *salutes condescendingly and exits at back.* MOTHER HOLLUNDER *carries the plate into the dark-room* YOUNG HOLLUNDER, *after pushing the camera back in place, follows her*]

MOTHER HOLLUNDER [*muttering angrily as she passes* FICSUR *and* LILIOM]. You hang around and dirty the whole place up! Why don't you go take a walk? Things are going so well with you that you have to sing, eh? [*Confronting* FICSUR *suddenly*] Weren't you frightened sick when you saw the policeman?

FICSUR [*with loathing*]. Go 'way, or I'll step on you. [*She exits into the dark-room*]

LILIOM. They like Hollinger at the carousel?

FICSUR. I should say they do.

LILIOM. Did you see the Muskat woman, too?

FICSUR. Sure. She takes care of Hollinger's hair.

LILIOM. Combs his hair?

FICSUR. She fixes him all up.

LILIOM. Let her fix him all she likes.

FICSUR [*urging him toward the kitchen door*]. Go on. Now's your chance.

LILIOM. What for?

FICSUR. To get the knife.

LILIOM. What knife?

FICSUR. The kitchen knife. I've got a pocket-knife, but if he shows fight, we'll let him have the big knife.

LILIOM. What for? If he gets ugly, I'll bat him one over the head that'll make him squint for the rest of his life.

FICSUR. You've got to have something on you. You can't slit his throat with a bat over the head.

LILIOM. Must his throat be slit?

FICSUR. No, it *mustn't*. But if he asks for it. [*There is a pause*] You'd like to sail on the big steamer, wouldn't you? And you want to see the factories over there, don't you? But you're not willing to inconvenience yourself a little for them.

LILIOM. If I take the knife, Julie will see me.

FICSUR. Take it so she won't see you.

LILIOM [*advances a few paces toward the kitchen. The* POLICEMAN *enters at back.* LILIOM *knocks on the door of the dark-room*]. Here's the policeman!

MOTHER HOLLUNDER [*coming out*]. One minute more, please. Just a minute. [*She reënters the dark-room.* LILIOM *hesitates a moment, then exits into the kitchen. The* POLICEMAN *scrutinizes* FICSUR *mockingly.* FICSUR *returns his stare, walks a few paces toward him, then deliberately turns his back. Suddenly he wheels around, points at the* POLICEMAN *and addresses him in a teasing, childish tone*] Christiana Street at the corner of Retti!

POLICEMAN [*amazed, self-conscious*]. How do you know that?

FICSUR. I used to practice my profession in that neighborhood.

POLICEMAN. What is your profession?

FICSUR. Professor of pianola—

[*The* POLICEMAN *glares, aware that the man is joking with him, twirls his moustache indignantly.* YOUNG HOLLUNDER *comes out of the dark-room and gives him the finished pictures*]

YOUNG HOLLUNDER. Here you are, sir.

[*The* POLICEMAN *examines the photographs, pays for them, starts to go, stops, glares at* FICSUR *and exits. When he is gone,* FICSUR *goes to the doorway and looks out after him.* YOUNG HOLLUNDER *exits.* LILIOM *reënters, buttoning his coat*]

FICSUR [*turns, sees* LILIOM]. What are you staring at?

LILIOM. I'm not staring.

FICSUR. What then are you doing?

LILIOM. I'm thinking it over.

FICSUR [*comes very close to him*]. Tell me then—what will you say to him?

LILIOM [*unsteadily*]. I'll say—"Good evening— Excuse me, sir— Can you tell me the time?" And suppose he answers me, what do I say to him?

FICSUR. He won't answer you.

LILIOM. Don't you think so?

FICSUR. No. [*Feeling for the knife under* LILIOM's *coat*] Where is it? Where did you put it?

LILIOM [*stonily*]. Left side.

FICSUR. That's right—over your heart. [*Feels it*] Ah—there it is—there—there's the blade—quite a big fellow, isn't it—ah, here it begins to get narrower. [*Reaches the tip of the knife*] And here is its eye—that's what it sees with. [JULIE *enters from the kitchen, passes them slowly, watching them in silent terror, then stops.* FICSUR *nudges* LILIOM] Sing, come on, sing!

LILIOM [*in a quavering voice*].

"Look out for the damn police."

FICSUR [*joining in, cheerily, loudly, marking time with the swaying of his body*].

"Look out, look out, my pretty lad."

LILIOM. "—look out, my pretty lad." [JULIE *goes out at back.* LILIOM's *glance follows her. When she has gone, he turns to* FICSUR] At night—in my dreams—if his ghost comes back—what will I do then?

FICSUR. His ghost won't never come back.

LILIOM. Why not?

FICSUR. A Jew's ghost don't come back.

LILIOM. Well then—afterwards—

FICSUR [*impatiently*]. What do you mean—afterwards?

LILIOM. In the next world—when I come up before the Lord God—what'll I say then?

FICSUR. The likes of you will never come up before Him.

LILIOM. Why not?

FICSUR. Have you ever come up before the high court?

LILIOM. No.

FICSUR. Our kind comes up before the police magistrate—and the highest we *ever* get is the criminal court.

LILIOM. Will it be the same in the next world?

FICSUR. Just the same. We'll come up before a police magistrate, same as we did in this world.

LILIOM. A police magistrate?

FICSUR. Sure. For the rich folks—the Heavenly Court. For us poor people—only a police magistrate. For the rich folks—fine music and angels. For us—

LILIOM. For us?

FICSUR. For us, my son, there's only justice. In the next world there'll be lots of justice, yes, nothing but justice. And where there's justice there must be police magistrates; and where there're police magistrates, people like us get—

LILIOM [*interrupting*]. Good evening. Excuse me, sir, can you tell me the time? [*Lays his hand over his heart*]

FICSUR. What do you put your hand there for?

LILIOM. My heart is jumping—under the knife.

FICSUR. Put it on the other side then. [*Looks out at the sky*] It's time we started—we'll walk slow—

LILIOM. It's too early.

FICSUR. Come on.

[*As they are about to go,* JULIE *appears in the doorway at back, obstructing the way*]

JULIE. Where are you going with him?

LILIOM. Where am I going with him?

JULIE. Stay home.

LILIOM. No.

JULIE. Stay home. It's going to rain soon, and you'll get wet.

FICSUR. It won't rain.

JULIE. How do you know?

FICSUR. I always get notice in advance.

JULIE. Stay home. This evening the carpenter's coming. I've asked him to give you work.

LILIOM. I'm not a carpenter.

JULIE [*more and more anxious, though she tries to conceal it*]. Stay home. Marie's coming with her intended to have their picture taken.

She wants to introduce us to her intended husband.

LILIOM. I've seen enough intended husbands—

JULIE. Stay home. Marie's bringing some money, and I'll give it all to you.

LILIOM [*approaching the door*]. I'm going —for a walk—with Ficsur. We'll be right back.

JULIE [*forcing a smile to keep back her tears*]. If you stay home, I'll get you a glass of beer—or wine, if you prefer.

FICSUR. Coming or not?

JULIE. I'm not angry with you any more for hitting me.

LILIOM [*gruffly, but his gruffness is simulated to hide the fact that he cannot bear the sight of her suffering*]. Stand out of the way—or I'll— [*He clenches his fist*] Let me out!

JULIE [*trembling*]. What have you got under your coat?

LILIOM [*produces from his pocket a greasy pack of cards*]. Cards.

JULIE [*trembling, speaks very low*]. What's under your coat?

LILIOM. Let me out!

JULIE [*obstructing the way. Speaks quickly, eagerly, in a last effort to detain him*]. Marie's intended knows about a place for a married couple without children to be caretakers of a house on Arader Street. Rent free, a kitchen of your own, and the privilege of keeping chickens—

LILIOM. Get out of the way!

[*JULIE stands aside. LILIOM exits. FICSUR follows him. JULIE remains standing meditatively in the doorway. MOTHER HOLLUNDER comes out of the kitchen*]

MOTHER HOLLUNDER. I can't find my kitchen knife anywhere. Have you seen anything of it?

JULIE [*horrified*]. No.

MOTHER HOLLUNDER. It was on the kitchen table just a few minutes ago. No one was in there except Liliom.

JULIE. He didn't take it.

MOTHER HOLLUNDER. No one else was in there.

JULIE. What would Liliom want with a kitchen knife?

MOTHER HOLLUNDER. He'd sell it and spend the money on drink.

JULIE. It just so happens—see how unjust you are to him—it just so happens that I went through all of Liliom's pockets just now—I wanted to see if he had any money on him. But he had nothing but a pack of cards.

MOTHER HOLLUNDER [*returns to the kitchen, grumbling*]. Cards in his pocket—cards! The fine gentlemen have evidently gone off to their club to play a little game. [*She exits*]

[*After a pause MARIE, happy and beaming, appears in the doorway at back, and enters, followed by WOLF*]

MARIE. Here we are! [*She takes WOLF by the hand and leads him, grinning shyly, to JULIE, who has turned at her call*] Hello!

JULIE. Hello.

MARIE. Well, we're here.

JULIE. Yes.

WOLF [*bows awkwardly and extends his hand*]. My name is Wolf Beifeld.

JULIE. My name is Julie Zeller.

[*They shake hands. There is an embarrassed silence. Then, to relieve the situation, WOLF takes JULIE's hand again and shakes it vigorously*]

MARIE. Well—this is Wolf.

WOLF. Yes.

JULIE. Yes.

[*Another awkward silence*]

MARIE. Where is Liliom?

WOLF. Yes, where is your husband?

JULIE. He's out.

MARIE. Where?

JULIE. Just for a walk.

MARIE. Is he?

JULIE. Yes.

WOLF. Oh!

[*Another silence*]

MARIE. Wolf's got a new place. After the first of the month he won't have to stand outside any more. He's going to work in a club after the first of the month.

WOLF [*apologetically*]. She don't know yet how to explain these things just right—hehehe— Beginning the first I'm to be second steward at the Burger Club—a good job, if one conducts oneself properly.

JULIE. Yes?

WOLF. The pay—is quite good—but the main thing is the tips. When they play cards there's always a bit for the steward. The tips, I may say, amount to twenty, even thirty kronen every night.

MARIE. Yes.

WOLF. We've rented two rooms for ourselves to start with—and if things go well—

MARIE. Then we'll buy a house in the country.

WOLF. If one only tends to business and keeps honest. Of course, in the country we'll miss the city life, but if the good Lord sends us children—it's much healthier for children in the country.

[*There is a brief pause*]

MARIE. Wolf's nice looking, isn't he?

JULIE. Yes.

MARIE. And he's a good boy, Wolf.

JULIE. Yes.

MARIE. The only thing is—he's a Jew.

JULIE. Oh, well, you can get used to that.

MARIE. Well, aren't you going to wish us luck?

JULIE. Of course I do. [*She embraces MARIE*]

MARIE. And aren't you going to kiss Wolf, too?

JULIE. Him, too. [*She embraces* WOLF, *remains quite still a moment, her head resting on his shoulder*]

WOLF. Why are you crying, my dear Mrs.— [*He looks questioningly at* MARIE *over* JULIE'S *shoulder*]

MARIE. Because she has such a good heart. [*She becomes sentimental, too*]

WOLF [*touched*]. We thank you for your heartfelt sympathy— [*He cannot restrain his own tears*]

   [*There is a pause before* MOTHER HOLLUNDER *and her son enter.* YOUNG HOLLUNDER *immediately busies himself with the camera*]

MOTHER HOLLUNDER. Now if you don't mind, we'll do it right away, before it gets too dark. [*She leads* MARIE *and* WOLF *into position before the background-screen. Here they immediately fall into an awkward pose, smiling mechanically*] Full length?

MARIE. Please. Both figures full length.

MOTHER HOLLUNDER. Bride and groom?

MARIE. Yes.

MOTHER HOLLUNDER, YOUNG HOLLUNDER [*speak in unison, in loud professionally expressionless tones*]. The lady looks at the gentleman and the gentleman looks straight into the camera.

MOTHER HOLLUNDER [*poses first* MARIE, *then* WOLF]. Now, if you please.

YOUNG HOLLUNDER [*who has crept under the black cloth, calls in muffled tones*]. That's good—that's very good!

MARIE [*stonily rigid, but very happy, trying to speak without altering her expression*]. Julie, dear, do we look all right?

JULIE. Yes, dear.

YOUNG HOLLUNDER. Now, if you please, hold still. I'll count up to three, and then you must hold perfectly still. [*Grasps the cover of the lens and calls threateningly*] One—two—three! [*He removes the cover; there is utter silence. But as he speaks the word "one" there is heard, very faintly in the distance, the refrain of the thieves' song which* FICSUR *and* LILIOM *have been singing. The refrain continues until the fall of the curtain. As he speaks the word "three" everybody is perfectly rigid save* JULIE, *who lets her head sink slowly to the table. The distant refrain dies out*]

THE CURTAIN FALLS

SCENE FOUR

SCENE: *In the fields on the outskirts of the city. At back a railroad embankment crosses the stage obliquely. At center of the embankment stands a red and white signal flag, and near it a little red signal lamp which is not yet lighted. Here also a wooden stairway leads up to the embankment.*

   At the foot of the embankment to the right is a pile of used railroad ties. In the background a telegraph pole, beyond it a view of trees, fences and fields; still further back a factory building and a cluster of little dwellings.

   It is six o'clock of the same afternoon. Dusk has begun to fall.

   LILIOM *and* FICSUR *are discovered on the stairway looking after the train which has just passed.*

LILIOM. Can you still hear it snort?

FICSUR. Listen! [*They watch the vanishing train*]

LILIOM. If you put your ear on the tracks you can hear it go all the way to Vienna.

FICSUR. Huh!

LILIOM. The one that just puffed past us— it goes all the way to Vienna.

FICSUR. No further?

LILIOM. Yes—further, too.

   [*There is a pause*]

FICSUR. It must be near six. [*As* LILIOM *ascends the steps*] Where are you going?

LILIOM. Don't be afraid. I'm not giving you the slip.

FICSUR. Why should you give me the slip? That cashier has sixteen thousand kronen on him. Just be patient till he comes, then you can talk to him, nice and polite.

LILIOM. I say, "Good evening—excuse me, sir; what time is it?"

FICSUR. Then he tells you what time it is.

LILIOM. Suppose he don't come?

FICSUR [*coming down the steps*]. Nonsense! He's got to come. He pays off the workmen every Saturday. And this is Saturday, ain't it? [LILIOM *has ascended to the top of the stairway and is gazing along the tracks*]. What are you looking up there?

LILIOM. The tracks go on and on—there's no end to them.

FICSUR. What's that to stare about?

LILIOM. Nothing—only I always look after the train. When you stand down there at night it snorts past you, and spits down.

FICSUR. Spits?

LILIOM. Yes, the engine. It spits down. And then the whole train rattles past and away— and you stand there—spat on—but it draws your eyes along with it.

FICSUR. Draws your eyes along?

LILIOM. Yes—whether you want to or not, you've got to look after it—as long as the tiniest bit of it is in sight.

FICSUR. Swell people sit in it.

LILIOM. And read newspapers.

FICSUR. And smoke cigars.

LILIOM. And inhale the smoke.

   [*There is a short silence*]

FICSUR. Is he coming?

LILIOM. Not yet. [*Silence again.* LILIOM *comes down, speaks low, confidentially*] Do you hear the telegraph wires?

FICSUR. I hear them when the wind blows.

LILIOM. Even when the wind doesn't blow you can hear them humming, humming—People talk through them.

FICSUR. Who?

LILIOM. Jews.

FICSUR. No—they telegraph.

LILIOM. They talk through them and from some other place they get answered. And it all goes through the iron strings—that's why they hum like that—they hum-m—

FICSUR. What do they hum?

LILIOM. They hum! ninety-nine, ninety-nine. Just listen.

FICSUR. What for?

LILIOM. That sparrow's listening, too. He's cocked one eye and looks at me as if to say: "I'd like to know what they're talking about."

FICSUR. You're looking at a bird?

LILIOM. He's looking at me, too.

FICSUR. Listen, you're sick! There's something the matter with you. Do you know what it is? Money. That bird has no money, either; that's why he cocks his eye.

LILIOM. Maybe.

FICSUR. Whoever has money don't cock his eye.

LILIOM. What then does he do?

FICSUR. He does most anything he wants. But nobody works unless he has money. We'll soon have money ourselves.

LILIOM. I say, "Good evening. Excuse me, sir, can you tell me what time it is!"

FICSUR. He's not coming yet. Got the cards? [LILIOM *gives him the pack of cards*] Got any money?

LILIOM [*takes some coins from his trousers pocket and counts*]. Eleven.

FICSUR [*sits astride on the pile of ties and looks off left*]. All right—eleven.

LILIOM [*sitting astride on the ties facing him*]. Put it up.

FICSUR [*puts the money on the ties; rapidly shuffles the cards*]. We'll play twenty-one. I'll bank. [*He deals deftly*]

LILIOM [*looks at his card*]. Good. I'll bet the bank.

FICSUR. Must have an ace! [*Deals him a second card*]

LILIOM. Another one. [*He gets another card*] Another. [*Gets still another*] Over! [*Throws down his cards.* FICSUR *gathers in the money*] Come on!

FICSUR. Come on what? Got no more money, have you?

LILIOM. No.

FICSUR. Then the game's over—unless you want to—

LILIOM. What?

FICSUR. Play on credit.

LILIOM. You'll trust me?

FICSUR. No—but—I'll deduct it.

LILIOM. Deduct it from what?

FICSUR. From your share of the money. If *you* win you deduct from my share.

LILIOM [*looks over his shoulder to see if the cashier is coming; nervous and ashamed*]. All right. How much is bank?

FICSUR. That cashier is bringing us sixteen thousand kronen. Eight thousand of that is mine. Well, then, the bank is eight thousand.

LILIOM. Good.

FICSUR. Whoever has the most luck will have the most money. [*He deals*]

LILIOM. Six hundred kronen. [FICSUR *gives him another card*] Enough.

FICSUR [*laying out his own cards*]. Twenty-one. [*He shuffles rapidly*]

LILIOM [*moves excitedly nearer to* FICSUR]. Well, then, double or nothing.

FICSUR [*dealing*]. Double or nothing.

LILIOM [*gets a card*]. Enough.

FICSUR [*laying out his own cards*]. Twenty-one. [*Shuffles rapidly again*]

LILIOM [*in alarm*]. You're not—cheating?

FICSUR. Me? Do I look like a cheat? [*Deals the cards again*]

LILIOM [*glances nervously over his shoulder*]. A thousand.

FICSUR [*nonchalantly*]. Kronen?

LILIOM. Kronen. [*He gets a card*] Another one. [*Gets another card*] Over again!

[*Like an inexperienced gambler who is losing heavily,* LILIOM *is very nervous. He plays dazedly, wildly, irrationally. From now on it is apparent that his only thought is to win his money back*]

FICSUR. That makes twelve hundred you owe.

LILIOM. Double or nothing. [*He gets a card. He is greatly excited*] Another one. [*Gets another card*] Another. [*Throws down three cards*]

FICSUR [*bends over and adds up the sum on the ground*]. Ten—fourteen—twenty-three—You owe two thousand, four hundred.

LILIOM. Now what?

FICSUR [*takes a card out of the deck and gives it to him*]. Here's the red ace. You can play double or nothing again.

LILIOM [*eagerly*]. Good. [*Gets another card*] Enough.

FICSUR [*turns up his own cards*]. Nineteen.

LILIOM. You win again. [*Almost imploring*] Give me an ace again. Give me the green one. [*Takes a card*] Double or nothing.

FICSUR. Not any more.

LILIOM. Why not?

FICSUR. Because if you lose you won't b

able to pay. Double would be nine thousand six hundred. And you've only got eight thousand altogether.

LILIOM [*greatly excited*]. That—that—I call that—a dirty trick!

FICSUR. Three thousand, two hundred. That's all you can put up.

LILIOM [*eagerly*]. All right, then—three thousand, two hundred. [FICSUR *deals him a card*] Enough.

FICSUR. I've got an ace myself. Now we'll have to take our time and squeeze 'em. [LILIOM *pushes closer to him as he takes up his cards and slowly, intently unfolds them*] Twenty-one. [*He quickly puts the cards in his pocket. There is a pause*]

LILIOM. Now—now—I'll tell you now—you're a crook, a low-down— [*Now* LINZMAN *enters at right. He is a strong, robust, red-bearded Jew about 40 years of age. At his side he carries a leather bag slung by a strap from his shoulder.* FICSUR *coughs warningly, moves to the right between* LINZMAN *and the embankment, pauses just behind* LINZMAN *and follows him.* LILIOM *stands bewildered a few paces to the left of the railroad ties. He finds himself facing* LINZMAN. *Trembling in every limb*] Good evening. Excuse me, sir, can you tell me the time?

[FICSUR *springs silently at* LINZMAN, *the little knife in his right hand. But* LINZMAN *catches* FICSUR'S *right hand with his own left and forces* FICSUR *to his knees. Simultaneously* LINZMAN *thrusts his right hand into his coat pocket and produces a revolver which he points at* LILIOM'S *breast.* LILIOM *is standing two paces away from the revolver. There is a long pause*]

LINZMAN [*in a low, even voice*.] It is twenty-five minutes past six. [*Pauses, looks ironically down at* FICSUR] It's lucky I grabbed the hand with the knife instead of the other one. [*Pauses again, looks appraisingly from one to the other*] Two fine birds! [*To* FICSUR] I should live so—Rothschild has more luck than you. [*To* LILIOM] I'd advise you to keep nice and quiet. If you make one move, you'll get two bullets in you. Just look into the barrel. You'll see some little things in there made of lead.

FICSUR. Let me go. I didn't do anything.

LINZMAN [*mockingly shakes the hand which still holds the knife*]. And this? What do you call this? Oh, yes, I know. You thought I had an apple in my pocket, and you wanted to peel it. That's it. Forgive me for my error. I beg your pardon, sir.

LILIOM. But I—I—

LINZMAN. Yes, my son, I know. It's so simple. You only asked what time it is. Well, it's twenty-five minutes after six.

FICSUR. Let us go, honorable sir. We didn't do anything to you.

LINZMAN. In the first place, my son, I'm not an honorable sir. In the second place, for the same money, you could have said Your Excellency. But in the third place you'll find it very hard to beg off by flattering me.

LILIOM. But I—*I* really didn't do anything to you.

LINZMAN. Look behind you, my boy. Don't be afraid. Look behind you, but don't run away or I'll have to shoot you down. [LILIOM *turns his head slowly around*] Who's coming up there?

LILIOM [*looking at* LINZMAN]. Policemen.

LINZMAN [*to* FICSUR]. You hold still, or— [*To* LILIOM *teasingly*] How many policemen are there?

LILIOM [*his eyes cast down*]. Two.

LINZMAN. And what are the policemen sitting on?

LILIOM. Horses.

LINZMAN. And which can run faster, a horse or a man?

LILIOM. A horse.

LINZMAN. There, you see. It would be hard to get away now. [*Laughs*] I never saw such an unlucky pair of highway robbers. I can't imagine worse luck. Just today I had to put a pistol in my pocket. And even if I hadn't—old Linzman is a match for four like you. But even that isn't all. Did you happen to notice, you oxen, what direction I came from? From the factory, didn't I? When I *went* there I had a nice bit of money with me. Sixteen thousand crowns! But now—not a heller. [*Calls off left*] Hey, come quicker, will you? This fellow is pulling pretty strong. [FICSUR *frees himself with a mighty wrench and darts rapidly off. As* LINZMAN *aims his pistol at the vanishing* FICSUR, LILIOM *runs up the steps to the embankment.* LINZMAN *hesitates, perceives that* LILIOM *is the better target, points the pistol at him*] Stop, or I'll shoot! [*Calls off left to the* POLICEMEN] Why don't you come down off your horses? [*His pistol is leveled at* LILIOM, *who stands on the embankment, facing the audience.*

[*From the left on the embankment a* PO-LICEMAN *appears, revolver in hand*]

FIRST POLICEMAN. Stop!

LINZMAN. Well, my boy, do you still want to know what time it is? From ten to twelve years in prison!

LILIOM. You won't get me! [LINZMAN *laughs derisively.* LILIOM *is now three or four paces from the* POLICEMAN *and equally distant from* LINZMAN. *His face is uplifted to the sky. He bursts into laughter, half defiant, half self-pitying, and takes the kitchen knife from under his coat*] Julie—

[*The ring of farewell is in the word. He*

turns sideways, thrusts the knife deep
in his breast, sways, falls and rolls down
the far side of the embankment. There is
a long pause. From the left up on the
embankment come the TWO POLICE-
MEN]

LINZMAN. What's the matter? [The FIRST
POLICEMAN comes along the embankment as
far as the steps, looks down in the opposite
side, then climbs down at about the spot where
LILIOM disappeared. LINZMAN and the other
POLICEMAN mount the embankment and look
down on him] Stabbed himself?

VOICE OF FIRST POLICEMAN. Yes—and he
seems to have made a thorough job of it.

LINZMAN [excitedly to the SECOND POLICE-
MAN]. I'll go and telephone to the hospital. [He
runs down the steps and exits at left]

SECOND POLICEMAN. Go to Eisler's grocery
store and telephone to the factory from there.
They've a doctor there, too. [Calling down to
the other POLICEMAN] I'm going to tie up the
horses. [Comes down the steps and exits at
left]

[The stage is empty. There is a pause. The
little red signal lamp is lit]

VOICE OF FIRST POLICEMAN. Hey, Stephan!
VOICE OF SECOND POLICEMAN. What?
VOICE OF FIRST POLICEMAN. Shall I pull the
knife out of his chest?

VOICE OF SECOND POLICEMAN. Better not, or
he may bleed to death.

[There is a pause]

VOICE OF FIRST POLICEMAN. Stephan!
VOICE OF SECOND POLICEMAN. Yes.
VOICE OF FIRST POLICEMAN. Lot of mos-
quitoes around here.

VOICE OF SECOND POLICEMAN. Yes.
VOICE OF FIRST POLICEMAN. Got a cigar?
VOICE OF SECOND POLICEMAN. No.

[There is a pause. The FIRST POLICEMAN
appears over the opposite side of the
embankment]

FIRST POLICEMAN. A lot of good the new
pay-schedule's done us—made things worse
than they used to be—we get more but we
have less than we ever had. If the Government
could be made to realize that. It's a thankless
job at best. You work hard year after year,
you get gray in the service, and slowly you
die—yes.

SECOND POLICEMAN. That's right.
FIRST POLICEMAN. Yes.

[In the distance is heard the bell of the
signal tower]

THE CURTAIN FALLS

SCENE FIVE

SCENE: The photographic "studio" a half
hour later that same evening.

[MOTHER HOLLUNDER, her son, MARIE and
WOLF stand in a group back right, their
heads together. JULIE stands apart
from them, a few paces to the left]

YOUNG HOLLUNDER [who has just come in,
tells his story excitedly]. They're bringing him
now. Two workmen from the factory are carrying him on a stretcher.

WOLF. Where is the doctor?

YOUNG HOLLUNDER. A policeman telephoned to headquarters. The police-surgeon
ought to be here any minute.

MARIE. Maybe they'll pull him through after
all.

YOUNG HOLLUNDER. He stabbed himself too
deep in his chest. But he's still breathing. He
can still talk, too, but very faintly. At first he
lay there unconscious, but when they put him
on the stretcher he came to.

WOLF. That was from the shaking.

MARIE. We'd better make room.

[They make room. Two workmen carry
in LILIOM on a stretcher which has four
legs and stands about as high as a bed.
They put the stretcher at left directly
in front of the sofa, so that the head is
at right and the foot at left. Then they
unobtrusively join the group at the
door. Later, they go out. JULIE is standing at the side of the stretcher, where,
without moving, she can see LILIOM's
face. The others crowd emotionally together near the door. The FIRST POLICE-
MAN enters]

FIRST POLICEMAN. Are you his wife?

JULIE. Yes.

FIRST POLICEMAN. The doctor at the factory
who bandaged him up forbade us to take him
to the hospital.—Dangerous to move him that
far. What he needs now is rest. Just let him be
until the police-surgeon comes. [To the group
near the door] He's not to be disturbed.

[They make way for him. He exits. There
is a pause]

WOLF [gently urging the others out]. Please
—it's best if we all get out of here now. We'll
only be in the way.

MARIE [to JULIE]. Julie, what do you
think? [JULIE looks at her without answer-
ing] Julie, can I do anything to help? [JULIE
does not answer] We'll be just outside on the
bench if you want us.

[MOTHER HOLLUNDER and her son have
gone out when first requested. Now
MARIE and WOLF exit, too. JULIE sits on
the edge of the stretcher and looks at
LILIOM. He stretches his hand out to
her. She clasps it. It is not quite dark
yet. Both of them can still be plainly
seen]

LILIOM [raises himself with difficulty,
speaks lightly at first, but later soberly, defi

antly]. Little—Julie—there's something—I want to tell you—like when you go to a restaurant—and you've finished eating—and it's time—to pay—then you have to count up everything—everything you owe—well—I beat you—not because I was mad at you—no—only because I can't bear to see anyone crying. You always cried—on my account—and, well, you see,—I never learned a trade—what kind of a caretaker would I make? But anyhow—I wasn't going back to the carousel to fool with the girls. No, I spit on them all—understand?

JULIE. Yes.

LILIOM. And—as for Hollinger—he's good enough—Mrs. Muskat can get along all right with him. The jokes he tells are mine—and the people laugh when he tells them—but I don't care.—I didn't give you anything—no home—not even the food you ate—but you don't understand.—It's true I'm not much good—but I couldn't be a caretaker—and so I thought maybe it would be better over there—in America—do you see?

JULIE. Yes.

LILIOM. I'm not asking—forgiveness—I don't do that—I don't. Tell the baby—if you like.

JULIE. Yes.

LILIOM. Tell the baby—I wasn't much good—but tell him—if you ever talk about me—tell him—I thought—perhaps—over in America—but that's no affair of yours. I'm not asking forgiveness. For my part the police can come now.—If it's a boy—if it's a girl.—Perhaps I'll see the Lord God today.—Do you think I'll see Him?

JULIE. Yes.

LILIOM. I'm not afraid—of the police Up There—if they'll only let me come up in front of the Lord God Himself—not like down here where an officer stops you at the door. If the carpenter asks you—yes—be his wife—marry him. And the child—tell him he's his father.—He'll believe you—won't he?

JULIE. Yes.

LILIOM. When I beat you—I was right.—You mustn't always think—you mustn't always be right.—Liliom can be right once, too.—It's all the same to me who was right.—It's so dumb. Nobody's right—but they all think they are right.—A lot they know!

JULIE. Yes.

LILIOM. Julie—come—hold my hand tight.

JULIE. I'm holding it tight—all the time.

LILIOM. Tighter, still tighter—I'm going— [*Pauses*] Julie—

JULIE. Good-bye.

[LILIOM *sinks slowly back and dies.* JULIE *frees her hand.* THE DOCTOR *enters with the* FIRST POLICEMAN]

DOCTOR. Good evening. His wife?

JULIE. Yes, sir.

[*Behind the* DOCTOR *and* POLICEMAN *en-*

ter MARIE, WOLF, MOTHER HOLLUNDER, YOUNG HOLLUNDER *and* MRS. MUSKAT. *They remain respectfully at the doorway. The* DOCTOR *bends over* LILIOM *and examines him*]

DOCTOR. A light, if you please. [JULIE *fetches a burning candle from the dark-room. The* DOCTOR *examines* LILIOM *briefly in the candle-light, then turns suddenly away*] Have you pen and ink?

WOLF [*proffering a pen*]. A fountain-pen—American—

DOCTOR [*takes a printed form from his pocket; speaks as he writes out the death-certificate at the little table*]. My poor woman, your husband is dead—there's nothing to be done for him—the good God will help him now—I'll leave this certificate with you. You will give it to the people from the hospital when they come—I'll arrange for the body to be removed at once. [*Rises*] Please give me a towel and soap.

POLICEMAN. I've got them for you out here, sir. [*Points to door at back*]

DOCTOR. God be with you, my good woman.

JULIE. Thank you, sir.

[*The* DOCTOR *and* POLICEMAN *exit. The others slowly draw nearer*]

MARIE. Poor Julie. May he rest in peace, poor man, but as for you—please don't be angry with me for saying it—but you're better off this way.

MOTHER HOLLUNDER. He is better off, the poor fellow, and so are you.

MARIE. Much better, Julie . . . you are young . . . and one of these days some good man will come along. Am I right?

WOLF. She's right.

MARIE. Julie, tell me, am I right?

JULIE. You are right, dear; you are very good.

YOUNG HOLLUNDER. There's a good man—the carpenter. Oh, I can speak of it now. He comes here every day on some excuse or other—and he never fails to ask for you.

MARIE. A widower—with two children.

MOTHER HOLLUNDER. He's better off, poor fellow—and so are you. He was a bad man.

MARIE. He wasn't good-hearted. Was he, Wolf?

WOLF. No, I must say, he really wasn't. No, Liliom wasn't a good man. A good man doesn't strike a woman.

MARIE. Am I right? Tell me, Julie, am I right?

JULIE. You are right, dear.

YOUNG HOLLUNDER. It's really a good thing for her it happened.

MOTHER HOLLUNDER. He's better off—and so is she.

WOLF. Now you have your freedom again. How old are you?

JULIE. Eighteen.

WOLF. Eighteen. A mere child! Am I right?

JULIE. You are right, Wolf. You are kind.

YOUNG HOLLUNDER. Lucky for you it happened, isn't it?

JULIE. Yes.

YOUNG HOLLUNDER. All you had before was bad luck. If it weren't for my mother you wouldn't have had a roof over your head or a bite to eat—and now Autumn's coming and Winter. You couldn't have lived in this shack in the winter time, could you?

MARIE. Certainly not! You'd have frozen like the birds in the fields. Am I right, Julie?

JULIE. Yes, Marie.

MARIE. A year from now you will have forgotten all about him, won't you?

JULIE. You are right, Marie.

WOLF. If you need anything, count on us. We'll go now. But tomorrow morning we'll be back. Come, Marie. God be with you. [Offers JULIE his hand]

JULIE. God be with you.

MARIE [embraces JULIE, weeping]. It's the best thing that could have happened to you, Julie, the best thing.

JULIE. Don't cry, Marie.

[MARIE and WOLF exit]

MOTHER HOLLUNDER. I'll make a little black coffee. You haven't had a thing to eat today. Then you'll come home with us.

[MOTHER HOLLUNDER and her son exit.
MRS. MUSKAT comes over to JULIE]

MRS. MUSKAT. Would you mind if I—looked at him?

JULIE. He used to work for you.

MRS. MUSKAT [contemplates the body; turns to JULIE]. Won't you make up with me?

JULIE. I wasn't angry with you.

MRS. MUSKAT. But you were. Let's make it up.

JULIE [raising her voice eagerly, almost triumphantly]. I've nothing to make up with you.

MRS. MUSKAT. But I have with you. Everyone says hard things against the poor dead boy—except us two. You don't say he was bad.

JULIE [raising her voice yet higher, this time on a defiant, wholly triumphant note] Yes, I do.

MRS. MUSKAT. I understand, my child. But he beat me, too. What does that matter? I've forgotten it.

JULIE [from now on answers her coldly, drily, without looking at her] That's your own affair.

MRS. MUSKAT. If I can help you in any way—

JULIE. There's nothing I need.

MRS. MUSKAT. I still owe him two kronen, back pay.

JULIE. You should have paid him.

MRS. MUSKAT. Now that the poor fellow is dead I thought perhaps it would be the same if I paid you.

JULIE. I've nothing to do with it.

MRS. MUSKAT. All right. Please don't think I'm trying to force myself on you. I stayed because we two are the only ones on earth who loved him. That's why I thought we ought to stick together.

JULIE. No, thank you.

MRS. MUSKAT. Then you couldn't have loved him as I did.

JULIE. No.

MRS. MUSKAT. I loved him better.

JULIE. Yes.

MRS. MUSKAT. Good-bye.

JULIE. Good-bye. [MRS. MUSKAT exits. JULIE puts the candle on the table near LILIOM's head, sits on the edge of the stretcher looks into the dead man's face and caresses it tenderly] Sleep, Liliom, sleep—it's no business of hers—I never even told you—but now I'll tell you—now I'll tell you—you bad, quick tempered, rough, unhappy, wicked—dear boy—sleep peacefully, Liliom—they can't understand how I feel—I can't even explain to you—not even to you—how I feel—you'd only laugh at me—but you can't hear me any more [Between tender motherliness and reproach yet with great love in her voice] It was wicked of you to beat me—on the breast and on the head and face—but you're gone now.—You treated me badly—that was wicked of you—but sleep peacefully, Liliom—you bad, bad boy—I love you—I never told you before—was ashamed—but now I've told you—I love you. Liliom—sleep—my boy—sleep. [She rises gets a Bible, sits down near the candle and reads softly to herself, so that, not the words but an inarticulate murmur is heard]

[The CARPENTER enters at back]

CARPENTER [stands near the door; in the dimness of the room he can scarcely be seen] Miss Julie—

JULIE [without alarm]. Who is that?

CARPENTER [very slowly]. The carpenter.

JULIE. What does the carpenter want?

CARPENTER. Can I be of help to you in any way? Shall I stay here with you?

JULIE [gratefully, but firmly]. Don't stay carpenter.

CARPENTER. Shall I come back tomorrow?

JULIE. Not tomorrow, either.

CARPENTER. Don't be offended, Miss Julie but I'd like to know—you see, I'm not a young man any more—I have two children—and I'm to come back any more—I'd like to know —if there's any use—

JULIE. No use, carpenter.

CARPENTER [as he exits]. God be with you.

[JULIE resumes her reading. FICSUR enters, slinks furtively sideways to the stretcher, looks at LILIOM, shakes his head. JULIE looks up from her reading. FICSUR takes fright, slinks away from the stretcher, sits down at right, biting his nails. JULIE rises. FICSUR rises, too, and looks at her half fearfully. With her piercing glance upon him he slinks to the doorway at back, where he pauses and speaks]

FICSUR. The old woman asked me to tell you that coffee is ready, and you are to come in.

[JULIE goes to the kitchen door. FICSUR withdraws until she has closed the door behind her. Then he reappears in the doorway, stands on tiptoes, looks at LILIOM, then exits. Now the body lies alone. After a brief silence music is heard, distant at first, but gradually coming nearer. It is very much like the music of the carousel, but slower, graver, more exalted. The melody, too, is the same, yet the tempo is altered and contrapuntal measures of the thieves' song are intertwined in it. Two men in black, with heavy sticks, soft black hats and black gloves, appear in the doorway at back and stride slowly into the room. Their faces are beardless, marble white, grave and benign. One stops in front of the stretcher, the other a pace to the right. From above a dim violet light illuminates their faces]

THE FIRST [to LILIOM]. Rise and come with us.

THE SECOND [politely]. You're under arrest.

THE FIRST [somewhat louder, but always in a gentle, low, resonant voice]. Do you hear? Rise. Don't you hear?

THE SECOND. We are the police.

THE FIRST [bends down, touches LILIOM's shoulder]. Get up and come with us.

[LILIOM slowly sits up]

THE SECOND. Come along.

THE FIRST [paternally]. These people suppose that when they die all their difficulties are solved for them.

THE SECOND [raising his voice sternly]. That simply by thrusting a knife in your heart and making it stop beating you can leave your wife behind her with a child in her womb—

THE FIRST. It is not as simple as that.

THE SECOND. Such things are not settled so easily.

THE FIRST. Come along. You will have to give an account of yourself. [As both bow their heads, he continues softly] We are God's police.

[An expression of glad relief lights upon LILIOM's face. He rises from the stretcher] Come.

THE SECOND. You mortals don't get off quite so easy as that.

THE FIRST [softly]. Come. [LILIOM starts to walk ahead of them, then stops and looks at them] The end is not as abrupt as that. Your name is still spoken. Your face is still remembered. And what you said, and what you did, and what you failed to do—these are still remembered. Remembered, too, are the manner of your glance, the ring of your voice, the clasp of your hand and how your step sounded—as long as one is left who remembers you, so long is the matter unended. Before the end there is much to be undone. Until you are quite forgotten, my son, you will not be finished with the earth—even though you are dead.

THE SECOND [very gently]. Come.

[The music begins again. All three exit at back, LILIOM leading, the others following. The stage is empty and quite dark save for the candle which burns by the stretcher, on which, in the shadows, the covers are so arranged that one cannot quite be sure that a body is not still lying. The music dies out in the distance as if it had followed LILIOM and the two POLICEMEN. The candle flickers and goes out. There is a brief interval of silence and total darkness before

THE CURTAIN FALLS

SCENE SIX

SCENE: In the Beyond. A whitewashed courtroom. There is a green-topped table; behind it a bench. Back center is a door with a bell over it. Next to this door is a window through which can be seen a vista of rose-tinted clouds.

Down right there is a grated iron door. Down left another door.

Two men are on the bench when the curtain rises. One is richly, the other poorly dressed.

From a great distance is heard a fanfare of trumpets playing the refrain of the thieves' song in slow, altered tempo.

Passing the window at back appear LILIOM and the two policemen.

The bell rings.

An old guard enters at right. He is bald and has a long white beard. He wears the conventional police uniform.

He goes to the door at back, opens it, exchanges silent greetings with the two policemen and closes the door again.

LILIOM looks wonderingly around.

THE FIRST [to the old guard]. Announce us. [The guard exits at left]

LILIOM. Is this it?

THE SECOND. Yes, my son.

LILIOM. This is the police court?

THE SECOND. Yes, my son. The part for suicide cases.

LILIOM. And what happens here?

THE FIRST. Here justice is done. Sit down.

[LILIOM *sits next to the two men. The* TWO POLICEMEN *stand silent near the table*]

THE RICHLY DRESSED MAN [*whispers*]. Suicide, too?

LILIOM. Yes.

THE RICHLY DRESSED MAN [*points to the* POORLY DRESSED MAN]. So's he. [*Introducing himself*]. My name is Reich.

THE POORLY DRESSED MAN [*whispers, too*]. My name is Stephen Kadar.

[LILIOM *only looks at them*]

THE POORLY DRESSED MAN. And you? What's your name?

LILIOM. None of your business.

[*Both move a bit away from him*]

THE POORLY DRESSED MAN. I did it by jumping out of a window.

THE RICHLY DRESSED MAN. I did it with a pistol—and you?

LILIOM. With a knife.

[*They move a bit further away from him*]

THE RICHLY DRESSED MAN. A pistol is cleaner.

LILIOM. If I had the price of a pistol—

THE SECOND. Silence!

[*The* POLICE MAGISTRATE *enters. He has a long white beard, is bald, but only in profile can be seen on his head a single tuft of snow-white hair. The* GUARD *re-enters behind him and sits on the bench with the dead men. As the* MAGISTRATE *enters, all rise, except* LILIOM, *who remains surlily seated. When the* MAGISTRATE *sits down, so do the others*]

THE GUARD. Yesterday's cases, your honor. The numbers are entered in the docket.

THE MAGISTRATE. Number 16,472.

THE FIRST [*looks in his notebook, beckons the* RICHLY DRESSED MAN] Stand up, please.

[*The* RICHLY DRESSED MAN *rises*]

THE MAGISTRATE. Your name?

THE RICHLY DRESSED MAN. Doctor Reich.

THE MAGISTRATE. Age?

THE RICHLY DRESSED MAN. Forty-two, married, Jew.

THE MAGISTRATE [*with a gesture of dismissal*]. Religion does not interest us here— why did you kill yourself?

THE RICHLY DRESSED MAN. On account of debts.

THE MAGISTRATE. What good did you do on earth?

THE RICHLY DRESSED MAN. I was a lawyer—

THE MAGISTRATE [*coughs significantly*]. Yes —we'll discuss that later. For the present I shall only ask you: Would you like to go back to earth once more before sunrise? I advise you that you have the right to go if you choose. Do you understand?

THE RICHLY DRESSED MAN. Yes, sir.

THE MAGISTRATE. He who takes his life is apt, in his haste and his excitement, to forget something. Is there anything important down there you have left undone? Something to tell someone? Something to undo?

THE RICHLY DRESSED MAN. My debts—

THE MAGISTRATE. They do not matter here. Here we are concerned only with the affairs of the soul.

THE RICHLY DRESSED MAN. Then—if you please—when I left—the house—my youngest son, Oscar—was asleep. I didn't trust myself to wake him—and bid him good-bye. I would have liked—to kiss him good-bye.

THE MAGISTRATE [*to* THE SECOND]. You will take Dr. Reich back and let him kiss his son Oscar.

THE SECOND. Come with me, please.

THE RICHLY DRESSED MAN [*to* The MAGISTRATE]. I thank you. [*He bows and exits at back with* THE SECOND]

THE MAGISTRATE [*after making an entry in the docket*]. Number 16,473.

THE FIRST [*looks in his note-book, then beckons* LILIOM]. Stand up.

LILIOM. You said *please* to him. [*He rises*]

THE MAGISTRATE. Your name?

LILIOM. Liliom.

THE MAGISTRATE. Isn't that your nickname?

LILIOM. Yes.

THE MAGISTRATE. What is your right name?

LILIOM. Andreas.

THE MAGISTRATE. And your last name?

LILIOM. Zavoczki—after my mother.

THE MAGISTRATE. Your age?

LILIOM. Twenty-four.

THE MAGISTRATE. What good did *you* do on earth? [LILIOM *is silent*] Why did you take your life? [LILIOM *does not answer.* THE MAGISTRATE *addresses* THE FIRST] Take that knife away from him. [THE FIRST *does so*] It will be returned to you, if you go back to earth.

LILIOM. Do I go back to earth again?

THE MAGISTRATE. Just answer my questions.

LILIOM. I wasn't answering then, I was asking if—

THE MAGISTRATE. You don't ask questions here. You only answer. Only answer, Andreas Zavoczki! I ask you whether there is anything on earth you neglected to accomplish? Anything down there you would like to do?

LILIOM. Yes.

THE MAGISTRATE. What is it?

LILIOM. I'd like to break Ficsur's head for him.

THE MAGISTRATE. Punishment is our office. Is there nothing else on earth you'd like to do?

LILIOM. I don't know—I guess, as long as I'm here, I'll not go back.

THE MAGISTRATE [*to* THE FIRST]. Note that He waives his right. [LILIOM *starts back to the bench*] Stay where you are. You are aware that you left your wife without food or shelter?

LILIOM. Yes.

THE MAGISTRATE. Don't you regret it?

LILIOM. No.

THE MAGISTRATE. You are aware that your wife is pregnant, and that in six months a child will be born?

LILIOM. I know.

THE MAGISTRATE. And that child, too, will be without food or shelter? Do you regret that?

LILIOM. As long as I won't be there, what's it got to do with me?

THE MAGISTRATE. Don't try to deceive us, Andreas Zavocki. We see through you as through a pane of glass.

LILIOM. If you see so much, what do you want to ask me for? Why don't you let me rest —in peace?

THE MAGISTRATE. First you must earn your rest.

LILIOM. I want—only—to sleep.

THE MAGISTRATE. Your obstinacy won't help you. Here patience is endless as time. We can wait.

LILIOM. Can I ask something—I'd like to know—if Your Honor will tell me—whether the baby will be a boy or a girl.

THE MAGISTRATE. You shall see that for yourself.

LILIOM [*excitedly*]. I'll see the baby?

THE MAGISTRATE. When you do it won't be a baby any more. But we haven't reached that question yet.

LILIOM. I'll see it?

THE MAGISTRATE. Again I ask you: Do you not regret that you deserted your wife and child; that you were a bad husband, a bad father?

LILIOM. A bad husband?

THE MAGISTRATE. Yes.

LILIOM. And a bad father?

THE MAGISTRATE. That, too.

LILIOM. I couldn't get work—and I couldn't bear to see Julie—all the time—all the time—

THE MAGISTRATE. Weeping! Why are you ashamed to say it? You couldn't bear to see her weeping. Why are you afraid of that word? And why are you ashamed that you loved her?

LILIOM [*shrugs his shoulders*]. Who's ashamed? But I couldn't bear to see her—and that's why I was bad to her. You see, it wouldn't do to go back to the carousel—and Ficsur came along with his talk about—that other thing—and all of a sudden it happened, I don't know how. The police and the Jew with the pistol—and there I stood—and I'd lost the money playing cards—and I didn't want to be put in prison. [*Demanding justification*] Maybe I was wrong not to go out and steal when there was nothing to eat in the house? Should I have gone out to steal for Julie?

THE MAGISTRATE [*emphatically*]. Yes.

LILIOM [*after an astounded pause*]. The police down there never said that.

THE MAGISTRATE. You beat that poor, frail girl; you beat her because she loved you. How could you do that?

LILIOM. We argued with each other—she said this and I said that—and because she was right I couldn't answer her—and I got mad—and the anger rose up in me—until it reached here—[*points to his throat*] and then I beat her.

THE MAGISTRATE. Are you sorry?

LILIOM [*shakes his head, but cannot utter the word "no"; continues softly*]. When I touched her slender throat—then—if you like—you might say— [*Falters, looks embarrassed at* THE MAGISTRATE]

THE MAGISTRATE [*confidently expectant*]. Are you sorry?

LILIOM [*with a stare*]. I'm not sorry for anything.

THE MAGISTRATE. Liliom, Liliom, it will be difficult to help you.

LILIOM. I'm not asking any help.

THE MAGISTRATE. You were offered employment as a caretaker on Arader Street. [*To* THE FIRST] Where is that entered?

THE FIRST. In the small docket. [*Hands him the open book*]

[THE MAGISTRATE *looks in it*]

THE MAGISTRATE. Rooms, kitchen, quarterly wages, the privilege of keeping poultry. Why didn't you accept it?

LILIOM. I'm not a caretaker. I'm no good at caretaking. To be a caretaker—you have to be a caretaker—

THE MAGISTRATE. If I said to you now: Liliom, go back on your stretcher. Tomorrow morning you will arise alive and well again. Would you be a caretaker then?

LILIOM. No.

THE MAGISTRATE. Why not?

LILIOM. Because—because that's just why I died.

THE MAGISTRATE. That is not true, my son. You died because you loved little Julie and the child she is bearing under her heart.

LILIOM. No.

THE MAGISTRATE. Look me in the eye.

LILIOM [*looks him in the eye*]. No.

THE MAGISTRATE [*stroking his beard*]. Liliom, Liliom, if it were not for our Heavenly patience— Go back to your seat. Number 16,474.

THE FIRST [*looks in his note-book*]. Stephan Kadar.

[THE POORLY DRESSED MAN *rises*]

THE MAGISTRATE. You came out today?

THE POORLY DRESSED MAN. Today.

THE MAGISTRATE [*indicating the crimson sea of clouds*]. How long were you in there?

THE POORLY DRESSED MAN. Thirteen years.

THE MAGISTRATE. Officer, you went to earth with him?

THE FIRST. Yes, sir.

THE MAGISTRATE. Stephan Kadar, after thirteen years of purification by fire you returned to earth to give proof that your soul had been burned clean. What good deed did you perform?

THE POORLY DRESSED MAN. When I came to the village and looked in the window of our cottage I saw my poor little orphans sleeping peacefully. But it was raining and the rain beat into the room through a hole in the roof. So I went and fixed the roof so it wouldn't rain in any more. My hammering woke them up and they were afraid. But their mother came in to them and comforted them. She said to them: "Don't cry! It's your poor, dear father hammering up there. He's come back from the other world to fix the roof for us."

THE MAGISTRATE. Officer?

THE FIRST. That's what happened.

THE MAGISTRATE. Stephan Kadar, you have done a good deed. What you did will be written in books to gladden the hearts of children who read them. [*Indicates the door at left*] The door is open to you. The eternal light awaits you. [THE FIRST *escorts the* POORLY DRESSED MAN *out at left with great deference*] Liliom! [LILIOM *rises*] You have heard?

LILIOM. Yes.

THE MAGISTRATE. When this man first appeared before us he was as stubborn as you. But now he has purified himself and withstood the test. He has done a good deed.

LILIOM. What's he done, anyhow? Any roofer can fix a roof. It's much harder to be a barker in an amusement park.

THE MAGISTRATE. Liliom, you shall remain for sixteen years in the crimson fire until your child is full grown. By that time your pride and your stubbornness will have been burnt out of you. And when your daughter—

LILIOM. My daughter!

THE MAGISTRATE. When your daughter has reached the age of sixteen—

[LILIOM *bows his head, covers his eyes with his hands, and to keep from weeping laughs defiantly, sadly*]

THE MAGISTRATE. When your daughter has reached the age of sixteen you will be sent for one day back to earth.

LILIOM. Me?

THE MAGISTRATE. Yes—just as you may have read in the legends of how the dead reappear on earth for a time.

LILIOM. I never believed them.

THE MAGISTRATE. Now you see they are true. You will go back to earth one day to show how far the purification of your soul has progressed.

LILIOM. Then I must show what I can do—

like when you apply for a job—as a coachman?

THE MAGISTRATE. Yes—it is a test.

LILIOM. And will I be told what I have to do?

THE MAGISTRATE. No.

LILIOM. How will I know, then?

THE MAGISTRATE. You must decide that for yourself. That's what you burn sixteen years for. And if you do something good, something splendid for your child, then—

LILIOM [*laughs sadly*]. Then? [*All stand up and bow their heads reverently. There is a pause*] Then?

THE MAGISTRATE. Now I'll bid you farewell, Liliom. Sixteen years and a day shall pass before I see you again. When you have returned from earth you will come up before me again. Take heed and think well of some good deed to do for your child. On that will depend which door shall be opened to you up here. Now go, Liliom. [*He exits at left*]

[THE GUARD *stands at attention. There is a pause*]

THE FIRST [*approaches* LILIOM]. Come along, my son. [*He goes to the door at right; pulls open the bolt and waits*]

LILIOM [*to the old* GUARD, *softly*]. Say, officer.

THE GUARD. What do you want?

LILIOM. Please—can I get—have you got—?

THE GUARD. What?

LILIOM [*whispers*]. A cigarette?

[*The old* GUARD *stares at him, goes a few paces to the left, shakes his head disapprovingly. Then his expression softens He takes a cigarette from his pocket and crossing to* LILIOM—*who has gone over to the door at right*—*gives him the cigarette.* THE FIRST *throws open the door An intense rose-colored light streams in The glow of it is so strong that it blinds* LILIOM *and he takes a step backward and bows his head and covers his eyes with his hand before he steps forward into the light*]

THE CURTAIN FALLS

SCENE SEVEN

SCENE: *Sixteen years later. A small, tumble down house on a bare, unenclosed plot o ground. Before the house is a tiny garden en closed by a hip-high hedge.*

At back a wooden fence crosses the stage in the center of it is a door large enough t admit a wagon. Beyond the fence is a view o a suburban street which blends into a broa vista of tilled fields.

It is a bright Sunday in Spring.

In the garden a table for two is laid.

JULIE, *her daughter* LOUISE, WOLF *and* MARIE *are discovered in the garden.* WOLF *is prosperously dressed,* MARIE *somewhat elaborately, with a huge hat.*

JULIE. You could stay for lunch.

MARIE. Impossible, dear. Since he became the proprietor of the Café Sorrento, Wolf simply has to be there all the time.

JULIE. But you needn't stay there all day, too.

MARIE. Oh, yes. I sit near the cashier's cage, read the papers, keep an eye on the waiters and drink in the bustle and excitement of the great city.

JULIE. And what about the children?

MARIE. You know what modern families are like. Parents scarcely ever see their children these days. The four girls are with their governess, the three boys with their tutor.

LOUISE. Auntie, dear, do stay and eat with us.

MARIE [*importantly*]. Impossible today, dear child, impossible. Perhaps some other time. Come, Mr. Beifeld.

JULIE. Since when do you call your husband, 'Mister'?

WOLF. I'd rather she did, dear lady. When we used to be very familiar we quarreled all the time. Now we are formal with each other and get along like society folk. I kiss your hand, dear lady.

JULIE. Good-bye, Wolf.

MARIE. Adieu, my dear. [*They embrace*] Adieu, my dear child.

LOUISE. Good-bye, Aunt Marie. Good-bye, Uncle Wolf.

[WOLF *and* MARIE *exit*]

JULIE. You can get the soup now, Louise dear.

[LOUISE *goes into the house and reënters with the soup. They sit at the table*]

LOUISE. Mother, is it true we're not going to work at the jute factory any more?

JULIE. Yes, dear.

LOUISE. Where then?

JULIE. Uncle Wolf has gotten us a place in big establishment where they make all kinds of fittings for cafés. We're to make big curtains, you know, the kind they hang in the windows, with lettering on them.

LOUISE. It'll be nicer there than at the jute factory.

JULIE. Yes, dear. The work isn't as dirty and pays better, too. A poor widow like your mother lucky to get it.

[*They eat.* LILIOM *and the two* HEAVENLY POLICEMEN *appear in the big doorway at back. The* POLICEMEN *pass slowly by.* LILIOM *stands there alone a moment, then comes slowly down and pauses at the opening of the hedge. He is dressed as he was on the day of his death. He is very pale, but otherwise unaltered.*

JULIE, *at the table, has her back to him.* LOUISE *sits facing the audience*]

LILOM. Good day.

LOUISE. Good day.

JULIE. Another beggar! What is it you want, my poor man?

LILOM. Nothing.

JULIE. We have no money to give, but if you care for a plate of soup— [LOUISE *goes into the house*] Have you come far today?

LILIOM. Yes—very far.

JULIE. Are you tired?

LILIOM. Very tired.

JULIE. Over there at the gate is a stone. Sit down and rest. My daughter is bringing you the soup.

[LOUISE *comes out of the house*]

LILIOM. Is that your daughter?

JULIE. Yes.

LILIOM [*to* LOUISE]. You are the daughter?

LOUISE. Yes, sir.

LILIOM. A fine, healthy girl. [*Takes the soup plate from her with one hand, while with the other he touches her arm.* LOUISE *draws back quickly*]

LOUISE [*crosses to* JULIE]. Mother!

JULIE. What, my child?

LOUISE. The man tried to take me by the arm.

JULIE. Nonsense! You only imagined it, dear. The poor, hungry man has other things to think about than fooling with young girls. Sit down and eat your soup.

[*They eat*]

LILIOM [*eats, too, but keeps looking at them*]. You work at the factory, eh?

JULIE. Yes.

LILIOM. Your daughter, too?

LOUISE. Yes.

LILIOM. And your husband?

JULIE [*after a pause*]. I have no husband. I'm a widow.

LILIOM. A widow?

JULIE. Yes.

LILIOM. Your husband—I suppose he's been dead a long time. [JULIE *does not answer*] I say—has your husband been dead a long time?

JULIE. A long time.

LILIOM. What did he die of?

[JULIE *is silent*]

LOUISE. No one knows. He went to America to work and he died there—in the hospital. Poor father, I never knew him.

LILIOM. He went to America?

LOUISE. Yes, before I was born.

LILIOM. To America?

JULIE. Why do you ask so many questions? Did you know him, perhaps?

LILIOM [*puts the plate down*]. Heaven knows! I've known so many people. Maybe I knew him, too.

JULIE. Well, if you knew him, leave him and

us in peace with your questions. He went to America and died there. That's all there is to tell.

Liliom. All right. All right. Don't be angry with me. I didn't mean any harm.

[*There is a pause*]

Louise. My father was a very handsome man.

Julie. Don't talk so much.

Louise. Did I say anything—?

Liliom. Surely the little orphan can say that about her father.

Louise. My father could juggle so beautifully with three ivory balls that people used to advise him to go on the stage.

Julie. Who told you that?

Louise. Uncle Wolf.

Liliom. Who is that?

Louise. Mr. Wolf Beifeld, who owns the Café Sorrento.

Liliom. The one who used to be a porter?

Julie [*astonished*]. Do you know him, too? It seems that you know all Budapest.

Liliom. Wolf Beifeld is a long way from being all Budapest. But I do know a lot of people. Why shouldn't I know Wolf Beifeld?

Louise. He was a friend of my father.

Julie. He was not a friend. No one was.

Liliom. You speak of your husband so sternly.

Julie. What's that to you? Doesn't it suit you? I can speak of my husband any way I like. It's nobody's business but mine.

Liliom. Certainly, certainly—it's your own business. [*Takes up his soup plate again*]

[*All three eat*]

Louise [*to* Julie]. Perhaps he knew father, too.

Julie. Ask him, if you like.

Louise [*crosses to* Liliom. *He stands up*]. Did you know my father? [Liliom *nods.* Louise *addresses her mother*] Yes, he knew him.

Julie. [*rises*]. You knew Andreas Zavoczky?

Liliom. Liliom? Yes.

Louise. Was he really a very handsome man?

Liliom. I wouldn't exactly say handsome.

Louise [*confidently*]. But he was an awfully good man, wasn't he?

Liliom. He wasn't so good, either. As far as I know he was what they called a clown, a barker in a carousel.

Louise [*pleased*]. Did he tell funny jokes?

Liliom. Lots of 'em. And he sang funny songs, too.

Louise. In the carousel?

Liliom. Yes—but he was something of a bully, too. He'd fight anyone. He even hit your dear little mother.

Julie. That's a lie.

Liliom. It's true.

Julie. Aren't you ashamed to tell the child

such awful things about her father? Get out of here, you shameless liar. Eats our soup and our bread and has the impudence to slander our dead!

Liliom. I didn't mean—I—

Julie. What right have you to tell lies to the child? Take that plate, Louise, and let him be on his way. If he wasn't such a hungry-looking beggar, I'd put him out myself.

[Louise *takes the plate out of his hand*]

Liliom. So he didn't hit you?

Julie. No, never. He was always good to me.

Louise [*whispers*]. Did he tell funny stories, too?

Liliom. Yes, and *such* funny ones.

Julie. Don't speak to him any more. In God's name, go.

Louise. In God's name.

[Julie *resumes her seat at the table and eats*]

Liliom. If you please, Miss—I have a pack of cards in my pocket. And if you like, I'll show you some tricks that'll make you split your sides laughing. [Louise *holds* Liliom's *plate in her left hand. With her right she reaches out and holds the garden gate shut*] Let me in, just a little way, Miss, and I'll do the tricks for you.

Louise. Go, in God's name, and let us be. Why are you making those ugly faces?

Liliom. Don't chase me away, Miss; let me come in for just a minute—just for a minute— just long enough to let me show you something pretty, something wonderful. [*Opens the gate*] Miss, I've something to give you. [*Takes from his pocket a big red handkerchief in which is wrapped a glittering star from Heaven. He looks furtively about him to make sure that the* Police *are not watching*]

Louise. What's that?

Liliom. Pst! A star! [*With a gesture he indicates that he has stolen it out of the sky*]

Julie [*sternly*]. Don't take anything from him. He's probably stolen it somewhere. [*To* Liliom] In God's name, be off with you.

Louise. Yes, be off with you. Be off. [*She slams the gate*]

Liliom. Miss—please, Miss—I've got to do something good—or—do something good—a good deed—

Louise [*pointing with her right hand*] That's the way out.

Liliom. Miss—

Louise. Get out!

Liliom. Miss! [*Looks up at her suddenly and slaps her extended hand, so that the slap resounds loudly*]

Louise. Mother!

[*Looks dazedly at* Liliom, *who bows his head dismayed, forlorn.* Julie *rises and looks at* Liliom *in astonishment. There is a long pause*]

JULIE [*comes over to them slowly*] What's the matter here?

LOUISE [*bewildered, does not take her eyes off* LILIOM]. Mother—the man—he hit me—on the hand—hard—I heard the sound of it—but it didn't hurt—mother—it didn't hurt—it was like a caress—as if he had just touched my hand tenderly. [*She hides behind* JULIE]

[LILIOM *sulkily raises his head and looks at* JULIE]

JULIE [*softly*]. Go, my child. Go into the house. Go.

LOUISE [*going*]. But mother—I'm afraid—it sounded so loud— [*Weepingly*] And it didn't hurt at all—just as if he'd—kissed my hand instead—mother! [*She hides her face*]

JULIE. Go in, my child, go in.

[LOUISE *goes slowly into the house.* JULIE *watches her until she has disappeared, then turns slowly to* LILIOM]

JULIE. You struck my child.

LILIOM. Yes—I struck her.

JULIE. Is that what you came for, to strike my child?

LILIOM. No—I didn't come for that—but I did strike her—and now I'm going back.

JULIE. In the name of the Lord Jesus, who are you?

LILIOM [*simply*]. A poor, tired beggar who came a long way and who was hungry. And I took your soup and bread and I struck your child. Are you angry with me?

JULIE [*her hand on her heart; fearfully, wonderingly*]. Jesus protect me—I don't understand it—I'm *not* angry—not angry at all—

[LILIOM *goes to the doorway and leans against the doorpost, his back to the audience.* JULIE *goes to the table and sits*]

JULIE. Louise! [LOUISE *comes out of the house*] Sit down, dear, we'll finish eating.

LOUISE. Has he gone?

JULIE. Yes. [*They are both seated at the table.* LOUISE, *her head in her hands, is staring into space*] Why don't you eat, dear?

LOUISE. What has happened, mother?

JULIE. Nothing, my child.

[*The* HEAVENLY POLICEMEN *appear outside.* LILIOM *walks slowly off at left. The* FIRST POLICEMAN *makes a deploring gesture. Both shake their heads deploringly and follow* LILIOM *slowly off at left*]

LOUISE. Mother, dear, why won't you tell me?

JULIE. What is there to tell you, child? Nothing has happened. We were peacefully eating, and a beggar came who talked of bygone days, and then I thought of your father.

LOUISE. My father?

JULIE. Your father—Liliom.

[*There is a pause*]

LOUISE. Mother—tell me—has it ever happened to you—has anyone ever hit you—without hurting you in the least?

JULIE. Yes, my child. It has happened to me, too.

[*There is a pause*]

LOUISE. Is it possible for someone to hit you —hard like that—real loud and hard—and not hurt you at all?

JULIE. It is possible, dear—that someone may beat you and beat you and beat you,—and not hurt you at all.—

[*There is a pause. Nearby an organ-grinder has stopped. The music of his organ begins*]

THE CURTAIN FALLS

GREEN GROW THE LILACS

A Play in Six Scenes

By LYNN RIGGS

PEOPLE

Curly McClain
Aunt Eller Murphy
Laurey Williams
Jeeter Fry
Ado Annie Carnes
A Pedler
Cord Elam
Old Man Peck
and Others of the Countryside

SCENES

Scene I—*The "front" room of the Williams farmhouse, a June morning.*
Scene II—*Laurey's bedroom.*
Scene III—*The smoke-house.*
Scene IV—*The porch of Old Man Peck's house, that night.*
Scene V—*The hayfield, a month later.*
Scene VI—*The "front" room, three nights later.*
The action of the play takes place in Indian Territory in 1900.

GREEN GROW THE LILACS

SCENE ONE

It is a radiant summer morning several years ago, the kind of morning which, enveloping the shapes of earth—men, cattle in a meadow, blades of the young corn, streams—makes them seem to exist now for the first time, their images giving off a visible golden emanation that is partly true and partly a trick of imagination focussing to keep alive a loveliness that may pass away.

The unearthly sunlight pours through the crocheted curtains of a window in the living room—the "front room"—of a farm house in Indian Territory. It rests upon, and glorifies, scrubbed floors of oak, bright rag rugs, rough hide-bottomed hairy chairs, a rock fireplace, a settee, an old organ magnificently mirrored, ancestral enlargements in their gilt and oval frames. A double sliding door of pine, now closed, is at the back of the room; other heavier doors of oak lead to other parts of the house and to the outside. Somewhere a dog barks twice and stops quickly, reassured; a turkey gobbler makes his startled, swallowing noise.

And, like the voice of the morning, a rich male voice outside somewhere begins to sing:

VOICE
As I walked out one bright sunny morning,
I saw a cowboy way out on the plain.
His hat was throwed back and his spurs was a-jingling,
And as I passed by him, he was singing this refrain:

Ta whoop ti aye ay, git along, you little dogies!
Way out in Wyoming shall be your bright home—
A-whooping and a-yelling and a-driving those dogies,
And a-riding those bronchos that are none of my own.

The people all say we're goin' to have a picnic,
But I tell you, my boy, they've got 'er down wrong,
For 'f it hadn't a-been for those troublesome dogies,
I never woulda thought of composing this song.

Ta whoop ti aye ay, git along, you little dogies!
Way out in Wyoming shall be your bright home—
A-whooping and a-yelling and a-driving those dogies,
And a-riding those bronchos that are none of my own.

[Before the first verse is finished, part of the singer comes into sight at a window —a tall, waggish, curly-headed young cowboy in a checked shirt and a ten-gallon hat. He looks about the room singing. Just as he finishes he withdraws, hearing footsteps. A moment later, AUNT ELLER MURPHY, a buxom, hearty woman about fifty, with a tall wooden brass-banded churn in her arms, comes in from the kitchen. She puts the churn down quickly by the fireplace, goes over to the window and looks out, squinting. She grins, good-humoredly]

AUNT ELLER. Oh, I see you, Mr. Curly McClain! Don't need to be a-hidin' 'hind that horse of your'n. Couldn't hide them feet of your'n even if yer head wasn't showin'. So you may as well come on in.

[She turns away from the window, takes off her apron, and comes back into the room. CURLY appears again at the window]

CURLY. Hi, Aunt Eller.

AUNT ELLER *[shortly]*. Skeer me to death! Whut're you doin' around here?

CURLY. Come a-singin' to you only you never give me no time to finish.

[Their speech is lazy, drawling, not Southern, not "hick"—but rich, half-conscious of its rhythms, its picturesque imagery]

AUNT ELLER. Go on and finish then. *[She smiles at him]* You do sing purty, Curly.

CURLY. Nobody never said I didn't.

AUNT ELLER. Yeah, purty. If I wasn't an old womern, and if you wasn't so young and smart-alecky—why, I'd marry you and git you to set around at night and sing to me.

CURLY. No, you wouldn't, neither. If I was to marry—anyone—I wouldn't set around at night a-singin'. They ain't no tellin' *whut* I'd do. But I wouldn't marry you ner none of yer kinfolks, I could he'p it.

515

AUNT ELLER [*wisely*]. Oh! None of my kin-folks neither, huh?

CURLY. And you c'n tell 'em that, *all* of 'em, includin' that niece of your'n, Miss Laurey Williams, if she's about anywhurs.

AUNT ELLER. Mebbe I will, and mebbe I won't. Whut you doin' over this-a-way, Curly? Thought you was over at Skidmore's ranch, tother side of Justus. Well, air you comin' in or gonna stay there like a Jack-in-the-box?

[CURLY *vaults into the room. He wears dark trousers stuffed into high boots. His heavy rowelled spurs clink against the floor*]

CURLY [*deliberately*]. Aunt Eller, if you was to tell me whur Laurey was at—*whur* would you tell me she was at?

AUNT ELLER. I wouldn't tell you a-tall, less'n you sung me another song.

CURLY. Must think I'm a medicine man a-singin' and passin' the hat around, the way you talk! Got to save my voice, got to take keer of it, so I'll have it. Don't want to do the way ole man Comer done. When he was a kid he squalled so much, and when he was growed he sung so much, now he's a ole man he cain't git a squawk out of him, nary a squawk. 'Cept a whistle. And a whistle don't mean nuthin'—the way a song do.

AUNT ELLER [*unimpressed*]. Sing me a song, Curly McClain.

CURLY. Aw, I *cain't* sing now! I *told* you. Not if I tried and tried, and even et cat-gut. And even 'f I drunk the gall of a turkey gobbler's liver, I couldn't sing a-tall.

AUNT ELLER. Liar and a hypocrite and a shikepoke! Ain't I heared you? Jist now. *You sing!* Er I'll run you off the place.

CURLY. I cain't sing, I told you! 'Ceptin' when I'm lonesome. Out in the saddle when it ain't so sunny, er on a dark night close to a fa'r when you feel so lonesome to God you could die. Looky here, you're old, my, you're old, you'd orter be so smart! Whur you been, anyhow, whose side meat you been eatin' all yer life, not to know nobody cain't sing good 'ceptin' when he's lonesome?

AUNT ELLER. Lonesome? Then if I was you I'd be a-singin' and a-singin' then. A long song, with forty 'leven verses and a chorus 'tween ever' verse. Fer as fur as I c'n make out, Laurey ain't payin' you no heed a-tall. You might jist as well be ridin' the rails as ridin' that range of your'n. So sing yer head off, you lonesome dogie, 'cause you shore have got into a lonesome side-pocket 'thout no grass, you dehorned maverick, you!

CURLY. Whut'd I keer about that? [*He takes cigaret papers out of his hat-band, Bull Durham from his shirt pocket, and begins to roll a cigaret with elaborate unconcern*]

AUNT ELLER. She goes around with her head some'eres else, don't she?

CURLY. How'd I know? Ain't looked at her nary a time since Christmas.

AUNT ELLER. 'Twasn't yore fault though, if you didn't. [*Jeering, good-naturedly*] She don't see you, does she, Mr. Adam's Off Ox! You've got onto the wrong side of the wagon tongue!

CURLY. Go on, you mean ole womern! Brand a steer till you burn a hole in his hide!

AUNT ELLER. *Mr.* Cowboy! A-ridin' high, wide and handsome, his spurs a-jinglin', and the Bull Durham tag a-whippin' outa his pocket! Oh, *Mr.* Cowpuncher! 'Thout no home, ner no wife, ner no one to muss up his curly hair, er keep him warm on a winter's night!

CURLY [*swelling up, defensively*]. So she don't take to me much, huh? Whur'd you git sich a uppity niece 'at wouldn't pay no heed to *me?* Who's the best bronc buster in this yere state?

AUNT ELLER. You, I bet.

CURLY. And the best bull-dogger in seventeen counties? *Me,* that's who! And looky here, I'm handsome, ain't I?

AUNT ELLER. Purty as a pitcher.

CURLY. Curly-headed, ain't I? And bow-legged from the saddle fer God knows how long, ain't I?

AUNT ELLER [*agreeing*]. Couldn't stop a pig in the road.

CURLY. Well, whut else does she want then, the damn she-mule?

AUNT ELLER. I don't know. But I'm shore sartin it ain't *you.*

CURLY. Anh! Quit it, you'll have me a-cryin'!

AUNT ELLER [*triumphantly*]. You better sing me a song then, like I told you to in the first place!

CURLY. Aw, whut'll I sing then?

AUNT ELLER. "A-ridin' ole Paint."

CURLY. And nen whut'll I sing?

AUNT ELLER. Lands, you better git one sung 'fore you start in on another'n!

[*But* CURLY *has already leaned against the wall with his head thrown back, and his feet crossed, and begun to sing in his rich, liquid, mock-heroic voice*]

CURLY [*singing*].
A-ridin' ole Paint and a-leadin' old Dan,
I'm goin' to Montana for to throw the hoolian.
They feed in the hollers and they water in the draw,
Their tails are all matted and their backs are all raw.

Ride around the little dogies, ride around them slow,
For the fiery and the snuffy are a-rarin' to go.

Ole Bill Jones had two daughters and a son,

One went to Denver and the other went wrong,
One was killed in a pool room fight,
But still he goes singing from morn till night:

Ride around the little dogies, ride around them
 slow,
For the fiery and the snuffy are a-rarin' to go.

When I die take my saddle from the wall,
Put it on my pony, lead him out of his stall,
Tie my bones to the saddle, turn our faces to
 the west,
And we'll ride the trail that we love best.

Ride around the little dogies, ride around them
 slow,
For the fiery and the snuffy are a-rarin' to go.

Now whur's Laurey at?

AUNT ELLER [*pointing*]. Settin' in there in her room a-sewin' er sump'n, when she orta be in here a-churnin' like I told her. Ain't you gonna sing another song?

CURLY. Ain't you a bother though—keep on a-pesterin'! You go and tell Laurey to drop a stitch, and see whut Sandy Claus brung her.

AUNT ELLER. Meanin' you, I guess. Whut'd you want with her, Curly, nohow? I'm her aunt, so you better tell me first, and see if I like the looks of it.

CURLY. You're jist nosy. Well, if you have to know my business, ole man Peck over acrost Dog Crick's givin' a play-party and I come to ast if Laurey ud go with me.

AUNT ELLER. And me, too, huh?

CURLY. Yeow, you too. If you'll go and knock on the door there, and bring Laurey out whur a man c'n git a look at her.

AUNT ELLER [*knocking*]. Laurey! Peck's is givin' a play-party.

LAUREY [*inside*]. Who's givin' a play-party?

AUNT ELLER. Ole man Peck acrost Dog Crick.

LAUREY. Cain't hear a word you say. Who?

AUNT ELLER [*shouting*]. Come on out. Someone's come to see you. He'll tell you.

LAUREY. Who's come to see me? Who's givin' a party?

AUNT ELLER. Well, open up the door, you crazy youngun, I cain't holler my head off!

[*The door slides back, and* LAUREY *comes out. She is a fair, spoiled, lovely young girl about eighteen in a long white dress with many ruffles. She sees* CURLY]

LAUREY. Oh! Thought you was somebody. [*To* AUNT ELLER] Is this all that's come a-callin' and it a'ready ten o'clock of a Satiddy mornin'?

CURLY [*sullenly*]. You knowed it was me 'fore you opened the door.

LAUREY. No sich of a thing.

CURLY. You did, too! You heared my voice and knowed it was me.

LAUREY. I did not, I tell you! Heared a voice a-talkin' rumbly along with Aunt Eller. And heared someone a-singin' like a bull-frog in a pond—

CURLY. I don't talk rumbly. And I don't sing like no bull-frog—

LAUREY. Bull-frog in a pond, I told you. But how'd I know it was you, Mr. Curly McClain? You ain't so special. All men sounds alike to me.

CURLY [*doggedly*]. You knowed it was me, so you set in there a-thinkin' up sump'n mean to say. I'm a good mind not to tell you nuthin' about the play-party now. You c'n jist stay at home, for yer tongue. Don't you tell her whur it is, Aunt Eller. Me'n you'll go and leave her at home.

LAUREY. If you *did* ast me, I wouldn't go with you. Besides, how'd you take me? You ain't bought a new buggy with red wheels onto it, have you?

CURLY. No, I ain't.

LAUREY. And a spankin' team with their bridles all jinglin'?

CURLY. No.

LAUREY. 'Spect me to ride on behind ole Dun, I guess. You better ast that ole Cummins girl you've tuck sich a shine to, over acrost the river.

CURLY. If I was to ast you, they'd be a way to take you, Miss Laurey Smarty.

LAUREY. Oh, they would?

CURLY. A bran' new surrey with fringe on the top four inches long—and *yeller!* And two white horses a-rarin' and faunchin' to go! You'd shore ride like a queen settin' up in *that* carriage! Feel like you had a gold crown set on yer head, 'th diamonds in it big as goose eggs.

LAUREY. Look out, you'll be astin' me in a minute!

CURLY. I ain't astin' you, I'm *tellin'* you. And this yere rig has got four fine side-curtains, case of a rain. And isinglass winders to look out of! And a red and green lamp set on the dashboard, winkin' like a lightnin' bug!

LAUREY. Whur'd you git sich a rig at? [*With explosive laughter*] Anh, I bet he's went and h'ard it over to Claremore, thinkin' I'd go with him!

CURLY. 'S all you know about it—

LAUREY [*jeering*]. Went and h'ard it! Spent all his money h'arin' a rig, and now ain't got nobody to ride in it.

CURLY. Have, too! Did *not* h'ar it. Made the whole thing up outa my head—

LAUREY. What! Made it up?

CURLY. Dashboard and all!

LAUREY [*flying at him*]. Oh! Git outa the house, you! Aunt Eller, make him git hisself outa here 'fore I take a stove arn to him! Tellin' me lies—!

CURLY [*dodging her*]. Makin' up a few— Look out, now! Makin' up a few purties ain't agin no law 'at I know of. Don't you wish they *was* sich a rig, though? Nen you could go to the party and do a hoe-down till mornin' 'f you was a mind to. Nen drive home 'th the sun a-peekin' at you over the ridge, purty and fine.

LAUREY. I ain't wantin' to do no hoe-down till mornin'. And whut would I want to see the sun come up fer, a-peekin' purty and fine— alongside of you, anyhow?

AUNT ELLER. Whyn't you jist grab her and kiss her when she acts that-a-way, Curly? She's jist achin' fer you to, I bet.

LAUREY [*with mock fury*]. Oh! I won't even *speak* to him, let alone 'low him to kiss me, the braggin', saddle-awk'ard, wish-'t-he-had-a-sweetheart bum! [*She flounces into her room, and bangs the sliding door*]

AUNT ELLER [*turning to* CURLY, *sagely*]. She likes you—quite a little.

CURLY. Whew! 'F she liked me quite a *lot*, she'd sic the dogs onto me, or shoot me full of buckshot!

AUNT ELLER. No, come 'ere, Curly, while I tell you sump'n. A womern that won't let you tetch her 'th a ten foot pole like that is jist dyin' fer you to git closer'n *that* to her.

CURLY. Mebbe. But they's women and women. And some of 'em is accordin' to the rules, and some of 'em ain't never *heard* no rules to be accordin' *to*. Guess I better be movin' my camp some'eres else.

AUNT ELLER. No, look here, Curly. I've knowed Laurey all her born days, ain't I? And since her paw and maw died five year ago, I been paw and maw both to her. And whutever I tell you about her way of feelin' is the truth. Er if it *ain't*, I'll give her a everlastin' good spankin', nen it *will* be! Fer I don't know whur her eyes was set in her head 'f she didn't see you, you purty thing, right from the start, the time you come over of a Sunday a year ago and broke them three broncs all in one evenin', 'thout tetchin' leather er yellin' calf-rope. 'Member?

CURLY [*feeling a little better*]. Yeah, I remember. Mean as sin they was, too! That one-eyed un 'th the star in his forehead liked to set me over his head right smack into them lilac bushes the first crack outa the bucket, didn't he? Yeah, onct I break 'em, they're purty apt to stay broke, fer a fact. [*Cryptically*] You c'n *count* on a horse. [*Suddenly*] Look here, Aunt Eller, I wanta know sump'n and if you lie to me, I'll ketch thirteen bulgy-eyed toad-frogs and put 'em in yer bed—

AUNT ELLER. Laws a-mercy!

CURLY. Er make you chew Indian turnip till yer tongue feels like a thousand needles run through it, and no way of pullin' 'em out—

AUNT ELLER. Feel 'em a'ready.

CURLY. Listen, whut low, filthy, sneakin' man has Laurey got her cap set fer?

AUNT ELLER. You.

CURLY. Now!—

AUNT ELLER. Fer a fact, I'm tellin' you! From the way she flew at you jist now, I got my mind all made up. 'F she don't git *you*, Curly, she'll waste away to the shadder of a pin point. Yes, sir. Be put in a sateen coffin dead of a broke heart.

CURLY [*ironically*]. I wouldn't want her to do *that*. I'd consider lettin' her *have* me, 'f that ud keep her from dyin'.

AUNT ELLER [*wisely*]. She's a young girl— and don't know her mind. She don't know her feelin's. You c'n he'p her, Curly—and they's few that can.

CURLY. They must be plenty of men a-tryin' to spark her. And she shorely leans to one of 'em, now don't she?

AUNT ELLER. Ain't no one a-sparkin' her. Well, they is that ole widder man at Claremore, makes out he's a doctor er a vet'nary. And that fine farmer, Jace Hutchins, jist this side of Lone Ellum—

CURLY. That's whut I thought!

AUNT ELLER. Not to say nuthin' about some-one nearer home that's got her on his mind most of the time, till he don't know a plow from a thrashin' machine—

CURLY. Who'd you mean by that?

AUNT ELLER. Jeeter.

CURLY. Jeeter who?

AUNT ELLER. Don't you know Jeeter Fry, our h'ard hand?

CURLY. What! That bullet-colored growly man 'th the bushy eyebrows that's alwys order-in' the other hands how to work the mowin' machine er sump'n!

AUNT ELLER. Now you don't need to go and say nuthin' agin him! He's a big help around here. Jist about runs the farm by hisself. Well, two women couldn't do it, you orta know that.

CURLY. Laurey'd take up 'th a man like that!

AUNT ELLER. I ain't said she's tuck up with him.

CURLY. Well, he's around all the time, ain't he? Eats his meals with you like one of the fambly, don't he? Sleeps around here some-'eres, don't he?

AUNT ELLER. Out in the smoke-house.

CURLY. Laurey sees him all the time, then, don't she? Whyn't you say so in the first place! Whur is this Jeeter, till I git a look at him and mebbe black his eyes fer him?

AUNT ELLER [*slyly*]. Thought you'd moved yer camp some'eres else?

CURLY [*with exaggerated bravado*]. My camp's right here till I git ready to break it. And moreover—whoever puts his foot in it's liable to git shot fer a stinkin' skunk er a sneakin' wildcat!

[*As if waiting for this declaration, the front door bangs open, and the bullet-colored, growly man, with an armful of wood for the fireplace, comes in. He throws the wood in the wood-box, and turns to* AUNT ELLER]

JEETER. Whur's Laurey at?

AUNT ELLER. In her room there.

[JEETER *gives a surly grunt by way of response, and without another word goes out again, leaving the door wide open behind him*]

CURLY. Now is that Jeeter?

AUNT ELLER. Yeah.

CURLY. Thought it was. [*He goes over and and looks out after him*] Why ain't he a-workin'?

AUNT ELLER. It's Satiddy.

CURLY. Oh! I'd forgot. He's went in the smoke-house.

AUNT ELLER. It's *his* house. Used to be the *dog*-house.

CURLY [*chuckling*]. That's the place fer him!

[*The sliding door opens a crack, and* LAUREY *sticks her head out*]

LAUREY. I forgot to tell you, Aunt Eller, you'll have to do the churnin' yerself, less'n you c'n git someone to do it fer you.

AUNT ELLER. Why, you lazy youngun, I'll do no sich of a thing! I got dinner on the stove—

LAUREY. It takes time fer a girl to git herself fixed up, it looks to me like. I'm goin' to a party tonight.

AUNT ELLER. To a party?

LAUREY. Well, stand there 'th yer mouth open! Didn't I tell you?—At ole man Peck's over acrost Dog Crick.

AUNT ELLER. Now whoever went and—Did you, Curly?

LAUREY. I heared about it a week ago. Jeeter told me. I'm goin' with Jeeter.

[*She withdraws.* CURLY *stands very still*]

CURLY [*after a moment*]. Ever hear that song, Aunt Eller?

AUNT ELLER [*frowning*]. A thousand pins it takes 'em to dress—

CURLY [*grins, ruefully*]. Now wouldn't that jist make you bawl!

[*He goes over, touches a few chords on the organ soberly, and then recovering, seats himself, and after a moment begins to sing, half-satirically. But by the time he has reached the first chorus, the song with its absurd yet plaintive charm has absorbed him. And he sings the rest of its sentimental periods, his head back, his eyes focussed beyond the room, beyond himself—upon the young man having his sad say, the young man who'll go into*

the army, by God, and put an end to his distemper, his unrequited fervor]

CURLY [*singing*].
I used to have a sweetheart, but now I've got none,
Since she's gone and left me, I care not for one,
Since she's gone and left me, contented I'll be,
For she loves another one better than me.

Green grow the lilacs, all sparkling with dew,
I'm lonely, my darling, since parting with you,
And by the next meeting I hope to prove true
To change the green lilacs to the red, white and blue.

I passed my love's window, both early and late,
The look that she gave me, it made my heart ache,
The look that she gave me was harmful to see,
For she loves another one better than me.

Green grow the lilacs, all sparkling with dew,
I'm lonely, my darling, since parting with you,
And by the next meeting I hope to prove true
To change the green lilacs to the red, white and blue.

I wrote my love a letter in red rosy lines,
She sent me an answer all twisted in twines,
Saying "Keep your love letters and I will keep mine,
Just write to your sweetheart and I'll write to mine."

Green grow the lilacs, all sparkling with dew,
I'm lonely, my darling, since parting with you,
And by the next meeting I hope to prove true
To change the green lilacs to the red, white and blue.

[*He swings off the organ stool, miraculously healed, and makes for the door*]

AUNT ELLER [*following him over*]. Now don't you be discouraged none, Curly. Laurey's good. She's got sense. She don't let you know too much—keeps you guessin'. And you shore got *her* to wonderin', too! You're shore a pair—full of life—made for each other! Got to have each other. *Got* to. [*She laughs*] Thought I'd die when you made up all that about the rig and told her—

CURLY [*whistles softly*]. Jesus! [*He turns round with a grin*] Well, we got a date together, you and me, Aunt Eller.

AUNT ELLER. We have?

CURLY. We shore have. We goin' to that party we've heared so much about.

AUNT ELLER. How we goin', Curly? In that rig you made up? [*She chuckles*] I'll ride a-straddle of them lights a-winkin' like lightnin' bugs, myself!

CURLY. That there rig ain't no made-up rig, you hear me? I h'ard it over to Claremore.

AUNT ELLER. Lands, you did!

CURLY. And when I come callin' fer you right after supper, see that you got yer beauty spots fastened onto you proper, so you won't lose 'em off, you hear? Now then. [*He strides away to the door again, enigmatically*] I think I'll jist go out here to the smoke-house a while.

AUNT ELLER [*puzzled*]. Whur Jeeter's at?

CURLY. Yeow, whur Jeeter's at. Thought mebbe I'd play a game of pitch with him, 'fore I mosey on home. You reckon he'd like that?

[*He goes out the door.* AUNT ELLER *stares after him, figuring out things*]

CURTAIN

SCENE TWO

LAUREY'S *bedroom, behind its sliding doors is small, primitive, but feminine. There's a bed, covered with a beautiful crazy-quilt, a dresser, very ornate, with little souvenir shell boxes, combs, hair receivers, hair-pins, a vase of butter-cups and daisies, etc. There's a small table with pitchers of water under it, and comfortable chairs. A small window looks out into the bril-liant day. At the left is a door which goes out to the swept yard in front of the kitchen. The walls are papered, and several small photo-graphs are tacked up—one of a man on horse-back, obviously for the first time, one of a young girl with enormous sleeves in her dress.*

LAUREY *is combing her hair. She seems, in this setting, younger, more glowing, more com-plete than before, as if the room were necessary to her. It is immediately after* SCENE ONE. AUNT ELLER *has come in from the door at the left to see what* LAUREY *is up to.*

AUNT ELLER. Is that all you got to do?

LAUREY [*abstractedly*]. When I was a little girl I had my hair in pig-tails. It hung down and down, till I'd wrap it around my head. Nen I'd look like sump'n crawled out of a hole.

AUNT ELLER. I ain't got time to listen to sich craziness.

LAUREY. When I got a little older, I cut it off. Maw licked me.

AUNT ELLER. Well, she'd orta licked you.

LAUREY. Why?

AUNT ELLER. Fer cuttin' yer hair off. Don't you know that ain't right?

LAUREY. I ast you fer a answer and all I git is another question.

AUNT ELLER. Oh, I'm goin' back in the kitchen. You ain't started on that churnin'. I

jist come in to see what you was up to so long. Here I find you a-primpin' and a-talkin' crazy.

LAUREY. Wait a minute. Why don't you set down here a minute?

AUNT ELLER. They's work to do. Ain't time to set.

LAUREY. Then redd up that table if you won't set. And put some fresh water onto them flowers I picked day before yistiddy. Them buttercups. In the meader back of the wheat field—walkin' in the tall grass and the sumakes, you know what I seen? A snake 'th its tail in its mouth—

AUNT ELLER. And a terrapin carryin' a ele-phant, too, didn't you?

LAUREY. Won't hurt you none to put some water on them flowers.

AUNT ELLER [*acquiescing, judicially*]. Well. You ain't always so lazy, I must say.

LAUREY. Dance at yer weddin'.

AUNT ELLER. I don't know whut's got into you, though.

LAUREY. You don't?

AUNT ELLER [*wisely*]. Yes, I do.

LAUREY [*cryptically*]. I thought you did.

[*Silence.* AUNT ELLER *fills the vase.* LAUREY *combs her hair slowly, and be-gins to sing*]

One morning as I rambled o'er
The fields I took my way
In hopes of meeting my miner boy
And for a while to stray,
In hopes of meeting my miner boy,
My hope, my joy, my own.
My heart was blessed, it could find no rest
For the thoughts of my miner boy.

The mother to her daughter,
"I'll comfort you to your room,
You never shall marry a miner boy,
It will certainly be your doom.
They're never, never satisfied,
But always on a drunk.
And all they have in this wide wide world
Is a satchel and a trunk."

The daughter to her mother,
"What makes you be unkind?
I never shall marry another one
But the one that suits my mind.
His trousers are made of corduroy,
His jacket of true blue.
I'd rather marry a miner boy
As to reign with the waters true."

Then fill your glasses to the brim,
Let's all go merry round,
And drink to the health of the miner boy
Who works down in the ground,
When work is o'er comes whistling home
With a heart so full of joy,

And happy, happy is the girl
That marries a miner boy.

Would you marry a miner boy, Aunt Eller?
AUNT ELLER. I don't know no miner boys.
LAUREY. Oh, 'f you did, you would, I bet.
[*After a moment*] Wish 't I lived in the White
House, and had diamonds on my shoes, and a
little nigger boy to fan me—when it was hot.
Does it git hot in the White House, Aunt Eller?
AUNT ELLER. How do I know?
LAUREY. Er I wish't I lived in Virginia or
Californie. In Californie, they's oranges growin',
and snow fallin' at the same time. I seen a
pitcher of it. In the Verdigree bottom the other
day, a man found thirty-three arrow heads—
thirty-three—whur they'd been a Indian
battle—
AUNT ELLER. Whut's that got to do with the
White House and livin' in Californie?
LAUREY. Who said anything about Californie?
AUNT ELLER [*whistles*]. Land's alive! [*After
a moment*] Curly's out in the smoke-house.
LAUREY. Who is?
AUNT ELLER. Curly. Him and Jeeter.
LAUREY [*as if she hadn't heard*]. Bet they'll
be a hundred people at Peck's. They'll come in
buggies and surries, a-horseback, in the wagon,
and some'll come afoot. Gracie Denham will
come all the way from Catoosie to be there, I
bet. When she married Dan Denham, everbody
thought—"Goodbye, good times"—fer Gracie.
She fooled 'em, though. How big is Indian Territory, Aunt Eller?
AUNT ELLER. Oh, big.
LAUREY. It's a funny place to live, ain't it?
AUNT ELLER. Whut's funny about it?
LAUREY. Well, take me, if paw and maw
hadn't come here, I'd a-been livin' in Missouri
now, 'stid of here. I'd a-had education, I'll bet.
[*She puts down her comb and stares thoughtfully out the window*] I lied about the White
House, Aunt Eller. I'd ruther be married to a
man—if he was a real good man—than to live
in the old White House.
AUNT ELLER [*chuckling*]. Hope you do one
of the two!
LAUREY. Wouldn't you, Aunt Eller?
AUNT ELLER. I've done about all the marryin'
I'm gonna do. Onct is quite a plenty. [*She
chortles with delight*] Less'n I marry Curly
and bring him up right. Me and Curly, we're
a-goin' to that there party—
LAUREY [*jumps up, runs over and begins
shaking the astounded* AUNT ELLER]. You ain't,
you air not! He ain't got no way to take you
to no party. You got to go with Jeeter and
me—
AUNT ELLER. Curly's h'ard a rig. That un he
told you about. [LAUREY *drops her hands, backs
away, and looks at* AUNT ELLER *with such an
amazed and startled expression, that the older

woman cries out:] Why, you look so funny!—
Like you'd saw sump'n. [LAUREY *goes over to
the windows, hangs on to the curtains*] Besides,
you turned him down. [*Teasing her*] If you jist
got to go with Jeeter, they ain't no way out of
it, I reckon. Well, me'n Curly, we'll make out—
LAUREY [*quietly, strangely*]. Onct I passed
by a farm house and it was night. Paw and
maw and me was in a covered wagon on our
way to here. And this farm house was burnin'
up. It was burnin' bright, too. Black night, it
was like I said. Flames licked and licked at the
red-hot chimbley and finally it fell, too, and
that was the last of that house. And that was
turrible! I cried and cried. [*A sudden slightly-
hysterical note in her voice*] And the farmer's
wife jist set there by the side of the road,
moanin' and takin' on. Had on a sunbonnet,
a *sunbonnet*, and it night! She kept sayin' over
and over—"Now my home's burnt up. 'F I'd
jist a-give him a piece of cold pork or sump'n.
If I'd jist a-fed him!—" [*She shakes her head,
as if shutting it out*] Now ain't that silly!—
Don't you listen to a word I said. Ever onct
in a while sump'n makes me think about it,
the way that womern cried, and said whut she
did. Don't you pay no attention to me—
AUNT ELLER. I b'lieve to my soul you got
sump'n worryin' on yer mind. Never seen you
ack before like a chicken 'th its head cut off,
Laurey.
LAUREY [*flippantly*]. Worried to death.
AUNT ELLER. Whut about? Now tell yer ole
Aunt. Whut is it, honey?
LAUREY. Ain't got a thing to wear tonight.
AUNT ELLER. You make me so mad—!
LAUREY. Well, I ain't. That ole flowered
dew-dad of a dress looks like sump'n the cat
drug in. And my sash is tore. Sylvie Roberts
has got a new kind of a shoe with high heels
onto 'em like stilts—and I ain't got none.
AUNT ELLER. You'd shore look purty
a-wearin' stilts—like a sandhill crane a-wadin'
shaller water! That ain't whut's a-worryin'
you, though—
LAUREY. I thought it was. Listen to that
mockin' bird a-singin'! Ever' mornin' he sets
in that ellum and sings like a tree full of birds
all by hisself.
AUNT ELLER. He's lonesome.
LAUREY. He's hungry.
AUNT ELLER. Well, it's the same thing.
LAUREY [*with real passion*]. If we ever had
to leave this here place, Aunt Eller, I'd shore
miss it. I like it. I like that thicket down by
the branch whur the 'possums live, don't you?
And the way we set around in the evenings
in thrashin' time, a-eatin' mushmelons and
singin', and oh! lots of things! Runnin' to the
cellar in a storm, and them yeller trumpet
tomaters even, you make jam out of, and the
branch and the pond to skate on— They's

only one thing I don't to say *like*. And that's Sunday in fall, when it's windy, and the sun shines, and the leaves piles up thick agin the house. I'm 'fraid of my life to go from here to the kitchen—like sump'n was gonna ketch me!

AUNT ELLER. Well, you *air* a silly.

LAUREY. But I'd shore hate to leave here, though, and go some'eres else—like to a town or some place—

AUNT ELLER. Well, the ole Scratch! Whut makes you keep talkin' about leavin' here?

LAUREY. Whut if we had to?

AUNT ELLER. Won't have to. We got money in the bank.

LAUREY. Bank might break.

AUNT ELLER. Well, let it. It's gonna be another good year fer corn and oats, like it's been now fer three year—

LAUREY. Whut if sump'n happened?

AUNT ELLER. Like whut?

LAUREY. Oh, things change. Things don't last the way they air. Besides, whut if they'd be a prairie f'ar—like the one that burnt up a thousand acres by Chambers School House five year ago?

AUNT ELLER. Ain't apt to be no prairie f'ar.

LAUREY. Or a cyclone ud come, like that un did at Sweetwater. Made hash outa three whole sections.

AUNT ELLER. Cain't stop a cyclone by worryin'.

LAUREY. No? Well, whut if Jeeter ud set the house on f'ar?

AUNT ELLER. Jeeter set the— Whut in the name of Jerusalem air you talkin' about! Jeeter set the— My goodness, git yer things ready, gonna start you right off to Vinita to the crazy house!

LAUREY. Well, I told you, anyway—

AUNT ELLER. Git 'em ready!

LAUREY. You don't have to listen.

AUNT ELLER. Whut if I'd put rat poison in the turnip greens? Now whut on earth would Jeeter want to set the house on f'ar fer?

LAUREY. I jist said he might.

AUNT ELLER. Might take a notion to rope a freight train, too. Fiddlesticks! I got my dinner on the stove a-cookin'. [*She makes for the door, slows her pace, and turns around again*] Now, whut do you mean, anyway—Jeeter set the house on f'ar?—

LAUREY. They's a horse and buggy turnin' off up the road this-a-way.

AUNT ELLER. I won't look till you tell me whut you're a-meanin'.

LAUREY. It's a roan horse 'th a long tail. He's string-haltered. Look at the way he walks—

AUNT ELLER. Not *gonna* look, I tell you!

LAUREY. You know whut a f'ar is, don't you? And you know Jeeter?

AUNT ELLER. That's jist it.

LAUREY [*gravely, queerly*]. Sump'n funny

about him. Sump'n black a-pilin' up. Ever since a year ago. Sump'n boilin' up inside of him—*mean*.

AUNT ELLER [*relieved*]. Is that it! Well, I guess you don't mind that so much—goin' to parties with him, and all.

LAUREY [*her face white—in a low voice*]. I'm afraid to tell him I won't, Aunt Eller. 'F I done what I wanted to, I'd f'ar him off the place so quick! Whut're we gonna do, Aunt Eller! He'd do sump'n turrible, he makes me shiver ever' time he gits close to me— [*With a frightened look around, as if he were in the room*] Have you ever looked out there in the smoke-house—whur he sleeps?

AUNT ELLER. Course I have, plenty of times.

LAUREY. Whut'd you see?

AUNT ELLER. Nuthin'—but a lot of dirt. Why, whut's out there?

LAUREY [*her voice tight with excitement—creating it*]. I don't know, sump'n awful. I hook my door at night and fasten the winders agin it. Agin *it*—and the sound of feet a-walkin' up and down out there under that tree, and around the corner of the house, and down by the barn—and in the front room there!

AUNT ELLER. Laurey!

LAUREY [*as before*]. I wake up and hear the boards creakin', I tell you! The rafters jist over my head here shakes a little—*easy*. Next mornin', he comes to his breakfast and looks at me out from under his eyebrows like sump'n back in the bresh some'eres. I know what I'm talkin' about—

AUNT ELLER. Why, I didn't have an idy you felt that-a-way about him! Why, we'll run him off the place if you're skeered of him—

LAUREY [*with deep premonition*]. Don't you do it! Don't you say nuthin' to him! *That's* whut skeers me—he'd do sump'n, I tell you! He'd set the house on f'ar, like I told you!

AUNT ELLER. Land's sakes! Jist let me ketch him at it! [*She laughs*] Now you've went and made all this up, and I don't believe a word of it—

LAUREY. You'll find out some day—

AUNT ELLER. Onct when you was a little girl you know what you done? Looked outa the winder and seen a cow standin' in the tool shed, and you said to yer Maw, "I knowed it, I knowed it! I knowed the cow ud eat the grindstone up!" Didn't you? But the cow didn't, though!

LAUREY [*smiling with great relief*]. No, the cow didn't.

AUNT ELLER. *Well*, then! You didn't know's much's you thought you did. [*She goes and looks out the window*] Now who'd you reckon that is drove up? [*A dog begins barking angrily*] Why, it's that ole pedler! The one that sold me that egg-beater. Jist let me git my hands onto him—'f I don't fix him—! [*She rushes toward the door*]

LAUREY. He's got someone with him. Why, it's Ado Annie Carnes! Now ain't she a sight! Ridin' around with that ole pedler.

AUNT ELLER. I'll th'ow him in the branch, that's whut I'll do to him! You know whut he done? Told me that egg-beater ud beat up eggs, and wring out dish rags, and turn the ice cream freezer, and I don't know whut all!—[*She dashes out the door*]

LAUREY [*leaning out the window*]. Yoohoo! Ado Annie! C'm here. And bring yer pedler man in too, 'f you ain't afeard I'll take him away from you. [*She snickers with delight*] I want to buy some things. [*She flies to the dresser, catches up her hair in the back, straightens her dress, and by the time* ADO ANNIE CARNES *appears in the door is humming softly to herself, apparently having forgotten her uneasiness of the moment before*]

ADO ANNIE [*coming in*]. Hi. [*She is an unattractive, stupid-looking farm girl, with taffy-colored hair pulled back from a freckled face. Her dress is of red gingham, and very unbecoming*]

LAUREY. Hi, yerself. Ridin' a piece?

ADO ANNIE [*non-committally*]. Rode over yere.

LAUREY. Well, set. Whur's yer pedler?

ADO ANNIE [*hiding a grin*]. Aw, he ain't mine. He's out there fightin' with Aunt Eller 'bout that ole egg-beater.

LAUREY [*teasing her*]. Now listen here, have you tuck up with a pedler that ud sell a pore old womern a egg-beater that wasn't no good? Ado Annie Carnes, I'm plumb ashamed of you! You ort to be strapped.

ADO ANNIE. Ain't tuck up with him. Rode a piece in his ole buggy for I was comin' over here, anyway, to ast about—to ast you sump'n.

LAUREY. Whut was you gonna ast me, then?

ADO ANNIE. 'F you was goin' to that there party over to Peck's.

LAUREY. Course I am.

ADO ANNIE. Well.

LAUREY. Don't I go to all the parties?

ADO ANNIE. I guess. You got fellers, lots of fellers.

LAUREY. Three hundred and fifty.

ADO ANNIE. Oh, you ain't!

LAUREY. Oh, I have.

ADO ANNIE. I kinda wondered 'f you wouldn't take *me*.

LAUREY. *Me*, take *you*? [*She becomes strange and thoughtful*]

ADO ANNIE. Well, someone's takin' you, ain't they? You could take me along.

LAUREY. Why, my goodness! [*She beams ecstatically*]. Why, I'd jist love to have you, Ado Annie! You git yerself over here to supper all diked up and fancy, and I'll see that you

got a way to go, all right. I'll put myself out!— [*She has another brilliant idea, which amuses her very much*] Oh, and I'm gonna buy you sump'n so purty the fellers'll all fall over a wagon tongue a-lookin' at you! Whur *is* that man! [*She rushes to the door, in a fever of delight*] Aunt Eller, Aunt Eller! Quit a-botherin' that man from his business! I want to buy some of his dewdads. [*To* ADO ANNIE, *with mock gravity*] You don't want to git to like a pedler man *too* good, Ado Annie. You hear me? They got wives in ever' state in the union.

ADO ANNIE. Oh, foot!

LAUREY. They have! And other places besides. Why, Alaska's jist full of women a-livin' in ice-houses, and freezin' to death 'cause of pedlers runnin' off and leavin' 'em 'thout no kindlin' er nuthin'—

ADO ANNIE. Aw!

LAUREY. A man *told* me! Shore as shootin'! He knowed a Eskimo womern that a pedler up there went off and left, and she had to sell her hair—a hundred hairs at a time—jist cut it right off—to keep from starvin' to death. Finally, she looked like a ole shave head, baldheaded as a turkey buzzard, and she tuck cold and died.

ADO ANNIE. *Who* did?

LAUREY. The *womern*!

ADO ANNIE. My goodness!

[AUNT ELLER *and the* PEDLER *come in. He is a little wiry, swarthy Syrian, neatly dressed, and with a red bandanna around his neck. He is very acquisitive, very cunning. He sets down his bulging suitcases, his little beady eyes sparkling professionally. He rushes over and, to* LAUREY'S *alarm, kisses her hand*]

PEDLER. My, oh my! But you are grown lady, Miss Laurey! [*He gives a grunt of surprised pleasure. His speech is some blurred European tongue with Middle Western variations, from dealing almost entirely with farmers*]

LAUREY [*backing away*]. Heavens and earth!

PEDLER. Growed up, and sich a be-*youty*, too! My, oh my! I don't see you in a whole year. Last time you was little, like that, all sunburnt and bony, and now you've turned into a be-*you*tiful young lady. Yum, yum! [*He kisses her hand again*]

LAUREY. Quit it, a-bitin' me! 'F you ain't had no breakfast go and eat yerself a green apple. Lands a goodness! You'd think I was angel food cake er sump'n. [*But she is a little pleased, in spite of herself*]

PEDLER. Angel cake, that's jist whut you air! Angel cake, and jist hot outa the oven!

LAUREY. My, listen at him! Shet up yer mouth, and show me sump'n. Is that the way he talks to you, Ado Annie?

ADO ANNIE. Aw, he don't talk to me!

LAUREY. Mercy, whut does he *do* to you!

PEDLER. Now Aunt Eller, jist listen at the way she does me—

AUNT ELLER [*snapping at him*]. I ain't yer *Aunt Eller!* Don't you *call* me Aunt Eller, you little wart! I'm mad at you.

PEDLER. Don't you go and be mad with me. Tell you what. I'll give you sump'n—give you another egg-beater.

AUNT ELLER. Don't you go and say *egg-beater* to me *again!*

PEDLER. Well, I'll give you sump'n—sump'n purty.

AUNT ELLER. Whut'll it be, and it'd better be good?

PEDLER. You wait. Sump'n purty fer to wear.

AUNT ELLER [*snorting*]. Foot! I got things fer to wear. Wouldn't have it. Whur is it?

PEDLER. You wait. I'll show you.

AUNT ELLER. Biggest liar I ever knowed! You'll be tellin' me next you got it hid some-'eres, tied onto the horse's belly band—

PEDLER. That's whur it is, exactly! You guessed it!

AUNT ELLER. Lands, you big—I won't listen at you, won't stay in the same room whur you're at. [*She marches out of the room and slams the door. Then she opens it and comes back in*] Thought I was gone, didn't you? Well, I ain't. I'm gonna stay right here, fer spite. Not gonna leave you and two girls in no bedroom, all by yerselves. [*She sits down, in the corner*]

LAUREY [*in a kind of abstracted ecstasy*]. Want some hair-pins, a fine-tooth comb, a pink un. Want a buckle made out of shiny silver to fasten onto my shoes! Want a dress with lace! Want pe'fume, face whitenin'! Wanta be purty, wanta smell like a honeysuckle vine!

AUNT ELLER [*from her corner*]. Give her a cake of soap.

LAUREY [*her mood rising*]. Want things I c'n see and put my hands on. Want things I've heared of and never had before—pearls in a plush box, diamonds, a rubber-t'ard buggy, a cut glass sugar bowl. Want things I caint tell you about. Cain't see 'em clear. Things nobody ever heared of. [*Passionately, in a low voice*] Not only things to look at and hold in yer hands. Things to *happen* to you! Things so nice if they ever did happen yer heart ud quit beatin', you'd fall down dead. They ain't no end to the things I want. Everything you got wouldn't be a starter fer me, Mister Pedler Man! [*Breaking off*] So jist give me a bottle of shoe blackin', and make it quick!

PEDLER [*on his knees, at his suitcases, handing them out*]. Some nice garters? Silk in 'em, real silk, too, and bows on 'em! Look at 'em. Made in Persia. Brought to this country—

AUNT ELLER [*satirically*]. Brought to this country at great riskin' of life and limb—like them Monsters from Madagascar. [*She giggles*] Lemme look at 'em.

LAUREY [*taking them*]. Jist whut I was a-wantin'—

PEDLER. Try 'em on.

LAUREY. Fer Ado Annie.

ADO ANNIE [*overcome*]. Aw!

PEDLER. Four bits apiece.

LAUREY. Four bits a pair.

PEDLER. Apiece.

LAUREY. Keep 'em, then.

PEDLER. Oh, take 'em.

LAUREY [*taking them*]. Here, Ado Annie. Put 'em on when no one ain't a-lookin'. [*To the* PEDLER] You got any face whitenin'?

PEDLER [*finding it*]. The best they is, Miss Laurey. Liquid powder. Smells like the Queen of Egyp'! Put it on you, they cain't no one stay away from you. Reg'ler love drops! And only six bits a bottle—with a sponge throwed in.

LAUREY. Lemme see it. C'm here, Ado Annie. [*She puts* ADO ANNIE *in a chair*] Now be still, I'm gonna try it on you. Now don't scrooge around like you had a ring worm or sump'n. Gonna hide them freckles 'f I have to put it on a inch thick.

[*She begins putting the liquid powder on a sponge and dabbing at* ADO ANNIE'S *face.* AUNT ELLER *leans back in her chair and begins to sing, in derision*]

AUNT ELLER [*singing*].
Young men they'll go courting, they'll dress up
    so fine,
To cheat the poor girls is all their design,
They'll hug and they'll kiss and they'll cheat and
    they'll lie,
They'll keep the girls up till they're ready to die.
    Sing down, hidery down!

Those girls will get angry, they'll rise up and
    say:
"I am so sleepy, I wish you'd go 'way."
Those boys will get angry to hear the girl's
    scorn—
Before they'll go home, they'll sleep in some
    barn.
    Sing down, hidery down!

Oh, early next morning those laddies will rise,
Brush off the straws and rub up their eyes,
They'll saddle their horses and away they will
    ride
Like all true lovers dressed up in their pride.
    Sing down, hidery down!

Let us turn from those boys and turn from those
    lads
And turn to those girls which are twice as bad.
They'll flour up their faces and comb up their
    hair

Till they look like an owl in the bresh, I'll
    declare!
    Wo, larry, wo!

It's two long hours they'll stand at the glass,
And a thousand pins it will take them to dress,
They'll dress up so neat, and vanish away,
The devil himself couldn't look half so gay.
    Wo, larry, wo!

You can tell a good girl wherever she goes—
No foolish marks about her clothes,
No ribbons or rings or any such things,
But an old straw bonnet tied under her chin.
    Wo, larry, wo!

Of all the good lives 'tis bachelor's best.
Be drunk or be sober, lie down and take rest,
No wife to scold, no children to squall—
How happy's the man that keeps bachelor's hall.
    Wo, larry, wo!

[*She gets up from her chair to see what*
LAUREY *is doing*] Let's see whut you're a-doin
to her. [*She turns* ADO ANNIE *about in her
chair, and bursts into a loud guffaw.* ADO
ANNIE's *face is plastered with white*] Mercy!
She's plum whitewashed you! Look like a nigger
angel turned all white and shinin'. Whur's yer
wings at, Angel?

ADO ANNIE [*scrubbing at her face*]. I'll take
ever' bit of it off! Won't have no sich of a mess
on me. I'm goin' right home! You've made a
plum sight outa me! [*She makes for the
door, flustered to death*]

LAUREY [*holding on to her*]. Don't you
b'lieve her, Ado Annie! Why, you look purty
as one of them rider ladies in the circus—'cept
fer not havin' on no pink tights. Well, jist look
in the lookin' glass, you don't b'lieve me.
    [*There is a muffled pistol shot somewhere
      outside. They all start violently*]

AUNT ELLER. Now, whut in the name of—

PEDLER. Shootin'—

ADO ANNIE. I'm goin' home—

LAUREY [*her face white*]. Wait a minute!
Whur was that shot, Aunt Eller? It wasn't out
there—out there—?

AUNT ELLER. Sounded like it come from the
smoke-house—

LAUREY. Don't you say it! It couldn't be,
couldn't!

AUNT ELLER. It *was*, I tell you.
    [*There is another shot*]

LAUREY [*shaken with fear*]. Curly!

AUNT ELLER [*looking at her in alarm*]. Why,
you're 's white as a sheet, Laurey!

LAUREY [*rushing toward the door*]. Why'd
you let him go out there whur Jeeter is!

AUNT ELLER. It couldn't be nuthin', honey!

LAUREY. We got to go see!
    [*She hurries out the door,* AUNT ELLER

and the PEDLER *following.* ADO ANNIE
*takes out her garters, puts them on hast-
ily, and flies out after them*]

CURTAIN

SCENE THREE

   *It is immediately after Scene One—at the
same time as Scene Two.*
   *The smoke-house is a dark, dirty building
where the meat was once kept. But now, the
floor is full of holes; at night the field mice
scurry about the room. The rafters are worn
and decayed, smoky, covered with dust and cob-
webs. On a low loft, many things are stored—
horse-collars, plowshares, bridles, jars of fruit,
a saddle, binder twine, a keg of nails. Under it,
the four-poster bed is grimy and never made.
A pair of muddy shoes and a pair of gum boots
are lying on their sides under the bed. On the
walls, of unpainted two-by-twelves, soiled
clothes are hanging, also tobacco advertise-
ments, an enlisting poster, a pink cover off the
Police Gazette, a large framed picture of Dan
Patch, several postcard pictures of teams pulling heavy loads of logs, etc. In one corner,
there are hoes, rakes and an axe. In another, a
bale of hay covered with a red saddle blanket.
In the room also, a tool box, several rough
chairs, a table, a spittoon, a wash-stand, several
farm lanterns, a rope, a mirror for shaving. A
small window lets in a little light, but not much.
The door at back is closed.*

   JEETER *sits in a low chair looking at some
postcards, leaning forward now and then to
spit at the spittoon. He is about thirty-five, with
a curious earth-colored face and hairy hands.
He wears heavy brogans, a greasy pair of
trousers, two shirts open at the neck, and both
dirty. He is always absorbed, dark, and sullen.
Hearing a knock, he shifts about in his chair,
spits again, shoves the pictures quickly back
into his pocket, and says crossly:*

JEETER. Well, cain't you open it?
    [CURLY *opens the door and comes in*]

CURLY. Howdy—

JEETER [*unpleasantly*]. Is that yore plug tied
to that peach tree?

CURLY. 'F you mean that horse, that's my
horse. He ain't no plug.

JEETER. Plug or no plug, you mighta tied him
some'eres else.

CURLY. They ain't nary a peach on that tree.

JEETER. And they *won't* be, if everbody's
gonna tie his saddle horse to it.

CURLY. I'll go and move him.

JEETER. 'S too late, pardner. I done moved
him.

CURLY. Whur'd you put him at?

JEETER. Turned him a-loose.

CURLY [*unruffled*]. That's all right.

JEETER. He's prob'ly tuck off up the road by this time, and serve you right.

CURLY. Left the reins a-draggin', didn't you?

JEETER. Yes, I did.

CURLY. Well, that's a cow pony, that is. He'll stand all day if the reins is down.

JEETER [*disappointed*]. You orten't to go around a-tyin' him to peach trees.

CURLY. You know, I don't know a peach tree from a corn stalk.

JEETER. Better learn, then. Whut'd you want around here, anyhow?

CURLY. I done got th'ough my business—up here at the house. I jist thought I'd come in and see you.

JEETER. I ain't got time to see no one. I'm a-takin' a bath.

CURLY [*facetiously*]. Thought you was balin' hay.

JEETER. How's that?

CURLY. I say, that's a good-lookin' rope you got there. [*He points*] Buy it at Claremore?

JEETER. Cain't see that that's none of *yore* business.

CURLY. I know you didn't steal it.

JEETER [*shortly*]. That rope was *give* to me. It's a used un.

CURLY. Ort to spin, then. [*He goes over, takes it down and begins spinning it*] You know Will Parker?

JEETER. Never heared of him.

CURLY. Ole man Parker's boy up here by Claremore? He can shore spin a rope. Chews gum when he spins it. Gum ain't healthy, I always say. [*Holding on to one end of the rope, he tosses the other over a rafter, and catches it. He pulls down on both ends, tentatively*] 'S a good strong rafter you got there. You could hang yerself on that, Jeeter.

JEETER. I could—what?

CURLY [*cheerfully*]. Hang yerself. It ud be easy as fallin' off a log! Fact is, you could stand on a log—er a cheer if you'd ruther—right about here, see, and put this here around yer neck. Tie that good up there first, of course. Then, all you'd have to do would be to fall off the log—er the cheer, whichever you'd ruther fall off of. In five minutes, er less, with good luck, you'd be dead as a door nail.

JEETER [*suspiciously*]. Whut'd you mean by that?

CURLY. The folks ud all gether around and sing. *Sad* songs, of course. And some of 'em ud say whut a good man you was, and others ud say what a pig-stealer and a hound dog you was, and you'd orter been in the penitentiary long ago, fer orneriness.

JEETER. You better be keerful, now!

CURLY. *I* ain't sayin' it. I'm sayin' *they'd* say it. You know the way people talks—like a swarm of mud wasps. [*Looking about the room*] So this is whur *you* live? Always like to see whur a man's a-livin' at. You got a fine place here, Mr. Jeeter. Matches you. [*He grins mischievously.* JEETER *gets up, goes over close to him, dangerously*]

JEETER. I don't know who you air er nuthin' —but I think you'd better tell me whut you come bustin' in here fer, makin' free 'th my things and talkin' the way you talk.

CURLY. Why, my name's Curly. Thought you knowed. Curly McClain. Born on a farm in Kansas. Cowpuncher by trade and by profession. I break broncs, mean uns. I bull-dog steers. I ain't never been licked, and I ain't never been shot. Shot *at,* but not *shot.* I got a good disposition, too, and when anything seems like to me it's funny, why I let loose and laugh till my belt breaks in two and my socks falls down. Whut on earth air *you* doin' 'th a pitcher of Dan Patch? [*He points to the picture*]

JEETER [*nonplussed*]. Got a right to have a pitcher of Dan Patch, ain't I?

CURLY. Yeah, and you shore have. And that there pink pitcher there, now that's a naked womern, ain't it?

JEETER. Yer eyes don't lie to you.

CURLY. Plumb stark naked as a jaybird! No. No, she ain't, not *quite.* Got a couple of thingumabobs tied on to her.

JEETER. That's a cover off the Police Gazette.

CURLY. Wouldn't do fer me to have sich a pitcher around.

JEETER. Whut's wrong with it?

CURLY. I never seen sich a pitcher! That ud give me idys, that would!

JEETER [*at home now and at ease with his guest*]. Shucks, that ain't a thing to whut I got here! [*He draws out his postcards*]

CURLY [*covering his eyes*]. I'll go blind! Whew! Lose my eyesight in a minute! I wonder now if we couldn't have a little game of pitch?

JEETER. Look at this here un. That's a dinger, that is!

CURLY [*looking at it gravely*]. Yeah, that shore *is* a dinger.

JEETER. The girls these is tuck of can shore make it interestin' for a man! God! cain't they! Over at Tulsa, I had me another whole pack of these—but I lost 'em—

CURLY. That's too bad. That was sump'n to lose.

JEETER. Yeah, stole off me over to a dance at Bushyhead. Shore, I'll play a game of pitch with you, all right. Here, set down.

[*They sit at the table.* JEETER *fishes in the drawer and pulls out two pistols and a pack of dirty Bicycle playing cards, and lays them on the table*]

CURLY. You—you got pistols, too?

JEETER. Good uns. Colt 45.

CURLY. Whut do you do 'th pistols?

JEETER. Shoot things.

CURLY. Oh. You deal.

JEETER. No, you deal.

CURLY. Shore, I'll deal. [*He shuffles the cards and begins to deal*] Is this draw?

JEETER. Suit yourself.

CURLY. Draw, then. With the Jick, and not the left Jack. It's yore first bid.

JEETER. Two.

CURLY. Three.

JEETER. It's your'n.

CURLY. Spades. [*He takes up the deck again*] How many?

JEETER. One.

[*CURLY deals one to JEETER, two to himself, picks up his hand. They begin to play*]

CURLY [*with lyric warmth—for he is stating something about his own life—and his feeling about life*]. Outside, the sun's jist crazy 'th the heat, beatin' on the prairie and the corn stalks. Passed a field in the bottom this mornin' whur the backwater had been. Ground all cracked and blistered and bakin' in the sun. Likin' it, though! Likin' it good. The crawfish put up their pinchers and hustled about, 'cause their holes is all goin' dry. Seen fields of wheat and oats—fine as a fiddle! The crows went to honkin' at me when I rode th'ough the Dog Crick timber, and I could see hundreds of squirrels friskin' in the blackjacks. I could smell them green walnuts, too, whenever old Dun ud tromp on 'em. Shore the purtiest mornin' in a long time! Felt like hollerin' and shoutin'. I raired away back in my saddle and ole Dun stepped out a-prancin' and we come th'ough Claremore like a streak of forked lightnin'! An' it's shore a funny end to a fine purty mornin' to find yerself shet up in a dark hole bent over a table a-fingerin' a pack of cards 's greasy 's a ole tin spoon, ain't it? Yeah, that's the way it is, though, in this here life. Got to git used to it. [*He begins to sing*]

Oh, my name it is Sam Hall, it is Sam Hall,
My name it is Sam Hall, it is Sam Hall,
My name it is Sam Hall, and I hate you one and all,
I hate you one and all, damn yer eyes!

To the gallows I must go, I must go,
To the gallows I must go, I must go,
To the gallows I must go, for I've killed a man you know,
Because he loved her so, damn his eyes!

I must hang till I am dead, I am dead,
I must hang till I am dead, I am dead,

I must hang till I am dead, for I killed a man, they said,
And I left him there for dead, damn his eyes!

I saw Mollie in the crowd, in the crowd,
I saw Mollie in the crowd, in the crowd,
I saw Mollie in the crowd, and I hollered right out loud:
"Hey, Mollie, ain't you proud, damn yer eyes!"

[*As he sings the game goes slower and slower, CURLY interested in the song and in JEETER, JEETER frowning and strangely excited. Suddenly a dog begins barking angrily. JEETER goes to the door quickly and looks out*]

JEETER. Who would that be, I wonder? In a buggy. Got a girl with him. Oh! [*He is relieved*] It's that Syrian pedler. Yeah, that's who. [*He closes the door and comes down again. After a moment*] Did that—did that Sam Hall kill the feller? [*CURLY nods*] He'd orta killed the girl, too.

CURLY. They wouldn't a-been much fun in that.

JEETER. Fun! Whut was fun about it, anyway! [*Strangely, darkly, his tongue unloosed*] I knowed a feller onct killed a girl. He'd been keepin' comp'ny with her and aimed to marry her. One day he found her up in the barn loft with another man. He didn't do nuthin' at first. But this girl lived on a farm with her folks. One night her paw and maw couldn't sleep fer the dog a-barkin' so. Next mornin' the old man went down to feed the stock like he always did, and when he come to the horse troft, he seen sump'n white a-layin' there. It was his daughter, in her nightgown, layin' there in the water all covered with blood, dead. They never did find out who done it. But I met up with a man onct on the road-gang a-makin' that road from here to Collinsville, and he told me he done it. Only—you know what he done? Made out this murder tuck place ten year ago back in Missouri. It didn't, though! It was up here by Sweetwater not two year ago—and I'd saw all about it in the paper! But I didn't let on. Whut a liar he was!

CURLY. And a kind of a—a kind of a murderer, too, wasn't he?

JEETER [*absorbed*]. I couldn't make out why he cut her throat and then throwed her in the horse troft, too. Less'n—he thought—why, that's why! He'd got blood all over him, and he couldn't stand havin' blood on him, so that's why he done it! I knowed another case, too, of a man got a girl in trouble—

CURLY. I was jist goin' to ast you 'f you didn't know some other stories.

JEETER. This man was a married farmer, and

he knowed this girl. It had been goin' on a long time till the man it looked like he couldn't live 'thout her. He was kinda crazy and wild if she'd even speak to anyone. One night, it was moonlight, and they'd met out back of an old mowin' machine left in the meader a-rustin' — She told him about the way she was, gonna have a baby. He went jist hog-wild, and found a piece of old rope in the tool box of the mowin' machine, tied her hands and feet with it, nen throwed her up on top of a stack of hay, and set f'ar to it. Burned her to death! Do you know why? He didn't keer about her goin' to have the baby, that wasn't it. He jist didn't know how he was goin' to live 'thout *havin'* her all the time while she was carryin' it! So he killed her. Yeow, it's funny the things people do, like that.

[CURLY *gets up, goes over, throws the door open. A shaft of brilliant sunlight pours in, alive with millions of dust motes*]

CURLY. Git a little air in here. [*He goes back and sits down*] Yore mind seems to run on two things, don't it? Before you come here to work fer the Williams', whur did you work?

JEETER [*hostile again*]. I don't know as that concerns no one but me.

CURLY. That's right, pardner. That's yore look-out.

JEETER. I'll tell you, though. Up by Quapaw. And before that over by Tulsa. Bastards to work fer, both of 'em!

CURLY. Whut'd they do?

JEETER. Alws makin' out they was *better*. Yeah, lots better! Farmers they was, like me, wasn't they? Only not half as good.

CURLY. And whut'd you do—git even?

JEETER [*looks up at him, suspiciously*]. Who said anything about gittin' even?

CURLY. No one, that I recollect. It jist come in my head.

JEETER. Oh, it did? [*He gets up, goes over and shuts the door, turns in the gloom, comes and sits down again, and looks at* CURLY] Whut was that business you had up here at the house?

CURLY [*after a moment*]. I don't know as that concerns you, does it?

JEETER. It does, though! If it's anything to do with this farm.

CURLY. I forgot you owned it.

JEETER. Never mind that! It couldn't be to buy hay, fer you got plenty of hay.

CURLY. How'd you know that?

JEETER. You work for Skidmore, don't you, tother side of Justus?

CURLY. Thought you didn't know me.

JEETER. I know you, all right. If he's sent you over to buy up the oat crop, why it's done spoke fer.

CURLY. Glad to find that out.

JEETER. We ain't got no cattle to sell, ner no cow ponies, you know that. And the farm ain't fer sale, and won't be.

CURLY. You shore relieved my mind considerable.

JEETER. They's only one thing left you could come snoopin' around here fer. And it ud better not be that!

CURLY [*easily*]. That's exactly whut it is!

JEETER [*white with anger*]. Better not be!

CURLY. It *is*, I tell you.

JEETER. I wouldn't come on the place if I was you! I wouldn't come here—

CURLY. Whut'll happen if I decide that's jist the right thing fer me to do?

JEETER. I'd git on my horse and go quick! Don't you come around that girl, you hear me?

CURLY [*scornfully*]. You shore got it bad. So you're takin' her to that party tonight? Jesus! She's got a taste. I don't know as it's worth fightin' about if she'd ruther go with you. I step out—cheerful as anything. You're welcome. [*Thoughtfully*] Only—somebody ort to tell her whut you air. And fer that matter somebody ort to tell you onct about yerself.

JEETER. I've had jist about enough!

CURLY. If you'd like to do anything to me, now's the best chanct you'll ever have. [*Softly*] You got two pistols, good uns, all loaded and ready to bark. They's a axe a-standin' in the corner. A bright sickle, right off the grindstone hangs over there on a nail and shines. Yer hoes is sharp, yer razor's got two edges onto it, and nary a one of 'em is rusty. And it ain't very light in here, is it? Not half light enough. A feller wouldn't feel very safe in here 'th you, 'f he didn't know you. [*Acidly*] But I *know* you, Jeeter. I've knowed you fer a long time.

JEETER [*half rising*]. You don't know a thing about me—

CURLY. The country's full of people like you! I been around. [*His voice rises dramatically*] In this country, they's two things you c'n do if you're a man. Live out of doors is one. Live in a hole is the other. I've set by my horse in the bresh some'eres and heared a rattlesnake many a time. Rattle, rattle, rattle!—he'd go, skeered to death. Skeered—and *dangerous!* Somebody comin' close to his hole! Somebody gonna step on him! Git his old fangs ready, full of pizen! Curl up and wait! Fer as long's you live in a hole, you're skeered, you got to have pertection. You c'n have muscles, oh, like arn—and still be as weak as a empty bladder—less'n you got things to barb yer hide with, [*Suddenly, harshly, directly to* JEETER] How'd you git to be the way you air, anyway—settin' here in this filthy hole—and thinkin' the way you're thinkin'? Why don't you do sump'n healthy onct in a while, 'stid of stayin' shet up here a-crawlin' and festerin'!

JEETER. Shet up, you!

CURLY. You'll die of yer own pizen, I tell you!

JEETER. Anh! [*He seizes a gun in a kind of reflex, a kind of desperate frenzy, and pulls the trigger. The wall across the room is splintered by the shot*]

CURLY. Jesus! What was you shootin' at, Jeeter?

JEETER [*his hands on the two pistols, hoarsely*]. Never mind, now!

CURLY [*in a high excitement, but apparently cool and calm*]. You orta feel better now. Hard on the wall, though. I wish 't you'd let me show you sump'n. Jist reach me one of them pistols acrost here a minute— [JEETER *does not move, but sits staring into* CURLY's *eyes*] They's a knot-hole over there about as big as a dime. See it a-winkin'? I jist want to see if I c'n hit it. [*He leans over unhurriedly, with cat-like tension, picks up one of the pistols, turns in his chair, and fires at the wall high up. He turns in triumph*] Didn't make a splinter! Bullet right through the knot-hole, 'thout tetchin', slick as a whistle, didn't I? I knowed I could do it. You saw it, too, didn't you? Somebody's comin', I 'spect. It's my play, ain't it?

[*He throws down a card.* JEETER *looks at the floor.* LAUREY, AUNT ELLER, *and the* PEDLER, *followed a moment later by* ADO ANNIE, *come running in at the door without knocking*]

AUNT ELLER [*gasping for breath*]. Whut's this? Who's been a-shootin'? Skeer the liver and lights out of a feller! Was that you, Curly? Don't set there, you lummy, answer when you're spoke to!

CURLY. Well, I shot onct.

AUNT ELLER. What was you shootin' at?

CURLY. See that knot-hole over there?

AUNT ELLER. I see lots of knot-holes.

CURLY. Well, it was one of them.

AUNT ELLER. Don't tell me you was shootin' at a knot-hole!

CURLY. I was, though.

AUNT ELLER [*exasperated*]. Well, ain't you a pair of purty nuthin's, settin' here a-pickin' away at knot-holes 'th a pair of ole pistols and skeerin' everybody to death! You've give that ole turkey gobbler conniption fits. Ort to give you a good Dutch rub and arn some of the craziness out of you! Come 'ere, you all, they ain't nobody hurt. Jist a pair of fools a-swappin' noises.

ADO ANNIE [*dumbly*]. Did someone shoot, Aunt Eller?

AUNT ELLER. Did someone *shoot!*

ADO ANNIE. Whut'd they shoot *at*, Aunt Eller?

AUNT ELLER. Yer grandmaw, silly! [*She goes out*]

ADO ANNIE. My lands!

[*She follows her out.* LAUREY *and the* PEDLER *stand in the door*]

LAUREY [*after a moment*] Curly.

CURLY. Yeah.

LAUREY. Did you *hit* that knot-hole?

CURLY. How's that?

LAUREY. I say, did you *hit* that knot-hole?

CURLY [*puzzled*]. Yeah, I—I hit it.

LAUREY [*cryptically*]. Well. That was good, wasn't it?

[*She goes out, smiling. The* PEDLER *bounds into life and comes forward with great animation*]

PEDLER. Well, well. Mr. Jeeter! Don't trouble yerself. Fine day, and a good crop comin'. You too, Mr. Curly. [*Lowering his voice*] Now then, we're all by ourselves, I got a few little purties, private knick-knacks for to show you. Special for the men folks. [*He winks mysteriously, and draws out of his inside coat pocket a thin flat box and opens it out on the table*] Yes sir, special. The things you cain't get and 've got to have. All them little things a man needs in his business, eh? [*He points*] Jist look at them things. Agin the law, ever one of 'em! There's brass knucks, lay a man out jist like he was dead in one good hard hit. Fit any knuckle and break any head. And —in the little package, well, I won't tell you!— Jist open her up, and you'll see— The little dinguses that you got to have. Fancy! Lots of colors and jiggers onto 'em. French! Yes, sir! French—right out of Paris. And jackknives and frog-stickers. Steel and never rusty. Kill a hog or a bastard eh, it's all the same to them little ones! And postcards! Kansas City Best. Made right. Take 'em away, they're hard on the eyes! And here's dice, playing cards. Everything you need, everything a man could want. Look 'em over and if they's any little thing you need, jist point, jist make the signs, and I'm right here— Now then, how's that?

JEETER [*rousing himself*]. How much is that frog-sticker?

PEDLER [*taking out a long wicked-looking knife and opening it*]. That frog-sticker. That's reasonable, reasonable. I won't charge you much for a knife like that. 'F you got it in Claremore, you know whut you pay? Twice my price, yes twice. 'F you could get it. That's a good frog-sticker, that is, and I'm sellin' it cheap to you, Mr. Jeeter—fer a man hadn't ort to be *without* a good frog-sticker, it ain't safe, he might need it. He never knows why and he never knows when. Don't see nuthin' to interest you, Mr. Curly?

CURLY [*slowly*]. I was jist thinkin' myself— that mebbe—jist fer the looks of the thing— and to kinda have it around—I might consider —buyin'—if they're good and not too high— and can be depended on—a nice hard pair of them brass knucks you got there— [*He reaches over and picks them up*]

CURTAIN

SCENE FOUR

Lead her up and down the little brass wagon,
Lead her up and down the little brass wagon,
Lead her up and down the little brass wagon,
For she's the one, my darling!

One wheel off and the axle draggin',
One wheel off and the axle draggin',
One wheel off and the axle draggin',
For she's the one, my darling!

Spokes all broke and the tongue a-waggin',
Spokes all broke and the tongue a-waggin',
Spokes all broke and the tongue a-waggin',
For she's the one, my darling!

Blistered brakes and sides all saggin',
Blistered brakes and sides all saggin',
Blistered brakes and sides all saggin',
For she's the one, my darling!

The party is in full swing in the back yard of OLD MAN PECK'S *place across Dog Creek. There are a few benches on the porch and a large coalstove. A primitive, rough-hewn built-in cabinet runs along one end of the porch and on it are piled all manner of miscellaneous things—ropes, cans of nails, a vinegar bottle, sacks of salt and sugar, home-dried apricots and peaches, a guitar, a fiddle, jars of home-made preserves. On the walls are hanging strings of popcorn on the cob, red peppers, onions hanging by their tops, the dried pelt of a possum, etc. Kerosene lanterns hung to the wall light up the yard. Light streams out from the house. Around the corner of the house can be seen the stone well with its wide arch of iron and its pulley, a tremendous walnut tree and the night sky.*

The farm boys and the cowboys have forgotten their corn plowing, their day in the hay field, their day on the range. They have put up the mules, doused themselves at the pump, bolted a supper of fried salt pork, potatoes and gravy and hot biscuits, and now in their store clothes and their chaps and their overalls they grin and sweat and stomp, their voices loud and harsh in the singing. Those who are not playing at the moment lounge in the doorway, chewing tobacco and smoking; some have gone out behind the barn or to their buggies and saddle pockets for a shot of liquor.

Most of the girls are dressed in white and wear bright bows. Some have tiny watches pinned to their dresses, and carry handkerchiefs. OLD MAN PECK *is clapping his hands. He is an old timer, grizzled and genial, about seventy.*

He has gone to play-parties and dances now for fifty years, and knows every trick, every extra stomp, every variation in the songs, every sly elaboration of the do si do.

The voices crack on the high notes, the feet pound, hands clap, the jars on the high cabinet rattle, dust clouds the air. "*The Little Brass Wagon*" *ends in a burst of high, excited, exhausted laughter. Immediately, on a peak of gaiety, hardly stopping to mop their brows, the men begin getting partners for a square dance, calling loudly, grabbing the girls carelessly around the waist and getting slapped for their temerity.*

OLD MAN PECK [*leaping out into the middle of the floor and holding up his hands*]. Hey! Boys and gals! Git in the kitchen fer the candy pullin'.

[*The crowd breaks, and dashes in the house noisily.* OLD MAN PECK *is about to follow*]

AUNT ELLER [*calling from the darkness off left*]. Lands sake, I'm all tangled up in it. Curly, help me, cain't you?

CURLY [*off*]. Well, be still, quit a-buckin' up.

AUNT ELLER. Mr. Peck! Mr. Peck, you ole fool, come an' help a lady, cain't you!

OLD MAN PECK. Is that you, Aunt Eller? Whut's the matter?

AUNT ELLER [*entering with* CURLY]. Matter! Say, do you have to have barbed w'ar layin' around all over the yard? Gettin' me all tangled up in it! 'F it hadn't a-been fer *me* I'd a-lost a leg. Whur's Mary?

OLD MAN PECK. Oh, I got the ole womern out in the smoke-house.

AUNT ELLER. Doin' all the work, I bet.

OLD MAN PECK. Yep, that's right. You're kinda late, ain't you?

AUNT ELLER. Got here quick 's I could make it. Say, is this whur the party's at—out here in the yard?

OLD MAN PECK. It's too hot in the house.

AUNT ELLER. Well, it's kinda purty out here, I must say. Here—hang this up.

OLD MAN PECK [*taking the lamp she holds out*]. Whur'd you get that?

AUNT ELLER [*grinning*]. Pulled it off the dashboard. Guess I'll go in and take off my fascinator. [*Taking* CURLY *by the arm*] How'd you like my feller I went and ketched?

CURLY [*smiling, and taking her by the arm*] How'd you like my girl I went and ketched?

OLD MAN PECK. Both of you is all right, I reckon. Whur's Laurey at?

CURLY [*pausing as he realizes what this means*]. Laurey, ain't she here yit?

OLD MAN PECK. *Course* not. Thought you was gonna bring her.

CURLY [*concerned*]. They ort to be here, Aunt Eller. Whutta you reckon's happened? They started 'fore we did—half a hour before.

Good

AUNT ELLER [*quieting him*]. Aw, they're jist poky. They're drivin' Old Eighty, and that fool mare is alwys wantin' to graze 'long side the road. Now don't look so worried, Curly, they'll git here. Come on in, and le's see *who's* come with *who*.

[*They go in. A burst of greeting floats out*]

SHORTY [*a cowboy, staggers in, drunk*]. Say, Mr. Peck, is that yore big old white cow standin' out there by the grainary?

OLD MAN PECK. Hi, Shorty. Yeah, she's mine. Give two gallon and a half a day.

SHORTY. Whew, she like to skeered me to death. Thought she was a ghost—till she said *Moo*.

OLD MAN PECK. You must be drinkin' a little, Shorty.

SHORTY [*speaking as he makes for the door*] Me? I ain't drinkin'. I'm drunk. [*He goes into the house*]

OLD MAN PECK [*spying JEETER, ADO ANNIE and LAUREY. JEETER is carrying a lighted lantern which he hangs up*]. Oh, here you are. We been wonderin' whur you was.

ADO ANNIE *and* LAUREY. Hi, Mr. Peck.

OLD MAN PECK. Most everbody's here that's comin', I 'spect. I got to go out to the smoke-house, and see about the ice cream freezin'. Go on in, and git yer pardners for the next set. [*He disappears around the corner of the house as LAUREY starts in the house*]

JEETER [*stopping her*]. I wanta see you.

LAUREY [*a little frightened*]. Well, here I am, so look yer eyes full.

JEETER. Ado Annie, go inside.

LAUREY [*grabbing her*]. Ado Annie, you stay here a minute.

ADO ANNIE [*pulling loose*]. Shoot! I wanta see 'f I cain't git me a pardner, 'fore they're all gone. [*She dashes in*]

JEETER. Whut'd you ast that Ado Annie to ride with us fer?

LAUREY. She didn't have no way to go.

JEETER. That ain't yore lookout. Why don't you wanta be with me by yerself?

LAUREY. Why, I don't know whut you're talkin' about! I'm with you by myself now, ain't I?

JEETER. You wouldn't a-been, you coulda got out of it.

LAUREY [*impatiently*]. Well, now 'at I *am*, whut'd you want?

JEETER. Nuthin'—but—

LAUREY. Well, fer land's-a-livin'! [*She makes for the door*] Of all the crazies!

JEETER [*getting in front of the door*]. Mornin's you stay hid in yer room all the time. Nights you set in the front room and won't git outa Aunt Eller's sight— [*In a strange hoarse excitement*] Ain't saw you by yerself in a long time! Why ain't I? First time was last year's thrashin'. You was watchin' the chaff fly and

them knives a-cloppin' at the bundles. I come around the corner of the stack and you stood there a-wavin' yer sunbonnet to keep some of the dust offen you, and you said to me to git you a drink of water. I *got* you a drink of water. I brung the jug around. I give it to you. I *did* give it to you, didn't I?

LAUREY [*frightened*]. I don't know whut you mean.

JEETER [*as before*]. Last time it was winter 'th snow six inches deep in drifts when I was sick. You brung me that hot soup out to the smoke-house and give it to me, and me in bed. I hadn't shaved in two weeks. You ast me 'f I had any fever and you put yer hand on my head to see. Why'd you do that? Whut'd you tetch me for! [*He suddenly seizes her in his arms, his voice thick with excitement*] You won't git away from me—!

LAUREY [*trying to free herself*]. You better le' me alone!

JEETER. You've kep' outa my way, and kep' outa my way—

LAUREY. Quit it, quit it—!

JEETER. Cain't think of nuthin' else! It's killin' me. Lay awake at nights. God damn you, quit a-tryin' to git away—I got you now—[*He holds her closer*]

LAUREY [*in revulsion*]. Oh! [*She turns her head aside, frightened and shaken*]

JEETER. So goddamned purty!

[*She frees an arm and strikes him in the face, with desperate strength. He releases her, and stands uncomprehending, tranced. She backs away, watching him*]

LAUREY [*almost hysterically*]. Now le' me go, le' me outa here 'fore I holler and tell on you!

JEETER [*after a moment, slowly*]. You hit me— [*Breaking out, violently*] Like 'em all! I ain't good enough, am I? I'm a h'ard hand, ain't I? Got dirt on my hands, pig slop—Ain't fitten to tetch you! You're better, so goddamned much better! Yeah, we'll see who's better—we'll see who's better, Miss Laurey! Nen you'll wish't you wasn't so free 'th yer airs, you're sich a fine lady—!

LAUREY [*suddenly so angry, all her fear vanishes*]. Air you makin' threats—to me? Air you standin' there tryin' to tell me 'f I don't 'low you to slobber over me like a hog, why you're gonna do sump'n about it! Why, you're a mangy dog and somebody'd orta shoot you! [*With enormous scorn*] Yeah, I ort to 'low you yer own way, I reckon. Sich a great, big, fine strappin' man so full of dazzle I ort to git down on my knees to him! Christ all hemlock! [*Sharply, her eyes blazing*] You think so much about bein' h'ard hand. Well, I'll jist tell you sump'n that'll rest yer brain, Mr. Jeeter! You ain't a h'ard hand for me, no more! You c'n jist pack up yer duds and scoot! Oh, and I even got better idys 'n that! You ain't to come on the place again, you hear me? I'll send yer stuff any place you say, but don't you 's much 's set foot inside the pasture gate or I'll sic the dogs onto you! Now then, next time you go makin' threats to people, you better think a few thinks first and spit on yer hands fer good luck!

JEETER [standing quite still, absorbed, dark, his voice low]. Said yer say. Brought it on yerself. [In a voice harsh with an inner frenzy] Cain't he'p it, I tell you! Sump'n brung it on you. On me, too. Cain't never rest. Cain't be easy. That's the way it is. Ay, I told you the way it was! You wouldn't listen—

[He goes out, passes the corner of the house and disappears. LAUREY stands a moment, held by his strangeness, then she starts toward the house, changes her mind and sinks onto a bench, a frightened little girl again. ADO ANNIE bounds out of the house, excited. She sees LAUREY]

ADO ANNIE [worried]. Laurey, I got sump'n to tell you.

LAUREY [standing up quickly]. Ado Annie, is Curly in there?

ADO ANNIE. Yes he's in there, but . . . Laurey, now look, Laurey, it's turrible—I gotta tell you—

LAUREY [starting swiftly towards the house]. Don't bother me.

ADO ANNIE [catching at her]. Now, Laurey, please, my lands, it's all yore fault, so you gotta tell me whut to do.

LAUREY. Well, whut is it?

ADO ANNIE. Them ole garters is 's tight they 'bout cut my laigs plum in two.

LAUREY. Well, take 'em off.

ADO ANNIE. Take 'em off? Have my stockings rollin' down onto my shoes? Wouldn't I be a purty sight?

LAUREY. You'd have all the boys a-runnin' after you right, you done that.

ADO ANNIE. You shore?

LAUREY. Shore, I'm shore.

ADO ANNIE. Aw, I wouldn't do it fer nuthin'.

LAUREY. Well I told you whut to do, you won't mind me. [She makes for the door]

ADO ANNIE [stopping her]. Laurey! Them ole boys worries me. The minute I got in the house they started grabbin' at me. Whut'd they mean a-tellin' me, "Come out 'hind the barn 'th me?" That ole Payne boy said that.

LAUREY. Whyn't you ast him whut he meant?

ADO ANNIE. I was skeered he'd tell me.

LAUREY. Fiddlesticks! [She starts again for the door, turns quickly, struck with an idea] Ado Annie, will you do sump'n fer me?

ADO ANNIE. 'F it ain't too hard.

LAUREY. Go in there and find Curly, and tell him to come out here. I want to see him, I got to see him!

[A man runs out of the house calling out "Whee! Here's my girl! Come on here, Ado Annie, I'm goin' to swing you till you're dizzy as a loon!" He whirls her around and around. LAUREY, distressed, starts for the house]

A MAN [coming out boisterously]. Here, Laurey's my partner. Come on, Laurey, you promised me away back last August, purt' near. [He swings her into position for the next dance]

OLD MAN PECK [coming from the house].
Git yore pardners like you done before,
Two big rings in the middle of the floor.
[The others all sweep out, paired off and take their places for the square dance]

CROWD [falling into position].
I hope there'll be a big fight!
Be lots of work for the shoemaker, tomorrow!
Watch yer honey, watch her close,
When you meet her, double the dose!
Eight hands up, and circle to the west!
[They start to dance]

OLD MAN PECK [stopping them before they begin]. Whoa, whoa, back, Maud! My you're like a gang of mule colts! Quiet down, cain't you, they ain't no a-stoppin' you! Wanta tell you sump'n!

CROWD. Let 'er rip, grampaw!
Say yer say and git it outa you 'fore you choke on it!
Open up yer mouth and holler yer head off, see 'f I keer!

OLD MAN PECK. Now then, listen to me a minute! We gonna have a little singin' to give us a rest. You all 'll be so broke down in a minute you'll be blowin' like a thrashin' machine. Quiet down now, see 'f we cain't git somebody to sing sump'n— Time we sing a little bit, got a s'prise for you. You all know whur the smoke-house is, don't you?

CROWD. 'Hind that ellum out there.
Shore, we know. Settin' on its foundations!

OLD MAN PECK. Well, I got the ole womern out there a-turnin' the ice cream freezer, and a-makin' popcorn balls. And jist as soon as we sing a little bit, everthing ort to be ready. Er 'f it ain't ready, take a scantlin' to the ole womern, I will, and blister her good! Now then, who'll give us a song?

CROWD.
Sing one yerself, Mr. Peck.
You ain't winded, air you?
Sing one of them ole ballets—
Sing "The Dyin' Cowboy." Oh, bury me not on the lone prairie!
Sing that there un 'bout the blind child, while we cry and take on, the pore little son of a gun, didn't have no mammy!

OLD MAN PECK [humorously]. Aw, I'm bashful 's a blushin' bride! Anyways, all I know is sad songs, make you cry. No, cain't I git someone else—how 'bout you, Lizzie?

CROWD. The sadder the better!

Go on, you start things, git everbody limbered up—!

OLD MAN PECK. Tell you whut I'll do, then! Sing you "Custer's Last Charge" an' 'f I ketch airy grin on any of you, gonna do sump'n, I'm tellin' you. And you better keep quiet and respectable-like, 'cause this yere is a serious piece.

CROWD. Go to it, Mr. Peck!

Serious 's a church.

Got my mouth sewed up like a button hole. Sh!

OLD MAN PECK [*singing in a high, thin voice*].

'Twas just before brave Custer's charge,
Two soldiers drew the rein,
In parting words and clasping hands,
They may never meet again.

One had blue eyes and curly hair,
Just nineteen years ago,
With rosy cheeks and down on his chin,
He was only a boy, you know.

The other was a tall and a dark slim form
With eyes that glittered like gold,
With coal-black hair and brown moustache,
Just twenty-five years old.

The tall dark form was the first to speak,
Saying, "Charley, our hour has come,
We will ride together up on yonder's hill,
But you must ride back alone.

"We have rode together on many a raid,
We have marched for many a mile,
But, comrade dear, I fear the last
Has come with a hopeless smile.

"I have a face, it's all this world to me,
And it shines like a morning's light,
Like a morning's light it has been to me
To cheer my lonesome life.

"Like a morning's light it has been to me
To cheer my lonesome life,
And little did I care for the flow of fate
When she promised to be my wife.

"Write to her, Charley, when I am gone,
Send back this fair-formed face,
And gently tell her how I died
And where is my resting place.

"And tell her I'll meet her on the other shore,
In the bordering land between
Yes, heaven and earth, I'll meet her there,
And it won't be long, I mean."

Then tears filled the eyes of the blue-eyed boy
And his kind heart filled with pain—

"I'll do your bidding, my comrade dear,
Though we never meet again.

"If I get killed and you ride back,
You must do as much for me,
For I have a praying mother at home,
She is all the world to me.

"She has prayed at home like a waiting saint,
She has prayed both night and morn,
For I was the last the country called,
She kissed and sent me on."

Just then, the orders came to charge,
An instant with clasped hands,
Then on they went, then on they rode,
This brave and devoted band.

They rode till they come to the crest of the hill
Where the Indians shot like hail,
They poured death's volley on Custer's men,
And scalped them as they fell.

They turned from the crest of the bloody hills
With an awful gathering gloom,
And those that were left of the faithful band
Rode slowly to their doom.

There was no one left to tell the blue-eyed girl
The words that her lover said,
And the praying mother will never know
That her blue-eyed boy is dead.

[*The crowd applauds and exclaims*]

CROWD. Shore a good un!

Sings plumb like a church choir, don't he?

Whur's Curly McClain?

Git him to sing.

Here you, Curly, you c'n sing—one of them cowpuncher ones.

CURLY [*appearing from the crowd*]. Well. Hand me down that guitar, will you?

[*Someone gets the guitar off the cabinet, and hands it to him. He drags forward a stool and sits down*]

CROWD. "Railroad Man."

"Levee Dan."

"Whistlin' Rufus."

"The Girl I Left Behind Me."

"The Pore Lost Dogie."

"Shoot the Buffalo."

Sump'n lively!

"The Mohawk Trail."

CURLY [*he strums a few notes, and begins to sing, very simply*]

There is a lady, sweet and kind,
Was never face so pleased my mind,
I did but see her passing by,
And yet I love her till I die.

Her gestures, motion, and her smiles,
Her wit, her voice, my heart beguiles,
Beguiles my heart I know not why,
And yet I love her till I die.

Cupid is wingèd and doth range
Her country so my love doth change,
But change she earth or change she sky,
Yet will I love her till I die.

CROWD [*applauding*]. Sing another'n, Curly.
You shore fooled us. Funny song fer *you* to
be a-singin'!

Now, Aunt Eller—

Aunt Eller, come on, you, it's yore time.

AUNT ELLER. Ketch me a-singin'! Got a frog
in my throat—I'm t'ard, too. Got a ketch in
my leg and cain't sing. Land's alive! Whyn't
you git Ado Annie—? Here, Ado Annie, sing
one of them songs of your'n.

[*They drag* ADO ANNIE *forward, squirm-
ing*]

CROWD. Here, quit it a-pullin' back, you don't
git out of it—

ADO ANNIE [*awkwardly, standing first on one
foot, then on the other*]. Done forgot! Done
forgot!

CROWD. Well, hurry up and remember—

ADO ANNIE. Don't know none, nary a one.
Done forgot ever one, I tell you!

CROWD. Well, whistle then, you got to do
sump'n.

AUNT ELLER. Forgot yer foot! Sing that un
about when you was young and single—

ADO ANNIE. Shoot! My th'oat's plumb sore—

AUNT ELLER. Sump'n else 'll be sore you don't
start. Hurry up, now—

ADO ANNIE [*singing in a flat mournful voice*].

When I was young and single,
At home by my own f'ar side,
With my loving brother and sister,
My mother she never would chide.

Then there came a young man
His smiles enticèd me.
—And I was young and foolish
And easy led astray.

I don't see why I love him,
He does not keer for me,
But my thoughts are alwys of him
Wherever he may be.

They tell me not to believe him,
Say "He don't keer fer you."
How little I think that ever
Them words would ever come true!

Some say that love is pleasure.
What pleasure do I see?

For the one I love so dearly
Has now gone back on me!

The night is dark and dreary,
A little incline to rain—
O God, my heart is weary
For my lover's gone off on a train!

OLD MAN PECK. All out fer the smoke-house
now! Git some ice cream in you, you feel better! Got vanilla and strawberry both, so don't
be bashful!

[*The crowd begins to stream noisily out,
disappearing past the corner of the
house*]

LAUREY [*catching* CURLY *away from his
partner, and dragging him back till the others
are all gone*]. Curly!

CURLY [*astonished*]. Now what on earth is
ailin' the belle of Claremore? By gum, if you
ain't a-cryin'!

[LAUREY *runs over to him, leans against
him*]

LAUREY. Curly—I'm 'fraid, 'fraid of my
life—!

CURLY [*in a flurry of surprise and delight*].
Jumpin' toadstools! [*He waves his hat, then
throws it away wildly, and puts his arms around*
LAUREY, *muttering under his breath*] Great
Lord—!

LAUREY. Don't you leave me—

CURLY. Great Godamighty—!

LAUREY. Don't mind me a-crying, I cain't
he'p it—

CURLY. Jesus! Cry yer eyes out—!

LAUREY. Oh, I don't know whut to do!

CURLY. Here. I'll show you. [*He lifts her
face and kisses her. She puts her arms about his
neck. He exclaims softly*] Laurey, Laurey—!
[*He kisses her again and again, then takes a
step away from her, disengaging her arms
gently*]

LAUREY [*in alarm*]. Curly—

CURLY. My goodness! [*He shakes his head as
if coming out of a daze, gives a low whistle, and
backs away*] Whew! 'Bout all a man c'n stand
in public—! Go 'way from me, *you!*

LAUREY. Oh, you don't like me, Curly—

CURLY. *Like* you? My God! Git away from
me, I tell you, plumb away from me! [*He
strides across the room and sits down on the
stove*]

LAUREY [*crying out*]. Curly! You're settin'
on the stove!

CURLY [*leaping up*]. Godamighty! [*He turns
round, puts his hand down gingerly on the lids*]
Aw! 'S cold 's a hunk of ice! [*He sits down
again*]

LAUREY [*pouting*]. Wish 't ud burnt a hole
in yer pants—

CURLY [*grinning at her, understandingly*].
You do, do you?

LAUREY [*turning away, to hide her smile*]. *You* heard me.

CURLY. Laurey, now looky here, you stand over there right whur you air, and I'll set over here—and you tell me whut you wanted with me.

LAUREY [*grave again*]. Well— Jeeter was here. [*She shudders*] He skeered me—he's crazy. I never saw nobody like him—

CURLY [*harshly*]. Whut'd he do? Aunt Eller told me all about the way you felt—whyn't you tell *me*—why didn't you? Whut'd he do?

LAUREY. Tried to kiss me— Wouldn't let me out of here. Said he'd tried to see me all by myself fer months. He talked wild—and he threatened me.

CURLY. The bastard!

LAUREY. I f'ard him! Told him not to come on the place again. I got mad to see him standin' there like a black cloud, and I told him what! I wish 't I hadn't-a! They ain't no tellin' whut he'll do now! 'F I'd jist a-kep' my head! Now whut am I gonna do!

CURLY. You f'ard him?

LAUREY. Yes, but—

CURLY. *Well,* then! That's all they is to it! He won't do nuthin'! Tomorrow, I'll git you a new h'ard hand. I'll stay on the place myself tonight, 'f you're nervous about that hound-dog. [*Putting an end to it*] That's the end of Jeeter, and about time. Now quit yer worryin' about it, er I'll spank you. Hey, while I think of it—how—how 'bout marryin' me?

LAUREY [*flustered*]. Gracious, whut'd I wanta marry *you* fer?

CURLY [*getting down off the stove and going to her, gravely, like a child*]. Laurey, please, ma'am—marry me. I—I don't know whut I'm gonna do if you—if you don't.

LAUREY [*touched*]. Curly—why, you—why, I'll marry you—'f you want me to—

CURLY [*he takes her in his arms, kisses her gently*]. I didn't think you would, I didn't dream you'd ever—!

LAUREY. Sh!

[*He leads her over, and lifts her up on the stove. Then he lets down the oven door and sits on it, at her feet*]

CURLY [*humbly*]. I ain't got no right to ast you—a good-fer-nuthin' cowpuncher like me—

LAUREY. Don't say things like that.

CURLY. If I'd ever a-thought—! Oh, I'd orta been a farmer, and worked hard at it, and saved, and kep' buyin' more land, and plowed and planted, like somebody—'stid of doin' the way I've done! Now the cattle business'll soon be over with. The ranches are breakin' up fast. They're puttin' in barbed w'ar, and plowin' up the sod fer wheat and corn. Purty soon they won't be no more grazin'—thousands of acres—no place fer the cowboy to lay his head.

LAUREY. Don't you worry none, Curly—

CURLY. Yer paw done the right way. He knowed. He could see ahead.

LAUREY. But Pap ain't alive now to enjoy it. But we're alive, Curly. Alive! Enjoy all we can! Case things happen.

CURLY. Nuthin' cain't happen now—nuthin' bad—if you—if you love me—and don't mind a-marryin' me.

LAUREY. Sh! I'll marry you. Somebody's comin', don't you reckon?

CURLY. I don't keer. When *will* you marry me?

LAUREY. Oh, purty soon. I'll have to ast Aunt Eller, first.

CURLY. I'll ast her myself! [*Gaily*] Oh, I 'member the first time I ever seen you! You was pickin' blackberries long side the road here years and years ago—you was a little tyke. [*He laughs*] You'd been a-eatin' berries as fast as you could pick 'em, and yer mouth was black as a coal shovel!—'F you wasn't a sight!

LAUREY [*embarrassed*]. Curly!

CURLY. Nen I seen you onct at the Fair—a-ridin' that little gray filly of Blue Starr's, and I says to someone—"Who's that little thing with a bang down on her forehead?"

LAUREY. Yeow, I 'member. You was ridin' broncs that day, and one th'owed you.

CURLY. Did *not* th'ow me!

LAUREY. Guess you jumped off, then.

CURLY. Shore I jumped off.

LAUREY. Yeow, you shore did!

CURLY [*lyrically, rapturously*]. Anh, and I seen you once—the Sunday a year ago, I'll never forget. I come over to break them broncs. You'd been out a-pickin' flowers next to that sorghum mill standin' in the cane patch. And you had a whole armful of Sweet Williams and wild roses and mornin' glories, and I don't know what all. My, I nearly fell off my horse a-lookin' at you! And I thought to myself—"if this yere bronc th'ows me, I won't land anywhurs near no Sweet Williams and wild roses. No sir! No sich luck! I'll find myself 'th my face plowin' up a patch of cuckle burrs and jimson weeds—er most likely a ole cow pile!"—

LAUREY. Curly! The way you talk!

CURLY [*as before*]. Be the happiest man a-livin', soon 's we're married! [*Frowning*] Oh, but I'll shore be a unsettled man, though, you're so blame purty, worried somebody'll run off with you! 'F I ever have to leave home to be gone all day, gonna shore tie you up to the hitchin' post, so you'll be there 'gin I git back, you hear? [*He shakes her playfully*] Ain't gonna take no chances! [*Mischievously*] And looky here, whut're you gonna give me fer a weddin' present? Well, you gonna marry a good-fer-nothin' cow hand, 'thout a red cent in his breeches, 's yer own fault, they come high! How 'bout a pair of spurs? Er a nice new saddle blanket, eh, 'th red stripes onto it, and 'nitials stitched inside of a bleedin' heart on the corner? Whut's the use of gettin' married, don't git a saddle blanket er sump'n purty out of it!—

LAUREY. Curly! Now I'll know why you married me—to git a saddle blanket!

CURLY. Yeow, out in the open, that's me! A man's got to watch out fer hisself even 'f he has to marry him a homely critter like you—'th a face like a windmill, make you dizzy to look at it! Come 'ere and kiss me, why don't you?

LAUREY [*gravely, touching his hair shyly*]. I jist set here and listen at you, and don't keer whut you say about me. Say I'm homely 's a mud fence, you want to—why then, I *am* homely 's a mud fence. 'F you say I'm purty, why I'm purty as anything, and got a voice like Jenny Lind. I never thought of anything like this! But I always wondered and wondered, after the first time I ever seen you— [*Her eyes fill with tears, absurdly*] And here we set, you and me, on the kitchen stove like a pair of skillets, and I don't know whut's come over us to act so silly—and I'm gonna cry in a minute—and it's all yore fault, you orten't to a-made love to me this-a-way—

[CURLY *jumps up, puts his arms around her*]

CURLY. Laurey— Cry 'f you want to, then. [*He kisses her tenderly*] Laurey, sweet— [*After a moment*] Now, then. [*Crying out, suddenly*] Why, my lands of goodness! I plumb forgot! You ain't had nothin' to eat! No pop-corn er ice cream er nuthin'! You pore thing! Wait a minute. I'll git you sump'n 'fore it's all gone! [*He runs and looks down the well, and comes back quickly very much amused*] Hey! Look in the cupboard there and see 'f you cain't find two glasses. [*He goes back to the well and can be seen hauling up a rope*]

LAUREY. Whut're you up to, Curly?

[*She flies to the cupboard, finds some glasses.* CURLY *has drawn up a small tin bucket, detached it from the rope, and come back, the bucket dripping. He sets it down on the stool, takes off the cover*]

CURLY. Cream! Good ole rich cream, right outa the well! Cold as ice! Freeze yer wish-bone, might' nigh, a-slidin' down yer throat!

[LAUREY *brings the glasses. He pours them full. They are drinking when the* CROWD, *already paired off, sweeps down into the yard hilariously*]

CROWD [*calling out in excitement*]. Hey! Whut's this!

Two little love birds!

Jist a-dyin' to git on the nest, too, from the look of 'em!

Gonna be a weddin'—

Gonna be a shivoree—

How'd a girl ever take to a feller like you, Curly?

AUNT ELLER [*appearing*]. Land sakes, I feel turrible! I went and ketched me a feller and here he is makin' up to another girl!

A MAN. Let's start the lovin' couple off right!

[JEETER *has leaned against a post and stands brooding. He has been drinking and has a bottle in his hand*]

JEETER [*with dark scorn*]. Yay, start 'em off right! To the bride and groom—

[*He lifts the bottle, darkly, insultingly, and hurls it across the yard, where it breaks with a loud crash.* CURLY *starts toward him angrily,* LAUREY *clinging to him.* OLD MAN PECK, *seeing the situation, grabs the hands of the people nearest him, and they form a circle which quickly grows, shunting* CURLY *and* LAUREY *off from* JEETER *on one side of the yard. Someone begins to sing; the crowd joins in.* LAUREY *and* CURLY *are hoisted up on chairs, the circle around them*]

CROWD [*singing*].

Gone again, skip to my Lou,
Gone again, skip to my Lou,
Gone again, skip to my Lou,
Skip to my Lou, my darling!

Cain't git a redbird, bluebird'll do,
Cain't git a redbird, bluebird'll do,
Cain't git a redbird, bluebird'll do,
Skip to my Lou, my darling!

My girl wears a number ten shoe,
My girl wears a number ten shoe,
My girl wears a number ten shoe,
Skip to my Lou, my darling!

Flies in the buttermilk, two by two,
Flies in the buttermilk, two by two,
Flies in the buttermilk, two by two,
Skip to my Lou, my darling!

CURTAIN

SCENE FIVE

A July moon is over the hayfield, making silver tents of the mounds of unbaled hay which recede in irregular formation far into the distance, crossing a low hill. A gaunt wire rake with enormous wheels stands at one side. The sky is powdered with stars, but low clouds drift often in front of them and the moon, blotting out the stubble. A soft summer wind, creeping about the meadow, lifts the spears of grass that have escaped the sickle. A low hay stack, very near, has a ladder leaning against it.

After a moment, CURLY *and* LAUREY *steal into sight, looking around cautiously. They stop, move forward a little, breathless, begin to speak in hushed voices.*

CURLY [*softly*]. D'you hear anything?

LAUREY [*softly*]. No.

CURLY. Listen. [*They listen. Then he turns to her with relief*] Not a sound. We've give 'em the slip.

LAUREY. Sh! Whut was that?

[*There is not a sound*]

CURLY. Don't hear nuthin'.

LAUREY [*relieved*]. Jist the wind, I guess.

CURLY. Listen. We'll leave Old Eighty standin' whur we tied her. We cain't drive up to the house, 'cause 'f anybody's watchin' out fer us, they'd see us. We'll sneak acrost the hayfield and th'ough the plum thicket—and go in the back door. Come on now. Watch whur you step.

LAUREY [*taking his hand, stopping him, hesitantly*]. Curly,—if they ketch us, whut'll happen? Will it be bad?

CURLY [*soberly*]. You know about shivorees, honey. They git purty rough.

LAUREY. I'm afeard.

CURLY. Don't be afeard, honey. Aunt Eller says fer shore nobody seen us gittin' hitched.

LAUREY. They mighta s'pected sump'n, though. [*Her voice low*] That's the ketch about gittin' married—

CURLY [*reassuringly*] But here we air, honey. Married—and purt' nigh home. And not a soul in sight.

LAUREY [*after a moment of registering this, relievedly*]. Yeah. We fooled 'em, didn't we?

CURLY. Shore we did.

LAUREY. Course. [*Her voice full of wonder*] Curly—we're—we're married now.

CURLY [*softly*]. Yeah. Plumb hitched.

LAUREY. Was you skeered when the preacher said that about "Will you take this here wo-mern—"?

CURLY. Skeered he wouldn't *say* it.

LAUREY. I was skeered you'd back out on me.

CURLY. I *couldn't* back out on you—'f I *wanted* to. Could you *me*?

LAUREY [*smiling tenderly*]. Not if I tried and tried.

[*They kiss, and embrace for a moment. Then still holding her hand, CURLY turns, looking out over the moonlight field*]

CURLY [*lyrically, feeling the moment*]. Look at the way the hayfield lays out purty in the moonlight. Next it's the pasture, and over yander's the wheat and the corn, and the cane patch next, nen the truck garden and the timber. Ever'thing laid out fine and jim dandy! The country all around it—all Indian Territory —plumb to the Rio Grande, and north to Kansas, and 'way over east to Arkansaw, the same way, with the moon onto it. Trees ain't hardly a-movin'. Branch bubbles over them limestone rocks, you c'n hear it. Wild flower pe'fume smellin' up the air, sweet as anything!

A fine night fer anyone to remember fer a weddin' night! A fine night—fer anyone.

[*Caught up in the spell of the night and their feelings, they move softly away across the stubble, and disappear. There is a moment of silence.*

Then there is a subdued titter, followed by shishing sounds, then more titters and smothered laughter. There pop into sight on top of, and from behind the stacks, dozens of men carrying noise-making instruments—tin lids, pots, washboilers, cow bells, gourd rattles, tambourines, pans, iron triangles, whistles, drums. They are an excited, huddled, whispering group, nervous at their long wait for the return of the bride and groom from town, disturbed and hysterical with conjecture on the marital scene they have come to despoil. Veterans of the "shivoree," hardly a bridal couple within twenty miles around, for years and years, has escaped their bawdy ministrations. They look off toward the retreating and oblivious couple, holding their voices down]

1ST MAN. Sh! They'll hear you!

3RD MAN [*satirically, mockingly*]. "Fine night to remember fer a weddin' night!"

[*Laughter*]

5TH MAN. Fine night fer anyone. Whee! [*Hushing them*] Quiet down now! They'll hear you 'fore they git to the house!

9TH MAN. Tee hee! Bet they'll go to bed in the dark!

[*Laughter*]

10TH MAN [*severely*]. Be keerful! They'll hear us, you hoodlums!

1ST MAN. Sh!

7TH MAN. Cain't you keep yer mouth still a minute!

3RD MAN. Whee! High ole doin's!

5TH MAN. Ketch 'em in the act!

YOUNG FARMER. Whut're we waitin' fer?

OLD FARMER. Give 'em time to git to the house, cain't you?

CORD ELAM. Don't want to give 'em too much time!

10TH MAN. Wish't I uz in his shoes. God-amighty!

3RD MAN. He shore got him sump'n there!

1ST MAN. Couple of sections!

2ND MAN. Grazin' and timber and plowed land!

4TH MAN. Money!

6TH MAN. Scads of it in the bank, and more comin'!

5TH MAN. And God! She's a purty un, too!

3RD MAN. Got a face fer kissin'!

7TH MAN. Hands white as snow!

5TH MAN. And that ain't all, brother!

YOUNG FARMER. No, and that ain't all! Jesus!

Wish't I uz in Curly's shoes! 'F I uz Curly, ud be in my bare feet by this time!

1ST MAN [in great excitement]. Look! They's a light!

[They crowd in an excited frenzy begins jumping off the stacks]

3RD MAN. In the bedroom!

4TH MAN. Look at the way them curtains blow!

2ND MAN. Lace curtains!

3RD MAN. Blowin' out like a shirt-tail a-poppin' in the breeze!

CORD ELAM. Wonder whut they're a-seein', them curtains?

1ST MAN. Bridal couple! Onct in a life-time—

3RD MAN. By theirselves!

4TH MAN. Night come on!

YOUNG FARMER. Ay, the good ole black night —'th nobody to spy on you, nobody to see whut you're up to!

8TH MAN. Look at them shadders a-movin'!

1ST MAN. It's them, they're there! See that there un!

2ND MAN. Gittin' ready!

3RD MAN. Got to hurry now, 'come on! Give 'em a s'prise!

CORD ELAM. Don't fergit now, right by this here stack whur the ladder is, like we said!

3RD MAN. Don't make so goddamned much noise!

[They go out. An OLD MAN stumbles into the moonlight, shaking his head, dismally]

OLD MAN. Listen at that ole owl a-hootin' in the timber, and that there coyote away off yander towards the Verdigree River! [He goes out]

[A YOUNG FARMER, flushed and drinking, staggers darkly out of the gloom]

YOUNG FARMER. Bridegroom a-waitin' and a-waitin'! Don't you wait now, Mr. Bridegroom! The moon's a-shinin'! Yer time has came! Yes, sirree, bob! No time to wait now. Time to git goin'. See that there bride a-glimmerin' there in her white! Waitin' fer you. Been a-standin' there with her hair down her back and her lips a-movin'! Git next to her, brother! Gonna be high ole times, gonna be Jesus into yer heart!

[The sound of raucous noise and excitement begins. CORD ELAM runs from around a stack shoving the YOUNG FARMER out of the way]

CORD ELAM. Git outa the way now, Homer! [To the approaching noisy party] Hey! Over this-a-way. Yere's the place!

[The noise of the shivoree grows louder and louder. Voices rise out of the bedlam, in sharp exclamations and cries. A few men drag CURLY in, struggling and angry, his hair in his eyes. His shirt has been ripped off in the struggle]

CURLY. God damn you, leave her alone! Don't ary son of a bitch put his hands onto her, I'll kill him—!

A MAN. Aw, nobody's a-hurtin' her, Curly—

CURLY. Better hadn't. I tell you. Make 'em git away from her, plumb away from her!

A MAN [shouting off]. Git away from her, you all! Bring her on in!

[CURLY relaxes, but his captors still hold him tightly. A wide circle of men, shouting, whistling, beating their various noise implements, advances across the stubble. In the middle of the group, walking alone, pale and shaken is LAUREY, in a nightgown, her hair down about her shoulders. The crowd goes over to the foot of the ladder and stops]

5TH MAN. Quiet down now, a minute! [To LAUREY] Right up the ladder with you, you purty thing!

[The noise stops]

6TH MAN. Go on, boost her up!

7TH MAN. Right up on the stack—!

8TH MAN. Make out it's a bed, why don't you!

[LAUREY looks around at CURLY, then climbs up the short ladder, the crowd shouting at her]

9TH MAN. Watch it!

10TH MAN. Put yer foot in the right place.

CORD ELAM. Don't wanta fall and break yer neck—cheat pore Curly outa his rights!

10TH MAN. All right, Curly—

6TH MAN. You're next.

10TH MAN. Bring him on over here.

[THE MEN holding CURLY lead him over to the foot of the ladder, and let go of him. THE CROWD begins to call out in more jubilant, crazier derision]

1ST MAN. Go, on, Mr. Bridegroom, there's yer bride—!

3RD MAN. Purty's a new bronc a-standin' and a-lookin', cain't hardly keep off her!

7TH MAN. Mane like silk and eyes a-shinin'!

CORD ELAM. Git on, there, cowpuncher—! [After a moment, CURLY starts up the ladder, the crowd continuing to shout] 'F you ain't a world-beater fer bashful!

3RD MAN. Better be glad we didn't ride you on no fence rail!

1ST MAN. Th'ow the ladder down when he gits up.

10TH MAN. Try to git off, you'll break yer neck, so watch out!

[CURLY reaches the top. Someone throws the ladder down]

CURLY [deeply troubled]. Laurey, honey— [She looks at him, in dumb misery] I'd give my eye-sight, honey—! Try to stand it—I done all I could. I cain't he'p it—

[He takes her in his arms. The men break out into derisive and lascivious guffaws, *and begin the deafening noises again, circling the hay stack, kicking up their heels, in an orgy of delight*]

3RD MAN. Give us a little kiss, honey lamb, do a man good, taint a-askin' much!

CORD ELAM. Give us a lick and a promise!— Quick's these bad ole mens goes away,—they ain't no a-tellin', no, siree!

5TH MAN. 'Taint right to stand there like that— Blush to look at you!

7TH MAN. Ain't no right to be in no night-gown!

10TH MAN. Go on, Mr. Moon Man, hide yer face fer shame!

YOUNG FARMER. How's it feel to be married, Laurey, sugar, all safe and proper, to sich a fine purty man with curly hair and a dimple on his chin! Whee! Got you whur I want you—!

1ST MAN. Scrunch you to death, purt' near!

CORD ELAM. Bite them shoulders—

3RD MAN. Eat 'er alive!

5TH MAN. Yay, Curly, and it's one more river to cross!

[*One of the men cries out, excitedly, snickering*]

A MAN. Hey, Curly! Hey, Laurey! One baby! [*He tosses a grotesque straw baby high in the air and onto the stack*] Two! [*He tosses another quickly*] Three! [*He tosses another*]

ANOTHER MAN [*holding up admonishing hands, grinning delightedly*]. Hold it! Not so many! That'll give Curly *idys, that* will!

[*There is raucous laughter, and beating of instruments. The glow and smoke of something burning which has already crept quietly over the hayfield, now leaps up. A hay stack is burning*]

CURLY [*startled, pointing*]. Look! Fer God's sake, that hay stack's on fire [THE MEN *rush toward it*] Get us a ladder someone, quick! The whole hayfield 'll be on fire!

[*Suddenly a dark figure comes into sight, carrying a flaming torch. It is* JEETER]

JEETER [*crying out*]. Yanh, you thought you had it over me so big, didn't you? And you, too, Missy! Wanted sump'n purtier to sleep with. Yanh, you won't be a-havin' it long. Burn you to cracklin's!

[*He springs forward like a maddened animal to apply the torch to the stack.* LAUREY *screams.* THE MEN *start rushing back, as* CURLY *leaps down, knocking the torch out of* JEETER's *hand*]

CURLY. Godamighty!

[*They struggle. The crowd exclaims*]

1ST MAN. It's Jeeter Fry! Thought he'd flew the country!

3RD MAN. Drunk as a lord—

4TH MAN. Godamighty, he's crazy drunk!

5TH MAN. He was sweet on her too, they tell me. Stop him, somebody!

7TH MAN. Man seen him last week 'way off in Joplin.

8TH MAN. Jeeter, you goddamned—

[A MAN *beats at the torch with his bare hands, till* ANOTHER MAN *runs up and smothers it quickly with his coat. Someone picks up the torch, stamping out the flames, and runs out to the branch with it*]

[JEETER *has backed away in the struggle, and drawn out a knife. He throws himself upon* CURLY. *The crowd mutters in excitement and fear. The men struggle over the knife, their arms gripping each other desperately. Suddenly,* JEETER *trips and they go down in the stubble.* JEETER *groans and whimpers and lies very still*]

CURLY. Now, now—Christ— [*He shakes his hand, crazily, helplessly, in horror*] Look at— look at him! Fell on it— Stuck it th'ough his ribs! [*He backs away, shaken, horrified. Some of* THE MEN *bend over the prostrate man*]

YOUNG FARMER. Pull that knife out!

MEN. What's the matter?

Don't you tech it!

Turn him over—

He's breathin', ain't he?

Feel his heart.

How'd it happen?

9TH MAN [*wildly*]. Anh, it's went right th'ough his heart—

4TH MAN. Whut'll we do? Ain't he all right?

10TH MAN. 'S he jist stunned?

CORD ELAM [*pushing into the crowd*]. Git away, some of you! Lemme look at him. [*He bends down, the men crowding around.* CURLY *has slumped back against the stack, like a sick man.* LAUREY *stands dazed, watching. After a moment, standing upright*] Cain't do a thing now. Try to git him to a doctor, but I don't know—

9TH MAN [*hysterically*]. Pull the knife out, cain't you? Leave a knife stuck in a—! [*He springs forward*]

CORD ELAM [*grabbing him*]. You can't pull it out, you fool! Git away from there! [*The man staggers away, weakly*] Here, you, some of you! Carry him down to the branch. Quick! I'm 'fraid it's too late!

[*The men lift* JEETER *up*]

10TH MAN. Handle him easy!

6TH MAN. Don't shake him!

3RD MAN. Hold on to him careful, there!

5TH MAN. Godamighty! Whut a thing to happen!

[*They carry him out*]

CORD ELAM [*to* CURLY]. I don't know, Curly. You better give yourself up, I 'spect. They ain't no a-tellin'. You better go in with me, as I go, and tell 'em how it was. Tonight. It might go hard with you, you don't. [CURLY *stands dazed, as if unhearing*] 'D you hear me, Curly?

You know the way ever'body feels about shivo-reein'. You got to take it right.

CURLY [*in desperation*]. But f'ar—f'ar! He was tryin' to burn us up!

CORD ELAM. I know. But you got to tell the *law.* It'll be easier that way. I'll come back fer you. [*He goes out toward the branch*]

LAUREY [*in a fever of horror*]. Curly, Curly—

CURLY [*hardly able to speak*]. Laurey—

LAUREY. Is he—is he—?

CURLY. Don't say anything—

LAUREY. It cain't be that-a-way!

CURLY. I didn't *go* to.

LAUREY. *Cain't* be! Like that—to happen to us!

CURLY. Sh! Be quiet!

LAUREY. Whyn't they do sump'n? Why'd they let him—lay there—? Cain't git over the way he—

CURLY. Laurey, Laurey!

LAUREY [*in mounting hysterical feeling*]. He laid there in the stubble, so quiet, 'th his eyes open, and his eyeballs white and starin'! He laid there in the stubble—'th his eyes open—!

[*She buries her face in her hands, shuddering.* CURLY *turns away, numb, speechless, his shoulders hunched up, like one shielding himself from the wind. The howl of a coyote drifts in on the summer air—near and desperate and forlorn*]

CURTAIN

SCENE SIX

A few nights later ADO ANNIE *and* AUNT ELLER *are sitting in the front room, sewing. An oil lamp makes an amber pool of light about them. The sliding doors are closed, but a thin crack of light comes from underneath.* ADO ANNIE, *with a piece of plaid across her knees, is snipping at it with scissors.* AUNT ELLER *is very busy over a flour sack; she pushes her iron spectacles up off her nose and looks over at* ADO ANNIE.

AUNT ELLER [*in astonishment*]. In the name of Doodlebug—whut *air* you a-doin'?

ADO ANNIE [*looking up from her work*]. Makin' a button-hole, cain't you see?

AUNT ELLER. A *round* button-hole?

ADO ANNIE. Course.

AUNT ELLER [*amused*]. Whyn't you make a square one? Er I tell you—make one looks like a four-leaf clover, why don't you?

ADO ANNIE [*shortly*]. Guess I know how to make button-holes.

AUNT ELLER. Yeah, you shore do. Cuttin' a round hole in that plaid. [*They sew in silence. After a moment* AUNT ELLER *glances up toward the closed door, and says*] She ain't went to bed yit.

ADO ANNIE. 'S nine o'clock about.

AUNT ELLER [*shaking her head*]. Worried about her. She don't eat ner sleep sence Curly was tuck away.

ADO ANNIE. She'll git pore she don't eat.

AUNT ELLER. Well, *course* she'll git pore.

ADO ANNIE. That's whut I said.

AUNT ELLER [*slightly irritated*]. I *heared* you say it.

ADO ANNIE [*blandly*]. Well.

AUNT ELLER. Looky here, Ado Annie Carnes, don't you ever marry.

ADO ANNIE [*self-consciously*]. Gracious, who'd I marry?

AUNT ELLER. Don't you *ever!* *I* did. And *look* at me. [*Half-seriously*] First yer man—he'll die—like mine did. Nen the baby—*she'll* die. The rest of yer younguns'll grow up and marry and leave you, the way mine did. Nen you'll be all by yerself. Time you're old as me, you'll be settin' around, jist the way *I* am, 'th a wooden leg and a bald head, and a-rippin' up old flour sacks to make yerself a pair of drawers out of. [*She holds up her work for* ADO ANNIE *to see*]

ADO ANNIE [*overcome with mirth*]. Hee! Hee!

AUNT ELLER. Trouble shore starts, you git married. Look at Laurey. Better *not* git married, I tell you.

ADO ANNIE. Well, I won't then, if you say so.

AUNT ELLER. Anh, but trouble starts nohow, so you might jist as well *git* married as *not.*

ADO ANNIE [*bewildered*]. Well, which'll I do, then?

AUNT ELLER. *Both!* I mean—I don't *keer!* [*Her voice sinking to a grave half-whisper, as she says what is really on her mind*] They *cain't* stick him—

ADO ANNIE. Stick who?

AUNT ELLER. Curly. They *cain't* stick him. Self-defense. Plain's the nose on yer face. Wish't they'd git it over with, that's whut I wish—

ADO ANNIE. Did—did Curly *kill* Jeeter—'th that old knife?

AUNT ELLER. Naw! 'Course not! Jeeter *fell* on his ole knife—and died. And he *ort* to 'a.

ADO ANNIE. They ain't no fair a-holdin' Curly fer it, then?

AUNT ELLER. 'Course it ain't fair! It's jist the law. They got to have their old hearin' first. Them *town* fools! First the shivoreein'—that was bad enough. And on top of it—Jeeter. Now Laurey all broke up, and Curly settin' in the cooler at Claremore. Shore a happy weddin', I *must* say. Why, them two ain't *railly* married yit.

ADO ANNIE [*her mouth open*]. Ain't they married, Aunt Eller!

AUNT ELLER. Well, they're married, all right, but they ain't— My, 'f you don't know whut I mean, I shore ain't gonna tell you! [*She gets up, and goes over to the window*] Looks blackened up over yander. "More rain, more rest, more niggers from the West." Hope it don't come a rain er a big wind-storm 'th all that forty of wheat in the shock. Ort to a-stacked it, I reckon. [*She turns back*] Does yer Maw need you tomorrow, Ado Annie?

ADO ANNIE. Naw, she said I could stay all week, 'f you ud feed me.

AUNT ELLER. I'll feed you, all right. Grease-eye gravy and cracklin' corn-bread! And roas'n'ears. Tomorrow we'll start in to can them peaches—clings and all. 'Spect we better be gittin' to bed. Only, I kinda hate to go to bed 'th Laurey still— [*She taps softly at* LAUREY'S *door, and calls gently*] Laurey—

LAUREY [*after a moment, inside*]. Yes.

AUNT ELLER. Ain't you gone to bed yit, honey?

[*The door slides back and* LAUREY *stands there in the lamplight, looking very pale and changed, years older, a woman now*]

LAUREY. I cain't sleep—so—they ain't no sense in goin' to bed. [*She comes down into the room*] Whut're you makin', Ado Annie?

ADO ANNIE. Me a dress. Ain't it purty?

LAUREY. Yes. [*Gravely*] Aunt Eller, did they— Whut *did* they say?

AUNT ELLER. I *told* you, honey. Jist said the hearin' was comin' up tomorrow. Now, I don't want you to worry about it no more. They'll let him off, all right, they got to.

LAUREY. Curly ort to a-let me went into Claremore with him like I wanted to—to testify for him.

AUNT ELLER. Don't you know they wouldn't a-let you say nuthin', Laurey? You're his wife, ain't you?

LAUREY [*slowly*]. Yes. I'm his wife.

AUNT ELLER. Well.

[LAUREY *sinks back in her chair with a disheartened little moan*]

LAUREY. Oh, I don't see why—I don't see why—when ever'thing was so fine, this had to happen!

AUNT ELLER [*comfortingly*]. Oh, Laurey—now nuthin' ain't happened.

LAUREY [*distressed*]. Ain't no tellin' whut they'll do to him! And he couldn't he'p it. He *couldn't*. [*Seeing it again*] It was over in a minute, and Jeeter lay there—dead. He'd a-killed Curly. He *tried* to kill him.

AUNT ELLER [*soothingly*]. Now, now—

LAUREY. Why'd they have to th'ow Curly in jail? Anyone could see how it happened—

AUNT ELLER. Shore they could, honey. But you know the way everbody feels about shiv-

oreein'. They got a right to it somehow. And a thing like this a-happenin' in the middle of a shivoree—why, it looks *bad,* that's all. But Curly'll go free. Why, it's only been three days. They jist got to git everthing straight. [*She gestures to indicate freedom and happiness for them both*]

LAUREY. You shore, Aunt Eller?

AUNT ELLER. *Course* I am!

LAUREY. I cain't stand to think of Curly bein' in jail!

AUNT ELLER. Why, it won't be no time now, till it's all over with—and forgot.

LAUREY [*strangely, a new element coming into her concern*]. No, *not* over with, *not* forgot. You didn't see. Other things. Things you cain't git outa yer mind. [*She shudders*]

AUNT ELLER. What is it, honey?

LAUREY. Over and over! The way them men done. The things they said. Oh—why'd it have to be that-a-way!

AUNT ELLER. Don't let yer mind run on it. Men is always like that at shivorees. Sump'n gits into 'em.

LAUREY. The one time in a body's life—!

AUNT ELLER. Sh! I know. It musta been bad.

LAUREY. Cain't ferget it, I tell you! I've tried and tried!

AUNT ELLER [*gravely, wisely*]. Don't try, honey. Don't *try*. They's things you cain't git rid of—lots of things. Not if you live to be a hundred. You got to learn. You got to look at all the good on one side and all the bad on the other, and say: "Well, all right, then!" to both of 'em.

LAUREY [*unheeding*].—On top of ever-thing!—

AUNT ELLER [*with great compassion*]. Yeah, you've had yer troubles. I know, Laurey. But they's been good things, too. Think about that. You ain't had to slave away a-workin' fer others, the way some girls has to do,—things like that. You've had you a good home—

LAUREY [*her mind temporarily diverted to another trouble*]. Paw and maw—

AUNT ELLER. Yeah, right when you needed 'em most, both gone. But you lived on, didn't you? You been happy since, ain't you? Course. You been strong about it. Why, when yer Paw died—and you thought the world of him—you was all by yerself here—and you stood it. When they sent fer me to Pryor, 'fore I could git here, why he was dead, and in his coffin.

LAUREY [*raising her head, and looking back into the room*]. It set right there—on two cheers. The head towards the door.

AUNT ELLER. Yeah. [*Quietly, without self-pity, stating the fact*] When yore Paw died, and laid there—it was *my brother* in his coffin, too. Oh, and they's lots more, Laurey! I couldn't tell you all. Yer Uncle Jack, the children, both of my sisters, my paw and maw. Troubles thick and fast, you got to put up with. My husband—yer Uncle Jack. When *he* died. 'D you know how? A crazy way to die. No use in it! He'd bought some hogs off Lem Slocum, and they turned out to be full of cholery—and all died. Jack walked over jist acrost the pasture to see Lem about it. Didn't show up and it got night. I tuck a lantern and went out to see. When I come to the worm fence, I found him, in a corner, all huddled down, all bloody from a gun-shot. Laid there all doubled up—dead—in a patch of yeller daisies. Lem Slocum musta shot him. I didn't know *who* done it. All I knowed was —*my husband was dead.* Oh, lots of things happens to a womern. Sickness, bein' pore and hungry even, bein' left alone in yer old age, bein' afraid to die—it all adds up. That's the way life is—cradle to grave. And you c'n stand it. They's one way. You got to be hearty. You *got* to be.

LAUREY [*moved*]. Oh, Aunt Eller, I'm sich a baby—!

AUNT ELLER. There, there!

LAUREY. Ashamed of myself! I want to be the way you air.

AUNT ELLER [*breaking off*]. Fiddlesticks! Fat—and *old?* You couldn't *h'ar* me to be the way *I* am! Why, in a year's time, you'll git so t'ard even of lookin' at me, you and Curly'll run me off the place, 'th a tin can tied onto my tail—

[LAUREY *half-smiles at the spectacle, and leaning over, gives* AUNT ELLER *an affectionate hug*]

LAUREY [*through tears*]. Oh, whut ud I do 'thout you, you're sich a crazy!—

AUNT ELLER. Shore's you're borned!—

LAUREY. I never could live. I never could. [*Rising, happier*] I'll go to bed now.

AUNT ELLER. And sleep, huh?

LAUREY [*smiling*]. Tight.

AUNT ELLER. And eat hearty from now on, huh? Fried chicken and everthing?

LAUREY. Tomorrow.

AUNT ELLER. Tomorrow, yer foot! [*She gets an apple out of a basket on the organ*] Here, eat that.

LAUREY. I don't want it.

AUNT ELLER. *Eat* it, I said.

[LAUREY *takes it, nibbles at it. A dog begins to bark. They all stop abruptly, listening*]

AUNT ELLER. Now, who could that— [*She stands up, looks at* LAUREY, *questioningly*] This hour of night—

[LAUREY *stands up, quite still, straight and pale*]

LAUREY. Curly—

AUNT ELLER. Couldn't be Curly, 'th ole Shep a-actin' up like a— He's stopped barkin'. [*The*

dog's barks stop suddenly. AUNT ELLER goes over to the window. ADO ANNIE has put down her work. All three women are in a breathless tranced state—suspended, curiously conjecturing*] It's pitch black—

LAUREY [*with quiet conviction*]. 'S Curly come back.

ADO ANNIE [*with a nervous giggle*]. Ole Shep stopped a-barkin' like he was shot!

AUNT ELLER [*angrily—because of her nervous apprehension*]. Sh! Be still, cain't you!

LAUREY. It's Curly!

AUNT ELLER. 'Taint *no* one. That dog's jist got the colic, I bet. [*There is a noise as of someone trying the door*] What's that!

ADO ANNIE [*rising*]. I'm goin' home.

AUNT ELLER. Be still. [*She picks up a shovel standing in the fireplace. She calls out sharply*] Now then. Whoever's there, answer, and answer quick!

[*The door opens quickly, and* CURLY, *dishevelled and worn, appears there*]

CURLY. Laurey!

AUNT ELLER [*joyfully*]. Why, it's Curly!

LAUREY. Curly! [*She runs to meet him half-way across the room as he comes forward. They go into each other's arms, and cling to each other*]

AUNT ELLER [*with extravagant delight*]. My, oh my! Look whut the old cat's drug in! Thought we had him safe in jail and here he turns up like a bad penny! Laws a me! Whutta you mean tryin' to skeer us wall-eyed?

ADO ANNIE [*astonished*]. Why, it's Curly!

AUNT ELLER [*gaily*]. Naw! It's Sandy Claus, cain't you see nuthin'! They've let him off! I knowed they would, I knowed it, I knowed it!

[CURLY *backs out of* LAUREY'S *arms, looks round quickly*]

LAUREY. Curly! Whut is it!

CURLY. Whut was that noise?

LAUREY [*with premonitory alarm*]. Whut's the matter? Everything's all right, ain't it? They've let you off, ain't they? Curly! Tell me and be quick, I—

CURLY. No. They ain't let me off.

LAUREY. Curly! [*Running to him*] They couldn't a-sent you up! It wasn't yore fault. They couldn't, I won't let 'em—I won't, I—

CURLY. Sh! [*As they become silent*] They're after me. [*He goes swiftly across and pulls down the window shade*]

AUNT ELLER. Never heared of sich a— Who's after you, the old Booger Man?

LAUREY. Curly!

CURLY. When I clumb th'ough the fence jist by that little bridge, I seen lights 'way over towards Clarmore. I knowed they'd got onto which way I was headin', so I run acrost the back of the—

AUNT ELLER. Whut *air* you jabberin' about?

[*Light dawning on her*] Oh! I mighta knowed a curly-headed cowhand like him ud come to a bad end! He's went and broke outa jail.

CURLY [*quickly*]. I *had* to see Laurey. I *had* to! I knowed she'd be a-worryin' about everthing, and I couldn't stand it her a-worryin' and nobody to help her none— [*He takes* LAUREY *in his arms again*]

AUNT ELLER [*severely*]. Worryin'! I ort to take a hick'ry to you and beat you plumb to a frazzle! Here you'd a-got off tomorrow, you crazy youngun—everbody *said* so. Now you'll prob'ly git sent up fer five year fer breakin' loose—and I hope you do!

LAUREY. Aunt Eller, they cain't send him up, they *cain't*!

AUNT ELLER. Oh, cain't they? You wait and see. [*To* CURLY] Didn't you know they'd know whur you was headin' fer, and find you 'fore a cat could lick his front paw?

CURLY. I didn't think.

AUNT ELLER. I reckon you hain't got nuthin' to think *with*. [*Giving him a swat*] I'd like to give you a good beatin'! [*Smiling at him tolerantly*] Aw, I reckon you jist had to see yer girl, didn't you?

CURLY. My wife.

AUNT ELLER. Yeow? Well, *call* her that 'f it does you any good. How fur back was it you seen 'em comin' after you?

CURLY. 'Bout half a mile.

AUNT ELLER. You got jist about two minutes to tell Laurey "Goodbye" then.

CURLY. They won't ketch me! Hide me till mornin', Aunt Eller. I cain't let 'em take me now, Aunt Eller!

AUNT ELLER. You'll stay *right* here till they come! You've already caused enough trouble to last us all out to doomsday. Now then. Ado Annie, come on out in the kitchen, and git yerself sump'n to eat. Bet you're hungry.

ADO ANNIE. I hain't hungry, Aunt Eller. I jist had a piece of—

AUNT ELLER. Not hungry! Why, you're all fallin' to staves. Feel ever' rib you got! [*She shoves* ADO ANNIE *out and follows her. As she goes out*] They'll come any minute now.

CURLY [*after a moment, not knowing how to begin*]. You all right, honey?

LAUREY. Yes. I guess. [*She puts her hand to her forehead as if brushing away her darkness*] I git to thinkin'.

CURLY [*gently*]. I know. Me, too. Thinkin' and thinkin' about you—and be bringin' sich trouble on you. All my fault.

LAUREY. Nobody could he'p it.

CURLY. Listen, Laurey. [*She goes to him, questioningly, disturbed at something in his manner*] I had to see you 'fore the hearin' tomorrow. That's why I broke out. Fer whut if they'd send me up, and I not see you fer a long time?

LAUREY. Curly! It *couldn't* be. Don't you say that.

CURLY. *Anything* can be. You got to be ready.

LAUREY [*alarmed*]. Have you heared anything, Curly? Tell me, whut'd you hear?

CURLY. Nuthin', honey. Ain't heared nuthin' —but *good*.

LAUREY [*with glad relief*]. Oh, it's all right, then!

CURLY [*gravely*]. That ain't it. I'm shore myself, honey. Er I *was* shore, till I broke out. I never thought whut *that* might do. But sump'n's always happenin' in this here world. Cain't count on a thing. So you got to promise me sump'n. Whutever happens—*whutever* it is —you got to bear up, you hear me? [*Smiling*] Why, I'm a purty one to go a-losin' sleep over, ain't I?

LAUREY [*ruefully*]. Oh, a fine start *we* got, ain't it? [*With an effort, painfully working it out in her mind*] Oh, I've worried about you, shet up in that filthy jail—

CURLY. Don't mind about that.

LAUREY.—And I've thought about that awful night, too, till I thought I'd go crazy—

CURLY. Pore Laurey.

LAUREY. Looked at it time and again, *heared* it—ringin' in my ears! *Cried* about it, cried about everthing! A plumb baby! And I've tried to figger out how it ud be if sump'n *did* happen to you. Didn't know how I could stand it. That was the worst! And nen, I tried to figger out how I'd go on. Oh, I've went th'ough it all, Curly, from the start. Now I feel shore of sump'n, anyway—I'll be growed up—like everbody else. [*With conviction*] I'll put up with everthing now. You don't need to worry about me no more. Why, I'll stand it— if they send you to the pen fer life—

CURLEY [*with mock alarm*]. Here! Don't know's I like that very well!

[LAUREY *bursts out into a peal of amused, hearty, infectious laughter*]

LAUREY. The look on yore face! 'S the first time I laughed in three days!

CURLY [*his old self again*]. *I* ain't goin' to no pen fer life—a-poundin' up rocks, and a-wearin' stripes around my legs!

LAUREY. Wouldn't you look purty!

CURLY [*with delight*]. You *air* a devil, ain't you? I don't think you even *like* me.

LAUREY [*playfully*]. Like you? Oh, I like you a little bit. [*They stand looking at each other, shyly, happily*] Whur on earth'd you git them clothes you got on?

CURLY [*gaily*]. Old Man Peck went and got 'em fer me. Shore a good ole man! Thinks the world of you. Shirt come outa Rucker's Dry Goods Store. Brand new, too! He thought I must be a-needin' clean clothes, I reckon, shet up in that ole jail! My, they's things a-crawlin' there, got legs on both sides! Cell next to mine's got a couple of horse thieves into it, the A. H. T. A. caught up by Sequoyah. They gimme a blanket and one of 'em said, "Tain't so purty-fer-nice but it's hell-fer-warm."

LAUREY [*amused*]. Curly!

CURLY. 'Nother cell's got a womern into it that smokes and cusses like a mule driver. Caught her stealin' from the Turf Exchange. Don't know whut's got into Indian Territory nohow! They puttin' everbody in jail—women and all!

LAUREY. I think you like yer ole jail!

CURLY. Jist rairin' to git back. Cain't wait! Lay back on that arn cot and dream about featherbeds!

LAUREY [*softly, happily*]. Ever time I pass by the barn lot, ole Dun lopes acrost and nickers at me, fer all get-out! Shows his teeth. He's astin' about you, I reckon.

CURLY. Oh, he's apt to fall dead of the heaves when he hears about me—settin' in jail 'stid of on the range! Feels like I ain't set in the saddle in a month of Sundays! Listen, Laurey. I been a-thinkin'— Everthing from now on is gonna be different.

LAUREY. Different?

CURLY. It come to me settin' in that cell of mine. [*Dreamily, out of a visionary absorption —like a song, growing in intensity*] Oh, I got to learn to be a farmer, I see that! Quit a-thinkin' about dehornin' and brandin' and th'owin' the rope, and start in to git my hands blistered a new way! Oh, things is changin' right and left! Buy up mowin' ma-chines, cut down the prairies! Shoe yer horses, drag them plows under the sod! They gonna make a state outa this, they gonna put it in the Union! Country a-changin', got to change with it! Bring up a pair of boys, new stock, to keep up 'th the way things is goin' in this here crazy country! Life jist startin' in fer me now. Work to do! Now I got you to he'p me—I'll 'mount to sump'n yit! Come here, Laurey. Come here, and tell me "Good-bye" 'fore they come fer me and take me away.

LAUREY [*wryly*]. All we do is say "Howdy" and "So long." [*Gravely*] Goodbye, Curly. If you come back tomorrow, I'll be here a-waitin'. If you don't come back, I'll be here a-waitin' anyhow.

CURLY. I'll come back, honey. They couldn't hinder me 'th bird-shot!

LAUREY. Promise me.

CURLY. Oh, I hate to go away and leave you! I cain't. [*He takes her in his arms, hungrily. After a moment, there are* VOICES *and sounds of an approaching party. The couple listen breathlessly*] They're here. Oh, I cain't go, I cain't leave you!

LAUREY [*anguishedly, clinging to him*]. I cain't let you go.

[AUNT ELLER *comes in*]

AUNT ELLER [*gravely*]. Well, here they air, I guess. They's a whole crowd. I seen the lan-terns. You all ready, Curly?

CURLY [*in anguish*]. I guess—I—

AUNT ELLER [*tenderly*]. Goodbye, honey. I'm sorry it has to be like this. [*There is a knock at the door.* AUNT ELLER *goes over and calls, her hand on the latch*] Who is that a-knockin'?

VOICE [*outside*]. It's me, Ed Peck—and I got to see you about—

AUNT ELLER [*opening the door, in astonish-ment*]. Why, Mr. Peck! Come on in. Whutta *you* want around here?

OLD MAN PECK [*coming in, his eyes going to* CURLY]. Curly knows whut I want. I've come fer him.

AUNT ELLER. *You* have? You ain't no marshal.

OLD MAN PECK. I know. But Mr. Burnett, the federal marshal, deputized me and some of the boys to come out and find Curly and bring him back. Come on, Curly.

AUNT ELLER. Well, I *must* say! Sidin' with the federal marshal!

OLD MAN PECK. I ain't sidin' with him, Aunt Eller. Curly's hearin' ain't come up yit, and he hadn't no right to run off this-a-way.

AUNT ELLER. No right! Say, looky here, he wanted to see his wife. That ain't agin the *law* in this country, is it?

OLD MAN PECK. No. But breakin' outa *jail* is agin the law.

AUNT ELLER [*disgusted*]. Well, of all the— When'd you go and git so respectful of the law? Looky here, if a law's a *good* law—it can stand a little breakin'. And them out there— Who's out there? Hey, you all! [*She has gone to the window and thrown up the shade*] Go on home. Nobody's wantin' *you* around here!

VOICES [*outside*]. We've come fer Curly, Aunt Eller. We got to take him back. [*Snicker-ing*] He's a plumb criminal, he is, breakin' outa jail this-a-way!

AUNT ELLER. Who's that? That you, Zeb? I mighta knowed! Say, you're a purty nuthin' —a ole pig-stealer like you tryin' to represent the govament!

VOICE [*outside, offended, protesting*]. Who's a pig-stealer?

AUNT ELLER. *You* air, Mr. Zeb Walkley.

VOICE. I ain't, either!

AUNT ELLER. You *air*! Why, you gittin' so that—'stid of talkin'—you plumb grunt like a ole sow! And say, Dave Tyler—you'll feel funny when I tell yer wife you're carryin' on 'th another womern, won't you?

VOICE [*outside*]. I ain't carryin' on 'th no one.

AUNT ELLER. Mebbe not. But you'll shore feel funny when I tell yer *wife* you air.

VOICES. Now, Aunt Eller, we've come fer Curly.

We cain't stand here and listen to you—
Send him on out!

AUNT ELLER [*indignantly*]. Oh, you'll listen to me! I'm gittin' mad! You cain't *take* Curly, that's all they is to it!

VOICES. We *got* to, Aunt Eller.

He'll git off tomorrow, won't he?

Make him come on out, and le's git started!

AUNT ELLER [*severely*]. All right, 'f you won't listen to me, I plumb warsh my hands of all of you. I thought you was a fine bunch of neighbors. Now I see you're jist a gang of fools. Tryin' to take a bridegroom away from his bride! Why, the way you're sidin' with the federal marshal, you'd think us people out here lived in the United States! Why, we're territory folks—we ort to hang together. I don't mean *hang*—I mean *stick*. Whut's the United States? It's jist a furrin country to me. And *you* supportin' it! Jist dirty ole furriners, ever last one of you!

VOICES [*outside, grumbling, protesting*]. Now, Aunt Eller, we hain't furriners.

My pappy and mammy was *both* borned in Indian Territory! Why, I'm jist plumb full of Indian blood myself.

Me, too! And I c'n prove it!

AUNT ELLER [*full of guile*]. Well, maybe you *ain't* furriners. I musta made a mistake. [*Slyly, smiling*] Anyway, I ain't astin' you to let Curly *off*. That's up to them ole United Statesers at the hearin'. *I* mean—you don't have to take Curly back *tonight*. Take him in the mornin' jist as well.

VOICES [*uncertainly*]. Well, I don't know— I ain't no furriner!

Whut does Mr. Peck say?

He's the boss. Ast *him*.

I wouldn't wanta stand in the way of lettin' Curly—

AUNT ELLER [*triumphantly, to* MR. PECK]. See there! They said it was all right to let him stay tonight.

OLD MAN PECK. No, they didn't.

AUNT ELLER. Did too! Cain't you hear nuthin'? I'll take a blacksnake whip to you!

OLD MAN PECK [*sheepishly*]. Well, I— If my men is gonna back out on me this-a-way— I reckon I better let Curly stay.

AUNT ELLER [*overjoyed*]. I knowed you'd see daylight, I knowed it, I knowed it!

OLD MAN PECK [*self-consciously, not looking at* CURLY, *and twirling his hat in his hands, sheepishly*]. I was young onct myself. [*He hugs* AUNT ELLER]

AUNT ELLER. Why, you ole devil! Tell yer wife on you!

CURLY. 'D you want me to stay, Laurey?

[*She backs away, flushed and embarrassed and joyous at the same time, flings an arm about his neck and kisses him quickly, whirls over to* OLD MAN PECK, *gives him a quick hug and flies into her room.* CURLY *grins and starts after her*]

OLD MAN PECK [*as* CURLY *reaches the door*].

Curly. I'll be here right after breakfast to fetch you. I'll be here bright and early.

[CURLY *goes in. The door shuts*]

AUNT ELLER [*slyly, owlishly*]. Well, not *too* early. [*Then, gravely*] Younguns has a turrible time, don't they? [*She throws it off*] Oh, well —they git to be old timers soon enough. *Too* soon. [*She shows* MR. PECK *out with a lantern. She marches over to the window, calling out*] Hey, you all! Go on home. They ain't nuthin' *you* c'n do around here. Curly's stayin'!

[*She jerks the shade down. The voices outside exclaim delightedly and move away. From the bedroom has come the sound of* CURLY *beginning to sing softly,* "Green Grow the Lilacs."]

AUNT ELLER [*going to the window*]. Mr. Peck! [*With delight*] Listen to that fool cowpuncher! His weddin' night—and there he is singin'!

CURTAIN

THE END

GLOSSARY

dogies—specifically, an orphaned calf, but used often, affectionately, as a synonym for cattle.

shikepoke—a mythical Middle West bird, whose activities (unprintable) are embarrassing to everyone. A term of opprobrium.

side meat—bacon.

maverick—an unbranded, and hence ownerless, calf or steer.

off-ox—the ox on the off-side (the right side) of the wagon tongue.

bronc buster—a rider of bucking bronchos.

bull-dogger—one who leaps off a running horse, swings on the horns of a bull or steer, and throws and ties him.

stove arn—that is, stove iron, or handle for lifting the lids.

tetchin' leather—to ride a bronc without touching leather is to ride without hanging on to the saddle horn or any other part of the saddle.

yellin' calf-rope—to yell calf-rope signifies defeat.

to change the green lilacs to the red, white and blue—means, "I'm going to join the army."

string-haltered—a corruption of spring-halted,

a convulsive movement of the hind legs of a horse.

Dan Patch—a celebrated racing horse, a pacer.

Jick—the joker in a pack of cards.

bottom—that is, river bottom, the low land along a river.

backwater—the water backed up, from being unable to empty into a swollen stream now higher than its tributaries.

shivoree—a corruption of the French charivari, a wedding celebration.

the A. H. T. A.—the Anti-Horse Thief Association.

HOTEL UNIVERSE

A Play

By PHILIP BARRY

The acting rights of this play are fully protected by law. For permission to perform, either by professionals or amateurs; to read in public, to broadcast by radio, or in any way reproduce them, application must be made to Samuel French, at 25 West 45th St., New York, N. Y., or at 811 West 7th St., Los Angeles, Calif.
Reprinted by permission of the author and Samuel French.

CHARACTERS

STEPHEN FIELD
ANN FIELD
PAT FARLEY
LILY MALONE
TOM AMES
HOPE AMES
NORMAN ROSE
ALICE KENDALL
FELIX

ACTION AND SCENE

The action of the play is continuous, and takes place in the course of about two hours, upon the terrace of a house in the south of France, near Toulon.
The time is an evening in early July, last summer.

HOTEL UNIVERSE

The Terrace is like a spacious, out-door room, irregularly paved with flags of gray stone. The house itself forms one wall on the left, a wall from which two screened doors open—the first from a hall, the second from a sitting-room. Down left, against this wall a flight of outside stairs, guarded by a slender iron railing, mounts to a balcony.

The other entrance is at right, down from the garden by stone steps. A three-foot wall follows the back and left sides of the terrace just to where the row of small cypresses, which screens the garden terrace, begins. Over and beyond the wall nothing is visible: sea meets sky without a line to mark the meeting. There, the angle of the terrace is like a wedge into space.

Down right, a small but ancient fig-tree in full leaf rises from the pavement. There is a large fan-back chair beneath it. Upon the wall at back, there are two folding-cushions. A small upright piano stands against the wall of the house. Near it, there is a table, upon which stand a carafe of brandy, a bottle of Cointreau. a bottle of champagne, and glasses. A few straw and wicker chairs and a sofa complete the furniture. It is about nine o'clock in the evening, and still quite light.

ANN FIELD sits at a small table at left, a silver-coffee-service before her. She is about twenty-eight, and lovely. Near her, taking their coffee, sit TOM and HOPE AMES, LILY MALONE and NORMAN ROSE. On the other side of the terrace, half asleep upon a cushion with a coffee-cup beside her, ALICE KENDALL reclines. She is twenty-six, very smart and rather pretty. PAT FARLEY is at the piano. He is thirty-two, medium tall, slight, likable looking. NORMAN ROSE is the handsomest of the men, and about thirty-eight. TOM AMES is forty, of amiable good looks. HOPE, his wife, is four years younger, in full bloom. LILY MALONE is small, slight and thirty. Without a feature to remark upon, she is able to impart to her small, impudent face a certain prettiness. All are browned by the sun and wear light summer clothes. The women, except LILY, who is in a linen day-dress, wear simple evening-dresses. The men are in flannels]

PAT.—And this is a cheerful number from the heart of Old Provence: "Le Roy a fait battre Tambour." Yvette Guilbert used to do it. [*He plays and sings the song, with its threatening,* repeated refrain "Rat-a-plan, rat-a-plan, rat-a-plan-plan-plan-plan"]

TOM [*at the conclusion*]. Sad.

HOPE. Oh, isn't it!

LILY. Lovely, though.

ALICE. But Ann said to play something gay.

PAT. Yes? How gay, Ann—very gay? [*He looks at* ANN. *She meets his eyes for a moment, then averts her head sharply*] Well, here's how the monks tried to be gay at Easter. It's Gregorian—eleventh century—rejoice, rejoice— God, how gay. [*He begins to intone the chant:* "Halleluiah! Halleluiah!"] Can't you see the lines of them, shuffling along, heads down, hands in sleeves, rejoicing, rejoicing? [*He continues to sing* "Halleluiah! Halleluiah!"]

[*Suddenly* ANN *rises*]

ANN. Pat! [*But he goes on singing*]

[ANN *mounts the steps to the balcony and goes into the house.* HOPE *rises and goes to* PAT]

HOPE. Pat—

PAT. What?

HOPE. Quit it!

PAT. Why?

HOPE. Why must we take our nerves out on Ann?

PAT. "Nerves" did you say?

HOPE.—You heard what I said. And you've been the worst. Knowing what you used to be to her, I suppose the torture's great fun.

PAT. Go away, Hope.

HOPE.—Then why do you suppose she suddenly leaves us this way?

PAT. It's her own house, isn't it?

HOPE. Yes—and a fine time we've been giving her in it! The wonder to me is that she's endured our bad manners as long as she has.

TOM. Oh come now, darling—

HOPE. I mean it! All we've done for three mortal days has been to sit around and make bitter cracks about anything we could put our tongues to.—Don't you realize that we're the first Americans she's seen since she's been here? She begged us to come. It meant so much to her to have us. And now, on our very last night with her, we still behave like—oh, I'm so ashamed. [*She returns to her chair*]

TOM. What do you want us to do, Hope?

NORMAN. Yes, what shall we?

HOPE. I don't know—something—anything but what we have been. It must be horrible for her, living here. She had a right to expect we'd bring some breath of life with us. And what have we given her?

PAT. Say it: the breath of death.

LILY [to HOPE]. You know the reason for our so-called "nerves," don't you?

TOM [quickly]. Now don't start that, Lily. We agreed when we left Antibes not to speak of that again.

NORMAN. Yes—Ann's got enough to depress her, without adding the sad story of a person she never knew or heard of.

LILY. Nobody's going to burden Ann with it. The point is, what it did to us. Every time I close my eyes I see him: a bright, sweet, utterly unimaginative boy of twenty-six—

HOPE. Don't—

LILY.—Standing up there, brown as a berry in a pair of blue swimming-pants on the highest rock over the sea, and— Pat, did you really hear him say that?

PAT. Of course I did. He said: "Look, Farley, I'm off for Africa!"

TOM. It was the most beautiful dive I've ever seen.

ALICE. He couldn't have meant it. I'm sure it was an accident.

PAT. Accident nothing. It was suicide.

LILY. Just five minutes before, I was rubbing his back with oil. He asked me to. He couldn't reach between the shoulders.

PAT. Little mother—

LILY. Shut up.

HOPE. He had a daisy behind his ear, the way a grocer-boy wears a pencil—

TOM. And didn't look silly, either.

LILY. Not he!

NORMAN. Of course there must have been some reason for what he did.

HOPE. Please, let's not talk about it any more. It isn't safe to dwell on things like that. It makes you morbid.

TOM. There was something grand about the way he did it.

LILY. He laughed up at me—the way his teeth gleamed from the water!—Did he have unusually white teeth?

PAT.—Brushed them night and morning. Promised nurse he would.

HOPE. Pat—

PAT. Oh, what the hell—you all make me sick. None of us gave a hang for him. We scarcely knew him.

TOM. We do now.

PAT. A neat job, I call it—no body to dispose of. You know, it's the devil getting a body out of France. The export duty's enormous. And I think there's a luxury-tax.—Do I offend you? Sorry.

LILY. Why did he do it? Why did he do it?

PAT. He'd just had enough, that's all. Eleven o'clock in the morning, up on a rock in the blazing sun— [He looks away, his eyes narrowing] "I'm off for Africa" and that's all. Lord, it's magnificent. It's scored for drums, that. [He sings again] "Rat-a-plan, rat-a-plan, rat-a-plan, plan, plan."

TOM. Look here, if we don't get that boy off our minds—

LILY. I know. There's something contagious about it. It's like having been in a room with a person with—

HOPE. Lily.

LILY. All right.

TOM. No one is to mention it again. We're here on this visit to dispense cheer to Ann, aren't we? Isn't that why we came? Well, then—

LILY. Hopeless, hopeless, hopeless.—As cheer-makers I'd sell the lot of us at a nickel a pound, on the hoof.

TOM. We can keep the ball in the air until we go, at any rate.

HOPE. We've simply got to. Think of her—buried down here for three years in this fake, rootless country, dying of homesickness with a half-mad father—

ALICE. I saw him, you know.

HOPE. You did!

NORMAN. When?

TOM. Where, Alice?

ALICE. It must have been him. Last night I woke up and couldn't get back to sleep again. I thought I heard someone down here, so I came out on the balcony. It was a funny light. Everything was—I don't know—awfully pale. For instance that fig-tree didn't seem to have any color.

TOM. But where was he? Here?

ALICE. Yes. At least there was a man—quite a nice-looking man, with gray hair. He was all in white. He was standing here at the wall, looking out over. The lighthouse was lit, and every now and then it would light him all up.

PAT [unimpressed]. Was there a very bright star in the sky?

ALICE. I didn't notice.

LILY. You ought to look out for those things, Alice, you really ought.

ALICE. I can see it all so distinctly, even to the way a button on his coat caught the light and a lace on his shoe that was untied and dragged along after him.

PAT. Then what did he do—ride off on a unicorn?

ALICE. No, he just went up there into the garden, the rooster after him.

HOPE. The what?

ALICE. Didn't I tell you? He had a white rooster with him.—After awhile I heard it crow, quite far away.

HOPE. It must have been dawn then—

ALICE. No—it was nowhere near it.

LILY. Well, it must have been dawn somewhere—

PAT. It usually is—

TOM. You dreamed all that, Alice.

ALICE. I saw it.

PAT.—While we're here he's staying down at the what-do-you-call-it—the little house—the bastide. I imagine he's sicker than he thinks. A fine end for one of the foremost electrical experts in the country, eh? A swell finish for the only first-rate physicist we've ever had.

ALICE. But hasn't he always been a little—you-know?

PAT. He never seemed so to me.—Who'll have a drink? [*He refills his glass*]

NORMAN. But when was it he began to crack?

PAT. Only about five or six years ago.—This is a noble brandy.

TOM. I heard something about his haranguing a crowd in Central Park once—

PAT. He can't take people casually—that was part of his trouble. He's supposed to have some kind of power over them. Somebody said it's because he always seems so close to death.—It tastes like cucumbers.

LILY. I've never known anyone to seem further from it than that boy standing there on that rock, and—

HOPE. Lily!

LILY. Oh, all right.—Only I never have—not anyone.

PAT. Finally Ann had to bring him here, where he doesn't see anyone but her, and seems to be all right. It's a swell deal for Ann. [*His tone changes*] So we thought we'd come and put on a show for her, did we? We thought we'd remind her of what a big, gay, exciting life exists outside these walls—rub a little salt in, just so she'd be really content to stay on here—is that it?

TOM. Lord, you can be a louse.

PAT. You bet I can.—If Ann has any illusions about what goes on in the great big wonderful world back home, *I* haven't. [*He goes to the wall and sits there, looking out*]

HOPE. Just the same, Pat—

PAT.—Oh, go ahead. Do as you like. Be bright, be merry.

[*A silence.* LILY *looks about her*]

LILY. I'm not happy in this old place. It's too violent, it's too dramatic. I know I'm an actress but hang it, I'm on a holiday. You get a sense of things being born all the time. They come bursting out of the ground. There's too much raw life about.

TOM. The house used to be a small hotel—the Hotel de l'Univers, it was called. I heard a tale or two about it down at the port to-day. It had been deserted for quite awhile before Ann and her father took it.

HOPE. Deserted? Why?

TOM. The boatman said things began to happen.

[PAT *laughs*]

PAT. The man in 608 had a nightmare, and the lady in 609 rang for ice-water.

ALICE. Things! What things?

TOM. The idea seemed to be that people began to resemble other people and the place itself other places. And time went sort of funny. Their pasts kept cropping up.

LILY.—Excuse me, friends, but *I'm* taking the night-boat for Albany.

TOM. I'm only telling you what I heard at the port.

NORMAN. There may be something in it.—When *I* stepped out on this terrace the other night, it was for all the world like the Grand Central the first time I saw it, when I was fifteen. I don't mean just the way it looked. I mean—

LILY. I know—and now it's a hill-top in New Hampshire. We played Concord once. I used to climb out my window at night when Father had drunk enough to sleep—and up it, and lie on my back there. [*She closes her eyes*]

TOM. Maybe what you call the "raw life" here makes people children again.—Lord, I remember the way Under the Piano became as many places in as many moments: a boat to London, and then London. An airship, and a grocery-store. A circus-tent, and 'way down cellar.—And it was—for the moment it really was.

[*A silence. Then:*]

HOPE. Tom, I wonder how the children are? I'm worried. I think I'll cable.

[*Another silence. Then:*]

LILY. Dear, dear Father—how I miss him.

ALICE. Oh, she's got her father on the brain. Every theatre we went to in Paris, she did nothing but talk about how he used to play—

LILY. That's enough, Alice.

ALICE. Of course we're sorry he's dead, but why we should be bored with endless accounts of his—

LILY. I say it's enough!

TOM. This is pleasant.

HOPE. I tell you, you're all in a state.

PAT. I don't doubt that the people who used to come here were, too. Lord knows it's on the edge of the world.

[HOPE *glances toward the house*]

HOPE. Here she is. Now for Heaven's sake—

[ANN *comes in from the house*]

ANN.—That was foolish of me. Please don't mind. [*She goes to the coffee-table*] More coffee, anyone?

TOM. *I* will.

HOPE. Me too. It's so delicious.

ANN. It took me two years to discover why French coffee was so vile.

HOPE. *I* could have told you. They load it full of chickory.

ANN. But the real trouble is in the roasting.

They roast it black, till it looks like shoe-buttons.

NORMAN. That was the spirit that won the War.

TOM [*reflectively*].—When I was a child, I used to have a pair of button-shoes that I wore Sundays.

LILY [*to* NORMAN]. Has there been a war? I've been away—

TOM. I don't think they make them any-more.

ANN.—So what did I do, but buy a roasting-machine of my own. It makes a very fine smell of a morning. More, Pat?

[PAT *turns*]

PAT. Thanks, I'll take another brandy.

TOM. So will Tom. I like my good things to-gether.

[PAT *fills two glases for them and returns to the wall with his*]

HOPE. It stays light so late, doesn't it?

ANN. Wasn't the beach a glory to-day? Wasn't it? Oh, I love that beach! It's my mother.—Why do you go? Why don't you all stay on with me? I'll be good to you—

LILY. If we could—

ANN. You're really splendid, you know. You are so splendid!

LILY. Don't make me cry, Ann.

ANN. You? [*She laughs*] Imagine! [*And turns to* PAT] What *are* you doing there, Pat?

PAT. Me? Oh, just looking—

ANN. But I thought you didn't like views.

PAT. This isn't a view. For a view you've got to have a horizon. There's not a sign of one out there. The sea meets the sky without a line to mark the meeting. The dome begins under your feet. The arc's perfect.

ANN. But I want to see your face. I'm fond of your lean, brown face— [*He turns to her*] That's better!—Pat, you're older. [*He turns away again*]—But I like you better older!

LILY [*after a slight pause*]. It's fantastic, this terrace. It just hangs here. Someday it'll float off in space—and anchor there, like an island in time.—I'm full of whimsies to-night. I need a good dose at bed-time.

ANN. Lily, why do you spoil everything you say?

LILY. Do I?

ANN. Yes. What are you afraid of?

LILY. Oh—these people's gibes.

ANN. I don't understand it.

LILY. Ah, Ann—come on home with us! We do need you so.

HOPE. Yes, Ann! To Paris to-night—sail with us Wednesday. Just as a farewell-present. Oh, do!

ANN. What a grand idea!—Tied up in a box —ribbons! Lovely!

HOPE. Isn't it even possible?

[ANN *laughs*]

ANN. No dear, it's not—not possibly possible.

[LILY *picks up a book and begins to read it*]

HOPE. But surely you could leave your father for a month, say. You could get a good nurse in Marseilles or Toulon, and—

ANN. Father doesn't need a nurse.

HOPE. I'm sorry. I'm stupid.

ANN. No you're not. You're sweet. You're all sweet. But I'm like that theoule tree—um, smell it!—I live here.

NORMAN. Three years is quite a while in one place—

ANN. Not here. Ever since we came my sense of time's been confined to music.

[PAT *lights a cigarette*]

PAT.—Look, everyone: there's nothing trav-els so fast as light—thirty million miles a minute. But by the time they see this match on Orion we'll all have been dead fifty years, maybe more.

[FELIX, *a French butler of about fifty, in a white summer uniform, comes in from the house*]

ANN [*laughing*]. There's a modest man!— He thinks they're hanging out of windows on Orion, to see him light a little match! [*She turns to* FELIX]—Oui, Felix?

FELIX [*to* PAT]. Pardon, Monsieur—

PAT. Oui?

FELIX. Il est neuf heure juste, Monsieur.

PAT. Bon. Merci.

[FELIX *traverses the terrace and goes out into the garden*]

ALICE.—And why was that, may I ask?

PAT. We've got to leave before eleven. I told him to let me know every half-hour from nine until then.

ANN. That was perfectly dear of you, Pat. That will help. [*A moment. Then impulsively*] Oh, I don't see why you at least can't stay on! I want you to. Pat—stay—

PAT. I wish I could, but I've got dates with mountains.

[TOM *pours himself a glass of champagne*]

TOM. If you had any sense at all you'd know you ought to train for mountain-climbing.

PAT. I feel pretty good, thanks.—Oh, by the way, would you mail some letters for me in New York?

TOM. Sure.

[PAT, *from a book on the wall takes several small envelopes and one large one and gives them to* TOM]

TOM.—The big one's got no address.

PAT. There are four or five others inside it. I thought they'd be easier to carry.

[TOM *puts the envelopes in his pocket, the large one with difficulty*]

TOM. You were wrong.

[LILY *slams her book shut and tosses it upon the sofa*]

LILY.—Another blonde heroine who won't take her milk, and Mama will throw up.

[*There is a silence, which* ALICE *finally breaks*]

ALICE.—Did I tell you?—I saw the most amusing boat this afternoon: all white, with sienna sails, and a thin white prow—

[*Another silence*]

TOM.—Gondolas are built in a rather curious way. You know how they seem to pivot—well— [*But he relapses into silence*]

HOPE. The air's so heavy—give me a glass of water, someone.

[TOM *gives her his glass of champagne.* HOPE *takes a swallow, and chokes*]

HOPE. This isn't water.

TOM. The water in France isn't safe. It's full of Frenchmen.

PAT.—And sometimes an American, who swims out too far.

[LILY *turns on him, angrily*]

LILY. Oh damn you, Pat! Shut your trap, will you?

NORMAN [*quickly*]. How long is the drive to Toulon?

TOM. Fifty minutes, Mr. Rose.

HOPE [*reflectively*].—Bags to be packed.

ANN. No, no—please—there's all the time in the world!

[*Another brief silence. Then* PAT *speaks*]

PAT. It was funny motoring over here. We passed the old Hotel Beau-Site in Cannes. Lord, how it took me back. I had an English tutor there, named Briggs, when I was twelve. He fell in love with my mother.

ALICE. What did she do? Fire him?

PAT. Heavens, no.—Mother?

[NORMAN *starts a record on a portable gramophone which stands upon the wall —it is the "Nailla" of Delibes*]

LILY. Dear God, not that again. If you knew what that tune does to me.

[NORMAN *promptly turns it off and returns to his chair. Silence is again about to descend upon them, but* HOPE *will not have it*]

HOPE. Seriously, Ann—how did you know we were at Antibes?

ANN. I told you: I had a hunch.

[TOM'S *elbow catches on the bulky envelope, protruding from his coat pocket. Unnoticed by* PAT, *he takes it out, opens it and extracts four smaller envelopes from it*]

HOPE. I know you said that. But seriously—

ANN. I have them, I tell you! It's not my first one about Pat, is it Pat?—Do you remember my cable to London once, years ago?

PAT. What? Oh yes—yes, sure.

ANN. I got a feeling that he was in some kind of trouble, so I cabled.—But what the trouble was, I never knew.

[TOM *is distributing the letters in his inside pockets and his wallet*]

LILY [*to* PAT]. Don't tell me anything's ever gone against *you*, darling. I couldn't bear it.

ANN.—I asked you about it once before, didn't I?

PAT. Did you?

ANN. Yes. Don't you know what you said?

PAT. What?

[*Now* TOM *has but one letter without a place for it. He reads the address upon it, starts slightly, frowns, and looks from it to* PAT, *and back again*]

ANN. You said: "I'll tell you that the day before I die."

PAT. All right, That still goes.

NORMAN. It sounds ominous.

ANN. Doesn't it!

[TOM *taps the letter reflectively. Then:*]

TOM [*suddenly*]. Pat—this letter—

[PAT *turns swiftly, goes to him, and takes it from his hand*]

PAT. Oh—oh, that—I'll tell you about that later.

TOM. I think you'd better.

[LILY *is watching* ANN]

LILY.—I wish I was like Ann.—Ann, I do wish I was like you. I feel so inadequate near you.

[ANN *laughs and blows her a kiss*]

ANN. Darling! You're famous—I'm nobody. I do nothing but read of your triumphs.

LILY.—The triumph of trash. You can have my public, if you'll give me your heart.

ANN. But you have it already!

LILY. I'd like to think that.

TOM. You may.

LILY. I want to play Cordelia in King Lear.

NORMAN. Cordelia?! You?

LILY.—And Booth turns a handspring in his grave. All right, but somehow that part fascinates me. Whenever I think of it I go absolutely cold. And still I know that if ever I have the guts to do Cordelia, my life will be a different thing.

PAT. Then why not try it? I'll back you, Lily.

LILY [*in fright*]. No! No! I wouldn't dare. [*Then she laughs*]—No. I start my farewell tour any day now. I'm going to play the Styx instead.—That's a joke, the *river* Styx.

NORMAN. Everybody laugh.

[LILY *springs up*]

LILY. Norman, there are times when I can't stand this damned Jewish superiority of yours, and this is one of them.

NORMAN. Really? I'm so sorry.

LILY.—The way you look down from your eminence of three thousand years—honestly, who do you think you are, some Disraeli?

NORMAN. He was later, wasn't he?

LILY [*to the others*]. You see?

NORMAN. Besides, I've always considered him enormously overrated.

LILY. I wouldn't mind so much if it made you happy. But you're one of the most wretched men I know.

TOM. Go on—bankers are always happy.

ALICE. Norman's more than a banker. He's a financial genius. My uncle says so.

[ANN *laughs*]

ANN. There, Norman! Now are you happy?

[*A moment. Then:*]

NORMAN. No.—I'll tell you, Ann: here's how I see my life—

LILY. Tune in on Norman Rose Hour.

NORMAN.—There are several angles to it: When a man decides he wants to accumulate a fortune—

TOM. It's going to be a speech.

PAT.—I can't speak to Mr. Morgan just now. Tell him I'll call him back.

TOM.—Nine-thirty A. M. The great Norman Rose enters his office— [*He goes to the table*]

LILY [*in three tones of voice*]. Good morning, Mr. Rose. Good morning, Mr. Rose! Good morning, Mr. Rose!

[TOM *grunts, seats himself at the table and contemplates the bottles and glasses*]

TOM. I see my desk is piled with work again.

LILY. You must learn to depute the smaller duties to underlings, Mr. Rose.

TOM. I have to think of my stock-holders. [LILY *knocks three times upon her book.* TOM *turns*] Who's there?

LILY. It's me, Mr. Rose. Little Lily Malone. You know *me*.

TOM [*wearily*]. Come in, come in!

[LILY *enters the great man's office*]

LILY.—A gentleman to see you, sir.

TOM. I don't like gentlemen. It's ladies I like.—Come closer, Miss Malone.

[LILY *stiffens*]

LILY.—A Mr. Patrick Farley. Morgan and Company. Sleighs and Violins Mended.

TOM. Show him in.

LILY.—Mr. Rose will see you now, Mr. Farley. [PAT *comes in,* LILY *announces him*] Mr. Farley, Mr. Rose.—I know you'll like each other.

[LILY *retires.* TOM *indicates a chair.* PAT *seats himself*]

TOM. Well, Farley, what is it?

PAT. It's—just about everything, Doctor. I feel awful.

TOM. Your Chemistry is down. C-minus.

PAT. Yes, sir.

TOM. Your Physics is down. D.

PAT. Yes, sir.

TOM. Your English is down.

PAT. Yes, sir. I can keep everything down now, sir.

TOM. You were not so good at that last night, Farley.

PAT. I think you are forgetting your place, Rose. Please remember that my grandfather kept slaves, and your grandfather was one of them.

TOM. Yes, and a good one!

PAT [*sneering*].—Pride of race, eh?

TOM. If you like.

PAT. And if I don't?

TOM. Farley, I am a busy man.

PAT.—Just so. And that is why I want to ask you a question:—That shipment of ear-marked gold for Sweden—

TOM. My God.

PAT. Don't temporize, Mr. Rose. He is my God as well as yours.

TOM. But I must have a moment to myself, to think. [*Suddenly*] I know what! I'll telephone about it! [*He takes a long spoon from the table and holds the handle to his ear*]

PAT.—That was the old Norman Rose speaking. That was the Norman Rose we once knew, and loved.

[TOM *speaks into the other end of the spoon*]

TOM. Get me Equitable Trust. [*Then to* PAT] What ever became of your Aunt Jessie Sprague?

PAT. None of that now! Don't try to get me off on sex.

TOM [*to the telephone*]. Hello?

PAT. Say this to him first: Say "what *is* ear-marked gold?"

[TOM *nods and waits a moment. Then:*]

TOM. Hello, is that you, Trust? Yes. This is Norman Rose speaking—the old Norman Rose. Listen now, Eq—about that gold for Sweden—Sweden, yes.—Look here, old man maybe you can tell me: what *is* ear-marked gold? [PAT *nods approvingly. There is a silence.* TOM *holds his hand over the end of the spoon and turns to* PAT] He's bluffing. [*Another moment, then again to the spoon*] Oh it *is*, is it? That's what it is, is it? Well, let me tell *you* something: you're not a big enough man to bluff Norman Rose. No sir!—Well, it's your *business* to know! [*To* PAT]—Still bluffing. [*To the telephone*] All right, all right—that's all right with me! But if you think you can—hello! Hello, are you there? Hello—hello— [*He puts down the spoon and turns to* PAT] He's gone. He's hung up, the big bluffer.

[PAT *fixes him with his eye*]

PAT. It's you who are bluffing, Rose. [*He points his finger at him*] What *is* ear-marked gold?

TOM [*confused*]. I—why, it's—I'm not sure, but I *think* it's—

PAT. We have no place here for men who are not sure.

TOM. Don't be hard on me, boy.

PAT. I'll give you two alternatives.

TOM. Make it three.

PAT. I'll give you three alternatives.

TOM. Four.

PAT. Four and a half.

TOM. Five. Five twenty-five!

[PAT's *fist descends upon the table*]

PAT. Sold!—To the gentleman in the straw hat, for five twenty-five!

TOM. But who—who are you?

[PAT *rises, opens his coat, and points to his badge*]

PAT. The Chairman of your Board of Directors. [TOM *covers his face.* PAT *speaks quietly*] Good afternoon, Mr. Rose. [TOM *rises, and makes one mute gesture of appeal*] Good *afternoon*, Mr. Rose.

[TOM *hulks out of his office, a broken man.* PAT *seats himself at the table and pours a drink*]

NORMAN [*laughing*]. All right! I'll resign!

HOPE. Silly—they are so silly.

ANN. It was lovely! Do another—

HOPE. No, they mustn't. I'm always afraid they'll slip over the line and turn into the people they're pretending to be.

LILY. It would be grand just to let yourself go sometime. I wonder what would happen?

HOPE. I hate to think.

LILY. It couldn't be any worse than it is. [*She closes her eyes*] Hopeless, hopeless—

NORMAN. What?

LILY. Hopeless.

PAT [*humming*]. Rat-a-plan, rat-a-plan, rat-a-plan-plan-plan.

NORMAN [*to* LILY]. But while there's life, my dear—

LILY.—There's the rent to pay.

PAT.—And what's the big premium on life, I'd like to know?

NORMAN. Well, it does look like all we've got.

PAT. There was a great big war, Pet, and we survived it. We're living on borrowed time.

TOM. Lost: one battalion.

PAT. We're not lost. Our schedule is different, that's all.—What I mean is, we'll have had the works at forty instead of eighty.

NORMAN. I've got a theory people expect too much from life.

ANN. But you can't! That's one thing that's not possible!

LILY. Then why is everyone so disappointed in it?

ANN. Because all they concern themselves with are its probabilities. Think of the things that might happen, can happen, do happen! The possibilities!

LILY. There might be a ray of hope in that. Who, for instance, would ever have thought that the little backstage rat I was, would spend a week-end with the King of Spain?—Not that I enjoyed it.

ALICE.—Snob.

ANN [*laughing*]. You might spend a week-end with yourself sometime, Lily. You just might have a lovely time.

LILY. I'd bore myself stiff. I'd get to showing myself card-tricks.

TOM. A person's got to look for disillusionment all the way along. It's the price paid by everyone who uses his head for anything but a hat-rack.

ANN. But Tom! What do you want with illusions in the first place?

LILY. Oh—just to make himself feel important. That's why he quit his business with such a great big gesture.

TOM. I quit publishing because it seemed ridiculous to devote my life to bringing out books about life.

LILY. Exactly—and how important the gesture made you feel. Sure. That's what we're all after—and that's all we're after.

ANN. You know, Lily, you're so completely de-bunked, there's very little of you left.

LILY. I tell you, to beat this game you've got to be born rich and healthy, and preferably a Farley—with Pat's private slant that nothing matters a damn anyway.

PAT. Is that my slant?

LILY. Isn't it?

ANN. It wasn't when I knew him.

PAT. People change, they say.

ANN. It breaks my heart to have you change, Pat.

[PAT *glances at her, then looks away.* ALICE *stretches upon her cushion*]

ALICE. Oh, you all think too much. Why don't you be like me?

LILY. Need you ask, dear?

ALICE. I know that when I die, I die. But in the meantime I hope to keep my days and nights fairly full.

LILY. Of what?

ALICE. I may not be as clever as you, Lily, but I'm a whole lot happier. [*She yawns luxuriously*]

LILY. I have a cat that is, too.

ALICE. I love cats. Cats have the right idea.

PAT. They also have kittens.

[NORMAN *clears his throat*]

NORMAN. It all resolves itself into the fundamental problem of the location of Man in the Universe.

PAT. Really? Is that all?

TOM. Oh Lord, how can anyone believe he matters any, when he knows that in a few years he'll be dead and done with?

ANN. You honestly think that *this* is all there is, then?

TOM. This what?

ANN. This life.

TOM. Why, of course. Don't you?

[ANN *laughs*]

ANN. Oh no, no, *no!* Of course not! Not possibly.

[*They all look at her in astonishment. Even* ALICE *raises herself upon her elbow on the cushion.* LILY *murmurs*]

LILY.—She's marvellous. She's really marvellous.

TOM. Chemistry is chemistry, Ann.

ANN [*still laughing*]. Heavens, Tom, is that as far as you've got?

LILY. There's always the next step. Look: you see that nice little white scar there? [*She holds one hand out for her to see, wrist upward*]

[ANN *is serious in a moment*]

ANN. Lily—what do you mean!

HOPE. Lily! You didn't!

LILY.—Didn't I, though.—At last a real use for old razor-blades.

HOPE. But when?

LILY. Oh—about a year ago. I forget, exactly.

HOPE. But my dear—*why?*

LILY. I just got sick of myself. [*She apologizes*]—It wasn't very successful. I know too much. I made the tourniquet myself.

PAT. That's right, Actress, do your stuff. God's out front to-night.

LILY.—Will you tell the Kind Gentleman I enjoyed his little piece, but found no part in it for me?

TOM. Don't talk that way, Lily.

LILY. Why not?

TOM. It's blasphemy. I was born a Catholic, and I don't like it.

[LILY *stares at him, finds him quite serious*]

LILY. "Blasph—"? I haven't heard that word in years. Say another.

NORMAN. I thought you'd given up your religion?

TOM. So I have. But all the same, the only real dope on life I ever got was from an old priest at school. I'd like to see that old fellow again. He was a nice old fellow. Father Francis, his name was.

ANN. There's been a great space left in you, Tom. It will take some filling.

TOM. And with what?

LILY. They say cyanide is quite satisfactory.

HOPE. Don't, Lily—

LILY. Why? Don't tell me *you've* never thought of it. [HOPE *is about to reply, but does not*] Ha-ha! Caught you—

TOM. Darling—you haven't really—

HOPE. Well, haven't you?

TOM. I know, but—

HOPE. Is it anyone's special privilege? Am I not worthy?

[LILY *laughs, and turns to* ALICE]

LILY. Alice?

[ALICE *sits up*]

ALICE. Yes, dear?

LILY. No, there'd be no point in it for you —it would be too little change.—But what about you, Norman? Do you ever yearn out windows?

[NORMAN *smiles*]

NORMAN. I can't say I've ever seriously contemplated it, no.

LILY. Then go on and contemplate it.

[*A brief pause. Then*]

NORMAN. Well, I wouldn't do anything positive—but if I knew I could save my life by changing from this chair to that one, I doubt if I'd move.

[*Again* LILY *laughs.* ANN *is gazing at them in amazement*]

LILY. This is grand! [*To* ANN] I suppose we can count you out, though.

ANN [*briefly*]. Yes, I'm out.

LILY.—And as for you, Patrick? How long since *your* last confession?

PAT. I'm sorry to disappoint you, but it's never crossed my mind.

LILY. And if I were you, I'd take precious good care it never did.

PAT. Thanks. You're kind. I'll remember.

LILY.—Because I don't think it would cross yours. I think it would stick there. [*She looks about her. Then, to* ANN] Four out of six. Not a bad average, is it?

TOM. Pat, why was that letter addressed to me?

[PAT *smiles*]

PAT. Suppose my foot should slip on an Alp?

TOM. Do you expect it to?

PAT. Not particularly, but there's always the hope.

TOM. You're not usually so foresighted.

PAT. But this time I am.

TOM.—I don't like it. May I read it now?

PAT. It would make me feel a little foolish. It's signed "oceans of love, Patrick."

ANN. What letter are you talking about?

PAT. One that he—

ALICE [*suddenly*]. Oh, good Lord—

HOPE. What's the matter?

ALICE. Suddenly I had the most abominable chill.

LILY. On a night like this?

ALICE. What a fool I am, really.

[NORMAN *wraps a thin beach-blanket about her*]

LILY [*sweetly*]. Please dear, let *me* say that.

NORMAN. I wouldn't give two francs for any of our nervous systems.

HOPE. It's probably too much sun and too little sleep for a week.

[PAT *pours himself another brandy*]

PAT.—And the grape—the grape and the grain. [*And drains the glass*]

[*Again silence descends upon them.* HOPE *finally breaks it*]

HOPE. Is it always so heavenly here, Ann?

ANN.—Except for some overcast nights in the

Autumn with no moon, no stars. Then there's such blackness as you wouldn't believe.—Only the light from the lighthouse on the Ile de Port-Cros, crossing the terrace here—like the finger of God, Father says.

[*It has got darker, but the atmosphere possesses a luminous quality that imparts a strange definiteness of outline to the objects and the people upon the terrace. Again, silence. Then:*]

LILY. I'm sad.—I could cry.—I am crying. —Oh, behave yourself.

[*Suddenly* ANN *stands bolt upright, rigid*]

HOPE. What is it?

ANN. Wait a minute.

HOPE. Honestly, Ann, I do wish—

ANN. Wait! [*For a moment they wait, silent, tense. Then from the distance is heard one muffled report*]—There. It's all right. Don't worry.

HOPE. But what on earth *was* it?

ANN. It's Father. He's at the bastide. Sometimes he fires a sunset-gun. I get to expect it.

ALICE [*awed*]. He won't do it again to-night, will he?

ANN. I said a sunset-gun. It sets only once a day as a rule. [*There is a silence. She rises, abruptly*] Well, why shouldn't he, if he likes? I think it's splendid of him! [*A moment. Then she laughs shortly*] Sorry! [*Waits another moment, and continues*]—I imagine he'd seem a trifle strange to you, but to me it's a pretty grand sort of strangeness. I believe he is a very wise man.

TOM. I don't doubt it.

ANN. I don't always understand him, but that's my fault. I understand better than I used to, and sometime I hope to understand all. So I just try to follow him wherever his mind leads. I've been beautiful places there with him.

TOM [*after a pause*]. I unearthed a marble tablet in the lower garden to-day. It was in Latin and said: "To Semptronius who, at age 12, danced here, and pleased."

ANN. But how charming that is!—Can't you see him?—Semptronius—

[TOM *rises. All at once he is as excited as a child*]

TOM. I'd like to dance here, too. [*To* PAT] Will you play? And would anyone mind?

HOPE.—Now that's what I mean! Really, we're not acting at all sensibly, don't you realize it?

[TOM *looks at her, and returns to the wall*]

TOM.—Ten years ago I wouldn't even have asked. It's a rotten feeling, knowing your youth's gone—knowing that all the brave things you once dreamed of doing, somehow just won't get done.

PAT [*as a small boy would say it:*] I wanna go out to the South Seas like Father *D*amien!

TOM [*soberly*]. I did, at that.

ALICE. Who is Father Damien?

TOM [*reciting*]. Father Damien was a noble priest who went to the South Seas to help the lepers and got it himself.

HOPE. Sometimes I don't know his voice from little Tommy's.

[*Suddenly* TOM *stands up upon the wall*]

TOM. Look, Mummy! Look where *I* am!

HOPE. Get down, Tom, you'll fall.

TOM. Don't punish me, Mummy.—Reason with me.

HOPE.—Acting like that! I don't know where you think you are.

[TOM *descends from the wall*]

TOM.—Under the piano. [*He moves away from them, toward the table*]—Under the apple tree— [*He seats himself cross-legged beside the table, whistling a tune softly through his teeth and trying to wrench the top from a wooden champagne-stick. A moment, then he calls, as a small boy would*] Hey, Pat! Pat! C'mon over!

[PAT *comes forward to him*]

PAT. Hello Tom.

TOM. Hello, yourself.

PAT. Where're the other fellows?

TOM. How should I know? I got better things to do than follow *them* all over everywheres. [*He examines his stick with interest*]

[PAT *seats himself on the ground beside him*]

HOPE. Don't, Tom.—Make them stop, Ann. They go too far with it.

[*But* ANN *is silent, watching them intently*]

PAT.—Gosh, I feel good, don't you?

TOM. I feel all right.

PAT.—But don't you ever feel—gosh, I don't know—*good?*

TOM. You don't feel very good when you've got things the matter with you, like I have.

PAT. What have you got? [*No answer*] Aw, come on, Tom—is it really bad?

[TOM's *head bends lower over his stick*]

TOM. It's awful.

PAT. Aw gosh, I'm sorry—tell me, Tom— [*A moment, then:*]

TOM. Will you promise never so long as you live— [PAT *nods eagerly*]—I think I've got something, Pat.

PAT. What?

TOM. I think I got the leprosy.

PAT [*appalled*]. You've—? Gosh, Tom, why do you think that?

TOM. I read a book last night about Father Damien in the South Seas and he got the leprosy and I think I've got it.

PAT. How—how do you suppose you ever—

TOM. I gave a old woman a dime the other day, and she went and kissed my hand, and

I think it must of been her that gave it to me.

PAT. But didn't you wash or anything?

TOM. I couldn't till I got home. And it takes awful fast. Look at that— [*He shows his wrist*]

PAT. Where? [*He almost touches* TOM's *wrist—but draws his hand back, fearfully*]

TOM. Doesn't it look sort of—white to you?

PAT. It does, sort of.

TOM.—And scaly. That's the way it starts. My foot's the same way. I could tell for sure by putting it in hot water.

PAT. Hot water!

TOM. If you've got it, you don't feel anything, not even the water, even. Father Damien didn't. That's the way he knew.

[NORMAN *is drawn over to them. He too, has begun whistling softly. His tune is "Pony Boy"*]

PAT. Oh, he was prob'ly just a crazy ole priest.—H'lo, Norman.

[TOM *scowls.* NORMAN *gestures "Hello," and goes on whistling, hands in pockets*]

TOM.—A *what*, did you say?

PAT. Well, there *are* crazy priests. Anyways, I bet there have been, sometime.

TOM. Never. Never one. God wouldn't let there be.

NORMAN. What about Theo-philus?

TOM. Who?

NORMAN. Theo-philus.

TOM. What did he do that was so crazy?

NORMAN. Just burnt the libary at Alexandria, that's all.

TOM. I never even heard of it.

PAT. I did. Alexander the Great built it, quite a long time ago, to please his vanity.

NORMAN [*reciting*].—And Theo-philus was a crazy Christian monk that burnt up the libary which was the greatest in the whole world and which history tells us contained over seventy thousand volumes.

TOM. Well, if he did, I bet he had some good reason. I bet they were impure books, or something.

NORMAN. He was crazy.

TOM. I bet he knew they were good and lashivious and he just burnt 'em to the honor and glory of God.

NORMAN. He was crazy.

PAT [*pointedly*]. Of course you'd say so, anyway. I guess you'd say any Christian holy man of God was crazy.

NORMAN. I wouldn't either. [*A moment*] Why would I?

PAT. I suppose you think we didn't notice you didn't eat that ham-sandwich the other day and asked for a sardine.

NORMAN. I wanted a sardine. I like sardines better. I like their taste better.

PAT. Yes, you do!

TOM [*to* PAT].—Anyone says sardines taste better'n ham says so for some good alterior reason, you bet.

NORMAN. You know what *you* are, don't you?

TOM. What?

NORMAN. Cath'lic! Cath'lic!

TOM [*soberly*] I am a Catholic. Yes. I am proud to be a Catholic.

NORMAN. Yes—well, before *I'd* go to confession and things—

TOM. You know why?—You wouldn't get the chance. They wouldn't let you in. See, Mr. Jew?

PAT. You are a Jew, aren't you?

[NORMAN *raises his head proudly*]

NORMAN. Of course I am. What about it?

TOM. You crucified our Lord, that's what about it.

NORMAN. Oh, no I didn't.

PAT. Who did, then?

NORMAN.—The Roman soldiers. See?

PAT. Oh, you think you know everything. All you do is sit around and read books, little Ikey.

NORMAN. I'm not an Ikey! Don't you call me that!

TOM [*to* PAT].—You're just as bad as he is. A heretic's what *you* are— Protestant-dog-sit-on-a-log-and-eat-meat-on-*Friday!*

PAT. I'll eat anything I like any day I like— see? *And* ham.

TOM. It's all right now, only wait'll you die. Just wait'll then.

PAT [*to* NORMAN]. Pooh, "when I die." That's what the priest tells him—

TOM. Well, just let me tell *you:* when I grow up maybe *I'm* going to be a priest. See? Maybe I've got a vacation right this minute. See?

PAT. A what?

TOM. A vacation—a call.

[PAT *looks at him in wonder*]

PAT. Gosh.

TOM [*closer to him*]. Just think that over, Mr. Fresh.—And when you hear of me going out to the South Seas and places like Father Dami— [*Awestruck, he remembers his malady. In fear he peers at his wrist again*]

PAT. Is it any worse?

TOM. I—I think it's spread a little.

PAT. Listen—

TOM. What—

PAT. I know a fellow's got a doctor-book. Only he won't lend it. You got to look at it at his house. Shall we—?

TOM. All right. [*A moment. Then:*] Pat—

PAT. What?

TOM. What would you do if *you* had the— the you-know?

PAT [*after thought*]. I'd kill myself.

TOM. You couldn't. You'd go straight to hell. And the tortures of the you-know are as nothing to the tortures of hell.

PAT. Just the same I'd do it, though. I certainly wouldn't go around with the lepr—
[TOM *claps his hand over his mouth*] Let go!

TOM.—You promised! [*To* NORMAN]—You get out. Get out, now!—If you know what's good for you—

[NORMAN *leaves them.* PAT *struggles*]

PAT. Let go! I'm—I can't breathe. Let go—!
[*Still* TOM *holds him.* PAT *struggles harder. He begins to beat at him with his fists. Finally freeing himself, he goes at him more violently.* TOM *retaliates. They go up and down the terrace, advancing, retreating, clinching, separating, raining blows upon each other in dead earnest.* HOPE *suddenly realizes that they are no longer playing, and cries:*]

HOPE. Stop it! [*But they go on. She begins to strike at* PAT] Stop! Stop it, do you hear me? [*She turns imploringly to* NORMAN] Norman!

[NORMAN *goes to* TOM]

NORMAN. Come on, now—that's enough!
[*He holds his arms from behind*] What's got into you two?

[HOPE *stands between* PAT *and* TOM, *protecting* TOM. *They are gasping for breath, glaring at each other.* TOM *lurches forward once more*]

HOPE. Stop, Tom!—How often must I tell you— [*Then she takes him in her arms*] Oh, didn't I beg you not to!

[ANN *goes to* PAT]

ANN. Pat—Pat, dear—

[PAT *stares at her blankly for a moment, then suddenly slumps down into a chair*]

PAT. I'm—I don't know—

[NORMAN *releases* TOM, *who stares first at* HOPE, *then at* PAT, *amazement growing in his eyes*]

ALICE. Well, of all the—

ANN. Wait!—Are you all right, Pat?

PAT [*weakly*]. Sure.

[HOPE *covers her face*]

HOPE. Oh, I'm scared—I'm so scared.

ANN. Of what, Hope—of seeing life burst the walls of the little room we try to keep it in?

[*Suddenly* TOM *turns upon her*]

TOM. Well, Ann—if you know so much, what's the answer to the whole works?

ANN. If I could tell you—

HOPE [*gently*]. Tom—listen—

TOM [*suddenly savage*]. I say, what's the answer? I want to know! [*He averts his head, sharply*] God help me, I've got to know!

ANN.—But I can't tell you!—I don't know how.—Oh my dears—what is to become of you? How can I let you go to rove the world like ghosts this way? You're so pitiful, and I love you so!

[FELIX *comes in from the garden*]

FELIX [*to* ANN]. Pardon, Mademoiselle—

ANN. Oui? Qu'est-ce-que c'est?

FELIX. C'est le père de Mademoiselle qui fait demander si elle a besoin de lui.

ANN. Ou est-il?

FELIX. À la bastide, Mademoiselle.

[*A moment.* ANN *looks about her, at the others. Then:*]

ANN. I'll go to him. [*She turns and goes out, up the garden steps*]

[FELIX *turns to* PAT]

FELIX. Pardon, Monsieur—il est neuf heures-et-demi, Monsieur.

PAT. Merci.

[FELIX *bows and goes out, into the house, taking the coffee-service with him. There is a long silence, then* LILY *collects herself and speaks*]

LILY. What did he say to Ann?

ALICE. Her father sent to ask if she needed him. She's gone to him.

HOPE. Needed him!—For what, I wonder.

[*Another pause.* LILY *ventures hopefully:*]

LILY. It is not generally known that polo was invented by Chinese women.—An interesting fact, is it not? [*No one replies*]—Nope.

NORMAN [*reflectively*].—I'd like to go all alone to Andora.

ALICE. Where's that?

NORMAN. I don't know.

ALICE. Then what do you want to go for?

NORMAN. No Federal Reserve—no "giant mergers."—Time to think—Lord, time to think!

LILY. About what?

NORMAN. Lily, I'm sorrier for you than for anyone I know.

LILY. I don't want your pity, Mr. Rose. I just want your money.

NORMAN [*pondering*]. When I was working in that fur shop on Twenty-third Street, I was a free man. [*A moment. Then he rises abruptly*] I think I'll go in and pack. [*And goes out into the house*]

TOM. Of course *I* think the trouble with Norman is, he's caught and he knows it. He'd like to retire now, but he can't. Too much depends on him.

[PAT *laughs shortly*]

PAT.—All looking for the answer, when there isn't any answer. [*A moment*]—Unless maybe it's "Off for Africa."

HOPE.—That will do, Pat. Don't even start it.

ALICE. I still don't see why men like you three can't enjoy life.

LILY. Promise me something, dear—

ALICE. What?

LILY.—When you die, leave your head to the Rockefeller Institute. It's a little gem.

[ALICE *rises and moves toward the house*]

ALICE. Oh, you're always so bright—

LILY. I know. Isn't it the devil?

ALICE. If you weren't, *au fond,* such a common little piece—

LILY.—*N'est ce pas?* [*To the others*]—She thinks in French.

[*At the door* ALICE *turns and contemplates them*]

ALICE. Honestly, it's all so boring— [*And goes out*]

LILY. The trouble with that girl is complete lack of vitamins A to Z.

HOPE. Do you suppose Norman is really in love with her?

LILY. I don't know. Anyhow, there's a chink in that fine Semitic pride of his. It would never risk a refusal.

HOPE. But surely if she cared for him—

LILY. She doesn't—too much effort.

[*A pause,* TOM *rises*]

TOM. Oh Lord, if only I'd died at fifteen.

PAT. Maybe you did.

HOPE. It's been a ghastly week all around. No wonder we're depressed.

[TOM *looks at her*]

TOM. Hope, sometimes I feel I don't know you at all. [*He mounts the steps to the house*] —And we're supposed to be the lucky ones! We're the ones who've got the world by the top of the head.—I'll let you know when I'm packed, Hope. [*And goes out*]

HOPE. I'm coming now. [*To* PAT *and* LILY] —He came abroad this time to study the origins of Ecclesiastical Precedence in Rome. He got as far as Antibes. He gets vaguer all the time. I'm so worried about him I can't see straight.

PAT. Of course *I* think Tom's trouble is having too much time on his hands.

HOPE. But it's his time to himself he always said he wanted! That would solve everything. And now that he's got it, *it's* not enough. I wish to heaven we were home with the children and he was still rushing madly for the 8:22. He cursed it, but it kept him going.

PAT. You're just travel-worn, that's all. Why not let him make his crusades for Truth by himself?

HOPE.—And get sent for the first day he's lonely? That's what's always happened.—Except once, just once, when he did go to Canada for a month. [*She rises*] He accomplished two things toward his soul's salvation there—two great things.

PAT. What?

HOPE.—He grew a red beard and learned to whistle through his teeth. [*She moves toward the stairs*]—Talk about children! He's the worst one I've got. Oh, if you *knew* how I want to stay home with my *real* babies! [*And goes into the house*]

LILY.—Which is the answer, of course, to Hope.

PAT. What is?

LILY. She's so peaceful, so normal. She's all home and babies.

PAT. That's not a bad thing to be.

LILY. It's a grand thing to be.—And so is it to be the fine, free, roving soul that Tom might. It's the combination that's wrong. Of course *I* think the real trouble with them both is— [*Suddenly she stops, and laughs*] Do you realize what we've been doing?

PAT. What?

LILY.—When I go in, what will you say about me?—The trouble with Lily is what? What's wrong with Lily?

PAT. Is there anything?

LILY. Plenty. But Pat—

PAT. What?

LILY. I think we've been good for each other, don't you?

PAT. I suppose so.

LILY. You lie, you don't!

[PAT *looks at her mildly*]

PAT. Don't be violent, Lily.

[LILY *groans*]

LILY.—Now he's going to turn gent on me again. That's the catch with you: you were born a gent and you can't get over it.

PAT. I think I've done pretty well.

LILY. Oh you do, do you? Well, listen to me—

PAT. Lily, I'm sunk.—And low, deep, full fathom five.

[*She looks at him curiously. There is a silence. Then she speaks in a different tone:*]

LILY. Have a drink.

PAT. No, thanks.

LILY. Pat, when I first knew you, your spine had turned to jelly—

PAT. Yes?

LILY. Yes. And your slant was all wrong. You'd been expecting too much of something —I don't know what—and hadn't got it. You were a mass of sobs.

PAT. That's a pretty picture.

LILY. It was you.—I'd knocked around enough, man and boy, to know what people really are. I taught you to expect nothing, didn't I?

PAT. Yes.

[*She raises her glass*]

LILY.—And what a dandy little mother's-helper *this* is— [*She drinks*]

PAT. Yes.

LILY.—And that there's no de-lousing station big enough to pass the whole world through.

PAT. That's right.

LILY. Well—have a drink.

[*But he decides not to*]

PAT.—I suppose they're good things to have learned.

LILY. I've changed your slant, haven't I?

PAT. Something has.

LILY. You've done a lot for me, too. How is it I don't fall in love with you, I wonder—

PAT. I don't know. Have you tried very hard?

LILY. Awfully hard.

PAT. I'm sorry. Maybe I'm just not your type.

LILY. Would you like to be?

PAT. I never gave it much thought.

LILY. Don't I attract you at all, Pat?

PAT. You might, if I thought about it.

LILY. Think about it. [*He does so. They look intently into each other's eyes*] Have you thought?

PAT. Um.

LILY. What's the answer?

PAT. I'm attracted.

LILY. Much?

PAT. Quite a lot.

LILY. Would you mind kissing me, Pat?

PAT. On the contrary.

LILY. Then do, please. [*He kisses her. She clings to him briefly, then turns away*] Oh, it's so awful—

PAT. Thanks! [*Then:*]—What is?

LILY. I don't feel anything. I don't feel anything at all.

PAT. No. I thought not.

[*She turns quickly*]

LILY. You knew about me?

PAT. I imagined.

LILY. Don't get me wrong, Pat. I'm not one of the girls, either.

PAT. I never supposed you were.

LILY. I just—don't feel anything for anyone.

PAT. Some people have all the luck.

LILY. Oh, no—don't say that! I want to, so much— [*A moment*] It seems to me—dimly—way back somewhere, I loved someone terribly. I don't know who—my father, maybe.

PAT. There you go about your father again.

LILY.—All I know is, that since, there's been nothing.

PAT. Maybe that did the trick, Lily.

LILY. How?

PAT. Maybe that's all you get.

LILY. You're a wise guy, in a way.

PAT. You think?

LILY [*touching his forehead*].—The Farley brow, eight months gone with Minerva. Where do you get all your dope?

PAT. The ravens feed me.

LILY. Oh, hell—nothing happens anymore.

PAT. Buck up, Lily. Something will before you know it.

LILY. A broken neck would be welcome.

PAT. Give things a chance. Don't try so hard for them.

LILY. All right, teacher.—Have another drink?

PAT. Later—when the night wears on a bit.

LILY. Yes—and won't it, though—

[*ALICE appears on the balcony*]

ALICE [*lowly*]. Listen, you two—

[*LILY puts on her humorless smile*]

LILY. Yes, Angel? [*To PAT*] Reach me my Winchester, will you?

ALICE. Honestly, I've got the queerest feeling.

LILY. I told you a week ago you swallow too fast.

ALICE.—I don't suppose we could decently leave *before* eleven—

PAT. No, I don't suppose we could.

ALICE. I was afraid we couldn't. [*She moves toward the doorway, but sways against the railing. She exclaims, weakly:*] Oh—come up here a minute, someone—will you? I feel awful.

LILY. Right away, dear.

[*ALICE goes out, into the house again*]

PAT. You'd better go. She may be ill.

[*LILY is looking off into the garden*]

LILY. Ann's coming back. One thing, Pat—

PAT. What?

LILY [*as she moves to follow ALICE*]. If I were you, I'd be careful to-night.

PAT. About what?

LILY. About Ann. You may not know it, but you're still the world to that girl.

PAT. You're talking tripe, Lily.

LILY. Just the same, I'd be careful. [*PAT turns abruptly and looks out over the wall. FELIX has come out upon the balcony, with three or four small candle-lamps, unlighted, which he arranges upon the balcony wall. ANN comes in from the garden*] Ann—do you suppose your maid could give me a hand with my things?

ANN. But of course! She's in my room. Call her.

[*LILY mounts the steps. FELIX takes out his watch*]

LILY.—And it isn't tripe, my Patrick.

[*From far in the distance beyond the wall a small pencil of light is cast. It performs an arc in space, sweeping across the terrace, flooding over the upper wall of the house and disappearing again in the garden above*]

FELIX. Pardon, Monsieur—il manque dix-sept minutes de dix heure, Monsieur.

PAT [*without turning*]. Bon.

[*FELIX goes into the house*]

LILY [*at the top of the steps*]. What happens when you forget to wind him up? [*She goes into the house by the other door*]

[*ANN stands silently watching PAT until the door has closed behind LILY. Then suddenly, swiftly, she goes to him, takes him by the shoulders and turns him about, facing her*]

PAT. Oh hello, Ann.

[*From the distance piano-music begins to be heard*]

ANN [*lowly, intensely*]. I won't have it, Pat. I just will not have it!

PAT. It?—What's that you won't have?

ANN. Something's burning you up. Tell me what it is!

PAT. I'm afraid you're imagining things. Where's the music from?

ANN. Réné Mayer has a house up the road. It's always full of musicians.—You've got to listen to me. I—

PAT. Have you heard Sandy Patch's new song? [*He moves toward the piano*]—It's called "Drunk and Disorderly." It goes like this—

ANN. Don't, Pat—we haven't time—

PAT. Then let's get the others down, shall we?—And enjoy what there is left. [*He makes a move toward the house. Her hand upon his arm stops him*]

ANN. Wait! [*She looks away, to control herself, her hand still upon his arm*]

PAT. I'm all right, my dear. Really I am.

ANN. We've known each other quite a few years, now—

PAT. We have, haven't we? I feel pretty spry, though, don't you?

ANN. We've always been able to talk.

PAT. They say I could talk when I was only—

[*Her hand tightens upon his arm*]

ANN.—Which we've always done directly, and honestly.

PAT. Yes?

ANN. Shan't we now?

PAT. If you like. Why not?

ANN. When you leave to-night I shan't see you again for at least a year—maybe more—

PAT. Oh—before I forget— [*From his pocket, in a fold of tissue-paper, he brings a very simple and fine ruby pendant, and gives it to her*]

ANN. What is it?

PAT. It was Mother's. I'm sure she'd want you to have it. I know I do.

ANN. Beautiful—

PAT. I think so.

ANN. But Pat—it's priceless—

PAT. So was she. So is Ann.

ANN. Oh, thank you for it! Put it on for me— [*He catches it around her throat. She turns again, facing him, then stands for a moment with her forehead against his breast*] Pat—my dear Pat—

PAT. Things don't go the way we'd like them to, Ann.

[*A moment, then she leaves him*]

ANN.—You've been dodging around corners, to get away from me.

PAT. I didn't know it.

ANN. I won't bite you, Pat.—What's been happening to you these past three years? I'm still a little interested.

PAT. It's been pretty much the same sort of life, thanks.

ANN. What are you doing with all that money?

PAT. Oh—spending some of it—giving away quite a lot of it. It's an awful pile to make a dent in.

ANN. You never found the job we used to talk so much about—

[*PAT smiles*]

PAT. How well she knows me.

ANN. There are only two people in this world who are really important to me, you and Father.

PAT. I'm—thanks, Ann. That's good to know.

ANN. I've been able to help him a little—

PAT. I should think you had.

ANN. I'd give the eyes right out of my head, if I could help you. [*He lifts her hand to his lips, kisses it, and turns away*] Oh Pat, Pat—whatever has happened to you?

PAT. Myself.

ANN.—Don't you go telling yourself you're no good! You're the best there is.

PAT. You don't know.

ANN. Oh, yes I do!

PAT. Anyhow, let's not get solemn about—

ANN.—And what do you suppose it means to me to know that a person I love as I love you is breaking up into little pieces over something I've no share in?

PAT. But Ann—you don't love me anymore.

ANN. I do, though. I've never got over it—never. I love you with all my heart. [*A silence. She smiles uncertainly*]—I don't suppose by any chance you love me back—

PAT [*with difficulty*]. There's something in the way. Nothing can ever come of you and me now. There's something in the— [*He turns away, with an exclamation*]

ANN. Tell me.

PAT. I can't.

ANN.—You'll be shocked to hear I'm living with you in my mind. I've taught myself to dream about you nearly every night. That gives me—rights.

PAT. Ah, Ann—let it go—please let it go.

ANN. I can't. I simply can't.—You've always been a life-and-death person. You take things terribly hard. I'm sure it's not as hopeless as it seems. [*But he does not answer*]—Do you remember the first time we met, on the Westbury Road?—me lost, with a sprained ankle, and you—

PAT.—When I forget anything about you and me—

ANN. I wish we could get back there. I wish we could start from the Westbury Road again.

PAT.—But we can't.

ANN.—Such a dear, serious boy you were.

All the time you were in college you used to come to me with your little troubles—
[*He laughs*]

PAT.—Would I row on the Crew?—I didn't make the Dramatic Club.—What if they passed me up on Tap Day.—Poor Ann—

ANN. I was important to you then—

PAT. You still are.

ANN. Come to me now with your big trouble, Pat.

PAT. I'm just a flop, darling.

ANN. It's a little soon to decide that, don't you think?

PAT. I told you my schedule was different.

ANN. Pat, whatever happened, happened four years ago. You came back from a year in England, and you were changed. It was a girl, wasn't it? I saw her picture in your study. What was it—wouldn't she have you?
[PAT *smiles*]

PAT. I forget. What did she look like?

ANN. Very young, quite English, very fair. A lovely face—pretty, oh, so pretty.

PAT. Funny—I've forgotten.

ANN. I haven't.—Then you went over again the next winter—for how long was it?

PAT. I don't know—three weeks—

ANN. That's when I had my hunch about you. It wasn't long after you'd sailed. I was walking up Madison Avenue and in a florist's window I saw a lot of hawthorn blossoms—
[PAT *starts slightly*]

PAT. Hawthorn—

ANN. Yes. They were lovely, and I was going in to get some when all at once I began to feel terribly queer. It was as if the bottom had dropped out of everything. I knew it had something to do with you, and I love you and I just went on home without them.

PAT. I don't get it at all.

ANN. Nor do I.—But the next morning I passed the same shop and saw that the hawthorn was gone. Somehow, that was terrible. I couldn't get warm again all day. I love you and I had to cable you.

PAT. I don't get it.

ANN. I've never known such a change in a person, as in you when you came back. Suddenly you were as hard as nails, and so bitter. I hated leaving you that way when I came here with Father. But I was sure you'd get through it somehow, back to yourself. Now I see that you haven't. I see that it's worse than it ever was, it's destroying you. Oh, Pat—it can't be just some fool of a girl who wouldn't have you.—What has done it?

PAT. Honestly, Ann—it's all so long ago.

ANN. But I've *got* to know. Tell me!
[PAT *shakes his head*]

PAT. It's all too ridiculous. Really. I never even think of it anymore.

ANN. Whether you do or not, it's got **you**

still. Something awful's got you. Tell me—it will help to tell me. Ah, *please*—because I love you—

PAT. I would if I could. I want to. I simply can't.

ANN. I'll find out!

PAT. All right, Ann.

ANN.—But can't you *accept* it, somehow? Can't you take life whole—all of it—for what it is, and be glad of it? Why do you have to go at it with a tin box of paints, daubing it up pretty? You're grown-up, now.—Why, my dear! What have I said? What is there in that, to hurt you so?

PAT. Listen: you can have your marvellous life. I'm not taking any.

ANN. What are you talking about?

PAT.—The lot of you—clutching, grabbing at some little satisfaction that lasts a day or two—a swell business.

ANN. You dare talk to me about my life like that!

PAT. Yours—theirs—anyone's—

ANN. Oh, you're horrible—
[PAT *looks at her intently*]

PAT. So you're the last to go. You fail me too—

ANN [*a cry*].—You?—And who are you, that you shouldn't be failed sometime?

PAT. I don't know, Ann. I've often wondered. [*Again he moves to the wall and stands looking out over it, the light from the lighthouse breaking over his head.* ANN *sinks into a corner of the sofa. From the distance, the piano-music begins to be heard more clearly, For a long time they are silent. Then* PAT *speaks. His voice is one of wonder, almost of fright*]—They're right about this place—it *is* so, you-know—it's really so—

ANN. What is?

PAT.—Like other places—like another place—

ANN. Where?

PAT.—A house my mother had in Florida, four years ago, when I came back from England—

ANN. That was the second time—

PAT. Yes. It was in March. I came straight down here from New York—I mean straight down there. Mother was in the patio all alone, having coffee— [*Still he looks out over the wall, without turning*]—I had so much to tell her—I'll never forget it—I thought if only I could talk to someone who—
[ANN *speaks, softly:*]

ANN. Hello, Son. It's good to have you back.

PAT.—Could talk to someone who might, just might, have some little faint idea of what I—

ANN. Hello, Son. It's good to have you back.
[*A moment. Then:*]

PAT [*a murmur*]. Hello, Mother. It's good to be back. [*He comes forward to her, slowly*]

ANN. I didn't expect you quite so soon.

PAT. I know. [*He sinks down upon a cushion on the floor beside her. The eyes of both are straight ahead, not looking at each other*]

ANN. You're looking tired.

PAT. It was a rotten trip. [*He goes on in a low voice, almost mechanically*]—I think I'll stay awhile this time.

ANN. I'm glad.

PAT. It seems like a pleasant place.

ANN. It's peaceful.

PAT. That's good.

ANN. Ah, Pat—what is it, dear? I've worried so about you.

PAT. Yes. I suppose.

ANN. I've wanted to ask, but—

PAT. I know. I just couldn't talk.

ANN. Are you so very much in love?

PAT. Yes.

ANN. Tell me about her. Who is she?

PAT. Oh, it's all over now.

ANN. Over?

PAT. Yes.

ANN. But are you sure?

PAT. I'm certain.

[*A moment. Then:*]

ANN. Who was she, then?

PAT.—Mary Carr—the niece of one of my dons at Cambridge. [*A moment. His voice hardens*]—Cambridge—another of Father's fake ideas. Finish me off, eh? Turn me into the little gentleman. Every inch a Farley—God!

ANN. Hush, Pat—

PAT.—Be good at everything. Shine! Always shine! And if you can't, don't play.—I can still hear his voice.

ANN.—Mary Carr, I've seen her photograph. She's very lovely.

PAT. Yes.

ANN.—And young.

PAT. She was eighteen in November. [*A pause. Then suddenly*] God, that is young. Father was right *there*, at least.

ANN. What happened when he went over to you last year—

PAT. I cabled I wanted to get married. He cabled me to wait, he was coming. I waited. He came. He talked me out of it. [*Bitterly*]—She wasn't suitable.

ANN. But that wasn't *your* reason—

PAT. I tell you I let him talk me out of it!

ANN. You agreed to put it off, that's all.

PAT. Yes—that's what I told myself—and that's what I told Mary.—That's what the little swine I was, grunted at Mary—just put it off awhile, that's all. But somehow the point missed Mary—somehow she didn't get me.—She just stopped talking in the middle of a word, and went into the house. And I took a train, and sailed with *him*. He was ill then—or said he was—we couldn't wait a day.

ANN [*hesitantly, after a pause*]. You—I suppose you and she—you'd been a good deal to each other.

PAT. We'd been everything.

ANN. I see.

PAT.—But there wasn't to be a baby, if that's what you mean— [*Again the bitter voice returns*] Wise boy, young Farley. He knows his way around!

ANN. But you wrote her. Surely you wrote her.

PAT. All the time, but I never had one little word from her. A dozen times I'd have gone over, but how could I with Father dying and then all that tangle settling the estate? [*He concludes, lowly*]—It was a year and three months since I'd seen her, when I'd sailed. I didn't even wire—I was afraid she'd run away somewhere.

ANN. But she hadn't, had she?

PAT. No.

ANN. She was there—

PAT. She was there.

[*A moment. Then:*]

ANN.—And she just won't have you. [*Her hand reaches to comfort him*]

[*He turns to her*]

PAT. Mother, she just won't have me. [*Suddenly he stares at her*] You're not—oh, damn you, Ann— [*He rises, and leaves her*]

[*She follows him*]

ANN. All right! But tell me. You've got to finish now! [*In another voice*]—Surely it isn't hopeless. Surely you can—

PAT. But it is, you see.

ANN. I don't believe it. Where is she now?

PAT. Down in the ground.

ANN. Pat—she isn't—?

PAT. She is, though—as a doornail.

ANN. Oh, my poor boy—

PAT. My poor Mary.

ANN. But listen to me—listen—!

PAT. No. *You* do. [*He points his finger at her, and speaks*] Three days before I came, she walked out under a tree where—she'd walked out under a hawthorn-tree at the end of a very sweet lane we knew, and stood there and shot herself.

ANN. Pat—Pat—

[*He moves away from her*]

PAT. You wanted to know, didn't you?

[*She looks at him. Then:*]

ANN.—So I lose you to a dead girl.

PAT. I've lost myself to her.

ANN. You loved me first!

PAT. But she died— [*He goes to the piano and seats himself, running his fingers silently over the keys*]—If only I could get back to her somehow. If I could just let her know I did come back.

ANN. How much of it is losing her—and how much the loss of yourself?

PAT. I don't understand that.

ANN.—You used to have a fair opinion of Pat Farley. That was essential to you—that *was* you.

PAT. All I know is that nothing's been any good to me since. I'm licked, Ann.

ANN. Well, what are you going to do about it?

[*Unnoticed by them* STEPHEN FIELD *has appeared at the top of the garden steps, where he stands, a figure in white, watching them. He is about fifty-eight, slight in build, gray-haired, with a face uncommonly strong, fine and sensitive, lined and worn as it is, gray, too, as it is*]

PAT. What is there to?

ANN. [*suddenly, sharply*]. Pat!

PAT [*without turning*]. What?

ANN. You said you'd tell me this the day before you died—

[*As she reaches the word, he strikes a chord and drowns it*]

PAT.—But I changed my mind, didn't I?— And told you now! [*He turns toward the house, and calls:*] What'll I play? Call your tunes, gents—almost closing-time!

ANN.—And the letter to Tom—. Oh my dear —what is it?

PAT. Don't be a fool.

[*A moment, then* STEPHEN *speaks*]

STEPHEN. Pat—

PAT [*without turning*]. What do you want? [*He is completely unnerved now*]

STEPHEN. I wouldn't do it, if I were you.

PAT. Do what?

STEPHEN. I really wouldn't. Things may change. [*He speaks with a clear, incisive strength*]

PAT.—Change? How? Who wants things changed? [*He turns, stares at him a moment, then rises*] Oh, how do you do, Mr. Field. How are you?—Everything's fine with me. Everything is—

STEPHEN.—And yet I wouldn't do it. I wouldn't go from here to those high places— to that strange accident. I really wouldn't.

[PAT *laughs shortly*]

PAT. Honestly!—If you think just because a fellow's planned a trip to climb an Alp or two—

[ANN *takes his shoulders in her hands, turns him about and gazes into his eyes*]

ANN. Pat!

PAT. I don't know what he's talking about. [*To* STEPHEN] I don't know what you're talking about. You're beyond me. I can't follow all this—

ANN. Oh, my poor Sweet, why do you want to do it? [*She shakes his shoulders*] Why?

PAT. Why not?—Maybe you can tell me that!—why not?—I should have three years ago, but I was too yellow then. [*Still she stares.*

Another silence, then he pulls away from her, mumbling:]—All right. Don't worry about me. It's all right. Small brain-storm, that's all.— Over now—

ANN. Promise it!

[*He gestures vaguely*]

STEPHEN. It is not so easy. He is in love with death.

[PAT *turns to him and sings, beating time with his finger*]

PAT.—Rat-a-plan, rat-a-plan, rat-a-plan-plan-plan-plan—[*He stops on the high note, holds out his arms, and cries:*] Yes! [*And goes to the point of the wall, where he stands with his back to them*]

ANN. Father—Pat's mine—I can't lose Pat!

[FELIX *comes out upon the balcony, watch in hand.* STEPHEN *descends the steps and comes upon the terrace*]

STEPHEN. I know, dear. [*He is watching the house*]—But let us take it quietly. Let us take it very quietly—

FELIX [*to* PAT]. Pardon, Monsieur—il est dix heure, juste.

[PAT *does not reply.* FELIX *goes out*]

STEPHEN.—Here are your other friends.

[TOM *and* HOPE *enter*]

TOM [*to* HOPE, *on the balcony*].—No, no— what's the good of talking?

HOPE. Well maybe if you'd—[*She sees* STEPHEN, *and stops*]

ANN. This—these are Tom and Hope Ames. —My Father, Hope.

HOPE. How do you do, Mr. Field?

TOM. How do you do, sir?

[STEPHEN *murmurs a greeting.* LILY *enters from the house*]

LILY.—I gave Alice a bromide, and she's sleeping like a log. She's—[*She sees* STEPHEN, *and stops*]

STEPHEN. What a beautiful color you all are. You look like savages. People don't realize that the sun here in the Midi is—

TOM. Didn't I meet you once with Father Francis at St. Luke's?

STEPHEN. I'm afraid not.

TOM. Perhaps it's just that your voice reminds me of him.

[LILY, *eyes wide, stands staring at* STEPHEN]

STEPHEN [*to* HOPE]. What do you think of our little retreat here?

HOPE. It's lovely. The days have gone so quickly.

STEPHEN.—Quickly—so quickly. [*To* LILY] —Why do you stare at me so?

LILY. Why I—I'm terribly sorry. I—

STEPHEN. But what is it?

LILY. It's just that you're so like my own father—

STEPHEN. Yes?

LILY. He was an actor in a touring-company.

He died years ago in Cleveland. He wanted me to be a dancer. I used to dance for him, often. It was a great pleasure to him. I mean to say—

STEPHEN [*gently*]. I am sure it was.

[NORMAN *comes in from the house*]

LILY [*in a burst*].—He was superb! He was so kind, so loving. He was the most beautiful man I've ever—! [*She stops suddenly, then continues:*]—But he deserted my mother, you know. He was simply foul to her.—Hell, I suppose he was just a ham actor—yes, and a drunkard, to boot. [*Again she stops*]—What am I spilling all this for? What's biting me now?

[STEPHEN *turns inquiringly to* ANN]

ANN.—Lily Malone, Father.

STEPHEN. Poor child. [*To* NORMAN]—And this?

NORMAN [*advancing*]. I'm Norman Rose, sir.

[*They shake hands*]

STEPHEN. I understand that you must leave us soon.

NORMAN. I'm afraid we must, sir.—At eleven, to be exact.

STEPHEN. That is unfortunate. [*Again he smiles*] Well—let us set the hour-glass on its side, and ask the Old Gentleman to put his sickle by, and sit down with us and rest a moment. [*He seats himself*] Before you go I want you all to see my bed of white phlox in the lower garden. In the moonlight it is white as white was never. I have banked the petunias near it—

HOPE [*delightedly*]. But *I* did that at home!

[STEPHEN *is watching the balcony.* ALICE *has appeared upon it*]

STEPHEN. The odor at night is so sweet, so pungent—cinnamon and gunpowder.—And is this Alice?

[ALICE *comes down the stairway without touching the railing, eyes far away, walking as in a dream.* ANN *rises*]

ANN. Yes—

LILY. Go back to bed, you foolish girl.

[ALICE *approaches them, unseeing*]

ANN.—This is my father.—Alice Kendall, Father.

STEPHEN. How do you do, my dear?

[*But she does not regard him*]

NORMAN. She's—!

ANN. Father, what is it?

STEPHEN. Sh! Be gentle with her—

HOPE. Oh, I don't like it!

LILY. I told you about that time she walked out into the hall, in Paris.

[ANN *goes to* ALICE]

ANN.—There, dear, it's all right. Just be quiet—quiet—

[PAT *is watching her, fascinated*]

PAT. Take her back. It's horrible—

[*Swiftly, directly* ALICE *walks to the angle of the wall*]

HOPE. Norman—don't let her hurt herself!

[NORMAN *and* ANN *have followed her*]

ANN. Alice—*Alice*—

[ALICE *turns to her. In a moment her eyes uncloud*]

ALICE.—But hello, my dear. They didn't tell me you were coming down. Divine house, isn't it? [*She speaks as if she were reading aloud*]

ANN. Listen to me a moment, dear—

ALICE. They're right. There's nothing like May in England. Who's on the party, do you know?

ANN. Oh—lots of people, But Alice, listen—

ALICE. Any extra men?

ANN. I think so.

[PAT *goes to the wall and stands there with his back to them*]

ALICE. I like this Norman person—

ANN. Yes, he's very nice. But—

[ALICE *laughs shrilly*]

ALICE. I know!—But not too nice! [*Her voice lowers, confidentially*] My dear, he burns me up. He looks so strong—so strong. I'll bet he'd give a girl a roll for her money, don't you? [*A moment. Then to herself, with real feeling:*]—Why can't he tell?—Why doesn't he know the way I ache for him?

PAT. Take her back, take her *back*—

ALICE.—Which one shall I wear?—I think the blue one, with the ruffle down the front— [*She unfastens a shoulder-clasp, and steps out of her dress*]

HOPE. But she mustn't—!

[ANN *turns to* NORMAN *with a helpless gesture*]

NORMAN. I'll speak to her.—Alice!

[ALICE *whispers:*]

ALICE. Who's that?—Is that you, Norman?

NORMAN. Hello, Alice—

ALICE. It was naughty of you to bring me here, you know it was—[*She leans toward him*] What did you tell the clerk at the desk?

NORMAN. Why, I just said that—

ALICE. Oh, I'm a pretty girl! [*She extends her arms.* NORMAN *takes one of her hands in his*] Why does no one want me? What are they afraid of?

NORMAN. Maybe they do. [*He turns to the others, painfully*] I love this girl. I've been crazy about her for years.

STEPHEN. Humble yourself before her beauty, sir.

ALICE. Come—there are people in the next room. I can hear them. They may come in— [*Suddenly she drags her hand from his and cries in terror:*]—Ann—Ann! [ANN *goes to her swiftly*]—This man's—been following me everywhere—

ANN. It's all right, darling, he won't hurt you. He's a nice man.

[ALICE *begins to whimper*]

ALICE. Is he? [*She turns to* NORMAN, *fearfully*] Are you? [*He nods, speechless. She darts a glance at* ANN *and huddles herself in her arms*]—But look at me—out on the street like this. Where's my little jacket? I want my little jacket—

[NORMAN *wraps a thin beach-blanket about her, and gives her her dress*]

NORMAN. Here you are, dear. [*He leads her gently to the steps. She looks up at him with a smile of childlike trust*]

ALICE. You *are* a nice man—

[*They mount the steps. There is a silence until they have gone out, into the house*]

LILY. She seemed to be so many places all at once.

STEPHEN. Sleep has freed her from time and space. One day sleep's sister will free her further. [*He hums a measure of a song, laughs softly, and concludes:*]—And near the white phlox I have a dappled pink variety which I developed by crossing a strain of crimson—

TOM [*an appeal*]. Mr. Field—What's the—? Mr. Field—!

STEPHEN.—Yes. It does bewilder one at first. I know. I too used to believe life had one aspect only. I was so sure that sleep and dreaming was—well, sleep and dreaming. And of course I knew that with death it was all over—

PAT. Well?

STEPHEN. Well, now I know I was mistaken.

PAT. How?

STEPHEN. I have found out a simple thing: that in existence there are three estates. There is this life of chairs and tables, of getting up and sitting down. There is the life one lives in one's imagining, in which one wishes, dreams, remembers. There is the life past death, which in itself contains the others. The three estates are one. We dwell now in this one, now in that —but in whichever we may be, breezes from the others still blow upon us.

PAT. I'm sorry, I don't follow you.

STEPHEN. There are no words for it. It is a sense, a knowing. It may come upon you in a field one day, or as you turn a corner, or one fine morning, as you stoop to lace your shoe [*A brief pause*]—Or even as it came on me.

TOM. How was that, sir?

STEPHEN. Here on this terrace.

ANN. Father—

STEPHEN. I know, dear.

PAT.—So life does go on, does it?

STEPHEN. Oh, yes. Of course.

PAT. How, for instance?

[STEPHEN *smiles*]

STEPHEN.—As it was in the beginning, is now, and ever shall be—

PAT.—World without end, eh?

STEPHEN. Without end.

PAT. Hah! That'd be a good joke.

LILY. Look out, Pat.

[NORMAN *comes out again upon the balcony and stands there, watching them*]

STEPHEN.—Let us be bold and change the "world" to "universe."—A fine night, isn't it? [*His gesture includes the sky*]—There is the space we one day shall inhabit, with all our memories and all our dreams. I ask you to admire this, gentlemen—

LILY. It's not always so fine, is it?

STEPHEN. But I ask you to admire that, too! [*To* PAT] If one could but once see his life whole, present and past together in one living instant, he would not wish to leave it before his time—oh no!

PAT. I know my time.

STEPHEN. I thought I knew mine once. My mind was quite made up, that night. Nothing was to deter me.—But the light from the Ile de Port-Cros described its arc as it does now. [*He stands erect*] It stopped me, held me.— How long I stood here, I don't know. But when I was aware again—

ANN. Father—

TOM.—What had happened to you? [HOPE *goes to him and tries to draw him away from the wall, murmuring* "Tom—Tom!" *but he does not answer and will not come*] Say what had happened!

[*The terrace, in a brief space, has become flooded with moonlight. There is a silence. Then* STEPHEN *begins to speak again, this time more softly, gently, coaxingly*]

STEPHEN. I had walked back in time. It is a very interesting excursion. You merely lift your foot, place it so, and there you are—or are you? One thinks one is going forward and one finds instead the remembered touch of water somewhere—the odor of geranium— sight of a blowing curtain—the faint sound of snow—the taste of apples. One finds the pattern of his life, traced with the dreadful clarity of dream. Then he knows that all that comes in remains—nothing is lost—all is important.

ANN [*a small voice*]. Father—

STEPHEN. Are you afraid?

[*A moment. Then:*]

ANN. No.

HOPE [*in a whisper*]. But I am, I am! Tom —Tom, listen—

[TOM *does not stir.* HOPE *leaves him*]

STEPHEN. Here is the moon at last, you see? —Here is our day's reflection, hung in space. [*He hums another measure and again laughs softly*] Space is an endless sea, and time the waves that swell within it, advancing and re-treating. Now and again the waves are still and one may venture any way one wishes. [*A moment*] They seem to be still now—quite still. So which way would you go—where would you travel?

[*A silence. Then* TOM *moves into the angle of the wall*]

TOM. To what I was—

[*Another silence.* LILY *moves towards* STEPHEN]

LILY. To him I love—

NORMAN [*after a moment*]. Wherever I should go— [*He turns and goes into the house again*]

HOPE. Nowhere. I'm happy as I am—or would be, if Tom were—

[*A silence. Then:*]

PAT [*a murmur*]. To Mary—Mary—

ANN [*a cry*]. No, no!—To the Westbury Road!

[PAT *hums softly*]

PAT.—Rat-a-plan-plan-plan-plan.

STEPHEN [*to* LILY]. Listen: there is a turn-ing. All things are turned to a roundness. Wherever there is an end, from it springs the beginning.

PAT [*barely audible*].—Ta-plan-plan-plan-plan.

[LILY *moves to the garden steps and out, following the movement of* STEPHEN's *hand.* TOM *turns and gazes at* HOPE *with a curious expression*]

HOPE. What's the matter with you?

STEPHEN. Pat—Ann—it was not so long ago. Was it so long ago?

[ANN *shakes her head hopelessly, and moves toward the garden, mounts the steps and goes out. Slowly* PAT *crosses the terrace in the opposite direction, and enters the house*]

HOPE [*to* TOM]. What are you staring at?

[TOM *smiles, but does not reply.* STEPHEN *turns to* TOM *and* HOPE]

STEPHEN. And for us—shall we see my white phlox, first?

HOPE. Oh, Mr. Field—you mustn't let them go on like this! It's so frightening. [*She turns and sees* TOM *still staring at her*] Tom's look-ing at me in the queerest way.—It's as if he didn't know me.

STEPHEN. Possibly you have changed.

HOPE. I—?

STEPHEN.—In his eyes. Perhaps you have one child too many.

HOPE. I don't know what you mean.

STEPHEN. It may be that he sees you not as a mother, but as a woman that he loves. I should not discourage that.

[TOM *goes to* HOPE *and gently turns her about, facing him. He looks at her with a curious smile*]

HOPE. Tom, what's the matter with you, anyhow? [*His answer is to take her in his arms and kiss her. She frees herself*] Honestly, I don't know what you're thinking of! What on earth has— [*He takes her face in his hands and kisses her again. She averts her head*] I can't imagine what's come over you. I want to talk to Mr. Field. [*To* STEPHEN] It seems to me that you're all— [TOM *comes to her again, takes both her hands in his and smiles into her eyes*] I'm not fooling. I really mean it.

PAT [*from the house*]. Mary? Mary!

HOPE [*to* STEPHEN]. Who's he calling?—I tell you it isn't good for people to let them-selves go that way— [TOM *draws her into his arms, and holds her there*] It's a form of self-indulgence.—Stop, Tom! It's a— [*Again* TOM *kisses her*] Tom, will you let me go!

[*He opens his arms suddenly and she is freed, almost falling. She recovers her-self and turns once more, with dignity, to* STEPHEN]

PAT [*from the house*]. Mary! Where are you?

HOPE. The things that are happening here to-night aren't natural, and what's not natural must be wrong.

STEPHEN. To me they are more natural than nature.

HOPE. Of course I don't pretend to follow *your* extraordinary— [*From behind her,* TOM *is taking the hair pins from her hair. She stamps her foot in exasperation*] Honestly! This is *too* much! [*To* STEPHEN] I hope you realize that goings on of this sort are not at all usual with us.

STEPHEN. I think that is a pity.

[*Tenderly, lovingly,* TOM *kisses the back of her neck*]

HOPE. Tom—don't be an utter fool! [*To* STEPHEN]—To me, life is a very simple thing—

STEPHEN. Is it?

HOPE. One has one's home, one's children and one's husband—

STEPHEN. Or has one home and children only?

[HOPE *looks at him, startled.* TOM *returns to the wall*]

HOPE. You mean you think that to me, Tom's just another—?

STEPHEN. What do *you* think?

[HOPE *turns to* TOM]

HOPE. Tom, darling—*surely* you must know that I—

[LILY's *voice is heard from the garden, calling as a little girl would*]

LILY. Good-bye, Pa! Good-bye!—Come right home after, won't you, Pa?

HOPE [*to* STEPHEN]. You see? That's Lily. Oh I know she'll hurt herself! [*To* TOM] Now you stay right here, won't you? Please, Tom

—like a good boy. [*She hurries off to the garden, calling*] Lily! Wait, dear!

[*A moment, then* TOM *speaks from the depths of his wretchedness*]

TOM. Oh, Father Francis—can't a fellow do anything without it's being sinful?

[STEPHEN *goes to a chair and seats himself*]

STEPHEN. What have you to tell me?

TOM.—So much. I know it's after hours. I know you're tired, but—

STEPHEN. Come—

[TOM *comes, head down, hands clasped. He kneels beside* STEPHEN's *chair and makes the Sign of the Cross*]

TOM.—Bless me, Father, for I have sinned. It is about three months ago since my last confession. Since then, I accuse myself of the following sins: Father, I've cursed and sworn and taken the name of the Lord in vain. I've neglected my morning prayers and missed Mass once, and been distracted during Mass seven times—

STEPHEN. Yes—but what is really wrong?

TOM. I've been drunk, and had immodest thoughts, and eaten meat on an Ember-Day, and committed acts of impurity four times—

STEPHEN. But what is really wrong?

[TOM *chokes*]

TOM. Oh, Father Francis—I don't believe any more! Nothing's got any meaning for me. I look around me, and nothing means anything at all—and I want it to! It must—it's got to—or I'll, or I'll—

STEPHEN. Your childhood faith is gone—

TOM. It wasn't true.

STEPHEN. Are you so sure?

TOM. Yes, and it meant so much to me. I even thought I ought to be a priest, but I lost my faith.

STEPHEN. Perhaps in order that you need not be one.

TOM. I know I've got no soul—nobody has.

STEPHEN. Look closer.

TOM. I have. It isn't there. There isn't any. There never was.

STEPHEN. At some time there is a soul born to every body—and like it, subject to many ills. But the soul's life is the only life there is, so the world is peopled with the living and with the dead. We know the living. Sometimes the dead deceive us.

TOM. You mean that maybe mine is—?

STEPHEN. No. The dead do not deceive me. —I mean that birth is painful. The infant suffers too.

TOM. It's awful—I can't stand it. Let me be damned!

STEPHEN. No.

TOM. But now I'm nothing—let me be *something*!

STEPHEN. Now you begin to be.

TOM. I keep wanting to do great things—too great for what I am—

STEPHEN. There are many men who would go to the ends of the earth for God—

TOM. I would! I keep starting to—

STEPHEN.—And cannot get through their own gardens.

TOM. Oh, don't! I'm such a weak soul—

STEPHEN.—Such a human being.

TOM. Something always stops me, always—

STEPHEN. Your own humanity.—But there are strong souls who never leave their gardens. Their strength is not in the doing, but in the wish to do. There is no strength anywhere, but in the wish. Once realized, it has spent itself, and must be born again.

TOM. But I don't know what I'm here at all for—

STEPHEN. To suffer and to rejoice. To gain, to lose. To love, and to be rejected. To be young and middle-aged and old. To know life as it happens, and then to say, "this is it."

TOM. Yes—but who *am* I? And what shall *I* be when it's over?

STEPHEN. You are the sum of all your possibilities, all your desires—each faint impression, each small experience—

TOM.—But when it's *over?*

STEPHEN. You will be what your spirit wants and takes of them. Life is a wish. Wishing is never over.

[*A brief silence.* TOM *rises to his feet*]

TOM.—Then everything about me *has* a meaning!—Everything I see and feel and think and do—dream, even!

[STEPHEN *closes his hand over* TOM's]

STEPHEN. Great heaven, yes!

TOM. I've got a feeling that I'm dreaming now.

STEPHEN. It may be.

PAT [*from the house*]. Mary!

TOM.—But Father Francis—are you ill?

STEPHEN. Why?

TOM. You look awfully white—and your hand—it was as cold as ice. I'm afraid I've been a strain for you. Good Lord, Father—you do look white. Here—take this— [*He goes to the table and pours a glass of brandy.* STEPHEN *goes to the fan-back chair in the shadow in the corner of the terrace.* TOM *turns with the glass*] This will fix you. This—why, where are you, Father? [*He looks about him*] Confound it, where's he gone to? He looked sick— [*He calls*] Father Francis!

[STEPHEN *does not answer.* TOM *moves toward the house, with the brandy. As he reaches the steps,* NORMAN *darts out with a small, white fur-rug in his hands*]

NORMAN. One minute, Mister!

TOM. What do you want? Have you seen Father Francis?

NORMAN [*in a moderate Jewish accent*]. How'd you like to buy a nice fur neck-piece?

TOM. Don't be a fool.

NORMAN.—Make a present to your lady-friend, eh? You can have it cheap—

TOM. No, thanks. Let me by—I'm in a hurry.

NORMAN. All right—I resign—I quit!—I'll get a job as runner in a bank. In five years I'll be rich—I'll be the biggest man in Wall Street! [*Again he offers the rug*] Look—five dollars—it's worth fifty—

[TOM *tries to pass him*]

TOM. Oh, for God's sake, Norman—Father Francis is ill—

NORMAN. I'll have money, power—that's what makes you happy—that's the life! [*Again, the rug*] Look: It's a bargain. Buy it. An inside tip: the National City's taken half the issue at 91, and Pritchard, Ames is bidding for another hundred thousand at—

TOM [*suddenly*]. I know—the bastide!

NORMAN. Don't you call me that, you leper!

[TOM *pulls away from him*]

TOM. Get away, I'm not fooling. Let me by! [*He crosses the terrace quickly, and goes up the garden steps and out*]

NORMAN. But what a bargain! [*He shrugs*] I should care. [*Then he turns and speaks to the empty chair in front of him*] Look here, Mr. Sterner—I resign—I'm through!

STEPHEN [*from the corner of the terrace, hidden in his chair*]. When I've given you such a fine opportunity, when I have even—?

NORMAN. Oh, I'll pay you back!—But I'm quitting, see? I've got better things to do than this. I'll educate myself. I'll—

STEPHEN. So ambitious, eh? Ah, you're all alike, you young people.—And next you marry a Gentile girl I suppose, and have her despise you—ruin you.

NORMAN. Oh no!—Say, am I such a fool as that? Marry a *schiksa*—me? Whose uncle is a rabbi—? I guess not! But what I'll do is get an honest job—yes! "White fox"—this cat-fur! I'm sick of it—I'm through. I'll get up in the world. You watch me! Have educated people for my friends—

STEPHEN. May you be happy with them.

NORMAN.—Happy and strong and rich and honest! Watch me! [*He offers the despised rug to another unseen client, is refused, and shrugs again*] No?—I should care! [*And re-enters the house, whistling*]

[*For a moment* STEPHEN *is alone upon the terrace.* PAT's *voice is heard from the house, in growing alarm*]

PAT.—Aren't you here?—It's me—it's Pat, Mary!

[STEPHEN *passes his hand over his brow*]

STEPHEN. My head—my head. [*A moment. Then:*]—But this is very strange. What is this mist that closes in around me? This is a win-ter mist, and it is summer. Wait a bit, you, I am not ready yet!

[*The distant music changes to "L'Enfant et ses Sortieeges" from Ravel's ballet "Five o'Clock."* LILY, *her hair flying about her shoulders, runs down the steps from the garden. She is crossing in the direction of the house, when the music stops her. She listens intently for a moment, then with a swift motion slips the belt from her dress and drops it upon a chair. Her appearance has changed to that of a girl of thirteen. She begins to rise up and down upon her toes, in a formal movement of ballet-practice. Her breath becomes a little short. Frowning, she bends and feels her instep.* STEPHEN *rises from his chair, and turns to her. She exclaims in joy*]

LILY. Pa! Oh Pa, you *did* come right home! [*She runs and kisses him. He strokes her head*]

STEPHEN. Well, well, well—and how has my little sprite endured her prison? [*He speaks in the eloquent voice of an old-fashioned actor*]

LILY.—Prison? Oh, I've been all right. I like it here. I think it's a nice hotel—nicer than the one in Harrisburg was, much nicer, warmer. —Pa, were you good to-night?

STEPHEN. I was splendid. [*He seats himself in another chair, facing her*]

LILY. How many curtain-calls were there?

STEPHEN. Alas, none. But I was magnificent.

LILY. I wish I'd gone. I wish you'd of let me. Could I maybe come tomorrow aft?

STEPHEN. Say "afternoon," child. Do not clip your words.

LILY. "Afternoon."—But could I?

STEPHEN. We shall see. [*With a gesture*] Fix me my drink— [LILY *goes to the table and makes a brandy-and-soda*]—And one for yourself.

LILY. I—I don't want any.

STEPHEN. And one for yourself, I said!—'Twill do you good.

LILY. Just a little one, then—it makes me feel so funny.

[STEPHEN's *manner begins to change*]

STEPHEN. I like you funny.

LILY. Can I put sugar in it?

STEPHEN. Put anything you like in it. Put salt in it.

LILY. Oh—I wouldn't like that! [*She brings him the glass, and a small one for herself*]

[*He seizes her glass and tastes it*]

STEPHEN. Water!

LILY [*in fright*]. But Pa, I—

STEPHEN.—Your mother's daughter, eh? Lying, deceiving—

LILY. I'm not! I just didn't want—

STEPHEN [*the actor*]. Whose child are you, eh? Are you my child, at all?

LILY. Oh yes, yes! Pa—I *am* your child! Truly I am!

STEPHEN. Then obey me—without question, without equivocation. [*He drains his glass and gives it to her*] Fill them both.

LILY. All right. I'll put some in—I'll put a lot in. [*Again she goes to the table with the glasses, refills them and returns to him*]

STEPHEN. Let me taste— [*He tastes her glass, and gives it back to her*] That's better. You are your old man's daughter. Give me a kiss— [*She kisses his cheek*]

[*He takes a swallow from his glass and she does likewise*]

LILY.—But you aren't an old man! You aren't old at all. And look, Pa: I don't ever lie to you. I love you too much to. I just can't tell you how much I— [*She strikes a posture, and declaims:*] "Then poor Cordelia!—And yet, not so; since, I am sure, my love's more richer than my tongue . . . good, my Lord, you have begot me, bred me, loved me: I return those duties back as are right fit—obey you, love you, and most honor you."

STEPHEN. "Pray, do not mock me: I am a very foolish, fond old man. Fourscore and upward, and, to deal plainly, I fear I am not in my perfect mind. . . . Do not laugh at me: for, as I am a man, I think this lady to be my child, Cordelia."

LILY. "And so I am, I am!"

STEPHEN.—Not bad, not half bad. You get the feeling well enough, but you lack voice. You need filling out everywhere. You're thin all over. I don't like you thin.—What did you do while I was playing?

LILY. Well, you know how it snowed—

STEPHEN. Yes?

[*She is sipping from her glass*]

LILY. Well, I got a whole shoe-box full off the window-sill and I was making a little girl out of it, only as fast as I made her she melted.

STEPHEN. What else?

LILY. Well, I did my toe-exercises.

STEPHEN. For how long?

LILY. A whole hour.—Well, almost a whole hour.

STEPHEN. You're lying to me.

LILY. Oh no, Pa!

STEPHEN. Don't you ever lie to me.

LILY. Oh, no.

STEPHEN. If you do, I'll treat you the way I did your mother.

LILY. Pa! You wouldn't ever leave me!

STEPHEN. Just let me catch you lying once.

LILY. But I never, never!

STEPHEN. See that you don't.

LILY. I don't know what I'd do if ever you should leave me—

STEPHEN.—Pick up with some cheap tout, most likely, and go off with him.

[*LILY turns her innocent eyes upon him*]

LILY. What?

STEPHEN. Never mind. [*She passes her hand vaguely over her eyes*]—What ails you?

LILY. It's—beginning to feel, in my head.

STEPHEN. Drink it down.

LILY. I can't. My throat won't turn over any more. And—and things are going round—

STEPHEN. Then start the music and go around with them.

[*She giggles*]

LILY. Oh, that's funny! That's so funny. You're such a funny man.

STEPHEN. Stop laughing.

LILY. I—I can't stop.

STEPHEN. Go start the music— [*Struggling hard to control her hysterics,* LILY *starts the gramophone. Again, it is the "Nailla" of Delibes. He follows the introductory bars with his hand, as if conducting an orchestra.*] Now then—

[*With difficulty, she empties her glass, and begins to dance, haltingly*]

LILY [*an appeal*]. Oh, Pa—

STEPHEN. What?

LILY. I don't want to.

STEPHEN. Why not?

LILY. My foot hurts. I hurt my foot practising.

STEPHEN. If you'd done it right, you wouldn't have hurt it. Go on and dance.

LILY. I can't, truly I can't.

STEPHEN. Is a man to have no amusement when he comes home of nights after playing his heart out to silly fools who don't know art from turnips? Come on—get going.

LILY [*almost in tears*]. Pa—this isn't like you. This isn't my you at all. My you tells me stories about queens and palaces and you hold me on your knee and rock me off to sleep and you tuck me in at night and say God love you, little daughter. That's what *you* do.

STEPHEN. Oh I do, do I? And how often? In my tender moments twice a year.—Not like me, is it? I'll show you what's like me. Will you dance?

LILY. Oh yes, yes. See? I'm dancing— [*Again she begins to dance, this time more haltingly*]

[*He stands over her*]

STEPHEN. Faster—Wasn't Burbage amused when he came home? Wasn't Barrett and wasn't Booth? Is it too much to ask, eh?

LILY. Oh no, Pa! See me, Pa?

STEPHEN. That's better.

[*She goes on, as well as she is able. At length*]

LILY [*panting*].—My hurt foot—it won't go up any more—

STEPHEN. No? Try it.

[*HOPE appears at the top of the garden steps, where she stands unseen by them, watching them in horror*]

LILY. But I *am* trying!—Is it all right if I just—? [*Again she tries to rise upon her toes, and cannot. She attempts a pitiful pas seul, fails in it, falls to the floor. Then, all at once she turns into a raging fury and screams:*] God damn! Hell!

[*He laughs*]

STEPHEN. Good!

LILY. Oh, I hate you. I hate you. I don't *love* you anymore!

STEPHEN. Splendid! Go on—more!

[*She rises to her feet and confronts him, trembling with rage*]

LILY. You're a dirty drunk! You left my mother when she was sick. You can't act. You're just a super, that's all you are. You can't act any!

[*Laughing, he holds his arms out to her*]

STEPHEN. Come here. Give us a kiss.

LILY. No. You smell of whisky and nasty grease-paint. You're dirty—I hate you! I won't stay with you any longer—I'll run away, that's what I'll do!

PAT [*from the house*]. Mary! I've come back. Where are you?

STEPHEN's *voice changes back to his own voice. Suddenly he seems very tired*]

STEPHEN.—Then go quickly. Go very quickly. See—there is the door. It is open. Go in, and up the stairs, and to your room.

[*She gazes at him for a moment, then turns and walks directly to the steps and into the house. Again* STEPHEN *sinks into a chair, his hand over his eyes. There is a slight pause, then* HOPE *comes down from the garden*]

HOPE. Oh, that was terrible! Why did you do it?

STEPHEN. I—? I did nothing. Tell me what happened—

HOPE. You know perfectly well what happened!—And she adored him. She— [*She turns and follows* LILY *into the house, calling:*] Lily!

[STEPHEN *is alone. He rises from his chair with effort, and moves toward the garden steps. He stiffens suddenly, then exclaims in wonder:*]

STEPHEN. What's this? [*Another moment. Then, more sharply:*] Come now! What is it? [*He slumps against the wall, and plucks at his left arm, which has gone limp, then tries to raise his right hand to his head, and cannot*]—Cerebral hemorrhage, is that it? That's very interesting, I'm sure. The left side is quite numb—the lesion must be in the right lobe, in the Area of— God, when we crack we crack, don't we? [*A moment. Then summoning his remaining strength:*]—But I am not ready, yet! [*He makes his way to the fan-back chair in the corner of the terrace and slowly lets himself into it. He calls:*] Pat! Ann! [*Another moment*]

There—there's the pulse—it is quite hard, quite stringy—[*Again he calls:*] Ann!—But the breathing is regular, Doctor—difficult, but regular.—I say, not yet! I'll go, but in my proper time.—Curious there is no pain—only a sense of— [*He catches his breath*]—No pain, did I say? [*And collects his strength for a final cry:*] Ann! [*And sinks lower into his chair*]

[*From the distance piano-music begins to be heard again. It is a popular waltz, of ten years ago. A moment, then* ANN *comes down the steps from the garden. She is limping. As she crosses the terrace she murmurs to herself*]

ANN. Poor dear—poor darling—what can I do for him? [*As she reaches the sofa her ankle gives way under her and she sinks down upon the floor, exclaiming:*] Ouch—ouch—oh, where is that road?

[PAT *comes in from the house, calling softly*]

PAT. Mary! Where are you, Mary?

ANN. Ouch—ouch—

[PAT *hesitates a moment, then comes up to her*]

PAT. Excuse me. Is there anything the—?

[ANN *starts in alarm*]

ANN.—Oh!

PAT. I'm all right. I'm harmless.—But I was just wandering around here and I saw you from across the field and I thought something might be the matter, and—

ANN.—There is. Plenty.

PAT. What? Can I help?

ANN. Well, for one thing, I've probably broken my ankle. And for another, I'm lost. And for another—no, I'm not sure you can.

PAT. Does your ankle hurt?

ANN. Oh no, it feels wonderful. They do, you know.—Ouch!

PAT. Maybe if I could get a car up into this field for you—

ANN. Have you got one that climbs fences?

PAT. What are you lost from?

ANN. The Westbury Road.

[*A breeze brings the music closer*]

PAT. That's easy.

ANN. It hasn't been.

PAT. You're practically on it. It's just over there—

ANN. No!

PAT. Honest.

ANN. Then what's that music I've been hearing. Isn't it the Club?

PAT. No. It's from a party I'm at.

ANN. At?

PAT. Well, one I got away from.

ANN. Whose?

PAT. Mine. At my house.

ANN. I'm impressed. Why wasn't *I* asked?

PAT. You would have been.—Where do you live?

ANN. I'm staying down here with some people named Ames. But I got the wanders and had to walk.

PAT. So did I.—Tom and Hope Ames?

ANN. That's right.

PAT. They said they couldn't come.

ANN. Maybe they don't like parties. Or maybe they didn't want people to see me. In the Spring I get freckled.—Oh, this *damned* ankle!

PAT. Quit talking about your ankle. What's your name?

ANN. Ann Field. What's yours?

PAT. Don't laugh—

ANN. No.

PAT. Patrick— [*She laughs*] You said you wouldn't.

ANN. But I've always wanted to know one! —What was it you said to Mike?

PAT. That's not very new, you know.—My last name's Farley.

ANN.—Not one of the great, enormous, important, rich ones!

PAT. Well—

ANN.—Please, forget everything I've said. You're beautiful. You'll get me home all right.

PAT. I'm—er—I came down for the Spring holidays, and I thought I'd swing a little party, and—

ANN. Why, bless his heart, he's embarrassed! Lovely!

PAT. Oh, go to hell.

ANN. You're sweet. I think you're really sweet.

[PAT *seats himself beside her*]

PAT. Foolish to stay indoors a night like this. Foolish to sleep even.—You've got awfully pretty hands.

ANN. Thanks. My eyes are nice, too. They don't cross, or anything.

PAT. Say—you come right back at a fellow, don't you?

ANN. Do I?

PAT.—Ever read a poem called "Pale hands I loved beside the Shal-i-mar"?

ANN [*suspiciously*]. What about it?

PAT. I just wondered. Didn't you like it?

ANN. I thought it was awful.

PAT. Why?

ANN. I don't know. I just did.

PAT. You're a funny girl. Maybe you don't like poetry.

ANN.—Maybe I do! [*He laughs*] I like the way you laugh.

PAT. I'll hire me a couple of expert ticklers.

[*And then they both laugh*]

ANN. You have awfully white teeth, haven't you?

[*Suddenly* PAT *frowns*]

PAT.—What?

ANN. I said, you have—

PAT [*slowly*]. I know—I'm trying to think: there was someone with white teeth that gleamed from the water—oh, never mind. [*Another moment. Then:*]—Funny, our meeting like this. I suppose that's the way good things happen.

ANN. Maybe.—I wish you'd brought a crutch, though, or a wheel-chair.

[*He eyes her reflectively*]

PAT. How much do you weigh?

ANN. Something fairly serious—or I did. To-night I've walked a good deal of it off.

PAT. We've got to do something about moving you.

ANN. I hoped you'd get around to that.

PAT. That is, eventually. There's lots of time.—Say, are you moody?

ANN. Maybe.—Am I?

PAT. Because I am. That's why I got to walking to-night. I had something on my mind.

ANN. So had I.

PAT. Really? What?

ANN. My father.

PAT. Is he—is he sick?

ANN. I don't know.—What is it that worried you?

PAT [*a moment*].—Well, you see, at Christmas I came down with the Copes—

ANN. Are they like the measles?

[PAT *laughs, and explains:*]

PAT.—Down here, with Johnny and Nora Cope. Well, one night we were coming home quite late from somewheres and we stopped in at the dog-wagon in the village to get— [*He stops suddenly and stares at her*] Jerusalem! I believe you're her!

ANN. "She," you should say.—Who?

PAT [*overcome with awe*]. Good Lord Almighty—

ANN. I wonder if it's the same dog-wagon I know.

PAT. Of course!—But this is— Gosh! Do you know what this means to me?

ANN. I'm trying awfully hard to follow, but—

PAT [*still staring*]. I had a Western, with a lot of onions, and we got up to go and there was a girl there sitting at the counter with a couple of other people and a great big glass of milk and she looked up as I went by, and—

[ANN *smiles*]

ANN. I did, didn't I?

PAT [*excitedly*]. Yes!—and the milk had made a little white rim along your upper lip and—

ANN [*distressed*]. Oh dear—

PAT. It was beautiful.—And ever since, I've seen your face the whole time, in my mind, and I could never find you. It's been terrible. —And now— Oh Lord!—Imagine!

[ANN *smiles*]

ANN. Well—here I am.

PAT. It's just miraculous, that's all, it's miraculous. Gosh, I don't know what to say. You know this isn't like the usual—there's something terribly right about it.—Ever since that night I've been longing to— Jeez, I thought I'd go crazy if I couldn't find you—been longing to take your face in my hands like this, and— [*He takes her face between his hands*]

ANN. Wait. Let me look at you. [*She looks*]

PAT. I'm not much on looks—

ANN. Shhh! [*She looks a longer time*] Why —it's the queerest thing. I think I—

PAT.—And to kiss that lovely mouth that had the white rim along the top of it—

ANN. But somehow—I don't think you'd better—yet—

PAT. No, I suppose not.—But I don't see why! [*A moment. Still they gaze at each other. Then:*] Look: do you ever get a feeling that you—oh, Lord—that you know all about it?

ANN. Sometimes.

PAT. I do now! I've never felt alive before! Everything's as clear as— [*Suddenly, directly*] Look: I'll be at the Ameses for lunch tomorrow. Tell 'em I like steak.

[ANN *laughs*]

ANN. I like *you*!

PAT.—As much as I like steak?

ANN. How much do you like steak?

PAT. I'm crazy for it. I dream about it. Well—?

[*Again* ANN *laughs, and rises*]

ANN. Come on.

[*He catches her hand in his*]

PAT. Ah, Ann—tell me, Ann!

ANN. No, no! This is ridiculous. It's— [*She frees herself*]

PAT. Oh, please! Tell me—do you like me? [*A moment. Then:*]

ANN. Yes.

PAT. Much?

ANN. A lot. Terribly!

[*For* PAT *this is almost too much to bear*]

PAT. Gosh, I'm glad.

ANN. I hope I'll be.—Come on—shall we?

PAT. Look: You've got to come up to the Spring Dance with me, and the ball games, and the boat races—I row Number Seven—and—oh, Ann—

ANN. What, Pat?

PAT. It's wonderful.

ANN. It is, it is.—Do come—come on— [*They go on another step or two, toward the garden steps, where again her ankle gives way. He catches her in his arms. She recovers herself and, still in his arms, turns and looks at him. For a long moment their eyes hold them together. At length they kiss. For an instant*

ANN *clings to him, then leaves him*] Pat—Pat —we're crazy.

PAT. No!

ANN [*breathlessly*]. Come on—. We must— [*She takes his hand. He turns*]

PAT. First, let's look back at our meadow. [ANN *frowns, half puzzled, half in alarm. Then:*]

ANN [*suddenly, sharply*]. No! That's wrong! [*He had not said that. The spell is breaking*]

PAT. What is? [*He takes a deep breath*]— Um! Doesn't it smell good, though! What is it? Hawthorn?

ANN. No!

PAT [*slowly, from very far away*]. But I—I guess they're right. I guess there's nothing like May in England— [*Suddenly he stops, releasing her hand. His face becomes troubled. He looks at the house, frowning*] What's that house?

ANN [*a sudden cry*]. Don't think, Pat! Don't think at all! Come with me—

PAT.—But there's something I've got to do in this house.

ANN. No!

PAT. Yes. And I can't think what. And it's terribly important. I've waited too long. It's got to be done at once. It's getting late.—I know!—I've got to pack a bag. It's late. I've got to get that bag packed. I've got to pack a bag and catch a boat and go to England.

[ANN *is still at the garden steps. His eyes have not left the house*]

ANN. Stay with me, Pat! I'll lose you there!

PAT. I tell you she's waiting, and it's getting late. [*Again he moves toward the house*]

ANN. Oh, why must I always lose you? [*She goes up the garden steps and out*]

[PAT *advances further toward the house, but* STEPHEN *rises—*]

STEPHEN. Pat!

[PAT *halts, turns slowly, looks at him, then goes to him*]

PAT. Why—why how do you do, Mr. Carr! I feel as if I'd been away for—I came across the fields and down the lane—the hawthorn's early, isn't it? I didn't wire. I thought I'd surprise her. How has she been?

STEPHEN. You cannot surprise her.

PAT. You mean she had a hunch that I was—? But where is she, then? I've been calling her all over everywhere. [STEPHEN *does not reply. Suddenly* PAT *becomes alarmed*] Say, what is this—a joke? Because if it is— yes, and what about my letters? Why didn't she answer them? Did you and Father fix it so she wouldn't get them? I've been almost crazy. I've been—where is she? She's here—I know she's here— [*He calls:*] Ann! [*Then feeling something wrong whispers:*]—Mary

[*Then, more confidently:*] It's Pat, Mary! [*He turns again to* STEPHEN]—And you needn't think we're going to stay on with people who fixed it up to separate us, either. Not for one minute. I'm going to take her with me this very night, and—

STEPHEN. That is too soon.

PAT. It's not. Haven't we waited years already? We'll be wanting to get married right away. Tomorrow, most likely—or the next day—

STEPHEN.—Too soon.

PAT. Look here, Mr. Carr— [*Then correcting himself:*] Mr. Field.—I know you're a sick man. But Ann's got her whole life ahead of her. You can't take it from her. You've taken too much of it already. I don't hold with those old ideas. Ann and I are in love, and if you don't grant that that's the most important thing, it's time you did. I'm sorry to have to put it this way, but I've got to speak as I feel. I'll certainly never expect a child of mine to—to—

STEPHEN.—To what?

PAT.—To give her whole life up to me, and I don't think you should.

STEPHEN. I see.

PAT. You let her bring you here, away from all the—

STEPHEN.—She has needed me as much these last three years as I have needed her.

PAT. That may be. But—

STEPHEN. Wait! [*He looks at* PAT *intently, then speaks with a slow emphasis:*]—But now she does not need me any longer.

PAT. What are you looking like that for? What do you mean? [*Then suddenly, wildly:*] She's not! That's not true—you're lying. It's not possible—it can't be! She's here—I know she's here! [*Again he calls:*] Ann! Ann!

STEPHEN. She does not come.

PAT. Ann, dear! It's Pat, Ann!

STEPHEN. And still she does not come.

PAT. Oh, don't keep saying that! She's here —I can feel her all about me. [*He wheels about and looks around him*] What kind of a deal is this, anyway? What am I doing—dreaming? [*Then one last despairing cry:*] Ann! [*And a long silence. Finally:*]—Because she thought I wasn't coming back— [*Another moment. Then, in anguish:*] —I can't believe—but how? *How* did she? She couldn't have hurt that sweet place at her temple, that lovely breast. What has death to do with her?

STEPHEN.—With anyone.

PAT. But I did come back! I wasn't the swine she thought me. I did come—she must know that. I'm sure she knows it!

STEPHEN. So then, you have your picture back—

PAT. My picture?

STEPHEN. The one you love so—your picture

of yourself. Now your pet illusion is whole again, and all is well, eh?

PAT. I don't know what you're—

STEPHEN. You built your whole life upon an illusion—and it went—and still you want it back—from death, even!

PAT. I don't know what you're talking about.

STEPHEN. Your idea of your own perfection.

PAT. That's not true—

STEPHEN. No?—You came back, yes—but in your own time. A swine? Indeed you are!— But what brought you? How much of it was the self-contempt you felt for having left her?

PAT. None of it.

STEPHEN.—And how much your love of her, your want of her?

PAT. All!

STEPHEN. Which is it you can't live with, now? Which is it that spoils your picture?

PAT. Oh, be still about my picture! You're talking about a spoiled boy, stuffed with what he thought were fine ideals. Fakes, all of them! I've left that boy behind. I've got no picture anymore. I know I'm what I am—myself!

STEPHEN. Then can you face yourself—say good-bye to your last illusion, and come through alive?

PAT. Go—will you?

STEPHEN. If you cannot—what else is there for you?

[*A moment. Then:*]

PAT [*to himself*].—Off to Africa.

STEPHEN. Well—?

[PAT *moves toward the garden steps*]

PAT. Off to—! [*But half way up the steps, he stops. When he speaks, it is with a fine, saving scorn:*]—One big last shining gesture, eh? Watching myself go by. Another pretty picture: "He died for love." [*He raises his head*] No!—That's for the weak ones. I stay.

STEPHEN [*a murmur*]. That's right, that's right. [*He leaves him, and moves painfully toward his corner*]

PAT. But I want her so. Ann—Ann—

[FELIX *comes in from house*]

FELIX. Pardon, Monsieur—je regrette que j'avais laissé passer l'heure. Maintenant, il est onze heures moins douze. Je regrette beaucoup, Monsieur. C'est ma faute.

[PAT *does not reply.* FELIX *goes out. A moment, then* ANN's *voice is heard softly, from the garden:*]

ANN. Pat?

PAT [*a cry of joy*]. Ann! [*In an instant he is up the garden steps and out*] I'll find you this time. Ann!

[STEPHEN *gropes for his chair in the corner and seats himself*]

STEPHEN.—All right, you. Very well—I am ready. This ends, and that begins.—Oh, so you'd like to end it, would you? All of it, eh? [*He half rises, gasping for breath*] Well, you can't!

—I tell you—you cannot! [*Gasping*] I tell you—!

> [*There is a slight shuffling sound, as he slumps into death. A moment. Then* TOM *comes in from the garden with the brandy-glass, as* FELIX *enters from the house and crosses the terrace toward him, with three traveling-bags*]

FELIX. Pardon, Monsieur— [*He goes up the garden steps and out*]

> [HOPE *comes in from the house. She is dressed to leave. She sees* TOM *and goes to him quickly*]

HOPE. Tom, Tom—

TOM.—I beg your pardon, but have you by any chance seen an old priest called Father— [*Then he recognizes her*] Why—why, hello, Hope—

HOPE.—Who, did you say?

TOM. Why—I don't know— [*He frowns at the brandy-glass*] I thought I—I had this for someone—who was it? I was taking it to him, to—Lord, *I* don't know— [*He looks at her closer*]—How are the children?

> [LILY *comes in from the house, also dressed for departure*]

HOPE.—The children—that's good, that is! —Do you realize that that's just what you've been acting like?

TOM [*to himself*].—Under the piano. Under the—

> [ALICE *comes down the stairs from the balcony. She wears a coat and carries a small traveling-bag.*

ALICE. Listen: could anyone tell me what's got into the Rose man?

HOPE. Not Norman, too!

ALICE.—I opened my door into the hall, and there he was, stretched on the floor outside it, fast asleep on a fur-rug. [*She looks back over her shoulder*].—And now he's—

> [NORMAN *appears upon the balcony, the fur-rug still over his arm*]

NORMAN [*heartily*]. Well, everyone—how goes it?

TOM. What's that you've got?

NORMAN. How'd you like to—? [*He stops and frowns at the rug*] Why, it's a — [*His accent leaves him*] Damned if I know. [*He drops it, and cleans his fastidious hands of it*]

TOM. Was it a bargain?

> [NORMAN *looks at him sharply*]

NORMAN.—Am I right in believing that some pretty funny business went on here to-night?

> [*All look troubled, eyeing one another furtively, trying to figure out how much the other remembers, how much one remembers oneself*]

LILY [*finally*]. Well, I don't know if you'd call it funny—but suddenly everything seems possible.—It's like beginning all over again.

> [ALICE *stretches upon her cushion*]

ALICE. I hope I didn't miss anything. I had a delicious nap.

LILY.—And did you dream?

ALICE. Dream?—I should say not. I was too dead. [*Another silence. All stare in front of them. Finally* ALICE *speaks again, this time as if from a distance:*] Did I tell you?—Once when I was in England staying with the Potters, they had a— [*Then suddenly, with an air of discovery*]—Why, Norman! That was where I met you, wasn't it?

NORMAN. Yes.

ALICE.—Strange.

> [*Again silence. Then:*]

TOM. At school the big idea used to be to sneak off in the afternoons and smoke real tobacco in real pipes.—Lord, how big that made us feel.

NORMAN [*after another moment*].—I often wonder what happened to old Morris Sterner. He gave me my first real job.—Once he told me that—

> [*But he relapses into silence, which* LILY *at length breaks*]

LILY. It's fantastic, this terrace. It just hangs here. Some day it will float off into space, and anchor there, like an island in time.

HOPE. Don't!

ALICE. Don't what?

HOPE. Please, everyone make sense. It must be nearly time to leave.

TOM. Hope— [*She turns to him*] Would you mind awfully if I don't sail with you?

HOPE. Why?

TOM. I want to go off somewhere by myself for awhile. I think at last I've really got a line on something that may be the answer for me.

HOPE [*unconvinced*]. Yes?

TOM.—In a way it's a kind of faith, in place of the old one—maybe it's the same. Anyhow, I want to work it out.

HOPE. Sweet Tom.

> [PAT *and* ANN *are nearing the terrace from the garden.* PAT'S *voice is heard:*]

PAT. There's so much I'd have gone without—

> [*They come in, her hand in his, and stand together upon the garden steps*]

TOM [*to* HOPE].—I don't know how long it will take—but if I send for you—

> [HOPE *smiles*]

HOPE. Don't come—

TOM. Don't come.

> [*Now everyone is talking in concert:*]

PAT.—Without so many good, quiet things—

TOM. I'm excited about this, Hope.

HOPE. So am I, Tom—if you do it.

PAT [*to* ANN]. I want to sit with the wife I love, and read books, and look at maps—

LILY. You won't believe me when I tell you—

ALICE. What?

LILY. Next year I'm going to play Cordelia in King Lear.

PAT.—And fish trout-streams with my boys, and take my daughter walking—

HOPE.—What time is it, Norman? Oughtn't we be starting?

NORMAN. I'm not going to Paris.

[ALICE glances at him in alarm]

HOPE. Really!—And who was it who simply had to be home by the tenth for a corporation meeting?

NORMAN. They can meet without me. They can whistle for me. I'll be in Andora.

PAT [to ANN].—And build a house and mend a fence, and be tired of a good day's work, and sleep—

[Now they have come down the steps and joined the others, ALICE moves toward NORMAN]

ALICE. Norman—

NORMAN. What, Alice?

ALICE. I'll miss you.—Take me with you!

[NORMAN starts forward]

NORMAN. You'd come?

ALICE. Just ask me.

NORMAN. Alice—

ALICE.—Darling.

[Then:]

NORMAN. That's the way to see Andora!

[ALICE and NORMAN keep on gazing at each other as if they could never look their fill]

TOM [suddenly]. Now I know how it happened! [To ANN] Where's your father?

[LILY rises quickly, and stares toward STEPHEN's chair, which conceals him from their view.

ANN. He must have gone down to the bastide. —Why?

TOM. Hotel Universe!—He'll know.

ANN. What?

TOM. Don't you know the story?

ANN. Oh—you mean about Réné Mayer's nouse—

TOM. I mean about this house—

ANN. You must be mixed, Tom. This was built in nineteen-twelve by a man from Lyons.

[A moment. TOM gazes at her. Then:]

TOM. Are you sure?

ANN. Oh, yes. Father leased it from him.

[LILY starts back from STEPHEN's chair with a sudden cry]

LILY. Pa!

HOPE. Don't, Lily—please don't again—

LILY. Pat—Pat!

[He goes to her]

PAT. What is it, Lily?

LILY [a moan].—I don't know, I don't know—

ANN. Lily—darling—

LILY.—I feel as if all that held me together had suddenly let go. [She begins to cry, softly]

ANN. Lily—darling—don't!

LILY. It's all right—I'll be all right—

[FELIX re-enters from the garden and goes to PAT]

FELIX. Pardon, Monsieur—il est onze heure juste, Monsieur.

[HOPE jumps up]

HOPE. Eleven! We've got to fly!

[They all talk together:]

ALICE. We'll probably be late at that.

NORMAN. Oh, no—not if we hurry.

TOM. You can make good time on these roads at night.

FELIX [to ANN]. Pardon, Mademoiselle, les valises sont dans les voitures.

ANN.—Your bags are all in.

TOM. Where's yours, Pat? Are you ready?

LILY. No! You've got to stay! Do you understand that?—You've got to stay!

PAT. Why yes, of course.—I'm not going.

[ANN glances at him quickly]

ANN. Pat!

PAT. I'm staying, Ann.

TOM. Now there's a good idea!

HOPE. I had a hunch Pat was no mountain-climber!

NORMAN. That's the stuff, Pat.

[HOPE goes to ANN and kisses her. ALICE slips her arm through NORMAN's]

HOPE. Good-bye, Ann.

ANN. Good-bye, dear.

TOM. Good-bye, Pat. Take it easy for awhile.

PAT. Yes, Good-bye, Tom.

LILY. Hurry, hurry!

[TOM kisses ANN]

TOM. Good-bye and thanks, Ann.—Say good-bye to your father for me.

HOPE. Yes.

NORMAN. Yes!

[TOM frowns]

TOM. Say to him, that—

LILY. Hurry, hurry!

TOM.—Say good-bye to him.

NORMAN. Do you want to come with us, Tom?

[TOM turns upon the garden steps]

TOM. To Andora? Why, it sounds like a good idea.

HOPE. No, no! Alone! You've got to go alone!

TOM. But Hope—you know what a friendly soul I am. You know how I need company.

HOPE [to the others]. What can you do with him?

[They go out. NORMAN and ALICE mount the steps, calling over their shoulders:]

NORMAN AND ALICE. Good-bye! Thanks! Good-bye!

[PAT, ANN and LILY are left]

LILY. You two—you're for each other, aren't you?

PAT. I hope so.

ANN. Then we are.

LILY [to ANN]. Your father—remember what he said? It does go on. [ANN looks at her] Wherever we may be—breezes from the other fields still blow upon us—

ANN. Why, yes. Why do you—?

LILY. I think that's good to know. God love him. God love you. Good-bye—

[She mounts the steps, pauses for one brief instant to glance down at STEPHEN, then goes out into the garden. PAT and ANN are left alone. ANN touches his cheek]

ANN. Dear love.

PAT. I want to make love to you for years. Oh, it's a life, Ann!

ANN. I know, dear—don't I know! [She murmurs]—Thank you, Father.

PAT. Yes—thanks! [In the distance, far off in the garden, a cock crows hoarsely. PAT starts] What's that? What time is it?

ANN. Hush, darling, never mind.—It's just an old white rooster—one of Father's pets—his cock he calls him.

PAT. It must be dawn somewhere.

ANN. But of course, dear—always!

PAT. Wherever there is an end, he said—

ANN.—From it the beginning springs.

[She stares straight in front of her, her apprehension growing in her eyes. Slowly, fearfully, her head turns in the direction of STEPHEN. Silence. Then again the cock exults]

CURTAIN

MICHEL AUCLAIR

A Play in Three Acts

By CHARLES VILDRAC

FREELY TRANSLATED FROM THE FRENCH BY
SIDNEY HOWARD

CHARACTERS

MICHEL AUCLAIR, *Clerk in a book-selling establishment, aged 26*
SUZANNE CATELAIN, *aged 23*
MADAME CATELAIN, *aged 50*
LOUIS CATELAIN, *an infantry sergeant, aged 21*
ARMAND BLONDEAU, *a non-commissioned officer, later an adjutant, aged 28*
COLSON, *a cantinier*
PIERROT, *a little boy*

SCENE

The action takes place in the little provincial town of Saint-Serge in France and before 1914.

ACT I: *The garden of Madame Catelain's house. An afternoon in Spring.*
ACT II: *Blondeau's cottage. Twenty months later.*
ACT III: *The same as Act II. Several days later.*

(*The curtain falls for a moment during Act III to denote the passing of an hour.*)

MICHEL AUCLAIR

ACT ONE

SCENE: *A garden before a little house. At the back and in the center is the door of the house. Two windows, gay with window boxes filled with geraniums, flank the door. Flat borders of flowers run along the wall of the house. In front, and on the right, is an iron table with iron chairs and an arbutus in full bloom. It is a bright afternoon in Springtime.*

[MADAME CATELAIN *knits, seated at the back before the door of the house. At the table,* SUZANNE *is sewing busily.* MICHEL *stands in front of her, his feet wide spread, his hands in his pockets*]

MICHEL. Madame Catelain!

MADAME CATELAIN. Michel?

MICHEL. Be a reasonable woman, now, and tell your daughter to come for a walk along the river?

SUZANNE. Listen to him! Haven't I told you, Michel, that I've got this chemisette to finish? You can't have everything, you know. If you expect me to be dancing with you tonight. . . .

MADAME CATELAIN. Her brother's just coming home, too, Michel. He's not off duty until five. I think it would be nice if he could find you both right here. The poor boy never sees his sister.

MICHEL. Well, it's nice here, too.

SUZANNE. If you were really nice, you'd sit down there and read to me.

MICHEL [*He strides up and down*]. Ah, I can't do that today, Suzon. Not that I shouldn't like to. But it's my last Sunday here before I go away—and—

SUZANNE. That isn't settled.

MICHEL. Perhaps not. . . . But it's more than likely. . . . I was thinking this morning. I said to myself: This must be exactly like every other Sunday. Not a word about my going away. Just the regular things. Reading with Suzon. Laughing with Suzon. And some silence with Suzon, too. . . .

MADAME CATELAIN. Don't I come in on this Sunday, too, Michel?

MICHEL. Of course, you do. Only I don't seem to be able to get this leave-taking out of my head . . . A whole week, now . . . ever since I stopped work— I've been like a man waiting on the station platform for his train to come in. You know how it is. . . . If he leaves the station for a moment just to get a cup of coffee across the way, he's sure he's going to miss that train and he burns his tongue. . . .

SUZANNE. Come now, Monsieur! You aren't quite at the station yet!

MICHEL. No. . . . But I've already embarked on my enterprise, Suzon. I've already taken the first step. I did that when I resigned from the Demoiselles Montifroy's book-shop . . . At least I'm clear of that boneyard. At least, I've washed my hands of that mould. . . . For a whole week now, I haven't touched one of their wretched books; a whole blessed week since I served my last portion of their skimmed milk to the blessed tabbies of Saint-Serge!

[SUZANNE *laughs*]

MADAME CATELAIN. Don't get so excited, Michel!

MICHEL. A whole week that I haven't known what to do with myself. . . . I've been too nervous to read or to go fishing. And too preoccupied to see any of my friends. . . . Oh, I might have been out rambling all over the countryside. Only the weather's been too fine. . . .

SUZANNE. Too fine!

MICHEL. Much too fine for me to go gamboling over the fields while a certain young lady I could mention has to sit behind a post office wicket and write in a stupid ledger. . . . [SUZANNE *lifts her eyes to him with a look so tender that it seems to blow him a kiss*] Day before yesterday, Madame Catelain, your son got me to play billiards with him. What do you think of that?

MADAME CATELAIN. I didn't know you played billiards.

MICHEL. I don't. But I pretended I did. And how I annoyed that friend of Louis!! You know. The one with the moustaches. That would-be officer.

SUZANNE. Blondeau?

MICHEL. Yes, Blondeau.

SUZANNE. Why do you always call him that would-be officer? I don't see why he hasn't a perfect right to look smart if his uniform suits him. I only wish I could see Louis as well turned out as that. A black tunic, well cut, fine material and a high collar . . . Mm. . . .

MICHEL. Now Suzon. That uniform, on a sergeant, is the sign of the military vocation. And that's just what ails Blondeau. He's got the military vocation. He's just the kind who re-enlists because he fancies himself in a uniform. . . . Louis tells me that Blondeau teaches all the recruits to recognize him as a superior brand of sergeant. The Blondeau brand. Something special. Not quite an officer maybe, but *much* more than a sergeant.

MADAME CATELAIN. They tell me he's working very hard to get himself a commission.

MICHEL. I should say that whether he turns out a colonel or a gendarme depends entirely on how his moustaches turn out.

SUZANNE. Oh, Michel!

MICHEL. Oh, let him be a colonel by all means! As well he as another. He's not a bad sort and he *is* a good billiard player. Only I hope he doesn't infect Louis with his military ambitions.

MADAME CATELAIN. You needn't be afraid. If Louis enlisted, it was simply to be in garrison here. Louis has his profession.

MICHEL. Louis will belong to the new Saint-Serge with us, Suzon.

SUZANNE [*after a moment of silence*]. Alas, Michel, while I wait for the new Saint-Serge, I have to live in the old!

MICHEL. That's not true. It only seems that way. That's blasphemous, Suzon! . . . Well, of course, you've got to go on with the Post Office; stamping the money orders Guerbois sends off to pay for his butter—registering samples—

SUZANNE. From Legris and Company—

MICHEL. And don't you be forgetting my letters, Suzon. . . . From the moment I set foot in Paris, you'll have my opinions of Paris. My letters will bring Paris to you. You'll be able to follow every step I take there. You'll watch me begin my work for this real book-seller I'm going to. You'll learn what I learn there. You'll meet the men I meet and hear the ideas I hear and read the books I read. No skimmed milk, either. I'll tell you how I explore all the highways and byways of literature, ancient and modern, French and foreign. I'll read. I'll read and I'll absorb all the newest authors, all those fellows people are talking about out in the world, those remarkable fellows whose names we never even hear in Saint-Serge.

SUZANNE [*a hand of protest*]. Oh . . .

MICHEL. And what I can't share with you by letter, my dear, that I'll bring back with me.

SUZANNE. And you'll send me all the nicest books you find?

MICHEL. Of course. . . . And then, one fine day, only a year from now, I'll be home again in Saint-Serge, poor town! It doesn't dream what's in store for it! [*A little pause*] Oh, I shan't upset people too much at first. To begin with, I'll have to realize on my capital. I shall sell my mill at Preuillant. And we shall be married, Suzon. . . . You don't object, Madame Catelain?

MADAME CATELAIN. It's quite a while since you asked me that question, Michel. Last year I couldn't so much as ask you to split me a stick of wood or light a lamp for me without your coming back at me with: On one condition . . . Let me marry Suzon. . . . You've been more reserved lately.

MICHEL. Matters have grown more serious.

SUZANNE. Now he asks me direct.

MADAME CATELAIN. I suppose he thinks it's no more of my affair!

MICHEL [*going to her*]. But you gave your consent! . . . What was I saying?

SUZANNE. We shall be married, Suzon. . . .

MICHEL. To be sure! We shall be married, Suzon, and commence our life together by travelling to all the most beautiful places in the world. I shall take you by your little hand and we shall set out across the fields and through the forests, running or loitering as we please. And when Suzon's tired— Down to rest on the fresh grass of summer! Oh yes! And there'll be flowers everywhere. . . . And those eyes of Suzon's will be looking at the fine marvels of a universe which doesn't show much of itself through a Post Office wicket in Saint-Serge. I promise to keep Suzon's eyes busy with looking. . . . Provence. . . . Marseille. . . .

SUZANNE. Nice, Michel!

MICHEL. Nice, the Alps, Savoie; the sea, the trees, the towers of the great churches; the mountains, the snows and the clouds! Then we shall come home again to Saint-Serge,—my wife and I, with our great plans before us.

SUZANNE [*exultant*].—Oh!

MADAME CATELAIN. Where is it you're going to install this people's university of yours?

SUZANNE. No, Maman! A book-shop first!

MICHEL [*turning* MADAME CATELAIN]. I'll come back from Paris a book-seller.—Bookselling's a trade that wants studying, a trade I haven't begun to learn.—I'll open my book-shop here. A real book-shop. Stationery, penwipers, art postal cards— I'll leave all that sort of thing to the Demoiselles Montifroy. And the young ladies' collections and those milk and water magazines the old ones love—those, too. I'll have none of them either. I'll sell books, rent books, lend books . . . I'll set myself up right near the Place de la Fontainerie. There's a crossing there. Everyone goes by. All the workmen and the clerks from up town, all the soldiers who come down from the garrison, all the housewives on their way to market, all the idlers when they go up to the observatory for the view. My book-shop will have one room where you can read, free of charge, every kind of newspaper and review . . . oh, things people in Saint-Serge have no idea of!

SUZANNE. And of course, you understand, Maman, there'll be sales and subscriptions. . . .

MADAME CATELAIN. If only the people come. . . .

MICHEL. They will come . . . Little by little, they'll come. . . . Oh, not without a little persuasion, perhaps . . . I shall go out after them. And I'll have my friends help me. . . .

SUZANNE. They'll come fast enough once they hear there's something new to do in Saint-Serge.

MICHEL. Poor people! How dull they are now! How bored! Look at them, any afternoon at five o'clock, how they loll around the Café du Commerce, not even drinking! Nothing to do but browse through the Gazette de Saint-Serge. They've got so used to being bored that they don't *know* the state they're in. I'll show them. I'll make their empty heads spin for them! . . . They aren't all incurable, you know. I shall print a catalogue announcement to stir them up all over town: in the café, at the barber shop, at the church door when they come out of mass, with their coffee on Sunday mornings—my catalogue announcement! . . . I'll wear them down slowly, without their catching on. Our aim, Maman Catelain, will be to make them read what we want them to read when they think they're choosing for themselves. It goes without saying we shall have to begin by amusing them and be satisfied with that. But, give us three years! five years! You'll see Saint-Serge! You'll see! The Free-thinking University of Saint-Serge! The Lecture Courses of Saint-Serge! The Concerts of Saint-Serge! And, oh, the friendliness of Saint-Serge!— Suzon, I shall end by placing the same book with Hilbruner's workmen, and with Ricard the hatter—who's nobody's fool—and on the desk of that old mess of vermouth and stupidity, what's his name, the Justice of Peace with his two happy daughters, and who knows?— perhaps with the young lady who's coming to replace Suzon at the Post Office. All these people who now share only the dullness of Saint-Serge will have the flame of this book in common! And when they walk down the street, they'll be humming a song with their heads in the air, and not dragging along as they do these days. . . .

MADAME CATELAIN. Dear me! Is it possible?

SUZANNE. Listen, Michel! For the circulating library I think we ought to get up a uniform binding with . . .

MICHEL. Oh, no, Suzon!

SUZANNE. Wait! With "Bibliothèque Michel Auclair" on the back in gold letters. Then you might put some sort of a motto underneath. . . .

MICHEL. What sort?

SUZANNE. I don't know . . . "Cultivate your mind" . . . or . . . "Wisdom is wealth" . . . Of course, that has to be thought out. . . .

MICHEL. No! In the first place, I don't believe in dressing books like so many soldiers. Books are individuals. One should be able to go straight to any book just as one goes straight to any person. The most we can do is to bind

all the books of one author alike . . . then, too . . . when a customer takes one of the books out of the library . . . takes it home with him for his week . . . he must be made to feel that it's his book . . . his very own. While he's reading it and enjoying it, it *will* be his book and have its place on the shelf with his other books. . . . It mustn't look strange there,—on his shelf. . . . No! The label of the "Bibliothèque Michel Auclair" will be found discreetly pasted in the back with a little number and nothing assertive about it.

SUZANNE. You know, I suppose. . . .

MICHEL. As to maxims or mottoes . . . You're quite wrong. Why, when I was in school, it was my greatest pleasure to write to my mother. But all over the walls they had signs: "WRITE YOUR MOTHER TO-DAY!" Well, after you read one of those, you couldn't write to anybody. . . . But I've got another idea. At the end of each book we can leave a few pages blank. Then, whoever reads the book will write his name down. That way, the names of Saint-Serge will be meeting one another, and the people, when they meet, if they've seen each other's names in the same fine books, they'll have something in common worth talking about. Why, in the end, we'll be responsible for discussions and public lectures.

SUZANNE. Oh, yes, Michel! And we can give a prize to the first book with a hundred readers on its list—if it's a really good book.

MADAME CATELAIN. Ah, your books will be making matches in Saint-Serge.

MICHEL. Who knows? If poets made marriages they might do a better job than the priests and the old ladies.

[LOUIS CATELAIN *and* BLONDEAU *enter from the right. They wear the uniforms of the days before the War; red pantaloons; tunics; kepis, epaulettes*]

LOUIS [*shaking* MICHEL'S *hand*]. Hello, there! What's this I hear about marrying the priest to an old lady? Well, that's an idea! Good evening, Mother. [*He kisses* MADAME CATELAIN] Hello, Suzon! [*He kisses* SUZANNE] [MICHEL *and* BLONDEAU *shake hands*] See! I've fetched Blondeau home to supper. He's going with us tonight. [*He removes his belt and bayonet and leans them against the tree. Then he loosens his tunic*]

SUZANNE [*she has risen and extends her hand to* BLONDEAU]. Good evening, Monsieur.

BLONDEAU. Mademoiselle. [*He turns and salutes* MADAME CATELAIN] Catelain invited me, Madame, but I wouldn't wish to cause you any trouble.

MADAME CATELAIN. It is always a pleasure to see my son's friends, Monsieur, and it's no trouble to lay another place. Please feel perfectly at home.

[*She goes into the house and during the*

rest of the scene, appears and vanishes as her duties require her presence here or there. SUZANNE *resumes her place*]

LOUIS [*grouping chairs*]. Sit down, Blondeau. Make yourself comfortable. [*He takes* BLONDEAU's *kepi and places it on the table.*]

[BLONDEAU *sits, holding his sabre stiffly between his knees*]

MICHEL. Give me that weapon, too. You're not going to take it with you tonight, I hope?

BLONDEAU [*gives the sabre up to* MICHEL *who places it on the table*]. I can't very well go without it.

SUZANNE. I hope you don't have to wear it while you're dancing!

BLONDEAU. Oh, no, Mademoiselle! I shall check it at the door.

MICHEL. That seems a pity.

BLONDEAU. You needn't laugh. In the old days they danced with their sabres. Have you never seen "La Fille de Madame Angot"? Well, in "La Fille de Madame Angot" the huzzars of Augereau do a waltz with their sabres swinging against their calves. I remember how the effect struck me.

LOUIS. Oh, but those were little sabres very curved and . . .

BLONDEAU. Ah, and there was the sabretache, too! What uniforms they did wear in those days!

MICHEL. With their long spurs clanking along the pavements, clanking into their horses' sides, clanking into the ladies' hearts! Of course, they were fine. They got even finer in Napoleon's time. . . . [*To* MADAME CATELAIN *who has come out on the threshold of the door to peel her potatoes*] Madame Catelain, give me your potatoes to peel.

MADAME CATELAIN. Get along with you, Michel!

LOUIS. Let's see your chemisette, Suzon.

SUZANNE. Wait, now, I haven't finished.

LOUIS. Come, on! Just one look!

SUZANNE. Wait a minute! [LOUIS *snatches it out of her hands*] Oh, Louis! Look out! My needle! Make him behave, Michel.

LOUIS. La . . . la . . . I saw anyway!

SUZANNE. Now I can't find where I left off. You make him behave, Monsieur Blondeau.

BLONDEAU. Mademoiselle, I have no right to give him orders. I'm not his superior. At least, not in rank. . . .

LOUIS [*pointing his finger at* BLONDEAU]. Oh, that reminds me! Have you heard the news?

BLONDEAU [*modestly*]. Never mind about that, Louis.

SUZANNE. What news?

MICHEL. Don't tell us you've passed an examination!

BLONDEAU. No. . . . It's nothing much. . . .

LOUIS. He soon *will* be giving me orders. They're going to make him an adjutant!

MADAME CATELAIN. Oh! How nice, Monsieur!

SUZANNE. Congratulations!

MADAME CATELAIN. Adjutant. Does that mean he's an officer at last?

BLONDEAU. Hmm . . . Nearly. . . .

MICHEL. It's a rank one doesn't often reach at your age. When I was a soldier, I never saw an adjutant who wasn't a man of ripe years and generally awe inspiring.

BLONDEAU [*beaming*]. I'll be the youngest adjutant in the regiment. But my case is rather a special one, because, being an adjutant, for me, is more a means to an end rather than an end in itself . . . I'm studying. . . .

LOUIS. For a real commission. . . .

MICHEL. Will you go to the officers' school at Saint-Maixent?

BLONDEAU. Hmm . . . Hardly . . . Admission there is . . . Well it's more difficult than you'd imagine. They have so many applicants, you see, and, besides that . . . well . . . I tried there four years ago and . . . Hmm . . . so now I've decided to try another tack . . . What I'm after now is a commission in the gardes-forestiers. People don't know so much about that, and so you have a chance at some mighty pleasant jobs. . . . I don't look for much trouble with the examination, either, although it isn't easy by any means . . . I've got the Colonel to thank for the idea. He noticed me. That's why he made me an adjutant. To help me along. He told me as much yesterday morning. They look up the rank and record of any applicant, you know. . . .

SUZANNE. Your colonel must be quite a nice man after all.

LOUIS. He's an old fogey, but he does know a good soldier from a bad one.

BLONDEAU. Yes, he does that! Why, one night as I'm coming out of quarters, I pass him going in—him and Captain Philippi. I'm wearing my dress parade—like today. I snap to attention and salute, and he stops and looks me over. Then he says to Philippi: "You might make an officer out of that boy." Then he asks me my name and tells me he remembers about my trying for Saint-Maixent. He never spoke a word to me before and three days after that he sends for me and gives me this forestry proposition.

MICHEL. I suppose you're coaching for it?

BLONDEAU. Oh, yes! With a young soldier who's been to college. He gives me an hour every night on condition that I get him off labor details.

MICHEL. He's in luck.

LOUIS. When do you go, Michel?

MICHEL. Any day. I'm waiting.

LOUIS. Some people are born lucky! Think of getting out of this hole and into Paris!

MICHEL. I shall fill up this hole when I

come back to it. We'll all fill it up together, if you're willing.

BLONDEAU. By the time you come back, I hope to be riding over some government forest reserve, making my inspection . . . in my green uniform. . . .

[BLONDEAU *and* MICHEL *converse in a low tone*]

LOUIS [*to* SUZANNE]. Are you never going to be done with that, sister?

SUZANNE. Why?

LOUIS. So we can get a stroll in before dinner. We've nearly an hour.

SUZANNE. I need about fifteen minutes more . . . half an hour, at the most. . . .

BLONDEAU. We can wait, Mademoiselle.

MADAME CATELAIN. Let me see how much more there is, Suzon, and I'll finish it for you. You young people must make the most of your Sunday.

SUZANNE. I can finish, Maman.

MICHEL. Where do you want to walk?

LOUIS. Oh, around the ramparts. We might stop at the Guerins' on the way to find out if they're coming with us tonight.

SUZANNE. You two go on ahead slowly, Louis, you and Monsieur Blondeau. Michel and I can join you at the Guerins'. I'm almost done.

LOUIS. That's an idea. Come along, Blondeau.

BLONDEAU [*takes up his kepi and his sword*]. Then I won't say good-bye, Mademoiselle.

SUZANNE. We shan't be long.

MICHEL. No.

BLONDEAU [*to* MADAME CATELAIN]. Au revoir, Madame.

MADAME CATELAIN. Au revoir, Monsieur. Get them back here by half past seven, Louis.

LOUIS. I'll do that, Maman. [*To* BLONDEAU, *as they go out*] This little Guerin we're going to see—there's a girl who can dance. . . .

[*A short silence*]

MICHEL. Perhaps the little Guerin can dance, but not like Suzanne Catelain.

SUZANNE. Oh, Michel, won't we dance tonight, though! We'll have a whole year to dance away tonight!

MICHEL. Yes.

SUZANNE. And you won't tease me, will you? Not like the last time when you told me you were going to kiss me right in front of everybody? Going to count three and then kiss me!

MICHEL. But I didn't kiss you.

SUZANNE. No. But you might have.

MICHEL. Tonight, when we're dancing together, Suzon, I sha'n't say a word to you. I don't think I shall even so much as look at you. We'll dance tonight for the joy of feeling ourselves together. Have you ever noticed how wonderful that is about dancing? How you and I do the very same thing at the very same moment, just as if we'd planned it all out before hand?

SUZANNE. Yes, but, isn't it that way with any good dancer?

MICHEL. Yes, That's true. I've danced with others and I suppose it must have been the same. Only I never thought of it with them. With you, it's different. It isn't just an amusement to dance with you. It's a real joy. Dancing with you is more than just ordinary dancing. . . .

SUZANNE. You know that I never really dance with any one but you.

[*A silence. The voice of a small boy, off-stage, left*]

THE VOICE. Monsieur Auclair!

MICHEL. It's my little neighbor, Pierrot. Come in, Pierrot.

PIERROT [*coming in*]. Here's a telegram that just came for you. I thought I'd find you here.

MICHEL [*takes the telegram*]. Thank you, Pierrot. You're a good boy. I know what it is. Thank you.

PIERROT. Good night.

MICHEL. Good night, Pierrot.

[MADAME CATELAIN *and* SUZANNE *press close to* MICHEL *as he reads*]

MADAME CATELAIN. Is it from Paris?

SUZANNE. Is it? . . . are you going?

MICHEL. Yes. I'm going.

SUZANNE. When, Michel? When?

MICHEL. Tonight.

SUZANNE. Tonight?

MICHEL. Yes. Oh, I've been expecting this telegram. Yesterday and this morning, too. I'd given it up. . . . They wrote me they might need me Monday morning. That's tomorrow. . . . They said they'd let me know by telegram.

SUZANNE. You didn't tell us!

MICHEL. No. Suzon. It wasn't absolutely sure. I didn't want to spoil our party last night or our Sunday today with this idea of farewell. So I packed my valise. . . .

MADAME CATELAIN. Oh, but, you can't go tonight, this way!

SUZANNE. Tomorrow. You can go tomorrow.

MICHEL. I've got to begin work tomorrow. I can, you see, and so I've simply got to.

MADAME CATELAIN. But your supper!

SUZANNE. But, look, Michel! If that telegram had come two hours later, you wouldn't have been able to leave before tomorrow.

MICHEL. But it didn't come two hours later. It's here . . . and in time for me to catch the train, Suzon. Since I've got to go in any case, the sooner I go, the sooner I'll get back!

MADAME CATELAIN. I'll get your supper ready for you.

SUZANNE. And your baggage! What about that?

MICHEL. Listen to me, both of you. It isn't as though we hadn't expected this. Oh, it may seem a little sudden now that it's happened. But, if you ask me, I think it's better so.

SUZANNE. It *isn't* better so!

MADAME CATELAIN. It's much *too* sudden!

MICHEL. My baggage and my overcoat are all ready. I've got everything in order. If Maman Catelain can spare me something to eat on my way—a little something I can take along with me—I'll have my supper on the train. So we'll have plenty of time. We can go and find Louis and pass by my place for my things.

SUZANNE [*stunned*]. And then go straight to the station?

MICHEL. Yes, Suzon! But there's plenty of time. And nothing to be so upset about, either. My going off, like this . . . it's just as it should be, just as we wanted it to be, Suzon . . . Maman Catelain, I won't water the geraniums while the sun is still so high. But you mustn't forget them in the morning.

MADAME CATELAIN. You needn't be afraid. I'll go and get your supper.

MICHEL. Just a bite!

SUZANNE. No! a nice little dinner! In my basket, Maman!

MADAME CATELAIN [*as she goes into the house*]. Leave that to me.

SUZANNE. You're going . . . You're going. . . .

MICHEL. Remember, now! We agreed to say good-bye with a smile. A great, big kiss and a smile! Why, you've been brave and calm enough about this. . . . All that you've been saying. . . .

SUZANNE. I don't think I knew what I was saying, Michel.

MICHEL. You don't really know yet. You've been thinking of nothing but my going away. Now just try thinking of my coming home again.

SUZANNE. I wasn't thinking so much of your going away because I still had you here. [*A little silence*] I used to see you for a minute every morning. And every morning I'd think: he'll be here for his coffee after lunch. . . . And our evenings when you'd read to me, Michel! And all those little surprises you thought of for me . . . You've taught me what a nice thing it is to have a Michel around thinking of me all the time even when he didn't seem to be thinking of anything! And now . . .

MICHEL. I believe you think that's all over! Why, it's only just beginning! If you had any idea of the grand life in store for you, Madame Suzon! All this nonsense, all these surprises—they're nothing, Madame, compared to what's coming! Where's your imagination? Just think of the travelling we've got ahead of us!

SUZANNE. All that's so far away!

MICHEL. You'll see! You'll see! . . . Once you really begin to think seriously about happiness. . . . You know . . . wonderful happiness . . . happiness that has wings to fly on. All kinds of wings, the softest and the strongest. . . . Once you put your mind on that you won't have time to count the days.

SUZANNE. Oh, when you come home again!

MICHEL. When I come home again it will be a beautiful day just as it is today! Can't you see us, together, the very first morning, out in the fields by our mill of Preuillant, in our own fields, under our apple tree? We'll be looking at each other and laughing and talking of everything wonderful at once. . . . Then we can say: No more partings! Nothing now, but to throw ourselves into our great adventures; nothing more but our wedding and our work to begin. . . . The year of separation will disappear like a puff of smoke. We shall take up the spring again where we leave it off today. The meadow at Preuillant will be just as we left it yesterday, with the apple blossoms and the bridal veil and the tips of the poplar trees so pale and gold: only, it will be morning then and more Spring than ever.

SUZANNE. Yes!

MICHEL. And then, remember, you'll be running down to our shop to keep your eye on the carpenter and the painter while we're getting settled. . . . You know, I think I may get Lecuyer's place. He'll find another to store his truck in. . . . It's big and right on the square. I'll pull the partitions down. We'll have a lecture hall upstairs larger than the grande salle at the Hôtel de Ville.

SUZANNE. We'll paint it all pale gray.

MICHEL. Yes. Or white.

SUZANNE [*a silence again*]. But it's so far away, Michel!

MICHEL. I can't go any faster than I'm going now. . . . Tonight . . . on the train. . . .

SUZANNE. Don't say that!

MICHEL. I'll be back to see you two or three times. Just give me a holiday and watch me jump on the train. I'll be here in the morning and off again at night.

SUZANNE. Oh, come in two months for the Fourteenth of July!

MICHEL. Perhaps. And you, Suzon . . . if you could only come to Paris! Just once, even for one day. . . . Ah, but you'd be tired out with two nights on the train.

SUZANNE. I could sleep in the train. And the day after. Oh, if Maman would only let me!

MICHEL. She will. I'll ask her myself. We'll go all over Paris together, you and I. . . . You won't forget to bring everything along?

SUZANNE. Everything?

MICHEL. Yes. . . . Those two eyes, for instance. You simply must bring those two eyes along. What could you see, how could you laugh, without them? and those little curls over your ears and that wrinkled little nose; and that mouth . . . you're always trying to make that mouth so serious; oh, and your voice, Suzon, your precious, precious voice that comes all warm out of your throat, skipping and flying like a little bird. . . . You must bring them along, Suzon, all those hundred, nameless lovely things that *are* Suzon!

SUZANNE. Michel! [*They kiss*] Very well, Sir, we shall be most happy to bring everything with us.

[MADAME CATELAIN *brings the basket and sets it on the table*]

MADAME CATELAIN. That's right. Keep on laughing.

MICHEL. Your daughter can't seem to get this parting through her head. She thinks it's sad.

MADAME CATELAIN. You may think it's gay, my boy, but come home soon and write us often. A great oaf like you leaves a hole to be filled.

MICHEL [*inspecting the basket*]. What have you put in here?

MADAME CATELAIN. There'll be time enough to find out on the train. Don't go poking about now. And bring the basket back . . . oh, and my jelly glass, too, if you think of it.

MICHEL. Oh, I like jelly!

MADAME CATELAIN. You'd best be going along, now, children.

SUZANNE. All right. [*She runs into the house. While she is gone,* MICHEL *and* MADAME CATELAIN *talk together in low tones. She returns*] Ready?

[MICHEL *goes to the table to pick up his basket. Instead he holds out* SUZANNE'S *chemisette*]

MICHEL [*imperiously*]. Suzon, you're going with the rest of them tonight.

SUZANNE. No, Michel!

MICHEL. I won't have any of that! I'll tell Louis and his friend to take you. Don't you think she ought to go, Maman Catelain?

MADAME CATELAIN. Of course! We can't have her moping here.

SUZANNE. But I don't feel like dancing.

MADAME CATELAIN. Then don't dance. But go and have some fun anyway.

MICHEL. No! No! I want her dancing! Go and dance for my sake, Suzon! So that, in the train, I can say to myself: She's dancing . . . she's laughing . . . she isn't one bit sad . . . she's thinking of my letters already . . . of my letters from Paris . . . she's thinking of what she's going to write me! Who is there to tell me about tonight if you don't go? You will go? Say you will—

SUZANNE. Perhaps I'll go.

MICHEL. No, I've got to be sure. Otherwise, I won't know what you're doing, and if I don't know that—why— I simply won't be able to

stand it. Why, even if the compartment is filled with the jolliest people on earth, I shall be miserable.

SUZANNE [*smiling*]. But, . . . my chemisette isn't done.

MADAME CATELAIN [*inspecting that article*]. Let's see. What more is there?

SUZANNE. The hem on the sleeve. . . .

MADAME CATELAIN. I'll attend to that. She'll go, Michel. I promise you. Be off now! [*She urges them off, left*]

MICHEL. Ah, Maman Catelain, kiss me good-bye! [*They go out*]

MADAME [*off-stage*]. La! La! Au revoir, dear little Michel!

MICHEL [*in the distance*]. Au revoir! Au revoir, Maman Catelain!

[MADAME CATELAIN *returns wiping her eyes furtively. She goes to the table, picks up the chemisette and begins to sew busily*]

CURTAIN

ACT TWO

The modest home of BLONDEAU *and* SU-ZANNE, *now married. At the left a door gives on the vestibule. At the back, the door to the kitchen is open. A sideboard, with shelves, rush bottom chairs furnish the room. There is an enlarged photograph of* BLONDEAU. *Other photographs are exhibited in "videpoches" of plush. Against a shield, covered with cotton imitation oriental stuff, a fan of fencing foils and cavalry pistols. In the center a table. Some dishtowels and handkerchiefs are suspended from a clothes line which cuts the right upstage corner of the room. At that end of the table* SUZANNE *is ironing.* BLONDEAU *is seated at the other end, facing the audience, and bent over a newspaper which is spread out in front of him. He is reading very attentively. His kepi on the table and his adjutant's uniform pierce the atmosphere of the room with their showy elegance.*

SUZANNE [*a moment of silence, then she puts down her iron*]. Armand, would you mind fetching me the hot iron off the stove? And put this one back on. [*Hastily she arranges the clothes in front of her*]

BLONDEAU. What? All right. Just a minute. [*Another pause*]

SUZANNE. Very well. I'll go myself.

BLONDEAU [*irritably*]. I'm going. [*He rises, takes the iron, goes out into the kitchen and returns with the other which he sets down in front of* SUZANNE]

SUZANNE. Thanks.

BLONDEAU [*sitting down again*]. Now, I've lost my place. . . .

SUZANNE. Oh, I'm sorry! . . . I didn't realize you were so busy. If I expect to get to see the baby after work tomorrow, I've got to finish my ironing today. That's why. . . .

BLONDEAU. The thing I can't understand is why you take such delight in washing and ironing when your mother's perfectly willing to do it for you!

SUZANNE. I dare say you think it's silly of me to do anything for myself. I've already turned my baby off on Maman to take care of and I might just as well give her our dirty clothes, too, and let her wash them with Louis' and her own and the baby's. . . . No, my friend. I will not ask my mother to do my washing for me.

BLONDEAU. Well, then, send it to a laundry. . . . For a few cents. . . .

SUZANNE. For a few cents! . . . Precious few cents we've got to spare these days! When you get your forestry commission, perhaps, but that's a long time coming, isn't it?

BLONDEAU. A long time? You needn't rub it in. I'll pass the next examination all right. Much I care whether I pass it or not. All I think of is the quickest way out of this miserable fix we're in. . . .

SUZANNE. The trouble, my poor friend, is that your nerve isn't up to your ambitions.

BLONDEAU. So it's my nerve now! Don't I work as hard as I can with all my duties to think of?

SUZANNE. If you worked half as hard on your studying as you do on the races, you'd pass in spite of. . . .

BLONDEAU. I like that!

SUZANNE. I haven't been able to make you do two lessons this whole week.

BLONDEAU. This is the last straw! Look out, now, Suzanne! You're not being fair. You know well enough that if I play the races . . . if *we* play the races, it's only to make a little extra money. You certainly can't accuse me of getting any pleasure out of it!

SUZANNE. Oh, can't I! Don't tell me, my friend! You love to gamble and you live in the hope of something for nothing.

BLONDEAU. Something for nothing! Do you call my statistics nothing? And the way I figure everything out? Is that your idea of nothing? And all my systems? Aren't they work? Haven't you worked on them with me, night after night? Nothing! . . . What if I do like to gamble? That doesn't mean gambling for the sake of gambling. Not necessarily, you know. I weigh all the chances. I shift my system about to meet every circumstance. I pick my winners absolutely scientifically. And you call that pleasure! I'd a lot rather be playing billiards. Yes, or even studying!

SUZANNE. Look what it does for you!

BLONDEAU. You're too impatient. Mathematics can *not* go wrong. If you keep your winnings even with your losses, sooner or later the big day comes and the long odds, and there you are . . . rich!

SUZANNE. Whenever you do win anything, you eat it all up with your friends. . . .

BLONDEAU. Only once!

SUZANNE. . . . and we live so badly. We're always in debt and with your pay and what I earn we could be perfectly comfortable . . . if it weren't for the races. . . . I could have a girl to help me, or a nurse maid, even. . . .

BLONDEAU. You'll have your nurse maid yet. . . . Yes, and what's more you'll have my orderly wait on you. [*A pause*] If you were in such a hurry to have a servant, it's a real pity you didn't marry Michel Auclair. He'd have given you a cook and made you the queen of a book-shop.

SUZANNE. We won't discuss that, if you please. You always think of such delicate things to say! [*A pause*]

BLONDEAU. Speaking of Michel, I suppose we'll be running into him again, at your mother's on Sundays.

SUZANNE. Since Michel came home two months ago, we've seen him there three times. Is that too much?

BLONDEAU. Yes, it is.

SUZANNE. I don't see that you have any cause to dislike him.

BLONDEAU. I haven't. Nobody could have anything against Michel. That's just the trouble with him. He's too nice. When he came back he'd have done much better to keep his distance instead of rushing up to me with open arms the way he did, and being such a good sport and your little playmate and your big brother and all. . . .

SUZANNE. Michel wasn't putting that on, Armand. Michel's always just himself. He always means what he says and says what he means. It wouldn't have been like him to keep his distance. Not when I wrote him myself, that he would always be my big brother. . . . Why shouldn't he spend his Sundays at Maman's? Hasn't he always been one of the family? Don't we all—Maman and Louis and I—love to see him? Even if you don't? . . . He could only have one reason for not coming. If he were still in love with me. . . . Do you dislike Michel because he was my old sweetheart?

BLONDEAU. Certainly not! It's the man himself. He's the kind of man I can't stand. I've seen plenty like him in the army. And I've always had it in for them. . . . The way he has of passing judgment on you! Who does he think he is? What's he know about me? That I haven't got my commission yet. But he hasn't any idea of what I really am.

SUZANNE. You'll have plenty of chance to show him. . . . It's true. . . . He doesn't know you. . . . He wrote me that. . . . But he said you *must* amount to something or I shouldn't have married you.

BLONDEAU. Oh, he said that, did he! [*A pause*] He never did anything to me, only with all his books and his wild ideas . . . well . . . he's not my style. . . .

SUZANNE. He loves his books and he has great ideas.

BLONDEAU. That may all be. But he and I haven't got much in common.

SUZANNE. Nothing. . . . If you're not doing anything, won't you fetch my other iron back again?

BLONDEAU [*as he obeys*]. I've got to be off to barracks. I'm not going to bet any money today. I don't know these yearlings. [*His glance falls on the newspaper*] But just the same, I've got tips enough to . . . well . . .

SUZANNE. What?

BLONDEAU. Why, the Captain gave me a louis to put on a horse that hasn't got a chance. Not a chance in the world. That's twenty francs to the good anyway.

SUZANNE. You're not going to bet them for him?

BLONDEAU. I'd be a fool if I did.

SUZANNE [*shocked*]. Oh, Armand!

BLONDEAU. The Captain picks the horse with the prettiest name. That's his system. Today it's Hidalgo. Hidalgo! [*He laughs*]

SUZANNE. Armand, please go right down now and place the Captain's bet.

BLONDEAU. What for? If Hidalgo doesn't fall down it'll be because his jockey falls off. I'd as soon bet a louis on a wheelbarrow.

SUZANNE. But, Armand, you can't be sure! And it's not honest. Oh dear me! Doing such things for people, too!

BLONDEAU. Why isn't it honest? I take whatever risk there is, don't I? I ought to have known better than tell you about it.

SUZANNE [*goes to him and puts her two hands on his shoulders*]. But you did tell, Armand, and if you don't place this bet for the Captain, I shall die. If you won't do it for me, then do it for our little Riquet's sake.

BLONDEAU. Well, if that's the way you feel, I'll go down to the bookie now. It isn't worth fighting over.

SUZANNE. Right now?

BLONDEAU. Yes. Right now. You get so excited over trifles.

SUZANNE. This isn't a trifle.

BLONDEAU. It's time I started for quarters anyway. Where's the brush? [*He takes a brush from the sideboard to brush the front of his tunic*]

SUZANNE. You'll go by Julien's on the way and settle up Hidalgo?

BLONDEAU [*impatiently*]. I said I would.

SUZANNE. Wait till I brush your back. [*She does*] Oh, here's a great spot on your breeches!

BLONDEAU. How did I get that?

SUZANNE. You must have rubbed against the stove when you went for my iron.

BLONDEAU. I must have. You can't brush it out, you know.

SUZANNE. Wait a minute. [*She fetches a bottle and a rag. She kneels in front of him and rubs the spot*] I shouldn't have made you do such a thing.

BLONDEAU. No. You shouldn't. A soldier in uniform is like a lady in evening dress. He hasn't any business around stoves! Is it out?

SUZANNE. It's out.

BLONDEAU. Good-bye, Suzanne. Kiss me. Tell me you're not angry.

SUZANNE [*languidly*]. Of course not. [*She kisses him*]

BLONDEAU [*holding her*]. You know if you were still angry I couldn't go away. I'd feel all upset inside. I shouldn't be good for anything.

SUZANNE. Really? [*She lifts her eyes to him and proffers her lips*]

[*He kisses her*]

BLONDEAU. I know things aren't going as well as they should. But I do have such rotten luck! I know I'm not perfect. But who is? My intentions are good, though, and I always do everything for the best. The best for both of us. You know that? [*A pause*] Say you know that, Suzanne.

SUZANNE. Of course I do. Run along now. [*He goes out.* SUZANNE *takes the clothes off the line and removes the line*]

BLONDEAU [*off-stage*]. Yes. I'm going out. But that doesn't matter. Come in anyway! [*He reappears to usher in* MICHEL]

MICHEL. Well, Suzanne. How are you?

SUZANNE. Ah, Michel! Michel! [*She runs to him*]

[*They shake hands*]

MICHEL. I couldn't go past your door without coming in for a minute, could I?

SUZANNE. I'm so glad. . . .

BLONDEAU. We were just talking about you. Not ten minutes ago.

MICHEL. Were you?

SUZANNE. Yes. Just now.

BLONDEAU. We were talking . . . we were talking about books! I was saying that we should hardly have time to take much advantage of your library, because if my commission comes along pretty soon now, as I expect it will, we shall be leaving Saint-Serge for good.

[*Embarrassed,* SUZANNE *pretends to arrange her washing*]

MICHEL. When is the examination?

BLONDEAU. In three weeks.

MICHEL. It will be no trouble for me to

send you any books you want wherever you
go.

SUZANNE. Oh, is the book-shop open,
Michel?

MICHEL. Since Monday.

BLONDEAU. I must beg you to excuse me.
I was late when you came in and I've got to
be off.

MICHEL. But I'm going too. I only dropped
in. I'm going. . . . I . . .

BLONDEAU. You're not in such a hurry, are
you?

SUZANNE. Armand has to go, Michel, but
you stay. You've only just come.

BLONDEAU. Excuse me.

MICHEL [shaking hands]. I'll see you some
Sunday soon?

BLONDEAU [going]. I hope so.

[MICHEL examines the room while SU-
ZANNE carries her ironing board into the
kitchen]

SUZANNE [coming back to him]. I'm
ashamed, Michel. The first time you come to
my house and you find everything upside
down.

MICHEL. No!

SUZANNE. Yes . . . I've been doing . . .
a little ironing . . .

MICHEL. So this is Suzanne's home!

SUZANNE. You mustn't look at it, Michel.
You mustn't look at anything. It's all just
temporary. It's just what Armand had in his
old room up at the barracks. [She sees MICHEL
looking at the books on the sideboard] Do
you recognize them? They're the books you
gave me.

MICHEL. Yes. . . . Tell me . . . Was I
wrong to come?

SUZANNE. Oh, no, Michel! Why? I'm so
glad to see you!

MICHEL. Your husband may not be so glad.

SUZANNE. Nonsense! It's all one to him. Sit
down. [She sits]

MICHEL [sitting beside her]. Ever since I
came home, I've been longing for a visit alone
with you, Suzanne. I didn't expect such good
luck today.

SUZANNE. And I've been wanting to see you.
You know, whenever I do have a minute, I
run to Maman's to see the baby. I always
hope I'm going to see you there. The fates
have been against me. So I've been waiting for
your shop to open so that I could call on you
there some morning. I wanted . . . well, I
wanted you to tell me something that you
left out of your letters . . . unless what they
did say was really the truth . . . I want you
to tell me that you haven't any hard feelings
against me, Michel . . . that you don't think
my marrying Armand was . . . was betraying
you. . . .

MICHEL. Suzanne . . .

SUZANNE. And then, I haven't had a chance,
yet, to ask you to forgive me for hurting you,
because I'm afraid I must have hurt you
dreadfully. . . .

MICHEL [a pause. He leans toward her].
Are you happy, Suzanne?

SUZANNE [a low voice]. Yes.

MICHEL. Really happy? That's what I
wanted most to ask you: Tell me! You're
really happy?

SUZANNE [with some effort]. Yes, Michel.

MICHEL [rises and commences walking
about]. Why should I be hurt then, Suzanne,
and what have I to forgive? . . . Oh, I had a
bad time for a while. I felt that I should never
have gone away; that I had made a fatal mistake in trying to establish myself before my
marriage . . . I should have married first of
all and taken you to Paris with me. But afterwards I realized that our separation had
really been a blessing to both of us, a sort of
test that we both needed. . . . You'd always
known me, Suzon. You'd always been with
me, even more, perhaps, than with your own
brother. I wonder if you've had so much as
one single pair of shoes since the first step you
ever took, that you haven't worn out at my
side!—trotting from home to school and from
school back home again; playing Saturdays in
the old quarry; running wild with me over the
countryside; dancing with me . . . I'd got to
be a habit. You began telling me you loved
me when we were two children playing father
and mother. When the time came for you to
say it in all seriousness, you believed it, Suzon.
You believed that such a long seasoned friendship must be love. How could you think that
love would call itself Michel! [A pause. SU-
ZANNE, her chin resting in her hand, stares
straight before her] When those last empty
letters came, always with less and less of
Suzon in them, and that unforgettable very
last one. . . . I said to myself: She's got over
loving me. But the truth was, I'd always been
wrong about us. And I soon came to see I
hadn't any right to say: She's got over loving
me. I should have said: Now she's just beginning to love me . . . Because, as we can both
see, now, Suzon, you never really had any
feeling for me except the quiet, deep affection
one should have for a friend. Why, if you had
really loved me, could anyone have taken you
from me, in a few months, when I had only
just left you, and when every post brought my
letters to you? [He pauses a moment before
BLONDEAU's photograph] You never loved me,
my dear Suzon.

SUZANNE [after a silence, still a little trou-
bled]. You're only thinking of me. Was that
how you felt too?

MICHEL [uneasily]. How I felt? . . .
Surely. . . . Didn't I write you? . . . I

couldn't have felt otherwise, could I? . . . You haven't any flowers here! If I'd only thought! And I've got so many roses now! You still like flowers, don't you?

SUZANNE. I usually have plenty . . . from Maman's garden. . . .

MICHEL. You ought to make your husband put in some book shelves. I'll be giving you more books from time to time. Three or four boards, a couple of brackets and a screw or two. . . . Does he like doing such things? Does he read sometimes? Eh?

SUZANNE. Of course he does! He loves to do anything like that. And we're going to have a library. He wants one just as much as I do.

MICHEL. Does he! I'm glad. I was afraid. . . .

SUZANNE. Only, right now he's got this examination to think of and all our plans for moving away.

MICHEL. Do you expect him to pass this time?

SUZANNE. We're both sure this time. . . .

MICHEL. Then you'll be leaving the Post Office?

SUZANNE. Of course. I shall stop at home then.

MICHEL. And have your son with you?

SUZANNE. As soon as ever we're settled.

MICHEL. He'll have to begin at the beginning, you know.

SUZANNE. I know. But there are no end of little things to help. Free lodging, his pay. . . . Oh, you've no idea!

MICHEL. Then we needn't worry about the future. And for the present . . . Everything's all right now, I hope? . . . Couldn't be better?

SUZANNE. Of course, Michel . . . Of course. . . .

MICHEL. You're embarrassed, Suzon. I want you to reassure me . . . and my questions embarrass you. Why?

SUZANNE. But they don't, Michel!

MICHEL. One thing you must understand. No matter what has happened, no matter what may yet happen, I shall never think of you except as my own little Suzon and I shall always be asking you questions about yourself and your life and saying whatever comes into my head. . . . But the one thing that could really hurt me Suzon, would be to feel that you were . . . uncomfortable with me, that you weren't quite frank with me. . . .

SUZANNE. My dear Michel! [She goes to him and kisses him on both cheeks]

MICHEL [returning the kiss]. There! . . . I needn't have been asking myself—as I have since I came home—"How am I going to speak to her?" . . . "What am I going to say to her?" . . . "What is she going to be like?" . . . I couldn't imagine a changed Suzon. No, nor any but my own way of talking to Suzon!

SUZANNE. Then it wasn't on my account that you stayed on six months longer in Paris?

MICHEL. On your account, no. Things turned out that way. That was all. I stayed on because . . . because . . . well, there wasn't any hurry any more, was there? . . . And the longer I stayed, the more I learned.

SUZANNE. Maman heard that you wanted to keep on in Paris always.

MICHEL. Ah!

SUZANNE. Yes. And I don't mind telling you that, when I heard that, I was afraid you'd given up all your fine plans for Saint-Serge . . . and that I was to blame.

MICHEL. No! Why, look! The book-shop's open, just as I always said it would be, in Lecuyer's place. . . . You'll see what I've done. . . . You'll recognize everything. . . .

SUZANNE. Are you satisfied? Are people coming?

MICHEL. Not many yet. We're hardly started. I'm in no hurry. I haven't even begun to advertise the library. . . . I'll be having my troubles, I dare say, more than I looked for. But such things want time, don't they? And work. Still, I shall do all that I said I should do. I've got to.

[A pause]

SUZANNE. And I shall be going away. . . .

MICHEL. Had you rather stay here in Saint-Serge?

SUZANNE. Yes.

[Another pause with MICHEL walking back and forth]

MICHEL. I hope you're not going to take Maman Catelain with you.

SUZANNE. Oh, no! At least, not right away. I don't believe she'd want to go. Louis will marry and settle down here. . . .

MICHEL. That's good! That means you'll come back now and then and see us. Maman Catelain will be wanting her grandson and you'll have to bring him and she'll be able to keep you for a few days every time. . . . And your husband will come on leave. . . . You may not be so far from us, either. . . .

SUZANNE. I hope not.

MICHEL. Suzon, when a man's young, as I am, and loves young people, like himself, like you and Louis, he always has one comfort: that he has plenty of time always to know his friends better and to follow what they do and to see them. He can always feel that they're a part of his own world. He can always call on them for help and . . . go to them, when . . . they need him . . . no matter how many months or years slip by. . . . That's a comfort always, Suzon. A real comfort. . . . It does a man good to think of it. . . .

SUZANNE. Yes. . . . Yes. . . .

MICHEL. People of our age need never be separated, Suzon, unless they want to be!

SUZANNE. That's true, Michel!

MICHEL. . . . Unless they're the kind who forget.

SUZANNE [*excited*]. That's true. . . . Only the forgetting kind. Not the others. Not our kind!

MICHEL. You see?

[*A knock at the door.* SUZANNE *goes to answer.* MICHEL *is inspecting her books as* COLSON *enters*]

COLSON [*peevishly, as he comes in*]. Good-day, Madame. Is this where Adjutant Blondeau lives?

SUZANNE. Yes, Monsieur.

COLSON. Well, is he home?

SUZANNE. No. He's gone up to the barracks.

COLSON. I just came from the barracks. He isn't there.

SUZANNE. That's because he hasn't got there yet. He only just left.

COLSON. I can't seem to put my finger on him anywhere. It's beginning to look funny.

SUZANNE. What do you want with him? Who are you?

COLSON. I'm Colson. I run the canteen for the dragoons. I suppose you're Blondeau's wife?

SUZANNE. Yes.

COLSON. I guess he's told you about me?

SUZANNE. No.

COLSON. No? Well, then, I'll tell you myself that your husband owes me ninety-four francs fifty centimes. And you just tell him, if you don't mind, that I want my money tonight. Tonight, do you hear? Before taps, too. And if he doesn't deliver—what's to prevent me from going to his major about it? I know the old boy well. I was his orderly ten years ago.

SUZANNE. But, Monsieur!

COLSON. Now, none of that! . . . Two weeks ago your husband comes over to our canteen for a drink with one of our corporals. I'm there and I hear them fixing up a small bet on the races. "Don't happen to know a bookie in Saint-Serge, do you?" I'm asking. "Certainly I know one," he says to me, "but if you've got any money to bet, put it in my hands because the bookie don't want people coming and going around his place."

SUZANNE [*a frightened glance toward* MICHEL]. My husband will come to see you tonight without fail.

COLSON. Just a minute! . . . Last week I'm coming after your Adjutant Blondeau and giving him fifteen francs to place on a particular horse. Oh, there's no mistake about that. I put my bet down in good clear writing, on a nice clean bit of paper. . . . Yes . . . And, what's more, my horse is a winner! . . .

SUZANNE [*another frightened glance at* MICHEL]. I tell you my husband will come. . . .

COLSON. Just a minute. . . . Just a minute! . . . My horse is a winner, I'm telling you, and the odds give me thirty-one francs fifty for every five franc piece I put up. That makes ninety-four francs fifty that's coming to me, and it ought to have come to me five days ago. I waited two days. After that I began looking for Blondeau. And not hide nor hair of him can I find anywhere. I leave him messages and still he don't turn up. Lady, he's lost to me! [*Indignantly*] I don't know what you expect me to think about him, but if you want me to tell you what I do think. . . .

MICHEL [*coming forward*]. Look here, we've heard enough of this! You can see perfectly well that Madame doesn't know anything about your story. I'm a friend of Adjutant Blondeau's. I happen to know that he's looking for you today. He's been busy. They're giving him a commission. . . .

COLSON [*impressed*]. Oh! Are they?

MICHEL. . . . And he's got more important things on his mind than worrying about you and your winnings. [*He turns his back on* COLSON]

COLSON. Well! In that case! . . . It wasn't the money, you know. . . . It was only the principle . . . [*Moving shiftily toward the door*] You tell him that, Madame. You tell him I didn't know what to think and it's all right. . . . It's all right. . . . I just didn't know. [*He goes out*]

SUZANNE [*following him*]. Yes. . . . Yes. . . . Of course . . .

COLSON [*off-stage*]. Good day, Madame . . .

SUZANNE [*returns and sits at table, burying her face on her arms*]. Oh, Michel! I'm ashamed . . . I'm ashamed . . .

MICHEL. Didn't you know that your husband . . .

SUZANNE. Oh, yes, I knew. . . . Not about this business. . . . But there have been others . . . [*She breaks down completely*] I didn't want you to find out, Michel! . . . oh, Michel, our life is so ugly and miserable! [*She weeps soundlessly*]

MICHEL. Suzon! It isn't possible. . . .

SUZANNE. A minute ago you told me I was embarrassed at you for asking me if I was happy. I *was* embarrassed. No wonder. I was lying to you, Michel. I'm not happy. I'm wretched.

[*A long silence*]

MICHEL [*deeply moved*]. Doesn't he love you?

SUZANNE. Yes.

MICHEL. Then you don't love him?

SUZANNE. I don't know . . . I don't know . . . I couldn't live without him. . . .

MICHEL. Ah! [*Another pause*] Do you respect him?

SUZANNE. Sometimes.

[*Another pause*]

MICHEL [*holding his head in his hands*]. Tell me about it, now. Tell me all about it. . . .

SUZANNE [*woebegone*]. You shouldn't have found out!

MICHEL. He came to your house after I went away. Often. Nearly every evening. . . . They don't go to houses where women aren't to be found, those fellows. They don't know any other kind of amusement. He made love to you, Suzon. What he calls love. You'd never been made love to that way before, had you? . . . Well? Am I wrong?

SUZANNE. Oh, Michel, you mustn't think he made love to me for the fun of it. Please don't say that, Michel. . . . Maman didn't want me to marry Armand. She gave me all sorts of reasons. Every word she said was true and right. I knew that, Michel, and half the time I was furious and half the time I was miserable. But I think that all the things about Armand that aren't so nice, even his worst faults, only bound me closer to him and made me defend him harder to Maman and to myself. So, I married him. Oh, I couldn't marry him quickly enough. He wanted to wait for his commission. I was the impatient one. I hurried him into it because I was so sure of myself then, and yet I was afraid, too, that I might weaken. And afterwards, afterwards, when there wasn't any escape, when I began to lead this dreadful life, then I wept for you, Michel. . . . Then I did nothing but weep for you and wonder how I could ever have done such a thing.

MICHEL. Poor Suzanne! [*A pause*] Oh . . . and I . . . I shed a few tears for you, my dear. [*He turns away from her*] It's quite true that for a while, I did think of settling in Paris.

SUZANNE [*weeping*]. My poor Michel! [*She leans towards him and buries her head on his shoulder*]

MICHEL. We've had bad luck, we two. Don't cry any more. We mustn't let people see that you've been crying. Give me your handkerchief and I'll dry your eyes. There! We stand together, anyway, don't we? And I'll help you. I'll always be able to help you. Eh?

SUZANNE [*a sad smile*]. Yes, Michel.

MICHEL. Let me ask you one thing more, Suzon. Your husband—he's kind and considerate with you, isn't he?

SUZANNE. Kind? Yes. In his way. Considerate? No. That is, he doesn't think of some things, and I have to remind him. I shouldn't call him a bad fellow, though. Not a bad fellow.

MICHEL. I know him so little. But he shows some good qualities. He loves his son.

SUZANNE. And he's so proud of him!

MICHEL. When I go to see your mother she seems to avoid speaking of him. I think she considers him a little self-centered.

SUZANNE. Maman doesn't like Armand. And he is self-centered and lazy, and—oh, so domineering—just like a child. But he's affectionate too—like a child.

MICHEL. Do you really expect him to pass his examination?

SUZANNE. I don't know.

MICHEL. He plays the races?

SUZANNE. Yes.

MICHEL. Much?

SUZANNE. A good deal.

MICHEL. Does he lose?

SUZANNE. Yes, Michel, and runs into debt.

MICHEL. We must put a stop to that. Whatever happens, we must.

SUZANNE. I often make him promise to stop playing. But then he does it on the sly. And he has to confess afterwards, that he's been losing and he begs my pardon. He's full of good intentions and he lies about them, to me and to himself. Soldiers get used to big talk.

MICHEL. . . . How does all this affect you? That's what I want to know. . . . Why, there must be days when . . . when . . .

SUZANNE [*thoughtfully*]. There are days when I'm hard and cruel with him. . . . Then there are others when I make all kinds of allowances, when he just breaks my heart and I want to excuse him and everything he does. He hasn't had a fair chance. He hardly knew his father. His mother never paid any attention to him. He never did a stroke of work until he was eighteen and enlisted. . . . It seems to me that I've just *got* to look after him. It's as though I'd adopted a child.

MICHEL [*thoughtfully*]. You're fond of him.

SUZANNE. Yes. . . . Isn't that love?

MICHEL. There are degrees and kinds of love. Many degrees and many kinds. [*A pause*] I understand. I understand the tie between you. [*Half to himself*] It's a strong tie. A tie of pain and humiliation. But strong. . . . [*To her again*] The strongest thing between you is your baby and there's nothing painful or humiliating about him! [*Another pause. Then* MICHEL *rises resolutely with a deep sigh*] Well, Suzon, that's the way of things. We have to build upon what's gone before. You've got your happiness to build, in spite of everything . . . your happiness with him, do you hear? [SUZANNE *shakes her head dubiously*] It's no great task to be happy, thank God, with love such an easy matter! . . . You'll have to find just what it is you love in him and make fast to that. You'll have to nourish your love on what is best in him, and most worthy of you. There's always something!

SUZANNE. No doubt.

MICHEL. . . . The best in him must be the

child you see in him, the child you've been talking about. . . . It isn't right that you should have to look upon him as a child. A man should have the prestige of manhood. . . . And you . . . you were the child, Suzon. . . .

SUZANNE. The spoiled child. . . .

MICHEL. My poor Suzon, it's all very well for you to play the mother. I wonder if you've got quite used to being stronger and wiser than your husband?

SUZANNE. Oh, that depends!

MICHEL. It's clear enough that you're better armed against life than he is. Far better armed than your soldier whom you're inclined to judge so severely for the weaknesses that make you love him, which make him so much less strong than you. And here you are, consecrated to him because . . . because he happens to be your husband. . . .

SUZANNE. That's true.

MICHEL. But that's nothing to be desperate about. You owe it to yourself and all of us to be strong and to take action, to be happy and to desire happiness. You must use a stern hand with this child of yours, Suzon. . . .

SUZANNE [interrupting him]. That isn't always easy.

MICHEL. You have a gentle power. He has his vanity. And I'll help you, Suzon. Ah, I've got my own responsibilities in this. I'm through with bitterness now and I only feel distress. I can make myself his friend. If need be, I can work my way into your affairs. He may hate the sight of me. It doesn't matter. I shall help you none the less. And we must begin with the races. We cannot have him a bookie's agent any longer. If he were a strong character, it would be dangerous enough. But he is not strong and he comes against the worst temptation and risks the most terrible disasters and next. . . . [He completes his thought with a gesture] Oh, my poor little Suzon! . . . Your mother knows what a hard time you're having. She doesn't guess why. But it worries her. She's told me so.

SUZANNE. Has she, Michel!

MICHEL. Before long she'll be asking questions. And . . . who knows? . . . Your husband's friends may take to calling on her!

SUZANNE. Oh!

MICHEL. You must say all this to your husband, Suzon. And, if that doesn't turn the trick, Louis or I will take him in hand.

SUZANNE. He'll listen to me, Michel. I'll make him listen to me.

MICHEL. Have you ever quarrelled?

SUZANNE. Yes.

MICHEL. That must not be! That would make me, too, unhappy! Talk to him, Suzon. Talk a long time with him . . . every day. . . . Firmly, but never angrily, or reproachfully.

That will make you really the stronger. Promise me to try, Suzon?

SUZANNE. Yes, Michel. With all my might.

[A pause]

MICHEL [taking his hat]. Now that I've seen you again and know how you are and what you're doing, I must be off. I'll need to think a great deal about all this.

SUZANNE. We'll see each other soon again, won't we? I'll come to call on you.

MICHEL. Yes. I insist on that. Soon. This very week.

SUZANNE. I will. Some morning.

MICHEL [preoccupied]. That's right. I'm going now. You don't want anything more of me?

SUZANNE. No. Oh, yes! You mustn't be upset on my account.

MICHEL. You aren't holding any other troubles back?

SUZANN. No, dear old Michel.

MICHEL [brusquely]. Suzon, Suzon, tell me the truth. Will Blondeau pay this canteen fellow, this Colson tonight?

SUZANNE. . . . Yes, Michel. . . . Yes, he will . . . certainly. . . .

MICHEL. Are you sure he has the money? Come now, Suzon, you can tell me! He hasn't got it, has he? And neither have you?

SUZANNE. But he has, Michel. Or at least, we have, between us. The end of the month's coming anyway. . . .

MICHEL. Bad, bad Suzon! You'd have let me go without telling me. [He takes a bank note out of his wallet and places it on the table]

SUZANNE [trying to stop him]. No! No, Michel! Please don't do that! I can't let you do that!

MICHEL. You see how simple it is? I happened to be here when that man came. It won't do Blondeau any harm to know it. You can pay me back any time.

SUZANNE. No, Michel! [She tries to give him back the note, but he takes her two hands and drags her with him out through the door]

MICHEL. Good-night. . . . Good-night . . . dear Suzon!

CURTAIN

ACT THREE

The same scene as the second act.

BLONDEAU *sits in deep gloom, his elbows on his knees, his head in his hands.* SUZANNE *stands near him, leaning on the table.*

BLONDEAU [after a silence]. All I want now is to get out of here. . . . I'm going to make my application for the customs service.

SUZANNE. You've been saying that for a week now and you haven't even bothered to find out what to do about it.

BLONDEAU. That's because I'm fed up on everything.

SUZANNE. You haven't any more time to lose. It's a pity you didn't think of the customs a year ago, the first time you failed. This last forestry examination was much too hard for you.

BLONDEAU. You think so? Well, I don't. These examinations are just a matter of pull. Whether you pass or not depends on who your friends are.

SUZANNE. Let's not think about it any more. You can go right into the customs with your own rank and I can stay right on in the post office. If any of them go on calling you "Lieutenant" up at the barracks, just be the first to laugh. They'll soon get tired of that joke.

BLONDEAU. I could stand that all right.

SUZANNE. Is there anything else?

BLONDEAU. I should say there is. I tell you, when a man's luck turns against him, he hasn't got a chance.

SUZANNE. What's the matter? You haven't been reprimanded or punished or . . .

BLONDEAU. No. Not that.

SUZANNE. Well, then, what? Not the races?

BLONDEAU. Yes, The races.

SUZANNE. Oh, I might have guessed it just from looking at you! Armand! Didn't you promise me not to play them any more? Didn't you promise not to go near them again without telling me? . . . Didn't you?

BLONDEAU. I owe the captain two hundred and eighty francs.

SUZANNE. Two hundred and eighty francs! . . . Does this come from those twenty francs we were talking about last week?

BLONDEAU. No. I promised you to place that bet and I did place it. Those twenty were lost. This is another horse he told me to play for him. Four days ago. Another pretty name. Girandole.

SUZANNE. Oh, I give you up! You'll ruin us, Armand! You are ruining us! I don't wonder you want to get away!

BLONDEAU. I was going to use those twenty francs to buy you a little surprise.

SUZANNE. Two hundred and eighty francs! . . . And four days ago. . . . Then the captain knows that he won? Has he asked for the money?

BLONDEAU. Day before yesterday, he did. I told him I forgot it and left it at home. Yesterday he didn't say anything. This morning I said to him: "Captain, I've forgotten you again. Excuse me."

SUZANNE. What did he say to that?

BLONDEAU. He said: "As long as you've got the money, that's the main thing."

SUZANNE. Two hundred and eighty francs!

BLONDEAU. Yes. That's four times seventy. You see the odds were . . .

SUZANNE. And we've only got a hundred and twenty-five to our name.

BLONDEAU. I've got twenty-five on me. [He rises] I've got to find the rest somehow. I've got my honor to think o'. The honor of a soldier. . . . And my future. . . .

SUZANNE. You might have thought of them a little sooner.

BLONDEAU. This time really is the last, Suzanne. I swear it is. Don't you see how bad I feel?

[A pause]

We'll pick up twenty francs here and thirty francs there and . . .

SUZANNE. I'm going to tell Louis about it.

BLONDEAU. Louis hasn't got any money.

SUZANNE. Michel told me we gave him back his hundred francs much too soon. Perhaps I might. . . .

BLONDEAU. No, you might not! It was bad enough last time. . . . We'll just have to. . . .

SUZANNE. Listen, Armand. Suppose we could borrow enough, we wouldn't have a sou left for food. . . . I can only see one way out. Go right up to your captain and tell him you were . . . foolish enough to keep his money and beg him to excuse you for not being able to make it up all at once and ask him if he'll let you do it in three or four payments.

BLONDEAU. What?! Tell him right out, I did such a thing as that? Why, he trusts me and I'm counting on him to endorse my transfer to the customs!

SUZANNE. He may think you were foolish but he'll know you're honest, won't he?

BLONDEAU. You don't know him! He may be a fine fellow, but he's not as easy as all that. He might just raise the devil with me. You don't stop to think I told him I had the money. I told him that in so many words, twice. I didn't want him thinking maybe I wasn't square, did I? I might have tried out your scheme three days ago. But it's too late now. I can't go up to him whining . . . like a naughty little boy. . . .

SUZANNE. That's just what you are . . . a naughty little boy. . . . [She sits, dejectedly, her elbows on the table]

BLONDEAU. I know I'm not much good. I know that. You don't have to rub it in. I'm disgusted enough with myself. . . . But we've got to think of something else.

SUZANNE [after a pause]. I'll tell you what. Let's say it was my fault. Let's say that I was supposed to take the money down for you and that I kept it and never told you a word about it and that I lied to you and pretended I had the money and that you were acting in perfect good faith.

BLONDEAU. Now that's an idea! That might fix up everything!

SUZANNE. Will you do it?

BLONDEAU. Well, I don't like to put it off on you, but . . . of course, it's a fact men don't mind what a woman does. About such things, I mean.

SUZANNE. Your captain will just tell you you ought to have known better. He'll say: "You can't trust a woman any more than you can a child."

BLONDEAU. Oh, certainly, he won't think any less of you! Men don't expect much of a woman's word of honor, you know. They take it for granted a woman's going to lie if she feels like it. . . . A woman isn't responsible in money matters, either. If her general behavior's all right, well, then she's all right. . . . My dear, you've saved the day for us again.

SUZANNE [with a sigh]. Well, then, go along! Go along and see your captain! And make your first payment of . . . fifty francs?

BLONDEAU. Not enough.

SUZANNE. A hundred, then. Give him a hundred.

BLONDEAU. All right. . . . What if he refuses to take it? What if he says: "Give me back the twenty and call it square?" Oh, I'll argue with him, but . . .

SUZANNE. You've got to insist on his taking it. You've got to, Armand! You've got to make him see that it's just as much of a bet whether you really placed the money or not. You've got to show him there isn't any difference. . . . It's a gambling debt, Armand.

BLONDEAU. Yes. Of course it is. [Another silence] Listen, Suzanne! This was your idea and you're in a better position than I am because you haven't done anything to be ashamed of. How about your going to see the captain?

SUZANNE. Me?

BLONDEAU. Yes. Go on, Suzanne. Please!

SUZANNE. Really, now. . . .

BLONDEAU. Listen: You go. If I go, I'll just be a sergeant talking to a captain. And that will make me guilty. There's no two ways about it. I know! The better I get at making my own men stand around, the worse I am at standing up for myself. You understand how it is. Go on, Suzanne! You do it! Why it would be terrible for me, but, for you, it just isn't anything at all. You're a woman, too. And don't I know you've got a better head than I have?

SUZANNE [after a silence]. All right. I'll go.

BLONDEAU. That's the way! Thank you! My good little Suzette! But I don't want you feeling too unhappy about it!

SUZANNE. I can't feel very happy. But I guess I'd better go. Will he be home now?

BLONDEAU [while SUZANNE makes ready to go]. Yes. He's almost always home at this time. You know where it is? You ring at the garden gate and . . . You've got the hundred francs, haven't you?

SUZANNE [moving toward the door]. Yes. . . .

BLONDEAU. Understand, I don't know anything about this. Not anything.

SUZANNE. I understand, Armand.

BLONDEAU. Well, come back soon. I'll be waiting. Go along now. Kiss me. [They embrace. SUZANNE goes out. BLONDEAU calls from the door] Look here! If you don't want to take all the blame, tell him you gave the money to someone else to place and she didn't place it. [Silence. He comes back] She's off.

[He sighs, sits, looks at his hands, takes his knife out of his pocket and begins to clean his nails. Then he rises, walks to and fro, halts, extracts the day's racing sheet from the inside of his tunic and sits again to study it. In a few seconds he is figuring odds on the margin of the paper with a pencil. The curtain falls. It rises immediately denoting the passing of an hour's time. There is a knock at the door. BLONDEAU rises, his racing sheet in his hand, and goes to admit MICHEL]

BLONDEAU [uncomfortably]. Hello!

MICHEL [furiously]. Aren't you ashamed!

BLONDEAU. What of?

MICHEL. I'm asking you if you're not ashamed of the way you're behaving?

BLONDEAU. What are you talking about? What do you want here?

MICHEL. I just left Suzanne. She went up to your captain's door all right and then, thank Heaven, she lost her nerve. So she ran to me. I gave her the money and now she's gone to leave it in your name.

BLONDEAU. I don't see why Suzanne. . . .

MICHEL. It wasn't Suzanne's place to see your Captain. And it seems to me that you've been behaving contemptibly like . . . like the weakling you are . . . and I've come to tell you so.

BLONDEAU. Look out! Don't talk that way to me!

MICHEL [snatching the racing sheet out of his hands and throwing it on the table]. I expected to find you a little conscience stricken, at least . . . and here you are deep as ever in this filthy truck!

BLONDEAU. Monsieur!

MICHEL. And she running here . . . running to tell you you've nothing more to fear. . . . And you sit here up to the same old game. . . .

BLONDEAU. That's a lie! Get out! Get out of here! I order you to get out of my house!

MICHEL. I'm not through yet!

BLONDEAU. What right have you got to interfere in my affairs?

MICHEL. It's not a right. It's a duty.

BLONDEAU. I'd like to know what Suzanne means by running to you! I'm going to ask her what she means by it! This is the second time you've taken advantage of our troubles and her trust in you and your . . . your money . . . to put me under obligations and humiliate and insult me!

MICHEL. You don't matter. I haven't done what I have from any interest in you. Can't you understand that if I'm here now I'm here simply to hold you to account for. . . .

BLONDEAU. I don't have to account to you for anything. What happens in my house is none of your business. I tell you to keep away from here. I don't want you hanging around. I don't want anything to do with you. You've just lent me some money. If I had it here I'd throw it in your face!

MICHEL. If you don't want to be rescued then keep yourself out of trouble or, at least, don't drag others in with you! [BLONDEAU *shrugs his shoulders*] If you didn't want to see me in your house; if you didn't want to have anything to do with me, then . . . well, you did steal my fiancée and you'd have done better to make her happy. You'd have done better to give some thought to her peace of mind and her well-being and her health. You'd have done better to . . .

BLONDEAU [*seizing the back of a chair*]. That's enough! You don't know what you're talking about!

MICHEL [*driving at him*]. You'd have done better to spare her these degrading worries instead of allowing her to take on herself the blame for your cheats and your lies. [*A real cry of despair*] God, why couldn't you have made her happy!

BLONDEAU [*his voice strangled*]. Who says she isn't happy?

MICHEL. She isn't. It isn't enough for her to love you. That won't make her happy unless you're worthy of her. Worthy of her, do you hear? And you're not worthy. . . .

BLONDEAU. You've got no right to be talking to me this way! Just because you've got a better education than I have,—and more money! Just because she thinks you're a better man than I am! You've got no right. . . . Get out! [*He brandishes the chair*] Get out of my house or I'll . . .

[MICHEL *snatches the chair out of his hand and throws it across the room. At this instant* SUZANNE *enters*]

SUZANNE [*terrified*]. What are you doing here, Michel?

[MICHEL *stands motionless and contrite*]

BLONDEAU. He's insulting me!

SUZANNE [*to* BLONDEAU]. How awful you look! Dear me! You weren't coming to blows, were you? . . . Ah, and it's my fault, too!

MICHEL. No it isn't, Suzanne. It's my fault. I came over here because . . . well, you know how upset I was just now and, anyway, I'd always wanted to speak my mind out. And

then, as luck would have it, your husband met me at the door with this thing [*Indicating the racing sheet*] in his hand and I got so angry that. . . .

BLONDEAU. Haven't I got a right to read what I choose and do what I please in my own house?

SUZANNE. Of course you have, Armand! Only please don't get so excited. You know perfectly well that if Michel . . .

BLONDEAU. He better get out of here! [*He sits, elbows on the table, chin in hands, and remains so during the following*]

MICHEL. Very well. I'll be off.

SUZANNE. No! You mustn't go like this! If you go like this, Michel, you and Armand will never be friends again. I couldn't stand that.

MICHEL [*after a moment's reflection*]. When I came in here I didn't know what I was doing. My one idea was to hurt you, Blondeau. . . . Suzanne wanted my help. She trusted me. She wouldn't have believed me capable of running here the way I did, like a crazy man, to . . . to throw her very confidences right back at you. . . . Isn't that so, Suzanne? [*He sits, his elbows on his knees*] The fact that she trusted me ought to have held me back. . . .

BLONDEAU [*after a silence*]. Yes.

MICHEL [*firmly*]. I apologize to both of you. If you'd been here just now, Suzanne, you'd have seen how easy it is for a man to give advice to others and go against it himself. . . . If you'd been here. . . .

SUZANNE. You wouldn't have quarrelled.

MICHEL. Some things wouldn't have been spoken. [*He rises and turns to* BLONDEAU] Look here, Blondeau, we don't always know just where we're headed for. We *do* go wrong, don't we?

[*A pause*]

SUZANNE. Who doesn't go wrong sometimes?

MICHEL. From the day I first heard about your playing the races and how they were getting you in deeper and deeper, I've wanted to have a talk with you. Many's the time I've thought about it, but I didn't plan anything like what we just finished. I didn't want it here. I wanted to run into you on the street. Then we'd have stepped into a café like the time you and Louis and I played billiards together. . . . I was going to talk to you, right out, just the way I talk to Suzanne, just as if we'd always been friends. . . . I wasn't going to ask for any confidences. I was going to confide in you! I was going to tell you how uneasy I was about this gambling. "Nothing of the sort"! you'd have said. Then, . . . I hoped I'd be able to show you that there's no good in gambling. And we'd have gone on that way, a long time, friendly and comfortable . . . talking about this and that, . . . and then . . . this is what I wanted most of all

. . . we'd have come to know one another, and even if we didn't quite agree, still we'd be able to discuss matters, and even argue a bit. And we'd have got rid of hard words for good and all.

SUZANNE. Of course you would.

MICHEL. Just think! If only we could have had such a talk before to-day and got a little acquainted with each other, would it have been possible for me to say the things I said just now? . . . We really don't know each other at all!

BLONDEAU [troubled]. No, you don't know me and that's just why you oughtn't to have. . . .

MICHEL. That's just what I mean!

SUZANNE. Well, then! Shake hands and make up.

MICHEL [with decision]. Will you, Blondeau? Eh? Try to forget what I said. Don't refuse to shake hands. [He holds out his hand. BLONDEAU hesitates a second, then takes it]

SUZANNE. There. That's right! [She presses MICHEL's other hand, then goes to kiss BLONDEAU]

BLONDEAU [with dignity]. Only . . .

MICHEL. Only what?

BLONDEAU. All that money we owe you. I wish . . .

MICHEL. Don't let's bother with that to-day! You take all the time you want about it. I don't need it.

SUZANNE [to BLONDEAU]. Owing money to Michel is just like owing it to Louis or Maman.

MICHEL. You ought to know that, Blondeau. I've always been like the eldest of the Catelain family.

BLONDEAU. I know that.

MICHEL. When I came of age, I was the man of the household, wasn't I Suzanne? And I took my job seriously! Didn't you always run to me when anything came up?

SUZANNE. Indeed we did!

MICHEL. They didn't have to run far either. I always looked out for everybody. It was my nature. Do you think I could stand off and do nothing to-day with you and Suzanne really in trouble? Wasn't it natural for her to come to me? On your account as much as on her own? And could I help running here to tell you to look out?

BLONDEAU. Oh, I understand that. . . .

MICHEL [half smiling, half tearful]. And I might as well tell you that this child—she's got a child of her own, now!—I've never seen her worried before. I've never seen a real frown on her little forehead. . . .

SUZANNE. I wasn't always laughing, Michel!

MICHEL. No, but when you did take life seriously, you were just a little girl with a beautiful romance to read— [He turns back to BLONDEAU] Don't you see what a shock it was to me to find a new Suzanne, all wretched and unhappy? Don't you see how that would have frightened me? Do you wonder I lost my head for a minute? . . . This little fracas of ours—don't let's think of it again—

SUZANNE. I don't believe Armand's going to cherish any hard feelings.

BLONDEAU [troubled more deeply]. No, I haven't any hard feelings. I wouldn't have any reason for them. I've been thinking quite a bit. I can see I ought to be a different kind of a fellow for Suzanne's sake. I ought to take hold on life better and look ahead more, and all that. I ought to make plans, too. . . .

MICHEL [protesting]. Well, but . . .

BLONDEAU. I started out on the wrong foot and now I'm just plain good for nothing. I know that. I'm good for nothing. [He bursts into sudden sobs, flinging himself across the table, burying his face in his arms]

SUZANNE. Armand, my dear!

BLONDEAU. How can I do the right thing by you!

SUZANNE. Don't, Armand! Don't!

BLONDEAU. I'm good for nothing.

MICHEL [patting his shoulder]. Don't say that, Blondeau! It isn't so! Not for a minute, it isn't!

BLONDEAU [sits up and gently pushes SUZANNE away from him]. I'll have to admit you weren't so far wrong about me when you said. . . .

MICHEL. I was angry, Blondeau!

BLONDEAU. There are some things, though, I just can't help thinking about . . . since . . .

SUZANNE. Don't think about them any more. They're over.

MICHEL [touched]. I may have been unfair. I've only got to look at you now to see that I was judging you according to my own idea of you, and I may have missed the real Blondeau altogether.

BLONDEAU. Whatever he is, I'm in a bad way now!

MICHEL. How so?

BLONDEAU. Well, I've been taken in by all these plans and ideas of mine, and . . . that way, I've taken in other people. I guess you know I failed again in this last examination?

MICHEL. Yes, I knew.

SUZANNE [to MICHEL]. That nearly broke his heart.

BLONDEAU. And what did it do to her? Even if she won't own up. . . . Our future isn't exactly what you'd call rosy. You can see that.

SUZANNE. Armand, it wasn't half as hard on me as it was on you. And we're going to be all right. As long as you stop the races. . . . [He promises with a gesture] We've nothing to worry about. We can just sit quietly and wait for things to improve. As they will, in time.

MICHEL [nervously]. As they will in time.

. . . That's the way to look at it! Honestly, to hear you talk, you two, anybody would think you'd both lost everything and been stricken with paralysis into the bargain!

BLONDEAU. Suzanne means we can go on living this kind of a life with her slaving, and no way out yet a while!

MICHEL. But I don't mean that. I mean you can change matters for the better right here and now. You can start in fresh now. Only you've got to believe in yourself more—and in a new way. [*He begins to walk animatedly up and down, stopping, from time to time in front of* BLONDEAU *and* SUZANNE *who sit side by side*] Do you remember the time your colonel saw you turned out in your very best? And called you a boy who might make an officer? Maybe he was right, but what an idea! Officer or not, the finest thing you can ever be is a happy man who makes other people happy! Have you got the stuff in you to be that? My dear Blondeau, I'm sure you have! I've just now seen you turned out in your very best. . . . Oh, Suzanne! Blondeau! Is it fair to say that happiness is a matter of ranks and promotions?

BLONDEAU. Just the same . . .

MICHEL [*a little uneasy*]. Think for yourself! Haven't you got everything you really need already? The rest is easy! Tell me, what is your next move?

SUZANNE. Armand's applying for a transfer to the customs.

BLONDEAU. Yes. I may get some chance there to. . . .

MICHEL [*unenthusiastically*]. The customs . . . the customs . . . well, that's an idea, too. . . . You might have the good luck to draw a nice mountain post and, on the other hand, you might find yourself in some horrid sea port town. . . .

SUZANNE. In a sea port town. Oh, we never thought of that!

MICHEL. No, the customs aren't bad. But if I were you, I'd try something quite different.

BLONDEAU. What?

MICHEL. Let's see. You've been ten years in the service, haven't you?

BLONDEAU. In three more months.

MICHEL. And that ends your enlistment, doesn't it?

BLONDEAU. Of course, I've got to reënlist for the customs.

MICHEL. See here, now! After ten years in the army, you're eligible for the civil service.

BLONDEAU. I never thought about the Civil Service.

SUZANNE. Armand's so bent on staying with the army.

BLONDEAU. I know the Civil Service, though. I've got one friend who's a guard in one of the state prisons and another who's. . . .

SUZANNE [*delighted*]. Oh, Armand!

MICHEL. I wasn't thinking of quite that sort of thing. There are other jobs, you know, in the Civil Service. Plenty of others! There are jobs to suit any taste and any talent and any ambition! I've seen a great, thick book about them. You can look up the kind of job you want and find out all about it. For instance, you might fancy the highway commission? Or the inspection of bridges? Or the bureau of weights and measures? Or the mine control bureau? Or the harbor police? Or . . . oh, almost anything!

BLONDEAU. I had no idea!

SUZANNE. Are you sure of this, Michel?

MICHEL. Absolutely!

SUZANNE. To think of your looking all that up for us!

MICHEL. I didn't look it up for you. It just happened that—well, I do have to know something about the books I sell! [*To* BLONDEAU] To be sure, these jobs, most of them, well, you have to pass more or less of an examination before you get them—but, if you don't aim too high at the start, there's one job you've got a right to—not a half bad one either—in the post office. The same thing Suzanne's doing now!

SUZANNE [*surprised into laughing*]. My partner!

BLONDEAU [*a trifle dashed*]. Hm. . . . Well, I don't see . . .

MICHEL. You will! Just wait! Suppose you are, both of you in the postal service. Married as you are, you ought to be able to get a whole post office of your own in some town or other where Suzanne could hold down the job of chief clerk. . . .

SUZANNE. That's an idea. Do you think we could?

MICHEL. It's possible anyway. I don't know much about the details, or how to start, but just think how nice it would be! You're in the country in some nice section. You've got a pleasant home at the government's expense,— a dear little house with a garden behind, right in the center of the village. . . .

BLONDEAU. That's not bad. . . .

MICHEL. You're your own masters as much as any independent tradesman and a lot more independent than the school teacher or anyone like that. And I'll bet you don't have any more red tape to bother with than you'd have as lieutenant of the customs. . . .

SUZANNE. The fact is . . .

MICHEL [*to* BLONDEAU]. How does the idea strike you?

BLONDEAU. It's not bad. I have to get used to it. I can't exactly see myself as a civilian, but it's not bad. . . .

MICHEL. My dear man, you can't imagine the comfort of civilian clothes! They'll make

you see the whole world on a larger scale!
You'll be like a horse when they take off his
blinders! . . . Then, think: you'll have that
feeling of being really useful every minute of
the day, in every single thing you do. . . . A
little post office with its telegraph wires marching down the street and along the highroad—
that's what links the village to the rest of the
world. . . .

SUZANNE. It's true! Sometimes we send tele-
grams to the most outlandish places! To places
you've never heard of!

MICHEL. Everybody depends on the postmaster and his wife and if you're pleasant and
obliging you'll have everybody's good will.
And you'll make friends. Oh, it's a job where
you can be of use to the world. Isn't that so,
Suzanne?

SUZANNE. Indeed, it is, Michel!

MICHEL. Not to mention the promotions
that will come in time.

SUZANNE. For both of us.

MICHEL. And, what's more, you could have
the baby with you!

SUZANNE. That's what I was just going to
say.

BLONDEAU [waking up]. A garden would be
good for Riquet. It certainly would be
good. . . .

SUZANNE. We'd have him right under our
noses, Armand! There'd be room for Maman
to come and visit now and then. . . .

MICHEL. Don't you see yourselves? In a
bright, clean, little post office? Not a useless
thing in it? And you in sole charge with the
whole responsibility? Your telegraph instrument there! Your telephone there! At the back
a door that's always left open so you can look
into your own dining room?

SUZANNE. Or out into the garden. . . .

BLONDEAU. Yes. . . . Yes. . . .

MICHEL. Or out into the garden where Suzanne is sewing in the shade with the baby
playing all around her, while you, Blondeau,
run the office. And when things get too busy for
you, you just turn in your chair and call Suzanne in to lend a hand. . . .

SUZANNE. Even if the work always kept both
of us busy, I wouldn't feel like an ordinary em-
ployee. . . .

MICHEL. But it won't always keep both of
you busy, if you know how to manage.

BLONDEAU. In those country places there are
hours every day when nobody comes near the
post office.

SUZANNE. Oh, it ought to be *much* nicer
than here!

MICHEL. And in summer, in the fine weather
—you don't open till eight—you'll have time
for your gardening or a ride on your bicycle.
People get up early in the country, you know.

SUZANNE. I shall grow *both* flowers and vegetables.

BLONDEAU. Do you think we can pick a place
where the fishing's good?

SUZANNE. And in winter I'll fix up my house
and begin reading again.

BLONDEAU. The only reason I never took to
reading was I never could find an interesting
book.

MICHEL. I'll send you all you want and
you can lend them to your friends. You can
get up a little club.

SUZANNE. Oh, yes! We'll be well situated for
that. . . . Oh, Michel! I'll found a branch of
your Saint-Serge Library!

MICHEL. Oh, thank you, thank you, Suzon!
That was part of my program but I was waiting for you to think of it.

BLONDEAU. Oh, we'll have to look into this
very carefully. [*To* MICHEL] Is the information
all in this book of yours, Michel?

MICHEL. I think so.

SUZANNE. Oh, we must get this book, Michel.
I want to make sure! It would be so nice!
So nice! Don't you think it would, Armand?

BLONDEAU. Of course I do. But we mustn't
count our chickens too soon.

MICHEL. Well, just let me run up to the
shop and I'll be back with the book in a jiffy.
[*He snatches up his hat*]

BLONDEAU. Now? Oh, we hate to trouble
you!

SUZANNE. We can wait till tomorrow, Michel.

MICHEL. No! Now! Now! I'm going! [*He
starts*]

BLONDEAU [*following him toward the door*].
All I hope is we're both eligible.

MICHEL. If you're not, we'll find something
else.

SUZANNE. No! No, Michel! I want my little
post office and my branch library. . . . Why,
I can see them both already!

BLONDEAU. It certainly is a comforting idea!

MICHEL. Go on and make your plans, then,
both of you! Make whole gardens of plans!
Fill all the air with your air castles! Cut loose,
now, if you want to! Things aren't so bad
after all, are they?

SUZANNE. And when you think that an hour
ago. . . .

BLONDEAU. I was desperate, too. . . .

MICHEL. Will you be desperate again if you
have to give up your little post office in the
country? Your little post office that you had
never dreamed of an hour ago?

SUZANNE. Be still, Michel! I want my post
office!

MICHEL. I'll fetch the book, Suzanne. I'll
run for the book. But whatever happens,
you've dreamed of the joys of life out there
in the country and that shows me you've got

the joys of life in yourselves, both of you, wherever you go!

BLONDEAU. There's no good in being desperate. I can see that. And a man isn't licked because he failed once.

MICHEL [*in the doorway*]. Bravo! And, anyway, we're young! You two haven't begun yet! You haven't even begun! I'll be back in a minute.

SUZANNE [*holding him by the hand*]. Quickly, Michel! And thank you! Thank you! Thank you! Oh, I feel so much better already!

[MICHEL *goes.* BLONDEAU *walks excitedly up and down*]

BLONDEAU. What I see, Suzanne, is a village of—well, say, three thousand. Not more! In a farming district where there's a fine river full of fish. . . .

SUZANNE [*setting the chairs to rights*]. Yes, Armand. . . . Yes. . . .

BLONDEAU. And we'll soon get to know all the nice people. . . . Oh, not *all* of them, maybe . . . still, a postmaster *is* somebody. . . .

SUZANNE [*Her eyes far away*]. The very first thing I do, I'll set aside two evenings a week for the library. People who live too far away can come on Sundays. . . .

CURTAIN